www.wadsworth.com

wadsworth.com is the World Wide Web site for
Wadsworth Publishing Company and is your direct
source to dozens of online resources.

At *wadsworth.com* you can find out about
supplements, demonstration software, and
student resources. You can also send e-mail to
many of our authors and preview new publications
and exciting new technologies.

wadsworth.com
Changing the way the world learns®

PHILOSOPHY OF RELIGION: TOWARD A GLOBAL PERSPECTIVE

Gary E. Kessler
California State University, Bakersfield

Wadsworth Publishing Company
I(T)P® *An International Thomson Publishing Company*

Belmont, CA • Albany, NY • Boston • Cincinnati • Johannesburg • London • Madrid • Melbourne
Mexico City • New York • Pacific Grove, CA • Scottsdale, AZ • Singapore • Tokyo • Toronto

Philosophy Editor: Peter Adams
Assistant Editor: Kerri Abdinoor
Editorial Assistant: Mindy Newfarmer
Print Buyer: Stacey Weinberger
Permissions Editor: Robert Kauser
Production: Matrix Productions
Copy Editor: Connie Day
Cover Designer: Laurie Anderson
Cover Image: Mandala of Avalokiteshvara, nineteenth century Tibet, Asian Art Museum, Avery Brundage Collection
Compositor: Circle Graphics
Printer: Webcom

I(T)P   The ITP logo is a registered trademark under license.

Printed in Canada
3 4 5 6 7 8 9 10

For more information, contact Wadsworth Publishing Company, 10 Davis Drive, Belmont, CA 94002, or electronically at
http://www.wadsworth.com

International Thomson Publishing Europe
Berkshire House
168–173 High Holborn
London, WC1V 7AA, United Kingdom

Nelson ITP, Australia
102 Dodds Street
South Melbourne
Victoria 3205 Australia

Nelson Canada
1120 Birchmount Road
Scarborough, Ontario
Canada M1K 5G4

International Thomson Publishing Southern Africa
Building 18, Constantia Square
138 Sixteenth Road, P.O. Box 2459
Halfway House, 1685 South Africa

International Thomson Editores
Seneca, 53
Colonia Polanco
11560 México D.F. México

International Thomson Publishing Asia
60 Albert Street #15-01
Albert Complex
Singapore 189969

International Thomson Publishing Japan
Hirakawa-cho Kyowa Building, 3F
2-2-1 Hirakawa-cho, Chiyoda-ku
Tokyo 102 Japan

Library of Congress Cataloging-in-Publication Data

Philosophy of religion : toward a global perspective / [compiled by]
   Gary E. Kessler.
      p.   cm.
   ISBN 0-534-50549-X
   1. Religion—Philosophy.   2. Religions.   I. Kessler, Gary E.
   BL51.P5454   1999
   210—dc21   98-27276

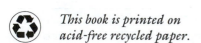

*This book is printed on
acid-free recycled paper.*

In memory of my father,
who first challenged me to think more deeply about religion.

Contents

Preface

THIS BOOK CAN BE used either as the main textbook or as a supplemental anthology in philosophy of religion courses. What primarily distinguishes it from other texts in the field is its breadth.

Most academic philosophy of religion in the West has focused on the kind of theism found in the Christian and Jewish religious traditions, with an occasional nod to Islam. As a consequence, most textbooks and most anthologies focus on "Judeo-Christian" theism. It is time for a change. It is time to broaden the scope so that the philosophy of religion becomes more than philosophical reflection on theistic issues influenced by a few religious traditions.

I wrote this book to provide students and instructors with a wide variety of philosophical material from different religious traditions. My hope is that this book will foster a more global perspective on philosophical issues related to some of the many religions of the world.

Coverage

A glance at the Contents for this book will indicate the different religious traditions that are represented. There are too many different religions to include a selection from each and still restrict this book to a reasonable length. However, the reader will find selections from some of the most influential traditions, including the Native American, African, Buddhist, Hindu, Islamic, Christian, Jewish, Confucian, and Taoist. Feminist, African American, Atheist, and Latin American viewpoints are also represented, not to mention different varieties within the major traditions, such as Protestant and Roman Catholic Christianity, Zen and Theravada Buddhism, and different strands of Confucianism.

I have *not* included scriptural texts, because my focus is on the philosophical reflection that has arisen in various traditions. Scriptural texts are, in many cases, the inspiration for such reflection, but their philosophical implications are frequently latent and need to be made explicit by subsequent interpretation. Thus Avicenna's explication of the nature of God (Chapter 2), though it is based on the Qur'an, is permeated with philosophical concepts, definitions, and arguments.

There is not one philosophical approach to religion but many. It is more accurate to speak of the philosoph*ies* of religions than of the philosophy of religion. I have included a variety of different philosophical approaches to the study of religion so that the student will get a feel for the range in the field. The student will learn something about different ways (such as the existential, phenomenological, linguistic, and comparative) in which philosophers analyze and evaluate religious beliefs and practices. The topics—the nature of religion, ultimate reality, God's existence, the problem of evil, and immortality, to mention only a few—are topics that have emerged in many of the different traditions as people have thought about religious matters and wondered about the nature and purpose of human existence.

Because of space limitations, I have not been able to pursue every position or select representatives of all the different kinds of arguments. Not every sort of theodicy, for example, could be covered in the chapter on evil (Chapter 5). However, I have selected material that represents most of the major positions. For instance, arguments for (and against) the immortality of the soul, resurrection of the body, rebirth, and extinction are examined in Chapter 7.

Organization

The selections are organized around key questions such as "Do Faith and Reason Conflict?" (Chapter 9). I begin with a consideration of the nature of religion, then focus on the notion of ultimate reality, and move on to a consideration of religious experience. After dealing with the problem of evil, with morality, and with immortality, I examine linguistic and epistemological topics. Students often find these latter two topics somewhat difficult, so I have placed them later in the text, assuming that students will have become accustomed to the way philosophers go about their business by that point.

I explore the relationships among religion, humanism, and science in Chapter 10. It is often said that science reflects a "humanistic" spirit, although students will soon learn that the relationships among religion, humanism, and science are quite complex. To provide a more concrete focus, I discuss miracles in this chapter, because some argue that the very idea of miracles is antithetical to the scientific spirit.

Questions surrounding religious truth and religious pluralism are addressed at the end. By now students should be ready to tackle the difficult question of whether any one particular religious viewpoint can be said to be true and other viewpoints false. How are we to think about the relationships among the various religious traditions? Are they all equally valid?

The order in which the chapters appear reflects what experience has taught me is effective pedagogically, but I know each instructor will have her or his own preferences. Thus the chapters have, for the most part, been written as independent units that instructors can rearrange to suit their particular needs.

Pedagogical Features

As I wrote this book, I kept in mind student needs and certain pedagogical problems that I have encountered in the past when teaching the philosophy of religion. I also consulted with others who teach the course and found, in many cases, that we had had similar experiences. I have tried to meet the needs and solve the problems that often arise in the teaching of philosophy of religion. The following list highlights some of the pedagogical features I have incorporated.

- *Global perspective.* Because I believe that philosophy of religion as usually taught has too narrow a focus, given the variety and complexity of world religions, I have broadened the range of religions represented. Teaching has taught me that we learn by contrasts. To paraphrase Max Müller, students who know only one kind of philosophy of religion really know none.
- *Starting in the right place.* Student preparation for a course in philosophy of religion varies greatly. Some students know some philosophy but little of religion. Some know something about religion but little philosophy. There is no simple way to rem-

edy this situation, but I have selected readings that college students to whom both philosophy and religious studies are new can understand with minimal background. I have also supplied background information, in my introductions, where necessary.

- *Learning to philosophize.* Students need to learn to philosophize, not just to learn about the philosophizing of others. My introductions invite students to think through the issues and the arguments, to explore different perspectives, to ask the unusual question, and to probe beneath the surface. In short, this book encourages and helps students to *do* philosophy.

- *Reading philosophy of religion.* At first students often have to rely heavily on the instructor to interpret texts for them. However, they need to learn how to read and interpret texts on their own, and this book helps them develop that skill by providing specific reading questions before each selection. If the students refer to these questions and keep them in mind as they read, they will be led step by step through the most important ideas and arguments of the texts. Answering these questions requires students to learn the skill of analysis, but many of the questions also invite open-ended critical responses.

- *Context, context, context.* Many textbooks provide only small excerpts from different authors in the hope of giving students some exposure to a lot of different positions. I think it is more valuable to provide fewer but longer selections so that students can see more of the immediate context and watch how authors develop the subtleties of their arguments. The selections in this book are long enough to provide the necessary context for students to understand, at a deeper level, the nuances of a position.

- *Research projects.* I have encouraged students to continue investigating these issues on their own by suggesting avenues they may want to explore and by providing a list of suggested readings at the end of each chapter.

Acknowledgments

I owe special thanks to Katy Kessler, whose research, suggestions, and advice were invaluable. My students in philosophy of religion provided a live audience on which I could try out some of this material. I thank them for their patience and aid. The faculty of the Department of Philosophy and Religious Studies were supportive and encouraging, and my colleagues Norman Prigge and Stafford Betty, in particular, made helpful suggestions. Tammy Goldfeld, former religion editor at Wadsworth, helped me conceive this project, and Peter Adams saw it through. A sabbatical from California State University Bakersfield and a fellowship at the Centre for Studies in Religion and Society at the University of Victoria provided time to add some finishing touches. The comments of reviewers were enormously helpful. I wish especially to thank Brian B. Clayton, Gonzaga University; R. Douglas Geivett, Biola University; Clevis Headley, Florida Atlantic University; George A. James, University of North Texas; Arnold E. Johanson, Moorhead State University; T. McK. Lounsbury, Loyola University, Chicago; Robert D. Maldonado, California State University, Fresno; Michael Myers, Washington State University, Pullman; Robert Nielson, D'Youville College; Kerry S. Walters, Gettysburg College; Mark Owen Webb, Texas Tech University; David Wilson, UCLA; and Linda Zagzebski, Loyola Marymount University.

It is not easy to weave the great diversity of philosophical reflection on religion into a coherent unity, and although many have helped me in my efforts to do this, any shortcomings are solely my responsibility. I do not think that the field of philosophy of religion has yet achieved a genuine global perspective. But it is on its way, and my hope is that this book will contribute to the journey.

Gary E. Kessler
California State University, Bakersfield
E-mail: gary_kessler@firstclass1.csubak.edu

Introduction
What Is Philosophy of Religion?

PHILOSOPHY OF RELIGION IS in transition, and my hope is that this book will contribute to the changes that are taking place. The transition is from a narrow focus on issues related primarily to theism to a broader focus that takes into account the diversity of the world's religions. Because the field is changing, it is difficult to introduce it to someone who may know little about it. Perhaps a brief look at its past, present, and possible future will help.

Philosophical reflection on religious issues is very old. In the West, the Greek philosopher Xenophanes (570–480 B.C.E.) noted that people portray their gods in their own image. The gods of Greece look like Greeks, and the gods of Egypt look like Egyptians. If horses could draw, what do you think their gods would look like? In India, the *Upanishads* (800–400 B.C.E.) show that philosophical reflection on the meaning and purpose of human life dates a long way back into history. Who are we? Where did we come from? Where are we going?

The contours of the field of philosophy of religion in the modern period in the West were drawn by Georg Wilhelm Friedrich Hegel (1770–1831) in a series of lectures entitled "Philosophy of Religion." In his lectures of 1824, Hegel asserts that the philosophy of religion has as its goal nothing less than knowledge of absolute truth. Absolute truth is God. Hence the goal of the philosophy of religion is to know God.[1]

Since Hegel, philosophy of religion in the West has, in effect, been the philosophy of theism. Hegel identified God as the proper object of study. God is of central concern to the religions of Judaism, Christianity, and Islam, so those religions have provided the primary data for philosophical reflection. Because Hegel believed that all actual or positive religions shared a common core or essence, he used the word *religion* in the singular, and that has been the custom ever since.

Things have changed, though, since Hegel defined the field. For one thing, we have learned more about the diversity of religious traditions. This knowledge indicates that God, understood primarily in a theistic and personal sense, is by no means the central concern of all religions.[2] We have also come to question whether there is any such thing as "religion" in the singular. Given the variety of human faiths, it now appears more accurate to talk about "religions." However, the vast and growing knowledge about the world's religions is only now beginning to change the field of philosophy of religion. It is slowly being transformed into what might more accurately be described as the philosophy of religions.[3]

The increase in our knowledge about the religions of the world has also led to a new appreciation for the diversity of what counts as philosophical reflection on religious matters. Many people think of philosophy as primarily an invention of the Greeks, who passed it along to modern Western culture. But on the contrary, we are discovering that philosophy is global. European and American philosophy are not all there is to philosophy. There are also African, Indian, Chinese, and Native American philosophy (the list could go on), and these systems of thought have much to do with religion. Buddhist philosophizing about religious matters, for example, seldom finds its way into university textbooks on philosophy of religion. However, Buddhism is a religion that has a long and distinguished philosophical tradition. Similarly, Indian philosophizing about religious matters is not widely represented in university textbooks on philosophy of religion. Yet Hinduism too is a religion that has a distinguished philosophical tradition. I could go on, but you get the point. Philosophy of religion, as traditionally practiced since Hegel, has been not only the philosophy of theism but also a type of philosophy that reflects the problems, values, ideas, and concerns of Western culture. Our present knowledge indicates that it is time for a change, and I hope this book contributes in a positive way to that change.

But what exactly constitutes philosophical reflection on religious matters? The first chapter in this book focuses on the debate about how best to define religion. In this introduction, I wish to focus on the term *philosophy*. Those who do philosophy are not in agreement about exactly what the word means. However, we do need to start somewhere. The following definition will do for our purposes. *Philosophy is the rational attempt to formulate, understand, and answer fundamental questions.* By extension, philosophy of religion can be characterized as the rational attempt to formulate, understand, and answer fundamental questions about religious matters. Like any brief definition, this one needs some unpacking.

Philosophy is an activity. It is something people do. It is not a set of beliefs, dogmas, doctrines, or ideas. It is a way of thinking about things. This way of thinking I characterize as "rational." But what is it to think rationally?

This is not an easy question to answer, and it is one of the most hotly debated topics in contemporary philosophy. In Hegel's day, it was customary to make a distinction between "natural theology" and "revealed theology." Natural theology deals with what can be known about the divine through human reason alone, whereas revealed theology deals with what can be known about the divine through revelation. Philosophy of religion, as Hegel understood it, continued the tradition of natural theology. Its goal is to discover, by means of reason alone, truths about God. To use one's reason is to be rational. Hence philosophy in general—and philosophy of religion in particular—rests on the foundation of *rationality*. However, what seems rational to me might seem irrational to you. There's the rub.

As we learn more about diverse cultures and religions, we learn more about the amazing flexibility of human rationality. It may make perfect sense in one culture to ascribe unfortunate events to demons, but in another such an explanation is regarded as irrational superstition. Even within cultures, what counts as a good reason for one person to believe in the healing powers of crystals may strike another as nonsense. Many find reincarnation a reasonable belief; others find such a belief unreasonable.

Few of us would claim to be irrational. We all like to think of ourselves as rational. However, we also know that what counts as rational is deeply influenced by social and cultural factors. Some have suggested that this influence is so strong that the best way to think of rationality is to think of it as a social construction.

If rationality is, at least in part, socially constructed, then are there as many rationalities as there are societies? Is rationality a hopelessly ethnocentric concept? Some philosophers have concluded that it is—that what counts as rational is determined by the intersubjective agreement of various human communities. Other philosophers have argued that rationality is trans-cultural and objective—that it is constituted by universal laws of logic and evidence, whether or not any particular individual arrives at her or his beliefs by the application of such laws.

It is best to avoid ethnocentrism as much as we possibly can. It is not fair to impose one's own standards of rationality on others. However, we cannot just abandon our standards and adopt different ones. Is there any common ground? Many people, from diverse traditions and cultures, might agree that rational beliefs are beliefs supported by good reasons. The reasons make the belief credible to us. However, what reasons count as *good* reasons?

We must be aware of our biases and the biases of others. This seems to be part of being rational. Charles Taylor remarks, "The sober and rational discourse which tries to understand other cultures has to become aware of itself as one among many possibilities in order properly to understand these others."[4] Conversing with those who differ can reveal biases and enlarge our understanding of rationality. Such conversation teaches us that what constitutes a good reason for a belief is embedded in a context of presuppositions. That context is provided by what we can call a *tradition*. Traditions may be secular in the sense that they reflect no loyalty to some particular religious heritage, or they may be explicitly religious. If the tradition is religious, then it might be Buddhist or Christian, Islamic or Confucian, or some other tradition. The more we know about such traditions, the more we understand about the rationality of those who are different, and the more we come to understand our own rationality (or lack of it).[5]

A good example of the way a tradition (in this case a secular tradition) structures our thinking is this textbook and the very idea of philosophy of religion as I am explaining it here. I begin with a Western conception of philosophy of religion. It is, I suggest, the rational quest for a critical understanding of religious beliefs and practices. My perspective is shaped by the Western philosophical "research tradition."[6] The very issues I discuss are determined to a large extent by that tradition. However, I am bringing that perspective into dialogue with other traditions and thereby broadening the horizons and extending the boundaries of what has traditionally counted as philosophy of religion in the West. Once again, Charles Taylor puts it well when he claims that this broader understanding comes about "in comparison and contrasts which let the other be."[7]

It would be possible to begin somewhere else—with, let us say, an Indian or a feminist perspective.[8] Certainly these perspectives are instructive, but to begin with these research traditions would by no means be to escape the influence of a tradition. There is no completely tradition-neutral, absolutely objective perspective. There is, to borrow a term from Nagel, no such thing as "a view from nowhere."[9] And even if there *were* a tradition-neutral view, this would not, in itself, guarantee rationality.

Rationality is an ideal. It is a future possibility. It beckons us. It demands that we present the best arguments and the best evidence we can, given our situation. Philosophy of religion uses reason to criticize and evaluate religious beliefs and practices. However, its task is more than critical. It also seeks to articulate the best understanding presently possible of religious matters. One important way to characterize philosophy of religions is to think of it as the *critical analysis* of religions. The goal of analysis is to describe and elucidate religious beliefs and practices. The goal of criticism is rational assessment.[10]

Philosophical students of religions must be willing to follow the argument wherever it leads. They must be prepared to present the best reasons they can for their critical interpretations. They must also understand that today's "good" reasons may seem not so good in the future. At one time most people believed the earth was flat. They had good reasons. Scientific theory of the day supported their belief, religious ideas reinforced it, and their own experiences confirmed it. It was rational for them to hold this belief. But they were wrong. So too might we be wrong. Nevertheless, right or wrong, our rationality is measured by our willingness to seek what we take to be the truth on the basis of the best evidence and arguments available to us.

Philosophers seek rational answers to fundamental questions by using the best tools reason has to offer. However, formulating and understanding questions is as important as answering them. Do we survive the death of our bodies? Before we can answer, we must know what might constitute meaningful survival. Who or what survives? Is life without a body even imaginable? Is it desirable? If our eyes, ears, and brains cease to function when we die, will we be able to know anything at all of our life beyond this world? How? The question of survival involves a host of other questions. How we formulate these and understand them will determine how we answer that question about the possibility of survival.

Philosophers are not concerned with any and all questions but with questions I have characterized as *fundamental*. What are fundamental questions? Traditionally, in the West, philosophy is divided into the fields of metaphysics, epistemology, and axiology. A brief look at each of these will give us some idea of what is meant by fundamental questions. *Metaphysics* deals with the distinction between reality and appearance. What is real, and how does it differ from what appears to be real? *Epistemology* focuses on the distinction between knowledge and opinion. What constitutes knowledge, and how does it differ from opinion? *Axiology* is concerned with the distinction between fact and value. What constitutes artistic or aesthetic value (beauty) or moral value (ethics), and how do such values differ from what we call facts? I can *describe* a painting or a medical case of a baby born with only a brain stem, but when I ask for a *normative* judgment on your part (Is that a good painting? Should the organs of the baby be taken and used for purposes of transplantation?) you are required to make a judgment that goes beyond the facts and draws on a set of values or norms. We need to distinguish carefully between the description of facts and normative judgments that reflect values.

These questions about reality, knowledge, and value are fundamental in the sense that they are basic to our thinking. They are also *universal* questions. The minds of many ages and many cultures have pondered them, and they will continue to provoke inquiry in the future.

If we focus on the philosophy of religion, then a variety of fundamental questions immediately come to our attention. A brief glance at the table of contents of this book will illustrate many of them. They cut across the fields of metaphysics, epistemology, and axiology. Is God the most perfect reality that exists? If there is some ultimate reality, is the word *god* the best way to name it? Can we know about life after death, about some ultimate reality, or about the meaning of life? Do we just have opinions about these things, but no genuine knowledge? How is religion related to morality? Can there be a purely secular ethics? Do moral values require some sort of divine sanction? Can an atheist do good? Can a theist do good?

Philosophy of religion not only forms part of the field that we call philosophy but is also part of a discipline usually called religious studies. In fact, the field of religious studies has contributed a great deal to the transition that is underway in the philosophy of religion, because it has provided a wealth of data about the diversity of religious beliefs and practices throughout the world. Two areas of religious studies have been particularly influential in enlarging the concerns of philosophy of religion.

The first area is called *history of religions* (it is also referred to as the comparative study of religions). History of religions seeks to describe, interpret, explain, compare, and evaluate, using the best historical methods available, the development of religious traditions. How did Christianity get started? What took place in the first five centuries of its history?

Developmental patterns are important to understand, but history of religions is also concerned with comparative issues. Do the developmental patterns of sectarian movements in Christianity share any similarities with Buddhist sectarian movements? What are the major differences between the practices of Taoists and Muslims? How do the views of the afterlife in Judaism differ from Hindu views?

The second area of religious studies that has had a significant influence on the philosophical study of religions is *the social scientific study of religions*. This area uses the methods and theories of anthropology, sociology, and psychology to describe, interpret, explain, compare, and evaluate religious phenomena. How are religions related to cultures? Are religions symbolic expressions of cultural values that function to socialize people into a particular way of life? How does my religious upbringing or lack of it influence my personality? Are social class and religious affiliation correlated? Are women more or less religious than men? Can we empirically measure religiosity? Do tribal or national social structures influence the type of religion that is practiced? What are the primary differences between patriarchal and matriarchal religions?

Both the history of religions and the social scientific study of religions have much to contribute to philosophical reflection on religious matters. It is becoming increasingly clear that philosophy of religion needs to draw on a variety of resources to reach the goal Hegel set for it—the truth. It needs to be interdisciplinary, drawing on the resources of philosophy, religious studies, history, the social sciences, and other fields of study. It needs to listen to and participate in interreligious dialogue. It needs to be comparative and global. Cross-cultural studies provide first-order data about the religious beliefs and practices found in diverse cultures and times. These data are indispensable to philosophy if it is to carry on its second-order task, or *meta-task*, of independent, rational reflection on what these data mean. Philosophy of religion, I believe, needs to develop a multicultural perspective. Increased global awareness and understanding are important for the development of human civilization, and philosophy of religions can contribute to that awareness and understanding by seriously engaging the variety of religious traditions and ideas.

Hegel, I think, would be happy with these developments and future possibilities. Indeed, he could be no less than happy with global understanding. He wrote that the object of religion (God) is "the region in which all the riddles of the world, all contradictions of thought, are resolved, and all griefs are healed, the region of eternal truth and eternal peace, of absolute satisfaction, of truth itself."[11]

We are a long way from "truth itself." Many would find Hegel's search for absolute truth completely naive in the post-modern world in which we live—a world in which the word *truth* seems to have lost all objective meaning. We must avoid being pretentious and claiming more for philosophy of religion than it can deliver. There are few certainties, and truth, especially in religious matters, may forever elude mere mortals. However, its pursuit can produce greater understanding, and it is in that spirit that I commend its study to you.

NOTES

1. See Hegel, *Lectures on the Philosophy of Religion*, Vol. 1, edited by Peter C. Hodgson (Berkeley, CA: University of California Press, 1984).

2. In fairness to Hegel, it should be noted that he did not think of God primarily in personal terms. God is for Hegel the absolute, unconditioned (infinite) truth.

3. The traditional term *philosophy of religion*, used in Western philosophy, has the advantage of emphasizing the unity of the field. The term *philosophy of religions* has the advantage of emphasizing the plurality and diversity of what is studied. Thomas Dean and others have used the term *cross-cultural philosophy of religion* in an effort to reflect both the unity and the plurality. See "Introduction: Cross-Cultural Philosophy of Religion," in *Religious Pluralism and Truth: Essays on Cross-Cultural Philosophy of Religion*, edited by Thomas Dean (Albany, NY: State University of New York Press, 1995). Others prefer the term *comparative philosophy of religions*. See *Religion and Practical Reason: New Essays in the Comparative Philosophy of Religions*, edited by Frank E. Reynolds and David Tracy (Albany, NY: State University of New York Press, 1994). I will continue to use the term *philosophy of religion*, but I will occasionally use the term *philosophy of religions* when it seems more appropriate.

4. See Taylor's "Comparison, History, Truth," in *Myth and Philosophy*, edited by Frank E. Reynolds and David Tracy (Albany, NY: State University of New York Press, 1990), p. 40.

5. The actual situation is more complex than I indicate here. Human reasoning is often influenced by a variety of different traditions that can be characterized in terms of time (traditional or modern), in terms of class (folk or elite), in terms of worldviews (religious or scientific) and so on. Hence the standards we use for judging what counts as good reasoning are often complex and are not always consistent. For a more thorough discussion of some of this complexity in the context of doing philosophy of religions, see Mikael Stenmark, *Rationality in Science, Religion, and Everyday Life: A Critical Evaluation of Four Models of Rationality* (Notre Dame, IN: University of Notre Dame Press, 1995).

6. Larry Laudan defines a research tradition as "a set of general assumptions about the entities and processes in a domain of study, and about the appropriate methods to be used for investigating the problems and constructing the theories in that domain." See *Progress and Its Problems: Toward a Theory of Scientific Growth* (Berkeley, CA: University of California Press, 1977), p. 81.

7. "Comparison, History, Truth," p. 42.

8. See, for example, Arvind Sharma, *A Hindu Perspective on the Philosophy of Religion* (New York: St. Martin's Press, 1990), and *Indian Philosophy of Religion*, edited by Roy W. Perrett (Dordrecht, The Netherlands: Kluwer Academic Publishers, 1989). Although the interest of feminist philosophers in the philosophy of religion is relatively recent, a good introduction can be found in a special issue of *Hypatia: A Journal of Feminist Philosophy* 9 (Fall 1994). See in particular Nancy Frankenberry's "Introduction: Prolegomenon to Future Feminist Philosophies of Religions," pp. 1–14.

9. See T. Nagel, *The View from Nowhere* (New York: Oxford University Press, 1985).

10. Wayne Proudfoot, I think, draws the distinction between descriptive analysis and criticism too sharply when he claims that the first aims at "understanding" and the second at criticism. I would prefer to think of understanding as the ideal result of both analysis and evaluation. See "Philosophy of Religion," *The Encyclopedia of Religion*, Vol. 11 (New York: Macmillan, 1987), pp. 305–311.

11. Hegel, *Lectures on the Philosophy of Religion*, p. 83.

CHAPTER 1

What Is Religion?

Introduction

WHAT IS RELIGION? That seems to be an easy enough question. Religion is _____. Go ahead; fill in the blank with your definition of religion before you continue reading.

This question is deceptively simple, as you may have discovered in trying to answer it. I will wager that anything you put in that blank will prove problematic for one reason or another. For example, many people in our culture think of religion in terms of belief. Hence they classify it as a kind of belief and then try to distinguish it from other kinds, as in saying, "Religion is belief in a god or gods." This focus on the single dimension of belief is probably due to the influence of certain kinds of Protestant Christianity on our culture, which emphasize beliefs as a key component in salvation. But what about the other dimensions of religion, such as its ritual, moral, experiential, and institutional aspects? Someone has remarked that Native American religion is not so much a matter of belief as a matter of dancing. Religion is not unidimensional but multidimensional, and, although one tradition may emphasize one of these dimensions more than the others, it may not be valid to emphasize one of these dimensions over others in our definition.

Then there is the matter of a god or gods. For some religions (such as early Buddhism), divine beings are not particularly important, and, of course, what religions mean by the divine can vary greatly. What is meant by such divine beings can range all the way from supernatural beings to superior (but not necessarily supernatural) beings. For some, God is not a being among many beings, but the ground or source of all being—thus we may need a more Inclusive term such as *ultimate reality* or *transcendent reality*. Yet the more we search for an inclusive term, the vaguer our definition becomes.

There are also things that we do not normally call religion but that nevertheless function very much like religion for some people. Certain political movements come to mind: Nazism, fascism, and nationalism. What about Marxism? Is it a religion? Is functioning like a religion sufficient to make something a religion? If it cuts like a knife, is it a knife?

1

The purpose of definitions is to draw boundaries that focus our attention on what is inside the boundaries and to help us distinguish what is inside from what is outside the boundaries. In an important sense, definitions are not true or false, but more or less useful given our purposes.

What, then, is our purpose when we ask, "What is religion?" Is our goal to describe the variety of ways in which the word *religion* is and has been used? Is our purpose to capture the essence of the reality of religion? Are we looking for some set of necessary and sufficient traits that "religion" must exhibit in order to fulfill the criteria we have established. Perhaps there *is* no essence. Perhaps the best we can do is list a series of characteristics that most things we usually call religion possess, while at the same time we acknowledge that not all religions necessarily possess all of these characteristics. Then again, is our goal descriptive and historical? Do we seek a definition that will tell us what religion has been and what it is now? Or is our goal normative and ideal? Are we seeking to find out what religion ought to be?

How can we best formulate and understand this question about religion? What if I had asked, "What are religions?" Would your answer have been different? What if I had asked, "What does religion mean to you personally?" Would that question elicit yet a different answer?

I ask these questions in order to get you started thinking about the problems involved in defining religion and in order to introduce you to the kinds of issues and questions the authors of the selections that follow grapple with and try to answer.

1.1 The Nature of Religion

Is it more fruitful to look for a definition of religion in general, or should we start on a more concrete level with particular examples of what we usually call religions? On the concrete level, there appears to be so much variety that generalizations prove difficult. If we focus on a single aspect or dimension then one person might appear to be religious on that dimension (say, belief in the supernatural), whereas a different person might appear to be nonreligious when we held up the same measuring stick. Yet the latter person (who does not believe in the supernatural) might appear to be quite religious on a different dimension (say, religious experiences). Thus a multidimensional approach would seem best—but how many dimensions are there, and can we describe them?

Then again, where do we draw the boundaries? Can so-called secular worldviews be religious? If so, how? And if they are, why call them secular? What is the difference between the secular and the religious?

Does a person have to belong to one of the religions in order to be religious? How many of the different dimensions of religions must I participate in to be religious? If these dimensions are aspects of organized religions, are they even useful in characterizing the religiosity of individuals?

Ninian Smart, author of the selection on "The Nature of Religion," teaches religious studies at the University of California, Santa Barbara. He has done important work in both the philosophy of religions and the comparative study of religions. In this selection, he tackles some of the questions we have raised and offers some answers. As you read, answer the following questions.

Reading Questions

1. Why does Smart think it is more practical to try to find out what a religion is than what religion in general is?
2. What are the seven dimensions of a religion? Give an example of each.
3. What is the difference between numinous and mystical experiences?
4. How does the ethical or legal dimension differ from the narrative and the doctrinal dimensions?
5. What are some examples of the ritual dimension of nationalism and the doctrinal dimension of Marxism?
6. Do you agree or disagree with Smart that although it is inappropriate to call nationalism and Marxism religions, they "play in the same league," as it were? Why?

The Nature of Religion*

NINIAN SMART

IN THINKING ABOUT RELIGION, it is easy to be confused about what it is. Is there some essence which is common to all religions? And cannot a person be religious without belonging to any of the religions? The search for an essence ends up in vagueness—for instance in the statement that a religion is some system of worship or other practice recognizing a transcendent Being or goal. Our problems break out again in trying to define the key term "transcendent." And in answer to the second question, why yes: there are plenty of people with deep spiritual concerns who do not ally themselves to any formal religious movement, and who may not themselves recognize anything as transcendent. They may see ultimate spiritual meaning in unity with nature or in relationships to other persons.

It is more practical to come to terms first of all not with what religion is in general but with what *a* religion is. Can we find some scheme of ideas which will help us to think about and to appreciate the nature of the religions?

Before I describe such a scheme, let me first point to something which we need to bear in mind in looking at religious traditions such as Christianity, Buddhism or Islam. Though we use the singular label "Christianity," in fact there is a great number of varieties of Christianity, and there are some movements about which we may have doubts as to whether they count as Christian. The same is true of all traditions: they manifest themselves as a loosely held-together family of subtraditions. Consider: a Baptist chapel in Georgia is a very different structure from an Eastern Orthodox church in Romania, with its blazing candles and rich ikons; and the two house very diverse services—the one plain, with hymns and Bible-reading, prayers and impassioned preaching; the other much more ritually anchored, with processions and chanting, and mysterious ceremonies in the light behind the screen where the ikons hang, concealing most of the priestly activities. Ask either of the religious specialists, the Baptist preacher or the Orthodox priest, and he will tell you that his own form of faith corresponds to original Christianity. To list some of the denominations of Christianity is to show something of its diverse

*From *The World's Religions* by Ninian Smart. Copyright © 1989 by Ninian Smart. Reprinted by permission of Prentice-Hall, Inc., Upper Saddle River, NJ, pp. 10–25.

practice—Orthodox, Catholic, Coptic, Nestorian, Armenian, Mar Thoma, Lutheran, Calvinist, Methodist, Baptist, Unitarian, Mennonite, Congregationalist, Disciples of Christ—and we have not reached some of the newer, more problematic forms: Latter-Day Saints, Christian Scientists, Unificationists, Zulu Zionists, and so forth.

Moreover, each faith is found in many countries, and takes color from each region. German Lutheranism differs from American; Ukrainian Catholicism from Irish; Greek Orthodoxy from Russian. Every religion has permeated and been permeated by a variety of diverse cultures. This adds to the richness of human experience, but it makes our tasks of thinking and feeling about the variety of faiths more complicated than we might at first suppose. We are dealing with not just traditions but many subtraditions.

It may happen, by the way, that a person within one family of subtraditions may be drawn closer to some subtradition of another family than to one or two subtraditions in her own family (as with human families; this is how marriage occurs). I happen to have had a lot to do with Buddhists in Sri Lanka and in some ways feel much closer to them than I do to some groups within my own family of Christianity.

The fact of pluralism inside religious traditions is enhanced by what goes on between them. The meeting of different cultures and traditions often produces new religious movements, such as the many black independent churches in Africa, combining classical African motifs and Christianities. All around us in Western countries are to be seen new movements and combinations.

Despite all this, it is possible to make sense of the variety and to discern some patterns in the luxurious vegetation of the world's religions and subtraditions. One approach is to look at the different aspects or dimensions of religion.

THE PRACTICAL AND RITUAL DIMENSION

Every tradition has some practices to which it adheres—for instance regular worship, preaching, prayers, and so on. They are often known as ritu-als (though they may well be more informal than this word implies). This *practical* and *ritual* dimension is especially important with faiths of a strongly sacramental kind, such as Eastern Orthodox Christianity with its long and elaborate service known as the Liturgy. The ancient Jewish tradition of the Temple, before it was destroyed in 70 C.E., was preoccupied with the rituals of sacrifice, and thereafter with the study of such rites seen itself as equivalent to their performance, so that study itself becomes almost a ritual activity. Again, sacrificial rituals are important among Brahmin forms of the Hindu tradition.

Also important are other patterns of behavior which, while they may not strictly count as rituals, fulfill a function in developing spiritual awareness or ethical insight: practices such as yoga in the Buddhist and Hindu traditions, methods of stilling the self in Eastern Orthodox mysticism, meditations which can help to increase compassion and love, and so on. Such practices can be combined with rituals of worship, where meditation is directed towards union with God. They can count as a form of prayer. In such ways they overlap with the more formal or explicit rites of religion.

THE EXPERIENTIAL AND EMOTIONAL DIMENSION

We only have to glance at religious history to see the enormous vitality and significance of experience in the formation and development of religious traditions. Consider the visions of the Prophet Muhammad, the conversion of Paul, the enlightenment of the Buddha. These were seminal events in human history. And it is obvious that the *emotions* and *experiences* of men and women are the food on which the other dimensions of religion feed: ritual without feeling is cold, doctrines without awe or compassion are dry, and myths which do not move hearers are feeble. So it is important in understanding a tradition to try to enter into the feelings which it generates—to feel the sacred awe, the calm peace, the rousing inner dynamism, the perception of a brilliant emptiness within, the outpouring of love, the sensations of hope, the gratitude for favors which have been received. One of the main reasons why music is so potent in religion is that it has mysterious powers to express and engender emotions.

Writers on religion have singled out differing experiences as being central. For instance, Rudolf Otto (1869–1937) coined the word "numinous." For the ancient Romans there were *numina* or spirits all around them, present in brooks and streams, and in mysterious copses, in mountains and in dwelling-places; they were to be treated with awe and a kind of fear. From the word, Otto built up his adjective, to refer to the feeling aroused by a *mysterium tremendum et fascinans,* a mysterious something which draws you to it but at the same time brings an awe-permeated fear. It is a good characterization of many religious experiences and visions of God as Other. It captures the impact of the prophetic experiences of Isaiah and Jeremiah, the theophany through which God appeared to Job, the conversion of Paul, the overwhelming vision given to Arjuna in the Hindu Song of the Lord (*Bhagavadgītā*). At a gentler level it delineates too the spirit of loving devotion, in that the devotee sees God as merciful and loving, yet Other, and to be worshiped and adored.

But the numinous is rather different in character from those other experiences which are often called "mystical." Mysticism is the inner or contemplative quest for what lies within—variously thought of as the Divine Being within, or the eternal soul, or the Cloud of Unknowing, emptiness, a dazzling darkness. There are those, such as Aldous Huxley (1894–1963), who have thought that the imageless, insight-giving inner mystical experience lies at the heart of all the major religions.

There are other related experiences, such as the dramas of conversion, being "born again," turning around from worldly to otherworldly existence. There is also the shamanistic type of experience, where a person goes upon a vision quest and acquires powers to heal, often through suffering himself and vividly traveling to the netherworld to rescue the dying and bring them to life again. Shamans are common to many small-scale societies and peoples that make their living by hunting, but many of the marks of the shamanistic quest have been left upon larger religions.

THE NARRATIVE OR MYTHIC DIMENSION

Often experience is channeled and expressed not only by ritual but also by sacred narrative or myth. This is the third dimension—the *mythic* or *narrative*. It is the story side of religion. It is typical of all faiths to hand down vital stories: some historical; some about that mysterious primordial time when the world was in its timeless dawn; some about things to come at the end of time; some about great heroes and saints; some about great founders, such as Moses, the Buddha, Jesus, and Muhammad; some about assaults by the Evil One; some parables and edifying tales; some about the adventures of the gods; and so on. These stories often are called myths. The term may be a bit misleading, for in the context of the modern study of religion there is no implication that a myth is false.

The seminal stories of a religion may be rooted in history or they may not. Stories of creation are before history, as are myths which indicate how death and suffering came into the world. Others are about historical events—for instance the life of the Prophet Muhammad, or the execution of Jesus, and the enlightenment of the Buddha. Historians have sometimes cast doubt on some aspects of these historical stories, but from the standpoint of the student of religion this question is secondary to the meaning and function of the myth; and to the believer, very often, these narratives *are* history.

This belief is strengthened by the fact that many faiths look upon certain documents, originally maybe based upon long oral traditions, as true scriptures. They are canonical or recognized by the relevant body of the faithful (the Church, the community, Brahmins and others in India, the Buddhist Sangha or Order). They are often treated as inspired directly by God or as records of the very words of the Founder. They have authority, and they contain many stories and myths which are taken to be divinely or otherwise guaranteed. But other documents and oral traditions may also be important—the lives of the saints, the chronicles of Ceylon as a Buddhist nation, the stories of famous holy men of Eastern Europe in the Hasidic tradition, traditions concerning the life of the Prophet (*ḥadīth*), and so forth. These stories may have lesser authority but they can still be inspiring to the followers.

Stories in religion are often tightly integrated into the ritual dimension. The Christian Mass or communion service, for instance, commemorates and presents the story of the Last Supper, when Jesus celebrated with his disciples his forthcoming fate, by which (according to Christians) he saved humankind and brought us back into harmony with the Divine Being. The Jewish Passover ceremonies commemorate and make real to us the events of the Exodus from Egypt, the sufferings of the people, and their relationship to the Lord who led them out of servitude in ancient Egypt. As Jews share the meal, so they retrace the story. Ritual and story are bound together.

THE DOCTRINAL AND PHILOSOPHICAL DIMENSION

Underpinning the narrative dimension is the *doctrinal* dimension. Thus, in the Christian tradition, the story of Jesus' life and the ritual of the communion service led to attempts to provide an analysis of the nature of the Divine Being which would preserve both the idea of the Incarnation (Jesus as God) and the belief in one God. The result was the doctrine of the Trinity, which sees God as three persons in one substance. Similarly, with the meeting between early Christianity and the great Graeco-Roman philosophical and intellectual heritage it became necessary to face questions about the ultimate meaning of creation, the inner nature of God, the notion of grace, the analysis of how Christ could be both God and human being, and so on. These concerns led to the elaboration of Christian doctrine. In the case of Buddhism, to take

another example, doctrinal ideas were more crucial right from the start, for the Buddha himself presented a philosophical vision of the world which itself was an aid to salvation.

In any event, doctrines come to play a significant part in all the major religions, partly because sooner or later a faith has to adapt to social reality and so to the fact that much of the leadership is well educated and seeks some kind of intellectual statement of the basis of the faith.

It happens that histories of religion have tended to exaggerate the importance of scriptures and doctrines; and this is not too surprising since so much of our knowledge of past religions must come from the documents which have been passed on by the scholarly elite. Also, and especially in the case of Christianity, doctrinal disputes have often been the overt expression of splits within the fabric of the community at large, so that frequently histories of a faith concentrate upon these hot issues. This is clearly unbalanced; but I would not want us to go to the other extreme. There are scholars today who have been much impressed with the symbolic and psychological force of myth, and have tended to neglect the essential intellectual component of religion.

THE ETHICAL AND LEGAL DIMENSION

Both narrative and doctrine affect the values of a tradition by laying out the shape of a worldview and addressing the question of ultimate liberation or salvation. The law which a tradition or subtradition incorporates into its fabric can be called the *ethical* dimension of religion. In Buddhism for instance there are certain universally binding precepts, known as the five precepts or virtues, together with a set of further regulations controlling the lives of monks and nuns and monastic communities. In Judaism we have not merely the ten commandments but a complex of over six hundred rules imposed upon the community by the Divine Being. All this Law or Torah is a framework for living for the Orthodox Jew. It also is part of the ritual dimension, because, for instance, the injunction to keep the Sabbath as a day of rest is also the injunction to perform certain sacred practices and rituals, such as attending the synagogue and maintaining purity.

Similarly, Islamic life has traditionally been controlled by the Law or *Sharī'a,* which shapes society both as a religious and a political society, as well as the moral life of the individual—prescribing that he should pray daily, give alms to the poor, and so on, and that society should have various institutions, such as marriage, modes of banking, etc.

Other traditions can be less tied to a system of law, but still display an ethic which is influenced and indeed controlled by the myth and doctrine of the faith. For instance, the central ethical attitude in the Christian faith is love. This springs not just from Jesus' injunction to his followers to love God and their neighbors: it also flows from the story of Christ himself who gave his life out of love for his fellow human beings. It also is rooted in the very idea of the Trinity, for God from all eternity is a society of three persons, Father, Son and Holy Spirit, kept together by the bond of love. The Christian joins a community which reflects, it is hoped at any rate, the life of the Divine Being, both as Trinity and as suffering servant of the human race and indeed of all creation.

THE SOCIAL AND INSTITUTIONAL DIMENSION

The dimensions outlined so far—the experiential, the ritual, the mythic, the doctrinal, and the ethical—can be considered in abstract terms, without being embodied in external form. The last two dimensions have to do with the incarnation of religion. First, every religious movement is embodied in a group of people, and that is very often rather formally organized—as Church, or Sangha, or *umma.* The sixth dimension therefore is what may be called the *social* or *institutional* aspect of religion. To understand a faith we need to see how it works among people. This is one reason why such an important tool of the investigator of religion is that subdiscipline which is known as the sociology of religion. Sometimes

the social aspect of a worldview is simply identical with society itself, as in small-scale groups such as tribes. But there is a variety of relations between organized religions and society at large: a faith may be the official religion, or it may be just one denomination among many, or it may be somewhat cut off from social life, as a sect. Within the organization of one religion, moreover, there are many models—from the relative democratic governance of a radical Protestant congregation to the hierarchical and monarchical system of the Church of Rome.

It is not however the formal officials of a religion who may in the long run turn out to be the most important persons in a tradition. For there are charismatic or sacred personages, whose spiritual power glows through their demeanor and actions, and who vivify the faith of more ordinary folk—saintly people, gurus, mystics and prophets, whose words and example stir up the spiritual enthusiasm of the masses, and who lend depth and meaning to the rituals and values of a tradition. They can also be revolutionaries and set religion on new courses. They can, like John Wesley, become leaders of a new denomination, almost against their will; or they can be founders of new groups which may in due course emerge as separate religions—an example is Joseph Smith II, Prophet of the new faith of Mormonism. In short, the social dimension of religion includes not only the mass of persons but also the outstanding individuals through whose features glimmer old and new thoughts of the heaven towards which they aspire.

THE MATERIAL DIMENSION

This social or institutional dimension of religion almost inevitably becomes incarnate in a different way, in *material* form, as buildings, works of art, and other creations. Some movements—such as Calvinist Christianity, especially in the time before the present century—eschew external symbols as being potentially idolatrous; their buildings are often beautiful in their simplicity, but their intention is to be without artistic or other images which might seduce people from the thought that

God is a spirit who transcends all representations. However, the material expressions of religion are more often elaborate, moving, and highly important for believers in their approach to the divine. How indeed could we understand Eastern Orthodox Christianity without seeing what ikons are like and knowing that they are regarded as windows onto heaven? How could we get inside the feel of Hinduism without attending to the varied statues of God and the gods?

Also important material expressions of a religion are those natural features of the world which are singled out as being of special sacredness and meaning—the river Ganges, the Jordan, the sacred mountains of China, Mount Fuji in Japan, Eyre's Rock in Australia, the Mount of Olives, Mount Sinai, and so forth. Sometimes of course these sacred landmarks combine with more direct human creations, such as the holy city of Jerusalem, the sacred shrines of Banaras, or the temple at Bodh Gaya which commemorates the Buddha's Enlightenment.

USES OF THE SEVEN DIMENSIONS

To sum up: we have surveyed briefly the seven dimensions of religion which help to characterize religions as they exist in the world. The point of the list is so that we can give a balanced description of the movements which have animated the human spirit and taken a place in the shaping of society, without neglecting either ideas or practices.

Naturally, there are religious movements or manifestations where one or other of the dimensions is so weak as to be virtually absent: nonliterate small-scale societies do not have much means of expressing the doctrinal dimension; Buddhist modernists, concentrating on meditation, ethics and philosophy, pay scant regard to the narrative dimension of Buddhism; some newly formed groups may not have evolved anything much in the way of the material dimension. Also there are so many people who are not formally part of any social religious grouping, but have their own particular worldviews and practices, that we can observe in society atoms of religion which do not possess any well-formed social dimension. But of course in forming a phenomenon within society they reflect certain trends which in a sense form a shadow of the social dimension (just as those who have not yet got themselves a material dimension are nevertheless implicitly storing one up, for with success come buildings and with rituals ikons, most likely).

If our seven-dimensional portrait of religions is adequate, then we do not need to worry greatly about further definition of religion. In any case, I shall now turn to a most vital question in understanding the way the world works, namely to the relation between more or less overtly religious systems and those which are commonly called secular: ideologies or worldviews such as scientific humanism, Marxism, Existentialism, nationalism, and so on. In examining these worldviews we shall take on some of the discussion about what count as religious questions and themes. It is useful to begin by thinking out whether our seven-dimensional analysis can apply successfully to such secular worldviews.

The Nature of Secular Worldviews

NATIONALISM

Although nationalism is not strictly speaking a single worldview or even in itself a complete worldview, it is convenient to begin with it. One reason is that it has been such a powerful force in human affairs. Virtually all the land surface of the globe, together with parts of the world's water surface, is now carved up between sovereign states. Nationalism has given shape decisively to the modern world, because its popularity in part stems from the way in which assembling peoples into states has helped with the processes of industrialization and modern bureaucratic organization. Countries such as Britain, France, the United States, Germany, and Italy pioneered the industrial revolution, and the system of national governments spread from Western to Eastern Europe after World War I and from Europe to Asia, Africa, and elsewhere after World War II. Ethnic identity was sometimes demarcated by language and therefore cultural heritage, sometimes by religion, sometimes both, and sometimes simply by shared history. Examples of each of these categories can be seen in the cases of Germany (shared language), the two parts of Ireland (distinctive religion), Poland (both distinctive language and religion), and Singapore (shared history of Chinese, Malay, and other linguistic groups). Colonialism often helped to spread nationalism by reaction: the British conquest of India fostered an Indian nationalism, and there are signs of national awakening in parts of the Soviet Union, once colonized by Tsarist Russia, and in Tibet, conquered by China.

The nation-state has many of the appurtenances of a religion. First of all (to use the order in which we expounded the dimensions of religion in the previous section), there are the *rituals* of nationhood: speaking the language itself; the national anthem; the flying and perhaps saluting of the flag; republic and memorial days, and other such festivals and holidays; the appearance of the Head of State at solemn occasions; military march-pasts; and so on. It is usual for citizens to make secular pilgrimages to the nation's capital and other significant spots—Washington (the Lincoln Memorial, the Vietnam Memorial, the White House, and so on); Plymouth Rock; Mount Rushmore; natural beauties exhibiting "America the Beautiful." Memorials to the nation's dead are of special significance, and often religious language is used about the sacrifices of the young on the altar of national duty.

The experiential or *emotional* side of nationalism is indeed powerful—for the sentiments of patriotism, pride in the nation, love of its beauties and powers, and dedication to national goals, can be very strong. Especially in times of national crisis, such as war, such sentiments rise to the surface. But they are reinforced all the time by such practices as singing the national anthem and other patriotic songs.

The *narrative* dimension of nationalism is easily seen, for it lies in the history of the nation, which is taught in the schools of the country, and which in some degree celebrates the values of the great men and women of the nation—for Italians, such great forebears as Julius Caesar (Giulio

Cesare), Dante, Galileo, Leonardo, Garibaldi, Cavour, Verdi, Leopardi, Alcide de Gasperi and others. History is the narrative that helps to create in the young and in citizens at large a sense of identity, of belonging, of group solidarity.

Of *doctrines* nationalism is somewhat bereft, unless you count the doctrine of self-determination. But often, too, nations appeal to principles animating the modern state, such as the need for democracy and the rights of the individual in a freedom-loving nation, etc.; or a nation may appeal to the doctrine of a full-blown secular ideology, such as Marxism. Or it may hark back to the teachings of its ancestral religion, and so represent itself as guarding the truths and values of Christianity, or of Buddhism, or of a revived and revolutionary Islam.

The *ethical* dimension of nationalism consists in those values which are inculcated into citizens. Young people are expected to be loyal people, taxpayers, willing to fight if necessary for the country, law-abiding, and hopefully good family people (supplying thus the nation with its population). There is of course a blend between ethical values in general and the particular obligations to one's own kith and kin, one's fellow-nationals.

The *social* and *institutional* aspect of the nation-state is of course easily discerned. It culminates in a head of state who has extensive ceremonial functions—especially with monarchy, as in Britain, where the Queen is an important ritual object—and on whom sentiments of patriotism also focus. The state has its military services which also perform ceremonial as well as fighting tasks. There are the public schools, with the teachers imparting the treasured knowledge and rules of the nation. Even games come to play an institutional role; loyalty is expressed through Olympics and various other contests, and the ethos of the athlete comes to be blended with that of the ideal citizen. In some countries loyalty to religion or to a secular ideology blends with loyalty to one's nation, and those who do not subscribe to it are treated as disloyal. State occasions are shown on television, which itself comes to have a role in transmitting and focusing the values of the nation.

Finally, there is of course much *material* embodiment of the nation in its great buildings and memorials, its flag, its great art, its sacred land, its powerful military hardware.

In all these ways, then, the nation today is like a religion. If you have a relative who has died for a cause, it is not like the old days when he might have died for his religion, maybe at the stake; now he is most likely to have died for his country.

It is, then, reasonable to treat modern nationalism in the same terms as religion. It represents a set of values often allied with a kind of modernism, which is natural to the thinking of many of our contemporaries, and which stresses certain essentially modern concerns: the importance of economic development; the merits of technology; the wonders of science; the importance of either socialism or capitalism, or some mixture, in the process of modernization; the need for the state to look after the welfare of its citizens; the importance of universal education; and so on.

There are some growing limitations on nationalism: the fact that in many countries which were once reasonably homogeneous there are now increasing ethnic mixes, the growth of transnational corporations, the developing economic interdependence of nations, the impossibility of older ways of conceiving sovereignty in the context of modern warfare, and so on. But nevertheless, nationalism remains a very strong and alluring ingredient in the world, and many of the trouble spots are so because of unfulfilled ethnic expectations and ethnic rivalries—in Cyprus, Northern Ireland, Israel and Palestine, South Africa, Sri Lanka, Kurdistan, Afghanistan, and elsewhere.

THE DIMENSIONS OF MARXISM

It is because Marxism has itself become more than a movement of ideas but has become embodied in many states that its analysis too needs to follow the general outlines I have sketched. It has a coherent set of *doctrines,* modified variously by leaders such as Stalin, Mao, Hoxha and Ceauşescu; it has a *mythic* dimension in the analysis of historical events in accordance with the principles of the dialectic (so that then the history of

the Russian Revolution or the German Democratic Republic gets fitted into a more general salvation-history of the human race). Its *rituals* combine with those of nationalism but have their own symbolisms, such as the widespread use of the color red, the adoption of festivals such as May Day and the anniversary of the October Revolution, the adulation of the Party leader, etc. The *emotions* it encourages are those of patriotism, internationalism, and revolutionary commitment; its *ethics* those of solidarity; its *institutions* those of the Party; and its *artistic* style is that of socialist realism, which glorifies the ideals of the Party, state, and country, with more than a hint of that pietism which can characterize religious painting. Its music is heroic and rousing. State Marxism, then, has a distinctly religious-type function, and moves men by theory, symbols, rituals, and Party energy. Like many religions it may not ultimately prove to be successful, for the people may not be inwardly and deeply moved by the embodied values of Marxism as an ideology: indeed much evidence shows the hollowness of Marxism in a number of Eastern European countries, and even in the Soviet Union. It is always faced with the struggle against local patriotisms, against religions, against the humanist desire for freedom of enquiry, and so on.

Some other secular worldviews are less clearly like traditional religions in so far as they tend not to wield the symbols of power: for instance, scientific humanism, which is influential in one form or another among many intellectuals in the West, and which in rather inarticulate form expresses something of the worldview of ordinary folk in secularized circumstances. It holds to human and democratic values, and it stresses science as the source of knowledge. It repudiates the doctrines of religion, especially of Jewish and Christian theism. It sees human individuals as of ultimate value. But it does not, as I have said, embody itself in a rich way as a religious-type system. Its *rituals* are slight, beyond those which reinforce other aspects of modernity. Perhaps the modern passion for games and sports is one sign of a kind of persistence of interest in activities pursued according to ritual rules. Its *myths* are not extensive, beyond a feel for the clash between science and religion during the modern period from Galileo Galilei (1564–1642) onwards. Its *doctrines* can be complex, especially in the formulations of contemporary humanistic (analytical and linguistic) philosophy. Its profoundest *experiences* are maybe those of culture, such as music and the arts. Its *ethics* are generally speaking those of utilitarianism, which sees morality as maximizing happiness and minimizing suffering. Its *institutions* are found in secular education. Its *material* symbols are perhaps the sky-scraper and the stadium. But it is hard to disentangle its manifestations from many other aspects of modern living.

Though to a greater or lesser extent our seven-dimensional model may apply to secular world-views, it is not really appropriate to try to call them religions, or even "quasi-religions" (which by implication demotes them below the status of "real" religions). For the adherents of Marxism and humanism wish to be demarcated strictly from those who espouse religions—they conceive of themselves, on the whole, as antireligious. However, we have seen enough of the seven-dimensional character of the secular worldviews (especially nationalism and state Marxism) to emphasize that the various systems of ideas and practices, whether religious or not, are competitors and mutual blenders, and can thus be said to play in the same league. They all help to express the various ways in which human beings conceive of themselves, and act in the world.

1.2 Religion as a Cultural System

Some definitions of religion focus on what religion *is,* its so-called essence or substance. However useful this approach may be, many social scientists have found it more empirically useful to focus on what religion *does* or how it functions. What does religion do to and for people? How does it function in society and culture?

In the next selection, Clifford Geertz, a distinguished and influential anthropologist, describes how he believes religion functions. His definition has been widely influential, in part because he conceives of religion as a system of symbols. People are symbol makers. They do not just live in the world. They interpret that world, and they give it meaning by symbolically representing it.

All definitions make certain assumptions. One might, for example, assume that the object of religious worship is real and, accordingly, define religious symbols as representations of that reality. Or one might assume that the object of religious worship is not real and thus define religious symbols as misleading attempts to represent as real that which is not. The question of the reality represented by religious symbols is an important philosophical issue, and we shall be dealing with it later. For now, let us simply note that because it does not seem possible to settle the issue of the truth of religious symbolic references on scientific grounds, many sociologists, psychologists, and anthropologists find it congenial to their methods (and what they take to be the limits of those methods) to focus on the human use of symbols instead. Hence Geertz seeks to uncover the ways in which religious symbols *work* to *persuade* people of the reality and factuality of that to which the symbols appear to refer.

Reading Questions

1. What does Geertz mean by "a system of symbols"?
2. What is the main difference between moods and motivations, and how are they related to a symbol system?

3. What does Geertz mean by a "general order of existence," and how is this related to the three limit situations he describes?
4. How does the religious perspective differ from the common-sense perspective, the scientific perspective, and the aesthetic perspective?
5. Is Geertz's definition too broad? Would it apply to things we do not normally call religion? Can you give an example?

Religion as a Cultural System*

CLIFFORD GEERTZ

As WE ARE TO DEAL with meaning, let us begin with a paradigm: viz. that sacred symbols function to synthesize a people's ethos—the tone, character, and quality of their life, its moral and aesthetic style and mood—and their world-view—the picture they have of the way things in sheer actuality are, their most comprehensive ideas of order (Geertz, 1958). In religious belief and practice a group's ethos is rendered intellectually reasonable by being shown to represent a way of life ideally adapted to the actual state of affairs the world-view describes, while the world-view is rendered emotionally convincing by being presented as an image of an actual state of affairs peculiarly well arranged to accommodate such a way of life. This confrontation and mutual confirmation has two fundamental effects. On the one hand, it objectivizes moral and aesthetic preferences by depicting them as the imposed conditions of life implicit in a world with a particular structure, as mere common sense given the unalterable shape of reality. On the other, it supports these received beliefs about the world's body by invoking deeply felt moral and aesthetic sentiments as experiential evidence for their truth. Religious symbols formulate a basic congruence between a particular style of life and a specific (if, most often, implicit) metaphysic, and in so doing sustain each with the borrowed authority of the other.

Phrasing aside, this much may perhaps be granted. The notion that religion tunes human actions to an envisaged cosmic order and projects images of cosmic order onto the plane of human experience is hardly novel. But it is hardly investigated either, so that we have very little idea of how, in empirical terms, this particular miracle is accomplished. We just know that it is done, annually, weekly, daily, for some people almost hourly; and we have an enormous ethnographic literature to demonstrate it. But the theoretical framework which would enable us to provide an analytic account of it, an account of the sort we can provide for lineage segmentation, political succession, labor exchange, or the socialization of the child, does not exist.

Let us, therefore, reduce our paradigm to a definition, for, although it is notorious that definitions establish nothing, in themselves they do, if they are carefully enough constructed, provide a useful orientation, or reorientation, of thought, such that an extended unpacking of them can be an effective way of developing and controlling a novel line of inquiry. They have the useful virtue of explicitness: they commit themselves in a way

---

*From *Anthropological Approaches to the Study of Religion*, edited by Michael Banton. Copyright © 1966 by Association of Social Anthropologists of the Commonwealth. Reprinted by permission of Routledge. Footnotes deleted.

discursive prose, which, in this field especially, is always liable to substitute rhetoric for argument, does not. Without further ado, then, a *religion* is:

(1) a system of symbols which acts to (2) establish powerful, pervasive, and long-lasting moods and motivations in men by (3) formulating conceptions of a general order of existence and (4) clothing these conceptions with such an aura of factuality that (5) the moods and motivations seem uniquely realistic.

1. *a system of symbols which acts to . . .*

Such a tremendous weight is being put on the term "symbol" here that our first move must be to decide with some precision what we are going to mean by it. This is no easy task, for, rather like "culture," "symbol" has been used to refer to a great variety of things, often a number of them at the same time. . . .

So far as culture patterns, i.e. systems or complexes of symbols, are concerned, the generic trait which is of first importance for us here is that they are extrinsic sources of information (Geertz, 1964a). By "extrinsic," I mean only that—unlike genes, for example—they lie outside the boundaries of the individual organism as such in that intersubjective world of common understandings into which all human individuals are born, in which they pursue their separate careers, and which they leave persisting behind them after they die (Schutz, 1962). By "sources of information," I mean only that—like genes—they provide a blueprint or template in terms of which processes external to themselves can be given a definite form (Horowitz, 1956). As the order of bases in a strand of DNA forms a coded program, a set of instructions, or a recipe, for the synthesization of the structurally complex proteins which shape organic functioning, so culture patterns provide such programs for the institution of the social and psychological processes which shape public behavior. Though the sort of information and the mode of its transmission are vastly different in the two cases, this comparison of gene and symbol is more than a strained analogy of the familiar "social heredity" sort. It is ac-

tually a substantial relationship, for it is precisely the fact that genetically programmed processes are so highly generalized in men, as compared with lower animals, that culturally programmed ones are so important, only because human behavior is so loosely determined by intrinsic sources of information that extrinsic sources are so vital (Geertz, 1962). To build a dam a beaver needs only an appropriate site and the proper materials—his mode of procedure is shaped by his physiology. But man, whose genes are silent on the building trades, needs also a conception of what it is to build a dam, a conception he can get only from some symbolic source—a blueprint, a textbook, or a string of speech by someone who already knows how dams are built, or, of course, from manipulating graphic or linguistic elements in such a way as to attain for himself a conception of what dams are and how they are built. . . .

2. *. . . to establish powerful, pervasive, and long-lasting moods and motivations in men by . . .*

So far as religious activities are concerned . . ., two somewhat different sorts of disposition are induced by them: moods and motivations.

The major difference between moods and motivations is that where the latter are, so to speak, vectorial qualities, the former are merely scalar. Motives have a directional cast, they describe a certain overall course, gravitate toward certain, usually temporary, consummations. But moods vary only as to intensity: they go nowhere. They spring from certain circumstances but they are responsive to no ends. Like fogs, they just settle and lift; like scents, suffuse and evaporate. When present they are totalistic: if one is sad everything and everybody seems dreary; if one is gay, everything and everybody seems splendid. Thus, though a man can be vain, brave, willful and independent at the same time, he can't very well be playful and listless, or exultant and melancholy, at the same time (Ryle, 1949, p. 99). Further, where motives persist for more or less extended periods of time, moods merely recur with greater or lesser frequency, coming and going for what are often quite unfathomable reasons. But perhaps the most important difference, so far as we are concerned, between moods and motivations is that motivations are "made meaningful" with reference to the ends toward which they are conceived to conduce, whereas moods are "made meaningful" with reference to the conditions from which they are conceived to spring. We interpret motives in terms of their consummations, but we interpret moods in terms of their sources. We say that a person is industrious because he wishes to succeed, we say that a person is worried because he is conscious of the hanging threat of nuclear holocaust. And this is no less the case when the interpretations invoked are ultimate. Charity becomes Christian charity when it is enclosed in a conception of God's purposes; optimism is Christian optimism when it is grounded in a particular conception of God's nature. The assiduity of the Navaho finds its rationale in a belief that, since "reality" operates mechanically, it is coercible; their chronic fearfulness finds its rationale in a conviction that, however "reality" operates, it is both enormously powerful and terribly dangerous.

3. . . . *by formulating conceptions of a general order of existence and . . .*

That the symbols or symbol systems which induce and define dispositions we set off as religious and those which place those dispositions in a cosmic framework are the same symbols ought to occasion no surprise. For what else do we mean by saying that a particular mood of awe is religious and not secular except that it springs from entertaining a conception of all-pervading vitality like mana and not from a visit to the Grand Canyon? Or that a particular case of asceticism is an example of a religious motivation except that it is directed toward the achievement of an unconditioned end like nirvana and not a conditioned one like weight-reduction? If sacred symbols did not at one and the same time induce dispositions in human beings and formulate, however obliquely, inarticulately, or unsystematically, general ideas of order, then the empirical

differentia of religious activity or religious experience would not exist. A man can indeed be said to be "religious" about golf, but not merely if he pursues it with passion and plays it on Sundays: he must also see it as symbolic of some transcendent truths. And the pubescent boy gazing soulfully into the eyes of the pubescent girl in a William Steig cartoon and murmuring, "There is something about you, Ethel, which gives me a sort of religious feeling", is, like most adolescents, confused. What any particular religion affirms about the fundamental nature of reality may be obscure, shallow, or, all too often, perverse, but it must, if it is not to consist of the mere collection of received practices and conventional sentiments we usually refer to as moralism, affirm something. If one were to essay a minimal definition of religion today it would perhaps not be Tylor's famous "belief in spiritual beings," to which Goody (1961), wearied of theoretical subtleties, has lately urged us to return, but rather what Salvador de Madariaga has called "the relatively modest dogma that God is not mad."

Usually, of course, religions affirm very much more than this: we believe, as James (1904, Vol. 2, p. 299) remarked, all that we can and would believe everything if we only could. The thing we seem least able to tolerate is a threat to our powers of conception, a suggestion that our ability to create, grasp, and use symbols may fail us, for were this to happen we would be more helpless, as I have already pointed out, than the beavers. The extreme generality, diffuseness, and variability of man's innate (i.e. genetically programmed) response capacities means that without the assistance of cultural patterns he would be functionally incomplete, not merely a talented ape who had, like some under-privileged child, unfortunately been prevented from realizing his full potentialities, but a kind of formless monster with neither sense of direction nor power of self-control, a chaos of spasmodic impulses and vague emotions (Geertz, 1962). Man depends upon symbols and symbol systems with a dependence so great as to be decisive for his creatural viability and, as a result, his sensitivity to even the remotest indication that they may prove unable to cope with one or another aspect of experience raises within him the gravest sort of anxiety . . .

There are at least three points where chaos—a tumult of events which lack not just interpretations but *interpretability*—threatens to break in upon man: at the limits of his analytic capacities, at the limits of his powers of endurance, and at the limits of his moral insight. Bafflement, suffering, and a sense of intractable ethical paradox are all, if they become intense enough or are sustained long enough, radical challenges to the proposition that life is comprehensible and that we can, by taking thought, orient ourselves effectively within it—challenges with which any religion, however "primitive," which hopes to persist must attempt somehow to cope.

Of the three issues, it is the first which has been least investigated by modern social anthropologists (though Evans-Pritchard's (1937) classic discussion of why granaries fall on some Azande and not on others, is a notable exception). Even to consider people's religious beliefs as attempts to bring anomalous events or experiences—death, dreams, mental fugues, volcanic eruptions, or marital infidelity—within the circle of the at least potentially explicable seems to smack of Tyloreanism or worse. But it does appear to be a fact that at least some men—in all probability, most men—are unable to leave unclarified problems of analysis merely unclarified, just to look at the stranger features of the world's landscape in dumb astonishment or bland apathy without trying to develop, however fantastic, inconsistent, or simple-minded, some notions as to how such features might be reconciled with the more ordinary deliverances of experience. Any chronic failure of one's explanatory apparatus, the complex of received culture patterns (common sense, science, philosophical speculation, myth) one has for mapping the empirical world, to explain things which cry out for explanation tends to lead to a deep disquiet—a tendency rather more widespread and a disquiet rather deeper than we have sometimes supposed since the pseudo-science view of religious belief

was, quite rightfully, deposed. After all, even that high priest of heroic atheism, Lord Russell, once remarked that although the problem of the existence of God had never bothered him, the ambiguity of certain mathematical axioms had threatened to unhinge his mind. And Einstein's profound dissatisfaction with quantum mechanics was based on a—surely religious—inability to believe that, as he put it, God plays dice with the universe.

But this quest for lucidity and the rush of metaphysical anxiety that occurs when empirical phenomena threaten to remain intransigently opaque is found on much humbler intellectual levels. Certainly, I was struck in my own work, much more than I had at all expected to be, by the degree to which my more animistically inclined informants behaved like true Tyloreans. They seemed to be constantly using their beliefs to "explain" phenomena: or, more accurately, to convince themselves that the phenomena were explainable within the accepted scheme of things, for they commonly had only a minimal attachment to the particular soul possession, emotional disequilibrium, taboo infringement, or bewitchment hypothesis they advanced and were all too ready to abandon it for some other, in the same genre, which struck them as more plausible given the facts of the case. What they were *not* ready to do was abandon it for no other hypothesis at all; to leave events to themselves. . . .

The second experiential challenge in whose face the meaningfulness of a particular pattern of life threatens to dissolve into a chaos of thingless names and nameless things—the problem of suffering—has been rather more investigated, or at least described, mainly because of the great amount of attention given in works on tribal religion to what are perhaps its two main loci: illness and mourning. Yet for all the fascinated interest in the emotional aura that surrounds these extreme situations, there has been, with a few exceptions such as Lienhardt's recent (1961, pp. 151ff) discussion of Dinka divining, little conceptual advance over the sort of crude confidence-type theory set forth by Malinowski: viz. that religion helps one to endure "situations of emotional stress" by "open[ing] up escapes from such situations and such impasses as offer no empirical way out except by ritual and belief into the domain of the supernatural" (1948, p. 67). The inadequacy of this "theology of optimism," as Nadel (1957), rather drily called it, is, of course, radical. Over its career religion has probably disturbed men as much as it has cheered them; forced them into a head-on, unblinking confrontation of the fact that they are born to trouble as often as it has enabled them to avoid such a confrontation by projecting them into sort of infantile fairy-tale world where—Malinowski again (1948, p. 67)—"hope cannot fail nor desire deceive." With the possible exception of Christian Science, there are few if any religious traditions, "great" or "little," in which the proposition that life hurts is not strenuously affirmed and in some it is virtually glorified . . .

As a religious problem, the problem of suffering is, paradoxically, not how to avoid suffering but how to suffer, how to make of physical pain, personal loss, worldly defeat, or the helpless contemplation of others' agony something bearable, supportable—something, as we say, sufferable. . . .

The problem of suffering passes easily into the problem of evil, for if suffering is severe enough it usually, though not always, seems morally undeserved as well, at least to the sufferer. But they are not, however, exactly the same thing—a fact I think Weber, too influenced by the biases of a monotheistic tradition in which, as the various aspects of human experience must be conceived to proceed from a single, voluntaristic source, man's pain reflects directly on God's goodness, did not fully recognize in his generalization of the dilemmas of Christian theodicy Eastward. For where the problem of suffering is concerned with threats to our ability to put our "undisciplined squads of emotion" into some sort of soldierly order, the problem of evil is concerned with threats to our ability to make sound moral judgements. What is involved in the problem of evil is not the adequacy of our symbolic resources to govern our affective life, but the adequacy of those resources to provide a workable

set of ethical criteria, normative guides to govern our action. The vexation here is the gap between things as they are and as they ought to be if our conceptions of right and wrong make sense, the gap between what we deem various individuals deserve and what we see that they get—a phenomenon summed up in that profound quatrain:

> The rain falls on the just
> And on the unjust fella;
> But mainly upon the just,
> Because the unjust has the just's umbrella.

Or if this seems too flippant an expression of an issue that, in somewhat different form, animates the Book of Job and the *Baghavad Gita,* the following classical Javanese poem, known, sung, and repeatedly quoted in Java by virtually everyone over the age of six, puts the point—the discrepancy between moral prescriptions and material rewards, the seeming inconsistency of "is" and "ought"—rather more elegantly:

> We have lived to see a time without order
> In which everyone is confused in his mind.
> One cannot bear to join in the madness,
> But if he does not do so
> He will not share in the spoils,
> And will starve as a result.
> Yes, God; wrong is wrong:
> Happy are those who forget,
> Happier yet those who remember and
>   have deep insight.

Thus the problem of evil, or perhaps one should say the problem *about* evil, is in essence the same sort of problem of or about bafflement and the problem of or about suffering. The strange opacity of certain empirical events, the dumb senselessness of intense or inexorable pain, and the enigmatic unaccountability of gross iniquity all raise the uncomfortable suspicion that perhaps the world, and hence man's life in the world, has no genuine order at all—no empirical regularity, no emotional form, no moral coherence. And the religious response to this suspicion is in each case the same: the formulation, by means of symbols, of an image of such a genuine order of the world which will account for, and even celebrate, the perceived ambiguities, puzzles, and paradoxes in human experience. The effort is not to deny the undeniable—that there are unexplained events, that life hurts, or that rain falls upon the just—but to deny that there are inexplicable events, that life is unendurable, and that justice is a mirage. The principles which constitute the moral order may indeed often elude men, as Lienhardt puts it, in the same way as fully satisfactory explanations of anomalous events or effective forms for the expression of feeling often elude them. What is important, to a religious man at least, is that this elusiveness be accounted for, that it be not the result of the fact that there are no such principles, explanations, or forms, that life is absurd and the attempt to make moral, intellectual or emotional sense out of experience is bootless. . . .

4. . . . and clothing those conceptions with such an aura of factuality that . . .

There arises here, however, a profounder question: how is it that this denial comes to be believed? how is it that the religious man moves from a troubled perception of experienced disorder to a more or less settled conviction of fundamental order? just what does "belief" mean in a religious context? . . .

In tribal religions authority lies in the persuasive power of traditional imagery; in mystical ones in the apodictic force of supersensible experience; in charismatic ones in the hypnotic attraction of an extraordinary personality. But the priority of the acceptance of an authoritative criterion in religious matters over the revelation which is conceived to flow from that acceptance is not less complete than in scriptural or hieratic ones. The basic axiom underlying what we may perhaps call "the religious perspective" is everywhere the same: he who would know must first believe.

But to speak of "the religious perspective" is, by implication, to speak of one perspective among others. A perspective is a mode of seeing, in that extended sense of "see" in which it means "discern," "apprehend," "understand," or "grasp." It is a particular way of looking at life, a particular manner of construing the world, as when we speak of an historical perspective, a scientific perspective, an aesthetic perspective, a common-sense perspective, or even the bizarre perspective embodied in dreams and in hallucinations. The question then comes down to, first, what is "the religious perspective" generically considered, as differentiated from other perspectives; and second, how do men come to adopt it.

If we place the religious perspective against the background of three of the other major perspectives in terms of which men construe the world—the common-sensical, the scientific, and the aesthetic—its special character emerges more sharply. What distinguishes common sense as a mode of "seeing" is, . . . a simple acceptance of the world, its objects, and its processes as being just what they seem to be—what is sometimes called naive realism—and the pragmatic motive, the wish to act upon that world so as to bend it to one's practical purposes, to master it, or so far as that proves impossible, to adjust to it. The world of everyday life, itself, of course, a cultural product, for it is framed in terms of the symbolic conceptions of "stubborn fact" handed down from generation to generation, is the established scene and given object of our actions. Like Mt. Everest it is just there and the thing to do with it, if one feels the need to do anything with it at all, is to climb it. In the scientific perspective it is precisely this givenness which disappears. . . . Deliberate doubt and systematic inquiry, the suspension of the pragmatic motive in favor of disinterested observation, the attempt to analyze the world in terms of formal concepts whose relationship to the informal conceptions of common sense become increasingly problematic—there are the hallmarks of the attempt to grasp the world scientifically. And as for the aesthetic perspective, which under the rubric of "the aesthetic attitude" has been perhaps most exquisitely examined, it involves a different sort of suspension of naive realism and practical interest, in that instead of questioning the credentials of everyday experience that experience is merely ignored in favor of an eager dwelling upon appearances, an engrossment in surfaces, an absorption in things, as we say, "in themselves": "The function of artistic illusion is not 'make-believe' . . . but the very opposite, disengagement from belief—the contemplation of sensory qualities without their usual meanings of 'here's that chair,' 'That's my telephone' . . . etc. The knowledge that what is before us has no practical significance in the world is what enables us to give attention to its appearance as such." And like the common-sensical and the scientific (or the historical, the philosophical, and the autistic), this perspective, this "way of seeing," is not the product of some mysterious Cartesian chemistry, but is induced, mediated, and in fact created by means of symbols. It is the artist's skill which can produce those curious quasi-objects—poems, dramas, sculptures, symphonies—which, dissociating themselves from the solid world of common sense, take on the special sort of eloquence only sheer appearances can achieve.

The religious perspective differs from the common-sensical in that, as already pointed out, it moves beyond the realities of everyday life to wider ones which correct and complete them, and its defining concern is not action upon those wider realities but acceptance of them, faith in them. It differs from the scientific perspective in that it questions the realities of everyday life not out of an institutionalized scepticism which dissolves the world's givenness into a swirl of probabilistic hypotheses, but in terms of what it takes to be wider, non-hypothetical truths. Rather than detachment, its watchword is commitment; rather than analysis, encounter. And it differs from art in that instead of effecting a disengagement from the whole question of factuality, deliberately manufacturing an air of semblance and illusion, it deepens the concern with fact and seeks to create an aura of utter actuality. It is this sense of the "really real" upon which the religious perspective rests and which the symbolic activities of religion as a cultural system are devoted to producing, intensifying, and, so far as possible, rendering inviolable by

the discordant revelations of secular experience. It is, again, the imbuing of a certain specific complex of symbols—of the metaphysic they formulate and the style of life they recommend—with a persuasive authority which, from an analytic point of view is the essence of religious action. . . .

5. . . . *that the moods and motivations seem uniquely realistic*

But no one, not even a saint, lives in the world religious symbols formulate all of the time, and the majority of men live in it only at moments. The everyday world of common-sense objects and practical acts is, as Schutz (1962, pp. 226ff.) says, the paramount reality in human experience—paramount in the sense that it is the world in which we are most solidly rooted, whose inherent actuality we can hardly question (however much we may question certain portions of it), and from whose pressures and requirements we can least escape. A man, even large groups of men, may be aesthetically insensitive, religiously unconcerned, and unequipped to pursue formal scientific analysis, but he cannot be completely lacking in common sense and survive. The dispositions which religious rituals induce thus have their most important impact—from a human point of view—outside the boundaries of the ritual itself as they reflect back to color the individual's conception of the established world of bare fact. The peculiar tone that marks the Plains vision quest, the Manus confession, or the Javanese mystical exercise pervades areas of the life of these peoples far beyond the immediately religious, impressing upon them a distinctive style in the sense both of a dominant mood and a characteristic movement. The interweaving of the malignant and the comic, which the Rangda-Barong combat depicts, animates a very wide range of everyday Balinese behavior, much of which, like the ritual itself, has an air of candid fear narrowly contained by obsessive playfulness. Religion is sociologically interesting not because, as vulgar positivism would have it, . . . it describes the social order (which, in so far as it does, by cultural gaps across which Kierkegaardian leaps must be made in both directions. . . . it does not only very obliquely but very incompletely), but because, like environment, political power, wealth, jural obligation, personal affection, and a sense of beauty, it shapes it.

The movement back and forth between the religious perspective and the common-sense perspective is actually one of the more obvious empirical occurrences on the social scene, though, again, one of the most neglected by social anthropologists, virtually all of whom have seen it happen countless times. Religious belief has usually been presented as an homogeneous characteristic of an individual, like his place of residence, his occupational role, his kinship position, and so on. But religious belief in the midst of ritual, where it engulfs the total person, transporting him, so far as he is concerned, into another mode of existence, and religious belief as the pale, remembered reflection of that experience in the midst of everyday life are not precisely the same thing, and the failure to realize this has led to some confusion, most especially in connection with the so-called "primitive mentality" problem. Much of the difficulty between Lévy-Bruhl (1926) and Malinowski (1948) on the nature of "native thought," for example, arises from a lack of full recognition of this distinction; for where the French philosopher was concerned with the view of reality savages adopted when taking a specifically religious perspective, the Polish-English ethnographer was concerned with that which they adopted when taking a strictly common-sense one. Both perhaps vaguely sensed that they were not talking about exactly the same thing, but where they went astray was in failing to give a specific accounting of the way in which these two forms of "thought"—or, as I would rather say, these two modes of symbolic formulation—interacted, so that where Lévy-Bruhl's savages tended to live, despite his postludial disclaimers, in a world composed entirely of mystical encounters, Malinowski's tended to live, despite his stress on the functional importance of religion, in a world composed entirely of practical actions. They became reductionists (an idealist is as much of a reductionist as a materialist) in spite of themselves because they failed to see man as moving more or less easily, and very frequently, between radically contrasting ways of looking at the world, ways which are not continuous with one another but separated. For an anthropologist, the importance of religion lies in its capacity to serve, for an individual or for a group, as a source of general, yet distinctive conceptions of the world, the self, and the relations between them, on the one hand—its model *of* aspect—and of rooted, no less distinctive "mental" dispositions—its model *for* aspect—on the other. From these cultural functions flow, in turn, its social and psychological ones.

Religious concepts spread beyond their specifically metaphysical contexts to provide a framework of general ideas in terms of which a wide range of experience—intellectual, emotional, moral—can be given meaningful form. The Christian sees the Nazi movement against the background of The Fall which, though it does not, in a causal sense, explain it, places it in a moral, a cognitive, even an affective sense. An Azande sees the collapse of a granary upon a friend or relative against the background of a concrete and rather special notion of witchcraft and thus avoids the philosophical dilemmas as well as the psychological stress of indeterminism. A Javanese finds in the borrowed and reworked concept of *rasa* ("sense-taste-feeling-meaning") a means by which to "see" choreographic, gustatory, emotional, and political phenomena in a new light. A synopsis of cosmic order, a set of religious beliefs, is also a gloss upon the mundane world of social relationships and psychological events. It renders them graspable.

But more than gloss, such beliefs are also a template. They do not merely interpret social and psychological processes in cosmic terms—in which case they would be philosophical, not religious—but they shape them. In the doctrine of original sin is embedded also a recommended attitude toward life, a recurring mood, and a persisting set of motivations. The Zande learns from witchcraft conceptions not just to understand apparent "accidents" as not accidents at all, but to react to these spurious accidents with hatred for the agent who caused them and to proceed against him with appropriate resolution. *Rasa,* in addition to being a concept of truth, beauty, and goodness, is also a preferred mode of experiencing, a kind of affectless detachment, a variety of bland aloofness, an unshakeable calm. The moods and motivations a religious orientation produces cast a derivative, lunar light over the solid features of a people's secular life.

The tracing of the social and psychological role of religion is thus not so much a matter of finding correlations between specific ritual acts and specific secular social ties—though these correlations do, of course, exist and are very worth continued investigation, especially if we can contrive something novel to say about them. More, it is a matter of understanding how it is that men's notions, however implicit, of the "really real" and the dispositions these notions induce in them, color their sense of the reasonable, the practical, the humane, and the moral. . . .

1.3 The Search for Family Resemblances of Religion

Since Aristotle and before, many philosophers have assumed that the goal of any good definition is to state the essence of the thing being defined. Accordingly, we might ask what are the necessary and sufficient characteristics that something must have before we can call it religion? Of course, some characteristics (such as belief in a god or gods) might be sufficient but not necessary (there are some nontheistic religions). Again, some characteristics (such as a moral code) might be necessary, but not sufficient (there are secular moral codes). Whatever the essence is, if there is one, it must be a set of characteristics that are both necessary and sufficient. Are there any?

Some philosophers have abandoned the search for essences. They argue that it may not be possible to provide essential or analytic definitions for things, simply because things do not have essences. Rather, they propose that we look for "cluster" definitions that state the resemblances among things that belong to a certain family. Thus a list of the important characteristics of religions might show no single common characteristic or essence but enough resemblances and similarities to warrant the designation "religion."

In this selection, Rem B. Edwards, a professor of philosophy at the University of Tennessee, explores the possibility of providing a cluster definition of religion. One of his discoveries is that the meaning of the English word *religion* reflects the influence of Western religions on our culture. This raises the interesting question of whether our definitions are so culture-bound that cross-cultural usage may be very misleading.

Reading Questions

1. What is the difference between the search for "family resemblances" and the search for a "common essence"?
2. Why is the attempt to find a common essence of religion difficult?
3. If all supernatural beings are superior beings, why are not all superior beings supernatural beings?
4. Of family traits 3–14, which one appears to be common to all the family members and why? Which two appear to be common to nearly all the members and why?
5. What four general conclusions does Edwards draw?

6. Do you agree with the claim that although there are many traits sufficient for calling something a religion, none of them is a necessary trait? Why? If you think there are some traits that are both necessary and sufficient, what are they and why do you think they are both necessary and sufficient?

The Search for Family Resemblances of Religion*

REM B. EDWARDS

THE INFLUENTIAL TWENTIETH-CENTURY philosopher Ludwig Wittgenstein thought that there are many perfectly meaningful, useful words in our language that have no "common essence" of connotation. These words are not used to name some characteristic or set of characteristics common to and distinctive of all the objects to which we normally apply such words. Wittgenstein thought that the common-sense assumption that there has to be a common essence where there is a common name is exceedingly naive, and he recommended that instead of making this assumption uncritically we should "look and see" if it is so. He believed that we would not always find a common essence for many perfectly useful words, such as *game, language, knowledge,* and so on. That he was correct with respect to *all* the words he used to illustrate his point may be questioned, but his general idea that some words have only "family resemblances" instead of "common essences" is a very fruitful one to explore, especially in its application to the word *religion.* Wittgenstein himself did not apply it to *religion,* but others who have been influenced by him have made preliminary studies of its possible application in this area. We shall first discuss briefly what is meant by "the search for family resemblances," and then we shall see if the search throws any light on our understanding of *religion.*

Not all objects called by a common name have a common essence, but they are frequently related to one another by "a complicated network of similarities overlapping and criss-crossing: sometimes overall similarities, sometimes similarities of detail," according to Wittgenstein. He compared this web of resemblances to the complicated way in which members of a human family resemble one another and are recognizable as members of the same family. Suppose that there are five brothers and sisters who are easily recognizable as members of the same family, but among whom there is not a single family trait that each has in common with *all* the others, as illustrated by the following diagram. Their resemblance to one another may depend not on a common essence, but on a complicated web of traits shared with one or more, but not with all, of the other members of the family. (In the diagram, the presence of a family trait is indicated by *P* and the absence by A.)

FAMILY TRAITS	FAMILY MEMBERS				
	Alex	Bill	Cathy	Dave	Enid
Over 6 feet tall	P	P	P	P	A
Blue eyes	P	P	P	A	P
Blond hair	P	P	A	P	P
Pug nose	P	A	P	P	P
Irritability	A	P	P	P	P

The obvious weakness of the family resemblance comparison is that if we were to add one additional family trait to our diagram, namely "Having the same parents," we would have a characteristic that was both common to and distinctive of each member of the family. But even this trait would not necessarily be common to all; suppose that Enid resembles all her brothers and sisters in all the respects indicated and yet is an adopted child! Nevertheless, there is always the possibility that such an additional family trait has been overlooked and will later turn up in any attempt to explore the meaning of a word in terms of family resemblances. When such a trait is discovered, this would seem to mean that our search for family resemblances has turned up a common essence as well and that the two approaches complement rather than conflict with each other. Perhaps this will turn out to be the case with the concept of "religion."

Family Traits of Religion

Many college students in the Western world who register for their first course in World Religions or Comparative Religions have some weird misconceptions about the non-Christian religions. They may think, for example, that in most of the non-Christian religions it is really the supernatural Christian God who is known and worshiped, but he is called by some other name such as the Buddha, the Brahman, or Allah, and that this knowledge is somewhat perversely distorted, since the devotees of these religions have not received all the benefits of the Christian revelation. Many students assume that most of the world religions teach that the individual human "soul" is created by God and is destined to everlasting existence in some place of reward or punishment, and that a program of "salvation" from the latter and for the former is invariably provided. Many students further assume that all world religions include a moral program—again somewhat distorted, of course—which contains the essentials of the Ten Commandments and the Sermon on the Mount and which is derived from and sanctioned by the Supreme Being. In short, it is typical for Westerners to assume at the outset of a study of the concept of "religion" or the phe-

nomena of the world religions that the field of inquiry is considerably less diversified than it in fact turns out to be. Yet it is precisely this diversity that makes it so difficult to discover some common essence for "religion" and that has suggested that the search for family resemblances might be a more fruitful approach to the concept of "religion." Let us see how such a search can be conducted.

We shall now look at a selected list of family traits and family members for the concept of "religion." In the chart on the following page, the family traits listed in the column on the left are all prominent characteristics of at least some of the things that we call religions, and the list of family members is a partial list of some of the things to which we apply the word with some degree of regularity. Neither list is in any way complete, especially the list of family members, and you can add to each list as you see fit. This chart and the discussion that follows are *not* to be construed as a survey of the field of comparative religion. The family members that are included were selected mainly because they permit us to introduce a preliminary discussion of the difficulties involved in discovering a common essence. The exercise as a whole is valuable because it allows us to make a place for the richness and concreteness of meaning that *religion* normally has and that we realized were missing at the end of our discussion of the search for a common essence, and because it may suggest a way of providing for the differentia of "religion" that we lacked earlier. . . .

General Conclusions of "The Search for Family Resemblances"

1. The only family members in our chart that clearly exhibit all the family traits are Christianity, Judaism, and Islam, though Hinduism comes very close. This suggests that these Western religions have had a definitive influence on our very conception of religion. We do in fact take them as paradigms for the application of the concept, since they exhibit *all* the important traits that we ascribe to a "religion." We might conjecture that if we were making an ordinary-language analysis

Selected Family Traits of Some Religions

FAMILY TRAITS	Christianity, Judaism, Islam	Vedanta Hindu Pantheism	Early Buddhism and Hinayana Buddhism	Early Greek Olympian Polytheism	Aristotle's Concept of Unmoved Mover	Communism	Moral Naturalistic Humanism	Spinozistic Pantheism	Success, Wealth, Golf, Fishing, etc.
1. Belief in a *supernatural* intelligent being or beings	P	A?	A	A	P	A	A	A	A
2. Belief in a *superior* intelligent being or beings	P	P	A	P	P	A	A	A?	A
3. Complex world view interpreting the significance of human life	P	P	P	P	P	P	P	P	A
4. Belief in experience after death	P	P	P	P?	A	A	A	A	A
5. Moral code	P	P	P	A	P	P	P	A	A
6. Belief that the moral code is sanctioned by a *superior* intelligent being or beings	P	P	A	A	A	A	A	A	A
7. An account of the nature of, origin of, and cure for evil	P	P	P	P?	P	P	P	P	A
8. Theodicy	P	P?	A	A	A	A	A	A	A
9. Prayer and ritual	P	P	P	P	A	P?	A	A?	A
10. Sacred objects and places	P	P	P	P	A	P	A	A	A?
11. Revealed truths or interpretations of revelatory events	P	P	P?	P	A	A	A	A	A
12. Religious experience—awe, mystical experience, revelations	P	P	P	P	A	A	A	A	P
13. Deep, intense concern	P	P	P	P	P?	P	P	P	P
14. Institutionalized social sharing of some of traits 1–13	P	P	P	P	A?	P	A?	A?	A?
15.									
16.									
17.									

Key: P = Present, A = Absent, ? = Unclear.

of religion in Ceylon we would have set up our list of family traits in such a way as to get a P in each case for Hinayana Buddhism, or in India a clear-cut P in each case for Hinduism—and in the languages of these countries it would be the Western religions that would be found wanting! If this is the case, then *religion* in English is only an approximate translation of any corresponding words in these other languages.

2. The family members on the chart are arranged in such a way that fewer and fewer P's appear as we move to the right in the direction of

success, wealth, golf, and fishing, and get further and further away from our paradigms of Christianity, Judaism, and Islam. This suggests that as we Westerners become acquainted with other cultures and new developments in our own cultures, we are willing to extend the application of *religion* to those phenomena that bear some significant similarities to our own standard religions. It further suggests that as these similarities become fewer and fewer in particular cases, we come to have more and more reservations about the legitimacy of extending *religion* to cover these cases. This explains why we are uneasy about calling success, wealth, golf, and fishing religions—they are like Christianity *only* in that they involve deep, intense concern. We say that such "religions" are only "borderline cases," or that in speaking of them as religions we are only speaking metaphorically.

3. In deciding whether to call something a religion, it is not merely the *number* of respects in which it resembles our paradigms that guides us, it is also the *importance* of these traits. Other traits besides deep, intense concern, such as a complex world view interpreting the significance of human life or an account of the nature of, origin of, and cure for evil, are nearly universal in the religions, and this may be one clue that guides us in assessing their importance. What other traits are of crucial importance? To us Westerners belief in God and in experience after death weigh heavily, though even these are not deemed absolutely necessary. A typical Western atheist who passionately denies God and immortality, who never indulges in anything resembling prayer, ritual, or mysticism, and whose principles we regard as less than moral would not be called a religious man; but a dedicated Hinayana Buddhist who

fails to affirm God and immortality and yet does engage in something resembling prayer, ritual, mysticism, and morality is called a religious man, mainly because his situation does exhibit a significant number of important resemblances to our paradigmatic religions.

4. The traits provide the differentia of "religion." We are willing to call a religion only a finite set of beliefs and practices through which we express our ultimate concerns, not a limitless set of them. . . . The list of family traits on our chart represents the hard core of the traits that the "religions" must manifest, and although it is by no means complete, it nevertheless could not be indefinitely extended. Neither could the list of family members be indefinitely extended. There are many sufficient but no necessary conditions for calling something a religion if the Wittgensteinian approach is correct. So long as there are family resemblances, it is not necessary that there be common essences in order for there to be limits on the correct application of a concept and rules to guide us in making those applications. However, is the contention that there are *only* family resemblances completely correct? What shall we say about the several nearly universal traits of religion that we have discovered? Would we call something a religion that completely failed to involve deep concern, answers to questions about the significance of human life, and perhaps even some account of the origin of, nature of, and cure for evil? Is the search for family resemblances completely at odds with the search for common essences? In looking to see, have we not found? In being nearly if not completely universal, these traits come as close to being necessary conditions for calling something a religion as we could expect to find for such a complex ordinary-language concept.

1.4 The Meaning and End of Religion

The English word *religion* derives from the Latin word *religio*. Balbus, a Roman Stoic, thought *religio* derived from *relegere,* a word that applies to people who are careful rather than neglectful in their worship. Lactantius, an early Christian writer, thought it derived from the Latin *religare;* meaning "to bind." Hence religion is an obligation. It is one's duty. Modern scholars differ in their interpretation of the earliest meanings of *religio.* Some argue that it was first used to designate powers obligating people to exhibit certain behaviors on pain of retribution. Others think it designated the feelings people have about such powers.

Early Christian writers in Latin adopted the term *religio* and focused on how it is possible to distinguish true religion from false. The term *religion* did not refer to "the religions" as we think of them today but primarily meant worship. Hence St. Augustine's book *De Vera Religione,* which is usually translated "On the True Religion," might be more accurately rendered as "On Genuine Worship." During the Middle Ages the term was not in wide use. When it was used, it was used to distinguish "the religious" (those who took up the monastic life) from the laity. Only during the modern period did the word begin to be used to name distinct institutions, traditions, and communities, such as the Christian, Jewish, and Islamic religions.

Today *religion* and its cognates are often used in at least four distinct ways. First, the adjective is frequently used to refer to the personal piety someone exhibits, as in "She is a very religious person." Second, the noun in singular or plural form is used to refer to actual historical traditions that involve systems of beliefs and practices: "There are many different religions." Third, the noun can refer to some ideal essence of one or more of "the religions" as in "This is the true Christian religion." Fourth, the singular noun is used as a generic summation or with reference to religion in general: "What is religion?" The first sense distinguishes the religious from the less religious or nonreligious person. The second distinguishes one religion from another, the third a true version of one religion from a false version. The fourth distinguishes religion from other areas of life and thought, such as politics, economics, and science.

This brief history of the changing uses of *religion* is a summary of information presented in Chapter 2 of Wilfred Cantwell Smith's book *The Meaning and End of Religion.* It precedes the following selection from that book and sets the stage for Smith's revisionist proposals. Smith concludes from his study that the term has become increasingly reified and abstracted from reality to the point where it is no longer useful. It misleads more than it helps. He proposes replacing it with the more concrete concepts of faith and cumulative tradition. Religion is, in actuality, the faith by which people live— a faith shaped, informed, and reformed by an evolving historical tradition.

Wilfred Cantwell Smith (1916–   ) was until his retirement a professor of world religions and director of the Center for the Study of World Religions at Harvard University. His scholarly career and interests center on the history of religions, with special emphasis on Islam.

Reading Questions

1. What two reasons does Smith give for abandoning the concept of "a religion"?
2. Do you agree or disagree with Smith's claim that "Whatever exists mundanely cannot be defined; whatever can be defined does not exist." Why?
3. What does Smith mean by "faith" and by "cumulative tradition," and why does he think these are better terms than such words as *Christianity, Judaism, Buddhism,* and so on?
4. Smith claims that there is no essence to religion that a definition can capture. Yet he also claims that the concepts of faith and cumulative tradition make it possible to "describe anything that has ever happened in the religious life of mankind." Is this a contradiction? If an essence is what is common to all, and if faith and cumulative tradition are common to all so-called religions, do they not constitute an essence?

The Meaning and End of Religion*

WILFRED CANTWELL SMITH

LET US TURN, next, to theoretical analysis. My own reasons to be urged for abandoning the concept altogether, are basically two. There are two considerations in the light of which a notion of the religions can be seen to be inherently and necessarily inadequate for interpreting man's religious life. Aphoristically, these are God and history.

Not all observers believe in God, and not all the devout are concerned with history; but it is difficult to escape both.

In the European Age of Reason, when these concepts were developed and flourished, men might think to conceptualize their world without much tremulous sense of the numinous or much dissolvent sense of historical flux. Now that the presuppositions of that particular time and place are superseded or outflanked, we may well seek more appropriate terms than theirs in which to depict man's variegated and evolving encounter with transcendence. In our final synthesis we shall argue that the two considerations are two faces of a single issue, with both of which my essentially personalistic interpretation will endeavour simultaneously to cope. In the meantime, we may look at the points one by one.

The first score on which I see the concept of a religion as tending to deceive the observer of a community's religious life is, basically, that the concept is necessarily inadequate for the man who believes and therefore cannot but be misleading for the outsider who does not. There is a serious and tricky problem here. We noted in our introductory chapter the position of those who hold that only a Christian can understand the Christian faith, only a Muslim can understand Islam, and so on. Although I hope to surmount this problem presently, I do not wish to under-estimate it. The observer's concept of a religion is beautifully suited to ignore it. The participant can see very clearly that the outsider may know *all about* a religious system, and yet may totally miss the point. The outsider may intellectually command all the details of its external facts, and yet may be—indeed, as an outsider, presumably must be or demonstrably is—untouched by the heart of the matter.

There is a difference between knowing a doctrine of salvation, and being saved. There is a difference between knowing that Islam involves submitting one's will to God's will as revealed in the Qur'an, and actually submitting one's will. There is a difference between having in one's mind an accurate picture of a sacrificial pattern, and actually sacrificing what one values, or being sacrificed. All this is evident enough (though it has sometimes not been stressed). And indeed the student may not merely know the doctrines and patterns, but know also that that difference exists. The relevant point here is that the significance of their involvement for those who are religiously involved lies on the far side of that difference. To know "a religion" is not yet to know the religious life of him whom one observes.

Christian life is a new life, lived in a supernatural context. To understand Christianity, or to think that one does, is not yet to understand Christians. This latter requires an understanding of that supernatural context, in which what the outsider calls Christianity enables them now to live. The Christian may affirm that no one can understand it who has not known it, and that no one can know it who has not been salvaged out of men's innate limitations by the only procedure in the universe capable of doing that. One may challenge the validity of either of these two propositions; but not their relevance. No amount of attention to the procedure's outward form, which is what concerns the outside student of Christianity, can give, or is even designed to give, an understanding of that transformed life in its spiritual dimensions.

The above argument will in most cases not carry much weight with those who are not believing Christians—a fact that in itself illustrates the very point that I am making. We shall return to this. In the meantime, one may make the further point that the outsider, if he is a sceptic, may reject the statement that the Christian life is lived in a supernatural context on the grounds that no supernatural exists. If so, then for him the Christian is induced by something called Christianity to live in an illusion. Here one must insist that the significant point to understand about this Christian is still not that something called Christianity but what it is like living in an illusion.

The important matter in the life of any religious community is what their religious tradition does to them. This is not easy for an outsider to ascertain. Yet if he is to succeed at all, he will need to conceptualize it in personal, not impersonal, terms.

What is profoundly important in the religious life of any people, and elemental to all our discussions, is that, whatever else it may be, religious life is a kind of *life*. Participants know this, consciously or unconsciously. Observers may have to learn it. In learning it, they find that they must leave behind the distraction of congealed concepts postulating entities different from the living persons before them, or even theoretically independent of them.

Not only do reifying concepts of "a religion," in terms such as "Buddhism" and "Zoroastrianism," misrepresent by freezing the inherently personal, living quality of men's religiousness. Further, they do so by omitting not only the vitality but the most significant of all factors in that vitality, namely its relation with transcendence. The observer's concept of a religion is by definition constituted of what can be observed. Yet the whole pith and substance of religious life lies in its relation to what cannot be observed.

The significant thing about a Christian's life, we have remarked, is that it is lived in a supernatural context. What signifies is not what the Christian does, but that he does it as a child of God; not what he believes, but that God has granted him the gift of believing; not that he is in the Church, but that in the Church he is in living communion with Christ as a personal friend and with fellow members in a fellowship not merely human, not merely social; not that he loves, but that he loves because of Christ; not that he sins, but that he sins to Christ's hurt, and yet forgivably.

The same consideration applies with equal force to other communities. The Muslim theologian al-Ghazzali learned (he phrases it, "God taught me") something of the shallowness of mere theology from an old peasant woman who, unlike al-Ghazzali with his formidable dialectic by which he controlled a score of proofs for the existence of God, knew no proofs at all and yet lived in God's presence.

It is quite possible and even easy for a modern Western graduate student to know more "about Islam" than that woman with her simple faith ever knew—or ever wanted to know. The question as to whether he understands *her* is a different sort of question.

Being a Muslim means living in a certain context, sociological, historical, ideological, *and transcendent*. The significance of being a Muslim lies in this fact, not in some prolegomenon to it. The concern of the observer with something that he calls Islam shifts attention from the heart of the matter, namely people's living within this context, to the context itself, which is damaging enough; and disrupts the whole procedure still farther by omitting from his purview the context's transcendence. It does this not perversely but inherently; since the observer by the very fact of being an outsider, a non-acceptor of the context, has ruled out its transcendent quality in theory *a priori*. He has conceptualized what for the man of faith does not exist, namely a context for his life shorn of its most significant dimension. The concept "Islam" in the mind of a nonbeliever has represented at best an element in the life of such Muslims as have lost their faith.

"Islam" comes alive for the Muslim through faith, which is not an item in a religion but a quality in some men's hearts—a personal quality in several senses, including that of varying from person to person and even from day to day. Once it has come alive, it is *ipso facto* no longer what it appears to be to him for whom it is not alive. The commands of God, for instance, which for an observer appear to control and even to confine a Muslim's behaviour, for the Muslim himself, in accord with the degree of vitality of his faith, rather liberate that behaviour. They free it from the confines of purely human floundering and the ignorance of mundane device; and elevate it to a quite new plane—the in one sense unbounded, certainly eternal plane of cosmic appropriateness and validity. To live a life of which even the apparently petty details now have ultimate significance, of which even the humdrum routine has been raised to cosmic stature and touched with divine splendour; to live in a community of which only the less interesting, mundane side is open to outsiders' observation while one can oneself catch at least a glimpse of its real import, its cosmic role; all this, at least, is part of the meaning of a Muslim's faith. Those of us on the outside who would interpret to ourselves the Muslim must understand not his religion but his religiousness.

So for the Hindu, the Buddhist, the Tierra del Fuegan. If we would comprehend these we must look not at their religion but at the universe, so far as possible through their eyes. It is what the Hindu is able to see, by being a Hindu, that is significant. Until we can see it too, we have not come to grips with the religious quality of his life. And we may be sure that as he looks around him, he does not see "Hinduism." Like the rest of us, he sees his wife's death, his child's minor and major aspirations, his moneylender's mercilessness, the calm of a starlit evening, his own mortality. He sees these things through coloured glasses, if one will, of a "Hindu" brand. He sees also certain gods and institutions that may carry this label, though the deeper and more sophisti-

cated his faith, the more he sees through these. His neighbour, also Hindu, sees the foreground differently; if their vision finally converges, it is because both have been sufficiently penetrating to see through and beyond their foreground to a Reality that, if not yet altogether attributeless, is certainly quite without the attribute of being in any sense *Hindu*.

Of primitive peoples the religious system often seems, to sophisticated outsiders, grotesque. They have not appreciated the religious life of such peoples if they have not grasped the point that it is constituted not only of that system but at least equally of the fact that through it the participants are enabled, one might be tempted to say, to feel at home in the universe (which is anything but grotesque!). Yet one has not truly construed the situation unless one can go beyond this and recognize their life as one in which, by being religious, they not only feel at home in the universe but indeed are at home in it. To omit this fact from one's apprehension is sorely to misconceive.

We return, then, to the Christian's flat assertion: "The Christian faith is not one of the religions of the world." Students of comparative religion have been wont to decry such sentiments, even dismissing them as ridiculous. I, in contrast, would argue vigorously that the Christian who says this—for instance, Brunner—is profoundly and critically right. Only, I would go on to assert, with equal vigour: *Neither is the faith of any other people.*

Those who ridicule have failed to understand all faith. Brunner has failed, as has his community generally, only to understand the faith of other men.

We are now in a position to recognize that it was not fortuitous that the religion concepts, having arisen in Western Europe, are inherently depreciative. For the Christian tradition, particularly in its Protestant form, has historically been unusually disparaging of other religious traditions; and the rationalist academic tradition has been skeptical, if not disparaging, of all. The concept "a religion," and the conceptualizing of named religions, omit, we have argued, the transcendent dimension from what they seek to represent. This has to do with the fact that Christians have regularly failed or refused to recognize that the faith of non-Christians has that transcendence; that God does in fact encounter men in Buddhist, Muslim and Hottentot forms, as he does in the Christian. Secular academics have regularly failed or refused to recognize that there is a transcendent dimension to human life at all. (The very notion of transcendence will, I realize, disquiet them not a little.)

Both these groups, therefore, surveying the religious history of man, could attempt to interpret it, leaving out of account the very quality that gives it significance. They have suspected, or affirmed, that that significance just is not there.

All religions are illusory, they have held; or, all religions other than ours.

Thus also many Muslims. More appreciative or tolerant traditions, on the other hand, such as those of India or farther East, have accordingly not developed this sort of concept not only for interpreting their own faith but also not for interpreting that of their neighbours. (Something similar has been true also of the mystics of all traditions—including Sufis and Christians—who, it is well known, have been the one type in their communities most successful in understanding men of divergent faiths.) Hindus, Buddhists, and their like, whatever their other faults, have usually not failed to recognize those who differed from them in outward pattern and formal grouping as nevertheless engaged on fundamentally the same enterprise, as attuned to the same kind of melody. In the positive hypothesis that I shall proffer in our subsequent chapters, in an attempt to handle religious diversity without distorting it, informed students will perhaps detect elements suggesting the influence on my thinking of certain Indian and Chinese orientations. At the same time I hope that the concepts proposed will also be serviceable within the Western academic tradition, and will be recognized as methodologically continuous with it, and indeed in part derived from it.

Among the Christian writers cited above as protesting sharply against the application of the concept "religion" to their own faith, none was hesitant to apply it to other people's. These men have not criticized or protested against the concept in itself, but have been content to reject it as applied to themselves, insisting that it does not do justice to that in which their own group is involved. Indeed they reject it in their own case because it compromises, and apply it to others because it compromises. Emil Brunner writes: "The God of the 'other religions' is always an idol." This judgement can be seen as expressing the arrogance of a narrow-minded Christian. I would suggest that it can also be seen as a perceptive remark, more universal than its author himself intended—but at another level.

The concept "other religions," religions of other people, inherently turns their gods into idols, into false deities, the product of human phantasy. This applies also to the Christian case. For those for whom Christianity is an *other* religion, for example Muslims, the Christian God is an idol, at least the second person of the Trinity.

Once again the concept serves those who would deny to the religious life of those whom they observe transcendent involvement. Actually, no one in the whole history of man has ever worshipped an idol. Men have worshipped God—or something—in the form of idols. That is what idols are for. Yet that is quite a different thing. "The heathen in his blindness," sang the nineteenth-century hymn, "bows down to wood and stone." Yet it is not the heathen here who is blind, but the observer. Even at his most restricted, the "idolator" worships not the stone that I see, but the stone that he sees.

Outsiders, then, in their conception of other men's religions, have tended to drain these of any but mundane content. They have done this by throwing a conceptual boundary around their interpretation, thus imposing on other people a limit to which their own mind has given birth. Yet the point of man's religious life lies in man's being introduced in it to that which is without limits. Any attempt to conceptualize a religion is a contradiction in terms.

The student's first responsibility is to recognize that there is always and in principle more in any man's faith than any other man can see. . . .

So much for my first point. My second is at a more mundane level. Those down-to-earth readers who may have been restless at my concern for transcendence will be the first to recognize the cogency of our next, historical consideration. If one rejects the fixity and neatness of formulated patterns because they presuppose some definite upper limit to men's faith, one rejects them also because they presuppose definiteness all round, whereas every historian now knows that in fact there is flux.

Neither the believer nor the observer can hold that there is anything on earth that can legitimately be called "Christianity" or "Shintoism" or "religion" without recognizing that if such a thing existed yesterday, it existed in a somewhat different form the day before. If it exists in one country (or village), it exists in somewhat different form in the next. The concepts were formed before the ruthlessness of historical change was recognized, in all its disintegrating sweep. They have in practice been being abandoned as awareness has since grown. It is time now definitely to reject them theoretically, as inherently inept.

Aristotle, in his *Posterior Analytics,* remarks of a mythical animal that one may give the meaning of the word that names it but it is not possible to give a definition, since there is actually no such animal. A term such as "unicorn" is used, and its meaning can therefore be stated; but there is no entity in the objective world to which it corresponds, and therefore no statement of what a unicorn is is possible. The implications of this analysis and the outlook that it implies were fundamental for much of Greek thought, and have been influential throughout much of Western civilization since, not least among those not self-consciously philosophizing: the idea that reality is definable. Language, in such a view, consists of words that can be explained; the real world, of things that can be defined.

In the modern age our embarrassment is the other way around. We are learning to reverse Aristotle's assessment; though confusion reigns when we do so unwittingly, or in a fashion that falls short of being explicit or rigorous. For us, words and concepts are to be defined, while things cannot be. We can speak with precision and elegance in our definition of imaginary constructs: an irrational number, or any of the notions in mathematics; model types in sociological theory; concepts in physics; abstractions of all kinds. In the realm of ideals something similar may perhaps obtain. The world of objective reality, on the other hand, is recalcitrant to our schematizations. We may define anything at all, provided only that it does not exist. Once we are talking of empirical objects, our minds move from the neatness of rational intelligibilities to the more humble approximations of an awareness of what always transcends our exact apprehension—and, in any case, is changing even while we try to apprehend it.

The sciences, while developing their own modified or novel meanings of definition, have abandoned the concept of *essence,* its original concomitant. Science is not interested in essences. A modern physicist cannot define matter; but he can handle it, and can do so because his predecessors eventually learned that the essence does not signify. He understands the behaviour of matter not because he knows what matter is—for he does not; but because he has learned how it operates, and how it changes.

The world of the natural sciences, however, is itself considerably less complex, less phased, than that of man and society. Here more than ever we have discovered that on close scrutiny boundaries shift if they do not actually dissolve. We are learning that we do not live in a universe that can be tidily and finally arrayed in a series of packaged items each intellectually dominable, and the whole kept in neat and docile order. The philosophic revolt against essentialism has followed the discovery that the objective world itself revolts against its pigeonholing dominance.

The point is valid generally, it would seem; it may be illustrated lavishly in the area of man's religious history. Understanding in this realm was seriously disrupted, we suggest, when last-century thinkers set out in chase of an essence of religion, an essence of Christianity, of Hinduism, and so on. The knowledge that has accrued over the past century or so as the reward of massive work in the academic field called History of Religions, has made those essences not more but less ascertainable. That work and that knowledge have not unearthed what religion, or one of the religions, is; but they have contributed something else, of revolutionary import. The History of Religions has taught man incontrovertibly that "the religions" have a history. This may sound tautological but actually is crucial. Many religious people have realized it, if at all, only peripherally. Even scholars have not taken it quite seriously.

For essences do not have a history. Essences do not change. Yet it is an observable and important fact that what have been called the religions do, in history, change.

What exists cannot be defined. What obstructs a definition of Hinduism, for instance, is precisely the richness of what exists, in all its extravagant variety from century to century and from village to village. The empirical religious tradition of the Hindus developing historically in the minds and hearts and institutions and literatures and societies of untold millions of actual people is not a form, but a growing congeries of living realities. It is not to be compressed within or eviscerated into or confused with any systematic intellectual pattern.

As an ideal, "Hinduism" might conceivably be defined (though only by a Hindu), but not as an historical reality. The sheer facts, in all their intractable toughness, stand in the way.

"Hinduism" refers not to an entity; it is a name that the West has given to a prodigiously variegated series of facts. It is a notion in men's minds—and a notion that cannot but be inadequate. To use this term at all is inescapably a gross oversimplification. There is an inherent contradiction between history and this order of idea.

I do not mean merely that to define Hinduism, or Taoism, or Protestantism is difficult. That, everyone knows. My point rather is that it is in principle impossible, and almost perverse.

One has radically misunderstood our world if one imagines that things can be defined; and especially living things, and especially human involvements. Not to have recognized that mundane reality—in its complexity, its particularity, and its givenness—outpaces our conceptualizations of it is not yet to have adopted that humility before facts that normatively characterizes modern study.

Obviously, I am not suggesting that what men have called the religions do not exist. The point is rather that, as every historian of them knows almost to his bewilderment, they exist all too copiously. It is the richness, the radical diversity, the unceasing shift and change, the ramification and complex involvement, of the historical phenomena of "religion" or of any one "religion" that create the difficulty. What has been called Christianity is, so far as history is concerned, not one thing but millions of things, and hundreds of millions of persons. "Islam" could perhaps fairly readily be understood if only it had not existed in such abundant actuality, at differing times and in differing areas, in the minds and hearts of differing persons, in the institutions and forms of differing societies, in the evolving of differing stages.

And even if somehow one came to know all that Judaism has been, how is one to make room for what Judaism may yet become?

For there is this further point, of great significance. Not only has the past been various; a future also must somehow be taken into account. And it is inherently unknowable. There is no more befuddling misconception of human history than not to recognize that it is free; if not absolutely, at least free from any limitations that our intellects may attempt to impose upon it. To define is to set limits; but no man can set limits that other men cannot transcend.

To define Hinduism is to deny the Hindu his right to the freedom and integrity of his faith. What he may do tomorrow no man can say today.

It might be felt that, by considering the Hindu case, I have unduly favoured my contention, selecting the admittedly freest, least definable, most amorphous of all the world's "religions." Let us look, then, at "Christianity." Some might hold that St. Thomas Aquinas, or the framers of the Westminster Confession, or someone, has defined Christianity. I myself would not phrase this so, nor would those named; but we have already treated at sufficient length the question of the inadequacy of these concepts for the man of faith, and I do not wish here to press into service again that side of the argument. For present purposes, let it even be conceded; it would still be an ideal Christianity that was defined, not the empirical Christianity of history, not the actual religious life or the actual institutions of Christians in all their ramifying and diverse objectivity.

This would corroborate my contention that one cannot define what exists. A Christian theologian who attempted to define Christianity would be attempting to define it as it truly is in an idealistic sense, up in the sky; not as it historically has been in concrete actuality. The definable is the pure; and purity is to be found only in theory and in God. Whatever exists mundanely cannot be defined; whatever can be defined does not exist.

Some few have indeed taken refuge in this kind of intellectualist idealism, conceiving a religion unsullied by the world, a transcendent form. To the unserviceability of such a concept for the historian's purpose, on many counts, we shall return. For the moment, we simply note that it evades rather than solves our problem, which would then become that of understanding (and somehow conceptualizing) the ever varying impingement of such a transcendent entity on man, caught in the sublunar flux. In the ambiguity between the ideal and the actual, not only is the manward side of even the most transcendentally conceived "religion" involved. More heroically, to be involved in it is presumably its very business and significance. . . .

The Cumulative Tradition

THE MAN of religious faith lives in this world. He is subject to its pressures, limited within its imperfections, particularized within one or another of its always varying contexts of time and place, and he is observable. At the same time and because of his faith or through it, he is or claims to be in touch with another world transcending this. The duality of this position some would say is the greatness and some the very meaning of human life: the heart of its distinctive quality, its tragedy and its glory. Others would dismiss the claim as false, though not uninteresting. However that may be, the duality raises problems not only for the man of faith himself, for the formulator of faith whether theologian or artist, and for the philosopher. It raises problems also, we have seen, for the student of religious history. My suggestion is that these latter issues might be treated differently from what has been customary and more effectively, in such a way as to enable the more ultimate questions to be appreciated in truer perspective, and not prejudged.

We speak of the life of religious man seeming to be somehow in two worlds, the mundane realm of limiting and observable and changing actuality and a realm transcending this. What is the nature of that transcendent sphere, and what the nature of its relation to this mundane one, are questions on which, to put it mildly, there is no general agreement. Whether the transcendence is the human imagination at work or the fantasy of subconscious neuroses, or the meaningless patter of language gone awry, or the ideological superstructure of a particular economic situation; or whether it is a real world, or more real than this immediate one, or is this immediate one perceived more truly; and whether, if it is real, it is personal, Jesus-like, rational, formless, moral, punitive, unknowable—all these are questions on which intelligent men have taken varying stands. It would seem evident that if the study of man's religious history is to make progress at all as a cogent scholarly pursuit, it must do so without waiting for, or presupposing, agreement on these matters. In fact the divergence of answers is one part of the very matter that one is trying to understand. Room for this multiplicity must therefore be provided in the conceptual framework with which one approaches the task.

The nature of the mundane world, on the other hand, is becoming increasingly known, in a fashion that admits less and less of divergence. This is true also of the mundane aspect of man's own living. Men may differ as to the content of faith or as to its validity, but there is in principle little room for differing as to its overt manifestations across the centuries in their resplendent or grotesque variety. The unobservable part of man's history, especially his religious history, may and indeed must be acknowledged an open question so far as scholarship is concerned. Meanwhile the observable part, including that of his religious history, is because of that very scholarship accessible to open scrutiny.

From this ambivalent quality of religious life, our difficulty ineluctably stems. What is needed, then, is a device to give the ambivalence full play. Such a device is in fact fairly readily to hand. It may seem disarmingly simple, and at first blush just a trifle evasive, although this in fact is part of its virtue. For as scholars we cannot but also as scholars we need not and must not begin by "solving" the problem of the relation between transcendence and the world. It is both possible and rewarding to postpone it. Our academic and intellectual skills are not capable of letting us climb over a mountain whose summit is in the skies. While staying on the ground we may, if the road that I discern does not deceive me, quietly outflank it, and so get on with our task.

This is because, whatever the relation between our two realms may be metaphysically or theologically, so far as the historian is concerned the link is quite clear. It is man.

The history of what has been called religion in general and of each religion, is the history of man's participation in an evolving context of observable actualities, and in a something, not directly observable by historical scholarship.

Any historiography, we suggest, distorts what it is reporting if it omits either of these two aspects; and yet is doomed to flounder if it attempts to combine them. My suggestion is the basically rather simple one that we separate them in intellectual analysis, retaining both.

Phrased more historically: the study of man's religious life has in the past been inadequate in so far as its concept of religion has neglected either the mundane or the transcendent element in what it has studied, and has been confused in so far as its concept has attempted to embrace both. I ask whether these studies may not proceed more satisfactorily in future if, putting aside the concept "religion" or "the religions" to describe the two, we elect to work rather with two separate concepts.

I propose to call these "cumulative tradition," on the one hand, and "faith," on the other. The link between the two is the living person.

By "faith" I mean personal faith. I shall endeavour to elucidate this in our next chapter. For the moment let it stand for an inner religious experience or involvement of a particular person; the impingement on him of the transcendent, putative or real. By "cumulative tradition" I mean the entire mass of overt objective data that constitute the historical deposit, as it were, of the past religious life of the community in question: temples, scriptures, theological systems, dance patterns, legal and other social institutions, conventions, moral codes, myths, and so on; anything that can be and is transmitted from one person, one generation, to another, and that an historian can observe.

It is my suggestion that by the use of these two notions it is possible to conceptualize and to describe anything that has ever happened in the religious life of mankind, whether within one's own religious community (which is an important point) or in others' (which is also an important point). Also, so far as I can see, it is possible for these concepts to be used equally by sceptic or believer, by Muslim or Buddhist, Episcopalian or Quaker, Freudian or Marxist or Sufi.

These are rather sweeping claims. They would seem pretentious, did one not remember that I do not pretend to have solved vast problems that have outwitted better men; I am suggesting rather a method that will humbly yet deliberately allow man's long wrestling with those problems to be investigated without prior solution.

1.5 What Is Religion?

What we mean by religion is undoubtedly influenced by our culture and the religion or religions with which we are most familiar. It is also influenced by the scholarly point of view we take. Philosophical interests may point us in one direction, historical interests in another.

Keiji Nishitani (1900–1990) was a Japanese philosopher who had a foot in two cultures. He was educated in both Japan and Germany and was strongly influenced by the Buddhist tradition (especially Zen Buddhism) and European philosophy (especially idealism and existentialism). He was a member of the Kyoto School of philosophy that developed in the departments of philosophy and religion at Kyoto State University. This philosophical school combines loyalty to the Buddhist philosophical tradition with openness to Western philosophy and seeks to synthesize the philosophical and religious insights of East and West.

The editors of a volume entitled *Lectures on Contemporary Religion* initially invited Nishitani to write the selection that follows. Nishitani concedes that what the editors had in mind was a historical viewpoint that analyzed the range of phenomena associated with what we normally call religion. In other words, they wanted an objective account that reached conclusions based on the facts of history. Nishitani does not offer such an account. Instead he seeks to elucidate the "home-ground" of religion. This ground, he argues, is where religion emerges as a vital, personal question for the individual who asks about the meaning of religion. He is interested not so much in the meaning of the word but in the meaningfulness of religion for our lives. Thus he directs our attention to what religion *ought to be* rather than to what it *has been.* He is convinced that pondering what religion ought to be can and does illuminate, at a deeper level than an objective historical approach, what religion has been and truly is. The question "What is religion?" he interprets as a question about what religion is for me. Not "for me" in the sense of what I might *think,* but "for me" in the sense of what I *feel* when I realize that religion raises the question of the purpose of my existence.

Reading Questions

1. What does Nishitani mean when he says, "the relationship we have to religion is a contradictory one"?
2. Why should we not consider religion from the viewpoint of its utility?
3. Why is religion, in Nishitani's view, primarily an "individual affair," and why is it a mistake to ask about its purpose for us?
4. What does Nishitani mean by "nihility" and by self-being becoming a question mark?
5. What does Nishitani mean by "self-awareness of reality" and by the religious quest?
6. What is the field of consciousness, and why does it prevent us from truly getting in touch with reality?
7. According to Nishitani, what is the major difference between the modern, post-Cartesian view of the world and the pre-modern, pre-Cartesian view?
8. Compare Nishitani's approach to the question "What is religion?" with the previous approaches presented in this chapter. Which account do you consider most helpful in understanding religion and why?

What Is Religion?*

KEIJI NISHITANI

I

"What is religion?" we ask ourselves, or, looking at it the other way around, "What is the purpose of religion for us? Why do we need it?" Though the question about the need for religion may be a familiar one, it already contains a problem. In one sense, for the person who poses the question, religion does not seem to be something he needs. The fact that he asks the question at all amounts to an admission that religion has not yet become a necessity for him. In another sense, however, it is surely in the nature of religion to be necessary for just such a person. Wherever questioning individuals like this are to be found, the need for religion is there as well. In short, the relationship we have to religion is a contradictory one: those for whom religion is *not* a necessity are, for that reason, the very ones for whom religion *is* a necessity. There is no other thing of which the same can be said.

When asked, "Why do we need learning and the arts?" we might try to explain in reply that such things are necessary for the advancement of mankind, for human happiness, for the cultivation of the individual, and so forth. Yet even if we can say why we need such things, this does not imply that we cannot get along without them. Somehow life would still go on. Learning and the arts may be indispensable to living well, but they are not indispensable to living. In that sense, they can be considered a kind of luxury.

Food, on the other hand, is essential to life. Nobody would turn to somebody else and ask him why he eats. Well, maybe an angel or some other celestial being who has no need to eat might ask such questions but men do not. Religion, to judge from current conditions in which many people are in fact getting along without it, is clearly not the kind of necessity that food is. Yet this does not mean that it is merely something we need to live *well*. Religion has to do with life itself. Whether the life we are living will end up in extinction or in the attainment of eternal life is a matter of the utmost importance for life itself. In no sense is religion to be called a luxury. Indeed, this is why religion is an indispensable necessity for those very people who fail to see the need for it. Herein lies the distinctive feature of religion that sets it apart from the mere life of "nature" and from culture. Therefore, to say that we need religion for example, for the sake of social order, or human welfare, or public morals is a mistake, or at least a confusion of priorities. Religion must not be considered from the viewpoint of its *utility*, any more than life should. A religion concerned primarily with its own utility bears witness to its own degeneration. One can ask about the utility of things like eating for the natural life, or of things like learning and the arts for culture. In fact, in such matters the question of utility should be of constant concern. Our ordinary mode of being is restricted to these levels of natural or cultural life. But it is in breaking through that ordinary mode of being and overturning it from the ground up, in pressing us back to the elemental source of life where life itself is seen as useless, that religion becomes something we need—a *must* for human life.

Two points should be noted from what has just been said. First, religion is at all times the individual affair of each individual. This sets it apart from things like culture, which, while related to the individual, do not need to concern each individual. Accordingly, we cannot understand what religion is from the outside. The religious quest alone is the key to understanding it; there is no other way. This is the most important point to be made regarding the essence of religion.

Second, from the standpoint of the essence of religion, it is a mistake to ask "What is the purpose of religion for us?" and one that clearly betrays an attitude of trying to understand religion apart from the religious quest. It is a question that must be broken through by another question coming from within the person who asks it. There is no other road that can lead to an understanding of what religion is and what purpose it serves. The counterquestion that achieves this breakthrough is one that asks, "For what purpose do I myself exist?" Of everything else we can ask its purpose for us, but not of religion. With regard to everything else we can make a *telos* of ourselves as individuals, as man, or as mankind, and evaluate those things in relation to our life and existence. We put ourselves as individuals/man/mankind at the center and weigh the significance of everything as the *contents* of our lives as individuals/man/mankind. But religion upsets the posture from which we think of ourselves as *telos* and center for all things. Instead, religion poses as a starting point the question: "For what purpose do I exist?"

We become aware of religion as a need, as a must for life, only at the level of life at which everything else loses its necessity and its utility. Why do we exist at all? Is not our very existence and human life ultimately meaningless? Or, if there is a meaning or significance to it all, where do we find it? When we come to doubt the meaning of our existence in this way, when we have become a question to ourselves, the religious quest awakens within us. These questions and the quest they give rise to show up when the mode of looking at and thinking about everything in terms of how it relates to *us* is broken through, where the mode of living that puts us at the center of everything is overturned. This is why the question of religion in the form, "Why do we need religion?" obscures the way to its own answer from the very start. It blocks our becoming a question to ourselves.

The point at which the ordinarily necessary things of life, including learning and the arts, all lose their necessity and utility is found at those times when death, nihility, or sin—or any of those situations that entail a fundamental negation of our life, existence, and ideals, that undermine the roothold of our existence and bring the meaning of life into question—become pressing personal problems for us. This can occur through an illness that brings one face-to-face with death, or through some turn of events that robs one of what had made life worth living.

Take, for example, someone for whom life has become meaningless as a result of the loss of a loved one, or of the failure of an undertaking on which he had staked his all. All those things that had once been of use to him become good for nothing. This same process takes place when one comes face to face with death and the existence of the self—one's "self-existence"—stands out clearly in relief against the backdrop of nihility. Questions crowd in upon one: Why have I been alive? Where did I come from and where am I going? A void appears here that nothing in the world can fill; a gaping abyss opens up at the very ground on which one stands. In the face of this abyss, not one of all the things that had made up the stuff of life until then is of any use.

In fact, that abyss is always just underfoot. In the case of death, we do not face something that awaits us in some distant future, but something that we bring into the world with us at the moment we are born. Our life runs up against death at its every step; we keep one foot planted in the vale of death at all times. Our life stands poised at the brink of the abyss of nihility to which it may return at any moment. Our existence is an existence at one with nonexistence, swinging back and forth over nihility, ceaselessly passing away and ceaselessly regaining its existence. This is what is called the "incessant becoming" of existence.

Nihility refers to that which renders meaningless the meaning of life. When we become a question to ourselves and when the problem of why we exist arises, this means that nihility has emerged from the ground of our existence and that our very existence has turned into a question mark. The appearance of this nihility signals nothing less than that one's awareness of self-existence has penetrated to an extraordinary depth.

Normally we proceed through life, on and on, with our eye fixed on something or other, always caught up with something within or without ourselves. It is these engagements that prevent the deepening of awareness. They block off the way to an opening up of that horizon on which nihility appears and self-being becomes a question. This is even the case with learning and the arts and the whole range of other cultural engagements. But when this horizon does open up at the bottom of those engagements that keep life moving continually on and on, something seems to halt and linger before us. This something is the meaninglessness that lies in wait at the bottom of those very engagements that bring meaning to life. This is the point at which that sense of nihility, that sense that "everything is the same" we find in Nietzsche and Dostoevski, brings the restless, forward-advancing pace of life to a halt and makes it take a step back. In the Zen phrase, it "turns the light to what is directly underfoot."

In the forward progress of everyday life, the ground beneath our feet always falls behind as we move steadily ahead; we overlook it. Taking a step back to shed light on what is underfoot of the self—"stepping back to come to the self," as another ancient Zen phrase has it—marks a conversion in life itself. This fundamental conversion in life is occasioned by the opening up of the horizon of nihility at the ground of life. It is nothing less than a conversion from the self-centered (or man-centered) mode of being, which always asks what *use* things have for us (or for man), to an attitude that asks for what *purpose* we ourselves (or man) exist. Only when we stand at this turning point does the question "What is religion?" really become our own.

II

Being the multi-faceted reality that it is, religion can be approached from any number of different angles. It is commonly defined as the relationship of man to an absolute, like God. But as that def-inition may already be too narrow, there are those who prefer, for example, to speak in terms of the idea of the Holy. If this relationship is taken more concretely, however, still other possible angles of approach suggest themselves. For instance, the relationship of man to God may be spoken of as the abandonment of self-will in order to live according to the will of God; as the vision or knowledge of God; or, as the unveiling of God to the self, or in the self. Again, it may be thought of as the immediate perception of the absolute dependency of self-existence on divine existence, or as man's becoming one with God. One might as well pursue the view that it is only in religion that man becomes truly himself, that the self encounters its "original countenance." Furthermore, it is possible to regard the essence of religion, as Schleiermacher does in his *Reden über die Religion,* as the intuition of the infinite in the finite, as "feeling the Universe." On a variety of counts, of course, each of these views is open to criticism. Rather than enter any further into their discussion here, I should like instead to approach religion from a somewhat different angle, as the self-awareness of reality, or, more correctly, the *real* self-awareness of reality.

By the "self-awareness of reality" I mean both our becoming aware of reality and, at the same time, the reality realizing itself in our awareness. The English word "realize," with its twofold meaning of "actualize" and "understand," is particularly well suited to what I have in mind here, although I am told that its sense of "understand" does not necessarily connote the sense of reality coming to actualization in us. Be that as it may, I am using the word to indicate that our ability to perceive reality means that reality realizes (actualizes) itself in us; that this in turn is the only way that we can realize (appropriate through understanding) the fact that reality is so realizing itself in us; and that in so doing the self-realization of reality itself takes place.

It follows that realization in its sense of "appropriation" differs from philosophical cognition. What I am speaking of is not theoretical knowledge but a real appropriation (the *proprium* taken here to embrace the whole man, mind and body). This real appropriation provides our very mode of being with its essential determination. The real perception of reality is our real mode of being itself and constitutes the realness that is the true reality of our existence. This perception of reality can constitute the realness of our existence because it comes into being in unison with the self-realization of reality itself. In this sense, the realness of our existence, as the appropriation of reality, belongs to reality itself as the self-realization of reality itself. In other words, the self-realization of reality can only take place by causing our existence to become truly real.

The question will no doubt arise as to what this "reality" signifies. If the question is posed merely in the form of the usual request for knowledge, in expectation of a simple, conceptual response, then it is inappropriate to the reality I am speaking of here. In order for it to become a *real* question, one that is asked with the whole self, body and mind, it must be returned to reality itself. The question that *asks about* reality must itself become something that *belongs to* reality. In that vein, I should like to try to interpret the religious quest as man's search for true reality in a *real* way (that is, not theoretically and not in the form of concepts, as we do in ordinary knowledge and philosophical knowledge), and from that same angle to attempt an answer to the question of the essence of religion by tracing the process of the real pursuit of true reality.

When we think of "reality" from an everyday standpoint, we think first of all of the things and events *without* us: the mountains and streams, the flowers and forests, and the entire visible universe all about us. We think, too, of other people, other societies and nations, and of the whole skein of human activities and historical events that envelop them. Next, we think of reality as the world *within* us: our thoughts, our feelings, and our desires.

When we pass from the everyday standpoint to that of natural science, we find that it is the atoms, or the energy that makes them up, or the scientific laws that regulate that energy, rather

than individual events and phenomena, that are now regarded as reality. In contrast, the social scientist, for his part, might posit that economic relations provide all human activity with its basis in reality. Or again, a metaphysician might argue that all those things are only the appearances of a phenomenal world, and that the true reality is to be found in the Ideas that lie behind them.

The problem with these various "realities" is that they lack unity among themselves and even seem to contradict one another. On the one hand, even if one assumes that things in the outer world are real, they cannot at bottom be separated from the laws of mathematics and natural science. The space the things of the outer world occupy and the movements they make conform to the laws of geometry and dynamics. Indeed, things cannot even exist apart from these laws. Moreover, our grasp of these laws obviously underlies the technology we have developed for controlling things and improving them. In a similar way, conscious phenomena such as feelings and desires cannot be separated from the laws of physiology and psychology; nor, as the stuff of concrete human existence, can they be considered apart from the kind of relationships that the social sciences take to be real.

On the other hand, no natural scientist would deny that the food he eats or the children seated at his table are all individual realities. No modern social scientist can help considering as very real the admiration he feels for a piece of Greek sculpture or the gloom he feels during the rainy season. On this point the scientist differs not in the least from men of ancient times. The same holds true for the metaphysician. Indeed, the relationship between ideas and sense objects, which has long been the most-debated problem in metaphysics, comes down to the question of deciding what is real.

In short, while the various standpoints of everyday life, science, philosophy, and the like all tell us what is real, there are grave discrepancies and contradictions among them. What the scientist takes to be real from the viewpoint of his science and what he takes to be real from the viewpoint of his everyday experience are completely at odds with each other, and yet he is unable to deny either of them. It is no simple matter to say what is truly real.

In addition to the things mentioned so far, death and nihility are also very real. Nihility is absolute negativity with regard to the very being of all those various things and phenomena just referred to; death is absolute negativity with regard to life itself. Thus, if life and things are said to be real, then death and nihility are equally real. Wherever there are finite beings—and all things are finite—there must be nihility; wherever there is life, there must be death. In the face of death and nihility, all life and existence lose their certainty and their importance as reality, and come to look unreal instead. From time immemorial man has continually expressed this fleeting transience of life and existence, likening it to a dream, a shadow, or the shimmering haze of the summer's heat.

This brings us, then, to another sense of the real altogether different from the various meanings discussed so far. As an example of this sense of the real, I recall a passage from Dostoevski's *The House of the Dead,* recording how, one summer day during the author's term of imprisonment, while he was at work carrying bricks by the banks of a river, he was suddenly struck by the surrounding landscape and overcome with profound emotion. Reflecting on the wild and desolate steppes, the sun blazing overhead in the vast blue vault of heaven, and the distant chanting of the Khirgiz that floated his way from across the river, he writes:

> Sometimes I would fix my sight for a long while upon the poor smokey cabin of some *baigouch;* I would study the bluish smoke as it curled in the air, the Kirghiz woman busy with her sheep. . . . The things I saw were wild, savage, poverty-stricken; but they were free. I would follow the flight of a bird threading its way in the pure transparent air; now it skims the water, now disappears in the azure sky, now suddenly comes to view again, a mere point in space. Even the poor wee floweret fading in a cleft of the bank, which would show itself when spring began, fixed my attention and would draw my tears.

As Dostoevski himself tells us, this is the only spot at which he saw "God's world, a pure and bright horizon, the free desert steppes"; in casting his gaze across the immense desert space, he found he was able to forget his "wretched self."

The things that Dostoevski draws attention to—the curling smoke, the woman tending her sheep, the poor hut, the bird in flight—are all things we come in touch with in our everyday lives. We speak of them as real in the everyday sense of the word, and from there go on to our scientific and philosophical theories. But for such commonplace things to become the focus of so intense a concentration, to capture one's attention to that almost abnormal degree, is by no means an everyday occurrence. Nor does it spring from scientific or metaphysical reflection. Things that we are accustomed to speak of as real forced their reality upon him in a completely different dimension. He saw the same real things we all see, but the significance of their realness and the sense of the real in them that he experienced in perceiving them as real are something altogether qualitatively different. Thus was he able to forget his wretched self and to open his eyes to "God's world."

Later, in *A Raw Youth* and *The Brothers Karamazov,* Dostoevski tells us that God may be found in a single leaf at daybreak, in a beam of sunlight, or in the cry of an infant. This way of speaking suggests a great harmony among all things in the universe that brings them into being and sustains them in mutual dependence and cooperation, a mystical order that rules over all things so that God can be seen in the most trivial of things. This is, we might say, the backdrop against which the author's profound sense of the real in everyday things came into being. We know from *The House of the Dead* that his remarkable sensibility was connected with the prison life that had deprived him of his freedom; but the experience of such a sense of the real does not require such singular circumstances. On the contrary, it is an experience open to anyone and everyone. It is something to which poets and religious men and women have attested down through the ages.

Although we ordinarily think of things in the external world as real, we may not actually get in touch with the reality of those things. I would venture to say that in fact we do not. It is extremely rare for us so to "fix our attention" on things as to "lose ourselves" in them, in other words, to *become* the very things we are looking at. To see through them directly to "God's world," or to the universe in its infinitude, is even rarer. We are accustomed to seeing things from the standpoint of the self. One might say that we look out at things from within the citadel of the self, or that we sit like spectators in the cave of the self. Plato, it will be recalled, likened our ordinary relationship to things to being tied up inside a cave, watching the shadows passing to and fro across its walls, and calling those shadows "reality."

To look at things from the standpoint of the self is always to see things merely as objects, that is, to look at things *without* from a field *within* the self. It means assuming a position vis-à-vis things from which self and things remain fundamentally separated from one another. This standpoint of separation of subject and object, or opposition between within and without, is what we call the field of "consciousness." And it is from this field that we ordinarily relate to things by means of concepts and representations. Hence, for all our talk about the reality of things, things do not truly display their *real* reality to us. On the field of consciousness, it is not possible really to get in touch with things as they are, that is, to face them in their own mode of being and on their own home-ground. On the field of consciousness, self always occupies center stage.

We also think of our own selves, and of our "inner" thoughts, feelings, and desires as real. But here, too, it is doubtful whether we properly get in touch with ourselves, whether our feelings and desires and so forth are in the proper sense really present to us as they are, and whether those feelings should be said to be present on their own home-ground and in their own mode of being. Precisely because we face things on a field separated from things, and to the extent that we do so, we are forever separated from ourselves. Or, to put it in positive terms, we can get in touch with ourselves only through a mode of being that puts us in touch with things from the very midst of those things themselves. We are of course accustomed to set ourselves against what is *without* by looking at it from *within,* and then to think of ourselves as being in our own home-ground and in touch with ourselves when we do so. Such is the bias of consciousness. In fact, however, the self that is self-centered in its relation to the *without* is a self that is separated from things and closed up *within* itself alone. It is a self that continually faces itself in the same way. That is, the self is set ever against itself, as some *thing* called "self" and separated from other things. This is the self of self-consciousness, wherein a representation of the self in the shape of some "thing" or other is always intervening, keeping the self from being really and truly on its own home-ground. In self-consciousness, the self is not really and truly in touch with itself. The same can be said in the case of the internal "consciousness" of feelings, desires, and the like.

Things, the self, feelings, and so forth are all real, to be sure. On the field of consciousness where they are ordinarily taken for real, however, they are not present in their true reality but only in the form of representations. So long as the field of separation between *within* and *without* is not broken through, and so long as a conversion from that standpoint does not take place, the lack of unity and contradiction spoken of earlier cannot help but prevail among the things we take as real. This sort of contradiction shows up, for example, in the opposition between materialism and idealism; but even before it shows up on the level of thought, it is already there beneath the surface of our everyday modes of being and thought. The field that lies at the ground of our everyday lives is the field of an essential separation between self and things, the field of consciousness, within which a real self-presentation of reality cannot take place at all. Within it, reality appears only in the shape of shattered fragments, only in the shape of ineluctable self-contradictions.

This standpoint, which we may best call the self-contradiction of reality, has come to exercise a powerful control over us, never more so than since the emergence of the subjective autonomy of the ego in modern times. This latter appears most forcefully in the thought of Descartes, the father of modern philosophy. As is commonly known, Descartes set up a dualism between *res cogitans* (which has its essence in thought or consciousness) and *res extensa* (which has its essence in physical extension). On the one hand, he established the ego as a reality that is beyond all doubt and occupies the central position with regard to everything else that exists. His *cogito, ergo sum* expressed the mode of being of that ego as a self-centered assertion of its own realness. Along with this, on the other hand, the things in the natural world came to appear as bearing no living connection with the internal ego. They became, so to speak, the cold and lifeless world of death. Even animals and the body of man himself were thought of as mechanisms.

That such a mechanistic view of the world would come into being and that the world itself would turn into a world of death were, we might say, already implicit in Descartes' identification of matter with extension and his consideration of that extension as the essence of things. This did enable the image of the world we find in modern natural science to come about and did open the way for the control of nature by scientific technology. But it had other consequences. To the self-centered ego of man, the world came to look like so much raw material. By wielding his great power and authority in controlling the natural world, man came to surround himself with a cold, lifeless world. Inevitably, each individual ego became like a lonely but well-fortified island floating on a sea of dead matter. The life was snuffed out of nature and the things of nature; the living stream that flowed at the bottom of man and all things, and kept them bound together, dried up.

The idea of life as a living bond had been central to the prescientific, pre-Cartesian view of the world. Life was *alive* then not only in the sense of the individual lives of individual people, but, at the same time and in a very real way, as something uniting parents and children, brothers and sisters, and thence all men. It was as if each individual human being were born from the same life, like the individual leaves of a tree that sprout and grow and fall one by one and yet share in the same life of the tree. Not only human beings, but all living beings belonged to the larger tree of life. Even the soul (or psyche) was nothing more than life showing itself. Appearing as men, life took the form of a human soul; appearing as plants and animals, that of a plant or animal soul—for plants and animals, too, were thought to have their own souls.

Furthermore, on the basis of the life that linked individual things together at bottom, a sympathetic affinity was thought to obtain between one man's soul and another's. This "sympathy" was meant to bespeak a contact prior to and more immediate than consciousness. It was meant to point to the field of the most immediate encounter between man and man, at the ground of the instincts and drives that underlie all thought, feeling, and desire. More than that, this same sympathy was thought to exist not only among men, but among all living things. In other words, the vital connective that bound individual beings to one another was thought to appear as a field of "psychic sympathy" between souls. Of course, this view seems to have all but been wiped out completely by the modern mechanistic view of nature. But is that cause enough simply to dismiss it as antiquated?

On a summer's night, a mosquito flies into my room from the outside. It buzzes about merrily, as if cheering itself for having found its prey. With a single motion I catch it and squash it in the palm of my hand, and in that final moment it lets out a shrill sound of distress. This is the only word we can use to describe it. The sound it makes is different from the howling of a dog or the screams of a man, and yet in its "essence" it is the selfsame sound of distress. It may be that each of these sounds is but vibrations of air moving at different wavelengths, but they all possess the same quality or essence that makes us hear them as signals of distress. Does not our immediate intuition of the distress in the sound of the mosquito take place on a field of psychic sympathy? Might we not also see here the reason that the ancients believed animals to have souls? In this sense, whatever modern mechanistic physiologists or functionalist psychologists, who are busy trying to erase the notion of soul, might make of it, let it be said that there is something, even in animals, that we have no other name for than the one that has come down to us from the past: soul.

Just what this "something" ought to be said to consist of is, of course, another problem. It may no longer be necessary to think of the soul as some special substance. Perhaps it is not even possible to continue to think of it as something with an independent existence that takes up lodging "within" the body. This view requires us to look on the body, too, as something independent, a lifeless object with an existence all its own apart from the soul. It means considering body and soul as distinct substances, and then trying to determine how they come to be joined together.

It is also possible to approach the question from the opposite direction. For instance, Schopenhauer takes "the Will to Live" as the thing-in-itself and considers the body, as an organism, to be the objectification of that will, the form under which it appears to the eye of man. Bergson expresses a similar idea when he says that in its material aspect the body represents a point of relaxation for the tension inherent in life as it advances creatively. In both cases, individuals appear as individualizations of something else—be it "will" or "life"—that is at work within them. This is another possible way of viewing the soul. Along this same line, ancient peoples imagined that one soul could take on a variety of different animal bodies in succession, which belief then led to such notions as reincarnation and metempsychosis. We may wish to dismiss such ideas as extravagant fantasies, but we should still see behind them the view of soul just referred to.

Even granting that we cannot really get in touch with reality on the fields of consciousness and self-consciousness, neither can we stop short at the viewpoint of preconscious life and sympathy that we have described above. More than a few religions have in fact based themselves on a return to just such a preconscious level; but at that level, it is impossible to get deeply in touch with reality. Instead of regressing from the field of consciousness to a preconscious or subconscious one, we need rather to seek a new and more encompassing viewpoint that passes through, indeed *breaks through*, the field of consciousness to give us a new perspective. . . .

Suggestions for Further Reading

Abelson, Raziel. "Definition." In *The Encyclopedia of Philosophy,* vol. 2. Edited by Paul Edwards, pp. 314–324. New York: Macmillan and The Free Press, 1967.

Alston, William P. "Religion." In *The Encyclopedia of Philosophy,* vol. 7. Edited by Paul Edwards, pp. 140–145. New York: Macmillan and The Free Press, 1967.

Comstock, Richard. "Toward Open Definitions of Religion." *Journal of the American Academy of Religion* LII (September 1984):499–515.

Durkheim, Emile. *The Elementary Forms of Religious Life.* London: Allen and Unwin, 1915.

Eliade, Mircea. *The Sacred and the Profane: The Nature of Religion.* New York: Harcourt, 1959.

Evans-Pritchard, E. E. "Religion." In *The Institutions of Primitive Society.* Edited by E. E. Evans-Pritchard *et al.,* pp. 37–56. Oxford: Basil Blackwell, 1956.

Hegel, G. W. "The Concept of Religion." In *Lectures on the Philosophy of Religion,* vol. 1. Edited by Peter C. Hodgson, pp. 185ff. Berkeley, CA: University of California Press, 1984.

King, Winston L. "Religion." In *The Encyclopedia of Religion,* vol. 12. Edited by Mircea Eliade, pp. 282–292. New York: Macmillan, 1987.

Smith, Jonathan A. *Imagining Religion.* Chicago: The University of Chicago Press, 1982.

Stark, Rodney; and Bainbridge, William Sims. "The Nature of Religion." In *The Future of Religion: Secularization, Revival, and Cult Formation,* pp. 1–10. Berkeley: University of California Press, 1985.

Streng, Frederick J. *Understanding Religious Life.* 3d ed. Belmont, CA: Wadsworth, 1985.

Tillich, Paul. *Dynamics of Faith.* New York: Harper & Row, 1958.

Whitehead, Alfred N. *Religion in the Making.* New York: Macmillan, 1926.

Yinger, Milton J. *Religion, Society and the Individual,* pp. 6–17. New York: Macmillan, 1957.

CHAPTER 2

Diverse Views of Ultimate Reality

Introduction

MANY ARGUE THAT the idea of an ultimate reality is central to religion. This, however, need not be the case. For example, totemism (worship of a plant or animal thought to be an ancestor of the tribe), animism (worship of spirits thought to inhabit and animate aspects of nature), polytheism (worship of many gods) and henotheism (recognition that many gods exist, but worship of only one of them) characterize many religions. The totem, the spirit, and the god are real, but should we think of them as *ultimately* real or simply as *superior* powers? The whole notion of some ultimate, absolute, infinite, unconditioned, and highest reality probably would not make much sense from the totemic, animistic, polytheistic, and henotheistic viewpoints. From these viewpoints, any reality or power greater than humans and related to human beings and nature in important ways is worth worshipping.

However, many religions do claim that there is an ultimate reality (although they disagree about its nature). Some claim it is God in the sense of a personal being. This outlook is usually called theism. Others claim it is nonpersonal or transcends the categories of personal/nonpersonal. We could call this outlook nontheism. However, the use of the word *God* is tricky and often confusing. By "God" some mean simply that which is ultimate, in which case "God" designates whatever is understood by the term *ultimate reality*. Others restrict the use of the term to a personal being. I will use the term *ultimate reality* to designate whatever religions take to be ultimate insofar as they recognize that there *is* something ultimate. Hence, from my viewpoint, the idea of an ultimate reality can be understood both theistically and nontheistically.

What, if anything, is ultimate? In the history of religious thought, there have been many different answers to that question. Some hold that ultimate reality is the way nature operates. Thus Taoism holds that the Tao, or the Way of Nature, is ultimate. This view is sometimes called pantheism, but that word is misleading. Literally, *pantheism* means "everything is divine or God." Yet philosophical Taoism does not explicitly identify the Tao with the divine and holds that it is not only the Way of Nature but also the source or origin of nature. Is the source of something identical to it? Is such an ultimate personal? Certainly it includes persons, because persons are part of nature, but it includes much more as well.

Some argue that the term *panentheism* ("everything is *in* God") better characterizes the view that ultimate reality is the source of the universe (and hence not identical to the universe) and that the universe is also the self-expression of this source. However, according to Taoism, the Tao is subtle and elusive. It is the "Nameless" (see Reading 2.1).

Some Indian philosophers think of ultimate reality as *Satchitanada* (Being, Consciousness, Bliss). *Satchitanada* is the sole reality, and once humans realize this truth, they are released from suffering, thereby attaining bliss (see Reading 2.2). This reality may include a notion of a personal God as a lower manifestation, but ultimate reality is greater than a personal God or Lord. This is not unlike the distinction some Christian theologians have made between the Godhead (the essence of divinity or ultimate reality in itself) and God (the manifestation or expression of the Godhead apprehended by humans).

Monotheism usually insists that ultimate reality is personal (see Reading 2.3). There is only one personal God, and that God is either an absolute unity (unitarianism) or a tri-unity (trinitarianism). Typically Judaism and Islam emphasize the former, and Christianity (with some notable exceptions) the latter. In addition, God is said to possess all possible perfections (and hence to be ultimate). Thus God's knowledge, power, will, mercy, justice, and so on are of the greatest possible magnitude. Indeed God is infinite (unconditioned) in all respects, whereas the universe and humans are finite (conditioned).

If God is personal, does God have a gender? Certainly personal beings do. Is God a "he" or a "she"? Either answer appears both to reinforce sexism by elevating one sex over another and to limit God and thereby contradict the claim that God is an infinite, ultimate reality (see Reading 2.5).

The search for an ultimate reality takes human thought in a variety of different directions. Some Buddhist philosophers maintain that nothing less than "emptiness" will do as an adequate characterization of ultimacy. Ultimate reality is not a god, for *a* god is a limited being. True ultimacy cannot be a particular thing. If it were, it would be finite, or conditioned. Thus it must be a no-thing in the sense that it is not just another item in the universe. Then what are the items that make up the universe? Are they too empty? Ultimately they too are empty in the sense that they have no independent substantial existence (see Reading 2.4).

"Wait a minute," you might be saying, "this is going too fast. You have not even defined *ultimate reality* yet. What is it, anyway? Is it the most perfect actual being or the most perfect possible being? Is it even a being at all?"

These are very good questions, and they are not easy to answer. If reality is measured on a scale from 1 to 10, then the most perfect actual being might be an 8, because 8 is very high on the scale of perfection and is much greater than the second-most-perfect actual reality (say, a 4). But if a 10 is the top of the scale and there cannot ever be anything higher, then would not what is ultimate have to rank a 10? Yet could a mere being ever rank so high? Would not *being itself* or the ground or *source* of being rank higher? And if there is a source of both being and non-being, would not this be higher still? Is there a highest? If there is, can we even think it, let alone define it? Perhaps our language is just carrying us off into a never-never land of paradoxes (if not contradictions) when we try to talk about the nature of ultimate reality. Let's see.

2.1 The Tao

Scholars of Chinese religion use the term *Taoism* to refer to a complex interweaving of religious practices and philosophic thought. In 142 Chang Tao-ling had a vision of Lao-tzu, a legendary sage, as an Immortal being, who gave him the title of Heavenly Master. In this vision, Lao-tzu instructed Tao-ling to institute new forms of worship and to teach people to abandon the old gods. The group Tao-ling founded eventually combined with other reform movements that stressed meditation, breathing exercises, doing good deeds, diet, various healing practices, and alchemical searches for an elixir of immortality. The idea of a future heavenly state of peace and harmony that could be achieved on earth became part of the mix. Over time these elements coalesced into Taoism, one of the three major strands of Chinese religion (the other two are Confucianism and Buddhism)

But who was Lao-tzu? According to tradition, he was the author of a book called the *Tao Te Ching* (*The Book of the Way and Its Excellence*). There are stories about Lao-tzu and when he lived, but we have very little firm historical information. Some claim he was a contemporary of Confucius (551–479 B.C.E.), but others have placed his book later (403–221 B.C.E.).

The *Tao Te Ching* is a classic of world literature. However, its meaning is very obscure, and it has been interpreted in a wide variety of ways. Scholars have argued it is a treatise on how one should live, that it is a political manual offering advice to government officials on how best to govern, that it is a metaphysical discussion of the ultimate source of reality, that it is a collection of anti-Confucian sayings, and so on. I have selected those chapters of the *Tao Te Ching* that have to do with the Tao, which literally means "way or road," because our concerns here are with different views of ultimate reality. The word *Tao* is used by Taoists to refer to the Way of Nature. This Way is indescribable. It transcends human thought and vocabulary. The best humans can do is hint at its nature by the use of metaphors and analogies. Thus it is compared to a valley, the empty space between mountains that makes mountains possible. It is compared to water that is weak in its fluidity, yet strong in its ability to bring about change. It is like the empty space inside a bowel. Without that space, the bowel would be useless. It acts by "not acting," (*wu-wei* means "no action"); that is, its actions are spontaneous, free, and natural, unlike the formal, rigid, and artificial actions, manners, and customs that the Confucians (according to the Taoists) maintain are necessary for a peaceful society.

The Tao is the source of all things and pervades all things. It is the *Te* ("excellence, power, or virtue") of nature. If all things could realize their full potential, they would actualize their *te* and would thereby be living in harmony with the Way of nature (Tao).

The world generated by Tao is an ever-changing flow of oppositions. At times the *yin,* or the passive, dominates. At other times the *yang,* or the active, dominates.

Yin and *yang* stand for *complementary* opposites. You cannot have one without the other. The seasonal cycle is an example. Winter is the most *yin* season. Life processes are slow. It is cold and dark. However, winter contains an element of *yang* that develops until we reach spring, with its warmth, light, and flourishing life. *Yang* reaches its zenith in summer. Yet summer contains an element of *yin* that expands into fall and then winter again.

According to Lao-tzu, Tao is prior to the gods. It is the most basic and fundamental reality. It is that which is truly real. It is the organic harmony that is the foundation of all things.

Reading Questions

1. Why do you think the Tao is called the Nameless?
2. According to Chapter 2, what is the nature of opposites?
3. Why do you think the Tao is called the invisible, inaudible, and formless?
4. What do you think "reversion is the action of the Tao" means?
5. If to exist is to exist as a some-thing distinguishable from other things, can the Tao exist? Why or why not?

The Tao*

LAO-TZU

1

The Tao that can be told of is not the
   eternal Tao;
The name that can be named is not the
   eternal name.
The Nameless is the origin of Heaven and
   Earth;
The Named is the mother of all things.

Therefore let there always be non-being,
   so we may see their subtlety,
And let there always be being, so we may
   see their outcome.
The two are the same,
But after they are produced, they have
   different names.

They both may be called deep and
   profound.
Deeper and more profound,
The door of all subtleties!

2

When the people of the world all know
   beauty as beauty,
   There arises the recognition of ugliness.
When they all know the good as good,
   There arises the recognition of evil.
Therefore:
   Being and non-being produce each
     other;

* From *A Source Book of Chinese Philosophy*, translated by Wing-tsit Chan. Copyright © 1963 by Princeton University Press. Reprinted by permission of Princeton University Press, Princeton, NJ. Footnotes edited.

Difficult and easy complete each other;
Long and short contrast each other;
High and low distinguish each other;
Sound and voice harmonize each
    other;
Front and behind accompany each
    other.

Therefore the sage manages affairs
    without action
And spreads doctrines without words.
All things arise, and he does not turn
    away from them.
He produces them but does not take
    possession of them.
He acts but does not rely on his own
    ability.
He accomplishes his task but does not
    claim credit for it.
It is precisely because he does not claim
    credit that his accomplishment
    remains with him.

4

Tao is empty (like a bowl).
    It may be used but its capacity is never
        exhausted.
    It is bottomless, perhaps the ancestor
        of all things.
    It blunts its sharpness,
    It unties its tangles.
    It softens its light.
    It becomes one with the dusty world.
    Deep and still, it appears to exist
        forever.
    I do not know whose son it is.
    It seems to have existed before the
        Lord.

6

The spirit of the valley never dies.
    It is called the subtle and profound
        female.
The gate of the subtle and profound
    female
    Is the root of Heaven and Earth.

It is continuous, and seems to be always
    existing.
Use it and you will never wear it out.

8

The best (man)[1] is like water.
    Water is good; it benefits all things and
        does not compete with them.
It dwells in (lowly) places that all
    disdain.
This is why it is so near to Tao.

(The best man) in his dwelling loves the
    earth.
In his heart, he loves what is profound.
In his associations, he loves humanity.
In his words, he loves faithfulness.
In government, he loves order.
In handling affairs, he loves competence.
In his activities, he loves timeliness.
It is because he does not compete that he
    is without reproach.

11

Thirty spokes are united around the hub
    to make a wheel,
    But it is on its non-being that the
        utility of the carriage depends.
Clay is molded to form a utensil,
    But it is on its non-being that the
        utility of the utensil depends.
Doors and windows are cut out to make
    a room,
    But it is on its non-being that the
        utility of the room depends.
Therefore turn being into advantage, and
    turn non-being into utility.

14

We look at it and do not see it;
    Its name is The Invisible.
We listen to it and do not hear it;
    Its name is The Inaudible.
We touch it and do not find it;
    Its name is The Subtle (formless).

These three cannot be further inquired
    into,
And hence merge into one.
Going up high, it is not bright, and
    coming down low, it is not dark.
Infinite and boundless, it cannot be given
    any name;
It reverts to nothingness.
This is called shape without shape,
Form without objects.
It is The Vague and Elusive.
Meet it and you will not see its head.
Follow it and you will not see its back.
Hold on to the Tao of old in order to
    master the things of the present.
From this one may know the primeval
    beginning (of the universe).
This is called the bond[2] of Tao.

25

There was something undifferentiated
    and yet complete,
Which existed before heaven and earth.
Soundless and formless, it depends on
    nothing and does not change.
It operates everywhere and is free from
    danger.
It may be considered the mother of the
    universe.
I do not know its name; I call it Tao.
If forced to give it a name, I shall call it
    Great.
Now being great means functioning
    everywhere.
Functioning everywhere means
    far-reaching.
Being far-reaching means returning to the
    original point.

Therefore Tao is great.
Heaven is great.
Earth is great.
And the king[3] is also great.
There are four great things in the universe,
    and the king is one of them.
Man models himself after Earth.
Earth models itself after Heaven.
Heaven models itself after Tao.
And Tao models itself after Nature.

34

The Great Tao flows everywhere.
It may go left or right.
All things depend on it for life, and it does
    not turn away from them.
It accomplishes its task but does not claim
    credit for it.
It clothes and feeds all things but does not
    claim to be master over them.
Always without desires, it may be called
    The Small.
All things come to it and it does not master
    them; it may be called The Great.
Therefore (the sage) never strives himself
    for the great, and thereby the great is
    achieved.

37

Tao invariably takes no action, and yet
    there is nothing left undone.
If kings and barons can keep it, all things
    will transform spontaneously.
If, after transformation, they should desire
    to be active,
I would restrain them with simplicity,
    which has no name.
Simplicity, which has no name, is free of
    desires.
Being free of desires, it is tranquil.
And the world will be at peace of its own
    accord.

40

Reversion is the action of Tao.
Weakness is the function of Tao.
All things in the world come from being.
And being comes from non-being.[4]

42

Tao produced the One.
The One produced the two.
The two produced the three.

And the three produced the ten
thousand things.
The ten thousand things carry the yin and
embrace the yang, and through the
blending of the material force they
achieve harmony.

People hate to be children without
parents, lonely people without spouses,
or men without food to eat,
And yet kings and lords call themselves by
these names.
Therefore it is often the case that things
gain by losing and lose by gaining.

What others have taught, I teach also:
"Violent and fierce people do not die a
natural death."
I shall make this the father of my teaching.

NOTES

1. Most commentators and translators have understood the Chinese phrase literally as "the highest good," but some commentators and translators, including Lin Yutang, Cheng Lin, and Bynner, have followed Wang Pi and taken the phrase to mean "the best man." Both interpretations are possible. The former interpretation has a parallel in chapter 38, which talks about the highest virtue, while the latter has a parallel in chapter 17, where both Wang Pi and Ho-shang Kung interpret *the best* to mean "the best ruler." I have followed Wang Pi, not only because his commentary on the text is the oldest and most reliable, but also because the *Lao Tzu* deals with man's way of life more than with abstract ideas.

2. *Chi,* literally "a thread," denotes tradition, discipline, principle, order, essence, etc. Generally it means the system, principle, or continuity that binds things together.

3. The Fu I and Fan Ying-yüan texts have *man* in place of *king*. This substitution has been accepted by Hsi T'ung, Ma Hsü-lun, Ch'en Chu, Jen Chi-yü, and Ch'u Ta-kao. They have been influenced, undoubtedly, by the concept of the trinity of Heaven, Earth, and man, without realizing that the king is considered here as representative of men. Moreover, in chapters 16 and 39, Heaven, Earth, and the king are spoken of together.

4. Cf. chapter 1. This seems to contradict the saying "Being and non-being produce each other" in chapter 2. But to produce means not to originate but to bring about.

2.2 Non-Dualism

Philosophical reflection on religion in India is ancient, rich, and diverse. The *Veda* is the name for the oldest scriptures of India, and the *Upanishads* form the last section. Hence they are called *Vedanta,* which means "the end of the *Veda.*" One of the many philosophical schools of India became known as *Vedanta* because its primary concern was to elaborate on the philosophical implications of the *Upanishads.* The most influential members of this school were Shankara, Ramanuja, and Madhva.

Shankara (c. 788–820) developed ideas that constitute *Advaita* (non-dualistic) *Vedanta.* Shankara was a philosopher, a religious reformer, a founder of an order of monks, a teacher, and an author. He presents his system as an explication of the meaning of the saying *tat tvam asi* ("Thou art That") found in the *Upanishads.*

According to Shankara, our task, when dealing with metaphysical questions related to the nature of reality, is to distinguish among reality, appearance, and unreality. To do this, we need a principle of discrimination called sublation.

Sublation is an act whereby a previous experience or judgment is corrected in light of a subsequent experience or judgment. For example, upon waking you reinterpret your previous experiences as dreaming. Your dream experiences are corrected, or sublated, by your waking experiences. Sublatability refers to the qualities something has that allow it to be sublated. These qualities are three. (1) It must be an object of the awareness of some subject. (2) It must be distinguishable from other objects, so the category of multiplicity is applicable to it. (3) It must be impermanent and hence subject to time and change.

If we define reality as what cannot be sublated, appearance as what can be sublated, and unreality as neither sublatable nor unsublatable (because nonexistent), then our philosophical task is to analyze our experiences in order to see into which of the three categories our experiences fall.

Shankara argues that everything experienced as internal—sensations, emotions, desires, thoughts, mind, intelligence, our ego or individual self—is sublatable. These are all objects of awareness, they are distinguishable from one another, and they change. But is consciousness itself sublatable? Shankara contends that consciousness in and of itself, pure consciousness, it not sublatable. He calls it the Atman (the true Self).

Let us now consider those objects of our experience that seem to be external. Are they appearance or reality? According to Shankara, they are sublatable by the divine because the divine is permanent, in contrast to the temporal and changing objects we experience as external. *Isvara* (Lord) is the name Shankara uses for the divine that has attributes (*saguna*) such as creator, good, merciful, and so on. *Isvara*, in turn, is sublatable by Brahman. Brahman is without attributes (*nirguna*). A reality without qualities is a non-dual reality beyond any multiplicity because nothing qualifies it.

Are there two ultimates, Atman and Brahman? There cannot be two ultimates. That is a contradiction in terms. Therefore Atman must be Brahman. This is the meaning of the saying in the *Upanishads tat tvam asi*. Atman and Brahman are non-dual.

Why, then, do we experience plurality—a world made up of many things? Plurality is an illusion or appearance (*maya*) that is due to our ignorance of the true nature of reality as non-dual. But whence comes such ignorance or nescience (*avidya*)?

It is due to superimposition. We superimpose on non-dual Brahman the images of many things. For example, we superimpose on a coiled rope the image of a snake. But do not our experiences show us that reality is plural, not non-dual?

Shankara distinguishes between lower knowledge—whose six sources are perception, inference, testimony, comparison, postulation, and noncognition (immediate cognition of the nonexistence of an object)—and higher knowledge—the immediate intuitive awareness of the identity of Atman with Brahman. Lower knowledge yields only knowledge of appearances: the way things seem to be to us. Higher knowledge gives us reality.

When we awake from our dreams, we think we know the way things really are rather than the way they appeared to be in our dreams. However, what we call being awake is just dreaming on another level. Beyond this is another awakening, and from the point of view of that higher knowledge, this will all appear to be a dream.

Shankara's views about what is ultimately real seemed so counterintuitive that they did not go unchallenged. Ramanuja (eleventh century) argued for a qualified non-dualism. He contended that the universe, the self, and God are all equally real, although the world and the self depend on God in an important way. Brahman or God has two forms: selves and matter. Yet these forms constitute irreducible realities. This viewpoint is a "qualified" non-dualism in the sense that both selves and matter are "forms" of Brahman although not reducible to Brahman.

Madhva (1197–1276) argued for dualism. There is God (Brahman) who is the eternally real and perfect. In addition, there are individual selves and matter. The distinctions among God and the individual self, God and matter, individual selves, selves and matter, and individual material substances are all fundamental and irreducible. The material universe and individual selves are not forms or aspects of Brahman, although they are dependent on Brahman for their existence.

Shankara, Ramanuja, and Madhva have differing notions of reality, but all three agree that true knowledge of reality can release or free (*mokhsa*) one from what appeared to many people in their society to be an endless round of painful reincarnations or transmigrations. Thus their philosophical reflections, however abstract, have a practical application.

The following selection represents Shankara's views. It is from his book *A Thousand Teachings*. The book consists of a metrical part in which he explains his key ideas and a prose part in which he engages in a dialogue with a pupil who wants to know how he can be released from "transmigratory existence." As Shankara answers, the pupil raises various objections, and Shankara (the teacher) provides a response. Do the responses convince you?

Reading Questions

1. Why will knowledge of Brahman, not action, destroy ignorance?
2. Why must we abandon the whole universe, our bodies, and even what we call our "I" in order to grasp Atman?
3. How is the highest Brahman characterized?
4. Who are we really, according to Shankara?
5. What is nescience (ignorance)?
6. How does the teacher (Shankara) respond to the objection by the pupil that "non-Atman cannot be superimposed upon Atman because Atman is not fully known"?
7. In paragraph 55 of the prose part, the pupil raises a crucial objection. What is the objection and how does the teacher answer? Do you find the teacher's answer adequate or not? Why?
8. Why is the pupil in doubt about being "transcendentally changeless," and how does the teacher respond?

Non-Dualism*

SHANKARA

A. *Metrical Part*

CHAPTER 1 PURE CONSCIOUSNESS

1. Salutation to the all-knowing Pure Consciousness which pervades all, is all, abides in the hearts of all beings, and is beyond all objects [of knowledge].

2. Having completed all the rituals, preceded by the marriage ceremony and the ceremony of installing the sacred fire, the *Veda* has now begun to utter knowledge of *Brahman*.

3. *Karmans* [as the results of actions, good or bad, in the past existence] produce association with a body. When there is association with a body, pleasant and unpleasant things are inevitable. From these result passion and aversion [and] from them actions.

4. [From actions] merit and demerit result [and] from merit and demerit there results an ignorant man's association with a body in the same manner again. Thus this transmigratory existence rolls onward powerfully forever like a wheel.

5. Since the root cause of this transmigratory existence is ignorance, its destruction is desired. Knowledge of *Brahman* therefore is entered on. Final beatitude results from this knowledge.

6. Only knowledge [of *Brahman*] can destroy ignorance; action cannot [destroy it] since [action] is not incompatible [with ignorance]. Unless ignorance is destroyed, passion and aversion will not be destroyed.

7. Unless passion and aversion are destroyed, action arises inevitably from [those] faults. Therefore, for the sake of final beatitude, only knowledge [of *Brahman*] is set forth here [in the Vedānta]. . . .

CHAPTER 6 HAVING CUT

1. *Ātman* Itself is not qualified by a hand which has been cut off and thrown away. Likewise, none of the rest [of the body] qualifies [*Ātman*].

2. Therefore, every qualification is the same as a hand which has been thrown away, since it is non-*Ātman*. Therefore, the Knower (= *Ātman*) is devoid of all qualifications.

3. This whole [universe] is qualification, like a beautiful ornament, which is superimposed [upon *Ātman*] through nescience. Therefore, when *Ātman* has been known, the whole [universe] becomes non-existent.

4. One should always grasp *Ātman* alone as the Knower, disconnected [from all qualifications], and abandon the object of knowledge. One should grasp that what is called "I" is also the same as a part which has been abandoned.

5. As long as the "this"-portion is a qualification [of *ātman*], that ["I"-portion] is different from [*Ātman*] Itself. When the qualification has been destroyed, the Knower is established [independently from it], as a man who owns a brindled cow [is established independently from it].

6. The learned should abandon the "this"-portion in what is called "I," understanding that it is not *Ātman*. ["I" in the sentence of the *Śruti*] "I am *Brahman*" (Brh. Up. I,4,10) is the portion which has been left unabandoned in accordance with the above teaching.

CHAPTER 8 THE NATURE OF PURE CONSCIOUSNESS

1. I Myself have the nature of Pure Consciousness, O Mind; [My apparent] connection with taste, etc., is caused by your delusion.

Therefore no result due to your activity would belong to Me, since I am free from all attributes.

2. Abandon here activity born of illusion and come ever to rest from search for the wrong, since I am forever the highest *Brahman*, released, as it were, unborn, one alone, and without duality.

3. And I am always the same to beings, one alone; [I am] the highest [*Brahman*] which, like the sky, is all-pervading, imperishable, auspicious, uninterrupted, undivided and devoid of action. Therefore no result from your efforts here pertains to Me.

4. I am one alone; No other than that [*Brahman*] is thought to be Mine. In like manner I do not belong to anything since I am free from attachment. I have by nature no attachment. Therefore I do not need you nor your work since I am non-dual.

5. Considering that people are attached to cause and effect, I have composed this dialogue, making [them] understand the meaning of the truth of their own nature, so that they may be released from [their] attachment to cause and effect.

6. If a man ponders on this dialogue, he will be released from ignorance, the origin of great fears. And such a man is always free from desire; being a knower of *Ātman*, he is ever free from sorrow, the same [to beings], and happy.

CHAPTER 10   SEEING

1. The highest [*Brahman*]—which is of the nature of Seeing, like the sky, ever-shining, unborn, one alone, imperishable, stainless, all-pervading, and non-dual—That am I and I am forever released. Om.[1]

2. I am Seeing, pure and by nature changeless. There is by nature no object for me. Being the Infinite, completely filled in front, across, up, down, and in every direction, I am unborn, abiding in Myself.

3. I am unborn, deathless, free from old age, immortal, self-effulgent, all-pervading, non-dual; I am neither cause nor effect, altogether stainless, always satisfied and therefore [constantly] released. Om.

4. Whether in the state of deep sleep or of waking or of dreaming, no delusive perception appears to pertain to Me in this world. As those [three states] have no existence, self-dependent or other-dependent, I am always the Fourth, the Seeing and the non-dual.

5. The continuous series of pains due to the body, the intellect and the senses is neither I nor of Me, for I am changeless. And this is because the continual series [of pain] is unreal; it is indeed unreal like an object seen by a dreaming man.

6. It is true that I have neither change nor any cause of change, since I am non-dual. I have neither good nor bad deeds, neither final release nor bondage, neither caste nor stages of life, since I am bodiless.

7. Since I am beginningless and attributeless, I have neither action nor result [of action]. Therefore I am the highest [*Ātman*], non-dual. Just as the ether, though all-pervading, is not stained, so am I not either, though abiding in the body, since I am subtle.

8. And I am always the same to [all] beings, the Lord, for I am superior to, and higher than, the perishable and the imperishable. Though I have the highest *Ātman* as my true nature and am non-dual, I am nevertheless covered with wrong knowledge which is nescience.

9. Being perfectly stainless, *Ātman* is distinguished from, and broken by, nescience, residual impression, and actions. Being filled with powers such as Seeing, I am non-dual, standing [perfect] in my own nature and motionless like the sky.

10. He who sees *Ātman* with the firm belief "I am the highest *Brahman*" "is born no more" (Kaṭh. Up. I,38), says the *Śruti*. When there is no seed, no fruit is produced. Therefore there is no birth, for there is no delusion.

11. "This is mine, being thus," "That is yours, being of such kind," "Likewise, I am so, not superior nor otherwise"—[such] assumptions of people concerning *Brahman*, which is the same [to all beings], non-dual and auspicious, are nothing but their stupidity.

12. When there is completely non-dual and stainless knowledge, then the great-souled experiences neither sorrow nor delusion. In the absence

of both there is neither action nor birth. This is the firm belief of those who know the *Veda*.

13. He who, in the waking state, like a man in the state of deep sleep, does not see duality, though [actually] seeing, because of his non-duality, and similarly he who, though [in fact] acting, is actionless—he [only] is the knower of *Ātman*, and nobody else. This is the firm conclusion here [in the Vedānta].

14. This view which has been declared by me from the standpoint of the highest truth is the supreme [view] as ascertained in the Vedānta. If a man has firm belief in it, he is released and not stained by actions, as others are.

CHAPTER 13   EYELESSNESS

1. As I am eyeless, I do not see. Likewise, as I am earless, how shall I hear? As I have no organ of speech, I do not speak. As I am mindless, how shall I think?

2. As I am devoid of the life principle,[2] I do not act. Being without intellect, I am not a knower. Therefore I have neither knowledge nor nescience, having the light of Pure Consciousness only.

3. Ever-free, pure, transcendentally changeless, invariable, immortal, imperishable, and thus always bodiless.

4. [All-] pervading like ether, I have neither hunger nor thirst, neither sorrow nor delusion, neither decay nor death, since I am bodiless.

5. As I have no sense of touch, I do not touch. As I have no tongue, I do not perceive taste. As I am of the nature of constant knowledge, I never have [either] knowledge or ignorance.

6. The modification of the mind, which is caused by the eye and takes on form-and-color [of its object], is certainly always seen by the constant Seeing of *Ātman*.

7. In like manner the modifications [of the mind] which are connected with the senses other [than the eye] and are colored by [external] objects; also [the modification of the mind] in the form of memory and in the forms of passion and the like; which is unconnected [from the senses], located in the mind;

8. and the modifications of the mind in the dreaming state are also seen to be an other's. The

Seeing of the Seer is, therefore, constant, pure, infinite, and alone.

9. The Seeing is [wrongly] taken to be inconstant and impure because of the absence of discriminating knowledge with regard to It. Similarly, I experience pleasure and pain through [a seeing] which is the object and adjunct [of the Seeing].

10. Through deluded [seeing] all people think, "[I am] deluded," and again through a pure [seeing] they think, "[I am] pure"; for this reason they continue in transmigratory existence.

11. If one is a seeker after final release in this world, he should always remember *Ātman* which is ever-free, described in the scripture as eyeless, etc. [which] includes the exterior and the interior, and is unborn.

12. And as the scripture says that I am eyeless, etc., no senses at all belong to Me. And there are the words in the [Muṇḍ. Up. (II,1,2)] belonging to the *Atharvaveda,* "[He is . . .] breathless, mindless, pure."

13. As it is stated in the Kaṭh. Up. (I,3,15) that I do not have sound, etc., and [in the Muṇḍ. Up. (II,1,2) that I am] "without breath, without mind," I am indeed always changeless.

14. Therefore, mental restlessness does not belong to Me. Therefore, concentration does not belong to Me. Both mental restlessness and concentration belong [only] to the changeable mind.

15. As I am without mind and pure, how can those two (= restlessness and concentration) belong to Me? Freedom from mind and freedom from change belong to Me who am bodiless and [all-]pervading.

16. Thus, as long as I had this ignorance, I had duties to perform, though I am ever-free, pure, and always enlightened.

17. How can concentration, non-concentration, or anything else which is to be done belong to Me? For, having meditated on and known Me, they realize that they have completed [all] that had to be done.

18. "I am *Brahman*" (Bṛh. Up. I,4,10). I am all, always pure, enlightened and unfettered, unborn, all-pervading, undecaying, immortal, and imperishable.

19. In no being is there any Knower other than Myself; [I am] the Overseer of deeds, the Witness, the Observer, constant, attributeless, and non-dual.

20. I am neither existent nor non-existent nor both, being alone and auspicious. To Me, the Seeing, there is neither twilight nor night nor day at any time.

21. Just as ether is free from all forms, is subtle and non-dual, so am I devoid even of this [ether], I am *Brahman,* non-dual.

22. My separatedness, *i.e.,* in the form "my *ātman,*" "his *ātman,*" and "your *ātman,*" is what is falsely constructed [on Me], just as the difference of one and the same ether arises from the difference of holes [in various objects].

23. Difference and non-difference, one and many, object of knowledge and knower, movement and mover—how can these [notions] be falsely constructed on Me who am one alone?

24. Nothing to be rejected or accepted belongs to Me, for I am changeless, always released and pure, always enlightened, attributeless, and non-dual.

25. Thus, with concentrated mind, one should always know everything as *Ātman.* Having known Me to be abiding in one's own body, one is a sage, released and immovable.

26. If a *Yogin* thus knows the meaning of the truth, he is one who has completed all that was to be done, a perfected one and knower of *Brahman.* [If he knows] otherwise, he is a slayer of *Ātman.*

27. The meaning of the *Veda* herein determined, which has been briefly related by me, should be imparted to serene wandering ascetics by one of disciplined intellect.

B. *Prose Part*

CHAPTER 2   AWARENESS

45. A certain student, who was tired of transmigratory existence characterized by birth and death and was seeking after final release, approached in the prescribed manner a knower of *Brahman* who was established in *Brahman* and sitting at his ease, and asked him, "Your Holiness, how can I be released from transmigratory existence? I am aware of the body, the senses and [their] objects; I experience pain in the waking state, and I experience it in the dreaming state after getting relief again and again by entering into the state of deep sleep again and again. Is it indeed my own nature or [is it] due to some cause, my own nature being different? If [this is] my own nature, there is no hope for me to attain final release, since one cannot avoid one's own nature. If [it is] due to some cause, final release is possible after the cause has been removed."

46. The teacher replied to him, "Listen, my child, this is not your own nature but is due to a cause."

47. When he was told this the pupil said, "What is the cause? And what will remove it? And what is my own nature? When the cause is removed, the effect due to the cause no [longer] exists; I will attain to my own nature like a sick person [who recovers his health] when the cause of his disease has been removed."

48. The teacher replied, "The cause is nescience; it is removed by knowledge. When nescience has been removed, you will be released from transmigratory existence which is characterized by birth and death, since its cause will be gone and you will no [longer] experience pain in the dreaming and waking states."

49. The pupil said, "What is that nescience? And what is its object? And what is knowledge, remover of nescience, by which I can realize my own nature?"

50. The teacher replied, "Though you are the highest *Ātman* and not a transmigrator, you hold the inverted view, 'I am a transmigrator.' Though you are neither an agent nor an experiencer, and exist [eternally], [you hold the inverted view, 'I am] an agent, an experiencer, and do not exist [eternally]'—this is nescience."

51. The pupil said, "Even though I exist [eternally], still I am not the highest *Ātman.* My nature is transmigratory existence which is characterized by agency and experiencership, since it is known by sense-perception and other means of

knowledge. [Transmigratory existence] has not nescience as its cause, since nescience cannot have one's own *Ātman* as its object.

Nescience is [defined as] the superimposition of the qualities of one [thing] upon another. For example, fully known silver is superimposed upon fully known mother-of-pearl, a fully known person upon a [fully known] tree trunk, or a fully known trunk upon a [fully known] person; but not an unknown [thing] upon [one that is] fully known nor a fully known [thing] upon one that is unknown. Nor is non-*Ātman* superimposed upon *Ātman* because *Ātman* is not fully known, nor *Ātman* [superimposed] upon non-*Ātman*, [again] because *Ātman* is not fully known."

52. The teacher said to him, "That is not right, since there is an exception. My child, it is not possible to make a general rule that a fully known [thing] is superimposed only upon a fully known [thing], since it is a matter of experience that [a fully known thing] is superimposed upon *Ātman*. [For example,] if one says, 'I am white,' 'I am dark,' this is [the superimposition] of qualities of the body upon *Ātman* which is the object of the 'I'-notion. And if one says, 'I am this,' this is [the superimposition of *Ātman*,] which is the object of the 'I'-notion, upon the body."

53. The pupil said, "In that case *Ātman* is indeed fully known as the object of the 'I'-notion; so is the body as 'this.' If so, [it is only a case of] the mutual superimposition of body and *Ātman*, both fully known, just like [the mutual superimposition] of tree-trunk and person, and of mother-of-pearl and silver. So, is there a particular reason why Your Holiness said that it is not possible to make a general rule that two fully known [things] are mutually superimposed?"

54. The teacher replied, "Listen. It is true that the body and *Ātman* are fully known; but they are not fully known to all people as the objects of distinct notions like a tree-trunk and a person."

"How [are they known] then?"

"[They are] always [known] as the objects of constantly non-distinct notions. Since nobody grasps the body and *Ātman* as two distinct no-

tions, saying, "This is the body, that is *Ātman*,' people are deluded with regard to *Ātman* and non-*Ātman*, thinking, '*Ātman* is thus' or '*Ātman* is not thus.' This is the particular reason why I said that it is impossible to make a general rule."

55. [The pupil raised another objection:] "Is it not experienced that the thing which is superimposed [upon something] else through nescience does not exist [in the latter]? For example, silver [does not exist] in a mother-of-pearl nor a person in a tree-trunk nor a snake in a rope; nor the dark color of the earth's surface in the sky. Likewise, if the body and *Ātman* are always mutually superimposed in the form of constantly non-distinct notions, then they cannot exist in each other at any time. Silver, etc., which are superimposed through nescience upon mother-of-pearl, etc., do not exist [in the latter] at any time in any way and *vice versa;* likewise the body and *Ātman* are mutually superimposed through nescience; this being the case, it would follow as the result that neither the body nor *Ātman* exists. And it is not acceptable, since it is the theory of the Nihilists.[3]

If, instead of mutual superimposition, [only] the body is superimposed upon *Ātman* through nescience, it would follow as the result that the body does not exist in *Ātman* while the latter exists. This is not acceptable either since it is contradictory to sense-perception and other [means of knowledge]. For this reason the body and *Ātman* are not superimposed upon each other through nescience."

"How then?"

"They are permanently connected with each other like bamboo and pillars [which are interlaced in the structure of a house]."

56. [The teacher said,] "No; because it would follow as the result that [*Ātman* is] non-eternal and exists for another's sake; since [in your opinion *Ātman*] is composite, [*Ātman* exists for another's sake and is non-eternal] just like bamboo, pillars, and so forth. Moreover, the *Ātman* which is assumed by some others to be connected with the body exists for another's sake since it is composite. [Therefore,] it has been

first established that the highest [*Ātman*] is not connected with the body, is different [from it], and is eternal.

57. [The pupil objected:] "Although [the *Ātman*] is not composite, It is [regarded] merely as the body and superimposed upon the body; from this follow the results that [the *Ātman*] does not exist and that [It] is non-eternal and so on. Then there would arise the fault that [you will] arrive at the Nihilists' position that the body has no *Ātman*."

58. [The teacher replied,] "Not so; because it is accepted that *Ātman*, like space, is by nature not composite. Although *Ātman* exists as connected with nothing, it does not follow that the body and other things are without *Ātman*, just as, although space is connected with nothing, it does not follow that nothing has space. Therefore, there would not arise the fault that [I shall] arrive at the Nihilists' position.

59. "Your further objection—namely that, if the body does not exist in *Ātman* [although *Ātman* exists], this would contradict sense-perception and the other [means of knowledge]: this is not right, because the existence of the body in *Ātman* is not cognized by sense-perception and the other [means of knowledge]; in *Ātman* — like a jujube-fruit in a pot, ghee in milk, oil in sesame and a picture on a wall—the body is not cognized by sense-perception and the other [means of knowledge]. Therefore there is no contradiction with sense-perception and the other [means of knowledge]."

60. [The pupil objected,] "How is the body then superimposed upon *Ātman* which is not established by sense-perception and the other [means of knowledge], and how is *Ātman* superimposed upon the body?"

61. [The teacher said,] "That is not a fault, because *Ātman* is established by Its own nature. A general rule cannot be made that superimposition is made only on that which is adventitiously established and not on that which is permanently established; for the dark color and other things on the surface of the earth are seen to be superimposed upon the sky [which is permanently established]."

62. [The pupil asked,] "Your Holiness, is the mutual superimposition of the body and *Ātman* made by the composite of the body and so on or by *Ātman*?"

63. The teacher said, "What would happen to you, if [the mutual superimposition] is made by the composite of the body and so on, or if [it] is made by *Ātman*?"

64. Then the pupil answered, "If I am merely the composite of the body and so on, then I am non-conscious, so I exist for another's sake; consequently, the mutual superimposition of body and *Ātman* is not effected by me. If I am the highest *Ātman* different from the composite [of the body and so on], then I am conscious, so I exist for my own sake; consequently, the superimposition [of body] which is the seed of every calamity is effected upon *Ātman* by me who am conscious."

65. To this the teacher responded, "If you know that the false superimposition is the seed of [every] calamity, then do not make it!"

66. "Your Holiness, I cannot help [it]. I am driven [to do it] by another; I am not independent."

67. [The teacher said,] "Then you are non-conscious, so you do not exist for your own sake. That by which you who are not self-dependent are driven to act is conscious and exists for its own sake; you are only a composite thing [of the body, etc.]."

68. [The pupil objected,] "If I am non-conscious, how do I perceive feelings of pleasure and pain, and [the words] you have spoken?"

69. The teacher said, "Are you different from feelings of pleasure and pain and from [the words] I have spoken, or are you identical [with them]?"

70. The pupil answered, "I am indeed not identical."

"Why?"

"Because I perceive both of them as objects just as [I perceive] a jar and other things [as objects]. If I were identical [with them] I could not perceive either of them; but I do perceive them, so I am different [from both of them]. If [I were] identical [with them] it would follow that the modifications of the feelings of pleasure and pain exist for their own sake and so do [the words] you have spoken; but it is not reasonable that any of them exists for their own sake, for the pleasure and pain produced by a sandal and a thorn are not for the sake of the sandal and the thorn, nor is use made of a jar for the sake of the jar. So, the sandal and other things serve my purpose, *i.e.,* the purpose of their perceiver, since I who am different from them perceive all the objects seated in the intellect."

71. The teacher said to him, "So, then, you exist for your own sake since you are conscious. You are not driven [to act] by another. A conscious being is neither dependent on another nor driven [to act] by another, for it is not reasonable that a conscious being should exist for the sake of another conscious being since they are equal like two lights. Nor does a conscious being exist for the sake of a non-conscious being since it is not reasonable that a nonconscious being should have any connection with its own object precisely because it is non-conscious. Nor does experience show that two non-conscious beings exist for each other, as for example a stick of wood and a wall do not fulfill each other's purposes."

72. [The pupil objected,] "Is it not experienced that a servant and his master, though they are equal in the sense of being conscious, exist for each other?"

73. [The teacher said,] "It is not so, for what [I] meant was that you have consciousness just as fire has heat and light. And [in this meaning I] cited the example, 'like two lights.' This being the case, you perceive everything seated in your intellect through your own nature, *i.e.,* the transcendentally changeless, eternal, pure consciousness which is equivalent to the heat and light of fire. And if you admit that *Ātman* is always without distinctions, why did you say, 'After getting relief again and again in the state of deep sleep, I perceive pain in the waking and dreaming states. Is this indeed my own nature or [is it] due to some cause?' Has this delusion left [you now] or not?"

74. To this the pupil replied, "Your Holiness, the delusion has gone thanks to your gracious as-

sistance; but I am in doubt as to how I am transcendentally changeless."

"How?"

"Sound and other [external objects] are not self-established, since they are not conscious. But they [are established] through the rise of notions which take the forms of sound and other [external objects]. It is impossible for notions to be self-established, since they have mutually exclusive attributes and the forms [of external objects] such as blue and yellow. It is, therefore, understood that [notions] are caused by the forms of the external objects; so, [notions] are established as possessing the forms of external objects, *i.e.,* the forms of sound, etc. Likewise, notions, which are the modifications of a thing (= the intellect), the substratum of the 'I'-notion, are also composite, so it is reasonable that they are non-conscious; therefore, as it is impossible that they exist for their own sake, they, like sound and other [external objects], are established as objects to be perceived by a perceiver different in nature [from them]. If I am not composite, I have pure consciousness as my nature; so I exist for my own sake. Nevertheless, I am a perceiver of notions which have the forms [of the external objects] such as blue and yellow [and] so I am indeed subject to change. [For the above reason, I am] in doubt as to how [I am] transcendentally changeless."

75. The teacher said to him, "Your doubt is not reasonable. [Your] perception of those notions is necessary and entire; for this very reason [you] are not subject to transformation. It is, therefore, established that [you] are transcendentally changeless. But you have said that precisely the reason for the above positive conclusion—namely, that [you] perceive the entire movement of the mind—is the reason for [your] doubt [concerning your transcendental changelessness]. This is why [your doubt is not reasonable].

If indeed you were subject to transformation, you would not perceive the entire movement of the mind which is your object, just as the mind [does not perceive] its [entire] object and just as the senses [do not perceive] their [entire] objects, and similarly you as *Ātman* would not perceive even a part of your object. Therefore, you are transcendentally changeless."

76. Then [the pupil] said, "Perception is what is meant by the verbal root, that is, nothing but change; it is contradictory [to this fact] to say that [the nature of] the perceiver is transcendentally changeless."

77. [The teacher said,] "That is not right, for [the term] 'perception' is used figuratively in the sense of a change which is meant by the verbal root; whatever the notion of the intellect may be, that is what is meant by the verbal root; [the notion of the intellect] has change as its nature and end, with the result that the perception of *Ātman* falsely appears [as perceiver]; thus the notion of the intellect is figuratively indicated by the term, "perception." For example, the cutting action results [in the static state] that [the object to be cut] is separated in two parts; thus [the term, "cutting," in the sense of an object to be cut being separated in two parts,] is used figuratively as [the cutting action] which is meant by the verbal root."

78. To this the pupil objected, "Your Holiness, the example cannot explain my transcendental changelessness."

"Why not?"

"'Cutting' which results in a change in the object to be cut is used figuratively as [the cutting action] which is meant by the verbal root; in the same manner, if the notion of the intellect, which is figuratively indicated by the term 'perception' and is meant by the verbal root, results also in a change in the perception of *Ātman*, [the example] cannot explain *Ātman*'s transcendental changelessness."

79. The teacher said, "It would be true, if there were a distinction between perception and perceiver. The perceiver is indeed nothing but eternal perception. And it is not [right] that perception and perceiver are different as in the doctrine of the logicians."

80. [The pupil said,] "How does that [action] which is meant by the verbal root result in perception?"

81. [The teacher] answered, "Listen, [I] said that [it] ends with the result that the perception

[of *Ātman*] falsely appears [as perceiver]. Did you not hear? I did not say that [it] results in the production of any change in *Ātman*."

82. The pupil said, "Why then did you say that if I am transcendentally changeless I am the perceiver of the entire movement of the mind which is my object?"

83. The teacher said to him, "I told [you] only the truth. Precisely because [you are the perceiver of the entire movement of the mind], I said, you are transcendentally changeless."

84. "If so, Your Holiness, I am of the nature of transcendentally changeless and eternal perception whereas the notions of the intellect, which have the forms of [external objects] such as sound, arise and end with the result that my own nature which is perception falsely appears [as perceiver]. Then what is my fault?"

85. [The teacher replied,] "You are right. [You] have no fault. The fault is only nescience as I have said before."

86. [The pupil said,] "If, Your Holiness, as in the state of deep sleep I undergo no change, how [do I experience] the dreaming and waking states?"

87. The teacher said to him, "But do you experience [these states] continuously?"

88. [The pupil answered,] "Certainly I do experience [them], but intermittently and not continuously."

89. The teacher said [to him,] "Both of them are adventitious [and] not your nature. If [they] were your nature [they] would be self-established and continuous like your nature, which is Pure Consciousness. Moreover, the dreaming and waking states are not your nature, for [they] depart [from you] like clothes and so on. It is certainly not experienced that the nature of anything, whatever it may be, departs from it. But the dreaming and waking states depart from the state of Pure Consciousness-only. If one's own nature were to depart [from oneself] in the state of deep sleep, it would be negated by saying, 'It has perished,' 'It does not exist,' since the adventitious attributes which are not one's own nature are seen to consist in both [perishableness and non-existence]; for example, wealth, clothes,

and the like are seen to perish and things which have been obtained in dream or delusion are seen to be non-existent."

90. [The pupil objected,] "[If so, Your Holiness, it follows [either] that my own nature, *i.e.,* Pure Consciousness, is also adventitious, since [I] perceive in the dreaming and waking states but not in the state of deep sleep; or that I am not of the nature of Pure Consciousness."

91. [The teacher replied,] "No, Look. Because that is not reasonable. If you [insist on] looking your own nature, *i.e.* Pure Consciousness, as adventitious, do so! We cannot establish it logically even in a hundred years, nor can any other (*i.e.* non-conscious) being do so. As [that adventitious consciousness] is composite, nobody can logically deny that [it] exists for another's sake, is manifold and perishable; for what does not exist for its own sake is not self-established, as we have said before. Nobody can, however, deny that *Ātman,* which is of the nature of Pure Consciousness, is self-established; so It does not depend upon anything else, since It does not depart [from anybody]."

92. [The pupil objected,] "Did I not point out that [It] does depart [from me] when I said that in the state of deep sleep I do not see?"

93. [The teacher replied,] "That is not right, for it is contradictory."

"How is it a contradiction?"

"Although you are [in truth] seeing, you say, 'I do not see.' This is contradictory."

"But at no time in the state of deep sleep, Your Holiness, have I ever seen Pure Consciousness or anything else."

"Then you are seeing in the state of deep sleep; for you deny only the seen object, not the seeing. I said that your seeing is Pure Consciousness. That [eternally] existing one by which you deny [the existence of the seen object] when you say that nothing has been seen, [that precisely is the seeing] that is Pure Consciousness. Thus as [It] does not ever depart [from you] [Its] transcendental changelessness and eternity are established solely by Itself without depending upon any means of knowledge. The knower, though self-established, requires

means of knowledge for the discernment of an object to be known other [than itself]. And that eternal Discernment, which is required for discerning something else (= non-*Ātman*) which does not have Discernment as its nature—that is certainly eternal, transcendentally changeless, and of a self-effulgent nature. The eternal Discernment does not require any means of knowledge in order to be Itself the means of knowledge or the knower since the eternal Discernment is by nature the means of knowledge or the knower. [This is illustrated by the following] example: iron or water requires fire or sun [to obtain] light and heat since light and heat are not their nature; but fire and sun do not require [anything else] for light and heat since [these] are always their nature. . . .

109. [The pupil said,] "If so, Your Holiness, Apprehension is transcendentally changeless, eternal, indeed of the nature of the light of *Ātman,* and self-established, since It does not depend upon any means of knowledge with regard to Itself; everything other than This is non-conscious and exists for another's sake, since it acts together [with others].

And because of this nature of being apprehended as notion causing pleasure, pain, and delusion, [non-*Ātman*] exists for another's sake; on account of this very nature non-*Ātman* exists and not on account of any other nature. It is therefore merely non-existent from the standpoint of the highest truth. Just as it is experienced in this world that a snake [superimposed] upon a rope does not exist, nor water in a mirage, and the like, unless they are apprehended [as a notion], so it is reasonable that duality in the waking and dreaming states also does not exist unless it is apprehended [as a notion]. In this manner, Your Holiness, Apprehension, *i.e.,* the light of *Ātman,* is uninterrupted; so It is transcendentally changeless, eternal and non-dual, since It is never absent from any of the various notions. But various notions are absent from Apprehension. Just as in the dreaming state the notions in different forms such as blue and yellow, which are absent from that Apprehension, are said to be non-existent from the standpoint of the highest truth, so in the waking state also, the various notions such as blue and yellow, which are absent from this very Apprehension, must by nature be untrue. And there is no apprehender different from this Apprehension to apprehend It; therefore It can Itself neither be accepted nor rejected by Its own nature, since there is nothing else."

110. [The teacher said,] "Exactly so it is. It is nescience that is the cause of transmigratory existence which is characterized by the waking and dreaming states. The remover of this nescience is knowledge. And so you have reached fearlessness. From now on you will not perceive any pain in the waking and dreaming states. You are released from the sufferings of transmigratory existence."

111. [The pupil said,] "Om."

NOTES

1. *Om* is the sacred syllable called *praṇava* and sometimes compared with *Amen*. It is used at the opening of most Hindu works and as a sacred exclamation may be uttered at the beginning and end of Vedic recitation or before any prayer.

2. According to Śankara, the individual consists of the following six components: (1) the body, gross (*sthūla*) and subtle (*sūkṣma*), (2) the five senses (*buddhindriya*), (3) the five organs of action (*karmendriya*), (4) the internal organ (*antaḥkaraṇa*), (5) the principal vital air (*mukhya prāṇa*), and (6) *Ātman*. The term *prāṇa* in its wider sense comprises (2)–(5), and the term is probably used here in this wider sense. In the first stanza, (2) (eye and ear), (3) (organ of speech), and (4) (mind) are referred to.

3. "The Nihilists" (*Vaināśika*) indicates the Buddhists, especially the Śūnyavādins (or Mādhyamikas), who hold the view that everything is empty (*śūnya*) and who have Nāgārjuna (150–250) as their founder.

2.3 The Nature of God

Islam is the name of a religion that stems from a book of sacred scriptures called the *Qur'an*. Muslims (followers of Islam) believe that the *Qur'an* contains revelations from Allah (God) given to the prophet Muhammad (570–623). Muhammad, Muslims maintain, is the last in a long series of prophets stretching back to Abraham and including Jesus. Hence Jews and Christians are called "People of the Book."

Islam teaches a strict monotheism. There is one God (Allah), and Allah constitutes an absolute unity. Hence the tri-unity (Trinity) that Christians affirm is rejected. Allah is the absolute, ultimate, and unique divine reality:

Say: He is the One God;
God, the Eternal, the Uncaused Cause of all being.
He begets not, and neither is he begotten
and there is nothing that could be compared to him.
(*Qur'an* 112).

This monotheism is clearly stated in the first of the five pillars (the central practices) of Islam. A faithful Muslim must

1. Witness that there is no God but Allah and that Muhammad is his Prophet.
2. Perform mandatory prayers (*salat*).
3. Give mandatory alms (*zakat*).
4. Fast during the month of Ramadan.
5. At least once during life make a pilgrimage (*hajj*) to Mecca.

There is no doubt that Islam regards ultimate reality to be God or Allah. Exactly what this means, however, became a point of theological and philosophical debate as Islam developed. Some theologians (the *mujassima*) thought of God in anthropomorphic terms. They taught that God is very much like humans, who, after all, are created in God's image. Thus they attribute to God characteristics such as hearing, seeing, and speaking (all mentioned in the *Qur'an*). Of course God is vastly more powerful and more wise than humans. The difference, however, between God and humans is not one of kind, but one of degree.

These views of the *mujassima* were condemned by other Muslims as little more than idol worship. They (the *mu'attila*) argued that such attributes as hearing, seeing, and speaking apply only to physical things. God is not physical; hence they do not literally apply to God. When the *Qur'an* speaks in an anthropomorphic manner, it is doing so because that is the only kind of language humans are able to grasp.

In addition to the anthropomorphic view and that of the "negators" (*mu'attila*), there is also the affirmers' view. These theologians (the *muthbita*) argue that when the *Qur'an* speaks of God as though he had human-like qualities, it means it. God really does speak and has a real face and real hands. However, because there is "nothing like Him," these attributes are not like the attributes of humans or any other created thing. One wonders, of course, just exactly what a divine hand is if it is not like any other hand we know about. Such talk invites philosophical analysis.

Islamic philosophers entered this debate by using the resources of Greek philosophy to analyze the idea of ultimacy. There is no question that Allah is ultimate. But what does that mean? There appears to be a tension between an anthropomorphic and personal understanding of the divine and the philosophic view. As early as the sixth century B.C.E., Xenophanes claimed God is "in no way similar to mortals." Later Greek philosophers would describe God very impersonally and abstractly as an Unmoved Mover, as an eternal unchanging divine power, and as Pure Intelligence or Thought.

This tension between anthropomorphic and philosophical views is found in Judaism, Christianity, and Hinduism as well. Tertullian, a second-century Christian theologian, asked, "What has Athens to do with Jerusalem?" Much later, the French mathematician and philosopher Blaise Pascal (1623–1662) wondered what the God of the philosophers had to do with the God of Abraham, Isaac, and Jacob? Hinduism portrays God as male and female as well as beyond all personal and human-like traits. So how should we think of God? Is God at all like the sorts of beings we know?

Ibn Sina (known as Avicenna in the West), the author of the next selection, is a tenth-century Islamic philosopher who was very much concerned with the relationship between the God described in the *Qur'an* and the God described by the philosophers. He attempted to use philosophical reason to discover (as nearly as mortals can) the exact nature of God. He divided beings into two kinds: necessary and contingent. A necessary being is completely uncaused and unconditioned. All contingent beings, by contrast, are caused and conditioned. Hence God could not be reckoned among their numbers. God is a necessary being. All of God's other attributes—oneness, uncausedness, pure benevolence, true perfection, complete self-sufficiency, absolute knowledge, omnipotence and so on—can be logically deduced from the fact of God's necessity.

This philosophical analysis did not entirely relieve the tension between the anthropomorphic viewpoint and the philosophical. If God is unchanging, then how could God have created the universe, an act that seems to require a change from a state of not creating to a state of creating? If God is unchanging, how can God be compassionate and forgiving? If God has perfect foreknowledge, how can humans be free? If God is all-powerful, can God create a stone that even God cannot lift?

The idea of an ultimate reality combined with the idea of a loving, forgiving, creating God seems threatened with incoherence. It is not surprising to find al-Ghazali, a hundred years after Avicenna, writing a book called *The Incoherence of the Philosophers* and Averroes responding in the twelfth century with *The Incoherence of the Incoherence.* The debate goes on.

Reading Questions

1. What is the difference between a necessary being and a contingent being, and why would there be an infinite succession of beings if there were no necessary being?
2. Why is it, according to Avicenna, that it is impossible that "the Necessary Being should be two"?
3. What does it mean to say that a necessary being has no cause?
4. Why does the multiplicity of God's attributes *not* destroy God's unity?
5. How does Avicenna "prove" that God has one unchanging knowledge of all objects of knowledge? Do you find this "proof" convincing or not? Why?

The Nature of God*

AVICENNA

That there Is a Necessary Being

Whatever has being must either have a reason for its being, or have no reason for it. If it has a reason, then it is contingent, equally before it comes into being (if we make this mental hypothesis) and when it is in the state of being—for in the case of a thing whose being is contingent the mere fact of its entering upon being does not remove from it the contingent nature of its being. If on the other hand it has no reason for its being in any way whatsoever, then it is necessary in its being. This rule having been confirmed, I shall now proceed to prove that there is in being a being which has no reason for its being.

Such a being is either contingent or necessary. If it is necessary, then the point we sought to prove is established. If on the other hand it is contingent, that which is contingent cannot enter upon being except for some reason which sways the scales in favour of its being and against its not-being. If the reason is also contingent, there is then a chain of contingents linked one to the other, and there is no being at all; for this being which is the subject of our hypothesis cannot enter into being so long as it is not preceded by an infinite succession of beings, which is absurd. Therefore contingent beings end in a Necessary Being.

Of the Unicity of God

It is not possible in any way that the Necessary Being should be two. Demonstration: Let us suppose that there is another necessary being:

* From *Avicenna on Theology.* Translated by Arthur J. Arberry. Copyright © 1951 John Murray. Reprinted by permission of John Murray.

one must be distinguishable from the other, so that the terms "this" and "that" may be used with reference to them. This distinction must be either essential or accidental. If the distinction between them is accidental, this accidental element cannot but be present in each of them, or in one and not the other. If each of them has an accidental element by which it is distinguished from the other, both of them must be caused; for an accident is what is adjoined to a thing after its essence is realized. If the accidental element is regarded as adhering to its being, and is present in one of the two and not in the other, then the one which has no accidental element is a necessary being and the other is not a necessary being. If, however, the distinction is essential, the element of essentiality is that whereby the essence as such subsists; and if this element of essentiality is different in each and the two are distinguishable by virtue of it, then each of the two must be a compound; and compounds are caused; so that neither of them will be a necessary being. If the element of essentiality belongs to one only, and the other is one in every respect and there is no compounding of any kind in it, then the one which has no element of essentiality is a necessary being, and the other is not a necessary being. Since it is thus established that the Necessary Being cannot be two, but is All Truth, then by virtue of His Essential Reality, in respect of which He is a Truth, He is United and One, and no other shares with Him in that Unity: however the All-Truth attains existence, it is through Himself.

That God is Without Cause

A necessary being has no cause whatsoever. Causes are of four kinds: that from which a thing has being, or the active cause; that on account of which a thing has being, or the final and completive cause; that in which a thing has being, or the material cause; and that through which a thing has being, or the formal cause.

The justification for limiting causes to these four varieties is that the reason for a thing is either internal in its subsistence, or a part of its being, or external to it. If it is internal, then it is either that part in which the thing is, potentially and not actually, that is to say its matter; or it is that part in which the thing becomes actually, that is to say its form. If it is external, then it can only be either that from which the thing has being, that is to say the agent, or that on account of which the thing has being, that is to say its purpose and end.

Since it is established that these are the roots and principles of this matter, let us rest on them and clarify the problems which are constructed upon them.

Demonstration that He has no active cause: This is self-evident: for if He had any reason for being, this would be adventitious and that would be a necessary being. Since it is established that He has no active cause, it follows on this line of reasoning that His Quiddity is not other than His Identity, that is to say, other than His Being; neither will He be a subsistence or an accident. There cannot be two, each of which derives its being from the other; nor can He be a necessary being in one respect, and a contingent being in another respect.

Proof that His Quiddity is not other than His Identity, but rather that His Being is unified in His Reality: if His Being were not the same as His Reality, then His Being would be other than His Reality. Every accident is caused, and every thing caused requires a reason. Now this reason is either external to His Quiddity, or is itself His Quiddity: if it is external, then He is not a necessary being, and is not exempt from an active cause; while if the reason is itself the Quiddity, then the reason must necessarily be itself a complete being in order that the being of another may result from it. Quiddity before being has no being; and if it had being before this, it would not require a second being. The question therefore returns to the problem of being. If the Being of the Quiddity is accidental, whence did this Being supervene and adhere? It is therefore established that the Identity of the Necessary Being is His Quiddity, and that He has no active cause; the necessary nature of His Being is like the quiddity of all other things. From this it is evident that the Necessary Being does not resemble any other thing in any respect whatsoever; for with all other things their being is other than their quiddity.

Proof that He is not an accident: An accident is a being in a locus. The locus is precedent to it, and its being is not possible without the locus. But we have stated that a being which is necessary has no reason for its being.

Proof that there cannot be two necessary beings, each deriving its being from the other: Each of them, in as much as it derives its being from the other, would be subsequent to the other, while at the same time by virtue of supplying being to the other, each would be precedent to the other: but one and the same thing cannot be both precedent and subsequent in relation to its being. Moreover, if we assume for the sake of argument that the other is non-existent: would the first then be a necessary being, or not? If it were a necessary being, it would have no connexion with the other: if it were not a necessary being, it would be a contingent being and would require another necessary being. Since the Necessary Being is One, and does not derive Its being from any one, it follows that He is a Necessary Being in every respect; while anything else derives its being from another.

Proof that He cannot be a Necessary Being in one respect and a contingent being in another respect: Such a being, in as much as it is a contingent being, would be connected in being with something else, and so it has a reason; but in as much as it is a necessary being, it would have no connexions with anything else. In that case it would both have being and not have being; and that is absurd.

Demonstration that He has no material and receptive cause: The receptive cause is the cause for the provision of the place in which a thing is received; that is to say, the place prepared for the reception of being, or the perfection of being. Now the Necessary Being is a perfection in pure actuality, and is not impaired by any deficiency; every perfection belongs to Him, derives from Him, and is preceded by His Essence, while every deficiency, even if it be metaphorical, is negated to Him. All perfection and all beauty are of His Being; indeed, these are the vestiges of the perfection of His Being; how then should He derive perfection from any other? Since it is thus estab-

lished that He has no receptive cause, it follows that He does not possess anything potentially, and that He has no attribute yet to be awaited; on the contrary, His Perfection has been realized in actuality; and He has no material cause. We say "realized in actuality", using this as a common term of expression, meaning that every perfection belonging to any other is non-existent and yet to be awaited, whereas all perfection belonging to Him has being and is present. His Perfect Essence, preceding all relations, is One. From this it is manifest that His Attributes are not an augmentation of His Essence; for if they were an augmentation of His Essence, the Attributes would be potential with reference to the Essence and the Essence would be the reason for the Attributes. In that case the Attributes would be subsequent to a precedent, so that they would be in one respect active and in another receptive; their being active would be other than the aspect of their being receptive; and in consequence they would possess two mutually exclusive aspects. Now this is impossible in the case of anything whatsoever; when a body is in motion, the motivation is from one quarter and the movement from another.

If it were to be stated that His Attributes are not an augmentation of His Essence, but that they entered into the constitution of the Essence, and that the Essence cannot be conceived of as existing without these Attributes, then the Essence would be compound, and the Oneness would be destroyed. It is also evident, as a result of denying the existence of a receptive cause, that it is impossible for Him to change; for the meaning of change is the passing away of one attribute and the establishment of another; and if He were susceptible to change, He would possess potentially an element of passing-away and an element of establishment; and that is absurd. It is clear from this that He has no opposite and no contrary; for opposites are essences which succeed each other in the occupation of a single locus, there being between them the extreme of contrariety. But He is not receptive to accidents, much less to opposites. And if the term "opposite" is used to denote one who disputes with Him in His Rulership, it is clear too on this count that He has no opposite. It is further clear that it is impossible for Him not to be; for since it is established that His Being is necessary, it follows that it is impossible for Him not to be; because everything which exists potentially cannot exist actually, otherwise it would have two aspects. Anything which is receptive to a thing does not cease to be receptive when reception has actually taken place; if this were not so, it would result in the removal of both being and not-being, and that is untenable. This rule applies to every essence and every unified reality, such as angels and human spirits; they are not susceptible to not-being at all, since they are free from corporeal adjunctions.

Demonstration that He has no formal cause: A formal, corporeal cause only exists and is confirmed when a thing is possessed of matter: the matter has a share in the being of the form, in the same way that the form has a part in the disposition of the matter in being in actuality; such a thing is therefore caused. It is further evident as a result of denying this cause to Him, that He is also to be denied all corporeal attributes, such as time, space, direction, and being in one place to the exclusion of all other; in short, whatever is possible in relation to corporeal things is impossible in relation to Him.

Proof that He has no final cause: The final cause is that on account of which a thing has being; and the First Truth has not being for the sake of anything, rather does everything exist on account of the perfection of His Essence, being consequent to His Being and derived from His Being. Moreover the final cause, even if it be posterior in respect of being to all other causes, yet it is mentally prior to them all. It is the final cause which makes the active cause become a cause in actuality, that is to say in respect of its being a final cause.

Since it is established that He is exalted above this last kind of cause too, it is clear that there is no cause to His Attributes. It is also evident that He is Pure Benevolence and True Perfection; the meaning of His Self-Sufficiency likewise becomes manifest, namely that he approves of nothing and disapproves of nothing. For if He approved of anything, that thing would come into being and would continue to be; while if He disapproved of anything, that thing would be converted into not-being and would be annulled. The very divergency of these beings proves the nullity of such a proposition; for a thing which is one in every respect cannot approve of a thing and of its opposite. It is also not necessary for Him to observe the rule of greater expediency or of expediency, as certain Qualitarians have idly pretended; for if His acts of expediency were obligatory to Him, He would not merit gratitude and praise for such acts, since He would merely be fulfilling that which it is His obligation to perform, and He would be to all intents and purposes as one paying a debt; He would therefore deserve nothing at all for such benevolence. In fact His acts proceed on the contrary from Him and for Him, as we shall demonstrate later.

His Attributes as Interpreted According to the Foregoing Principles

Since it is established that God is a Necessary Being, that He is One in every respect, that He is exalted above all causes, and that He has no reason of any kind for His Being; since it is further established that His Attributes do not augment His Essence, and that He is qualified by the Attributes of Praise and Perfection; it follows necessarily that we must state that He is Knowing, Living, Willing, Omnipotent, Speaking, Seeing, Hearing, and Possessed of all the other Loveliest Attributes. It is also necessary to recognize that His Attributes are to be classified as negative, positive, and a compound of the two: since His Attributes are of this order, it follows that their multiplicity does not destroy His Unity or contradict the necessary nature of His Being. Pre-eternity for instance is essentially the negation of not-being in the first place, and the denial of causality and of primality in the second place; similarly the term One means that He is indivisible in every respect, both verbally and actually. When it is stated that He is a Necessary Being, this means that He is a Being without a cause, and that He is the Cause of other than Himself: this is a combination of the negative and the positive. Examples of the positive Attributes are His being Creator, Originator, Shaper, and the entire

Attributes of Action. As for the compound of both, this kind is illustrated by His being Willing and Omnipotent, for these Attributes are a compound of Knowledge with the addition of Creativeness.

God's Knowledge

God has knowledge of His Essence: His Knowledge, His Being Known and His Knowing are one and the same thing. He knows other than Himself, and all objects of knowledge. He knows all things by virtue of one knowledge, and in a single manner. His Knowledge does not change according to whether the thing known has being or not-being.

Proof that God has knowledge of His Essence: We have stated that God is One, and that He is exalted above all causes. The meaning of knowledge is the supervention of an idea divested of all corporeal coverings. Since it is established that He is One, and that He is divested of body, and His Attributes also; and as this idea as just described supervenes upon Him; and since whoever has an abstract idea supervening upon him is possessed of knowledge, and it is immaterial whether it is his essence or other than himself; and as further His Essence is not absent from Himself; it follows from all this that He knows Himself.

Proof that He is Knowledge, Knowing and Known: Knowledge is another term for an abstract idea. Since this idea is abstract, it follows that He is Knowledge; since this abstract idea belongs to Him, is present with Him, and is not veiled from Him, it follows that He is Knowing; and since this abstract idea does not supervene save through Him, it follows that He is Known. The terms employed in each case are different; otherwise it might be said that Knowledge, Knowing and Known are, in relation to His Essence, one. Take your own experience as a parallel. If you know yourself, the object of your knowledge is either yourself or something else; if the object of your knowledge is something other than yourself, then you do not know yourself. But if the object of your knowledge is yourself, then both the one knowing and the thing known are your self. If the image of your self is impressed

upon your self, then it is your self which is the knowledge. Now if you look back upon yourself reflectively, you will not find any impression of the idea and quiddity of your self in yourself a second time, so as to give rise within you to a sense that your self is more than one. Therefore since it is established that He has intelligence of His Essence, and since His Intelligence is His Essence and does not augment His Essence, it follows that He is Knowing, Knowledge and Known without any multiplicity attaching to Him through these Attributes; and there is no difference between "one who has knowledge" and "one who has intelligence", since both are terms for describing the negation of matter absolutely.

Proof that He has knowledge of other than Himself: Whoever knows himself, if thereafter he does not know other than himself this is due to some impediment. If the impediment is essential, this implies necessarily that he does not know himself either; while if the impediment is of an external nature, that which is external can be removed. Therefore it is possible—nay, necessary—that He should have knowledge of other than Himself, as you shall learn from this chapter.

Proof that He has knowledge of all objects of knowledge: Since it is established that He is a Necessary Being, that He is One, and that the universe is brought into being from Him and has resulted out of His Being; since it is established further that He has knowledge of His Own Essence, His Knowledge of His Essence being what it is, namely that He is the Origin of all realities and of all things that have being; it follows that nothing in heaven or earth is remote from His Knowledge—on the contrary, all that comes into being does so by reason of Him: He is the causer of all reasons, and He knows that of which He is the Reason, the Giver of being and the Originator.

Proof that He knows all things by virtue of one knowledge, in a manner which changes not according to the change in the thing known: It has been established that His Knowledge does not augment His Essence, and that He is the Origin of all things that have being, while being exalted above accident and changes; it therefore follows that He knows things in a manner unchanging. The objects of knowledge are a consequence of His Knowledge; His Knowledge is not a consequence of the things known, that it should change as they change; for His Knowledge of things is the reason for their having being. Hence it is manifest that Knowledge is itself Omnipotence. He knows all contingent things, even as He knows all things that have being, even though we know them not; for the contingent, in relation to us, is a thing whose being is possible and whose not-being is also possible; but in relation to Him one of the two alternatives is actually known. Therefore His Knowledge of genera, species, things with being, contingent things, manifest and secret things— this Knowledge is a single knowledge. . . .

2.4 Emptiness and God

If you were in search of two categories that you could use to characterize everything, the ideas of being and non-being might do nicely. Everything that exists, however diverse, has at least being or existence in common. Everything that does not exist has non-being in common. This, of course, is an odd way of talking, because presumably nothing exists in the category of non-being. In other words, non-being refers to nothing (although, somewhat paradoxically, we might characterize this nothing as everything that is not being). Some philosophers argue that because something (what has being) cannot come from nothing (non-being) and because non-being is the negation of being (and therefore grammatically and logically dependent on it), being has priority over non-being.

This line of reasoning has inspired much philosophical reflection on God among Jews, Christians, and Muslims. If the term *God* does refer to what is ultimate, then does it refer to being or to non-being? Surely, some argue, it must refer to being, because non-being is dependent on being and hence less than ultimate. Further, because all particular beings are dependent on being, being itself must be independent in the sense of not conditioned by anything else. Even further, being must be good and somehow concerned with the welfare of particular beings; otherwise, we would live in a totality nihilistic universe with no point or purpose.

It is something of a shock to those who think of God as ultimate reality and as being rather than non-being to encounter Buddhist philosophical reflection on ultimate reality. The religion known as Buddhism stems from the teachings and experiences of Siddhartha Gautama, a sixth- or possibly fifth-century B.C.E. Indian of the Sakya clan. He was called the Buddha, or Enlightened One, because he realized nirvana or release from suffering.

The core of the Buddha's teachings is the Four Noble Truths. First, life is suffering. All living creatures suffer to one degree or another during their lives. This suffering may be physical (disease, for example) or psychological (unhappiness, for example). Second, suffering is caused by desire. Attachment to pleasures and to life itself means that we live wanting more and more of what we do not have. It also means that we try to prevent things from changing. We cling to what we like and to what gives us pleasure and joy. Everything, however, eventually changes. Impermanence characterizes life. Ultimately we grow old and die, no matter how much we wish it were otherwise. Third, the release from suffering (nirvana) can be achieved by following the Eightfold Path or Middle Way. This Eightfold Path constitutes the fourth Noble Truth and it involves cultivating right views, right thought, right speech, right action, right livelihood, right effort, right mindfulness, and right concentration. Exactly what these phrases mean was worked out (and argued over) as the Buddhist tradition developed.

One of the right views that those who would overcome suffering needed to develop was an understanding of the Buddha's teaching known as "dependent co-origination." Everything that exists is dependent on something else that exists. Animals are dependent on food. Food is dependent on sunlight and water. Sunlight is dependent on the sun, and water on rain. Later Buddhist philosophers, reflecting on this teaching, came to a startling conclusion. If we mean by *being* that which can exist independently, then, if the doctrine of dependent co-origination is true, nothing can exist independently. Hence being is not ultimate. What is ultimate is empty of being. Further, if nirvana is the realization of release from all suffering, then it must be the realization of ultimate reality—that is, emptiness (*sunyata*).

What, however, is emptiness? Is it non-being? It would seem so, because being and non-being are ultimate categories. But perhaps not. Perhaps emptiness should be understood as no-thingness. If so, then it is very much like being, because being is also no-thingness in the sense that it is no particular being (it is not one of the beings) but is rather the source or ground of all beings. Emptiness is not a thing and neither is being, so it seems we have different words for the same reality. It is, however, not that simple, because Buddhist philosophers maintain that emptiness is beyond both being and non-being. It is, if you will, the source or ground of both. Thus those who might like to equate God and emptiness face a more difficult task than it first appears.

John B. Cobb, Jr. (1925–   ), Ingraham Professor of Theology at Claremont University and author of the following essay, is very much concerned with how the Buddhist conception of ultimate reality as emptiness is related to the Christian conception of God. He is a process theologian. Much Christian theology reflects a metaphysical viewpoint that assumes ultimate reality is static and substantive. The permanent is more real than process or change. Process theologians assume just the opposite and try to rethink the Christian theological tradition on a metaphysical basis that emphasizes process. Cobb finds this sort of metaphysics more like the metaphysical assumptions found in Buddhism. Hence he is particularly interested in that tradition and in the resources it may offer for understanding ultimacy.

Reading Questions

1. What is dualism?
2. What is being?
3. What does it mean to say that an event is empty?
4. What is dependent co-origination?
5. How does the "principle of rightness" differ from emptiness?
6. Why is that which is "ultimate" more easily conceived as a principle than as a personality?
7. Why, according to Cobb, must God be identified with the "principle of rightness rather than with the metaphysical ultimate"?
8. How might the duality between Emptiness and God be overcome, according to Cobb?
9. Cobb says that the affirmation of two different ultimates (Emptiness and God) is not contradictory. Do you agree or disagree? Why?

Emptiness and God*

JOHN B. COBB, JR.

MY TOPIC IS quite ambitious: it is the ultimate. In Buddhism the ultimate is often designated as Emptiness. In Christendom, at least traditionally, the ultimate has been declared to be God. One view of this situation is that Emptiness and God are but two names of the same reality, such that understanding between East and West is a matter of clarifying terminology. Another view is that these two names express opposing views of what the one ultimate reality is. In that case we can either engage in disputation or seek some sort of dialectical reconciliation. My own view is that Emptiness and God name two quite different ultimates to which we are related in two quite different ways. Indeed, there may be still other ultimates, such as the Whole or Cosmos, in relation to which segments of humanity have taken their bearings. If so, the question is whether human beings can develop their relations to this multiplicity of ultimates in ways that are not mutually exclusive. In this paper this question will be pressed only in terms of the Buddhist and Christian ultimate.

I propose to develop my position as follows. First, I will consider briefly the quest for the ultimate as it has led to Being in the West and to Brahman in the East. I will note how in Buddhism and in twentieth century philosophy Brahman or Being has been dissolved into Emptiness. Second, I will discuss the sense of rightness as pointing to another ultimate that has come most clearly to expression in Confucianism and Judaism. I will evaluate the efforts that have been made by the heirs of these traditions to assimilate the metaphysical ultimate to this ultimate principle of rightness. Third, I will consider the status of the idea of God in light of the dissolution of the ultimate into two ultimates, urging its renewal

as a designation of the principle of rightness. Fourth, I will consider whether the realization of Emptiness and faith in God are mutually exclusive states, or whether they can be achieved in unity.

I. Being and Emptiness

Our efforts to understand reality in the West have led us again and again to dualism. This has grown out of our preoccupation with the subjective experience of the external object. The visual experience of a table, for example, has been a typical starting point of philosophical inquiry. This experience readily lends itself to analysis in terms of the one who sees and the entity that is seen. The one who sees is the subject; what is seen is the object. The subject is mental, the object, physical or material. The world, therefore, seems to be made up of mind and matter.

The philosophical problems generated by dualism are notorious. Hence Western philosophy is full of efforts to escape dualism. The easiest ways are by declaring the primacy either of the mental or of the material. Either mind can be viewed as the one source and locus of the data that are interpreted as matter, or mind can be viewed as an epiphenomenal by-product of changes in position of material particles. In these ways we can achieve idealist and materialist monisms, but since the ideal and the material are defined against each other, the taint of dualism is in fact not overcome.

There has been in the West a deeper response to the threat of dualism, a response which probes behind the differences between mind and matter to what they have in common. If both mental and material entities *are*, then what they have in common is existence or being. The tendency in

* From "Buddhist Emptiness and the Christian God" by John B. Cobb, Jr. *Journal of the American Academy of Religion* XLV (March 1977): 11–25. Reprinted by permission of the American Academy of Religion.

the West is often to suppose that this only means that existence or being names what is ultimate in the hierarchy of abstractions. That is, whereas only some entities are characterized by such particular qualities as squareness or redness, and whereas on the dualistic view thinking and extension are mutually exclusive characterizations of entities, existence or being characterizes all. But to view existence or being as simply the most abstract of characteristics, so abstract that it can be predicated of all things, is to misunderstand. Existence or being is not one more characteristic or essence that can be posited of things. It is that by virtue of which anything whatever can be posited. Hence it is related to things in a way totally different from the way in which abstractions or essences or forms are related to them. These differentiate types of things, but no combination of forms constitutes an existent thing: it constitutes only a more complex form. The existence of the existing thing is an entirely different matter. Hence existence as such, or being itself, is the ultimate reality by and through which every particular entity is or exists as qualified in its distinctive way.

The recognition of being itself as beyond and above all dualism and indeed all distinctions has played an important role in human thought. It is perceived as radically superior to all contingent things that have their being only through it. All things that are exist only by participation or derivation from being itself, whereas being itself is unaffected by them. As that by virtue of which all things are, as the ground of the being of all beings, it appears as infinitely more excellent than even the greatest being could be. It is absolute, immutable, omnipotent, and ineffable.

In the East the admiration for pure being went even further. As Brahman, its contrast with all contingent things led to viewing these things not merely as phenomenal but even as unreal or illusory. The goal for human life could be construed as release from involvement in this unreal and illusory world so as to be one with the real and changeless Brahman. This release could be affected by the realization of the identity of the being of the self and the being of all things.

Western mysticism at times came close to this position. Meister Eckhart identified being with the Godhead, and he was able to realize his own identity with this Godhead. But he did not draw conclusions about the unreality or illusoriness of the world comparable in their negations to those that can be found in the school of Sankara.

The point of these brief comments is to argue that the ultimate of metaphysical thought and of mysticism is one. In the Hindu tradition this is clear; for the greatest metaphysicians and the greatest mystics are often one. In the West it is less clear, but Rudolf Otto has pointed out how closely Meister Eckhart follows the metaphysics of Thomas Aquinas. This unity suggests that critics of metaphysics are wrong when they suppose that it deals only with abstractions remote from human experience. On the contrary, insofar as metaphysics penetrates to the ground of the being of beings it moves in tandem with the mystical penetration into ultimate reality. Metaphysics and mysticism inform one another. Mystical experience seems to confirm the metaphysical vision of Being Itself, the Ground of Being, or Brahman underlying and transcending the world of flux and expressing itself in that world.

The mystical literature both of the West and of Hinduism is full of negations as well as affirmations. Being or Brahman is utterly other than all things of which we can think, for all concepts are of forms rather than of being itself. Our habit of conceptual thinking can be broken only by repeated negations of all our efforts to conceive. The appeal can only be to intuition or experiential realization. Nevertheless, the mysticism of Being and of Brahman employs negations in support of affirmation. Being is not real as contingent things are real, but this is because it has an eminently superior reality of a wholly different order. Being is no-thing, because to be a thing is to be finite, and Being is without limitations of any kind. Being is empty in that it lacks all definition by forms; for such definition too is a mark of limitation and finitude.

Nevertheless, in Western and Hindu mysticism the negation served the cause of the affirmation of ultimate reality as Being or Brahman, the infinite source or ground of all things. Buddhism, on the other hand, from its origins insisted that the quest for the source or ground of things is idle, and this quickly came to be understood to imply that there is no such ground. Ultimate reality is not Being but Nothingness, Nirvana.

Even this was not radical enough to undergird the Buddhist requirement of total detachment. Nirvana could still be viewed as a blessed state or condition to be discovered or attained in contrast with the misery of Samsara, the phenomenal world. As long as this duality was allowed, one could be repelled by Samsara and crave Nirvana. Hence in the Madhyamika school, the distinction of Nirvana and Samsara was also negated, and in the Mahayana vision the identity of these opposites became fundamental. Nirvana is Samsara and Samsara is Nirvana; for both Nirvana and Samsara are "sunya" or empty. All that is, is Emptiness.

The dissolution of Being into Emptiness is also a dissolution of metaphysics into the language of things and of mysticism into the sheer immediacy of the world. We may, as a result, speak of the Buddhist denial or rejection of Being, of metaphysics, and of mysticism. But this would be misunderstood in the West where such denial usually arises by refusing the questions and the experiential probing that lead to Being, to metaphysics, and to mysticism. Buddhism overcomes Being by its analysis, metaphysics by metaphysical subtlety, and mysticism by mystical discipline. Hence it will be less confusing to continue to speak of Being, metaphysics, and mysticism, recognizing that in the Buddhist penetration they are dissolved and transformed.

The dissolution of Being into Emptiness is not designed to restore primacy to the finite things and events. Just as for Western and Hindu metaphysics and mysticism the finite things and events are nothing but expressions of Being; so for Buddhism they are nothing but expressions of Emptiness. Disengagement from attachment to things is as strong in Buddhism as in Hinduism. But this disengagement is not for the sake of a new engagement with ultimate reality. The ultimate that comes to expression in things, events, or experiences is Emptiness.

These Buddhist assertions are, and are intended to be, mind-boggling. As Buddhists insist, there is no simple way to explain them to those of us who have not experientially realized their truth. Still, much can be said, and I will try to indicate what I have understood or believe myself to have understood. What does it mean to say that an event, such as a moment of human experience, is empty?

First, it is empty of substance. There is no underlying self or "I" that unites separate moments of experience. Even in the single moment there is no subject to which the experience occurs. The happening of the experience brings into being the only subject that in any sense exists, and this subject is nothing other than the happening.

Second, the experience lacks all possession. That which makes up the experience does not belong to the experience. Its constituent elements are given to it. The experience is nothing but the coming together of that which is other than the experience.

Third, the experience is empty of form. It does not possess a form which it imposes on what constitutes it. The form is nothing but the result of the constitution, which is carried out by the constituting elements.

Fourth, it is empty of being. There is not, in addition to the coming together of the constituting elements something else which is the being of the new experience. Those constituting elements become the new experience, or rather, this becoming is the experience. Further, these elements, in their turn do not have being; for they in their turn are empty in the same way. There is no being—only Emptiness.

This explanation indicates that the Emptiness of an experience is the obverse side of the mode of its constitution. This mode is called *pratitya-samutpada* or dependent co-origination. That is, all the elements jointly constitute the new event which is then an element in the constitution of others. Both as event and as an element in other events it is empty.

The doctrine of Emptiness is not developed for the purpose of destroying all possible happiness and engendering bleak pessimism. On the contrary, it is developed to encourage the attainment of bliss through experiential realization of Emptiness. Indeed, there is no doubt that Buddhism succeeds in leading its adepts into a state of remarkable serenity and inner peace. Furthermore, just because all events are empty, they are also spontaneous and free.

The serenity and spontaneity attained by realization of Emptiness do not lead away from the awareness of what is occurring in one's world or reduce effectiveness of action. On the contrary, Buddhist meditation has been cultivated successfully for the sake of greater effectiveness in normal life. The Buddhist adept is able to be aware of every feature of her or his environment, responding to it freshly with enjoyment and appreciation without imposing upon it any meaning or emotional tone not immediately derived from it. Recent tests have vindicated this claim. In most meditative states persons are shown to respond differentially to stimuli. If a simple stimulus is frequently repeated, they respond with strong emotion initially, but eventually they become accustomed to it and do not respond at all. In a state of Zen meditation, however, persons respond to each repetition of the stimulus identically.

I mention this recent verification of Buddhist claims, not because Buddhist metaphysics is thereby proven, but to make it clear that we are not simply playing word-games. The experiential realization of being as Emptiness has definite effects, experienced as salvific by those who know them inwardly, and profoundly impressive to observers.

My knowledge of comparative religious practice and the results is not sufficient to allow me to judge between Western-Hindu mysticism and Buddhist meditation. But whereas until recently Western thought tended to support the view of being as Being Itself and the Ground of Being, in the twentieth century it has engaged in a dissolution of Being comparable to that of Buddhism. Hence there is special importance today in the encounter with Buddhism.

This reference to twentieth century development is especially focused on Martin Heidegger and Alfred North Whitehead. It is Heidegger who has done the major work in recovering for Western thought the question of being. It is he who has insisted upon the ontological difference between being and beings and worked through the history of Western philosophy in terms of his cognitive-experiential grasp of this difference. The results follow Buddhism in the insistence that there is no Being other than the being of the beings, and he goes far toward ridding this being of substantial character. Like Buddhism, he has dissolved metaphysics as onto-theo-logic.

Whitehead's work is remarkably compatible with that of Heidegger. He noted that every philosophy requires an ultimate that is actual only in its instantiations. In *Science and the Modern World* he called this ultimate "substantial activity," and he related it specifically to Spinoza's substance. But by the time he wrote *Process and Reality* the note of substantiality was gone. The ultimate is creativity, and creativity is nothing other than the many becoming one and being increased by one. Creativity is neither a being nor Being. It is remarkably like the ancient Buddhist dependent co-origination.

II. *The Principle of Rightness*

The dissolution of Being itself into Emptiness highlights the presence in the history of religions of another ultimate. Alongside the drive to go beyond the conditioned multiplicity of things to their common ground, which turns out to be groundlessness, there is another drive rightly to order action and experience. One finds this concern reflected in all the religious literatures of humankind, although in the religions of India it seems to be finally subordinated to the other concern for release through experiential realization of ultimate reality. In Judaism and in Confucianism it is paramount.

The rightness in question expresses itself in diverse ways. There is a rightness of style or form, propriety, appropriateness, good judgment, wisdom. Only in special circumstances is it expressed in clear-cut moral dualities of "ought" and "ought not." More often it functions as a discrimination of excellence from mediocrity. Still it is always bound up with norms of conduct that are broadly ethical.

It is particularly instructive to the Westerner to observe the struggle of the two ultimates in China. The first is represented by Taoism and is supported and strengthened subsequently by Buddhism. In Taoism efforts to improve society or to mold moral character are either ridiculed or viewed as clearly secondary to the fundamental goal of human beings, the realization of Tao. The embodiment of the second ultimate in Confucianism led to occasional attacks upon the escapism and amorality of Taoism. For the Confucian the goal must be rightly to order individual life and through it the corporate life. Moral considerations should never be subordinated to a mystical fulfillment of the private individual. They are as ultimate for the Confucian as is the unnamable Tao for the Taoist. But they are a radically different kind of ultimate.

Confucian thought was directed primarily to social theory and ethics. Hence it did not depend on agreed clarification of the metaphysical status of the ground or principle of rightness. Nevertheless, even a cursory reading of the texts allows one to say that in an important sense this principle is both immanent and transcendent for most Confucian thinkers. It is immanent in that it can be found by the sage through self-knowledge. The sense of rightness is a part of lived experience. We can grow in our ability to discern it well and to conform ourselves to it. But it is not imposed on us by alien authority. It is our own deepest nature.

At the same time, rightness is transcendent. It is not transcendent in the sense of having to be revealed or existing apart from human experience. But it is transcendent in that it is not created or chosen by human beings. It is given for us. It belongs to the nature of reality. It is prior to our acknowledgment of it or conformity to it. We individually derive it from beyond ourselves, and societies derive it from beyond themselves. The source or ground of its presence in our experience and nature is its prior characterization of heaven or of Tao. In its ultimacy it commands respect and even devotion, and that devotion is directed toward the cosmic ground of what is within.

All of this is familiar to the Westerner. Only in the last century have we come to see how even the most immanental interpretations of Western morality have in fact grounded themselves upon the transcendent. For only in the last century have we had radical critics of this transcendence who have argued that all appraisal of rightness is in fact a creation of norms rather than a recognition of a rightness already there. Kant's "moral law within" is as transcendent of human choice as is the prophet's "Thus says the Lord." The question is how to understand this transcendence. And to this question there has been far greater attention in the West than in China.

In Christianity there has been a transcending of morality. But this transcendence of morality should not be confused with the mystical transcending. In Paul morality is transcended because the effort to be righteous fails, not because being righteous is unimportant. What comes in the place of human fulfillment of the requirements of rightness is true righteousness as a gift. This involves conceiving of the principle of rightness as giving what it demands so that the believer can live out of this gift. It does not involve turning from the ultimate source of rightness to another ultimate that is beyond, or indifferent to, the distinctions of better and worse.

Just as it has proved possible to ignore and even to deny the metaphysical and mystical ultimate, so also it has proved possible to ignore and deny the ultimate of rightness. Cognitive confusion about both ultimates has contributed its share to the "positivistic" spirit. Nevertheless, these denials, however brilliant and important they have been, are best seen as phases in the process of cleansing our thought of these ultimates from conceptual accretions. Both remain present and functioning in human life when unrecognized, and in new forms they are recognized again and again. Our present experience as much as that of any previous epoch witnesses to the presence of a rightness in things more or less conformed to, just as the deepest intellectual and experiential penetration leads to the realization of a being that is Emptiness.

Clarification of each of the two ultimates and of what each means for human existence has taken place in separate traditions. I have suggested that the metaphysical-mystical ultimate is most fully clarified precisely in that tradition in which it is most fully freed of the last remnants of substantiality, namely Buddhism. But much can be learned of it in Hindu Brahmanism and Chinese Taoism as well. The ethical ultimate received its fullest development in the biblical and Confucian traditions.

In China the two ultimates were cultivated for centuries in partly separate traditions. Many Chinese embodied both in their lives, but an attempt at full synthesis in an inclusive philosophy awaited the advent of Neo-Confucianism. Chu Hsi is the greatest figure in this movement, and his synthesis can be treated in terms of the two concepts of T'ai-chi, the Great Ultimate, and Li, the principle of heaven and earth and the thousand things. Chu-Hsi declares that T'ai-chi is Li. This means that the metaphysical ultimate and the ultimate of rightness are one and the same. This identification does not, however, subordinate the directive character of Li to the transcendence of good and evil of the metaphysical ultimate. On the contrary, in Chu Hsi the metaphysical ultimate is viewed as characterized by the directivity derived from the ultimate principle of rightness.

In the West contact between Jewish and metaphysical thinking quickly drove Jewish thought to the claim that the ultimate principle of rightness to which it was directed must also be the metaphysical ultimate. Philo is the first great figure in this synthesis, and he has been followed by the major traditions of Christian theology. This synthesis could not be postponed or avoided as in China, because already in its dealings with the ultimate principle of rightness Israel had identified this as the creator of heaven and earth, and her praise of this creator heaped upon him every superlative attribute. It would be unthinkable to allow another ultimate beside this one. In later Christian theology, notably that of St. Thomas, the metaphysical ultimate was recognized as *esse,* the act of being, or Being Itself, but in Jewish and Christian thought, as in that of Neo-Confucian-

ism, the metaphysical ultimate is suffused with a directivity derived from the ultimate of rightness.

Hinduism and Buddhism have from the beginning dealt with the principle of rightness as well as with the metaphysical ultimate. In general, however, they have done so by distinguishing levels of human existence and attainment. The level at which considerations of rightness are relevant is finally transcended by the level at which the metaphysical ultimate is experientially realized. This final subordination of the ethical to the metaphysical is unacceptable to Confucianists and to heirs of the biblical tradition.

The question that confronts us now is whether the synthesis of the two ultimates effected in Neo-Confucianism and in most Western theology can be vindicated. Does the directivity in things, the orientation toward rightness, arise out of the relation to the metaphysical ultimate, or is the metaphysical ultimate finally neutral? If it is neutral, then is the ethical ultimate in fact not ultimate at all? Or is there an ultimate that is just as ultimate in its way as the metaphysical ultimate but that differs fundamentally from it?

The history of both Neo-Confucianism and of Western thought reveals a fundamental instability in the efforts to identify the two ultimates as one. To show that would be to retrace the history of these traditions in a way for which I have neither the knowledge nor the time. But the work of Heidegger and Whitehead indicates that the Buddhist analysis of the metaphysical-mystical ultimate as Emptiness carries us more fully into truth than any other. This emptiness cannot be identified with the ultimate of rightness. Hence either the ultimacy of this ultimate must be denied, or we are left with a duality of ultimates.

III. *God*

In the two preceding sections the word God has been avoided because it carries such heavy freight of meaning that it is difficult to discuss topics dispassionately once it is introduced. However, it is time now to ask to what this word has referred and what are its equivalents in other traditions and languages.

"God" is best used, first, to refer to whatever is worshipped. In this sense there are, superficially at least, many gods, and a god need have no ultimacy. But there is a drive in the act of worship itself to attribute ultimacy to what is worshipped, and this calls forth an effort to think through the specific object of worship to the ultimate that is worshipped in it. Hence "God," wherever the thought functions strongly, tends to name what is felt in some important way to be ultimate.

That "God" belongs with worship not only leads to association with ultimacy but also with actuality or concreteness. Within the context of worship there is a strong tendency to personalize the divine. But this tendency comes into tension with the other tendency toward ultimacy. What is actual, concrete, or personal seems always necessarily delimited and therefore limited. What is ultimate is more easily conceived as principle than as personality.

One solution to this problem is to hold that all worship is in fact directed to the metaphysical ultimate, but that it is psychologically necessary for all except the mystic to worship this ultimate through particular embodiments. The word God then can continue to attach to the supreme embodiment or embodiments of the ultimate, and some other word, such as "Godhead," can name the ultimate itself. This usage in Meister Eckhart was noted in Section I. It corresponds to the relation of Isvara and Brahman in Sankara, and to the relation of the Buddhas to the Buddha-nature or Emptiness in much Buddhist thought.

In Confucian thought much less attention is given to the object of worship, but this could be identified as T'ai-yi, the Great One. In the Neo-Confucian philosophy of Chu Hsi, the Great One is explicitly identified with Li, the principle of rightness that functions as the directivity of all things. Li is also identified with the metaphysical ultimate, T'ai-chi, but in such a way that the metaphysical ultimate is assimilated to the ethical rather than the reverse. Hence, the God of Confucianism is the principle of rightness which may or may not also be viewed as metaphysically ultimate. The reality of God for Confucianism is bound up with the reality of a principle of rightness that is transcendent as well as immanent. But because worship is of minor importance to the Confucian, the identification of this principle as God is optional.

In the West God has meant the Ultimate, and the Ultimate has been both ethically and metaphysically ultimate. Hence belief in God faces a crisis when the one Ultimate is divided into two. The crisis has been precipitated especially by Heidegger, whose profound investigation of being led him to the conclusion that being is not God. If theologians are to continue to speak of God, they must identify God in another way. Heidegger lent his blessing to the proposal of Heinrich Ott that God is to faith as being is to thought, but this suggestive opening to a new mode of theology has thus far not been developed among Heideggerians.

On the contrary, the most influential philosophical theologian of our century, Paul Tillich, in spite of Heidegger's warning, identified God with Being. He recognized with Heidegger that this meant that God is not in any sense a being. Hence he was forced to remove from the idea of God much that had clung to the earlier understanding of Being when *esse* had been assimilated to an established understanding of deity. That is, in Tillich the classical identification of God and Being was continued, but whereas in Thomism the understanding of Being has been assimilated to the understanding of God, in Tillich the understanding of God was assimilated to the understanding of Being.

The contrast here should not be exaggerated. The understanding of God in philosophical theology had long been profoundly affected by its assimilation of Being. And in Tillich the understanding of Being as the Ground of Being and Depth of Being and much of his rhetoric and even doctrine shows the influence of an understanding of God shaped by the principle of rightness. Nevertheless, once the ontological difference between being and beings is unequivocally accepted, as it is by Tillich, the reversal is in principle effected.

The English theologian, John Macquarrie, made still more explicit and specific use of

Heidegger's renewal of the understanding of being. He freed being largely from the connotations of Ground of Being and Depth of Being that reflected Schelling and the Protestant mystics rather than Heidegger. Certainly much that he says about God as Being betrays the tension between the principle of rightness and the metaphysical ultimate. But he goes one step further in displaying the cost to Christianity of the identification of God with the metaphysical ultimate as this is progressively freed from the connotations of the principles of rightness. Although this kind of theological response to Heidegger continues, it appears to have decreasing power.

Whitehead agreed with Heidegger that the metaphysical ultimate is not God. This ultimate, creativity, was nevertheless appropriated by some of those influenced by him as God. Usually they coordinated his doctrine of creativity with that of Henry Nelson Wieman, thus restoring to it the association with the principle of rightness from which his own analysis freed it. Nevertheless, since Whitehead not only allowed and encouraged a different identification of God but himself developed it, Whitehead's primary theological influence has been the emergence of a school, process theology, that dissociates God from the metaphysical ultimate.

Even within the mainstream of process theology, however, the dissociation has been very incomplete. Charles Hartshorne has engaged more in a new interpretation of the metaphysical ultimate that introduces process into it than in a dissolution of the historic identification of the ultimate of metaphysics with the ultimate principle of rightness. For years I struggled to subordinate creativity to God, rather than to allow their radical difference to stand out clearly. It has required an encounter with Eastern thought to clarify the religious meaning of the work of both Heidegger and Whitehead and to force the issue of God. When that issue is forced, at least within process theology, but also wherever biblical faith is primary, God must be identified with the principle of rightness rather than with the metaphysical ultimate. The problem for Christian theology is then the right understanding of this principle in

its purity and distinctness instead of the effort to unite with it the metaphysical ultimate. To this task Whitehead has himself made a contribution whose full meaning has not yet been grasped or appropriated by his followers.

IV. The Realization of Emptiness and Faith in God

The analysis thus far has been primarily designed to show that an adequate account of the deepest level of human experience requires us to recognize that there are two ultimates, the metaphysical ultimate and the ultimate principle of rightness. I have also argued that the metaphysical ultimate is best understood precisely in its dissolution into dependent co-origination or Emptiness, and that the principle of rightness is properly designated as God.

The discussion has shown that the affirmation of these two ultimates is not contradictory. Indeed, the double affirmation is allowed and clarified in Heidegger and actually developed in Whitehead. Heidegger's being and Whitehead's creativity correspond remarkably with Buddhist Emptiness. And Whitehead has developed a cosmology in which God as the principle of rightness is clearly distinguished from and related to creativity as the metaphysical ultimate.

It is not so evident, however, that Buddhism can allow this dual ultimate. The question posed by Buddhism to this affirmation of God is whether it fully recognizes that God, too, insofar as God is, must be empty. That would mean recognizing that God does not possess a being different in kind from the being of other entities, which has been displayed as Emptiness. God, too, must be empty, just as the self, and all things are empty—empty of substantiality or own-being, and lacking in any given character of their own. God like all things must be an instance of dependent co-origination.

Whitehead's doctrine of God is open to this interpretation. God, like all things, is an instance of creativity, that is, of the many becoming one, which is his formulation of dependent co-origination. God is as much a creature of creativ-

ity as is any other entity, and God is not an exception to the categories. The principle of universal relativity includes God. Furthermore, God as understood by Whitehead supremely embodies the characteristics that follow from enlightenment. Accordingly God my be conceived as the totally enlightened one, the supreme and everlasting Buddha.

Whereas the unenlightened one discriminates, accentuating some stimuli and shutting out others, the enlightened one receives all for just what they are. Whereas the unenlightened one juxtaposes self-interest and the good of others, the enlightened one is equally benevolent toward all. Emptiness is freedom from all distorting perceptions and concerns and perfect openness to all that is, human and nonhuman alike.

Whitehead conceives God in much this way. God is constituted by the progressive unification of all actuality with all possibility. Each actuality and every possibility is allowed to be just what it is in the process of dependent co-origination or concrescence. God is undiscriminatingly benevolent towards all. There are no distortions in God's perceptions and concerns preventing God's perfect openness toward all that is, human and nonhuman alike. Thus "God" can be freed from the note of substantiality and dualism that makes this concept offensive to the Buddhist. Whether Buddhists can accept the remaining distinction between the one cosmic Buddha, the ultimate principle of rightness, and the many creaturely Buddhas is not yet clear.

Religiously some such acceptance seems to function in some Buddhist schools. The Christian conviction that personal trust in God, present in the world as Christ, is essential to salvation is paralleled in those Buddhist schools that teach salvation by the power of the Other, especially Amida Buddha, rather than by one's own efforts. Nevertheless, there is a profound difference.

For the Buddhists, even in those schools that emphasize total dependence on the power of the Other, the goal is that of enlightenment, or the realization of the ultimate reality of one's situation. This is the realization of the identity of one's true self as the Emptiness that is open to be filled by everything impartially. For Christians the goal is for the self to be progressively conformed to the gracious promptings or call of God, trusting the creative outcome of that surrender of the resistant selfhood to the divine wisdom and purpose.

We can now see that either goal is attainable, or rather that either may be approximated. For the Buddhist, even the Buddhist who stresses faith in the Other, the final goal is to attain freedom from the other power in becoming oneself a Buddha. For the Christian the final goal is to experience freedom as the perfect conformation to God, the principle of rightness.

When compared with ordinary states of self-centeredness, anxiety, isolation, and ambition, the Buddhist and Christian goals seem very much alike. But they overcome our ordinary pettiness and misery in fundamentally distinct ways. The differences can be stated as follows. Buddhists realize that they are at each and every moment, and hence without qualification, instances of dependent co-origination or, in Whitehead's language, concrescent processes. The actual standpoint of experience is never that of a completed entity, whereas all of our conceptuality, even about ourselves, turns us into such entities. This actual, existential realization frees the concrescent process of distortion and illusion, and it opens experience to what is as it is. Christians on the other hand, attend to God's aim for the concrescence, a directivity toward rightness that is the divine immanence in the concrescent process. This aim is both at an immediate achievement in that concrescence and at its appropriate effects beyond itself. These effects are upon other events and especially upon other human experiences.

I have tried to show in this presentation that the respective attainments of Buddhism and Christianity are not contradictory, but that they yet differ profoundly. Christians can agree that what is ultimate in the metaphysical sense is dependent co-origination, the many becoming one, creativity, or concrescence as such. They can understand, therefore, why metaphysicians and mystics have so often pushed through and past God to the metaphysical-mystical ultimate which can be called Being, Brahman, or God-head. But they need not be intimidated. Buddhism teaches that this ultimate is indeed devoid of form and beyond good and evil, as mystics have often said. It is exemplified without discrimination in a cockroach, a human child, God, and an atomic explosion. It is not evident that this is the one ultimate that should guide all human attention, effort, and reflection. If there is importance in the shape that dependent co-origination or concrescence takes, if it matters whether the universe is full of life or allowed to die, then we should attend to God. God is not that ultimate that is actual only in its instantiations, but God is the ultimate instantiation of the ultimate. It is meaningless to speak of Emptiness as superior to God or of God as superior to Emptiness. They are incommensurable.

In this way the encounter with Buddhist Emptiness can free Christians to distinguish the Emptiness of God from the Emptiness which is the Godhead, without claiming for God the kind of ultimacy that belongs to Emptiness or to Godhead as such. But a still deeper question remain. How are Christians to relate themselves to that other form of human realization and perfection exemplified so purely in Buddhist enlightenment? Having recognized the possibility and reality of this fulfillment as well as its difference from Christian trust in God, are they to envy it in its superiority, condemn it as an inferior rival, recognize it as a legitimate option to be chosen by those so inclined, or attempt to appropriate it?

The argument of this paper counts against the first two of these options. That is, it finds no neutral grounds from which the respective worth of the two ultimates can be appraised. It opposes any claim to superiority between them. This implies that the orientation of human beings may be equally to Emptiness or to God. World history shows that the results of both orientations have been impressive, despite all their ambiguities, and that each exercises a certain attraction on the practitioners of the other. But the argument thus far has left fully open the question whether we are confronted here by existentially exclusive alter-

natives or whether this duality can in turn be transcended.

There are encouraging indications that the duality can be transcended. The hope that a synthesis of Buddhist and Christian achievements is possible is strengthened by the observation that the Buddhist saint appears to live and act as the Christian would expect one to live and act who is fully responsive to God. Although there is much talk of transcending the duality of good and evil, and although cheap imitations of Buddhism sometimes lead to amorality and immorality, authentic Buddhism does not have this character. The result of transcending the duality of good and evil is a pure and spontaneous goodness. It seems that when all discrimination and objectifying conceptualization are overcome, when one realizes what is as it is, the resultant concrescent process conforms effortlessly, without naming it, to the divine impulse.

Much Buddhist literature, indeed, witnesses to the conviction that Emptiness is not really neutral toward rightness. For example, in the treatment of the *Dharmakaya*, the Buddha-body or Buddha-nature, which is the truth and reality of all things, Buddhist writers employ notions of rightness, and especially of wisdom and compassion. Also, they attribute to the *Dharmakaya* the effecting of good works in those who realize it. Although the personalistic and value-laden language may be interpreted as a concession to popular understanding, it reflects a deep sense that what is realized in the realization of the metaphysical ultimate has its directivity toward wisdom and compassion.

This can be understood in terms of the double ultimate discussed above. Ultimate reality is the process of dependent co-origination in which the many that constitute the given world become a new, but ephemeral and insubstantial, one. Among these many, one is God, functioning in all things as a directivity toward rightness. The Buddhist who is completely empty is by that token completely open. To be completely open is to allow each element in the many to be what it is in the new one, that is, to function appropriately according to its own potentiality. To allow God so to function is to be spontaneously formed by the rightness appropriate in that moment. Thus to be truly open is to be spontaneously good. By being wholly indifferent to right and wrong the Buddhist achieves a perfect conformation to the immanent principle of right. It seems, therefore, that Buddhist enlightenment contains a synthesis of the two ultimates.

There is also a Christian approach to this synthesis. This is through attention to the principle of rightness. The Christian goal is to achieve sensitivity and responsiveness to the inner promptings of God. Spiritual discipline consists in discerning the spirits so as to discriminate the divine urge from the many other urges that affect us. Response to this directivity leads away from concern primarily with oneself to a broader concern and to sensitivity to the needs and feelings of others. In short, it leads toward openness to what occurs as it occurs and to self-constitution that is appropriate thereto. Perhaps when this is combined with the recognition that the reality of the self *is* this dependent co-origination, what is achieved through cultivated responsiveness to the directivity that is God's presence will converge with what is achieved through Buddhist enlightenment.

2.5 The Female Nature of God

Recently the press has reported controversy about using female terms for God. God is Mother or God is Goddess, or God is She. One might wonder what all the fuss is about. The sacred scriptures of Judaism, Christianity, and Islam, and many other religious traditions, affirm that God created human beings in the image of God. Women as well as men are human beings. Adam in Hebrew means "human being." So why do we not speak of God as mother as well as father, and why do we not use the pronoun *She* as well as *He* to refer to God?

The reason is that male and masculine metaphors have not only deeply infected our conception of God, but they have also infected our very thinking about ultimate reality. We live in a sexist society. Nearly everything we read or see on television or in the movies reinforces the notion that males are superior to females. We are comfortable with male metaphors for the divine but uncomfortable with female metaphors. Male images mask the sexuality of God. To say that God is "Father" has sexual connotations. Yet these connotations do not become obvious until we speak of God as "Mother."

Why do we not pray to "Mother–Father" God? "Well," you might say, "because we are taught by scripture and tradition to pray to a Father God." So? Does that which is ultimate, that which is the creator of the world—including both male and female— play favorites? If so, what we call "God" is not God.

One might argue that male metaphors for God are innocent. After all, in English, the pronoun *he* often is used to refer to any antecedent subject whose gender is not explicitly female. Is this really so innocent? Language and the symbols employed by language have profound and deep influences on how people think and act. How many of you think of God in primarily masculine terms?

Some scholars argue that we should substitute female and feminine terms for God. God is the Goddess, the Mother of all life. She is the eternal womb of all that is. Others argue that we must get beyond sexual metaphors entirely. God is the source of all that is. As such, God is neither male nor female but the ultimate reality that creates both.

Rosemary Radford Reuther, the author of the following essay, contends that we should conceive of God or ultimate reality as beyond the dualities of sex.

Dr. Reuther is Georgia Harkness Professor of Applied Theology at Garrett-Evangelical Theological Seminary and Northwestern University in Evanston, Illinois. She is the author or editor of over 17 books and has written extensively on topics relating to feminist theology.

Reading Questions

1. What is the problem with regarding God as male?
2. What is the point of Reuther's survey of "suppressed feminine images in patriarchal theology"?
3. According to Reuther, what is wrong with the "Goddess Movement"?
4. Why will bringing to the surface the suppressed "feminine" side of God not help the situation?
5. According to Reuther, how should we best envision God?
6. What do you think? Is Reuther right or not? Why?

The Female Nature of God*

ROSEMARY RADFORD REUTHER

THE EXCLUSIVELY MALE IMAGE of God in the Judaeo-Christian tradition has become a critical issue of contemporary religious life. This question does not originate first of all in theology or in hermeneutics. It originates in the experience of alienation from this male image of God experienced by feminist women. It is only when this alienation is taken seriously that the theological and exegetical questions begin to be raised.

1. What Is the Problem?

The problem of the male image of God cannot be treated as trivial or an accidental question of linguistics. It must be understood first of all as an ideological bias that reflects the sociology of patriarchal societies; that is, those societies dominated by male, property-holding heads of families. Although not all patriarchal societies have male monotheist religions, in those patri-

archal societies which have this view of God, the God-image serves as the central reinforcement of the structure of patriarchal rule. The subordinate status of women in the social and legal order is reflected in the subordinate status of women in the cultus. The single male God is seen not only as creator and lawgiver of this secondary status of women. The very structure of spirituality in relation to this God enforces her secondary status.

What this means quite simply is the following. When God is projected in the image of one sex, rather than both sexes, and in the image of the ruling class of this sex, then this class of males is seen as consisting in the ones who possess the image of God primarily. Women are regarded as relating to God only secondarily and through inclusion in the male as their "head." This is stated very specifically by St. Augustine in his treatise *On the Trinity* (7, 7, 10).

* From "The Female Nature of God" by Rosemary Radford Reuther. *Concilium* 143: 1981. Reprinted by permission of Concilium.

The male monotheist image of God dictates a certain structure of divine-human relationship. God addresses directly only the patriarchal ruling class. All other groups—women, children, slaves—are addressed by God only indirectly and through the mediation of the patriarchal class. This hierarchal order of God/Man/Woman appears throughout Hebrew law. But it also reappears as a theological principle in the New Testament. Thus Paul (despite Gal. 3:28) in I Cor. 11:3 and 7 reaffirms this patriarchal order of relationships:

> But I want you to understand that the head of every man is Christ, the head of a woman is her husband, and the head of Christ is God. . . . For a man ought not to cover his head, since he is the image and glory of God; but the woman is the glory of man.

Thus the woman is seen as lacking the image of God or direct relation to God, in herself, but only secondarily, as mediated through the male.

2. The Suppressed "Feminine" in Patriarchal Theology

Recognising the fundamentally ideological, and even idolatrous, nature of this male-dominant image of God, some recent scholars have sought to show that this was never the whole story. God is not always described as a male. There is a small number of cases where God is described as a female. These texts occur in the Scriptures, particularly in the context of describing God's faithfulness to Israel and suffering on behalf of Israel. Here the labours of a woman in travail, giving birth to a child, and the fidelity of a mother who loves the child unconditionally, seemed to be more striking human analogies for these attributes of God than anything to be found in male activity. Thus in Isaiah we find:

> Yahweh goes forth, now I will cry out like a woman in travail, I will gasp and pant. (Isa. 42:13, 14).
>
> For Zion said, "Yahweh has forsaken me; my Lord has forgotten me. Can a woman forget her suckling child, that she should have no compassion on the son of her womb? Even these may forget, yet I will not forget you." (Isa. 49:14, 15).

These analogies of God as female in Scripture have been collected in Leonard Swidler's *Biblical Affirmation of Woman* (Philadelphia: Westminster 1979).

There is a second use of the female image for God in Scripture. The female image also appears as a secondary *persona* of God in the work of mediation to creation. In biblical thought this is found primarily in the Wisdom tradition. Here Holy Wisdom is described as a daughter of God through whom God mediates the work of creation, providential guidance, revelation, and reconciliation to God. In relation to the Solomon, the paradigmatic royal person, Wisdom is described as a "bride of his soul." Of her Solomon says:

> I loved her and sought after her from my youth, and I desired to take her for my bride, and I became enamoured of her beauty. . . . Therefore I determined to take her to live with me, knowing that she would give me good counsel (Wisd. of Sol. 8:2, 9).

The same view of Wisdom as mediating creatrix is found in Proverbs (8:23–31). Here she is imaged as the mother who mediates wisdom to her sons.

Behind this powerful image of Divine Wisdom undoubtedly lies remnants of the ancient Near Eastern Goddess, Isis or Astarte. These Goddesses were imaged as creators and redeemers. They are linked particularly with Wisdom, defined as both social justice and harmony in nature, over against the threatening powers of Chaos. Raphael Patai, in his book, *The Hebrew Goddess* (Ktav 1967), has delineated the heritage of this ancient Near Eastern Goddess as she appeared in suppressed form in Hebrew theology.

Although the Sophia image disappears in rabbinic thought after the advent of the Christian era, possibly because of its use in gnosticism, a new image of God's mediating presence as female appears in the form of the *Shekinah*. The *Shekinah* is both the mediating presence of God in the midst of Israel, but also the reconciler of Israel with God. In rabbinic mystical speculation on the *galut* (exile), the *Shekinah* is seen as going into exile with Israel when God-as-father has turned away his face in anger. Each Shabbat celebration is seen as a mystical connubial embrace of God with his *Shekinah,* anticipating the final reuniting of God with creation in the messianic age. The exile of Israel from the land is seen ultimately as an exile within God, divorcing the masculine from the feminine "side" of God.

In Christianity this possibility of the immanence of God as feminine was eliminated. Christianity translated the Sophia concept into the Logos concept of Philo, defined as "son of God." It related this masculine mediating *persona* of God to the human person, Jesus. Thus the maleness of Jesus as a human person is correlated (or even fused into) the maleness of the Logos as "son of God." All possible speculation on a "female side" of God within trinitarian imagery was thus cut off from the beginning.

Some Sophia speculation does get revived in the Greek Orthodox tradition in relation to creation, the Church and Mariology. One somewhat maverick modern Orthodox thinker (Sergius Bulgakov *The Wisdom of God,* London 1937) even relates this sophiological aspect of God to the *ousia* or Being of God. Sophia is the matrix or ground of Being of the three (male) persons of God! But it is doubtful if most Orthodox thinkers would be comfortable with that idea.

In western thought speculation on feminine aspects of God were probably rejected early because of links with gnosticism. Some recent Catholic thinkers (i.e., Leonard Swidler) have tried to revive the Sophia/*Shekinah* idea and link it with the Holy Spirit. But this does not have roots in western trinitarian thought. Basically the Spirit is imaged as a "male" but non-anthropomorphic principle. As the power of God that "fecundates" the waters at creation and the womb of Mary, its human referent would seem to be closer to the male semen as medium of male power.

This means that in western Christian theology, the female image is expelled from any place within the doctrine of God. It appears instead on the creaturely side of the God/creation relation. The female is used as the image of that which is created by God, that which is the recipient of God's creation; namely, Nature, Church, the soul, and, finally, Mary as the paradigmatic image of the redeemed humanity.

One partial exception to this rule is found in the Jesus mysticism of the middle ages that finds its culmination in Juliana of Norwich. Here Jesus, as the one who feeds us with his body, is portrayed as both mother and father. Eucharistic spirituality particularly seems to foster this mothering, nurturing image of Jesus. However since both the divine and the human person of Jesus is firmly established in the orthodox theological tradition as male, this feminine reference to Jesus remains an attribute of a male person. Female-identified qualities, such as mothering and nurturing, are taken over by the male. But the female is not allowed "male" or "headship" capacities.

What I wish to argue then is that all of these suppressed feminine aspects of God in patriarchal theology still remain fundamentally within the context of the male-dominant structure of patriarchal relationships. The female can never appear as the icon of God in all divine fullness, parallel to the male image of God. It is allowed in certain limited references to God's faithfulness and suffering for Israel. Or it appears as a clearly subordinate principle that mediates the work and power of the Father, much as the mother in the family mediates to the children (sons) the dictates of the father. She can be daughter of the divine king; bride of the human king; mother of his sons; but never an autonomous person in her own right.

The "feminine" in patriarchal theology is basically allowed to act only within the same limited, subordinate or mediating roles that women are allowed to act in the patriarchal social order. The feminine is the recipient and mediator of male power to subordinate persons; i.e., sons, servants. In Christianity even these covert and marginal roles of the feminine as aspects of God disappear. Here the feminine is only allowed as image of the human recipient or mediator of divine grace, not as an aspect of the divine. In every relationship in which this "feminine" aspect appears in patriarchal theology, the dominant sovereign principle is always male; the female operating only as delegate of the male.

3. "Pagan Feminism": The Revolt Against the Biblical Patriarchal God

In the 1970s the feminist movement, particularly in the United States, began to develop an increasingly militant wing that identified patriarchal religion as the root of the problem of women's subordination. These women saw that efforts to create a more "androgynous" God within the biblical tradition would be insufficient. The female aspect of God would always be placed within this fundamentally male-centred perspective. They concluded that biblical religion must be rejected altogether.

In its place they would substitute a Goddess and nature religion that they believe to be the original human cult of matriarchal society before the rise of patriarchy. They believe that the witches of the European middle ages preserved this Goddess-centred nature religion. They were persecuted for this faith by the Christian Church who falsely accused them of malevolence and "devil worship." Feminist Wicca (or witchcraft) believes itself to be reviving this ancient Goddess religion. The book by Starhawk (Miriam Simos), *The Spiral Dance* (New York 1979), is a good expression of this feminist Goddess movement.

It is possible that we are witnessing in this movement the first strings of what may become a new stage of human religious consciousness. This possibility cannot be ruled out by the critical Christian. It may be that we have allowed divine revelation through the prophets and through Jesus to be so corrupted by an idolatrous androcentrism, that a fuller understanding of God that truly includes the female as person must come as superseding and judging patriarchal religion. However, Goddess religion in its present form manifests a number of immaturities that are open to criticism, even from the point of view of feminism.

Following outdated matriarchal anthropology from the nineteenth century, much of the pedigree claimed by this movement is of doubtful historicity. In fact, the patterns of Goddess religion reveal very clearly their roots in nineteenth-century European romanticism. The dualistic world view that sets the feminine, nature and immanence on one side, and the masculine, history and transcendence on the other, is fundamentally preserved in this movement. It simply exalts the feminine pole of the dualism and repudiates the masculine side. One must ask whether this does not entrap women in precisely the traditional stereotypes. The dualisms are not overcome, but merely given a reverse valuation. But, in practice, this still means that women, even in "rebellion," are confined to a powerless Utopianism in which males own and run "the world."

Moreover, within their own community, instead of transforming the male monotheist model, they have reversed it. Now the great Goddess is the predominant image of the Divine. Woman then becomes the one who fully images the Goddess and communicates directly with her. Males are either excluded or given a subordinate position that is analogous to the position traditionally accorded women in the patriarchal cult. This *coup d'etat* may feel satisfying in the short run, but in the long run would seem to reproduce the same fundamental pathology.

4. Does the Ancient Goddess Represent the Feminine?

Both biblical feminists, who search for the suppressed feminine in the Judaeo-Christian tradition, and Goddess worshipers, who wish to exalt the feminine at the expense of the masculine, share a common assumption. Both assume that the recovery of the female as icon of the divine means the vindication of the "feminine." Neither ask the more fundamental question of whether the concept of the feminine itself is not a patriarchal creation. Thus the vindication of the "feminine," as we have inherited that concept from patriarchy, will always be set within a dualistic scheme of complementary principles that segregate women on one side and men on the other. Even if this scheme is given a reversed valuation, the same dualism remains.

A recent study by Judith Ochshorn, *The Female Experience and the Nature of the Divine* (Indiana University Press 1980) raises some important questions about the appropriateness of identifying this patriarchally-defined feminine with the ancient goddesses of polytheistic cultures. What Ochshorn has discovered is that, in polytheistic cultures of the Ancient Near East, gods and goddesses do not fall into these stereotyped patterns of masculinity and femininity. A God or Goddess, when addressed in the context of their own cult, represents a fullness of divine attributes. The Goddess represents sovereignty, wisdom, justice, as well as aspects of sexual and natural fecundity. Likewise the God operates as a sexual and natural principle, as well as a principle for social relations. The Goddess displays all the fullness of divine power in a female image. She is not the expression of the "feminine." Ochshorn also believes that this more pluralistic schema allows women to play more equalitarian and even leading roles in the cultus.

The subordinate status of women, in which relation to God is mediated only through the patriarchal class, is absent from religions which have a plurality of divine foci in male and female forms. Although such a lost religious world is probably not revivable as an option today, such studies may help to point us to the relativity of our patriarchally-defined patterns of masculine or feminine. They alert us to the dangers of simply surfacing the suppressed "feminine side" of that dualism as part of the image of God, without further criticism.

5. *Towards an Image of God Beyond Patriarchy*

If we are to seek an image of God(ess) beyond patriarchy, certain basic principles must be acknowledged. First we must acknowledge that the male has no special priority in imaging God(ess). If male roles and functions; i.e., fathering, are only analogies for God, then those analogies are in no way superior to the parallel analogies drawn from female experience; i.e., mothering. God(ess) as Parent is as much Mother as Father.

But even the Parent image must be recognised as a limited analogy for God(ess), often reinforcing patterns of permanent spiritual infantilism and cutting off moral maturity and responsibility. God(ess) as creator must be seen as the Ground of the full personhood of men and women equally. A God(ess) who is a good parent, and not a neurotic parent, is one that promotes our growth towards responsible personhood, not one who sanctions dependency. The whole concept of our relation to God(ess) must be reimaged.

If God(ess) is not only creator, but also redeemer of the world from sin, then God(ess) cannot be seen as the sanctioner of the priority of male over female. To do so is to make God the creator and sanctioner of patriarchy. God becomes the architect of injustice. The image of God as predominantly male is fundamentally idolatrous. The same can be said of an image of God(ess) as predominantly female.

The God(ess) who can be imaged through the experience of men and women alike does not simply embrace these experiences and validate them in their traditional historical form. We cannot simply add the "mothering" to the "fathering" God, while preserving the same hierarchical patterns of male activity and female passivity. To vindicate the "feminine" in this form is merely to make God the sanctioner of patriarchy in new form.

God(ess) must be seen as beyond maleness and femaleness. Encompassing the full humanity of both men and women, God(ess) also speaks as judge and redeemer from the stereotyped roles in which men as "masculine" and women as "feminine" have been cast in patriarchal society. God(ess) restores both men and women to full humanity. This means not only a new humanity, but a new society, new personal and social patterns of human relationships. The God(ess) who is both male and female, and neither male or female, points us to an unrealised new humanity.

In this expanding image of God(ess) we glimpse our own expanding human potential, as selves and as social beings, that have remained truncated and confined in patriarchal, hierarchical relationships. We begin to give new content to the vision of the messianic humanity that is neither "Jew nor Greek, that is neither slave nor free, that is neither male nor female" (Gal. 3:28) in which God(ess) has "broken down the dividing wall of hostility" (Eph. 2:14).

2.6 Is the Concept of Ultimate Reality Coherent?

We have been looking at diverse views of ultimate reality (Tao, Brahman, God, Emptiness) in this chapter. As different as these views are and as incompatible as you may find them, they have in common the concern to describe or at least help us understand (however dimly) what is ultimate. It is time to take a step back from specific religious views and ask whether the notion of an ultimate reality makes any sense.

You might be inclined to argue that it does not. If that which is ultimate cannot be defined, if it transcends all names and forms, then we cannot form a clear conception of what it is. If we cannot form a clear conception, then why not conclude that the ultimate is incoherent or, at the very least, that we are not in a position to say one way or the other? As logicians have long pointed out, negative definitions do not help us very much. To say of the ultimate that it is "not this" and "not that," or to name it the Nameless, might seem like mere word play.

However, many find this strange way of talking very profound. How else could we talk (if we talk at all) about the ultimate? Yes, we should avoid negative definitions whenever possible. But perhaps there is just no other satisfactory way of proceeding when it comes to ultimacy. Still, questions remain.

What is it for something to be ultimate? Some support the "best widget" theory. What is ultimate is the best of all things that now exist. If we take this line of reasoning, then it would seem possible that at some future point, something better might come along. If so, *it* would then be ultimate. This raises the possibility that at some point in the past there was a better widget than there is now, even though the one we now have is the best of the present lot.

These sorts of speculations, others have argued, show that whatever is ultimate cannot be an *actual* being. They support the "best widget possible" theory. Ultimate reality is absolutely perfect. It is maximally perfect—the very best of all things that *might* exist. It is simply not possible for there to be a better widget.

If we follow this notion of ultimate reality as maximally perfect, then it seems that whatever is truly ultimate must have all possible perfections. Some perfections, however, are incompatible, such as being unchanging (a property frequently assigned to the ultimate) and being a perfect swimmer. Does it make sense to try to envision a reality that has all perfections? If some perfections are incompatible, then it would appear to be impossible for any being or reality to have all of them.

The next selection shows that other problems arise when we try to think through the concept of ultimate reality. William J. Wainwright (1935–   ) is a philosopher of religion teaching at the University of Wisconsin, Milwaukee. He supports the view that ultimate reality is best thought of as maximally perfect and defends its coherence in the face of critical objections.

Reading Questions

1. According to William James, what three beliefs characterize religious life?
2. What, according to Tillich, is the demand and the promise of an ultimate concern?
3. What reason does Wainwright give for concluding that "a *fully* appropriate object of ultimate concern must . . . be maximally perfect"?
4. How does Wainwright answer the objection that an appropriate object of ultimate concern need not be the most perfect *possible* reality, but only the most perfect *existing* (actual) reality?
5. What three reasons might lead us to think that the concept of a maximally perfect reality is incoherent, and what sort of response might be made to these objections?
6. What, according to Wainwright, conditions one's understanding of a maximally perfect reality as personal (theistic) or nonpersonal (nontheistic)?
7. What do you think? Does the concept of a maximally perfect reality make sense or not? Why?

Is the Concept of Ultimate Reality Coherent?*

WILLIAM J. WAINWRIGHT

ACCORDING TO WILLIAM JAMES (1842–1910), religious life includes three beliefs:

"that the visible world is part of a more spiritual universe from which it draws its chief significance;

that union or harmonious relation with that higher universe is our true end," and

that life can be transformed for the better by making proper contact with it.

Religious people believe that "prayer or inner communion with the spirit thereof—be that spirit 'God' or 'law'—is a process wherein work is really done, and spiritual energy flows in and produces effects, psychological or material, within the phenomenal world."

James thinks that religion also involves "a new zest which adds itself to life, and takes the form either of lyrical enhancement or of appeal to earnestness and heroism." It provides, he says, "an assurance of safety and a temper of peace,

and, in relation to others, a preponderance of loving affections."

Throughout history, men and women have turned to religion for comfort, strength, and assurance. Traditions like Buddhism, Christianity, and Islam give life depth and significance by explaining the nature of reality and our place in it, by assuring us of the possibility of victory over life's difficulties, and by providing means for achieving it.

Religion is rooted in human needs and yearnings—a conviction that ordinary life is flawed and that the powers of the "visible world" aren't sufficient to mend it. While suffering causes some to doubt the very existence of a "higher universe," it strengthens the convictions of many others. In Elizabeth Gaskell's novel *North and South*, a factory girl who is dying in miserable surroundings argues that this can't be all there is and that there must therefore be a "God to wipe away all tears from all eyes." The incompleteness and unsatisfactoriness of life—its inability to fully satisfy our yearnings or provide lasting happiness—leads many to hope or believe that the visible world isn't the whole of reality.

But religion isn't rooted only in needs and yearnings. The order and beauty of the world and even the fact that it exists at all seem to point to something beyond it. Furthermore, saints, mystics, prophets, and many ordinary men and women believe they have actually glimpsed a sovereign good that transcends life's contingencies and provides an answer to the quest for meaning and happiness.

Religion is thus rooted in human needs, yearnings, and experiences. The strength of conviction, hope, and commitment varies considerably from person to person. But, for the devout, the higher universe is a matter of what Paul Tillich (1886–1965) calls "ultimate concern."

Ultimate concern is "total." The self as a whole is caught up in it, and every other concern becomes secondary. The object of a person's ultimate concern is experienced as holy—distinct from all profane or ordinary realities. It is also experienced as a mystery. No matter how much one knows about it, it eludes one's grasp. One appears to be caught up in something so charged with power, so real and splendid that, in comparison, other things are empty and worthless. In short, the object of ultimate concern is experienced as overwhelming and supremely valuable. It thus demands total surrender and promises total fulfillment.

Whether ultimate concern is necessary for any kind of religious attitude is a matter of dispute. Nevertheless, it *is* characteristic of the religious attitudes idealized in Christianity, Buddhism, Islam, and other major religious traditions.

Ultimate concern can, however, take different forms. It often takes the form of worship and then involves praise, love, gratitude, supplication, confession, petition, and so on. It can also take the form of a quest for the ultimate good. The object of this quest is a knowledge of the ultimate good or a union with it that transfigures us and overcomes our wrongness. These forms of ultimate concern may be combined or they may exist

separately. Christianity, for example, combines both. In Buddhism, however, ultimate concern usually takes the second form but not the first.

The fact that ultimate concern is an aspect of religious attitudes may have an important implication. Perhaps nothing can be a completely worthy object of these attitudes unless it is so great that we can conceive of nothing greater.

Why think this? It isn't sufficient for the object of these attitudes to be the greatest reality that actually exists, for the most perfect existing reality might be limited or defective. Suppose, for example, that the most perfect existing thing was wiser and better than other existing things but was ignorant of a number of matters and somewhat selfish. It would not be appropriate to surrender totally to a being of this sort. The defects or limitations of the most perfect existing thing might not be this striking. Nevertheless, if there is a possible reality that surpasses the most perfect existing thing, then the latter is limited or imperfect in comparison with the former. It thus seems that our admiration, concern, and commitment shouldn't be unconditional and without reservation. A *fully* appropriate object of ultimate concern must therefore be maximally perfect in the sense that it is the most perfect possible reality.

This conclusion isn't certain, and some philosophers doubt it. They grant that an appropriate object of ultimate concern must be greater than other *existing* beings. If it weren't, it wouldn't be ultimate. If another existing being was greater, our concern, loyalty, and commitment should be directed toward *it*. Suppose, though, that a being *is* greater than other existing beings, that it created heaven and earth, and is perfectly righteous. Suppose also that its power and knowledge are vastly greater than that of other existing beings although not as great as they could possibly be. While such a being would be the most perfect existing reality, it wouldn't be the most perfect possible reality. For we can conceive of something greater—a perfectly righteous creator of heaven and earth with *unlimited* power and knowledge. But isn't a most perfect existing reality of this kind an appropriate object of ultimate concern? It surely isn't *morally* wrong to worship it. Nor does it seem unfitting to totally commit ourselves to it, making it the object of our ultimate loyalty.

This is a plausible objection. Nevertheless, two things suggest that a *fully* appropriate object of ultimate concern must be the greatest possible reality.

Suppose a being has many perfections and is greater than other existing beings but that we can conceive of something greater. If the second being *had* existed, we ought to have given ourselves to *it* rather than the first. If we admit this, however, can we say that our commitment to the first is totally unreserved? Wouldn't this be like saying, "I love her unreservedly, but I might have met someone more beautiful and affectionate and, if I had, I would have loved her instead"? If one's love depends on not having met someone more loveable, is it truly unreserved? Similarly, is one's commitment to something unreserved if it depends on there not having been something more perfect?

The second point is this. Ultimate concern includes a number of attitudes—love, loyalty, and commitment but also reverence, awe, and admiration. Each is unreserved. Suppose something is greater than other existing beings but less great than some possible being. Even if unreserved love, loyalty, and commitment are appropriate, are unreserved reverence, awe, and admiration appropriate? Not clearly. I don't *unreservedly* admire a painting or a ball player if I think it would be possible for a painting or ball player to be better. Do I, then, unreservedly admire a being if I think a better being might have existed?

There are thus reasons for thinking that an appropriate object of ultimate concern must be *maximally* perfect. Classical Western theology has usually thought of God in this way. The issue is, however, controversial. . . .

Is the Concept of a Maximally Perfect Reality Coherent?

Critics sometimes argue that the concept of a maximally perfect reality is incoherent. If it is, then a maximally perfect reality isn't possible: either the object of the religious attitudes of Christians, Buddhists, and others doesn't exist, or it could be more perfect than it is.

There are three reasons for thinking that the concept is incoherent. Some critics argue that there are no standards in relation to which something could be said to be more perfect than everything else. Others contend that a maximally perfect reality would have logically incompatible properties. Still others maintain that some perfections have no maximum. According to them, the concept of a maximally perfect reality is ill-formed like the concept of the largest possible number or the longest possible line.

THE LACK OF STANDARDS

Charles Crittendon (1933–) puts the first objection in this way: "Normally when we say that something is 'greatest,' 'best,' 'most perfect,' etc., we mean greatest of *a given kind*: greatest symphony, best tennis player . . . most perfect likeness. The kind in question dictates which characteristics count for or against something's being greater, better, more perfect than something else. . . . [Thus] the best ball point pen would be one which smudges least, lasts longest, looks nicest, and so on; the best tennis player would be the one who wins the most important matches or something of the kind." But while one ball point pen or tennis player can be better than another, it makes no sense to say that my ball point pen is better than the winner of Wimbledon. There is no class that includes both within which meaningful comparisons could be made. If I were to say that my ball point pen is better than the winner of Wimbledon, I would invite the question "A better what?" There is no clear answer to this question. Comparisons presuppose standards, and standards are possible only when there is a common class within which things can be ranked as better or worse.

Just as there is no significant class of comparison that includes ball point pens and tennis players, there is no significant class of comparison that includes everything. To say that something is as good as, or better than, everything else is thus nonsense. The notion of a reality that nothing surpasses is therefore incoherent.

This objection rests on a mistake. That some reality, *x,* is at least as perfect as every other possible reality does not entail that there is a class of comparison within which everything can be ranked. What *is* entailed is that, for every other possible reality, *y,* there are classes of comparison that include both *x* and *y;* and in each of these *x* ranks at least as highly as *y.* This can be true even if there is no *single* class within which *x* can be compared with everything else. For example, God might be more perfect than other minds in virtue of His greater wisdom and righteousness and might be more perfect than material objects in virtue of features like greater power, permanence, and beauty. If God is maximally perfect, then (1) every possible reality can be compared with God in *some* respect and (2) no possible reality is better than God in *any* respect. This does not imply that God is better than everything else in the *same* respect and thus doesn't imply that God and everything else can be included in a common class of comparison.

THE INCOMPATIBILITY OF SOME PERFECTIONS

The second objection hinges on the fact that some perfections are logically incompatible. Immutability is the property something has if it cannot change in any respect. Incorporeality is the property of being bodiless. Both properties have been traditionally regarded as perfections, and both are incompatible with such perfections as being able to dance or play tennis well.

Why does this create a problem? A maximally perfect reality is sometimes described as a being that possesses all perfections. If some perfections are incompatible, then no possible being has all of them. Hence, no possible being is maximally perfect. There are two ways of responding to this objection.

First Response

One can distinguish between imperfections, "mixed" perfections, and "pure" perfections. Some imperfections are defects like blindness or

unrighteousness. Others are limitations such as our inability to lift stones over a certain weight or the fact that our knowledge of the world can only be acquired piece by piece through time-consuming and difficult investigations. These properties are not defects since the fact that we are limited in these ways doesn't imply that we are imperfect specimens of humanity. Their possession does, however, imply that the human species is less perfect in these respects than are other species of being whose members could lift stones of any tonnage or whose knowledge of the world is intuitive and complete.

A mixed perfection is a property that makes something better but implies some defect or limitation. Repentance, for example, implies a defect (the moral failure that one repents). Being human or being corporeal implies limitations (susceptibility to physical damage, for example). A pure perfection, on the other hand, is a perfection that does not entail a defect or limitation. Being or actuality, goodness, love, power, knowledge, unity, and independence are sometimes mentioned as examples.

While theists have sometimes characterized a maximally perfect reality as a reality that possesses *every* perfection, they have implicitly meant "every *pure* perfection." Even if some perfections are mutually incompatible, pure perfections may be consistent with one another. If they are, the properties of a maximally perfect reality are mutually compatible.

Second Response

The concept of a maximally perfect reality is designed to pick out a *possible* reality that is at least as good as any other possible reality. If some perfections are incompatible, then a reality that possesses *all* perfections is not a *possible* reality and is thus not maximally perfect reality. A maximally perfect reality would possess a set of mutually consistent perfections that are as good as, or better than, any other set of mutually consistent perfections. However, it would not possess *all* perfections if there are some that are incompatible.

Both responses reject the assumption upon which the objection was based (that a maximally perfect reality must have all perfections). The first response insists that a maximally perfect reality need only have all *pure* perfections. The second insists that all that is needed is that it have an unsurpassable set of *mutually compatible* perfections.

THE LACK OF INTRINSIC MAXIMA

The third problem is created by the fact that certain perfections seem to lack "intrinsic maxima" (upper limits). Some properties admit of degrees and some do not. The sky can be more or less cloudy, but a tree can't be more or less of a maple. A day can be more or less hot, but it cannot be more or less in July. Some "degreed properties" have intrinsic maxima and others do not. Being cloudy, for example, has an upper limit (being completely cloudy). Being large, on the other hand, is a degreed property that does not have an upper limit. No matter how large an object is, it is logically possible that something can be larger.

Many of the perfections that have been ascribed to a maximally perfect reality are degreed properties—for example, knowledge, power, righteousness, love, and happiness. One being can know more than another, or be more powerful, and so on. Some of these appear to have intrinsic maxima. The knowledge of every true proposition or the power to bring about every contingent state of affairs may be the intrinsic maxima of knowledge and power respectively. Perhaps, too, nothing could be more righteous than a being whose dispositions and behavior never deviate from the appropriate moral standards—who is, for example, perfectly truthful, just, and faithful. Happiness, however, seems to lack an intrinsic maximum. No matter how happy a being is, it seems possible for it (or some other being) to be even happier.

The problem, then, is this. Most religions believe that a maximally perfect reality would be happy. But happiness doesn't seem to have an intrinsic maximum. Their notion of a maximally

perfect reality is therefore incoherent. Why is this the case? To be maximally perfect, a thing must be happy. But happiness has no upper limit. Hence, it is possible that the maximally perfect reality, or some other thing, be even happier and thus more perfect in that respect. This statement is incoherent. It is impossible for something to be *more* perfect than a thing that is *maximally* perfect (as perfect as anything could possibly be). Two responses are again possible.

First Response

One might deny that happiness has no intrinsic maximum. Theists, for example, have traditionally believed that God's happiness consists in the possession and enjoyment of the highest good (namely, Himself). That is, God's happiness consists in His delight in His own nature, activity, and splendor. Perhaps a happiness of this kind could not be surpassed.

Second Response

One might also respond to the objection by adopting a suggestion made by Charles Hartshorne (1897–). Hartshorne argues that a maximally perfect reality should be understood as a reality that (1) cannot be surpassed with respect to properties which have maxima and (2) with respect to properties which do not have maxima, can only be surpassed by itself. Suppose, for example, that a maximally perfect reality would be powerful and joyous. Since power has a maximum, it would possess it. It would thus be impossible for anything to be more powerful. On the other hand, if there really is no upper limit to happiness, its happiness cannot be maximal. Nevertheless, because it is maximally perfect, its joy is so intense that even though *it* could be still happier, its joy could not be surpassed by the joy of any *other* possible being.

CONCLUSION

If our discussion has been sound, then the concept of a maximally perfect reality is probably coherent. It is not, however, sufficient to determine our understanding of divine reality, for the concept doesn't tell us precisely *what* properties a maximally perfect reality would have. It does provide some direction. If a property (1) is a perfection and (2) no equal or greater perfection is incompatible with it, then a maximally perfect reality would presumably have it. Nevertheless, it may be difficult to determine whether these conditions are met in particular cases. For example, whether immutability should be ascribed to a maximally perfect reality depends upon whether change is an imperfection. It also depends upon whether immutability is compatible with such perfections as creative activity.

The remainder of this chapter will examine problems that arise when one attempts to determine precisely what properties a maximally perfect reality would have.

Is a Perfect Reality Personal?

The difficulties in ascribing properties to a maximally perfect reality can be illustrated by considering the fundamental question of whether such a reality is personal or nonpersonal. Theists believe that, even though ultimate reality transcends all finite realities, it is more like a person than anything else. That is, they believe that ultimate reality should be understood as God—an infinitely wise, good, and powerful ruler of heaven and earth. Many important religious traditions, however, are nontheistic—for example, Advaita Vedānta and Buddhism. These traditions believe that ultimate reality is impersonal. They don't think of it as a god.

Advaita Vedānta's rejection of theism is a consequence of its emphasis upon ultimate reality's unity and incomprehensibility. Advaita believes that Brahman (the first principle) is an absolute unity. "Brahman is without parts or attributes . . . one without a second. In Brahman there is no diversity whatsoever." "All difference in Brahman is unreal."

The Brahman contains no plurality and transcends every distinction. It thus has no properties. Why is this the case? If the Brahman had properties, we could *distinguish* between the

Brahman and its properties. This would be incompatible with its absolute unity. But since Brahman has no properties and since we can only understand things by grasping their properties, it is incomprehensible. "It is the reality beyond all thought . . . outside the range of any mental conception."

If ultimate reality transcends *all* properties, it transcends the property of being a person. However, even if the Brahman is not *literally* a person, it might be more like a person than anything else. Why, then, does Advaita reject theism?

Persons are rational agents—beings who have beliefs about themselves and the world and act on the basis of their beliefs. Believing and willing are essential to personhood. The major theistic traditions, accordingly, describe ultimate reality as an omniscient mind and an omnipotent and active will. Advaita Vedānta is nontheistic because its emphasis upon the divine unity leads it to deny that Brahman is either a knower or a causal agent.

Knowledge presupposes a distinction between the knower and what it knows. Advaita concludes that the first principle is beyond thought and cognition. Even self-knowledge involves a distinction between the self as knower and the self as known and is therefore incompatible with the Brahman's unity. Hence, "all specific cognition such as seeing, and so on, is absent."

Why can't the Brahman be a causal agent? If the Brahman is maximally perfect, it must be unlimited. It is limited, however, if something exists outside it. The Brahman must therefore be identical with the whole of reality. But if the Brahman is identical with the whole of reality and if the Brahman contains no plurality, then reality as a whole must be an undifferentiated unity. The space-time world, with its distinctions between times, places, and events, is therefore unreal. Since a real causal relation is a relation between two real things, Brahman is not the cause of the space-time world or the events in it. The Brahman is thus neither the world's creator nor its ruler. "The Lord's being a Lord, his omniscience, his omnipotence, etc., all depend on . . . ignorance; while in reality none of these qualities belong to the Self [Brahman]. . . . In reality the relation of ruler and ruled [creator and created], does not exist." The Brahman is the "ground" of the world, but only in the sense that it is the real thing upon which people project the illusion of spatio-temporal reality. (This is compared with the way in which a person who mistakes a rope for a snake projects the illusory idea of the snake onto the rope.)

Advaita does, however, contain what one might call "theistic elements." It describes Brahman as infinite, joyous consciousness (although the consciousness has no objects or contents and is thus "empty"). Advaita also admits that the idea of an omniscient and omnipotent cause of the space-time world is superior to most conceptualizations of ultimate reality—though, like all conceptualizations, it too must be transcended.

Nevertheless, because Advaita refuses to ascribe either knowledge or activity to ultimate reality, it is essentially nontheistic. The maximally perfect reality is not the God of the theistic traditions—all powerful, all knowing, all loving, the ruler of heaven and earth. It is, rather, an "infinite ocean" of empty, joyous consciousness—impersonal, inactive, and anonymous. Brahman is "pure consciousness and infinite bliss"—"beyond all attributes, beyond action."

Some nontheistic traditions are devoid of theistic elements. According to Hīnayāna Buddhism, a person is simply a collection of interrelated experiences and body states called "dharmas." The dharmas are causally conditioned and transient. (They last for at most a few moments.) Consciousness is as conditioned and impermanent as the other dharmas. Furthermore, the realm of the transient and causally conditioned is the realm of suffering or unsatisfactoriness (duhka). One cannot therefore construe a maximally perfect reality as a person. To do so would imply that it was impermanent, causally conditioned, and unhappy. Ultimate reality (Nirvāna) is not a substance, it is not conscious, and it does not act. It is more like a transcendent place or state than a transcendent person.

Our discussion illustrates the way in which one's understanding of a maximally perfect real-

ity is determined by one's philosophical ideas, one's evaluations, and (as we shall see) one's interpretation of religious attitudes and experiences.

For example, we have seen how Advaita's emphasis upon the idea of absolute unity and Buddhism's analysis of personhood lead them to reject theism. One's evaluations are also important. Traditional thought places a high value on unity, permanence, and stability and a correspondingly low value on plurality, impermanence, and change. Persons appear to be complex, changing realities. An emphasis upon the values of unity, permanence, and stability may therefore lead one to deny that ultimate reality should be understood as a person.

These ideas and evaluations, however, are controversial. The Buddhist's analysis of personhood may be unable to account for the self's unity. Classical theists argue that God's unity, permanence, and stability do not entail impersonality. Some modern theists place a high value on change and complexity and ascribe them to the first principle. They believe, for example, that God's knowledge grows progressively richer and that He changes in response to His creatures.

One's understanding of the nature of a maximally perfect reality will also be influenced by one's attitude toward certain religious experiences. For example, Advaita Vedānta places a high value on "monistic mystical consciousness"—a joyous state of consciousness in which the mind is emptied of its contents and distinctions disappear. . . . Advaita privileges this experience and treats it as a model of the unifying and transfiguring knowledge (jnāna) that is the goal of the religious quest. It is thus not surprising that Advaita views the appropriate object of religious attitudes as "one without distinctions"—neither a knower nor a doer and hence not a god.

But other types of religious experience have different implications. . . . some of these experiences seem to have a person as their object. An emphasis upon them usually leads to theistic interpretations of maximal perfection.

Even the basic claim that a maximally perfect reality is a kind of person is thus subject to dispute. Let us assume, however, that the dispute has been resolved in favor of theism and turn to problems connected with three perfections traditionally ascribed to God—impassibility, omnipotence, and omniscience. Examining these problems will further illustrate the difficulties involved in working out the implications of the concept of a maximally perfect reality.

Suggestions for Further Reading

Afnan, Soheil Muhsin. *Avicenna, His Life and Works.* London: George Allen & Unwin, 1958.

Al-Ghazzali. *The Foundations of the Articles of Faith.* Translated by Nabih Amin Faris. Lahore, Pakistan: Sh. Muhammad Ashraf, 1969.

Armstrong, Karen, *A History of God: The 4000-Year Quest of Judaism, Christianity and Islam.* New York: Knopf, 1994.

Carter, Robert E. *The Nothingness Beyond God: An Introduction to the Philosophy of Mishida Kitaro.* New York: Paragon House, 1989.

Christ, Carol P. "Why Women Need the Goddess: Phenomenological, Psychological, and Political Reflections." In *Womanspirit Rising,* edited by Carol P. Christ and Judith Plaskow. New York: HarperCollins, 1979.

Cobb, Jr., John B. *Beyond Dialogue: Toward a Mutual Transformation of Christianity and Buddhism.* Philadelphia, PA: Fortress Press, 1982.

Creel, Harrlee G. *What Is Taoism?* Chicago: University of Chicago Press, 1970.

Daly, Mary. *Beyond God the Father.* Boston: Beacon Press, 1973.

Deutsch, Eliot. *Advaita Vedanta: A Philosophical Reconstruction.* Honolulu: East-West Center Press, 1969.

Deutsch, Eliot, and van Buitenen, J.A.B., eds. *A Source Book of Advaita Vedanta.* Honolulu: The University Press of Hawaii, 1971.

Eckel, Malcolm. *To See the Buddha: A Philosopher's Quest for the Meaning of Emptiness.* San Francisco: HarperCollins, 1992.

Fakhry, Majid. *A History of Islamic Philosophy.* New York: Columbia University Press, 1970.

Graham, A.C. *Disputers of the Tao: Philosophical Argument in Ancient China.* LaSalle, IL: Open Court, 1989.

Hartshorne, Charles. *The Divine Relativity.* New Haven, CT: Yale University Press, 1948.

Jayatilleke, K.N. *The Message of the Buddha.* New York: The Free Press, 1975.

Lafargue, Michael. *The Tao of the Tao Te Ching: A Translation and Commentary.* Albany: State University of New York Press, 1992.

McFague, Sallie. *Models of God: Theology for an Ecological, Nuclear Age.* Philadelphia, PA: Fortress Press, 1987.

Morewedge, Parviz, ed. *Islamic Philosophical Theology.* Albany, NY: State University of New York Press, 1979.

Nozick, Robert. "The Nature of God, The Nature of Faith." In *The Examined Life.* New York: Simon and Schuster, 1989.

Owen, H.P. *Concepts of Deity.* New York: Herder and Herder, 1971.

Sharma, Arvind. *The Philosophy of Religion and Advaita Vedanta: A Comparative Study in Religion and Reason.* University Park, PA: The Pennsylvania State University Press, 1995.

Sontag, Fredrick. *Divine Perfection: Possible Ideas of God.* New York: Harper and Brothers, 1962.

Sontag, Fredrick, and Bryant, M. Darrol, eds. *God: The Contemporary Discussion.* New York: The Rose of Sharon Press, 1982.

Welbon, Guy Richard. *The Buddhist Nirvana and Its Western Interpreters.* Chicago, IL: The University of Chicago Press, 1968.

CHAPTER 3

Can We Prove That Some Kind of Ultimate Reality Exists?

Introduction

Is THERE ANY WAY of proving that some ultimate reality exists? Is there any evidence? Has ultimate reality left traces of itself that might give us clues about its existence?

Interestingly enough, most of the arguments philosophers and others have offered have to do with proving the existence of God. Those who offer such arguments understand ultimate reality in a theistic fashion (see Chapter 2). This may be because nontheistic interpretations of ultimacy usually claim that what is ultimately real is beyond all human categories of thought, including the category of existence. Ultimate reality is the source of the class of all things that exist, but it is not itself a member of that class. This should not be interpreted as equivalent to the claim that it does not exist in the sense that it is not real. Rather, it is meant to indicate that what is ultimate transcends, or goes beyond, the category of existing *things*.

If, however, we think of ultimate reality as a divine being who is the creator of the universe, then it seems to make sense to ask whether such a creator exists. It certainly makes sense to ask whether the creator of a particular type of computer exists, so why not ask whether the creator of the universe exists? The answer depends in large part on whether the universe is the sort of thing that is created. If it is, then there must be some creator or cause. Many different arguments have been offered that purport to show that there must be a divine cause of the cosmos. These arguments are grouped together under the heading "cosmological arguments for God's existence," because in one way or another they try to show that the existence of the universe (cosmos) can be adequately explained only by positing the existence of a divine being as its cause or originator.

Perhaps, in addition to the existence of the cosmos, there are other clues to the existence of a divine ultimate reality. The word *cosmos* means "order" in Greek, and the universe manifests an intricate and complex order. The universe exhibits greater order and complexity than, say, a watch. If a watch could not exist except for the intelligence of a watchmaker, surely there must be some intelligence that designed the vastly greater complexity and order of the universe. Arguments of this sort (and again there are a great variety) are classified as teleological arguments, or arguments from design.

Both the cosmological type of argument and the teleological type of argument are *a posteriori* arguments. That is, they infer their conclusions ("God exists as the cause of the universe" or "God exists as the intelligent designer of the order of the universe") from the experience people have of the existence and order of the universe. If we did not experience a universe or its order, a key premise in these arguments would not be established. It would be hard to argue that God created the universe if we had no experience of one.

Another set of arguments for God's existence is *a priori.* These arguments do not rely, in their premises, on any empirical or alleged empirical fact that people experience. These are ontological arguments. Such arguments begin with a particular definition of God and conclude that, given the definition, God must exist.

Before we look in some detail at *a posteriori* and *a priori* arguments for God's existence, it might be well to ask whether taking such a look is worth our time. Those who interpret ultimate reality nontheistically might argue not only that such arguments are beside the point but also that they lead to serious confusion in our thinking about what is ultimate. They lead us to believe that what is ultimate is a member of the class of existing things when, in fact, it transcends that class. Such arguments will not convince atheists (those who deny the existence of God and of any coherent notion of ultimacy), and theists don't need such arguments because they are already convinced on other grounds (such as personal experience) that God exists. Perhaps we should just skip this chapter!

I hope you will read it, though, because your thinking about the nature of ultimate reality and about God will be enhanced by doing so. These arguments and counterarguments are logically and philosophically interesting. They raise important questions about how the universe came to be, how it came to be the kind of universe it is, and what we mean by the words *God* and *ultimate.* They show believer and nonbeliever alike that religious belief is not totally devoid of rational support. Even when the arguments fail to convince, we can learn something important from them.

3.1 The Seven Ways

Imagine you are walking in a forest. Ahead on the path you see a coiled snake. You are afraid. "Should I go around it," you think, "or should I try to scare it off." Opting for the latter alternative, you pick up a rock and throw it at the coiled snake. It does not move. "Perhaps it is dead or sleeping," you think. You approach. It does not move. As you get closer, you realize that although some of its features appear to be those of a coiled snake, not all do. You get closer still. Now you see, much to your relief, that it is nothing but a coiled bit of rope.

What is going on here? You might say that you have made a mistake in your inference. You first believed, on the basis of your perceptions, that what you now know to be a coiled rope was a coiled snake. You thought (inferred) it was a snake, but now you know it to be a rope. A basic problem in epistemology (theory of knowledge) is ascertaining what rules or standards can help us distinguish between knowledge and mistaken opinion.

A school of Indian philosophy called Nyaya focused on this issue. Members of this school analyzed the case set forth above in terms of the knowing subject, the known object, the object as known, and the means by which the object comes to be known. According to Nyaya philosophy, knowledge is the disclosure of a real object, and the various means of this disclosure are perception, inference, analogy, and testimony.

Perceptual knowledge is the truth about some object that results from the contact of the senses with the object when they are not deceived or distorted in some way (illusions, dreaming, poor eyesight, or the like). Inference is also a way to gain knowledge, but it is different from perception. From perceptual knowledge it is possible to infer something true that has not actually been perceived. This inference takes place by the use of logical reasoning. According to Nyaya, the logical reasoning should ideally be arranged according to the following form:

1. Proposition: There is fire on that hill.
2. Reason: Because there is smoke on that hill.
3. Example: As in a kitchen (where there is fire and smoke).
4. Application: Wherever there is smoke there is fire.
5. Conclusion: Therefore, there is fire on that hill.

Typically, Nyaya logicians expressed their arguments using only the first three or four elements. Thus Udayana, a tenth-century Nyaya philosopher, expresses his arguments for the existence of God in a truncated form.

According to Nyaya philosophy, analogy is another path to knowledge. This knowledge comes about by means of comparison between the known and the unknown on the basis of similarities. Thus you come to know that the universe has a cause on the basis of similarities between it and other things you know to have a cause.

Testimony also can yield knowledge, provided that the persons giving the testimony are honest, that they know what they are talking about, and that you correctly understand what they are saying.

By the time Udayana wrote, Nyaya philosophy (the logic of knowing) had been combined with the Vaisheshika school of philosophy. Vaisheshika philosophers were particularly concerned with the nature of the known object. According to Vaisheshika, the objects of knowledge (what is known) can be categorized in a variety of ways. One important category is substance. Substance is made up of indivisible particles (atoms) or is the result of a combination of atoms. The book you see is a substance, but it is the product of a combination of atoms. Hence it is temporal, composite, and destructible. However, the atoms that make up the book are not temporal, composite, or destructible. How do atoms get combined? Who or what starts the process? Udayana thinks it is God. Read and see why.

Reading Questions

1. What do the first three arguments conclude?
2. Restate the sixth argument in your own words.
3. What does Udayana mean by "the all-knowing, imperishable God"?
4. What is the first of the five objections, and how does Udayana reply? Do you find the reply convincing? Why or why not?

The Seven Ways*

UDAYANA

I. *The Seven Ways*

From (1) effects, (2) atomic combinations, (3) the suspension and other states of the world, (4) the existence of human skills, (5) the existence of authoritative knowledge, (6) the existence of Revelation and (7) the numerical combination of atoms—from all these we can prove the existence of the all-knowing, imperishable God.

1. *Argument from effects*
Things like the earth must have a cause.
Because they are effects.
Like a pot.
By having a cause I mean active production by someone possessed of the intent to produce, and a direct knowledge concerning the matter from which the production is to be.

2. *Argument from atomic combinations*
[The world, it must be remembered, is a combination of atoms, in different degrees of complexity.] Combination is an action, and hence an action occurring at the beginning of creation that brings about the bonding of two atoms, thus originating a dyad. Such a combination is always consequent on the activity of a conscious agent.
Because it is action.
As, for instance, the action of our bodies.

3. *Argument from the suspension of the world*
The world is supported by an active being which impedes it from falling.
Because it has the character of something suspended.
Like a twig held in the air by a bird.
By "*suspension*" I mean the absence of falling in things that possess weight. When I say "the suspension and *other states* of the world," I mean destruction. For the world is destructible by an active being; because its nature is destructible; like that of a torn cloth.

4. *Argument from the existence of human skills* . . . or the arts of life.
Traditional arts, like weaving, need to be launched by an independent person.
Because of their character as human usages.
Like modern writing and such other usages.

5. *Argument from the existence of authoritative knowledge.* Authoritative knowledge, that is, knowledge through authoritative norms.
The knowledge produced by the Veda is due to positive qualities in the cause of that knowledge.
Because of its character as normative knowledge.
As in a norm such as experience.

* From Udayana, *Nyayakusumanjali.* Translated by E. B. Cowell and M. C. Nyayaratna. Calcutta.

6. *Arguments from the existence of Revelation.* Revelation, that is to say, the Veda.

a. The Veda is personally originant.

Because of its capacity to instruct [instruction being conveyed through one person dialoguing with another].

Like the Veda of medicine [which all accept to have been humanly, or personally, produced].

b. Again, the Veda is personally originant.

Because it is composed of sentences.

Like the *Mahābhārata* [epic of the Great Indian War].

c. And the Veda's sentences are personally originant.

Because they are sentences.

Like our own sentences.

7. *Argument from numerical augmentation*

[Physical objects, which have measure, are produced from combinations of atoms, beginning with the dyads. But atoms themselves have no measure. How then do dyads? For the following reasons:]

a. A dyad's measure is produced by *number.*

Because, though not produced through the aggregation of measures, it still remains a *produced* measure.

As, for instance [of pot sections of equal size], the measure of a pot composed of three sections is greater than that of a pot composed of two such sections [the former's greater size thus being due to number alone].

b. An atomic measure does not produce measure.

Because its measure is eternal [and hence incapable of the temporal change that all production entails]; or because its measure is infinitesimal.

In this way, at the beginning of creation, the dual number—the reason for the dyad's measure—needs to be implanted in atoms. [According to the tenets of our combined Logicist-Atomist system, things exist singly, or monadically, and can be combined only by a faculty that reduces these monads to unity and order—the Methodizing Mind]. The combination cannot have been produced at that [primordial] time by the Methodizing Mind of beings like

ourselves [then non-existent]. Hence there exists such a Mind coeval with that time, that is to say, God's.

Finally, by the words "the all-knowing, imperishable God," I mean that the quality of imperishableness belongs to Him essentially [and is inconceivable apart]. It is certain then that an everlasting knowledge embracing all things exists.

II. Five Objections to the Argument from Effects

There are five fallacies in your inferent sign, "effectness."

a. Causality is qualified by corporeity. [A cause always has a body; the body is thus the qualifier and the cause the qualified.] To negate the qualifier is to negate the qualified. [You deny that God is corporeal: so you must deny that He is a cause.]

b. And there is the counter-syllogism [that serves to neutralize your argument]:

There is no production by a cause [in the case of things like the earth].

Because the invariable concomitance between "production by a cause" and "production by a body" is there lacking.

c. "The cause is always corporeal"—here is a concomitance that counters yours [that "effects always have causes"].

d. From a concomitance unfolded by the perception of things as they are, we infer that a cause is corporeal [for experience shows us that causes always have bodies]. In your argument, however, the inherence of the inferent sign "effectness" in the subject "the earth," does not serve to prove the inferendum ["God"] as qualified by incorporeity. There is, besides, a contradiction between qualifier [incorporeity] and qualified [the cause, always perceived as corporeal].

e. We can also introduce into your argument a vitiating contingency [a contingency which invalidates the concomitance, basic to your whole argument, between your inferent sign "effectness" and your inferendum "cause." It is as if you were to assume the concomitance between fire and smoke, and argue that "The mountain is smoky, because it has fire." But the concomitance is vitiated by the contingency of wet fuel, and I could contend that "The mountain is smoky, because it has wet fuel"]. Here this vitiating contingency is "being produced by a body" [and the argument could be presented thus: "Things like the earth must have a cause, because they are produced by a body"]. But then your concomitance between effect and causality [the causality of an incorporeal being] would be inconclusive.

III. *Reply to Objections*

Our argument is not invalidated, because of the efficacity of its inferent sign; and it is not contraposed, because of the feebleness of the disproofs. But whether demonstrative or not, our reasoning is free of contradiction, and its inconclusiveness is baselessly alleged.

a. The negation of corporeity, the qualifier, in God, the subject qualified, does not imply negation of causality. Without knowledge about the subject, there cannot be knowledge about what the subject lacks. [God, the subject, is as you say not known: so it cannot be known whether He has a body.] Greater cogency has that effectness which both demonstrates the existence of the qualified subject and generates a knowledge of it, since it is a reason we are all constrained to recognize. Our argument is also not overridden by your syllogism "God is not a cause, because He has no body."

b. "Things like the earth have no cause, because they are not produced by a body." This is not a valid contraposition to our argument because, for the purposes of a counter-syllogism, the qualification "body" has no probative relevance. [It is as if you argued: "The mountain is fiery, because it has golden-colored smoke." Smoke and fire are concomitant; the color qualifying the smoke is immaterial.] So qualified, your concomitant [between no production by cause and no production by body] is inconclusive; so your disproof is feeble.

c. As for your third objection, the effect-cause concomitance has the greater cogency, because of the inherence of the inferent sign "effectness" in the subject "earth," and because of the presence of reasons precluding all instances to the contrary [as there are no effects ever devoid of causes]. To this your own postulated concomitance "the cause is always corporeal" is too feeble to be a contrapositive.

d. As for your fourth objection [contradiction], the inherence of the inferent sign "effectness" in the subject "earth" either entails the incorporeity of the cause, in which case there cannot be contradiction, as the correlation between causality and incorporeity has been recognized; or it does not, in which case there can be no contradiction either, as there is no subject to which the contradiction can be predicated.

e. As for your fifth objection, since our argument has reasons preclusive of contrary instances, there cannot be any inconclusiveness in the shape of ignorance occasioned by their absence. Neither is there the inconclusiveness of concomitance [between cause and effect]. The vitiating contingency "being produced by a body," unable as it is to preclude contrary instances [such as God] can be disregarded.

IV. *Harmony Between Faith and Reason*

'If God is a cause, He must be corporeal. Thus we are confronted with adversative reasoning and the absence of supportive proof.'

To this I say: the flawed reasoning of some thinkers has only the semblance of logic, and so is no refutation at all. But the supportive reasoning from the absence of effects [resulting from absence of causes] is our own position's enhancement.

The adversative arguments, supposing God as unproved, are devoid of a subject [to which they can predicate corporeity, in which the main force of their reasoning lies]. Hence they have only the semblance of logic. On the other hand "There is no effect without a cause"—such a reasoning is an enhancement: in other words, efficacious.

Our view is supported by Sacred Tradition too:

> I am the source of all: all things evolve from Me. The wise know this, and filled with emotion worship Me.

[And as the sage Manu says:]

A man who determines the sages' teachings on the Law through a logic not discordant with Revelation and the sacred sciences, only he, no other, knows that Law.

These words evince the greater cogency of Sacred Tradition when reinforced by logic.

3.2 The Five Ways

Several hundred years after Udayana, St. Thomas Aquinas (1225–1274), a brilliant Roman Catholic theologian and philosopher, published five arguments for the existence of God in his masterful summation of theology (*Summa Theologica*). The first three of these arguments are versions of the cosmological argument. Aquinas knew nothing of Udayana and his arguments, but he did know previous Western arguments for God's existence.

The cosmological argument is an *a posteriori* argument; it argues from experience to God's existence. Typically the argument begins with our experience that a cosmos (universe, world) exists. Then, invoking the notion that what exists must have a cause of its existence, the argument concludes that only some absolute and ultimate reality such as God can provide a sufficient explanation for the existence of the universe.

This type of argument, in the West, goes back to the ancient Greek philosophers. Aristotle, for example, argued from the existence of motion in the universe to the existence of a prime unmoved mover as the explanation of motion. This he called "the god." Aristotle, however, thought that motion and the universe were eternal—that the cosmos had always been. When Islamic theologians and philosophers discovered his writings, his argument for God's existence impressed them, but his idea that the universe was eternal troubled them. According to the *Qur'an,* Allah created the universe. The cosmos has not always been, but came into existence at some point in the past. Therefore, Islamic theologians revised Aristotle's argument into the Kalam version of the cosmological argument. (*Kalam,* which means "speech," came to denote the statement of points in theological doctrines.) A simple version of this argument runs like this:

1. Whatever begins to exist has a cause of its existence.
2. The universe began to exist.
3. Therefore, the universe has a cause of its existence.

Although this argument alone does not prove that Allah (God) is the cause of the universe, it takes the first step by attempting to show that there must *be* a cause.

Moses ben Maimon, better known as Maimonides (1135–1204), was a great Jewish theologian and philosopher who, in his major work *Guide for the Perplexed,* attempted to harmonize Jewish religious tradition with the science and philosophy dominant in his day. He was critical of the Greek cosmological argument because it relies on an unproved assumption—namely, that the world is eternal. He was also critical of the Islamic version because it too relies on an unproved assumption—namely, that the world is not eternal. Therefore, he developed a version of the argument that he thought proved that the universe had a divine cause on either supposition. He argued that if the universe is created, some agent had to create it because it is absurd to think that an effect could be a cause of itself. Further, if the universe is eternal, there must be a cause of this "perpetual motion" that is neither a body nor a force residing in a body, and this cause is God.

St. Thomas was well aware of these developments and of the problem concerning the eternity of the universe. Like Maimonides, he believes that whether we think the universe is eternal or not, its existence needs an explanation. One can ask why an eternal universe exists just as much as one can ask why a temporal universe exists.

Reading Questions

1. What arguments appear to show that God does not exist?
2. State the argument from motion in your own words in premise-and-conclusion form.
3. According to the second way, why is it impossible for the order of efficient causes to be infinite?
4. State the third way in your own words in premise-and-conclusion form.
5. What are some of the differences between the fourth and fifth ways?
6. Why do you think St. Thomas calls an unmoved mover, a first cause, a necessary and maximally perfect being, and an intelligent governor of the world God?
7. How does St. Thomas reply to the first two objections? Do you find his reply convincing? Why or why not?

The Five Ways*

ST. THOMAS AQUINAS

Third Article.
Whether God Exists?

We proceed thus to the Third Article:—

Objection 1. It seems that God does not exist; because if one of two contraries be infinite, the other would be altogether destroyed. But the word "God" means that He is infinite goodness. If, therefore, God existed, there would be no evil discoverable; but there is evil in the world. Therefore God does not exist.

Obj. 2. Further, it is superfluous to suppose that, what can be accounted for by a few principles has been produced by many. But it seems

* From *The Summa Theologica of St. Thomas Aquinas*. Part 1. Translated by the Fathers of the English Dominican Province. Copyright 1911. New York: Genziger Brothers.

that everything that appears in the world can be accounted for by other principles, supposing God did not exist. For all natural things can be reduced to one principle, which is nature; and all things that happen intentionally can be reduced to one principle, which is human reason, or will. Therefore there is no need to suppose God's existence.

On the contrary, It is said in the person of God: *I am Who am* (Exod. iii. 14).

I answer that, The existence of God can be proved in five ways.

The first and more manifest way is the argument from motion. It is certain and evident to our senses that some things are in motion. Whatever is in motion is moved by another, for nothing can be in motion except it have a potentiality for that towards which it is being moved; whereas a thing moves inasmuch as it is in act. By "motion" we mean nothing else than the reduction of something from a state of potentiality into a state of actuality. Nothing, however, can be reduced from a state of potentiality into a state of actuality, unless by something already in a state of actuality. Thus that which is actually hot as fire, makes wood, which is potentially hot to be actually hot, and thereby moves and changes it. It is not possible that the same thing should be at once in a state of actuality and potentiality from the same point of view, but only from different points of view. What is actually hot cannot simultaneously be only potentially hot; still, it is simultaneously potentially cold. It is therefore impossible that from the same point of view and in the same way anything should be both moved and mover, or that it should move itself. Therefore whatever is in motion must be put in motion by another. If that by which it is put in motion be itself put in motion, then this also must needs be put in motion by another, and that by another again. This cannot go on to infinity, because then there would be no first mover, and, consequently, no other mover—seeing that subsequent movers only move inasmuch as they are put in motion by the first mover; as the staff only moves because it is put in motion by the hand. Therefore it is necessary to arrive at a First

Mover, put in motion by no other; and this everyone understands to be God.

The second way is from the formality of efficient causation. In the world of sense we find there is an order of efficient causation. There is no case known (neither is it, indeed, possible) in which a thing is found to be the efficient cause of itself; for so it would be prior to itself, which is impossible. In efficient causes it is not possible to go on to infinity, because in all efficient causes following in order, the first is the cause of the intermediate cause, and the intermediate is the cause of the ultimate cause, whether the intermediate cause be several, or one only. To take away the cause is to take away the effect. Therefore, if there be no first cause among efficient causes, there will be no ultimate cause, nor any intermediate. If in efficient causes it is possible to go on to infinity, there will be no first efficient cause, neither will there be an ultimate effect, nor any intermediate efficient causes; all of which is plainly false. Therefore it is necessary to put forward a First Efficient Cause, to which everyone gives the name of God.

The third way is taken from possibility and necessity, and runs thus. We find in nature things that could either exist or not exist, since they are found to be generated, and then to corrupt; and, consequently, they can exist, and then not exist. It is impossible for these always to exist, for that which can one day cease to exist must at some time have not existed. Therefore, if everything could cease to exist, then at one time there could have been nothing in existence. If this were true, even now there would be nothing in existence, because that which does not exist only begins to exist by something already existing. Therefore, if at one time nothing was in existence, it would have been impossible for anything to have begun to exist; and thus even now nothing would be in existence—which is absurd. Therefore, not all beings are merely possible, but there must exist something the existence of which is necessary. Every necessary thing either has its necessity caused by another, or not. It is impossible to go on to infinity in necessary things which have their necessity caused by another, as has been already proved in regard to efficient causes. Therefore we cannot but postulate the existence of some being having of itself its own necessity, and not receiving it from another, but rather causing in others their necessity. This all men speak of as God.

The fourth way is taken from the gradation to be found in things. Among beings there are some more and some less good, true, noble, and the like. But "more" and "less" are predicated of different things, according as they resemble in their different ways something which is in the degree of "most," as a thing is said to be hotter according as it more nearly resembles that which is hottest; so that there is something which is truest, something best, something noblest, and, consequently, something which is uttermost being; for the truer things are, the more truly they exist. What is most complete in any genus is the cause of all in that genus; as fire, which is the most complete form of heat, is the cause whereby all things are made hot. Therefore there must also be something which is to all beings the cause of their being, goodness, and every other perfection; and this we call God.

The fifth way is taken from the governance of the world; for we see that things which lack intelligence, such as natural bodies, act for some purpose, which fact is evident from their acting always, or nearly always, in the same way, so as to obtain the best result. Hence it is plain that not fortuitously, but designedly, do they achieve their purpose. Whatever lacks intelligence cannot fulfil some purpose, unless it be directed by some being endowed with intelligence and knowledge; as the arrow is shot to its mark by the archer. Therefore some intelligent being exists by whom all natural things are ordained towards a definite purpose; and this being we call God.

Reply Obj. 1. As Augustine says: *Since God is wholly good, He would not allow any evil to exist in His works, unless His omnipotence and goodness were such as to bring good even out of evil.* This is part of the infinite goodness of God, that He should allow evil to exist, and out of it produce good.

Reply Obj. 2. Since nature works out its determinate end under the direction of a higher agent, whatever is done by nature must needs be traced back to God, as to its first cause. So also whatever is done designedly must also be traced back to some higher cause other than human reason or will, for these can suffer change and are defective; whereas things capable of motion and of defect must be traced back to an immovable and self-necessary first principle.

3.3 The Cosmological Argument

Do you believe that everything must have an explanation? Could there be something that has no explanation? What about you? Must there be an explanation for your existence, characteristics, and qualities? What about the universe? Must it too have an explanation? Why?

According to the Big Bang theory of modern science, the universe originated in a massive explosion and has been expanding ever since. There is good scientific evidence for this theory. It explains many observations physicists and astronomers have made. What, however, caused the Big Bang? Does that itself need an explanation? Certainly many scientists think so, and very imaginative attempts have recently been made to push the clock back behind the Big Bang. Some scientists have speculated, on the basis of what we know about particle physics, that there may have existed a false vacuum (a vacuum devoid of matter, but not of energy). According to Einstein's general relativity theory, a region filled with energy but not with matter will expand suddenly and explosively. The Big Bang may have been nothing other than just such a sudden explosion.

"Where did the false vacuum come from?" I hear you say. That is a good question. If I answered, "From nowhere," would you be satisfied? Probably not, and neither are physicists. Hence some argue that before the false vacuum there was a true vacuum devoid of both matter and energy. According to quantum mechanics, a well-established theory, everything, including a true vacuum, is subject to fluctuations. If so, then a fluctuation in a true vacuum could produce a false vacuum and, lo and behold, the universe.

This is a highly simplified account, and these ideas are speculative. But let us say they are true. If a false vacuum comes from a fluctuation in a true vacuum, have we now reached a sufficient explanation of how the universe originated? You might ask, "Where did the true vacuum come from?" If you pressed the issue, you would seem to be a believer in what the German philosopher Gottfried Leibniz (1646–1716) called the Principle of Sufficient Reason (PSR). According to this principle, there must be an explanation for everything.

"Well, if that is true," you might argue, "then even if you told me God caused the true vacuum, there would have to be an explanation for God too." It would seem so. The answer Leibniz gave (an answer already there in St. Thomas's third way) is that God is a necessary being and hence is explained by nothing but itself. To put that a bit differently, whatever reality is ultimate, it must be an uncaused cause and consequently a reality that exists through itself or has, if you prefer, a sufficient reason of its existence in itself.

"Why call such a reality God?" you might respond. "Why not call it the universe or nature and be done with it?" This question echoes the sentiments of the famous French mathematician and astronomer Pierre Laplace (1749–1827), who, when asked why God played no role in scientific theories of the origin of the universe, replied, "We have no need of that hypothesis."

William Rowe (1931–   ), a professor of philosophy at Purdue University and the author of the next selection, explores some of these issues in his study of the cosmological argument and various objections to it. He wishes to examine critically the PSR and the role it plays in the cosmological argument for God's existence.

Reading Questions

1. What are the two parts of the cosmological argument?
2. What is the difference between a dependent being and a self-existent being?
3. How does the Principle of Sufficient Reason apply to the cosmological argument?
4. Briefly state the main criticisms of the second premise, and the response to those criticisms.
5. What is Rowe's conclusion? Do you agree? Why or why not?

The Cosmological Argument*

WILLIAM ROWE

THE FIRST PART of the eighteenth-century form of the Cosmological Argument seeks to establish the existence of a self-existent being. The second part of the argument attempts to prove that the self-existent being is the theistic God, that is, has the features which we have noted to be basic elements in the theistic idea of God. We shall consider mainly the first part of the argument, for it is against the first part that philosophers from Hume to Russell have advanced very important objections.

In stating the first part of the Cosmological Argument we shall make use of two important concepts, the concept of a *dependent being* and the concept of a *self-consistent being*. By *a dependent being* we mean *a being whose existence is accounted for by the causal activity of other things.* Recalling Anselm's division into the three cases: "explained by another," "explained by nothing," and "explained by itself," it's clear that a dependent being is a being whose existence is explained by another. By *a self-existent being* we mean *a being whose existence is accounted for by its own nature*. This idea, as we saw in the preceding chapter, is an essential element in the theistic concept of God. Again, in terms of Anselm's three cases, a self-existent being is a being whose existence is explained by itself. Armed with these two concepts, the concept of a dependent being and the concept of a self-existent being, we can now state the first part of the Cosmological Argument.

1. Every being (that exists or ever did exist) is either a dependent being or a self-existent being.
2. Not every being can be a dependent being.

Therefore,

3. There exists a self-existent being.

Deductive Validity

Before we look critically at each of the premises of this argument, we should note that this argument is, to use an expression from the logician's vocabulary, *deductively valid*. To find out whether an argument is deductively valid, we need only ask the question: If its premises were true, would its conclusion have to be true? If the answer is yes, the argument is deductively valid. If the answer is no, the argument is deductively invalid. Notice that the question of the validity of an argument is entirely different from the question of whether its premises are in fact true. The following argument is made up entirely of false statements, but it is deductively valid.

1. Babe Ruth is the President of the United States.
2. The President of the United States is from Indiana.

Therefore,

3. Babe Ruth is from Indiana.

The argument is deductively valid because even though its premises are false, if they were true its conclusion would have to be true. Even God, Aquinas would say, cannot bring it about that the premises of this argument are true and yet its conclusion is false, for God's power extends only to what is possible, and it is an absolute impossibility that Babe Ruth be the President, the President be from Indiana, and yet Babe Ruth not be from Indiana.

The Cosmological Argument (that is, its first part) is a deductively valid argument. If its premises are or were true, its conclusion would have to be true. It's clear from our example about

* From William L. Rowe, *Philosophy of Religion: An Introduction*. 2d ed. Copyright © 1993 by Wadsworth, Inc. Reprinted by permission of Wadsworth Publishing Company.

Babe Ruth, however, that the fact that an argument is deductively valid is insufficient to establish the truth of its conclusion. What else is required? Clearly that we know or have rational grounds for believing that the premises are true. If we know that the Cosmological Argument is deductively valid, and can establish that its premises are true, we shall thereby have proved that its conclusion is true. Are, then, the premises of the Cosmological Argument true? To this more difficult question we must now turn.

PSR and the First Premise

At first glance the first premise might appear to be an obvious or even trivial truth. But it is neither obvious nor trivial. And if it appears to be obvious or trivial, we must be confusing the idea of a self-existent being with the idea of a being that is not a dependent being. Clearly, it is true that any being is either a dependent being (explained by other things) or it is not a dependent being (not explained by other things). But what our premise says is that any being is either a dependent being (explained by other things) or it is a self-existent being (explained by itself). Consider again Anselm's three cases.

a. explained by another
b. explained by nothing
c. explained by itself

What our first premise asserts is that each being that exists (or ever did exist) is either of sort *a* or of sort *c*. It denies that any being is of sort *b*. And it is this denial that makes the first premise both significant and controversial. The obvious truth we must not confuse it with is the truth that any being is either of sort *a* or not of sort *a*. While this is true it is neither very significant nor controversial.

Earlier we saw that Anselm accepted as a basic principle that whatever exists has an explanation of its existence. Since this basic principle denies that any thing of sort *b* exists or ever did exist, it's clear that Anselm would believe the first premise of our Cosmological Argument. The eighteenth-century proponents of the argument also were convinced of the truth of the basic principle we attributed to Anselm. And because they were convinced of its truth, they readily accepted the first premise of the Cosmological Argument. But by the eighteenth century, Anselm's basic principle had been more fully elaborated and had received a name, the *Principle of Sufficient Reason*. Since this principle (PSR, as we shall call it) plays such an important role in justifying the premises of the Cosmological Argument, it will help us to consider it for a moment before we continue our enquiry into the truth or falsity of the premises of the Cosmological Argument.

The Principle of Sufficient Reason, as it was expressed by both Leibniz and Samuel Clarke, is a very general principle and is best understood as having two parts. In its first part it is simply a restatement of Anselm's principle that there must be an explanation of the *existence* of any being whatever. Thus if we come upon a man in a room, PSR implies that there must be an explanation of the fact that that particular man exists. A moment's reflection, however, reveals that there are many facts about the man other than the mere fact that he exists. There is the fact that the man in question is in the room he's in, rather than somewhere else, the fact that he is in good health, and the fact that he is at the moment thinking of Paris, rather than, say, London. Now, the purpose of the second part of PSR is to require an explanation of these facts, as well. We may state PSR, therefore, as the principle that *there must be an explanation (a) of the existence of any being, and (b) of any positive fact whatever*. We are now in a position to study the role this very important principle plays in the Cosmological Argument.

Since the proponent of the Cosmological Argument accepts PSR in both its parts, it is clear that he will appeal to its first part, PSRa, as justification for the first premise of the Cosmological Argument. Of course, we can and should enquire into the deeper question of whether the proponent of the argument is rationally justified in accepting PSR itself. But we shall put this question aside for the moment. What we need to see first is whether he is correct in thinking that *if* PSR is true then both of the premises of the Cosmological Argument are true. And what we have just seen is that if only the first part of PSR, that is, PSRa, is true, the first premise of the Cosmological Argument will be true. But what of the second premise of the argument? For what reasons does the proponent think that it must be true?

The Second Premise

According to the second premise, not every being that exists can be a dependent being, that is, can have the explanation of its existence in some other being or beings. Presumably, the proponent of the argument thinks there is something fundamentally wrong with the idea that every being that exists is dependent, that each existing being was caused by some other being which in turn was caused by some other being, and so on. But just what does he think is wrong with it? To help us in understanding his thinking, let's simplify things by supposing that there exists only one thing now, A_1, a living thing perhaps, that was brought into existence by something else, A_2, which perished shortly after it brought A_1, into existence. Suppose further that A_2 was brought into existence in similar fashion some time ago by A_3, and A_3 by A_4, and so forth back into the past. Each of these beings is a *dependent* being, it owes its existence to the preceding thing in the series. Now if nothing else ever existed but these beings, then what the second premise says would not be true. For if every being that exists or ever did exist is an A and was produced by a preceding A, then every being that exists or ever did exist would be dependent and, accordingly, premise two of the Cosmological Argument would be false. If the proponent of the Cosmological Argument is correct there must, then, be something wrong with the idea that every being that exists or did exist is an A and that they form a causal series. A_1 caused by A_2, A_2 caused by A_3, A_3 caused by A_4, . . . A_n caused by A_{n+1}. How does the proponent of the Cosmological Argument propose to show us that there is something wrong with this view?

A popular but mistaken idea of how the proponent tries to show that something is wrong with the view, that every being might be dependent, is that he uses the following argument to reject it.

1. There must be a *first* being to start any causal series.
2. If every being were dependent there would be no *first* being to start the causal series.

Therefore,

3. Not every being can be a dependent being.

Although this argument is deductively valid, and its second premise is true, its first premise overlooks the distinct possibility that a causal series might be *infinite,* with no first member at all. Thus if we go back to our series of A beings, where each A is dependent, having been produced by the preceding A in the causal series, it's clear that if the series existed it would have no first member, for every A in the series there would be a preceding A which produced it, *ad infinitum*. The first premise of the argument just given assumes that a causal series must stop with a first member somewhere in the distant past. But there seems to be no good reason for making that assumption.

The eighteenth-century proponents of the Cosmological Argument recognized that the causal series of dependent beings could be infinite, without a first member to start the series. They rejected the idea that every being that is or ever was is dependent not because there would then be no first member to the series of dependent beings, but because there would then be no explanation for the fact that there are and have always been dependent beings. To see their reasoning let's return to our simplification of the supposition that the only things that exist or ever did exist are dependent beings. In our simplification of that supposition only one of the dependent beings exists at a time, each one perishing as it produces the next in the series. Perhaps the first thing to note about this supposition is that there is no individual A in the causal series of dependent beings whose existence is unexplained—A_1 is explained by A_2, A_2 by A_3, and A_n by A_{n+1}. So the first part of PSR, PSRa, appears to be satisfied. There is no particular being whose existence lacks an explanation. What, then, is it that lacks an explanation, if every particular A in the causal series of dependent beings has an explanation? It is the *series itself* that lacks an explanation. Or, as I've chosen to express it, *the fact that there are and have always been dependent beings.* For suppose we ask why it is that there are and have always been As in existence. It won't do to say that As have always been producing other As—we can't explain why there have always been As by saying there always have been As. Nor, on the supposition that only As have ever existed, can we explain the fact that there have always been As by appealing to something other than an A—for no such thing would have existed. Thus the supposition that the only things that exist or ever existed are dependent things leaves us with a fact for which there can be no explanation; namely, the fact that there are and have always been dependent beings.

Questioning the Justification of the Second Premise

Critics of the Cosmological Argument have raised several important objections against the claim that if every being is dependent the series or collection of those beings would have no explanation. Our understanding of the Cosmological Argument, as well as of its strengths and weaknesses, will be deepened by a careful consideration of these criticisms.

The first criticism is that the proponent of the Cosmological Argument makes the mistake of treating the collection or series of dependent beings as though it were itself a dependent being, and, therefore, requires an explanation of its existence. But, so the objection goes, the collection of dependent beings is not itself a dependent being any more than a collection of stamps is itself a stamp.

A second criticism is that the proponent makes the mistake of inferring that because each member of the collection of dependent beings has a cause, the collection itself must have a cause. But, as Bertrand Russell noted, such reasoning is as fallacious as to infer that the human race (that is, the collection of human beings) must have a mother because each member of the collection (each human being) has a mother.

A third criticism is that the proponent of the argument fails to realize that for there to be an explanation of a collection of things is nothing more than for there to be an explanation of each of the things making up the collection. Since in the infinite collection (or series) of dependent beings, each being in the collection does have an explanation—by virtue of having been caused by some preceding member of the collection—the explanation of the collection, so the criticism goes, has already been given. As David Hume remarked, "Did I show you the particular causes of each individual in a collection of twenty particles of matter, I should think it very unreasonable, should you afterwards ask me, what was the cause of the whole twenty. This is sufficiently explained in explaining the cause of the parts."

Finally, even if the proponent of the Cosmological Argument can satisfactorily answer these objections, he must face one last objection to his ingenious attempt to justify premise two of the Cosmological Argument. For someone may agree that if nothing exists but an infinite collection of dependent beings, the infinite collection will have no explanation of its existence, and still refuse to conclude from this that there is something wrong with the idea that every being is a dependent being. Why, he might ask, should we think that everything has to have an explanation? What's wrong with admitting that the fact that there are and have always been dependent beings is a *brute fact,* a fact having no explanation whatever? Why does everything have to have an explanation anyway? We must now see what can be said in response to these several objections.

Responses to Criticism

It is certainly a mistake to think that a collection of stamps is itself a stamp, and very likely a mistake to think that the collection of dependent beings is itself a dependent being. But the mere fact that the proponent of the argument thinks that there must be an explanation not only for each member of the collection of dependent beings but for the collection itself is not sufficient grounds for concluding that he must view the collection as itself a dependent being. The collection of human beings, for example, is certainly not itself a human being. Admitting this, however, we might still seek an explanation of why there is a collection of human beings, of why there are such things as human beings at all. So the mere fact that an explanation is demanded for the collection of dependent beings is no proof that the person who demands the explanation must be supposing that the collection itself is just another dependent being.

The second criticism attributes to the proponent of the Cosmological Argument the following bit of reasoning.

1. Every member of the collection of dependent beings has a cause or explanation.

Therefore,

2. The collection of dependent beings has a cause or explanation.

As we noted in setting forth this criticism, arguments of this sort are often unreliable. It would be a mistake to conclude that a collection of objects is light in weight simply because each object in the collection is light in weight, for if there were many objects in the collection it might be quite heavy. On the other hand, if we know that each marble weighs more than one ounce, we could infer validly that the collection of marbles weighs more than an ounce. Fortunately, however, we don't need to decide whether the inference from 1 to 2 is valid or invalid. We need not decide this question because the proponent of the Cosmological Argument need not use this inference to establish that there must be an explanation of the collection of dependent beings. He need not use this inference because he has in PSR a principle from which it follows immediately

that the collection of dependent beings has a cause or explanation. For according to PSR, every positive fact must have an explanation. If it is a fact that there exists a collection of dependent beings then, according to PSR, that fact too must have an explanation. So it is PSR that the proponent of the Cosmological Argument appeals to in concluding that there must be an explanation of the collection of dependent beings, and not some dubious inference from the premise that each member of the collection has an explanation. It seems, then, that neither of the first two criticisms is strong enough to do any serious damage to the reasoning used to support the second premise of the Cosmological Argument.

The third objection contends that to explain the existence of a collection of things is the same thing as to explain the existence of each of its members. If we consider a collection of dependent beings where each being in the collection is explained by the preceding member which caused it, it's clear that no member of the collection will lack an explanation of its existence. But, so the criticism goes, if we've explained the existence of every member of a collection, we've explained the existence of the collection—there's nothing left over to be explained. This forceful criticism, originally advanced by David Hume, has gained considerable support in the modern period. But the criticism rests on an assumption that the proponent of the Cosmological Argument would not accept. The assumption is that to explain the existence of a collection of things it is *sufficient* to explain the existence of every member in the collection. To see what is wrong with this assumption is to understand the basic issue in the reasoning by which the proponent of the Cosmological Argument seeks to establish that not every being can be a dependent being.

In order for there to be an explanation of the existence of the collection of dependent beings, it's clear that the eighteenth-century proponents would require that the following two conditions be satisfied:

C1. There is an explanation of the existence of each of the members of the collection of dependent beings.

C2. There is an explanation of why there are *any* dependent beings.

According to the proponents of the Cosmological Argument, if every being that exists or ever did exist is a dependent being—that is, if the whole of reality consists of nothing more than a collection of dependent beings—C1 will be satisfied, but C2 will not be satisfied. And since C2 won't be satisfied, there will be no explanation of the collection of dependent beings. The third criticism, therefore, says in effect that if C1 is satisfied, C2 will be satisfied, and, since in a collection of dependent beings each member will have an explanation in whatever it was that produced it, C1 will be satisfied. So, therefore, C2 will be satisfied and the collection of dependent beings will have an explanation.

Although the issue is a complicated one, I think it is possible to see that the third criticism rests on a mistake: the mistake of thinking that if C1 is satisfied C2 must also be satisfied. The mistake is a natural one to make for it is easy to imagine circumstances in which if C1 is satisfied C2 also will be satisfied. Suppose, for example, that the whole of reality includes not just a collection of dependent beings but also a self-existent being. Suppose further that instead of each dependent being having been produced by some other dependent being, every dependent being was produced by the self-existent being. Finally, let us consider both the possibility that the collection of dependent beings is finite in time and has a first member, and the possibility that the collection of dependent beings is infinite in past time, having no first member. Using G for the self-existent being, the first possibility may be diagramed as follows:

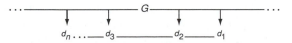

G, we shall say, has always existed and always will. We can think of d_1 as some presently existing dependent being, d_2, d_3, and so forth as dependent beings that existed at some time in the past, and d_n as the first dependent being to exist. The second possibility may be portrayed as follows:

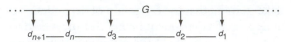

On this diagram there is no first member of the collection of dependent beings. Each member of the infinite collection, however, is explained by reference to the self-existent being G which produced it. Now the interesting point about both these cases is that the explanation that has been provided for the members of the collection of dependent beings carries with it, at least in part, an answer to the question of why there are any dependent beings at all. In both cases we may explain why there are dependent beings by pointing out that there exists a self-existent being that has been engaged in producing them. So once we have learned that the existence of each member of the collection of dependent beings has its existence explained by the fact that G produced it, we have already learned why there are dependent beings.

Someone might object that we haven't really learned why there are dependent beings until we also learn *why* G has been producing them. But, of course, we could also say that we haven't really explained the existence of a particular dependent being, say d_3, until we also learn not just that G produced it but *why* G produced it. The point we need to grasp, however, is that once we admit that every dependent being's existence is explained by G, we must admit that the fact that there are dependent beings has also been explained. So it is not unnatural that someone should think that to explain the existence of the collection of dependent beings is nothing more than to explain the existence of its members. For, as we've seen, to explain the collection's existence is to explain each member's existence and to explain why there are any dependent beings at all. And in the examples we've considered, in doing the one (explaining why each dependent being exists) we've already done the other (explained why there are any dependent beings at all). We must now see, however, that on the supposition that the whole of reality consists *only* of a collection of dependent beings, to give an explanation of each member's existence is not to provide an explanation of why there are dependent beings.

In the examples we've considered, we have gone *outside* of the collection of dependent beings in order to explain the members' existence. But if the only beings that exist or ever existed are dependent beings then each dependent being will be explained by some other dependent being, ad infinitum. This does not mean that there will be some particular dependent being whose existence is unaccounted for. Each dependent being has an explanation of its existence; namely, in the dependent being which preceded it and produced it. So C1 is satisfied: there is an explanation of the existence of each member of the collection of dependent beings. Turning to C2, however, we can see that it will not be satisfied. We cannot explain why there are (or have ever been) dependent beings by appealing to all the members of the infinite collection of dependent beings. For if the question to be answered is why there are (or have ever been) any dependent beings at all, we cannot answer that question by noting that there always have been dependent beings, each one accounting for the existence of some other dependent being. Thus on the supposition that every being is dependent, it seems there will be no explanation of why there are dependent beings. C2 will not be satisfied. Therefore, on the supposition that every being is dependent there will be no explanation of the existence of the collection of dependent beings.

The Truth of PSR

We come now to the final criticism of the reasoning supporting the second premise of the Cosmological Argument. According to this criticism, it is admitted that the supposition that every being is dependent implies that there will be a *brute fact* in the universe, a fact, that is, for which there can be no explanation whatever. For there will be no explanation of the fact that dependent beings exist and have always been in existence. It is this brute fact that the proponents of the argument were describing when they pointed out that if every being is dependent, the series or collection of dependent beings would lack an explanation of *its* existence. The final criticism asks what is wrong with admitting that the universe contains such a brute, unintelligible fact. In asking this question the critic challenges the fundamental principle, PSR, on which the Cosmological Argument rests. For, as we've seen, the first premise of the argument denies that there exists a being whose existence has no explanation. In support of this premise the proponent appeals to the first part of PSR. The second premise of the argument claims that not every being can be dependent. In support of this premise the proponent appeals to the second part of PSR, the part which states that there must be an explanation of any positive fact whatever.

The proponent reasons that if every being were a dependent being, then although the first part of PSR would be satisfied—every being would have an explanation—the second part would be violated; there would be no explanation for the positive fact that there are and have always been dependent beings. For first, since every being is supposed to be dependent, there would be nothing outside of the collection of dependent beings to explain the collection's existence. Second, the fact that each member of the collection has an explanation in some other dependent being is insufficient to explain why there are and have always been dependent beings. And, finally, there is nothing about the collection of dependent beings that would suggest that it is a self-existent collection. Consequently, if every being were dependent, the fact that there are and have always been dependent beings would have no explanation. But this violates the second part of PSR. So the second premise of the Cosmological Argument must be true: Not every being can be a dependent being. This conclusion, however, is no better than the principle, PSR, on which it rests. And it is the point of the final criticism to question the truth of PSR. Why, after all, should we accept the idea that every being and every positive fact must have an explanation? Why, in short, should we believe PSR? These are important questions, and any final judgment of the Cosmological Argument depends on how they are answered.

Most of the theologians and philosophers who accept PSR have tried to defend it in either of two ways. Some have held that PSR is (or can be) known *intuitively* to be true. By this they mean that if we fully understand and reflect on what is said by PSR we can see that it must be true. Now, undoubtedly, there are statements which are known intuitively to be true. "Every triangle has exactly three angles" or "No physical object can be in two different places in space at one and the same time" are examples of statements whose truth we can apprehend just by understanding and reflecting on them. The difficulty with the claim that PSR is intuitively true, however, is that a number of very able philosophers fail to apprehend its truth, and some even claim that the principle is false. It is doubtful, therefore, that many of us, if any, know intuitively that PSR is true.

The second way philosophers and theologians who accept PSR have sought to defend it is by claiming that although it is not known to be true, it is, nevertheless, a presupposition of reason, a basic assumption that rational people make, whether or not they reflect sufficiently to become aware of the assumption. It's probably true that there are some assumptions we all make about our world, assumptions which are so basic that most of us are unaware of them. And, I suppose, it might be true that PSR is such an assumption. What bearing would this view of PSR have on the Cosmological Argument? Perhaps the main point to note is that even if PSR is a presupposition we all share, the premises of the Cosmological Argument could still be false. For PSR itself could still be false. The fact, if it is a fact, that all of us *presuppose* that every existing being and every positive fact has an explanation does not imply that no being exists, and no positive fact obtains, without an explanation. Nature is not bound to satisfy our presuppositions. As the American philosopher

William James once remarked in another connection, "In the great boarding house of nature, the cakes and the butter and the syrup seldom come out so even and leave the plates so clear."

Our study of the first part of the Cosmological Argument has led us to the fundamental principle on which its premises rest, the Principle of Sufficient Reason. Since we do not seem to know that PSR is true, we cannot reasonably claim to know that the premises of the Cosmological Argument are true. They might be true. But unless we do know them to be true they cannot *establish* for us the conclusion that there exists a being that has the explanation of its existence within its own nature. If it were shown, however, that even though we do not *know* that PSR is true we all, nevertheless, *presuppose* PSR to be true, then, whether PSR is true or not, to be consistent we should accept the Cosmological Argument. For, as we've seen, its premises imply its conclusion and its premises do seem to follow from PSR. But no one has succeeded in *showing* that PSR is an assumption that most or all of us share. So our final conclusion must be that although the Cosmological Argument might be a *sound* argument (valid with true premises), it does not provide us with good rational grounds for believing that among these beings that exist there is one whose existence is accounted for by its own nature. Having come to this conclusion, we may safely put aside the second part of the argument. For even if it succeeded in showing that a self-existent being would have the other attributes of the theistic God, the Cosmological Argument would still not provide us with good rational grounds for belief in God, having failed in its first part to provide us with good rational grounds for believing that there is a self-existent being.

3.4 A Buddhist Critique

Many Indian philosophers adopted the idea of a created universe from the *Veda*. The God primarily responsible for its creation is Brahma. The universe created by Brahma, however, is only one of an infinite number. Hence, unlike the conception reflected in Western views, this universe in which we live is not the only one. It will eventually decline, and Brahma will create a new one, just as Brahma has created numerous universes before this one.

The idea that the universes are created was supported by versions of the cosmological argument. Every event must have a cause. A universe is an event. Therefore, it must have a cause (see Reading 3.1). However, not all Indian philosophers agreed. The Buddha (see Reading 2.4), for example, thought the universe is an infinite and eternal series of changes that could be explained in its own terms. No creative cause existing outside the universe need be posited to explain its existence.

The Buddha's rejection of the cosmological argument should not be construed as a rejection of all notions of an ultimate reality. The Buddha taught that nirvana, an ultimate state free from all suffering, is possible. Nor should his views be construed as a rejection of all notions of divinity. There may be gods, but they too are in need of release. Rather, we should understand his position as a specific denial of the logic embodied in the cosmological argument. It fails to prove what it claims to prove—namely, that there is a creator God.

Gunapala Dharmasiri is a professor of philosophy at the University of Sri Lanka. In the following selection, he combines Buddhist and non-Buddhist critiques of the cosmological argument. He argues that for all we know, the universe may be an exception to the principle of causality or that the explanation of its existence can be found within itself.

Reading Questions

1. In what specific way does Dharmasiri think religions should be compared?
2. What distinguishes the Buddha from the theist on the topic of "the world"?
3. Why would a Buddhist argue that the everlastingness of the world not only makes the idea of a creator God superfluous but also contradicts the ideas that such a God is unique and omnipotent?
4. What is wrong with claiming there is a necessary being?
5. How does the Buddhist answer the following questions: "What is the cause of all this?" and "Why does anything exist at all?" Do you find these answers convincing? Why or why not?

A Buddhist Critique*

GUNAPALA DHARMASIRI

THE BUDDHA DID NOT accept the existence of God. He also rejected the idea of a soul though he advocated the possibility of salvation. The present work is an attempt to elucidate the reasons that led the Buddha to such conclusions.

Here, the Buddha's arguments against theism are used for a critical evaluation of the concept of God in contemporary Christian theology and philosophy of religion. The early Buddhist teachings are used in two ways: I. When direct arguments against theism are found in early Buddhist works, they are directly applied to the present context. II. Elsewhere, the early Buddhist ideas have been used as bases to develop arguments critical of theistic ideas. In most cases, I have quoted from the early Buddhist Pali Canon itself and from other early Buddhist writings.

Though this is a critique of the Christian concept of God, my intention is not to disparage Christianity. In fact, the Buddha himself, on many occasions, has advised that one should not disparage other religions and faiths or flatter one's own religion by condemning another. He said that a good person, "because of his success in moral habit, does not exalt himself and does not disparage others." He advised his disciples: "Our mode of living must be perfectly pure, clear, open, and without defects controlled. But not on account of this perfectly pure mode of living will we exalt ourselves or disparage others." This does not mean that one cannot make criticisms of another religion if the concepts involved in that religion are unsatisfactory. The Buddha did so on many occasions, as this work illustrates.

Still, the criticism of one religion in terms of another may not be welcomed. It is the fashion today to see the similarities and parallels in religions, thus making "positive" comparisons rather than "negative" criticisms. From a humanitarian point of view such comparisons seem more justifiable, because it is always a nice thing to say that humanity agrees on fundamental things rather than differs. Criticisms, very often, breed only ill-feelings. But this attitude is wrong for some very important reasons. To make comparisons between religions is an easy task. To quote parallel passages from the texts of different religions is equally easy. But intellectually this is a very immoral exercise, since when we quote such apparently similar passages we quote them out of their proper contexts. It is the context that gives religious statements their meaning. Therefore, religions should be compared and contrasted in terms of their whole doctrinal and cultural contexts. It is only then that comparisons or contrasts between religions can be made. What is

attempted in this work is a comparison or a contrast of that type. . . .

2.1. "Creator" is an indispensable attribute of God because the whole doctrinal edifice of Christianity rests on the assumption that God created the world and man. In Christianity, God is able to offer salvation to man because it was he who created man. However, the ideas of salvation and creation are not necessarily bound together as is seen in the later theistic Samkhya philosophy, where God can offer salvation though he is not a creator. But in Christianity the two are inseparable particularly because God is conceived as omnipotent and unique. . . .

2.4 The starting point of the argument for a creator is the idea of contingency, or "existence" as another for contingency. The assumption behind the argument is that existence cannot be explained by itself. Smart clarifies, ". . . in attempting to argue ourselves beyond the cosmos we seem to be going beyond the observable, and outside space and time. This provides us with another lesson—namely that any attempted explanation of the cosmos is non-scientific." This permits one to speak of God as the Cosmos-Explaining-Being: "We can argue that somehow 'beyond' or 'behind' the cosmos there exists a Being which explains the existence of the cosmos."

2.5 It is here that the Buddha would strongly disagree with the theist. He was conversant with the view of creation and said that some "believed as their traditional doctrine that the beginning of things was the work of God or Brahma." But he did not think that such a view could explain anything about the world. Buddhism does not call the world contingent but only impermanent. Its central thesis emphasizes that everything is subject to an unceasing flow of change (*vipariṇā- madhamma*). One of his disciples once questioned the Buddha: "'The world! The world!' is the saying, lord. How far, lord, does this saying go? It crumbles away, brethren. Therefore it is called 'the world.' What crumbles away? The eye . . . objects . . . eye-consciousness . . . tongue . . . body . . . mind etc. It crumbles away, brethren. Therefore it is called 'the world.'" What distinguishes the Buddha from the theist is that the former strongly believed the world to be explainable in its own terms. To him the world was not a "thing" but only a vast series of evanescent changes. The law of causation (*idappaccayatā*) as affecting the physical and mental realms was regarded to be fully sufficient to explain this cosmic series of changes. But the question as to what is the cause of this causal series still remains. Buddhaghosa thinks that when the idea of a creator God is rejected this question remains yet to be answered. But he maintains that empirical causation and causal regularities, in turn, can explain the causal series. "To begin with, he considers thus: 'Firstly this mentality-materiality is not causeless, because if that were so, it would follow that (having no causes to differentiate it), it would be identical everywhere always and for all. It has no Overlord [God] etc., because of the non-existence of any Overlord, etc., over and above mentality-materiality. And because, if people then argue that mentality-materiality itself is its Overlord etc., then it follows that their mentality-materiality, which they call the Overlord, etc., would itself be causeless. Consequently there must be a cause and a condition for it. What are they?'

"Having thus directed his attention to mentality-materiality's cause and condition, he first discerns the cause and condition for the material body in this way. . . . When it is born thus, its causes (root-causes) are the four things namely, ignorance, craving, clinging, and Kamma: since it is they that bring about its birth; and nutriment is its condition, since it is that that consolidates it. So five things constitute its cause and condition." In the same way, as we shall see later, Buddhism maintains that one can give a self-sufficient causal account in empirical terms of the physical and mental aspects of the world. . . .

2.12 Now, our central problem is the idea of contingency. The concept of God as the creator is meant to explain and solve this problem. If the solution is meaningful and correct it is meant to serve two purposes. One is that is can account for the origin of the universe or the existence of the universe. The second is that if the first task is successful it would, in turn, prove the plausibility of the existence of God. For the Buddhist this prob-

lem would be of special interest because the starting point of Buddhism is the fact of impermanence and change in the world. What would be the Buddhist attitude towards the Christian solution?

2.13 The concept of creator, as we saw, tries to account for the contingent world in two ways. First by strict and literal creation. Second by positing a necessary being. The Buddhist would regard the first solution as irrelevant. As we shall see later . . ., the Buddha believed in an everlasting and oscillating theory of the universe (though not strictly *as a theory* but more as a possibility . . .). This, of course, does not logically rule out creation because the oscillating universe could have been created a long time ago by God. But in the absence of any evidence to the contrary it makes it logically conceivable that this oscillating universe goes back to an infinite past. In fact, the Buddhist can believe in an everlasting universe. If the universe is everlasting then the problem of creation becomes completely redundant. The idea of continuous creation cannot be introduced here because it leads to problems we have already raised.

2.14 Though Smart says that the eternity of the universe is compatible with the Five Ways and therefore with the existence of God, it poses a big problem for the theist because it affects God's uniqueness and perfections. This happens in two ways. Firstly, there is at least one thing that is not under God's power of strict, literal creation. This contradicts the Christian idea of God as Creator which Barth clarifies: ". . . creation does also denote a relationship between God and the world, i.e., the relationship of absolute superiority and lordship on the one hand and of absolute dependence on the other. Creation does not signify, however, only a mythological or speculative intensification of the concept of this relationship, but its presupposition and decisive meaning. That is, creation speaks primarily of a basis which is beyond this relationship and makes it possible; of a unique, free creation of heaven and earth by the will and act of God." Though Barth states the typical belief about the Christian Creator God one can still insist that it is not the only possible version of the Christian idea of the Creator God. But an eternal world still limits God in several important ways. God ceases to be the absolute creator but only a relative creator. He does not create the world from nothing but from the existing matter. God cannot destroy the world because the world is eternal. Even if he could destroy the world the fact remains that there has been a world from eternity outside his absolute, strict and literal creative power. One can still say that this type of limitation would not make a significant limitation upon God's omnipotence etc. But one has to accept necessarily that an eternal world is, at least to a certain extent, a limitation upon an absolutely unique and all perfect God. If one says that God need not be that unique then one already accepts the fact of, at least, certain limitations. In either case it raises the grave and uneasy question about the degree of limitations one wants to attribute to God. Within the Christian tradition it is not an easy problem to solve. The second way in which the eternity of the cosmos affects an all-perfect and unique God is that if the cosmos is eternal, then there is at least one thing that shares a divine perfection, i.e., eternity. Here one can make a distinction and say that this type of limitation affects only the abstract definition of God but not the working or practical definition of God, i.e., God can carry on his divine activities quite unhindered by the presence of an eternal world. But in Christianity, the practical definition gains its power and validity on the authority of the abstraction definition, and so the change in the abstract definition has decisive repercussions on the practical definition. Further, the attempt to give a practical definition would make the concept of God subject to the charges of unfalsifiability. A Buddhist would see the possibility of an everlasting world as not only making the idea of a creator God superfluous but also as contradicting the conception of a unique and omnipotent God.

2.15 The second way of accounting for the contingent world is by positing a necessary Being. This second way seems to be the more fundamental argument because the first way still leaves God within the realm of contingency and

makes it possible to ask the "why" of God. One has necessarily to end up in a necessary existence. According to the Christian standpoint, even though the world is eternal the problem of contingency remains. Hawkins emphasizes the necessity of the idea of a necessary Being. "Being is either dependent on other being or not. All being cannot be dependent on other being, for thus there would be no being upon which it could depend. Therefore there is some being which is independent of other being and necessary of itself." But the attempt to speak of the existence of a necessary being has been open to grave logical objections. One of the stock arguments against it is, as J.J.C. Smart states, that "No existential proposition can be logically necessary . . ." and he maintains, "'Logically necessary being' is a self-contradictory expression like 'round square.'" J.N. Findlay thinks that Anselm exposed the unfortunate predicament of the idea of a necessary being when the latter formulated his Argument. "It was indeed an ill day for Anselm when he hit upon his famous proof. For on that day he not only laid bare something that is of the essence of an adequate religious object, but also something that entails its necessary non-existence."

2.16 For a Buddhist, who also looks at the world as subject to change and impermanence, the argument from contingency may look fascinating. Though he would speak of the world as changing and impermanent, the concept of contingency is completely unfamiliar to him. This raises the question whether "contingency" is "a fact." The word "contingency" is a term that functions meaningfully within the realm of logic and mathematics. It is a relative term and always denotes a relation. "Contingency" and "necessity" derive their meaning and significance from each other and you call a proposition contingent only because you already have the conception of a necessary proposition. Because the idea of necessity functions only within the realm of *a priori* thinking and propositions, the idea of contingency too limits itself to that realm and therefore no existential fact can be contingent. Also, the idea of contingent existence or fact cannot have any meaning because one cannot make the idea of necessary existence meaningful, because one cannot talk of a necessary existence or a fact. . . . This argument does not, of course, apply to "change" and "impermanence" because the Buddha was making those two terms meaningful in terms of the empirical context, e.g., by illustrating "impermanence" by appealing to experience or contrasting it with apparent "permanence" etc. Therefore while "impermanence" can be empirically and factually meaningful, "contingency" cannot be so. If so, what does the Christian mean when he speaks of the world as contingent? What he is doing is expressing an attitude towards the world using the logical term "contingence" because he is already familiar with the illegitimate idea of a necessary Being.

2.17 It may happen the other way round too. Ian Crombie clarifies it this way: "'Finite' and 'infinite,' 'contingent' and 'necessary,' 'derivative' and 'non-derivative': all these are pairs. When we use either member of any of them in the theological context we cannot anatomize the meaning to be attached to it. When we speak of the world as finite we do not mean that it can be counted, or travelled across; when we speak of it as derivative, we do not think of it as extracted from its origin by any normal kind of derivation. But the meaning to be attached to the second member of each pair is to be got at by seeing what kind of judgment about the world is intended by the use of the first. The kind of judgment intended by the use of such expressions . . . is an intellectual dissatisfaction with the notion of this universe as a complete system, with, as corollary, the notion of a being with which one could not be thus dissatisfied." Thus, if he starts from "contingency" then he is trying to give a logical explanation or definition of the factual world. By using that term one is only begging the question in terms of a necessary being. A purely abstract logical relationship cannot explain or give an intellectually satisfying account of an existing factual world.

2.18 But, the theist can still object that the Buddhist's treatment still leaves two questions unanswered: (i) What is the cause of all this?

(ii) Why does anything exist at all? We shall take the first question first. The Buddha believed that an empirical theory of causation and the regularity of laws of nature etc., within the world could fully account for causation. It was the nature of the world. The Buddha explains: "What is causation? On account of birth arises death. Whether Tathagatas arise or not, this order exists namely the fixed nature of phenomena, the regular pattern of phenomena or conditionality. This the Tathagata discovers and comprehends; having discovered and comprehended it, he points it out, teaches it, lays it down, establishes, reveals, analyzes, clarifies it and says 'look.'" K.N. Jayatilleke illustrates and analyzes how the Buddha applied this theory of causation to explain both physical and mental phenomena in the world. The Buddha's central theory of causality was the regularity theory of causation but he accepted the possibility of other forms of empirical causation like relative causation (e.g. mind and body are caused by consciousness and vice versa; good exists because of bad and vice versa). We saw above, as Buddhaghosa explained, how the Buddhist thinker thought this was a sufficient explanation. But the theist may still insist on seeking the cause that originates or sustains this causal series. One might allow him to proceed further if he could give a satisfying and conclusive explanation of causation. Hawkins maintains, "The divine causality is . . . the source of all other causality and combines all that is positive in other modes of causation." But the fallacy here is that the argument from causation abruptly stops at God. Even an enriched form of the Cosmos-Explaining-Being still raises the question of its causation. To silence the problem of causation after coming to the idea of God is a fundamentally wrong attitude towards causation or as Schopenhauer puts it, "we cannot use the causal law as if it were a sort of cab, to be dismissed when we have reached our destination."

2.19 Here a theist, following St. Augustine, can object that we are misconceiving the idea of time in the context of creation. He would say that one cannot ask about what existed prior to creation because the idea of "prior" cannot be meaningful before creation began. "Prior" is a temporal concept and time starts only with creation. Actually this argument does make some sense to a certain extent. The idea of time is essentially related to matter or some form of existent. Time is derivative from the processes of change in matter or existents. Every time we try to conceive of any form of time, prior to creation etc., we do it always in terms of some form of existent. Therefore, in essence, it is true that time does not exist prior to any form of existent. Thus the theist can say that it is meaningless to ask about what existed prior to creation because the 'prior' is meaningless as time is created along with the existents or is a creation relative to the existents.

2.20 Two answers can be given to this argument. One is that the theist's argument is double-edged but he uses only one edge to the exclusion of the other. If the creation of existents creates time then it creates time retrospectively as well. Then it becomes meaningful to talk about the time prior to creation. Secondly, even if the theist's contention were correct, he cannot talk about the non-existence of any existent prior to creation because God himself is so existent. The theist's obvious reply would be that God is timeless etc. But it is not a logically satisfactory or valid answer because God exists in some form, transcendent or otherwise, prior to creation and so the idea of 'prior to creation' becomes a meaningful concept. Therefore the idea of creator validly raises the question of the creator of the creator and so on *regressus ad infinitum.*

2.21 The Buddha emphasized that one has to stop at the fundamental laws of nature and regularities of causation. To go beyond that would be both unnecessary and wrong. Buddhaghosa states, ". . . knowledge of (causal) origin forestalls wrong theories of cause that occur as finding a reason where there is none, such as 'The world occurs owing to an Overlord . . .' etc." Here we can ask three questions: (i) Is it necessary to go beyond this point of explanation? (ii) Is it meaningful to go beyond this point? (iii) Is it correct to go beyond this point? Flew thinks that it is not necessary to go beyond this point of explanation

because it is not a deficiency to stop at some fundamentals when one is giving an explanation. "In each and every case we must necessarily find at the end of every explanatory road some ultimates which have simply to be accepted as the fundamental truths about the way things are. And this itself is a contention, not about the lamentable contingent facts of the human condition, but about what follows necessarily from the nature of explanation." Is it meaningful to go beyond this point? If the theist goes beyond this point he will have to stop at some other ultimate which seems arbitrary, enigmatic and abrupt. For example, to stop at a necessary God is an arbitrary conclusion. Even before proceeding to that point he has to accept or stop at more enigmatic and uneasy ultimates. C.B. Martin points out one such ultimate: "This is one law of nature or one way of the world that would be beyond the power of God, namely, that the world should in fact go according to the will of God. God cannot ordain or will that his ordinations and will are effective. That, God's will is effective is just a fact (though a basic one) about how things happen. To ask why God's will is effective is to invite the answer 'That is just the way things are.'" The theist's ultimates become more and more meaningless as he proceeds further. Hence, to proceed beyond the empirical ultimates is progressively meaningless. Then we come to the third question. Is it correct to go beyond the ultimates of empirical explanation? Hume explains: "In such a chain too, or succession of objects, each part is caused by that which preceded it, and causes that which succeeds it. Where then is the difficulty? But the *whole,* you say, wants a cause. . . . Did I show you the particular causes of each individual in a collection of twenty particles of matter, I should think it very unreasonable, should you afterwards ask me, what was the cause of the whole twenty." Similarly, the Buddhist would say that once the empirical facts have been explained causally it would be positively wrong to ask the cause of the whole of it. That was why Buddhaghosa, as we saw above, maintained that the knowledge of the causal origin of things forestalls the theories of a creator God.

2.22 Now, coming to the second question of the theist, he can still ask "Why does anything exist at all?" The Buddhist can give four answers to this question. One is that, as he accepts the possibility of an everlasting cosmos, this question does not, in an important sense, arise to him. Here it should be emphatically stated that we should not drag in the idea of logical contingency into this context because it does not have any meaning as applied to empirical and factual contexts. Of existential propositions one can speak only of an empirical necessity. So, if the world is everlasting the fact that anything exists at all is an empirical necessity. One can *logically* think the world away, but it is not important at all because we are not talking about the realm of logic. The important thing is that one cannot *practically* think the world away because it exists as an empirical necessity. Therefore, to the Buddhist "why does anything exist at all?" does not pose any problem. One might still insist on a logical kind of explanation in terms of the idea of necessity, but such an explanation would not mean anything and therefore would fail to be an explanation at all.

2.23 The Buddhist can give yet another answer to this question. The Buddha answers Sunakkhatta, the Wanderer: "What think you, Sunakkhatta? Whether the beginning of things revealed, or whether it be not, is the object for which I teach the Dhamma (norm) this: that it leads to the thorough destruction of ill for the doer thereof?... If then, Sunakkhatta, it matters not to that object whether the beginning of things be revealed, or whether it be not, of what use to you would it be to have the beginning of things revealed?" The Buddha can give this answer because he starts from the fact that there is the world, as a given. (He did not preach the everlastingness of the cosmos *as a theory* about the origin of the universe etc., but only tried to explain certain moral problems with the help of this idea . . .). The main concern of religion is salvation and he discovered that it could be found without delving into all the mysteries of the world. A Christian cannot give this form of answer because in the context of Christianity the ideas of salvation and creator God are essentially bound to each other. Objectively

speaking, it is possible to think of a non-creator God of salvation as is found in the later theistic Samkhya system. But in Christianity the ideas of creation and salvation are inevitably bound together, or rather entail each other. Theologians like Tillich and Bultmann try to maintain that the idea of strict creation is not relevant for salvation. Tillich says that "The doctrine of creation does not describe an event. It points to the situation of creatureliness and to its correlate, the divine creativity." According to Bultmann, "This, then, is the primary thing about faith in creation: the knowledge of the nothingness of the world and of our own selves, the knowledge of our complete abandonment." Without clarifying the problem of the possibility of limitations upon God's power how can one, as they maintain, put absolute and unconditional faith in the salvific power of God? If the world can manage to exist from eternity it might be able to account for its own internal mechanism too. Tillich should not confidently maintain, "The doctrine of creation affirms that God is the creative ground of everything every moment." Or, Bultmann cannot safely conclude that faith in creation is "faith in man's present determination by God," because there can be other possible sources of man's determination other than God. Without ruling out these possibilities, i.e. without clearing the idea of absolute creator, one cannot keep an unconditional faith in the salvific power of an absolutely omnipotent God. A Mahayana cosmic Buddha or Bodhisattva might be quoted as an example to the contrary. However, they are not gods of salvation, they can only help and aid men to get their own salvation, and they have limitations which they know of and consequently they work very hard indeed. Out of compassion for suffering men Kwan Yin is supposed to be weeping all the time. In the later Samkhya it is not God, who openly accepts limitations, that matters in salvation but the following of the practical path as laid down in the Yoga. But in Christianity the unconditional faith in God's salvific power presupposes and therefore logically entails the factual truth of God as absolute literal creator and as all perfect unique Being. Or, as Crombie puts it, "Christianity, as a human activity, involves much more than simply believing certain propositions about matters of fact, such as that there is a God, that He created this world, that He is our judge. But it does involve believing these things, and this believing is, in a sense, fundamental. . . ." Though the Buddhist can hold that creation is not necessary for salvation, the Christian cannot claim so, and this conclusion makes Tillich's and Bultmann's attempts to ignore the problem of creation essentially wrong.

2.24 The Buddhist can give two more answers on the basis of the Buddha's teachings. The idea of "necessary being" that is advanced as a solution to the problem of the contingent world is fundamentally a logical conception based on *a priori* reasoning because, as we discussed before, "contingency" and "necessity" are concepts denoting a logical relationship. The Buddha was very critical of assertions based on *a priori* forms of reasoning . . . . He maintained that though a piece of logical reasoning may be self-evident and valid it does not say anything at all about the truth or falsity of the claims made by that type of reasoning. A valid argument can be, according to the Buddha, either true or false and this cannot be decided on grounds of logical reasoning alone. Therefore, *a priori* reasoning about logical relationships cannot lead to making any factual assertions.

2.25 The fourth answer stems from the Buddha's ideas about the universe. As we shall see later . . . , the Buddha spoke of the possibility of an infinite universe. If the universe is infinite then nobody can know the nature of the universe as a whole, and without knowing the universe fully and wholly one cannot arbitrarily decide that the concept of causation can be applied to the universe as a whole. We know that there are areas where the concept of causality is not applicable. As F. Waismann says, "It is only when we descend to the atomic level that the question of causality can be put to the test; and here all the facts speak decidedly against it. The only theory known at present capable of connecting and unifying an enormously wide range of phenomena, quantum theory, is in sharp logical contradiction with it." This in an important way shows that the sovereignty of causation is not all pervading. Therefore one cannot arbitrarily maintain that it should apply in each and every case of which we can think. If causality is not applicable to microcosmic entities like atoms, can we not conceive the possibility that it might not be applicable to macrocosmic phenomena as a whole? As in the case of atoms the universe may be an exception to the principle of causality. Because we do not know the universe as a whole, how do we know that it is not?

3.5 The Teleological Argument

Imagine yourself on a walk in the woods. You come upon a meadow that is breathtaking in its beauty. Red, purple, and golden flowers nestle among deep green grasses. Bumblebees move from flower to flower collecting pollen. Hummingbirds flit about, and meadowlarks sing wonderful songs. Each delicate flower has an intricate geometrical shape. You see a cool brook with a beaver dam. The trunks and limbs from trees have been carefully selected and arranged in ways that you yourself probably could not plan.

"Surely," you think, "this wonderful order could not have happened by chance. There must be some very intelligent designer who conceived and arranged this fragile, ecological balance."

You have not only stumbled on a beautiful meadow, but have also come up with the teleological argument. Like the cosmological argument, this is an *a posteriori* argument for God's existence. It begins with our experience of order in the world and proceeds to claim that this order is a design—that is, it has some purpose (*telos*) to it. The final step is to conclude that there is an intelligent designer (God) who is responsible for the order of the world. This type of argument has been around for a long time (see Reading 3.1 and St. Thomas's fifth way in Reading 3.2) and has enjoyed considerable popularity. The teleological argument, which is sometimes called the argument from design, centers on an analogy between designed things and the universe. When we use analogies, we compare different things and draw a conclusion about an unknown thing on the basis of what is known about another thing. Whatever similarities may exist between two different things, there are also differences. The trick is to figure out whether these differences are great enough to invalidate the conclusion. False analogies abound in the history of thought.

What do you think we could learn about the development of a human being from observing the growth of a hair? Could we reach sound conclusions about how humans develop from such observations? How many universes have you seen? Would we not have to compare different universes, just as we compare items within our universe, to see whether universes are the sorts of things that are designed? And how do we know that the universe was not made by many different beings, as a ship is, rather than by just one being?

The Scottish philosopher David Hume (1711–1776) raised such questions because, in his view, the argument from design is a false analogy. He published, posthumously in 1779, one of the most devastating philosophical critiques of the teleological argument. He presents his views in the form of a conversation among three people: Cleanthes, Demea, and Philo. Cleanthes is a natural theologian who believes that human reason can prove that God exists on the basis of the evidence provided by the natural world. Demea is also a theologian but does not believe that unaided human reason can prove much of anything about the God revealed in the Christian scriptures. The basis of theology, in his opinion, is revelation and faith. Philo is skeptical of the human ability to know much of anything when it comes to God. After Cleanthes states a version of the teleological argument, Philo raises a series of objections that undermine the conclusion of the argument.

Reading Questions

1. What is the "rule of analogy" to which Cleanthes appeals, and what does he conclude from it?
2. What is Demea's objection?
3. Philo's initial objection to Cleanthes's argument is that it is a weak analogy at best. Why is it weak?
4. At one point, Philo argues that the operations of a part cannot provide the basis for sound conclusions about the whole and that no one part can form a rule for another part if there is great dissimilarity between them. Provide two examples that support Philo's reasoning. Can you think of any counterexamples?
5. Why does Philo think that all the discoveries of modern science count as so many objections to the principle that like effects prove like causes?
6. Philo contends that several unwelcome consequences follow from Cleanthes's use of the principle "like effects prove like causes." What are these consequences?
7. How does Cleanthes respond?
8. What do you think of Philo's (Hume's) objections to the design argument? Do they undermine the argument? Why or not?

The Teleological Argument*

DAVID HUME

Cleanthes: Look round the world: Contemplate the whole and every part of it: You will find it to be nothing but one great machine, subdivided into an infinite number of lesser machines, which again admit of subdivisions to a degree beyond what human senses and faculties can trace and explain. All these various machines, and even their most minute parts, are adjusted to each other with an accuracy which ravishes into admiration all men who have ever contemplated them. The curious adapting of means to ends, throughout all nature, resembles exactly, though it much exceeds, the productions of human contrivance: of human design, thought, wisdom, and intelligence. Since therefore the effects resemble each other, we are led to infer, by all the rules of analogy, that the causes also resemble, and that the Author of Nature is somewhat similar to the mind of man, though possessed of much larger faculties, proportioned to the grandeur of the work which he has executed. By this argument *a posteriori,* and by this argument alone, do we prove at once the existence of a Deity and his similarity to human mind and intelligence.

Demea: I shall be so free, *Cleanthes,* said *Demea,* as to tell you that from the beginning I could not approve of your conclusion concerning the similarity of the Deity to men; still less can I approve of the mediums by which you endeavor to establish it. What! No demonstration of the Being of God! No abstract arguments! No proofs *a priori!* Are these which have hitherto been so much insisted on by philosophers all fallacy, all sophism? Can we reach no farther in this subject than experience and probability? I will say not that this is betraying the cause of a Deity; but surely, by this affected candor, you give advantages to atheists which they never could obtain by the mere dint of argument and reasoning.

Philo: What I chiefly scruple in this subject, said *Philo,* is not so much that all religious arguments are by *Cleanthes* reduced to experience, as that they appear not to be even the most certain and irrefragable of that inferior kind. That a stone will fall, that fire will burn, that the earth has solidity, we have observed a thousand and a thousand times; and when any new instance of this nature is presented, we draw without hesitation the accustomed inference. The exact similarity of the cases gives us a perfect assurance of a similar event, and a stronger evidence is never desired nor sought after. But wherever you depart, in the least, from the similarity of the cases, you diminish proportionably the evidence; and may at last bring it to a very weak *analogy,* which is confessedly liable to error and uncertainty. After having experienced the circulation of the blood in human creatures, we make no doubt that it takes place in *Titius* and *Maevius;* but from its circulation in frogs and fishes it is only a presumption, though a strong one, from analogy that it takes place in men and other animals. The analogical reasoning is much weaker when we infer the circulation of the sap in vegetables from our experience that the blood circulates in animals; and those who hastily followed that imperfect analogy are found, by more accurate experiments, to have been mistaken.

If we see a house, *Cleanthes,* we conclude, with the greatest certainty, that it had an architect or builder because this is precisely that species of effect which we have experienced to proceed from that species of cause. But surely you will not affirm that the universe bears such a resemblance to a house that we can with the same certainty infer a similar cause, or that the analogy is here entire and perfect. The dissimilitude is so striking that the utmost you can here

---

* From David Hume, *Dialogues Concerning Natural Religion* (1779).

pretend to is a guess, a conjecture, a presumption concerning a similar cause; and how that pretension will be received in the world, I leave you to consider.

Cleanthes: It would surely be very ill received, replied *Cleanthes;* and I should be deservedly blamed and detested did I allow that the proofs of a Deity amounted to no more than a guess or conjecture. But is the whole adjustment of means to ends in a house and in the universe so slight a resemblance? The economy of final causes? The order, proportion, and arrangement of every part? Steps of a stair are plainly contrived that human legs may use them in mounting; and this inference is certain and infallible. Human legs are also contrived for walking and mounting; and this inference, I allow, is not altogether so certain because of the dissimilarity which you remark; but does it, therefore, deserve the name only of presumption or conjecture?

Demea: Good God! cried *Demea,* interrupting him, where are we? Zealous defenders of religion allow that the proofs of a Deity fall short of perfect evidence! And you, *Philo,* on whose assistance I depended in proving the adorable mysteriousness of the Divine Nature, do you assent to all these extravagant opinions of *Cleanthes?* For what other name can I give them? or, why spare my censure when such principles are advanced, supported by such an authority, before so young a man as *Pamphilus?*

Philo: You seem not to apprehend, replied *Philo,* that I argue with *Cleanthes* in his own way, and, by showing him the dangerous consequences of his tenets, hope at last to reduce him to our opinion. But what sticks most with you, I observe, is the representation which *Cleanthes* has made of the argument *a posteriori;* and, finding that that argument is likely to escape your hold and vanish into air, you think it so disguised that you can scarcely believe it to be set in its true light. Now, however much I may dissent, in other respects, from the dangerous principle of *Cleanthes,* I must allow that he has fairly represented that argument, and I shall endeavor so to state the matter to you that you will entertain no further scruples with regard to it.

Were a man to abstract from everything which he knows or has seen, he would be altogether incapable, merely from his own ideas, to determine what kind of scene the universe must be, or to give the preference to one state or situation of things above another. For as nothing which he clearly conceives could be esteemed impossible or implying a contradiction, every chimera of his fancy would be upon an equal footing; nor could he assign any just reason why he adheres to one idea or system, and rejects the others which are equally possible.

Again, after he opens his eyes and contemplates the world as it really is, it would be impossible for him at first to assign the cause of any one event, much less of the whole of things, or of the universe. He might set his fancy a rambling, and she might bring him in an infinite variety of reports and representations. These would all be possible; but, being all equally possible, he would never of himself give a satisfactory account for his preferring one of them to the rest. Experience alone can point out to him the true cause of any phenomenon.

Now, according to this method of reasoning, *Demea,* it follows (and is, indeed, tacitly allowed by *Cleanthes* himself) that order, arrangement, or the adjustment of final causes, is not of itself any proof of design, but only so far as it has been experienced to proceed from that principle. For aught we can know *a priori,* matter may contain the source or spring of order originally within itself, as well as mind does; and there is no more difficulty in conceiving that the several elements, from an internal unknown cause, may fall into the most exquisite arrangement, than to conceive that their ideas, in the great universal mind, from a like internal unknown cause, fall into that arrangement. The equal possibility of both these suppositions is allowed. But, by experience, we find, according to *Cleanthes,* that there is a difference between them. Throw several pieces of steel together, without shape or form; they will never arrange themselves so as to compose a watch. Stone and mortar and wood, without an architect, never erect a house. But the ideas in a human mind, we see, by an unknown, inexplicable economy, arrange themselves so as to form the plan of a watch or house. Experience, therefore, proves that there is an original principle of order in mind, not in matter. From similar effects we infer similar causes. The adjustment of means to ends is alike in the universe, as in a machine of human contrivance. The causes, therefore, must be resembling.

I was from the beginning scandalized, I must own, with this resemblance which is asserted between the Deity and human creatures, and must conceive it to imply such a degradation of the Supreme Being as no sound theist could endure. With your assistance, therefore, *Demea,* I shall endeavor to defend what you justly call the adorable mysteriousness of the Divine Nature, and shall refute this reasoning of *Cleanthes,* provided he allows that I have made a fair representation of it.

When *Cleanthes* had assented, *Philo,* after a short pause, proceeded in the following manner.

That all inferences, *Cleanthes,* concerning fact are founded on experience, and that all experimental reasonings are founded on the supposition that similar causes prove similar effects, and similar effects similar causes, I shall not at present much dispute with you. But observe, I entreat you, with what extreme caution all just reasoners proceed in the transferring of experiments to similar cases. Unless the cases be exactly similar, they repose no perfect confidence in applying their past observation to any particular phenomenon. Every alteration of circumstances occasions a doubt concerning the event; and it requires new experiments to prove certainly that the new circumstances are of no moment or importance. A change in bulk, situation, arrangement, age, disposition of the air, or surrounding bodies; any of these particulars may be attended with the most unexpected consequences. And unless the objects be quite familiar to us, it is the highest temerity to expect with assurance, after any of these changes, an event similar to that which before fell under our observation. The slow and deliberate steps of philosophers here, if anywhere, are distinguished from the precipitate march of the vulgar, who, hurried on by the smallest similitude, are incapable of all discernment or consideration.

But can you think, *Cleanthes,* that your usual phlegm and philosophy have been preserved in so wide a step as you have taken when you compared to the universe houses, ships, furniture, machines; and, from their similarity in some circumstances, inferred a similarity in their causes? Thought, design, intelligence, such as we discover in men and other animals, is no more than one of the springs and principles of the universe, as well as heat or cold, attraction or repulsion, and a hundred others which fall under daily observation. It is an active cause by which some particular parts of nature, we find, produce alterations on other parts. But can a conclusion, with any propriety, be transferred from parts to the whole? Does not the great disproportion bar all comparison and inference? From observing the growth of a hair, can we learn anything concerning the generation of a man? Would the manner of a leaf's blowing, even though perfectly known, afford us any instruction concerning the vegetation of a tree?

But allowing that we were to take the *operations* of one part of nature upon another for the foundation of our judgment concerning the *origin* of the whole (which never can be admitted), yet why select so minute, so weak, so bounded a principle as the reason and design of animals is found to be upon this planet? What peculiar privilege has this little agitation of the brain which we call "thought," that we must thus make it the model of the whole universe? Our partiality in our own favor does indeed present it on all occasions, but sound philosophy ought carefully to guard against so natural an illusion.

So far from admitting, continued *Philo,* that the operations of a part can afford us any just conclusion concerning the origin of the whole, I will not allow any one part to form a rule for another part if the latter be very remote from the former. Is there any reasonable ground to conclude that the inhabitants of other planets possess thought, intelligence, reason, or anything similar to these faculties in men? When nature has so extremely diversified her manner of operation in this small globe, can we imagine that she incessantly copies herself throughout so immense a universe? And if thought, as we may well suppose, be confined merely to this narrow corner, and has even there so limited a sphere of action, with what propriety can we assign it for the original cause of all things? The narrow views of a peasant who makes his domestic economy the rule for the government of kingdoms is in comparison a pardonable sophism.

But were we ever so much assured that a thought and reason resembling the human were to be found throughout the whole universe, and were its activity elsewhere vastly greater and more commanding than it appears in this globe; yet I cannot see why the operations of a world constituted, arranged, adjusted, can with any propriety be extended to a world which is in its embryo-state, and is advancing towards that constitution and arrangement. By observation we know somewhat of the economy, action, and nourishment of a finished animal; but we must transfer with great caution that observation to the growth of a foetus in the womb, and still more to the formation of an animalcule in the loins of its male parent. Nature, we find, even from our limited experience, possesses an infinite number of springs and principles which incessantly discover themselves on every change of her position and situation. And what new and unknown principles would actuate her in so new and unknown a situation as that of the formation of a universe, we cannot, without the utmost temerity, pretend to determine.

A very small part of this great system, during a very short time, is very imperfectly discovered to us; and do we thence pronounce decisively concerning the origin of the whole?

Admirable conclusion! Stone, wood, brick, iron, brass, have not, at this time, in this minute globe of earth, an order or arrangement without human art and contrivance; therefore, the universe could not originally attain its order and arrangement without something similar to human art. But is a part of nature a rule for another part very wide of the former? Is it a rule for the whole? Is a very small part a rule for the universe? Is nature in one situation a certain rule for nature in another situation vastly different from the former?

And can you blame me, *Cleanthes*, if I here imitate the prudent reserve of *Simonides*, who, according to the noted story, being asked by *Hiero, What God was?* desired a day to think of it, and then two days more; and after than manner continually prolonged the term, without ever bringing in his definition or description? Could you even blame me if I had answered, at first, *that I did not know*, and was sensible that this subject lay vastly beyond the reach of my faculties? You might cry out skeptic and raillier, as much as you pleased; but, having found in so many other subjects much more familiar the imperfections and even contradictions of human reason, I never should expect any success from its feeble conjectures in a subject so sublime and so remote from the sphere of our observation. When two *species* of objects have always been observed to be conjoined together, I can *infer,* by custom, the existence of one wherever I see the existence of the other; and this I call an argument from experience. But how this argument can have place where the objects, as in the present case, are single, individual, without parallel or specific resemblance, may be difficult to explain. And will any man tell me with a serious countenance that an orderly universe must arise from some thought and art like the human because we have experience of it? To ascertain this reasoning it were requisite that we had experience of the origin of worlds; and it is not sufficient, surely, that we have seen ships and cities arise from human art and contrivance. . . .

Philo: But to show you still more inconveniences, continued *Philo,* in your anthropomorphism, please to take a new survey of your principles. *Like effects prove like causes.* This is the experimental argument; and this, you say too, is the sole theological argument. Now it is certain that the liker the effects are which are seen and the liker the causes which are inferred, the stronger is the argument. Every departure on either side diminishes the probability and renders the experiment less conclusive. You cannot doubt of the principle; neither ought you to reject its consequences.

All the new discoveries in astronomy which prove the immense grandeur and magnificence of the works of nature are so many additional arguments for a Deity, according to the true system of theism; but, according to your hypothesis of experimental theism, they become so many objections, by removing the effect still farther from all resemblance to the effects of human art and contrivance. For if *Lucretius,* even following the old system of the world, could exclaim:

> Who is strong enough to rule the sun, who to hold in hand and control the mighty bridle of the unfathomable deep? who to turn about all the heavens at one time, and warm the fruitful worlds with ethereal fires, or to be present in all places and at all times.

If Tully esteemed this reasoning so natural as to put it into the mouth of his Epicurean:

> What power of mental vision enabled your master Plato to descry the vast and elaborate architectural process which, as he makes out, the deity adopted in building the structure of the universe? What method of engineering was employed? What tools and levers and derricks? What agents carried out so vast an understanding? And how were air, fire, water, and earth enabled to obey and execute the will of the architect?

If this argument, I say, had any force in former ages, how much greater must it have at present when the bounds of nature are so infinitely enlarged and such a magnificent scene is opened to us? It is still more unreasonable to form our idea of so unlimited a cause from our experience of the narrow productions of human design and invention.

The discoveries by microscopes, as they open a new universe in miniature, are still objections, according to you; arguments, according to me. The farther we push our researches of this kind, we are still led to infer the universal cause of all to be vastly different from mankind, or from any object of human experience and observation.

And what say you to the discoveries in anatomy, chemistry, botany? . . . *Cleanthes:* These surely are no objections, replied *Cleanthes;* they only discover new instances of art and contrivance. It is still the image of mind reflected on us from innumerable objects. *Philo:* Add a mind *like the human,* said *Philo. Cleanthes:* I know of no other, replied *Cleanthes. Philo:* And the liker, the better, insisted *Philo. Cleanthes:* To be sure, said *Cleanthes.*

Philo: Now, *Cleanthes,* said *Philo,* with an air of alacrity and triumph, mark the consequences. *First,* by this method of reasoning you renounce all claim to infinity in any of the attributes of the Deity. For, as the cause ought only to be proportioned to the effect, and the effect, so far as it falls under our cognizance, is not infinite: What pretensions have we, upon your suppositions, to ascribe that attribute to the Divine Being? You will still insist that, by removing him so much from all similarity to human creatures, we give in to the most arbitrary hypothesis, and at the same time weaken all proofs of his existence.

Secondly, you have no reason, on your theory, for ascribing perfection to the Deity, even in his finite capacity; or for supposing him free from every error, mistake, or incoherence, in his undertakings. There are many inexplicable difficulties in the works of Nature which, if we allow a perfect author to be proved *a priori,* are easily solved, and become only seeming difficulties from the narrow capacity of man, who cannot trace infinite relations. But according to your method of reasoning, these difficulties become all real; and, perhaps, will be insisted on as new instances of likeness to human art and contrivance. At least, you must acknowledge that it is impossible for us to tell, from our limited views, whether this system contains any great faults or deserves any considerable praise if compared to other possible and even real systems. Could a peasant, if the *Aeneid* were read to him, pronounce that poem to be absolutely faultless, or even assign to it its proper rank among the productions of human wit, he who had never seen any other production?

But were this world ever so perfect a production, it must still remain uncertain whether all the excellences of the work can justly be ascribed to the workman. If we survey a ship, what an exalted idea must we form of the ingenuity of the carpenter who framed so complicated, useful, and beautiful a machine? And what surprise must we feel when we find him a stupid mechanic who imitated others, and copied an art which, through a long succession of ages, after multiplied trials, mistakes, corrections, deliberations, and controversies, had been gradually improving? Many worlds might have been botched and bungled, throughout an eternity, ere this system was struck out; much labor lost; many fruitless trials made; and a slow but continued improvement carried on during infinite ages in the art of world-making. In such subjects, who can determine where the truth, nay, who can conjecture where the probability lies, amidst a great number of hypotheses which may be proposed, and a still greater which may be imagined?

And what shadow of an argument, continued *Philo,* can you produce from your hypothesis to prove the unity of the Deity? A great number of men join in building a house or ship, in rearing a city, in framing a commonwealth; why may not several deities combine in contriving and framing a world? This is only so much greater similarity to human affairs. By sharing the work among several, we may so much further limit the attributes of each, and get rid of that extensive power and knowledge which must be supposed in one deity, and which, according to you, can only serve to weaken the proof of his existence. And if such foolish, such vicious creatures as man can yet often unite in framing and executing one plan, how much more those deities or demons, whom we may suppose several degrees more perfect?

To multiply causes without necessity is indeed contrary to true philosophy, but this principle applies not to the present case. Were one deity antecedently proved by your theory who were possessed of every attribute requisite to the production of the universe, it would be needless, I own (though not absurd), to suppose any other deity existent. But while it is still a question whether all these attributes are united in one subject or dispersed among several independent beings; by what phenomena in nature can we pretend to decide the controversy? Where we see a body raised in a scale, we are sure that there is in the opposite scale, however concealed from

sight, some counterpoising weight equal to it; but it is still allowed to doubt whether that weight be an aggregate of several distinct bodies or one uniform united mass. And if the weight requisite very much exceeds anything which we have ever seen conjoined in any single body, the former supposition becomes still more probable and natural. And intelligent being of such vast power and capacity as is necessary to produce the universe, or, to speak in the language of ancient philosophy, so prodigious an animal, exceeds all analogy and even comprehension.

But further, *Cleanthes,* men are mortal, and renew their species by generation; and this is common to all living creatures. The two great sexes of male and female, says *Milton,* animate the world. Why must this circumstance, so universal, so essential, be excluded from those numerous and limited deities? Behold, then, the theogeny of ancient times brought back upon us.

And why not become a perfect anthropomorphite? Why not assert the deity or deities to be corporeal, and to have eyes, a nose, mouth, ears, etc.? *Epicurus* maintained that no man had ever seen reason but in a human figure; therefore, the gods must have a human figure. And this argument, which is deservedly so much ridiculed by *Cicero,* becomes, according to you, solid and philosophical.

In a word, *Cleanthes,* a man who follows your hypothesis is able, perhaps, to assert or conjecture that the universe sometime arose from something like design: But beyond that position he cannot ascertain one single circumstance, and is left afterwards to fix every point of his theology by the utmost license of fancy and hypothesis. This world, for aught he knows, is very faulty and imperfect, compared to a superior standard; and was only the first rude essay of some infant deity who afterwards abandoned it, ashamed of his lame performance: It is the work only of some dependent, inferior deity, and is the object of derision to his superiors: It is the production of old age and dotage in some superannuated deity; and ever since his death has run on at adventures, from the first impulse and active force which it received from him. . . . You justly give signs of horror,

Demea, at these strange suppositions; but these, and a thousand more of the same kind, are *Cleanthes'* suppositions, not mine. From the moment the attributes of the Deity are supposed finite, all these have place. And I cannot, for my part, think that so wild and unsettled a system of theology is, in any respect, preferable to none at all.

Cleanthes: These suppositions I absolutely disown, cried *Cleanthes:* They strike me, how-ever, with no horror, especially when proposed in that rambling way in which they drop from you. On the contrary, they give me pleasure when I see that, by the utmost indulgence of your imagination, you never get rid of the hypothesis of design in the universe, but are obliged at every turn to have recourse to it. To this concession I adhere steadily; and this I regard as a sufficient foundation for religion.

3.6 Whence This Consciousness?

One might imagine that Hume's critique of the teleological argument (see Reading 3.5) put an end to the matter, but it didn't. In 1802 William Paley published, in *Natural Theology, or Evidences of the Existence and Attributes of the Deity Collected from the Appearances of Nature,* a version of the teleological argument that became very popular. At the heart of Paley's argument is an analogy between the natural order of the universe and a machine. Just as machines (such as watches) exhibit designed order because they are made by an intelligent agent, so too the natural order must be designed by a divine intelligence.

This argument had considerable weight until Darwin's theory of evolution (1850) provided a scientific alternative. According to Darwin, life is the result of a long history of changes. Each new generation inherits from the past those traits that have proved successful in adapting a life form to its environment.

Theological and philosophical responses to Darwin have varied. Some argue for "creation science," rejecting the notion that species can change and asserting that God is the cause of all distinct forms of life. Others opt for "guided evolution," maintaining that God uses evolution as the means to design and develop life. Still others rework the teleological argument into an argument from probability. They maintain that the odds against life as we know it coming about by the blind forces of evolution and chance are astronomical. Hence mathematical probability is on the side of there having been an intelligent designer.

Certain of the more recent probability versions of the design argument utilize the anthropic principle. This principle was developed in physics to explain why the universe in our region of space–time is the way it is. If it were not this way—that is, if nature did not exhibit certain laws—then humans (*anthropos* in Greek) would not have evolved. If human consciousness had not evolved, then human observation and hence physical science (among other things) would not be possible.

Some have generalized this anthropic principle to apply to the whole universe. They argue that so many things could have gone wrong in the development of the universe that chance alone cannot explain the existence of human consciousness. Someone has claimed that the probability of life evolving on earth by chance is roughly the same as the probability of a tornado assemblying the parts of a 747 spread across a field into a functioning airplane.

These neoteleologists interpret the anthropic design argument as showing that some kind of extracosmic intelligence (God) designed the universe in such a way that life—and eventually human life—would emerge. Perhaps, however, it does not show that God exists but rather that Brahman does.

"Brahman," you say. Who or what is that? According to Sri Aurobindo (1872–1950), Brahman is Infinite Consciousness. Brahman involutes (contracts) aspects of itself until it reaches an outer limit of "inconscient," or unconscious, matter. But Brahman cannot be content with total inconscience—a universe devoid of life and intelligence—because then the universe would be the total opposite of an Infinite Consciousness. Over time, an inconscient universe evolves into a conscient one. Life, awareness, and human consciousness eventually emerge out of what appears to be lifeless matter, reflecting their true source.

In the selection that follows, Aurobindo argues that Chance, Necessity, and Theism (here understood as a extracosmic Creator), cannot explain certain features of the universe. Only if the Divine is immanent in the universe can these features be explained. Although Aurobindo nowhere mentions the anthropic principle, his argument clearly anticipates those who use that principle to breathe new life into the teleological argument.

However, Aurobindo is himself not overly impressed with this line of reasoning. Granted, a case can be made for the hypothesis that an initial "Consciousness-Force" needs to be posited in order to account for the emergence of consciousness out of what appears to be unconscious matter. Nevertheless, this argument does not leave us with a great deal of certitude. We need in addition the mystical experience of unity with Brahman.

It is not surprising that Aurobindo finds personal mystical experience the most persuasive. It reflects the claims of his religious tradition and his own personal experiences. Aurobindo was born in India and educated in England. He was imprisoned in 1908 for participating in an Indian nationalist movement and, while in prison, had a powerful mystical experience. Upon his release, he settled in Pondicherry, India, and began an ashram (religious community). He wrote a massive book, *The Life Divine,* in which he set forth his principal ideas. What follows is a very small part of that 1000-page book.

Reading Questions

1. What is it, according to Aurobindo, that is fundamentally unintelligible about the "formulae of Science"?
2. According to Aurobindo, "Chance" and "mechanical Necessity" will not work as an explanation for the order of nature. Why?
3. Theistic explanations of nature that involve the positing of an "extracosmic Divinity" also are not adequate, according to Aurobindo. Why?
4. According to Aurobindo, what hypothesis makes the most sense, and why is it the best explanation of the emergence of consciousness in nature?
5. Do you find Aurobindo's arguments convincing? Why or why not?

Whence This Consciousness?*

SRI AUROBINDO

A CONSCIOUSNESS-FORCE, everywhere inherent in Existence, acting even when concealed, is the creator of the worlds, the occult secret of Nature. . . .

Actually to our Science this infinite or indeterminate Existence reveals itself as an Energy, known not by itself but by its works, which throws up in its motion waves of energism and in them a multitude of infinitesimals; these, grouping themselves to form larger infinitesimals, become a basis for all the creations of the Energy, even those farthest away from the material basis, for the emergence of a world of organised Matter, for the emergence of Life, for the emergence of Consciousness, for all the still unexplained activities of evolutionary Nature. On the original process are erected a multitude of processes which we can observe, follow, can take advantage of many of them, utilise; but they are none of them, fundamentally, explicable. We know now that different groupings and a varying number of electric infinitesimals can produce or serve as the constituent occasion—miscalled the cause, for here there seems to be only a necessary antecedent condition—for the appearance of larger atomic infinitesimals of different natures, qualities, powers; but we fail to discover how these different dispositions can come to constitute these different atoms,—how the differentiæ in the constituent occasion or cause necessitate the differentiæ in the constituted outcome or result. We know also that certain combinations of certain invisible atomic infinitesimals produce or occasion new and visible determinations quite different in nature, quality and power from the constituent infinitesimals; but we fail to discover, for instance, how a fixed formula for the combi-

nation of oxygen and hydrogen comes to determine the appearance of water which is evidently something more than a combination of gases, a new creation, a new form of substance, a material manifestation of a quite new character. We see that a seed develops into a tree, we follow the line of the process of production and we utilise it; but we do not discover how a tree can grow out of a seed, how the life and form of the tree come to be implied in the substance or energy of the seed or, if that be rather the fact, how the seed can develop into a tree. We know that genes and chromosomes are the cause of hereditary transmissions, not only of physical but of psychological variations; but we do not discover how psychological characteristics can be contained and transmitted in this inconscient material vehicle. We do not see or know, but it is expounded to us as a cogent account of Nature-process, that a play of electrons, of atoms and their resultant molecules, of cells, glands, chemical secretions and physiological processes manages by their activity on the nerves and brain of a Shakespeare or a Plato to produce or could be perhaps the dynamic occasion for the production of a *Hamlet* or a *Symposium* or a *Republic;* but we fail to discover or appreciate how such material movements could have composed or necessitated the composition of these highest points of thought and literature: the divergence here of the determinants and the determination becomes so wide that we are no longer able to follow the process, much less understand or utilise. These formulæ of Science may be pragmatically correct and infallible, they may govern the practical how of Nature's processes, but they do not disclose the intrinsic how or why; rather they have the air of the formulæ of a cos-

* From Part 1, Chapter 1, "Indeterminates, Cosmic Determinations and the Indeterminable," *The Life Divine*. 3d ed. New York, NY: India Library Society, 1965. Copyright © 1965 The Sri Aurobindo Ashram Trust. Used by permission.

mic Magician, precise, irresistible, automatically successful each in its field, but their rationale is fundamentally unintelligible.

There is more to perplex us; for we see the original indeterminate Energy throwing out general determinates of itself,—we might equally in their relation to the variety of their products call them generic indeterminates,—with their appropriate states of substance and determined forms of that substance: the latter are numerous, sometimes innumerable variations on the substance-energy which is their base: but none of these variations seems to be predetermined by anything in the nature of the general indeterminate. An electric Energy produces positive, negative, neutral forms of itself, forms that are at once waves and particles; a gaseous state of energy-substance produces a considerable number of different gases; a solid state of energy-substance from which results the earth principle develops into different forms of earth and rock of many kinds and numerous minerals and metals; a life principle produces its vegetable kingdom teeming with a countless foison of quite different plants, trees, flowers; a principle of animal life produces an enormous variety of genus, species, individual variations: so it proceeds into human life and mind and its mind-types towards the still unwritten end or perhaps the yet occult sequel of that unfinished evolutionary chapter. Throughout there is the constant rule of a general sameness in the original determinate and, subject to this substantial sameness of basic substance and nature, a profuse variation in the generic and individual determinates; an identical law obtains of sameness or similarity in the genus or species with numerous variations often meticulously minute in the individual. But we do not find anything in any general or generic determinate necessitating the variant determinations that result from it. A necessity of immutable sameness at the base, of free and unaccountable variations on the surface seems to be the law; but who or what necessitates or determines? What is the rationale of the determination, what is its original truth or its significance? What compels or impels this exuberant play of varying possibilities which seem to have no aim or meaning unless it

be the beauty or delight of creation? A Mind, a seeking and curious inventive Thought, a hidden determining Will might be there, but there is no trace of it in the first and fundamental appearance of material Nature.

A first possible explanation points to a self-organising dynamic Chance that is at work,—a paradox necessitated by the appearance of inevitable order on one side, of unaccountable freak and fantasy on the other side of the cosmic phenomenon we call Nature. An inconscient and inconsequent Force, we may say, that acts at random and creates this or that by a general chance without any determining principle,—determinations coming in only as the result of a persistent repetition of the same rhythm of action and succeeding because only this repetitive rhythm could succeed in keeping things in being,—this is the energy of Nature. But this implies that somewhere in the origin of things there is a boundless Possibility or a womb of innumerable possibilities that are manifested out of it by the original Energy,—an incalculable Inconscient which we find some embarrassment in calling either an Existence or a Non-Existence; for without some such origin and basis the appearance and the action of the Energy is unintelligible. Yet an opposite aspect of the nature of the cosmic phenomenon as we see it appears to forbid the theory of a random action generating a persistent order. There is too much of an iron insistence on order, on a law basing the possibilities. One would be justified rather in supposing that there is an inherent imperative Truth of things unseen by us, but a Truth capable of manifold manifestation, throwing out a multitude of possibilities and variants of itself which the creative Energy by its action turns into so many realised actualities. This brings us to a second explanation—a mechanical necessity in things, its workings recognisable by us as so many mechanical laws of Nature;—the necessity, we might say, of some such secret inherent Truth of things as we have supposed, governing automatically the processes we observe in action in the universe. But a theory of mechanical Necessity by itself does not elucidate the free play of the endless unaccountable variations which are visible in the evolution: there must be behind the Necessity or in it a law of unity associated with a co-existent but dependent law of multiplicity, both insisting on manifestation; but the unity of what, the multiplicity of what? Mechanical Necessity can give no answer. Again the emergence of consciousness out of the Inconscient is a stumbling-block in the way of this theory; for it is a phenomenon which can have no place in an all-pervading truth of inconscient mechanical Necessity. If there is a necessity which compels the emergence, it can be only this, that there is already a consciousness concealed in the Inconscient, waiting for evolution and when all is ready breaking out from its prison of apparent Nescience. We may indeed get rid of the difficulty of the imperative order of things by supposing that it does not exist, that determinism in Nature is imposed on it by our thought which needs such an imperative order to enable it to deal with its surroundings, but in reality there is no such thing; there is only a Force experimenting in a random action of infinitesimals which build up in their general results different determinations by a repetitive persistence operative in the sum of their action; thus we go back from Necessity to Chance as the basis of our existence. But what then is this Mind, this Consciousness which differs so radically from the Energy that produced it that for its action it has to impose its idea and need of order on the world she has made and in which it is obliged to live? There would then be the double contradiction of consciousness emerging from a fundamental Inconscience and of a Mind of order and reason manifesting as the brilliant final consequence of a world created by inconscient Chance. These things may be possible, but they need a better explanation than any yet given before we can accord to them our acceptance.

This opens the way for other explanations which make Consciousness the creator of this world out of an apparent original Inconscience. A Mind, a Will seems to have imagined and organised the universe, but it has veiled itself behind its creation; its first erection has been this screen of an inconscient Energy and a material form of substance, at once a disguise of its presence and a plastic creative basis on which it could work as an artisan uses for his production of forms and patterns a dumb and obedient material. All these things we see around us are then the thoughts of an extra-cosmic Divinity, a Being with an omnipotent and omniscient Mind and Will, who is responsible for the mathematical law of the physical universe, for its artistry of beauty, for its strange play of samenesses and variations, of concordances and discords, of combining and intermingling opposites, for the drama of consciousness struggling to exist and seeking to affirm itself in an inconscient universal order. The fact that this Divinity is invisible to us, undiscoverable by our mind and senses, offers no difficulty, since self-evidence or direct sign of an extracosmic Creator could not be expected in a cosmos which is void of his presence: the patent signals everywhere of the works of an Intelligence, of law, design, formula, adaptation of means to end, constant and inexhaustible invention, fantasy even but restrained by an ordering Reason might be considered sufficient proof of this origin of things. Or if this Creator is not entirely supracosmic, but is also immanent in his works, even then there need be no other sign of him,—except indeed to some consciousness evolving in this inconscient world, but only when its evolution reached a point at which it could become aware of the indwelling Presence. The intervention of this evolving consciousness would not be a difficulty, since there would be no contradiction of the basic nature of things in its appearance; an onmipotent Mind could easily infuse something of itself into its creatures. One difficulty remains; it is the arbitrary nature of the creation, the incomprehensibility of its purpose, the crude meaninglessness of its law of unnecessary ignorance, strife and suffering, its ending without a denouement or issue. A play? But why this stamp of so many undivine elements and characters in the play of One whose nature must be supposed to be divine? To the suggestion that what we see worked out in the world is the thoughts of God, the retort can be made that God could well have had better thoughts and the best thought of all would have been to refrain from the creation of an unhappy and unintelligible universe. All theistic explanations of existence starting from an extra-cosmic Deity stumble over this difficulty and can only evade it; it would disappear only if the creator were, even though exceeding the creation, yet immanent in it, himself in some sort both the player and the play, an Infinite casting infinite possibilities into the set form of an evolutionary cosmic order.

On that hypothesis, there must be behind the action of the material Energy a secret involved Consciousness, cosmic, infinite, building up through the action of that frontal Energy its means of an evolutionary manifestation, a creation out of itself in the boundless finite of the material universe. The apparent inconscience of the material Energy would be an indispensable condition for the structure of the material world-substance in which this Consciousness intends to involve itself so that it may grow by evolution out of its apparent opposite; for without some such device a complete involution would be impossible. If there is such a creation by the Infinite out of itself, it must be the manifestation, in a material disguise, of truths or powers of its own being: the forms or vehicles of these truths or powers would be the basic general or fundamental determinates we see in Nature; the particular determinates, which otherwise are unaccountable variations that have emerged from the vague general stuff in which they originate, would be the appropriate forms or vehicles of the possibilities that the truths or powers residing in these fundamentals bore within them. The principle of free variation of possibilities natural to an infinite Consciousness would be the explanation of the aspect of inconscient Chance of which we are aware in the workings of Nature,—inconscient only in appearance and so appearing because of the complete involution in Matter, because of the veil with which the secret Consciousness has disguised its presence. The principle of truths, real powers of the Infinite imperatively fulfilling themselves would be the explanation of the opposite aspect of a mechanical Necessity which we see in Nature,—mechanical in appearance only

and so appearing because of the same veil of Inconscience. It would then be perfectly intelligible why the Inconscient does its works with a constant principle of mathematical architecture, of design, of effective arrangement of numbers, of adaptation of means to ends, of inexhaustible device and invention, one might almost say, a constant experimental skill and an automatism of purpose. The appearance of consciousness out of an apparent Inconscience would also be no longer inexplicable.

All the unexplained processes of Nature would find their meaning and their place if this hypothesis proved to be tenable. Energy seems to create substance, but, in reality, as existence is inherent in Consciousness-Force, so also substance would be inherent in Energy,—the Energy a manifestation of the Force, substance a manifestation of the secret Existence. But as it is a spiritual substance, it would not be apprehended by the material sense until it is given by Energy the forms of Matter seizable by that sense. One begins to understand also how arrangement of design, quantity and number can be a base for the manifestation of quality and property; for design, quantity and number are powers of existence-substance, quality and property are powers of the consciousness and its force that reside in the existence; they can then be made manifest and operative by a rhythm and process of substance. The growth of the tree out of the seed would be accounted for, like all other similar phenomena, by the indwelling presence of what we have called the Real-Idea; the Infinite's self-perception of the significant form, the living body of its power of existence that has to emerge from its own self-compression in energy-substance, would be carried internally in the form of the seed, carried in the occult consciousness involved in that form, and would naturally evolve out of it. There would be no difficulty either in understanding on this principle how infinitesimals of a material character like the gene and the chromosome can carry in them psychological elements to be transmitted to the physical form that has to emerge from the human seed; it would be at bottom on the same principle in the objectivity of Matter as that which we find in our subjective experience,—for we see that the subconscient physical carries in it a mental psychological content, impressions of past events, habits, fixed mental and vital formations, fixed forms of character, and sends them up by an occult process to the waking consciousness, thus originating or influencing many activities of our nature.

On the same basis there would be no difficulty in understanding why the physiological functionings of the body help to determine the mind's psychological actions: for the body is not mere unconscious Matter; it is a structure of a secretly conscious Energy that has taken form in it. Itself occultly conscious, it is, at the same time, the vehicle of expression of an overt Consciousness that has emerged and is self-aware in our physical energy-substance. The body's functionings are a necessary machinery or instrumentation for the movements of this mental Inhabitant; it is only by setting the corporeal instrument in motion that the Conscious Being emerging, evolving in it can transmit its mind formations, will formations and turn them into a physical manifestation of itself in Matter. The capacity, the processes of the instrument must to a certain extent reshape the mind formations in their transition from mental shape into physical expression; its workings are necessary and must exercise their influence before that expression can become actual. The bodily instrument may even in some directions dominate its user; it may too by a force of habit suggest or create involuntary reactions of the consciousness inhabiting it before the working Mind and Will can control or interfere. All this is possible because the body has a "subconscient" consciousness of its own which counts in our total self-expression; even, if we look at this outer instrumentation only, we can conclude that body determines mind, but this is only a minor truth and the major Truth is that mind determines body. In this view a still deeper Truth becomes conceivable; a spiritual entity ensouling the substance that veils it is the original determinant of both mind and body. On the other side, in the opposite order of process,— that by which the mind can transmit its ideas and commands to the body, can train it to be an instrument for new action, can even so impress it with its habitual demands or orders that the physical instinct carries them out automatically even when the mind is no longer consciously willing them, those also more unusual but well attested by which to an extraordinary and hardly limitable extent the mind can learn to determine the reactions of the body even to the overriding of its normal law or conditions of action,—these and other otherwise unaccountable aspects of the relation between these two elements of our being become easily understandable: for it is the secret consciousness in the living matter that receives from its greater companion; it is this in the body that in its own involved and occult fashion perceives or feels the demand on it and obeys the emerged or evolved consciousness which presides over the body. Finally, the conception of a divine Mind and Will creating the cosmos becomes justifiable, while at the same time the perplexing elements in it which our reasoning mentality refuses to ascribe to an arbitrary fiat of the Creator, find their explanation as inevitable phenomena of a Consciousness emerging with difficulty out of its opposite—but with the mission to override these contrary phenomena and manifest by a slow and difficult evolution its greater reality and true nature.

But an approach from the material end of Existence cannot give us any certitude of validity for this hypothesis or for that matter for any other explanation of Nature and her procedure: the veil cast by the original Inconscience is too thick for the Mind to pierce and it is behind this veil that is hidden the secret origination of what is manifested; there are seated the truths and powers underlying the phenomena and processes that appear to us in the material front of Nature. To know with greater certitude we must follow the curve of evolving consciousness until it arrives at a height and largeness of self-enlightenment in which the primal secret is self-discovered; for presumably it must evolve, must eventually bring out what was held from the beginning by the occult original Consciousness in things of which it is a gradual manifestation.

3.7 The Ontological Argument

Is the existence of this book necessary? Is Canada's existence necessary? Is it necessary that you exist? Could this world exist and this book, Canada, and you not be items existing in this world?

The answer seems obvious. Of course this book, Canada, and you need not exist. Existence, as we normally think of it, is contingent or conditional. The existence of things is dependent on a number of complex factors and causes. Take away the causes, and those things that are contingent on them would not be. Hence it is possible for them not to exist.

Is the existence of ultimate reality also contingent? St. Anselm (1033–1109) thought that it was not. Ultimate reality is the greatest possible reality that we can think of. Nothing greater than it can be conceived. That is why we call it ultimate. If St. Anselm is right, then there is at least one thing whose existence is not contingent. Its existence is necessary. It is impossible that it not exist.

Unlike the cosmological and teleological arguments for God's existence (see Readings 3.1–3.6), the ontological argument is purely *a priori*. It depends entirely on how we define God. If we define God as ultimate reality, and if we mean by that the greatest possible that can be thought, then God must exist. Only a fool would think otherwise.

Let us define God as that than which nothing greater can be conceived. In other words, God is the greatest possible being of whom we can think. If we think of existing things in terms of a scale of perfection ranging from the least perfect to the most perfect, God is at the top of the scale. If you understand this definition, then God exists as an idea in your mind or understanding. Which is greater, to exist as a concept in the mind or to exist both in the mind and outside the mind? "Both inside and outside," you might reply. St. Anselm would agree.

His version of the ontological argument, as we shall soon see, takes the form of a *reductio ad absurdum* ("reduction to absurdity"). Suppose that the greatest conceivable being (God) exists *only* in your mind. This, however, cannot be. It is a contradiction, because you have already admitted it is greater to exist both in and outside the mind. Therefore, if God is a being that is truly ultimate (the greatest possible that can be thought), God must exist independently of your idea of God.

"Something is fishy here," you might well say. You are not alone. A Christian monk named Gaunilo, a contemporary of Anselm, thought there was something fishy too. Suppose there is an island that no one knows about. Suppose further that this island is perfect. It is the greatest possible island—an ultimate island, if you will. Should we conclude with confidence that it must exist just because it is the most perfect? Gaunilo thinks not, but St. Anselm cries, "False analogy!"

Before you work through the ins and outs of this debate, note that the ontological argument, unlike either the cosmological or the teleological argument, is an argument whose conclusion clearly leads to the other great-making attributes of God, such as omnipotence, omniscience, omnibenevolence, and the like. If the cosmological argument succeeds, the most it proves is that the cosmos had a cause or causes. Need this cause be God? If the teleological argument succeeds, the most it proves is that the order of the world results from intelligent design. Need this intelligence(s) be all-powerful, all-knowing, and all-good? If the ontological argument succeeds, then all the other perfections traditionally associated (at least in classic Western theism) with God follow.

Reading Questions

1. What role does St. Anselm's distinction between what exists in the understanding and what exists outside the understanding play in his argument?
2. What do you think is the key notion in the ontological argument?
3. What is Gaunilo's criticism, and how does St. Anselm respond?
4. Who do you think is right, St. Anselm or Gaunilo? Why?

The Ontological Argument*

ST. ANSELM AND GAUNILO

Truly there is a God, although the fool hath said in his heart, There is no God.

And so, Lord, do thou, who dost give understanding to faith, give me, so far as thou knowest it to be profitable, to understand that thou art as we believe; and that thou art that which we believe. And, indeed, we believe that thou art a being than which nothing greater can be conceived. Or is there no such nature, since the fool hath said in his heart, there is no God? (Psalms xiii, 1). But, at any rate, this very fool, when he hears of this being of which I speak—a being than which nothing greater can be conceived—understands what he hears, and what he understands is in his understanding; although he does not understand it to exist.

For, it is one thing for an object to be in the understanding, and another to understand that the object exists. When a painter first conceives of what he will afterwards perform, he has it in his understanding, but he does not yet understand it to be, because he has not yet performed it. But after he has made the painting, he both has it in

his understanding, and he understands that it exists, because he has made it.

Hence, even the fool is convinced that something exists in the understanding, at least, than which nothing greater can be conceived. For, when he hears of this, he understands it. And whatever is understood, exists in the understanding. And assuredly that, than which nothing greater can be conceived, cannot exist in the understanding alone. For, suppose it exists in the understanding alone: then it can be conceived to exist in reality; which is greater.

Therefore, if that, than which nothing greater can be conceived, exists in the understanding alone, the very being, than which nothing greater can be conceived, is one, than which a greater can be conceived. But obviously this is impossible. Hence, there is no doubt that there exists a being, than which nothing greater can be conceived, and it exists both in the understanding and in reality.

God cannot be conceived not to exist.—God is that, than which nothing greater can be con-

* Reprinted by permission of Open Court Publishing Company, a division of Carus Publishing Company, Peru, IL, from *Anselm's Basic Writings.* 2d ed. Tranlated by S. W. Deane. Copyright © 1962 by Open Court Publishing Company.

ceived.—That which can be conceived not to exist is not God.

And it assuredly exists so truly, that it cannot be conceived not to exist. For, it is possible to conceive of a being which cannot be conceived not to exist; and this is greater than one which can be conceived not to exist. Hence, if that, than which nothing greater can be conceived, can be conceived not to exist, it is not that, than which nothing greater can be conceived. But this is an irreconcilable contradiction. There is, then, so truly a being than which nothing greater can be conceived to exist, that it cannot even be conceived not to exist; and this being thou art, O Lord, our God.

So truly, therefore, dost thou exist, O Lord, my God, that thou canst not be conceived not to exist; and rightly. For, if a mind could conceive of a being better than thee, the creature would rise above the Creator; and this is most absurd. And, indeed, whatever else there is, except thee alone, can be conceived not to exist. To thee alone, therefore, it belongs to exist more truly than all other beings, and hence in a higher degree than all others. For, whatever else exists does not exist so truly, and hence in a less degree it belongs to it to exist. Why, then, has the fool said in his heart, there is no God (Psalms xiii, 1), since it is so evident, to a rational mind, that thou dost exist in the highest degree of all? Why, except that he is dull and a fool?

How the fool has said in his heart what cannot be conceived.—A thing may be conceived in two ways: (1) when the word signifying it is conceived: (2) when the thing itself is understood. As far as the word goes, God can be conceived not to exist; in reality he cannot.

But how has the fool said in his heart what he could not conceive; or how is it that he could not conceive what he said in his heart? since it is the same to say in the heart, and to conceive.

But, if really, nay, since really, he both conceived, because he said in his heart; and did not say in his heart, because he could not conceive; there is more than one way in which a thing is said in the heart or conceived. For, in one sense, an object is conceived, when the word signifying it is conceived; and in another, when the very entity, which the object is, is understood.

In the former sense, then, God can be conceived not to exist; but in the latter, not at all. For no one who understands what fire and water are can conceive fire to be water, in accordance with the nature of the facts themselves, although this is possible according to the words. So, then, no one who understands what God is can conceive that God does not exist; although he says these words in his heart, either without any or with some foreign, signification. For, God is that than which a greater cannot be conceived. And he who thoroughly understands this, assuredly understands that this being so truly exists, that not even in concept can it be non-existent. Therefore, he who understands that God so exists, cannot conceive that he does not exist.

I thank thee, gracious Lord, I thank thee; because what I formerly believed by thy bounty, I now so understand by thine illumination, that if I were unwilling to believe that thou dost exist, I should not be able not to understand this to be true.

Gaunilo's Criticism

For example: it is said that somewhere in the ocean is an island, which, because of the difficulty, or rather the impossibility, of discovering what does not exist, is called the lost island. And they say that this island has an inestimable wealth of all manner of riches and delicacies in greater abundance than is told of the Islands of the Blest; and that having no owner or inhabitant, it is more excellent than all other countries, which are inhabited by mankind, in the abundance with which it is stored.

Now if some one should tell me that there is such an island, I should easily understand his words, in which there is no difficulty. But suppose that he went on to say, as if by a logical inference: "You can no longer doubt that this island which is more excellent than all lands exists somewhere, since you have no doubt that it is in your understanding. And since it is more excellent not to be in the understanding alone, but to exist both in the understanding and in reality, for this reason it must exist. For if it does not exist, any land which really exists will be more excellent than it; and so the island already understood by you to be more excellent will not be more excellent."

If a man should try to prove to me by such reasoning that this island truly exists, and that its existence should no longer be doubted, either I should believe that he was jesting, or I know not which I ought to regard as the greater fool: myself, supposing that I should allow this proof; or him, if he should suppose that he had established with any certainty the existence of this island. For he ought to show first that the hypothetical excellence of this island exists as a real and indubitable fact, and in no wise as any unreal object, or one whose existence is uncertain, in my understanding.

St. Anselm's Rejoinder

A criticism of Gaunilo's example, in which he tries to show that in this way the real existence of a lost island might be inferred from the fact of its being conceived.

But, you say, it is as if one should suppose an island in the ocean, which surpasses all lands in its fertility, and which, because of the difficulty, or rather the impossibility, of discovering what does not exist, is called a lost island; and should say that there can be no doubt that this island truly exists in reality, for this reason, that one who hears it described easily understands what he hears.

Now I promise confidently that if any man shall devise anything existing either in reality or in concept alone (except that than which a greater cannot be conceived) to which he can adapt the sequence of my reasoning, I will discover that thing, and will give him his lost island, not to be lost again.

But it now appears that this being than which a greater is inconceivable cannot be conceived not to be, because it exists on so assured a ground of truth; for otherwise it would not exist at all.

Hence, if any one says that he conceives this being not to exist, I say that at the time when he conceives of this either he conceives of a being than which a greater is inconceivable, or he does not conceive at all. If he does not conceive, he does not conceive of the non-existence of that of which he does not conceive. But if he does conceive, he certainly conceives of a being which cannot be even conceived not to exist. For if it could be conceived not to exist, it could be conceived to have a beginning and an end. But this is impossible.

He, then, who conceives of this being conceives of a being which cannot be even conceived not to exist; but he who conceives of this being does not conceive that it does not exist; else he conceives what is inconceivable. The non-existence, then, of that than which a greater cannot be conceived is inconceivable.

3.8 Problems and Possibilities for the Ontological Argument

Since Anselm and Gaunilo (see Reading 3.7) went head to head over the ontological argument in the eleventh century, discussions of the argument have taken many twists and turns. Some have found it puzzling, some unconvincing, some convincing, and most fascinating.

René Descartes (1596–1650) found the argument convincing and introduced a version of it into modern philosophical discussion. He interpreted it as an argument from perfection. God, Descartes said, is by definition the most perfect being and hence has all perfections. Because existence is a perfection, God must have it.

Immanuel Kant (1724–1804) was unconvinced by the argument and is thought by many to have provided the definitive critique. If you heard the word *unicorn* but did not know what it meant and asked me for a definition, I would tell you that it is a horse-like creature that is white and has one horn in the middle of its forehead. You might then ask me whether any such creatures exist. Your question about whether there are any unicorns makes sense. Just because there is an answer to the question "What is *x*?" does not mean there are any *x*s.

Should God be any different? Just because we can define God as the greatest possible that can be thought or, as Descartes preferred, as supremely perfect, does it follow, any more than it does for unicorns, cabalots (whatever they are), chairs, dogs, witches, angels, and so on, that there *are* any? Kant did not think so.

But what precisely is wrong? Kant thought that the argument illicitly treats existence as a "real" predicate. *Orange* is an attribute of a cat in the sentence "My cat is orange," and because this attribute is predicated of my cat, we may call it a real predicate in the sense that it tells us something more about the cat than we knew before. Existence, however, is not, according to Kant, a predicate in the same sense that orange is. When we define something, we state its predicates, properties, or attributes. For example, the sentence "A unicorn is a white horse-like animal with one horn in the middle of its forehead" states the attributes of a unicorn. When we claim such a thing exists, we are not adding another predicate or attribute (that is, we are not answering the question "What is it?") but are merely claiming that it is exemplified or instantiated in the world (we are answering the logically different question "Are there any?") Hence we cannot any more conclude there is a God from a definition of God than we can conclude there is a unicorn from our definition of a unicorn.

Kant found other problems beside this one, and others have offered versions that they think escape Kant's "definitive" critique. Lurking behind much of the discussion is the question whether *any* definition of God that might yield a genuinely convincing argument is coherent. It would seem that God would have to be defined as maximally perfect in some sense in order to get any ontological argument to work. But does the concept of maximal perfection or greatest possible that can be thought or a being who necessarily exists even make sense? If it does not, then we cannot even get past the answer to the question "What is God?" to the question "Is there one?" If the answer to the first question is incoherent, then the only possible answer to the second question is "There is not."

Yeager Hudson (1931–   ) is Dana Professor of Philosophy at Colby College. In the following selection, he surveys something of the history of the discussion, points out areas of difficulties, and concludes that the jury is still out.

Reading Questions

1. State Descartes's version of the ontological argument in your own words.
2. What are Kant's objections to the ontological argument?
3. State the modal version of the ontological argument in your own words.
4. According to Hudson, what might be wrong with the modal version?

5. What is the "ontological disproof," and why does it raise the question of whether the concept of a maximally great being is intelligible?
6. What conclusions does Hudson draw from his study of ontological proofs and disproofs? Do you agree? Why or why not?

Problems and Possibilities for the Ontological Argument*

YEAGER HUDSON

THE **ONTOLOGICAL ARGUMENT** for the existence of God attempts to demonstrate that the existence of God is a necessary truth on grounds that the denial of God's existence is self-contradictory. What is perhaps most distinctive about the **ontological argument** is that it is alleged to be an *a priori* argument. That means that the proponents of the argument claim that it does not depend in any way on empirical evidence. Since many philosophers, especially those before the twentieth century, have shown considerable suspicion about sense impressions and the evidence they provide, the fact that this argument does not depend on such evidence has been regarded as a very great advantage. The ontological argument is also supposed to be deductive, the kind of argument that, if it is valid and its premises are true, provides conclusive evidence for the truth of its conclusion. Thus it would appear to be the ideal kind of argument for the theist. Yet, as we will see, it has also been one of the most controversial.

The Claim That God Does Not Exist Is Self-Contradictory

The ontological argument has been formulated in a variety of ways. Indeed, it might be better to say that a cluster of arguments with certain similarities are collectively referred to as the ontological argument. Some thinkers, Descartes for example, have said that the argument amounts to pointing out that the claim that God does not exist is contradictory. God means "the supremely perfect being." But to deny that such a being exists is like saying, "The supremely perfect being lacks a perfection." Stated in this way, the contradiction becomes blatant. Another way of putting it is to say that God is a being whose essence includes existence; to deny the existence of such a being is to contradict oneself. God allegedly is the kind of being who could not possibly not exist—whose nonexistence is inconceivable. We know that there are some kinds of things whose existence is inconceivable and that therefore do not exist because it is impossible for them to exist. For example, no square circles exist because there could not be any; the very concept is contradictory, the nature of such a thing is inconceivable, and its existence is impossible. Conversely, so the argument goes, God is the sort of thing that could not fail to exist. The very concept of God includes the notion of existence as the concept of square circle includes nonexistence. Thus the nonexistence of God is inconceivable and God's actual nonexistence is impossible.

Existence Is Inseparable from God's Essence

René Descartes (1596–1650) argues that existence is an inseparable part of the essence of God and for this reason God must exist.

> I find it manifest that we can no more separate the existence of God from his essence than we can separate from the essence of a triangle the fact that the size of its three angles equals two right angles. . . . It is no less self-contradictory to conceive of a God, a supremely perfect Being, who lacks existence—that is, who lacks some perfection—than it is to conceive of a mountain for which there is no valley.

This argument does not prove that triangles or mountains must exist, but only that they must have all the features that are parts of their essence. It does, so it is claimed, prove that God must exist, because existence *is* a part of God's essence. To be a triangle means to have the sum of internal angles add up to 180 degrees; similarly to be God means to exist. Thus "God does not exist" is as much a self-contradiction as "A triangle has internal angles that add up to more than two right angles," or "There is a mountain with no valley."

Anselm's "Something Than Which No Greater Can Be Conceived"

The classic statement of the ontological argument comes from St. Anselm (1033–1109), although it was Immanuel Kant who gave the argument its name. Anselm tells us that God means that than which nothing greater can be conceived. We understand something by that expression, and thus that being exists in our thought. But a being that exists only in thought is less great than a being that exists in thought and in reality. To deny that this being exists in reality is to say, in effect, that the being than which no greater can be conceived is not as great as another that can be conceived (the one existing both in thought and reality). That is clearly a contradiction. Thus God must exist not only in thought but also in reality.

Anselm argues further that a being than which no greater can be conceived cannot be conceived as nonexistent. This means that God is a necessary being, one that could not possibly fail to exist—or, in the parlance of contemporary philosophy, one that exists in every possible world. Clearly a being that only happens to exist but that might not have existed—that is, a being that is contingent or that exists in some but not all possible worlds—is less great or less perfect than one that exists necessarily in every possible world. So the existence of God is not contingent like that of a human or a horse; rather, God's existence is necessary. Indeed, as some theologians expressed it, God *is* his existence just as God *is* his goodness, his power, and all of the other aspects of his essence.

Criticisms of the Ontological Argument

The ontological argument has had a checkered career. Some have regarded it as the decisive argument that succeeds in proving conclusively the existence of God. Others have thought it little better than sophistry. But there is something intriguing about this position, and philosophers have returned to it again and again to see whether it might not be made to do what it is supposed to do—or to see whether it might be turned against itself to prove that God does not, or even could not, exist. It is the traditional argument to which scholars in the twentieth century have probably devoted most attention.

St. Thomas Aquinas (1225–1275) held that it was a valid argument but that only God could realize that it is a proof in the strict sense, for only an omniscient being could possess the knowledge necessary to know that the premises of the argument are true. Finite humans cannot know the essence of God; the ontological argument turns on claims about God's essence; thus only God and not humans can know the truths that make the ontological argument a conclusive proof. Aquinas elected as a consequence to rely on other arguments than the ontological.

One of the most formidable critics of the ontological argument was Immanuel Kant

(1724–1804). One of the objections that Kant pressed against Anselm's version had already been raised by Gaunilo, a contemporary of Anselm. Gaunilo argued that if Anselm's argument was valid, it could be used to prove the existence of any conceivable excellent thing. For example, we can conceive of an island idyllic in every way, an island paradise "than which no greater could be conceived." Because we understand the description, the island exists in our minds. But this island "than which no greater could be conceived" must also exist in reality; otherwise, we could conceive of a greater one existing both in thought and in reality, an obvious contradiction. Thus this most excellent island— or anything else conceived along similar lines— must exist. But an argument that proves the existence of all sorts of absurd things is not a sound argument. Thus Gaunilo insisted that the ontological argument fails.

A possible reply to Gaunilo, one that Anselm himself attempted in part, is to insist that God is the only being to whom the title "that than which nothing greater can be conceived" applies. It is a mistake to suppose that we could conceive an island that is supremely idyllic in every way. No matter how many varieties of luscious fruit it might have, we could always imagine adding one more or improving the flavor slightly. But God is the supremely perfect being in the sense that every perfection is actualized fully and harmonized completely in God's essence. God is not merely a being than whom feeble human intellect cannot think of a better; God is *the* being than which a greater is inconceivable. Thus God is the only being for which the ontological argument works.

Kant was not impressed by this response. He raises two objections to the ontological argument. One, which resembles Gaunilo's, is that Anselm mistakenly assumes that existence is a real predicate. A *predicate* is a word that attributes some property or characteristic to a subject. When we say that God is powerful, we predicate the property of power to God. But when we say that God exists, we do not attribute a property, for existence is not a property a subject can or

cannot have. We would make a similar error if we think that in saying, "American eagles are rare," we are attributing a property to eagles. What we are actually saying is that there are not very many American eagles. Descartes makes the same error when he argues that God must exist because to deny that God exists is to say that the supremely perfect being lacks a perfection. But existence is not a perfection that can be added to or subtracted from the other perfections or properties that something may have. To say that something exists is not to say that it has some additional characteristic, existence, but rather to say that there is such a thing, that the subject named or described is present in the real world.

Kant puts it this way: "A hundred real dollars do not contain one penny more than a hundred imaginary dollars." No doubt we prefer the real to the imaginary dollars, but that is beside the point; the essential nature of the two is in no way different. And this, according to Kant, is the error of the ontological argument. If existence is not an attribute that a subject can either have or fail to have, then it cannot be argued that God must exist because existence is an inseparable aspect or perfection of God's essence. Given the coherence of the *notion* of a supremely perfect being (a point not everyone would grant), like that of an idyllic island or a hundred dollars, the question remains whether or not any of them exists. The existence of God can no more be inferred from God's definition as the supremely perfect being than can that of the island from its definition as the island than which no greater can be imagined.

Kant's other major objection to this argument is grounded in the claim that no existential proposition is logically necessary. The ontological argument attempts to derive the existence of God from the definition of God, by way of the claim that a being so defined is a necessary being, but Kant is convinced that no such derivation is possible. Necessity applies to propositions and not to beings. Every existential proposition— that is, every proposition that asserts the existence of something—must be grounded on empirical evidence. Thus Kant rejects the whole notion of necessary being as incoherent.

It seems, however, that the nonexistence of some things can be derived from their definition and thus that some sense can be given to the notion of necessary nonbeing. The nonexistence of four-sided triangles can be derived from their definition as four-sided plane figures that have three sides, because such a definition is incoherent. Thus we say not just that such things do not exist, as we claim that unicorns do not exist; rather, we say that they *necessarily* do not exist. The proposition, "Four-sided triangles do not exist," seems to be an existential proposition that is logically necessary. Richard Swinburne claims that there are also affirmative existential propositions that are logically necessary or, in other words, that there are some things that necessarily exist. "There exists a number greater than one million—and it is a logically necessary truth that there does." We might say that a plain figure with more sides than anyone has ever counted exists or that the ratio between two numbers larger than anyone has ever calculated exists, and so on. Thus it seems to be too much to claim that no existential proposition can be logically necessary or that the concept of necessary existence is incoherent.

It might be claimed that an eternal being is a necessary being because such a being could not begin to exist or cease to exist. Such a beginning or ending is inconsistent with the meaning of "eternal being." But this necessity is not quite like the kind of necessity we have been discussing. Even if we admit that it is proper to designate such a being as necessary, we are still justified in asking whether or not any such being exists. The statement, "Eternal beings are necessary beings," can thus be understood to mean not, "There are eternal beings that are necessary beings," but rather, "If anything is an eternal being, then it is a necessary being." Similarly, the ontological argument may be taken to mean not "God exists," but rather, "If anything is God, then it exists." Granted, if there is an eternal being, it is a necessary being, but to call it necessary does not prove that it exists. Likewise, we may grant that if there is a God, that is, a supremely perfect being—if anything answers to

that description—then it exists. The question is whether or not there is anything that answers to the description. We will look more closely at the concept of necessary being when we examine the so-called ontological disproof later in this chapter.

The Modal Version of the Ontological Argument

The most popular formulation of the ontological argument among contemporary philosophers, advanced by such thinkers as Charles Hartshorne, Norman Malcolm, and Alvin Plantinga, is grounded in **modal logic,** the logic of necessity, possibility, and impossibility, and is usually stated in possible world language. Its various advocates state it in slightly different ways, but all versions seem to have essentially the same strengths and weaknesses.

The modal version of the ontological argument attempts to infer God's existence from the claim that God's existence is logically possible, together with certain allegedly necessary truths about God's nature and the laws of modal logic. It is the assertion of the possibility of God's existence that sharply differentiates this from the classic versions of the ontological argument, which argued from the definition or from certain allegedly necessary traits of God without explicitly asserting that a being with those traits was possible.

It is a principle of modal logic that contingent truths vary from one possible world to another, but that necessary truths obtain in every possible world. This means that contingent truths such as "Horses exist" and "Logicians are fond of verbal puzzles" could not be necessary truths in any possible world, but that necessary truths such as "Unicorns have one horn" and "It is false that $2 + 2 = 7$" are necessarily true in every possible world. This is another way of saying that the modal status—whether something is necessary or possible—is a universal fact and not one that applies only to specific worlds. Unicorns may exist in one world and not in another, but in every possible world they have a single horn, that is, their existence is contingent, but their nature is not contingent. If we can say of anything that its existence is necessary, then it must exist in every possible world.

The argument begins, then, with the claim that if it is possible that God's existence is necessary, then God exists in every possible world, including the actual world. But is it possible? That it is allegedly follows from the nature of God. God is defined by certain contemporary philosophers of religion as a maximally great or maximally perfect being. It seems to be possible that such a being exists; that is, it seems that there is a possible world in which a maximally perfect being exists, even if we think this being does not exist in the actual world. But a being that exists in every possible world is more perfect than a being that exists in only one or some possible worlds. Indeed, to be maximally perfect means to exist in every possible world or, in other words, to be a necessary being. Thus if it is possible for a maximally perfect being to exist—that is, if God exists in some possible world—then it is necessarily true that God exists—that is, that God exists in every possible world. But we have already remarked that the existence of a maximally perfect being seems to be possible. There is nothing contradictory in the notion and no absurdity seems to follow from it. The conclusion is that "God exists" is necessarily true, that is, true not just in some possible world but in every possible world. But the actual world is one possible world. From all this it follows that "God exists" is true of the actual world or, in other words, that God actually does exist.

The modal argument is more complex than the earlier versions of the ontological argument. It can be stated in several different ways, and some constructions of the argument are more intuitively appealing than others. There is fairly widespread agreement among contemporary modal logicians that at least some versions of the argument are valid. But considerable disagreement remains concerning what the argument, even if it is valid, proves. One of the most serious problems lies in the premise that asserts that the existence of a maximally perfect being is possible.

Some philosophers believe that perfection or greatness is like numbers; there is no such thing as a maximum. Just as there is no highest number than which none higher is possible; just as there is no island so perfect that some alteration cannot improve it; so there may be no coherent concept of a being than which no greater can be conceived. Thus if there is no such conceivable thing as a maximally perfect being, the existence of such a being is not possible. In that case, since the modal argument depends on the assumption that the existence of God is possible, it fails to establish its conclusion not because it is invalid, but because one of its premises is false.

Even if the situation is not quite this bad for the argument, we may still not be justified in claiming that the argument proves that God exists, because even if it is valid and even if all its premises are true, it may not be possible for any humans to know that the premises are true. This was St. Thomas's point about the ontological argument. He maintained that the argument is valid and that its premises are true, and thus God can recognize that it establishes its conclusion, but we humans cannot have sufficient knowledge of the characteristics of God to justify our making any confident use of the argument. Even Alvin Plantinga, one of the most able contemporary defenders of the argument, is unwilling to claim that it proves the existence of God. "What I claim for this argument, therefore, is that it establishes, not the *truth* of theism, but its rational acceptability." Even that is a lot to claim, and a great many contemporary philosophers would insist that it is too much.

The So-Called Ontological Disproof

We have examined briefly the argument by which Gaunilo attempted by a **reductio ad absurdum** to refute the ontological argument by showing that, taken to its logical conclusion, it implied an absurdity. Gaunilo and Kant both tried to discredit the argument by demonstrating that parallel reasoning could establish the existence of anything that we wish to conceive of as perfect, such as the perfect island. In recent times even more radical responses to this argument have appeared. We will briefly examine just one, by David and Marjorie Haight, that purports to use the ontological argument to prove the existence of a devil.

The Haight argument is similar to Gaunilo's except that it parodies the ontological argument by arguing for the existence of a supremely evil being rather than an idyllic island. We have a concept of a being than which no worse can be conceived. If this being did not actually exist, it would not be that than which no worse could be conceived, since we could conceive such a being as existing, and this being would clearly be worse. Now this being than which a worse is inconceivable is called the devil. Therefore the devil exists.

The Haights point out that this argument is exactly parallel to the ontological argument. If the ontological argument is valid, so must this one be; if it establishes the existence of God, this one must establish the existence of the devil. They suggest that what the argument really proves, if it proves anything at all, is the existence of one greatest thing that might be called either God or devil. The argument, as stated by Anselm, does not prove that the being than which no greater can be conceived is a good being, unless an implicit assumption has been made identifying greatness with goodness or including goodness in greatness. But such an assumption would be question begging. And if the argument is formulated in such a way that the conception on which it turns is of a supremely perfect being, the counterargument might be made to hinge on the concept of a supremely imperfect being and the parallel would still obtain.

If the ontological argument is to work and also avoid criticisms like those of Gaunilo and the Haights, it must be supplemented somehow to show that God is the only being to which such an argument can apply. This Anselm attempted to do in his reply to Gaunilo. He first argued that any being that can be conceived to exist but does not exist can be conceived as having a beginning. But any being that can be conceived as having a beginning or an end is not that being than which a greater is inconceivable. Now an island, how-ever perfect, or anything else whose nonexistence is conceivable, can be conceived as having a beginning. Thus the argument does not prove the existence of imagined perfect things such as islands or hundred dollars, but does prove the existence of the one thing than which no greater is conceivable, namely, God.

But this response will not work against the Haight argument. For the devil, as the supremely evil being, is a being that need not be conceived as having a beginning or an end. Indeed, his chief difference from God is only that he is evil and God is good. Anselm maintains that his argument can apply only to the one thing than which any greater is inconceivable. If God is conceived as the greatest good being and the devil as the greatest evil being, the question would still need to be raised of which is the greater of these two, that is, the single being than which no greater is conceivable. Perhaps a case could be made for the claim that to be good is greater than to be evil, but it would require an additional argument, one that Anselm does not supply and one that does not readily present itself. Wanting such an argument, the claim that to be good is greater than to be evil becomes question begging, assuming without supplying grounds a point that need not be accepted unless grounds are supplied.

The upshot of the dispute between Anselm and the Haights seems to be that the ontological argument might establish the existence of some supreme being but leave us uncertain whether it is God or the devil. This is what the Haights themselves suggest. Many theists would be pleased to welcome this concession and would regard this outcome of the Haights' argument as friendly rather than hostile to theism. These theists would then resort to empirical arguments, such as the argument from design and beauty in the world, to support their further contention that the being whose existence the ontological argument has been conceded to establish is God and not the devil. They would have to face, however, a potentially formidable counterargument based on the existence of evil in the world.

What seems really to be at issue with the ontological argument and its counterarguments, the so-called **ontological disproofs,** is the question of whether the concept of a necessary being or a maximally great being is intelligible and whether any proposition asserting the existence of such a being can be necessarily, and not merely contingently, true. The conventional view of necessity follows Hume and Kant in the assumption that no existential statement can be necessary. All existential propositions are regarded as contingent, empirical claims, and all necessary propositions as nonexistential. If "God exists" were a necessary proposition, then it could not be about existence—a patent absurdity. And if it is to be about existence, then it will be contingent or nonnecessary.

We have already questioned the claim that no necessity proposition can make an assertion about what exists. We noted that propositions such as "No four-sided triangles exist" seem to be both necessary and existential. If these are indeed examples of propositions that are both existential and necessary, they would seem to be just the kind of proposition one would need to formulate an ontological proof or disproof successfully. An ontological disproof claims to be an analogue of the ontological proof that attempts to establish the existence of God on the basis of an analysis of the concept's meaning. An ontological disproof therefore would proceed by analyzing the concept of God and showing that it is incoherent—from which the disproof would infer that no such being could exist. If, for example, an analysis of the attributes of God . . . turned up convincing reasons to believe that these attributes are mutually inconsistent, and if no consistent set of modified or attenuated attributes still compatible with the notion of deity could be discovered, we would have to conclude that the concept of God is incoherent.

Now if the concept of a necessary being or a supremely perfect being really is incoherent—like the concept of a seven-sided square—the ontological disproof would seem to be successful. We believe that when we show that the concept of a seven-sided square is self-contradictory, we demonstrate not only that the concept is incoherent but also that no seven-sided squares could

possibly exist. In other words, we acknowledge that such statements are both necessary and existential. An appropriate proposition of this sort about God is just what an advocate of an ontological disproof needs. If we recognize that there can be necessary existential propositions, this opens up the possibility of an ontological disproof. But we must notice that such a recognition cuts both ways: It also opens up the possibility of an ontological proof. This is the possibility that such contemporary supporters of the ontological argument as Swinburne seek to exploit.

Are we in a position to draw any conclusions about the ontological argument? One seems to be that the advocates of the ontological argument have not been able by means of the argument to demonstrate the existence of God. Another is that its critics have equally failed to demonstrate God's nonexistence and have not even been able to show decisively that the ontological argument itself completely fails. Indeed, the Haights interpret the argument in a way that amounts to a substantial concession to the theist. Many would say that theirs is much too much of a concession.

Perhaps one of the most important things we have discovered in examining the ontological argument is the plausibility of the claim that necessary judgments can have existential import. If such necessary propositions as the basic laws of logic and mathematics are admitted to have implications about what cannot exist, why may not certain necessary propositions have implications about what can or must exist? But if this point clears the way for either an ontological proof or an ontological disproof, at the same time a fully satisfactory formulation of either of these arguments remains to be discovered. The ontological argument continues to exert great powers of fascination, however. There can be little doubt that philosophers will continue to refine it and to attempt to find new ways to formulate it in hope of making it work. Up to this time, however, it seems not yet to have contributed in any substantial way to settling the question whether or not God exists. . . .

Suggestions for Further Reading

Angeles, Peter, ed. *Critiques of God.* Buffalo, NY: Prometheus Books, 1976.

Betty, L. Stafford, and Cordell, Bruce. "God and Modern Science: New Life for the Teleological Argument." *International Philosophical Quarterly* XXVII (December 1987):409–435.

Craig, William. *The Cosmological Argument from Plato to Leibniz.* New York: Barnes & Noble, 1980.

———. *The Kalam Cosmological Argument.* London: Macmillan, 1979.

Flew, Anthony. *God and Philosophy.* New York: Dell, 1966.

Gale, Richard. *On the Nature and Existence of God.* Cambridge, England: Cambridge University Press, 1992.

Hartshorne, Charles. *Anselm's Discovery: A Re-examination of the Ontological Proof for God's Existence.* La Salle, IL: Open Court, 1965.

Hick, John. *Arguments for the Existence of God.* London: Macmillan, 1971.

Iqbal, Mohammad. *The Reconstruction of Religious Thought in Islam.* Delhi, India: Oriental Publishers, 1975.

Jacobson, John R., and Mitchell, Robert Lloyd, eds. *Existence of God: Essays from the Basic Issues Forum.* Lewiston, NY: Mellen Press, 1988.

Kenny, A. *The Five Ways.* London: Routledge and Kegan Paul, 1968.

Kung, Hans. *Does God Exist? An Answer of Today.* New York: Vintage Books, 1981.

Leslie, John. "Anthropic Principle, World Ensemble, Design." *American Philosophical Quarterly* 19 (April 1982): 141–151.

Mackie, J. L. *The Miracle of Theism.* Oxford, England: Oxford University Press, 1982.

Malcolm, Norman. "Anselm's Ontological Arguments." *The Philosophical Review* LXIX (January 1960): 41–62.

Martin, Michael. *Atheism.* Philadelphia: Temple University Press, 1990.

Matson, Wallace I. *The Existence of God.* Ithaca, NY: Cornell University Press, 1965.

McPherson, Thomas. *The Argument from Design.* London: Macmillan, 1972.

Parsons, Keith M. *God and the Burden of Proof: Plantinga, Swinburne, and the Analytic Defense of Theism.* Buffalo, NY: Prometheus, 1989.

Plantinga, Alvin, ed. *The Ontological Argument from St. Anselm to Contemporary Philosophers.* Garden City, NY: Doubleday, 1965.

Ross, James. *Philosophical Theology.* New York: Bobbs-Merrill, 1969.

Rowe, William L. *The Cosmological Argument.* Princeton, NJ: Princeton University Press, 1975.

Swinburne, Richard. *The Existence of God.* Oxford, England: Oxford University Press, 1979.

Taylor, Richard. *Metaphysics.* Englewood Cliffs, NJ: Prentice-Hall, 1963.

Tennant, R. R. *Philosophical Theology.* Cambridge, England: Cambridge University Press, 1928.

Wainwright, William J. *Philosophy of Religion.* Belmont, CA: Wadsworth, 1988.

CHAPTER 4

Religious Experience: What Is It and What Does It Prove?

Introduction

WHAT ARE RELIGIOUS EXPERIENCES? Can you define the term *religious experience* with enough accuracy and precision to distinguish it clearly from experience that is not religious? What kinds of religious experiences are there? We know that there are a great variety—visions of the Virgin Mary, of Krishna, of Buddha, hearing angelic voices, spirit possession, conversion, speaking in tongues, union with God, oneness with Brahman, and many more. Can this variety be reduced to a few general types? Do they overlap enough so that we can find some common thread?

What should we make of naturalistic explanations of these experiences? Suppose we said, following the founder of psychoanalysis, Sigmund Freud, that God is a projection of the human father-figure on the sky, resulting from our desire and need to feel as adults the security we felt as children. God is a cosmic security blanket that helps us cope with fear and anxiety in the face of death. According to this interpretation, experiences of the divine have specific and describable psychological causes.

Suppose that by giving certain drugs to people under the right conditions we can produce visions of what they think are spirits and cause them to hear what they take to be supernatural voices. Are naturalistic explanations incompatible with the claim that religious experiences have supernatural causes?

Are religious experiences veridical? That is, are they cases of genuine cognition of reality, or are they cases of only apparent cognitions? Do people really experience the Tao, or is the Tao a product of overactive imaginations seeking confirmation of what their religious tradition has taught?

Are certain kinds of religious experiences everywhere the same? Do people have the same experiences but interpret and express them in different ways? Widespread agreement across cultures would be powerful evidence for veridicality. But do Buddhists see the Virgin Mary? Do Catholics hear the voice of Krishna? Would you be more impressed if Joseph Smith, the founder of the Church of the Latter Day Saints, had had a vision of Muhammad rather than of the Angel Maroni?

Many questions and issues arise when philosophical reflection turns to the topic of religious experience. The modern interest in this topic begins with the nineteenth-century German theologian Friedrich Schleiermacher. Schleiermacher was dismayed that many cultured and well-educated people of his day had come to despise religion. He felt that they misunderstood what religion really is. They confused it with dogmas, rituals, repressive moral codes, and institutions. They had put their faith in rational arguments for the existence of God, only to be disappointed when such arguments were shown to be defective. But, according to Schleiermacher, the heart of religion is to be found in experience, not in dogmas, rituals, or rational argumentation. It is in experience that true religion moves and breathes and has its being. And what is this experience? Schleiermacher characterized it as the feeling of absolute dependence. This feeling is the irreducible essence of all religion.

Rudolf Otto (1896–1937) in his book *The Idea of the Holy* continued the examination of religious experience begun by Schleiermacher. He thought that Schleiermacher had identified an important feature of religion but that he had erred by making it too subjective (an awareness of one's feelings rather than of some transcendent object) and by excluding the possibility that people might have direct experiences of the divine. Given Schleiermacher's account, the divine could only be inferred as the cause of the feeling of absolute dependence.

Like Schleiermacher, however, Otto had theological motives. He wanted to show that there is an element in religious experience, which he called the numinous, that could not be explained away. Religious experience, he maintained, is not reducible to mere wish fulfillment, need for security, or chemical reactions in the brain.

Since Otto, we have come to realize that religious experience is far more complex than either he or Schleiermacher thought. Hence we must be careful to distinguish among its various types. Also, we do not necessarily have to fear naturalistic explanations. For one thing, they may not be adequate. For another, they may be quite compatible with religious explanations. Ninian Smart considers some of these issues in the first selection in this chapter.

The next three selections present examples of what appear to be very different types of religious experiences. We begin with the grand and awe-inspiring vision of Black Elk, a great Native American medicine man. There follows an example from Judaism that affirms the irreducible personal element in religious experience. Finally, we turn to the East and study the marks of satori—the Zen Buddhist experience of enlightenment.

For many people, their religious experiences confirm what they already believe to be true on other grounds. They do not erect their beliefs after the fact or even use their experiences as proof for others who do not share them. Some theologians and philosophers, however, have tried to use religious experience as evidence from which we can infer the existence of some type of ultimate reality. Following the lead of Schleiermacher, they realize that the purely rational arguments for the existence of some ultimate reality such as God (see Chapter 3) fail to convince most people. Perhaps arguments from experience will prove more satisfactory. Such arguments appear to be in keeping with the scientific appeal to experience and hence should resonate for people who live in a scientific age. Some people who have religious experiences do claim that, even if their experiences do not prove that God exists, they are noetic in the sense that they include the conviction that one is directly apprehending some vital religious truth or reality. This noetic quality makes it worthwhile to investigate whether the conviction that such experiences yield genuine knowledge is only a subjective feeling or is a fact. These issues are explored in the last two selections.

In a sense, religious experience is both too rich and too poor. On the one hand, the commonality of certain general features and the richness for human life and culture that such experiences produce, combined with their persistence throughout history, suggest that they cannot all be delusions. It is hard to believe that none of these experiences has a foundation in truth. If it is all delusion, then it would be a truly massive hallucination. It seems, then, too rich to be discounted. On the other hand, if we try to support all religious beliefs and practices by an appeal to religious experience alone, it appears too poor. Religious traditions aspire to say much more about the nature of ultimate reality, the afterlife, how we should live, and so on than these experiences would allow. Religious experiences cannot bear the whole weight of all religious claims. However, they can strengthen the faith of people who have already come to believe on other grounds, and for those who do not believe, the hymns, poetry, art, and culture that these experiences inspire make for fascinating study and a deeper appreciation of the hopes and dreams of human beings.

4.1 The Experiential Dimension

If you made a list of all the sorts of experiences you would normally think of as religious experiences, would some of those experiences exhibit characteristics that would allow you to group them together? For example, do all experiences that involve what the person having the experience calls "God" fall into one group and all experiences that involve what the person having the experience calls "nirvana" fall into another group?

Would you say religious experiences are veridical? Would you argue that they are delusions? Are people who claim to be born again really born again, or do they just think they are? How would you go about deciding? Suppose a person who recounts her experience of being born again says it is due to the grace of God, but a psychologist says it is due to the eruption into consciousness of a repressed conflict between her desire to do right and her desire to do wrong. Could you decide who was right? Could both explanations be right?

These are some of the questions and issues that Ninian Smart (see also Reading 1.1) deals with in the next selection. As you may recall, he defines religion in terms of various dimensions. Here he elaborates on the experiential dimension, explicating a way of classifying religious experiences and discussing whether psychological explanations of religious experiences are adequate.

Reading Questions

1. What are the characteristics of the numinous experience?
2. Why, according to Smart, did Otto wish to "drive a path between physics and ethics"?
3. How, according to Smart, does mystical experience differ from the numinous?
4. How do the *Upanishads* weave together the mystical and numinous threads?
5. What is the "panenhenic" experience?
6. How does the right wing of Shamanism differ from the left wing?
7. From Smart's point of view, what is wrong with depth psychology's explanation of religious experience?
8. Do you agree with Smart that how we answer the question about the truth of religious experiences depends "in part" on the worldview with which we start? Why or why not?

The Experiential Dimension*

NINIAN SMART

WHEN PEOPLE THINK of the cosmos as the work of a great God it is perhaps partly because they reason that the cosmos must have come from somewhere, and its beauties and design suggest a Creator of vast intelligence. Or it may be that they accept the word of others—as found, for instance, in such tremendous scriptures as the *Bhagavadgītā* or the Bible or the Qur'ān. But it may also be because they have some feelings in their own experience of a majestic, terrifying, overwhelming, loving Being, a divine Reality. Indeed, if we look in the Song of the Lord (the *Gītā*) we find there the most dramatic account of how Arjuna, the hero of the narrative, is confronted by the Lord in all his many-formed glistening power, like a very personal nuclear explosion. And running like a thread through the Qur'ān is the sense of the experiences of the mighty and compassionate Allah who came to Muhammad and set him on his amazing prophetic quest. The Bible, too, echoes with a sense of the mighty presence of the Lord—for Isaiah in the Temple, for Job in his complaining despair, for the apostle Paul as he plodded along the road to Damascus, ready to deal death to the disciples of that very Christ who now suddenly blinded him and crashed around his scared skull.

Not all religious people have such dramatic encounters. But people frequently do experience feelings that softly echo these great turning points in human history. Indeed, much of religious ritual is designed to express and to stimulate such feelings. The soaring columns of a great European cathedral, the dim religious light, the high-flying solemn choral music, the sanctity of slow procession, the clashing of the mysterious bells, the dark features of the great judge Christ depicted in the wondrous colored windows: All these things are meant to give us the feel of the Lord, the feel of the numinous God.

And in the humbler chapels of Protestantism, which are plain and without all the expensive and

*From Ninian Smart, *Worldviews: Crosscultural Explorations of Human Beliefs.* 2d ed. Copyright © 1995. Prentice-Hall, Inc., pp. 58–73. Reprinted by permission of Prentice-Hall, Inc., Upper Saddle River, NJ.

highly organized aids to experience, there is the intense feeling of the hymn, and the thundering voice of the preacher. It sometimes seems as if the preacher is possessed by some force outside of him and beyond him. That is as it ought to be, for he speaks and thunders not in his own name but in the name of the Lord to whom he has devoted his life, and it is this Lord whose majesty and mercy he seeks to express.

One can get a sense of the numinous God outside the cathedral, church, or temple—in nature. Religious thinkers and believers have long heard the "voice of God" in the wind on the tips of the soaring mountains, for instance, or in the churning of the ocean.

And sometimes the sense of presence comes to a person for no obvious outer reason at all. So we find many instances of people who are awed by an unseen force that seems to approach them wordlessly.

Numinous and Mystical Religious Experience

All this is one important strand of religious experience for which Rudolf Otto (1869–1937) in *The Idea of the Holy* coined the word "numinous." This he derived from the Latin word *numen,* a spirit— the sort of spirit that in Roman religion haunted the rivers and the copses and strange places and the threshold and the hearth— unseen forces sending a thrill of fear and power down one's back. For Otto the numinous experience is at the heart of religion. He defined it as the experience of something that is a *mysterium tremendum et fascinans*—a mystery that is fearful, awe-inspiring (*tremendum,* literally meaning "to be trembled at"), and fascinating, and that, for all its fearfulness, draws you toward it. You get something of this feeling looking over a cliff. Doesn't the great drop inspire fear, and yet aren't you also drawn toward it, so much so that sometimes you have to make a conscious effort to draw back? But above all, the sense of presence that confronts a person in the numinous experience is majestic: marvelous in power and glory. In their rather different ways the experiences of Arjuna, Isaiah,

Job, Paul, and Muhammad are all numinous in character.

As I have said, for Rudolf Otto this kind of experience lay at the heart of religion. Through it he tried to explain the meaning of the Holy, and he saw holiness as the key category we use in defining religion. God is not just good: He is *holy,* and religion, for Otto, concerns that which is holy.

Otto also referred to the Holy as the Wholly Other—both because it was something completely other than the person encountering it, and because it was mysteriously other in quality from the things and people of this world. It is thus *different* and other-worldly, a description that fits in with many accounts of God in living religious contexts.

Otto was attempting to depict the central experience of religion. Since feelings were involved in the numinous experience he thought that the reader of his book would not understand it unless he too had had such an experience—and indeed, empathy would require at least some inkling of the nature of numinous feelings. But I think most people do understand: Who has not felt awe before a storm? Who has not had ghostly intimations of a strange presence? Who has not felt dread? These may not amount to a full experience of the Holy but they are a step along the way.

Otto stressed feeling and the sense of the numinous because he wished to drive a path between physics and ethics, between the natural world and the world of value. If we go back to Immanuel Kant (1724–1804), chief figure of the European Enlightenment and the one who set the agenda for so much of Western philosophy since, we find a philosopher who wished to make sense of science—to try and see what the foundations of science are. But he wished to do this in a way which still left room for the moral agent; his philosophy recognized freedom of will outside the absolute constraints of the laws of physics. In so doing, however, it divided reality into two categories: science and ethics. Otto wanted to show how religion comes *in between:* It is in part about the cosmos, but it is not science; it is about action, but it is not just ethics—

it is also worship. Worship comes in because the appropriate response to the Holy is indeed worship and adoration. Religion, in Otto's view, may also express itself as moral action, but at its heart worship is expression of a feeling of reverence for the numinous. Indeed, a typical characteristic of religion is that it involves the worship of God or gods. But is worship universal? And is it always of central importance? Are there religions, in other words, where worship is only secondary? The answer is yes.

There is another kind of religious experience—mystical experience—that has been very important for the history of humanity, and that does not seem to have the qualities Otto ascribes to the numinous. Thus, in the Indian tradition particularly and especially in Buddhism we find the practice of yogic meditation, aimed at purifying the consciousness of the individual to such a degree that all images and thoughts are left behind. It is as if the meditator is ascending a kind of inner ladder where at the highest rungs he or she gains a kind of pure bliss and insight, free from the distractions of ordinary experience. Very often this higher state is spoken of as being "non-dual," in other words, it is not like our usual experiences. In ordinary perception if I am looking at something, say a flower, then I am here and the flower is over there. I am the subject who sees; the flower is the object that is seen. But this distinction between subject and object seems to disappear in the higher mystical states, if we can judge from many reports. Also, such an ascent of stages of consciousness is usually said to involve the stilling of all feelings and the attainment of a perfect quietness. This is very different from the dynamic and shattering experience of the numinous.

As we shall see, there are some problems with the contrast that I am here trying to draw, but the contrast is nevertheless an important one. To sum it up, very often the mystical experience that arises in the process of contemplation or meditation is non-dual, but the numinous experience is very much dual; the mystical is quiet, but the numinous experience is powerful and turbulent; the mystical seems to be empty of images, while

the numinous experience is typically clothed in ideas of encounter with a personal God: the mystical does not give rise to worship or reverence, in so far as there is nothing "other" to worship or revere.

This theory of mystical experience as "pure consciousness" helps to explain why we find systems of belief in the Indian tradition, most notably Buddhism, that do not give much importance to God or the gods but put the highest value on personal liberation. The saintly yogi achieves the highest detachment and serenity, typically as a consequence of meditation that brings him to a state in which no distinctions can be made, in which the usual world of objects disappears. At the same time, however, this purity of consciousness usually is thought to bring about a kind of knowledge or insight. When a person sees the permanent, the impermanence of the world of objects is seen: when a person achieves the highest welfare, the truly unsatisfactory and suffering quality of ordinary life is known. Gaining true serenity, a person can reenter the ordinary world with equanimity and know things and people in the new light shed by the higher state he or she has reached.

Thus it is that the central figure in the Buddhist faith, Gautama, left his wife, child, and luxurious life (according to the received story) to pursue the quest for the truth about the suffering of the world. After sitting at the feet of various teachers and practicing various kinds of self-control and fasting, he finally attained a state of enlightenment while sitting beneath a tree—the famous Bodhi, or Enlightenment Tree (an offshoot of which is still to be seen at Bodh-Gaya in northern India). He became thus the ideal expression of wisdom, who sought—and found—insight in the upper reaches of his consciousness, having tested in his mind various theories about the cosmos. As a result of his experience, he taught his new insight to a group of former associates, also yogis and seekers after truth, and spent more than forty years setting forth the doctrines and the path to liberation. Gautama did not teach worship. He did not speak of the Other. He did not prophesy in the name of the Lord. He did not put the mighty creator of the world at the center of his teaching and life. On the contrary, he treated with irony the creator god (Brahmā) of those who conserved the ancient tradition of the Vedas, the priestly caste known as Brahmins. According to the Buddha, Brahmā was merely under the illusion he had created the world—a mistake arising from the fact that after a period in which the cosmos lies dormant, asleep between two vast ages of dynamism, the first living being to rise in the cosmic cycle is the god Brahmā, who ignorantly thinks that because he is the first living being to emerge he caused what came after. But what came after was already programmed to emerge, independently of Brahmā's activity. This irony about the great god is an indication of how Buddhism, while not denying the gods outright, sought to put them down, to show that they were at best of secondary value. In fact, at the heart of the Buddha's message lies not the experience of gods or God but the non-dual experience of liberation. Virtually all the later teachings and variations of Buddhism can be seen as so many different ways of captivating human beings, through religious myths and practices, to set them forth on a path that will bring them freedom. This freedom consists of an experience of "emptiness," or purity of consciousness, together with the perception that this emptiness is the underlying nature of things, that they are without permanent substance.

But another strand in Indian thinking is worth consideration and helps to open up the debate about the contrast between the numinous and the mystical experiences. In those mysterious collections of writings known as the Upanishads, which came into being about the time of the Buddha, there are some famous so-called identity statements. These say "I am the divine Being," and "That art Thou" (usually interpreted to mean "Thou, as having within thee the eternal Self, art one with the divine Being"). The key words used in Sanskrit are *Brahman,* meaning the divine Being or Power, and Ātman, meaning "Self." The two are said to be the same. Now, if we spell this out in more concrete terms, what the Upanishads appear to be saying in such passages is as follows: "That divine Being which lies behind the whole

cosmos, which creates it and sustains it and constitutes its inner nature, is the same as what you will discover in the depths of your own Self, if you will voyage inward through self-control and the methods of meditation and purification of your consciousness."

Here, in effect, the two strands of religious experience and thinking are being woven together. On the one hand, there is the numinous Brahman, seen as divine Power behind the cosmos and dimly visible through nature. This numinous Being in later Indian thought is portrayed in a more personal and dramatic way, as the great gods Shiva and Vishnu and as the divine female Kali, replete with power, terror, and love. On the other hand, there is the mystical search within. The Upanishads in a flash of insight bring the two together: The divine Being is found not only out there but also within the heart. This is a theme of much mysticism elsewhere—among Christians, for instance, who adopt the path of contemplation in order to seek God at the depths of their souls.

But in doing this such Christians are seeing the inner path in the light of a previously accepted numinous God who is the object of worship and devotion. In the case of Buddhism there was no such prior assumption: Buddhism was interested more in pursuing the inner path without believing in the Creator and the Wholly Other.

Let us see how far we've come in setting out a theory about the types of religious experience. Some religious traditions or phases of traditions stress the powerful Other, the great Creator. Others stress more the inner quest, without reference to God. Others combine the two quests. Before going on to see the questions that stem from this theory, it may be useful to see whether there are other strands of religious experience to consider.

The British writer R.C. Zaehner (1919–1975) drew attention, as others have done, to the fact that in a number of cultural contexts people may have a very powerful sense of unity with nature—with the cosmos around them. This sense of being lost to oneself but yet united to the world around, this sense of being part of a whole, Zaehner referred to as the "panenhenic" experience. The word derived from Greek means "all (*pan*) in (*en*) one (*hen*) ish (*ic*)." This concept may have been important for teachers of early Taoism. It came to be important in the development of Chinese and Japanese Buddhism, for instance in Zen, where themes from Taoism were blended with the spirit of Buddhist meditation. Thus, often we find in Zen art the idea of the disappearance of all distinctions between oneself and the world around one. The Zen poem—haiku—attempts in brief compass to bring out something of this strange and yet also beautiful way of perceiving the world.

Another form of religious experience, prevalent among small-scale and hunting societies, is that of the shaman. The shaman is a person who, because of his special personality, can make contact with the supernatural world. He will go into a trance and is thought to ascend to the heavenly world and to descend into the world of the dead. His ability to be in contact with spirits and his capacity to come back from the realm of death give him the power, it is thought, not only to tell where game can be found but also to cure disease. He can reenact dramatically the death and restoration to life of the sick person, and restore him to health. Much attention has been given to shamanism by the modern historian of religions, Mircea Eliade (1907–1986), who saw it as a key phenomenon of archaic religion. This may be so because shamanism may have influenced early techniques of producing special states of consciousness such as methods of breathing and mind control in the Indian and Chinese traditions—and out of this came the whole yoga tradition. On the other hand, a strand of the shamanistic experience is found in the phenomenon of being "possessed." In trance the shaman may be "occupied" by a god and so come to speak the words of the god. He thus becomes a crucial link between the world of spirits and the community to which he belongs. Out of this strand of shamanism there may have developed the tradition in which the prophet not only is confronted by God as the numinous Other but also speaks in the name of the Lord as though he is, so to say, "possessed" by God. Thus God says

to Jeremiah that he has "put words in his mouth" after mysteriously touching his lips.

So one model that we can propose about the way religious experience has developed is as follows: There are two developments of shamanism, which we might call the right wing and the left wing. The right wing focuses on the numinous experience of the Other, and the experience of the prophet is a special form of this. Institutionally, the successor to the prophet is the preacher, who tries to recapture something of the spirit of prophecy. The left wing focuses on the mystic or yogi, the one who practices the art of contemplation; institutionally, the successor of the mystical teachers of the past is the monk or nun.

This way of looking at religious experience, polarized into the numinous and mystical experiences, suggests that somehow mysticism is the same in differing religions, and that the difference between, say, the Christian and the Buddhist mystic is found in the kind of interpretation each places on her or his experience. Thus, the Christian finds in the light of the purity of her consciousness a sense of union with Christ, while the Buddhist sees the non-dual light as insight into the Emptiness, the Void, which lies in the midst of everything. But are the differences just a matter of interpretation? There has been much debate in recent times about this, for a number of reasons.

One is that, like Zaehner, some scholars think that there is a distinctive kind of mysticism that is different from the non-dual type (which he referred to as "monistic"). Zaehner thought that there is an inner experience the Christian and other God-oriented mystics undergo that involves the feeling of a loving relationship (he called this "theistic" mysticism). In this Zaehner was defending belief in God, for he thought of the non-dual experience as being at a lower level and so not as important or revealing. But once we talk about levels we usually are talking about value judgments. Why is the loving experience better than the non-dual one? It depends on your point of view. For many modern Westerners the idea of a personal relationship with God is at the heart of religion, but for the Buddhist we have to get away from preoccupation with personhood, which is only a mask of the ego, of selfishness. Who is right?

Another consideration is this: How do we tell what belongs to the experience itself and what to the interpretation? If I see a rope on the ground and perceive it as a snake and so become frightened, isn't it true to say I experienced a snake? So, if a mystic sees the inner light of consciousness as manifesting the divine being, does he not then experience God?

It may be so. But still, the idea of the single type of mystical experience is useful, for it enables us to understand that there are recurrent patterns of inner consciousness into which, according to context, people of differing religious and cultural traditions read differing messages.

This idea also helps explain some other things. It helps explain why mysticism in the West and in Islam has helped to promote what has been called "negative theology," or the way of thinking about God that stresses what cannot be said: God is beyond language, beyond thought. This side of belief chimes in with the experience of pure consciousness; if indeed God is found within—in what contains no images or thoughts or distinctions, in this bright and purifying blank—then God cannot be spoken of as this or that. This "negative theology" is a counterweight to the positive, sometimes very human ways, in which God is spoken of, for instance, in the Bible. Many preachers talk of God as though he is a human being, larger than life, who tells us to do this or that and worries about moral rules and whether there should be abortions or war. We should indeed see these important issues in the light of the highest values that we know, and for the Christian or Jew that means seeing them in the light of Eternity, of God. And since God is infinite, he has so much energy that it is not especially tiresome for him to worry about our minor human concerns. But even so there is often a need to counterbalance this human language about the divine Being with negativity: God may be like us but he is also very unlike us. He may be wise but it is not in the way in which a person would be wise. His goodness goes beyond all our ideas of goodness. And so on. Thus "negative" and mystical language helps to balance the other talk of God.

Also, our theory of two strands of experience helps explain a tension that appears from time to time between mystics and orthodoxy in traditions that believe in God. The orthodox stress the holiness and otherness of God. The orthodox Muslim or Christian conceives of God as Other and of us merely as creatures. It is blasphemous to put ourselves on a par with God. But if the mystical experience is, as we have seen, non-dual, and if by contrast the numinous God is Other, different from us, then there is a problem about the mystic's non-dual experience of God. The mystic often is led by the experience to say that he becomes one with God. He loses his sense of otherness from God. And this may even lead to the paradox of saying that one becomes or is God (as the Upanishads indeed say). This happened in the case of al-Hallaj (ca. 858–922), a famous Sufi mystic within Islam. He thought that all duality between himself and Allah was washed away and so said "I am the Real," using here one of the titles of Allah himself. For his blasphemy, for that was how the orthodox saw it, he was put to death—crucified, in fact, for he was an admirer of Jesus and crucifixion seemed a suitably ironic punishment.

Our theory of types of experience is also useful in helping to explain differing patterns of doctrine. If you stress the numinous, you stress that our salvation or liberation (our becoming holy) must flow from God the Other. It is he who brings it to us through his grace. You also stress the supreme power and dynamism of God as creator of this cosmos. If, on the other hand, you stress the mystical and the non-dual, you tend to stress how we attain salvation or liberation through our own efforts at meditation, not by the intervention of the Other. You also tend to stress the emptiness of things, the idea of a liberation that takes us beyond this impermanent life. If we combine the two but accentuate the numinous, we see mystical union as a kind of close embrace with the other—like human love, where two are one and yet the "two-ness" remains. If the accent is on the mystical rather than the numinous, then God tends to be seen as a being whom we worship, but in such a way that we get beyond the duality, until even God disappears in the unspeakable non-dual higher consciousness. This is the position of Advaita Vedānta, as we have noted; it is also in rather a different way the position of Mahāyāna or Greater Vehicle Buddhism (which developed out of early Buddhism and became the dominant kind of Buddhism in China and Japan) in its mainstream.

There is another way in which we may look at the distinction between the numinous and the mystical. In the numinous, the eternal lies, so to speak, beyond the cosmos and outside the human being. In the mystical, the Eternal somehow lies within us. In the first case we need to be dependent on the Other; in the second case we may rely upon our own powers, though the task of penetrating to the Eternal may be very hard. The numinous, in encouraging worship, encourages a loving dependence on the Other. The mystical, in encouraging meditation, encourages a sense of self-emptying. As we have seen, the two can go together. But there are differing accents.

In this discussion I have, of course, been oversimplifying. Because of the richness of ideas and myths in which experiences tend to be clothed, the feelings and insights people gain can vary subtly and widely in character. I have tried to combine Otto's theory with other theories which in modern times have emphasized the unity of mystical experiences across the religions. The famous writer Aldous Huxley (1894–1963) also emphasized such mystical unity. In his book *The Perennial Philosophy* he did much to influence Western thinking about the inner searches of Eastern religions, and so contributed to that flowering of mystical interests and gentleness that accompanied the otherwise turbulent 1960s.

Questions of Value and Truth

But a question is likely to remain in our minds. Is there after all any basis to these experiences? It is true that we may feel a sense of awe before the glories of the cosmos, or may from time to time experience a sense of the overpowering presence of God. It is true that yogis may purify their consciousness and feel thereby a sense of illumination and freedom. But so what? Could these experiences perhaps be delusions? Is the mystical, non-dual experience in the last analysis just a very interesting state of mind? And isn't the sense of presence of God just like a waking dream? We may feel that someone confronts us: Arjuna in the Song of the Lord may think himself in front of Vishnu in all his dramatic and terrifying glory. But is this not something that can be explained by some theory of projection? Couldn't we say that Arjuna projected his vision outward onto the screen of the world and then took it to be something real?

From one point of view we should not be concerned about what the value of various religious experiences is or might be. They have the effects that they have quite independently of how we may view them. But many writers in one way or another have tried to argue that religion is indeed a projection; and if this is true, it would follow that key religious experiences are also projections. The projection theory is one explanation of how so pervasive a feature of human history arose and how it maintains itself.

Consider one way in which the numinous experience, or one of its offshoots, is quite common in modern life: the experience of being "born again." The person who feels this, in the Christian context, often has feelings not unlike those of the great reformer, Martin Luther (1483–1546)—a deep sense of sin and powerlessness. These are the mirror images, so to speak, of the power and holiness of God as the Other. In the face of the Holy the individual feels unholy, Christ comes to such a person, giving a marvelous reassurance. If she repents, then the Savior will overcome the sin and give the person new power in her life. Some would argue that it is the circumstances of the person's life and times that created in her the sense of sin, and that the threatening figure of God was something projected from her unconscious out of a sense of guilt, arising from infantile conflicts in the nuclear family. To say this is to echo the thinking of psychoanalysis, going back to Freud's influential book *Totem and Taboo* (1915). Freud gives a psychological interpretation to then current theories of totemism in archaic religion, in which each clan or group has a totem or sacred animal, which is normally forbidden or taboo. So wouldn't we, by Freud's explanation, be suggesting that the sense of the numinous (with the *tremendum*— "to be trembled at"—aspect being played by the Father and the *fascinans* by Christ) comes from her own psyche, triggered by the circumstances of her life? If we could manage such explanation consistently, it would no doubt be a great advance in trying to understand the power of religion and the ways in which it works.

But for the explanation to be valid certain conditions have to be met. For one thing, Freud's theory on the dynamics of the psyche would have to be confirmed in a variety of cultures. Here there is a problem with Freud's *Totem and Taboo* and his later ideas about religion. He did not have access to the wide knowledge of other religions that we now possess. The fact is that his stress upon the role of the father figure in religion (which is, as it were, the heavenly image of the real-life father) is relevant only to some religions and not others. Moreover, the data which Freud drew on in late nineteenth- and early twentieth-century Vienna were largely related to a very special and not very typical society whose preoccupations were Christianity and Judaism.

For Freud himself religion was an illusion. His position has been influential not only because of the fruitful way in which he made use of the idea of the unconscious mind but also because his picture of human nature and the path of self-understanding became itself an alternative to religion. The analyst was able to take over something of the priest's role: He was a new kind of pastor, very much in the modern idiom. The new teachings of psychoanalysis could deal with guilt and promise a new kind of spiritual health. The patient, in undergoing the process of analysis, went through a new form of religious initiation and renewal.

This leads us to see a problem about theories of the origins of religious experience. Such theories may, like Freud's, begin from the assumption that there is no ultimate religious reality—that there is no God. So they already begin from a particular worldview—a humanist one in the sense in which we used this term in the previous chapter. But what is the reason for starting with that worldview rather than with one that accepts the existence of something lying beyond the visible cosmos? Or is there perhaps some neutral standpoint between rejection of God and acceptance of him? (Or between acceptance of nirvana and rejection of it?)

To spell out further the problem about the Freudian position on traditional religion: Isn't Freud using one worldview to judge another— like the Christian missionary we referred to earlier, who judges Hinduism from the assumptions of the Bible? Freud was—with part of himself at any rate—claiming to be engaged in science. However, it is not scientific simply to begin with assumptions that would make a rival theory false before the evidence is properly examined. And once we begin to look at Freud's major writings on the origin of religion in the light of the evidence from the history of religions, we find that his theories break down. For instance, he thought totemism, or the worship of sacred animals, was a universal early phenomenon. He was relying on some contemporary anthropology that is now out of date. His idea that the leader of a primitive human horde had been killed by his sexually jealous sons was pure speculation derived in part from an aside in the writings of Charles Darwin. It is a remarkable thing that so speculative a theory should have won so much intelligent support in the 1920s. We can perhaps explain it the way many have chosen to explain the popularity of religion: It is a case of appeal, rather than truth.

I shall come back to the question of how we judge religious experiences, but first let us look at two further depth psychological approaches. One is that of Carl Gustav Jung, who broke with Freud in the early days of psychoanalysis and took a positive view of the value of religion and of the symbols people use in myth and ritual, the symbols that, so to speak, well up from the human race's unconscious. Jung's attitude toward religious experience was ambiguous. Although he did not affirm any particular religious doctrine, he nevertheless considered that religion could be useful in helping people reach balance and maturity, and achieve an integrated personality.

Erich Fromm (1900–1980), who belongs to the Freudian tradition, considered that religion could be a good force if it were humanistic. For him religion is unavoidable, or it represents for a group a common outlook and a common focus of devotion—and every group needs these. Fromm believed, however, that an authoritarian and rigid religion is bad for us. For one thing, all that is good and reasonable in ourselves is projected outward onto God, and we are left merely with a sense of sin and powerlessness. We are alienated from our own goodness.

It thus appears that from Fromm's perspective the numinous experience of the powerful Other is unhealthy. When he wrote about Luther (and Luther's religion was permeated with the sense of the numinous), he remarked:

> Thus, while Luther freed people from the authority of the Church, he made them submit to a much more tyrannical authority, that of a God who insisted on complete submission of man and annihilation of the individual self as the essential condition of his salvation. *Luther's faith was the conviction of being loved upon the condition of surrender.* . . .

And this was because:

> If you get rid of your individual self with all its shortcomings and doubts by utmost self-effacement, you free yourself from the feeling of your own nothingness and can participate in God's glory.[1]

There have been others who also looked at Luther from the perspective of psychoanalysis, and there seems to be some ground for thinking that the numinous awareness of God was able to play a key role in resolving conflicts arising acutely within Luther's soul. In other words, we have here a typical religious equation: a type of experience that had part of its dynamic from factors outside the individual, encountering the psychological condition inside the individual.

Luther's outlook, with its undue respect for power and authority and its sense of the complete sinfulness and evil in the human being when left alone and without the intervening power and grace of God, is, for Fromm, unhealthy. It is not humanistic, because it fails to mobilize what is good in human nature. By contrast, Fromm is more favorable toward the religion of the mystic and of Jesus as he, Fromm, interpreted it. For Fromm, the Oedipus complex that Freud saw as resulting from a child's sexual jealousy of the parent is not so much sexual as a craving to free herself from dependence on the parent. The adult, like the child, wishes to prolong childhood and to avoid freedom. But a truly humanistic approach is one that stresses freedom. When Jesus said "For I am come to set a man at variance against his father and the daughter against her mother," what he meant, according to Fromm, was that the individual must throw off the craving to be a child. Whether he is right in his feeling for what the Gospel means is another matter.

Fromm's way of looking at religion is quite openly judgmental. He distinguishes the good and valuable in religion from what he regards as dangerous and unhealthful. As I have said before with some force, it is important for us to look first not to questions of value but to questions of power and meaning—to see how worldviews actually operate and what their significance is for human beings. But if I may comment on the question of evaluation, then I think we must look at religious experience in a wider context than the psychology of the individual, important though this is. We need to see the degree to which religion and its core experiences have been creative and destructive. Fromm, in writing the words quoted above, was trying to set the debate in a wider context, for he saw in Luther's attitudes some of the seeds of later Nazism. And it cannot be denied that sometimes the numinous and wrathful character of the experience of God can lean in the direction of hostility. Often the preacher "possessed" by the numinous also expresses hatreds. And, in particular, Luther was highly abusive of the Jews, and so contributed to that stream of anti-Semitism that was so destructive to Europe.

But on the other hand there are things to be said regarding the creativity of Luther the prophet. For one thing, Luther's revolution itself prepared the way for a critique of authority and for a new vision of the individual that has done much to shape Western culture. By a paradox, the human relationship with a powerful and merciful God can give the individual a source of independence against the powerful and often unmerciful pressures of the state, economic power, and prevailing values.

But perhaps the main thing we can learn from this brief look at some of the depth psychologists is that they too bring a worldview to bear in estimating religious experience. Their worldview is not that of any of the traditional religions. It tends to be humanist by denying the transcendent realm, the other depth that lies beyond the cosmos, which the older religions see as the abode of the divine, or of nirvana. The depth psychologists tend to start from a picture of the human being trapped, as it were, within the material cosmos. In so doing, they beg the question of whether religious experience tells us anything about the way things are—the question of whether religious visions and insights "tell the truth." If there is only this cosmos, then nothing, however dramatic in experience, will make us aware of something outside the cosmos. The experience of what transcends or goes beyond the cosmos will always be interpreted as having its origins inside us. So the question of whether religious experience tells us the truth at all is a question that depends in part on the worldview with which we start. It looks like a circle. But it is not a circle to be trapped in, for what it shows is that questions of religious truth are a matter of the perspective with which they are viewed. And which perspective—the humanist or the religious—is more convincing depends on a whole array of details.

Initially, in worldview analysis, we are concerned with the power of religion and its varieties of experience. One of the things we can learn from psychology is that personal factors will be important in determining the degree to which a type of religion "catches on." And depth psychology helps to explore how symbolic patterns, of which we are at best only half aware, help shape our feelings and actions and thus prepare seed beds upon which the differing worldviews may grow.

NOTE

1. The quotations are from J. Milton Yinger, ed., *Religion, Society and the Individual* (New York: Macmillan, 1957), p. 392.

4.2 Black Elk's Vision

If a man told you about a vision he believed had been given him by a sacred power, what would you think? Suppose this vision involved being transported in supernormal ways from the earth to the sky, traveling roads in four directions, and journeying to the center of the earth. Suppose the person (let's call him Nicholas) who recounted this vision claimed to have encountered sacred and mysterious beings that taught him sacred songs and gave him the powers to heal. What sort of explanation would you offer for this vision? Would you take it seriously or dismiss it as pure fantasy?

Suppose further that Nicholas's description involved highly complex symbolism that derived from the religious tradition in which he was raised. According to that tradition, the Thunder-beings who live in the sky engage in cosmic warfare with the waters below, and Nicholas tells you that in part of this vision, he vanquishes the spirit of the water by turning it into a turtle. Would you think that his vision had been strongly influenced by his religious tradition? Perhaps he "saw" what he had been taught to expect? But then, what did he actually see? Is his account a pure description of what actually happened to him or a description mixed with interpretation?

Are these kinds of questions really relevant? Perhaps we should believe what Nicholas tells us. Perhaps we miss the point and meaning of the vision if we become too concerned about its truth.

If you have just finished Reading 4.1, you might just say that this is a rather typical shamanistic experience. Nicholas believes that the spirit world has made contact with him, revealed future events, and given him the power to cure disease. Does this classification, however, tell us very much? Does it help us understand the philosophical implications of such experiences? Let's turn to a concrete example.

Black Elk (1863–1950), a great medicine man of the Oglala Lakota Sioux, lived in two worlds. The world into which he was born was the world of the Lakota at a time when the sacred myths, legends, and rituals of the Lakota tradition were still very much alive. The whites destroyed that world. Black Elk, like so many other Native Americans, had to learn to adjust to the white world. He did. He became a Roman Catholic, was given the name Nicholas, and professed Christianity as his new faith. He put aside the "old ways" as the work of Satan and did not practice the rituals of the Lakota. The old Lakota religion, however, lived on in him, and eventually he realized that it was his sacred duty to transmit the "old ways" to a new generation.

John G. Neihardt interviewed Black Elk and immortalized his teachings in two books, *Black Elk Speaks* (1932) and *When the Tree Flowered* (1951). These books, according to Vine Deloria, Jr., have become a kind of "American Indian Bible."

Central to Black Elk's life was a great vision he received in 1873 from the six grandfathers who symbolize the power of the six directions (above, below, west, north, east, and south) and *Wakan Tanka,* the Great Mysteriousness. What follows is my edited version of the notes Neihardt took as Black Elk recounted his vision.

Although this account reveals little philosophical reflection on the meaning of the vision, Black Elk spent the rest of his life reflecting on its meaning for his people and their future. He believed that the vision placed a sacred duty on him to realize its meaning in his life. He felt obliged to do all in his power to restore the sacred hoop of his people that the invasion of the whites so brutally broke. This vision helped Black Elk bridge the world of the "old ways" and the new world brought by the whites. It laid the foundation for finding a way to preserve, and to make meaningful again, a rich culture and religion that were in danger of dying. What Black Elk saw in 1873 led to a renaissance of Native American religion and culture in the last half of the twentieth century.

Reading Questions

1. What do you think Black Elk's vision means?
2. What do you consider the most important part of the vision? Why?
3. What role do traditional Sioux symbols play in this vision?
4. Is it possible to develop criteria that would allow one to distinguish description from interpretation in this vision? If so, what might they be?

Black Elk's Vision*

BLACK ELK

The Two Men Take Black Elk up into the Clouds

As I lay in the tipi I could see through the tipi the same two men whom I saw before and they were coming from the clouds. Then I recognized them as the same men I had seen before in my first vision. They came and stood off aways from me and stopped, saying: "Hurry up, your grandfather is calling you." When they started back I got up and started to follow them. Just as I got out of the tipi I could see the two men going back into the clouds and there was a small cloud coming down toward me at the same time, which stood before me. I got on top of the cloud and was raised up, following the two men, and when I looked back, I saw my father and mother looking at me. When I looked back I felt sorry that I was leaving them.

Black Elk is Shown the Horses of the Four Directions

I followed those men on up into the clouds and they showed me a vision of a bay horse standing there in the middle of the clouds. One of the men said: "Behold him, the horse who has four legs, you shall see." I stood there and looked at the horse and it began to speak. It said: "Behold me; my life history you shall see. Furthermore, behold them, those where the sun goes down, their lives' history you shall see."

I looked over there and saw twelve black horses toward the west, where the sun goes down. All the horses had on their necks necklaces of buffalo hoofs. [*I saw above the twelve head of horses birds.*] I was very scared of those twelve head of horses because I could see the light[ning] and thunder around them.

Then they showed me twelve white horses with necklaces of elks' teeth and said: "Behold them, those who are where the giant lives [the north]." Then I saw some white geese flying around over the horses.

Then I turned around toward the east, where the sun shines continually. The men said: "Behold them, those where the sun shines continually." I saw twelve head of horses, all sorrels [*and these sorrels had horns and there were some eagles flying above the sorrels*].

Then I turned to the place where you always face, the south, and saw twelve head of buckskin horses. They said: "Behold him, those where you always face." These horses had horns.

[*At the beginning of the vision they were all horses, only two* (sets) *had necklaces* (the blacks and the whites) *and two had horns* (the sorrels and the buckskins).]

When I had seen it all, the bay horse said to me: "Your grandfathers are having a council, these shall take you; so take courage." Then these horses went into formation of twelve abreast in four lines—blacks, whites, sorrels, buckskins. As they stood, the bay horse looked to the west and neighed. I looked over there and saw great clouds of horses in all colors and they all neighed back to this horse and it sounded like thunder. Then the horse neighed toward the north and the horses came through there and neighed back again. These horses were in all colors also. Then the bay looked toward the east and he neighed and some more horses neighed back. The bay looked southward and neighed and the horses neighed back to him from there.

The bay horse said to me: "Behold them, your horses come dancing." I looked around and saw millions of horses circling around me—a sky full

*Reproduced from *The Sixth Grandfather: Black Elk's Teachings Given to John G. Neihardt,* edited by Raymond J. DeMallie, copyright 1984 by the University of Nebraska Press, by permission of the University of Nebraska Press. Footnotes edited and renumbered.

of horses. Then the bay horse said: "Make haste." The horse began to go beside me and the forty-eight horses followed us. I looked around and all the horses that were running changed into buffalo, elk, and all kinds of animals and fowls and they all went back to the four quarters.

The Bay Horse Leads Black Elk to the Cloud Tipi of the Six Grandfathers

I followed the bay horse and it took me to a place on a cloud under a rainbow gate and there were sitting my six grandfathers, sitting inside of a rainbow door, and the horses stopped behind me. I saw on either side of me a man whom I recognized as those of the first vision. The horses took their original positions in the four quarters.

One of the grandfathers said to me: "Do not fear, come right in" (through the rainbow door). So I went in and stood before them. The horses in the four quarters of the earth all neighed to cheer me as I entered the rainbow door.

The grandfather representing where the sun goes down said: "Your grandfathers all over the world and the earth are having a council and there you were called, so here you are. Behold then, those where the sun goes down; from thence they shall come, you shall see. From them you shall know the willpower of myself, for they shall take you to the center of the earth, and the nations of all kinds shall tremble.[1] Behold where the sun continually shines, for they shall take you there."

The first grandfather then showed me a wooden cup with water, turning it toward me. He said: "Take courage and be not afraid, for you will know him. And furthermore, behold him, whom you shall represent. By representing him, you shall be very powerful on earth in medicines and all powers. He is your spirit and you are his body and his name is Eagle Wing Stretches."

When I looked up I saw flames going up from the rainbow. The first grandfather gave me a cup of water and also a bow and arrow and said: "Behold them, what I give you shall depend on, for you shall go against our enemies and you shall be a great warrior." Then he gave me that cup of water and said: "Behold, take this, and with this you shall be great." (This means that I should kill all sickness on earth with this water.)

After this he got up and started to run toward where the sun goes down and as he ran he changed into a black horse as he faced me. The five men left said: "Behold him." And this black horse changed into a poor horse.

The second grandfather rose and said: "Take this and make haste." So I took an herb out of the second grandfather's hand. And as [*I turned to the dying horse*] I held it toward the black horse [*and this holy herb*] cured the black horse, making him strong and fat once again.

The second grandfather represented the north. He said: "Behold the mother earth, for you shall create a nation." (This means that I am going to cure lots of sickness with this herb—bring children back to life.) The bay horse stood with the black horse and said to me: "Father, paint me, for I shall make a nation on the earth." [The] second grandfather of the north said again: "Take courage and behold, for you shall represent the wing of the great giant that lives."[2] The second grandfather stood up and ran toward the north and as he turned around he changed himself again into a white goose. I looked toward where the black horses were and they were thunders and the northern white horses turned into white geese. The second grandfather said: "Behold then, your grandfather, for they shall fly in circles from one end of the earth to the other." [*Through this power of the north I will make everybody cry as geese do when they go north in the spring because the hardship is over.*]

First grandfather's song:

> They are appearing, may you behold.
> They are appearing, may you behold.
> The thunder nation is appearing, may you
>   behold.

Second grandfather's song:

> They are appearing, may you behold.
> They are appearing, may you behold
> The white geese nation is appearing, may
>   you behold.

The third grandfather, where the sun continually shines, says: "Younger brother, take courage, for across the earth they shall take you. Behold them" (pointing to the morning star and below the star there were two men flying), "from them you shall have power. All the fowls of the universe, these he has wakened and also he has wakened the beings on the earth" (animals, people, etc.). As the third grandfather said this, he held in his hand a peace pipe, which had a spotted eagle outstretched on the handle of the pipe; apparently the eagle was alive for it was moving. He said: "Behold this, for with this you shall walk across the earth. Behold this, for with this whatever is sick on this earth you shall make well."

Then the third grandfather pointed to a man who was solid red in color and said: "Behold him." Then the red man lay down and changed into a buffalo before he got up. When he was standing up, the third grandfather said "Behold him" again. The buffalo ran back to the east and when he looked at the horses in this direction they all turned into buffalo.

The fourth grandfather said to me: "Younger brother, behold me; a nation's center of the earth I shall give you with the power of the four quarters. With the power of the four quarters like relatives you shall walk. Behold the four quarters." And after he said this I looked and saw that at each of the four quarters there was a chief. [*At the time I grew up to manhood there was no war and the Indians all became white men and if there had been the right feeling among the Indians I would have been the greatest, most powerful medicine man of the ages.*]

The fourth grandfather had a stick in his hand and he said: "Behold this, with this to the nation's center of the earth, many you shall save." I looked at the stick and saw that it was sprouting out and at the top there were all kinds of birds singing. The fourth grandfather said: "With this you shall brace yourself as a cane and thus your nation shall brace themselves with this as a cane and upon this cane you shall make a nation. Behold the earth, for across it there are two roads. Behold the sacred road from where the giant is to where we always face. Behold, this road shall be your nation. From this road you shall

receive good." (Meaning red sacred road from north to south, a good road for good spirits.)

Next the fourth grandfather pointed to the road from where the sun shines continually to where the sun goes down and said: "Behold the black road, for it is the road of the Thunder-beings" (road of fearfulness); or, "Behold the black road for it shall be a fearful road. With this road you shall defend yourself." (Whenever I go to war I shall get powers from this fearful road and will be able to destroy any enemies. From the red road I get power to do good. From east to west I have power to destroy and from north to south power to do good.)

"Behold the earth with four ascents you shall walk." (This power will be with me for four generations.) The fourth grandfather turned around and started to the south and then he rolled on the ground and became a horse and he rolled once more and became an elk. He then stood among the buckskins and they too turned into elks.

The fifth grandfather represented the Great Spirit above. He said: "Boy, I sent for you and you came. Behold me, my power you shall see." He stretched his hands out and turned into a spotted eagle. Then he said: "Behold them; they, the fowls of the universe, shall come to you. Things in the skies shall be like relatives" (meaning stars). "They shall take you across the earth with my power. Your grandfathers shall attack an enemy and be unable to destroy him, but you will have the power to destroy. You shall go with courage. This is all." Then the eagle flew up over my head and I saw the animals and birds all coming toward me to perform a duty.

Then the sixth grandfather said: "Boy, take courage, you wanted my power on earth, so you shall know me. You shall have my power in going back to the earth. Your nation on earth shall have great difficulties. There you shall go. Behold me, for I will depart." (The sixth grandfather was a very old man with very white hair.) I saw him go out the rainbow gate. I followed him out the rainbow gate. I was on the bay horse now that had talked to me at the first. I stopped and took a good look at the sixth grandfather and it seemed that I recognized him. I stood there for awhile very scared and then as I looked at him longer I knew it was myself as a young man. At the first he was an old man, but he got younger and younger until he was a little boy nine years old. This old man had in his hand a spear.

Black Elk Walks the Black Sacred Road from West to East and Vanquishes the Spirit in the Water

I remembered that the grandfather of the west had given me a wooden cup of water and a bow and arrow and with this bow and arrow I was going to destroy the enemy with the power of the fearful road. With the wooden cup of water I was to save mankind. This water was clear and with it I was to raise a nation (like medicine).

My horse turned around and faced the west and all the black horses went and stood behind me in four ranks, twelve abreast—blacks, whites, sorrels, buckskins. They turned around toward the north. "Behold your wind from the north; this wind and an herb they have given you. With this herb and the wind you shall go back to the earth." (With the herb I was to have power to save horses and the wind was included. Whenever I would own a horse, it would be able to run for weeks and weeks without getting out of wind.) We swung around to the east in formation. The grandfather of the east let the pipe go which he was holding and it flew to me: "Behold it, for with this you shall be peaceful with the nations. Behold it, for you shall possess this for the nations on earth." I took the pipe. The eastern grandfather said again: "Behold him who shall appear; from him you shall have power." The morning star was coming up in the east as I looked this way. As I faced them, I noticed that the sorrels of the east had stars on their foreheads and they were very bright. Then we faced the south and the eastern grandfather said: "Behold your black sacred road you shall walk." As I turned around the buckskins lined up into formation and turned around facing the east to take me down the road of destruction. "As you walk your nation, the beings all over the universe shall fear you."

They began to go toward the east. They were all following me. I was the leader. I could see ahead of me a lot of birds in the air and behind me they were all fearful of me. There were twelve riders—all right-handed except one and he was called Left Hand Charger. The rider of the white horse was called One Horn Red and they gave me the name of Eagle That Stretches Its Wing.

Going east from the highest peak in the west— Pike's Peak. As we went along I noticed that everything on the earth was trembling with fear. I looked back and saw my twelve horseback riders and the horses' manes and tails were decorated with hail and the men had hail all over them. I was riding along as the chief of all the heavens and I looked down and saw the hail falling from these men and horses. I could see the country as I went and I remember well seeing in the forks of the Missouri River a man standing amid a flame with the dust around him in the air. I knew then that this was the enemy which was going to attack me. I could see all kinds of creatures dying beneath me, as he had destroyed everything.

As we neared this place we sang a sacred song concerning the peace pipe and the eagle, and all the riders had this for a weapon. [*The sorrels sang first.*] The song that represents the four quarters:

> I, myself, have sent them a-fleeing
> Because I wore the feather of an eagle.
> I, myself, sent them a-fleeing.

> I, myself, have sent them a-fleeing
> For I wore the relic of the wind.
> I, myself, have sent them a-fleeing.

[The] Thunder-beings sang then:

> I, myself, send them a-fleeing
> For I wore the relic of the hail.
> I, myself, send them a-fleeing.

Then the ones on the west sang:

> I, myself, send them a-fleeing.
> I, myself, send them a-fleeing.

Then the water splashed up as a result of something scared of me, and the flames came rolling out of this same place. The twelve riders from the west attacked this man but could not destroy him. He attacked them and forced them back toward the south. The white riders from the north attacked him but failed also to kill him. The eastern riders attacked him and also failed [*as he drove them back. They stood facing north*]. The buckskins from the south also attacked him and failed. After they all had attacked this man and failed, I looked at the splashing water and saw a man painted blue coming out. Then they all hollered: "He is coming!" and ran. They said: "Eagle Wing Stretches, make haste, for your nation all over the universe is in fear, make haste." I could hear, at this time, everything in the universe cheering for me. At this time my bow and arrow turned into a big spear. With the spear and the cup of water in the other hand, I immediately charged on the enemy myself. As I attacked, everybody cheered for me, telling me to "Make haste!" Just as the man got to the water, I swooped down on him and stabbed him through the heart. You could see the lightning from my spear as I stabbed him. I took him and threw him quite a distance. Just as I took the spear out, the man turned into a turtle. After I had killed the enemy the horse troops came by and hit [couped] the enemy [*and then they went back*]. Everything that had been dead came back to life and cheered me for killing that enemy. (This means that sometime in the future I was going to kill an enemy in some future battle.) . . .

Black Elk Receives the Healing Herb of the North and the Sacred Tree Is Established at the Center of the Nation's Hoop

As I looked down upon the people, there stood on the north side a man painted red all over his body and he had with him a lance (Indian spear) and he walked into the center of the sacred nation's hoop and lay down and rolled himself on the ground and when he got up he was a buffalo standing right in the center of the nation's hoop. The buffalo rolled and when he got up there was an herb there in his place. The herb plant grew up and bloomed so that I could see what it looked like—what kind of an herb it was from the bloom.

After the buffalo's arrival the people looked better and then when the buffalo turned into an herb, the people all got up and seemed to be well. Even the horses got up and stretched themselves and neighed. Then a little breeze came from the north and I could see that the wind was in the form of a spirit and as it went over the people all the dead things came to life. All the horses pulled up their tails and neighed and began to prance around.

[The southern?] spirit said: "Behold you have seen the powers of the north in the forms of man, buffalo, herb and wind. The people shall follow the man's steps; like him they shall walk and like the buffalo they shall live and with the herb they shall have knowledge. They shall be like relatives to the wind." (From the man in the illustration they should be healthy, from the buffalo they shall get meat, from the herb they shall get knowledge of diseases. The north wind will give them strong endurance.)

[The southern?] spirit speaks again: "Behold him they have sent forth to the center of the nation's hoop." Then I saw the pipe with the spotted eagle flying to the center of the nation's hoop. The morning star went along with the pipe. They flew from the east to the center. "With this your nation's offering as they walk. They will be like unto him. With the pipe they shall have peace in everything. Behold your eagle, for your nation like relatives they shall be. Behold the morning star, relative-like they shall be, from whence they shall have wisdom." Just then the morning star appeared and all the people looked up to it and the horses neighed and dogs barked.

(The flowering stick was in the middle of the nation's hoop again.) [The southern?] spirit said: "Behold the circle of the sacred hoop, for the people shall be like unto it; and if they are like unto this, they shall have power, because there is no end to this hoop and in the center of the hoop these raise their children." (The sacred hoop means the continents of the world and the people shall stand as one. Everything reproduces here inside the hoop.)

They put the sacred stick into the center of the hoop and you could hear birds singing all kinds of songs by this flowering stick and the people and animals all rejoiced and hollered. The women were sending up their tremolos. The men said: "Behold it; from there we shall multiply, for it is the greatest of the greatest sticks." This stick will take care of the people and at the same time it will multiply. We live under it like chickens under the wing. We live under the flowering stick like under the wing of a hen. Depending on the sacred stick we shall walk and it will be with us always. From this we will raise our children and under the flowering stick we will communicate with our relatives—beast and bird—as one people. This is the center of the life of the nation.

The sacred stick is the cottonwood tree ("rustling tree," waga chun [*wagacan*]). The nation represents this tree [*and if they grow up they will multiply like birds, etc.*]. This tree never had a chance to bloom because the white men came. The trunk is the chief of the people. If this tree had seen a bloom probably I or some of my descendants would be great chiefs.

The people camped there. I was on the bay horse again on the west side and was with another man. (This man is still living today and probably I could have made him a medicine man, but I never did it as yet, because I have never seen him. This man lives at Grass Creek and he knows nothing about this, nevertheless. This man's name was One Side.) One Side had [a] bow and arrow in one hand and a cup of water in the other. I saw that the people were getting ready for a storm and they were fixing their tipis to make them stronger for the storm. The storm cloud was approaching and swallows were coming under the cloud and I, myself, and One Side were coming on top of the cloud. (We were traveling on the fourth ascent and I saw the people on the third ascent from the fourth ascent.)

It was raining on earth now. A spirit [southern?] said to me that they had shown me everything there was to do on earth and that I was to do it myself now. He sang this song and it went like this:

> A good nation I will make over.
> The nation above has said this to me.
> They have given me the power to make
>   over this nation.

The cloud then swept over the village and they [the people?] stood in the west. When they turned around, the cloud was all gone. The cloud christened them with water. They all hollered: "Eagle Wing Stretches, A-ha-hey!" (meaning "Thanks to Eagle Wing Stretches!"). The people on earth started on the good road again, the red road, and I was forced to give all my relics to the people with the exception of the bow and arrow. The horses were all very fat now, so the people began to break camp. The people accepted what I gave them and I went ahead on the good road. (The bow and arrow represent lightning.) . . .

Black Elk Is Taken to the Center of the Earth and Receives the Daybreak Star Herb

[The] western black spirit said: "Behold this day, for this day is yours." [*I will have the power to shed many happy days on people, they tell me.*] "Take courage, for we shall take you to the center of the earth." They [the spirits] said: "Behold the center of the earth for we are taking you there." As I looked I could see great mountains with rocks and forests on them. I could see all colors of light flashing out of the mountains toward the four quarters. Then they took me on top of a high mountain where I could see all over the earth. Then they told me to take courage for they were taking me to the center of the earth. All the sixteen riders of the four quarters were with me going to the center of the earth and also this man by the name of One Side.

We were facing the east and I noticed something queer and found out that it was two men coming from the east and they had wings. On each one's breast was a bright star. The two men came and stood right in front of us and the west black spirit said: "Behold them, for you shall depend upon them." Then as we stood there the daybreak star stood between the two men from the east. There was a little star beside the daybreak star also.[3] They had an herb in their hands and they gave it to me, saying: "Behold this; with this on earth you shall undertake anything and accomplish it." As they presented the herb to me they told me to drop it on earth and when it hit the earth it took root and grew and flowered. You could see a ray of light coming up from the flower, reaching the heavens, and all the creatures of the universe saw this light. (Herbs used by Black Elk are in four colors—yellow, blue, red, white flowers all on one bush. The four-colored flowers represent the four quarters of the earth. This herb is called daybreak star herb.)

[The] western black spirit said: "Behold all over the universe." As I looked around I could see the country full of sickness and in need of help. This was the future and I was going to cure these people. On the east and north people were rejoicing, and on the south and west they were sick and there was a cloud over them. They said: "Behold them who need help. You shall make them over in the future." After a while I noticed the cloud over the people was a white one and it was probably the white people coming.

The western black spirit sang:

> Here and there may you behold. (twice)
> All may you behold.
> Here and there may you behold. (twice)

They had taken me all over the world and showed me all the powers. They took me to the center of the earth and to the top of the peak they took me to review it all. This last song means that I have already seen it. I was to see the bad and the good. I was to see what is good for humans and what is not good for humans. . . .

NOTES

1. "Willpower" (*tawacin*) is an important concept for understanding Lakota religion, for it is the power of mind—which is not merely passive, but creative—that is enriched ("made wise") by the vision experiences. Here the western grandfather promises that Black Elk will share in his willpower, thus giving him power to use on earth. To receive such power—or to activate it once one has it—requires "clarity of understanding" (*waableza*), a focusing of mental energies on the psychic gifts of the spirits. It is probably this to which the Lakotas refer when they say that mastery of a vision requires "effort and study" (Densmore, *Teton Sioux Music*, p. 85). See Brown, *The Sacred Pipe*, p. 64, no. 5.

2. The "great giant that lives" is *Waziya*, personification of the north. His "wing" (winged) is the white goose.

3. *Anpo wicahpi* (daybreak star) and *anpo wicahpi sunkaku* (daybreak star's younger brother).

4.3 I and Thou

Which are more important, individuals or the relationships among individuals? Among the sorts of relationships that are possible, which are primary? How, for example, can I relate to a tree? As a logger, my relationship may be purely instrumental. The tree represents to me so many board feet of lumber from which I can make a profit. The tree for me is an it—a thing.

I might, however, relate to a tree in a more personal way. I might marvel at the tree's immensity, complexity, and power. I might contemplate the life of the tree. Perhaps the tree will inspire me to write a poem. For me the tree is no longer an it—a thing to be used for my own benefit—but has become more like a person. It has become more like a you or a thou than like an it.

How can I relate to God? How should I relate to God? Should God be for me as the tree is for the logger, an impersonal it that I can use to my advantage? Or should the divine be for me as the tree is for the poet, an intimate friend?

Martin Buber (1878–1965) was an Austrian–Jewish theologian and philosopher. Hasidism, a Jewish mystical movement that flourished in Eastern Europe before spreading elsewhere, inspired his religious thought and life. Buber himself had a mystical experience that he initially interpreted as union with "the primal being." Later he decided that he had experienced the unity of his own soul. This reinterpretation coincided with traditional Jewish notions that however intimate the relationship a person has with God, there always remains an important and real difference.

In the selection that follows, Buber does not describe his religious experiences but rather shares with us his philosophical and theological reflections on the meaning of his religious experiences. Buber uses the term I-It to denote impersonal relationships, and he uses the term I-Thou to denote personal relationships. According to Buber, these two types of relationships are fundamental to our existence. The English word *thou* translates the German word *du. Du* is an informal pronoun (as opposed to the formal *Sie*) used with intimate friends and loved ones. At one time the English word *thou* was equivalent to *du.* That is why the King James Version of the Bible uses *thou* (*thee, thine*) instead of *you.* Today, the word *thou* is no longer used, or if it is, has an archaic ring to it. So Buber's I-Thou relationship is in German *Ich und Du* ("I and You"). The *Du* indicates mutuality, trust, sharing, openness, and intimacy.

Buber's religious experiences and his reflections on the Jewish tradition taught him that God is an eternal Thou who is present in every genuine I-Thou relationship. To treat God as It (an all-too-human tendency, according to Buber) amounts to idolatry—trying to use the divine for one's own personal ends. His ideas appear to reflect what Smart might call both numinous and mystical elements (see Reading 4.1).

Reading Questions

1. What do you think Buber means when he says that "*I-Thou* can only be spoken with the whole being" but "*I-It* can never be spoken with the whole being"?
2. What do you think Buber means when he says, "all real living is meeting"?
3. How can God be both "wholly Other" and "wholly the Same"?
4. What does Buber mean when he calls God an absolute Person?
5. Do you agree with Buber when he says that in all genuine I-Thou relationships we meet God? Why or why not?

I and Thou*

MARTIN BUBER

TO MAN THE WORLD IS TWOFOLD, in accordance with his twofold attitude.

The attitude of man is twofold, in accordance with the twofold nature of the primary words which he speaks.

The primary words are not isolated words, but combined words.

The one primary word is the combination *I-Thou.*

The other primary word is the combination *I-It;* wherein, without a change in the primary word, one of the words *He* and *She* can replace *It.*

Hence the *I* of man is also twofold.

*Reprinted with permission of Scribner, a division of Simon & Schuster, from *I and Thou,* by Martin Buber, translated by Ronald Gregor Smith. Translation copyright © 1958 by Charles Scribner's Sons.

For the *I* of the primary word *I-Thou* is a different *I* from that of the primary word *I-It*.

Primary words do not signify things, but they intimate relations.

Primary words do not describe something that might exist independently of them, but being spoken they bring about existence.

Primary words are spoken from the being.

If *Thou* is said, the *I* of the combination *I-Thou* is said along with it.

If *It* is said, the *I* of the combination *I-It* is said along with it.

The primary word *I-Thou* can only be spoken with the whole being.

The primary word *I-It* can never be spoken with the whole being.

There is no *I* taken in itself, but only the *I* of the primary word *I-Thou* and the *I* of the primary word *I-It*.

When a man says *I* he refers to one or other of these. The *I* to which he refers is present when he says *I*. Further, when he says *Thou* or *It,* the *I* of one of the two primary words is present.

The existence of *I* and the speaking of *I* are one and the same thing.

When a primary word is spoken the speaker enters the word and takes his stand in it.

The life of human beings is not passed in the sphere of transitive verbs alone. It does not exist in virtue of activities alone which have some *thing* for their object.

I perceive something, I am sensible of something. I imagine something. I will something. I feel something. I think something. The life of human beings does not consist of all this and the like alone.

This and the like together establish the realm of *It*.

But the realm of *Thou* has a different basis.

When *Thou* is spoken, the speaker has no thing for his object. For where there is a thing there is another thing. Every *It* is bounded by others; *It* exists only through being bounded by others. But when *Thou* is spoken, there is no thing. *Thou* has no bounds.

When *Thou* is spoken, the speaker has no *thing;* he has indeed nothing. But he takes his stand in relation.

If I face a human being as my *Thou,* and say the primary word *I-Thou* to him, he is not a thing among things, and does not consist of things.

Thus human being is not *He* or *She,* bounded from every other *He* and *She,* a specific point in space and time within the net of the world; nor is he a nature able to be experienced and described, a loose bundle of named qualities. But with no neighbour, and whole in himself, he is *Thou* and fills the heavens. This does not mean that nothing exists except himself. But all else lives in *his* light.

Just as the melody is not made up of notes nor the verse of words nor the statue of lines, but they must be tugged and dragged till their unity has been scattered into these many pieces, so with the man to whom I say *Thou.* I can take out from him the colour of his hair, or of his speech, or of his goodness. I must continually do this. But each time I do it he ceases to be *Thou.*

And just as prayer is not in time but time in prayer, sacrifice not in space but space in sacrifice, and to reverse the relation is to abolish the reality, so with the man to whom I say *Thou.* I do not meet with him at some time and place or other. I can set him in a particular time and place; I must continually do it; but I set only a *He* or a *She,* that is an *It,* no longer my *Thou.*

So long as the heaven of *Thou* is spread out over me the winds of causality cower at my heels, and the whirlpool of fate stays its course.

I do not experience the man to whom I say *Thou.* But I take my stand in relation to him, in the sanctity of the primary word. Only when I step out of it do I experience him once more. In the act of experience *Thou* is far away.

Even if the man to whom I say *Thou* is not aware of it in the midst of his experience, yet relation may exist. For *Thou* is more than *It* realises. No deception penetrates here; here is the cradle of the Real Life.

This is the eternal source of art: a man is faced by a form which desires to be made through him into a work. This form is no offspring of his soul, but is an appearance which steps up to it and demands of it the effective power. The man is concerned with an act of his being. If he carries it through, if he speaks the primary word out of his being to the form which appears, then the effective power streams out, and the work arises.

The act includes a sacrifice and a risk. This is the sacrifice: the endless possibility that is offered up on the altar of the form. For everything which just this moment in play ran through the perspective must be obliterated; nothing of that may penetrate the work. The exclusiveness of what is facing it demands that it be so. This is the risk: the primary word can only be spoken with the whole being. He who gives himself to it may withhold nothing of himself. The work does not suffer me, as do the tree and the man, to turn aside and relax in the world of *It;* but it commands. If I do not serve it aright it is broken, or it breaks me.

I can neither experience nor describe the form which meets me, but only body it forth. And yet I behold it, splendid in the radiance of what confronts me, clearer than all the clearness of the world which is experienced. I do not behold it as a thing among the "inner" things nor as an image of my "fancy," but as that which exists in the present. If test is made of its objectivity the form is certainly not "there." Yet what is actually so much present as it is? And the relation in which I stand to it is real, for it affects me, as I affect it.

To produce is to draw forth, to invent is to find, to shape is to discover. In bodying forth I disclose. I lead the form across—into the world of *It.* The work produced is a thing among things, able to be experienced and described as a sum of qualities. But from time to time it can face the receptive beholder in its whole embodied form.

—What, then, do we experience of *Thou?*
—Just nothing. For we do not experience it.

—What, then, do we know of *Thou?*
—Just everything. For we know nothing isolated about it any more.

The *Thou* meets me through grace—it is not found by seeking. But my speaking of the primary word to it is an act of my being, is indeed *the* act of my being.

The *Thou* meets me. But I step into direct relation with it. Hence the relation means being chosen and choosing, suffering and action in one; just as any action of the whole being, which means the suspension of all partial actions and consequently of all sensations of actions grounded only in their particular limitation, is bound to resemble suffering.

The primary word *I-Thou* can be spoken only with the whole being. Concentration and fusion into the whole being can never take place through my agency, nor can it ever take place without me. I become through my relation to the *Thou;* as I become *I,* I say *Thou.*

All real living is meeting.

The extended lines of relations meet in the eternal *Thou.*

Every particular *Thou* is a glimpse through to the eternal *Thou;* by means of every particular *Thou* the primary word addresses the eternal *Thou.* Through this mediation of the *Thou* of all beings fulfilment, and non-fulfilment, of relations comes to them: the inborn *Thou* is realised in each relation and consummated in none. It is consummated only in the direct relation with the *Thou* that by its nature cannot become *It.*

Men have addressed their eternal *Thou* with many names. In singing of Him who was thus named they always had the *Thou* in mind: the first myths were hymns of praise. Then the names took refuge in the language of *It;* men were more and more strongly moved to think of and to address their eternal *Thou* as an *It.* But all God's names are hallowed, for in them *He* is not merely spoken about, but also spoken to.

Many men wish to reject the word God as a legitimate usage, because it is so misused. It is indeed the most heavily laden of all the words used by men. For that very reason it is the most imperishable and most indispensable. What does all mistaken talk about God's being and works (though there has been, and can be, no other talk about these) matter in comparison with the one truth that all men who have addressed God had God Himself in mind? For he who speaks the word God and really has *Thou* in mind (whatever the illusion by which he is held), addresses the true *Thou* of his life, which cannot be limited by another *Thou,* and to which he stands in a relation that gathers up and includes all others.

But when he, too, who abhors the name, and believes himself to be godless, gives his whole being to addressing the *Thou* of his life, as a *Thou* that cannot be limited by another, he addresses God.

Every real relation with a being or life in the world is exclusive. Its *Thou* is freed, steps forth, is single, and confronts you. It fills the heavens. This does not mean that nothing else exists; but all else lives in *its* light. As long as the presence of the relation continues, this its cosmic range is inviolable. But as soon as a *Thou* becomes *It,* the cosmic range of the relation appears as an offence to the world, its exclusiveness as an exclusion of the universe.

In the relation with God unconditional exclusiveness and unconditional inclusiveness are one. He who enters on the absolute relation is concerned with nothing isolated any more, neither things nor beings, neither earth nor heaven; but everything is gathered up in the relation. For to step into pure relation is not to disregard everything but to see everything in the *Thou,* not to renounce the world but to establish it on its true basis. To look away from the world, or to stare at it, does not help a man to reach God; but he who sees the world in Him stands in His presence. "Here world, there God" is the language of *It;* "God in the world" is another language of *It;* but to eliminate or leave behind nothing at all, to include the whole world in the *Thou,* to give the

world its due and its truth, to include nothing beside God but everything in him—this is full and complete relation.

Men do not find God if they stay in the world. They do not find Him if they leave the world. He who goes out with his whole being to meet his *Thou* and carries to it all being that is in the world, finds Him who cannot be sought.

Of course God is the "wholly Other"; but He is also the wholly Same, the wholly Present. Of course He is the *Mysterium Tremendum* that appears and overthrows; but He is also the mystery of the self-evident, nearer to me than my *I.*

If you explore the life of things and of conditioned being you come to the unfathomable, if you deny the life of things and of conditioned being you stand before nothingness, if you hallow this life you meet the living God.

The eternal *Thou* can by its nature not become *It;* for by its nature it cannot be established in measure and bounds, not even in the measure of the immeasurable, or the bounds of boundless being; for by its nature it cannot be understood as a sum of qualities, not even as an infinite sum of qualities raised to a transcendental level; for it can be found neither in nor out of the world; for it cannot be experienced, or thought; for we miss Him, Him who is, if we say "I believe that He is"—"He" is also a metaphor, but "Thou" is not.

And yet in accordance with our nature we are continually making the eternal *Thou* into *It,* into some thing—making God into a thing. Not indeed out of arbitrary self-will; God's history as a thing, the passage of God as Thing through religion and through the products on its brink, through its bright ways and its gloom, its enhancement and its destruction of life, the passage away from the living God and back again to Him, the changes from the present to establishment of form, of objects, and of ideas, dissolution and renewal—all are one way, are *the* way.

Meeting with God does not come to man in order that he may concern himself with God, but in order that he may confirm that there is meaning in the world. All revelation is summons and sending. But again and again man brings about, instead of realisation, a reflexion to Him who reveals: he wishes to concern himself with God instead of with the world. Only, in such a reflexion, he is no longer confronted by a *Thou,* he can do nothing but establish an It-God in the realm of things, believe that he knows of God as of an *It,* and so speak about Him. Just as the "self" seeking man, instead of directly living something or other, a perception or an affection, reflects about his perspective or reflective *I,* and thereby misses the truth of the event, so the man who seeks God (though for the rest he gets on very well with the self-seeker in the one soul), instead of allowing the gift to work itself out, reflects about the Giver—and misses both.

God remains present to you when you have been sent forth; he who goes on a mission has always God before him: the truer the fulfilment the stronger and more constant His nearness. To be sure, he cannot directly concern himself with God, but he can converse with Him. Reflexion, on the other hand, makes God into an object. Its apparent turning towards the primal source belongs in truth to the universal movement away from it; just as the apparent turning away of the man who is fulfilling his mission belongs in truth to the universal movement towards the primal source.

In this context only one question more must be discussed, but it must be discussed since it is incomparably the most important of all.

The question is, how can the eternal *Thou* in the relation be at once exclusive and inclusive? How can the *Thou*-relationship of man to God, which is conditioned by an unconditioned turning to him, diverted by nothing, nevertheless include all other *I-Thou* relations of this man, and bring them as it were to God?

Note that the question is not about God, but about our relation to him. And yet in order to be able to answer I must speak of him. For our relation to him is as above contradictions as it is, because he is as above contradictions as he is.

Of course we speak only of what God is in his relation to a man. And even that is only to be expressed in paradox; more precisely, by the paradoxical use of a concept; more precisely still, by the paradoxical combination of a substantive concept with an adjective which contradicts its normal content. The assertion of this contradiction must yield to the insight that the indispensable description of the object by this concept can be justified only in this way. The content of the concept is revolutionised, transformed, and extended—but this is indeed what we experience with every concept which we take out of immanence—compelled by the reality of faith—and use with reference to the working of transcendence.

The description of God as a Person is indispensable for everyone who like myself means by "God" not a principle (although mystics like Eckhart sometimes identify him with "Being") and like myself means by "God" not an idea (although philosophers like Plato at times could hold that he was this): but who rather means by "God," as I do, him who—whatever else he may be—enters into a direct relation with us men in creative, revealing and redeeming acts, and thus makes it possible for us to enter into a direct relation with him. This ground and meaning of our existence constitutes a mutuality, arising again and again, such as can subsist only between persons. The concept of personal being is indeed completely incapable of declaring what God's essential being is, but it is both permitted and necessary to say that God is *also* a Person. If as an exception I wished to translate what is meant by this into philosophical language, that of Spinoza, I should have to say that of God's infinitely many attributes we men do not know two, as Spinoza thinks, but three: to spiritual being (in which is to be found the source of what we call spirit) and to natural being (which presents itself in what is known to us as nature) would be added the attribute of personal being. From this attribute would stem my and all men's being as person, as from those other attributes would stem my and all men's being as spirit and being as nature. And only this third attribute of personal being would be given to us to be known direct in its quality as an attribute.

But now the contradiction appears in the appeal to the familiar content of the concept person. This says that it is indeed the property of a person that its independence should consist in itself, but that it is limited in its total being by the plurality of other independent entities; and this can of course not be true of God. This contradiction is countered by the paradoxical description of God as the absolute Person, i.e., the Person who cannot be limited. It is as the absolute Person that God enters into direct relation with us. The contradiction yields to deeper insight.

As a Person God gives personal life, he makes us as persons become capable of meeting with him and with one another. But no limitation can come upon him as the absolute Person, either from us or from our relations with one another; in fact, we can dedicate to him not merely our persons but also our relations to one another. The man who turns to him therefore need not turn away from any other *I-Thou* relation; but he properly brings them to him, and lets them be fulfilled "in the face of God."

One must, however, take care not to understand this conversation with God—the conversation of which I have to speak in this book and in almost all the works which followed—as something happening solely alongside or above the everyday. God's speech to men penetrates what happens in the life of each one of us, and all that happens in the world around us, biographical and historical, and makes it for you and me into instruction, message, demand. Happening upon happening, situation upon situation, are enabled and empowered by the personal speech of God to demand of the human person that he take his stand and make his decision. Often enough we think there is nothing to hear, but long before we have ourselves put wax in our ears.

The existence of mutuality between God and man cannot be proved, just as God's existence cannot be proved. Yet he who dares to speak of it, bears witness, and calls to witness him to whom he speaks—whether that witness is now or in the future.

4.4 Satori

What is the most important thing about religion? Is it the beliefs? The rituals? The moral codes? The experiences? According to Zen Buddhism, the most important thing about Buddhism is experience—in particular, the experience of satori, or enlightenment.

Zen Buddhism is a school within the Mahayana Buddhist tradition. The word *Zen* is the Japanese term for *Ch'an,* the Chinese word for "meditation." *Ch'an* began in China in the fifth century, although its roots go back to the Buddha's own enlightenment and the Indian practice of *dhyana,* or meditation. Around 1200 Eisei brought *Ch'an* to Japan, where Zen has flourished. It has had a profound impact on all aspects of Japanese culture from painting to poetry. Zen has continued to spread West and has attracted followers throughout the United States and Europe.

Daisetz Teitaro Suzuki (1870–1966), author of the next selection, awakened the interest of the English-speaking world in Zen with the 1927 publication of his book *Essays in Zen Buddhism.* He underwent Zen training at the Zen monastery at Kamakura and later became a professor of Buddhist philosophy (a somewhat ironic title because Suzuki believed that in essence Buddhism was not a philosophy, but an experience) at Otani University in Kyoto. He was also a visiting professor at many universities in the United States, including Columbia University in New York. He became interested in comparative mysticism and found similarities between the experience of satori and the experiences of other mystics, such as the German Roman Catholic Meister Eckhart (c. 1260–1328). However, he also found differences, especially when the Christian mystics characterized their experience as "union with God."

Ineffability is one of the hallmarks of mystical experiences. The experience cannot be described accurately in words. Exactly what is meant by ineffability and why mystical experiences are said to be ineffable are widely debated. This characteristic captures some of the paradox of mysticism, because words are used by mystics to characterize an experience that they claim words cannot characterize.

Although satori is ultimately something one must personally experience to understand fully and, in that sense, is ineffable, Suzuki does believe that its "chief" characteristics can be described. In this selection he discusses those characteristics, emphasizing that satori is an intuitive insight into the nature of things.

Max Weber, an important and influential twentieth-century sociologist, drew a distinction between an "emissary prophet" and an "exemplary prophet." The difference is this: The emissary prophet has a religious experience and sees her task as getting others to believe the message given in that experience, whereas the exemplary prophet sees her task as getting others to have her experience. Suzuki would think it inaccurate to label the Buddha a prophet, but he does argue that the most important thing about the Buddha and Buddhism is the experience of enlightenment. It is not what the Buddha said that is important (though it is not totally irrelevant, either), but what he experienced. Believing the message without the experience does little good. The Buddha is an example of someone who has had an experience potentially available to all of us: the experience of awakening to the truth (satori).

Reading Questions

1. How does Suzuki define *satori,* and how does it differ from analytical understanding?
2. What does Suzuki mean by "intuitive insight," and how is this characteristic related to "authoritativeness"?
3. How does the "impersonal tone" of satori make it different from Christian mystical experiences?
4. What is the difference between the characteristic "sense of the Beyond" and the "feeling of exaltation"?
5. Do you think it is possible to have a direct and immediate experience of reality that is not filtered by or influenced by either our senses or our concepts? Why or why not?

Satori*

D. T. SUZUKI

I

The essence of Zen Buddhism consists in acquiring a new viewpoint on life and things generally. By this I mean that if we want to get into the inmost life of Zen, we must forgo all our ordinary habits of thinking which control our everyday life, we must try to see if there is any

*Excerpts from D.T. Suzuki, "Satori or Enlightenment" in *Zen Buddhism: Selected Writings of D.T. Suzuki.* Edited by William Barrett. Copyright © 1956 by William Barrett. Reprinted by permission of Susan Barrett. Footnotes deleted.

other way of judging things, or rather if our ordinary way is always sufficient to give us the ultimate satisfaction of our spiritual needs. If we feel dissatisfied somehow with this life, if there is something in our ordinary way of living that deprives us of freedom in its most sanctified sense, we must endeavour to find a way somewhere which gives us a sense of finality and contentment. Zen proposes to do this for us and assures us of the acquirement of a new point of view in which life assumes a fresher, deeper, and more satisfying aspect. This acquirement, however, is really and naturally the greatest mental cataclysm one can go through with in life. It is no easy task, it is a kind of fiery baptism, and one has to go through the storm, the earthquake, the overthrowing of the mountains, and the breaking in pieces of the rocks.

This acquiring of a new point of view in our dealings with life and the world is popularly called by Japanese Zen students "satori" (*wu* in Chinese). It is really another name for Enlightenment (*anuttara-samyak-sambodhi*), which is the word used by the Buddha and his Indian followers ever since his realization under the Bodhitree by the River Nairanjana. There are several other phrases in Chinese designating this spiritual experience, each of which has a special connotation, showing tentatively how this phenomenon is interpreted. At all events there is no Zen without satori, which is indeed the Alpha and Omega of Zen Buddhism. Zen devoid of satori is like a sun without its light and heat. Zen may lose all its literature, all its monasteries, and all its paraphernalia; but as long as there is satori in it it will survive to eternity. I want to emphasize this most fundamental fact concerning the very life of Zen; for there are some even among the students of Zen themselves who are blind to this central fact and are apt to think when Zen has been explained away logically or psychologically, or as one of the Buddhist philosophies which can be summed up by using highly technical and conceptual Buddhist phrases, Zen is exhausted, and there remains nothing in it that makes it what it is. But my contention is, the life of Zen begins with the opening of satori (*kai wu* in Chinese).

Satori may be defined as an intuitive looking into the nature of things in contradistinction to the analytical or logical understanding of it. Practically, it means the unfolding of a new world hitherto unperceived in the confusion of a dualistically-trained mind. Or we may say that with satori our entire surroundings are viewed from quite an unexpected angle of perception. Whatever this is, the world for those who have gained a satori is no more the old world as it used to be; even with all its flowing streams and burning fires, it is never the same one again. Logically stated, all its opposites and contradictions are united and harmonized into a consistent organic whole. This is a mystery and a miracle, but according to the Zen masters such is being performed every day. Satori can thus be had only through our once personally experiencing it.

Its semblance or analogy in a more or less feeble and fragmentary way is gained when a difficult mathematical problem is solved, or when a great discovery is made, or when a sudden means of escape is realized in the midst of most desperate complications; in short, when one exclaims "Eureka! Eureka!" But this refers only to the intellectual aspect of satori, which is therefore necessarily partial and incomplete and does not touch the very foundations of life considered one indivisible whole. Satori as the Zen experience must be concerned with the entirety of life. For what Zen proposes to do is the revolution, and the revaluation as well, of oneself as a spiritual unity. The solving of a mathematical problem ends with the solution, it does not affect one's whole life. So with all other particular questions, practical or scientific, they do not enter the basic life-tone of the individual concerned. But the opening of satori is the remaking of life itself. When it is genuine—for there are many simulacra of it—its effects on one's moral and spiritual life are revolutionary, and they are so enhancing, purifying, as well as exacting. When a master was asked what constituted Buddhahood, he answered, "The bottom of a pail is broken through." From this we can see what a complete revolution is produced by this spiritual experience. The birth of a new man is really cataclysmic.

In the psychology of religion this spiritual enhancement of one's whole life is called "conversion." But as the term is generally used by Christian converts, it cannot be applied in its strict sense to the Buddhist experience, especially to that of the Zen followers; the term has too affective or emotional a shade to take the place of satori, which is above all noetic. The general tendency of Buddhism is, as we know, more intellectual than emotional, and its doctrine of Enlightenment distinguishes it sharply from the Christian view of salvation; Zen as one of the Mahayana schools naturally shares a large amount of what we may call transcendental intellectualism, which does not issue in logical dualism. When poetically or figuratively expressed, satori is "the opening of the mind-flower," or "the removing of the bar," or "the brightening up of the mind-works." . . .

V. *Chief Characteristics of Satori*

1. *Irrationality.* By this I mean that satori is not a conclusion to be reached by reasoning, and defies all intellectual determination. Those who have experienced it are always at a loss to explain it coherently or logically. When it is explained at all, either in words or gestures, its content more or less undergoes a mutilation. The uninitiated are thus unable to grasp it by what is outwardly visible, while those who have had the experience discern what is genuine from what is not. The satori experience is thus always characterized by irrationality, inexplicability, and incommunicability.

Listen to Tai-hui once more: "This matter [i.e. Zen] is like a great mass of fire; when you approach it your face is sure to be scorched. It is again like a sword about to be drawn; when it is once out of the scabbard, someone is sure to lose his life. But if you neither fling away the scabbard nor approach the fire, you are no better than a piece of rock or of wood. Coming to this pass, one has to be quite a resolute character full of spirit." There is nothing here suggestive of cool reasoning and quiet metaphysical or epistemological analysis, but of a certain desperate will to break through an insurmountable barrier, of the will impelled by some irrational or unconscious power behind it. Therefore, the outcome also defies intellection or conceptualization.

2. *Intuitive insight.* That there is noetic quality in mystic experiences has been pointed out by James in his *Varieties of Religious Experience,* and this applies also to the Zen experience known as satori. Another name for satori is "ken-sho" (*chien-hsing* in Chinese) meaning "to see essence or nature," which apparently proves that there is "seeing" or "perceiving" in satori. That this seeing is of quite a different quality from what is ordinarily designated as knowledge need not be specifically noticed. Hui-k'e is reported to have made this statement concerning his satori which was confirmed by Bodhidharma himself: "[As to my satori], it is not a total annihilation; it is knowledge of the most adequate kind; only it cannot be expressed in words." In this respect Shen-hui was more explicit, for he says that "the one character *chih* (knowledge) is the source of all mysteries."

Without this noetic quality satori will lose all its pungency, for it is really the reason of satori itself. It is noteworthy that the knowledge contained in satori is concerned with something universal and at the same time with the individual aspect of existence. When a finger is lifted, the lifting means, from the viewpoint of satori, far more than the act of lifting. Some may call it symbolic, but satori does not point to anything beyond itself, being final as it is. Satori is the knowledge of an individual object and also that of Reality which is, if I may say so, at the back of it.

3. *Authoritativeness.* By this I mean that the knowledge realized by satori is final, that no amount of logical argument can refute it. Being direct and personal it is sufficient unto itself. All that logic can do here is to explain it, to interpret it in connection with other kinds of knowledge with which our minds are filled. Satori is thus a form of perception, an inner perception, which takes place in the most interior part of consciousness. Hence the sense of authoritativeness, which means finality. So, it is generally said that Zen is like drinking water, for it is by one's self

that one knows whether it is warm or cold. The Zen perception being the last term of experience, it cannot be denied by outsiders who have no such experience.

4. *Affirmation*. What is authoritative and final can never be negative. For negation has no value for our life, it leads us nowhere; it is not a power that urges, nor does it give one a place to rest. Though the satori experience is sometimes expressed in negative terms, it is essentially an affirmative attitude towards all things that exist; it accepts them as they come along regardless of their moral values. Buddhists call this *kshanti*, "patience," or more properly "acceptance," that is, acceptance of things in their suprarelative or transcendental aspect where no dualism of whatever sort avails.

Some may say that this is pantheistic. The term, however, has a definite philosophic meaning and I would not see it used in this connection. When so interpreted the Zen experience exposes itself to endless misunderstandings and "defilements." Tai-hui says in his letter to Miao-tsung: "An ancient sage says that the Tao itself does not require special disciplining, only let it not be defiled. I would say: To talk about mind or nature is defiling; to talk about the unfathomable or the mysterious is defiling; to practise meditation or tranquillization is defiling; to direct one's attention to it, to think about it is defiling; to be writing about it thus on paper with a brush is especially defiling. What then shall we have to do in order to get ourselves oriented, and properly apply ourselves to it? The precious vajra sword is right here and its purpose is to cut off the head. Do not be concerned with human questions of right and wrong. All is Zen just as it is, and right here you are to apply yourself." Zen is Suchness—a grand affirmation.

5. *Sense of the Beyond*. Terminology may differ in different religions, and in satori there is always what we may call a sense of the Beyond; the experience indeed is my own but I feel it to be rooted elsewhere. The individual shell in which my personality is so solidly encased explodes at the moment of satori. Not, necessarily, that I get unified with a being greater than myself or

absorbed in it, but that my individuality, which I found rigidly held together and definitely kept separate from other individual existences, becomes loosened somehow from its tightening grip and melts away into something indescribable, something which is of quite a different order from what I am accustomed to. The feeling that follows is that of a complete release or a complete rest—the feeling that one has arrived finally at the destination. "Coming home and quietly resting" is the expression generally used by Zen followers. The story of the prodigal son in the *Saddharmapundarika,* in the *Vajra-samadhi,* and also in the New Testament points to the same feeling one has at the moment of a satori experience.

As far as the psychology of satori is considered, a sense of the Beyond is all we can say about it; to call this the Beyond, the Absolute, or God, or a Person is to go further than the experience itself and to plunge into a theology or metaphysics. Even the "Beyond" is saying a little too much. When a Zen master says, "There is not a fragment of a tile above my head, there is not an inch of earth beneath my feet," the expression seems to be an appropriate one. I have called it elsewhere the Unconscious, though this has a psychological taint.

6. *Impersonal Tone*. Perhaps the most remarkable aspect of the Zen experience is that it has no personal note in it as is observable in Christian mystic experiences. There is no reference whatever in Buddhist satori to such personal and frequently sexual feelings and relationships as are to be gleaned from these terms: flame of love, a wonderful love shed in the heart, embrace, the beloved, bride, bridegroom, spiritual matrimony, Father, God, the Son of God, God's child, etc. We may say that all these terms are interpretations based on a definite system of thought and really have nothing to do with the experience itself. At any rate, alike in India, China, and Japan, satori has remained thoroughly impersonal, or rather highly intellectual.

Is this owing to the peculiar character of Buddhist philosophy? Does the experience itself take its colours from the philosophy or theology?

Whatever this is, there is no doubt that in spite of its having some points of similitude to the Christian mystic experience, the Zen experience is singularly devoid of personal or human colourings. Chao-pien, a great government officer of the Sung dynasty, was a lay-disciple of Fach'uan of Chiang-shan. One day after his official duties were over, he found himself leisurely sitting in his office, when all of a sudden a clash of thunder burst on his ear, and he realized a state of satori. The poem he then composed depicts one aspect of the Zen experience:

> "Devoid of thought, I sat quietly by the
>   desk in my official room,
> With my fountain-mind undisturbed, as
>   serene as water;
> A sudden clash of thunder, the mind-
>   doors burst open,
> And lo, there sitteth the old man in all his
>   homeliness."

This is perhaps all the personal tone one can find in the Zen experience, and what a distance between "the old man in his homeliness" and "God in all his glory," not to say anything about such feelings as "the heavenly sweetness of Christ's excellent love," etc.! How barren, how unromantic satori is when compared with the Christian mystic experiences!

Not only satori itself is such a prosaic and non-glorious event, but the occasion that inspires it also seems to be unromantic and altogether lacking in supersensuality. Satori is experienced in connection with any ordinary occurrence in one's daily life. It does not appear to be an extraordinary phenomenon as is recorded in Christian books of mysticism. Someone takes hold of you, or slaps you, or brings you a cup of tea, or makes some most commonplace remark, or recites some passage from a sutra or from a book of poetry, and when your mind is ripe for its outburst, you come at once to satori. There is no romance of love-making, no voice of the Holy Ghost, no plenitude of Divine Grace, no glorification of any sort. Here is nothing painted in high colours, all is grey and extremely unobtrusive and unattractive.

7. *Feeling of Exaltation*. That this feeling inevitably accompanies satori is due to the fact that it is the breaking-up of the restriction imposed on one as an individual being, and this breaking up is not a mere negative incident but quite a positive one fraught with signification because it means an infinite expansion of the individual. The general feeling, though we are not always conscious of it, which characterizes all our functions of consciousness, is that of restriction and dependence, because consciousness itself is the outcome of two forces conditioning or restricting each other. Satori, on the contrary, essentially consists in doing away with the opposition of two terms in whatsoever sense—and this opposition is the principle of consciousness as before mentioned, while satori is to realize the Unconscious which goes beyond the opposition.

To be released of this, therefore, must make one feel above all things intensely exalted. A wandering outcast maltreated everywhere not only by others but by himself finds that he is the possessor of all the wealth and power that is ever attainable in this world by a mortal being—if this does not give him a high feeling of self-glorification, what could? Says a Zen master, "When you have satori you are able to reveal a palatial mansion made of precious stones on a single blade of grass; but when you have no satori, a palatial mansion itself is concealed behind a simple blade of grass."

Another Zen master, evidently alluding to the *Avatamsaka*, declares: "O monks, lo and behold! A most auspicious light is shining with the utmost brilliancy all over the great chiliocosm, simultaneously revealing all the countries, all the oceans, all the Sumerus, all the suns and moons, all the heavens, all the lands—each of which number as many as hundreds of thousands of kotis. O monks, do you not see the light?" But the Zen feeling of exaltation is rather a quiet feeling of self-contentment; it is not at all demonstrative, when the first glow of it passes away. The Unconscious does not proclaim itself so boisterously in the Zen consciousness.

8. *Momentariness*. Satori comes upon one abruptly and is a momentary experience. In fact,

if it is not abrupt and momentary, it is not satori. This abruptness (*tun*) is what characterizes the Hui-neng school of Zen ever since its proclamation late in the seventh century. His opponent Shen-hsiu was insistent on a gradual unfoldment of Zen consciousness. Hui-neng's followers were thus distinguished as strong upholders of the doctrine of abruptness. This abrupt experience of satori, then, opens up in one moment (*eka-muhurtena*) an altogether new vista, and the whole existence is appraised from quite a new angle of observation.

4.5 Perceiving God

Are religious experiences veridical or delusory? Do they provide correct information about the nature of reality? Are there any good reasons to doubt that they provide knowledge about the way things really are? Are there good reasons to doubt Black Elk's vision (see Reading 4.2), Buber's encounter with a personal God (see Reading 4.3), or the Zen experience of satori (see Reading 4.4)? Granted, such experiences happen, but do they provide good evidence for the claims to truth based on them?

Over 90 years ago William James (1842–1910) drew three conclusions from what has proved to be one of the most influential studies of mystical experience in this century. He wrote

1. Mystical states, when well developed, usually are, and have the right to be absolutely authoritative over the individuals to whom they come.
2. No authority emanates from them which should make it a duty for those who stand outside of them to accept their revelations uncritically.
3. They break down the authority of the nonmystical or rationalistic consciousness, based upon the understanding and the senses alone. They show it to be only one kind of consciousness. (*Varieties of Religious Experience*)

That seems to be a fair conclusion, granting to those who have religious experiences a right to believe on the basis of such experiences and granting to those who do not share such experiences a right to withhold belief. James was much impressed by the diversity and variety of religious experiences, as the title of his Gifford Lectures suggests. But he was also impressed by the apparent agreement among many different mystics from different religious traditions and different times and places. If there is considerable agreement among mystics about the nature of their experiences, that must count for something.

Bertrand Russell (1872–1970) agreed with James that a great deal of unanimity could be found among mystics, but he did not think this fact counted for much. In *Religion and Science* (1935) he argued that unlike the scientist, who changes the means of observation, the mystic changes his or her physiology by fasting, meditation, prolonged prayer, and the like. Further, he argued, we know that altered physiological states are often associated with unreliable perceptions if not downright delusions. Therefore, he concluded that "from a scientific point of view, we can make no distinction between the man who eats little and sees heaven and the man who drinks much and sees snakes."

Bertrand Russell was an English philosopher much impressed with the results of the physical sciences, and C.D. Broad (1887–1971), another English philosopher, was equally impressed by science. Like Russell, he believed there was widespread and impressive agreement among mystics around the world, but he drew a very different conclusion from this assumption. He argued that given widespread agreement, unless there is some positive reason to think mystics delusive, it is reasonable to conclude that their experiences are veridical. Of course, Russell thought he had positive reasons to think mystical experiences delusive (the disanalogy with scientific observation), but Broad does not think such reasons decisive. Why assume, as Russell seems to, that mental states that may interfere with reliable observations of the physical world also interfere with reliable experiences of some spiritual reality?

Richard Swinburne, a contemporary English philosopher, echoes Broad's argument by suggesting that we employ the "Principle of Credulity" in such matters (see his *The Existence of God,* Oxford University Press, 1979, Chapter 13). Swinburne argues that we should regard apparent cognitions as true until they are proved false. If we do not have some special reason for discounting the veridicality of religious and mystical experiences, then why not accept them at face value? After all, we normally give people "the benefit of the doubt." If I ask you how you know this book exists, it seems plausible to respond that you see it. Of course, you may not really see it; you might be deceived in some way. A pencil appears bent when put in a glass of water, but it is not. Water appears to be on the road up ahead, but it turns out to be the light reflecting off the pavement. Magicians appear to produce rabbits out of empty hats, but they don't really do that. It is a trick. In the cases of the bent pencil, the mirage, and the magic trick, we have some good reasons to doubt what we see. However, in the case of your seeing the book, do we have good reasons to doubt?

You might reasonably respond that "religious experiences are rather extraordinary." Indeed they are. The more an experience is in keeping with our everyday experiences, the more likely it is to be veridical. But spirit visions and voices, ineffable intuitive insights into the nature of reality, encounters with divine beings—all these seem very much out of the ordinary. There are other considerations as well.

Thomas Hobbes (1588–1679) once remarked that there is no difference between the statements "Last night God spoke to me in a dream" and "Last night I dreamed that God spoke to me." If Hobbes is right, then appealing to religious and mystical experiences in order to prove the existence of some ultimate reality will not work. The fact that someone has a certain type of psychological or subjective experience does not prove that what he or she thought he or she experienced really exists apart from that experience. Consider: "Last night I had a mystical experience" and "There is no ultimate reality." The truth of the first statement is logically compatible with the truth of the second statement. We all have experiences (dreams) that are perfectly compatible with statements about the content of our experiences (dreambeings) not existing. When we call something a dream or a hallucination or a mirage or a delusion, we do not deny that the experiences referred to occur, but the very fact that we give certain experiences these names indicates that we do not think what they were about exists outside our mental state at the time.

C.B. Martin (1924–   ) agrees with Hobbes. Arguments like "I have had a direct experience of God; therefore, God exists" do not work because without additional checking procedures, one cannot infer, from psychological claims, existence claims about what is experienced. "I have had a direct experience of God" is logically like "I seem to have had a direct experience of God," or so Martin argues.

The fact that you *seem* to be reading this book does not prove that you are. The only way to prove that you are is to introduce verification procedures of one sort or another: for someone to take a video of you reading, for example, or for others to observe you and agree that you are indeed reading this book, or for people to quiz you afterwards on its content.

Although religions do have checking procedures (a transformed moral life after an encounter with Jesus; meditate and you too may realize satori; pray and Allah may grant your wish), no such verification is totally adequate and none is as good as the checking procedures we have for sense experience, or so Martin thinks.

However, are religious experiences exactly like sensory experiences? Is the object of religious experiences (God, let us say) like material objects such as a book? Are the checking procedures adequate? Are not all of them just further experiences (looking at the video, talking to others, peering through a microscope, and so on)? Why should we think that these additional psychological claims provide any better proof for existence claims?

One should be cautious, perhaps, about trying to prove too much. Perhaps the existence of religious experiences (be they putatively of God, Allah, the Tao, Nirvana, or Atman/Brahman) does not provide evidence for the existence of these alleged ultimate realities and hence Martin is right in a way. We cannot argue successfully from religious experience to the existence of God. Yet people's tendency to rely on religious experiences to form and justify their beliefs may be no less rational than the tendency to rely on perceptual experiences to form and justify beliefs about physical objects. William P. Alston, author of the first part of the next selection, thinks it is quite reasonable to rely on experience in religious matters.

Alston is Professor of Philosophy Emeritus at Syracuse University. In the selection that follows, he enters the debate we have been tracing about the epistemic value of religious experiences. Do religious experiences provide us with some kind of knowledge? Whereas James, Russell, and Broad believe that the apparent unanimity among mystics is a significant element in any argument about the epistemic value of religious experiences, Alston believes that the strong analogy between experiences of what he calls "perceiving God" and perceiving physical objects is sufficient to support the conclusion that religious experiences can provide justification for religious beliefs. He does not argue that such experiences prove that God exists, but he does take up part of Martin's challenge. If there is a strong enough analogy between religious experiences and sense experiences, and if sense experiences are cognitive (provide knowledge), then we should also expect religious experiences to be cognitive.

Terence Penelhum of the University of Calgary in Canada wonders whether the analogy Alston wishes to draw proves too much and proves too little. Read and see. How strong is the analogy between perceiving physical objects and religious experience?

Reading Questions

1. What is Alston's main contention?
2. What is the central analogy Alston wishes to draw between the perception of physical objects and the perception of God?
3. How does Alston respond to the first two objections?

4. What is "epistemic circularity," and what role does it play in Alston's argument?

5. How does Alston deal with the claim that naturalistic explanations of RE do not require us to bring God into the picture at all?

6. How does Alston explain the "limited distribution" of RE and the "cognitively unsatisfactory features of the doxastic output" of RE when compared to SP?

7. What is an "overrider system," and why is this concept important to the debate about how close the analogy is between RE and SP?

8. What is "epistemic chauvinism," and what role does it play in Alston's reply to objection VI?

9. What objection does Alston regard as the most serious, and how does he respond to it?

10. What critical issues does Penelhum raise?

11. Do you think the analogy Alston wishes to defend is a false analogy? Why or why not?

Perceiving God*

WILLIAM P. ALSTON WITH A RESPONSE BY TERENCE PENELHUM

I WANT TO EXPLORE and defend the idea that the experience, or, as I shall say, the *perception,* of God plays an epistemic role with respect to beliefs about God importantly analogous to that played by sense perception with respect to beliefs about the physical world. The nature of that latter role is, of course, a matter of controversy, and I have no time here to go into those controversies. It is admitted, however, on (almost) all hands that sense perception provides us with knowledge (justified belief) about current states of affairs in the immediate environment of the perceiver and that knowledge of this sort is somehow required for any further knowledge of the physical world. The possibility I wish to explore is that what a person takes to be an experience of God can provide him/her with knowledge (justified beliefs) about what God is doing, or how God is "situated," vis-à-vis that subject at that moment. Thus, by experiencing the presence and activity of God, *S* can come to know (justifiably believe)

that God is sustaining her in being, filling her with His love, strengthening her, or communicating a certain message to her. Let's call beliefs as to how God is currently related to the subject *M-beliefs* ("M" for manifestation); these are the "perceptual beliefs" of the theological sphere. I shall suppose that here too the "perceptual" knowledge one acquires from experience is crucial for whatever else we can learn about God, though I won't have time to explore and defend that part of the position; I will have my hands full defending the claim that M-beliefs are justified. I will just make two quick points about the role of M-beliefs in the larger scheme. First, just as with our knowledge of the physical world, the recognition of a crucial role for perceptual knowledge is compatible with a wide variety of views as to just how it figures in the total system and as to what else is involved. Second, an important difference between the two spheres is that in the theological sphere perceptual beliefs as to what

*From *The Journal of Philosophy*, Vol. LXXXIII, 11 (November 1986): 655–666. Reprinted by permission of *The Journal of Philosophy* and the authors.

God has "said" (communicated, revealed) to one or another person play a major role.

I have been speaking alternatively of perceptual *knowledge* and of the *justification* of perceptual beliefs. In this paper I shall concentrate on justification, leaving to one side whatever else is involved in knowledge. It will be my contention that (putative) experience of God is a source of justification for M-beliefs, somewhat in the way that sense experience is a source of justification for perceptual beliefs. Again, it is quite controversial what this latter way is. I shall be thinking of it in terms of a direct-realist construal of sense perception, according to which I can be justified in supposing that my dog is wagging his tail just because something is visually presenting itself to me as (looks like) my dog wagging his tail; that is, it looks to me in such a way that I am thereby justified in thereby supposing it to be my dog wagging his tail. Analogously I think of the "experience of God" as a matter of something's presenting itself to one's experience as God (doing so and so); so that here too the subject is justified in believing that God is present to her, or is doing so and so vis-à-vis her, just because that is the way in which the object is presented to her experience. (For the purposes of this paper let's focus on those cases in which this presentation is not via any *sensory* qualities or sensorily perceivable objects. The experience involved will be nonsensory in character.) It is because I think of the experience of God as having basically the same structure as the sense perception of physical objects that I feel entitled to speak of "perceiving God." But though I construe the matter in direct-realist terms, most of what I have to say here will be relevant to a defense of the more general claim that the experiential justification of M-beliefs is importantly parallel to the experiential justification of perceptual beliefs about the physical environment, on any halfway plausible construal of the latter, at least on any halfway plausible realist construal.

I shall develop the position by way of responding to a number of objections. This procedure reflects my conviction that the very considerable incidence of putative perceptions of God creates a certain initial presumption that these experiences are what they seem to be and that something can thereby be learned about God.

Objection I. What reason do we have for supposing that anyone ever does really perceive God? In order for *S* to perceive God it would have to be the case that (1) God exists, and (2) God is related to *S* or to his experience in such a way as to be perceivable by him. Only after we have seen reason to accept all that will we take seriously any claim to perceive God.

Answer. It all depends on what you will take as a reason. What you have in mind, presumably, are reasons drawn from some source other than perceptions of God, e.g., metaphysical arguments for the existence and nature of God. But why do you think you are justified in that restriction? We don't proceed in this way with respect to sense perception. Although in determining whether a particular alleged perception was genuine we don't make use of the results of *that* perception, we do utilize what has been observed in many other cases. And what alternative is there? The conditions of veridical sense perception have to do with states of affairs and causal interactions in the physical world, matters to which we have no cognitive access that is not based on sense perception. In like fashion, if there is a divine reality why suppose that the conditions of veridically perceiving it could be ascertained without relying on perceptions of *it*? In requiring external validation in this case but not the other you are arbitrarily imposing a double standard.

Objection II. There are many contradictions in the body of M-beliefs. In particular, persons report communications from God that contradict other reported communications. How, then, can one claim that all M-beliefs are justified?

Answer. What is (should be) claimed is only *prima facie* justification. When a person believes that God is experientially present to him, that belief is justified *unless* the subject has sufficient reasons to suppose it to be false or to suppose that the experience is not, in these circumstances, sufficiently indicative of the truth of the belief. This is, of course, precisely the status of individual perceptual beliefs about the physical environment. When, seeming to see a lake, I believe there to be a lake in front of me, my belief is thereby justified unless I have sufficient reason to suppose it false or to suppose that, in these circumstances, the experience is not sufficiently indicative of the truth of the belief.

Objection III. It is rational to form beliefs about the physical environment on the basis of the way that environment appears to us in sense experience (call this practice of belief formation *SP*) because that is a generally reliable mode of belief formation. And it is reliable just because, in normal conditions, sense experience varies concomitantly with variations in what we take ourselves to be perceiving. But we have no reason to suppose any such regular covariation for putative perception of God. And hence we lack reason for regarding as rational the parallel practice of forming M-beliefs on the basis of what is taken to be a perception of God (call that practice *RE*).

Answer. This is another use of a double standard. How do we know that normal sense experience varies concomitantly with perceived objects? We don't know this a priori. Rather, we have strong empirical evidence for it. That is, by relying on sense perception for our data we have piled up evidence for the reliability of SP. Let's call the kind of circularity exhibited here *epistemic circularity*. It is involved whenever the premises in an argument for the reliability or rationality of a belief-forming practice have themselves been acquired by that practice.[1] If we allow epistemically circular arguments, the reliability of RE can be supported in the same way. Among the things people have claimed to learn from RE is that God will enable people to experience His presence and activity from time to time in a veridical way. By relying on what one learns from the practice of RE, one can show that RE is a reliable belief-forming practice. On the other hand, if epistemically circular arguments are not countenanced, there can be no significant basis for a reliability claim in either case.

Objection IV. A claim to perceive *X*, and so to form reliable perceptual beliefs about *X* on the basis of this, presupposes that the experience involved is best explained by the activity of *X*, *inter alia*. But it seems that we can give adequate explanations of putative experiences of God in purely naturalistic terms, without bringing God into the explanation at all. Whereas we can't give adequate explanations of normal sense experience without bringing the experienced external objects into the explanation. Hence RE, but not SP, is discredited by these considerations.

Answer. I do not believe that much of a case can be made for the adequacy of any naturalistic explanation of experiences of God. But for present purposes I want to concentrate on the way in which this objection once more depends on a double standard. You will have no case at all for your claim unless you, question-beggingly, restrict yourself to sources of evidence that exclude RE. For from RE and systems built up on its output we learn that God is involved in the explanation of every fact whatever. But you would not proceed in that way with SP. If it is a question of determining the best explanation of sense experience you will, of course, make use of what you think you have learned from SP. Again, you have arbitrarily applied different standards to the two practices.

Here is another point. Suppose that one could give a purely psychological or physiological explanation of the experiences in question. That is quite compatible with God's figuring among their causes and, hence, coming into an ideally complete explanation. After all, it is presumably possible to give an adequate causal explanation of sense experience in terms of what goes on within the skull, but that is quite compatible with the external perceived objects' figuring further back along the causal chain.

Objection V. You have been accusing me of *arbitrarily* employing a double standard. But I maintain that RE differs from SP in ways that make different standards appropriate. SP is a pervasive and inescapable feature of our lives. Sense experience is insistent, omnipresent, vivid, and richly detailed. We use it as a source of information during all our waking hours. RE, by contrast, is not universally shared; and even for its devotees its practice is relatively infrequent. Moreover, its deliverances are, by comparison, meager, obscure, and uncertain. Thus when an output of RE does pop up, it is naturally greeted with more skepticism, and one properly demands more for its validation than in the case of so regular and central part of our lives as SP.

Answer. I don't want to deny either the existence or the importance of these differences. I want to deny only that they have the alleged bearing on the epistemic situation. Why should we suppose that a cognitive access enjoyed only by a part of the population is less likely to be reliable than one that is universally distributed? Why should we suppose that a source that yields less detailed and less fully understood beliefs is more suspect than a richer source? A priori it would seem just as likely that some aspects of reality are accessible only to persons that satisfy certain conditions not satisfied by all human beings as that some aspects are equally accessible to all. A priori it would seem just as likely that some aspects of reality are humanly graspable only in a fragmentary and opaque manner as that some aspects are graspable in a more nearly complete and pellucid fashion. Why view the one sort of cognitive claim with more suspicion than the other? I will agree that the spotty distribution of RE calls for explanation, as does the various cognitively unsatisfactory features of its output. But, for that matter, so does the universal distribution and cognitive richness of SP. And in both cases explanations are forthcoming, though in both cases the outputs of the practices are utilized in order to achieve those explanations. As for RE, the limited distribution may be explained by the fact that many persons are not prepared to meet the moral and other "way of life" conditions that God has set for awareness of Himself. And the cognitively unsatisfactory features of the doxastic output are explained by the fact that God infinitely exceeds our cognitive powers.

Objection VI. When someone claims to see a spruce tree in a certain spot, the claim is check-able. Other people can take a look, photographs can be taken, the subject's condition can be diagnosed, and so on. But there are no comparable checks and tests available in RE. And how can we take seriously a claim to have perceived an objective state of affairs if there is, in principle, no intersubjective way of determining whether that claim is correct?

Answer. The answer to this objection is implicit in a point made earlier, viz., that putative experience of God yields only prima facie justification, justification (unqualifiedly) provided there are no sufficient overriding considerations. This notion has a significant application only where there is what we may call an *overrider system,* i.e., ways of determining whether the facts are such as to indicate a belief from the range in question to be false and ways of determining whether conditions are such that the basis of the belief is sufficiently indicative of its truth. SP does contain such a system. What about RE? Here we must confront a salient difference between the two spheres. If we consider the way in which a body of beliefs has been developed on the basis of SP we find pretty much the same system across all cultures. But our encounters with God have spawned a number of different religious communities with beliefs and practices of worship which are quite different, though with some considerable overlap. These differences carry with them differences in overrider systems. But it remains true that if we consider any particular religious community which exhibits a significant commonality in doctrine and worship it will feature a more or less definite overrider system. For concreteness let's think of what I will call the *mainline Christian community.* (From this point onward I will use the term "RE" for the practice of forming M-beliefs as it goes on in this community.) In that community a body of doctrine has developed concerning the nature of God, His purposes, and His interactions with mankind, including His appearances to us. If an M-belief contradicts this system that is a reason for deeming it false. Moreover there is a long and varied history of experiential encounters with God, embodied in written accounts as well as oral transmission. This provides bases for regarding particular experiences as more or less likely to be veridical, given the conditions, psychological or otherwise, in which they occurred, the character of the subject, and the effects in the life of the subject. Thus a socially established religious doxastic practice like RE will contain a rich system of overriders that provides resources for checking the acceptability of any particular M-belief.

But perhaps your point is rather that there are no *external* checks on a particular report, none that do not rely on other claims of the same sort. Let's agree that this is the case. But why suppose that to be any black mark against RE? Here is the double standard again. After all, particular claims within SP cannot be checked without relying on what we have learned from SP. Suppose I claim to see a fir tree in a certain spot. To check on this one would have to rely on other persons' perceptual reports as to what is at that spot, our general empirical knowledge of the likelihood of a fir tree in that locality, and so on. Apart from what we take ourselves to have learned from SP, we would have nothing to go on. One can hardly determine whether my report was accurate by intuiting self-evident truths or by consulting divine revelation. But if SP counts as having a system of checks even though this system involves relying on some outputs of the practice in order to put others to the test, why should RE be deemed to have no such system when its procedures exhibit the same structure? Once more you are, arbitrarily, setting quite different requirements for different practices.

Perhaps your point was that RE's system of checks is unlike SP's. In particular, the following difference can be discerned. Suppose I report seeing a morel at a certain spot in the forest. Now suppose that a number of qualified observers take a good look at that spot at that time and report that no morel is to be seen. In that case my report would have been decisively disconfirmed. But nothing like that is possible in RE. We can't lay down any conditions (of a sort the satisfaction of which we can determine) under which a properly qualified person will experience the presence of God if God is "there" to be experienced. Hence

a particular report cannot be decisively disconfirmed by the experience of others.

But what epistemic relevance does this difference have? Why should we suppose that RE is rendered dubious for lacking checkability of this sort? Let's consider what makes this kind of intersubjective test possible for SP. Clearly it is that we have discovered fairly firm regularities in the behavior of physical things, including human sense perception. Since there are stable regularities in the ways in which physical objects disclose themselves to our perception, we can be assured that if X exists at a certain time and place and if S satisfies appropriate conditions then S is sure to perceive X. But no such tight regularities are discoverable in God's appearances to our experience. We can say something about the way in which such matters as the distribution of attention and the moral and spiritual state of the subject are conducive to such appearances; but these most emphatically do not add up to the sort of lawlike connections we get with SP. Now what about this difference? Is it to the epistemic discredit of RE that it does not enable us to discover such regularities? Well, that all depends on what it would be reasonable to expect if RE does put us into effective cognitive contact with God. Given what we have learned about God and our relations to Him (from RE, supplemented by whatever other sources there be), should we expect to be able to discover such realities if God really exists? Clearly not. There are several important points here, but the most important is that it is contrary to God's plans for us to give us that much control, cognitive and practical. Hence it is quite understandable, if God exists and is as RE leads us to suppose, that we should not be able to ascertain the kinds of regularities that would make possible the kinds of intersubjective tests exhibited by SP. Hence, the epistemic status of RE is in no way diminished by its lack of such tests. Once more RE is subjected to an inappropriate standard. This time, however, it is not a double standard, but rather an inappropriate single standard. RE is being graded down for lacking positive features of other practices, where these features cannot reasonably be supposed to be generally necessary conditions of epistemic excellence, even for experiential practices. Thus my critic is exhibiting what we might term *epistemic chauvinism,* judging alien forms of life according to whether they conform to the home situation, a procedure as much to be deplored in the epistemic as in the political sphere.

Objection VII. How can it be rational to take RE as a source of justification when there are incompatible rivals that can lay claim to that status on exactly the same grounds? M-beliefs of different religious communities conflict to a considerable extent, particularly those concerning alleged divine messages, and the bodies of doctrine they support conflict even more. We get incompatible accounts of God's plans for us and requirements on us, of the conditions of salvation, and so on. This being the case, how can we pick out just one of these communal practices as yielding justified belief?

Answer. I take this to be by far the most serious difficulty with my position. I have chosen to concentrate on what I take to be less serious problems, partly because their consideration brings out better the main lineaments of the position, and partly because any serious treatment of this last problem would spill beyond the confines of this paper. Here I shall have to content myself with making one basic point. We are not faced with the necessity of choosing only one such practice as yielding prima facie justified M-beliefs. The fact that there are incompatibilities between systems of religious beliefs, in M-beliefs and elsewhere, shows that not all M-beliefs can be true, but not that they cannot all be prima facie justified. After all, incompatible beliefs *within* a system can all be prima facie justified; that's the point of the prima facie qualification. When we are faced with a situation like that, the hope is that the overrider system and other winnowing devices will weed out the inconsistencies. To be sure, intersystem winnowing devices are hazier and more meager than those which are available within a system; but consistency, consonance with other well-entrenched beliefs and doxastic practices, and general reasonability and plausibil-

ity give us something to go on. Moreover, it may be that some religious ways of life fulfill their own promises more fully than others. Of course, there is never any guarantee that a unique way of resolving incompatibilities will present itself, even with a system. But where there are established practices of forming beliefs on the basis of experience, I believe the rational course is to regard each such belief as thereby prima facie justified, hoping that future developments, perhaps unforeseeable at present, will resolve fundamental incompatibilities.

In conclusion I will make explicit the general epistemological orientation I have been presupposing in my defense of RE. I take our human situation to be such that we engage in a plurality of basic doxastic practices, each of which involves a distinctive sort of input to belief-forming "mechanisms," a distinctive range of belief contents (a "subject matter" and ways of conceiving it), and a set of functions that determine belief contents as a function of input features. Each practice is socially established: socially shared, inculcated, reinforced, and propagated. In addition to experiential practices, with which we have been concerned in this paper, there are, e.g., inferential practices, the input of which consists of beliefs, and the practice of forming memory beliefs. A doxastic practice is not restricted to the formation of first-level beliefs; it will also typically involve criteria and procedures of criticism of the beliefs thus formed; here we will find the "overrider systems" of which we were speaking earlier. In general, we learn these practices and engage in them long before we arrive at the stage of explicitly formulating their principles and subjecting them to critical reflection. Theory is deeply rooted in practice.

Nor, having arrived at the age of reason, can we turn our back on all that and take a fresh start, in the Cartesian spirit, choosing our epistemic procedures and criteria anew, on a purely "rational" basis. Apart from reliance on doxastic tendencies with which we find ourselves, we literally have nothing to go on. Indeed, what Descartes did, as Thomas Reid trenchantly pointed out, was arbitrarily to pick one doxastic practice he

found himself engaged in—accepting propositions that seem self-evident—and set that as a
judge over all the others, with what results we are
all too familiar. This is not to say that we must acquiesce in our prereflective doxastic tendencies in
every respect. We can tidy things up, modify our
established practices so as to make each more internally consistent and more consistent with the
others. But, on the whole and for the most part,
we have no choice but to continue to form beliefs
in accordance with these practices and to take
these ways of forming beliefs as paradigmatically
conferring epistemic justification. And this is the
way that epistemology has in fact gone, except
for some arbitrary partiality. Of course it would
be satisfying to economize our basic commitments by taking one or a few of these practices as
basic and using them to validate the others; but
we have made little progress in this enterprise
over the centuries. It is not self-evident that sense
perception is reliable, nor can we establish its reliability if we restrict ourselves to premises drawn
from introspection; we cannot show that deductive reasoning is valid without using deductive
reasoning to do so; and so on. We are endowed
with strong tendencies to engage in a number of
distinct doxastic practices, none of which can be
warranted on the basis of others. It is clearly the
better part of wisdom to recognize beliefs that
emerge from these practices to be rational and
justified, at least once they are properly sifted
and refined.

In this paper I have undertaken to extend this
account to doxastic practices that are not universally practiced. Except for that matter of distribution and the other peripheral matters mentioned in Objection V and except for being faced
with actually existing rivals, a religious experiential doxastic practice like RE seems to me to be
on all fours with SP and other universal practices.
It too involves a distinctive range of inputs, a
range of belief contents, and functions that map
features of the former onto contents of the latter. It is socially established within a certain community. It involves higher-level procedures of
correction and modification of its first-level beliefs. Though it *may* be acquired in a deliberate

and self-conscious fashion, it is more typically
acquired in a practical, prereflective form. Though
it is obviously evitable in a way SP, e.g., is not,
for many of its practitioners it is just about as
firmly entrenched.

These similarities lead me to the conclusion
that if, as it seems we must concede, a belief is
prima facie justified by virtue of emerging from
one of the universal basic practices, we should
also concede the same status to the products of
RE. I have sought to show that various plausible-
sounding objections to this position depend on
the use of a double standard or reflect arbitrary
epistemic chauvinism. They involve subjecting
RE to inappropriate standards. Once we appreciate these points, we can see the strength of the
case for RE as one more epistemically autonomous practice of belief formation and source of
justification.

On "Perceiving God"

I agree with Professor Alston that many of the
objections he discusses to the epistemic legitimacy of religious experience involve a double
standard. That is, those who offer them (and I
here include my own past self) ought, if consistent, to express parallel doubts about the credentials of sense perception, though they usually do
not. Alston therefore joins that important group
of apologists who demand that the theist be accorded parity of treatment with other nonskep-
tics. But although I agree with him about this, I
must use my space in this symposium to spell out
what I see to be the apologetic limitations of his
argument.

Alston recognizes that he establishes only that
putative perceptions of God provide *prima facie*
(or defeasible) justification of M-beliefs, and concedes that this leaves us with the need for overriders within religious systems and with a serious
problem of religious balkanization. The demand
for parity makes us accord rights to apparently
incompatible religious systems. Alston does not
exclude the possibility that we may have to settle
for living in the Balkans to avoid epistemic chauvinism. I am not Cartesian enough to deny this

possibility either, but, if it is accepted as real, it is hard to see any grounds for refusing to extend rights to such anti-religious systems as Marxism, Freudianism, Sociobiology, and many versions of secular humanism, each equipped with its own battery of putative insights and overriders. Although perhaps none of these systems can undermine the *autonomy* of a system built on RE, there is no way of denying the "adequacy" of their naturalistic accounts of RE which is not, in its own way, chauvinistic.

The identification of putative perceptions of God is not as clear from Alston's general account as it might be. While drawing an analogy with sense perception, he asks us to focus on those cases in which something presents itself as God doing something, but not via any sensory qualities or sensorily perceivable objects. This seems to exclude putative perceptions of God that people get from reading the Scriptures, encountering natural wonders, or escaping physical dangers—in fact the whole range of phenomena in which believers think they encounter God, whereas unbelievers (who agree that the phenomena occur) deny they do. Whatever Alston intends, these are the occasions of very many supposed perceptions of God, and cases to which believers particularly apply their overrider systems. They are also the cases to which naturalistic accounts will also be applied—since believers will not deny the natural causes that such accounts mention. REs of this kind can be accommodated both to systems that include M-beliefs and to systems that exclude them. Like other forms of human experience, they are religiously ambiguous.

There is another dimension to this ambiguity. The existence of so many naturalistic belief systems in our culture causes many who *have* putative perceptions of God to be rationally disinclined ever to admit that these are real perceptions. Alston's arguments may encourage such persons to be less dismissive of the rationality of their religious acquaintances, but they do nothing to address this disinclination. . . .

NOTE

1. See my "Epistemic Circularity," *Philosophy and Phenomenological Research* XLVII, 1(September 1986): 1–30.

4.6 Feminists, Philosophers, and Mystics

There has been much debate among contemporary philosophers about the nature of religious experiences in general and mystical experiences in particular and about what, if anything, they prove about the reality of God or some other religious reality. William James (see Reading 4.5) thought that all, or nearly all, mystical experiences are characterized by ineffability, a noetic quality, transiency, and passivity. Walter Stace (1961) thought there were two main types: introvertive and extrovertive. The former (and in Stace's estimation the "highest") is a unitary conscious state from which all multiplicity of content (either sensory or conceptual) is absent, and the latter (and lesser) involves a "unifying vision" in which the multiplicity perceived through the senses is experienced as one or unified. R.C. Zaehner (1961) took exception to Stace's typology, maintaining that the literature clearly showed at least three distinct types: theistic, monistic, and nature mysticism. The first, as far as Zaehner is concerned (and contrary to Stace's evaluation), is by far the best. Union with God far surpasses, in spiritual and moral stature, the experiences of an absolute impersonal oneness or experiences of intense and intimate unity with nature. I could continue the account of revisionary typologies, but all of them appear to share the assumption that mystical experiences are intense, subjective, ineffable states of consciousness having to do with experiences of unity.

Even though the typologies of mysticism constructed by scholars vary somewhat, many philosophers assumed that there is a common core to these experiences that transcend religion and culture. Thus mystical experiences seemed to be a promising foundation on which to rest an argument for religious truth (see Reading 4.5). In 1978 the "common core" assumption came under attack when Steven Katz published a collection of essays by different scholars entitled *Mysticism and Philosophical Analysis.* In the essay that Katz contributed, he argued that there is no common core and, more strongly, that there could not ever be a common core, because all experiences, including mystical and religious experiences, are constructed out of the beliefs systems, cultural values, religious traditions, and practices that individuals learn from their social and religious environment and training.

Katz's claims were met by a host of critics led by Robert Forman (1990), who argued, among other things, that it seems totally arbitrary to rule out *a priori* the possibility that some mystical experiences might be everywhere the same without carefully examining the evidence. Certainly some experiences—those called Pure Consciousness Events—that are devoid of all content must be culturally and religiously independent, because there is no content that could be constructed by the mystic out of the influences of his or her environment.

Wait! There appears to be something wrong with this picture. These arguments may not rest on careful historical analysis and do not take into account the role that gender plays in religious experiences. Grace M. Jantzen, John Rylands Senior Research Fellow at the University of Manchester and an expert on Christian mysticism (especially the female mystics of the Christian tradition), argues in the next selection that the contemporary philosophical discussion of mystical experiences is woefully misguided because it ignores the ways in which mysticism is socially constructed and ignores the role that gender plays in the development of mysticism and in the debate about its cognitive significance.

Reading Questions

1. Why does Jantzen suspect that mysticism may not be best characterized as an "intense, ineffable, subjective experience"?
2. Why does Jantzen think that much of "the modern construction of mysticism" stems from an attempt to "circumvent Kantian strictures on epistemology"?
3. According to Jantzen, what mistakes do contemporary philosophers of religion make when dealing with the issue of mystical experience?
4. Why, from a "feminist perspective," does Jantzen find the contemporary interest, especially on the part of women, in New Age spirituality, mysticism, and psychological self-help books "deeply worrying"?
5. What three conclusions does Jantzen draw?
6. How does Jantzen respond to the question "Why should philosophers of religion who investigate it [mysticism] not use the resources that the mystics provide [as evidence for God's existence], even if that was not the original intention behind their writings?" Do you find her response adequate? Why or why not?

Feminists, Philosophers, and Mystics*

GRACE M. JANTZEN

WHAT IS MYSTICISM? Is it an experience of direct communion with God? Or is it just a human phenomenon, at its best benign piety and at its worst muddleheaded fanaticism claiming divine authority for intolerant behavior? Is mysticism something shared by all world religions, which could serve as a link between different ways of life and belief? Or is the idea of a mystical core of religion misguided—perhaps yet another of the totalizing discourses of modernity? What does mysticism have to do with justice? Is mystical experience private and subjective, or does it have political and social implications? Is mysticism related to gender, perhaps especially available to women? Or is feminist mysticism impossible? Is mysticism essentially patriarchal?

Implicit in all these questions is an agenda of power. The fascination of the subject of mysticism is not, I suggest, simply a fascination with intense psychological experiences for their own sake: rather, what fascinates is that the answers to each of these questions are also ways of defining or delimiting authority. The connection of questions of power to questions of mysticism is obvious as soon as one stops to consider that a person who was acknowledged to have direct access to God would be in a position to challenge any form of authority, whether doctrinal or political, which she saw as incompatible with the divine will. If defining mysticism is a way of defining power, then the question of who counts as a mystic is of immediate political importance. From the early days of the Christian church, struggles for authority were prominent, and throughout the medieval period, the struggles increased. It was crucial to the ecclesiastical establishment that those who claimed knowledge of the mysteries of God should be contained within the structures of the church, since the power of the church would

be severely threatened if it should be acknowledged that access to divine authority was possible outside its confines.

In modern times, the issues of power in relation to mysticism have shifted less than we might think. If, for instance, mystical experience (or religious experience more generally) is to be trusted, it could be used to provide an authoritative basis for knowledge of the existence and nature of God (Swinburne 1979; Alston 1991); if this were to be established and acknowledged, it would accord enormous authority to those whose experience was deemed to be veridical. Or, from another perspective, if mystical experience could be delimited as private and subjective, that would be a way of ensuring that it did not have to be taken into account by those making social and political decisions: in this respect, at least, religion could be kept well out of politics (while implicitly reinforcing the status quo). If mystical experience is seen as gender-related, especially available to women, and at the same time as private and subjective, then this can be used to reinforce stereotypes of women as the spiritual nurturers of humanity while keeping both women and spirituality firmly domesticated.

Contemporary philosophers and theologians, feminists among them, regularly speak of mysticism as though the term is clearly understood: it stands for a subjective psychological state, perhaps a state of "altered consciousness," in which an individual undergoes a private, intense, and ineffable experience, usually of a religious nature. A study of the historical records, however, shows that such an understanding of mysticism is a relatively recent one which bears little resemblance to those who are taken paradigmatically as mystics of the Christian tradition. I begin with a brief sketch of some of the ways in which mysticism

*From "Feminists, Philosophers, and Mystics," *Hypatia: Special Issue Feminist Philosophy of Religion* 9 (Fall 1994):186–206. Reprinted by permission.

has been socially constructed in the Christian West. Then I discuss the bearing of this historical diversity on some of the issues preoccupying philosophers of religion who think and write about mysticism. In the final section, I raise questions about contemporary uses of mysticism from a feminist perspective sharpened by the recognition of the interconnection of issues of power and gender. I suggest that this interconnection is not restricted to the single topic of mysticism, but can be generalized much more widely within the philosophy of religion and beyond it.

Who Counts as a Mystic?

Histories of Christian mysticism often base themselves on the dubious premise that there is something like an "essence" of mysticism which can be seen to have a beginning in the biblical writings, to develop in the patristic and medieval era, to make progress toward its full flowering in the thirteenth and fourteenth centuries, and then to send out seeds for new developments in the Protestant and Catholic reformations (Bouyer et al. 1968; McGinn 1991). Taking a cue from the work of Michel Foucault (1965, 1973), I find it worthwhile to ask instead how the mystical has been understood in a variety of times and places within the Christian West.

Even a brief look results in sketches toward a counterhistory, which render improbable the traditional linear picture of what constitutes mysticism and its history as presented by historians such as Bouyer and McGinn, and as accepted by philosophers of religion such as Swinburne and Alston. Far from having a constant meaning, the ideas surrounding the mystical and about who counts as a mystic have undergone major changes. In the classical context in which Christian theology had its beginnings, mystics were simply those who had been initiated into the mystery religions, who had undergone a rite of initiation about which they kept silent. There was nothing particularly "ineffable" about the experience; the point was simply that the ritual was to be kept secret, it was *not* to be talked about with the uninitiated. Clearly, the assumption behind the

injunction to silence is that without such a rule, the ritual might have been talked about: the assumption, in other words, is diametrically opposite to any assumption that the ritual is "ineffable" (Bouyer 1981). From this idea of mystics as those who keep their mouths shut came the further idea, linked with Platonic philosophy, that mystics are those whose knowledge of the divine comes by shutting *all* the senses: mystical knowledge is knowledge available only to the mind or spirit that is as detached as possible from bodily concerns. Thus the mystical or spiritual comes to mean, in this context, that which is beyond ordinary sense perception and the normal means of human knowledge (Louth 1981). Except for one brief exception in Plato's *Republic*, Plato and all in his train took for granted that women were identified with bodiliness and that knowledge, especially in its highest forms, was the prerogative of men. In Christian spirituality as influenced by Plato, this meant that if there were women whose spiritual knowledge could not be denied, they would have to be reclassified as "honorary males" (Miles 1989, 53–77).

The concept of the mystical as having to do with special knowledge underwent a considerable change of construction as the Christian tradition came to increase its emphasis on the Bible and, in particular, on the notion that every part of the Bible at its deepest level really refers to Christ. This deepest level became known as the spiritual or mystical meaning of Scripture, as contrasted with the literal or historical meaning. The "mystical ones," therefore, were those who could discern the spiritual meaning of Scripture underneath the literal meaning: "The letter kills, but the spirit gives life." The mystical meaning of Scripture was not some special, intense, psychological experience imparted to the reader but rather the perception of its hidden depths, its reference to Christ even in passages that in literal terms were speaking of something quite different. Similarly, the sacraments, whether baptism or the Eucharist, were to be understood not merely as literal water or bread or wine but as the mystical entry into the church by the washing away of sins or as the mystical body and blood of Christ. And it was not held to be the case that receiving them in their mystical sense either required or effected a psychological transformation of the people concerned. Indeed, the whole point of *faith* in their efficacy was that no such intense subjective experiences need take place, but that the sacraments are valid, nevertheless. Such an understanding of the mystical is obviously a far cry from current discussions regarding altered states of consciousness and ineffability as essential characteristics of mystical experiences (Jantzen 1986, Smalley 1983).

Once again, however, the mystical under this description was largely the domain of men. Women, on the whole, did not have the education necessary to study the text and its multiple glosses; and even in exceptional cases where they did have the requisite education and access to the manuscripts, they were not considered suitable to teach or to have the authority that discernment of the mystical meaning would confer (Newman 1987, 37–41; Flanagan 1989, 53). An alternative source of authority about the mysteries of God might come by visions, a direct communication from God to the most humble creatures of divine creation. Since women were those who could be seen as most like "the handmaiden of the Lord," they might, ironically, be most likely to be privileged with a vision of the mysteries of God. Thus Hildegard of Bingen in the twelfth century marks an important transition in the social construction of mysticism: whereas, as she insists, it is men who should be the mystical ones, expounding the knowledge of God by their insight into the mystical meaning of Scripture, because of their laxity God has had to turn to Hildegard herself, a woman, and give her the message to be communicated, doing so by means of visions rather than by the "normal" method of years of prayerful study of the Scriptures (Hildegard [c. 1142] 1990, 67). In the high and late Middle Ages, numerous women visionaries across the European continent, including among many others the famous Gertrude the Great and Mechthild of Helfta, Mechtild of Magdeburg, Hadewijch of Antwerp, Bridget of Sweden, Catherine of Siena, Julian of Norwich, and Teresa of Avila claimed authority for themselves as spiritual teachers and

based that claim at least in part on the visions they had received. The construction of mysticism could no longer exclude women (Bynum 1987, 13–30).

What is apparent in the high Middle Ages, however, is the increasing wariness of the male ecclesiastical authorities of visionaries, usually but not exclusively women. Strict criteria were set down for the assessment of their claims. Many of those who today are counted as the male mystics of the medieval period decried visions and other such putative direct communications from God altogether (Eckhart [c. 1320] 1979, 127, 117; *Cloud* [c. 1350] 1981, 231, 223; Ruusbroec [c. 1350] 1985, 89, 231). At the very least, strict adherence to the male-defined doctrines and practices of the church was expected of any woman who claimed spiritual authority. Among the requirements were obedience to the counsel of her (male) spiritual director, strict physical enclosure, and absolute chastity. Thus for instance the relatively unregulated movement in thirteenth-century Rhineland of religious women known as Beguines escaped charges of heresy only by giving up their independent living arrangements, entering enclosure, and accepting the direction of a male ecclesiastic, usually a Dominican friar.

Even this, however, was not enough to guarantee that women would be counted as genuine mystics, as likely as men to be recipients of divine communication. As the controls were more tightly drawn throughout western Europe from the time of Pope John XXII onward, many women and men were tried and condemned as heretics, often on charges of false mysticism—another notable shift in the possibilities included in the term. False mysticism was seen as the demonic counterpart of communication with God and was regularly characterized in terms of sexual obscenities and murderous evil (Cohn 1976; Russell 1980). Within the prevailing misogyny of the late medieval and early modern periods, this took the horrendous form of the execution of thousands of women and some men as witches. The connection of power and gender in the social construction of mysticism could hardly have been made more clear than in the condemnation and slaughter of those who were considered, as false mystics, to be a threat to church and society sufficient to justify their extermination (Hester 1992).

Only with the development of the secular state, when religious experience was no longer perceived as a source of knowledge and power, did it become safe to allow women to be mystics. Schleiermacher, for example, in his *Speeches on Religion,* is happy to proclaim the greater religious consciousness of women, whom he also saw as ideally maintaining domestic bliss (Schleiermacher [1799] 1958, 37; Briggs 1985, 227–29). In the next century Tennyson presented his ideal woman as

> Not learned, save in gracious household
>   ways,
> Not perfect, nay, but full of tender wants,
> No Angel, but a dearer being, all dipt
> In Angel instincts, breathing Paradise,
> Interpreter between the Gods and men.
> (Tennyson [1847] 1906, 89)

This ideal woman would, of course, never venture into the sordid public world. Both mysticism and women, then, became constructed as private and personal, having nothing to do with politics; hence mystical raptures were quite compatible with a woman's role as the "angel in the house," servicing her husband and children not only physically but spiritually as well. The decline of gender as an issue in the definition of who should count as a mystic occurred in direct relation to the decline in the perception of mystical experience, and religion generally, as politically powerful. At the same time, such experience came to be described as "ineffable"—a notion that would have simply baffled many of the medieval women from Hildegard of Bingen to Teresa of Avila who are standardly included in histories of mysticism and who wrote about their insights and experiences with great fluency and creativity, and at great length (James [1902] 1960). It is plausible to suspect that the characterization of mystical experience as ineffable has much more to do with the construction of modern epistemology than with what those who are counted as mystics have

actually said about their experiences. Furthermore, the alleged inexpressibility of mystical experience correlates neatly with the silencing of women in the public arena of the secular world: women may be mystics, but mysticism is a private, intense experience not communicable in everyday language and not of political relevance.

Given the interconnection of power and gender in the social construction of mysticism in the past, it is hardly farfetched to ask what sorts of power and gender issues are at work in this modern construction. The ineffability and privacy of mystical experience are uniformly taken as its central features by philosophers including Stace (1961), Alston (1991), Pike (1992), and Franks Davis (1989), even though in other respects their understandings of mysticism differ from one another. Feminists have every reason, both historical and current, to be suspicious of an understanding of mysticism which allows that women may be mystics, but which makes mysticism a private and ineffable psychological occurrence and which detaches it from considerations of social justice.

Although it is clear that to a very large extent the definition and control of who should count as a mystic have been in the hands of powerful males intent on retaining ecclesiastical or intellectual dominance, and that they have exercised that control to their own advantage, it is also evident that women were not simply passive victims. Even women who had strongly internalized male ideals of womanhood as passive and humble, and who fully accepted the authority of the ecclesiastical establishment, often pushed back the boundaries of what could be counted as genuinely mystical by the courageous integrity of their lives and writings. Women such as Hildegard of Bingen and Julian of Norwich cannot be studied without recognizing their strength and insight. Furthermore, it is obvious that at least in some respects that strength and insight are directly related to their gender. Julian's theology of God as Mother, for example, and her insistence that her recognition of God's love shall be available to all God's children, not only those in a religious community, are hardly detachable from her experiences as a woman. Hadewijch of Antwerp speaks of spiritual growth using the metaphor of the nine months of pregnancy and urges that when one is gestating God, it is best not to give birth prematurely: it is hardly a metaphor that male writers would use. Although the women in the Christian tradition were in many respects bounded by male definition and authority, they still found unconventional possibilities of working within those boundaries and indeed in pushing them back in ways that remain instructive for contemporary feminists: Julian of Norwich raised radical questions about whether God could be thought of as wrathful or punishing; Teresa of Avila refused to tolerate the equation between wealth and worthiness to belong to a religious community; the visionary women already named challenged the idea that authority was necessarily conjoined with education and ecclesiastical privilege. The many women and men who were willing to stand against the ecclesiastical structures of authority that were often corrupt and self-serving, and who, like Marguerite Porete and Meister Eckhart, were liable to be defined as heretics or witches because of it, showed radical ways of taking responsibility for what they would count as genuinely religious, whether or not it was approved by those with the power of the sword. It is appropriate that the dangerous memory of these women and men should be preserved in studies of who counts as a mystic and that their lives should be included in the parameters of the question of power and gender in the Christian mystical tradition.

The Philosophical Uses of Mysticism

The changes in the meaning of the idea of the mystical, and the fact that the changes were not innocent of considerations of power and gender, are readily apparent in the historical sources. None of this, however, would be guessed by reading contemporary philosophical literature about mysticism. Modern philosophers of religion are seduced by a particular picture of mysticism, inherited largely from William James, which involves them in a stately dance of claims and

counterclaims about experience and interpretation, language and ineffability, credulity and doubt. The movements of this dance are by now well defined; but what is hardly ever noticed is how little resemblance they bear to the things that preoccupied the medieval men and women whom they themselves would consider to be paradigm mystics: discernment of the mystical meaning of Scripture, ministry to the needs of the destitute, the lepers, and the ignorant, and development of rich new genres and modes of language to sing of the love of God (Jantzen 1989, 1990; Bynum 1987). Nor is it at all usual for philosophers of religion discussing mysticism to pay close attention to the issues of power, let alone gender, which feminists consider essential to adequate analysis. I shall illustrate this by noting some issues to which contemporary philosophers of religion do pay close attention: the nature of mystical experience and its evidential value.

Contemporary philosophers of religion have a clear presupposition that mystical experiences are private, subjective, intense psychological states. Whatever else is open to question about mysticism, this, at least, continues to be assumed, even though contemporary writers on mysticism caution that the word is notoriously difficult to define. Thus Nelson Pike in *Mystic Union* (1992) concentrates wholly on the variety of intense psychological states that he believes certain mystics have described as union with God. Taking seriously the need to look at primary sources, Pike spends considerable time trying to analyze the various stages of mystical development as presented by Teresa of Avila. He then uses this analysis as a basis for his philosophical discussion about the relationship between experience and interpretation in mystical experiences. Because he has already assumed that what is of fundamental importance are the experiential psychological states of the mystic, however, his whole account is focused on those states and their similarities and differences. He never asks whether this focus might seriously distort what the mystic herself considered to be essential; yet as Rowan Williams has argued, Teresa's own concern was with the "contemplative's missionary vocation in a way far removed from the individualistic and slightly precious ambience" fostered by concentration on her psychological states (Williams 1991, ix).

At one point, to be sure, Pike comes very close to seeing that his concern does not coincide with the concern of the mystics whom he is discussing. In his preface, he asks, "What, then, do we find when we turn to the primary literature?" and in response he says, "Comments about the states of union are often embedded in contexts in which mystics are less concerned to describe features of mystical phenomena than to extol the majesty of God, decry the sinful states of the soul, warn against the dangers of deception, etc." (Pike 1992, xii). Exactly so. But instead of taking this as a warning that the project of philosophical analysis of mysticism strictly in terms of psychological states might be in any way misguided, Pike simply takes it as adding to the difficulties that a philosopher who discusses mysticism must face. The central question he sets himself is, "What is it to experience union with God?" And he immediately adds the following gloss: "More precisely, what are the experiential or phenomenological features of the various experiences traditionally included in the union class?" (x). Union with God is here *assumed* to be a subjective psychological state. Accordingly, there is no consideration of moral issues, for example, or of the social and political contexts in which certain people were allowed to count as mystics while others were not. Pike lifts passages out of the writings of Teresa of Avila, Jan van Ruusbroec, Eckhart and other mystics, and then treats these passages as describing "experiences of God" that can be known and identified as such without any reference to the ecclesiastical and social climate in which they occurred, and that can be analyzed by a modern philosopher of religion strictly in terms of the psychological phenomena involved.

The assumption of the subjective and psychological nature of mysticism occurs also in the work of John Hick, whose *An Interpretation of Religion* (1989) discusses the question of whether the mystical experiences of adherents of various world religions are at their core the same. Throughout, Hick relies on the basic understanding of mysticism as centrally involving a subjective state of consciousness, usually brief in duration, which would be quite different from ordinary consciousness. Similarly, Michael Stoeber, in his interesting search for a mystical theodicy, characterizes an "authentic" mystic as one who "grants the experiences extraordinary status as a central premise of his or her life" because of their psychological impact on subjective consciousness (Stoeber 1992, 80). Again, most of the contributors to Steven Katz's volume on *Mysticism and Language* (Katz 1992) assume that mystical experience is an intense subjective state. The discussion never challenges this assumption but only questions the extent to which such a state is expressible in language. These recent authors stand in a long line of writers, among them Anthony O'Hear (1984, chap. 2), J.L. Mackie (1982, chap. 10), and Richard Swinburne (1979, chap. 13), who, following William James, have interpreted mystical experience as essentially involving the four characteristics of ineffability, noetic quality, transiency, and passivity (James [1902] 1960, 367–8) even while fundamentally disagreeing with one another about the significance of such experiences.

Moreover, investigation reveals that much of the modern construction of mysticism derives from an attempt to circumvent Kantian strictures on epistemology, strictures whose effect would be to render genuine religious experience impossible. Kant's understanding of rationality and his theory of knowledge stand at the summit of the Enlightenment project. In Kant's view, human knowledge can never extend to knowledge of things as they are in themselves; the best we can hope for is accurate knowledge of things as they appear to us. Knowledge of ultimate reality, including knowledge of God, must therefore remain forever beyond human capability: we can never circumvent the categories of our perception which entail that any human experience will be seen strictly in terms of these categories. The price of the Enlightenment project of making the human subject the center and foundation of all knowledge is to foreclose forever knowledge of any transcendent reality.

Postmodern thinkers have taken the Kantian turn to the rational subject as one of the most objectionable aspects of modernity, and much has been written about "the death of the subject." Whether this is to be welcomed or not is another question. Feminists in particular have reason to be wary of announcements of the "death of autonomous man" in a world in which autonomous women have hardly had a chance to be born (Braidotti 1991; Flax 1990). Contemporary Anglo-American philosophers of religion, however, remain largely untouched by postmodern concerns, and conduct their discussion of mysticism, wittingly or not, under the long shadow of Kant. This shadow stretches through the work of Schleiermacher and William James, who try to retrieve religious and mystical experience from Kantian strictures by seeing such experiences as unique, intense, subjective states of consciousness occurring "on the verges of the mind" (James [1902] 1960, 406), different from normal consciousness and thus escaping Kant's critical theory. Not all modern philosophers acknowledge their indebtedness to Schleiermacher and James, although many do; but it is clear that without their emphasis on the subjectivity of religious experience generally and mystical experience in particular, the contemporary discussion would be very different.

The classical mystics of the Christian tradition had not read Kant, and their preoccupations were quite different from what one might think if one read only modern philosophical discussions of them. Even when they did speak of experience, they were focusing on something much broader and more nuanced than is captured by the characteristics given by James and accepted by subsequent philosophers. Furthermore, even mystics in a common tradition cannot all be piled into one monolithic heap, as though their experiences and concerns were homogenized. Female mystics were much more concerned with visions and locutions and intense experiences than were the dominant male mystics. Indeed, the disparagement of intense experiences on the part of these men can be read as an attempt to discredit the women visionaries and the authority they claimed. Ironically, post-Kantian characterizations of mysticism are more accurate to female visionaries than to male mystics, since it was only by way of visions and other acute psychological states that women of spirit could hope to be accorded spiritual authority.

Moreover, once the characterization of mysticism in terms of intense experiences is taken as definitive, then a further question presents itself: Is there any reason to suppose that the mystical experiences of people of other religions (or none) need be any different from those of Christian mystics? Could there be a mystical core of religion—an inward, personal experience that people in all religions have in common, although it is then overlaid with culture-specific beliefs and practices?

Opinions are sharply divided. Caroline Franks Davis, following Richard Swinburne, uses the "principle of credulity" to argue that in the absence of considerations that defeat the claims of those who have religious experiences, their claims should be taken as evidence for the truth of religious doctrines (Franks Davis 1989, chaps. 4 and 9; Swinburne 1979, chap. 13; see also Alston 1991). That is, just as we standardly accept that a person who claims to see a tree or a flower really does see a tree or a flower unless there is serious reason to doubt the person's trustworthiness or the reliability of her senses, so also we should accept that if a person claims to have seen or otherwise experienced God, that is in itself good reason to believe that her experience is veridical unless we have serious reason to call it into doubt. On the other side, Richard M. Gale argues that the parallels between mystical experience and sense experience are too weak to allow for such an application of the principle of credulity and that therefore mystical experience cannot serve as evidence for the truth of religious claims, particularly the claim that God exists (Gale 1991, chap. 8).

It is obvious that this is another preoccupation that those who are counted as mystics hardly shared, living as they did under the "sacred canopy" in which God's existence was taken for granted. Although they were indeed concerned that their experiences should not be self-induced or, worse, of demonic origin, the basis for this concern was not a need for evidence for the existence of God. What today is essentially contested was to them completely clear. Philosophers who use the accounts of mystical writers to argue about the existence of God or the truth of the doctrines of Christianity are using these accounts in ways that would have been foreign and in some cases abhorrent to the people who wrote them.

Of course, it is proper to recognize that when modern philosophers ask questions different from those asked by the mystics themselves, it does not follow that modern philosophers are wrong to do so. Although the mystics were convinced of the truth of God's existence, that claim has now become problematic: Why should philosophers of religion who investigate it not use the resources that the mystics provide, even if that was not the original intention behind their writings? It would be courtesy (to put it no higher) to notice that this is a different use of the mystical writings than that which their authors intended, but in itself there is nothing particularly devious about finding resources in a text which were not part of the author's designs. One can, for instance, quite legitimately use the Icelandic sagas as evidence that certain species of birds mentioned in the text must have been resident in Iceland at the time of the Viking era, even though providing that evidence was only incidental to the text and not what was important to those who developed the sagas. Similarly, if the experiences of the mystics in the Christian tradition as described in the books they wrote give evidence for the existence of God, then it is legitimate for modern philosophers to recognize that evidence, even when the original writers were not making that their main point and indeed would have been astounded that anyone should need such evidence.

But now another problem arises, and it is this one that I am concerned to highlight. If mystical experience is indeed used as evidence for the truth of religious claims (or rejected as providing such evidence), *which* mystical experiences are we talking about? Contrary to what would be as-

sumed from reading philosophical discussions of mysticism, we saw in the first section of this paper that what counts as mystical experience has gone through enormous variations and that these variations have been essentially connected with issues of power and gender. Accordingly, if philosophers are going to use "mysticism" as part of their argument, it is first necessary for them to decide what they mean by that term, and whom they will count as a mystic. At this point, philosophers typically do two incompatible things. The first is that they employ the understanding of mysticism largely derived from the work of William James, an understanding that I have indicated is highly problematic, at least in a historical sense. And second, in doing so they suppose themselves to be discussing the experiences of the classical mystics of Christianity, all of whom, they suppose, had experiences characterizable in roughly Jamesian terms. Given these assumptions, it is not surprising that issues of power and gender go unnoticed; and feminists have been quick to point out in other areas that where such issues are unnoticed, they are reinforced.

If, however, philosophers of religion do wish to ask whether certain altered states of consciousness can provide evidence for the existence of God, that may be a legitimate question, although one that feminists would do well to probe. But it is necessary to be clear that this is a very *different* question from asking whether "mystical experience" (which ones? whose?) provides such evidence, let alone whether "mysticism" does. If my argument is correct, then one thing stands out: James and his followers notwithstanding, there is no such thing as an "essence" of mysticism, a single type of experience which is characterizable as mystical while others are excluded. All these terms have long histories of social construction; they are not unproblematic terms with clear referents, not are their variations innocent of the shifting machinations of power. Philosophers who pick on any one construction—usually one that involves intense subjective states of consciousness—to provide the evidential data for their discussion have not usually recognized that it *is* a construction, rather than "what mysticism really is," let alone that it is constructed out of differentials of power and gender relations.

Thus, for example, Caroline Franks Davis tries to find a common thread in religious experiences which will enable her to use them as part of a cumulative case for the truth of religious beliefs. Franks Davis is well aware that mysticism is not monolithic and recognizes this as a problem to be resolved in her effort to use the claims of mystics as evidence for religious doctrines. The problem, put bluntly, is that the claims of mystics of various religions, and even within religions, on the face of it contradict one another. She argues, however, that the apparent conflict can often be reconciled and that even where differences remain with regard to specific doctrinal claims, what the mystics have in common is more important than what divides them. For example, while it is true that a Christian mystic such as Teresa of Avila might experience Jesus as the Son of God, whereas a Muslim mystic would reject this claim, and a Buddhist mystic would experience "emptiness," all three, despite these differences, would agree that "the mundane world of physical bodies . . . is not the whole or ultimate reality" and that "whatever *is* the ultimate reality is holy, eternal, and of supreme value" (Franks Davis 1989, 191). These agreements on what Franks Davis calls "relatively unramified" doctrines are then given very great importance in her cumulative case for a broad theism, even though she recognizes that the people who make such claims are not themselves "broad theists" but rather holders of specific doctrines.

There are a variety of problems with Franks Davis's argument here. In the first place, even granting the terms of the argument, it is far from clear that her conclusion holds. After all, the more highly ramified beliefs that are in conflict with one another are often held, according to Franks Davis, on the basis of *exactly the same* mystical or religious experiences as those that produce the less ramified, compatible beliefs. If she wishes to use those experiences as evidence for the truth of the latter, how is it that they can be sidestepped (or reinterpreted) when it comes to the former?

Her strategy of response involves the even more doubtful move, familiar since Walter Stace's

book *Mysticism and Philosophy* (1961), of distinguishing between interpretation and experience. During the experience, she says, "mystics generally admit that little interpretation is possible." When we look closely at what they say after the fact, we find, however, that "mystics very probably have the same sort of experience, viz. freedom from all sense of time, space, personal identity, and multiplicity, which leaves them with a blissful, 'naked awareness' of perfect unity and a sense that 'this is it,' the ultimate level of reality" (1989, 178). It is only upon emerging from their experiences that mystics interpret them in accordance with their prior "doctrinal set," and it is this, rather than the experiences themselves, which causes the apparent conflict.

By this time we should be alert to how problematic such a line of argument is. In the first place, Caroline Franks Davis concentrates exclusively on intense subjective experiences, as though that is what is important about mysticism. I have already shown how such a concentration is a modern selection, having more to do with a modern philosophical agenda than with accuracy to the mystical tradition of Christianity, within which the focus on intense experiences was for long periods absent altogether. I have done nothing to show that the same would be true in the case of other world religions, but I suspect that in them, too, the "discovery" of mystical experience by Western scholars has more to do with the preoccupation of post-Enlightenment philosophy than with the indigenous religious traditions themselves. (While not concentrating on the issue of mystical experience, Wilfred Cantwell Smith has argued that the concept of religion is itself a Western, post-Enlightenment monster foisted on other traditions and societies rather than drawn out of a genuine understanding of them [Smith 1978, 1981; Byrne 1989]). For Franks Davis and other modern philosophers to take intense experiences as central to mysticism is thus simply inaccurate, at least to the Christian tradition, and since it is this tradition which most concerns them, their conclusions must be highly suspect.

Furthermore, even in those cases where Franks Davis could indeed appeal to intense experiences in the Christian mystical tradition, such as, for example, the visions of Hildegard of Bingen, Hadewijch of Antwerp, or Julian of Norwich, they would tend to cast doubt on her case rather than assist it. These women, and others like them, kept their wits about them during their intense experiences, sometimes taking part in the visions, not as though they were watching a film, but as full participants in a drama. Julian, for example, asked pointed questions of God about the evil and suffering in the world, and objected when she felt that the responses she received were inadequate. To claim, as Franks Davis does, that "mystics generally admit that little interpretation is possible *during* such an experience" simply betrays unawareness of the descriptions of the experiences given by the women themselves. Of course they were not *writing down* their "interpretations" during the time of the experiences, but that is not to say that they were having some sort of undifferentiated ecstasy, and only later invented the narrative of their experiences, cutting it out of whole cloth. The only alternative would be to say that these women were not *really* mystics, or at least that these experiences are not paradigmatically mystical. But to make that sort of move would only repeat in modern philosophical guise the same sorts of power/gender strategies that we have seen active in ecclesiastical dress in the medieval period. It is obviously not legitimate both to *stipulate* that only certain sorts of experience shall count as genuinely mystical (e.g., those which are ineffable [Stace 1961], or those which display a sense of "naked awareness" [Franks Davis 1989]), and at the same time to suppose that it is an *empirical* claim that all mystics have experiences of roughly this nature; yet this is the sort of circular reasoning that too often characterizes projects of showing that mystical experiences have a common core that can serve as part of a cumulative case for religious belief. The modern enterprise of fitting mystics into a procrustean bed has many antecedents, as we have seen, and such a move still has a strong appeal for contemporary philosophers of religion. The issues of power and gender which operated so powerfully in medieval defini-

tions of who should count as a mystic are still with us, albeit in modern liberal costume.

A Feminist Response

In the philosophical study of mysticism, with its assumption that mystical experience is an essentially private, subjective matter which, as such, does not connect with issues of social justice, feminism has yet to make an impact. If this amounted only to there being a small academic enclave which had not taken feminist scholarship into account and which insisted on defining and studying mysticism in male-dominated ways, that would be bad enough, though feminists might well decide that in a world of starving children, battered women, and rising fascism we had more important things to do than to spend energy trying to change the minds of philosophers of religion. But the situation is very much more serious. No social construction is the property of only one small group of people; rather, the nature of a social construction is that the definition imposed in the interests of a powerful group in society becomes constitutive of the society as a whole, as part of received knowledge. The assumption, therefore, that spirituality and social justice are separate, or, in more colloquial terms, that religion doesn't mix with politics, is one that is accepted and reinforced not only by many philosophers of religion but also far more widely. And if, as I have already suggested, it is also deemed that women are "naturally" more spiritual than men, then only a small step is necessary to confine both the "feminine" and the "spiritual" to a context in which they are rendered thoroughly ineffectual.

Largely escaping feminist scrutiny, in the past decade there has been a strong resurgence of interest in mysticism and spirituality outside academia as well as inside, in the churches as well as in secular society. Devotional and New Age books, and volumes containing selected readings from the mystics which can be read for a few minutes at the beginning or end of the day, sell thousands of copies and help keep religious publishers solvent. Retreat centers flourish; institutes of spirituality are set up; more and more of the writings of medieval mystics are available in modern translation; and theology and religious studies departments at universities are offering courses—often heavily subscribed—on mysticism and spirituality.

Feminists have paid astonishingly little attention to this widespread and culturally significant phenomenon. Although there has been some new feminist scholarship on particular medieval mystics, and themes arising from them, we have yet to evaluate the social needs to which this resurgent interest in them bears witness. Why and how does such interest arise and make itself felt in a male-dominated, capitalist, and increasingly fascist society characterized by consumerism, greed, and racist and sexist violence? Nor have we asked many questions about whether or how spirituality, either in its popular manifestations or in its academic study, connects with efforts for social justice. Still less have we inquired whether involvement in spirituality movements might actually deflect attention from the real needs of people, offering palliatives to individuals rather than solutions to the social causes of injustice. A feminist analysis of the patriarchal social construction of mysticism has hardly begun.

One place to start is to look at some of the most widely sold books on prayer and spirituality. Here, we find a huge emphasis on personal psychological well-being. Topics such as anxiety, depression, and loneliness are regularly addressed, along with such matters as suffering, bereavement, and sexual desires, all treated as essentially private issues for an individual to work through in her or his own way, guided by the insights offered by the author of the book. Prayer and spiritual exercises are advocated as bringing an increase of peace and tranquillity, and courage for the hard things in life. Thus, for example, Henri Nouwen, whose books have sold many thousands of copies, concentrates on woundedness, suffering, and healing through solitude and silence, prayer and meditation (Nouwen 1979, 1981). Gerard Hughes, in his enormously popular *God of Surprises,* guides readers through meditations on their own self-worth and seeks to help people deal with crippling guilt and make life-affirming decisions (Hughes 1985). Even

Matthew Fox, in his many popular books on creation-centered spirituality, emphasizes personal well-being and the blessings of sexuality and growth, but beyond bland assurances that this approach will be good for women and the earth, he has little specific to say about structural or political injustice or the ways in which spirituality or mysticism might have a bearing on it (Fox 1983, 1988). Perhaps most striking of all are the writings of M. Scott Peck, especially *The Road Less Traveled* (1978), which in the *New York Times Book Reviews* in August 1993, still stood at the top of the paperback list after 508 weeks. The book begins, "Life is difficult." Its theme is how to meet that difficulty through personal discipline, healing, love, and trust, characterized as "spiritual growth" in "traditional values."

While it is certainly no part of a feminist agenda to minimize the importance of personal psychological well-being, healthy sexuality, or creative decision making, several features of the spirituality industry need critique. First, the immense success of such devotional and spiritual self-help books, measured in numbers of sales, shows how urgent is the felt need for psychospiritual well-being, for inner resources to cope with the distresses of life. Second, while at least some of these books may indeed be helpful for the empowering of women, as the cliché goes, this by itself does not begin to address the question of where the stresses of life originate, or whether there are unjust structures in society which generate the oppression and anxiety for which help is sought. Except insofar as the psychospiritual well-being of an individual has an impact on her society (and this should not be minimized), there is as little indication in the popular literature as there is in scholarly treatments that mysticism and spirituality have anything to do with politics and social justice. Instead, they provide a private religious way of coping with life, whatever the external circumstances.

From a feminist perspective, this is deeply worrying. To the extent that prayer and meditation and books on spirituality actually help people cope with the distresses of life that arise out of unjust social conditions but fail to challenge those conditions themselves, to that extent they act as a sedative that distracts attention from the need to dismantle the structures that perpetuate the misery. If books and practices of spirituality help calm jangled nerves and release anxieties and renew courage to re-enter the world as it is, then despite the good intentions of the authors and practitioners (and these are usually not in doubt) the actual effect is unwittingly to reinforce the structures of injustice. The social and political policies that make for starving children, battered women, and the evils of rising fascism remain in place as people learn through prayer to find the tranquillity to live with corrupt political and social structures instead of channeling their distress and anger and anxiety into energy for constructive change.

In this connection it is instructive to consider the way in which the writings of medieval Christian mystics have been domesticated for a privatized spirituality. In almost any book of short readings from the mystics, the selections predominantly emphasize love of God, trust in God, humility, submission to God's will, dependence on providence, and cultivation of inner peace and tranquillity. Women who are aware of how regularly such themes of trust and humility and submission have been used to keep women "in their place" in church and society will immediately find their suspicions raised. It is clear that while a person who uses these readings as a basis for daily meditation may well find herself calmed and encouraged, it is unlikely that they will provoke her to think hard about the social causes of her stress or to detect the ways in which the structures of capitalist society produce the stresses she feels, threaten the survival of our sisters and brothers in economically deprived countries, and undermine the life-sustaining capacities of the earth. As Margaret Miles has pointed out, it was one thing for people to meditate trustingly on exhortations to submit to divine providence in the fourteenth century when the plague might come at any moment and no one knew how to avoid it; it is quite another thing to take those texts as blueprints for consolation and inactivity in the late twentieth century when the very survival of the planet depends on informed and concerted effort (Miles 1988, 176–84).

In summary, with some notable exceptions, books of popular Christian spirituality treat prayer and spiritual exercises as strictly private, having to do with the relationship between the individual and God. For all their differences in style and intention from philosophical explorations of mysticism and spirituality, they share the same assumptions of the privacy and subjectivity of religious experience, including mystical experience. In both cases, the privatizing of spirituality obscures its relation to social justice. The net result, whatever the conscious intention of the authors and compilers, is the reinforcement of the societal status quo, as intellectual and religious energy pours into an exploration of private religiosity rather than into social and political action for change. This in turn has the effect not only of diverting the attention of those seeking deepened spirituality away from issues of justice but also of leaving the efforts for justice to those who have abandoned concern with spirituality, seeing it as severed from the work for structural change.

It is, however, one thing for feminists to recognize that there is considerable need for analysis of the social construction of mysticism as it is reflected both in popular spirituality and in philosophical accounts of mysticism; it is quite another to provide such an analysis. We can quite easily come to suspect that the agenda with which philosophers have studied the lives and writings of medieval mystics is not an agenda that the mystics themselves would have shared. We can recognize, as well, that one of the primary effects of the current social construction of mysticism has been a focus on its personal psychological dimensions, deflecting attention away from its political and social dynamic. But even a feminist philosophy of religion that would retrieve the lives and writings of the mystics and expose their concerns for political and social justice would need to proceed cautiously. It is manifestly not the case that the tradition of Christian spirituality uniformly nurtures wholeness and justice, let alone sexual egalitarianism! There is racism and classism, sexism and homophobia, as deep in the hearts of many of the paradigm mystics of Western Christianity as it is deep in the heart of the

Christian church itself. None of the mystical writers were unambiguous: we find levels of tension within each individual, as strength and integrity struggled with deeply internalized misogyny and suspicion of the body and sexuality (Newman 1987; Jantzen 1987). And yet, while oppression runs deep, it is also true that from within the mystical tradition, especially (but not only) from some of the women mystics, came creative and courageous efforts at pushing back the boundaries of thought and action so that liberation could be achieved.

Conclusion

As feminist/womanist philosophers of religion struggle toward our identities, the study of power and gender in the social construction of mysticism offers a fruitful set of reflections. I wish to draw out three that have particular significance for the emergence of feminist philosophy of religion.

The first is that feminists who study mysticism and religious experience have much to gain by being more alert than philosophers of religion have usually been to the social context, including the gendered structures of authority, within which the lives and writings of the classical mystics took form. Rather than falling into the trap of universalizing discourse, or measuring all the mystics according to a single procrustean bed, we can learn to respect and celebrate difference by resurrecting the dangerous memories of individuals who resisted such homogenization. Luce Irigaray has written of women's urgent need for positing new, female, values for the divine (Irigaray 1993, 67). The women mystics offer such values in their colorfully inclusive language, their unconventional concepts of God (often spoken of as female), and the costly integrity of their lives as they claimed the authority of their experiences against the grain of convention.

Second, feminist philosophers of religion can use a study of the social construction of mysticism to become aware of current areas in philosophy of religion (and beyond it) where concepts are bandied about as though they were objective and universally applicable when in fact they are products of particular, gendered, constellations

of authority. What power relations are concealed, for example, in philosophical discourses about religious pluralism and interreligious dialogue, in which there may also be an appeal to a mystical core of religion? Who benefits and who loses, not only from the contemporary construction of mysticism, but also from other conceptions in the philosophy of religion, most notably the conceptions of God and the divine attributes, which have regularly been fashioned after a male ideal and used to legitimate oppression? To whom, finally, are feminists accountable in our own highly privileged philosophical pursuits, and is that accountability to be reckoned in terms of truth only or also in terms of justice?

This connects with a third implication that a study of the social constructions of mysticism, past and present, opens out for feminist/womanist philosophy of religion. The women's movements of this century have taken women's experience as central, validating women who spoke their truth, perhaps for the first time, in contexts such as consciousness-raising groups. For many women, the experience of being heard in such a group was utterly life-changing, and sometimes felt as near to a disclosure of the divine as they had ever come. It has become obvious that "women's experience" is neither so uniform nor so unproblematic as it at first may have appeared and that these experiences themselves are not immune from social construction. Nevertheless, feminists are, I expect, much more likely to ground our philosophies of religion in women's experiences as the source of religious knowledge than in the traditional categories of revelation and reason: I cannot quite imagine what a feminist rendition of the ontological argument might look like. As we look to women's experiences for such grounding, however, we need to be alert to the parameters within which such experiences are constructed, even while being open to the epiphanies which they may disclose. It is only as we are critically alert to the dangers of a privatized and psychologized construction of experience that we will also be able to use our experiences creatively in feminist/womanist philosophies of religion that preserve vital connections to the urgent issues of social justice.

REFERENCES

Alston, William A. 1991. *Perceiving God: The epistemology of religious experience*. Ithaca: Cornell University Press.

Bouyer, Louis, et al. 1968. History of Christian spirituality, 3 vols. London: Burns and Oates; New York: Seabury.

———. 1981. Mysticism: An essay on the meaning of the word. In *Understanding mysticism,* ed. Richard Woods. London: Athlone Press.

Braidotti, Rosi. 1991. *Patterns of dissonance: A study of women in contemporary philosophy*. Cambridge: Polity Press; New York: Routledge.

Briggs, Sheila. 1985. Images of Women and Jews in Nineteenth- and Twentieth-Century German Theology. In *Immaculate and powerful: The female in sacred image and social reality,* ed. Clarissa W. Atkinson, Constance H. Buchanan, and Margaret R. Miles. Boston: Beacon Press.

Bynum, Caroline Walker. 1987. *Holy feast and holy fast: The religious significance of food to medieval women*. Berkeley: University of California Press.

Byrne, Peter. 1989. *Natural religion and the nature of religion*. New York and London: Routledge.

Cloud of Unknowing. [c. 1350] 1981. Edited by James Walsh. New York: Paulist Press; London: SPCK.

Cohn, Norman. 1976. *Europe's inner demons*. London: Paladin.

Eckhart. [c. 1320] 1979. *Sermons and treatises,* 3 vols. Trans. and ed. M. O'C. Walshe. London: Watkins.

Flanagan, Sabina. 1989. *Hildegard of Bingen: A visionary life*. New York: Routledge.

Flax, Jane. 1990. *Thinking fragments: Psychoanalysis, feminism and postmodernism in the contemporary West*. Los Angeles: University of California Press.

Foucault, Michel. 1965. *Madness and civilization: A history of insanity in the age of reason*. Trans. Richard Howard. New York: Random House.

———. 1973. *The order of things: An archaeology of the human sciences*. New York: Vintage.

Fox, Matthew. 1983. *Original blessing*. Santa Fe: Bear and Company.

———. 1988. *The coming of the cosmic Christ*. San Francisco: Harper and Row.

Franks Davis, Caroline. 1989. *The evidential force of religious experience*. Oxford: Clarendon Press.

Gale, Richard M. 1991. *On the nature and existence of God*. Cambridge: Cambridge University Press.

Hester, Marianne. 1992. *Lewd women and wicked witches: A study of the dynamics of male domination*. New York: Routledge.

Hick, John. 1989. *An interpretation of religion: Human responses to the transcendent*. New York: Macmillan.

Hildegard of Bingen. [c. 1142] 1990. *Scivias.* Trans. Columba Hart and Jane Bishop. New York: Paulist Press.

Hughes, Gerard W. 1985. *God of surprises*. London: Darton, Longman and Todd.

Irigaray, Luce. 1993. *Sexes and genealogies.* Trans. Gillian C. Gill. New York: Columbia University Press.

James, William. [1902] 1960. *The varieties of religious experience*. Glasgow: Collins.

Jantzen, Grace. 1986. The mystical meaning of scripture: Medieval and modern presuppositions. *King's Theological Review* 7.2.

———. 1987. *Julian of Norwich: Mystic and theologian*. London: SPCK; New York: Paulist Press.

———. 1989. Mysticism and experience. *Religious Studies* 25.

———. 1990. Could there be a mystical core of religion? *Religious Studies* 26.

Julian of Norwich. [c. 1370] 1978. *Showings.* Trans. Edmund Colledge and James Walsh. London: SPCK; New York: Paulist Press.

Katz, Steven T., ed. 1992. *Mysticism and language*. Oxford: Oxford University Press.

Louth, Andrew. 1981. *The origins of the Christian mystical tradition: From Plato to Denys*. Oxford: Clarendon Press.

Mackie, J. L. 1982. *The miracle of theism: Arguments for and against the existence of God*. Oxford: Clarendon Press.

McGinn, Bernard. 1991. *The foundations of mysticism: Origins to the fifth century*. London: SCM.

McNay, Lois. 1992. *Foucault and feminism: Power, gender and the self*. Cambridge: Polity.

Miles, Margaret. 1988. *The image and practice of holiness: A critique of the classic manuals of devotion*. London: SCM Press.

———. 1989. *Carnal knowing: Female nakedness and religious meaning in the Christian West*. Boston: Beacon Press.

Newman, Barbara. 1987. *Sister of wisdom: St. Hildegard's theology of the feminine*. Berkeley: University of California Press.

Nouwen, Henri J. M. 1979. *The wounded healer: Ministry in contemporary society*. New York: Doubleday.

———. 1981. *The way of the heart*. New York: Ballantine.

O'Hear, Anthony. 1984. *Experience, explanation, and faith: An introduction to the philosophy of religion*. London: Routledge and Kegan Paul.

Peck, M. Scott. 1978. *The road less traveled: A new psychology of love, traditional values and spiritual growth*. New York: Simon and Schuster.

Pike, Nelson. 1992. *Mystic union: An essay in the phenomenology of mysticism*. Ithaca: Cornell University Press.

Russell, Jeffrey B. 1980. *A history of witchcraft: Sorcerers, heretics and pagans*. London: Thames and Hudson.

Ruusbroec, John. [c. 1350] 1985. *The spiritual espousals and other works*. Trans. James A. Wiseman. New York: Paulist Press.

Schleiermacher, Friedrich. [1799] 1958. *Speeches on religion to its cultured despisers*. New York: Harper Torchbooks.

Smalley, Beryl. 1983. *The study of the Bible in the Middle Ages*. 3d ed. Oxford: Blackwell.

Smith, Wilfred Cantwell. 1978. *The meaning and end of religion*. London: SPCK.

———. 1981. *Toward a world theology*. London: Macmillan.

Stace, Walter Terence. 1961. *Mysticism and philosophy*. London: Macmillan.

Stoeber, Michael. 1992. *Evil and the mystics' God: Towards a mystical theodicy*. London: Macmillan.

Swinburne, Richard. 1979. *The existence of God*. Oxford: Clarendon Press.

Tennyson, Alfred, Lord. [1847] 1906. The Princess. In *In Memoriam and other poems*. London: Macmillan.

Williams, Rowan. 1991. *Teresa of Avila*. London: Geoffrey Chapman.

Suggestions for Further Reading

Alston, William. *Perceiving God*. Ithaca, NY: Cornell University Press, 1991.

Baillie, John. *The Sense of the Presence of God*. London: Oxford University Press, 1962.

Broad, C. D. *Religion, Philosophy, and Psychical Research*. New York: Humanities Press, 1969.

Brown, Joseph Epes, recorder and editor. *The Sacred Pipe: Black Elk's Account of the Seven Rites of the Oglala Sioux*. Norman: University of Olahoma Press, 1963.

Donovan, Peter. *Interpreting Religious Experience*. New York: Seabury, 1975.

Faure, Bernard. *The Rhetoric of Immediacy: A Cultural Critique of Chan/Zen Buddhism*. Princeton: Princeton University Press, 1991.

———. *Chan Insights and Oversights: An Epistemological Critique of the Chan Tradition*. Princeton, NJ: Princeton University Press, 1993.

Forman, Robert K. C. *The Problem of Pure Consciousness: Mysticism and Philosophy*. New York: Oxford University Press, 1990.

Freud, Sigmund. *The Future of an Illusion*. New York: Norton, 1976.

Friedman, Maurice. *Martin Buber: The Life of Dialogue*. 3d. ed. Chicago: The University of Chicago Press, 1976.

Gale, Richard. *On the Nature and Existence of God*. Cambridge, England: Cambridge University Press, 1991.

Gutting, Gary. *Religious Belief and Religious Skepticism*. Notre Dame, IN: University of Notre Dame Press, 1982.

Hardy, Alister. *The Spiritual Nature of Man*. Oxford, England: Clarendon Press, 1979.

Hollenback, Jess Byron. *Mysticism: Experience, Response, and Empowerment*. University Park, PA: The Pennsylvania State University Press, 1996.

Holler, Clyde. *Black Elk's Religion: The Sun Dance and Lakota Catholicism*. Ithaca, NY: Syracuse University Press, 1995.

Inge, William R. *Mysticism in Religion*. Chicago: University of Chicago Press, 1948.

James, William. *The Varieties of Religious Experience*. New York: Longmans, Green and Co., 1902.

Jantzen, Grace M. *Power, Gender, and Christian Mysticism*. Cambridge, England: Cambridge University Press, 1995.

Jones, Richard H. *Mysticism Examined: Philosophical Inquiries Into Mysticism.* Albany, NY: State University of New York Press, 1993.

Katz, Steven T., ed. *Mysticism and Philosophical Analysis.* New York: Oxford University Press, 1978.

Lewis, H. G. *Our Experience of God.* New York: Macmillan, 1959.

Martin, C. B. *Religious Belief.* Ithaca, NY: Cornell University Press, 1959.

Mavrodes, George. *Belief in God.* New York: Random House, 1970.

Merton, Thomas. *The Seven Story Mountain.* New York: Harcourt, 1948.

———. *Mystics and Zen Masters.* New York: Dell, 1967.

Miles, T. R. *Religious Experience.* New York: St. Martin's Press, 1972.

Neihardt, John G. *Black Elk Speaks: Being the Life Story of a Holy Man of the Oglala Sioux.* Lincoln: University of Nebraska Press, 1961, 1979.

———. *When the Tree Flowered: An Authentic Tale of the Old Sioux World.* New York: Macmillan, 1951.

Otto, Rudolf. *Mysticism: East and West.* New York: Macmillan, 1932.

———. *The Idea of the Holy.* New York: Oxford University Press, 1958.

Powers, William K. *Oglala Religion.* Lincoln: University of Nebraska Press, 1977.

———. *Yuwipi: Vision and Experience in Oglala Ritual.* Lincoln: University of Nebraska Press, 1982.

Proudfoot, Wayne. *Religious Experience.* Berkeley: University of California Press, 1985.

Russell, Bertrand. *Religion and Science.* London: Oxford University Press, 1939.

Staal, Frits. *Exploring Mysticism.* Berkeley: University of California Press, 1975.

Stace, W. T. *Mysticism and Philosophy.* Philadelphia: Lippincott, 1960.

———. *The Teachings of the Mystics.* New York: New American Library, 1960.

Suzuki, D. T. *Essays in Zen Buddhism: First Series.* London: Rider & Co., 1949.

———. *Essays in Zen Buddhism: Second Series.* London: Rider & Co., 1950.

———. *Essays in Zen Buddhism: Third Series.* London: Rider & Co., 1953.

———. *The Zen Doctrine of No-Mind.* London: Rider & Co., 1949.

———. *Mysticism: Christian and Buddhist: The Eastern and Western Way.* New York: Greenwood Press, 1975.

Underhill, Evelyn. *Mysticism.* New York: Dutton, 1961.

Wainwright, W. J. *Mysticism.* Madison: University of Wisconsin Press, 1981.

Wall, George B. *Religious Experience and Religious Belief.* Lanham, MD: University Press of America, 1996.

Zaehner, R. C. *Mysticism: Sacred and Profane.* New York: Oxford University Press, 1961.

———. *Zen, Drugs and Mysticism.* New York: Pantheon, 1973.

CHAPTER 5

Why Do Suffering and Evil Occur?

Introduction

ALL HUMAN BEINGS SHARE the experiences of suffering and evil. Often, these experiences impel them to engage in philosophical and religious thought. Children are born with horrible birth defects. Teenagers die in the streets. Young men and women are killed in war. People are tortured, maimed, and tormented. Earthquakes bury thousands. Fires destroy animals, hunters kill them, and cars wound them. There is a staggering amount of suffering and pain in the world in which we live. It touches all of us in one way or another.

Evil is a problem for human existence. It is a complex problem with many dimensions. There is the concrete existential and personal dimension. How do *I* cope with evil and suffering? And then there is the intellectual dimension. Can we make sense of evil? Is suffering the sort of thing that can be explained? How? These two dimensions—the existential and the intellectual—are not totally separate. They are closely interrelated because part of how I might cope with my suffering is by discovering an explanation that makes it meaningful.

We can explain the causes and origins of some specific evils. The Azande (an African tribe) know that termites weaken the structures of granaries. These granaries occasionally fall down. They also know people like to seek the shade of these granaries on hot days. Sometimes the granaries fall on the people, and sometimes the people are injured or killed. Knowing all of this, however, does not explain why this particular person was under this particular granary at the particular time it fell. What can account for this unique combination of events? For the Azande the answer is witchcraft (see E. E. Evans-Pritchard, *Witchcraft, Oracles, and Magic among the Azande,* Oxford, 1937). For others it may be chance, for still others Fate, and for many just plain bad luck. Whatever the answer, the question is never one of general causation. We know why automobile accidents occur and that a crash can kill a family of five. But why did it happen to my relatives? To my neighbors? To my friends? Why me, Lord, why me? This is the "why" we want addressed, and this "why" is much harder to answer than questions about general, abstract, and depersonalized causation. Explaining that the accident occurred because a drunk driver hit the family of five does not address the deeper question that the problem of evil raises.

It is helpful to distinguish the problem of evil in its broad and narrow senses. In the broad sense, the problem is to give an account of where evil comes from, why it happens, and what might be done about it. It has long been debated in many cultures whether evil stems primarily from human nature or is due to society. Is society corrupt because individuals are corrupt, or are individuals corrupt because society is? Is it one or the other? Or is it both? Are people born nasty? Is evolution to blame?

The narrow sense of the problem is often called the theological problem of evil. The broad problem of the "why" of evil becomes the theological problem when a concept of God is brought into the picture. Why does God permit evil? Is the existence of evil compatible with the existence of God? How can it be that God loves us, and yet all these terrible things happen to us? Is the divine too weak to do anything about evil? If there is some ultimate reality, perhaps it does not really care about suffering and evil, or if it does, it has some secret reason for permitting them.

Two types of arguments related to the problem of evil and God can be distinguished. One (called the deductive or logical argument from evil) attempts to show that the existence of evil is *logically* incompatible with the existence of a God who is perfectly good, all-powerful, and the all-knowing creator of this world. The other (called the inductive or evidential argument from evil) tries to demonstrate that the variety and amount of evil in the world constitute good evidence that such a God may well not exist.

Once God is introduced into the picture, many have argued that what is required is some sort of theodicy, or theory, that will show God's purposes in permitting evil. Thus some philosophers, like John Hick, support what is called a "soul-making" theodicy. For Hick and others, any complete theodicy must account for both natural evils (suffering caused by natural events such as hurricanes, floods, and earthquakes) and moral evils (suffering that results from the conscious decision of some moral agent). Both sorts of evils, Hick argues, serve good. Evil provides an opportunity for humans to develop themselves both morally and spiritually. If we lived in an evil-free paradise, then this good would be lost.

Hick's "soul-making" theodicy is just one example of the many different kinds of theodicies proposed. All have been criticized, and many philosophers argue that theodicy is impossible. We simply cannot know why God (if there is one) permits evil. We might desperately want to know. Perhaps such knowledge would give us a special comfort. But we cannot know.

However, as Job demonstrated so long ago, humans cannot help asking why. Why do evil and suffering occur, and what are the religious implications of the fact that we live in a world that has a great profusion of evil?

5.1 Night

All you need to do is read the newspaper to find examples, on a daily basis, of human and animal suffering. Much of it seems senseless. Why is a small child brutally tortured and murdered? Why is a helpless baby beaten to death? What brings someone to blow up a building, killing many innocent people?

Dealing with natural disasters—floods, earthquakes, tornadoes—is one thing. We know that these things happen and that people suffer as a result. But moral evils— evils deliberately inflicted on other humans and on other-than-human animals by human beings—that is something else. It is harder to deal with.

There are magnitudes to evil and suffering. What is reported routinely in the newspapers pales in comparison to events such as the Holocaust. Over six million Jews and others were enslaved, tortured, and deliberately and systematically murdered by the Nazis, who desired to exterminate all of the Jews. Fortunately the Nazis did not succeed. They did, however, inflict horrific suffering on millions of women, men, and children.

As time passes, people forget. Just as we often deal with the evils we hear about on a daily basis by depersonalizing them, so we let the narcotic waves of forgetfulness dull our empathic pain. Some go so far as to deny it happened at all!

As painful as it may be, we must personalize the suffering of others. It is not some number that suffers, but persons who have hopes, fears, and dreams. Persons who deserve better than dying in gas chambers, on the gallows, or by the bullet. Persons like you and me.

Those who were there, those who witnessed, those who survived, can help us remember. They can personalize the face of evil for us and thereby help us all recover something of our lost humanity.

Elie Wiesel is a survivor and witness to the events that occurred in the Nazi concentration camps. He was born in Romania in 1928. The Nazis sent him and his family to the death camps simply because they were Jewish. His family was murdered. In countless stories and essays, he has explored with insight and power what such evil is like. It is a journey into night.

Reading Questions

1. Try to give a satisfactory answer to Wiesel's question "How could it be possible for them to burn people, children, and for the world to keep silent?"
2. What is the significance of Wiesel's comment that after the first hanging he found the soup excellent and that after the hanging of the young *pipel* the "soup tasted of corpses"?
3. Interpret the meaning of the comment "He is hanging here on this gallows" that Wiesel hears in response to the question "Where is God now?"
4. What is your emotional reaction to this true story of Wiesel's experiences at the hands of the Nazis?

Night*

ELIE WIESEL

THE CHERISHED OBJECTS we had brought with us thus far were left behind in the train, and with them, at last, our illusions.

Every two yards or so an SS man held his tommy gun trained on us. Hand in hand we followed the crowd.

An SS noncommissioned officer came to meet us, a truncheon in his hand. He gave the order:

"Men to the left! Women to the right!"

Eight words spoken quietly, indifferently, without emotion. Eight short, simple words. Yet that was the moment when I parted from my mother. I had not had time to think, but already I felt the pressure of my father's hand: we were alone. For a part of a second I glimpsed my mother and my sisters moving away to the right. Tzipora held Mother's hand. I saw them disappear into the distance; my mother was stroking my sister's fair hair, as though to protect her, while I walked on with my father and the other men. And I did not know that in that place, at that moment, I was parting from my mother and Tzipora forever. I went on walking. My father held onto my hand.

Behind me, an old man fell to the ground. Near him was an SS man, putting his revolver back in its holster.

My hand shifted on my father's arm. I had one thought—not to lose him. Not to be left alone.

The SS officers gave the order:

"Form fives!"

Commotion. At all costs we must keep together.

"Here, kid, how old are you?"

It was one of the prisoners who asked me this. I could not see his face, but his voice was tense and weary.

"I'm not quite fifteen yet."

"No. Eighteen."

"But I'm not," I said. "Fifteen."

"Fool. Listen to what *I* say."

Then he questioned my father, who replied: "Fifty."

The other grew more furious than ever.

"No, not fifty. Forty. Do you understand? Eighteen and forty."

He disappeared into the night shadows. A second man came up, spitting oaths at us.

"What have you come here for, you sons of bitches? What are you doing here, eh?"

Someone dared to answer him.

"What do you think? Do you suppose we've come here for our own pleasure? Do you think we asked to come?"

A little more, and the man would have killed him.

"You shut your trap, you filthy swine, or I'll squash you right now! You'd have done better to have hanged yourselves where you were than come here. Didn't you know what was in store for you at Auschwitz? Haven't you heard about it? In 1944?"

No, we had not heard. No one had told us. He could not believe his ears. His tone of voice became increasingly brutal.

"Do you see that chimney over there? See it? Do you see those flames? (Yes, we did see the flames.) Over there—that's where you're going to be taken. That's your grave, over there. Haven't you realized it yet? You dumb bastards, don't you understand anything? You're going to be burned. Frizzled away. Turned into ashes."

He was growing hysterical in his fury. We stayed motionless, petrified. Surely it was all a nightmare? An unimaginable nightmare?

I heard murmurs around me.

"We've got to do something. We can't let ourselves be killed. We can't go like beasts to the slaughter. We've got to revolt."

There were a few sturdy young fellows among us. They had knives on them, and they tried to incite the others to throw themselves on the armed guards.

One of the young men cried:

"Let the world learn of the existence of Auschwitz. Let everybody hear about it, while they can still escape. . . ."

But the older ones begged their children not to do anything foolish:

"You must never lose faith, even when the sword hangs over your head. That's the teaching of our sages. . . ."

The wind of revolt died down. We continued our march toward the square. In the middle stood the notorious Dr. Mengele (a typical SS officer: a cruel face, but not devoid of intelligence, and wearing a monocle); a conductor's baton in his hand, he was standing among the other officers. The baton moved unremittingly, sometimes to the right, sometimes to the left.

I was already in front of him:

"How old are you?" he asked, in an attempt at a paternal tone of voice.

"Eighteen." My voice was shaking.

"Are you in good health?"

"Yes."

"What's your occupation?"

Should I say that I was a student?

"Farmer," I heard myself say.

This conversation cannot have lasted more than a few seconds. It had seemed like an eternity to me.

The baton moved to the left. I took half a step forward. I wanted to see first where they were sending my father. If he went to the right, I would go after him.

The baton once again pointed to the left for him too. A weight was lifted from my heart.

We did not yet know which was the better side, right or left; which road led to prison and which to the crematory. But for the moment I was happy; I was near my father. Our procession continued to move slowly forward.

Another prisoner came up to us:

"Satisfied?"

"Yes," someone replied.

"Poor devils, you're going to the crematory."

He seemed to be telling the truth. Not far from us, flames were leaping up from a ditch, gigantic flames. They were burning something. A lorry drew up at the pit and delivered its load—little children. Babies! Yes, I saw it—saw it with my own eyes . . . those children in the flames. (Is it surprising that I could not sleep after that? Sleep had fled from my eyes.)

So this was where we were going. A little farther on was another and larger ditch for adults.

I pinched my face. Was I still alive? Was I awake? I could not believe it. How could it be possible for them to burn people, children, and for the world to keep silent? No, none of this could be true. It was a nightmare. . . . Soon I should wake with a start, my heart pounding, and find myself back in the bedroom of my childhood, among my books. . . .

My father's voice drew me from my thoughts:

"It's a shame . . . a shame that you couldn't have gone with your mother. . . . I saw several boys of your age going with their mothers. . . ."

His voice was terribly sad. I realized that he did not want to see what they were going to do to me. He did not want to see the burning of his only son.

My forehead was bathed in cold sweat. But I told him that I did not believe that they could burn people in our age, that humanity would never tolerate it. . . .

"Humanity? Humanity is not concerned with us. Today anything is allowed. Anything is possible, even these crematories. . . ."

His voice was choking.

"Father," I said, "if that is so, I don't want to wait here. I'm going to run to the electric wire. That would be better than slow agony in the flames."

He did not answer. He was weeping. He body was shaken convulsively. Around us, everyone was weeping. Someone began to recite the Kaddish, the prayer for the dead. I do not know if it has ever happened before, in the long history of the Jews, that people have ever recited the prayer for the dead for themselves.

"*Yitgadal veyitkadach shmé raba*. . . . May His Name be blesssed and magnified. . . ." whispered my father.

For the first time, I felt revolt rise up in me. Why should I bless His name? The Eternal, Lord of the Universe, the All-Powerful and Terrible, was silent. What had I to thank Him for?

We continued our march. We were gradually drawing closer to the ditch, from which an infernal heat was rising. Still twenty steps to go. If I wanted to bring about my own death, this was the moment. Our line had now only fifteen paces to cover. I bit my lips so that my father would not hear my teeth chattering. Ten steps still. Eight. Seven. We marched slowly on, as though following a hearse at our own funeral. Four steps more. Three steps. There it was now, right in front of us, the pit and its flames. I gathered all that was left of my strength, so that I could break from the ranks and throw myself upon the barbed wire. In the depths of my heart, I bade farewell to my father, to the whole universe; and, in spite of myself, the words formed themselves and issued in a whisper from my lips: *Yitgadal veyitkadach shmé raba.* . . . May His name be blessed and magnified. . . . My heart was bursting. The moment had come. I was face to face with the Angel of Death. . . .

No. Two steps from the pit we were ordered to turn to the left and made to go into a barracks.

I pressed my father's hand. He said:

"Do you remember Madame Schächter, in the train?"

Never shall I forget that night, the first night in camp, which has turned my life into one long night, seven times cursed and seven times sealed. Never shall I forget that smoke. Never shall I forget the little faces of the children, whose bodies I saw turned into wreaths of smoke beneath a silent blue sky.

Never shall I forget those flames which consumed my faith forever.

Never shall I forget that nocturnal silence which deprived me, for all eternity, of the desire to live. Never shall I forget those moments which murdered my God and my soul and turned my dreams to dust. Never shall I forget these things, even if I am condemned to live as long as God Himself. Never.

[Time passes; setting shifts from the Auschwitz camp to the Buna camp.]

A week later, on the way back from work, we noticed in the center of the camp, at the assembly place, a black gallows.

We were told that soup would not be distributed until after roll call. This took longer than usual. The orders were given in a sharper manner than on other days, and in the air there were strange undertones.

"Bare your heads!" yelled the head of the camp, suddenly.

Ten thousand caps were simultaneously removed.

"Cover your heads!"

Ten thousand caps went back onto their skulls, as quick as lightning.

The gate to the camp opened. As SS section appeared and surrounded us: one SS at every three paces. On the lookout towers the machine guns were trained on the assembly place.

"They fear trouble," whispered Juliek.

Two SS men had gone to the cells. They came back with the condemned man between them. He was a youth from Warsaw. He had three years of concentration camp life behind him. He was a strong, well-built boy, a giant in comparison with me.

His back to the gallows, his face turned toward his judge, who was the head of the camp, the boy was pale, but seemed more moved than afraid. His manacled hands did not tremble. His eyes gazed coldly at the hundreds of SS guards, the thousands of prisoners who surrounded him.

The head of the camp began to read his verdict, hammering out each phrase:

"In the name of Himmler . . . prisoner Number . . . stole during the alert. . . . According to the law . . . paragraph . . . prisoner Number . . . is condemned to death. May this be a warning and an example to all prisoners."

No one moved.

I could hear my heart beating. The thousands who had died daily at Auschwitz and at Birkenau in the crematory ovens no longer troubled me. But this one, leaning against his gallows—he overwhelmed me.

"Do you think this ceremony'll be over soon? I'm hungry. . . ." whispered Juliek.

At a sign from the head of the camp, the Lagerkapo advanced toward the condemned man. Two prisoners helped him in his task—for two plates of soup.

The Kapo wanted to bandage the victim's eyes, but he refused.

After a long moment of waiting, the executioner put the rope round his neck. He was on the point of motioning to his migrants to draw the chair away from the prisoner's feet, when the latter cried, in a calm, strong voice:

"Long live liberty! A curse upon Germany! A curse . . .! A cur—"

The executioners had completed their task.

A command cleft the air like a sword.

"Bare your heads."

Ten thousand prisoners paid their last respects.

"Cover your heads!"

Then the whole camp, block after block, had to march past the hanged man and stare at the dimmed eyes, the lolling tongue of death. The Kapos and heads of each block forced everyone to look him full in the face.

After the march, we were given permission to return to the blocks for our meal.

I remember that I found the soup excellent that evening. . . .

I witnessed other hangings. I never saw a single one of the victims weep. For a long time those dried-up bodies had forgotten the bitter taste of tears.

Except once. The Oberkapo of the fifty-second cable unit was a Dutchman, a giant, well over six feet. Seven hundred prisoners worked under his orders, and they all loved him like a brother. No one had ever received a blow at his hands, nor an insult from his lips.

He had a young boy under him, a *pipel*, as they were called—a child with a refined and beautiful face, unheard of in this camp.

(At Buna, the *pipel* were loathed; they were often crueller than adults. I once saw one of thirteen beating his father because the latter had not made his bed properly. The old man was crying softly while the boy shouted: "If you don't stop crying at once I shan't bring you any more bread. Do you understand?" But the Dutchman's little servant was loved by all. He had the face of a sad angel.)

One day, the electric power station at Buna was blown up. The Gestapo, summoned to the spot, suspected sabotage. They found a trail. It eventually led to the Dutch Oberkapo. And there, after a search, they found an important stock of arms.

The Oberkapo was arrested immediately. He was tortured for a period of weeks, but in vain. He would not give a single name. He was transferred to Auschwitz. We never heard of him again.

But his little servant had been left behind in the camp in prison. Also put to torture, he too would not speak. Then the SS sentenced him to death, with two other prisoners who had been discovered with arms.

One day when we came back from work, we saw three gallows rearing up in the assembly place, three black crows. Roll call. SS all round us, machine guns trained: the traditional ceremony. Three victims in chains—and one of them, the little servant, the sad-eyed angel.

The SS seemed more preoccupied, more disturbed than usual. To hang a young boy in front of thousands of spectators was no light matter. The head of the camp read the verdict. All eyes were on the child. He was lividly pale, almost calm, biting his lips. The gallows threw its shadow over him.

This time the Lagerkapo refused to act as executioner. Three SS replaced him.

The three victims mounted together onto the chairs.

The three necks were placed at the same moment within the nooses.

"Long live liberty!" cried the two adults.

But the child was silent.

"Where is God? Where is He?" someone behind me asked.

At a sign from the head of the camp, the three chairs tipped over.

Total silence throughout the camp. On the horizon, the sun was setting.

"Bare your heads!" yelled the head of the camp. His voice was raucous. We were weeping.

"Cover your heads!"

Then the march past began. The two adults were no longer alive. Their tongues hung swollen, blue-tinged. But the third rope was still moving; being so light, the child was still alive. . . .

For more than half an hour he stayed there, struggling between life and death, dying in slow agony under our eyes. And we had to look him full in the face. He was still alive when I passed in front of him. His tongue was still red, his eyes were not yet glazed.

Behind me, I heard the same man asking:

"Where is God now?"

And I heard a voice within me answer him:

"Where is He? Here He is—He is hanging here on this gallows. . . ."

That night the soup tasted of corpses.

5.2 Does Evil Stem from Society or from Human Nature?

Are humans good or evil by nature? Are people born with a fundamental disposition to do good and to show kindness and compassion? Are people born with a fundamental disposition to do evil, and do they seek to maximize their own pleasure at the expense of others? Is society good or bad? Does our social environment teach us evil and corrupt us? Does our social environment teach us goodness and make us more virtuous?

Were the Nazis who ran the death camps just plain evil people from birth? Did they learn to be cold-blooded murderers? If their social environment had been different, would they have acted differently?

The debate about how and where moral evil arises knows the bounds of neither time nor space. It is a universal debate because evil is a universal experience. Whether it be the atrocities of modern genocide or the sufferings experienced by the people of ancient China that prompt the question, human reflection eventually gets around to asking where evil originates. Somehow, we seem to believe, if we can figure out where it comes from, we can figure out what to do about it.

The grandson of Confucius instructed Mencius (371–289 B.C.E.) in philosophy. Central to Confucius's philosophy is the idea that humans ought to cultivate a virtuous life. Among the many virtues that are worth developing, *jen* (humaneness, benevolence, kind-heartedness) is central.

Although Confucius nowhere explicitly says so, Mencius believed that his teachings definitely implied that human nature is good. That is, it is *originally* good before being subjected to the corrupting influence of society. Mencius made this teaching the cornerstone of his moral philosophy and argued that education must center on recovering the innate knowledge of the good and the innate ability to do the good that has been lost through corrupting influences. In the first selection that follows, he presses this point in debate with Kao Tzu (420–350 B.C.E.). If Mencius were alive today, he would argue that the Holocaust stemmed from a corrupt political and social order that did not educate people to seek their original goodness and, in fact, deliberately encouraged them to lose it.

Mencius represents the idealistic wing of Confucianism. Hsün-tzu (298–238 B.C.E.) represents the naturalistic wing and took direct and vigorous exception to

Mencius's claim that human beings are good by nature. He repeatedly attacks Mencius's views in the second selection that follows, arguing that humans are evil by nature and that only society—through education—can change them into virtuous people.

In the translation I use, Hsün-tzu argues that goodness is the result of "activity." The word translated as *activity* (*wei*) can mean both *doing* and *artifice.* Hence it refers to that which human society cultivates through proper education and culture, in contrast to what humans are like prior to such education.

For Mencius, Heaven (a good cosmic power or force) bestows human nature on us, and hence human nature must be good. Hsün-tzu thinks Heaven is morally neutral. The course of events is not meant to go either for or against humans. Heaven did not intend the seasons to produce evil (as in drought) or the earth to destroy human cities (as in earthquakes). Thus Heaven did not intend (Heaven is a nonpersonal force, so it is misleading to speak of it as intending anything) that the conflicting desires with which humans are born should lead to strife, suffering, and violence. These things, however, can be the result when humans fail to learn to control their conflicting tendencies.

Although there are clear differences between Mencius and Hsün-tzu, there are also areas of agreement. Both agree, for example, on the nature of virtue and that proper education is essential to the cultivation of virtue. For Mencius, the role of education is to help us recover our "lost mind." For Hsün-tzu, its role is to teach us how to gain control over our conflicting desires. Thus, in one sense, both Mencius and Hsün-tzu would blame Nazi society, politics, and ideology for the evils of the Holocaust. The Nazis failed to educate properly. The ultimate source of the evil, however, they would characterize differently. For Mencius it rests finally in the failure of the social environment, whereas for Hsün-tzu it stems ultimately from human nature.

A note of caution for those who are used to thinking about the issue of the relationship between human nature and evil in the context of Christian theology. This debate from ancient China is not a debate over what Christians call "original sin." In the Christian scheme, humans are created good by a good God, but sin originates when the first humans rebel against God. Hence humans "fell" from an original goodness, and all humans since the first live under the influence of that original sin. There is no "fall" for either Mencius or Hsün-tzu. Indeed there is no personal creator God who intended to make humans a certain way. Rather, the issue centers on original human nature prior to social influences. For Mencius, this original nature has an innate tendency to do good, and this tendency will flourish if not corrupted by external influences. For Hsün-tzu, this original nature lacks the ability to control its many conflicting desires and can gain such control only through proper education.

Reading Questions

1. What is at issue in the exchange between Kao Tzu and Mencius in section 2?
2. Why, according to Mencius, is becoming bad not the fault of the native endowment of humans?
3. What reasons does Mencius present in support of the claim that no human is devoid of a heart sensitive to the suffering of others?

4. According to Hsün-tzu, why was Mencius wrong when he said, "Man learns because his nature is good"?

5. Where, according to Hsün-tzu, do propriety and righteousness come from?

6. What does Hsün-tzu mean by good and evil, and why are discrimination and evidence important when discussing such matters?

7. Do you agree with Mencius or Hsün-tzu? Why?

Human Nature Is Good*

MENCIUS

Book VI Part A

1. Kao Tzu said, "Human nature is like the *ch'i* willow. Dutifulness is like cups and bowls. To make morality out of human nature is like making cups and bowls out of the willow."

"Can you," said Mencius, "make cups and bowls by following the nature of the willow? Or must you mutilate the willow before you can make it into cups and bowls? If you have to mutilate the willow to make it into cups and bowls, must you, then, also mutilate a man to make him moral? Surely it will be these words of yours men in the world will follow in bringing disaster upon morality."

2. Kao Tzu said, "Human nature is like whirling water. Give it an outlet in the east and it will flow east; give it an outlet in the west and it will flow west. Human nature does not show any preference for either good or bad just as water does not show any preference for either east or west."

"It certainly is the case," said Mencius, "that water does not show any preference for either east or west, but does it show the same indifference to high and low? Human nature is good just as water seeks low ground. There is no man who is not good; there is no water that does not flow downwards.

"Now in the case of water, by splashing it one can make it shoot up higher than one's forehead, and by forcing it one can make it stay on a hill. How can that be the nature of water? It is the circumstances being what they are. That man can be made bad shows that his nature is no different from that of water in this respect."

3. Kao Tzu said, "The inborn is what is meant by 'nature.'"

"Is that," said Mencius, "the same as 'white is what is meant by "white"'?"

"Yes."

"Is the whiteness of white feathers the same as the whiteness of white snow and the whiteness of white snow the same as the whiteness of white jade?"

"Yes."

"In that case, is the nature of a hound the same as the nature of an ox and the nature of an ox the same as the nature of a man?"

6. Kung-tu Tzu said, "Kao Tzu said, 'There is neither good nor bad in human nature,' but others say, 'Human nature can become good or it can become bad, and that is why with the rise of King Wen and King Wu, the people were given to goodness, while with the rise of King Yu and King Li, they were given to cruelty.' Then there are

---

*Reprinted with permission from *Mencius,* translated by D. C. Lau, volume 2. Copyright © D. C. Lau, 1970. Reprinted by permission of Penguin Books Ltd. Footnotes deleted.

others who say, 'There are those who are good by nature, and there are those who are bad by nature. For this reason, Hsiang could have Yao as prince, and Shun could have the Blind Man as father, and Ch'i, Viscount of Wei and Prince Pi Kan could have Tchou as nephew as well as sovereign.' Now you say human nature is good. Does this mean that all the others are mistaken?"

"As far as what is genuinely in him is concerned, a man is capable of becoming good," said Mencius. "That is what I mean by good. As for his becoming bad, that is not the fault of his native endowment. The heart of compassion is possessed by all men alike; likewise the heart of shame, the heart of respect, and the heart of right and wrong. The heart of compassion pertains to benevolence, the heart of shame to dutifulness, the heart of respect to the observance of the rites, and the heart of right and wrong to wisdom. Benevolence, dutifulness, observance of the rites, and wisdom do not give me a lustre from the outside, they are in me originally. Only this has never dawned on me. That is why it is said, 'Seek and you will find it; let go and you will lose it.' There are cases where one man is twice, five times or countless times better than another man, but this is only because there are people who fail to make the best of their native endowment. The *Odes* say,

> Heaven produces the teeming masses,
> And where there is a thing there is a
>   norm.
> If the people held on to their constant
>   nature,
> They would be drawn to superior virtue.

Confucius commented, 'The author of this poem must have had knowledge of the Way.' Thus where there is a thing there is a norm, and because the people hold on to their constant nature they are drawn to superior virtue."

8. Mencius said, "There was a time when the trees were luxuriant on the Ox Mountain, but as it is on the outskirts of a great metropolis, the trees are constantly lopped by axes. Is it any wonder that they are no longer fine? With the respite they get in the day and in the night, and the moistening by the rain and dew, there is certainly no lack of new shoots coming out, but then the cattle and sheep come to graze upon the mountain. That is why it is as bald as it is. People, seeing only its baldness, tend to think that it never had any trees. But can this possibly be the nature of a mountain? Can what is in man be completely lacking in moral inclinations? A man's letting go of his true heart is like the case of the trees and the axes. When the trees are lopped day after day, is it any wonder that they are no longer fine? If, in spite of the respite a man gets in the day and in the night and of the effect of the morning air on him, scarcely any of his likes and dislikes resembles those of other men, it is because what he does in the course of the day once again dissipates what he has gained. If this dissipation happens repeatedly, then the influence of the air in the night will no longer able to preserve what was originally in him, and when that happens, the man is not far removed from an animal. Others, seeing his resemblance to an animal, will be led to think that he never had any native endowment. But can that be what a man is genuinely like? Hence, given the right nourishment there is nothing that will not grow, while deprived of it there is nothing that will not wither away. Confucius said. 'Hold on to it and it will remain; let go of it and it will disappear. One never knows the time it comes or goes, neither does one know the direction.' It is perhaps to the heart this refers."

15. Kung-tu Tzu asked, "Though equally human, why are some men greater than others?"

"He who is guided by the interests of the parts of his person that are of greater importance is a great man; he who is guided by the interests of the parts of his person that are of smaller importance is a small man."

"Though equally human, why are some men guided one way and others guided another way?"

"The organs of hearing and sight are unable to think and can be misled by external things. When one thing acts on another, all it does is to attract it. The organ of the heart can think. But it will find the answer only if it does think; otherwise, it will not find the answer. This is what Heaven has given me. If one makes one's stand on what is of greater importance in the first instance, what is of smaller importance cannot displace it. In this way, one cannot but be a great man."

16. Mencius said, "No man is devoid of a heart sensitive to the suffering of others. Such a sensitive heart was possessed by the Former Kings and this manifested itself in compassionate government. With such a sensitive heart behind compassionate government, it was as easy to rule the Empire as rolling it on your palm.

"My reason for saying that no man is devoid of a heart sensitive to the suffering of others is this. Suppose a man were, all of a sudden, to see a young child on the verge of falling into a well. He would certainly be moved to compassion, not because he wanted to get in the good graces of the parents, nor because he wished to win the praise of his fellow villagers or friends, nor yet because he disliked the cry of the child. From this it can be seen that whoever is devoid of the heart of compassion is not human, whoever is devoid of the heart of shame is not human, whoever is devoid of the heart of courtesy and modesty is not human, and whoever is devoid of the heart of right and wrong is not human. The heart of compassion is the germ of benevolence; the heart of shame, of dutifulness; the heart of courtesy and modesty, of observance of the rites; the heart of right and wrong, of wisdom. Man has these four germs just as he has four limbs. For a man possessing these four germs to deny his own potentialities is for him to cripple himself; for him to deny the potentialities of his prince is for him to cripple his prince. If a man is able to develop all these four germs that he possesses, it will be like a fire starting up or a spring coming through. When these are fully developed, he can tend the whole realm within the Four Seas, but if he fails to develop them, he will not be able even to serve his parents."

Human Nature Is Evil*

HSÜN-TZU

THE NATURE OF man is evil; his goodness is the result of his activity.[1] Now, man's inborn nature is to seek for gain. If this tendency is followed, strife and rapacity result and deference and compliance disappear. By inborn nature one is envious and hates others. If these tendencies are followed, injury and destruction result and loyalty and faithfulness disappear. By inborn nature one possesses the desires of ear and eye and likes sound and beauty. If these tendencies are followed, lewdness and licentiousness result, and the pattern and order of propriety and righteousness disappear. Therefore to follow man's nature and his feelings will inevitably result in strife and rapacity, combine with rebellion and disorder, and end in violence. Therefore there must be the civilizing influence of teachers and laws and the guidance of propriety and righteousness, and then it will result in deference and compliance, combine with pattern and order, and end in discipline. From this point of view, it is clear that the nature of man is evil and that his goodness is the result of activity.

Crooked wood must be heated and bent before it becomes straight. Blunt metal must be ground and whetted before it becomes sharp.

*From Chan, W. ed., *A Source Book in Chinese Philosophy.* Copyright © 1963, Princeton University Press. Excerpt (pp. 128–132) reprinted by permission of Princeton University Press. Footnotes edited.

Now the nature of man is evil. It must depend on teachers and laws to become correct and achieve propriety and righteousness and then it becomes disciplined. Without teachers and laws, man is unbalanced, off the track, and incorrect. Without propriety and righteousness, there will be rebellion, disorder, and chaos. The sage-kings of antiquity, knowing that the nature of man is evil, and that it is unbalanced, off the track, incorrect, rebellious, disorderly, and undisciplined, created the rules of propriety and righteousness and instituted laws and systems in order to correct man's feelings, transform them, and direct them so that they all may become disciplined and conform with the Way (Tao). Now people who are influenced by teachers and laws, accumulate literature and knowledge, and follow propriety and righteousness are superior men, whereas those who give rein to their feelings, enjoy indulgence, and violate propriety and righteousness are inferior men. From this point of view, it is clear that the nature of man is evil and that his goodness is the result of his activity.

Comment. In the *Hsün Tzu,* rules of propriety and law are often spoken of together, giving the impression that, unlike Confucius and Mencius, who advocated propriety (*li*) as inner control, Hsün-tzu advocated it for external control. Thus rules of propriety shifted from being a means of personal moral cultivation to one of social control.

Mencius said, "Man learns because his nature is good." This is not true. He did not know the nature of man and did not understand the distinction between man's nature and his effort. Man's nature is the product of Nature; it cannot be learned and cannot be worked for. Propriety and righteousness are produced by the sage. They can be learned by men and can be accomplished through work. What is in man but cannot be learned or worked for is his nature. What is in him and can be learned or accomplished through work is what can be achieved through activity. This is the difference between human nature and human activity. Now by nature man's eye can see and his ear can hear. But the clarity of vision is not outside his eye and the distinctness of hearing is

not outside his ear. It is clear that clear vision and distinct hearing cannot be learned. Mencius said, "The nature of man is good; it [becomes evil] because man destroys his original nature." This is a mistake. By nature man departs from his primitive character and capacity as soon as he is born, and he is bound to destroy it. From this point of view, it is clear that man's nature is evil.

By the original goodness of human nature is meant that man does not depart from his primitive character but makes it beautiful, and does not depart from his original capacity but utilizes it, so that beauty being [inherent] in his primitive character and goodness being [inherent] in his will are like clear vision being inherent in the eye and distinct hearing being inherent in the ear. Hence we say that the eye is clear and the ear is sharp. Now by nature man desires repletion when hungry, desires warmth when cold, and desires rest when tired. This is man's natural feeling. But now when a man is hungry and sees some elders before him, he does not eat ahead of them but yields to them. When he is tired, he dares not seek rest because he wants to take over the work [of elders]. The son yielding to or taking over the work of his father, and the younger brother yielding to or taking over the work of his older brother—these two lines of action are contrary to original nature and violate natural feeling. Nevertheless, the way of filial piety is the pattern and order of propriety and righteousness. If one follows his natural feeling, he will have no deference or compliance. Deference and compliance are opposed to his natural feelings. From this point of view, it is clear that man's nature is evil and that his goodness is the result of his activity.

Someone may ask, "If man's nature is evil, whence come propriety and righteousness?" I answer that all propriety and righteousness are results of the activity of sages and not originally produced from man's nature. The potter pounds the clay and makes the vessel. This being the case, the vessel is the product of the artisan's activity and not the original product of man's nature. The artisan hews a piece of wood and makes a vessel. This being the case, the vessel is the product of the artisan's activity and not the original product of man's nature. The sages gathered together their ideas and thoughts and became familiar with activity, facts, and principles, and thus produced propriety and righteousness and instituted laws and systems. This being the case, propriety and righteousness, and laws and systems are the products of the activity of the sages and not the original products of man's nature.

As to the eye desiring color, the ear desiring sound, the mouth desiring flavor, the heart desiring gain, and the body desiring pleasure and ease—all these are products of man's original nature and feelings. They are natural reactions to stimuli and do not require any work to be produced. But if the reaction is not naturally produced by the stimulus but requires work before it can be produced, then it is the result of activity. Here lies the evidence of the difference between what is produced by man's nature and what is produced by his effort. Therefore the sages transformed man's nature and aroused him to activity. As activity was aroused, propriety and righteousness were produced, and as propriety and righteousness were produced, laws and systems were instituted. This being the case, propriety, righteousness, laws, and systems are all products of the sages. In his nature, the sage is common with and not different from ordinary people. It is in his effort that he is different from and superior to them.

It is the original nature and feelings of man to love profit and seek gain. Suppose some brothers are to divide their property. If they follow their natural feelings, they will love profit and seek gain, and thus will do violence to each other and grab the property. But if they are transformed by the civilizing influence of the pattern and order of propriety and righteousness, they will even yield to outsiders. Therefore, brothers will quarrel if they follow their original nature and feeling but, if they are transformed by righteousness and propriety, they will yield to outsiders.

People desire to be good because their nature is evil. If one has little, he wants abundance. If he is ugly, he wants good looks. If his circumstances are narrow, he wants them to be broad. If poor, he wants to be rich. And if he is in a low position, he wants a high position. If he does not have it himself, he will seek it outside. If he is rich, he does not desire more wealth, and if he is in a high position, he does not desire more power. If he has it himself, he will not seek it outside. From this point of view, [it is clear that] people desire to be good because their nature is evil.

Now by nature a man does not originally possess propriety and righteousness; hence he makes strong effort to learn and seeks to have them. By nature he does not know propriety and righteousness; hence he thinks and deliberates and seeks to know them. Therefore, by what is inborn alone, man will not have or know propriety and righteousness. There will be disorder if man is without propriety and righteousness. There will be violence if he does not know propriety and righteousness. Consequently by what is inborn alone, disorder and violence are within man himself. From this point of view, it is clear that the nature of man is evil and that his goodness is the result of his activity.

Mencius said, "The nature of man is good." I say that this is not true. By goodness at any time in any place is meant true principles and peaceful order, and by evil is meant imbalance, violence, and disorder. This is the distinction between good and evil. Now do we honestly regard man's nature as characterized by true principles and peaceful order? If so, why are sages necessary and why are propriety and righteousness necessary? What possible improvement can sages make on true principles and peaceful order?

Now this is not the case. Man's nature is evil. Therefore the sages of antiquity, knowing that man's nature is evil, that it is unbalanced and incorrect, and that it is violent, disorderly, and undisciplined, established the authority of rulers to govern the people, set forth clearly propriety and righteousness to transform them, instituted laws and governmental measures to rule them, and made punishment severe to restrain them, so that all will result in good order and be in accord with goodness. Such is the government of sage-kings and the transforming influence of propriety and righteousness.

But suppose we try to remove the authority of the ruler, do away with the transforming influence of propriety and righteousness, discard the rule of laws and governmental measure, do away with the restraint of punishment, and stand and see how people of the world deal with one another. In this situation, the strong would injure the weak and rob them, and the many would do violence to the few and shout them down. The whole world would be in violence and disorder and all would perish in an instant. From this point of view, it is clear that man's nature is evil and that his goodness is the result of his activity.

The man versed in ancient matters will certainly support them with evidences from the present, and he who is versed in [the principles of] Nature will certainly support them with evidences from the world of men. In any discussion, the important things are discrimination and evidence. One can then sit down and talk about things, propagate them, and put them into practice. But now Mencius said that man's nature is good. He had neither discrimination nor evidence. He sat down and talked about the matter but rose and could neither propagate it nor put it into practice. Is this not going too far? Therefore if man's nature is good, sage-kings can be done away with and propriety and righteousness can be stopped. But if his nature is evil, sage-kings are to be followed and propriety and righteousness are to be greatly valued. For bending came into existence because there was crooked wood, the carpenter's square and ruler came into existence because things are not straight, and the authority of rule is instituted and propriety and righteousness are made clear because man's nature is evil. From this point of view, it is clear that man's nature is evil and that his goodness is the result of his activity. Straight wood does not depend on bending to become straight; it is straight by nature. But crooked wood must be bent and heated before it becomes straight because by nature it is not straight. Now, the nature of man is evil. It has to depend on the government of sage-kings and the transforming influence of propriety and righteousness, and then all will result in good order and be in accord with goodness. From this point of view, it is clear that man's nature is evil and that his goodness is the result of his activity. . . .

NOTE

1. According to Yang Liang, *wei* ("artificial") is "man's activity." It means what is created by man and not a result of natural conditions. This is accepted by most commentators, including Hao I-hsing, who has pointed out that in ancient times *wei* (which ordinarily means "false or artificial") and *wei* ("activity") were interchangeable.

5.3 Evil and Omnipotence

If God is a perfectly good creator of this world in which we live, then why do evil and suffering exist? We consider people good if they try to eliminate evil as much as they possibly can without thereby producing a greater evil or eliminating a greater good. Of course people are not God. For one thing, the power people have to prevent or eliminate evil is much less than God's power. And there's the rub. God is all-powerful (omnipotent) as well as perfectly good. Surely such a God could and would eliminate evil. Maybe God does not know about all evil. God, however, is omniscient; God knows everything.

What are we to conclude? Perhaps evil does not really exist. Perhaps God does not exist. Perhaps God is not perfectly good, or omnipotent, or all-knowing. Perhaps there is nothing logically incompatible between the existence of a perfectly good, all-powerful, and all-knowing creator God and the existence of evil.

J. L. Mackie (1917–1981) taught at Oxford University and is the author of the next selection. He made important contributions to many different areas of philosophy and formulated the deductive or logical form of the theological problem of evil. According to this argument, the existence of evil is logically incompatible with the existence of a perfectly good, all-knowing, and all-powerful creator God. That is a rather strong claim, and we need to pay careful attention to how Mackie develops his case. We may not be able to prove that God exists (see Chapter 3), but even if we fail, it is still possible that God does exist. Mackie's argument takes us a step further, because if Mackie is right, then those who embrace traditional theism are caught in a contradiction.

Reading Questions

1. According to Mackie, what additional propositions are needed in order to show that asserting the existence of an omnipotent, totally good God along with the existence of evil constitutes a contradiction?
2. According to Mackie, why is the claim that good cannot exist without evil a fallacious solution to the problem of evil?
3. Why, according to Mackie, is the claim that evil is a necessary means to good inadequate for solving the problem of evil?
4. State as precisely as you can Mackie's *objection* to the claim that the universe is better with some evil than with no evil.
5. Why does Mackie think that ascribing evil to human free will does not avoid the contradiction in which the theist is caught?
6. Do you find Mackie's argument convincing? Why or why not?

Evil and Omnipotence*

J. L. MACKIE

THE TRADITIONAL arguments for the existence of God have been fairly thoroughly criticised by philosophers. But the theologian can, if he wishes, accept this criticism. He can admit that no rational proof of God's existence is possible. And he can still retain all that is essential to his position, by holding that God's existence is known in some other, non-rational way. I think, however, that a more telling criticism can be made by way of the traditional problem of evil. Here it can be shown, not that religious beliefs lack rational support, but that they are positively irrational, that the several parts of the essential theological doctrine are inconsistent with one another, so that the theologian can maintain his position as a whole only by a much more extreme rejection of reason than in the former case. He must now be prepared to believe, not merely what cannot be proved, but what can be *disproved* from other beliefs that he also holds.

The problem of evil, in the sense in which I shall be using the phrase, is a problem only for someone who believes that there is a God who is both omnipotent and wholly good. And it is a logical problem, the problem of clarifying and reconciling a number of beliefs: it is not a

*From *Mind*, Vol. LXIV, No. 254 (1955). Reprinted by permission of Oxford University Press.

scientific problem that might be solved by further observations, or a practical problem that might be solved by a decision or an action. These points are obvious; I mention them only because they are sometimes ignored by theologians, who sometimes parry a statement of the problem with such remarks as "Well, can you solve the problem yourself?" or "This is a mystery which may be revealed to us later" or "Evil is something to be faced and overcome, not to be merely discussed."

In its simplest form the problem is this: God is omnipotent; God is wholly good; and yet evil exists. There seems to be some contradiction between these three propositions, so that if any two of them were true the third would be false. But at the same time all three are essential parts of most theological positions: the theologian, it seems, at once *must* adhere and *cannot consistently* adhere to all three. (The problem does not arise only for theists, but I shall discuss it in the form in which it presents itself for ordinary theism.)

However, the contradiction does not arise immediately; to show it we need some additional premises, or perhaps some quasi-logical rules connecting the terms "good," "evil," and "omnipotent." These additional principles are that good is opposed to evil, in such a way that a good thing always eliminates evil as far as it can, and that there are no limits to what an omnipotent thing can do. From these it follows that a good omnipotent thing eliminates evil completely, and then the propositions that a good omnipotent thing exists, and that evil exists, are incompatible.

A. Adequate Solutions

Now once the problem is fully stated it is clear that it can be solved, in the sense that the problem will not arise if one gives up at least one of the propositions that constitute it. If you are prepared to say that God is not wholly good, or not quite omnipotent, or that evil does not exist, or that good is not opposed to the kind of evil that exists, or that there are limits to what an omnipotent thing can do, then the problem of evil will not arise for you.

There are, then, quite a number of adequate solutions of the problem of evil, and some of these have been adopted, or almost adopted, by various thinkers. For example, a few have been prepared to deny God's omnipotence, and rather more have been prepared to keep the term "omnipotence" but severely to restrict its meaning, recording quite a number of things that an omnipotent being cannot do. Some have said that evil is an illusion, perhaps because they held that the whole world of temporal, changing things is an illusion, and that what we call evil belongs only to this world, or perhaps because they held that although temporal things are much as we see them, those that we call evil are not really evil. Some have said that what we call evil is merely the privation of good, that evil in a positive sense, evil that would really be opposed to good, does not exist. Many have agreed with Pope that disorder is harmony not understood, and that partial evil is universal good. Whether any of these views is *true* is, of course, another question. But each of them gives an adequate solution of the problem of evil in the sense that if you accept it this problem does not arise for you, though you may, of course, have *other* problems to face.

But often enough these adequate solutions are only *almost* adopted. The thinkers who restrict God's power, but keep the term "omnipotence," may reasonably be suspected of thinking, in other contexts, that his power is really unlimited. Those who say that evil is an illusion may also be thinking, inconsistently, that this illusion is itself an evil. Those who say that "evil" is merely privation of good may also be thinking, inconsistently, that privation of good is an evil. (The fallacy here is akin to some forms of the "naturalistic fallacy" in ethics, where some think, for example, that "good" is just what contributes to evolutionary progress, and that evolutionary progress is itself good.) If Pope meant what he said in the first line of his couplet, that "disorder" is only harmony not understood, the "partial evil" of the second line must, for consistency, mean "that which, taken in isolation, falsely appears to be evil," but it would more naturally mean "that which, in isolation, really is evil." The second line, in fact, hesitates between two views, that "partial evil" isn't really evil, since only the universal quality is real, and that "partial evil" is really an evil, but only a little one.

In addition, therefore, to adequate solutions, we must recognise unsatisfactory inconsistent solutions, in which there is only a half-hearted or temporary rejection of one of the propositions which together constitute the problem. In these, one of the constituent propositions is explicitly rejected, but it is covertly re-asserted or assumed elsewhere in the system.

B. Fallacious Solutions

Besides these half-hearted solutions, which explicitly reject but implicitly assert one of the constituent propositions, there are definitely fallacious solutions which explicitly maintain all the constituent propositions, but implicitly reject at least one of them in the course of the argument that explains away the problem of evil.

There are, in fact, many so-called solutions which purport to remove the contradiction without abandoning any of its constituent propositions. These must be fallacious as we can see from the very statement of the problem, but it is not so easy to see in each case precisely where the fallacy lies. I suggest that in all cases the fallacy has the general form suggested above: in order to solve the problem one (or perhaps more) of its constituent propositions is given up, but in such a way that it appears to have been retained, and can therefore be asserted without qualification in other contexts. Sometimes there is a further complication: the supposed solution moves to and fro between, say, two of the constituent propositions, at one point asserting the first of these but covertly abandoning the second, at another point asserting the second but covertly abandoning the first. These fallacious solutions often turn upon some equivocation with the words "good" and "evil," or upon some vagueness about the way in which good and evil are opposed to one another, or about how much is meant by "omnipotence." I propose to examine some of these so-called solutions, and to exhibit their fallacies in detail. In-

cidentally, I shall also be considering whether an adequate solution could be reached by a minor modification of one or more of the constituent propositions, which would, however, still satisfy all the essential requirements of ordinary theism.

1. "Good cannot exist without evil" or "Evil is necessary as a counterpart to good."

It is sometimes suggested that evil is necessary as a counterpart to good, that if there were no evil there could be no good either, and that this solves the problem of evil. It is true that it points to an answer to the question "Why should there be evil?" But it does so only by qualifying some of the propositions that constitute the problem.

First, it sets a limit to what God can do, saying that God *cannot* create good without simultaneously creating evil, and this means either that God is not omnipotent or that there are *some* limits to what an omnipotent thing can do. It may be replied that these limits are always presupposed, that omnipotence has never meant the power to do what is logically impossible, and on the present view the existence of good without evil would be a logical impossibility. This interpretation of omnipotence may, indeed, be accepted as a modification of our original account which does not reject anything that is essential to theism, and I shall in general assume it in the subsequent discussion. It is, perhaps, the most common theistic view, but I think that some theists at least have maintained that God can do what is logically impossible. Many theists, at any rate, have held that logic itself is created or laid down by God, that logic is the way in which God arbitrarily chooses to think. (This is, of course, parallel to the ethical view that morally right actions are those which God arbitrarily chooses to command, and the two views encounter similar difficulties.) And *this* account of logic is clearly inconsistent with the view that God is bound by logical necessities—unless it is possible for an omnipotent being to bind himself, an issue which we shall consider later, when we come to the Paradox of Omnipotence. This solution of the problem of evil cannot, therefore, be consistently adopted along with the view that logic is itself created by God.

But, secondly, this solution denies that evil is opposed to good in our original sense. If good and evil are counterparts, a good thing will not "eliminate evil as far as it can." Indeed, this view suggests that good and evil are not strictly qualities of things at all. Perhaps the suggestion is that good and evil are related in much the same way as great and small. Certainly, when the term "great" is used relatively as a condensation of "greater than so-and-so," and "small" is used correspondingly, greatness and smallness are counterparts and cannot exist without each other. But in this sense greatness is not a quality, not an intrinsic feature of anything; and it would be absurd to think of a movement in favour of greatness and against smallness in this sense. Such a movement would be self-defeating, since relative greatness can be promoted only by a simultaneous promotion of relative smallness. I feel sure that no theists would be content to regard God's goodness as analogous to this—as if what he supports were not the *good* but the *better,* and if he had the paradoxical aim that all things should be better than other things.

This point is obscured by the fact that "great" and "small" seem to have an absolute as well as a relative sense. I cannot discuss here whether there is absolute magnitude or not, but if there is, there could be an absolute sense for "great," it could mean of at least a certain size, and it would make sense to speak of all things getting bigger, of a universe that was expanding all over, and therefore it would make sense to speak of promoting greatness. But in *this* sense great and small are not logically necessary counterparts: either quality could exist without the other. There would be no logical impossibility in everything's being small or in everything's being great.

Neither in the absolute nor in the relative sense, then, of "great" and "small" do these terms provide an analogy of the sort that would be needed to support this solution of the problem of evil. In neither case are greatness and smallness *both* necessary counterparts *and* mutually opposed forces or possible objects for support and attack.

It may be replied that good and evil are necessary counterparts in the same way as any quality and its logical opposite: redness can occur, it is suggested, only if non-redness also occurs. But unless evil is merely the privation of good, they are not logical opposites, and some further argument would be needed to show that they are counterparts in the same way as genuine logical opposites. Let us assume that this could be given. There is still doubt of the correctness of the metaphysical principle that a quality must have a real opposite: I suggest that it is not really impossible that everything should be, say, red, that the truth is merely that if everything were red we should not notice redness, and so we should have no word "red"; we observe and give names to qualities only if they have real opposites. If so, the principle that a term must have an opposite would belong only to our language or to our thought, and would not be an ontological principle, and, correspondingly, the rule that good cannot exist without evil would not state a logical necessity of a sort that God would just have to put up with. God might have made everything good, though we should not have noticed it if he had.

But, finally, even if we concede that this *is* an ontological principle, it will provide a solution for the problem of evil only if one is prepared to say, "Evil exists, but only just enough evil to serve as the counterpart of good." I doubt whether any theist will accept this. After all, the *ontological* requirement that non-redness should occur would be satisfied even if all the universe, except for a minute speck, were red, and, if there were a corresponding requirement for evil as a counterpart to good, a minute dose of evil would presumably do. But theists are not usually willing to say, in all contexts, that all the evil that occurs is a minute and necessary dose.

2. "Evil is necessary as a means to good."

It is sometimes suggested that evil is necessary for good not as a counterpart but as a means. In its simple form this has little plausibility as a solution of the problem of evil, since it obviously implies a severe restriction of God's power. It would be a *causal* law that you cannot have a certain end without a certain means, so that if God has to introduce evil as a means to good, he must be subject to at least some causal laws. This certainly conflicts with what a theist normally means by omnipotence. This view of God as limited by causal laws also conflicts with the view that causal laws are themselves made by God, which is more widely held than the corresponding view about the laws of logic. This conflict would, indeed, be resolved if it were possible for an omnipotent being to bind himself, and this possibility has still to be considered. Unless a favourable answer can be given to this question, the suggestion that evil is necessary as a means to good solves the problem of evil only by denying one of its constituent propositions, either that God is omnipotent or that "omnipotent" means what it says.

3. "The universe is better with some evil in it than it could be if there were no evil."

Much more important is a solution which at first seems to be a mere variant of the previous one, that evil may contribute to the goodness of a whole in which it is found, so that the universe as a whole is better as it is, with some evil in it, than it would be if there were no evil. This solution may be developed in either of two ways. It may be supported by an aesthetic analogy, by the fact that contrasts heighten beauty, that in a musical work, for example, there may occur discords which somehow add to the beauty of the work as a whole. Alternatively, it may be worked out in connexion with the notion of progress, that the best possible organisation of the universe will not be static, but progressive, that the gradual overcoming of evil by good is really a finer thing than would be the eternal unchallenged supremacy of good.

In either case, this solution usually starts from the assumption that the evil whose existence gives rise to the problem of evil is primarily what is called physical evil, that is to say, pain. In Hume's rather half-hearted presentation of the problem of evil, the evils that he stresses are pain and disease, and those who reply to him argue that the existence of pain and disease makes possible the existence of sympathy, benevolence, heroism, and the gradually successful struggle of doctors and reformers to overcome these evils. In fact, theists often seize the opportunity to accuse those who stress the problem of evil of taking a low, materialistic view of good and evil, equating these with pleasure and pain, and of ignoring the more spiritual goods which can arise in the struggle against evils.

But let us see exactly what is being done here. Let us call pain and misery "first order evil" or "evil (1)." What contrasts with this, namely, pleasure and happiness, will be called "first order good" or "good (1)." Distinct from this is "second order good" or "good (2)" which somehow emerges in a complex situation in which evil (1) is a necessary component—logically not merely causally, necessary. Exactly *how* it emerges does not matter: in the crudest version of this solution good (2) is simply the heightening of happiness by the contrast with misery, in other versions it includes sympathy with suffering, heroism in facing danger, and the gradual decrease of first order evil and increase of first order good.) It is also being assumed that second order good is more important than first order good or evil, in particular that it more than outweighs the first order evil it involves.

Now this is a particularly subtle attempt to solve the problem of evil. It defends God's goodness and omnipotence on the ground that (on a sufficiently long view) this is the best of all logically possible worlds, because it includes the important second order goods, and yet it admits that real evils, namely first order evils, exist. But does it still hold that good and evil are opposed? Not, clearly, in the sense that we set out originally: good does not tend to eliminate evil in general. Instead, we have a modified, a more complex pattern. First order good (*e.g.* happiness) *contrasts with* first order evil (*e.g.* misery): these two are opposed in a fairly mechanical way; some second order goods (*e.g.* benevolence) try to maximise first order good and minimise first order evil; but God's goodness is not this, it is rather the will to maximise *second* order good. We might, therefore, call God's goodness an example of a third order goodness, or good (3). While this account is different from our original one, it might well be held to be an improvement on it, to give a more accurate description of the way in which good is opposed to evil, and to be consistent with the essential theist position.

There might, however, be several objections to this solution.

First, some might argue that such qualities as benevolence—and *a fortiori* the third order goodness which promotes benevolence—have a merely derivative value, that they are not higher sorts of good, but merely means to good (1), that is, to happiness, so that it would be absurd for God to keep misery in existence in order to make possible the virtues of benevolence, heroism, etc. The theist who adopts the present solution must, of course, deny this, but he can do so with some plausibility, so I should not press this objection.

Secondly, it follows from this solution that God is not in our sense benevolent or sympathetic: he is not concerned to minimise evil (1), but only to promote good (2); and this might be a disturbing conclusion for some theists.

But, thirdly, the fatal objection is this. Our analysis shows clearly the possibility of the existence of a *second* order evil, an evil (2) contrasting with good (2) as evil (1) contrasts with good (1). This would include malevolence, cruelty, callousness, cowardice, and states in which good (1) is decreasing and evil (1) increasing. And just as good (2) is held to be the important kind of good, the kind that God is concerned to promote, so evil (2) will, by analogy, be the important kind of evil, the kind which God, if he were wholly good and omnipotent, would eliminate. And yet evil (2) plainly exists, and indeed most theists (in other contexts) stress its existence more than that of evil (1). We should, therefore, state the problem of evil in terms of second order evil, and against this form of the problem the present solution is useless.

An attempt might be made to use this solution again, at a higher level, to explain the oc-

currence of evil (2); indeed the next main solution that we shall examine does just this, with the help of some new notions. Without any fresh notions, such a solution would have little plausibility: for example, we could hardly say that the really important good was a good (3), such as the increase of benevolence in proportion to cruelty, which logically required for its occurrence the occurrence of some second order evil. But even if evil (2) could be explained in this way, it is fairly clear that there would be third order evils contrasting with this third order good: and we should be well on the way to an infinite regress, where the solution of a problem of evil, stated in terms of evil (*n*), indicated the existence of an evil (*n* + 1), and a further problem to be solved.

4. "Evil is due to human freewill."

Perhaps the most important proposed solution of the problem of evil is that evil is not to be ascribed to God at all, but to the independent actions of human beings, supposed to have been endowed by God with freedom of the will. This solution may be combined with the preceding one: first order evil (*e.g.* pain) may be justified as a logically necessary component in second order good (*e.g.* sympathy) while second order evil (*e.g.* cruelty) is not *justified*, but is so ascribed to human beings that God cannot be held responsible for it. This combination evades my third criticism of the preceding solution.

The freewill solution also involves the preceding solution at a higher level. To explain why a wholly good God gave men freewill although it would lead to some important evils, it must be argued that it is better on the whole that men should act freely, and sometimes err, than that they should be innocent automata, acting rightly in a wholly determined way. Freedom that is to say, is now treated as a third order good, and as being more valuable than second order goods (such as sympathy and heroism) would be if they were deterministically produced, and it is being assumed that second order evils, such as cruelty, are logically necessary accompaniments of freedom, just as pain is a logically necessary pre-condition of sympathy.

I think that this solution is unsatisfactory primarily because of the incoherence of the notion of freedom of the will: but I cannot discuss this topic adequately here, although some of my criticisms will touch upon it.

First I should query the assumption that second order evils are logically necessary accompaniments of freedom. I should ask this: if God has made men such that in their free choices they sometimes prefer what is good and sometimes what is evil, why could he not have made men such that they always freely choose the good? If there is no logical impossibility in a man's freely choosing the good on one, or on several, occasions, there cannot be a logical impossibility in his freely choosing the good on every occasion. God was not, then, faced with a choice between making innocent automata and making beings who, in acting freely, would sometimes go wrong: there was open to him the obviously better possibility of making beings who would act freely but always go right. Clearly, his failure to avail himself of this possibility is inconsistent with his being both omnipotent and wholly good.

If it is replied that this objection is absurd, that the making of some wrong choices is logically necessary for freedom, it would seem that "freedom" must here mean complete randomness or indeterminacy, including randomness with regard to the alternatives good and evil, in other words that men's choices and consequent actions can be "free" only if they are not determined by their characters. Only on this assumption can God escape the responsibility for men's actions; for if he made them as they are, but did not determine their wrong choices, this can only be because the wrong choices are not determined by men as they are. But then if freedom is randomness, how can it be a characteristic of *will*? And, still more, how can it be the most important good? What value or merit would there be in free choices if these were random actions which were not determined by the nature of the agent?

I conclude that to make this solution plausible two different senses of "freedom" must be confused, one sense which will justify the view that freedom is a third order good, more valuable than other goods would be without it, and another sense, sheer randomness, to prevent us from ascribing to God a decision to make men such that they sometimes go wrong when he might have made them such that they would always freely go right.

This criticism is sufficient to dispose of this solution. But besides this there is a fundamental difficulty in the notion of an omnipotent God creating men with free will, for if men's wills are really free this must mean that even God cannot control them, that is, that God is no longer omnipotent. It may be objected that God's gift of freedom to men does not mean that he *cannot* control their wills, but that he always *refrains* from controlling their wills. But why, we may ask, should God refrain from controlling evil wills? Why should he not leave men free to will rightly, but intervene when he sees them beginning to will wrongly? If God could do this, but does not, and if he is wholly good, the only explanation could be that even a wrong free act of will is not really evil, that its freedom is a value which outweighs its wrongness, so that there would be a loss of value if God took away the wrongness and the freedom together. But this is utterly opposed to what theists say about sin in other contexts. The present solution of the problem of evil, then, can be maintained only in the form that God has made men so free that he *cannot* control their wills.

This leads us to what I call the Paradox of Omnipotence: can an omnipotent being make things which he cannot subsequently control? Or, what is practically equivalent to this, can an omnipotent being make rules which then bind himself? (These are practically equivalent because any such rules could be regarded as setting certain things beyond his control, and *vice versa*.) The second of these formulations is relevant to the suggestions that we have already met, that an omnipotent God creates the rules of logic or causal laws, and is then bound by them.

It is clear that this is a paradox: the questions cannot be answered satisfactorily either in the affirmative or in the negative. If we answer "Yes," it follows that if God actually makes things which he cannot control, or makes rules which bind himself, he is not omnipotent once he has made them: there are *then* things which he cannot do. But if we answer "No," we are immediately asserting that there are things which he cannot do, that is to say that he is already not omnipotent.

It cannot be replied that the question which sets this paradox is not a proper question. It would make perfectly good sense to say that a human mechanic has made a machine which he cannot control: if there is any difficulty about the question it lies in the notion of omnipotence itself.

This, incidentally, shows that although we have approached this paradox from the free will theory, it is equally a problem for a theological determinist. No one thinks that machines have free will, yet they may well be beyond the control of their makers. The determinist might reply that anyone who makes anything determines its ways of acting, and so determines its subsequent behaviour: even the human mechanic does this by his *choice* of materials and structure for his machine, though he does not know all about either of these: the mechanic thus determines, though he may not foresee, his machine's actions. And since God is omniscient, and since his creation of things is total, he both determines and foresees the ways in which his creatures will act. We may grant this, but it is beside the point. The question is not whether God *originally* determined the future actions of his creatures, but whether he can *subsequently* control their actions, or whether he was able in his original creation to put things beyond his subsequent control. Even on determinist principles the answers "Yes" and "No" are equally irreconcilable with God's omnipotence.

Before suggesting a solution of this paradox, I would point out that there is a parallel Paradox of Sovereignty. Can a legal sovereign make a law restricting its own future legislative power?

For example, could the British parliament make a law forbidding any future parliament to socialise banking, and also forbidding the future repeal of this law itself? Or could the British parliament, which was legally sovereign in Australia in, say, 1899, pass a valid law, or series of laws, which made it no longer sovereign in 1933? Again, neither the affirmative nor the negative answer is really satisfactory. If we were to answer "Yes," we should be admitting the validity of a law which, if it were actually made, would mean that parliament was no longer sovereign. If we were to answer "No," we should be admitting that there is a law, not logically absurd, which parliament cannot validly make, that is, that parliament is not now a legal sovereign. This paradox can be solved in the following way. We should distinguish between first order laws, that is laws governing the actions of individuals and bodies other than the legislature, and second order laws, that is laws about laws, laws governing the actions of the legislature itself. Correspondingly, we should distinguish two orders of sovereignty, first order sovereignty (sovereignty (1)) which is unlimited authority to make first order laws, and second order sovereignty (sovereignty (2)) which is unlimited authority to make second order laws. If we say that parliament is sovereign we might mean that any parliament at any time has sovereignty (1), or we might mean that parliament has both sovereignty (1) and sovereignty (2) at present, but we cannot without contradiction mean both that the present parliament has sovereignty (2) and that every parliament at every time has sovereignty (1), for if the present parliament has sovereignty (2) it may use it to take away the sovereignty (1) of later parliaments. What the paradox shows is that we cannot ascribe to any continuing institution legal sovereignty in an inclusive sense.

The analogy between omnipotence and sovereignty shows that the paradox of omnipotence can be solved in a similar way. We must distinguish between first order omnipotence [omnipotence (1)], that is unlimited power to act, and second order omnipotence [omnipotence (2)], that is unlimited power to determine what powers to act things shall have. Then we could consistently say that God all the time has omnipotence (1), but if so no beings at any time have powers to act independently of God. Or we could say that God at one time had omnipotence (2), and used it to assign independent powers to act to certain things, so that God thereafter did not have omnipotence (1). But what the paradox shows is that we cannot consistently ascribe to any continuing being omnipotence in an inclusive sense.

An alternative solution of this paradox would be simply to deny that God is a continuing being, that any times can be assigned to his actions at all. But on this assumption (which also has difficulties of its own) no meaning can be given to the assertion that God made men with wills so free that he could not control them. The paradox of omnipotence can be avoided by putting God outside time, but the freewill solution of the problem of evil cannot be saved in this way, and equally it remains impossible to hold that an omnipotent God *binds himself* by causal or logical laws.

Conclusion

Of the proposed solutions of the problem of evil which we have examined, none has stood up to criticism. There may be other solutions which require examination, but this study strongly suggests that there is no valid solution of the problem which does not modify at least one of the constituent propositions in a way which would seriously affect the essential core of the theistic position.

Quite apart from the problem of evil, the paradox of omnipotence has shown that God's omnipotence must in any case be restricted in one way or another, that unqualified omnipotence cannot be ascribed to any being that continues through time. And if God and his actions are not in time, can omnipotence, or power of any sort, be meaningfully ascribed to him?

5.4 The Free-Will Explanation

A very popular and widespread response to the theological problem of evil is the free-will explanation. According to this argument, God is not responsible for evil (or at least moral evil), because humans are responsible. God created humans, however, and as Mackie pointed out in the last selection, there is nothing logically impossible about people freely choosing to do good on every occasion. Why didn't God create humans with the power to freely choose good all the time? After all, God is omnipotent.

At the heart of the free-will explanation is the claim that God, even though omnipotent, cannot do what is logically impossible. If it were logically possible for a person to be made to do x and at the same time do x freely, then there is no reason why a perfectly good God could not have created a world in which free human beings always do what is right. According to the free-will explanation, however, this is logically impossible.

The free-will explanation is directly relevant to the claim that Mackie and others make about the logical incompatibility of the existence of evil and the existence of the traditional theistic God. If an omnipotent, omniscient, and wholly good God exists, and if such a God cannot create a world in which there are no evils *and* free human beings, and if a world with free humans and some evil is *better* than a world with no free will, then God must have created the best world possible.

If God created the best possible world, then there is no logical inconsistency between the existence of the traditional theistic God and the existence of moral evil. Did God do that?

There is a vast body of philosophical literature in the West on the problem of evil and free will. This has led some philosophers to assume that the absence of written philosophical texts dealing with this particular issue amounts to the absence of philosophical thinking about it. This assumption is false, as Professor Kwame Gyekye demonstrates in the next selection.

Professor Kwame Gyekye of the University of Ghana has studied the Akan oral traditions, proverbs, and folktales and has interviewed Akan elders seeking to uncover the philosophical thinking underlying Akan culture. The Akan are the largest ethnic group in Ghana, and according to Professor Gyekye, they are concerned not only with the problem of evil in the broad sense but also with theological aspects of the problem. They recognize a potential contradiction between the existence of a Supreme Being and evil.

Because the Akan recognize other deities besides the supreme deity, they seem to have a way out that is not available to the monotheist: The lesser gods are responsible for evil. However, this response is not unlike Christians arguing that the source of evil is Satan and his demons (although Satan is a fallen angel, not a deity, in the Christian tradition). Both responses do not really solve the problem; they just move it back one step. So why does the supreme God allow the lesser deities (or fallen angels) to do evil?

The second Akan response is to ascribe evil, or at least moral evil, to human free will. It is here, according to Professor Gyekye, that Akan thinking and the traditional free-will explanation found in the Christian tradition become very similar. This line of argument assumes there is such a thing as free-will (an issue that is by no means settled), and it provides only a limited explanation. At best it shows that the existence of moral evil and a wholly good and omnipotent God are not necessarily contradictory. It stops far short of a fully developed theodicy that might explain God's purposes for permitting the profusion of natural evil in our world.

Reading Questions

1. Why, according to Gyekye, does making the deities responsible for evil fail to solve the theological problem of evil?
2. Why is the argument that evil stems from our inability to exercise the moral sense not persuasive?
3. What is the free-will explanation, and how does the author counter the objections to it?
4. Which are more persuasive, the objections to the free-will explanation or Gyekye's responses to those objections? Why?

The Free-Will Explanation*

KWAME GYEKYE

BECAUSE AKAN THINKERS hold that moral evil stems from the exercise of man's free will, it is appropriately treated here. The problem of evil appears to be more complex in Akan thought than Western thought. The reason is that whereas in Western thought the problem centers round God, in Akan thought the problem centers round both the Supreme Being (God: Onyame) and the deities (that is, lesser spirits). In Western thought the problem arises out of seeming conflicts between the attributes of God and the existence of evil. In Akan thought the problem is conceived in terms not only of the attributes of God but also of those of the deities. When the problem of evil in Akan thought is pushed to its logical limits, however, its philosophical nature is quite similar to that in Western philosophy and theology.

The problem of evil in Western philosophy arises out of the contradiction between God's attributes of omnipotence and goodness (benevolence) on the one hand and the existence of evil on the other hand. Thus, given the three propositions:

A. God is omnipotent,

B. God is wholly good,

C. evil exists,

C is considered to be incompatible with *A* and *B*, individually or jointly. If God is omnipotent, then He can completely eliminate evil, since there are no limits to what an omnipotent being can do, and if God is wholly good or benevolent then He would be willing to eliminate evil. Yet evil exists. The existence of evil, it is argued in Western philosophy, implies that either God does not exist or if He does exist He is not omnipotent or not wholly good or both. Of course various attempts have been made by philosophers and theologians to explain the sources of evil in this world.

In Akan philosophy and theology God is conceived as omnipotent and wholly good. Yet the Akan thinkers do not appear to find these attributes of God incompatible with the fact of the existence of moral evil. One might suppose that the Akan thinkers are dodging the philosophical issue here, but this is not so. Rather, they locate the source of the problem of evil elsewhere than in the logic of the relationships between the attributes of God and the fact of existence of evil.

For the Akan, evil is not a creation of God; that would be inconsistent with the goodness of God. Akan thinkers generally believe that it was not God who created evil . . . . Then how is the existence of evil explained? According to them, there are two main sources of evil: the deities (. . . including all supernatural forces such as magic forces, witches, etc.) and mankind's own will. About half a dozen assembled discussants were unanimous in asserting that "evil derives from evil spirits" . . . . The deities are held either to be good and evil or to have powers of good and evil. Thus, unlike Onyame (God), they are not wholly good, and hence they are the authors of evil things. Although the deities were created by God, they are considered in Akan theology and cosmology to have independent existence of some sort; they operate independently of God and in accordance with their own desires and intentions.

Since the deities that constitute one source of evil in this world are held not to be wholly good, one might suppose that the problem of evil is thereby solved. Busia, for instance, thought that

> . . . the problem of evil so often discussed in Western philosophy and Christian theology does *not* arise in the African concept of deity. It is when a God who is not only all-powerful and omniscient but also perfect and loving is

*Kwame Gyekye, *An Essay on African Philosophical Thought. The Akan Conceptual Scheme*, 1995 Rev.ed., pp. 123–128. Reprinted by permission of Temple University Press and the author. Footnotes deleted.

postulated that the problem of the existence of evil becomes an intellectual and philosophical hurdle. The Supreme Being of the African is the Creator, the source of life, *but between Him and man lie many powers and principalities good and bad, gods, spirits, magical forces, witches to account for the strange happenings in the world.*

It is not clear what Busia means by "deity" here; perhaps he means the Supreme Being, God. If so, his view of the attributes of the Supreme Being—a view that implies some limitation on the Supreme Being as conceived in African thought—is disputable. Be that as it may, the view that the African concept of the Supreme Being does not give rise to the problem of evil is of course predicated on the assumption that the lesser spirits created by Him are conceived of as good *and* bad, so that the quandaries arising out of the conflict of omnipotence and perfect goodness on the one hand and evil on the other hand cease to exist. But this conclusion is premature and unsatisfactory philosophically.

The immediate question that arises is this: Why should a wholly good God create a being that embodies in itself both good *and* evil powers or dispositions? One possible answer may be that it was not God who created the evil powers or actions of a lesser spirit, but that these result from the operations of the independent will of the spirit itself. But this answer is not wholly satisfactory either. First, God, being a higher entity, can destroy the lesser spirits as well as the other powers and forces. Consequently, God has the power to eliminate or control the evil wills and actions of the lower beings such as the lesser spirits and so to eliminate evil from the world. Second, since God is wholly good and eschews evil . . ., as an Akan proverb has it, he would not refrain from eliminating evil or controlling evil wills. Even if it were granted that God endowed the lesser spirits with independent wills, it might be expected that the wholly good God would be willing to intervene when he sees them using their wills to choose to act wrongly and so to cause evil. Would it have been wrong for God to intervene in the evil operations of the independent free wills of the lesser spirits in order to

eliminate evil? But if he had done so, would he not have disrupted the free wills with which he endowed them? (These questions come up again in discussing mankind as a source of evil.) Thus, contrary to Busia's assertion, it is clear that the Akan concept of deity does generate the philosophical problem of evil. Busia's assertion would be true only if a lesser spirit, held to be both good *and* bad, were considered as the supreme or ultimate spiritual being. But this . . . is not the case. It is Onyame who is the Supreme and Absolute Being.

The other source of evil, according to Akan thought, is human will. On this some of my discussants advanced the following views:

Evil comes from man's character.

In the view of this discussant, character determines the nature of our actions; bad character gives rise to evil actions, and good character gives rise to good actions. The person with bad character, he asserted, thinks evil, and it is such evil thoughts that translate or issue in morally evil actions. According to him, it is impossible for evil to come from Onyame (God) because (1) Onyame is good . . ., and (2) our character, from which evil proceeds, is of our own making; what a person's character is, or will be, is the person's responsibility, not God's. In a discussion with a different group of three elders, two of them also blamed evil on human character, but the third one, criticizing the other two, asked: "Is it not *Onyame* who created the world and us and all that we are?" He answered his own question by saying: "If Onyame made us what we are, then he created, along with everything else, evil too." To this one of the others retorted: "It is surely *not* Onyame who tells or forces a person to go and rape, steal, and kill. It is the person's own desires and mind" . . . . But the conception of the human source of moral evil was shared by two other discussants, both from different communities. One of them maintained that "Onyame did not create evil; evil comes from man's own actions" . . ., and the other that "Onyame is not the cause of evil, but our own thinking and deliberation". . . .

Arguing that God is not the author of evil, another discussant maintained that "evil comes from man's conscience" . . . . His position is that a human being has what is called *tiboa,* conscience (moral sense—that is, a sense of right and wrong), which enables one to see the difference . . . between good and evil. Putting it bluntly, he said, "Man is not a beast . . . to fail to distinguish between the good and evil." The comparison between man and beast is intended as a distinction between moral sense and amoral sense on the one hand, and between rationality (intelligence) and irrationality (nonintelligence) on the other hand. The implication is that it is only conscienceless, irrational beasts that cannot distinguish between good and evil. Since, according to this traditional thinker, our possession of *tiboa* enables (or, should enable) us to do correct moral thinking, evil stems from our inability to exercise the moral sense. But this argument is not persuasive. Having the ability to do correct moral thinking, or to distinguish between good and evil, does not necessarily imply possession of the moral will to carry out the implications of the distinction. This traditional wise man assumes that it does, but this assumption, I think, is mistaken. So that the statement "Evil comes from man's conscience" must perhaps be taken to mean that evil stems from the inability to exercise either our moral sense or our moral will.

In sum, the basic premise of the arguments of the Akan thinkers on the problem of evil is generally that God does not like evil . . . and hence did not create it . . . . Evil, according to most of them, proceeds from man's character, conscience, desires, and thoughts—all of which suggest, within the Akan conceptual system, that evil stems from the exercise by the person of his or her own free will . . ., as was in fact explicitly stated by a discussant. . . .

[T]he general nature of destiny . . . allows for the concept of human freedom, and therefore of choice, and that within the context of human actions—which are *not* to be considered as events—the concept of determinism is inapplicable. Thus the view of the human source of moral evil appears to stem from a set of related concepts in the Akan metaphysical system.

This argument seems to me a potent one. Nevertheless, some difficult questions might be raised against it. For instance: Why did not God, if he is omnipotent and wholly good, make human beings such that they always choose the good and avoid the evil? Or, having endowed them with freedom of the will, why does God not intervene when he sees them using this freedom to choose the wrong thing and so to cause evil? Is God unable to control human will? Is he unable to control what he has created? And if he is able, why does he not do so? Can the argument that evil results from the exercise of human free will really be sustained?

If God is omnipotent, then he certainly could have made human beings such that they always choose the good and avoid the evil, that he could also intervene in the event of human freedom of the will leading to evil, and that he could thus control human will. But if God had done all this, humans would act in a wholly determined way, without any choice whatever—a situation that would run counter to the *general* nature of the concept of destiny and the notion of human action as held by Akan thinkers. That would also have led to the subversion of rationality, which not only distinguishes human beings from beasts, but also enables human beings generally to judge before acting. The argument that God should have made humans such that they always choose the good implies that God should have made them nonrational and thus less human, wholly without the ability to choose. Thus, the subversion of rationality together with its concomitants of choice, deliberation, judgment, etc., constitutes a *reductio ad absurdum* of the view that the wholly good God should have created humans such that they always choose the good. The Akan thinkers, like thinkers in most other cultures, would rather have humankind endowed with rationality and conscience than to have them fashioned to behave like a beast. Hence, God's provision of rationality and freedom of the will and of choice is justified. If humans debase this provision, knowing that this would bring evil in its wake, then they, not their Creator, should be held responsible.

What if God [had] made humans such that they use their rationality always to choose the good? Would they have been free under such circumstances? The answer must be no, inasmuch as the choice of the good would have been predetermined, which means that no choice ever existed.

This discussion shows that the problem of evil does indeed arise in Akan philosophy and theology. The Akan thinkers, although recognizing the existence of moral evil in the world, generally do not believe that this fact is inconsistent with the assertion that God is omnipotent and wholly good. Evil, according to them, is ultimately the result of the exercise by humans of their freedom of the will with which they were endowed by the Creator . . . .

5.5 Atheism and Evil

Consider the following case. A child in a day-care center suffers horrendous burns when it is blown up by people who believe they have a righteous cause. The building collapses. The child is not immediately killed but rather is trapped in the rubble alive. She suffers for several days with severe burns and then dies. What might justify such suffering? Some might say that such intense suffering leads to a greater good. The baby will go to heaven to be with God to enjoy eternal bliss. Let's grant that eternal bliss awaits this unfortunate child. Does that erase the suffering? She suffered horribly, whatever her future, and such suffering is a clear-cut case of evil.

Consider the following case. A baby bunny lives in a forest that is set on fire by lightning. The baby bunny is terribly burned. It suffers intense pain for several days before the relief of death ends its misery. What might justify such suffering? You might argue that the environment will benefit from the cleansing fire. Perhaps it will and perhaps it will not. The point is that whatever justification you or I might propose, the baby bunny suffered intense pain for several days.

Whatever sorts of justification can be provided for such cases of suffering, it is clear that they constitute cases of suffering—and hence evil—and that they amount to evidence against the claim that a benevolent and merciful God rules the world. Cases like these (and countless more) indicate that the variety and profusion of evil in our world provide rational support for atheism, even if they do not prove that the existence of evil is logically inconsistent with the existence of God.

The evidential problem of evil (also called the inductive problem) is distinguished from the deductive, or logical, problem (see Reading 5.3) by the fact that it does not claim that the existence of evil is logically inconsistent with the existence of God, but only that the existence of the variety, intensity, and abundance of evil in this world provides good evidence in support of an atheistic conclusion.

In the next selection, William Rowe, professor of philosophy at Purdue University, presents the case for the evidential argument from evil. He believes the logical (or deductive) argument fails because it cannot be shown explicitly that the existence of evil is logically incompatible with the existence of an omnipotent, totally good God. That does not mean, however, that the existence of evil does not count as good evidence for the claim that an omnipotent, wholly good God does not exist. It does. Pay close attention to how he develops his case. Has he made a mistake?

Reading Questions

1. What is the difference between theism in the narrow sense and theism in the broad sense?
2. What is the difference between atheism in the narrow sense and atheism in the broad sense?
3. What, according to Rowe, is the argument for atheism based on evil?
4. Why does Rowe think the second premise of the argument for atheism based on evil is true?
5. Why are we not, according to Rowe, in a position to prove the truth of the first premise of the argument for atheism based on evil but, nonetheless, may have rational grounds for believing it true?
6. What is the difference between the "direct attack" and the "indirect attack," and why does the "direct attack" fail?
7. How does the "G. E. Moore shift" help the theist?
8. What are the differences among "unfriendly atheism," "indifferent atheism," and "friendly atheism," and why does Rowe think "friendly atheism" is the best alternative?
9. Has Rowe convinced you? Why or why not?

Atheism and Evil*

WILLIAM ROWE

THIS PAPER IS CONCERNED with three interrelated questions. The first is: Is there an argument for atheism based on the existence of evil that may rationally justify someone in being an atheist? To this first question I give an affirmative answer and try to support that answer by setting forth a strong argument for atheism based on the existence of evil.[1] The second question is: How can the theist best defend his position against the argument for atheism based on the existence of evil? In response to this question I try to describe what may be an adequate rational defense for theism against any argument for atheism based on the existence of evil. The final question is: What position should the informed atheist take concerning the rationality of theistic belief? Three different answers an atheist may give to this question serve to distinguish three varieties of atheism: unfriendly atheism, indifferent atheism, and friendly atheism. In the final part of the paper I discuss and defend the position of friendly atheism.

Before we consider the argument from evil, we need to distinguish a narrow and a broad sense of the terms "theist," "atheist," and "agnostic." By a "theist" in the narrow sense I mean someone who believes in the existence of an omnipotent, omniscient, eternal, supremely good being who created the world. By a "theist" in the broad sense I mean someone who believes in the existence of some sort of divine being or divine reality. To be a theist in the narrow sense is

* Reprinted from "The Problem of Evil and Some Varieties of Atheism," *American Philosophical Quarterly* 16 (1979) by permission. Footnotes edited.

also to be a theist in the broad sense, but one may be a theist in the broad sense—as was Paul Tillich—without believing that there is a supremely good, omnipotent, omniscient, eternal being who created the world. Similar distinctions must be made between a narrow and a broad sense of the terms "atheist" and "agnostic." To be an atheist in the broad sense is to deny the existence of any sort of divine being or divine reality. Tillich was not an atheist in the broad sense. But he was an atheist in the narrow sense, for he denied that there exists a divine being that is all-knowing, all-powerful and perfectly good. In this paper I will be using the terms "theism," "theist," "atheism," "atheist," "agnosticism," and "agnostic" in the narrow sense, not in the broad sense.

I

In developing the argument for atheism based on the existence of evil, it will be useful to focus on some particular evil that our world contains in considerable abundance. Intense human and animal suffering, for example, occurs daily and in great plentitude in our world. Such intense suffering is a clear case of evil. Of course, if the intense suffering leads to some greater good, a good we could not have obtained without undergoing the suffering in question, we might conclude that the suffering is justified, but it remains an evil nevertheless. For we must not confuse the intense suffering in and of itself with the good things to which it sometimes leads or of which it may be a necessary part. Intense human or animal suffering is in itself bad, an evil, even though it may sometimes be justified by virtue of being a part of, or leading to, some good which is unobtainable without it. What is evil in itself may sometimes be good as a means because it leads to something that is good in itself. In such a case, while remaining an evil in itself, the intense human or animal suffering is, nevertheless, an evil which someone might be morally justified in permitting.

Taking human and animal suffering as a clear instance of evil which occurs with great frequency in our world, the argument for atheism based on evil can be stated as follows:

1. There exist instances of intense suffering which an omnipotent, omniscient being could have prevented without thereby losing some greater good or permitting some evil equally bad or worse.[2]
2. An omniscient, wholly good being would prevent the occurrence of any intense suffering it could, unless it could not do so without thereby losing some greater good or permitting some evil equally bad or worse.
3. There does not exist an omnipotent, omniscient, wholly good being.

What are we to say about this argument for atheism, an argument based on the profusion of one sort of evil in our world? The argument is valid; therefore, if we have rational grounds for accepting its premises, to that extent we have rational grounds for accepting atheism. Do we, however, have rational grounds for accepting the premises of this argument?

Let's begin with the second premise. Let s_1 be an instance of intense human or animal suffering which an omniscient, wholly good being could prevent. We will also suppose that things are such that s_1 will occur unless prevented by the omniscient, wholly good (OG) being. We might be interested in determining what would be a *sufficient* condition of OG failing to prevent s_1. But, for our purpose here, we need only try to state a *necessary* condition for OG failing to prevent s_1. That condition, so it seems to me, is this:

Either (i) there is some greater good, G, such that G is obtainable by OG only if OG permits s_1,

   or (ii) there is some greater good, G, such that G is obtainable by OG only if OG permits either s_1 or some evil equally bad or worse,

   or (iii) s_1 is such that it is preventable by OG only if OG permits some evil equally bad or worse.

It is important to recognize that (iii) is not included in (i). For losing a good greater than s_1 is not the same as permitting an evil greater than s_1. And this because the *absence* of a good state of affairs need not itself be an evil state of affairs. It is also important to recognize that s_1 might be such that it is preventable by *OG without* losing *G* (so condition (i) is not satisfied) but also such that if *OG* did prevent it, *G* would be lost *unless OG* permitted some evil equal to or worse than s_1. If this were so, it does not seem correct to require that *OG* prevent s_1. Thus, condition (ii) takes into account an important possibility not encompassed in condition (i).

Is it true that if an omniscient, wholly good being permits the occurrence of some intense suffering it could have prevented, then either (i) or (ii) or (iii) obtains? It seems to me that it is true. But if it is true then so is premise (2) of the argument for atheism. For that premise merely states in more compact form what we have suggested must be true if an omniscient, wholly good being fails to prevent some intense suffering it could prevent. Premise (2) says that an omniscient, wholly good being would prevent the occurrence of any intense suffering it could, unless it could not do so without thereby losing some greater good or permitting some evil equally bad or worse. This premise (or something not too distant from it) is, I think, held in common by many atheists and nontheists. Of course, there may be disagreement about whether something is good, and whether, if it is good, one would be morally justified in permitting some intense suffering to occur in order to obtain it. Someone might hold, for example, that no good is great enough to justify permitting an innocent child to suffer terribly. Again, someone might hold that the mere fact that a given good outweighs some suffering and would be lost if the suffering were prevented, is not a morally sufficient reason for permitting the suffering. But to hold either of these views is not to deny (2). For (2) claims only that *if* an omniscient, wholly good being permits intense suffering *then* either there is some greater good that would have been lost, or some equally bad or worse evil that would have occurred, had the intense suffering been prevented. (2) does not purport to describe what might be a *sufficient* condi-

tion for an omniscient, wholly good being to permit intense suffering, only what is a *necessary* condition. So stated, (2) seems to express a belief that accords with our basic moral principles, principles shared by both theists and nontheists. If we are to fault the argument for atheism, therefore, it seems we must find some fault with its first premise.

Suppose in some distant forest lightning strikes a dead tree, resulting in a forest fire. In the fire a fawn is trapped, horribly burned, and lies in terrible agony for several days before death relieves its suffering. So far as we can see, the fawn's intense suffering is pointless. For there does not appear to be any greater good such that the prevention of the fawn's suffering would require either the loss of that good or the occurrence of an evil equally bad or worse. Nor does there seem to be any equally bad or worse evil so connected to the fawn's suffering that it would have had to occur had the fawn's suffering been prevented. Could an omnipotent, omniscient being have prevented the fawn's apparently pointless suffering? The answer is obvious, as even the theist will insist. An omnipotent, omniscient being could have easily prevented the fawn from being horribly burned, or, given the burning, could have spared the fawn the intense suffering by quickly ending its life, rather than allowing the fawn to lie in terrible agony for several days. Since the fawn's intense suffering was preventable and, so far as we can see, pointless, doesn't it appear that premise (1) of the argument is true, that there do exist instances of intense suffering which an omnipotent, omniscient being could have prevented without thereby losing some greater good or permitting some evil equally bad or worse?

It must be acknowledged that the case of the fawn's apparently pointless suffering does not *prove* that (1) is true. For even though we cannot see how the fawn's suffering is required to obtain some greater good (or to prevent some equally bad or worse evil), it hardly follows that it is not so required. After all, we are often surprised by how things we thought to be unconnected turn out to be intimately connected. Perhaps, for all we know, there is some familiar good outweighing the fawn's suffering to which that suffering is connected in a way we do not see. Furthermore, there may well be unfamiliar goods, goods we haven't dreamed of, to which the fawn's suffering is inextricably connected. Indeed, it would seem to require something like omniscience on our part before we could lay claim to *knowing* that there is no greater good connected to the fawn's suffering in such a manner that an omnipotent, omniscient being could not have achieved that good without permitting that suffering or some evil equally bad or worse. So the case of the fawn's suffering surely does not enable us to *establish* the truth of (1).

The truth is that we are not in a position to prove that (1) is true. We cannot know with certainty that instances of suffering of the sort described in (1) do occur in our world. But it is one thing to *know* or *prove* that (1) is true and quite another thing to have *rational grounds* for believing (1) to be true. We are often in the position where in the light of our experience and knowledge it is rational to believe that a certain statement is true, even though we are not in a position to prove or to know with certainty that the statement is true. In the light of our past experience and knowledge it is, for example, very reasonable to believe that neither Goldwater nor McGovern will ever be elected President, but we are scarcely in the position of knowing with certainty that neither will ever be elected President. So, too, with (1), although we cannot know with certainty that it is true, it perhaps can be rationally supported, shown to be a rational belief.

Consider again the case of the fawn's suffering. Is it reasonable to believe that there is some greater good so intimately connected to that suffering that even an omnipotent, omniscient being could not have obtained that good without permitting that suffering or some evil at least as bad? It certainly does not appear reasonable to believe this. Nor does it seem reasonable to believe that there is some evil at least as bad as the fawn's suffering such that an omnipotent being simply could not have prevented it without permitting the fawn's suffering. But even if it should somehow be reasonable to believe either of these things of the fawn's suffering, we must then ask whether it is reasonable to believe either of these things of *all* the instances of seemingly pointless human and animal suffering that occur daily in our world. And surely the answer to this more general question must be no. It seems quite unlikely that *all* the instances of intense suffering occurring daily in our world are intimately related to the occurrence of greater goods or the prevention of evils at least as bad; and even more unlikely, should they somehow all be so related, that an omnipotent, omniscient being could not have achieved at least some of those goods (or prevented some of those evils) without permitting the instances of intense suffering that are supposedly related to them. In the light of our experience and knowledge of the variety and scale of human and animal suffering in our world, the idea that none of this suffering could have been prevented by an omnipotent being without thereby losing a greater good or permitting an evil at least as bad seems an extraordinary absurd idea, quite beyond our belief. It seems then that although we cannot *prove* that it is true, it is, nevertheless, altogether *reasonable* to believe that (1) is true, that (1) is a *rational* belief.

Returning now to our argument for atheism, we've seen that the second premise expresses a basic belief common to many theists and nontheists. We've also seen that our experience and knowledge of the variety and profusion of suffering in our world provides *rational support* for the first premise. Seeing that the conclusion, "There does not exist an omnipotent, omniscient, wholly good being" follows from these two premises, it does seem that we have *rational support* for atheism, that it is reasonable for us to believe that the theistic God does not exist.

II

Can theism be rationally defended against the argument for atheism we have just examined? If it can, how might the theist best respond to that argument? Since the argument from (1) and (2) to (3) is valid, and since the theist, no less than the nontheist, is more than likely committed to (2), it's clear that the theist can reject this atheistic argument only by rejecting its first premise, the premise that states that there are instances of intense suffering which an omnipotent, omniscient being could have prevented without thereby losing some greater good or permitting some evil equally bad or worse. How, then, can the theist best respond to this premise and the considerations advanced in its support?

There are basically three responses a theist can make. First, he might argue not that (1) is false or probably false, but only that the reasoning given in support of it is in some way *defective*. He may do this either by arguing that the reasons given in support of (1) are *in themselves* insufficient to justify accepting (1), or by arguing that there are other things we know which, when taken in conjunction with these reasons, do not justify us in accepting (1). I suppose some theists would be content with this rather modest response to the basic argument for atheism. But given the validity of the basic argument and the theist's likely acceptance of (2), he is thereby committed to the view that (1) is false, not just that we have no good reasons for accepting (1) as true. The second two responses are aimed at showing that it is reasonable to believe that (1) is false. Since the theist is committed to this view. I shall focus the discussion on these two attempts, attempts which we can distinguish as "the direct attack" and "the indirect attack."

By a direct attack, I mean an attempt to reject (1) by pointing out goods, for example, to which suffering may well be connected, goods which an omnipotent, omniscient being could not achieve without permitting suffering. It is doubtful, however, that the direct attack can succeed. The theist may point out that some suffering leads to moral and spiritual development impossible without suffering. But it's reasonably clear that suffering often occurs in a degree far beyond what is required for character development. The theist may say that some suffering results from free choices of human beings and might be preventable only by preventing some measure of human freedom. But, again, it's clear that much intense suffering occurs not as a result

of human free choices. The general difficulty with this direct attack on premise (1) is two-fold. First, it cannot succeed, for the theist does not know what greater goods might be served, or evils prevented, by each instance of intense human or animal suffering. Second, the theist's own religious tradition usually maintains that in this life it is not given to us to know God's purpose in allowing particular instances of suffering. Hence, the direct attack against premise (1) cannot succeed and violates basic beliefs associated with theism.

The best procedure for the theist to follow in rejecting premise (1) is the indirect procedure. This procedure I shall call "the G. E. Moore shift," so-called in honor of the twentieth century philosopher, G. E. Moore, who used it to great effect in dealing with the arguments of the skeptics. Skeptical philosophers such as David Hume have advanced ingenious arguments to prove that no one can know of the existence of any material object. The premises of their arguments employ plausible principles, principles which many philosophers have tried to reject directly, but only with questionable success. Moore's procedure was altogether different. Instead of arguing directly against the premises of the skeptic's arguments, he simply noted that the premises implied, for example, that he (Moore) did not know of the existence of a pencil. Moore then proceeded indirectly against the skeptic's premises by arguing:

> I do know that this pencil exists.
> If the skeptic's principles are correct I cannot know of the existence of this pencil.

∴ The skeptic's principles (at least one) must be incorrect.

Moore then noted that his argument is just as valid as the skeptic's, that both of their arguments contain the premise "If the skeptic's principles are correct Moore cannot know of the existence of this pencil," and concluded that the only way to choose between the two arguments (Moore's and the skeptic's) is by deciding which of the first premises it is more rational to believe—Moore's premise "I do know that this pencil exists" or the skeptic's premise asserting that his skeptical principles are correct. Moore concluded that his own first premise was the more rational of the two.

Before we see how the theist may apply the G. E. Moore shift to the basic argument of atheism, we should note the general strategy of the shift. We're given an argument: *p, q,* therefore, *r.* Instead of arguing directly against *p,* another argument is constructed—not-*r, q,* therefore, not-*p*—which begins with the denial of the conclusion of the first argument, keeps its second premise, and ends with the denial of the first premise as its conclusion. Compare, for example, these two:

$$\begin{array}{ll} \text{I. } p & \text{II. not-}r \\ \underline{\quad q\quad} & \underline{\quad q\quad} \\ r & \text{not-}p \end{array}$$

It is a truth of logic that if I is valid II must be valid as well. Since the arguments are the same so far as the second premise is concerned, any choice between them must concern their respective first premises. To argue against the first premise (*p*) by constructing the counter argument II is to employ the G. E. Moore shift.

Applying the G. E. Moore shift against the first premise of the basic argument for atheism, the theist can argue as follows:

not-3. There exists an omnipotent, omniscient, wholly good being.

2. An omniscient, wholly good being would prevent the occurrence of any intense suffering it could, unless it could not do so without thereby losing some greater good or permitting some evil equally bad or worse.

therefore,

not-1. It is not the case that there exist instances of intense suffering which an omnipotent, omniscient being could have prevented without thereby losing some greater good or permitting some evil equally bad or worse.

We now have two arguments: the basic argument for atheism from (1) and (2) to (3), and the theist's best response, the argument from (not-3) and (2) to (not-1). What the theist then says about (1) is that he has rational grounds for believing in the existence of the theistic God (not-3), accepts (2) as true, and sees that (not-1) follows from (not-3) and (2). He concludes, therefore, that he has rational grounds for rejecting (1). Having rational grounds for rejecting (1), the theist concludes that the basic argument for atheism is mistaken.

III

We've had a look at a forceful argument for atheism and what seems to be the theist's best response to that argument. If one is persuaded by the argument for atheism, as I find myself to be, how might one best view the position of the theist? Of course, he will view the theist as having a false belief, just as the theist will view the atheist as having a false belief. But what position should the atheist take concerning the *rationality* of the theist's belief? There are three major positions an atheist might take, positions which we may think of as some varieties of atheism. First, the atheist may believe that no one is rationally justified in believing that the theistic God exists. Let us call this position "unfriendly atheism." Second, the atheist may hold no belief concerning whether any theist is or isn't rationally justified in believing that the theistic God exists. Let us call this view "indifferent atheism." Finally, the atheist may believe that some theists are rationally justified in believing that the theistic God exists. This view we shall call "friendly atheism." In this final part of the paper I propose to discuss and defend the position of friendly atheism.

If no one can be rationally justified in believing a false proposition then friendly atheism is a paradoxical, if not incoherent position. But surely the truth of a belief is not a necessary condition of someone's being rationally justified in having that belief. So in holding that someone is rationally justified in believing that the theistic God exists, the friendly atheist is not committed to thinking that the theist has a true belief. What he is committed to is that the theist has rational grounds for his belief, a belief the atheist rejects and is convinced he is rationally justified in rejecting. But is this possible? Can someone, like our friendly atheist, hold a belief, be convinced that he is rationally justified in holding that belief, and yet believe that someone else is equally justified in believing the opposite? Surely this is possible. Suppose your friends see you off on a flight to Hawaii. Hours after take-off they learn that your plane has gone down at sea. After a twenty-four hour search, no survivors have been found. Under these circumstances they are rationally justified in believing that you have perished. But it is hardly rational for you to believe this, as you bob up and down in your life vest, wondering why the search planes have failed to spot you. Indeed, to amuse yourself while awaiting your fate, you might very well reflect on the fact that your friends are rationally justified in believing that you are now dead, a proposition you disbelieve and are rationally justified in disbelieving. So, too, perhaps an atheist may be rationally justified in his atheistic belief and yet hold that some theists are rationally justified in believing just the opposite of what he believes.

What sort of grounds might a theist have for believing that God exists? Well, he might endeavor to justify his belief by appealing to one or more of the traditional arguments: Ontological, Cosmological, Teleological, Moral, etc. Second, he might appeal to certain aspects of religious experience, perhaps even his own religious experience. Third, he might try to justify theism as a plausible theory in terms of which we can account for a variety of phenomena. Although an atheist must hold that the theistic God does not exist, can he not also believe, and be justified in so believing, that some of these "justifications of theism" do actually rationally justify some theists in their belief that there exists a supremely good, omnipotent, omniscient being? It seems to me that he can.

If we think of the long history of theistic belief and the special situations in which people are sometimes placed, it is perhaps as absurd to think that no one was ever rationally justified in believing that the theistic God exists as it is to think that no one was ever justified in believing that human beings would never walk on the moon. But in suggesting that friendly atheism is preferable to unfriendly atheism, I don't mean to rest the case on what some human beings might reasonably have believed in the eleventh or thirteenth century. The more interesting question is whether some people in modern society, people who are aware of the usual grounds for belief and disbelief and are acquainted to some degree with modern science, are yet rationally justified in accepting theism. Friendly atheism is a significant position only if it answers this question in the affirmative.

It is not difficult for an atheist to be friendly when he has reason to believe that the theist could not reasonably be expected to be acquainted with the grounds for disbelief that he (the atheist) possesses. For then the atheist may take the view that some theists are rationally justified in holding to theism, but would not be so were they to be acquainted with the grounds for disbelief—those grounds being sufficient to tip the scale in favor of atheism when balanced against the reasons the theist has in support of his belief.

Friendly atheism becomes paradoxical, however, when the atheist contemplates believing that the theist has all the grounds for atheism that he, the atheist, has, and yet is rationally justified in maintaining his theistic belief. But even so excessively friendly a view as this perhaps can be held by the atheist if he also has some reason to think that the grounds for theism are not as telling as the theist is justified in taking them to be.

In this paper I've presented what I take to be a strong argument for atheism, pointed out what I think is the theist's best response to that argument, distinguished three positions an atheist might take concerning the rationality of theistic belief, and made some remarks in defense of the position called "friendly atheism." I'm aware that the central points of the paper are not likely to be warmly received by many philosophers. Philosophers who are atheists tend to be tough minded—holding that there are no good reasons for supposing that theism is true. And theists tend either to reject the view that the existence of evil provides rational grounds for atheism or to hold that religious belief has nothing to do with reason and evidence at all. But such is the way of philosophy.

NOTES

1. Some philosophers have contended that the existence of evil is *logically inconsistent* with the existence of the theistic God. No one, I think, has succeeded in establishing such an extravagant claim. Indeed, granted incompatibilism, there is a fairly compelling argument for the view that the existence of evil is logically consistent with the existence of the theistic God. (For a lucid statement of this argument see Alvin Plantinga, *God, Freedom, and Evil* (New York, 1974), 29–59.) There remains, however, what we may call the *evidential* form—as opposed to the *logical* form—of the problem of evil: the view that the variety and profusion of evil in our world, although perhaps not logically inconsistent with the existence of the theistic God, provides, nevertheless, *rational support* for atheism. In this paper I shall be concerned solely with the evidential form of the problem, the form of the problem which, I think, presents a rather severe difficulty for theism. . . .

2. If there is some good, G, greater than any evil, (1) will be false for the trivial reason that no matter what evil, E, we pick the conjunctive good state of affairs consisting of G and E will outweigh E and be such that an omnipotent being could not obtain it without permitting E. (See Alvin Plantinga, *God and Other Minds* (Ithaca, 1967), 167.) To avoid this objection we may insert "unreplaceable" into our premises (1) and (2) between "some" and "greater." If E isn't required for G, and G is better than G plus E, then the good conjunctive state of affairs composed of G and E would be *replaceable* by the greater good of G alone. For the sake of simplicity, however, I will ignore this complication both in the formulation and discussion of premises (1) and (2).

5.6 Karma and the Problem of Evil

Do you believe that there is justice in this world? Do you think that people who do good things eventually will have good things happen to them in return and that people who do bad and evil things will have evil inflicted on them in return? Do we reap what we sow? Is this a just world after all? If you answered "yes" to these questions, then you may be a believer in karma.

I am sure you have heard it said, when misfortune befalls someone, "Well, that's just bad karma." Perhaps you have said it yourself. What exactly is karma, and what role does it play in explaining evil?

The word *karma* has several meanings. It means deed or action—what you do. It also can mean what happens to you, and it can refer to the law of karma—an inevitable pattern of events linking what you do with what happens to you. Although we often think of karma in situations of misfortune and evil, it can explain both good fortune and bad. However, my primary concern here is with how the concept of karma might provide a solution to the problem of evil.

Karma provides a possible answer to the problem of evil in the broad nontheological sense and in the narrower theological sense. Why does evil happen to people? Is it due to chance? Is it due to God? Is it due to demons and evil deities? The doctrine of karma asserts that the evil (and good) that happens to us is primarily the result of what we have done in the past. We do reap what we sow—if not in this life, then in some future life.

How does karma work? There are a variety of different explanations. According to some explanations, karma is a principle of universal causality resulting from what we do. Every good deed as well as every negative act leaves a trace on our psyche. These traces or impressions solidify into habits and hence determine our character.

Our character embodies our dispositions to behave in certain ways in response to certain stimuli. If we develop good habits, we will reap good results. If we develop bad habits, we will suffer evil consequences. The results (good or bad) are proportionate to what is done, and hence justice prevails.

Justice may not prevail in this lifetime. Indeed, empirically, it appears that it does not. Hence the doctrine of karma is usually linked to the doctrine of rebirth. If you have developed the habit of honesty, but someone cheats you out of your retirement money and you die poor and in misery, you will be reborn to a life that may well lead to a rich and prosperous retirement. If you are a cheat and a liar, but you prosper and do well and then die, you will be reborn to a life that may well involve someone cheating you out of your riches and prospering as you die in poverty. What goes around, comes around.

Does this law of karma happen automatically, or is there some judicial administrator that keeps the books balanced? Is the law of karma a natural law like the law of gravity? Do natural laws discriminate on the basis of character? The naturalistic interpretation of the law of karma claims that value is part of the structure and pattern of the universe. There is no God or judicial administrator that tinkers with natural laws in order to ensure justice. Justice is automatic. If you drive over a cliff, you will fall. If you do bad things, negative things will result.

Others, however, have argued that a supernatural court must administer karma. Enter the divine. According to this view, the law of karma is a law of God's action in the world. God arranges things such that the good are rewarded, and the evil get their just deserts.

Bruce R. Reichenbach, professor of philosophy at Augsburg College, is the author of the next selection. He explores the potential of the doctrine of karma to offer a philosophically adequate explanation of what he terms the nontheistic and theistic problem of evil. A full assessment, he believes, requires a critical examination of doctrines such as rebirth and of both the naturalistic and the supernaturalistic explanation of how the law of karma works. In the book from which this selection is taken, he provides such an examination. Here I include only those sections that deal with the theistic and nontheistic problem and with the naturalistic interpretation.

Reading Questions

1. What two problems is the hypothesis of the law of karma designed to solve?
2. What is the difference between the deductive argument from evil and the inductive argument from evil?
3. What is the difference between the problem of evil as generally found in Indian philosophy and as found in Western philosophical theology?
4. What are the consequences of trying to use the law of karma to resolve the theistic problem of evil?
5. What is the major difficulty with karma understood subjectively?
6. Why does Reichenbach conclude that the naturalistic explanation of how the law of karma works is inadequate?
7. In your view, does the theory of karma solve the problem of evil? Why or why not?

Karma and the Problem of Evil*

BRUCE REICHENBACH

THE DOCTRINE OF KARMA continues to be significant because it provides an explanation for both pain, suffering and misfortune on the one hand, and pleasure, happiness and good fortune on the other. Consequently, an assessment of the success of the doctrine in resolving the problem of good and evil will go a long way in enabling us to evaluate the doctrine itself, for should it fail to resolve satisfactorily the problem which it is intended to meet, since as we have seen the law is an explanatory hypothesis proposed to resolve a problem and not empirically verifiable, there would seem to be little reason to advocate the doctrine.

The Problem of Evil

What is the problem that the law of karma was introduced to meet? Though we have no historical records on the matter, it seems to have been introduced to explain why it is that we experience happiness and unhappiness, pleasure and pain, good and bad. These experiences come to us apparently randomly; there is no obvious logic to them or equality in their distribution. Two people are walking down the road in a thunderstorm; one gets struck and killed by lightning, the other escapes unhurt. Two children contract influenza; one dies while the other survives. Two daughters of the same parents have different dispositions, the one obedient and helpful, the other obstinate and selfish. One thing that is obvious is that one's experiences often seem to have no necessary connection with one's present moral qualities or character. Good people sometimes experience good—birth into advantageous settings, healthy bodies, devoted spouses, wealth and prestige—but at other times

bad. On the other hand bad people sometimes have bad experiences, but often have good. This suggests that the world is governed by moral chance. But a world governed by moral chance is unacceptable. For one thing, it violates cosmic or universal justice, according to which each person should have an equal opportunity to achieve happiness and ultimately liberation. There is a reason behind the events which happen to us, a reason which is intrinsically joined to fairness and equality. For another, it eliminates a proffered primary sanction for keeping the moral law, for unless there is a necessary connection between the moral quality of the actions performed and pain and pleasure experienced by the doer of those acts, there is no reason for doing right and avoiding the wrong. Why should we do the right if it fails to bring us happiness or at least avoid pain, suffering and misery?

To avoid this some explanatory hypothesis has to be suggested, a hypothesis which is consistent with universal justice and the moral law. According to this hypothesis, universal justice is preserved by virtue of the fact that the good and bad that we experience are not the result of chance, nor of the acts of others, but of actions we performed at some time in our past. We have brought on our own misery or happiness. Though often there is no immediate or obvious empirical connection between our moral actions and our happiness and unhappiness or good and bad circumstances, the connection is there. Chance is excluded; cosmic justice upheld. Right actions and happiness, wrong actions and misery, are linked.

Likewise, this hypothesis preserves one suggested sanction for keeping the moral law. If we do right, we will be rewarded with pleasure or

*From *The Law of Karma: A Philosophical Study,* by Bruce R. Reichenbach. Copyright © 1990 by Bruce R. Reichenbach. Honolulu: University of Hawaii Press. Reprinted by permission. Footnotes deleted.

happiness sometime in the future, though not necessarily in this life; and if we do wrong, we will be punished. If we wish to escape punishment and experience pleasure, we have no choice but to opt for doing the right thing.

Those familiar with the so-called problem of evil as discussed in Western philosophy will immediately notice an obvious difference of focus. In Western thought, the problem of evil usually is formulated in terms of the questioned ability of the theist to justify the actions, character or very existence of God in light of the evil present in the world. Simply put, if God is omnipotent, omniscient and wholly good, why is there evil in the world? The argument from evil has two forms. In its deductive form, the argument asserts that the existence of evil *per se* is inconsistent with a God who is good, omnipotent and omniscient. Persons are considered good when they eliminate evil as far as they can without losing a greater good or producing a greater evil. Since God is omnipotent—the argument goes—one would expect God to eliminate all evil from the world. Since there is evil, God either does not exist or does not possess the properties ascribed to him, namely, omnipotence, omniscience or goodness. In its inductive form, it is not the mere existence of evil that matters, but rather the variety, degree and profusion of evil which make it improbable or unlikely that God exists. The likelihood of there being this much evil in the world given what we know about the world and that God exists is less than the likelihood of there being this much evil and God not existing. That is, if God existed, we should expect there to be much less evil than there currently is. Since there is so much evil and since it is so bad, it is unlikely that God exists or has certain ascribed properties.

It should be readily apparent that both kinds of arguments in Western philosophical theology have to do with the existence and character of God rather than with the question of moral chance. True, there is an attempt to provide an explanation for the evil that afflicts human persons. Yet what is of primary concern is the existence and nature of the deity. Given the presence of evil, does God exist? Is he good? Is he om-

nipotent? For this reason Western treatments of the problem attempt to construct either a defence of God's existence or possession of certain properties such as goodness, or a theodicy which justifies the ways or actions of God *vis-à-vis* the world and the evil found in it in terms of some morally sufficient reason for evil. Indeed, the very word "theodicy" (from the Greek for "God" and "justice"), which means vindicating the justice of God, indicates this.

But the problem of evil as generally found in Indian philosophical traditions rests not on the question of the existence and nature of God, but rather on the question whether there is universal justice. Evidence for this thesis can be found in the fact that the problem of evil in a theological guise (that is, with reference to God) is rarely treated directly in classical or medieval Indian literature. What this means in effect is that the question of the relation of God to pain, suffering and dysfunction is much less significant or even insignificant in Indian karmic systems. And the reason has to do not so much with the law of karma as with their respective views of God.

Paradoxically, evidence for this is found in the fact that the problem of evil is formulated in identical fashion in Indian philosophy, irrespective of whether the context is theistic or not. For example, the description of the problem to be solved by the law of karma in Theravāda Buddhism, which is not theistic, does not differ from that found in theistic Vedānta. Both want to understand why it is that persons experience pain and pleasure, fortune and misfortune in ways that seem unconnected with the moral quality of their present actions, and ultimately, how this cycle of suffering can be escaped. Justification of divine ways and action is rarely undertaken. . . .

The Theistic Problem of Evil

We have already noted that the law of karma is introduced to resolve the non-theistic problem of evil. Can it also be used to resolve the theistic problem, which attempts to defend or reconcile the existence of a good, omnipotent, omniscient deity with the presence of pain, suffering and misfortune in the world? Since some Western philosophers and theologians think so, it is worth reconstructing what such a solution might look like.

Let us begin with Śaṅkara's brief treatment of the theistic problem. As we noted above, the problem is raised in the context of an objection that God is not qualified to be the cause of the world because good and evil are dispensed unequally, there is great misery in the world, and he periodically destroys the world. Śaṅkara's reply involves an appeal to the law of karma. He contends that all three of these are explained as the recompense of individuals' acts. That is, the evil in the world is due to human merit and demerit accumulated from prior karmic actions. Though God causes what happens (since he is the sole material cause), he has no control over dispensing either fortune or misfortune. He simply acts according to the dictates of the law of karma. The solution to the theistic problem of evil, then, is that God is not morally responsible for the evil in the world because he simply administrates the consequences of our karmic acts. It is the individual agents which are morally accountable. This means, then, that all evil is moral evil, that is, evil for which human agents can be held morally accountable. There is no natural evil *per se*.

Three objections to this can be raised:

1. First, is this subjection of God's acts to the law of karma consistent with his omnipotence? The answer is affirmative, provided one carefully defines omnipotence. If God is omnipotent, then he can do anything which is not or does not entail a contradiction or which he is not excluded from performing. If he is omnipotent but cannot violate the law of karma, there must then be some contradiction in his doing so. There would be a contradiction if the law expresses a necessary truth. That it is treated as doing so we saw in chapter 3. As such, it would be impossible for anything, including God, to break the law. Hence, that God cannot do the impossible does not count against his omnipotence.

2. Second, if all evil ultimately is caused by human persons and if human persons are God's

creations, where did the original human desire to do evil come from, and why did God create human persons with the ability to desire and do evil? If the first humans did evil, not because they desired to do so, but accidentally, then they should not be held morally accountable for breaking the moral law and karma should not accumulate. If, on the other hand, they did evil because they were disposed to do evil, then God created them with that disposition and is morally responsible for it. It might be replied that they did evil, not because they were disposed to do so, but of their own free choice. But then why did God create humans with the ability freely to choose and do evil? Some justification of this action of granting persons morally significant choice is required in order to preserve God's goodness and wisdom.

So stated, it appears that the attempt to use a karmic theodicy in the theistic context depends upon a more basic theodicy, such as a free will or soul-building theodicy. That is, some explanation of why God created human persons with the ability to choose and do evil is required, and it is to this issue that non-karmic theodicies are directed.

Śaṅkara and Rāmānuja suggest two answers to the dilemma.

a. First, they maintain that God's causation of the world is not an intentional act. God causes (and in Rāmānuja, sustains and destroys) the world, not purposefully, but out of sport, and thus is not morally accountable for his acts. Generalized to the above problem, this means that the creation of persons with the freedom to make moral decisions was not intended or purposed by God. In fact, God has no intentions or purposes. It is merely the result of his non-intentional or sporting actions. And since he did not intend it, there is no answer to the "why" question, nor need a moral justification for his actions be sought.

Why do they argue in this fashion? The reason is to avoid a dilemma. On the one hand, if God acts from a purpose or goal, he wants to achieve something. But if he wants to achieve something, he lacks something; he is not self-sufficient, which contradicts his perfection. On the other hand, if he has no purpose, he cannot act except in senseless or spontaneous ways, which contradicts his omniscience. Thus, they want to suggest that there is a class of actions which is neither intentional (in that it has no purpose) nor unintentional (and hence not done senselessly). And this they see manifested in acting out of sport.

But is "doing something out of sport" equivalent to doing something for no purpose or nonintentionally? To do something out of sport is to do something either for pleasure (for the heck of it) or else to do it for its own sake. But in both cases, a purpose of some sort is involved. To use their example, when nobility engage in sporting activities, they do so for the pleasure they derive from them; from seeing the hounds chase and catch the fox, the falcon swoop down on its prey, or the billiard balls roll into the pocket. That the sport itself has no purpose does not entail that those who engage in it have no purpose in doing so.

What Śaṅkara and Rāmānuja require is an intentional act which is not done for a purpose (and hence out of any lack) and which frees the agent from moral accountability. Interestingly enough, they have such acts at their disposal. . . . [A]cts which are performed for their own sake, without any thought of or desire for the results, do not build karma. They are performed not out of desire, necessity or lack, but out of the fullness of being. The acts of God which are other than karma-implementing could be of this non-karma-producing nature. He would be seen as acting simply for the sake of acting, without desires for any end.

This view, of course, has implications for the nature of God. In particular, it removes from God any desires, goals or objectives concerning the world. This, of course, would be consistent with Śaṅkara's and (to a lesser extent) Rāmānuja's view of God. It becomes more problematic, however, for the theist who sees God actively involved in the world. For example, it would not be right to ascribe to him the desire that all persons be liberated. As such, on this account God could not be a God of grace, who intervenes telically on the behalf of those who worship him to relieve them of their suffering and bring liberation.

b. In their next response, they argue that to ask why God created persons as he did is a pseudo-problem because the world is beginningless. All effects are products of causes, which are themselves effects of other causes. Thus there is no question why God brought these particular beings into existence; they have always existed. God simply "arranges the diversity of the creation in accordance with the different Karman of the individual souls." God, then, is subject to the law of karma in his dealings with the universe. He is not the teleologically-efficient cause of what exists.

Again, for the theist who sees God involved telically with the creation, this raises the larger question concerning what can be said about God's acts and his relation to the world. Does God do anything but administer the law of karma? If not, and if the law of karma is a necessary truth, then of course the law of karma solves the theistic problem of evil, for all his acts are justified in terms of the karma accumulated by us. But what then happens to the nature of God? He becomes little more than a general cause in the universe. He is, as Śaṅkara notes, a general or "common" cause, like the god who dispenses rain everywhere regardless of where it is needed. God then creates everything (as a non-teleological material cause) but has no further role to play with the created as individuals.

But this God can hardly be the God of religious worship, the one to whom devotion is paid and requests made. It is not the God who out of love and compassion relieves the suffering of the petitioner or who liberates those who call on him. Indeed, in this view divine grace in any particularized sense is impossible. If the law of karma requires that each person receives his due, and if what is due a person is the result of the actions he has performed, then God can be of little direct aid in removing our acquired karma by divine intervention, mercy and forgiveness. In short, God's role is cosmogenic and administrative and little else.

3. Finally, there is the problem how God as the material cause can avoid sullying his perfection with the evil which evolves. Though the *Bhagavad-Gītā* at times appears nonchalant about the disassociation of God from evolved evil, other personal, theistic systems show more explicit concern. For example, Rāmānuja notes that "the Supreme *Brahman* is devoid of even the slightest trace of the evil that is found to exist in all the intelligent and non-intelligent things . . . . The Supreme *Brahman* is the opposite of all that is evil and the sole seat of all auspicious qualities. He is entirely distinct from all other things (than Himself)." The imperfection of the evolved does not affect the perfection of the evolver. However, how his panentheistic deity can remain separate enough from what evolves out of him, which includes evil and imperfection, to be perfect is unclear. *Brahman* and his body (souls and matter) are one, a unity.

It might be thought that the imperfection here is ontological and not moral, and hence not directly germane to the problem of evil. That something is not perfect in its being says nothing about its moral perfection. For example, being crippled and in a wheel chair implies nothing about moral character. But for Rāmānuja, God is the soul or self in each person, just as each is part of his body. But souls or selves perform karmic deeds, both good and bad. As such, it is hard to see how God can escape similar consequences.

In summation, the appeal to the law of karma to resolve the theistic problem of evil has important consequences. First, it either necessitates that the creation of the world and selves is the result of a desireless and purposeless act of God (so that he does not lack self-sufficiency) or that the world and selves are beginningless (so that the evil which we experience is always the result of our prior acts). The former not only leaves many questions unanswerable, including why God made what he did and why he made it as he did, but turns the universe into a grand sporting event. If anything, it trivializes and degrades human existence. The latter is possible, though unlikely, given what we know and can reasonably infer about the history of the universe and

life in it. But more importantly it accounts for no other divine acts. Secondly, either all God's acts are governed by the law of karma and hence justified thereby, or else he performs acts which are done to realize no end. Both make it impossible that God is gracious, having pity for miserable mankind and intervening on behalf of those he seeks to save. In effect, if one appeals to the law of karma to explain all evil, then we have a movement towards an impersonal theism, where God's primary roles are non-teleologically cosmogenic and/or administrative. Where we have a personal theism in which God brings selves into being or sustains their existence, or is motivated by a desire to show mercy and intervenes in behalf of their liberation, an appeal to the law of karma must be conjoined with other theodicies (such as the free will or soul-building theodicies) in order to justify either God's creation and sustenance of beings capable of free, moral choice or the degree to which he intervenes. However, this being said, the adequacy of the law of karma within the Hindu/Buddhist context should not be measured on this score, since, as we suggested at the outset, the theistic problem of evil was not the problem it was developed to resolve.

The Non-theistic Problem of Evil

It is time to return to the issue with which we began this chapter. Is the law of karma adequate to solve the non-theistic problem of evil? To evaluate its adequacy, two areas must be addressed. First, some defence of the doctrine of rebirth (in either the Hindu or Buddhist forms) must be made. . . . [T]his is a presupposition of the theory. . . . Secondly, the advocate of this explanation of evil must provide an account of the mechanism by which karma is implemented. That is, if the law of karma is to explain all kinds of fortune and misfortune and the evil that we do to one another as well as the evil that results from natural causes, some reasonable description of its workings is requisite. . . .

According to the law of karma, our actions have consequences which affect not only our dispositions and tendencies (*saṃskāras*), but also the non-dispositional aspects of our being (for example, our genetic make-up, our physical characteristics, our social status at birth, our length of life) and our environment. The environment is affected in such a way that in some future life it will be instrumental in rewarding or punishing us according to the merit or demerit resulting from our acts. For example, a person might be mauled by a grizzly bear either in retribution for a particular violent act he committed or because of his pool of accumulated karmic residues.

One can understand how desiring to act and then acting in accord with those desires would create dispositions in the person who wills and acts; and where a continuous, substantial self is presupposed, it is reasonable to hold that these dispositions would be preserved and bear fruit in that self at some later time. But that our acts also have cosmic or environmental effects of a specific character in subsequent existences is more problematic. How, it might be wondered, can the acts we performed in some past life affect the present material and physical conditions of our environment or other agents? With the exception of certain theistic systems, about which we shall speak later, karma is held to operate in a naturalistic fashion. That is, prior events effect subsequent events without the intervention of any supernatural agent. But if karma operates naturally, is it reasonable to believe that there is any causal link between the original cause (our doing either one or many acts) and the (pleasurable or painful, advantageous or disadvantageous) effects we experience in a subsequent life? What causal chain can be established between a person's doing good actions in a previous life and the fact that the person has the pleasure of owning a Cadillac, recovered from an attack of influenza, or had a tree blown down by the windstorm miss his house?

The problem is exacerbated by the contention that the law of karma is not empirically verifiable. Yet its constitutive process of cause (one's action) and effect (the pain or pleasure received) cannot be understood in any way other than empirical. . . .

The Environment and Natural Good and Evil

Were we to understand the workings of karma strictly subjectively, we could stop here. Our acts create dispositions or accumulations of merit and demerit which cause us to act in ways which bring us pleasure and pain, to interpret our experiences in terms of pleasure and pain, or to be vulnerable to certain things in the environment (such as diseases) which affect our body or mind and thus bring pleasure and pain. These accumulations or dispositions affect our experiences and their interpretations until we eliminate them, as the metaphor goes, burning out both the seed (using up the accumulated karma) and its roots (destroying the dispositions and not creating new ones). This is accomplished when we achieve a proper understanding of the self, no longer act out of desire for any fruits, have equanimity toward all events, or cease mental modifications.

That this is a reasonable explanation of karma interpreted subjectively does not however mean that it is without difficulty. The major difficulty is to be found in assuring that the produced dispositions, whether behavioural or bodily, and resultant pain and pleasure, are justly appropriate to the karmic act. We have no scale which correlates the amount of pleasure and pain to be received with the moral quality of the act performed. And even were we provided with one, it would be difficult if not impossible to carry out the relevant calculations. Pleasure and pain are notoriously difficult to quantify accurately. . . .

[S]ubjectively transmitted karma, the appeal to dispositions or special moral qualities, is only the first step in explaining how the law of karma operates naturalistically. Karma also affects us as embodied and the environment which mediates or is an instrument of karmic justice. Karmic residues, whether found as unique moral qualities (*adṛṣṭa*), as invisible material bodies (*kārmana-śarīra*), as dispositions (*saṃskāras*), or as karmic seeds (*karmabīja*), condition events in the environment which bring pain and pleasure to the agent. That is, they are in part responsible for certain events occurring as they do or things being as they are. What, then, is the relationship between this moral, material or dispositional quality which exists in the person and the material environment? The response is that this subtle karmic influence, at the appropriate time, disposes us to act or itself acts on the environment to produce the appropriate state which causally contributes to punishing or rewarding us for our prior action(s).

For example, the creative power of ethically relevant actions is as axiomatic to the Buddhists, as it is strange to us. The environment in which beings have to live is to a great extent, especially in regard to its pleasantness or unpleasantness, determined by their deeds (karma). The various hells, for instance, are *produced* by the deeds of the creatures who are reborn there. We have waterless deserts in our world because of our small merit. The world of things is really nothing more than a kind of reflex of peoples' deeds.

There is, it is held, a symbiotic relationship between human actions and the environment. And this is to be seen in terms of a causal chain. Our actions produce moral qualities or condition tendencies or dispositions to act. These bear fruit later in actions. These actions, in turn, create or causally condition events in our environment. These events in turn affect us, bringing us pleasure or pain according to our karmic merit or demerit. Thus our good and bad experiences and the ensuing pain and pleasure have been brought upon us by our own deeds.

But how do human actions condition the environment? We noted above that some Buddhists attempted to provide an explanation by postulating the existence of an unseen product of a volition (*avijñapti*) which resided in agents, where it functions as an invisible cause which emanated from persons to affect their environment. But the postulation of this unseen result helps us no better to explain how we can be a causal condition of our environment than the postulation of phlogiston helps us to understand how things burn. Clearly the *avijñapti* is a theoretical construct rather than something for which there is empirical evidence. Indeed, this

was precisely the Yogācārins' contention against the Sarvāstivādins; the former held that, due to the non-empirical character, it was only the product of a creative imagination.

Now it is true to say that my actions can affect my environment, and that my environment, in turn, has a bearing on my happiness. For example, in a fit of rage I might destroy a work of art, an act which, when I return to my senses, I greatly regret, or again, by our greedy timbering of the Amazon we are rapidly creating an inhospitable desert. But though we might affirm this connection for some of our experiences, it is difficult to see how our actions can have the cosmic implications necessary to account for all natural evils. How can our *saṃskāras* or *adṛṣṭas* have the causal efficacy to occasion natural evils such as earthquakes, tornadoes, genetic deficiencies and the like?

Vaiśeṣikas attempt to make this claim plausible by suggesting that the self or *ātman* is omnipresent and eternal. As omnipresent, its activity is not restricted by the particular body to which it is connected by the *manas*. It can act on all things. As eternal, its action can cover spans of time and incarnations. Since *adṛṣṭa* is a quality of the self, by means of this quality the self can causally affect all of nature, and thus bring about earthquakes, fires, diseases and the like. An illustration of this is given in Uddyotakara's *Nyāyavārttika* [4.1.47]: if somebody waters a tree, the success of his action, that is, the process of fertilization and growth, may be influenced by the karma of the person who at a later time will eat the fruits of the tree; it becomes the function of the tree, directed by the karmic potential of a soul which may or may not be that of the person who watered the tree, to provide an opportunity of retributive experience, of enjoyment. As such, the dispositions or moral qualities of the person directly affect things in the environment and function as a causal condition of their acting, both in general and on the agent. The gap between self and environment is overcome.

The viability of this solution depends on the adequacy of Vaiśeṣika's description of the self as pure substance, omnipresent and eternal. We shall argue in the next chapter that there are serious difficulties with this view. In particular, if each self is substance only, underlying cognitive qualities but itself possessing no essential psychological or physical qualities, how can there be a plurality of such substances? Are we not reduced to a monism Vaiśeṣika rejects in Advaita Vedānta?

Beyond the particular problems elucidated, the underlying and fundamental question concerns the claim that moral calculations can be preserved naturally. If one appeals to distinctive moral qualities, are there such things in the universe? How do karmic actions create them? And how do they affect the environment so as to produce precisely the appropriate experiences for the agent? If one appeals to dispositions and tendencies, to potencies and seeds, or to subtle material bodies, how are merits and demerits not only preserved in them but transferred to the environment and returned in *appropriate* and *just* proportions of happiness or unhappiness? For example, how can the postulation of the *avijñapti* assure that the external situation it conditions will cause the appropriate and just experience for the agent? That is, the naturalistic explanation of the implementation of precise moral calculations through the intermediating agency of the environment is inadequate. . . .

5.7 Theological Explanations

Do you think it is possible for humans to understand evil? Can we ever discover why it exists, what purposes it might serve, how best to deal with it, and how best to reduce the amount of it? Of course we do know some things about specific evils, such as the causes of disease and natural disasters. We have been able to reduce or eliminate specific types of suffering, such as various sorts of diseases. New diseases, however, always seem to be waiting just around the corner. AIDS has caused a vast amount of suffering, and unless an effective way of dealing with the disease is found soon, it will cause much more suffering. AIDS may do to modern civilization what the bubonic plague did to Medieval European civilization. Millions will die, and the economic cost could drastically affect the standard of living throughout the world.

The problem of evil, however, transcends specific instances. We know why earthquakes happen and what causes some cancers. But there is a deeper question. Why were my house and family destroyed in an earthquake? Why did my child get cancer? Evil is not just an intellectual problem; it is a personal and existential problem. The cry "Why me?" can be uttered without any belief or hope that there might be some benevolent ultimate reality that is concerned about one's welfare. The cry can also be uttered with a different awareness. "Why me, Lord?" adds an element of poignancy to the lament. If there is a Lord, a benevolent and kind ultimate reality concerned with my welfare and the welfare of all people, then the existential question becomes even harder to answer, although, for some perhaps, the suffering becomes easier to bear.

Is theodicy (an explanation of why God permits evil) possible? Can we know why God permits evil? Is evil punishment for sin? Is evil necessary in order for us to know good? Does evil contribute to the growth of character and virtue? No theodicy can tell us in detail what future goods might arise from a specific evil. We cannot read the mind of God. However, theodicies do endeavor to cast doubt on the idea that there are some evils that God could have prevented without thereby jeopardizing a greater good. They try to show that if obtaining some particular good is God's aim, then, as far as we know, it is reasonable to believe God has a good reason for permitting certain evils.

There are many different kinds of theodicies found among the world's religions. One kind of theodicy became particularly attractive to many Jewish thinkers. It derives from the Kabbalah. The word *Kabbalah* means "tradition." It refers to a type of Jewish mysticism that developed in Spain and France in the twelfth and thirteenth centuries.

The Crusades, beginning in 1095, brought occasional pogroms in many parts of Europe. Jews were expelled from England in 1290, and in 1492, they were expelled from Spain. These events renewed an ancient Jewish mystical tradition that emphasized inner piety and communion with God. God is characterized as Ein Sof—the eternally perfect, ineffable One from whom ten powers called the Sefirot emanate. These powers (such as Wisdom, Mercy, Justice, and Grandeur) play an important role in the creation of the world. Human acts can have effects on the divine. God needs human beings to accomplish the divine purpose, and humans need God to achieve the happiness and peace they seek. Israel, by its obedience, kindness, suffering, and faithfulness, can help restore the proper balance to a world plunged into disharmony by sin.

This message was particularly helpful during a time of increasing oppression and persecution by the dominant Christian society. It assured the Jews not only that there was a divine purpose to what was happening but also that God suffered along with them as they went through their trials and tribulations.

In the next selection, Professor Robert Nozick of Harvard University, winner of a National Book Award in 1975, reviews some of the theodicies that have been offered and some of the objections to them. He finds in the Jewish Kabbalistic tradition important resources for rethinking solutions to the theological problem of evil.

Reading Questions

1. Why, according to Nozick, do the ideas that evil is a privation, evil exists for soul-making purposes, and evil is due to free will fail to solve the problem of evil?
2. Why are the views on evil of Plato, Plotinus, and the Gnostics unsatisfactory?
3. Why do dualistic types of theodicies fail?
4. What is the virtue of the Kabbalistic view?
5. What does Leibniz mean by "best of all possible worlds"?
6. What is Schlesinger's argument for the necessity of a world of finite value, and even if it satisfies intellectual criteria, why does it fail to satisfy religious criteria?
7. What does Nozick mean by "net positive value," and how is this idea related to the problem of evil?
8. What criteria must any satisfactory theodicy meet?
9. In what three admittedly unsatisfactory ways does Nozick suggest that the Holocaust might parallel a divine trauma?
10. Do you think Nozick is right when he asserts that we need a daring theodicy that drives issues about evil "deep within the divine"? Why or why not?

Theological Explanations*

ROBERT NOZICK

NOT JUST METAPHYSICS but theology too has wrestled with darkness. A traditional theological question asks why God allows there to be evil in the world. I want to consider some untraditional answers. While for the religious this problem is a pressing one, the nonreligious too can find it interesting, or at least a challenging intellectual exercise.

"The problem of evil" is set up by the fact that God, as traditionally conceived, has certain attributes: omnipotence, omniscience, and goodness. Yet, evil exists. Eliminate one of those attributes and there remains no hard intellectual conflict. If God weren't omnipotent, then evil might exist because he (or she) could not prevent it. If God weren't omniscient, then evil might exist because God didn't know he was creating it in creating the world. If God weren't good, if God didn't mind there being evil (at least as we conceive it), or if God were malicious, then similarly evil might exist and there would be no (intellectual) problem. There seems to be no way to reconcile those characteristics of omnipotence, omniscience, and goodness with the existence of evil in the world, whether it is in people doing evil to others or in events—the standard example is earthquakes—causing great suffering to people who do not deserve it. There seems to be no religious explanation that can be offered for a world containing evil. At any rate, no adequate and internally satisfactory religious explanation (or theodicy) has yet been offered.

One path has been to deny that evil exists at all. According to some views, evil isn't a positive thing, it is a privation. What (and all) evil is is the lack of goodness. It is not that God made evil—he just didn't fit in enough good everywhere, he didn't fill up everything with goodness. (These theorists must have thought that if God didn't create evil but merely failed to create enough goodness to constitute goodness enough, then God would be less responsible morally for what evil exists.)

The view that evil is merely a lack of goodness has never seemed very plausible, especially to those who have undergone or suffered it. If goodness is a score above zero, then evil is not zero, not merely a lack of goodness, but a score below zero. It is something in its own right, something negative. One doctrine has seen evil as having a role in the world, to educate us. The world is a big school, what Keats called a vale of soul-making. We undergo evil and gain wisdom through suffering. Thus, a divine being has kindly provided for our education.

That raises a very serious question about why we weren't skipped in certain grades. Why weren't we made prefabricated or made with a more advanced status so that we didn't actually have to go through this complete learning process?

Another traditional doctrine sees evil as stemming from free will. A divine being created human beings with free will, realizing they sometimes would use it to do evil. Yet not all bad things occur to human beings as a result of the action of other human beings; there are natural disasters, earthquakes, storms, etc. The free-will theorist might in principle ascribe these events to the actions of other beings to whom God gave free will—(fallen) angels or demons; thereby, in one way or another, all evil would be accounted for by the actions of free agents.

But if God wanted to create beings with free will, couldn't he have predicted in advance which ones were going to (mis)use their free will by doing bad, and then just have left them out of the

---

* Reprinted with the permission of Simon & Schuster from *The Examined Life: Philosophical Meditations* by *Robert Nozick*. Copyright © 1989 by Robert Nozick. Footnotes omitted.

creation? (A large and delicate literature debates whether this is really a possibility.) Free will is valuable; only autonomous agents have moral virtue when they choose good rather than evil. But a theorist who explains evil via free will has to hold not only that free will is good and worthwhile, but that it is far and away more valuable than the next best alternative. Suppose the next best alternative to free will is beings who have goodness ingrained in them, so that they naturally and inevitably choose the good. Maybe that's not *as* good as beings with free will who face temptation and autonomously choose the good. But how much worse is it? Is the difference so great and important that it would justify having all of the evil and suffering this world contains? Is the extra value gained by having beings with free will, as compared to the next best alternative, enough to outweigh all the evil and suffering that (by hypothesis) free will brings in its wake? To say the least, it is unclear.

Let us recall some other positions taken about this problem. There's the view that the world was created out of preexistent material, not *ex nihilo* (as standardly interpreted). Plato (in the *Timaeus*) takes the view that a divine artificer acts in this way. One Kabbalist view, in the Jewish mystical tradition, holds that there were previous creations; shards left over from these earlier creations interact negatively with the current one. So God really isn't to blame for any evil or defect in creation, because such things are due to the character of the previous material left over. What could you expect given what he had to work with? However, this view places a limitation on the power of God. Even if preexistent material was utilized, why couldn't God have transformed it so as not leave the later residue of evil?

According to Plotinus and the neo-Platonists, a divine being (the One) emanates lower levels. It involuntarily gives forth these levels but doesn't know about them—you might say it secretes them. Since the divine being doesn't know about these lower levels, it doesn't do anything to prevent them. More and more levels are produced, each level giving forth another. When you get far enough away from the divine, you reach the level

that evil exists in. And unfortunately, that is the level *we* inhabit, or at least our material natures do. Whether or not the neo-Platonic view is theoretically appropriate, it does not leave a God worth worshiping. We are presented with a being that doesn't know what it's doing, that involuntarily gives forth things, that doesn't know what is going on. Such a theory might conceivably serve as metaphysics, but it won't do as a religion.

The Gnostics (whose doctrines, along with neo-Platonism, fed into Kabbalah) held that the divinity that created our world wasn't all-perfect and all-wise; it also wasn't the top divinity there was. A God higher than our creator exists who is more distant from our world. Our world was created by a helper or a rebellious divine spirit—at any rate, by somebody who botched the job in some way. This led Gnostic theorists to think their task was to escape this world, moving beyond the reign of the local lord to somehow make contact with the higher all-good divinity.

Dualist views of one kind or another have been frequent in the history of thought. Having more than one God enables you to say that there is one who is all-good—he's just not the one you're dealing with, who is responsible for all of this. But that merely postpones the problem; it pushes the same problem to another level. If the higher God really is a top divinity (let's stop with two, and not worry about three levels or an infinite number), then why does that higher being allow the one who's dominating our world to mess around with it in the way he has? If that topmost divine being is all-good and doesn't want suffering or evil to take place, then why does he allow this lesser divinity to make such a mess over here? (Doesn't he have the power to stop him?) If the higher being created the lesser one, why didn't he create him as one who wouldn't act wrongly? It is clear that Gnostic doctrines only postpone the questions, though no doubt it is satisfying to think for a while that *somewhere* there is a God who is not to be blamed for anything.

One strand of the Jewish tradition, Kabbalah, holds—I follow the descriptions of the great scholar Gershom Scholem—that within the divine being, within *einsof* (translated as without limits), there are attributes, realms (*sefirot*). Evil in the world results, in the standard Kabbalist view, through a tension between various divine attributes. These attributes each are good in themselves. No attribute is bad or evil or blameworthy. Only somehow in their interaction things don't work out so well. It is not an accident, I think, that for the two attributes which didn't work out so well, the Kabbalist writers focused on judgment (*din*) and loving kindness or mercy (*chesed*). These were in tension, they somehow couldn't reach the right balance; because of their tension and imbalance, trouble occurs in the created world.

You might ask: Why couldn't the divine being get them into the right balance? Isn't that an imperfection in the divine being? But between judgment and loving kindness, between justice and mercy, who knows what the right balance should be? These things are always in tension. (In certain views, it's hard to see how there would be room for mercy at all, if there's justice. If mercy means giving people less than they deserve—that is, less punishment that they deserve—then can that be just at all if they do deserve something bad? I ask this not to endorse the incompatibility of mercy and justice but to exhibit the tension, a tension that remains when they are given separate spheres: justice seeking to make right the past, mercy seeking to heal the future.)

Since there always has been a tension in the history of thought between justice and mercy, the Kabbalist thinkers did well to pick out these as the two in imbalance. That wouldn't indicate any flaw in the divine nature; those very attributes themselves, given *their* natures, couldn't fit together easily. Nevertheless, a divine being should contain both.

Still, why didn't the divine being work out the perfect balance? One might hold that there simply is no single right balance, even for God to work out, but the standard Kabbalist theory was that *din*, justice or judgment, overstepped its bounds in the right balance. In the view of Isaac Luria, when, in order to create the world, there is a contraction of the divine being into itself, some of the *din* coagulates or concentrates and is left

out, a little speck that eventually produces whatever bad things we encounter. Later, Nathan of Gaza, a follower of the discredited purported messiah Sabbatai Zevi, claimed that there were different components to God. There was God who was completely self-satisfied, and in no way wanted to create the world—he just wanted to be busy in contemplation, as a good Aristotelian. Another part of God, however, wanted to create the world. It is because the self-satisfied aspect of God resisted the creation of the world that there is evil in it.

All of these Kabbalist theories possess the following virtue: They try to explain evil's existence in the world in terms of some tension, conflict, or interactive process within the divine nature. In this way, they are, as Scholem pointed out, theosophical views in that they talk about the internal nature and life—"psyche" isn't quite right—and ongoing existence of a divine being. Within this realm, they find much room to maneuver, utilizing mystical experiences and interpretations, often esoteric, of traditional texts. Such theories are especially profound.

With their expulsion from Spain in 1492, the Jewish people underwent an enormous trauma. The Kabbalist picture of the *Shechinah* (an aspect of the divine presence) as displaced, in exile and having to return, mirrored the earthly situation of the Jewish people in exile from Jerusalem and their holy land. When suffering of the most traumatic sort beset the Jewish people on earth, the Kabbalists held that everything was not harmonious in the divine realm either. (A large part of Kabbalah's appeal to the Jewish people then, Scholem maintains, was due to this parallelism.) Unlike the standard views wherein God for his own reasons has created evil here (he wanted to create beings with free will or whatever) and is just whistling along happily, the Kabbalists said there was trouble up there as well. There was a parallel between the human realm, in which bad things were happening, and events in the divine realm, which didn't leave that realm untouched. A divine trauma corresponded to the exile of the Jewish people; an aspect of God was in exile and not in its proper place. It was thought that the

Jewish people had a particular function to perform, that by so doing they could help the divine *Shechinah* return to its proper place. We shall return to some features of the Kabbalist view later.

Leibniz's view of the problem of evil is best known from Voltaire's satire in *Candide*. Leibniz said that God created the best of all possible worlds. Voltaire presents us with a character encountering one disaster after another and saying, ridiculously, "Yes, it is the best of all possible worlds." How could somebody as smart as Leibniz, the coinventor of calculus, say something as dumb as what Voltaire attributes to him? (Recall the joke: The optimist thinks this is the best of all possible worlds and the pessimist agrees.)

What did Leibniz actually mean? Leibniz thought that God was going to create the most perfect of the possible worlds. The possible worlds are those that don't involve a contradiction; a world in which you're both reading now and not reading right now is not a possible world. Within the realm of logical possibility, God picked, according to Leibniz, the best and most perfect—but best and most perfect in what respect?

Leibniz's idea of the perfection of the world was one whereby a simple set of principles and laws gave rise to the wealth of the world's detail. The most perfect world would have the greatest diversity given rise to in the simplest possible way—that is, would have the greatest organic unity. In setting up a world you will want simple, natural laws, yet through their operation, occasionally, there will be earthquakes and natural accidents, sometimes with people wandering into them. However, God could have avoided that. He could have sprinkled in miracles—like raisins in a raisin cake—that would have intervened at just the right moments. (Maimonides discusses whether miracles are built in, preprogrammed, or popped in later.) Each disaster is avoided by a separate little wrinkle, if not by a miracle then by a separate little complication in the original natural laws. Although that could have been done, in Leibniz's view it would have resulted in a highly imperfect and unaesthetic world. A raisin-filled world would not have been perfect or desirable. So in Leibniz's view, in creation God was

creating the most perfect of all possible worlds; he—Leibniz and God both—viewed as best a world in which the greatest wealth and variety of facts (including a lot of good things) would be given rise to in a very simple way.

Clearly, this is not the notion Voltaire satirized. Still, we might wonder why we should worship a divine being who cares only about so aesthetic a perfection. If bad things occur, morally bad things, that being won't care about them at all except insofar as they mar the world's aesthetic perfection. (He might care to this extent: If two worlds were tied in having the most aesthetic perfection, he would prefer and pick the one that causes the least suffering for us.)

However, we can modify Leibniz's view to involve (as the economists say) trade-offs. In this altered view, God does not create the most perfect of all possible worlds (the one giving rise to the greatest diversity in the simplest possible way), but he creates the seventeenth most perfect of all the possible worlds. He sacrifices some metaphysical perfection in order to alleviate a large amount of suffering that otherwise would go on. Such a God cares about us; he hasn't just chosen that most perfect world growing out of the simplest possible laws. He has thrown in a few raisins here and there, complicating things. To be sure, he has not created the morally best world for us. This would involve very many little miracles and raisins dropped in, and that world, the 1695th most perfect, is *too* unaesthetic and imperfect for him. Yet he hasn't created the best world from his point of view, either. He has made some sacrifices, creating a world lower on his hierarchy of perfection in order to enhance moral goodness here. Such a being shouldn't be scorned for not caring at all about human welfare—he's made important sacrifices for our sake, although he doesn't care about it solely. However, I do not believe that even this modified Leibnizean view can provide an adequate religious explanation for the existence of evil, for a reason I shall come to soon.

Since the time of Leibniz, many philosophers have discussed possible worlds, even if not always the best. One recent philosopher, George

Schlesinger, has claimed there is no such thing as the best of all possible worlds. The only thing that could be best would be a world of infinite value, but the only thing that has infinite value is a divine being, God. (God, for reasons we needn't go into now, isn't going to create another being with infinite value just like himself.) So all God can do in creating a world is to create one of finite value.

But why does God want to create a world anyway? (We are aware of the warnings that one shouldn't speculate about certain things, and how those people who do will realize it would have been better had they not been born.) Usually theological discussions of creation are carried on apart from discussions of evil. People assume there are separate questions: Why create a world? Why create one with evil in it? But perhaps, if we understood the reasons for creation, why a perfect divine being would create any world at all rather than simply resting content all by itself, then we would understand why this world has the character it does, including evil.

God doesn't want to create a world to add to his or her own value (being already perfectly self-satisfied and infinitely valuable) or out of need (though the Jewish tradition often describes functions that individual human beings, or the Jewish people as a whole, can perform). A divine being is trying not to add to the total value there is—that's already infinite due to God's own presence—but to create other value for its own sake, and any created world can only have finite value.

God, in creating the world, is bringing about a certain magnitude of value, a finite magnitude. It's as if God is picking a number. God picks a number—suppose, 1,000,563—and that's the amount of value, merit, and goodness in the world. Then we ask God, "Why didn't you pick a higher number?" He asks what number he should have picked. We say, "Why not 5,000,222?" He says, "If I had picked that one, you'd say, 'Why didn't you pick a higher number?' Given that a world I create can't have infinite value, it will be of finite value. So any world I created would be criticizable in the same way for not being better." In theory, there's no best of all possible worlds—

just as there's no highest positive integer. For any world that God creates, there could always be a better one. God had to pick some world or other if he was going to create a world, and he picked this one.

Thus, Schlesinger's reply to the problem of evil asks (it feels like a technical trick): What are we complaining about? Why are we complaining about this world, asking why God didn't make it better, why there is evil in it? For any world he would have created, wouldn't we have said the same thing?

We want to reply that we wouldn't, because there is one natural line we can draw and ask why God didn't at least make the world better than that. We could draw a line at the existence of evil. Maybe that world without evil isn't as splendiferous a world as one can imagine; maybe there's no limit to how splendiferous a world can be. (Maybe if God really was making it splendiferous, the world wouldn't include us at all!) But at least God could have created a world without all the immense pain and suffering that now exist.

There is one line, marked by the existence of evil, yet the world is below that line in its score and value. Why didn't God cross that line at least? The counterreply to this, in Schlesinger's line of argument, is that there are an indefinite number of lines. We are noticing just one line, involving no evil, and asking why God didn't cross that line. But he has crossed a lot of other lines. There are many disastrous ways the world could have been that it isn't—it wasn't created that way. He did cross those lines. If he also had crossed this line (involving no evil) we would notice another line up ahead and ask why he didn't cross that one. The argument now has moved one level up, only this time with lines that can be drawn, instead of varying the amount of value to creation.

Someone might ask why God didn't at least prevent enormous magnitudes of evil. The answer similarly might be that he *did* prevent the most enormous magnitudes; for example, perhaps he has acted to avoid events and wars that would have killed 100,000,000 people. Whatever are the greatest of the evils remaining after God eliminated the most enormous will seem enormous to us since they are at the top of the scale with which we actually are acquainted; so we will, mistakenly, then ask why God didn't at least remove the most enormous evils. He did.

Perhaps this theory satisfies the intellectual criteria we would have listed, at first, in thinking about a satisfactory solution to the problem of evil. We might only have wanted something that would logically reconcile divine omniscience, omnipotence, and goodness with the existence of evil in the world. We might have thought any theory that reconciled these would be a satisfactory solution. Except that this one isn't.

One condition to impose on an adequate religious view of the existence of evil is that it provide something to say to somebody who is actually undergoing suffering or pain or evil. That doesn't mean that what is said would necessarily have to comfort the sufferer. Perhaps the true story isn't a comforting one. But it cannot be something to make one shrink in embarrassment. What the theory we have considered provides is not a possible, not a decent thing to say to somebody.

Another view of the existence of evil has the same defect, yet is worth describing. Consider the reason why God wants to create a world at all, rather than continuing alone in whatever situation he is in. Is this a reason for creating just *one* world? Recall the stories of a sequence of creations that were inadequate, and also the science fiction themes of parallel noninteracting universes.

God isn't going to create a world in order to increase his own value or goodness, or whatever—that's already infinite. Neither is the total amount of value there is going to be increased; adding a finite amount to an already infinite amount doesn't make that any bigger. The reason has to be to create that world, of finite value, for its own sake and value. But, then, why create just *one*? Why not create many worlds, many noninteracting universes?

If a divine being were going to do that, what would these worlds be like? Would he create the same one with the same details over and over and over again? Maybe there's no point to that, or maybe he would do so five times or twelve times or a million times. Still, adding a different world

also would introduce some variety, some value of its own, without subtracting from what already had been created. Perhaps, then, a divine being would create all worlds of net positive value. (A world has net positive value if when that world's amount of goodness or value or whatever is assessed and its amount of badness is subtracted, then the result is still a plus.) A world would get created if that world's existing was better than its not existing. Thus, we can imagine a divine being setting out to create multiple universes, all of which are valuable.

You say you see a lot of defects over here in this universe, and ask why God didn't make the universe better. He did make a better one; he made another one that was better, in just the ways you are imagining. He made that one *and* he made this one too. "Well, why didn't he make *only* that one?" Would it have been better if he had made only that one, instead of both that one plus this one? No, not if this one is worth existing also. "But why didn't he put me in that one rather than this one?" Of course, anybody he placed in this one would ask the same question. (Moreover, this universe or you yourself may be so structured that you could exist only in it or in similar ones.)

In this picture, there is a good, divine being that is creating all worlds of net positive value, and our world, although it contains some evil, is one of those. It is better that our world exist than that it not, and the answer to the question of why a good God didn't make the world better is that he did make a better world *also*. He created all possible good worlds, not only the best of all possible worlds (as Leibniz thought), not only any *one* world. He created a multitude of possible (good) worlds. Indeed, if he created an infinite number, then this might be his route to a creation of infinite value. For though the value of each individual created world is finite (and positive), the infinite summation of these finite values can itself be infinite.

While this theory, perhaps, is somewhat easier to present to someone who suffers evil, it is not clear that it ascribes a morally acceptable pattern of behavior to the deity. Because a world is of net positive value, is it automatically all right and morally permissible to create it? Consider how the comparable principle applies to creating children. Suppose there were a couple who otherwise didn't want to have a child but thought it would be handy to have a little servant around the house. They think, "We otherwise wouldn't create this child, being busy with careers or amusements, but if we had the child and then kept it semi-enslaved to serve us, even then its existence would be of net positive value. Nobody could criticize us for bringing it into existence, for it would be better off living, even that way, than not existing at all. So it's perfectly all right to have that child and keep it permanently as a servant. We are just following the policy of creating something so long as its existence is more valuable than not."

But clearly, it is not all right for the couple to have the child that way. Whatever explanation we ultimately give of why not, they cannot bring a child into such an existence and then repel criticism by saying, "But otherwise we wouldn't have made it exist at all. Its existence has net positive value, so what is it complaining about?" Once the child exists, it has a certain moral status. Others, including the parents, cannot just treat it any way they want compatible with its existence being a net plus.

Choices that affect the size of future populations raise these issues in an acute form. And moral theorists do not find it easy to delineate the correct moral principles to apply there. Even if each person in the growing population of India thinks his or her life better than not existing at all, we believe it would be better for the population there to be smaller, with fewer people living better. We don't think the total amount of happiness should be maximized if that would involve continuing to add massive numbers of people who each are barely positively happy or barely better off existing rather than not. That would lower the average happiness by too much. Yet neither do we think a situation desirable merely because the average happiness is at a maximum—that might occur because only one or two people existed at all, *extremely* happy people!

Parallel to issues about bringing new people, thus far nonexistent, into the world are issues (this time faced by a deity) about creating new universes. The question, How good does a universe have to be to make it worth creating? is parallel to the question, What does a person's life have to be like for us to think beforehand that it would be better if that person were here? (Afterward, though, the question is different; we won't say of each person outside the pale of the first answer that it would be better if that particular person weren't here.)

The topics are different, one involving people thinking about creating new people, the other involving a divine being thinking about creating universes, yet the problems have a similar structure. It's very difficult to figure out what the appropriate moral principles should be for such situations. But it seems the following is *not* an acceptable principle: It is always morally permissible to create something when its existence is of net positive value. So we cannot solve the problem of evil by saying that God created all universes of net positive value, and ours, though it contains much evil, is one of those.

Perhaps it would be acceptable, though, to create all universes that have a net value greater than a certain significantly large quantity. It is not sufficient merely if the net value of a universe is greater than zero; it must also be a certain substantial level above zero. It is difficult to know exactly what that threshold quantity should be. But plausibly our universe meets this more stringent condition and scores above the cutoff quantity.

When we're not sure what principles should govern choices about population numbers, can we do moral philosophy by turning to theology? To find the right population policy, should we formulate a general moral principle such that if God were following it in creating universes, he would have created this one? Can we test a moral principle for a structurally parallel realm by seeing whether it's a principle that God could have followed in creating our world? That would give religion a role in ethical theory, based upon the religious premise that God acted acceptably in creating this universe. An ethical theory then could be tested by whether it had this consequence, and only those passing this test would be candidates for use in deciding other hard moral questions.

Can we solve the problem of evil, then, by saying that God created all possible worlds of very significant net positive value, and ours is one of those? (Why didn't he create a world that was better? He did that too.) It seems to me that this too would be hard to say to people who are undergoing suffering. ("This is one of a basketful of worlds that God created. Don't complain that he didn't make a better one. He did. He created a lot of better ones, and some worse ones as well. You and your suffering are just somewhere along the line.") We might consider, too, the view that God creates not all worlds whose *value* is above a certain threshold, but rather all worlds whose *reality* is. That might, of course, leave more room for evil to enter in, but it is not clear whether it would leave God a fit object of our worship.

Other ethical distinctions might be used to get some leeway here: There is the distinction between doing something and letting it happen (or not preventing it); and the distinction between trying to maximize the best end result and just following certain moral restrictions. Someone might say that God isn't really obligated to maximize and create the best of all possible worlds or the best universe for us; so long as he doesn't *do* anything too terrible, and refrains from various things, then he's off the moral hook, even if he *allows* certain bad things to happen. However, the distinction between making something happen and merely standing by isn't a clear one when the Creator of the whole universe is involved.

What criteria then, must any satisfactory answer to the problem of evil meet? First, the obvious one that it must somehow reconcile those three attributes of God—omniscience, omnipotence, and goodness—with the existence of evil in the world. An answer has to intellectually fit those things together.

Second, the answer has to be something we can actually utter and bring ourselves to say to somebody who is undergoing suffering, or who has a loved one who is, or who has experienced and knows of suffering in the world.

I feel less certain about the third criterion, which involves a psychological speculation. It seems to me that we actually won't find a religious explanation satisfying unless something analogous to it also would serve to answer the more personal question of why our parents, who once seemed to us omnipotent, weren't better to us or even perfect. (I am not claiming that religious beliefs are merely family life projected large.) An answer is being sought, I think, that would satisfy at that level as well.

Fourth—and here I draw from the Kabbalist tradition—the explanation of evil should not leave a divine being untouched. It won't do to say that he or she is just proceeding along merrily doing what's best (maximizing some good function, creating the best of all possible worlds, giving us free will, or whatever), and it so happens that a consequence of its doing what's best is that things are sometimes pretty terrible for us down here. God cannot just proceed merrily along. For an explanation to be satisfying, at least concerning the traumatic evils that occur, it has to in some way show that flaw reflected up in the divine realm.

This condition is not satisfied by Leibniz's view that God creates the best of all possible worlds, or by various gimmicky modifications such as the view that God creates not just one universe but *all* the sufficiently good universes, including this one (hence jauntily replying to the question of why he didn't create a better one: He did that too). These theories all leave the divine being too detached from our plight and situation.

Fifth, a satisfactory explanation must talk about a divine being worth worshiping, a divine being that you can have a religion about. (Plotinus's theory that this realm is a lower one somehow emanated by a God that doesn't even know of it fails this test.) It cannot just be a detached metaphysical theory. Not only must God not be detached from what's happening here, the explanation must leave us attached to God in certain sorts of ways, not simply created by him. The "object relations" have to work well in both directions.

One other condition on an answer to the problem of evil is thrust upon us by the Holocaust. In theory, every and any evil, however slight—the suffering of one child—raises the theological question of why an all-powerful, all-knowing, and good God allows it. However, although the intellectual problem is the same when the evil has the traumatic magnitude of the Holocaust, the emotional problem is not. That raises a special problem.

It is, moreover, especially a problem for Jewish tradition, which holds that the Jewish people stand in a special relationship with the divine being. It is not enough for Jewish theology somehow to offer some story or explanation that reconciles a divine being with the existence of evil; it is this particular stupendous evil to the Jewish people that must be fitted within a religious picture. Some have wondered whether the creation of the State of Israel, so close in time afterward, might not redeem all, but (although these are not easy matters to speak of) this does not seem an acceptable answer, nor has it seemed so to Holocaust survivors living in Israel.

The Jewish theology of the future, I think, will have to do for the Holocaust what Kabbalah did for the Expulsion from Spain, where the situation of the *Shechinah* in exile mirrored and was mirrored by the situation of the Jewish people.

The Holocaust constitutes some kind of rift in the universe. This must be echoed by some rift in the divine life or realm. There must be some kind of trauma there as well. God is not left untouched.

We can mention three possibilities which, though not completely satisfactory, begin to get the flavor of the kind of explanation that is needed. Since the Holocaust *almost* ended the existence of the Jewish people, a theological view might hold that it corresponds to an event of that magnitude in God, to something that almost ended the divine existence. For instance—and I don't mean to say something offensive—an attempt at self-destruction on the part of God.

Why would something like that happen? Could something like that happen? Could the divine being choose to end its own existence? Does it have the power to do that? In the philosophical literature there is a somewhat gimmicky question known as the paradox of omnipotence: Could God create a stone so heavy that God could not lift it? If God couldn't create the stone, then there's something he or she couldn't do, so God isn't omnipotent. If God could create that stone, then there's something else God cannot do, namely, lift it. In either case, then, it seems that God is not omnipotent. Since the problem is a gimmicky one, I won't stop here to survey the attempts that have been made to work it through.

It is not very clear whether a divine being could end its own omnipotent powers. (I don't mean to conclude quickly—*à la* the paradox of omnipotence—that if it can't then it's not omnipotent.) As for those traits we think God has, could God stop having them? Could God stop being omnipotent? Could God stop existing, if he or she chose? Not only isn't the answer clear to us, it also might not be clear to the divine being himself or herself. Don't just *define* the divine being as omniscient; there might be certain facts about the limits of its own powers at that level that it doesn't know. Whether it could end its whole existence or not might be the last thing it didn't know about itself. It might be something, though, that it had to know, or to attempt, in order to accomplish some other task.

An attempt by God to end his own existence, then, is not excluded by the very concept of God, and it does have the right order of magnitude to correspond to an unparalleled rift in our universe. Although it has the right magnitude, nevertheless this theory is inadequate. If God's attempt at self-destruction is an experiment, done from intellectual curiosity about his own possible limits, then the event so motivated, however momentous, is not of the right sort to parallel the Holocaust, which fell upon the Jewish people involuntarily. Perhaps some other egodystonic motive might lead God to attempt self-destruction, but I have nothing appropriate to suggest.

Here is a second attempt, also inadequate. God, as traditionally conceived, has infinite power to do anything he chooses; he is omniscient and so knows every fact that there is and every fact that there will be. But although God has infinite knowledge of all truths, perhaps he doesn't have infinite wisdom. Wisdom is another kind of thing, not the same as (ordinary) knowledge. Think of the kinds of situations where people say, "If you haven't been in a war, you don't really know what it's like." You can read about it, you can see films, you can have it described to you, but there's still something that you don't know. There's a kind of knowledge you don't have, experiential knowledge, what the philosophical tradition sometimes calls "knowledge by acquaintance."

Are there some things which God can know only by undergoing them himself (or herself) or by experiencing what his creations undergo? Wisdom, the Greeks held, might be attainable only by undergoing certain experiences of suffering. Might a divine being need to gain wisdom in a similar way? In gaining this experience, God wouldn't be left untouched; the sufferings people experience here would in some way also be affecting the divine being. He too is undergoing these experiences, to gain a kind of knowledge not obtainable in any other way, knowledge he might need for some other important task. Does it make a divine being imperfect if it doesn't start out all-wise? Maybe it's better for a divine being to gain wisdom than to start out with it fully; maybe it's better for it to earn wisdom, in a certain way.

A third view would hold that God created (not man but) the world in his own image as a material representation of himself, perhaps as an act of self-expression. (Is the whole of the material world a representation of the divine being's emotions; are we living in, and part of, God's emotional life?) Without his goodness being diminished, God might have subsidiary parts whose tendency goes against the whole but which are well-controlled, just as good men can have under control passions or unconscious desires that are unexpressed or expressed only in acceptable ways. What then will be the character of a universe created in this God's image? This vast universe will contain small dissonant parts which do not prevent it from being excellent overall. God does not attempt, in this third view, to create the most perfect possible world but rather to create a world in his own image. (Or perhaps he creates many such worlds, all differently apt representations of himself.) Although the small parts God keeps under control do not make him imperfect, their representation in this universe does constitute a (moral) imperfection here. This universe is not a perfect likeness; it is only one possible image of God, capturing many but not all salient aspects. The mapping that makes our universe a representation of God does not preserve perfection. (Nonetheless, perhaps we can feel exalted in contributing to a representation of God, being a dab in his portrait, a vowel in his name.)

This third view does correlate something within the divine realm to evil here. However, that something may not be sufficiently upsetting there. A satisfying solution to the problem of evil, it seems, must place us in a universe where the image of the representational mapping preserves (but doesn't augment) upsettingness. Moreover, what is to be preserved is how upset *we* feel—the universe as a whole may not be terribly upset at the evil within it. (At this point, though, hasn't our demand for a satisfying solution to the problem of evil become too humanocentric?)

These three alternatives, concerning self-destruction, wisdom, and creation of the world in God's image, are not satisfactory theories of the internal life and motivation of the divine being. The concept of God, we already have seen, is not (restricted to) the most perfect possible being. Earlier we formulated the concept as: the most perfect actual being, far superior to the next most perfect, who also stands in a most significant relation to this world (such as being its creator). A slightly different definition would replace the notion of "most perfect" by "most real." God would then be the most real actual being, whose reality far surpasses that of the next most real being, who stands in a most significant relation to this world, etc. Apparent defects in God's perfection or goodness might then contribute to his greater *reality* overall. In any case, the next task of theology (especially of a Jewish theology) is to dare to speculate, as the Kabbalists did before, about a divine being's internal existence. A daring theory is needed to drive issues about evil deep within the divine realm or nature in some way, leaving it deeply affected yet not itself evil.

Suggestions for Further Reading

Adams, Marilyn McCord, and Adams, Robert Merrihew, eds. *The Problem of Evil.* Oxford, England: Oxford University Press, 1990.

Allen, Diogenes. "Natural Evil and the Love of God." *Religious Studies* 16 (1980), 439–456.

Alston, William. "The Inductive Argument from Evil and the Human Cognitive Condition." *Philosophical Perspectives* 5 (1991), 29–67.

Andre, Shane. "The Problem of Evil and the Paradox of Friendly Atheism." *International Journal for Philosophy of Religion* 17 (1985), 209–216.

Betty, L. Stafford. "Making Sense of Animal Pain: An Environmental Theodicy." *Faith and Philosophy* 9 (1992), 65–82.

Bilimoria, Purushottama. "Duhkha & Karma: The Problem of Evil," *Sophia* 34 (1995), 92–119.

Bowker, John. *Problems of Suffering in Religions of the World.* Cambridge, England: Cambridge University Press, 1970.

Buber, Martin. *Good and Evil.* New York: Charles Scribner's Sons, 1952.

Christlieb, Terry. "Which Theisms Face an Evidential Problem of Evil?" *Faith and Philosophy* 9 (1992), 45–64.

Davis, Stephen T. "A Defense of the Free Will Defense." *Religious Studies* 8 (1972), 335–343.

Fachenheim, Emil L. "The Holocaust and Philosophy." *Journal of Philosophy* 82 (1985), 505–514.

Frankenberry, Nancy. "Some Problems in Process Theodicy." *Religious Studies* 17 (1981), 179–197.

Geach, Peter. *Providence and Evil.* Cambridge, England: Cambridge University Press, 1977.

Griffin, David R. *Evil Revisited: Responses and Reconsiderations.* Albany, NY: State University of New York Press, 1991.

————. *God, Power, and Evil: A Process Theodicy.* Philadelphia: Westminster Press, 1976.

Halberstram, Joshua. "Philosophy and the Holocaust." *Metaphilosophy* 12 (1981), 277–283.

Herman, Arthur L. *The Problem of Evil and Indian Thought.* Delhi: Motilal Banarsidass, 1976.

Hick, John. *Evil and the God of Love.* London: Macmillan, 1966.

Howard-Snyder, Daniel, ed. *The Evidential Argument from Evil.* Bloomington, IN: Indiana University Press, 1996.

Hsu, Sung-peng. "Lao Tzu's Conception of Evil." *Philosophy East and West* 26 (1976), 301–316.

Jonas, Hans. "The Concept of God After Auschwitz: A Jewish Voice." In *Mortality and Morality: A Search for the Good After Auschwitz,* edited by Lawrence Vogel. Evanston, IL: Northwestern University Press, 1996, pp. 131–143.

Kekes, John. *Facing Evil.* Princeton, NJ: Princeton University Press, 1990.

Mackie, J. L. "Omnipotence." *Sophia* 1 (July 1962), 13–25.

Madden, Edward, and Hare, Peter. *Evil and the Concept of God.* Springfield, IL: Charles C. Thomas, 1968.

Malkani, G. R. "The Rationale of the Law of Karma." *The Philosophical Quarterly* (India) 37 (1965), 257–266.

Matilal, Bimal Krishna. *Logical and Ethical Issues of Religious Belief.* Calcutta: University of Calcutta, 1982.

Mbiti, John S. *African Religion and Philosophy.* Garden City, NY: Doubleday, 1969.

Perrett, Roy W. "Karma and the Problem of Suffering." *Sophia* 24 (April 1985), 54–72.

Peterson, Michael L., ed. *The Problem of Evil: Selected Readings.* Notre Dame, IN: University of Notre Dame Press, 1993.

Plantinga, Alvin. *God, Freedom, and Evil.* Grand Rapids, MI: Eerdmans, 1977.

Pradhan, Sudhir Chandra. "The Problem of Evil and Human Freedom." *Indian Philosophical Quarterly* 13 (1986), 15–24.

Reichenbach, Bruce R. *Evil and a Good God.* New York: Fordham Univeristy Press, 1982.

Rosenberg, Alan, and Myers, Gerald, eds. *Echoes from the Holocaust: Philosophical Reflections on a Dark Time.* Philadelphia: Temple University Press, 1988.

Roth, John K. *A Consuming Fire: Encounters with Elie Wiesel and the Holocaust.* Atlanta, GA: Knox Press, 1979.

Rubenstein, Richard L. *After Auschwitz: Radical Theology and Contemporary Judaism.* New York: Bobbs-Merrill, 1966.

Rubenstein, Richard L., and Roth, John K. *Approaches to Auschwitz: The Holocaust and Its Legacy.* Louisville, KY: John Knox Press, 1994.

Schlesinger, George. "The Problem of Evil and the Problem of Suffering." *American Philosophical Quarterly* 1 (1964), 244–247.

Schloegl, Irmgard. "Suffering in Zen Buddhism." *Theoria to Theory* 11 (1977), 217–227.

Sharma, R. P. "The Problem of Evil in Buddhism." *Journal of Dharma* 2 (1977), 307–311.

Sharma, Ursala. "Theodicy and the Doctrine of Karma." *Man* 8 (1973), 347–364.

Swinburne, Richard. "The Problem of Evil." In *The Existence of God.* Oxford, England: Clarendon Press, 1979.

Urban, Linwood, and Walton, Douglas N., eds. *The Power of God: Readings on Omnipotence and Evil.* New York: Oxford University Press, 1978.

Wadia, A.R., "Philosophical Implications of the Doctrine of Karma." *Philosophy East and West* 15 (April 1965), 145–152.

Wykstra, Stephen J. "The Humean Obstacle to Evidential Arguments from Suffering: On Avoiding the Evils of 'Appearance.'" *International Journal of Philosophy of Religion* 16 (1984), 73–94.

CHAPTER 6

How Are Religion and Morality Related?

Introduction

THE RELATIONSHIP BETWEEN RELIGION and morality is complex. On one level, we might characterize it as psychological. People find religious beliefs and practices morally inspiring. This inspiration can range from the morally admirable (the saint sacrificing her own self-interest to help others) to the morally objectionable (the person who does what is right only because he fears going to hell). Religion can motivate people to do what is right—sometimes for all the right reasons, and sometimes for all the wrong reasons.

On another level, we might think of this relationship sociologically. The institutional structures and ritual practices can and do perform the social function of reinforcing and encouraging conventional morality and behavior that is conducive to community solidarity. Participating in the public rituals (Christmas, the Hajj, Day of Atonement, sacrifices, devotion to Krishna)—thus fosters a sense of belonging to a moral community—a community of like-minded people who have mutual obligations.

We might think also of the relationship between religion and morality as historical. For example, in much of Asia, Confucian, Buddhist, and Hindu teachings have shaped the ethos, behavior, and values of many generations. Likewise, Judaism and Christianity have taught the Ten Commandments as basic moral values to many generations of people in the West. Many of us learn our first moral lessons from religious sources.

The relationship between religion and morality can also be thought of in logical and philosophical terms. There may be some type of logical connection such that morality can never be fully autonomous from religious belief. A purely secular morality, based on human reasoning guided by rational and philosophical principles independent of religious considerations, is simply not possible. This does not mean (as some assert) that atheists cannot do what is morally right. Rather it means that atheists are simply mistaken in thinking that their moral values are entirely independent of religion. This issue, however, is complicated enormously when we recall that religion may be nontheistic. Can even the atheistic be religious?

Some have claimed that such a towering and influential religious figure as Confucius was an atheist in the broad sense of the term, because he believed in no power greater than the universe or nature. Whether this is true is a matter of scholarly debate. However, there can be no doubt that Confucius was a moral genius of great insight and that he saw religious rituals and rites as vitally important to social well-being and stability.

Even an atheist such as the German philosopher Nietzsche was deeply concerned with matters of morality. For Nietzsche, genuine morality becomes possible only when humanity is freed from the illusion of some supernatural source of goodness. True morality must stem from humans assuming responsibility for their own destiny.

The complex relationship between theistic religion and morality and a variety of issues and arguments surrounding this relationship emerge when we consider the validity of the divine command theory of ethics. According to this theory, moral goodness is dependent on what God wills. However, as we shall shortly see, this is a problematic claim.

In the last two selections, we turn to political and social issues that revolve around the role religion plays in helping the oppressed and exploited find liberation from their suffering. Most people in this world are not privileged. They do not enjoy wealth, power, status, or education. They have little chance for a secure future. They live off garbage and, at night, huddle under cardboard boxes if they are lucky. What role does religion play in either keeping them oppressed and wretched or empowering them to take the action necessary for liberation from a life of misery?

6.1   Analects

We mentioned Confucius or Master K'ung (551–479 B.C.E.) in Section 2 of Chapter 5. One of the great religious traditions of China—Confucianism—bears his name, yet scholars dispute his own attitude toward religious matters. Some argue that Confucius should be interpreted as primarily concerned with moral, political, and social issues. Others argue that religion was important to him, as evidenced by his teachings about *li.*

Although *li* is often translated as "ceremony," its meaning is quite broad. It can refer to rites, good manners, customs, etiquette, and sacrifices to the ancestors. Some translate it as "propriety." The cultivated Confucian gentleman is carefully trained in the actions, words, music, and dance of sacred and artistic performances that form a part of *li. Li* also refers to the *efficacy* of sacred rites in transforming human relationships from brutish and uncivil to cultured and civilized.

Some critics of Confucius have accused him of confusing the ritualistic aspects of life with the moral. However, Confucius used the word *yi,* or "fitting," to talk about conduct that is appropriate to one's status (such as ruler and subject or mother and daughter), and he distinguished *yi* from *li.* Central to morality (or what is "fitting") is the idea of *jen,* which is commonly translated as "benevolence," "humanity," or "kind-heartedness." Benevolence is unselfish concern for the other person, and Confucius understood it, in part, in terms similar to what the West has come to know as the Golden Rule. Confucius formulated the principle of *shu* (reciprocity) in response to a question about whether there was a single word that one could act on all one's life.

"Wouldn't it be likening-to-oneself (*shu*)? What you do not yourself desire, do not do to others." Whereas *shu* appears to emphasize only the negative side of the Golden Rule, another principle *chung* (doing one's best for others) emphasizes the positive.

How are these moral insights related to religion? We can see how ritual behavior can reinforce and instruct in moral matters, but what about gods or God or spirits, or the ancestors, or supernatural beings in general? How important are they to morality? Some have portrayed Confucius as skeptical when it comes to belief in the existence of supernatural beings. Religious rites are important because they bring about political, social, and moral harmony, but there is no divine reality that is pleased by the sacrifices and bestows blessings on humans in response. I think it is misleading to paint Confucius as a skeptic in this matter. It is probably more accurate to say that he believed we should not be diverted from human concerns by matters either that do not concern us or that we cannot comprehend. It mattered little to him whether sacred power stems from some objective supernatural realm. We can know that sacred power is created by the performance of sacred rites and correct moral action. What more do we need to know?

The following selections come from *Analects*—sayings and stories attributed to Confucius by his students. It is difficult to know how much of this material records the words of Confucius, but much of it definitely does represent the spirit of his thought.

Reading Questions

1. What is the function of funeral rites, sacrifices, and rites of decorum?
2. How does Confucius characterize the person of virtue?
3. How do *superior* and *inferior* persons differ?
4. How can one achieve the "quality of humanity" (*jen*)?
5. What is the principle of reciprocity? Do you think it can "serve as a lasting principle for the conduct of one's whole life"? Why or why not?
6. From what you have read, do you think there is a connection between religion and morality for Confucius? Why or why not? If you think there is, what is that connection?

Analects*

CONFUCIUS

Book I

Confucius said: "Isn't it a pleasure to learn and then constantly carry into practice what has been learned? Isn't it a delight to have friends coming from afar, who cherish the same ideals and follow the same path? Isn't such a man one of established virtue as does not feel resentful even when others do not understand him?"

Youzi said: "There are few who have faith in filial and fraternal duties but should be fond of going against their superiors; there have been none who

*From *Confucius: The Analects of Confucius,* translated by Lao An. Jinan, China: Shandong Friendship Press, 1992. Reprinted by permission.

are not fond of going against their superiors but should be fond of standing up in rebellion. The superior man always tries to do what is radical; that being achieved, the highest principle will naturally be brought forth. So filial piety and respect and love for one's elder brothers are the fundamental principles of humanity, aren't they?"

Confucius said: "Those who are capable of sweet words and fine appearances are rarely men of true virtue."

Zengzi said: "Every day I make several self-examinations on the following points: whether I have or not exerted my utmost in helping others; whether I have or not been honest and sincere in intercourse with friends; whether I have or not practiced the instructions of my teacher." . . .

Confucius said: "The young people should be filial to parents at home and polite and respectful to their elders in society. They should be guarded in speech and true in words. While constantly keeping on good terms with all, they should foster closer ties with kindhearted men. With all this performed, if they still have energy to spare, they should engage themselves in studying the literature handed down from the ancients." . . .

Confucius said: "Even a man of virtue cannot stand on his dignity if he does not keep gravity in his conduct. Such a flaw can be overcome through learning. Focus your personal cultivation on the two principal virtues: faithfulness and truthfulness. Do not associate with those who are not equal to yourself. When you have made mistakes, be bold enough to correct them."

Zengzi said: "Through carefully performing funeral rites to parents and reverently offering sacrifices to remote ancestors, popular feelings can be molded into a higher moral stature of honesty, sincerity and faithfulness." . . .

Confucius said: "Let a man observe his father's aspirations when his father is alive, and study his father's concrete conduct when his father is dead. If a man can for long adhere to the correct principles formerly advocated by his father, he may be considered a filial son."

Youzi said: "The precious role that rites and the rules of decorum can play is that they can harmonize human relations. That has been the most

valuable experience drawn by the ancient sagacious kings in governing their states, who, in dealing with both their major and minor assignments, used to take that as their starting point. However, it is not advisable in all cases, for, without being regulated with certain rules of decorum, harmony for harmony's sake is not always practical."

Youzi said: "Commitments are honored only when they are in keeping with moral norms, while courtesy and politeness prevent shame and disgrace only when they are in keeping with the rules of decorum. Make friends with those who deserve your friendship and you will find a reliable backing."

Confucius said: "A man of virtue does not insist on gratifying his appetite in eating, nor does he indulge himself in seeking comforts in dwelling. He is diligent in work and careful in speech and associates with worthy men so as to follow their examples. Such a man may well be said as being eager to learn."

Zigong asked: "What would you say of a man who is poor but never flatters, and who is rich but is never arrogant?" Confucius said: "That is fairly good. But he is not yet as good as one who is poor but attaches great importance to moral cultivation, and who is rich but observes strict rules of decorum in his conduct." . . .

Confucius said: "I do not worry about people not knowing me; I am worrying that I myself do not know others."

Book II

Confucius said: "A sovereign who exercises government on moral principles may be likened to the polestar, which holds its place while all the lesser stars revolve around it." . . .

Confucius said: "Lead the people by laws and regulate them by penalties, and the people will try to avoid offenses and punishments, but will have no sense of shame; lead the people on moral principles and educate them with the rules of decorum, and the people will not only have a sense of shame, but also behave well."

Confucius said: "At fifteen, I set my heart on learning. At thirty, I had already a good grasp of the rites and morals. At forty, I could form my own judgments of things. At fifty, I began to know the objective laws of nature. At sixty, I could know a man from his words and make a clear distinction between right and wrong. At seventy, I could follow my inclinations without any of my words or deeds ever running counter to the rules."

Meng Yizi consulted Confucius on filial piety. Confucius said: "Do not violate the proprieties." Later when Fan Chi was driving for him Confucius told the man: "Mengsun asked me about filial piety, and I answered him 'Do not violate the proprieties.'" Fan Chi asked: "What did you mean by that?" Confucius replied: "I meant that parents, when alive, should be served according to the rules of propriety, that, when dead, they should be buried according to the funeral rites, and that they should be sacrificed to according to the sacrificial rites."

Meng Wubo asked about filial piety. Confucius said: "For a filial son, the biggest worry should be about his parents' health."

Ziyou asked about filial piety. Confucius said: "Nowadays filial piety is simply mistaken for supporting one's parents with food. But even dogs or horses are given food, too. If one practices filial piety without reverence and obedience to his parents, then, what is its difference from raising dogs or horses?"

Zixia asked about filial piety. Confucius said: "In attending one's parents, the most difficult thing for one to do is to constantly maintain an affable and pleasant manner. When anything has to be done, the young people undertake it; when there is wine and food, the elders are served— is this all there is to filial piety?" . . .

Zigong asked how to be a gentleman. Confucius said: "Let his deeds go before his words." . . .

Confucius said: "Do bear in mind, You, what I am now teaching you: when you know a thing, say that you know it; when you do not know a thing, admit you do not know it. That is wisdom." . . .

Book III

. . . Confucius said: "If a man is void of humanity, even though he perseveres in rites and decorum,

what's the good of that? If a man is void of humanity, even though he enjoys music, singing and dancing, what's the good of that?" . . .

Book IV

Confucius said: "It is indeed a privilege to live in a neighborhood where humanity is prevalent. If a man does not insist on such an environment in selecting his residence, how can he be counted as being wise?"

Confucius said: "Without humanity, a man cannot long endure adversity or poverty, nor can he long enjoy ease or prosperity. The humane feel relieved in carrying out humanity, while the wise find it beneficial to practice humanity."

Confucius said: "Only the kindhearted men can love the good and hate the evil."

Confucius said: "As long as one is resolved to bring about the spirit of humanity, there won't be any wickedness."

Confucius said: "Riches and honor are what every man desires; but if they can be obtained only by transgressing the right way, a virtuous man will disdain to hold them. Poverty and lowliness are what every man detests; but if they can be avoided only by transgressing the right way, a virtuous man will not try to evade them. If a man of true virtue should ignore humanity, how can he achieve his noble reputation? So not even for the lapse of a single meal does a man of true virtue depart from humanity. In moments of haste he cleaves to it; in seasons of peril he cleaves to it, too."

Confucius said: "I have not seen a person who hankered after humanity or a person who abhorred inhumanity. One who hankers after humanity would certainly be the best; one who abhors inhumanity would practice humanity in such a way that he would not allow any act of inhumanity in his own conduct. Is there anyone who can exert himself to achieve humanity for a whole day? I have never seen anyone who was willing to do so but did not have the ability; there might be such men, but I have not seen them." . . .

Confucius said: "Amidst the universe of men and events, the superior man does not set his mind either absolutely for anything or absolutely against anything. The sole measure of them all is morality and justice."

Confucius said: "The superior man takes pains in moral culture; the inferior man is sentimentally attached to his native soil. The superior man cares about the sanctions of law; the inferior man is concerned with small favors." . . .

Confucius said: "The superior man understands what is moral; the inferior man understands only what is profitable."

Confucius said: "When you have met a virtuous man, try to follow his example; when you have met an immoral man, try to examine yourself inwardly."

Confucius said: "In serving his parents, a son should express his different opinions in a mild tone. If he sees that his suggestions are not accepted, he should keep up his reverence and should not go against them. He should never complain even though he has a worried heart."

Confucius said: "While his parents are alive, the son should not go abroad to a great distance. If he does go on a long journey, he must tell his parents the definite place he is going to."

Confucius said: "If a man manages not to alter, for a number of years, from the correct principles formerly advocated by his dead father, he can be called a filial son."

Confucius said: "For the son, the ages of his parents should not be kept out of mind, for he should feel at once joyful for their healthiness and fearful for their aging." . . .

Confucius said: "A man of virtue never stands isolate; he will always have comrades." . . .

Book V

. . . Speaking of Zichan, Confucius said: "He has displayed in himself four characteristics of moral excellence: courtesy and gravity in the conduct of himself; loyalty and reverence in serving his prince; kindness and benevolence in nourishing the people; and morality and justice in ordering and employing the people." . . .

Book XI

. . . Zizhang asked about a man of moral excellence. Confucius said: "To be a man of moral excellence, although he doesn't have to follow in the footsteps of his predecessors, he can hardly attain to the lofty realm of a sage in the cultivation of his moral character." He added: "Isn't he a man whose words are truthful and sincere? Isn't he a man of moral integrity? Isn't he a man whose appearances are dignified and simple?" . . .

Book XII

Yan Yuan asked how to achieve the quality of humanity. Confucius said: "The quality of humanity consists in restraining yourself and making your words and deeds conform to decorum. Once you have restrained your personal desires and made your words and deeds conform to decorum, you will be universally acknowledged as bearing the virtue of humanity. To achieve the quality of humanity depends upon yourself; can it depend on others?" Yan Yuan said: "Allow me, sir, to further ask what the focal points are." Confucius said: "Do not look at what is contrary to decorum; do not listen to what is contrary to decorum; do not speak what is contrary to decorum; and do not do what is contrary to decorum." Yan Yuan said: "I will act upon these instructions although I am dull."

Zhonggong asked Confucius how to achieve the quality of humanity. Confucius said: "Behave with great respect and prudence when away from home as though you were receiving a distinguished guest. Preside over the common people with gravity and seriousness as though you were officiating at a grand sacrifice. Do not do to others what you would not want others to do to you. Try not to incur any dissatisfaction both in administrating the state and in managing your family affairs." Zhonggong said: "I will act upon these instructions although I am dull."

Sima Niu asked Confucius how to achieve the quality of humanity. Confucius said: "The humane are slow to talk." Sima Niu asked again: "Can it be counted as one of the characteristics of humanity to be slow to talk?" Confucius said: "It is no easy task to achieve the quality of humanity, and so one cannot but be slow to talk, can one?"

Sima Niu asked Confucius how to be a gentleman. Confucius said: "The gentleman has neither anxiety nor fear." Sima Niu said: "Neither anxiety nor fear—does that characterize a gentleman?" Confucius said: "Since he has a clear conscience, what has he to be anxious about, and what has he to fear?" . . .

Zizhang asked Confucius how to promote one's moral culture and dispel one's delusion. Confucius said: "Focus on the qualities of faithfulness and honesty, and act always upon the cardinal principles of morality and justice, and then your moral character will be improved. For the same person, you would wish him to enjoy a long life when you love him; you would wish him to die immediately when you hate him. So, you wish him a long life one moment, and you wish him to be short-lived the next—this is a case of delusion. Indeed, it is no good to yourself, and, besides, it will only make people feel absurd." . . .

Confucius said: "Study extensively the ancient literature, and regulate yourself with the rules of decorum, and then you won't go so far as to transgress the right way."

Confucius said: "The superior man seeks to enable people to succeed in what is good, but does not help them in what is evil. The inferior man does just the contrary." . . .

Fan Chi asked what humanity was. Confucius said: "Love men." Then Fan Chi asked about wisdom. Confucius said: "Know men." Fan Chi still could not understand thoroughly. Confucius said: "Promote upright men over those who are not upright, and you will be able to remold the latter into uprightness." When he retired, Fan Chi met Zixia and told him: "Just a moment ago, I saw our master and asked about wisdom. The master said: 'Promote upright men over those who are not upright, and you will be able to remold the latter into uprightness.' What did he mean by saying that?" Zixia said: "Oh, his statement has rich meanings in-

deed. When Emperor Shun gained the ruling power of his empire, he managed to select able persons from among all the people, and finally employed Gao Yao, and then all inhumane practices began to be kept away; when Emperor Tang gained the ruling power of his empire, he also managed to select able persons from among all the people, and finally employed Yi Yin, and then all inhumane practices began to be kept away." . . .

Zigong asked: "What would you say of a man who is loved by all the people of the whole village?" Confucius said: "That is not so good." Zigong asked again: "What would you say of a man who is hated by all the people of the whole village?" Confucius said: "That is not so good either. It would be better that all the good people of the whole village love him, and all the bad people there hate him." . . .

Confucius said: "The superior man is even-tempered and good-humored but never self-important. The inferior man is self-important but never even-tempered and good-humored."

Confucius said: "Those who possess such qualities as firmness, resolution, simplicity, and prudence in speech are close to the virtue of humanity." . . .

Book XIV

. . . Confucius said: "Virtuous men are sure to speak beautifully, but those who speak beautifully are not necessarily virtuous. Humane men are always found to be bold, but those who are bold are not necessarily humane." . . .

Confucius said: "The superior man loves morality and justice; the inferior man hankers after wealth and profits." . . .

Confucius said: "A gentleman feels ashamed of talking much but doing little."

Confucius said: "There are three principles a gentleman follows, but I myself have not been able to attain any of them: being humane, he has no anxieties; being wise, he has no perplexities: being brave, he has no fear."

Zigong said: "That is just our master's own way." . . .

Confucius said: "Do not worry about people not knowing your ability, but worry that you have not enough of it." . . .

Someone asked: "What do you think of requiting enmity with kindness?" Confucius said: "Then how will you requite kindness? Enmity should be requited with justice, and kindness should be requited with kindness." . . .

Book XV

. . . Confucius and his party ran out of food in the State of Chen, and all his followers fell ill and became so weak that they even could not stand up. Zilu came to see Confucius in resentment, saying, "Then, even the superior man can be driven to a wall?" Confucius said: "Yes, but the superior man when reduced to such straits can stick to his moral integrity, while the inferior man when thus reduced tends to do all manner of evil." . . .

Confucius said: "Men of lofty ideals and moral integrity will under no circumstance seek life at the expense of the principles of humanity. On occasion they will be brave enough to sacrifice their lives to accomplish the cultivation of the quality of humanity." . . .

Confucius said: "More blame on yourself and less blame on others, and you will be able to keep away from resentment." . . .

Confucius said: "A gentleman takes propriety as the cardinal principle in his conduct. He performs it according to the rule of decorum. He brings it forth in terms of modesty and magnanimity, and completes it with honesty and sincerity. Such a man is a true gentleman."

Confucius said: "The superior man merely worries that he himself is wanting in ability, and does not worry about people not knowing him." . . .

Confucius said: "The superior man always seeks the cause of any error in himself. The inferior man always finds an excuse for any error in others." . . .

Zigong asked Confucius: "Is there any one word that can serve as a lasting principle for the conduct of one's whole life?" Confucius said: "Perhaps it is the word 'reciprocity.' Do not do to others what you would not want others to do to you." . . .

Confucius said: "The superior man may not be observed and tested in small matters, but can be entrusted with great concerns. The inferior man cannot be entrusted with great concerns, but can be observed and tested in small matters." . . .

Confucius said: "When it comes to the cardinal principle of realizing the spirit of humanity, a man should not defer even to his master." . . .

Confucius said: "A gentleman is as good as his words on moral principles, but does not necessarily keep his promise in trifling matters." . . .

Book XVII

. . . Zizhang asked Confucius about the principles of humanity. Confucius said: "A man who is able to practice the five virtues everywhere at any moment is an adherent to the principles of humanity." Zizhang said: "I would like to ask what the five virtues are." Confucius said: "They are courtesy, magnanimity, good faith, diligence, and kindness. He who is courteous will not be humiliated; he who is magnanimous will win the multitude; he who is of good faith will be trusted by others; he who is diligent will achieve a great deal; and he who is kind will be able to get service from others." . . .

6.2 Master and Slave Morality

Does morality need some divine transcendent source? Might not moral values be generated by humans without reference to the divine or to some religious reality? Some have thought we really have only two alternatives when it comes to questions like this: Either morality is somehow based on a divine, objective, and hence absolute source, or morality is based on a human, subjective, and hence relative source. Thus, some argue, if there is no God, anything is morally permissible.

There is little question that some religious traditions (Judaism, Christianity, Islam) are closely associated with the moral values and rules we have all learned. What if this religious foundation for our morality crumbled? What might happen? Would we be plunged into moral chaos and nihilism? Let's go one step further. What if the kinds of moral values associated with our dominant religious traditions are themselves morally inappropriate? What if the values we have learned are wrong?

Friedrich Wilhelm Nietzsche (1844–1900) was a German philosopher and classicist who became convinced that the God of Western European civilization was "dead." He saw that God, who is the religious and metaphysical foundation of Western values, was increasingly becoming irrelevant to many people's lives. This alarmed Nietzsche because once God's funeral was made public, he thought, European civilization would be thrown into despair, nihilism, and moral chaos. Its conception of moral value was too closely tied to a divine, metaphysical source. In order to avoid this, we need a new morality, a morality suited to a new age in which God's reality is no longer required to secure moral value. This new morality must be shaped by those bold, creative, and masterful humans who dare themselves to become as "gods"— the sources of meaning and value. Such a new morality stands in contrast to the old "slave" morality taught by our religious past. This slave morality is a "cowardly" morality based on humility and subservience.

Nietzsche writes in a shocking, poetic, and enigmatic manner, so his meaning is not always clear. However, his style stimulates both thought and emotion. His passionate concern for a meaningful human future beyond the death of God is unmistakable. Even though he died in the first year of the twentieth century, his vision of the social and cultural chaos into which Europe (and indeed much of the world) would be plunged in this century was prophetic. His solution—the adoption of a "master-morality," the realistic acknowledgment that God is dead, and the claim that humans must now assume responsibility for their own lives and the fate of culture—has proved more controversial. Some argue that it is precisely the abandonment of God and traditional morality that has led us into this moral chaos and that what we need is to recover the traditions we have lost. Others, following Nietzsche, argue that we must bravely forge ahead, exploring not only new religious but also new moral options.

Reading Questions

1. What do you think the story of the Madman means?
2. What are some of the basic differences between slave-morality and master-morality?
3. Nietzsche characterized the morality of Judaism and Christianity as a slave-morality. Why do you think he did this, and how is such a morality related to the belief that God is alive, not dead?
4. Which morality do you prefer, the slave-morality or the master-morality? Why?

Master and Slave Morality*

FRIEDRICH NIETZSCHE

In the Horizon of the Infinite.—We have left the land and have gone aboard ship! We have broken down the bridge behind us,—nay, more, the land behind us! Well, little ship! look out! Beside thee is the ocean; it is true it does not always roar, and sometimes it spreads out like silk and gold and a gentle reverie. But times will come when thou wilt feel that it is infinite, and that there is nothing more frightful than infinity. Oh, the poor bird that felt itself free, and now strikes against the walls of this cage! Alas, if homesickness for the land should attack thee, as if there had been more *freedom* there,—and there is no "land" any longer!

The Madman.—Have you ever heard of the madman who on a bright morning lighted a lantern and ran to the market-place calling out unceasingly: "I seek God! I seek God!"—As there were many people standing about who did not believe in God, he caused a great deal of amusement. Why! is he lost? said one. Has he strayed away like a child? said another. Or does he keep himself hidden? Is he afraid of us? Has he taken a sea-voyage? Has he emigrated?—the people cried out laughingly, all in a hubbub. The insane man jumped into their midst and transfixed them with his glances. "Where is God gone?" he called out. "I mean to tell you! *We have killed him,*—you and I! We are all his murderers! But how have we done it? How were we able to drink up the sea? Who gave us the sponge to wipe away the whole horizon? What did we do when we loosened this earth from its sun? Whither does it now move? Whither do we move? Away from all suns? Do we not dash on unceasingly? Backwards, sideways, forewards, in all directions? Is there still an above and below? Do we not stray, as through infinite nothingness? Does not empty space breathe upon us? Has it not become colder? Does not night come on continually, darker and darker? Shall we not have to light lanterns in the morning? Do we not hear the noise of the grave-diggers who are burying God? Do we not smell the divine putre-faction?—for even Gods putrefy! God is dead! God remains dead! And we have killed him! How shall we console ourselves, the most murderous of all murderers? The holiest and the mightiest that the world has hitherto possessed, has bled to death under our knife,—who will wipe the blood from us? With what water could we cleanse our-selves? What lustrums, what sacred games shall we have to devise? Is not the magnitude of this deed too great for us? Shall we not ourselves have to become Gods, merely to seem worthy of it? There never was a greater event,—and on account of it, all who are born after us belong to a higher his-tory than any history hitherto!"—Here the mad-man was silent and looked again at his hearers; they also were silent and looked at him in surprise. At last he threw his lantern on the ground, so that it broke in pieces and was extinguished. "I come too early," he then said. "I am not yet at the right time. This prodigious event is still on its way, and is travelling,—it has not yet reached men's ears. Lightning and thunder need time, the light of the stars needs time, deeds need time, even after they are done, to be seen and heard. This deed is as yet further from them than the furthest star,—*and yet they have done it!*"—It is further stated that the madman made his way into different churches on the same day, and there intoned his *Requiem aeternam deo.* When led out and called to ac-count, he always gave the reply: "What are these churches now, if they are not the tombs and mon-uments of God?" . . .

---

*From Friedrich Nietzsche, *The Joyful Wisdom,* translated by Thomas Common, sections 124–125; *Be-yond Good and Evil,* translated by Helen Zimmern, section 260. In *The Complete Works of Nietzsche,* edited by Oscare Levy, Volumes 10 and 11. Edinburgh: T. N. Foulis, 1910, 1911.

In a tour through the many finer and coarser moralities which have hitherto prevailed or still prevail on the earth, I found certain traits recurring regularly together and connected with one another, until finally two primary types revealed themselves to me, and a radical distinction was brought to light. There is *master-morality* and *slave-morality:*—I would at once add, however, that in all higher and mixed civilisations, there are also attempts at the reconciliation of the two moralities: but one finds still oftener the confusion and mutual misunderstanding of them, indeed, sometimes their close juxtaposition—even in the same man, within one soul. The distinctions of moral values have either originated in a ruling caste, pleasantly conscious of being different from the ruled—or among the ruled class, the slaves and dependents of all sorts. In the first case, when it is the rulers who determined the conception "good," it is the exalted, proud disposition which is regarded as the distinguishing feature, and that which determines the order of rank. The noble type of man separates from himself the beings in whom the opposite of this exalted, proud disposition displays itself: he despises them. Let it at once be noted that in this first kind of morality the antithesis "good" and "bad" means practically the same as "noble" and "despicable";—the antithesis "good" and "*evil*" is of a different origin. The cowardly, the timid, the insignificant, and those thinking merely of narrow utility are despised; moreover, also, the distrustful, with their constrained glances, the self-abasing, the dog-like kind of men who let themselves be abused, the mendicant flatterers, and above all the liars:—it is a fundamental belief of all aristocrats that the common people are untruthful. "We truthful ones"—the nobility in ancient Greece called themselves. It is obvious that everywhere the designations of moral value were at first applied to *men*, and were only derivatively and at a later period applied to *actions;* it is a gross mistake, therefore, when historians of morals start with questions like, "Why have sympathetic actions been praised?" The noble type of man regards *himself* as a determiner of values; he does not require to be approved of; he passes the judgment: "What is injurious to me is injurious in itself"; he knows that it is he himself only who confers honour on things; he is a *creator of values*. He honours whatever he recognises in himself: such morality is self-glorification. In the foreground there is the feeling of plenitude, of power, which seeks to overflow, the happiness of high tension, the consciousness of a wealth which would fain give and bestow:—the noble man also helps the unfortunate, but not—or scarcely—out of pity, but rather from an impulse generated by the super-abundance of power. The noble man honours in himself the powerful one, him also who has power over himself, who knows how to speak and how to keep silence, who takes pleasure in subjecting himself to severity and hardness, and has reverence for all that is severe and hard. "Wotan placed a hard heart in my breast," says an old Scandinavian Saga: it is thus rightly expressed from the soul of a proud Viking. Such a type of man is even proud of *not* being made for sympathy: the hero of the Saga therefore adds warningly: "He who has not a hard heart when young, will never have one." The noble and brave who think thus are the furthest removed from the morality which sees precisely in sympathy, or in acting for the good of others, or in *désintéressement,* the characteristic of the moral; faith in oneself, pride in oneself, a radical enmity and irony towards "selflessness," belong as definitely to noble morality, as do a careless scorn and precaution in presence of sympathy and the "warm heart."—It is the powerful who *know* how to honour, it is their art, their domain for invention. The profound reverence for age and for tradition—all law rests on this double reverence,—the belief and prejudice in favour of ancestors and unfavourable to newcomers, is typical in the morality of the powerful; and if, reversely, men of "modern ideas" believe almost instinctively in "progress" and the "future," and are more and more lacking in respect for old age, the ignoble origin of these "ideas" has complacently betrayed itself thereby. A morality of the ruling class, however, is more especially foreign and irritating to present-day taste in the sternness of its principle that one has duties only to one's equals: that one may act towards beings of a lower rank, towards all that is foreign, just as seems good to one, or "as the heart desires," and in any case "beyond good and evil": it is here that sympathy and similar sentiments can have a place. The ability and obligation to exercise prolonged gratitude and prolonged revenge—both only within the circle of equals,—artfulness in retaliation, *raffinement* of the idea in friendship, a certain necessity to have enemies (as outlets for the emotions of envy, quarrelsomeness, arrogance—in fact, in order to be a good *friend*): all these are typical characteristics of the noble morality, which, as has been pointed out, is not the morality of "modern ideas," and is therefore at present difficult to realise, and also to unearth and disclose.—It is otherwise with the second type of morality, *slave-morality.* Supposing that the abused, the oppressed, the suffering, the unemancipated, the weary, and those uncertain of themselves, should moralise, what will be the common element in their moral estimates? Probably a pessimistic suspicion with regard to the entire situation of man will find expression, perhaps a condemnation of man, together with his situation. The slave has an unfavourable eye for the virtues of the powerful: he has a scepticism and distrust, a *refinement* of distrust of everything "good" that is there honoured—he would fain persuade himself that the very happiness there is not genuine. On the other hand, *those* qualities which serve to alleviate the existence of sufferers are brought into prominence and flooded with light; it is here that sympathy, the kind, helping hand, the warm heart, patience, diligence, humility, and friendliness attain to honour; for here these are the most useful qualities, and almost the only means of supporting the bur-

den of existence. Slave-morality is essentially the morality of utility. Here is the seat of the origin of the famous antithesis "good" and "*evil:*"—power and dangerousness are assumed to reside in the evil, a certain dreadfulness, subtlety, and strength, which do not admit of being despised. According to slave-morality, therefore, the "evil" man arouses fear: according to master-morality, it is precisely the "good" man who arouses fear and seeks to arouse it, while the bad man is regarded as the despicable being. The contrast attains its maximum when, in accordance with the logical consequences of slave-morality, a shade of depreciation—it may be slight and well-intentioned—at last attaches itself even to the "good" man of this morality; because, according to the servile mode of thought, the good man must in any case be the *safe* man: he is good-natured, easily deceived, perhaps a little stupid, *un bonhomme.* Everywhere that slave-morality gains the ascendency, language shows a tendency to approximate the significations of the words "good" and "stupid."—A last fundamental difference: the desire for *freedom,* the instinct for happiness and the refinements of the feeling of liberty belong as necessarily to slave-morals and morality, as artifice and enthusiasm in reverence and devotion are the regular symptoms of an aristocratic mode of thinking and estimating.—Hence we can understand without further detail why love *as a passion*—it is our European specialty—must absolutely be of noble origin; as is well known, its invention is due to the Provençal poet-cavaliers, those brilliant ingenious men of the "*gai saber,*" to whom Europe owes so much, and almost owes itself.

6.3 A Modified Divine Command Theory

Consider the following questions:

1. What is the ultimate source of ethical principles?
2. What is the authoritative basis of religious morality?
3. How can we know whether God is good?

These are not easy questions to answer. We must carefully make correct distinctions and consider the reasons offered for different answers. These questions all presuppose a theistic context. They assume that a "religious ethic" is somehow connected to the belief that there is a God, that God is morally good, and that God wills that humans also be morally good.

Many of the issues raised by these questions are related to the divine command theory of ethics. There are different versions of the theory, but central to the theory is the notion that God's will or commands form the basis of ethical value. Certainly the theistic traditions such as Sikhism, Islam, Judaism, and Christianity assert that we must obey God's will because that is the right thing to do. However, Socrates (470–399 B.C.E.) asked a crucial question centuries ago. Is something good because the divine wills it, or does the divine will it because it is good?

This deceptively simple question hides a complex dilemma. If we take the first horn of the dilemma and maintain that *x* is good solely because God wills it, then, it seems, we must admit that morality rests on the arbitrary fiat of some divine being. It follows that if such a being willed that torturing and killing innocent people was good, those practices would be good. Now you might say that a divine being would not will that, because to be divine is to be good. However, how would you know God is good independently of what God wills, given that, according to this version of the divine command theory, being good is equivalent to what God wills or commands?

Let's take the other horn of the dilemma. Suppose God wills *x* because *x* is good. If so, it would appear that God is subject to some moral law independent of what he or she commands. Hence not only is the supposed moral supremacy of God challenged, but God must, like humans, morally deliberate and exert an act of will to obey the call of moral duty. Hence, given the second horn, we seem compelled to admit some type of anthropomorphic conception of God as a moral agent who is subject to moral constraints, must decide what is right and wrong according to some set of moral principles, and must then find the moral courage to act according to what those principles dictate.

Neither alternative appears acceptable. The first horn leads in the direction of power worship. Do it because God said so! God is more powerful, and if you don't do what God wants, there will be hell to pay. The second horn leads to an anthropomorphic conception of God as struggling to figure out what is the right thing and then mustering the courage to do it. Can this dilemma be resolved?

Robert Merrihew Adams (1931–   ), professor of philosophy at Yale University and author of the following selection, wants to link the origin of ethical truth to the will of God. However, he denies that this implies that the believer is "committed to doing the will of God just because it is the will of God." God's commands are worthy of obedience only if certain conditions obtain. What are these conditions? Read and see.

Reading Questions

1. What is the divine command theory in its unmodified form?
2. What is the gravest objection to the divine command theory of ethical wrongness?
3. What is the modified form of the divine command theory of ethical wrongness, and how does this modified theory answer the gravest objection to the unmodified theory?
4. What are two philosophical objections to the modified divine command theory, and how does Adams respond to these objections? Do you find his response satisfactory? Why or why not?

5. What is the theological objection to the modified divine command theory, and how does Adams respond to this objection? Do you find his response satisfactory? Why or why not?
6. What sorts of problems does ascribing moral qualities to God cause, and how does Adams respond to these problems? Is his response adequate? Why or why not?
7. What are the conditions that make common moral discourse between believers and nonbelievers possible?

A Modified Divine Command Theory*

ROBERT MERRIHEW ADAMS

I

It is widely held that all those theories are indefensible which attempt to explain in terms of the will or commands of God what it is for an act to be ethically right or wrong. In this paper I shall state such a theory, which I believe to be defensible; and I shall try to defend it against what seem to me to be the most important and interesting objections to it. I call my theory a *modified* divine command theory because in it I renounce certain claims that are commonly made in divine command analyses of ethical terms. (I should add that it is *my* theory only in that I shall state it, and that I believe it is defensible—not that I am sure it is correct.) I present it as a theory of ethical *wrongness* partly for convenience. It could also be presented as a theory of the nature of ethical obligatoriness or of ethical permittedness. Indeed. I will have occasion to make some remarks about the concept of ethical permittedness. But as we shall see (in section IV) I am not prepared to claim that the theory can be extended to all ethical terms; and it is therefore important that it not be presented as a theory about ethical terms in general.

It will be helpful to begin with the statement of a simple, *unmodified* divine command theory of ethical wrongness. This is the theory that ethical wrongness *consists in* being contrary to God's commands, or that the word "wrong" in ethical contexts *means* "contrary to God's commands." It implies that the following two statement forms are logically equivalent.

(1) It is wrong (for A) to do X.
(2) It is contrary to God's commands (for A) to do X.

Of course that is not all that the theory implies. It also implies that (2) is conceptually prior to (1), so that the meaning of (1) is to be explained in terms of (2), and not the other way around. It might prove fairly difficult to state or explain in what that conceptual priority consists, but I shall not go into that here. I do not wish ultimately to defend the theory in its unmodified form, and I think I have stated it fully enough for my present purposes.

I have stated it as a theory about the meaning of the word "wrong" in ethical contexts. The most obvious objection to the theory is that the word "wrong" is used in ethical contexts by many people who cannot mean by it what the theory says they must mean, since they do not believe that there exists a God. This objection seems to me sufficient to refute the theory if it is presented as an analysis of what *everybody* means by "wrong" in ethical contexts. The theory cannot reasonably be offered except as a theory about what the word "wrong" means as used by *some but not all* people in ethical contexts. Let us say that the theory offers an analysis of the meaning of "wrong" in Judeo-Christian religious ethical discourse. This restriction of scope will apply to my modified divine command theory too. This restriction obviously gives rise to a possible objection. Isn't it more plausible to suppose that Judeo-Christian believers use "wrong" with the same meaning as other people do? This problem will be discussed in section VI.

In section II, I will discuss what seems to me the most important objection to the unmodified divine command theory, and suggest how the theory can be modified to meet it. Section III will be devoted to a brief but fairly comprehensive account of the use of "wrong" in Judeo-Christian ethical discourse, from the point of view of the modified divine command theory. The theory will be further elaborated in dealing with objections in sections IV to VI. In a seventh and final section, I will note some problems arising from unresolved issues in the general theory of analysis and meaning, and briefly discuss their bearing on the modified divine command theory.

II

The following seems to me to be the gravest objection to the divine command theory of ethical wrongness, in the form in which I have stated it. Suppose God should command me to make it my chief end in life to inflict suffering on other human beings, for no other reason than that he commanded it. (For convenience I shall abbreviate this hypothesis to "Suppose God should command cruelty for its own sake.") Will it seriously be claimed that in that case it would be wrong for me not to practice cruelty for its own sake? I see three possible answers to this question.

(1) It might be claimed that it is logically impossible for God to command cruelty for its own sake. In that case, of course, we need not worry about whether it would be wrong to disobey if he did command it. It is senseless to agonize about what one should do in a logically impossible situation. This solution to the problem seems unlikely to be available to the divine command the-

orist, however. For why would he hold that it is logically impossible for God to command cruelty for its own sake? Some theologians (for instance, Thomas Aquinas) have believed (a) that what is right and wrong is independent of God's will, *and* (b) that God always does right by the necessity of his nature. Such theologians, if they believe that it would be wrong for God to command cruelty for its own sake, have reason to believe that it is logically impossible for him to do so. But the divine command theorist, who does not agree that what is right and wrong is independent of God's will, does not seem to have such a reason to deny that it is logically possible for God to command cruelty for its own sake.

(2) Let us assume that it is logically possible for God to command cruelty for its own sake. In that case the divine command theory seems to imply that it would be wrong not to practice cruelty for its own sake. There have been at least a few adherents of divine command ethics who have been prepared to accept this consequence. William Ockham held that those acts which we call "theft," "adultery," and "hatred of God" would be meritorious if God had commanded them. He would surely have said the same about what I have been calling the practice of "cruelty for its own sake."

This position is one which I suspect most of us are likely to find somewhat shocking, even repulsive. We should therefore be particularly careful not to misunderstand it. We need not imagine that Ockham disciplined himself to be ready to practice cruelty for its own sake if God should command it. It was doubtless an article of faith for him that God is unalterably opposed to any such practice. The mere logical possibility that theft, adultery, and cruelty might have been commanded by God (and therefore meritorious) doubtless did not represent in Ockham's view any real possibility.

(3) Nonetheless, the view that if God commanded cruelty for its own sake it would be wrong not to practice it seems unacceptable to me; and I think many, perhaps most, other Jewish and Christian believers would find it unacceptable too. I must make clear the sense in which I find it unsatisfactory. It is not that I find an internal inconsistency in it. And I would not deny that it may

reflect, accurately enough, the way in which some believers use the word "wrong." I might as well frankly avow that I am looking for a divine command theory which at least might possibly be a correct account of how *I* use the word "wrong." I do not use the word "wrong" in such a way that I would say that it would be wrong not to practice cruelty if God commanded it, and I am sure that many other believers agree with me on this point.

But now have I not rejected the divine command theory? I have assumed that it would be logically possible for God to command cruelty for its own sake. And I have rejected the view that if God commanded cruelty for its own sake, it would be wrong not to obey. It seems to follow that I am committed to the view that in certain logically possible circumstances it would not be wrong to disobey God. This position seems to be inconsistent with the theory that "wrong" means "contrary to God's commands."

I want to argue, however, that it is still open to me to accept a modified form of the divine command theory of ethical wrongness. According to the modified divine command theory, when I say, "It is wrong to do X," (at least part of) what I *mean* is that it is contrary to God's commands to do X. "It is wrong to do X" *implies* "It is contrary to God's commands to do X." But "It is contrary to God's commands to do X" implies "It is wrong to do X" only if certain conditions are assumed—namely, only if it is assumed that God has the character which I believe him to have, of loving his human creatures. If God were really to command us to make cruelty our goal, then he would not have that character of loving us, and I would not say it would be wrong to disobey him.

But do I say that it would be wrong to obey him in such a case? This is the point at which I am in danger of abandoning the divine command theory completely. I do abandon it completely if I say both of the following things.

(A) it would be wrong to obey God if he commanded cruelty for its own sake.
(B) in (A), "wrong" is used in what is for me its normal ethical sense.

If I assert both (A) and (B), it is clear that I cannot consistently maintain that "wrong" in its normal ethical sense for me means or implies "contrary to God's commands."

But from the fact that I deny that it would be wrong to disobey God if He commanded cruelty for its own sake, it does not follow that I must accept (A) and (B). Of course someone might claim that obedience and disobedience would both be ethically permitted in such a case; but that is not the view that I am suggesting. If I adopt the modified divine command theory as an analysis of my present concept of ethical wrongness (and if I adopt a similar analysis of my concept of ethical permittedness), I will not hold either that it would be wrong to disobey, or that it would be ethically permitted to disobey, or that it would be wrong to obey, or that it would be ethically permitted to obey, if God commanded cruelty for its own sake. For I will say that my concept of ethical wrongness (and my concept of ethical permittedness) would "break down" if I really believed that God commanded cruelty for its own sake. Or to put the matter somewhat more prosaically, I will say that my concepts of ethical wrongness and permittedness could not serve the functions they now serve, because using those concepts I could not call any action ethically wrong or ethically permitted, if I believed that God's will was so unloving. This position can be explained or developed in either of two ways, each of which has its advantages.

I could say that by "X is ethically wrong" I mean "X is contrary to the commands of a *loving* God" (i.e., "There is a *loving* God and X is contrary to his commands") and by "X is ethically permitted" I mean "X is in accord with the commands of a *loving* God" (i.e., "There is a *loving* God and X is not contrary to his commands"). On this analysis we can reason as follows. If there is only one God and he commands cruelty for its own sake, then presumably there is not a *loving* God. If there is not a loving God then neither "X is ethically wrong" nor "X is ethically permitted" is true of any X. Using my present concepts of ethical wrongness and permittedness, therefore, I could not (consistently) call any action ethically wrong or permitted if I believed that God commanded cruelty for its own sake. This way of developing the modified divine command theory is the simpler and neater of the two, and that might reasonably lead one to choose it for the construction of a theological ethical theory. On the other hand, I think it is also simpler and neater than ordinary religious ethical discourse, in which (for example) it may be felt that the statement that a certain act is wrong is *about* the will or commands of God in a way in which it is not about his love.

In this essay I shall prefer a second, rather similar, but somewhat untidier, understanding of the modified divine command theory, because I think it may lead us into some insights about the complexities of actual religious ethical discourse. According to this second version of the theory, the statement that something is ethically wrong (or permitted) says something about the will or commands of God, but not about his love. Every such statement, however, *presupposes* that certain conditions for the applicability of the believer's concepts of ethical right and wrong are satisfied. Among these conditions is that God does not command cruelty for its own sake—or, more generally, that God loves his human creatures. It need not be assumed that God's love is the only such condition.

The modified divine command theorist can say that the possibility of God commanding cruelty for its own sake is not provided for in the Judeo-Christian religious ethical system as he understands it. The possibility is not provided for, in the sense that the concepts of right and wrong have not been developed in such a way that actions could be correctly said to be right or wrong if God were believed to command cruelty for its own sake. The modified divine command theorist agrees that it is logically possible that God should command cruelty for its own sake; but he holds that it is unthinkable that God should do so. To have *faith* in God is not just to believe that he exists, but also to trust in his love for mankind. The believer's concepts of ethical wrongness and permittedness are developed within the framework of his (or the religious community's) reli-

gious life, and therefore within the framework of the assumption that God loves us. The concept of the will or commands of God has a certain function in the believer's life, and the use of the words "right" (in the sense of "ethically permitted") and "wrong" is tied to that function of that concept. But one of the reasons why the concept of the will of God can function as it does is that the love which God is believed to have toward men arouses in the believer certain attitudes of love toward God and devotion to his will. If the believer thinks about the unthinkable but logically possible situation in which God commands cruelty for its own sake, he finds that in relation to that kind of command of God he cannot take up the same attitude, and that the concept of the will or commands of God could not then have the same function in his life. For this reason he will not say that it would be wrong to disobey God, or right to obey him, in that situation. At the same time he will not say that it would be wrong to obey God in that situation, because he is accustomed to use the word "wrong" to say that something is contrary to the will of God, and it does not seem to him to be the right word to use to express his own personal revulsion toward an act against which there would be no divine authority. Similarly, he will not say that it would be "right" in the sense of "ethically permitted," to disobey God's command of cruelty; for that does not seem to him to be the right way to express his own personal attitude toward an act which would not be in accord with a divine authority. In this way the believer's concepts of ethical rightness and wrongness would break down in the situation in which he believed that God commanded cruelty for its own sake; that is, they would not function as they now do, because he would not be prepared to use them to say that any action was right or wrong.

III

It is clear that according to this modified divine command theory, the meaning of the word "wrong" in Judeo-Christian ethical discourse must be understood in terms of a complex of relations which believers' use of the word has, not only to their beliefs about God's commands, but also to their attitudes toward certain types of action. . . .

IV

The modified divine command theory clearly conceives of believers as valuing some things independently of their relation to God's commands. If the believer will not say that it would be wrong not to practice cruelty for its own sake if God commanded it, that is because he values kindness, and has a revulsion for cruelty, in a way that is at least to some extent independent of his belief that God commands kindness and forbids cruelty. This point may be made the basis of both philosophical and theological objections to the modified divine command theory, but I think the objections can be answered.

The philosophical objection is, roughly, that if there are some things I value independently of their relation to God's commands, then my value concepts cannot rightly be analyzed in terms of God's commands. According to the modified divine command theory, the acceptability of divine command ethics depends in part on the believer's independent positive valuation of the sorts of things that God is believed to command. But then, the philosophical critic objects, the believer must have a prior, nontheological conception of ethical right and wrong, in terms of which he judges God's commandments to be acceptable— and to admit that the believer has a prior, nontheological conception of ethical right and wrong is to abandon the divine command theory.

The weakness of this philosophical objection is that it fails to note the distinctions that can be drawn among various value concepts. From the fact that the believer values some things independently of his beliefs about God's commands, the objector concludes, illegitimately, that the believer must have a conception of ethical right and wrong that is independent of his beliefs about God's commands. This inference is illegitimate because there can be valuations which do not imply or presuppose a judgment of ethical

right or wrong. For instance, I may simply like something, or want something, or feel a revulsion at something.

What the modified divine command theorist will hold, then, is that the believer values some things independently of their relation to God's commands, but that these valuations are not judgments of ethical right and wrong and do not of themselves imply judgments of ethical right and wrong. He will maintain, on the other hand, that such independent valuations are involved in, or even necessary for, judgments of ethical right and wrong which also involve beliefs about God's will or commands. The adherent of a divine command ethics will normally be able to give reasons for his adherence. Such reasons might include: "Because I am grateful to God for his love"; "Because I find it the most satisfying form of ethical life"; "Because there's got to be an objective moral law if life isn't to fall to pieces, and I can't understand what it would be if not the will of God." As we have already noted, the modified divine command theorist also has reasons why he would not accept a divine command ethics in certain logically possible situations which he believes not to be actual. All of these reasons seem to me to involve valuations that are independent of divine command ethics. The person who has such reasons wants certain things—happiness, certain satisfactions—for himself and others; he hates cruelty and loves kindness; he has perhaps a certain unique and "numinous" awe of God. And these are not attitudes which he has simply because of his beliefs about God's commands. They are not attitudes, however, which presuppose judgments of moral right and wrong.

It is sometimes objected to divine command theories of moral obligation, or of ethical rightness and wrongness, that one must have some reason for obeying God's commands or for adopting a divine command ethics, and that therefore a nontheological concept of moral obligation or of ethical rightness and wrongness must be presupposed, in order that one may judge that one ought to obey God's commands. This objection is groundless. For one can certainly have reasons for doing something which do not involve believing one morally ought to do it or believing it would be ethically wrong not to do it.

I grant that in giving reasons for his attitudes toward God's commands the believer will probably use or presuppose concepts which, in the context, it is reasonable to count as nontheological value concepts (e.g., concepts of satisfactoriness and repulsiveness). Perhaps some of them might count as moral concepts. But all that the defender of a divine command theory of ethical wrongness has to maintain is that the concept of ethical wrongness which occurs in the ethical thought and discourse of believers is not one of the concepts which are used or presupposed in this way. Divine command theorists, including the modified divine command theorist, need not maintain that *all* value concepts, or even all moral concepts, must be understood in terms of God's commands.

In fact some well-known philosophers have held forms of divine command theory which quite explicitly presuppose some nontheological value concepts. Locke, for instance, says in his *Essay,*

> Good and evil . . . are nothing but pleasure or pain, or that which occasions or procures pleasure or pain to us. *Morally good and evil,* then, is only the conformity or disagreement of our voluntary actions to some law, whereby good or evil is drawn on us from the will and power of the law-maker . . . (*Essay,* II, xxviii, 5).

Locke goes on to distinguish three laws, or types of law, by reference to which actions are commonly judged as to moral good and evil: "(1) The *divine* law. (2) The *civil* law. (3) The law of *opinion* or *reputation,* if I may so call it" (*Essay,* II, xxviii, 7). Of these three Locke says that the third is "the common *measure of virtue and vice*" (*Essay,* II, xxviii, 11). In Locke's opinion the terms "virtue" and "vice" are particularly closely attached to the praise and blame of society. But the terms "duty" and "sin" are connected with the commandments of God. About the divine law Locke says,

> This is the only true touchstone of *moral rectitude;* and by comparing them to this law, it is that men judge of the most considerable *moral*

good or *evil* of their actions: that is, whether, as *duties or sins,* they are like to procure them happiness or misery from the hands of the ALMIGHTY (*Essay,* II, xxviii, 8).

The structure of Locke's analysis is clear enough. By "good" and "evil" we *mean* (nontheologically enough) pleasurable and painful. By "morally good" and "morally evil" we *mean* that the actions so described agree or disagree with some law under which the agent stands to be rewarded or punished. By "duty" and "sin," which denote the most important sort of moral good and evil, we *mean* (theologically now) actions which are apt to cause the agent good or evil (in the nontheological sense) because they agree or disagree with the law of God. . . .

The modified divine command theory that I have in mind does not rely as heavily as Locke's theory does on God's power to reward and punish, nor do I wish to assume Locke's analysis of "good" and "evil." The point I want to make by discussing Locke here is just that there are many different value concepts and it is clearly possible to give one or more of them a theological analysis while giving others a nontheological analysis. And I do assume that the modified divine command theorist will give a nontheological analysis of some value concepts although he gives a theological analysis of the concept of ethical wrongness. For instance, he may give a nontheological analysis, perhaps a naturalistic one or a noncognitivist one, of the meaning of "satisfactory" and "repulsive," as he uses them in some contexts. He may even regard as *moral* concepts some value concepts of which he gives a nontheological analysis.

For it is not essential to a divine command theory of ethical wrongness to maintain that all valuing, or all value concepts, or even all moral concepts, depend on beliefs about God's commands. What is essential to such a theory is to maintain that when a believer says something is (ethically) *wrong,* at least part of what he means is that the action in question is contrary to God's will or commands. Another way of putting the matter is this. What depends on beliefs about God and his will is not all of the religious person's value concepts, nor in general his ability to value things, but only his ability to appraise actions (and possible actions) in terms of their relation to a superhuman, nonnaturally objective, law. Indeed, it is obvious that Judeo-Christian ethics presupposes concepts that have at least ethical overtones and that are not essentially theological but have their background in human social relations and political institutions—such as the concepts of promise, kindness, law, and command. What the specifically theological doctrines introduce into Judeo-Christian ethics, according to the divine command theory, is the belief in a law that is superior to all human laws.

This version of the divine command theory may seem *theologically* objectionable to some believers. One of the reasons, surely, why divine command theories of ethics have appealed to some theologians is that such theories seem especially congruous with the religious demand that God be the object of our highest allegiance. If our supreme commitment in life is to doing what is right just because it is right, and if what is right is right just because God wills or commands it, then surely our highest allegiance is to God. But the modified divine command theory seems not to have this advantage. For the modified divine command theorist is forced to admit, as we have seen, that he has reasons for his adherence to a divine command ethics, and that his having these reasons implies that there are some things which he values independently of his beliefs about God's commands. It is therefore not correct to say of him that he is committed to doing the will of God *just* because it is the will of God; he is committed to doing it partly because of other things which he values independently. Indeed it appears that there are certain logically possible situations in which his present attitudes would not commit him to obey God's commands (for instance, if God commanded cruelty for its own sake). This may even suggest that he values some things, not just independently of God's commands, but more than God's commands.

We have here a real problem in religious ethical motivation. The Judeo-Christian believer is supposed to make God the supreme focus of his loyalties; that is clear. One possible interpretation of this fact is the following. Obedience to whatever God may command is (or at least ought to be) the one thing that the believer values for its own sake and more than anything and everything else. Anything else that he values, he values (or ought to) only to a lesser degree and as a means to obedience to God. This conception of religious ethical motivation is obviously favorable to an *un*modified divine command theory of ethical wrongness.

But I think it is not a realistic conception. Loyalty to God, for instance, is very often explained, by believers themselves, as motivated by gratitude for benefits conferred. And I think it is clear in most cases that the gratitude presupposes that the benefits are valued, at least to some extent, independently of loyalty to God. Similarly, I do not think that most devout Judeo-Christian believers would say that it would be wrong to disobey God if he commanded cruelty for its own sake. And if I am right about that I think it shows that their positive valuation of (emotional/volitional pro-attitude toward) doing *whatever* God may command is not clearly greater than their independent negative valuation of cruelty.

In analyzing ethical motivation in general, as well as Judeo-Christian ethical motivation in particular, it is probably a mistake to suppose that there is (or can be expected to be) one only thing that is valued supremely and for its own sake, with nothing else being valued independently of it. The motivation for a person's ethical orientation in life is normally much more complex than that, and involves a plurality of emotional and volitional attitudes of different sorts which are at least partly independent of each other. At any rate, I think the modified divine command theorist is bound to say that that is true of his ethical motivation.

In what sense, then, can the modified divine command theorist maintain that God is the supreme focus of his loyalties? I suggest the following interpretation of the single-hearted loyalty to God which is demanded in Judeo-Christian religion. In this interpretation the crucial idea is *not* that some one thing is valued for its own sake and more than anything else, and nothing else valued independently of it. It is freely admitted that the religious person will have a plurality of motives for his ethical position, and that these will be at least partly independent of each other. It is admitted further that a desire to obey the commands of God (*whatever* they may be) may not be the strongest of these motives. What will be claimed is that certain beliefs about God enable the believer to integrate or focus his motives in a loyalty to God and his commands. Some of these beliefs are about what God commands or wills (contingently: that is, although he could logically have commanded or willed something else instead).

Some of the motives in question might be called egoistic; they include desires for satisfactions for oneself—which God is believed to have given or to be going to give. Other motives may be desires for satisfaction for other people—these may be called altruistic. Still other motives might not be desires for anyone's satisfaction, but might be valuations of certain kinds of action for their own sakes—these might be called idealistic. I do not think my argument depends heavily on this particular classification, but it seems plausible that all of these types, and perhaps others as well, might be distinguished among the motives for a religious person's ethical position. Obviously such motives might pull one in different directions, conflicting with one another. But in Judeo-Christian ethics beliefs about what God does in fact will (although he could have willed otherwise) are supposed to enable one to *fuse* these motives, so to speak, into one's devotion to God and his will, so that they all pull together. Doubtless the believer will still have some motives which conflict with his loyalty to God. But the religious ideal is that these should all be merely momentary desires and impulses, and kept under control. They ought not to be allowed to influence voluntary action. The deeper, more stable, and controlling desires, intentions, and psychic energies are supposed to be fused in devotion to God. As I interpret it, however, it need not be inconsistent with the Judeo-Christian ethical and religious ideal that this fusion of mo-

tives, this integration of moral energies, depends on belief in certain propositions which are taken to be contingent truths about God.

Lest it be thought that I am proposing unprecedented theological positions, or simply altering Judeo-Christian religious beliefs to suit my theories, I will call to my aid on this point a theologian known for his insistence on the sovereignty of God. Karl Barth seems to me to hold a divine command theory of ethics. But when he raises the question of why we should obey God, he rejects with scorn the suggestion that God's *power* provides the basis for his claim on us. "By deciding for God [man] has definitely decided not to be obedient to power as power." God's claim on us is based rather on his grace. "God calls us and orders us and claims us by being gracious to us in Jesus Christ." I do not mean to suggest that Barth would agree with everything I have said about motivation, or that he offers a lucid account of a divine command theory. But he does agree with the position I have proposed on this point, that the believer's loyalty is not to be construed as a loyalty to God *as* all-powerful, nor to God *whatever* he might conceivably have willed. It is a loyalty to God *as* having a certain attitude toward us, a certain will for us, which God was free not to have, but to which, in Barth's view, he has committed himself irrevocably in Jesus Christ. The believer's devotion is not to merely possible commands of God as such, but to God's actual (and gracious) will.

V

The ascription of moral qualities to God is commonly thought to cause problems for divine command theories of ethics. It is doubted that God, as an agent, can properly be called "good" in the moral sense if he is not subject to a moral law that is not of his own making. For if he is morally good, mustn't he do what is right *because* it is right? And how can he do that, if what's right is right because he wills it? Or it may be charged that divine command theories trivialize the claim that God is good. If "X is (morally) good" means roughly "X does what God wills," then "God is (morally) good" means only that God does what he wills—which is surely much less than people are normally taken to mean when they say that God is (morally) good. In this section I will suggest an answer to these objections.

Surely no analysis of Judeo-Christian ethical discourse can be regarded as adequate which does not provide for a sense in which the believer can seriously assert that God is good. Indeed an adequate analysis should provide a plausible account of what believers do in fact mean when they say, "God is good." I believe that a divine command theory of ethical (rightness and) wrongness can include such an account. I will try to indicate its chief features.

(1) In saying "God is good" one is normally expressing a favorable emotional attitude toward God. I shall not try to determine whether or not this is part of the meaning of "God is good"; but it is normally, perhaps almost always, at least one of the things one is doing if one says that God is good. If we were to try to be more precise about the type of favorable emotional attitude normally expressed by "God is good," I suspect we would find that the attitude expressed is most commonly one of *gratitude*.

(2) This leads to a second point, which is that when God is called "good" it is very often meant that he is *good to us*, or *good to* the speaker. "Good" is sometimes virtually a synonym for "kind." And for the modified divine command theorist it is not a trivial truth that God is kind. In saying that God is good in the sense of "kind," one presupposes, of course, that there are some things which the beneficiaries of God's goodness value. We need not discuss here whether the beneficiaries must value them independently of their beliefs about God's will. For the modified divine command theorist does admit that there are some things which believers value independently of their beliefs about God's commands. Nothing that the modified divine command theorist says about the meaning of ("right" and) "wrong" implies that it is a trivial truth that God bestows on his creatures things that they value.

(3) I would not suggest that the descriptive force of "good" as applied to God is exhausted

by the notion of kindness. "God is good" must be taken in many contexts as ascribing to God, rather generally, qualities of character which the believing speaker regards as virtues in human beings. Among such qualities might be faithfulness, ethical consistency, a forgiving disposition, and, in general, various aspects of love, as well as kindness. Not that there is some definite list of qualities, the ascription of which to God is clearly implied by the claim that God is good. But saying that God is good normally commits one to the position that God has some important set of qualities which one regards as virtues in human beings.

(4) It will not be thought that God has *all* the qualities which are virtues in human beings. Some such qualities are logically inapplicable to a being such as God is supposed to be. For example, aside from certain complications arising from the doctrine of the incarnation, it would be logically inappropriate to speak of God as controlling his sexual desires. (He doesn't have any.) And given some widely held conceptions of God and his relation to the world, it would hardly make sense to speak of him as *courageous*. For if he is impassible and has predetermined absolutely everything that happens, he has no risks to face and cannot endure (because he cannot suffer) pain or displeasure.

Believers in God's goodness also typically think he lacks some human virtues which would *not* be logically inapplicable to a being like him. A virtuous man, for instance, does not intentionally cause the death of other human beings, except under exceptional circumstances. But God has intentionally brought it about that all men die. There are agonizing forms of the problem of evil; but I think that for most Judeo-Christian believers (especially those who believe in life after death), this is not one of them. They believe that God's making men mortal and his commanding them not to kill each other, fit together in a larger pattern of harmonious purposes. How then can one distinguish between human virtues which God must have if he is good and human virtues which God may lack and still be good? This is an interesting and important question, but I will not attempt here to formulate a precise or adequate criterion for making the distinction. I fear it would require a lengthy digression from the issues with which we are principally concerned.

(5) If we accept a divine command theory of ethical rightness and wrongness, I think we shall have to say that *dutifulness* is a human virtue which, like sexual chastity, is logically inapplicable to God. God cannot either do or fail to do his duty, since he does not have a duty—at least not in the most important sense in which human beings have a duty. For he is not subject to a moral law not of his own making. Dutifulness is one virtuous disposition which men can have that God cannot have. But there are other virtuous dispositions which God can have as well as men. Love, for instance. It hardly makes sense to say that God does what he does *because* it is right. But it does not follow that God cannot have any reason for doing what he does. It does not even follow that he cannot have reasons of a type on which it would be morally virtuous for a man to act. For example, he might do something because he knew it would make his creatures happier.

(6) The modified divine command theorist must deny that in calling God "good" one presupposes a standard of moral rightness and wrongness superior to the will of God, by reference to which it is determined whether God's character is virtuous or not. And I think he can consistently deny that. He can say that morally virtuous and vicious qualities of character are those which agree and conflict, respectively, with God's commands, and that it is their agreement or disagreement with God's commands that makes them virtuous or vicious. But the believer normally thinks he has at least a general idea of what qualities of character are in fact virtuous and vicious (approved and disapproved by God). Having such an idea, he can apply the word "good" descriptively to God, meaning that (with some exceptions, as I have noted) God has the qualities which the believer regards as virtues, such as faithfulness and kindness.

I will sum up by contrasting what the believer can mean when he says, "Moses is good," with what he can mean when he says, "God is good,"

according to the modified divine command theory. When the believer says. "Moses is good," (a) he normally is expressing a favorable emotional attitude toward Moses (normally, though perhaps not always—sometimes a person's moral goodness displeases us). (b) He normally implies that Moses possesses a large proportion of those qualities of character which are recognized in the religious-ethical community as virtues, and few if any of those which are regarded as vices. (c) He normally implies that the qualities of Moses' character on the basis of which he describes Moses as good are qualities approved by God.

When the believer says, "God is good," (a) he normally is expressing a favorable emotional attitude toward God, and I think exceptions on this point would be rarer than in the case of statements that a man is good. (b) He normally is ascribing to God certain qualities of character. He may mean primarily that God is kind or benevolent, that he is *good* to human beings or certain ones of them. Or he may mean that God possesses (with some exceptions) those qualities of character which are regarded as virtues in the religious-ethical community. (c) Whereas in saying, "Moses is good," the believer was stating or implying that the qualities of character which he was ascribing to Moses conform to a standard of ethical rightness which is independent of the will of Moses, he is not stating or implying that the qualities of character which he ascribes to God conform to a standard of ethical rightness which is independent of the will of God.

VI

As I noted at the outset, the divine command theory of ethical wrongness, even in its modified form, has the consequence that believers and nonbelievers use the word "wrong" with different meanings in ethical contexts, since it will hardly be thought that nonbelievers mean by "wrong" what the theory says believers mean by it. This consequence gives rise to an objection. For the phenomena of common moral discourse between believers and nonbelievers suggest that they mean the same thing by "wrong" in ethical contexts. In the present section I shall try to explain how the modified divine command theorist can account for the facts of common ethical discourse.

I will first indicate what I think the troublesome facts are. Judeo-Christian believers enter into ethical discussions with people whose religious or antireligious beliefs they do not know. It seems to be possible to conduct quite a lot of ethical discourse, with apparent understanding, without knowing one's partner's views on religious issues. Believers also discuss ethical questions with persons who are known to them to be nonbelievers. They agree with such persons, disagree with them, and try to persuade them, about what acts are morally wrong. (Or at least it is normally *said*, by the participants and others, that they agree and disagree about such issues.) Believers ascribe, to people who are known not to believe in God, beliefs that certain acts are morally wrong. Yet surely believers do not suppose that nonbelievers, in calling acts wrong, mean that they are contrary to the will or commandments of God. Under these circumstances how can the believer really mean "contrary to the will or commandments of God" when he says "wrong"? If he agrees and disagrees with nonbelievers about what is wrong, if he ascribes to them beliefs that certain acts are wrong, must he not be using "wrong" in a nontheological sense?

What I shall argue is that in some ordinary (and I fear imprecise) sense of "mean," what believers and nonbelievers mean by "wrong" in ethical contexts may well be partly the same and partly different. There are agreements between believers and nonbelievers which make common moral discourse between them possible. But these agreements do not show that the two groups mean exactly the same thing by "wrong." They do not show that "contrary to God's will or commands" is not part of what believers mean by "wrong."

Let us consider first the agreements which make possible common moral discourse between believers and nonbelievers.

(1) One important agreement, which is so obvious as to be easily overlooked, is that they use many of the same ethical terms—"wrong," "right," "ought," "duty," and others. And they may utter many of the same ethical sentences, such as "Racial discrimination is morally wrong." In determining what people believe we rely very heavily on what they say (when they seem to be speaking sincerely)—and that means, in large part, on the words that they use and the sentences they utter. If I know that somebody says, with apparent sincerity, "Racial discrimination is morally wrong," I will normally ascribe to him the belief that racial discrimination is morally wrong, even if I also know that he does not mean *exactly* the same thing as I do by "racial discrimination" or "morally wrong." Of course if I know he means something *completely* different, I would not ascribe the belief to him without explicit qualification.

I would not claim that believers and nonbelievers use *all* the same ethical terms. "Sin," "law of God," and "Christian," for instance, occur as ethical terms in the discourse of many believers, but would be much less likely to occur in the same way in nonbelievers' discourse.

(2) The shared ethical terms have the same basic grammatical status for believers as for nonbelievers, and at least many of the same logical connections with other expressions. Everyone agrees, for instance, in treating "wrong" as an adjective and "Racial discrimination is morally wrong" as a declarative sentence. "(All) racial discrimination is morally wrong" would be treated by all parties as expressing an A-type (universal affirmative) proposition, from which consequences can be drawn by syllogistic reasoning or the predicate calculus. All agree that if X is morally wrong, then it isn't morally right and refraining from X is morally obligatory. Such grammatical and formal agreements are important to common moral discourse.

(3) There is a great deal of agreement, among believers and nonbelievers, as to what types of action they call "wrong" in an ethical sense and I think that that agreement is one of the things that make common moral discourse possible. It is certainly not complete agreement. Obviously there is a lot of ethical disagreement in the world.

Much of it cuts right across religious lines, but not all of it does. There are things which are typically called "wrong" by members of some religious groups, and not by others. Nonetheless there are types of action which everyone or almost everyone would call morally wrong, such as torturing someone to death because he accidentally broke a small window in your house. Moreover any two people (including any one believer and one nonbeliever) are likely to find some actions they both call wrong that not everyone does. I imagine that most ethical discussion takes place among people whose area of agreement in what they call wrong is relatively large.

There is probably much less agreement about the most basic issues in moral theory than there is about many ethical issues of less generality. There is much more unanimity in what people (sincerely) say in answer to such questions as "Was what Hitler did to the Jews wrong?" or "Is it normally wrong to disobey the laws of one's country?" than in what they (sincerely) say in answer to such questions as "Is it always right to do the act which will have the best results?" or "Is pleasure the only thing that is good for its own sake?" The issue between adherents and nonadherents of divine command ethics is typical of basic issues in ethical and metaethical theory in this respect.

(4) The emotional and volitional attitudes normally expressed by the statement that something is "wrong" are similar in believers and nonbelievers. They are not exactly the same; the attitudes typically expressed by the believer's statement that something is "wrong" are importantly related to his religious practice and beliefs about God, and this doubtless makes them different in some ways from the attitudes expressed by nonbelievers uttering the same sentence. But the attitudes are certainly similar, and that is important for the possibility of common moral discourse.

(5) Perhaps even more important is the related fact that the social functions of a statement that something is (morally) "wrong" are similar for believers and nonbelievers. To say that something someone else is known to have done is "wrong" is commonly to attack him. If you say that something you are known to have done is

"wrong," you abandon certain types of defense. To say that a public policy is "wrong" is normally to register oneself as opposed to it, and is sometimes a signal that one is willing to be supportive of common action to change it. These social functions of moral discourse are extremely important. It is perhaps not surprising that we are inclined to say that two people agree with each other when they both utter the same sentence and thereby indicate their readiness to take the same side in a conflict.

Let us sum up these observations about the conditions which make common moral discourse between believers and nonbelievers possible. (1) They use many of the same ethical terms, such as "wrong." (2) They treat those terms as having the same basic grammatical and logical status, and many of the same logical connections with other expressions. (3) They agree to a large extent about what types of action are to be called "wrong." To call an action "wrong" is, among other things, to classify it with certain other actions, and there is considerable agreement between believers and nonbelievers as to what actions those are. (4) The emotional and volitional attitudes which believers and nonbelievers normally express in saying that something is "wrong" are similar, and (5) saying that something is "wrong" has much the same social functions for believers and nonbelievers.

So far as I can see, none of this is inconsistent with the modified divine command theory of ethical wrongness. According to that theory there are several things which are true of the believer's use of "wrong" which cannot plausibly be supposed to be true of the nonbeliever's. In saying "X is wrong," the believer commits himself (subjectively, at least, and publicly if he is known to be a believer) to the claim that X is contrary to God's will or commandments. The believer will not say that anything would be wrong, under any possible circumstances, if it were not contrary to God's will or commandments. In many contexts he uses the term "wrong" interchangeably with "against the will of God" or "against the commandments of God." The heart of the modified divine command theory, I have suggested, is the claim that when the believer says, "X is wrong," one thing he means to be doing is stating a nonnatural objective fact about X, and the nonnatural objective fact he means to be stating is that X is contrary to the will or commandments of God. This claim may be true even though the uses of "wrong" by believers and nonbelievers are similar in all five of the ways pointed out above.

Suppose these contentions of the modified divine command theory are correct. (I think they are very plausible as claims about the ethical discourse of at least some religious believers.) In that case believers and nonbelievers surely do not mean exactly the same thing by "X is wrong" in ethical contexts. But neither is it plausible to suppose that they mean entirely different things, given the phenomena of common moral discourse. We must suppose, then, that their meaning is partly the same and partly different. "Contrary to God's will or commands" must be taken as expressing only part of the meaning with which the believer uses "wrong." Some of the similarities between believers' and nonbelievers' use of "wrong" must also be taken as expressing parts of the meaning with which the believer uses "wrong." This view of the matter agrees with the account of the modified divine command theory in section III, where I pointed out that the modified divine command theorist cannot mean exactly the same thing by "wrong" that he means by "contrary to God's commands."

We have here a situation which commonly arises when some people hold, and others do not hold, a given theory about the nature of something which everyone talks about. The chemist, who believes that water is a compound of hydrogen and oxygen, and the man who knows nothing of chemistry, surely do not use the word "water" in entirely different senses, but neither is it very plausible to suppose that they use it with exactly the same meaning. I am inclined to say that in some fairly ordinary sense of "mean," a phenomenalist, and a philosopher who holds some conflicting theory about what it is for a physical object to exist, do not mean exactly the same thing by "There is a bottle of milk in the refrigerator." But they certainly do not mean entirely different things, and they can agree that there is a bottle of milk in the refrigerator.

VII

These remarks bring us face to face with some important issues in the general theory of analysis and meaning. What are the criteria for determining whether two utterers of the same expression mean exactly the same thing by it, or something partly different, or something entirely different? What is the relation between philosophical analyses, and philosophical theories about the natures of things, on the one hand, and the meanings of terms in ordinary discourse on the other hand? I have permitted myself the liberty of speaking as if these issues did not exist. But their existence is notorious, and I certainly cannot resolve them in this essay. Indeed, I do not have resolutions to offer.

In view of these uncertainties in the theory of meaning, it is worth noting that much of what the modified divine command theorist wants to say can be said without making claims about the *meaning* of ethical terms. He wants to say, for instance, that believers' claims that certain acts are wrong normally express certain attitudes toward those acts, whether or not that is part of their meaning; that an act is wrong if and only if it is contrary to God's will or commands (assuming God loves us); that nonetheless, if God commanded cruelty for its own sake, neither obedience nor disobedience would be ethically wrong or ethically permitted; that if an act is contrary to God's will or commands that is a nonnatural objective fact about it; and that that is the only nonnatural objective fact which obtains if and only if the act is wrong. These are among the most important claims of the modified divine command theory—perhaps they include the very most important. But in the form in which I have just stated them, they are not claims about the *meaning* of ethical terms.

I do not mean to reject the claims about the meanings of terms in religious ethical discourse which I have included in the modified divine command theory. In the absence of general solutions to general problems in the theory of meaning, we may perhaps say what seems to us intuitively plausible in particular cases. That is presumably what the modified divine command theorist is doing when he claims that "contrary to the will or commands of God" is part of the meaning of "(ethically) wrong" for many Judeo-Christian believers.

And I think it is fair to say that if we have found unresolved problems about meaning in the modified divine command theory, they are problems much more about what we mean in general by "meaning" than about what Judeo-Christian believers mean by "wrong."

6.4 An Afro-American Revolutionary Christianity

When some people associate religion and morality, they think in terms of rules concerning "do's and don'ts" that individuals should follow in order to live a good life. However, we should not ignore the social and political dimensions of religions. The cry of the Jewish prophets for social justice and Jesus' teaching about loving one's neighbor clearly have political and social implications. This is the prophetic aspect of Judaism and Christianity. Other religions also contain prophetic elements. By "prophetic" I do not mean the foretelling of future events, but the demand that echoes throughout the *Bible,* the *Qu'ran,* and other sacred scriptures for social justice.

African Americans were brought to the Americas in chains to work as slaves. Many converted to Christianity and eventually developed their own distinctive styles of worship and preaching. Because they were and remain an oppressed people subject to discrimination and racism, the promise of justice and liberation from oppression found in the *Bible* became and remains central to their understanding of the Christian gospel.

The African American community has grasped with great clarity the prophetic dimension of Christianity and has, over the years, brought forth its own prophets. In the latter part of this century two are particularly well known: Martin Luther King, Jr. (1929–1968) and Malcolm X (1925–1965). King was a Baptist minister who drew on the Jewish prophets, the message of Jesus, and the teachings of Gandhi to lay a religious foundation for the civil rights movement. Racial injustice is morally intolerable for many different reasons, but one of them (and one that King found particularly important) is that it violates the basic moral norms of Judaism and Christianity. We are all children of God, and God has made it clear through the prophets and Jesus that social justice is a fundamental moral value.

Malcolm X was a Muslim minister who drew on the Islamic tradition in his demand for social justice, civil rights for African Americans, and an end to racism and discrimination. He came to traditional Islam by way of the Black Muslim movement, which preached, among other things, that the "white man is the devil." However, after a trip to Mecca, he realized that traditional Islam taught that all peoples, black or white, were children of the one God Allah. Malcolm X did not agree with Martin Luther King that nonviolence was the only acceptable means to achieve social justice, but both were inspired by their religious convictions.

Cornel West, author of the following selection, is a professor of religion and the director of the Afro-American Studies Program at Princeton University. He is the author of more than 12 books. He wants to forge links among Christianity, Marxism, and American pragmatism in order to find resources for developing a philosophical and religious foundation for the promotion of social justice.

Reading Questions

1. What is the basic contribution of prophetic Christianity to Afro-American critical thought?
2. What is the Christian dialectic of human nature and human history?
3. What is the difference between penultimate and ultimate liberation?
4. What is the second fundamental norm of prophetic Christianity, and how is it related to the Christian dialectic?
5. What is the difference between Christian and Marxist historicism?
6. What is the conception of philosophy that is characteristic of American pragmatists such as John Dewey?
7. How does pragmatism characterize knowledge?
8. How does West define Afro-American critical thought, and what, according to West, are its tasks?
9. How do you think West would respond to the argument that the African American community is best served by returning to, renewing, and strengthening its African religious roots and traditions instead of turning to Christianity for moral resources in the struggle for liberation and social justice?

An Afro-American Revolutionary Christianity*

CORNEL WEST

THE OBJECT OF INQUIRY for Afro-American critical thought is the past and the present, the doings and the sufferings of African people in the United States. Rather than a new scientific discipline or field of study, it is a genre of writing, a textuality, a mode of discourse that interprets, describes, and evaluates Afro-American life in order comprehensively to understand and effectively to transform it. It is not concerned with "foundations" or transcendental "grounds" but with how to build its language in such a way that the configuration of sentences and the constellation of paragraphs themselves create a textuality and distinctive discourse which are a material force for Afro-American freedom.[1]

First Source: Prophetic Christian Thought

Afro-American thought must take seriously the most influential and enduring intellectual tradition in its experience: evangelical and pietistic Christianity. This tradition began the moment that African slaves, laboring in sweltering heat on plantations owned and ruled primarily by white American Christians, tried to understand their lives and servitude in the light of biblical texts, Protestant hymns, and Christian testimonies.[2] This theological reflection—simultaneously building on and breaking with earlier African non-Christian theological reflection—is inseparable from the black

*From *Prophesy Deliverance! An Afro-American Revolutionary Christianity.* © 1982 Cornel West. Used by permission of Westminster John Knox Press.

church.[3] This "church," merely a rubric to designate black Christian communities of many denominations, came into being when slaves decided, often at the risk of life and limb, to "make Jesus their choice" and to share with one another their common Christian sense of purpose and Christian understanding of their circumstances. Like the tradition of other Christian communities, this took many forms, some more prophetic than others, and its multiplicity of streams made possible the rich diversity of contemporary black theological reflection which encompasses both prophetic and priestly streams, the visionary and quotidian components, of the tradition. Afro-American critical thought must focus on the former of these streams, the prophetic. This has been guided by a profound conception of human nature and human history, a persuasive picture of what one is as a person, what one should hope for, and how one ought to act.[4] It also proposes the two fundamental moral norms of individuality and democracy as the center of Afro-American thought. I will not stress here the obvious opposition of prophetic black Christianity to racism, but rather its character as an underlying prophetic world view.

The basic contribution of prophetic Christianity, despite the countless calamities perpetrated by Christian churches, is that every individual regardless of class, country, caste, race, or sex should have the opportunity to fulfill his or her potentialities.[5] This first and fundamental norm is the core of the prophetic Christian gospel. A transcendent God before whom all persons are equal thus endows the well-being and ultimate salvation of each with equal value and significance. I shall call this radical egalitarian idea *the Christian principle of the self-realization of individuality within community*. This is often interpreted as simply the salvation of *individual* souls in heaven, an otherworldly community. But such a truncated understanding of the core of the Christian gospel accents its otherworldly dimension at the expense of its this-worldly possibilities. The fuller prophetic Christian tradition must thus insist upon both this-worldly liberation and otherworldly salvation as the proper loci of Christianity.

The quite similar fundamental thrust of Marxism, despite the numerous brutalities perpetrated by Marxist regimes, is the self-fulfillment, self-development, and self-realization of harmonious personalities.[6] Marxism is a child of nineteenth-century Romanticism to the extent that it subscribes to a steadfast hope in an earthly paradise and invests in politics a passion previously monopolized by Christianity. Since Romanticism was, as M. H. Abrams demonstrated, a naturalization of the Christian world view, a secularization of the Christian gospel, it is no accident that Marxism and Christianity share a similar moral impulse.[7] Socioeconomic well-being has remained at the center of Marxist dogma, but the political liberties and diverse cultural activities of individuals have, for the most part, been ignored by it. Thus, the historical roots of the notion of individuality are found in the Christian gospel and the Romantic world view, a moral core which Marxism has also appropriated. The norm of individuality reinforces the importance of community, common good, and the harmonious development of personality. And it stands in stark contrast to those doctrinaire individualisms which promote human selfishness, denigrate the idea of community, and distort the holistic development of personality. The norm of individuality conceives persons as enjoyers and agents of their uniquely human capacities, whereas doctrinaire individualism views them as maximizers of pleasure and appropriators of unlimited resources.[8]

Two further fundamental elements in the Christian gospel are the dignity of persons and, likewise, the depravity of persons: human beings possess the capacity to transform prevailing realities for the better, and yet are prone to do so imperfectly. The dignity of persons is their ability to contradict what is, to change and be changed, and to act in the light of that which is not-yet. The depravity of persons is their proclivity to cling to the moment, to refuse to transform and to be transformed. The Christian gospel accents decision, commitment, engagement, and action which transform what is in the light of that which is to be. The Christian gospel also acknowledges that such contradiction and transformation are circumscribed by human imperfection.

Contradiction and transformation are at the heart of the Christian gospel. The former always presupposes what presently is; the latter, the prevailing realities. For Christians, this "what is" and these "prevailing realities" are products of fallen, finite creatures, products that bear the stamp of imperfection. *This dialectic of imperfect products and transformative practice, of prevailing realities and negation, of human depravity and human dignity, of what is and the not-yet constitutes the Christian dialectic of human nature and human history.* Each element of the dialectic is inextricably bound to the other, as are human nature and human history.

This emphasis on process, development, discontinuity, and even disruption precludes the possibility of human perfection and human utopias. Human beings possess the capacity to change their conditions and themselves, but not to perfect either their conditions or themselves. Human history dooms human beings to problems and problematics, obstacles and obstructions, to relative achievements and relative accomplishments.

For Christians, the realm of history is the realm of the pitiful and the tragic.[9] It serves as the context for passive persons who refuse to negate and transform what is and for active persons who reject and change prevailing realities. The pitiful are those who remain objects of history, victims manipulated by evil forces; whereas the tragic are those persons who become subjects of history, aggressive antagonists of evil forces. Victims are pitiful because they have no possibility of achieving either penultimate liberation or ultimate salvation; aggressive antagonists are tragic because they fight for penultimate liberation, and in virtue of their gallant struggle against the limits of history they become prime candidates for ultimate salvation. In this sense, to play a tragic role in history is positive: to negate and transform what is, yet run up against the historical limits of such negation and transformation, is candidacy for transcending those limits.

Penultimate liberation is the developmental betterment of humankind, the furtherance of the uncertain quest for human freedom in history. Ultimate salvation hopes for the transcendence of history, the deliverance of humankind from the treacherous dialectic of human nature and human history. The process of penultimate liberation can culminate within history, whereas the process of ultimate salvation is grounded in history but promises to proceed beyond it.

For prophetic Christianity, the two inseparable notions of freedom are existential freedom and social freedom. Existential freedom is an effect of the divine gift of grace which promises to sustain persons through and finally deliver them from the bondage to death, disease, and despair. Social freedom is the aim of Christian political practice, a praxis that flows from the divine gift of grace; social freedom results from the promotion and actualization of the norms of individuality and democracy. Existential freedom empowers people to fight for social freedom, to realize its political dimension. Existential freedom anticipates history and is ultimately trans-historical, whereas social freedom is thoroughly a matter of this-worldly human liberation.

The prophetic Christian dialectic of human nature and human history produces *democracy* as its second fundamental norm. Democracy requires that accountability—of institutions to populace, of leaders to followers, of preachers to laity—be the center of any acceptable social vision. This accountability exists when people have control over the leaders and institutions that serve them. Democratic participation of people in the decision-making processes of institutions that regulate and govern their lives is a precondition for actualizing the Christian principle of the self-realization of human individuality in community. The norms of individuality and democracy are in this way inseparable. The former rests upon the moral core of the Christian gospel, the latter upon its historical realism.

The prophetic Christian norm of democracy reflects the dignity of persons in that it accents potential for human betterment. It recognizes the depravity of persons in that it acknowledges human disabilities. The Christian dialectic of human nature and human history makes the norm of democracy necessary and possible; yet only the praxis of imperfect human beings renders it desirable and realizable.

As with the Christian gospel, negation and transformation lie at the heart of Marxism. What is must be overcome; prevailing realities must be changed. Instead of a dialectic of human nature and human history, Marxism posits a dialectic of human practice and human history: human nature is nothing other than human practice under specific historical conditions, conditions which themselves are both results of past human practice and preconditions for it in the present. This *collapse* of human nature into human practice and into human history—as opposed to a dialectical relation of human nature to human practice and to human history—is the distinctive difference between Christianity and Marxism. The Christian espouses a dialectical historicism which stresses the dignity and the depravity of persons, whereas the Marxist puts forward a full-blown historicism in which the eventual perfectability of persons within history is inevitable. The Christian world view is a clandestine complaint against history, the Marxist an avowed apotheosis of it.

The contribution of prophetic Christian thought as a source for Afro-American critical thought is twofold. First, it confronts candidly the tragic character of human history (and the hope for ultimate transhistorical triumph) without permitting the immensity of what is and must be lost to call into question the significance of what may be gained. In this way, it allows us to sidestep what Baudelaire called "the metaphysical horror of modern thought" and take more seriously the existential anxiety, political oppression, economic exploitation, and social degradation of actual human beings. Second, prophetic Afro-American Christian thought elevates the notion of struggle (against the odds!)—personal and collective struggle regulated by the norms of individuality and democracy—to the highest priority. To be a prophetic Afro-American Christian is to negate what is and transform prevailing realities against the backdrop of the present historical limits. In short, prophetic Afro-American Christian thought imbues Afro-American thinking with the sobriety of tragedy, the struggle for freedom, and the spirit of hope.

Second Source: American Pragmatism

The basic notions in American philosophy that ought to play a significant role in the formation of Afro-American critical thought are primarily the products of the reforming orientation of the pragmatic movement.[10] This began with a series of papers that Charles Peirce wrote in 1872, continued in a more visible manner after 1898 in William James, and was elaborated in detail by George Mead and, above all, by John Dewey. The pragmatic movement questioned the subjectivist turn in European philosophy, the idea that knowledge requires philosophical foundations in direct personal awareness, through intuition or unmediated insight. For American pragmatists, the quest for such certainties and foundations could only be misguided.

John Dewey recognized that philosophy is inextricably bound to culture, society, and history.[11] For Dewey, an autonomous philosophy would be culturally outmoded. Like its first cousin, theology, philosophy was once an autonomous discipline with its own distinct set of problems, most of which now lie at the mercy of psychology, sociology, history, and anthropology.

Despite this, however, the normative function of philosophy remains. It becomes the critical expression of a culture and the critical thought of a society, sacrificing in the process its delusions of autonomy. Philosophy is, thus, the interpretation of a people's past for the purpose of solving specific problems presently confronting the cultural way of life from which the people come. For Dewey, philosophy is critical in that it constantly questions the tacit assumptions of earlier interpretations of the past. It scrutinizes the norms these interpretations endorse, the solutions they offer, and the self-images they foster.

American pragmatism rejects the idea of knowledge as a private affair where one begins with uninterpreted givens, theory-free entities, self-authenticating episodes, or intrinsically credible beliefs, and builds all other knowledge upon them. Rather, it conceives of knowledge as within the conceptual framework of intersubjective, communal inquiry. Of course, some norms, premises, and procedures must be taken for granted, but these are never immune to revision. For American pragmatists, the myth of the given must be demythologized. Knowledge should not be a rummaging for foundations but a matter of public testing and open evaluation of consequences. Knowledge claims are secured by the social practices of a community of inquirers, rather than the purely mental activity of an individual subject. The community understands inquiry as a set of social practices geared toward achieving and warranting knowledge, a perennial process of dialogue which can question any claim but never all at once. This self-correcting enterprise requires neither foundations nor grounds. It yields no absolute certainty. The social or communal is thus the central philosophical category of this pragmatist conception of knowledge. It recognizes that in knowledge the crucial component is not intuition but social practice and communal norm.

The pragmatist movement also bursts the narrow conception of experience of the Cartesian tradition and its historical successors. In contrast to the narrowness of Cartesian individualism, the pragmatic conception of experience is broader in scope and richer in content. And, lastly, pragmatism's primary aim is to discern, delineate, and defend particular norms through highlighting desirable possibilities present in the practices of a specific community or society. The goal of reflection is amelioration, and its chief consequence is the transformation of existing realities. This process is guided by moral convictions and social norms, and the transformation is shaped by the interpretation and description of the prevailing communal practices.

Afro-American thought recognizes, of course, the major shortcomings of the pragmatist movement: its relative neglect of the self, its refusal to take class struggle seriously, and its veneration of scientific method and the practices of the scien-

tific community.[12] And, in contrast to this, Afro-American Christian thought must, for its part, emphasize the uniqueness of human personality, the centrality of the class struggle, and the political dimensions of knowledge. But pragmatism's contributions are still enormous. Through its historicist orientation, for example, Afro-American thought can avoid both absolutist dogmatism and paralysis in action. Pragmatism also dethroned epistemology as the highest priority of modern thought in favor of ethics: not the professional discipline of ethics but the search for desirable and realizable historical possibilities in the present. Despite its limitations, pragmatism provides an American context for Afro-American thought, a context that imparts to it both a shape and a heritage of philosophical legitimacy.

Following its sources, I shall define Afro-American critical thought as an interpretation of Afro-American history, especially its cultural heritage and political struggles, which provides norms for responding to challenges presently confronting black Americans. The particular historical phenomena interpreted and justified by it consist in religious doctrines, political ideologies, artistic expressions, and unconscious modes of behavior. These serve as raw ingredients to be utilized to interpret the Afro-American past and defend the existence of particular norms within it.

The Tasks

The two basic challenges presently confronting Afro-Americans are self-image and self-determination. The former is the perennial human attempt to define who and what one is, the issue of self-identity. The latter is the political struggle to gain significant control over the major institutions that regulate people's lives. These challenges are abstractly distinguishable, yet concretely inseparable. In other words, culture and politics must always be viewed in close relationship to each other.[13]

The major function of Afro-American critical thought is to reshape the contours of Afro-American history and provide a new self-understanding of the Afro-American experience which suggests guidelines for action in the present.[14] It attempts to make theoretically explicit what is implicit in history, to describe and demystify cultural and social practices and offer solutions to urgent problems besetting black Americans.

Afro-American thought is thus critical in character and historical in content. It is an interpretive activity which reveals new insights and uncovers old blindnesses about the complexity and richness of the Afro-American experience. Its first task is to put forward an overarching interpretive framework for the inescapable problematic of any such inquiry: What is the relationship between the African, American, and European elements in this experience? The prerequisite for a sophisticated response to this is an understanding of the emergence, development, and end of European modernity, the complex variation of it which evolved as American culture, and the intricate transactions between marginalized Africans—for the most part effectively excluded from the behavioral modes and material benefits of European life—and the American culture in which these dark bastard people were both participants and victims. . . .

The second task of an Afro-American religious philosophy is to engage in a genealogical inquiry into the cultural and linguistic roots—in addition to the economic, political, and psychological roots—of the idea of white supremacy which has shaped the Afro-American encounter with the modern world. What is the complex configuration of controlling metaphors, categories, and norms which shape and mold this idea in the modern West? . . .

The third task of Afro-American thought is to provide a theoretical reconstruction and evaluation of Afro-American responses to white supremacy. . . . [T]his takes the form of delineating four fundamental traditions in Afro-American thought and practice. I will endorse one of them.

The fourth task of Afro-American religious thought is to present a dialogical encounter between prophetic Afro-American Christian thought and progressive Marxist social analysis. The aim of this dialogue . . . is to demystify the deep misunderstanding and often outright ignorance each side has of the other. And since in Christianity and Marxism we are dealing with the most distorted traditions in the modern world, we have a difficult task before us. In my view, this effort is warranted by the fact that in an alliance between prophetic Christianity and progressive Marxism—both castigated remnants within their own worlds—lies the hope of Western civilization. The destiny of Afro-Americans is inextricably bound—as is most of the world—with the fate of this civilization.

The last task of Afro-American religious philosophy is to provide a political prescription for—or strategic intervention into—the specific praxis in the present historical moment of the struggle for liberation. . . . Afro-American critical thought begins in a broad theoretical mode by situating the life-worlds of Africans in the United States and ends in a narrow practical mode steeped in those same life-worlds. This philosophical journey is mediated by value-laden interpretations of the Afro-American struggle for freedom; the major bias of this inquiry is the desire for freedom.

The articulation of an Afro-American religious philosophy presupposes access to and acquisition of certain kinds of skills, training, and knowledge. The skills, interpretive and descriptive, make use of imagination, self-reflection, and logical analysis. The training requirements are open-ended and may range from those of a classical humanist to those of an autodidactic street philosopher. The crucial element is the ability for rigorous thought, clear exposition, and investment of one's whole self in one's thinking. Afro-American thought must also remove itself from the uncritical elements of mainstream Afro-American life. This is not a geographical or existential removal, but an intellectual one which acknowledges the demands of the discipline. Any critical and creative activity requires a certain degree of marginality. Intellectual activity certainly flourishes best when one is on the margin, not in an ivory tower but resolutely outside the world of aimless chitchat and gossip.

Afro-American philosophy expresses the particular American variation of European modernity that Afro-Americans helped shape in this country and must contend with in the future. While it might be possible to articulate a competing Afro-American philosophy based principally on African norms and notions, it is likely that the result would be theoretically thin. Philosophy is cultural expression generated from and existentially grounded in the moods and sensibilities of a writer entrenched in the life-worlds of a people. The life-worlds of Africans in the United States are conceptually and existentially neither solely African, European, nor American, but more the latter than any of the former. In fact, ironically, the attempt by black intellectuals to escape from their Americanness and even go beyond Western thought is itself very *American*.

NOTES

1. For the conception of philosophy as a kind of writing, rather than a science in search of certainty or professional area of study with a distinct subject matter, see Richard Rorty, "Philosophy as a Kind of Writing: An Essay on Derrida," *New Literary History*, Vol. 10, No. 1 (Autumn 1978), pp. 141–160. Needless to say, my perspective is deeply influenced by Richard Rorty's brilliant work, *Philosophy and the Mirror of Nature* (Princeton University Press, 1979). For my sympathetic yet hard-hitting critique of this book, see my review in *Union Seminary Quarterly Review*, Vol. 37, Nos. 1, 2 (Fall-Winter 1981–1982), pp. 179–185.

2. For the best full-length treatment of this neglected phenomenon, see Albert J. Raboteau, *Slave Religion: The "Invisible Institution" in the Antebellum South* (Oxford University Press, 1978).

3. It is important to note that black churches in the United States evolved as independent churches, separate from any white control. Therefore black religious leadership and black theological reflection could arise autonomous (or at least, relatively so) from white censorship, as is not the case for black people in Catholic and Anglican churches in Latin America and Africa. It is no accident that Pentecostalism—the denomination that vigorously promotes the development of indigenous religious leadership free from the control of church bureaucracies—was founded by black Baptists, principally Rev. W. J. Seymour in Los Angeles, California, in 1906. Pentecostalism is the only denomination of the Christian faith founded by black people and is one of the fastest-growing denominations in the world, especially among oppressed peoples. See James S. Tinney, "Black Origins of the Pentecostal Movement," *Christianity Today*, Oct. 8, 1971, pp. 4–6, and Richard Quebedeaux, *The New Charismatics* (Doubleday & Co., 1976), pp. 25–51.

4. For the complex relationship between the conception of a person and moral norms, see the superb essays by Samuel Scheffler, "Moral Skepticism and Ideals of the Person," and Norman Daniels, "Moral Theory and the Plasticity of Persons," *The Monist: An International Journal of General Philosophical Inquiry*, Vol. 62, No. 3 (July 1979), pp. 288–303 and pp. 266–287. I also touch on this difficult issue in "Ethics, Historicism and the Marxist Tradition," Ph.D. dissertation, Princeton University, 1980, pp. 3–26, 127–145, 259–274.

5. This claim is partly derived from Hegel's insight regarding the Christian principle of self-consciousness or subjectivity in his *The Philosophy of History*, trans. J. Sibree (Dover Publications, 1956), pp. 19, 319, 334. See also Colin Morris, *The Discovery of the Individual, 1050–1200* (Harper & Row, 1972), pp. 10–13.

6. For interesting treatments of Marx's own Romantic sensibilities as a young literary artist and thinker, see William M. Johnston, "Karl Marx's Verse of 1836–1837 as a Foreshadowing of His Early Philosophy," *Journal of the History of Ideas 28* (1967), pp. 259–268; Leonard P. Nessell, "Marx's Romantic Poetry and the Crisis of Romantic Lyricism," *Studies in Romanticism*, Vol. 16, No. 4 (Fall 1977), pp. 509–534; Donald R. Kelley, "The Metaphysics of Law: An Essay on the Very Young Marx," *American Historical Review*, Vol. 83, No. 2 (April 1978), pp. 350–367. Marx's own deep concern for individuality can be seen in the following three passages from three major works: "In bourgeois society, therefore, the past dominates the present; in Communist society, the present dominates the past. In bourgeois society capital is independent and has individuality, while the living person is dependent and has no individuality. . . . In place of the old bourgeois society, with its classes and class antagonisms, we shall have an association, in which the free development of each is the condition for the free development of all." (Karl Marx, "Manifesto of the Communist party," in *The Marx-Engels Reader*, ed. Robert C. Tucker, pp. 347, 353; W. W. Norton & Co., 1972.) "The communal relationship, into which the individuals of a class entered and which was determined by their common interests over against a third party, was always a community to which these individuals belonged only as average individuals, only insofar as they lived within the conditions of existence of their class—a relationship in which they participated not as individuals but as members of a class. On the other hand, it is just the reverse with the community of revolutionary proletarians who take their conditions of existence and those of all members of society under their control. The individuals participate in this

community as individuals." (Karl Marx, *The German Ideology, Writings of the Young Marx on Philosophy and Society,* trans. and ed. Lloyd D. Easton and Kurt H. Guddat, p. 460; Doubleday & Co., 1967.) "The barrier to capital is that this entire development proceeds in a contradictory way, and that the working-out of the productive forces, of general wealth, etc., knowledge etc., appears in such a way that the working individual alienates himself [*sich entäussert*]; relates to the conditions brought out of him by his labour as those not of his own but of an alien wealth and of his own poverty. But this antithetical form is itself fleeting, and produces the real conditions of its own suspension. The result is: the tendentially and potentially general development of the forces of production—of wealth as such—as basis; likewise, the universality of intercourse, hence the world market as a basis. The basis as the possibility of the universal development of the individual, and the real development of the individuals from this basis." (Karl Marx, *Grundrisse: Foundations of the Critique of Political Economy,* trans. Martin Nicolaus, pp. 541–542; Random House, 1973.)

7. M. H. Abrams, *Natural Supernaturalism: Tradition and Revolution in Romantic Literature* (W. W. Norton & Co., 1971). For his conception of Marx's "Romantic humanism" in the early *Manuscripts,* see pp. 313–316.

8. This central contrast—as well as the elaboration of the notion of individuality—is the major point of departure in the writings of C. B. MacPherson. This important Canadian political theorist deserves much more attention than he has received. See his *The Political Theory of Possessive Individualism: Hobbes to Locke* (Oxford University Press, 1962); *The Real World of Democracy* (Oxford University Press, 1966); *Democratic Theory: Essays in Retrieval* (Oxford University Press, 1973).

9. A distinctive feature of prophetic Afro-American Christianity is the African encounter with the absurd in the United States: an existential situation in which no reasons suffice to make any kind of sense or give any type of meaning to the personal circumstances and collective condition of Afro-Americans. With the "death of the African gods," the African appropriation of the Christian world view transformed a prevailing absurd situation into a persistent and present tragic one—a kind of "Good Friday state of existence"—with the hope for a potential and possible triumphant state of affairs. The relationship between this stress on the tragic and the relative absence of tragic themes in the ancient oral narratives of Dahomey (as noted by Melville Herskovits) remains unexplored. This creative appropriation, with African styles and forms within a new faith context, made new sense of the circumstances and gave new meaning to the lives of Afro-Americans by promoting a world view in which the

problem of evil—the utterly tragic character of life and history—sits at its center. Prophetic Afro-American Christianity is not simply an escapist pie-in-the-sky religion, nor a sophisticated political ideology in religious veil. Rather, it contains elements of both, plus an enduring emphasis on the deeply tragic quality of everyday life of a culturally degraded, politically oppressed, and racially coerced labor force and unique individuals who face the ultimate facts of human existence: death, disease, disappointment, dread, and despair. In fact, I suggest that the radically comic character of Afro-American life—the pervasive sense of joy, laughter, and ingenious humor in the black community—flows primarily from the Afro-American preoccupation with tragedy, a preoccupation significantly colored by the Black Christian world view. For as Walter Kerr has rightly noted: "Comedy is never the gaiety of things; it is the groan made gay. Laughter is not man's first impulse; he cries first. Comedy always comes second, late, after the fact and in spite of it or because of it." (Walter Kerr, *Tragedy and Comedy,* p. 19; Simon & Schuster, 1967.) Furthermore, as Prof. Dennis Dickerson, of Williams College, conveyed to me in conversation, the African sense of time, with its paradoxical poles of urgency and belatedness, in conjunction with this stress on tragedy may partly account for the phenomenon so deeply rooted in Afro-American Christian thought and practice: the aggressive waiting (or what I call revolutionary patience) for the Lord to intervene and the Kingdom of God to come. This "waiting" is not of the quietistic sort, but rather encourages action while tempering one's exorbitant expectations. I explore this matter as a pillar (among others) for a theory of Afro-American culture in my as yet unpublished essay (delivered at Haverford College), "Afro-American Christianity and the Quest for Cultural Identity."

10. For a recent philosophical plea for the importance of American pragmatism, see Richard J. Bernstein, "In Defense of American Philosophy," in *Contemporary American Philosophy,* Second Series, ed. John E. Smith (Humanities Press, 1970), pp. 293–311. For historical analyses of American pragmatism, see H. S. Thayer's detailed work, *Meaning and Action: A Critical History of Pragmatism* (Bobbs-Merrill Co., 1968), and John Dewey's classic essay "The Development of American Pragmatism," in his *Philosophy and Civilization* (Peter Smith, 1963), pp. 13–35. It is interesting that one of the leading African philosophers, Kwasi Wiredu, of the University of Ghana, is deeply influenced by American pragmatism—especially that of John Dewey. See his noteworthy book, *Philosophy and an African Culture* (Cambridge University Press, 1980).

11. I have in mind John Dewey's formulations in *Reconstruction in Philosophy* (Beacon Press, 1949). For

a comparison to the work of Heidegger and Wittgenstein, see Cornel West, "Philosophy and the Afro-American Experience," *The Philosophical Forum*, Vol. 9, Nos. 2–3 (Winter 1977–78), pp. 117–148.

12. For a penetrating critique of the neglect of the self in pragmatism, especially in the work of John Dewey (and treatment by the pragmatic psychologist George Mead), see Gordon Allport, "Dewey's Individual and Social Psychology," in *The Philosophy of John Dewey*, ed. Paul Arthur Schilpp (Northwestern University, 1939), pp. 265–290. For the pragmatic movement's refusal to take seriously class struggle, the early Sidney Hook's work is unsurpassed. As the work of a student and disciple of Dewey and a self-styled Marxist, Hook's writings in the '30s serve as a corrective to Dewey's. See Sidney Hook, "John Dewey and His Critics," *The New Republic*, Vol. 67 (June 3, 1931), pp. 73–74; *Towards the Understanding of Karl Marx* (John Day Co., 1933); "Experimental Naturalism," in *American Philosophy Today and Tomorrow,* ed. Horace M. Kallen and Sidney Hook (Lee Furman, 1935), pp. 205–225; and for a brief examination of the early Hook's work, note the critical essay by Lewis S. Feuer, "From Ideology to Philosophy: Sidney Hook's Writings on Marxism," in *Sidney Hook and the Contemporary World: Essays on the Pragmatic Intelligence,* ed. P. W. Kurtz (John Day Co., 1968), pp. 35–53. Other noteworthy treatments of the intersection of American pragmatism (especially Dewey) and Marx are: Max Eastman's polemic response to the early Hook, "The Americanization of Marx," in his *Marxism: Is It Science?* (W. W. Norton & Co., 1940), pp. 299–348; William English Walling, *The Larger Aspects of Socialism* (1913), pp. 1–29, 373–385; Jim Cork, "John Dewey and Karl Marx," in *John Dewey, Philosopher of Science and Freedom,* ed. Sidney Hook (Dial Press, 1950), pp. 331–350; Harry K. Wells, *Pragmatism: Philosophy of Imperialism* (International Publications Co., 1954); Howard Selsam, *Philosophy in Revolution* (International Publications Co., 1957), pp. 102–114,

146–148; George Novack, *Pragmatism vs. Marxism: An Appraisal of John Dewey's Philosophy* (Pathfinder Press, 1975); and the fine treatment by Richard J. Bernstein, *Praxis and Action: Contemporary Philosophies of Human Activity* (University of Pennsylvania Press, 1971), pp. 80–83, 227–229. I believe Bernstein hits the nail on the head when he writes, "The dialectic that can take place between Marx and Dewey is the political dialectic of our time" (p. 80). Lastly, for the pragmatic movement's veneration of scientific method (much more Peirce, Dewey, and Mead than James), see the standard critical treatment of this issue by Jürgen Habermas, *Knowledge and Human Interests* (Beacon Press, 1971), pp. 113–139.

13. A particular conception of the Afro-American self-image deeply affects the political strategy of Afro-American self-determination. Yet we must not assume *a priori* that certain correlations necessarily hold, such as that a positive self-image will always accompany the acquisition of power, or a negative self-image the absence of power. Afro-American philosophy must preserve the delicate symbiotic relationship between culture and politics without resorting to a simplistic and all too often incorrect reductionism.

14. Based on my conception of Afro-American philosophy, there have been few instances of it. Of course, there have been Afro-American philosophers, such as Alain Locke, Eugene Holmes, and William Fontaine, but, like most Afro-American intellectuals, they have exerted their energies either trying to convince the black middle class that the world of ideas should be taken seriously, serving as an ideologue for a particular political or cultural movement, or attempting to gain acceptance in the predominantly white academy. All three activities are essential for a potent intelligentsia, but leave little time for reflecting upon the basic assumptions of the theoretical frameworks wherein thinkers speculate. Effective propagandists and insecure academicians rarely question basic frameworks or ask fundamental questions with seriousness.

6.5 Popular Religion and Liberation

Many religions speak of some kind of release, liberation, or freedom from suffering as their goals. Hinduism calls it *moksha,* Buddhism names it *nirvana,* and Christianity calls it salvation. Often the release or liberation envisioned is an other-worldly type of freedom. It is something that will occur to our spirit or soul after we die and leave this body far behind. This other-worldly characterization of the religious goal led Marx to think that religion was a mechanism of the rich and powerful to keep the poor and powerless in their place.

In Latin America, the gap between rich and poor is so apparent and so appalling that a group of theologians began to formulate what they called *teologia de la liberación.* Central to liberation theology is the notion that the liberation from suffering preached by the Christian gospel must be this-worldly liberation as well as other-worldly. People are both bodies and souls, and to "save the soul" but neglect the body is to violate the basic moral principles of Christianity. The church must be with the poor, work with the poor, and help the poor achieve social justice and economic equality in this world. The Christian church must be responsive to the needs of the people. It must listen to the people and learn from them.

However, the religion of the people, or popular religion, in Latin America as elsewhere often appears to be just the sort of religion of which Marx was so critical. There is often an intense concern with the other-worldly heavenly kingdom where all will eventually be well, and the truly faithful will be rewarded for their patience in suffering. Indeed, there is a strong element of the intensification of suffering in popular religion. It is good to suffer as Jesus suffered. God wants us to suffer. Suffering will improve our character. Suffering is good. How, then, can the liberation theologian, who wishes to raise people's consciousness so that they can see how they are unfairly exploited by the rich, listen to and learn from the people? How can popular religion become a force for liberation? Must it not be abandoned or transformed in significant ways?

Michael Candelaria, author of the following selection, probes the dilemma that popular religion raises for liberation theology. In the process, he shows how the relationship between religion and moral concerns with social justice is subtle and complex. There is no simple correlation between what a religion teaches and its impact on moral values. Social, cultural, and historical factors play a large role in shaping the relationship between religions and morality.

Reading Questions

1. What is the double dimension of popular religion, and what does it account for?
2. What are alienation and false consciousness, and how are they related to popular religion?
3. What are the two streams of liberation theology, and how does each evaluate popular religion?
4. What two criteria might be used to evaluate popular religion?
5. Do you believe that genuine economic and social justice is easier to achieve without the aid of popular religion? Why or why not?

Popular Religion and Liberation*

MICHAEL R. CANDELARIA

LIBERATION THEOLOGIANS generally admit that popular religiosity plays a role in the liberation of the masses. But does it play a positive role? Is it just a question of the survival of folk religion in an increasingly secularized world? What is its capacity for real socio-historical liberation? Segundo Galilea

*From *Popular Religion and Liberation: The Dilemma of Liberation Theology* by Michael R. Candelaria. Copyright © 1990 State University of New York. Reprinted by permission. Footnotes deleted.

frames the question in precisely these terms: "the thrust of this questioning will not be whether folk religion is capable of surviving or keeping the people believing in a secularized world, as it would be in highly industrialized countries, but whether it is capable of being a positive factor in the liberation of the poor." Does popular religion endow believers with the capacity to enter into and take part in the temporal task of social transformation? Is it an obstacle to the process of liberation? Does it operate as a palliative inuring people to human suffering caused by structural oppression and institutionalized exploitation?

The Double Dimension of Popular Religion

Karl Marx, in *Contribution to the Critique of Hegel's Philosophy of Law*, "Introduction," underscores what I call the double dimension of religion as protest and opiate:

> Religious distress is at the same time the expression of real distress and also the protest against real distress. Religion is the sigh of the oppressed creature, the heart of a heartless world, just as it is the spirit of spiritless conditions. It is the opium of the people.

Stubbornly ambiguous, popular religion is potentially liberating or alienating. "Marx's well-known characterization of religion as a protest and false consolation of the 'enslaved creature' offers a good point of reference to locate the question of the meaning of popular piety in the process of political liberation in Latin America."

Can we deny that religion stimulates people to protest and to resist oppression, war, and repression? In 1976, for instance, over a hundred thousand people participated in a procession to the sanctuary at Lujan, Argentina, to pray for peace in the country. More recently, in February 1986, hundreds of campesinos, laborers, students, and clergy participated in a Via Crucis (The Way of the Cross) from Jalapa to Managua. They marched for peace and life against U.S. support of the contras. Our Lady of Guadalupe, as a na-

tional and cultural symbol, has often inspired the masses to rally for freedom. Miguel Hidalgo fought for independence under the banner of Nuestra Señora de Guadalupe. At Dolores, Mexico, "he snatched up from the local church a banner bearing a picture of the Virgin of Guadalupe. Behind it then rallied many thousands of peasants." Similarly, in the 1910 Mexican revolution. Emilio Zapata and his followers rallied under the protection of the Protectoress of Mexico. During the Morelos uprising the Zapatistas decorated their sombreros with embroideries of the Guadalupe. Cesar Chavez and hundreds of farm laborers marched from Delano to Sacramento behind the banner of Our Lady of Guadalupe. What can we glean from this brief survey? For one thing, religion can be a source of hope for liberation. Religious symbols like the Guadalupe remind the poor that God fights alongside them. With God on their side how can they lose? Thus, religion encourages oppressed people to stand up and be counted.

Yet in that religion is the religious expression of oppressed and dominated people it includes elements of alienation and generates an other-worldly consciousness that despises earthly realities. For example, these lines from a hymn popular among Latin American Protestants demonstrate the alienation from this-worldly historical tasks and the preoccupation with other-worldly interests:

> Ya no me importa que el mundo me
> desprecie por doquier,
> Ya no soy mas de este mundo,
> soy del reino celestial.
>
> Yo solo espero ese dia
> cuando me levantare de la tumba fria
> con un cuerpo ya inmortal.
>
> No longer do I care that this world
> despises me,
> No longer am I from this world,
> I'm from the celestial Kingdom.
> I only wait for that day
> when I shall rise from the cold tomb
> with an immortal body.

It is easy to see, therefore, why José Miguez Bonino, a Protestant liberation theologian from Argentina, claims that popular piety operates as a "substitute satisfaction" for historical change. He adds that popular religion has imbibed elements of the dominant ideology, supported the *status quo,* legitimized the hegemonic claims of the dominant classes, and has been utilized and manipulated by reactionary political forces that fear social change. Diego Irarrazaval, a Peruvian theologian and social scientist, highlights the double dimension of the religion of the poor:

> The poor, in Latin American reality, constitute an oppressed and believing people. In being oppressed, in its religiosity there are alienating elements that impede the way to liberty. The powers of domination penetrate and mold its religious vitality. But in the Christianity of the oppressed there are also dimensions of resistance and protest.

This double dimension of popular religion accounts for its ambiguity and complexity, and hence the difficulty in evaluating it.

This ambiguous nature accounts for much of the disagreement and the conflicting evaluations and interpretations among liberation theologians and social scientists. Some people stress its liberating potential, others emphasize its alienating features. For example, the symbol of Our Lady of Guadalupe is for some an alienating symbol for women. Cordelia Candelaria, a Chicana poet from New Mexico, interprets the symbol of the virgin negatively:

> What's the point of knowing
> that a Virgin Mary miracle founded Spain
> in century one, A.D., and that another one
> in Mexico made it easier to tranquilize
> the Aztecs in 1531? . . . I object to all
>   pornography:
> my mother sister daugher aunt and me
> as cheesecake icons of Kink or of church—

For others it is a symbol of liberation for the poor and dark-skinned peoples both men and women. For Virgilio Elizondo, a Mexican-American priest and director of the Mexican-American Cultural Center in San Antonio, Our Lady is a symbol of liberation for the poor. "Her presence," he says, "is not a pacifier but an energizer which gives meaning, dignity and hope to the peripheral and suffering people of today's societies. Her presence is the new power of the powerless to triumph over the violence of the powerful." He adds that she represents, for Mexicans and Mexican-Americans, "the temple in whom and through whom Christ's saving presence is continually incarnated in the soil of the Americas." Are we at an impasse? Is popular religion liberating or alienating? This is the dilemma confronting Liberation Theology and Marxism.

ALIENATION AND POPULAR RELIGION

Erich Fromm traces the idea of alienation back to antiquity, in Jewish and Christian denunciations of idolatry, but claims that Hegel originally coined the term. Alienation (*Entfremdung*) for Hegel refers to the separation between consciousness and the world of objects, between ideas and things, in which the external world appears as an alien reality for the mind (Geist). In Hegel's view, spirit or mind creates the external physical world. Ludwing Feuerbach inverted Hegel claiming that ideas, the mind, consciousness are dependent on material reality. The idea of God, for example, is the result of the projection of human desires and wishes. What is attributed to God is really characteristic of humans. Consequently, religion is alienating because it foments an otherworldly outlook which esteems as ultimately real what is only fanciful.

For Karl Marx, alienation was a major theme. It appears in *On the Jewish Question, A Critique of Hegel's Philosophy of Right,* and even *Capital.* His deepest and most penetrating treatment of alienation is contained in the *Economic and Philosophical Manuscripts of 1844.* In the manuscript entitled "Alienated Labor," Marx develops the concept of alienation at a high level of abstraction, assuming a simple wage-laborer-capitalist relationship. As a result, Marx discovers four levels of alienation:

1. the alienation of the worker from his or her product;

2. the alienation of the worker in the process of production;
3. the alienation of the individual from others; and
4. the alienation of the individual from species being.

The basic idea of alienation is the sense of loss or separation. For Marx the concept of alienation points to a disparity that exists between existence (what one is in reality) and essence (what one should be). It is only when religion aggravates the separation between existence and essence that we can meaningfully speak of alienation.

Corresponding to the sense of alienation there also results a false consciousness that identifies the social world, social relations, as the natural order of things. In *The Sacred Canopy,* sociologist Peter Berger says "put differently, alienation is the process whereby the dialectical relationship between the individual and his world is lost to consciousness." To the extent that religion fosters or maintains a false consciousness and a dualistic worldview that conceives of social reality as natural and the supernatural as the ultimately real, popular religion can be considered as alienating. Its fundamental manifestation is an otherworldly outlook.

The 1968 International Week of Catechists, held in Bogota, concluded that popular piety is vulnerable to alienation, commercialization, and exploitation. Furthermore, they decided that popular religion is an obstacle to social transformation:

> The manifestations of popular religiosity, though containing positive aspects, in the current accelerated evolution of society are expressions of an alienated group, that is, of a massified and depersonalized group; it is conformist and incapable of being critical, it does not commit itself to the transformation of the prevailing social system. This type of religion is, in fact, conservative, and to a certain extent, caused by the dominant superstructures of those who form part of the current ecclesial organization: for example, the implantation of new forms of religiosity, the commercialization of the same in sanctuaries, tourist exploitation of religious folklore, and the forms of the celebration of Eucharistic Congresses. Unfortunately, the foment of this type of religiosity functions as a brake to stop the change of social structures.

In the 1972 El Escorial meeting, pivotal in the history of Liberation Theology, theologians and social scientists gathered together to discuss matters of faith and social change. Segundo Galilea took a decidedly negative stance toward popular Catholicism. In his opinion, popular Catholicism bolsters a dualistic view of reality and an otherworldly religious attitude. "It is well known," he says, "that such Catholicism reinforces a dualistic vision of reality, and, therefore, a religious attitude foreign to temporal tasks." Moreover, he portrays folk piety as a *status quo* religion which legitimizes the prevailing social order. What Galilea seems to have in mind is the fatalistic attitude typical of the Latin American popular mentality. This attitude is expressed in sayings like "si Dios quiere" (if God wills), and "el que nace para el tamal, solo del cielo caen las hojas," (to him who is born for tamales, from heaven come only [tamale] leaves). In Oscar Lewis' *The Children of Sanchez,* one of the characters exemplifies this attitude:

> To me one's destiny is controlled by a mysterious hand that moves all things. Only for the select do things turn out as planned; to those of us who are born to be tamale-eaters, heaven sends only tamales. We plan and plan and some little thing happens to wash it all away. Like once, I decided to try to save and I said to Paula, "Old girl, put away this money so that some day we'll have a little pile." When we had ninety pesos laid away, pum! my father got sick and I had to give all to him for doctors and medicines. It was the only time I had tried to save. I said to Paula, "There you are! why should we save if someone gets sick and we have to spend it all!" Sometimes I even think that saving brings on illness! That's why I firmly believe that some of us are born to be poor and remain that way no matter how hard we struggle and pull this way and that. God gives us just enough to go on vegetating, no?

José Miguez Bonino acknowledges the potential for protest in popular religion, but concludes that this potential "is absorbed by religiosity and changed into a substitute satisfaction, that strips it of its transforming potential." For Dussel, popular Catholicism is but a passing, moribund phenomenon. Juan Luis Segundo considers popular religion as a mass phenomenon, and hence incapable of being disestablishing. Mass religion, in his mind, follows the line of least resistance. At the outset of his career, while a member of Christians for Socialism, Diego Irarrazaval, a liberation theologian from Peru, berated popular religion as a false praxis: "It appears as a false practice of liberation, because it departs from the consciousness and struggle of the oppressed. It is a false practice because it does not break free the chains that enslave the people." Popular religion, in his opinion, leads to social withdrawal and individualism. Thus, popular religion hinders people from participating in revolutionary practice:

> They are practices that separate Christians from the revolutionary attempt to destroy the capitalist roots of domination. Instead of taking history in their own hands, they trust that the solidarity of the oppressed will forge a linking solidarity with other knowing believers. Instead of taking history into their own hands, they trust in miracles. Instead of struggling with and for all, they want to receive something with and for a few. In the light of these facts, religious practice appears to separate the people from a true revolutionary praxis.

In sum, popular religion is considered alienating when its social efficacy is limited to being a conservative cohesive factor and when its major social role is ideological. To the extent that its characteristics include privatization of faith, social withdrawal, false consciousness, false praxis, ahistoricism, and belief in the miraculous, popular religion appears to many as conformist, uncritical, and an obstacle to liberation.

LIBERATION AND POPULAR RELIGION

Partly in reaction to this iconoclastic attitude, others have raised their voices defending the revolutionary potential of popular religion. To those who are overly critical of popular religion, Gutierrez responds that they are simply mistaken: "but one would mistake the way if, from a critical posi-

tion, it is not perceived that the believing dimension of the people also implies as its practice demonstrates, the presence of an immense liberating potentiality." A number of extremely competent theologians, especially from Argentina, would agree.

Exponents of the stream of Liberation Theology that I call the "Theology of the People" or "Populist Theology" include Lucio Gera, Juan Carlos Scannone, Fernando Boasso, and Aldo Büntig, just to name a few. These theologians rate popular religiosity as culturally liberating by virtue of its "popular" character. It is believed to be a reservoir of liberating values simply by virtue of its being of the people. Popular religiosity, they hold, is the kernel of the cultural heritage of the Latin American people and the essential element of their identity. Since folk piety is a constituting part of the people, their history, and their culture, it is necessary to take it into account in the struggle for cultural and national liberation. This perspective underlines the "Christian sense and religiosity" of the people as the "storehouse of the values" of the people. The exponents of this current of thought "acknowledge the liberative import of religious symbols" and "stress the distinctive contribution that faith can and does make to both the religious and the secular praxis of our people and their historico-cultural project."

Another stream of Liberation Theology, more closely following the lines opened up by Gutierrez, also acknowledges the revolutionary potential of popular religion but in a more critical manner. Here, the question of the role of popular religion is set within a socio-political frame of reference. "Though popular culture and its liberation are not to be neglected, they have to be set in the context of socio-political liberation." Religion has positive potential in its capacity to mobilize the people for political action and consciousness. "Folk religion is here seen as retaining its potential value, but less in relation to culture and more in relation to its capacity for strengthening the political consciousness and mobilization of the people."

Popular religiosity, according to this line of thought, will be alienating or liberating depending on the role the popular sectors play in specific historical situations. Critical to evangelization, then, is the task of purifying popular religion from alienating tendencies by means of raising political consciousness and creating a critical historical awareness. Thus, according to Irarrazaval, popular religion stands at a crossroads in which it will be revitalized by revolutionary construction or it will stagnate by withdrawal from historical responsibility into the individualistic search for security and mere religious salvation. In other words, we must confront popular piety in order to mobilize the popular sectors. "The ideology of the ascending class of modern Latin America has to take into account popular religiosity in order to mobilize all of the popular sectors, in the hope of forming a new society through a revolution."

Popular religiosity then is rated positively in two ways. First, it is liberating because it is of the people. Second, to the extent that it mobilizes the popular sectors to struggle for social change, it reveals a liberating dynamic.

Nevertheless, the ambiguity of popular religiosity remains and generates opposing standpoints among liberation theologians. The problem is complex; there are no simple answers and no black and white issues. Segundo Galilea aptly expresses the central questions preoccupying many liberation theologians:

> Is it [popular religion] a valid starting point for liberation? Does it lead to conformity and alienation? Can a critical and developing consciousness be developed from folk religion, or must it always be a stage of development that has to be surpassed? Do pastoral care of folk religion and liberating evangelization converge or diverge in their aims and practices? And supposing that folk religion is a factor that cannot be overlooked in the practice of liberation, is this purely for practical reasons? or because it really is a potentially liberating factor? . . .

SPIRITUAL TRANSFORMATION AND ETHICAL COMMITMENT

What criteria serve to separate the positive from the alienating elements of popular religion? Do any criteria exist? Of course, depending on the nature of the investigation the criteria will vary according to discipline—sociology, psychology, theology, etc. In the area of theology, different sets of criteria have been proposed. During the Reformation, the Protestant criteria were summed up in the following formulae: *sola scriptura, sola fidei, sola gratia,* and *solos Christo.* In Latin America, Leonardo Boff and Clodovis Boff offer a different set of criteria embodying the spirituality of Liberation Theology—spiritual transformation and ethical commitment.

Spirituality in this context is not opposed to the material. Rather it has to do with personal openness to transcendence. "Spiritual, in this sense, has nothing to do with the opposite of the material; it has to do with the worship of the heart, the consecration of the whole person."Religion centered on rites, rituals, and formulas is not a substitute for spiritual openness.

> If one is seeking God primarily instead of ties, the rites have meaning as expressions of the individual's search and as a celebration of the individual's encounter with God. Overemphasizing ritual music, and symbolism leads to a bastardization of religion and causes it to lose its true purpose for faith and experience.

If religion does not result in the personal edification and spiritual renewal of the believer it becomes mere ritualism and magic.

A corollary of spiritual transformation is ethical commitment. Its theological basis is the indissoluable unity between loving God and loving one's neighbor.

> The prophets highlighted the connection of the commandments of the first tablet (having to do with God) to those of the second tablet (pertaining to one's neighbor). The violation of the sacred law of humanity is included in the violation of the sacrosanct law of God. Whoever says that he loves God and yet hates his neighbor (I Jn. 4:20) is a liar and his worship is nothing more than idolatry.

In the New Testament, religion is defined by St. James in the following manner: "this is pure and undefiled religion (*threskeia,* the worship of God expressed in religious service of cult) in the sight of our God and Father, to visit orphans and widows in their distress, and to keep oneself unstained by the world" (Jas. 1:27). Thus popular religion satisfies the criterion of ethical commitment if it engenders and encourages the spirit of love.

THE ECONOMIC QUESTION

In any consideration of the problem of popular religion and liberation, certain questions undoubtedly loom large.

First, What is the economic role of popular religion in society? This question may at first appear to be posing a mismatch. Indeed, this is not so! Already, Marx, Max Weber, Durkheim and many others have brought out the connections between religion and the economy. Religion itself is a process of production, albeit, not to the full extent a material process of production; it is primarily an intellectual, mental, or spiritual process of production. At the same time, it is indissoluable from the material process of production. Consider, for example, the production of the Bible. On the one hand, there exists its material being resulting from centuries of historical transmission and translation. Beginning with a historical event, e.g., the Exodus or the crucifixion of Jesus of Nazareth, it passes through various stages—oral transmission, cultic formulation, transcription, editing, canonization, translation, distribution, etc. Finally, it emerges as a commodity to be consumed by the believer. In this sense, the Bible, the Word of God, Sacred Scripture, Holy Writ undergoes a material process of production. But it is simultaneously a spiritual product. It was initially conceived by persons sensitive to a spiritual interpretation of historical events accepted by a community of believers, accorded a hallowed place in tradition, and recognized as the rule and guide of faith and practice. . . .

6.6 Religion and Women's Human Rights

Alfred North Whitehead (1861–1947) spoke of the fallacy of misplaced concreteness in conjunction with the tendency of some philosophers to treat their abstractions from reality as though they were concrete. Hence Descartes abstracted mind and matter from the full concrete richness of experience and treated them as fundamental ontological categories. Adapting this notion from Whitehead, we might note the tendency on the part of philosophers of religion to abstract the categories "religion" and "morality" from the concrete world of everyday moral realities that impinge on people's lives. Perhaps it is better to speak of *religions* and *moralities* and to recall the social and political contexts in which they operate.

The need to remain concrete is particularly important when it comes to the question of human rights. The rights that people are afforded or denied directly affect the quality of their lives. Although we often think of human rights in a political context, this context cannot be divorced from the role that religions play for good or ill in people's lives. The question of religion and human rights becomes particularly pressing in the pluralistic age in which we live and in light of the political conviction, at least in some countries, that we must respect the freedom to practice religion, such freedoms as freedom of speech and of assembly, and the right to be treated equally.

Let's get more concrete still and talk about women's human rights. Women have been denied the rights afforded men for centuries, and this denial is often supported by religious views of one sort or another. St. Augustine of Hippo (354–430) seriously considered whether or not women had souls (and hence intelligence, spiritual value, and all the other good things that go along with having souls) because Genesis says in one place (3:22) that Eve was made out of Adam's rib. If this is so, then she and her female descendants must be primarily physical in nature. Only Adam, the man, is made directly in God's image, Augustine reasoned, and hence only men are directly endowed with souls. Augustine finally decides that Eve does have a soul (after all, she can talk and reason) but only indirectly through Adam. Hence men in general are more like God than are women. Augustine read his Bible selectively, ignoring the part (Genesis 1:27) that says God created both males and females in God's image.

We may think that we have come along way since Augustine and his misogynist machinations. But have we? Moral progress (if we may entertain such a radical notion) is uneven at best and is seldom guaranteed.

Martha C. Nussbaum is Ernst Freund Professor of Law and Ethics at the University of Chicago. In the next selection, she is very much concerned about the relationship between religions and women's human rights on a concrete level. She is also very much concerned with the political context in which issues that involve women's rights arise. Her discussion raises important questions about the relationship between "church and state," as it is often put, not only here but also around the world.

Reading Questions

1. What is the "liberal dilemma"?
2. Restate in your own words Nussbaum's argument that leads her to conclude that the religious liberty of any individual is not infringed by making available to all people "the basic menu of individual rights."
3. What is Will Kymlicka's argument, and how does Nussbaum counter it?
4. What does Nussbaum think can be done? Do you agree? Why or why not?

Religion and Women's Human Rights*

MARTHA C. NUSSBAUM

The *mullahs* say: "When they will die we shall not bury them." Villagers say, "Wherever they want, they go. They do not cover their heads. They talk with men. They will be sinners." I said: "If Allah does not see us when we stay hungry then Allah has sinned."[1]

—*A Bangladeshi wife, participant in a literacy and skills program sponsored by the Bangladesh Rural Advancement Committee*

The Liberal Dilemma

Political liberals, of whom I am one, characteristically defend two theses, which seem to be closely related. First, liberals hold that religious liberty, or more generally the liberty of conscience, is among the most important of the human freedoms, and must be given a very strong degree of priority in the basic structure of a political regime. This is frequently understood

*From "Religion and Women's Human Rights," *Criterion* 36 (Winter 1997), 2–13. This article is an extract from a longer article which appears in *Religion and Contemporary Liberalism* edited by Paul Weithman (University of Notre Dame Press, 1997) and appears in a revised form in Martha Nussbaum, *Sex and Social Justice* (NY: Oxford University Press, 1998). Reprinted by permission.

to entail that the freedom of religious exercise can permissibly be infringed only when there is an imminent threat to public order.[2] Second, liberals hold that human beings have various other rights, including rights to freedom of movement, freedom of assembly, freedom of speech, the right to equal political participation, the right to be treated as equals under the law, both civil and criminal, and, finally, various rights to the integrity and inviolability of the person.

In a sense, there would seem to be a strong complementarity between the first thesis and the second. For we know well that the rights on the list given in the second thesis have all too often been denied to individuals on grounds of religious membership; one clear sign of a regime's failure to honor the first thesis will be its discriminatory behavior toward religious groups, and individuals, with respect to a wider spectrum of human rights.

Thus, the German Nazi regime, unlike that of Mediaeval Spain, was not preoccupied with the specific task of impeding the Jews' freedom to worship. They pursued their campaign through the denial to others a whole venue of human rights, such as the equal right to contract a marriage, the right to mobility, assembly, and choice of occupation, and, of course, ultimately, the right to life. It would be correct to hold that true religious liberty required that these other basic freedoms not be impaired on a discriminatory basis.

On the other hand, the two theses can also generate a tension which poses difficult questions for contemporary law and political thought, especially in some constitutional democracies in the developing world. I will focus above all else on India. The major religions of the world, in their actual, human, politicized form have not always been outstanding respectors of certain basic human rights, or of the equal dignity and inviolability of persons. Some, indeed, have gone so far as to create systems of law that deny the equal rights of persons and justify violations of their dignity and their person. Apart from law, influential religious discourse in many parts of the world threatens the bodily integrity and equal dignity of persons—and sometimes, even their

equal liberty of worship. Tensions arise when the claims of religious groups to manage things their own way come into conflict with the rights of persons under the constitutions. Consider the following examples:

1. In a village in rural Bangladesh in the early 1980s, impoverished women leave their homes to meet in a group organized by the Bangladesh Rural Advancement Committee. They are learning to read, to keep accounts, and to pursue various forms of work outside the home—all important ingredients in improving their status—including nutrition and health for themselves and their children. The local *mullahs* (Islamic religious leaders) make speeches saying that women who work outside the house and talk with men other than their husbands are whores. They threaten them with religious and communal ostracism (refusal to officiate at any of the woman's social or religious functions, for example), and even with physical violence ("If you go into the field, your legs will be broken.")[3] Although most of the women do continue with the literacy project, they fear for their status in the community and their well-being.[4]

2. In Pakistan, again in the early 1980s, a young blind girl named Safia Bibi complained of rape. Since she was a minor, her father filed a complaint. Under the recently promulgated *Hudood* Ordinance, rape convictions require four male witnesses; and complainants who fail to produce the necessary testimony may then be prosecuted for fornication under the *zina* ordinance. The Sessions Court found Safia in violation of the *zina* ordinance, sentencing her to three years hard labor in prison, despite her blindness. After a storm of national and international protest, the Federal Shariat Court set the case aside on some technical quibble, but refused to prosecute the accused rapist.[5]

3. The last case is the most famous and most interestingly complex one. In Madhya Pradesh, India, in 1978, a Muslim woman named Shah Bano was thrown out of her home by her husband after forty-four years of marriage. In India, there's no uniform civil law. There is a uniform

criminal law, but in the place of a secular civil law, all your civil law matters must be dealt with by the religion of your origin. So Shah Bano had to be dealt with by the Islamic courts. As required by Islamic personal law, he had to return Rs. 3,000, which was about $300. This had been her marriage settlement from her family when she got married forty-four years ago. And of course, it had not increased in value during that time. Rather than accept this settlement (she was illiterate, she couldn't find employment; she was generally in a terrible situation), she sued for maintenance under Section 125 of India's Criminal Procedure Code, which requires a person of adequate means to protect certain specified relations from destitution and vagrancy.[6] As a result, she was awarded Rs. 180 (about $18.00) per month, hardly a princely sum, but an improvement. Her husband, however, who was quite well-off by the way, appealed this judgement to the Supreme Court of India, holding that as a Muslim he was bound only by Islamic law. In 1985, the Supreme Court held that the provisions of the Criminal Procedure Code requiring maintenance were applicable to members of all religions, and that a person should not lose simply by being a Muslim. In his opinion Chief Justice Chandrachud who was a Hindu (and this was an important part of the politics of the case) wrote at some length on the desirability of having a uniform civil code and on the inequalities (as well as the deplorable nature of these inequalities) done to women under Muslim law. The Muslim Personal Law Board and other religious leaders vehemently criticized the ruling, using public rhetoric to persuade followers that their religion was in grave danger unless the government should decide to exempt Muslim women from the provisions of Section 125.[7] Responding to this campaign, the government of Rajiv Gandhi passed the Muslim Women's Divorce Act of 1986, depriving divorced Muslim women and these alone of their right of maintenance under the criminal code.[8] At the same time he added a clause that it would be nice if by the year 2000 the nation did adopt a uniform civil code.[9] Hindu political activists subsequently complained that the new law discriminated against Hindus by giving Muslims "special privileges." . . .[10] So they were all arguing about how not to give this poor woman $18.00 a month. Eventually, the Muslim authorities brought enough pressure to bear on her that she signed a statement with her thumbprint in which she retracted her claim. It was a very sad case.

In each of these cases we see an apparent dilemma for the modern liberal regime. For if the people who claim to speak for the religious traditions in these examples are to be accepted as merely their representatives and their claims as legitimate claims of religious liberty (which is, of course, a big if), then there really does seem to be a tension between respect for religious liberty and respect for the basic human rights of many citizens. This tension finds its sharpest form wherever the religious traditions have been permitted the right to make law. They view it as part of their exercise of religious liberty that they should be able to make law and maintain these courts of family law. It arises, as well, in more informal ways when the highly influential discourse of religious leaders poses problems for the equal worth of basic liberties—usually already guaranteed in the constitutions (or the legal traditions) of the nations in question, as well as in their commitment to the Universal Declaration of Human Rights, and, in most cases, the Convention on the Elimination of All Forms of Discrimination Against Women, a multilateral treaty ratified by 131 countries.[11] If the government defers to the wishes of the religious group, a vulnerable group of individuals will lose basic rights; if the government commits itself to respecting equal human rights of all individuals, it will stand accused of indifference to the liberty of conscience. Often, government actors, for example Rajiv Gandhi, make a mere pretense of serious engagement with the problem. They strive to satisfy the religious group, since it is far more powerful than women, but say, at the same time, that something must surely be done about this by someone in the future.

Nor is this dilemma troubling only for the liberal state: it vexes the religions themselves. An especially poignant statement of its force can be found in the Pope's recent address to the United Nations. On the one hand, this address contained a very strong injunction to respect the world's major religions, and a ringing defense of "the fundamental right to freedom of religion and freedom of conscience as the cornerstones of the structure of human rights and the foundation of every truly free society."[12] At the same time, however, the Pope vigorously praises the U.N.'s Universal Declaration of Human Rights and the other recently adopted human rights instruments as "one of the highest expressions of the human conscience of our time," and spoke of a world-wide movement toward universal respect for the dignity and inviolability of the human person. His more recent "Letter to Women," issued just before the Beijing Women's Conference, makes it clear that he considers many of the rights at issue in the United Nations' Declaration for the Convention on the Elimination of All Forms of Discrimination Against Women to be central human rights (most of them, of course, with some very obvious exceptions): he mentions freedom from sexual violence (including marital rape), equality in family rights, equality in political duties and responsibilities, equality under the law, and equality in the workplace.[13] So there is tension here: how is one going to respect the liberties of the various religions and at the same time promote the respect of liberties for individuals and their equality under the law?

Although the dilemma I propose to study does arise in the U.S., as well as internationally, given that the United States has a bill of rights that is effective, not merely aspirational, and given that by now the major religions in the U.S. have long accepted some fundamental shared ideas about the equal dignity and liberty of persons, such a focus cannot address the most problematic aspects of the relationship between political liberalism and religion.[14] We simply do not hear any influential religious voice in the United States proposing, at this time, that women's legal testimony be judged unequal to that of men, that women be severely punished for dressing this way or that, that their legs be broken for working out-

side the house, that they be denied a right to divorce equal to that granted to a man. None of these cases is totally discontinuous with our own past and even present; the practical difficulty of complaining of rape, for example, and the punishment meted out to women who do so complain, are real and recent, in some cases current. Further back in our history all the mentioned inequalities in family law could be attested, often buttressed by appeals to religion.[15] Certainly Christianity and Judaism are far from blameless in the global history of women's unequal treatment; they have merely been on a rather short leash recently in Europe and America. My international examples manifest, I believe, what parts of most religious traditions (as well as many non-religious traditions) will try to do when they are not on such a short leash. I believe, therefore, that a focus on current international issues is valuable in order to give us a vivid sense of the reality of our topic. Without this focus, we might fail to acknowledge that religions can propose and seriously defend gross atrocities; we might therefore fail to ask what liberals who care about religion should say when they do.

Such atrocities frequently involve women, but they are obviously not limited to them; a similar paper could be written about the religions' treatment of other religions, or about issues of case and hierarchy with the religions. But the example of women will give us a very useful focus for debate.

It is useful to focus on this topic for another reason as well: because these atrocities do not always receive the intense public concern and condemnation that other systematic atrocities against groups often receive, and there is reason to think that liberal respect for religious difference is involved in this neglect.[16] The worldwide mobilization against South African apartheid has not been accompanied by any similar mobilization to divest stock holdings in nations that treat women as unequal under the law. Indeed, these inequalities are often cheerfully put up with, as part of legitimate difference—as when our troops were asked to fall in with Saudi customs regarding women's dress while serving in the Gulf. During a debate on South African divestiture at Harvard University in 1983, a prominent liberal political thinker argued that the case of apartheid was unique in today's world because a group of persons was not merely being discriminated against, but was being treated as systematically unequal under the law. Unique in the world? That was false in 1983 and is even more false today. One reason for the reluctance of Western liberals to face this fact and to take appropriate political action is surely the political hopelessness of it all: how could we hope to convince our nation to take economic action against so many oil-rich nations? There may be several other reasons. Among them, however, is surely the role of religion in the debate: liberals who do not hesitate to criticize a secular government that perpetrates atrocity are anxious and reticent when it comes to vindicating claims of justice against major religious leaders and groups. They are hesitant, I suggest, because they hold that the liberty of conscience is among the fixed points in our considered judgements of justice, and are at a loss to see how they could in good conscience ask religious people to acquiesce in a judgement about sex equality that is foreign to that religious tradition. This suggests that a sorting out of the liberal dilemma may contribute to a greater political clarity in an area where we urgently need clarity.

In this paper, and in the larger version out of which it came, I focus on cases in which religions threaten basic human rights, because it is these cases that generate the dilemma with which I am concerned, not because I believe that this is the primary relation religions have had to human rights. It is obvious that religious discourse has been among the major sources of support for human rights around the world, and I have focused on the Pope's statement partly in order to keep this fact before our minds. The dual role of the religions in these areas will concern me when I turn to the philosophical unraveling of the dilemma; for the time being, however, I shall continue to focus on cases where human rights are at risk.

In what follows, I do not ignore, though I shall not directly address, the difficulties involved in defining the notion of a "human right" or specifying the conditions under which a person can be said to have a right to a certain type of treatment. I do not accept a positivist analysis, according to which a person has a right if, and only if, the law in her country has recognized such a right. I understand a human right to be a claim of an especially urgent and powerful sort, one that can be justified by an ethical argument that can command a broad cross-cultural consensus, and one that does not cease to be morally salient when circumstances render its recognition inefficient. A human right, unlike many other rights people may have, derives not from a person's particular situation of privilege or power or skill, but, instead, just from the fact of being human. In my understanding, there is a very close relationship between a list of basic human rights and the Rawlsian list of "primary goods," that is, things that all persons may be presumed to need in order to carry out their life plans, whatever those plans are. Human rights are, in effect, justified claims to such basic goods. Other much-discussed questions, concerning the precise relationship between rights and interests, rights and theories of the good, rights and duties, do not affect the analysis to be presented here and can therefore be deferred.[17] If this way of proceeding leaves the philosopher open to accusations of woolly abstractness, she may justly reply that economists standardly use notions (such as "preference" and "development") that are similarly in need of clarification, and that have, unlike these much-analyzed philosophical notions, received, in the literature of the profession, relatively little of the clarification they need.

Women's Human Rights: One Problem Area

Cultures are complex. It is generally very difficult to determine to what extent the religions in a nation reflect influences from other aspects of the culture and to what extent they influence the culture. In nations such as Iran, we can contrast the situation prior to the control of religious fundamentalists with the current situation; usually such assessments are more elusive, and we must exercise caution in drawing conclusions. The problem is compounded, in a nation such as India, by sharp regional variations that reflect many different cultural and political factors; differences across religions are less sharp than such regional differences, though religion appears to have some independent explanatory weight.

Our assessments are made more complex by the fact that when religions act politically their religious discourse is often powerfully colored by issues of political power. Thus, the Hinduism represented today in India by the BJP (Bharatiya Janata Party, the leading Hindu nationalist party) is not very much like the inclusive, loosely defined, polytheistic Hinduism of earlier tradition; political and cultural forces are likely to have shaped the BJP's selection of religious principles and emphases.[18] Very different political aims shaped by Mahatma Gandhi's characterization of the essence of Hinduism, when he said, "If I were asked to define the Hindu creed, I should simply say: Search after the truth through non-violent means."[19] Where women are concerned, the same has been true over the years. The Hindu tradition offers many different and contradictory pictures of women's agency, from Draupadi's strength and sexual initiative in the Mahabharata (including a choice to marry five husbands simultaneously!) to the enlightened sensualism of the *Kama Sutra,* to the extremely negative portrayal of woman's nature in the *Laws of Manu,* in which women are depicted as both childish and whorish, totally unfit for independent choice.[20] An investigation of cultural context would be likely, here too, to reveal influences at work shaping and reshaping the religious tradition; more important for our purposes, the contemporary choice to stress one aspect of the tradition, rather than another, itself often betrays political aims.[21] This awareness must be followed in studying Islam, Judaism and Christianity as well, for these traditions contain complexities similar to that of the Hindu tradition.

Thus the criticisms we make of "religious practices" and "religious discourse" will be criticisms of human beings, often vying for political power; they do not presuppose that any of these religions has an unchanging and unchangeable core of misogyny, or even that the misogynistic elements are religiously central rather than political in origin. Nonetheless, since we are interested in the rights of individuals, we must approach the religions where they, or their representatives, threaten these rights.

The Right to Bodily Integrity[22]

Women suffer many abuses that violate their bodily integrity. These include domestic violence, rape, marital rape, sexual abuse and genital mutilation.

While religious discourse does not frequently call directly for violence against a disobedient spouse, it can frequently promulgate norms of male authority—and also pictures of female wantonness and childishness—that give support to these practices. This is as true of Western as of non-Western religions. Nations that allow the religions to take charge of family law often move very slowly to counter this problem. In India, women have long sought a civil law against domestic violence; a major obstacle to this is the fact that, in the absence of a uniform civil code, such laws would have to be separately made for Hindus, Muslims and Parsis.[23]

Stranger rape is, again, usually not directly urged by religious authorities; and yet norms of female purity and submissiveness are frequently used to justify the rape of women who defy such conventions. The Iranian Prosecutor-General believes that any woman who violates the dress code deserves death; he is not likely, then, to defer the common practice of police rape of women under detention for such violations. More generally, the requirements on rape evidence under Islamic Laws that prevail in many nations (four male witnesses) make an accusation a virtual impossibility; in Pakistan, with its Catch-22 according to which an unsuccessful accusation of rape constitutes a confession to fornication, very few women will complain of rape, and few men will be deterred from raping.

The very concept of marital rape is foreign to many religious traditions, which give a husband limitless sexual access to the wife. The concept of marital rape is a very recent one in European and North American culture and religion as well, a fact on which we should not pride ourselves. Indeed, the notion of "restoration of conjugal rights" that is frequently invoked in Indian family courts is of British origin, and was retained in the Hindu Marriage Act and the Special Marriage Act of 1954. Nonetheless, at this point, religious law and discourse, including the Hindu and Islamic, are heavily implicated in maintaining marital rape as an option for men.

There has been opposition. In *T. Sareetha v. T. Venkata Subhaiah* (1983),[24] a judge of the Andhra Pradesh High court claimed that the remedy of restitution of conjugal rights violates "The right to privacy and human dignity guaranteed by and contained in Article 21 of our Constitution." The measure, he continues, "deprives a woman of control over her choice as to when and by whom the various parts of her body should be allowed to be sensed" and "when and how her body is to become the vehicle for the procreation of another human being."[25] The Supreme Court of India reversed, however, saying the Hindu Marriage Act contains sufficient safe-guards to prevent such abuses, since a woman fleeing from the home could get out of this restoration decree by paying a fine. The decree of restoration was even praised as one that "serves a social purpose as an aid to the prevention of break-up of marriage."[26] The Court did not take cognizance of the likely financial position of such women, many of whom would be forced to return to marriages from which they had fled, or effectively respond to the constitutional questions raised by the lower court judge. In other related decisions, the Court opined that a Hindu woman's duty is to live with her husband in the matrimonial home.

Similar cases can be found on the Islamic side. In Bangladesh, another battered woman left the conjugal home and filed for divorce. Her husband brought suit for restitution of conjugal rights.[27] The lower court held that the woman had "no right to divorce at her own sweet will and without any reasonable excuse." In this case,

however, the High Court vindicated her rights, commenting on the inconsistency between the "restoration" remedy and the equality provisions in Bangladesh's constitution:

> The very concept of the husband's unilateral plea for forcible restitution of conjugal rights had become outmoded and . . . does not fit with the State and Public Principle and Policy of equality of all men and women being citizens equal before the law and entitled to be treated only in accordance with the law as guaranteed in Articles 27 and 31 of the Constitution . . . [not in talk] A reference to Article 28(2) of the Constitution of Bangladesh guaranteeing equal rights of women and men in all spheres of the State and public life would clearly indicate that any unilateral plea of the husband for forcible restitution of conjugal rights as against a wife unwilling to live with her husband is violative of the accepted State and Public Principle and Policy.

In these two contested cases we see our liberal dilemma. Both India and Bangladesh have sought to combine a secular liberal constitution, including guarantees of sex equality, with religious courts of family law. In both cases, it remains ambiguous to what extent the equality provisions of the constitution apply to the protected family sphere. In such a situation, women's constitutional rights are bound to be fragile and contestable; sometimes things will work out one way, sometimes the other.

Female genital mutilation is frequently defended with discourse that appeals to its basis in Islam. It would appear that these appeals are at the very least tendentious: the practice long preexisted the arrival of Islam in Africa, and the one textual reference to the practice in the *hadith* classifies it as a *makrama* or nonessential practice. Even here, the attitude expressed by Mohammed is ambiguous, and dissuasive of any extensive mutilation.[28] Nonetheless, the discourse is religious, and it is powerful in defending the practice and branding the attack on it as Westernizing. Female genital mutilation is usually performed on young girls, often as young as five or six years old, without their consent even were consent at that age a meaningful notion. Female genital mutilation, both in the form of clitoridectomy and in the form of infibulation,[29] involves, as commonly practiced, the permanent loss of capacity for orgasm, and is strongly linked with many other health problems: infection from the unsanitary conditions in which it is performed; hemorrhage and abscesses; later difficulties in urination and menstruation; stones in the urethra and bladder due to repeated infections; excessive growth of scar tissue at the site, which may become disfiguring; pain during intercourse, infertility (with its devastating consequences for a woman's other life-chances), obstructed labor.[30] It is not surprising that female genital mutilation is illegal in most of the nations in which it is practiced, or that international human rights activists should view it as a major violation of human rights.

The Dilemma in Intra-National Issues [31]

My examples suggest that there are some forms of religious discourse and practice that should be utterly unacceptable as constitutive structural elements within a society; others that should be criminalized within a society; and, finally, others that we should simply deem immoral and inappropriate. Deciding which practices should be treated in each way will properly involve prolonged analysis and political deliberation, hearing the voices of all parties concerned.

My starting point is a simple one: it is that human beings should not be violated, and that the protection of the basic human rights should have a very strong degree of priority, even when this interferes with traditional religious discourse and practice. To those who object that violating others is part of the free exercise of their religion, we should reply as we do when a murderer claims that God told him to do it (and he may sincerely believe this to be true): never mind, we say, there are some things we do not allow people to do to other people. Or, as the Bangladeshi wife said in my epigraph, if Allah really said that (as may be doubted) then he is dead wrong.[32]

I would suggest that the fundamental bearer of rights in all these cases should be thought of as the individual person. In that case we see that because a certain group, which of course in most cases is not just a religious group, but a highly politicized group, has been given the right to make law, individuals lose their rights. They lose the chance to choose what system they go under and they lose the basic rights of sex equality as well that they have been guaranteed under the constitution.

Even the claim that the protection of these individual rights infringes religious free exercise is a contentious and highly political claim that I do not accept. Religious liberty, I would say, is a right of individuals, like other basic rights. And it doesn't seem at all clear that the religious liberty of any individual is infringed by the determination to make available to all members of all religions the basic menu of individual rights. The liberty to treat your co-religionists unequally simply is not a legitimate provider of religious freedom. The fact that prominent spokesmen for the religions actually agree with this, and there is great controversy in all the religions about all of this, supports what I just said. How we should view religious free exercise is as the right of the individual to worship and freedom of conscience and we shouldn't think that the failure of the state to allow the religion to run the legal systems is an infringement of those rights of individuals.

Before concluding, I want to examine a claim from the opposing viewpoint. There is a recent philosophical book, by Will Kymlicka, called *Multicultural Citizenship,* which discusses, in a very interesting way, cases where it looks like we want to recognize some form of group rights. He's focusing on tribal populations in Canada and not on religious subsections of the population, but similar cases arise here because some of the tribal populations treat the sexes more unequally than they would be able to under Canada's constitution. Kymlicka urges that wider latitude be granted to such tribal subgroups that have historically suffered from discrimination to form distinct political communities. And he says that if such groups were to rule illiberally and violated individual rights, it is legitimate for the constitution to exempt them from a high level of judicial review at the Federal level. The idea is that their complaints of sexual discrimination from within the population should be treated differently because of the history of that subgroup. Liberals should hold that such a minority acts unjustly, should speak out against such injustices, and should promote the development of international human rights policies that would ultimately give international courts the power to handle complaints of rights violations from such communities. But in the meantime, intervention from the Federal level in the internal affairs of a minority would be justified, he argues, only in cases of "gross and systematic violation of human rights, such as slavery or genocide or mass torture and expulsions, just as these are grounds for intervening in foreign countries."[33] In other words, you treat the tribal group as a foreign country. Remarks elsewhere in the chapter indicate that Kymlicka does not regard the denial of legal and political rights to women as the type of "gross and systematic" violation that would justify intervention.[34]

This position seems to me completely inadequate. It is of course desirable that ultimately international courts should become strong defenders of individual rights, but what is to happen in the meantime with women who are not only suffering what ought to be called gross and systematic rights violations, but precisely on account of those deprivations (of political voice, mobility, assembly, education, often equal nutrition and health care) are unable to move their own community in the direction of change? If they are not able to work outside the home, they are not able to assemble, etc., it is much harder to move their own community, much less any other group. Should this subgroup within the nation even be thought of as "their" community, just because they are in it and are unable to leave? We think that the family is a type of community. Nonetheless, if a husband beats a wife, or tries to prevent her from voting or going out of the house, we do not hesitate to intervene—or if we do hesitate, we shouldn't. I see no reason why a tribal or religious group should have any more latitude legally than a family should in abridging the fundamental rights of adult citizens.

It is, of course, another matter to decide how we should implement that judgement politically. Kymlicka seems right that such cases are less tractable than the Indian case, where the two largest religious groups have been intertwined for years and each has considerable political power at the federal level. In today's India, given the real danger that the Muslim minority will suffer persecution, it seems appropriate for feminists to defend the continued autonomy of the Islamic legal system and the Islamic courts, even though the absence of a uniform civil code makes progress for women more difficult. Feminists in India now typically focus on achieving sex equality within each separate system of religious law, rather than on the abolition of the separate systems, because they sympathize with the plight of the Muslim minority in an India governed by a Hindu fundamentalist party that associates the goal of legal uniformity with the goal of declaring India a Hindu state. However, in each of the major religions there are prominent voices pressing for sex equality, so there is at least some hope of reform within the existing structure. Kymlicka's case is more difficult, because the tribal peoples are few, uninfluential, and bitterly opposed to cooperation with the former oppressor. All such cases should be approached with rich local knowledge and sensitivity to all the parties and the risks they are running. Nonetheless, it seems important to state that the sad history of a group can never provide a philosophical justification for the gross denial of equal rights and liberties. This seems to me another form of oppression that should not be allowed to continue. In India, it seems appropriate for defenders of a unified civil code to say, with Muslim jurist M.C. Chagla, that Muslims who wish to influence the law are already empowered to do so: "After all, fifty million Muslims[35] have a voice in the election of that Parliament through adult suffrage."[36] The election of 1996 showed the world exactly how decisive that power can be: Muslim parties form a major part of the coalition that eventually managed to form a government, after the BJP was unable to do so.

What Can Be Done

I am fully aware that some of my recommendations may sound like pie in the sky. And yet, this does not mean that there is no scope for action aimed at making these constraints real.

One form of action in which liberals concerned with religion can very definitely engage, is the encouraging of pluralistic and comparative religious discourse on these topics, discourse that brings to light and publicizes the plurality of views on all these matters within the religious traditions, and also brings members of the different traditions together for consultation and comparative discussion.[37] In the process, many appeals to religion that do violate women's rights will be exposed as, at the least narrow and partial accounts of a tradition, and often as simple misrepresentations—as has been happening with the relation of Islam to female genital mutilation. This is one area where the old adage that it is best to drive out bad speech with more speech seems to be just right. And this is why the general issue raised by our volume seems so urgent for the future of the world's women: for religious discourse, if a villain in many of my examples is also, in multiple and powerful ways, a major source of hope for women's futures. We should therefore not accept any solution to the liberal dilemma that unduly marginalizes religious speech, or asks people to cut themselves off from humanitarian motivations that may motivate them in a specifically religious form. I believe that my own proposal does not do this.

It is, moreover, a legitimate function of a liberal state to encourage the liberal elements in the religious traditions. Here I agree with John Courtney Murray and with Rawls: by giving prominence to the type of religious speech that accords with constitutional fundamentals and to its speakers, a state legitimately strengthens the political consensus around these fundamentals, and dramatizes to citizens the fact that religious argument in the major traditions can support them. Thus, in India, it would be highly advisable for major state actors to spend time insisting (as intellectuals such as Tariq Mahmood and Amartya Sen have long insisted) that both Islamic and Hindu traditions are diverse and plural, and contain prominent liberal elements. Such public emphasis weakens the claim of anti-liberal parties and individuals to speak for the entirety of a religious tradition.

Beyond this, it seems crucial for all who are concerned with these facts to promote and support local forms of group action that are the most promising avenues of change. The means supporting NGOs like Bangladesh Rural Advancement Committee (organizer of the literacy project), which are free from government pressure and able to pursue a highly effective grass roots agenda.[38] At the same time, we should also try to bring pressure to bear on our governments and on multinational corporations to alter this situation, as was done so successfully in the case of South Africa. Women who are fighting these injustices on the spot need such external reinforcement. Frequently, too, the fact that an international body or a foreign government has made compliance with certain human rights practices a condition of some form of economic or diplomatic cooperation, gives women a way to support such change without fear. Blaming change on the Americans is a convenient way out for people who are not in a position to risk personal defiance; we should create many such opportunities.

Meanwhile, in acute cases, individuals who suffer human rights violations on account of being female should be granted political asylum. This happened for the first time in the U.S. in June 1996, when a woman from Togo, about to be forced to undergo genital mutilation, was admitted by the INS, in a ruling that stated "that women have little legal recourse and may face threats or acts of physical violence, or social ostracization for refusing to undergo this harmful traditional practice, or attempting to protect their female children."[39] Obviously, however, we should not only rely on this remedy, which is arbitrary in its benefits (it helps only those people who can get on a plane and go somewhere), and which can hardly address problems that affect millions of people.

The best way to promote a liberal role for religious discourse is to produce active, unintimidated, educated, democratic citizens. Such citizens will demand that religious discourse play a role compatible with constitutional guarantees of human equality. And this means that their role toward their own religious tradition will also be active and reflective, not merely submissive to the powerful interpreters of the moment. In many parts of the world, women have not been encouraged to become such citizens. But this situation is changing. At the conclusion of the literacy project, some women said that they no longer took advice from the local religious leaders. One woman said that she still went to get advice. Asked whether she found the advice helpful, she replied:

> I will think myself whether he gives me good suggestions or bad ones. If he gives me a good suggestion, I will try to understand how far it is good for me. Or whether it is a bad suggestion.

This is exactly the response that a society truly committed to religious liberty should encourage.

NOTES

1. Cited in Martha A. Chen, *A Quiet Revolution: Women in Transition in Rural Bangladesh* (Cambridge, MA: Schenkman, 1983).

2. See John Rawls, *A Theory of Justice* (Cambridge, MA: Harvard University Press, 1971), pp. 205–221; on p. 213, Rawls holds that restrictions of religious liberty can be justified only when the consequences for the security of public order are "reasonably certain or imminent."

3. See Chen, *A Quiet Revolution,* pp. 172–8, 204, 217; this example is on p. 174.

4. In this case, the fact that the women were soon understood to be augmenting the family income won the day for them; husbands and in-laws soon ceased resistance, and the authority of the *mullahs* declined in importance. One woman concludes, "We do not listen to the *mullahs* any more. They . . . did not give us even a quarter kilo of rice. Now we get ten maunds of rice [i.e. through their employment]. Now, people help us" (176). Now, another woman adds, "the leaders

know that if they do anything bad with us they will face a problem" (177).

5. See the account of the case in Radhika Coomaraswamy, "Women, Ethnicity, and the Discourse of Rights," in *Human Rights of Women: National and International Perspectives* (hereafter *HRW*), ed. Rebecca J. Cook (Philadephia: University of Pennsylvania Press, 1994), pp. 39–57, at 50–51.

6. Relations enumerated are spouse, minor children, adult handicapped children and aged parents.

7. On the controversy, see Kavita R. Khory, "The Shah Bano Case: Some Political Implications," in Robert Baird, ed., *Religion and Law in Independent India* (Delhi: Manohar, 1993), pp. 121–37, which points out that in reality the Islamic community was highly divided about the judgement. See also Sen, "Secularism," pp. 22–23; Kirti Singh, "Obstacles to Women's Rights in India," in *HRW*, pp. 375–96, at 384-5; relevant documents are collected in Ashgar Ali Engineer, ed., *The Shah Bano Controversy* (Delhi: Ajanta Publishers, 1987). See also Veena Das, *Critical Events* (Delhi: Oxford University Press, 1992), Chapter 4. On general issues about the Indian legal system and its history, see John H. Mansfield, "The Personal Laws or a Uniform Civil Code?" in Baird, ed., *Religion and Law;* Tahir Mahmood, *Muslim Personal Law, Role of the State in the Indian Subcontinent* (Nagpur, second edition 1983).

8. The Act, however, contains an option: at the time of marriage, a couple may elect to submit themselves to the maintenance provisions of the Criminal Procedure Code instead of the Islamic law; previously, Islamic law was enforced toward all Muslims, regardless of their choice, and that is still the case, in effect, for most matters. Such options have been a matter of great dispute. Under the Shariat Act, individuals will be governed by the Shariat only if they make an election in its favor, but that choice will be binding on their descendants, who have no choice in the matter. See Mansfield, p. 169.

9. On the pros and cons of a uniform code, see Sen, "Secularism," 22ff., citing constitutional debates; Mahmood, pp. 115–130 on Muslim opinion. Although Dr. Ambedkar, the leader of the team of constitutional framers, expressed a preference for "uniformity of fundamental laws, civil and criminal," this uniformity was not incorporated in the constitution, and his preference was included only as an unenforceable "Directive Principle of State Policy," stating that "the State shall endeavour to secure for the citizens a uniform civil code throughout the territory of India." It was stated that this principle was "fundamental in the governance of the country," and that "it shall be the duty of the State to apply" it, but that it "shall not be enforceable by any court." (*Constitution of India,* Article 44). At the same time,

however, Article 13(1) provides that all "laws in force" shall be void insofar as they are in conflict with the constitutionally enumerated Fundamental Rights, among which (Articles 14 and 15) are the right of all persons to the equal protection of the laws and a guarantee of non-discrimination on the basis of "religion, race, caste, sex, place of birth or any of them." It is thus possible to hold that the personal laws were already rendered void by Article 13(1): see discussion below.

10. Cited in Sen, "Secularism," p. 22 who observes: "This line of reasoning has many problems. . . . Any unfairness that is there is surely one against *Muslim women*, rather than against *Hindu men.*"

11. Data as of January 1994, cited in *HRW*, p. 254. See also UN *Human Development Report 1995* (New York: UN Development Program, 1995), p. 43. Among the countries that will be discussed below, Iran, Pakistan, Saudi Arabia and the Sudan have not ratified the Convention; some of the others, including India, China and Bangladesh (and many European nations as well), have ratified it only with some "reservation"; the United States has signed it but not ratified it.

12. Pope John Paul II, "Address to the United Nations General Assembly," October 5, 1995. These sentiments are exactly those of John Rawls, who writes that "the question of equal liberty of conscience is settled. It is one of the fixed points of our considered judgements of justice." Rawls, *A Theory of Justice*, p. 206.

13. Pope John Paul II, "Letter to Women," dated June 29, 1995, released July 10. P. 2: "As far as personal rights are concerned, there is an urgent need to achieve real equality in every area: equal pay for equal work, protection for working mothers, fairness in career advancements, equality of spouses with regard to family rights and the recognition of everything that is part of the rights and duties of citizens in a democratic state. . . . The time has come to condemn vigorously the types of sexual violence which frequently have women as their object and to pass laws which effectively defend them from such violence." Elsewhere, the Pope has spoken explicitly about marital rape, making it clear that he believes it to fall among the violent acts that should be legally prohibited.

14. One of my reasons for focusing on international examples of this situation is that the other papers of the conference that this paper grew out of generally focused on similar issues in the United States. I saw, therefore, a need to introduce other elements into the discussion.

15. See Mary E. Becker, "The Politics of Women's Wrongs and the Bill of 'Rights': A Bicentennial Perspective," *University of Chicago Law Review* 59 (1992), pp. 453–517; reprinted in *The Bill of Rights*, ed. G. Stone, et al.

16. An honorable exception to the neglect is certainly Rawls, who in "The Law of Peoples" argued that women's equality was one area in which it was legitimate to interfere with the religious or traditional practices of a nation.

17. For a sense of my own relation to them, see my "Human Capabilities, Female Human Beings," in *Women, Culture and Development: A Study of Human Capabilities,* ed. M. Nussbaum and J. Glover (Oxford: Clarendon Press, 1993); and "The Good as Discipline, the Good as Freedom," forthcoming in *The Ethics of Consumption and Stewardship,* ed. D. Crocker, discussing the very close relationship between my list of the basic human capabilities and Rawls' list of primary goods.

18. See Amartya Sen, "Secularism and its Discontents," in *Unravelling the Nation,* ed. Kaushik Basu and Sanjay Subrahmanyam, 1995; and Sen, *On Interpreting India's Past* (Calcutta: The Asiatic Society, 1996).

19. Cited by Jawaharlal Nehru in *The Discovery of India* (Calcutta: Signet Press, 1956, centenary edition Oxford: Clarendon Press, 1989), p. 75; see discussion in Sen, *Interpreting,* pp. 13–14.

20. This work, which Westerners often encounter as a pornographic curiosity, is, of course, a central text of the religious tradition, of deeply serious pedagogical intent. For an account of the misogynist texts, see Roop Rekha Verma, "Femininity, Equality, and Personhood," in WCD, pp. 433–43. The reader of these texts will quickly discover that the tendency of some Hindu feminists to blame all repressive tendencies in Hinduism on the Islamic cultural influence is in error.

21. For one clear example of this, see Khory's study of reactions to the Shah Bano case, op. cit. She summarizes: "the Shah Bano case is representative of the way in which group divisions within Indian society are increasingly manipulated for political reasons."

22. Among the issues that I also focus on in the larger version of this paper are the right to life and health, the right to employment, mobility and assembly rights, the rights of political participation and speech, rights of property, nationality and education.

23. See Indira Jaising, "Violence Against Women: The Indian Perspective," in *Women's Rights, Human Rights, (WRHR),* ed. Julie Peters and Andrea Wolper (New York: Routledge, 1995), pp. 51–6.

24. A.I.R. (1983) A.P. 356.

25. Citations in Singh, in *HRW*, pp. 387–8.

26. A.I.R. 1984 S.C. 152; see Singh, in *HRW*, p. 388.

27. *Nelly Zaman v. Ghiyasuddin,* 34 D.L.R. 221 (1982), discussed in Sara Hossain, "Women's Rights and Personal Laws in South Asia," in *HRW*, pp. 465–494, at 478–9.

28. See Nahid Toubia, "Female Genital Mutilation," (FGM) in *WRHR,* pp. 224–37, at 36. Mohammed told his listeners to "circumcise" but not to "mutilate," for not destroying the clitoris would be better for the man and would make the woman's face glow—a directive that many interpret as calling for a "male-type circumcision where the prepuce is removed, making the clitoris even more sensitive to the touch" (236).

29. In clitoridectomy, part or all of the clitoris is removed, and frequently, part or all of the labia minora; in infibulation, the clitoris is removed, the labia minora are cut off, and incisions in the labia majora create raw surfaces which are then stitched together to heal as a hood of skin which covers the urethra and most of the vagina. In general, 85% of the women who undergo FGM have clitoridectomies, 15% infibulations. In countries such as the Sudan, Somalia and Djibouti, 80% to 90% of FGM is infibulation, and infibulation is also common in symbolic operations in which capacity for sexual functioning is not impaired. Worldwide, approximately 2 million girls per year suffer FGM—around 6,000 per day (see Toubia).

30. See Toubia, in *WRHR,* pp. 227–9. Toubia was the first female surgeon in the Sudan, is an advisor to the World Health Organization, Vice-chair of the Women's Rights Project of Human Rights Watch, and the director of the Global Action against FGM Project at the Columbia University School of Public Health.

31. This section was originally entitled "Addressing the Dilemma" and contained a philosophical development of my perspective. This version of the paper contains only a suggestion of my argument.

32. Compare a moment in Lincoln's Second Inaugural, where, commenting on the use of religious discourse by southern slaveholders, he observes that it "may seem strange that any men should dare to ask a just God's assistance in wringing their bread from the sweat of other men's faces."

33. Will Kymlicka, *Multicultural Citizenship: A Liberal Theory of Minority Rights* (Oxford: Clarendon Press, 1995).

34. See Kymlicka, p. 165, arguing that intervention with the policies of Saudi Arabia denying political rights to women and non-Muslims would be unjustified.

35. Today it's 110 million; this was written 10 years ago.

36. Chagla, "Plea for a Uniform Civil Code," in Mahmood, p. 116.

37. For one good example, see the volume *Religion and Human Rights,* ed. John Kelsay and Sumner B. Twiss for The Project on Religion and Human Rights.

38. It is for this reason that NGO's were regarded with much more alarm than governments by the powers that be in Beijing.

39. "U.S. Gives Asylum to Woman Who Fled Genital Mutilation," Celia W. Dugger, *The New York Times,* June 1996. She was unusual for two reasons: the woman was nineteen, old enough to take action for herself, rather than age five or six, the usual time for the operation, because her wealthy progressive father had forbidden the procedure during his lifetime; and, second, because, thanks to great sacrifices on the part of family members, she could get hold of enough money to purchase a plane ticket to Europe.

Suggestions for Further Reading

Abalos, David T. *Latinos in the United States: The Sacred and the Political.* Notre Dame, IN: University of Notre Dame Press, 1986.

Audi, Robert, and Wainwright, William J., eds. *Rationality, Religious Belief, and Moral Commitment: New Essays in the Philosophy of Religion.* Ithaca, NY: Cornell University Press, 1986.

Bartley, W.W., III. *Morality and Religion.* New York: Macmillan, 1971.

Chopp, Rebecca S. *The Praxis of Suffering: An Interpretation of Liberation and Political Theologies.* Maryknoll, NY: Orbis Books, 1986.

Cleaver, Eldridge. *Soul On Ice.* New York: Dell, 1968.

Cone, James H. *Black Theology and Black Power.* New York: The Seabury Press, 1969.

———. *A Black Theology of Liberation.* New York: J. B. Lippincott, 1970.

———. *For My People: Black Theology and the Black Church.* Maryknoll, NY: Orbis Books, 1984.

Cox, Harvey. *The Seduction of the Spirit: The Use and Misuse of People's Religion.* New York: Simon and Schuster, 1973.

Dharmasiri, Gunapala. *Fundamentals of Buddhist Ethics.* Antioch, CA: Golden Leaves Publishing Company, 1989.

Donagan, Allan. *The Theory of Morality.* Chicago: University of Chicago Press, 1977.

Dussel, Enrique. *Philosophy of Liberation.* Translated by Aquilina Martinez and Christine Morkowsky. Maryknoll, NY: Orbis Books, 1979.

Fingarette, Herbert. *Confucius–The Secular as Sacred.* New York: Harper & Row, 1972,

Frankena, William. *Ethics,* 2d ed. Englewood Cliffs, NJ: Prentice-Hall, 1973.

Freire, P. *Pedagogy of the Oppressed.* Translated by Myra Bergman Ramos. New York: Continuum, 1982.

Gill, Robin. *A Textbook of Christian Ethics.* Edinburgh, Scotland: TPT Clark, 1985.

Graham, A.C. *Disputers of the Tao: Philosophical Argument in Ancient China.* La Salle, IL: Open Court, 1989.

Grant, Jacquelyn. "Black Women and the Church." *All the Women Are White, All the Blacks are Men, but Some of Us are Brave: Black Women's Studies.* Edited by Gloria T. Hull, Patricia Bell Scott, and Barbara Smith. Old Westbury, NY: The Feminist Press, 1982.

Green, R. M. *Religion and Moral Reason: A New Method for Comparative Study.* New York: Oxford University Press, 1988.

Gutierrez, Gustavo. *A Theology of Liberation: History, Politics, and Salvation.* Revised edition. Edited and translated by Sister Caridad Inda and John Eagleson. Maryknoll, NY: Orbis Books, 1988.

———. *The Power of the Poor in History.* Translated by Robert R. Barr. Maryknoll, NY: Orbis Books, 1983.

Hall, David L., and Ames, Roger T. *Thinking Through Confucius.* New York: State University of New York Press, 1987.

Helm, Paul, ed. *The Divine Command Theory of Ethics.* Oxford, England: Oxford University Press, 1979.

Hudson, Yeager. *The Philosophy of Religion: Selected Readings.* Mountain View, CA: Mayfield Publishing Company, 1991.

Kierkegaard, Søren. *Fear and Trembling.* Translated by Howard V. Hong and Edna H. Hong. Princeton, NJ: Princeton University Press, 1983.

King, Martin Luther, Jr. *Why We Can't Wait.* New York: HarperCollins, 1963.

———. *The Trumpet of Conscience.* New York: HarperCollins, 1967.

Marty, Martin E., and Peerman, Dean G., eds. *New Theology No. 9.* New York: Macmillan, 1972.

McClendon, James W., Jr. *Ethics: Systematic Theology,* vol. 1, Nashville, TN: Abingdon, 1986.

Mouw, Richard J. *The God Who Commands.* Notre Dame, IN: University of Notre Dame Press, 1990.

Nielsen, Kai. *Ethics Without God.* Buffalo, NY: Prometheus Books, 1973.

Outka, Gene, and Reeder, John P., Jr., eds. *Religion and Morality.* Garden City, NY: Anchor Books, 1973.

Quinn, Philip. *Divine Commands and Moral Requirements.* Oxford, England: Oxford University Press, 1978.

Rouner, Leroy S., ed. *Human Rights and the World's Religions.* Notre Dame, IN: University of Notre Dame Press, 1988.

Schutte, Ofelia. *Cultural Identity and Social Liberation in Latin American Thought.* Albany, NY: State University of New York Press, 1993.

Tutu, Desmond Mpilo. *Hope and Suffering: Sermons and Speeches.* Grand Rapids, MI: Eerdmans, 1984.

West, Cornel. *Keeping Faith: Philosophy and Race in America.* New York: Routledge, 1993.

X, Malcolm. *The Autobiography of Malcolm X.* New York: Grove Press, 1967.

CHAPTER 7

Are We Immortal?

Introduction

THE QUESTION "ARE WE IMMORTAL?" is a difficult question to answer. It is difficult for a variety of reasons, not the least of which is the fact that it is not clear exactly what a "yes" answer affirms or what a "no" answer denies. This is so because of the ambiguity of the words *we* and *immortal.* Let's start with *we.*

Who are "we"? It seems natural to answer "human beings," although many of us would love our animal companions to accompany us into eternity. Let us not complicate the issue by considering other-than-human animals now. Let us say we mean human beings by "we." But who or what are human beings? We must be careful here. All human beings that we know of are persons, but not all persons are human beings. For example, we can well imagine some extraterrestrial intelligence (ET, for instance) who is not a human being from a biological point of view but nevertheless is a person. So do we mean persons, or do we mean only those that biologically count as belonging to the species we call human beings?

The question of who or what survives is important because it is obvious that all kinds of things survive our death—our atoms, for example. The things we have produced in our lifetime also survive for a while. Memories of us will survive among our friends and relatives after we die. So will things that belonged to us. The biological species *Homo sapiens* may also outlast us for a time. Is this the sort of immortality we are talking about? Many would say we are talking about personal immortality, the continued existence of persons after their bodies die. What is a person?

This too is not an easy question to answer. Some might say that persons are physical organisms who are conscious, are capable of self-motivated activity, have a capacity to communicate, are capable of reasoning, and possess a self-concept. Exactly what all these notions mean is a subject of intense philosophical debate. Let's focus on two issues: What are persons made of? And what constitutes personal identity through time?

We might argue that persons, so far as we know, are made of matter. Persons are physical creatures who have bodies and various organs. There is nothing more to them than that. Of course these physical components, including the brain, cease to function at death. That is what we mean by death. If this is what a person is made of, then it seems difficult to imagine any sort of immortality that would not involve either bringing the body back to life or creating a new body to house the mental life that persons also have. What about that mental life?

Some have argued that the existence of thoughts, feelings, consciousness, and so on demands that we think of the person as more complex than just a physical body. A person has both a body and a soul. But what is a soul? Some might say the soul refers simply to the mental life of a person. This mental life is a bundle or collection of experiences that characterize our inner or subjective lives. David Hume argued that he, when he looked inward at his mental life, could find no soul or mind above and beyond this bundle of thoughts, feelings, memories, and associations that constituted his subjective life. However, some philosophers argue that this "bundle theory" of the self will not do. They argue that there must be a center to this bundle, an I or ego that is the subject of all these thoughts and feelings. After all, we speak of *my* thoughts, *my* memories, or *my* feelings. Who is this "my"?

William James argued that there is no "I" above and beyond the stream of consciousness that characterizes persons. We use the term *I* to refer to ourselves because one part of this stream of consciousness feels connected to a previous part of the stream. Hence we have a sense of "ownedness." A sense of "I" comes, so to speak, with the bundle Hume described. Others argue that the "I" must be something more than this. It must be a substance—a mental and hence immaterial substance—that stands at the center of consciousness and constitutes the true subject of all experiences and of all bodily processes. It is this immaterial and hence spiritual substance that constitutes the soul and the true nature of the person. It is this that is immortal.

Let us turn to the question of self-identity through time. Am I the same person now at age 58 that I was at age 2? In one sense I am not. I do not have the same body. I look nothing like I did at 2. I have no memories of when I was 2, although I do know some rather unflattering stories my sister likes to tell about me at that age. My character is quite different, too. For one thing, I have outgrown the temper tantrums my sister likes to recount. In another sense, however, I *am* the same person. Although I look nothing like I did at 2, there is physical continuity between that 2-year-old and me. My body developed out of that body. And even though I have no memories of when I was 2, I have little doubt that my mental life is a continuation of the mental life of me at 2. My character has certainly changed. Yet the character traits I now possess and my present dispositions to act in certain ways are continuous with those of that toddler. It would be odd to claim that what I am now is totally and completely discontinuous with what I was at 2. If I did make such a claim, you might seriously consider the possibility that I was an entirely different person. It seems bizarre to say that there are two of me (or more!)

We can complicate this problem of self-identity through time by bringing in cases of multiple personalities, amnesia, or science fiction scenarios of dissolving my body and transporting "me" through space to another planet and reconstructing my body out of a fresh supply of atoms. And we can complicate it by bringing in death. Death, at the very least, is a discontinuity of some magnitude. What would entitle us to say that someone who has survived death is the same person as someone who once lived?

This brings us to the question of immortality. There are various conceptions of what it is, and to a large extent, these conceptions make sense (or don't make sense) depending on how we answer the philosophical questions about what persons are made of and what constitutes their self-identity through time. If, for example, we argue that persons are essentially souls, that souls are some type of immaterial substance, and that our identity consists in having the same soul, then we would be inclined to support some sort of theory about the immortality of the soul. There are a variety of possibilities. We might argue that the soul is immortal by nature, in which case it can both pre-exist this present incarnation and post-exist it. Then again, we might argue that souls are not immortal by nature but rather that God grants them immortality at death for the purposes of reward or punishment. Hence they post-exist this incarnation, but they do not pre-exist it. Or we might argue that this is only one of many incarnations of the soul. Our soul-selves pass from body to body to body until someday they find release. When they do, they may go to some paradise to exist eternally in their distinctive and unique identities. Perhaps, like rivers running into the sea, they dissolve into some universal soul of eternal bliss. All of these views raise serious questions about what personal existence means and about whether such an existence is possible without a body.

Those who find bodies essential to persons often argue for some kind of resurrection theory. However, what is resurrection? Is it a resuscitation of a corpse? That seems improbable. If I die of cancer at 75 and that corpse is brought back to life, I will die again of cancer. If my pre-cancerous body (say age 65) is resuscitated, is it really "my" body? What if I died at 2? Is my 2-year-old body brought back to life? If so, my enjoyment of the afterlife would seem to be severely restricted. If the potential 25-year-old body of the 2-year-old is brought back to life, in what sense can we say it is my body? What if my body is eaten by wild animals after I die? What if it totally decomposes?

These sorts of questions have led many to argue that resurrection refers not to a resuscitation of some corpse but to a re-creation of a totally new body. This would be a replica of me that would look like me, have my memories, and embody my character. But if it is a replica—a duplicate, so to speak—in what sense is it really me?

We have entered some deep waters here and have not even talked about what sort of evidence there might be for survival. Some argue philosophically from some kind of definition of the soul as spiritual that it must be immortal. Others argue scientifically that certain evidence about communicating with the dead, reincarnation memories, and near-death experiences point to the possibility of survival. Still others maintain that the weight of scientific evidence about the dependence of the mind on the brain points to extinction. Perhaps the strongest argument is the theological argument that if God exists, there must be eternal life because it would contradict God's purposes if those meant for divine fellowship perished. Of course, this argument contains an important "if"; it is by no means certain that God does exist.

How, then, do we answer the question "Are we immortal?" Read what follows and make up your mind for yourself—if you can. Who makes the best case?

7.1 Death and Immortality in African Religions

If you could live forever, would you? Is quality of life more important than quantity? If there is some immortal part of you that never dies, in what sense can it be said that *you* die? If we cannot help being immortal, then how should we conduct ourselves?

Can a person be both mortal and immortal? Does it make sense to regard an immortal soul-substance as a person? Why should you be saddened when friends and relatives die if you believe that what is most important about them, their personhood, lives on?

Can we communicate with the dead? If we can, in what sense are they dead? Can a person live on as an immaterial soul and yet be reborn in this physical world? How essential is your physical body to you? Would its destruction change who you essentially are? Do you think that what you do in this life influences what will happen to you after you die? Do culture and tradition influence our views about death and the afterlife?

These are just a few of the questions that traditional African religious thinkers address and try to answer. Because traditional African religious beliefs and practices were formulated in societies that, for the most part, did not have a written language, we must look to the myths, legends, folklore, and proverbs passed on from one generation to the next in order to uncover their philosophical reflection on themes related to death and the afterlife.

It is probably more accurate to speak of African religions than of African religion, because each tribal group has its own distinct views. There is Yoruba religion, Zulu religion, Neuer religion, and many more. In spite of this variety and diversity, there are common themes and similar values. In the next selection, Professor Kofi Asare Opoku, reader in religious studies at the University of Calabar, Nigeria, describes certain common themes and ideas about death and immortality found among different African tribes. He believes that traditional African thinking about life and death is both profound and sophisticated.

Reading Questions

1. What do you think is the meaning of the Nupe myth about how death entered the world?
2. Give examples of physical and nonphysical causes of death? Do you believe that there can be nonphysical causes? Why?
3. What is the *okra*?
4. What is "partial reincarnation"?
5. Who is an ancestor?
6. Do you agree with the judgment that African views of immortality are "not intended to encourage the illusion of escaping the reality of death"? Why or why not?

Death and Immortality in African Religions*

KOFI ASARE OPOKU

EVERY CULTURE SEEKS to provide meaningful answers to the ultimate questions about human existence and destiny, and these answers are born out of the experiences of the people within that cultural milieu and their mature reflection on those experiences. The important consideration here is that the answers given satisfy the needs of the human spirit and provide meaning and significance to human life and destiny.

The problem of life and death has received profound attention in the African cultural heritage, and has been the basis of much philosophical reflection and religious insight. Both life and death are viewed as given by the Creator, and once life is given, death must inevitably follow, as the Akan of Ghana say: *"obra twa 'wu"*: life must needs end in death, each person lives towards death.

African mythology abounds with innumerable accounts of how death entered the world, and although these stories may at first sight appear to be "mere" accounts or myths about the origin of death, they have a level of profundity at which they clearly inform us of the conception of the human condition held by the narrators of the myths. In some of the myths, human beings did not seem to have had a choice in the matter of death: two messengers were sent by God, one with the message of life and the other with the message of death.[1] The messenger with the message of death reached mankind first and the one with the message of life arrived rather too late.

In other myths however, human beings had a choice between immortality and mortality, and they chose the latter. The reason for their choice was clear: it conformed to the essential condition of mankind. A Nupe (Nigeria) myth recounts:

In the beginning God created tortoises, men and stones, and, with the exception of the stones, he made them male and female and provided them with life. However, none of the species reproduced. One day the tortoise wanted to have descendants and asked this of God, whose response was that he had granted life to the tortoise and to men but had not given them permission to have children. At this time, the story adds, men did not die; when they became old they were automatically rejuvenated. The tortoise renewed his appeal and God warned him against the danger of death which would result from a positive response on his part. But the tortoise took no notice and pressed his request. He was joined by men, who had decided to have children even at the risk of death, while the stones refused to join in with them. Thus God granted tortoises and men the ability to have posterity, and death entered the world, but the stones remained unaffected.[2]

Clearly, a choice of immortality would have led to a rejection of the human condition, and the choice of mortality affirms our nature as human beings.

Causes of Death and Religious Explanations of Death

African notions of death and immortality cannot be understood without first taking into account African conceptions of human personality.[3] Broadly speaking, the human being is made up of material and immaterial factors and either of them can cause death. There is a profoundly interactionist view of man that holds that the material and immaterial parts of man have a causal influence on each other; in other words, what

*From "Death and Immortality in the African Religious Heritage" by Kofi Asare Opoku in *Death and Immortality in the Religions of the World*, edited by Paul and Linda Badham. Copyright © 1987 by Paragon House Publishers. Reprinted by permission.

happens to the soul of man affects the body, and similarly, what happens to the body affects the condition of the soul. Death, therefore, has both physical and nonphysical, or physiological and psychological causes. Since the human being is considered to be a part of the whole universe, the visible and invisible influences that the rest of creation may have on him or her are seriously taken into consideration.

Physical causes of death may include childbirth, disease, famine, injury from wild animals, accidents or injury sustained during communal or personal disputes, execution, or old age. In addition to these, there are other kinds of physical causes that modern life has added to the stock of causes. But these physical explanations alone do not adequately explain all of the phenomenon of death, and this is where religious explanations come in.[4] And in this regard, the relationship with God, the ancestors or living-dead and spirits, and fellow members of the community are of crucial significance, for these nonphysical considerations can also cause death.

A curse by an elderly person could lead to suffering and death; those who are selfish and do not have the interest of the community at heart may suffer physically, even to the point of death. The breaking of taboos and established standards of religious behavior, dishonoring the ancestors, breaking a binding oath—all may result in physical disability and death. Witchcraft, magic, and sorcery are also recognized as causes of physical suffering and death. All of these religious explanations help to answer the question why, and enable people to accept, and to come to terms with, what would otherwise remain inexplicable.

The Meaning of Death

When death occurs, the immaterial part (the soul) separates itself from the body and survives the experience of death. The survival of a part of man after death is a certainty that is not doubted as much as the fact of human existence is not doubted, and is a stark reality. In African thought, this indestructible part of man has a divine origin and is sacred, and the attribute of immortality accorded to it stems from the fact that it is considered to be a spiritual substance or entity, and not "a bundle of qualities or perceptions," which would mean that nothing would be left when the qualities and perceptions are removed. On the contrary, there remains, after death, a substratum or "owner" of those qualities.[5]

To give an example from the Akan of Ghana, a human being possesses an *okra,* the part of *Onyame,* God, in every person, which is the essential part of being human.[6] Animals do not possess *okra.* The *okra* is divine in origin and has an antemundane existence and a postmortem existence. It is the presence of the *okra* that makes one a living human being and its departure from the body signifies death. At death, therefore, the *okra* returns to its source and is reunited with *Onyame.* Hence the Akan say, *"Onyame bewu na mawu"*: could God die, I will die, or I shall only die if God dies; which is a reference to the *okra,* the undying part of the human person. It is inconceivable to the Akan to imagine that the Creator could die, therefore the *okra* does not die when one dies physically. An Akan maxim also epigrammatically expresses the idea that when a man dies he is not (really) dead: *Onipa wu a, na onwui."* In other words, there is something that is eternal and indestructible in man, which continues to exist after death in the land of spirits.

The idea of death as a *return* underlies the funeral rites. The body of the person is prepared as if the person were going on a journey, and some personal belongings are put in the coffin so that the deceased may take them along. These may include the sponge, soap, comb, and towel with which the deceased was given his or her last bath, a cup or calabash for drinking water, some pieces of coins for buying things along the way, and some assorted clothing of which the deceased was particularly fond. Messages are also given to the deceased to carry to relatives in the other world, just as one sends messages with a person going on a journey. These messages are not only given verbally but are also contained in many of the dirges that are sung during funerals.[7]

Sending messages with the deceased presupposes the ability of the living to communicate with the dead, and this communication link is maintained even after burial. The deceased is believed to be united with his or her relatives who live in the abode of the dead, which is invisible but very close to that of the living. Death does not bring the deceased to a complete end. In a sense, it is only a channel through which the deceased passes to continue to live, albeit in the form of a spirit. But the dead retain features that describe them in physical terms. They maintain their identity, and there is no merging with the Absolute. In fact the deceased person:

> . . . retains most of the other features which were used to describe him during his physical existence . . . he retains his personal name, and his relatives continue to recognize him as one of the members of the family. Although he no longer lives in the flesh, he continues to hold the social, political and religious status which he held while he lived physically.[8]

But although the deceased is believed to continue to live and to interact with others, there is an important sense in which death brings an end to a person's physical participation in the community. The deceased ceases to be a physical being and separates from the community, and the funeral rites that are performed are symbols of separation between the dead and the living.

This physical separation, which interrupts normal life and robs families and the society of its members, largely accounts for the negative sentiments and attitudes towards death. Thus death is seen as a wicked destroyer, a killer and an implacable enemy who frustrates human effort; it drives men to sorrow and despair, and has no respect for intelligence, position, or beauty. The sense of frustration and utter helplessness in the face of death is expressed in a Yoruba funeral dirge:

> If death had requested for money, we would have given him money; if death had requested for meat, we would have bought ram for him. We made sacrifices without ceasing, yet we do not see the medicine that will prevent death from killing man. Death has done a wicked thing. Death has done a wicked thing.[9]

But the separation is only physical and does not terminate the life of the individual, and the expression of anxiety, frustration, despondency, and utter helplessness soon gives way to a more positive and lasting attitude, since the separation marks the beginning of the prolongation of the life of the individual and a change in status from a lesser to a higher authority.

A common practice among members of the immediate family of the deceased during funerals is to shave off their hair as a symbol of separation, showing that one of their members has been separated from them. But new hair will grow back, and that is an indication of the profound belief that death does not destroy life, since the growth of new hair indicates that life continues to spring up.[10]

After-death and Immortality

Death represents a transition from corporeal to incorporeal life in the religious heritage of Africa and the incorporeal life is taken to be as real as the corporeal. This attitude was held with such utter conviction that little anxiety was shown in the face of death. An authentication of this attitude could be found in Benin where servants and persons especially indulged by the king would compete with each other for the privilege of being buried alive with the body of the king when he died so that they could attend on him in the next world.[11] This firm belief in the reality of life after death represents a fundamental antidote to the threat of human extinction and the scare of nothingness, which have jointly "conspired" to render life utterly meaningless to many a modern person. In the African understanding, death does not rob life of meaning, on the contrary, it gives greater depth of meaning to life by prolonging it on the spiritual plane.[12]

Because the dead continue to live, communication with them is possible; and there are culturally accepted ways of maintaining the relationship between the living and the dead. Prayers, libations, offerings, and the observation of other religious rites are of crucial importance in this regard. And furthermore, as Zahan wrote:

Tradition for Africans is, then, a means of communicating between the dead and the living. It belongs to a vast network of communications between the two worlds which embodies "prayer" offerings, sacrifices and myths. In this relationship tradition possesses a real originality. At times it is direct, that is, it precludes any intermediary between man and the beyond. . . . At other times tradition is indirect, and in this case the human being perceives more or less clearly the reasons for his religious actions.

Whether in the form of one or the other of these two types of communication, tradition as the "word" of the dead remains the most vital link between the living and the dead.[13]

The relationship is not one-sided, for the dead, too, have a role to play in keeping it alive and real. It is a reciprocal relationship, and death, therefore, does not put a stop to one's obligation to the family and community. The dead have a duty to protect, intervene, and mediate on behalf of the living, and as it is believed that death increases one's powers, the dead are able to offer more help or assistance. This underscores the involvement of the dead in the affairs of the living; and the reciprocal permeability of the world of the living and that of the dead is accepted without disputation.

Return of the Dead

It is firmly believed that the dead come back into life and that this is in the nature of things. In African cultural practices the symbolism of death and resurrection or return to life is very pervasive. In the initiation rites, for instance, the neophytes die to their old selves and are born into new persons, they die only to be reborn. In the *Poro* initiation rites of the Mende of Sierra Leone, the young initiates are "swallowed" by the *Poro* spirit, and on the night before the end of the initiation rites, the *Poro* spirit groans like a woman in labor. Kenneth Little explains:

The initiation rite and the whole time spent in the bush which follows it symbolize the change in status. The young initiate is supposed to be "swallowed" by the [*Poro*] spirit when he enters,

and separation from his parents and kinsfolk signifies death. The marks on his back are evidence of the spirit's teeth. At the end of his time, he is "delivered" by the spirit and reborn. Thus, the period in the bush marks his transition from boyhood to manhood, and as a result of the experience he emerges a fully fledged member of Mende society.[14]

In the training for the priesthood, the same symbolism prevails. Even mystical ecstasy is a death followed by resurrection.

The Zulu express the belief that the dead are reborn by burying the dead in a squatting position in a symbolic repetition of the position of the embryo in the fetal membrane, and the niche into which the dead is put is called a "navel." The dead person is received in the grave as at birth. But this symbolism also extends to other members of the family, who also participate in the death and resurrection or death and rebirth syndrome. Sundermeier wrote:

. . . even the mourner is born again. A Zulu widow is only allowed to take baby food at the beginning of the mourning period and is slowly accustomed to a firmer diet. She is washed like a child, later gets the clothes of a bride, and after some last ritual washings which finally wash off death, receives the clothes of a grown-up.[15]

The belief that the dead come back into life and are reborn into their families is given concrete expression in the personal names that are given to children. The Yoruba, for example, have many names that suggest the return of the dead: *Iyabo*, Mother returns; *Yetunde*, Mother comes back a second time; and *Babatunde*, Father has come again. Ewe names that indicate the return of the dead are *Afetogbo*, the master has come back (given to children born after the death of a member of the family); *Degbo*, gone and returned; *Evakpo*, he has ventured to come again; and *Noviegbo*, sister has returned. Not only are parents and grown-ups believed to return; children, too, are believed to do likewise. Hence the Yoruba names, *Omotunde*, child comes back again; and *Omodeinde*, child turns back and is here. There are also other names that express the idea of waking up from sleep, for example,

Babajide, Father wakes up and is back; and *Babatunji,* Father wakes up again.

The belief in the return of the dead and its concrete expression in personal names suggest the idea of reincarnation, but it is one that differs significantly from the conventional understanding of the word. In African belief, even though a person is said to have returned to earth and to have been reincarnated in his or her grandchildren or great grandchildren, that person nevertheless continues to live in the afterlife and to keep his or her identity. What is reincarnated are some of the dominant characteristics of the ancestor and not his soul. For each soul remains distinct and each birth represents a new soul.

Idowu describes this as a "partial reincarnation," and observes that there are "certain dominant lineage characteristics which keep occurring through births and ensuring the continuity of the vital existence of the family or clan."[16]

The Fate of the Dead

There are areas in Africa where eschatological ideas similar to those in Judaism, Christianity, or Islam are found. The Yoruba, the Dogon, and the LoDagoa (Ghana) provide interesting insights into African eschatological thought. Among the Yoruba, for example, *Olodumare* (God), is believed to mete out judgment to individuals after death and each has to give an account of his or her earthly life before *Olodumare,* who then judges accordingly. The Yoruba say, "All that we do on earth we shall account for kneeling in heaven," and "We shall state our case at the feet of *Olodumare.*"[17] What *Olodumare,* the Searcher of Hearts, who sees and knows everything, and whose judgment is sure and absolutely inescapable, judges is *"iwa,"* character. Man's well-being here on earth depends on his character, his place in the Afterlife is determined by God according to his deserts. And by good character, the Yoruba mean "chastity before marriage, hospitality, generosity, the opposite of selfishness; kindness, justice, truth and rectitude as essential virtues; avoiding stealing; keeping a covenant and avoiding falsehood; protecting the poor and weak, especially women; giving honour and respect to older people, and avoiding hypocrisy."[18]

Those whose earthly life receives the approbation of *Olodumare* are sent to *Orun rere,* where they are reunited with their kin and where there is no sorrow or suffering. Those who enter this good heaven may choose to be reborn into their families. But those who led a bad life on earth will go to *Orun apaadi,* a place of broken potsherds, where it is unbearably hot and dry, and where they will feed on centipedes and earthworms. This is why the Yoruba express the wish in the final words of farewell to a dead person:

Be sure you do not feed on centipedes
Be sure you do not feed on earthworms
What people feed on in *Orun rere*
That you should feed on.[19]

But in most African societies, there is a marked absence of such clear-cut notions of heaven and hell, although there are notions of God judging the soul after death. The Song of Divine Judgment from the Fon of the Republic of Benin vividly describes God as the Final Judge:

Life is like a hill,
Mawu, the Creator, made it steep and
    slippery,
To right and left deep waters surround it,
You cannot turn back once you start to
    climb.
You must climb with a load on your head.
A man's arms will not help him for it is a
    trial,
The world is a place of trial.
At the gates of the land of the dead,
You will pass before a searching Judge,
His justice is true and he will examine
    your feet,
He will know how to find every stain,
Whether visible or hidden under the skin.
If you have fallen on the way, he will
    know,
If the judge finds no stains on your feet,
Open your belly to joy, for you have
    overcome
And your belly is clean.[20]

Other African people believe that the dead go to give an account of their earthly existence before God, and the Akan, for instance, believe that the *okra* of the deceased goes to give an account of its life before God and if the *okra* did not complete its destiny, it is sent back to complete it. There is also the belief that those who led good lives will join the ancestors, but others will not.

The Bini of Nigeria believe that God has ordered every human being to make fourteen tours throughout this life, and that the tours begin at birth and end at death. A person's place in the afterlife is determined by the way he or she has lived during the fourteen tours. As Ighodaro wrote:

> His purity, his love of his neighbour and
> God
> and his kindness will be taken into
> account.
> A man or woman is not judged until his
> or her
> last journey in this world, and so a person
> is never
> in a position to determine whether he is
> on his first
> or last tour. A man has only to presume
> that this may
> be his last tour, and therefore all the good
> he can do
> now, he must do them, as he may not pass
> this way again.[21]

Good people become ancestors and ancestorhood is a status that is attained, and not all who die achieve it. The notion of the ancestor hinges on important moral, social, and religious considerations, which make the ancestors into models worthy of emulation. Those who are accorded the status have their family life on earth extended into the supersensible world, and communion and communication are held with them regularly. Through these activities the continuity and identity of the family or community over time is maintained. The world of the dead is part of our world and the afterlife is linked up with the present life of the family or community in a dynamic way.

Absence of Eschatology?

Several writers have commented on the absence of eschatological thinking in African religion. Benjamin Ray wrote:

> There is little speculation about "last things"—that is, about the nature of the after life or about immortality or final judgement—for there are no "last things" towards which human life is headed. There is no vision of a culminating "end" to individual lives or to human history in general.[22]

Such viewpoints originate from the attempt, conscious or unconscious, to evaluate African religion and other religions and to view them through the prism of Western religions. This, of course, leads to gross distortions and value judgments that prevent us from fully appreciating the contribution that insights from non-Western religions and, in this particular instance, African traditional religion, can make to the present discussion. It may be worth our while to bear in mind that one cannot fully understand eschatological thinking in Western religions without taking into account the historical experiences of the Jews. As Huston Smith wrote:

> Judaism, the foundational religion of the West, was instigated by a concrete historical happening—the Exodus—as the religion of India and China were not. In addition, the basic concepts of Judaism were forged while the Jews, being either displaced or oppressed, were a people in waiting—first to cross over into the promised land, then to return to Jerusalem, then for the coming of the Messiah who was to deliver them. This built into Judaism a future-oriented character that was unique until it was duplicated by Christianity. . . .[23]

The experiences of the African peoples were quite different and their notions about death and the afterlife, as well as about time, must be viewed against their historical and other experiences. It is certainly not so difficult to see why eschatological thinking could be so pronounced in the Judeo–Christian heritage, but having said this, one must hasten to add that notions of a "culminating end" to individual lives or to human history, or about time as irreversibly headed towards a destination and more often than not, to a catastrophic end, are quite contrary to the experiences of other people. And although these eschatological speculations are grounded in faith in God, African views about time and history are also grounded in faith in God. In the African world view, time has no end, neither does the world have an end. The Creator sustains the universe and there is no thought that it will come to an end.[24]

The eschatological ideas of Christianity with respect to the resurrection of the body and life in the Kingdom of God certainly help to relieve the anxiety of believers who are facing death. To a large extent, the resurrection represents a future hope, an event that will occur at the end of time. In the religious heritage of Africa, however, the fate of the dead as it relates to their return to life is a present reality that has been and is still being experienced. It is a realized experience, which is given concrete expression in life, personal names, and rituals. This realized experience, which has already occurred in this life to fulfill our deepest ontological aspirations, it is believed, will continue through time.

The life of the dead is a reality and it does not even depend on the remembrance of them by those who are living on earth, Mbiti asserts.[25] On the contrary, the dead have their own independent existence, and they do not continue to live because they are remembered in the hearts of those who have been left behind. As Idowu wrote:

> . . . they do not for any reason fade into nothing or lapse into any kind of durational retirement. In the invocation of ancestors in certain African localities, the liturgy embraces those remembered and unremembered, those known and unknown. It is often said specifically, "we cannot remember all of you by name, nevertheless, we invoke you all." Further, ancestors connected with certain professions like medicine, crafts or priesthood are mentioned as far back as the first one who initiated the practice. . . . During annual festivals, or special rituals, ancestors are traced as far back as the beginning of things.[26]

African ideas about death and immortality are not intended to encourage the illusion of escaping the reality of death; on the contrary, while living in full awareness of our mortality, we are provided with its real meaning and significance within the context of the totality of human life, as well as with the tools to overcome our mortality. The genius of the African humanity reveals itself in the ideas about death and immortality even when we live in full cognizance of the transience of bodily existence. Life is not restricted to bodily existence, for the soul, which is distinct from the body and which is identified with the conscious self, continues to live after the death and disintegration of the physical body.[27]

NOTES

1. See Hans Abrahamsson, *The Origin of Death*, Studia Ethnographica Upsalensia, vol. 3 (Uppsala: Almquist and Wiksell, 1951); also Dominique Zahan, *The Religion, Spirituality and Thought of Traditional Africa* (Chicago: University of Chicago Press, 1979), pp. 36–52.

2. Leo Frobenius, *Atlantis*, vol. 12 (Jena: E. Diedrichs, 1928), p. 140, as cited by Dominique Zahan, *The Religion, Spirituality and Thought of Traditional Africa*, p. 41.

3. For a full discussion of African concepts of human personality, see Kofi Asare Opoku, *West African Traditional Religion* (Singapore: F. E. P. International, 1978) pp. 91–100; also E. B. Idowu, *Olodumare: God in Yoruba Belief* (London: Longman, 1962), chap. 13–14; also W. E. Abraham, *The Mind of Africa* (London: Weidenfeld and Nicolson, 1962).

4. For a discussion of African Concepts of Causality see J. O. Sodipo, "Notes on the Concept of Cause and Change in Yoruba Traditional Thought," *Second Order: An African Journal of Philosophy,* no. 2 (1973), pp. 12–20.

5. See Kwame Gyeke, "Akan Concept of Person," *International Philosophical Quarterly*, vol. 18, no. 3 (September 1978): pp. 277–287.

6. See Opoku, *West African Traditional Religion*, pp. 94–96.

7. See Joseph H. Nketia, *Funeral Dirges of the Akan People* (Achimoto, 1955).

8. J. Mugambi and N. Kirima, *The African Religious Heritage* (Nairobi: Oxford University Press, 1979), p. 101.

9. Wande Abimbola, "Burial of the Dead Among the Yoruba," *Staff Seminar Papers*, School of African and Asian Studies, (Nigeria: University of Lagos, 1968–69), pp. 108–9.

10. See John S. Mbiti, *An Introduction to African Religion* (London: Heinemann, 1975), p. 115.

11. See James G. Frazer, *The Golden Bough*, vol. 4 (London: Macmillan, 1937), p. 104; also David Lorimer, *Survival: Body, Mind and Death in the Light of Psychic Experience* (London: Routledge and Kegan Paul, 1984), p. 27.

12. Mbiti refers to the dead as "Living-dead," a term which vividly conveys the idea that life continues after death; see his *African Religions and Philosophy* (London: Heinemann, 1969).

13. Zahan, *The Religion, Spirituality and Thought of Traditional Africa*, p. 119.

14. Kenneth Little, *The Mende of Sierra Leone* (London: Routledge and Kegan Paul, 1967), p. 119.

15. Theo Sundermeier, "Death Rites Supporting Life: The Process of Mourning in Africa," *African Theological Journal*, vol. 9, no. 3 (November 1980), p. 60; also, A. I. Berglund, *Zulu and Symbolism*, unpublished doctoral dissertation, Kapstadt, 1972.

16. E. B. Idowu, *Olodumare: God in Yoruba Belief*, p. 159.

17. E. B. Idowu, p. 199.

18. Idowu, p. 154.

19. Idowu, p. 199.

20. John V. Taylor, *The Primal Vision* (London: S. C. M., 1963), p. 179.

21. S. O. Ighodaro, "The Benin High God," *Staff Seminar Papers*, School of African and Asian Studies (Nigeria: University of Lagos, 1967–68), pp. 43–61.

22. Benjamin C. Ray, *African Religions: Symbol, Ritual and Community* (Englewood Cliffs, N.J.: Prentice-Hall, 1976), p. 140.

23. One could also add the religions of Africa, like China and India, as not instigated by a concrete historical happening. T. William Hall, ed., "Accents of the World Religions," in *Introduction to the Study of Religion* (New York: Harper and Row, 1978), p. 129.

24. For further reading, see Kofi Asare Opoku, "The World View of the Akan," in *Tarikh* 26, vol. 7, no. 2, Historical Society of Nigeria, (London: Longmans, 1982), pp. 61–73.

25. John S. Mbiti, *African Religions and Philosophy* (London: Heinemann, 1969), p. 33.

26. E. B. Idowu, *African Traditional Religion: A Definition* (London: S. C. M., 1973), p. 188.

27. David Lorimer, *Survival: Body, Mind and Death in the Light of Psychic Experience*, pp. 9–28.

7.2 Jewish Views of the Afterlife

The Hebrew *Bible* (*Old Testament*) does not say much about a life after death. For Biblical Judaism, a complete, fulfilling, and pious earthly life is of primary importance. Immortality, if we can use that term, is found in the community of the faithful living on in the service of the Lord. There are some references to the place of the dead (Psalms 22:16, 28:1, 28:22, and 88:5; Job 28:22 and 30:23, for example), but the life of the dead is not pictured as desirable. The dead exist in a ghostly, dull, almost lifeless state much as do the Shades painted in Homer's *Iliad*.

In Greco-Roman times, Persian ideas about the afterlife influenced Jewish thinking. Some of the rabbis who belonged to the Pharisees began to teach the idea that the dead shall rise again at some future date. God would judge people by the faithfulness of their lives and reward those who were pious and punish those who did evil. Not all Jews accepted this teaching, however, on the grounds that scripture did not teach it. In time the Pharisaic view won out, and belief in resurrection of the dead, the return of the Messiah, and a final day of judgment became standard rabbinical teachings.

Today, Jewish traditionalists regard the notion of resurrection as essential to the faith, but modernists do not. Modernists argue that Judaism existed for a long time without such an idea, and there is no reason why it should be made an article of faith because some rabbis began teaching it during Greco-Roman times. Traditionalists would maintain that the doctrine of resurrection is not just a creation of the rabbis but can be found in scripture (Ezekiel's vision of dry bones coming to life, for example). Further, it makes sense theologically. In fact, a strong argument for some sort of afterlife can be made on theological grounds alone. If God is just, merciful, and good, and if God created humans for divine fellowship, then God's purposes would go unfulfilled if there were no afterlife. If a just, merciful, and good God exists, then it is certainly reasonable to believe in life after death.

What exactly is meant by resurrection of the dead? Are we talking about the rotting physical corpse coming back to life? What if there is no corpse any more? Does God create new bodies for the dead? If so, in what sense has my body been resurrected? If they are truly physical bodies, why won't they die again? Where will all those people live? Is overcrowding a concern?

The exact nature of resurrection is left vague in Jewish teaching. We cannot know exact details about the afterlife. However, this notion of life after death is clearly very different from the idea that the soul is the essential part of a person and is, by nature, immortal. The resurrection idea affirms the unity of body and mind, and it affirms the essential importance of the body to the person. Further, God is the one to grant or not grant life beyond the grave. We do not have it automatically by virtue of the nature of our soul. It is a gift of God's mercy and justice.

Reading Questions

1. Why is a precise conception of immortality not possible?
2. What are the basic Jewish views that the idea of resurrection symbolizes?
3. Why is the existence of a life after death a necessary corollary of the Jewish belief in a just, merciful, and good God?
4. Do you find convincing Lamm's argument that death has meaning only if life has meaning? Why or why not?

Jewish Views of the Afterlife*

MAURICE LAMM

The Concept of Immortality

The conception of an after-life is fundamental to the Jewish religion; it is an article of faith in the Jews' creed. The denial of the after-life constitutes a denial of the cornerstone of the faith. This concept is not merely an added detail that may lose its significance in some advanced age. It is an essential and enduring principle. Indeed, the Mishnah (*Sanhedrin* X, 1) expressly excludes from the reward of the "world beyond" he who holds that the resurrection of the dead is without biblical warrant. Maimonides considers this belief one of the 13 basic truths which every Jew is commanded to hold.

The concept of after-life entered the prayerbook in the philosophic hymns of *Yigdal* and *Ani Ma'amin*. Centuries later, hundreds of thousands of Jews, packed in cattle-cars, enroute to the crematoria, sang the *Ani Ma'amin*, the affirmation of the coming of the Messiah.

Philosophers, such as Hasdai Crescas in the fourteenth century, changed the formulation of the basic truths, but still kept immortality as a

*From Maurice Lamm, *The Jewish Way in Death and Mourning*. Copyright © 1969 by Maurice Lamm. New York: Jonathan David Publishers. Reprinted by permission.

fundamental principle without which the Jewish religion is inconceivable. Simon Ben Zemah Duran, in the early fifteenth century, reduced the fundamentals to three, but resurrection was included. Joseph Albo, in the same era, revised the structure of dogmas, and still immortality remained a universally binding belief. No matter how the basic principles were reduced or revised, immortality remained a major tenet of Judaism. Indeed, we may say of immortality what Hermann Cohen says of the Messiah, "If the Jewish religion had done nothing more for mankind than proclaim the messianic idea of the Old Testament prophets, it could have claimed to be the bed-rock of all the world's ethical culture."

Strange as it may appear, despite the historic unanimity of scholarly opinion on the fundamental belief, the practical details of immortality are ambiguous and vague. There is no formal eschatology in Judaism, only a traditional concensus that illuminates the way. The veil has never been pierced, and only shadowy structures can be discerned. But, as a renowned artist remarked, the true genius of a painting can be determined at dusk when the light fades, when one can see only the outline, the broad strokes of the brush, while the details are submerged in darkness. The beauty of the concept of immortality and its enormous religious significance does not lie in details. Maimonides denies that man can have a clear picture of the after-life and compares earth-bound creature with the blind man who cannot learn to appreciate colors merely by being given a verbal description. Flesh-and-blood man cannot have any precise conception of the pure, spiritual bliss of the world beyond. Thus, says Maimonides, the precise sequence in which the after-life will finally unravel is not a cardinal article of the faith, and the faithful should not concern themselves with the details. So it is often in Judaism that *abstract* principles must be held in the larger, conceptual sense, while the formal philosophic details are blurred. Contrariwise, pragmatic religious ideals—the observances of the faith—are worked out to their minutest detail, although the basic concept behind them may remain unknown forever.

For all that, there is a consensus of belief based on talmudic derivations from the Torah and philosophic analyses of statements uttered by the sages. The concept is usually discussed under the headings of "Messiah" and "Resurrection of the Dead." (Concepts such as *Ge-hinnom* and *Gan Eden* are too complicated for discussion in this work.) The term, *olam ha'ba*, the "world beyond," while relatively unclear, seems to have encompassed the two basic concepts of Messiah and Resurrection. Maimonides lists these two as cardinal principles of the Jewish creed. . . .

Resurrection: A Symbolic Idea

Some contemporary thinkers have noted that the physical revival of the dead is symbolic of a cluster of basic Jewish ideas:

First, man does not achieve the ultimate redemption by virtue of his own inherent nature. It is not because he, uniquely, possesses an immortal soul that he, *inevitably*, will be resurrected. The concept of resurrection underscores man's reliance on God who, in the words of the prayerbook, "Wakes the dead in great mercy." It is His grace and His mercy that rewards the deserving, and revives those who sleep in the dust.

Second, resurrection is not only a private matter, a bonus for the righteous individual. It is a corporate reward. *All* of the righteous of *all* ages, those who stood at Sinai, and those of our generation, will be revived. The *community* of the righteous has a corporate and historic character. It will live again as a whole people. The individual, even in death, is not separated from the society in which he lived.

Third, physical resurrection affirms unequivocally that man's soul *and* his body are the creations of a holy God. There is a tendency to assume that the affirmation of a spiritual dimension in man must bring with it the corollary that his physical being is depreciated. Indeed, such has been the development of the body-soul duality in both the Christian tradition and in Oriental religions, and accounts for their glorification of asceticism. Further, even the Greek philosophers who were enamored of the beauty of the body, came to denigrate the physical side of man. They crowned reason as man's noblest virtue. For them the spiritual-intellectual endeavor to perceive the unchanging truth was the highest function of man. Man's material existence, on the other hand, was always in flux, subject to change and, therefore, inferior. Thus, they accepted immortality of the soul—which to the Greeks was what we call mind—which survives the extinction of his physical being. But they could not understand physical resurrection because they did not, by any means, consider the body worthy of being reborn.

To the contrary, Judaism has always stressed that the body, as the soul, is a gift of God—indeed, that it belongs to God. *Ha'neshamah lach ve'haguf pa'alach,* the Jew declared, "The soul is yours, and the body is your handiwork." To care for the body is a religious command of the Bible. The practice of asceticism for religious purposes was tolerated, but the ascetic had to bring a sacrifice of atonement for his action. Resurrection affirms that the body is of value because it came from God, and it will be revived by God. Resurrection affirms that man's empirical existence is valuable in God's eyes. His activities in this world are significant in the scheme of eternity. His strivings are not to be deprecated as vain and useless, but are to be brought to fulfillment at the end of days.

The concept of resurrection thus serves to keep God ever in man's consciousness, to unify contemporary and historic Jewry, to affirm the value of God's world, and to heighten, rather than to depress, the value of man's worthy strivings in this world.

Which specific virtues might guarantee a person's resurrection is a subject of much debate. The method of resurrection is, of course, an open question that invites conjecture, but which can offer no definite answer.

While the details of the after-life are thus very much a matter of speculation, the traditional consensus must serve to illuminate the dark path. In the words of Rabbi Joshua ben Chanania (*Niddah* 70b): "When they come to life again, we will consult about the matter."

Life After Death: A Corollary of Jewish Belief

The existence of a life after death is a necessary corollary of the Jewish belief in a just and merciful and ethical God.

GOD IS JUST

The Jew is caught in a dilemma: He believes that God is righteous and just—He rewards the good and punishes the wicked. Yet, for all the strength of his belief, he lives in a world where he sees that life is unfair. He sees all too often the spiritual anomaly of *zaddik vera lo, rasha vetov lo,* the righteous who suffer and the wicked who prosper. The sages answer by saying that there is *spiritual* reward and *spiritual* punishment. The answer that religion gives is that the good, just, and eternal God revives the righteous dead, while the wicked remain in the dust. It is in life-after-death at which time the just God balances the scales and rewards or punishes those who truly deserve it. This doctrine of resurrection is, thus, a necessary corollary of our belief in a just God.

GOD IS MERCIFUL

But if we ask of God only that He be just, can we expect that we ourselves will be resurrected? Who is so righteous as to be assured of that glorious reward? Hence we call upon God's *mercy* that He revive us. The concept of resurrection is an affirmation of His mercy. Thus, Joseph Albo, a fifteenth-century philosopher, notes that in the prayer-book the concept of resurrection is associated with *rachamin rabim,* "*great* mercy," whereas God's gift of life and sustenance are considered only *chen, chessed* and *rachamim,* "grace, kindness and mercy." Says Rabbi Albo: "The life of man is divided into three portions: The years of rise and growth, the middle years or the plateau, and the years of decline." These are described by the three adjectives—grace, kindness and mercy. While one is young and vigorous one does not require an *extra* measure of assistance from God in being nourished. All that he needs is *chen,* Divine grace. In the second portion of life, man grows older, but he is still able and strong. He needs more than just Divine grace, he needs God's kindness, *chessed.* In the declining years, he is weak, dependent on others, and in desperate need of more than grace and kindness. He now needs *rachamim,* God's mercy. But there is also a fourth portion of life: life after death. For this man requires more than grace, kindness and mercy. He needs *rachamim rabim,* "great mercy"! Thus, in Albo's scheme, resurrection is only a natural, further development of God's providence. In the words of the prayerbook: *Mechalkal chayim bechessed, mechayeh metim berachamim rabim.* "He sustains the living with kindness and revives the dead with *great mercy.*"

GOD AS AN ETHICAL PERSONALITY

The concept of life-after-death also follows from a belief in God as the God of goodness. A great teacher of our generation supports this by citing the *amidah* prayer in the daily prayerbook, "You support the *falling,* and heal the *sick,* and free those who are *bound up,* and keep your faith with those who *sleep in the dust.*" The prayerbook lists a series of evils that befall man, and asserts that God will save man from them. Those who "fall" suffer financial failure, a defect in the structure of society. We believe that God who is good will overcome that defect. He will "support the falling." Worse than that is sickness, which is a flaw in the physical nature of man. We believe that God is good and will not tolerate such an evil forever. He will heal the sick. Worse yet is the disease of slavery, the sickness which man wishes upon his fellowman. God will overcome this, too, for He not only supports the falling and heals the sick, He is the great emancipator of man. The worst evil of all, however, the meanest scandal, the vilest disgrace to that being created in the image of God, is death, the end to all hope and all striving. But we believe in an ethical and good God. As He prevailed over the evils of lifetime, so will He prevail over the final evil, that of death. Thus, we conclude, you who support and heal, and free, will also keep your faith with those who are dead.

The Meaning of Death

What is death? Is it merely the cessation of the biological function of living? Is it but the tragedy to end all other tragedies? Is it simply the disappearance of the soul, the end of consciousness, the evaporation of personality, the disintegration of the body into its elemental components? Is it an end beyond which there is only black void? Or, is there a significance, some deep and abiding meaning to death—one that transcends our puny ability to understand?

With all of modern man's sophistication, his brilliant technological achievements, the immense progress of his science, his discovery of new worlds of thought, he has not come one iota closer to grasping the meaning of death than did his ancient ancestors. Philosophers and poets have probed the idea of immortality, but stubbornly it remains, as always, the greatest paradox of life.

In practice, however, we must realize that what death means to the individual depends very much on what life means to him.

If life is a stage, and we the poor players who strut and fret our hour upon the stage and then are heard no more; if life is a tale told by an idiot, full of sound and fury, signifying nothing; if life is an inconsequential drama, a purposeless amusement—then death is only the heavy curtain that fails on the final act. It sounds its hollow thud: *Finita la comedia,* and we are no more. Death has no significance, because life itself has no lasting meaning.

If life is only the arithmetic of coincidence, man a chance composite of molecules, the world an haphazard conglomeration without design or purpose, where everything is temporal and nothing eternal—with values dictated only by consensus—then death is merely the check-mate to an interesting, thoughtful, but useless game of chance. Death has no transcendent significance, since nothing in life has had transcendent significance. If such is the philosophy of life, death is meaningless, and the deceased need merely be disposed of unceremoniously, and as efficiently as possible.

If life is only nature mindlessly and compulsively spinning its complicated web, and man only a high-level beast, and the world—in Schopenhauer's phrase—*eine grosse shlachtfeld,* a great battlefield, and if values are only those of the jungle, aimed only at the satisfaction of animal appetites—then death is simply a further reduction to the basic elements, progress an adventure into nothingness, and our existence on this earth only a cosmic trap. In this scheme, life is surrounded by parentheses, dropped or substituted without loss of meaning to nature. Death, in this sense, is the end of a cruel match that pits man against beast, and man against man. It is the last slaughter. Furtively, irrevocably, despairingly, man sinks into the soil of a cold and impersonal nature, his life without purpose, his death without significance. His grave need not be marked. As his days were as a passing shadow, without substance and shape, so his final repose.

If life is altogether absurd, with man bound and chained by impersonal fate or ironbound circumstances, where he is never able to achieve real freedom and only dread and anguish prevail—then death is the welcome release from the chains of despair. The puppet is returned to the box, the string is severed, the strain is no more.

But if life is the creation of a benevolent God, the infusion of the Divine breath; if man is not only higher than the animal, but also "a little lower than the angels"; if he has a soul, as well as a body; if his relationship is not only the "I-it" of man and nature, but the "I-Thou" of creature with Creator; and if he tempers his passions with the moral commands of an eternal, transcendent God—then death is a return to the Creator at the time of death set by the Creator, and life-after-death the only way of a just and merciful and ethical God. If life has any significance, if it is not mere happenstance, then man knows that some day his body will be replaced, even as his soul unites with eternal God.

In immortality man finds fulfillment of all his dreams. In this religious framework, the sages equated this world with an ante-room to a great palace, the glorious realm of the future. For a truly religious personality, death has profound meaning, because for him life is a tale told by a saint. It is, indeed, full of sound and fury which sometimes signifies nothing, but often bears eloquent testimony to the Divine power that created and sustained him.

The rabbis say *hai alma k'bei hilula damya,* this world can be compared to a wedding. At a wedding two souls are united. In that relationship they bear the seed of the future. Ultimately, the partners to the wedding die—but the seed of life grows on, and death is conquered, for the seed of the future carries the germ of the past. This world is like unto a wedding.

Death has meaning if life had meaning. If one is not able to live, will he be able to die?

7.3 Human Destiny: Immortality and Resurrection

Although Christianity gradually absorbed the Greek idea of the immortality of the soul, the *New Testament* teaches that after we die we will be resurrected at some future date. In the debate over the afterlife among the Jews, Jesus appears to have sided with the Pharisees. Resurrection is the official dogma stated in the early Christian creeds, but no specific interpretation of what that dogma means has ever received official sanction.

Many have thought of resurrection as resuscitation of a corpse. Perhaps this idea arose because of the story of Jesus' apparent resuscitation of Lazarus (John 11). Also, the "empty tomb" tradition maintains that after Jesus' body had been entombed for three days he was brought back to life by God and walked out of his tomb (Mark 16). Other accounts, however, indicate that Jesus' resurrected body had qualities very different from those of physical bodies. It could, for example, pass through locked doors (John 20:19). St. Paul, in I Corinthians 15, refers to a resurrected body as a "spiritual body." By this he means a body not subject to the decay and corruption of the physical body. However, this notion of a "spiritual body" indicates that our present physical bodies are not resuscitated. Rather, at some future date we will have new, incorruptible bodies.

If I suppose that God will create a new being very similar to my present self, then such a being will be a duplicate or so it may seem. If there is little or no continuity between me and my future duplicate, is it really I who will enjoy eternal life? In fact, will it not be my successor (someone very similar, perhaps even exactly similar except for a new "spiritual body") who will be so rewarded? If that is so, I cannot take much comfort in the fact that someday there will be a duplicate of me enjoying a blessed life. *I* want to enjoy that life!

John Hick, a contemporary philosopher of religion who recently retired from Claremont Graduate School, presents his interpretation of resurrection in the next selection. He argues against the idea of the immortality of the soul and attempts to make the case that the resurrected you will really be you. He also examines possible evidence for survival from the area of parapsychology and near-death experiences.

In addition to the theological argument for some kind of immortality, there is the scientific argument. This argument rests, in part, on alleged cases of mediumship. There are a number of well-documented cases in which a medium goes into a trance state, apparently contacts a deceased person, and conveys precise information that seems to be attainable in no other way. What are we to make of this? Some believe such cases provide strong evidence for survival. Others do not think so. In either case, it is important to ask what sort of survival might be supported by such cases. Perhaps our shades or ghosts or energy fields of some kind hang around for a while after we die and the medium makes contact with this. Perhaps they fade away eventually into total oblivion. One must be cautious in using parapsychological cases. Even if true, most do not support the rich pictures of the afterlife painted by many religions.

Reading Questions

1. What arguments for the immortality of the soul did Plato develop, and what, according to Hick, is wrong with them?
2. How, according to Hick, does the Biblical conception of the human being differ from the views of Plato and Descartes?
3. What is the *religious* difference between the ideas of the immortality of the soul and the resurrection of the body?
4. What is the major problem with the idea of resurrection, and how does Hick propose to solve it? Do you think his theory of a replica solves the problem? Why or why not?
5. What is the basis for the belief in the re-creation of the human personality after death?
6. Why does Hick reject the idea of hell?
7. Hick suggests that the evidence of parapsychology may not support the idea that there is life after death. Why does he conclude this? Do you agree? Why or why not?

Human Destiny: Immortality and Resurrection*

JOHN HICK

The Immortality of the Soul

Some kind of distinction between physical body and immaterial or semimaterial soul seems to be as old as human culture; the existence of such a distinction is indicated by the manner of burial of the earliest human skeletons yet discovered. Anthropologists offer various conjectures about the origin of the distinction: perhaps it was first suggested by memories of dead persons, by dreams of them, by the sight of reflections of oneself in water and on other bright surfaces, or by meditation upon the significance of religious rites which grew up spontaneously in face of the fact of death.

It was Plato (428/7–348/7 B.C.), the philosopher who has most deeply and lastingly influenced Western culture, who systematically developed the body–mind dichotomy and first attempted to prove the immortality of the soul.[1]

Plato argues that although the body belongs to the sensible world[2] and shares its changing and impermanent nature, the intellect is related to the unchanging realities of which we are aware when we think not of particular good things but of Goodness itself, not of specific just acts but of Justice itself, and of the other "universals" or eternal Ideas by participation in which physical things and events have their own specific characteristics. Being related to this higher and abiding realm rather than to the evanescent world of sense, the soul is immortal. Hence, one who devotes one's life to the contemplation of eternal realities rather than to the gratification of the fleeting desires of the body will find at death that whereas the body turns to dust, one's soul gravitates to the realm of the unchanging, there to live forever. Plato painted an awe-inspiring picture, of haunting beauty and persuasiveness, which has moved and elevated the minds of men and women in many different centuries and lands. Nevertheless, it is not today (as it was during the first centuries of the Christian era) the common philosophy of the West; and a demonstration of immortality which presupposes Plato's metaphysical system cannot claim to constitute a proof for a twentieth-century person.

Plato used the further argument that the only things that can suffer destruction are those which are composite, since to destroy something means to disintegrate it into its constituent parts. All material bodies are composite; the soul, however, is simple and therefore imperishable. This argument was adopted by Aquinas and became standard in Roman Catholic theology, as in the following passage from the Catholic philosopher Jacques Maritain:

> A spiritual soul cannot be corrupted, since it possesses no matter; it cannot be disintegrated, since it has no substantial parts; it cannot lose its individual unity, since it is self-subsisting, nor its internal energy, since it contains within itself all the sources of its energies. The human soul cannot die. Once it exists, it cannot disappear; it will necessarily exist for ever, endure without end. Thus, philosophic reason, put to work by a great metaphysician like Thomas Aquinas, is able to prove the immortality of the human soul in a demonstrative manner.[3]

This type of reasoning has been criticized on several grounds. Kant pointed out that although it is true that a simple substance cannot disintegrate, consciousness may nevertheless cease to exist through the diminution of its intensity to

*From Hick, John H. *Philosophy of Religion*, 4th ed., © 1990, pp. 120–130. Reprinted by permission of Prentice-Hall, Upper Saddle River, New Jersey.

zero.[4] Modern psychology has also questioned the basic premise that the mind is a simple entity. It seems instead to be a structure of only relative unity, normally fairly stable and tightly integrated but capable under stress of various degrees of division and dissolution. This comment from psychology makes it clear that the assumption that the soul is a simple substance is not an empirical observation but a metaphysical theory. As such, it cannot provide the basis for a general proof of immortality.

The body–soul distinction, first formulated as a philosophical doctrine in ancient Greece, was baptized into Christianity, ran through the medieval period, and entered the modern world with the public status of a self-evident truth when it was redefined in the seventeenth century by Descartes. Since World War II, however, the Cartesian mind–matter dualism, having been taken for granted for many centuries, has been strongly criticized.[5] It is argued that the words that describe mental characteristics and operations—such as "intelligent," "thoughtful," "carefree," "happy," "calculating," and the like—apply in practice to types of human behavior and to behavioral dispositions. They refer to the empirical individual, the observable human being who is born and grows and acts and feels and dies, and not to the shadowy proceedings of a mysterious "ghost in the machine." An individual is thus very much what he or she appears to be—a creature of flesh and blood, who behaves and is capable of behaving in a characteristic range of ways—rather than a nonphysical soul incomprehensibly interacting with a physical body.

As a result of this development, much midtwentieth-century philosophy has come to see the human being as in the biblical writings, not as an eternal soul temporarily attached to a mortal body, but as a form of finite, mortal, psychophysical life. Thus the Old Testament scholar J. Pedersen said of the Hebrews that for them "the body is the soul in its outward form."[6] This way of thinking has led to quite a different conception of death from that found in Plato and the Neoplatonic strand in European thought.

THE RE-CREATION OF THE PSYCHOPHYSICAL PERSON

Only toward the end of the Old Testament period did afterlife beliefs come to have any real importance within Judaism. Previously, Hebrew religious insight had focused so fully upon God's covenant with the nation, as an organism that continued through the centuries while successive generations lived and died, that the thought of a divine purpose for the individual, a purpose transcending this present life, developed only when the breakdown of the nation as a political entity threw into prominence the individual and the question of personal destiny.

When a positive conviction arose of God's purpose holding each man and woman in being beyond the crisis of death, this conviction took the non-Platonic form of belief in the resurrection of the body. The religious difference between the Platonic belief in the immortality of the soul, and the Judaic-Christian belief in resurrection is that the latter postulates a special divine act of re-creation. This produces a sense of utter dependence upon God in the hour of death, a feeling that is in accordance with the biblical understanding of the human being as having been formed out of "the dust of the earth,"[7] a product (as we say today) of the slow evolution of life from its lowly beginnings in the primeval slime. Hence, in the Jewish and Christian conception, death is something real and fearful. It is not thought to be like walking from one room to another, or like taking off an old coat and putting on a new one. It means sheer unqualified extinction—passing out from a lighted circle of life into "death's dateless night." Only through the sovereign creative love of God can there be a new existence beyond the grave.

What does "the resurrection of the dead" mean? Saint Paul's discussion provides the basic Christian answer to this question.[8] His conception of the general resurrection (distinguished from the unique resurrection of Jesus) has nothing to do with the resuscitation of corpses in a cemetery. It concerns God's re-creation or reconstitution of the human psychophysical individual, not as the organism that has died but as a *soma pneumatikon,* a "spiritual body," inhabiting a spiritual world as the physical body inhabits our present material world.

A major problem confronting any such doctrine is that of providing criteria of personal identity to link the earthly life and the resurrection life. Paul does not specifically consider this question, but one may perhaps develop his thought along lines such as the following.[9]

Suppose, first, that someone—John Smith—living in the United States were suddenly and inexplicably to disappear before the eyes of his friends, and that at the same moment an exact replica of him were inexplicably to appear in India. The person who appears in India is exactly similar in both physical and mental characteristics to the person who disappeared in America. There is continuity of memory, complete similarity of bodily features including fingerprints, hair and eye coloration, and stomach contents, and also of beliefs, habits, emotions, and mental dispositions. Further, the "John Smith" replica thinks of himself as being the John Smith who disappeared in the United States. After all possible tests have been made and have proved positive, the factors leading his friends to accept "John Smith" as John Smith would surely prevail and would cause them to overlook even his mysterious transference from one continent to another, rather than treat "John Smith," with all of John Smith's memories and other characteristics, as someone other than John Smith.

Suppose, second, that our John Smith, instead of inexplicably disappearing, dies, but that at the moment of his death a "John Smith" replica, again complete with memories and all other characteristics, appears in India. Even with the corpse on our hands, we would, I think, still have to accept this "John Smith" as the John Smith who had died. We would just have to say that he had been miraculously re-created in another place.

Now suppose, third, that on John Smith's death the "John Smith" replica appears, not in India, but as a resurrection replica in a different world altogether, a resurrection world inhabited only by resurrected persons. This world occupies its own space distinct from that with which we are now familiar. That is to say, an object in the resurrection world is not situated at any distance or in any direction from the objects in our present world, although each object in either world is spatially related to every other object in the same world.

This supposition provides a model by which one may begin to conceive of the divine re-creation of the embodied human personality. In this model, the element of the strange and mysterious has been reduced to a minimum by following the view of some of the early Church Fathers that the resurrection body has the same shape as the physical body,[10] and ignoring Paul's own hint that it may be as unlike the physical body as a full grain of wheat differs from the wheat seed.[11]

What is the basis for this Judaic-Christian belief in the divine re-creation or reconstitution of the human personality after death? There is, of course, an argument from authority, in that life after death is taught throughout the New Testament (although very rarely in the Old Testament). More basically, though, belief in the resurrection arises as a corollary of faith in the sovereign purpose of God, which is not restricted by death and which holds us in being beyond our natural mortality. In a similar vein it is argued that if it be the divine plan to create finite persons to exist in fellowship with God, then it contradicts both that intention and God's love for the human creatures if God allows men and women to pass out of existence when the divine purpose for them still remains largely unfulfilled.

It is this promised fulfillment of God's purpose for the individual, in which the full possibilities of human nature will be realized, that constitutes the "heaven" symbolized in the New Testament as a joyous banquet in which all and sundry rejoice together. As we saw when discussing the problem of evil, it is questionable whether any theodicy can succeed without drawing into itself this eschatological[12] faith in an eternal, and therefore infinite, good which thus outweighs all the pains and sorrows that have been endured on the way to it.

Balancing the idea of heaven in Christian tradition is the idea of hell. This, too, is relevant to the problem of theodicy. Just as the reconciling of God's goodness and power with the fact of evil requires that out of the travail of history there shall come in the end an eternal good for humanity, so likewise it would seem to preclude eternal human misery. The only kind of evil that is finally incompatible with God's unlimited power and love would be utterly pointless and wasted suffering, pain which is never redeemed and worked into the fulfilling of God's good purpose. Unending torment would constitute precisely such suffering; for being eternal, it could never lead to a good end beyond itself. Thus, hell as conceived by its enthusiasts, such as Augustine or Calvin, is a major part of the problem of evil! If hell is construed as eternal torment, the theological motive behind the idea is directly at variance with the urge to seek a theodicy. However, it is by no means clear that the doctrine of eternal punishment can claim a secure New Testament basis.[13] If, on the other hand, "hell" means a continuation of the purgatorial suffering often experienced in this life, and leading eventually to the high good of heaven, it no longer stands in conflict with the needs of theodicy. Again, the idea of hell may be deliteralized and valued as a powerful and pregnant symbol of the grave responsibility inherent in our human freedom in relation to our Maker.

DOES PARAPSYCHOLOGY HELP?

The spiritualist movement claims that life after death has been proved by cases of communication between the living and the "dead." During the closing quarter of the nineteenth century and the decades of the present century this claim has been made the subject of careful and prolonged study by a number of responsible and competent persons.[14] This work, which may be approximately dated from the founding in London of the Society for Psychical Research in 1882, is known either by the name adopted by that society or, more commonly today, as parapsychology.

Approaching the subject from the standpoint of our interest in this chapter, we may initially divide the phenomena studied by the parapsychologist into two groups. There are those that involve no reference to the idea of a life after death, chief among these being psychokinesis (PK) and extrasensory perception (ESP) in its various forms (such as telepathy, clairvoyance, and precognition). There are also those phenomena that raise the question of personal survival after death, such as the apparitions and other sensory manifestations of dead persons and the "spirit messages" received through mediums. This division is, however, only of preliminary use, for ESP has emerged as a clue to the understanding of much that occurs in the second group. We shall begin with a brief outline of the reasons that have induced the majority of workers in this field to be willing to postulate so strange an occurrence as telepathy.

Telepathy is a name for the mysterious fact that sometimes a thought in the mind of one person apparently causes a similar or associated thought to occur to someone else when there are no normal means of communication between them, and under circumstances such that mere coincidence seems to be excluded.

For example, one person may draw a series of pictures or diagrams on paper and somehow transmit an impression of these to someone else in another room who then draws recognizable reproductions of them. This might well be a coincidence in the case of a single successful reproduction; but can a series consist entirely of coincidences?

Experiments have been devised to measure the probability of chance coincidence in supposed cases of telepathy. In the simplest of these, cards printed in turn with five different symbols are used. A pack of fifty, consisting of ten bearing each symbol, is then thoroughly shuffled, and the sender concentrates on the cards one at a time while the receiver (who of course can see neither sender nor cards) tries to write down the correct order of symbols. This procedure is repeated, with constant reshuffling, hundreds or thousands of times. Since there are only five different symbols, a random guess would stand one chance in five of being correct. Consequently, on the assumption that only "chance" is operating, the receiver should be right in about 20 percent of his or her tries and wrong in about 80 percent; the longer the series, the closer should be the approach to this proportion. However, good telepathic subjects are right in a larger number of cases than can be reconciled with random guessing. The deviation from chance expectation can be converted mathematically into "odds against chance" (increasing as the proportion of hits is maintained over a longer and longer series of tries). In this way, odds of over a million to one have been recorded. J. B. Rhine (Duke University) has reported results showing "antichance" values ranging from seven (which equals odds against chance of 100,000 to one) to eighty-two (which converts the odds against chance to billions).[15] The work of both these researchers has been criticized, and a complex controversy surrounds them; on the other hand, other researchers have recorded similar results.[16] In the light of these reports, it is difficult to deny that some positive factor, and not merely "chance," is operating. "Telepathy" is simply a name for this unknown positive factor.

How does telepathy operate? Only negative conclusions seem to be justified to date. It can, for example, be said with reasonable certainty that telepathy does not consist of any kind of physical radiation analogous to radio waves. First, telepathy is not delayed or weakened in proportion to distance, as are all known forms of radiation; second, there is no organ in the brain or elsewhere that can plausibly be regarded as its sending or receiving center. Telepathy appears to be a purely mental occurrence.

It is not, however, a matter of transferring or transporting a thought out of one mind into another—if, indeed, such an idea makes sense at all. The telepathized thought does not leave the sender's consciousness in order to enter that of the receiver. What happens would be better described by saying that the sender's thought gives rise to a mental "echo" in the mind of the receiver. This "echo" occurs at the unconscious level, and consequently the version of it that rises

into the receiver's consciousness may be only fragmentary and may be distorted or symbolized in various ways, as in dreams.

According to one theory that has been tentatively suggested to explain telepathy, our minds are separate and mutually insulated only at the conscious (and preconscious) level, but at the deepest level of the unconscious we are constantly influencing one another, and it is at this level that telepathy takes place.[17]

How is a telepathized thought directed to one particular receiver among so many? Apparently the thoughts are directed by some link of emotion or common interest. For example, two friends are sometimes telepathically aware of any grave crisis or shock experienced by the other, even though they are at opposite ends of the earth.

We shall turn now to the other branch of parapsychology, which has more obvious bearing upon our subject. The *Proceedings of the Society for Psychical Research* contain a large number of carefully recorded and apparently satisfactorily attested cases of the appearance of the figure of someone who has recently died to living people (in rare instances to more than one at a time) who were, in many cases, at a distance and unaware of the death. The S.P.R. reports also establish beyond reasonable doubt that the minds that operate in the mediumistic trance, purporting to be spirits of the departed, sometimes give personal information that the medium could not have acquired by normal means, and at times even give information, later verified, that had not been known to any living person.[18]

On the other hand, physical happenings such as the "materializations" of spirit forms in a visible and tangible form, are much more doubtful. However, even if we discount the entire range of physical phenomena, it remains true that the best cases of trance utterance are impressive and puzzling, and taken at face value are indicative of survival and communication after death. If, through a medium, one talks with an intelligence that gives a coherent impression of being an intimately known friend who has died and who establishes identity by a wealth of private information and indefinable personal characteristics—

as has occasionally happened—then we cannot dismiss without careful trial the theory that what is taking place is the return of a consciousness from the spirit world.

However, the advance of knowledge in the other branch of parapsychology, centering upon the study of extrasensory perception, has thrown unexpected light upon this apparent commerce with the departed, for it suggests that unconscious telepathic contact between the medium and his or her client is an important and possibly a sufficient explanatory factor. This was vividly illustrated by the experience of two women who decided to test the spirits by taking into their minds, over a period of weeks, the personality and atmosphere of an entirely imaginary character in an unpublished novel written by one of them. After thus filling their minds with the characteristics of this fictitious person, they went to a reputable medium, who proceeded to describe accurately their imaginary friend as a visitant from beyond the grave and to deliver appropriate messages from him.

An even more striking case is that of the "direct voice" medium (a medium in whose séances the voice of the communicating "spirit" is heard apparently speaking out of the air) who produced the spirit of one "Gordon Davis," who spoke in his own recognizable voice, displayed considerable knowledge about Gordon Davis, and remembered his death. This was extremely impressive until it was discovered that Gordon Davis was still alive; he was a real-estate agent and had been trying to sell a house at the time when the séance took place![19]

Such cases suggest that genuine mediums are simply persons of exceptional telepathic sensitiveness who unconsciously derive the "spirits" from their clients' minds.

In connection with "ghosts," in the sense of apparitions of the dead, it has been established that there can be "meaningful hallucinations," the source of which is almost certainly telepathic. To quote a classic and somewhat dramatic example: a woman sitting by a lake sees the figure of a man run toward the lake and throw himself in. A few days later a man commits suicide by throwing himself into this same lake. Presumably, the explanation of the vision is that the man's thought while he was contemplating suicide had been telepathically projected onto the scene via the woman's mind.[20]

In many of the cases recorded there is delayed action. The telepathically projected thought lingers in the recipient's unconscious mind until a suitable state of inattention to the outside world enables it to appear to the conscious mind in a dramatized form—for example, by a hallucinatory voice or vision—by means of the same mechanism that operates in dreams.

If phantoms of the living can be created by previously experienced thoughts and emotions of the person whom they represent, the parallel possibility arises that phantoms of the dead are caused by thoughts and emotions that were experienced by the person represented when he or she was alive. In other words, perhaps ghosts may be "psychic footprints," a kind of mental trace left behind by the dead but not involving the presence or even the continued existence of those whom they represent.

RESUSCITATION CASES

Yet another range of phenomena that have recently attracted considerable interest consists of reports of the experiences of people who have been resuscitated after having been declared dead.[21] The periods during which they were apparently dead vary from a few seconds to twenty minutes or even more. These reports include the following elements, though not usually all on the same occasion: an initial loud noise; a sensation as of being drawn through a dark tunnel-like space; emergence into a "world" of light and beauty; meeting with relatives and friends who had died; encounter with a "being of light" of immense moral or spiritual impressiveness, who is assumed by Christians to be Christ and by others to be an angel or a deity; an extremely vivid and almost instantaneous visual review of one's life; approach to a border, sensed to be the final division between this life and the next; and being sent or drawn back to the earthly body. Generally, those who have had this kind of experience are reluctant to speak about such hard-to-describe and hard-to-believe phenomena, but characteristically their attitude toward death has changed and they now think of their own future death without fear or even with positive anticipation.

Prior to such visual and auditory sequences there is also often an "out-of-the-body" experience, a consciousness of floating above one's own body and seeing it lying in bed or on the ground or the operating table. There is a growing literature concerning such "out-of-the-body" experiences, whether at the time of death or during life.[22]

Whether or not the resuscitation cases give us reports of the experiences of people who have actually died, and thus provide information about a life to come, it is at present impossible to determine. Do these accounts describe the first phase of another life, or perhaps a transitional stage before the connection between mind and body is finally broken; or do they describe only the last flickers of dream activity before the brain finally loses oxygen? It is to be hoped that further research may find a way to settle this question.

All these considerations suggest the need for caution in assessing the findings of parapsychology.[23] However, this caution should lead to further investigations, not to a closing of the issues. In the meantime one should be careful not to confuse absence of knowledge with knowledge of absence.

NOTES

1. *Phaedo.*
2. The world known to us through our physical senses.
3. Jacques Maritain, *The Range of Reason* (London: Geoffrey Bles Ltd. and New York: Charles Scribner's Sons, 1953), p. 60.
4. Kant, *Critique of Pure Reason, Transcendental Dialectic,* "Refutation of Mendelssohn's Proof of the Permanence of the Soul."
5. Gilbert Ryle's *The Concept of Mind* (London: Hutchinson & Co., Ltd., 1949, and New York: Barnes & Noble Books, 1975) is a classic statement of this critique.

6. J. Pedersen, *Israel* (London: Oxford University Press, 1926), I, 170.
7. Genesis 2:7; Psalms 103:14.
8. I Corinthians 15.
9. The following paragraphs are adapted, with permission, from a section of my article, "Theology and Verification," published in *Theology Today* (April 1960) and reprinted in *The Existence of God* (New York: The Macmillan Company, 1964) and elsewhere. A fascinating recent argument for the personal identity of an original and his or her replica is offered by Derek Parfitt in *Reasons and Persons* (New York: Oxford University Press, 1985).
10. For example, Irenaeus, *Against Heresies,* Book II, Chap. 34, para. 1.
11. I Corinthians 15:37.
12. From the Greek *eschaton,* end.
13. The Greek word *aionios,* which is used in the New Testament and which is usually translated as "eternal" or "everlasting," can bear either this meaning or the more limited meaning of "for the aeon, or age."
14. The list of past presidents of the Society for Psychical Research includes the philosophers Henri Bergson, William James, Hans Driesch, Henry Sidgwick, F.C.S. Schiller, C.D. Broad, and H.H. Price; the psychologists William McDougall, Gardner Murphy, Franklin Prince, and R.H. Thouless; the physicists Sir William Crookes, Sir Oliver Lodge, Sir William Barrett, and Lord Rayleigh; and the classicist Gilbert Murray.
15. J.B. Rhine, *Extrasensory Perception* (Boston: Society for Psychical Research, 1935), Table XLIII, p. 162. See also Rhine, *New Frontiers of the Mind* (New York: Farrar and Rinehart, Inc., 1937), pp. 69f.
16. The most comprehensive up-to-date account of the evidence for ESP, together with competent discussions of its significance, is to be found in Benjamin Wolman, ed., *Handbook of Parapsychology* (New York: Van Nostrand, 1977). For the important Russian work see L.L. Vasiliev, *Experiments in Distant Influence* (previously *Experiments in Mental Suggestion,* 1963) (New York: E.O. Dutton, 1976).
17. Whateley Carington, *Telepathy* (London: Methuen, 1945), Chaps. 6–8. See also H.L. Edge, R.L. Morris, J.H. Rushand, and J. Palmer, *Foundations of Parapsychology* (London: Routledge, 1986).
18. A famous example is the Chaffin will case, recounted in many books, such as C.D. Broad, *Lectures on Psychical Research* (London: Routledge & Kegan Paul and New York: Humanities Press, 1962), pp. 137–39. (This, incidentally, remains one of the best books on parapsychology.)
19. S.G. Soal, "A Report of Some Communications Received through Mrs. Blanche Cooper," Sec. 4, *Proceedings of the Society for Psychical Research,* XXXV, 560–89.

20. F.W.H. Myers, *Human Personality and Its Survival of Bodily Death* (London: Longmans, Green, & Co., 1903, and New York: Arno Press, 1975), I, 270–71. This is a classic work, still of great interest.

21. The recent wave of interest began with the publication in 1975 of Raymond Moody's *Life after Life* (Atlanta: Mockingbird Books), and has been fed by a growing number of other books, including Raymond Moody, *Reflections on Life after Life* (New York: Bantam Books, 1977); Karlis Otis and Erlendur Haraldsson, *At the Hour of Death* (New York: Avon Books, 1977); Maurice Rawlings, *Beyond Death's Door* (Nashville: Thomas Nelson, Inc., 1978, and London: Sheldon Press, 1979).

22. For example, Sylvan Muldoon and Hereward Carrington, *The Phenomena of Astral Projection* (London: Rider, 1951); Robert Crookall, *The Study and Practice of Astral Projection* (London: Aquarian Press, 1961); Celia Green, *Out-of-the-Body Experiences* (London: Hamish Hamilton, 1968); *Journeys Out of the Body* (New York: Doubleday & Co., Inc., 1971, and London: Souvenir Press, 1972); Benjamin Walker, *Beyond the Body* (London: Routledge & Kegan Paul, 1974).

23. Philosophical discussions of parapsychology can be found in: C.D. Broad, *Religion, Philosophy and Psychical Research* (London: Routledge & Kegan Paul, 1953); James Wheatley and Hoyt Edge, eds., *Philosophical Dimensions of Parapsychology* (Springfield, Ill.: Charles C Thomas, 1976); Shivesh Thakur, ed., *Philosophy and Psychical Research* (New York: Humanities Press, 1976); Jan Ludwig, ed., *Philosophy and Parapsychology* (Prometheus, 1978); Stephen Braude, *ESP and Psychokinesis: A Philosophical Examination* (Philadelphia: Temple University Press, 1980).

7.4 The Immortality of the Soul

Imagine living a totally disembodied existence. You have no eyes, no nose, no ears, no tongue, no flesh, and no nervous system. You have no brain to process all the information about your external environment that your sense organs feed you. Could you see anything? Could you smell, hear, taste, or feel anything? It seems unlikely. Nevertheless, a long tradition of philosophical argument has maintained that the afterlife consists in the existence of a disembodied soul.

Plato (427-347 B.C.E.) asserted that the shadowy and nearly lifeless existence of the Shades in Hades spoken about in Greek mythology is wrong. He argued that the afterlife is much more enjoyable than what the "poets" portrayed. He used a variety of arguments to support his position. One of those arguments, in one form or another, became a popular philosophical argument for an afterlife. According to Plato, the soul is the essence of our personhood. This soul is immortal because it has no parts or, to use the traditional terminology, is simple. The argument runs something like this:

1. The soul is a substance that has no parts.
2. The only way a substance can be destroyed is by separating its parts.
3. Therefore, the soul cannot be destroyed.

Plato believed that the soul is eternal. It existed before its present incarnation in some physical body and will continue to exist after the body dies. The eternality of the soul was not acceptable to Christian theologians because it threatened, in their view, the idea that God alone is eternal. Thus they adopted Plato's view with a twist. The soul does live on eternally after the death of the body, but it does not pre-exist its present embodiment. Exactly when the body became ensouled developed into something of a debate. Today the Roman Catholic Church, which adopted a modified form of Plato's views, argues that the soul joins with the body at conception. Hence they oppose abortion at any time after conception. St. Thomas Aquinas (see Reading 3.2), however, argued that the fetus does not become ensouled until the time when the mother can feel it move in the womb (roughly three months into a pregnancy). He reasoned that the soul makes dead matter alive and that the sign of being alive is self-movement.

Plato's argument for the immortality of the soul has been subject to intense philosophical criticism (see Hick, Reading 7.3). Some argue that we must make a distinction between extensive quantity and intensive quantity. If an immaterial substance, such as a soul, has no extensive quantity, then it cannot be destroyed by dissolution (separation into parts). However, it may have intensive quantity (nothing Plato says might make us think otherwise), in which case it may be subject to destruction through a reduction of its intensity to zero. If the soul is conscious (and one presumes that it is because it is the essence of our personhood), it can have degrees of consciousness. We certainly have degrees of consciousness in this life (wide awake, sleeping, dreaming, day-dreaming, groggy, and the like). If the soul's degree of consciousness diminishes to nothing and stays that way, why not say it has been destroyed?

Of course, one might object to Plato's arguments on the grounds that he assumes the soul is an immaterial substance. Maybe it is not. Maybe only physical things are real. Then again, maybe the soul is not a substance at all. Maybe the soul is a series of mental events that are related by ties of succession, association, and memory. There may be no underlying mental or soul substance that endures through time but simply a bundle of mental events that last for a time and then fade.

These sorts of objections did not prevent Jacques Maritain, author of our next selection, from pressing the case for the immortality of the soul in this century. Maritain, born in 1882 into a liberal Protestant family, converted to Catholicism in 1906. He became convinced that the Roman Catholic Christian scholastics (theologians of the Middle Ages) had it right when it came to immortality. The scholastics made their case by building on the ideas of Plato and Aristotle. Central to the views of the scholastics is the notion that our true personhood consists in an immaterial soul substance.

Reading Questions

1. What is Maritain's argument, following St. Thomas Aquinas, supporting the notion that the intellect is immaterial?
2. How is the intellect related to the body?
3. How is the intellect related to the soul?
4. How does Maritain define the human soul?
5. Why is the immortality of the human soul an immediate corollary of its spirituality?
6. What can philosophy, unaided by revelation, tell us about the condition of the immortal soul after death?
7. What can revelation tell us about the condition of the immortal soul after death?
8. Do you think that Maritain has proved the human soul is immortal? Why or why not? What might be wrong with his argument?

The Immortality of the Soul*

JACQUES MARITAIN

Personal Immortality

THE EXISTENCE OF THE SOUL

It is of this immortality, and of the way in which the Scholastics established its rational certainty, that I should now like to speak.

We must of course realize that we have a soul before we can discuss whether it is immortal. How does St. Thomas Aquinas proceed in this matter?

He observes first that man has an activity, the activity of the intellect, which is in itself immaterial. The activity of the intellect is immaterial because the proportionate or "connatural" object of the human intellect is not, like the object of the senses, a particular and limited category of things, or rather a particular and limited category of the qualitative properties of things. The proportionate or "connatural" object of the intellect is the nature of the sense-perceivable things considered in an all-embracing manner, whatever the sense concerned may be. It is not only—as for sight—color or the colored thing (which absorbs and reflects such or such rays of light) nor—as for hearing—sound or the sound-source; it is the whole universe and texture of sense-perceivable reality which can be known by the intellect, because the intellect does not stop at qualities, but pierces beyond, and proceeds to look at essence (that which a thing *is*). This very fact is a proof of the spirituality, or complete immateriality of our intellect; for every activity in which matter plays an intrinsic part is limited to a given category of material objects, as is the case for the senses, which perceive only those properties which are able to act upon their physical organs.

There is already, in fact, a certain immateriality in sense-knowledge; knowledge, as such, is an immaterial activity, because when I am in the act of knowing, I become, or am, the very thing that I know, a thing other than myself, insofar as it is other than myself. And how can I be, or become, other than myself, if it is not in a supra-subjective or immaterial manner? Sense-knowledge is a very poor kind of knowledge; insofar as it is knowledge, it is immaterial, but it is an immaterial activity intrinsically conditioned by, and dependent upon, the material functioning of the sense-organs. Sense-knowledge is the immaterial achievement, the immaterial actuation and product of a living bodily organ; and its very object is also something half material, half immaterial, I mean a physical quality *intentionally* or immaterially present in the medium by which it acts on the sense-organ (something comparable to the manner in which a painter's idea is immaterially present in his paintbrush).

But with intellectual knowledge we have to do with an activity which is in itself completely immaterial. The human intellect is able to know whatever participates in being and truth; the whole universe can be inscribed in it; this means that, in order to be known, the object known by the intellect has been stripped of any existential condition of materiality. This rose, which I see, has contours; but Being, of which I am thinking, is more spacious than space. The object of the intellect is universal, for instance that universal or de-individualized object which is apprehended in the idea of man, of animal, of atom; the object of the intellect is a universal which remains what it is while being identified with an infinity of individuals. And this is only possible because things, in order to become objects of the mind, have been entirely separated from their material existence. To this it must be added that the operation of out intellect does not stop at the knowledge of the nature of sense-perceivable things; it goes further; it knows by analogy the spiritual natures; it extends to the realm of merely possible things; its field has infinite magnitude.

Thus, the objects known by the human intellect, taken not as things existing in themselves, but precisely as objects determining the intellect and united with it, are purely immaterial.

Furthermore, just as the condition of the *object* is immaterial, so is the condition of the *act* which bears upon it, and is determined or specified by it. The object of the human intellect is, as such, purely immaterial; the act of the human intellect is also purely immaterial.

And, moreover, if the act of the intellectual power is purely immaterial, that *power* itself is also purely immaterial. In man, this thinking animal, the intellect is a purely spiritual power. Doubtless it depends upon the body, upon the conditions of the brain. Its activity can be disturbed or hindered by a physical disorder, by an outburst of anger, by a drink or a narcotic. But this dependence is an *extrinsic* one. It exists because our intelligence cannot act without the joint activity of the memory and the imagination, of the internal senses and external senses, all of which are organic powers residing in some material organ, in some special part of the body. As for the intellect itself, it is not *intrinsically* dependent upon the body since its activity is immaterial; the human intellect does not reside in any special part of the body. It is not contained by the body, but rather contains it. It uses the brain, since the organs of the internal senses are in the brain; yet the brain is not an organ of the intelligence; there is no part of the organism whose act is intellectual operation. The intellect has no organ.

Finally, since intellectual power is spiritual, or purely immaterial in itself, its *first substantial root,* the subsisting principle from which this power proceeds and which acts through its instrumentality, is also spiritual.

So much for the spirituality of the intellect. Now, thought or the operation of the intellect is an act and emanation of man as a unit; and when I think, it is not only my intellect which thinks: it is *I,* my own self. And my own self is a bodily self; it involves matter; it is not a spiritual or purely immaterial subject. The body is an essential part of man. The intellect is not the whole man.

Therefore the intellect, or rather the substantial root of the intellect, which must be as immaterial as the intellect, is only a part, albeit an essential part, of man's substance.

But man is not an aggregate, a juxtaposition of two substances; man is a natural whole, a single being, a single substance.

Consequently, we must conclude that the essence or substance of man is single, but that this single substance itself is a compound, the components of which are the body and the spiritual intellect: or rather matter, of which the body is made, and the spiritual principle, one of the powers of which is the intellect. Matter—in the Aristotelian sense of prime matter, or of that root potentiality which is the common stuff of all corporeal substance—matter, substantially united with the spiritual principle of the intellect, is ontologically molded, shaped from within and in the innermost depths of being, by this spiritual principle as by a substantial and vital impulse, in order to constitute that body of ours. In this sense, Saint Thomas, after Aristotle, says that the intellect is the form, the substantial form of the human body.

That is the Scholastic notion of the human soul. The human soul, which is the root principle of the intellectual power, is the first principle of life of the human body, and the substantial form, the *entelechy,* of that body. And the human soul is not only a substantial form or entelechy, as are the souls of plants and animals according to the biological philosophy of Aristotle; the human soul is also a spirit, a spiritual substance able to exist apart from matter, since the human soul is the root principle of a spiritual power, the act of which is intrinsically independent of matter. The human soul is both a soul and a spirit, and it is its very substantiality, subsistence and existence, which are communicated to the whole human substance, in order to make human substance be what it is, and to make it subsist and exist. Each element of the human body is human, and exists as such, by virtue of the immaterial existence of the human soul. Our body, our hands, our eyes exist by virtue of the existence of our soul.

The immaterial soul is the first substantial root not only of the intellect, but of all that which, in us, is spiritual activity; and it is also the first substantial root of all our other living activities. It would be inconceivable that a non-spiritual soul, that kind of soul which is not a spirit and cannot exist without informing matter—namely, the souls of plants or animals in Aristotelian biology—should possess a power or faculty *superior* to its own degree in being, that is, immaterial, or act through a supra-material instrumentality independent of any corporeal organ and physical structure. But when it is a question of a spirit which is a soul, or of a *spiritual soul,* as the human soul is, then it is perfectly conceivable that such a soul should have, aside from immaterial or spiritual faculties, other powers and activities which are organic and material, and which, relating to the union between soul and body, pertain to a level of being *inferior* to that of the spirit.

THE SPIRITUALITY OF THE HUMAN SOUL

Thus, the very way in which the Scholastics arrived at the existence of the human soul also established its spirituality. Just as the intellect is spiritual, that is to say intrinsically independent of matter in its operation and in its nature, so also, and for the same reason, the human soul, the substantial root of the intellect, is spiritual, that is, intrinsically independent of matter in its nature and in its existence; it does not live by the body, the body lives by it. The human soul is a spiritual substance which, by its substantial union with matter, gives existence and countenance to the body.

That is my second point. As we have seen, the Scholastics demonstrated it by a metaphysical analysis of the intellect's operation, carefully distinguished from the operation of the senses. They adduced, of course, much other evidence in support of their demonstration. In their consideration of the intellect, they observed, for instance, that the latter is capable of *perfect reflection,* that is, of coming back entirely upon itself—not in the manner of a sheet of paper, half of which can be folded on the other half, but in a complete manner, so that it can grasp its whole operation and penetrate it by knowledge, and can contain itself and its own principle, the existing self, in its own knowing activity, a perfect reflection or self-containing of which any material agent, extended in space and time, is essentially incapable. Here we are confronted with that phenomenon of self-knowledge, of *prise de conscience* or becoming aware of oneself, which is a privilege of the spirit, as Hegel (after St. Augustine) was to emphasize, and which plays so tremendous a part in the history of humanity and the development of its spiritual energies. . . .

THE IMMORTALITY OF THE HUMAN SOUL

The third point follows immediately from the second. The immortality of the human soul is an immediate corollary of its spirituality. A soul which is spiritual in itself, intrinsically independent of matter in its nature and existence, cannot cease existing. A spirit—that is, a "form" which needs nothing other than itself (save the influx of the Prime Cause) to exercise existence—once existing cannot cease existing. A spiritual soul cannot be corrupted, since it possesses no matter; it cannot be disintegrated, since it has no substantial parts; it cannot lose its individual unity, since it is self-subsisting, nor its internal energy, since it contains within itself all the sources of its energies. The human soul cannot die. Once it exists, it cannot disappear; it will necessarily exist forever, endure without end.

Thus, philosophic reason, put to work by a great metaphysician like Thomas Aquinas, is able to prove the immortality of the human soul in a demonstrative manner. Of course, this demonstration implies a vast and articulate network of metaphysical insights, notions and principles (relating to essence and nature, substance, act and potency, matter and form, operation, etc.) the validity of which is necessarily presupposed. We can appreciate fully the strength of the Scholastic demonstration only if we realize the significance and full validity of the metaphysical notions involved. If modern times feel at a loss in the face of metaphysical knowledge, I fancy that it is not metaphysical knowledge which is to blame, but rather modern times and the weakening of reason they have experienced.

It is not surprising, on the other hand, that the philosophical demonstration I have just summarized is an abstract and a difficult one. The great and fundamental truths which are spontaneously grasped by the natural instinct of the human mind are always the most arduous for philosophic reason to establish. . . .

THE CONDITION AND DESTINY
OF THE IMMORTAL SOUL

What can philosophy tell us about the natural condition of the immortal soul after the death of its body? That is my fourth and last point. Philosophy can tell us very little indeed on this subject. Let us try to summarize the few indications there are. All the organic and sensuous powers of the human soul remain dormant in a separated soul, for they cannot be brought into play without the body. The separated soul is itself engulfed in a complete sleep with regard to the material world; the external senses and their perceptions have vanished; the images of memory and imagination, the impulses of instinct and passion have vanished. But this sleep is not like the sleep we know, obscure and filled with dreams; it is lucid and intelligent, alive to spiritual realities. For now light shines from within. The intellect and the spiritual powers are awake and active. From the very fact of its separation from the body, the soul now knows itself through itself; its very substance has become transparent to its intellect; it is intellectually penetrated to its innermost depths. The soul knows itself in an intuitive manner; it is dazzled by its own beauty, the beauty of a spiritual

substance, and it knows other things through its own substance already known, in the measure in which other things resemble it. It knows God through that image of God which the soul itself is. And in accordance with its state of incorporeal existence, it receives from God, the sun of the spirits, certain ideas and inspirations which directly enlighten it, and help the natural light of the human intellect, of that intellect which is, as Saint Thomas Aquinas phrased it, the lowest in the hierarchy of spirits.

Saint Thomas teaches also that all that is of the intellect and the spirit, and especially the intellectual memory, which is but one with the intellect, keeps alive, in the separated soul, the whole treasure of knowledge acquired during our bodily life. The intellectual knowledge, the intellectual virtues acquired here below subsist in the separated soul. Whereas the images of the sense-memory, which had its seat in the brain, disappear, that which has penetrated into the intellectual memory is preserved. Thus, in an intellectual and spiritual manner, the separated soul ever knows those whom it loved. And it loves them spiritually. And it is able to converse with other spirits by opening to them what abides in its inner thoughts and is taken hold of by its free will.

We may thus imagine that, at the moment when it leaves the body, the soul is suddenly immersed into itself as into a shining abyss, where all that was buried within it, all its dead, rise up again in full light, insofar as all this was encompassed in the subconscious or supraconscious depths of the spiritual life of its intellect and will. Then all that is true and good in the soul becomes a blessing for it at the touch of this all-pervading revelatory light; all that is warped and evil becomes a torment for it under the effect of the very same light.

I do not believe that natural reason can go further in its understanding of the natural condition of the separated soul. What would be the life and happiness of souls if their state after death were a purely natural state? Their supreme good would consist in wisdom, untrammeled spiritual life, mutual friendship, and first and foremost in advancing constantly in their natural knowledge and love of God, Whom they would, however, never see face to face. It would be happiness in motion, never absolutely fulfilled—what Leibniz called *un chemin par des plaisirs,* "a road amidst spiritual pleasures."

But if we wish to know more, can we not go beyond philosophy? Philosophy itself will then entrust us to the guidance of a knowledge whose sources are superior to its own. Christians know that man does not live in a state of pure nature. They know that he was created in a state of grace, and that, after the first sin which wounded our race, he has been living in a state of fallen and redeemed nature; they know that he is made for supernatural blessedness. In answer to the question of the separated soul's destiny, the Scholastic doctors spoke not as philosophers, but as theologians whose knowledge rests on the data of Revelation.

Insofar as man participates in the metaphysical privileges of spirit and personality, he has aspirations which transcend human nature and its possibilities, and which consequently may be called transnatural aspirations: the longing for a state in which he would know things completely and without error, in which he would enjoy perfect communion with spirits, in which he would be free without being able to fail or to sin, in which he would inhabit a realm of unfading justice, in which he would have the intuitive knowledge of the First Cause of being.

Such a longing cannot be fulfilled by nature. It can be fulfilled by grace. The immortal soul is involved and engaged in the great drama of the Redemption. If, at the moment of its separation from the body, at the moment when its choice is immutably fixed forever, the immortal soul prefers its own will and self-love to the will and gift of God, if it prefers misery with pride to the blessing of grace, then it is granted what it has wished for. It has it, and it will never cease wanting and preferring it, for a free choice made in the condition of a *pure* spirit is an eternal choice. If the soul opens itself to the will and gift of God, Whom it loves more than its own existence, then it is granted what it has loved, it enters forever into the joy of the uncreated Being, it sees God face to face and knows Him as it is known by Him [cf. I Cor.

13:12], intuitively. Thus, it becomes God by participation, as Saint John of the Cross phrased it, and, through grace, it attains that communion in divine life, that blessedness for the sake of which all things have been created. And the degree of its blessedness itself, the degree of its vision, will correspond to the degree of the inner impetus which projects it into God, in other words, to the degree of love to which it has attained in its life on earth. In the last analysis, therefore, we must say with Saint John of the Cross: It is upon our love that we shall be judged. In its state of blessedness the immortal soul will know creation in the Creator, by that kind of knowledge which Saint Augustine called "matutinal" knowledge, because it is produced in the eternal morning of Creative Ideas; the immortal soul will be equal to the angels, and will communicate freely with the whole realm of spirits; it will love God, henceforth clearly seen, with a sovereign necessity; and it will exert free will with regard to all its actions concerning creatures, but its free will shall no longer be liable to failure and sin; the soul will inhabit the realm of unfading justice, that of the three divine Persons and of the blessed spirits; it will grasp and possess the divine Essence which, infinitely clearer and more intelligible than any of our ideas, will illumine the human intellect from within and will itself be the intelligible medium, the actuating form through which it will be known. According to a line of the Psalms [36:9] which Saint Thomas loved and often quoted: "In Thy light shall we see light."

Such are the teachings of Saint Thomas, both as a philosopher and as a theologian, about the condition and destiny of the human soul. Immortality is not a more or less precarious, successful or unsuccessful survival in other men, or in the ideal waves of the universe. Immortality is a nature-given, inalienable property of the human soul as a spiritual substance. And grace makes eternal life possible to all, to the most destitute as well as to the most gifted. The eternal life of the immortal soul is its transforming union with God and His intimate life, a union which is to be accomplished inchoatively here below, by love and contemplation and, after the body's death, in a definite and perfect manner, by the beatific vision.

For eternal life begins here upon earth, and the soul of man lives and breathes where it loves; and love, in living faith, has strength enough to make the soul of man experience unity with God— "two natures in a single spirit and love, *dos naturalezas en un espiritu y amor de Dios.*"

I do not believe that a philosopher can discuss the immortality of the soul without taking into consideration the complementary notions which religious thought adds to the true and inadequate answers which reason and philosophy can furnish by themselves.

7.5 The Problem of Rebirth

The idea of reincarnation is very old in both the East and the West. Presumably Pythagoras taught some version of it in the sixth century B.C.E. It is found in the oldest layers of Hindu literature, and the Bible shows traces of the belief. Though always more widespread in India than elsewhere, it is becoming increasingly popular in the West because of the influence of New Age thought. Parapsychology has studied cases of people who claim to remember their past lives, and hypnotic regression has become popular with many.

What exactly is reincarnation? There are a variety of different viewpoints. The most widespread and popular belief reflects views found in the Bhagavad Gita: "Just as a person casts off worn-out garments and puts on others that are new, even so does the embodied soul cast off worn-out bodies and take on others that are new" (2,13). Death amounts to the death of our physical bodies, but our souls survive and eventually are reborn in new bodies.

But how might we know this is so? There are usually three ways we use to identify someone as the same person: the physical criterion, the memory criterion, and the psychological criterion. According to the first, if there is sufficient physical continuity between someone at time T^1 and someone at time T^{60}, then we will probably consider them the same person. This criterion will not work, however, when it comes to the popular view of reincarnation, because there is no physical continuity between the various bodies. In theory people can remember their past lives, and cases of such memories provide important evidence for reincarnation. However, most people do not remember. If I claim to be the reincarnation of someone who lived in tenth-century China, but I have no memories of what that person experienced, in what sense can I be the same person? The psychological criterion suggests that someone is the same person if there is a continuity of a pattern of mental dispositions. Thus if the person in China was selfish, introverted and prone to outbursts of temper, and I am also like that, we might wish to say we are the same. However, this third criterion, in the absence of the other two, seems insufficient to carry all the weight. It is far too broad because there may have been, and may be now, millions of people who have similar characters and dispositions.

According to one version of reincarnation, however, the "sameness" consists in having the same soul. What is meant by *soul*? Does it mean mind or consciousness? But I have no memories of my previous lives. Is it some type of immaterial substance that stays the same from birth to birth? But why should we say this immaterial substance is a person? Is it really me? I do experience myself as a conscious person, but I have no experience of being an immaterial substance.

Hindu and Buddhist philosophers early recognized the problems associated with popular views of reincarnation, and so they developed more sophisticated versions. In India some of these philosophical theories utilized a distinction between *purusha* and *prakriti. Purusha* is the true Self or Person. It is pure consciousness in the sense that it is uncontaminated by anything that is not consciousness. *Prakriti* is everything that is not consciousness. Ghose Aurobindo (see Reading 3.6), author of the next selection, uses these concepts to explain what he believes is a more sophisticated view of reincarnation. He finds the Western desire for some type of personal immortality, even in the form of reincarnation, to be quite selfish and wrong-headed. Real salvation does not lie in endless personal existence (embodied or disembodied) but rather in escape from the illusion and ignorance that keep us tied to a false notion of ourselves and hence to the endless cycle of rebirth.

A variety of different views about reincarnation developed in India. Of these, Aurobindo discusses two: what he terms the Buddhist view and the Vedantist. According to Buddhism, there is no soul that reincarnates. However, there are connection and continuity between births. This connection is a causal one. What was done in a past life causes this life and what is done in this life causes the next. The word *karma* means both what is done and what happens. Hence we can speak of this causal connection between births as a karmic connection. Aurobindo uses the analogy of water flowing in a river or stream bed. He alludes to another analogy that Buddhists used, the analogy of the flame. If we use the flame from one lamp to light another and then use that flame to light another, and so on, there is a continuity connecting the lamps. This continuity is a causal one, but nothing (no soul) is passed from one lamp to the next.

Aurobindo does not discuss this Buddhist view at length and passes over it without criticism. However, many Hindus believed there had to be some vehicle that carried the karma from one life to the next. In the lamp analogy, there is contact between one lamp and the next. But where is the point of contact between one birth and the next?

Aurobindo favors the Vedantist view (although he does not say that here). One version of the Vedantist view that informs his discussion pictures the true immutable and undying Self (*Atman, purusha*) covered by five sheaths: food, vitality, mind, intellect, and bliss. These five sheaths are coordinated with three bodies: gross, subtle, and causal. Food is associated with the gross body, bliss with the causal body. Vitality, mind, and intellect are all associated with the subtle body. It is this body, the subtle, that is the vehicle for carrying karma from one lifetime to the next. However, this subtle body is not the true Self. As Aurobindo makes clear, the true Self does not change or reincarnate. It is the eternal witness of the events associated with the subtle body, including its cycles of rebirth. Although the subtle body is not the true Self, there is a connection. It reflects (especially the sheath of intellect) the true Self like a pool reflects light.

This picture of the self and its rebirths is clearly far more complex than the term *reincarnation of the soul* indicates. Aurobindo wishes to convey some of that complexity here in the hope of convincing us that we misidentify ourselves by overvaluing the importance of our personalities. Once we get straight who we are and who we are not, it is Aurobindo's hope, along with that of both Buddhists and Vedantists, that these rounds of rebirths can be brought to an end and that we will gain release from our ignorance and suffering.

Reading Questions

1. Do you agree that the loss of memory is a major objection to the "cruder" notion of reincarnation? Why or why not?
2. How does Aurobindo characterize the Buddhist view of reincarnation?
3. Why does "metempsychosis" better characterize the Vedantist view?
4. If your personality does not reincarnate, in what sense can we say that you reincarnate?
5. Are there any reasons to think that the Buddhist or Vedantist views on reincarnation might be any more reasonable than the more popular views? If so, what are these reasons?

The Reincarnating Soul*

SRI AUROBINDO

HUMAN THOUGHT IN THE generality of men is no more than a rough and crude acceptance of unexamined ideas; it is a sleepy sentry and allows anything to pass the gates which seems to it decently garbed or wears a plausible appearance or can mumble anything that resembles some familiar password. Especially is this so in subtle matters, those remote from the concrete facts of our physical life and environment. Even men who will reason carefully and acutely in ordinary matters, and there consider vigilance against error an intellectural or a practical duty, are yet content with the most careless stumbling when they get upon higher and more difficult ground. Where precision and subtle thinking are most needed, there they are most impatient of it and averse to the labour demanded of them. Men can manage fine thought about palpable things, but to think subtly about the subtle is too great a strain on the grossness of our intellects; so we are content with making a dab

at the truth, like the painter who threw his brush at his picture when he could not get the effect that he desired. We mistake the smudge that results for the perfect form of a verity.

It is not surprising then that men should be content to think crudely about such a matter as rebirth. Those who accept it, take it usually ready-made, either as a cut and dried theory or a crude dogma. The soul is reborn in a new body,—that vague and almost meaningless assertion is for them sufficient. But what is the soul and what can possibly be meant by the rebirth of a soul? Well, it means reincarnation; the soul, whatever that may be, had got out of one case of flesh and is now getting into another case of flesh. It sounds simple,—let us say, like the Djinn of the Arabian tale expanding out of and again compressing himself into his bottle or perhaps as a pillow is lugged out of one pillow-case and thrust into another. Or the soul fashions itself a

*From Sri Aurobindo, *The Problem of Rebirth*, 1952, pp. 20–27. Reprinted by permission of the Sri Aurobindo Ashram.

body in the mother's womb and then occupies it, or else, let us say, puts off one robe of flesh and then puts on another. But what is it that thus "leaves" one body and "enters" into another? Is it another, a psychic body and subtle form, that enters into the gross corporeal form,—the Purusha perhaps of the ancient image, no bigger than a man's thumb, or is it something in itself formless and impalpable that incarnates in the sense of becoming or assuming to the senses a palpable shape of bone and flesh?

In the ordinary, the vulgar conception there is no birth of a soul at all, but only the birth of a new body into the world occupied by an old personality unchanged from that which once left some now discarded physical frame. It is John Robinson who has gone out of the form of flesh he once occupied; it is John Robinson who tomorrow or some centuries hence will re-incarnate in another form of flesh and resume the course of his terrestrial experiences with another name and in another environment. Achilles, let us say, is reborn as Alexander, the son of Philip, a Macedonian, conqueror not of Hector but of Darius, with a wider scope, with larger destinies; but it is still Achilles, it is the same personality that is reborn, only the bodily circumstances are different. It is this survival of the identical personality that attracts the European mind today in the theory of reincarnation. For it is the extinction or dissolution of the personality, of this mental, nervous and physical composite which I call myself that is hard to bear for the man enamoured of life, and it is the promise of its survival and physical reappearance that is the great lure. The one objection that really stands in the way of its acceptance is the obvious non-survival of memory. Memory is the man, says the modern psychologist, and what is the use of the survival of my personality, if I do not remember my past, if I am not aware of being the same person still and always? What is the utility? Where is the enjoyment?

The old Indian thinkers,—I am not speaking of the popular belief which was crude enough and thought not at all about the matter,—the old Buddhistic and Vedantist thinkers surveyed the whole field from a very different standpoint. They were not attached to the survival of the personality; they did not give to that survival the high name of immortality; they saw that personality being what it is, a constantly changing composite, the survival of an identical personality was a non-sense, a contradiction in terms. They perceived indeed that there is a continuity and they sought to discover what determines this continuity and whether the sense of identity which enters into it is an illusion or the representation of a fact, of a real truth, and, if the latter, then what that truth may be. The Buddhist denied any real identity. There is, he said, no self, no person; there is simply a continuous stream of energy in action like the continuous flowing of a river or the continuous burning of a flame. It is this continuity which creates in the mind the false sense of identity. I am not now the same person that I was a year ago, not even the same person that I was a moment ago, any more than the water flowing past yonder ghaut is the same water that flowed past it a few seconds ago; it is the persistence of the flow in the same channel that preserves the false appearance of identity. Obviously, then, there is no soul that reincarnates, but only Karma that persists in flowing continuously down the same apparently uninterrupted channel. It is Karma that incarnates; Karma creates the form of a constantly changing mentality and physical bodies that are, we may presume, the result of that changing composite of ideas and sensations which I call myself. The identical "I" is not, never was, never will be. Practically, so long as the error of personality persists, this does not make much difference and I can say in the language of ignorance that I am reborn in a new body; practically, I have to proceed on the basis of that error. But there is this important point gained that it is all an error and an error which can cease; the composite can be broken up for good without any fresh formation, the flame can be extinguished, the channel which called itself a river destroyed. And then there is non-being, there is cessation, there is the release of the error from itself.

The Vedantist comes to a different conclusion; he admits an identity, a self, a persistent immutable reality,—but other than my personality, other than this composite which I call myself. In the Katha Upanishad the question is raised in a very instructive fashion, quite apposite to the subject we have in hand. Nachiketas, sent by his father to the world of Death, thus questions Yama, the lord of that world: Of the man who has gone forward, who has passed away from us, some say that he is and others "this he is not"; which then is right? What is the truth of the great passage? Such is the form of the question and at first sight it seems simply to raise the problem of immortality in the European sense of the word, the survival of the identical personality. But that is not what Nachiketas asks. He has already taken as the second of three boons offered to him by Yama the knowledge of the sacred Flame by which man crosses over hunger and thirst, leaves sorrow and fear far behind him and dwells in heaven securely rejoicing. Immortality in that sense he takes for granted as, already standing in that farther world, he must surely do. The knowledge he asks for involves the deeper, finer problem, of which Yama affirms that even the gods debated this of old and it is not easy to know, for subtle is the law of it; something survives that appears to be the same person, that descends into hell, that ascends into heaven, that returns upon the earth with a new body, but is it really the same person that thus survives? Can we really say of the man "He still is," or must we not rather say "This he no longer is"? Yama too in his answer speaks not at all of the survival of death, and he only gives a verse or two to a bare description of that constant rebirth which all serious thinkers admitted as a universally acknowledged truth. What he speaks of is the Self, the real Man, the Lord of all these changing appearances; without the knowledge of that Self the survival of the personality is not immortal life but a constant passing from death to death; he only who goes beyond personality to the real Person becomes the Immortal. Till then a man seems indeed to be born again and again by the force of his knowledge and works, name succeeds to name, form gives place to form, but there is no immortality.

Such then is the real question put and answered so divergently by the Buddhist and the Vedantin. There is a constant re-forming of personality in new bodies, but this personality is a mutable creation of force at its work streaming forward in Time and never for a moment the same, and the ego-sense that makes us cling to the life of the body and believe readily that it is the same idea and form, that it is John Robinson who is reborn as Sidi Hossain, is a creation of the mentality. Achilles was not reborn as Alexander but the stream of force in its works which created the momentarily changing mind and body of Achilles flowed on and created the momentarily changing mind and body of Alexander. Still, said the ancient Vedanta, there is yet something beyond this force in action, Master of it, one who makes it create for him new names and forms, and that is the Self, the Purusha, the Man, the Real Person. The ego-sense is only its distorted image reflected in the flowing stream of embodied mentality.

Is it then the Self that incarnates and reincarnates? But the Self is imperishable, immutable, unborn, undying. The Self is not born and does not exist in the body, rather the body is born and exists in the Self. For the Self is one everywhere,—*in* all bodies, we say, but really it is not confined and parcelled out in different bodies except as the all-constituting ether seems to be formed into different objects and is in a sense in them. Rather all these bodies are in the Self; but that also is a figment of space-conception, and rather these bodies are only symbols and figures of itself created by it in its own consciousness. Even what we call the individual soul is greater than its body and not less, more subtle than it and therefore not confined by its grossness. At death it does not leave its form, but casts it off, so that a great departing Soul can say of this death in vigorous phrase, "I have spat out the body."

What then is it that we feel to inhabit the physical frame? What is it that the Soul draws out from the body when it casts off this partial physical robe which enveloped not it, but part of its members? What is it whose issuing out gives this wrench, this swift struggle and pain of parting, creates this sense of violent divorce? The answer does not help us much. It is the subtle or psychical frame which is tied to the physical by the heart-strings, by the cords of life-force, of nervous energy which have been woven into every physical fibre. This the Lord of the body draws out and the violent snapping or the rapid or tardy loosening of the life-cords, the exit of the connecting force constitutes the pain of death and its difficulty.

Let us then change the form of the question and ask rather what it is that reflects and accepts the mutable personality, since the Self is immutable? We have, in fact, an immutable Self, a real Person, lord of this ever-changing personality which, again, assumes ever-changing bodies, but the real Self knows itself always as above the mutation, watches and enjoys it, but is not involved in it. Through what does it enjoy the changes and feel them to be its own, even while knowing itself to be unaffected by them? The mind and ego-sense are only inferior instruments; there must be some more essential form of itself which the Real Man puts forth, puts in front of itself, as it were, and at the back of the changings to support and mirror them without being actually changed by them. This more essential form is the mental being or mental person which the Upanishads speak of as the mental leader of the life and body . . . . It is that which maintains the ego-sense as a function in the mind and enables us to have the firm conception of continuous identity in Time as opposed to the timeless identity of the Self.

The changing personality is not this mental person; it is a composite of various stuff of Nature, a formation of Prakriti, and is not at all the Purusha. And it is a very complex composite with many layers; there is a layer of physical, a layer of nervous, a layer of mental, even a final stratum of supramental personality; and within these layers themselves there are strata within each stratum. The analysis of the successive couches of the earth is a simple matter compared with the analysis of this wonderful creation we call the personality. The mental being in resuming bodily life forms a new personality for its new terrestrial existence; it takes material from the common matter-stuff, life-stuff, mind-stuff of the physical world and during earthly life it is constantly absorbing fresh material, throwing out what is used up, changing its bodily, nervous and mental tissues. But this is all surface work; behind is the foundation of past experience held back from the physical memory so that the superficial consciousness may not be troubled or interfered with by the conscious burden of the past, but may concentrate on the work immediately in hand. Still that foundation of past experience is the bed-rock of personality; and it is more than that. It is our real fund on which we can always draw even apart from our present superficial commerce with our surroundings. That commerce adds to our gain, modifies the foundation for a subsequent existence.

Moreover, all this is, again, on the surface. It is only a small part of ourselves which lives and acts in the energies of our earthly existence. As behind the physical universe there are worlds of which ours is only a last result, so also within us there are worlds of our self-existence which throw out this external form of our being. The subconscient, the super-conscient are oceans from which and to which this river flows. Therefore to speak of ourselves as a soul reincarnating is to give altogether too simple an appearance to the miracle of our existence; it puts into too ready and too gross a formula the magic of the supreme Magician. There is not a definite psychic entity getting into a new case of flesh; there is a metempsychosis, a rein-souling, a rebirth of a new psychic personality as well as a birth of a new body. And behind is the Person, the unchanging entity, the Master who manipulates this complex material, the Artificer of this wondrous artifice.

This is the starting-point from which we have to proceed in considering the problem of rebirth. To view ourselves as such and such a personality getting into a new case of flesh is to stumble about in the ignorance, to confirm the error of the material mind and the senses. The body is a convenience, the personality is a constant formation for whose development action and experience are the instruments; but the Self by whose will and for whose delight all this is, is other than the body, other than the action and experience, other than the personality which they develop. To ignore it is to ignore the whole secret of our being.

7.6 A Naturalistic Case for Extinction

As we have seen (Reading 7.3), a scientific case based on parapsychical evidence, in particular the phenomenon of mediumship, can be made for survival of death. This evidence suggests that under certain circumstances, some kind of survival may occur—although this evidence falls far short of showing that eternal survival of a person beyond death occurs. The strength of this evidence needs to be assessed very carefully.

A scientific case for extinction can also be made. Central to this argument is the claim that the best scientific evidence available suggests that our mental life is dependent on bodily processes, particularly those associated with the brain. Damage to various parts of the brain, for example, results in loss of memories or a greatly reduced ability to remember. We know the brain ceases to function at death, and given the evidence for mind-brain dependence, it is reasonable to infer our that mental life also ceases at death.

One could acknowledge the dependence, however, and still argue for some kind of survival. Perhaps the brain is like the hardware of a computer and the mind like the software. Just as different computers can run the same software, so different brains might be able to run the same mind. This idea, however, is speculative (what isn't when it comes to an afterlife?) and requires some sort of resurrection or replica theory.

There are other possibilities. J. M. E. McTaggart (1866–1925) suggested that the relationship between the mind and the body used in the scientific argument for extinction might be based on a false analogy. Perhaps we should think of the situation as more like that of a person enclosed in a room with one window. Board up the window either partly or completely, and you will decisively affect the experiences of the person inside. By analogy, changes to the brain (window) will affect the mind (person in the room) while the mind is connected to the body. However, perhaps bodily death is more like the person gaining freedom from the room. The dependence on the body and brain is broken, and the mind is now free to experience independently. The fact that a person's perspective is dependent on the size of the window while the person is living in the room does not prove that the person ceases to experience once the room is destroyed. Similarly, the argument that our mental life is dependent on the brain while our minds are associated with a body does not prove that the mind ceases to function at death.

Perhaps there are other analogies one might draw. We have to remember that we are discussing a subject in which firm proof is, at least at this time, not possible. Maybe the best we can do is ask whether the preponderance of the scientific evidence tips the scales one way or another.

Linda Badham teaches mathematics at Aberaeron School and has long had an interest in the scientific evidence relevant to the question of survival. She is impressed by the strength of the case against survival that can be made on the basis of scientific information about the relationship between mind and body. She finds the parapsychological evidence not at all compelling and, given the philosophical problems associated with the replica theory and the idea of the soul, concludes that the case for surviving death is very weak and the case for extinction far more convincing.

Reading Questions

1. Why should modern evidence about the physiochemical conditions of living organisms render literal notions of bodily resurrection unacceptable?
2. What is the replica problem?
3. Why won't the idea that the soul survives physical death work to guarantee personal survival?
4. Why don't near-death experiences and OBEs prove that survival of physical death is possible?
5. Do you agree with Badham's conclusion? Why or why not?

A Naturalistic Case for Extinction*

LINDA BADHAM

Introduction

It is a popularly held view that science and religion are antithetical. And this view is supported by the sociological fact that leading scholars and scientists are significantly less likely to be Christian than other groups in society. Yet even so, there are a number of very eminent scientists, and particularly physicists, who claim that there is no real conflict between their scientific and religious beliefs. And many Christian apologists have drawn comfort from such claims in an age where the tide of secularism threatens to engulf the ancient citadel of Christian belief. However, I have my doubts as to whether or not Christianity is secure from attack by science in general on some of its most crucial tenets. And, in particular, what I want to argue in this chapter is that the implications of modern science are far more damaging to doctrines of life after death than many Christian writers have supposed.

Resurrection of the Body (This Flesh)

Although many might think that belief in the resurrection of this flesh at the end of time is now unthinkable, it has to be recognized that this is the form that orthodox Christian belief took from at least the second century onwards. Thus the Apostles' Creed affirms belief in the resurrection of the flesh; the Nicene Creed looks for the "upstanding of the dead bodies"; and the Christian Fathers were utterly explicit that the resurrection was definitely a physical reconstitution. Moreover, such belief is still Catholic orthodoxy: a recent *Catholic Catechism for Adults* declares that each one of us will rise one day "the same person he was, in the same flesh made living by the same spirit." And Wolfhart Pannenberg, one of the most influential continental Protestant theologians of our day, also affirms belief in the traditional doctrine. Hence it seems reasonable to suppose that this form of resurrection belief is

*From "A Naturalistic Case for Extinction" by Linda Badham. From *Death and Immortality in the Religions of the World* edited by Paul and Linda Badham. Copyright © 1987 by Paragon House Publishers. Reprinted by permission. Footnotes deleted.

still held among Christians. Yet a minimal knowledge of modern science seems sufficient to undermine it completely.

First, there is the problem that "this flesh" is only temporarily mine. I am not like a machine or artifact, which keeps its atoms and molecules intact throughout its existence, save for those lost by damage or replaced during repair. Rather, I am a biological system in dynamic equilibrium (more or less) with my environment, in that I exchange matter with that environment continually. As J. D. Bernal writes, "It is probable that none of us have more than a few atoms with which we started life, and that even as adults we probably change most of the material of our bodies in a matter of a few months." Thus it might prove an extremely difficult business to resurrect 'this' flesh at the end of time, for the atoms that will constitute me at the moment of death will return to the environment and will doubtless become part of innumerable other individuals. Augustine discussed the case of cannibals having to restore the flesh they had "borrowed" as an exception. But in the light of our current knowledge, shared atoms would seem the rule rather than the exception.

Morever, there is the further problem that even if the exact atoms that constituted me at death could all be reassembled without leaving some other people bereft of vital parts, then the reconstituted body would promptly expire again. For whatever caused the systems failure in my body, which led to my death originally, would presumably still obtain if the body exactly as it was prior to death were remade. But perhaps we can overcome this problem with a fairly simple proviso: the resurrection body should be identical to the body that died, malfunctions apart. After all, it might be said, we have no difficulty in accepting our television set returned in good working order from the repair shop after a breakdown as one and the same television set that we took to be repaired, even though some or even several of its components have been replaced. But people are not television sets. What counts as malfunction? Increasing age usually brings some diminution in physical and mental powers. Are all these to be mended too? How much change can a body take and still be the same person? Nor is it possible to suggest that the resurrection environment might be such as to reverse the effects of aging and disease. For this move implies such a great change in the properties of the matter that is "this flesh" as to make it dubious whether "this" flesh really had been resurrected. The more one actually fills out the vague notion of the resurrection of the same flesh that perished, the more problems arise.

And even if the problem of reconstituting each one of us to the same (healthy) flesh he was (or might have been) could be overcome, there would remain the question of where we could all be resurrected. There is a space problem. If the countless millions of human beings who have ever lived and may live in the future were all to be resurrected on this earth, then the overcrowding would be acute. Now there are at least two theological maneuvers that we could make to circumvent this embarrassment. If we want to retain resurrection on this earth, then we might say that only the chosen will be resurrected and thereby limit the numbers. But that solution raises insuperable problems about the morality of a God who would behave in such a way. Alternatively, it might be argued that the resurrection will be to a new life in heaven and not to eternal life on earth. But in that case it has to be noted that resurrected bodies would need a biological environment markedly similar to the one we now live in. This leads to the implication that heaven would have to be a planet, or series of planets, all suitable for human life. The further one pushes this picture, the more bizarre and religiously unsatisfying it becomes.

In sum, then, a little knowledge of the biochemistry of living organisms together with a brief consideration of the physicochemical conditions that such organisms require if they are to live, ought to have rendered the traditional notion of literal bodily resurrection unthinkable.

Resurrection of the Body (Transformed)

It might be argued, as John Polkinghorne claims, that all this is irrelevant: "We know that there is nothing significant about the material which at any one time constitutes our body. . . . It is the pattern they [the atoms] form which persists and evolves. We are liberated, therefore, from the quaint medieval picture of the reassembly of the body from its scattered components. In very general terms it is not difficult to imagine the pattern recreated (the body resurrected) in some other world."

At this point we should note that the doctrine being proposed here has shifted in a very significant way. The old doctrine of resurrection of the flesh guaranteed personal survival because the resurrected body was physically identical with the one laid in the grave. Physical continuity supplied the link between the person who died and the one who was resurrected. But Polkinghorne's version of the resurrection envisages recreation of a *pattern* in some other world. This is open to a host of philosophical problems about the sense in which the recreation of a replica can count as the survival of the person who died.

What would we say, for example, if the replica were created *before* my death? Would I then die happily knowing that someone was around to carry on, as it were, in my place? Would I think to myself that the replica really was me? Consider the possibility of cloning. Let us imagine that science reaches a stage where a whole adult human individual can be regenerated from a few cells of a person in such a way that the original—Jones I—and the copy—Jones II—are genetically identical, and that the clone knows everything that Jones I knows. We may imagine that the purpose of doing this is to give a healthy body to house the thoughts of the physically ailing, but brilliant Jones I. Now does Jones I die secure in the knowledge that he will live again? I would suggest that he might feel relieved to know that his life's work would carry on, and that his project would be entrusted to one incomparably suited to continue with it. He might also feel exceptionally close to Jones II and be deeply concerned for his welfare. But the other would not *be* him. In the end, Jones I would be dead and the other, Jones II, would carry on in his place. As far as Jones I was concerned, he himself would not live again, even though most other people would treat Jones II as if here were Jones I rejuvenated.

If these intuitions are correct, then they suggest that whatever it is that we count as essential for being one and the same person, it is not a "pattern." And I would suggest that all theories of resurrection that speak of our rising with new and transformed bodies fall foul of what I term the replica problem. For without some principle of continuity between the person who died and the one who was resurrected, then what was resurrected would only be something very similar to the one who died, a replica, and not a continuation of the dead person.

The Soul

Such considerations have led theologians at least from Aquinas onwards to argue that any tenable resurrection belief hinges on a concept of the soul. For even if we hold to a belief in the resurrection of some "new and glorious body," then we need the soul to avoid the replica problem. There has to be a principle of continuity between this world and the next if what is raised to new life really is one and the same person as the one who died. Moreover, this principle of continuity must encapsulate enough of the real "me" for both "old" and "new" versions to count as the same person. Might this requirement be fulfilled if we were to espouse a dualist concept of the person and say, with Descartes, that my essential personhood is to be identified with my mind, that is, with the subject of conscious experiencing? However, I want to argue that not even this move is sufficient to rescue the Christian claim.

First, there are all the practical problems of which contemporary dualists are very much aware. Our personal experience and emotions are intimately linked to our body chemistry. Indeed, the limits to what we are able to think at all are set by our genetic endowment; so that one man's physicochemical equipment enables him to be a brilliant mathematician, while another's lack condemns him to lifelong imbecility. If our diet is imbalanced and inadequate, or if certain of our organs are malfunctioning, then our bodies may be starved of essential nutrients or poisoned by the excessive production of some hormone. In such cases, the whole personality may be adversely affected. The "subject of my conscious experiences" would seem to be very much at the mercy of my physicochemical constitution.

A second difficulty lies in deciding which organisms count as having souls and which do not. And if God is to give eternal life to the former class and not to the latter, then even He has to be able to draw a line somewhere, and that nonarbitrarily. The problem occurs both in considering the evolution of the species *Homo sapiens* and the individual development of human beings. Even if we ignore the problem of nonhuman animals and restrict the possibility of possessing a soul to humans, there are still insuperable difficulties.

Consider first the evolutionary pathway that led from the early mammals to man. Somewhere along that line we would be fairly secure in denying that such and such a creature had any awareness of self. And it is also true to say that most normal adult humans possess such an awareness. But between these extremes lies a gray area. To have a nonarbitrary dividing line, it has to be possible for us to decide (at least in principle) where a sharp division can be drawn between the last generation of anthropoid apes and the first generation of true *Homo sapiens*. Are we to suppose that in one generation there were anthropoid apes who gave birth to the next generation of true *Homo sapiens*, and that the changes between one generation and the next were so great that the children counted in God's eyes as the bearers of immortality while their parents were "mere animals"? Yet unless dualists are prepared to fly in the face of evolutionary biology, how can they avoid this unpalatable conclusion?

The problems that we see in the evolution of the species are mirrored in the development of each fertilized human ovum. Somewhere in the path leading from conception to adulthood awareness of self develops. When exactly seems impossible to pinpoint (unless it turns out that awareness of self is a sort of quantum leap in a child's development). Nor can the difficulty be evaded by claiming that each fertilized ovum is a potential human being and therefore potentially self-aware, not least because some genetic combinations become cancerous and are in no sense even potential human beings.

Just as there were religious difficulties arising for the dualist's position from the lack of sharp divisions in evolutionary development, so too there are religious difficulties here. For if, as Descartes would have us believe, it is the ability to doubt that guarantees the existence of the "I", and if what survives is this subject of conscious experiences, then there is nothing to survive in any potential human being that has yet to develop the necessary level of mental life. Panpsychists apart, most of us would accept that a certain minimum of neurological equipment is a necessary condition of conscious experience. As Arturo Rosenblueth writes: "In the human species, the central nervous system, especially the cerebral cortex of the newborn baby, is very underdeveloped as compared with those of an adolescent or an adult. . . . The first signs of conscious behaviour do not appear until this anatomical and neurophysiological evolution reaches a sufficiently high level."

If this is right, then would we have to imagine God greeting two mothers in heaven and saying to one, "The soul of your long-lost infant is now fully mature and waits here to be reunited with you"; while to the other he mutters, "Well, I am sorry about this, but your baby didn't quite make it because he failed to develop self-consciousness before he died"? Nor is the problem to be circumvented by claiming that what survives has nothing to do with neural equipment. It is rather the immaterial soul, which admittedly had yet to manifest its presence in the infant. For what content could be given to claiming that this tabula rasa was the real child? This theory of the soul fails to satisfy not just because it seems incompatible with our scientific knowledge, but also because it has some undesirable religious implications.

There are, in addition, some further objections of a more purely philosophical nature, which I think need mentioning at this point. The subject of my conscious experiencing is singularly unconvincing as a principle of continuity that guarantees persistence of the "same" person through change. Moreover, defining the "real" me in this way actually misses a lot of what most of us would want to say is a part of the "real" me. I shall begin by discussing the question of a principle of continuity.

One great problem with my awareness of self is its lack of persistence, its transitoriness. My stream of consciousness is far from being a constant or even ever-present (though varying) flow. When I am unconscious, in a dreamless sleep, or even in a vacant mood, it just is not there. Yet *I* do not cease to exist whenever my conscious mind is, as it were, switched off temporarily. Secondly, we have to face the problem that this awareness of self is ever-changing. What I was as a child is very different from what I, as I am in myself, am today; and if I live to be an old lady, doubtless the subject of my conscious experiences will look back with a mixture of wry amusement and nostalgia at that other her of forty years ago. Now it might be thought that this problem of continual change is no greater a problem for the notion of same "self" than it is for the notion of same "body" since the body is also in a continual state of flux. But I would suggest that what supplies continuity through change is matter. It may be that all my constituent atoms will have changed in the next few months, but they will not have all changed simultaneously. Moreover, the physically-based blueprints from the chemistry that keeps my body going are passed on from one generation of cells to another in a direct physical line of succession. Thus, I would argue that what keeps the subject of my conscious experiencing belonging to one and the same person is this physical continuity.

The essential requirement of physical continuity can be illustrated if we return to the clone example. Let us modify the thought experiment a little, and makes Jones II a copy of a perfectly healthy Jones I. And let us also stipulate that the two Joneses emerge from the cloning laboratory not knowing who is the original and who the copy. In other words, Jones I and II are, seemingly, wholly similar. Neither they nor we can tell which is which, unless we trace the histories of the

two bodies to ascertain which grew from a fertilized ovum and which developed as the result of cloning. Now if we apply the implications of this to the question of what might live again after death, we see that being "the subject of my conscious experiences" is not sufficient to guarantee that I am one and the same person as the one who died. For what the clone example shows is that both Jones I and Jones II may believe (or doubt) equally that he really is the same person as Jones I while he relies solely on his personal experience of himself as Jones. Only when he traces the path of physical continuity can he know whether he truly is Jones I or not. (Of course, we might want to say that where there had been one person, Jones, there were now two distinct individuals, both of whom were physically continuous with the original. But in that case the possibility of defining "same person" in terms of "same stream of consciousness" does not even arise.)

Thus I contend, a dualist definition of what I really am fails because it cannot provide adequate criteria for recognizing the "same" person through change. I can think of no other case where we would even be tempted to accept something as transitory and ever-changing as "consciousness of self" to be the essential criterion for defining what it is that an entity has to retain if it is to count as remaining the same individual through change.

I move on now to the problems that arise from the restrictedness of defining me as the subject of my conscious experiences. A great deal of what I am does not involve my conscious thoughts at all, even when I am fully awake. Take the familiar example of driving a car. When I was learning to drive, I certainly employed a great amount of conscious effort. But nowadays my conscious thoughts are fairly free to attend to other matters when I am driving, even though, of course, intense conscious attention instantly returns if danger threatens. I certainly do not want to say "my body" drove here. *I* drove here, even though most of the time the subject of my conscious experiences was not much involved.

Moreover, we cannot ignore the possibility that the conscious subject might actually fail to recognize a significant part of all that I really am. To exemplify the point: imagine someone who believes himself to be a great wit, when most of his colleagues find him a crashing bore. If he were to arrive in the resurrection world without his familiar characteristics—clumsiness of speech, repetitiveness, triviality, self-centeredness—would he really be the person who had died? Yet could he bring these characteristics with him if the subject of his conscious experiences, the "real" him, was wholly unaware of having been like this?

In sum, what I have been arguing against dualism is that this concept of the soul cannot bear the weight put on it. Yet it has to bear this weight if it is to be the sine qua non of my surviving bodily death. Considerations from the natural sciences and philosophy, and even religious implications, combine to render it far from convincing. But, it might be countered, no amount of argument on the basis of current scientific theory, philosophy, or religious sentiments can count against hard empirical fact. So what about the reports that exist of near-death experiences, which seem to show that some people really do have experiences apart from their bodies?

Near-Death Experiences

Let me begin by stating quite clearly that I shall not be concerned to discuss the merits or otherwise of individual cases. I am going to suppose, for the purposes of discussion, that there is strong, bonafide evidence that some people come back from the brink of death fully convinced that they had left their bodies and had had apparently veridical experiences as if from a vantage point different from that of the body. The question then is, how do we interpret these "travelers tales."

I have three main points to make here. The first is that a present absence of satisfactory normal explanations for these cases does not imply that there are no such explanations ever to be found. We should not be hurried into a supernaturalist account merely because we can find no other, as if the God-of-the-gaps lesson had yet to

be learned. And I note that at least one worker in this field, Dr. Susan Blackmore, argues for a psychological approach to explaining out-of-the-body experiences (OBEs). Dr. Blackmore has spent the last decade researching OBEs and has moved from an initial belief that persons can leave their bodies to her present more skeptical position. She writes: "Everything perceived in an OBE is a product of memory and imagination, and during the OBE one's imagination is more vividly experienced than it is in everyday life." One limiting factor, for our purposes here, in Dr. Blackmore's work is that she has been researching primarily "astral projection" rather than near-death experiences. And clearly, if there is such a thing as a quasi-independent human soul, it is at least possible that such a soul cannot actually leave the body while the body is not near death. In that case, all the research in the world into astral projection may be wholly irrelevant. But we should be prepared to explore naturalistic accounts of OBEs before embracing a supernaturalistic hypothesis.

My second point is that even if we take near-death experiences as supplying empirical proof of the existence, nay persistence, of the human soul or mind, that would not smooth out all the difficulties. All the problems that I have discussed earlier would still be there, awaiting some kind of resolution. And there would arise yet further problems. Take, for example, the question of how the soul actually "sees" physical objects while it supposedly hovers below the ceiling. William Rushton puts the point thus: "What is this out-of-the-body eye that can encode the visual scene exactly as does the real eye, with its hundred million photoreceptors and its million signaling optic nerves? Can you imagine anything but a replica of the real eye could manage to do this? But if this floating replica is to see, it must catch light, and hence cannot be transparent, and so must be visible to people in the vicinity. In fact floating eyes are not observed, nor would this be expected, for they exist only in fantasy." And if it be countered that the soul perceives without using the normal physicochemical mechanisms, then we might ask why on earth did such a complicated organ as the eye ever evolve (or remain unatrophied) if human beings possess souls that can "see" without normal eyes. Moreover, one might expect that blind people, deprived of normal visual stimuli, would use this psychic ability, if it really existed. These, and kindred problems concerned with modes of perception, would need answers if we were to take seriously supernatural interpretations of OBEs.

Finally, I suggest that to accept the existence of some nonmaterial soul in man would be to embrace a notion fundamentally at variance with other well-founded convictions about the nature of reality. For we would then have to allow for events happening in the world that rest on no underlying physicochemical mechanisms. Now I am very well aware that scientists are continually changing their theories to accommodate new data, and that from time to time some wholesale replacement of outmoded ideas has been necessary. So, it might be asked, can we not envisage some new scientific outlook that embraces both the normal data and the paranormal? Just so. A new scientific outlook, which could encompass both normal and paranormal data, would clearly be more satisfactory than one which could in no way account for the paranormal. But it must be remembered that the whole scientific enterprise presupposes the existence of underlying mechanisms whose discovery enables us to understand the "how" of an event. So it is hard to see how any unified scientific theory could embrace both the notion that most events in the world depend on underlying physicochemical mechanisms, and also that there are some events that do not utilize any such mechanisms at all. And if paranormal data are taken as support for the belief in the existence of nonmaterial entities (like souls) then these data fly in the face of normal science. Thus I concur with C. D. Broad that "It is certainly right to demand a much higher standard of evidence for events which are alleged to be paranormal than those which would be normal. . . . For in dealing with evidence we have always to take into account the antecedent probability or improbability of the alleged event, i.e. its probability or improbability relative to all the rest of our knowledge and well-founded belief other than the special evidence adduced in its favour."

In sum then, it seems that at present paranormal data cannot be accommodated within naturalist science. But to move from that to claiming that we have empirical evidence for the existence of immaterial souls seems unwarranted, not least because to explicate the paranormal in terms of the activities of immaterial souls may appear to solve one explanatory difficulty, but only at the expense of raising a host of other problems.

Conclusion

When Christianity was originally formulated, man's entire world view was very different from our current beliefs. It was plausible to think in terms of a three-decker universe in which the center of God's interest was this Earth and its human population. The idea that God would raise man from the dead to an eternal life of bliss fitted neatly into this schema. However, the erosion of this picture, beginning from at least the time of Copernicus and Galileo, has cut the traditional Christian hope adrift from the framework of ideas in which it was originally formulated. What I have tried to show in this chapter is that various attempts, which have been made to try to accommodate some form of resurrection/immortality belief within our current world view, are inadequate and fail. I conclude, then, that a due consideration of man's place in nature leads us to the view that he belongs there and nowhere else.

Suggestions for Further Reading

Broad, C. D. *The Mind and Its Place in Nature.* London: Routledge and Kegan Paul, 1937.

————. *Lectures on Psychical Research.* New York: Humanities Press, 1962.

Chidester, David. *Patterns of Transcendence: Religion, Death and Dying.* Belmont, CA: Wadsworth, 1990.

Ducasse, C. J. *A Critical Examination of the Belief in a Life After Death.* Springfield, IL: Charles C Thomas, 1961.

Edwards, Paul, ed. *Immortality.* New York: Macmillan, 1992.

Flew, Antony. *God, Freedom, and Immortality.* Buffalo, NY: Prometheus Books, 1976.

————. "Immortality." In *Encyclopedia of Philosophy,* edited by Paul Edwards. Vol. 4. New York: Macmillan, 1967.

Fontinell, Eugene. *Self, God, and Immortality: A Jamesian Investigation.* Philadelphia: Temple University Press, 1986.

Geach, Peter. *God and the Soul.* New York: Schocken Books, 1969.

Habermas, Gary R., and Moreland, J. P., eds. *Immortality: The Other Side of Death.* Nashville, TN: Thomas Nelson Publishers, 1992.

Head, Joseph, and Cranston, S. L. *Reincarnation: The Phoenix Fire Mystery.* Julian Press, 1977.

Herbert, R. T. *Paradox and Identity in Theology.* Ithaca, NY: Cornell University Press, 1979.

Hick, John. *Death and Eternal Life.* New York: Harper & Row, 1976.

Kastenbaum, Robert. *Is There Life After Death?* Upper Saddle River, NJ: Prentice-Hall, 1984.

Küng, Hans. *Eternal Life.* New York: Doubleday, 1984.

Lamont, Corliss. *The Illusion of Immortality.* New York: Philosophical Library, 1965.

Lewis, Hywel D. *The Self and Immortality.* New York: Seabury Press, 1973.

MacGregor, Geddes. *Images of the Afterlife: Beliefs from Antiquity to Modern Times.* New York: Paragon House, 1992.

Moody, Raymond. *Life After Life.* Atlanta, GA: Mockingbird Books, 1975.

Neufeldt, Ronald W. *Karma and Rebirth: Post-Classical Developments.* Albany, NY: State University of New York Press, 1986.

O'Flaherty, Wendy Doniger, ed. *Karma and Rebirth in Classical Indian Traditions.* Berkeley: University of California Press, 1980.

Olan, Levi A. *Judaism and Immortality.* New York: Union of Hebrew Congregations, 1971.

Perry, John. *Personal Identity and Immortality.* Indianapolis, IN: Hackett, 1979.

Penelhum, Terence, ed. *Immortality.* Belmont, CA: Wadsworth, 1973.

————. *Survival and Disembodied Existence.* London: Routledge and Kegan Paul, 1970.

Phillips, D. Z. *Death and Immortality.* London: Macmillan, 1970.

Purtill, Richard. *Thinking about Religion.* Englewood Cliffs, NJ: Prentice-Hall, 1978.

Royce, Josiah. *The Conception of Immortality.* Boston: Houghton Mifflin, 1900.

Smart, Ninian. *Doctrine and Argument in Indian Philosophy.* London: George Allen & Unwin, 1964.

Steinberg, Milton. *Basic Judaism.* New York: Harcourt, 1947.

Stendahl, Krister, ed. *Immortality and Resurrection.* New York: Macmillan, 1965.

Stevenson, Ian. *Twenty Cases Suggestive of Reincarnation,* 2d ed. Charlottesville: University of Virginia Press, 1974.

Stewart, Roy A. *Rabbinic Theology.* Edinburgh, Scotland: Oliver and Boyd, 1961.

Swinburne, Richard. *The Evolution of the Soul.* Oxford, England: Oxford University Press, 1986.

Van Inwagen, Peter. "The Possibility of Resurrection." *International Journal of Philosophy and Religion* (1978):114–121.

Wolman, Benjamin, ed. *Handbook of Parapsychology.* New York: Van Nostrand, 1977.

CHAPTER 8

What Is the Meaning of Religious Language?

Introduction

THE IDEAS OF THE logical positivists in the 1930s decisively shaped Western reflection on the problem of religious language. The logical positivists distinguished between *analytic* statements such as "All bachelors are unmarried men," which are true by virtue of the meaning of the words (*bachelor* means "unmarried man," and hence this statement amounts to saying that All bachelors are bachelors), and *synthetic* statements such as "Some bachelors are less than 6 feet tall," which are about empirical states of affairs. They advanced a verification theory of meaning with respect to synthetic statements. This theory asserts that a statement's meaning consists in the conditions under which it can be verified. Scientific language provided the paradigm for the logical positivists. Science consists of nontrivial analytic statements such as those found in mathematics and synthetic statements whose meaning derives from specifying the conditions under which they would be empirically verified. According to the logical positivists, religious statements (especially "God-talk") must either be analytic, in which case they are trivial, or synthetic, in which case the empirical conditions under which they would be verified must be specified. However, empirical conditions cannot be specified because most religious language is about nonempirical matters. Hence, religious language is either trivial or empirically meaningless.

The debate about religious language took a variety of twists and turns in response to the work of the logical positivists. Ludwig Wittgenstein (1889–1951) an Austrian-born British philosopher whose early work expressed a logical positivist viewpoint, broke new ground in his later work. Wittgenstein admonished philosophers to stop trying to think up abstractly the various ways in which language might function and instead to "Look and see." Wittgenstein introduced the concept of "language games" and argued that language is used in a wide variety of ways. These ways are something like games. There are certain rules that govern what sorts of moves can be made. The language game of science may be very different from the language game of religion, just as tennis is very different from chess, but that does not mean that one game makes sense and the other does not if it does not follow the same rules. Is chess a meaningless activity because it is not tennis?

The hunt was now on to map the language game called religion. Much of the hunt centered on God-talk because a theistic model of religion dominated philosophers' attention. Some argued that religious language expresses a "vision of life" by which people live. Others maintained that religious utterances are disguised statements of moral policy or intentions to act in certain ways. Still others contended that religious language is a symbolic or expressive language used for the purposes of expressing a total life orientation. Some concentrated on distinctive types of religious discourse, such as myth, and tried to "demythologize" such discourse. Others argued for a depth dimension to religious symbols and viewed the symbolic character of religion as essential. Many turned their attention away from verifiability and focused on falsifiability. Are there any specific conditions that might show that "God loves me" is false?

Most of this debate about religious language drew on the theories of language and meaning developed by Western philosophers in Europe, the British Isles, and the United States. Little if any attention was paid to ideas about language and religion found in Asia. As far as Western philosophers were concerned, either there was no Asian thinking on this subject or, if there was, it was not worthy of attention. Thomas P. Kasulis (Reading 8.3) attempts to show not only that there is significant thinking about language in Japanese philosophy (not to mention Indian and Chinese philosophy) but also that much of this thinking centers on the meaning and understanding of religious discourse.

However, we do not have to travel to Asia to find significant alternatives to the standard Western approaches. We can find them in the West itself among Native Americans' reflections on religious symbols. For Native Americans, what counts as religious language goes far beyond the words people use. In fact, most words are inadequate when it comes to religious matters. However, we can look around us at the world in which we live and see symbols of great spiritual meaning, provided that we develop the right attitude about nature and life.

Renewed attention to science on the part of philosophers showed that scientific language is far more complex than the logical positivists imagined. Scientific theories build models and use elaborate metaphors to gain insight into nature. Religions also rely heavily on metaphor to convey their view of the world. These metaphors often reflect the cultural, historical, class, and gender contexts in which they arose. Many theists became interested in how the complex textures of context shape our images and ideas of God. We must pay attention to the context in order to understand the meaning of God-talk.

8.1 The Nature of Religious Language

In popular discourse, the word *myth* often means an untrue story. Hence people say, "That is *only* a myth." The word *myth* comes from the Greek word *mythos,* which means "story." Early Christian writers, concerned to distinguish their stories about God and Christ from the stories the Greeks told about Zeus, Apollo, and other gods and goddesses, argued that their stories were true, whereas the *mythoi* (stories) of the pagans were false. Today, we still speak of untrue stories as myths.

Modern students of religions, however, prefer to use the term *myth* in a technical manner to designate a particular kind of story that people have found to be authoritative and of sacred significance. There is disagreement about a precise definition of the term and about the types of stories that should be so classified, but generally, stories about the origin of the cosmos (creation) or the origin of significant events (where sin, evil, and death came from), stories about the exploits of divine or quasi-divine beings, and stories about the destruction or end of the world are called myths.

Myths are often associated with religious rituals, so some have argued that they should be seen as scripts for a sacred drama that ritual enacts. Thus the myth (story) of the Last Supper becomes the script for the Mass, or celebration of communion, in the Christian church.

Many scholars have pointed out that myths were originally *spoken* narratives. They were told by sacred storytellers who orally passed, from generation to generation, the legends, lore, and myths of the tribe. Once myths were removed from the live situation in which they were told and were written down, their character and function changed. Now organized as narratives in sacred scriptures (*Bible, Qur'an, Book of Mormon, Vedas, Lotus Sutra, Gita,* and so on), they are preserved in a form that invites commentary and interpretation. What do these stories mean? Why was this word used instead of that? Why does this event precede that event? Can all the accounts of the creation of the world found in all the so-called revealed scriptures be true?

Let us take Christianity as an example. We have already pointed out that some early Christian writers argued that the stories in the *Bible* were true whereas the pagan stories were false. Today some Christians (often called fundamentalists) go even further and suggest that the stories of the *Bible* are not only true but literally true. They need no interpretation because their meaning is obvious to anyone who can read. When it says that Jesus rose from the dead, that is what it means: He physically came back to life. Other Christians (often called liberals) think matters are not so simple as the fundamentalists make them out to be. First, the *Bible* appears to contain myths very much like those contained in other religions, and to call one set of myths true and the other false seems arbitrary and prejudicial. Second, it is not so obvious what these stories mean. It is difficult to talk about something being true or false if its meaning is obscure. Some sort of interpretation is necessary. Texts do not interpret themselves.

Part of the difficulty stems from the fact that religious scriptures and myths rely on the use of symbols to convey meaning. Much of the time, symbolic meaning is clear and unproblematic. We use the distinction between literal meaning and symbolic meaning frequently. Much of our language thrives on metaphor and analogy. Thus we say that someone is as wise as an owl or that someone is cool or spaced out or hot under the collar. We don't mean this sort of talk literally, as though someone who is cool really has a lower temperature than someone else. You would think me odd if I went around taking the temperature of those you called cool and those you called hot under the collar to see whether there really was a literal difference. If I did that, you would say that I just didn't understand what you meant.

However, it is not always very clear just *how* literal meaning differs from symbolic meaning. We seem to recognize the difference, and we usually know how to interpret what people say, but when pressed to give a precise general account, we probably would have difficulties. Is the literal meaning the "strict" meaning a word or sentence has in any given language by virtue of the dictionary definition? But what do we mean by "strict meaning" other than something like nonsymbolic or nonfigurative meaning? Does literal meaning have something to do with the intention of the person speaking or writing? Often philosophers give priority to literal meaning and claim the symbolic is dependent on it. If that is so, then should we not be able to translate symbolic and figurative language into literal? But can we translate poetry that is highly symbolic and metaphoric into literal language and still have it mean the same thing? What is the literal meaning of the following lines of poetry?

> Once when lifting sails
> on trains headed for camps
>   unwanted,
> a revealing mystery appeared
>   unwashed
>   unkept
> then disappeared like water
> down a dark drain into depths
>   unseen
> below.

Of course, we might offer a prose interpretation and analyze the use of language and comment on the layers of possible meaning, but such a prose account would not be the same as the poem, which is enhanced and enriched by the symbols it employs.

When we turn to the nature of religious language and ask whether we should take it literally or symbolically, our problems multiply. People often argue about whether religious language ought to be taken literally or symbolically. The literalist might claim that someone who says that "God is up in heaven" means that God is located in a space above the earth, a space called heaven. Others might argue that such words must be understood symbolically. God is infinite, and no infinite being can be "located" anywhere. If it were, it would not be infinite. Then there is that little matter of "above the earth." What direction is "above"? The earth rotates on an axis and revolves around the sun. There is literally no "above" or, for that matter, a "below." All these terms suggest a location *relative to* where we happen to be at any given time. Thus the sentence "God is up in heaven" must have a symbolic meaning. It must mean, the symbolist might argue, something like "God is greater or more powerful than humans or anything else in the universe," and "being in heaven" just means that God is a greater (greatest?) power.

Paul Tillich (1886–1965) was concerned with probing the meaning and nature of religious symbols. He was born and educated in Germany. He taught there until 1933, when Hitler dismissed him and he came to the United States to teach. He became one of the most influential philosophical theologians of his time and championed the view that religious language is primarily symbolic. In a country strongly influenced by a literalistic fundamentalism, his views proved very controversial. In this selection he wants to distinguish between signs and symbols and to analyze the function of symbols, the nature of religious symbols in particular, and the truth of symbols.

Reading Questions

1. How are signs and symbols alike, and how are they different?
2. What is the main function of symbols?
3. Why does Tillich claim symbols are born and die?
4. How do religious symbols function?
5. What is "demonization"?
6. What is the difference between taking God-talk literally and taking it symbolically?
7. What is the truth of religious symbols?
8. Does Tillich's assertion that "Being Itself" is the nonsymbolic element in the symbol God contradict his claim that symbols are necessary because they open up levels of reality that cannot be grasped in any other way?
9. In your view, is symbolic meaning dependent on literal meaning? Why or why not? What do you think Tillich would say?

The Nature of Religious Language*

PAUL TILLICH

THE FACT THAT THERE is so much discussion about the meaning of symbols going on in this country as well as in Europe is a symptom of something deeper, something both negative and positive in its import. It is a symptom of the fact that we are in a confusion of language in theology and philosophy and related subjects which has hardly been surpassed at any time in history. Words do not communicate to us any more what they originally did and what they were invented to communicate. This has something to do with the fact that our present culture has no clearing house such as medieval scholasticism was, Protestant scholasticism in the seventeenth century at least tried to be, and philosophers like Kant tried to renew. We have no such clearing house, and this is the one point at which we might be in sympathy with the present day so-called logical positivists or symbolic logicians or logicians generally. They at least try to produce a clearing house.

The only criticism is that this clearing house is a very small room, perhaps only a corner of a house, and not a real house. It excludes most of life. But it could become useful if it increased in reach and acceptance of realities beyond the mere logical calculus.

The positive point is that we are in a process in which a very important thing is being rediscovered: namely, that there are levels of reality of great difference, and that these different levels demand different approaches and different languages; not everything in reality can be grasped by the language which is most adequate for mathematical sciences. The insight into this situation is the most positive side of the fact that the problem of symbols is again taken seriously.

Let us proceed with the intention of clearing concepts as much as we are able, and let us take five steps, the first of which is the discussion of "symbols and signs." Symbols are similar to signs

*From Paul Tillich "Religious Symbols and Our Knowledge of God," *The Christian Scholar*, XXXVIII (3 September 1955):189–197. Reprinted by permission.

in one decisive respect: both symbols and signs point beyond themselves to something else. The typical sign, for instance the red light at the corner of the street, does not point to itself but it points to the necessity of cars stopping. And every symbol points beyond itself to a reality for which it stands. In this, symbols and signs have an essential identity—they point beyond themselves. And this is the reason that the confusion of language mentioned above has also conquered the discussion about symbols for centuries and has produced confusion between signs and symbols. The first step in any clearing up of the meaning of symbols is to distinguish it from the meaning of signs.

The difference, which is a fundamental difference between them is that signs do not participate in any way in the reality and power of that to which they point. Symbols, although they are not the same as that which they symbolize, participate in its meaning and power. The difference between symbol and sign is the participation in the symbolized reality which characterizes the symbols, and the non-participation in the "pointed-to" reality which characterizes a sign. For example, letters of the alphabet as they are written, an "A" or an "R" do not participate in the sound to which they point; on the other hand, the flag participates in the power of the king or the nation for which it stands and which it symbolizes. There has, therefore, been a fight since the days of William Tell as to how to behave in the presence of the flag. This would be meaningless if the flag did not participate as a symbol in the power of that which it symbolizes. The whole monarchic idea is itself entirely incomprehensible, if you do not understand that the king always is both: on the one hand, a symbol of the power of the group of which he is the king and on the other hand, he who exercises partly (never fully, of course) this power.

But something has happened which is very dangerous for all our attempts to find a clearing house for the concepts of symbols and signs. The mathematician has usurped the term "symbol" for mathematical "sign," and this makes a disentanglement of the confusion almost impossible.

The only thing we can do is to distinguish different groups, signs which are called symbols, and genuine symbols. The mathematical signs are signs which are wrongly called symbols.

Language is a very good example of the difference between signs and symbols. Words in a language are signs for a meaning which they express. The word "desk" is a sign which points to something quite different—namely, the thing on which a paper is lying and at which we might be looking. This has nothing to do with the word "desk," with these four letters. But there are words in every language which are more than this, and in the moment in which they get connotations which go beyond something to which they point as signs, then they can become symbols; and this is a very important distinction for any speaker. He can speak almost completely in signs, reducing the meaning of his words almost to mathematical signs, and this is the absolute ideal of the logical positivist. The other pole of this is liturgical or poetic language where words have a power through centuries, or more than centuries. They have connotations in situations in which they appear so that they cannot be replaced. They have become not only signs pointing to a meaning which is defined, but also symbols standing for a reality in the power of which they participate.

Now we come to a second consideration dealing with the functions of symbols. This first function is implied in what has already been said—namely, the representative function. The symbol represents something which is not itself, for which it stands and in the power and meaning of which it participates. This is a basic function of every symbol, and therefore, if that word had not been used in so many other ways, one could perhaps even translate "symbolic" as "representative," but for some reason that is not possible. If the symbols stand for something which they are not, then the question is, "Why do we not have that for which they stand directly? Why do we need symbols at all?" And now we come to something which is perhaps the main function of the symbol—namely, the opening up of levels of reality which otherwise are hidden and cannot be grasped in any other way.

Every symbol opens up a level of reality for which nonsymbolic speaking is inadequate. Let us interpret this, or explain this, in terms of artistic symbols. The more we try to enter into the meaning of symbols, the more we become aware that it is a function of art to open up levels of reality; in poetry, in visual art, and in music, levels of reality are opened up which can be opened up in no other way. Now if this is the function of art, then certainly artistic creations have symbolic character. You can take that which a landscape of Rubens, for instance, mediates to you. You cannot have this experience in any other way than through this painting made by Rubens. This landscape has some heroic character; it has character of balance, of colors, of weights, of values, and so on. All this is very external. What this mediates to you cannot be expressed in any other way than through the painting itself. The same is true also in the relationship of poetry and philosophy. The temptation may often be to confuse the issue by bringing too many philosophical concepts into a poem. Now this is really the problem; one cannot do this. If one uses philosophical language or scientific language, it does not mediate the same thing which is mediated in the use of really poetic language without a mixture of any other language.

This example may show what is meant by the phrase "opening up of levels of reality." But in order to do this, something else must be opened up—namely, levels of the soul, levels of our interior reality. And they must correspond to the levels in exterior reality which are opened up by a symbol. So every symbol is two-edged. It opens up reality and it opens up the soul. There are, of course, people who are not opened up by music or who are not opened up by poetry, or more of them (especially in Protestant America) who are not opened up at all by visual arts. The "opening up" is a two-sided function—namely, reality in deeper levels and the human soul in special levels.

If this is the function of symbols then it is obvious that symbols cannot be replaced by other symbols. Every symbol has a special function which is just it and cannot be replaced by more or less adequate symbols. This is different from signs, for signs can always be replaced. If one finds that a green light is not so expedient as perhaps a blue light (this is not true, but could be true), then we simply put on a blue light, and nothing is changed. But a symbolic word (such as the word "God") cannot be replaced. No symbol can be replaced when used in its special function. So one asks rightly, "How do symbols arise, and how do they come to an end?" As different from signs, symbols are born and die. Signs are consciously invented and removed. This is a fundamental difference.

"Out of what womb are symbols born?" Out of the womb which is usually called today the "group unconscious" or "collective unconscious," or whatever you want to call it—out of a group which acknowledges, in this thing, this word, this flag, or whatever it may be, its own being. It is not invented intentionally; and even if somebody would try to invent a symbol, as sometimes happens, then it becomes a symbol only if the unconscious of a group says "yes" to it. It means that something is opened up by it in the sense which I have just described. Now this implies further that in the moment in which this inner situation of the human group to a symbol has ceased to exist, then the symbol dies. The symbol does not "say" anything any more. In this way, all of the polytheistic gods have died; the situation in which they were born, has changed or does not exist any more, and so the symbols died. But these are events which cannot be described in terms of intention and invention.

Now we come to a third consideration—namely, the nature of religious symbols. Religious symbols do exactly the same thing as all symbols do—namely, they open up a level of reality, which otherwise is not opened at all, which is hidden. We can call this the depth dimension of reality itself, the dimension of reality which is the ground of every other dimension and every other depth, and which therefore, is not one level beside the others but is the fundamental level, the level below all other levels, the level of being itself, or the ultimate power of being. Religious symbols open up the experience of the dimension of this depth in the human soul. If a religious symbol has ceased to have this function, then it dies. And if new symbols are born, they are born out of a changed relationship to the ultimate ground of being, i.e., to the Holy.

The dimension of ultimate reality is the dimension of the Holy. And so we can also say, religious symbols are symbols of the Holy. As such they participate in the holiness of the Holy according to our basic definition of a symbol. But participation is not identity; they are not themselves *the* Holy. The wholly transcendent transcends every symbol of the Holy. Religious symbols are taken from the infinity of material which the experienced reality gives us. Everything in time and space has become at some time in the history of religion a symbol for the Holy. And this is naturally so, because everything that is in the world we encounter rests on the ultimate ground of being. This is the key to the otherwise extremely confusing history of religion. Those of you who have looked into this seeming chaos of the history of religion in all periods of history from the earliest primitives to the latest developments, will be extremely confused about the chaotic character of this development. The key which makes order out of this chaos is comparatively simple. It is that everything in reality can impress itself as a symbol for a special relationship of the human mind to its own ultimate ground and meaning. So in order to open up the seemingly closed door to this chaos of religious symbols, one simply has to ask, "What is the relationship to the ultimate which is symbolized in these symbols?" And then they cease to be meaningless; and they become, on the contrary, the most revealing creations of the human mind, the most genuine ones, the most powerful ones, those who control the human consciousness, and perhaps even more the unconsciousness, and have therefore this tremendous tenacity which is characteristic of all religious symbols in the history of religion.

Religion, as everything in life, stands under the law of ambiguity, "ambiguity" meaning that it is creative and destructive at the same time. Religion has its holiness and its unholiness, and the reason for this is obvious from what has been said about religious symbolism. Religious symbols point symbolically to that which transcends all of them. But since, as symbols, they participate in that to which they point, they always have the tendency (in the human mind, of course) to replace that to which they are supposed to point, and to become ultimate in themselves. And in the moment in which they do this, they become idols. All idolatry is nothing else than the absolutizing of symbols of the Holy, and making them identical with the Holy itself. In this way, for instance, holy persons can become a god. Ritual acts can take on unconditional validity, although they are only expressions of a special situation. In all sacramental activities of religion, in all holy objects, holy books, holy doctrines, holy rites, you find this danger which we will call "demonization." They become demonic at the moment in which they become elevated to the unconditional and ultimate character of the Holy itself.

Now we turn to a fourth consideration—namely, the levels of religious symbols. There are two fundamental levels in all religious symbols: the transcendent level, the level which goes *beyond* the empirical reality we encounter, and the immanent level, the level which we find *within* the encounter with reality. Let us look at the first level, the transcendent level. The basic symbol on the transcendent level would be God himself. But we cannot simply say that God is a symbol. We must always say two things about him: we must say that there is a non-symbolic element in our image of God—namely, that he is ultimate reality, being itself, ground of being, power of being; and the other, that he is the highest being in which everything that we have does exist in the most perfect way. If we say this we have in our mind the image of a highest being, a being with the characteristics of highest perfection. That means we have a symbol for that which is not symbolic in the idea of God—namely, "Being Itself."

It is important to distinguish these two elements in the idea of God. Thus all of these discussions going on about God being a person or not a person, God being similar to other things or not similar, these discussions which have a great impact on the destruction of the religious experience through false interpretations of it, could be overcome if we would say, "Certainly the awareness of something unconditional is in itself what it is, is not symbolic." We can call it "*Being Itself*," *esse qua esse, esse ipsum,* as the scholastics did. But in our relationship to this ultimate we symbolize and must symbolize. We could not be in communication with God if he were only "ultimate being." But in our relationship to him we encounter him with the highest of what we ourselves are, *person*. And so in the symbolic form of speaking about him, we have both that which transcends infinitely our experience of ourselves as persons, and that which is so adequate to our being persons that we can say, "Thou" to God, and can pray to him. And these two elements must be preserved. If we preserve only the element of the unconditional, then no relationship to God is possible. If we preserve only the element of the ego-thou relationship, as it is called today, we lose the element of the divine—namely, the unconditional which transcends subject and object and all other polarities. This is the first point on the transcendent level.

The second is the qualities, the attributes of God, whatever you say about him: that he is love, that he is mercy, that he is power, that he is omniscient, that he is omnipresent, that he is almighty. These attributes of God are taken from experienced qualities we have ourselves. They cannot be applied to God in the literal sense. If this is done, it leads to an infinite amount of absurdities. This again is one of the reasons for the destruction of religion through wrong communicative interpretation of it. And again the symbolic character of these qualities must be maintained consistently. Otherwise, every speaking about the divine becomes absurd.

A third element on the transcendent level is the acts of God, for example, when we say, "He has created the world," "He has sent his son," "He will fulfill the world." In all these temporal, causal, and other expressions we speak symbolically of God. As an example, look at the one small sentence: "*God*

has sent his son." Here we have in the word "has" temporality. But God is beyond *our* temporality, though not beyond every temporality. Here is space; "sending somebody" means moving him from one place to another place. This certainly is speaking symbolically, although spatiality is in God as an element in his creative ground. We say that he "has sent"—that means that he has caused something. In this way God is subject to the category of causality. And when we speak of him and his Son, we have two different substances and apply the category of substance to him. Now all this, if taken literally, is absurd. If it is taken symbolically, it is a profound expression, the ultimate Christian expression, of the relationship between God and man in the Christian experience. But to distinguish these two kinds of speech, the non-symbolic and the symbolic, in such a point is so important that if we are not able to make understandable to our contemporaries that we speak symbolically when we use such language, they will rightly turn away from us, as from people who still live in absurdities and superstitions.

Now consider the immanent level, the level of the appearances of the divine in time and space. Here we have first of all the incarnations of the divine, different beings in time and space, divine beings transmuted into animals or men or any kinds of other beings as they appear in time and space. This is often forgotten by those within Christianity who like to use in every second theological proposition the word "incarnation." They forget that this is not an especially Christian characteristic, because incarnation is something which happens in paganism all the time. The divine beings always incarnate in different forms. That is very easy in paganism. This is not the real distinction between Christianity and other religions.

Here we must say something about the relationships of the transcendent to the immanent level just in connection with the incarnation idea. Historically, one must say that preceding both of them was the situation in which the transcendent and immanent were not distinguished. In the Indonesian doctrine of "Mana," that divine mystical power which permeates all reality, we have some divine presence which is both immanent in everything as a hidden power, and at the same time transcendent, something which can be grasped only through very difficult ritual activities known to the priest.

Out of this identity of the immanent and the transcendent, the gods of the great mythologies have developed in Greece and in the Semitic nations and in India. There we find incarnations as the immanent element of the divine. The more transcendent the gods become, the more incarnations of personal or sacramental character are needed in order to overcome the remoteness of the divine which develops with the strengthening of the transcendent element.

And from this follows the second element in the immanent religious symbolism, namely, the sacramental. The sacramental is nothing else than some reality becoming the bearer of the Holy in a special way and under special circumstances. In this sense, the Lord's Supper, or better the materials in the Lord's Supper, are symbolic. Now you will ask perhaps, "only symbolic?" That sounds as if there were something more than symbolic, namely, "literal." But the literal is not more but less than symbolic. If we speak of those dimensions of reality which we cannot approach in any other way than by symbols, then symbols are not used in terms of "only" but in terms of that which is necessary, of that which we *must* apply. Sometimes, because of nothing more than the confusion of signs with symbols, the phrase "only a symbol" means "only a sign." And then the question is justified. "Only a sign?" "No." The sacrament is not only a sign. In the famous discussion between Luther and Zwingli, in Marburg in 1529, it was just this point on which the discussion was held. Luther wanted to maintain the genuinely symbolic character of the elements, but Zwingli said that the sacramental materials, bread and wine, are "only symbolic." Thus Zwingli meant that they are only signs pointing to a story of the past. Even in that period there was semantic confusion. And let us not be misled by this. In the real sense of symbol, the sacramental materials are symbols. But if the symbol is used as *only* symbol (i.e., only signs), then of course the sacramental materials are more than this.

Then there is the third element on the immanent level. Many things—like special parts of the church building, like the candles, like the water at the entrance of the Roman Church, like the cross in all churches, especially Protestant churches—were originally only signs, but in use became symbols; call them sign-symbols, signs which have become symbols.

And now a last consideration—namely, the truth of religious symbols. Here we must distinguish a negative, a positive, and an absolute statement. First the negative statement. Symbols are independent of any empirical criticism. You cannot kill a symbol by criticism in terms of natural sciences or in terms of historical research. As was said, symbols can only die if the situation in which they have been created has passed. They are not on a level on which empirical criticism can dismiss them. Here are two examples, both connected with Mary, the mother of Jesus, as Holy Virgin. First of all you have here a symbol which has died in Protestantism by the changed situation of the relation to God. The special, direct, immediate relationship to God, makes any mediating power impossible. Another reason which has made this symbol disappear is the negation of the ascetic element which is implied in the glorification of virginity. And as long as the Protestant religious situation lasts it cannot be reestablished. It has not died because Protestant scholars have said, "Now there is no empirical reason for saying all this about the Holy Virgin." There certainly is not, but this the Roman Church also knows. But the Roman Church sticks to it on the basis of its tremendous symbolic power which step by step brings her nearer to Trinity itself, especially in the development of the last decade. If this should ever be completed as is now discussed in groups of the Roman Church, Mary would become co-Saviour with Jesus. Then, whether this is admitted or not, she is actually taken into the divinity itself.

Another example is the story of the virginal birth of Jesus. This is from the point of view of historical research a most obviously legendary story, unknown to Paul and to John. It is a late creation, trying to make understandable the full possession of the divine Spirit of Jesus of Nazareth. But again its legendary character is not the reason why this symbol will die or has died in many groups of people, in even quite conservative groups within the Protestant churches. The reason is different. The reason is that it is theologically quasiheretical. It takes away one of the fundamental doctrines of Chalcedon, viz., the classical Christian doctrine that the full humanity of Jesus must be maintained beside his whole divinity. A human being who has no human father has no full humanity. This story then has to be criticized on inner-symbolic grounds, but not on historical grounds. This is the negative statement about the truth of religious symbols. Their truth is their adequacy to the religious situation in which they are created, and their inadequacy to another situation is their untruth. In the last sentence both the positive and the negative statement about symbols are contained.

Religion is ambiguous and every religious symbol may become idolatrous, may be demonized, may elevate itself to ultimate validity although nothing is ultimate but the ultimate itself; no religious doctrine and no religious ritual may be. If Christianity claims to have a truth superior to any other truth in its symbolism, then it is the symbol of the cross in which this is expressed, the cross of the Christ. He who himself embodies the fullness of the divine's presence sacrifices himself in order not to become an idol, another god beside God, a god into whom the disciples wanted to make him. And therefore the decisive story is the story in which he accepts the title "Christ" when Peter offers it to him. He accepts it under the one condition that he has to go to Jerusalem to suffer and to die, which means to deny the idolatrous tendency even with respect to himself. This is at the same time the criterion of all other symbols, and it is the criterion to which every Christian church should subject itself.

8.2 Does God-Talk Make Sense?

Language can do many things. I can use it to order someone to shut the door or to express how I feel about the outcome of a baseball game. I can question you, tease you, or crack a joke. Language can even create new states of affairs, as when a minister pronounces a couple married.

Language can also assert specific states of affairs to be the case, as in "My dog Arthur is thin." Statements that assert that some state of affairs is the case also deny that some state of affairs is the case. To assert that my dog Arthur is thin is also to deny that he is fat. This means that, in principle, every assertion is falsifiable (capable of being falsified) because if what it asserts (Arthur is thin) should turn out not to be the real state of things (Arthur is fat), then the assertion "My dog Arthur is thin" is false.

Some philosophers have argued that falsifiability is an essential characteristic of assertions. If it is, then any sentence that is unfalsifiable (not capable of being falsified) is not an assertion even if it looks or sounds like one grammatically. Please note that these philosophers are not claiming that every assertion is false. That would be absurd. Their claim is that for any sentence to be an assertion, it must, *in principle,* be capable of being falsified. We must know just what state of affairs *would* count against its truth, even if they do not obtain. If we can imagine no such state of affairs, then the sentence in question is not an assertion. It might be an order, or a joke, or an expression of emotion, but, whatever it is, it asserts nothing. Hence it is neither true nor false.

So what does falsifiability have to do with talk about God? When we say, "God forgives us our sins," are we asserting something to be true? If we are, then we need to be concerned not only about what evidence might count for it, but also about what evidence might count against it. Is there any evidence that would? If we cannot imagine any state of affairs that might count against it, then it asserts nothing, even though, on the surface, it seems to.

In the next selection, Antony Flew, R. M. Hare, and Basil Mitchell, three contemporary British philosophers, talk about God-talk. Interestingly, they all use allegorical tales or parables to try to illustrate their ideas about the meaning and function of religious language.

Reading Questions

1. What is the point of the story about the gardener?
2. What does Flew mean by "death by a thousand qualifications"?
3. Summarize Flew's argument in your own words. How would you respond to the question with which he concludes?
4. What is the point of the story about the lunatic and the dons?
5. What does Hare mean by a *blik*?
6. What mistake does Hare think Flew has made?
7. What is Mitchell's response to Flew's argument?
8. How does Flew respond to Mitchell and Hare, and why does he apply the notion of "doublethink" to theology?
9. As far as you are concerned, who won this debate—Flew, Hare, or Mitchell? Why?

Does God-Talk Make Sense?*

ANTONY FLEW, R. M. HARE, AND BASIL MITCHELL

A: Antony Flew

Let us begin with a parable. It is a parable developed from a tale told by John Wisdom in his haunting and revelatory article "Gods." Once upon a time two explorers came upon a clearing in the jungle. In the clearing were growing many flowers and many weeds. One explorer says, "Some gardener must tend this plot." The other disagrees, "There is no gardener." So they pitch their tents and set a watch. No gardener is ever

seen. "But perhaps he is an invisible gardener." So they set up a barbed-wire fence. They electrify it. They patrol with bloodhounds. (For they remember how H.G. Wells's *The Invisible Man* could be both smelt and touched though he could not be seen.) But no shrieks ever suggest that some intruder has received a shock. No movements of the wire ever betray an invisible climber. The bloodhounds never give cry. Yet still the Believer is not convinced. "But there is a gardener, invisible, intangible, insensible to electric shocks, a gardener

*Reprinted with the permission of Simon & Schuster from *New Essays in Philosophical Theology*, ed. Antony Flew and Alasdair Macintyre. Copyright © 1955 by Antony Flew and Alasdair Macintyre, renewed 1983, pp. 96–108. Foonotes deleted.

who has no scent and makes no sound, a gardener who comes secretly to look after the garden which he loves." At last the Sceptic despairs, "But what remains of your original assertion? Just how does what you call an invisible, intangible, eternally elusive gardener differ from an imaginary gardener or even from no gardener at all?'

In this parable we can see how what starts as an assertion, that something exists or that there is some analogy between certain complexes of phenomena, may be reduced step by step to an altogether different status, to an expression perhaps of a "picture preference." The Sceptic says there is no gardener. The Believer says there is a gardener (but invisible, etc.). One man talks about sexual behaviour. Another man prefers to talk of Aphrodite (but knows that there is not really a superhuman person additional to, and somehow responsible for, all sexual phenomena). The process of qualification may be checked at any point before the original assertion is completely withdrawn and something of that first assertion will remain (Tautology). Mr. Wells's invisible man could not, admittedly, be seen, but in all other respects he was a man like the rest of us. But though the process of qualification may be, and of course usually is, checked in time, it is not always judiciously so halted. Someone may dissipate his assertion completely without noticing that he has done so. A fine brash hypothesis may thus be killed by inches, the death by a thousand qualifications.

And in this, it seems to me, lies the peculiar danger, the endemic evil, of theological utterance. Take such utterances as "God has a plan," "God created the world," "God loves us as a father loves his children." They look at first sight very much like assertions, vast cosmological assertions. Of course, this is no sure sign that they either are, or are intended to be, assertions. But let us confine ourselves to the cases where those who utter such sentences intend them to express assertions. (Merely remarking parenthetically that those who intend or interpret such utterances as crypto-commands, expressions of wishes, disguised ejaculations, concealed ethics, or as anything else but assertions, are unlikely to succeed in making them either properly orthodox or practically effective.)

Now to assert that such and such is the case is necessarily equivalent to denying that such and such is not the case. Suppose then that we are in doubt as to what someone who gives vent to an utterance is asserting, or suppose that, more radically, we are sceptical as to whether he is really asserting anything at all, one way of trying to understand (or perhaps it will be to expose) his utterance is to attempt to find what he would regard as counting against, or as being incompatible with, its truth. For if the utterance is indeed an assertion, it will necessarily be equivalent to a denial of the negation of that assertion. And anything which would count against the assertion, or which would induce the speaker to withdraw it and to admit that it had been mistaken, must be part of (or the whole of) the meaning of the negation of that assertion. And to know the meaning of the negation of an assertion, is as near as makes no matter, to know the meaning of that assertion. And if there is nothing which a putative assertion denies then there is nothing which it asserts either: and so it is not really an assertion. When the Sceptic in the parable asked the Believer, "Just how does what you call an invisible, intangible, eternally elusive gardener differ from an imaginary gardener or even from no gardener at all?" he was suggesting that the Believer's earlier statement had been so eroded by qualification that it was no longer an assertion at all.

Now it often seems to people who are not religious as if there was no conceivable event or series of events the occurrence of which would be admitted by sophisticated religious people to be a sufficient reason for conceding "There wasn't a God after all" or "God does not really love us then." Someone tells us that God loves us as a father loves his children. We are reassured. But then we see a child dying of inoperable cancer of the throat. His earthly father is driven frantic in his efforts to help, but his Heavenly Father reveals no obvious sign of concern. Some qualification is made—God's love is "not a merely human love" or it is "an inscrutable love," perhaps—and we realize that such sufferings are quite compatible with the truth of the assertion that "God loves us as a father (but, of course, ...)." We are reassured again. But then perhaps we ask: what is this assurance of God's (appropriately qualified) love worth, what is this apparent guarantee really a guarantee against? Just what would have to happen not merely (morally and wrongly) to tempt but also (logically and rightly) to entitle us to say "God does not love us" or even "God does not exist"? I therefore put to the succeeding symposiasts the simple central questions, "What would have to occur or to have occurred to constitute for you a disproof of the love of, or of the existence of, God?"

B: R. M. Hare

I wish to make it clear that I shall not try to defend Christianity in particular, but religion in general—not because I do not believe in Christianity, but because you cannot understand what Christianity is, until you have understood what religion is.

I must begin by confessing that, on the ground marked out by Flew, he seems to me to be completely victorious. I therefore shift my ground by relating another parable. A certain lunatic is convinced that all dons want to murder him. His friends introduce him to all the mildest and most respectable dons that they can find, and after each of them has retired, they say, "You see, he doesn't really want to murder you; he spoke to you in a most cordial manner; surely you are convinced now?" But the lunatic replies "Yes, but that was only his diabolical cunning; he's really plotting against me the whole time, like the rest of them; I know it I tell you." However many kindly dons are produced, the reaction is still the same.

Now we say that such a person is deluded. But what is he deluded about? About the truth or falsity of an assertion? Let us apply Flew's test to him. There is no behaviour of dons that can be enacted which he will accept as counting against his theory; and therefore his theory, on this test, asserts nothing. But it does not follow that there is no difference between what he thinks about dons and what most of us think about them—otherwise we should not call him a lunatic and ourselves sane, and dons would have no reason to feel uneasy about his presence in Oxford.

Let us call that in which we differ from this lunatic, our respective *bliks*. He has an insane *blik* about dons; we have a sane one. It is important to realize that we have a sane one, not no *blik* at all; for there must be two sides to any argument—if he has a wrong *blik*, then those who are right about dons must have a right one. Flew has shown that a *blik* does not consist in an assertion or system of them; but nevertheless it is very important to have the right *blik*.

Let us try to imagine what it would be like to have different *bliks* about other things than dons. When I am driving my car, it sometimes occurs to me to wonder whether my movements of the steering-wheel will always continue to be followed by corresponding alterations in the direction of the car. I have never had a steering failure, though I have had skids, which must be similar. Moreover, I know enough about how the steering of my car is made, to know the sort of thing that would have to go wrong for the steering to fail—steel joints would have to part, or steel rods break, or something—but how do I know that this won't happen? The truth is, I don't know; I just have a *blik* about steel and its properties, so that normally I trust the steering of my car; but I find it not at all difficult to imagine what it would be like to lose this *blik* and acquire the opposite one. People would say I was silly about steel; but there would be no mistaking the reality of the difference between our respective *bliks*—for example, I should never go in a motor-car. Yet I should hesitate to say that the difference between us was the difference between contradictory assertions. No amount of safe arrivals or bench-tests will remove my *blik* and restore the normal one; for my *blik* is compatible with any finite number of such tests. It was Hume who taught us that our whole commerce with the world depends upon our *blik* about the world; and that differences between *bliks* about the world cannot be settled by observation of what happens in the world. That was why, having performed the interesting experiment of doubting the ordinary man's *blik* about the world, and showing that no proof could be given to make us adopt one *blik* rather than another, he turned to backgammon to take his mind off the problem. It seems, indeed, to be impossible even to formulate as an assertion the normal *blik* about the world which makes me put my confidence in the future reliability of steel joints, in the continued ability of the road to support my car, and not gape beneath it revealing nothing below; in the general non-homicidal tendencies of dons; in my own continued well-being (in some sense of that word that I may not now fully understand) if I continue to do what is right according to my lights; in the general likelihood of people like Hitler coming to a bad end. But perhaps a formulation less inadequate than most is to be found in the Psalms: "The earth is weak and all the inhabiters thereof: I bear up the pillars of it."

The mistake of the position which Flew selects for attack is to regard this kind of talk as some sort of *explanation,* as scientists are accustomed to use the word. As such, it would obviously be ludicrous. We no longer believe in God as an Atlas—*nous n'avons pas besoin de cette hypothèse.* But it is nevertheless true to say that, as Hume saw, without a *blik* there can be no explanation; for it is by our *bliks* that we decide what is and what is not an explanation. Suppose we believed that everything that happened, happened by pure chance. This would not of course be an assertion; for it is compatible with anything happening or not happening, and so, incidentally, is its contradictory. But if we had this belief, we should not be able to explain or predict or plan anything. Thus, although we should not be *asserting* anything different from those of a more normal belief, there would be a great difference between us; and this is the sort of difference that there is between those who really believe in God and those who really disbelieve in him.

The word "really" is important and may excite suspicion. I put it in, because when people have had a good Christian upbringing, as have most of those who now profess not to believe in any sort of religion, it is very hard to discover what they really believe. The reason why they find it so easy to think that they are not religious, is that they have never got into the frame of mind of one who suffers from the doubts to which religion is the answer. Not for them the terrors of the primitive jungle. Having abandoned some of the more picturesque fringes of religion, they think that they have abandoned the whole thing—whereas in fact they still have got, and could not live without, a religion of a comfortably substantial, albeit highly sophisticated, kind, which differs from that of many "religious people" in little more than this, that "religious people" like to sing Psalms about theirs—a very natural and proper thing to do. But nevertheless there may be a big difference lying behind—the difference between two people who, though side by side, are walking in different directions. I do not know in what direction Flew is walking; perhaps he does not know either. But we have had some examples recently of various ways in which one can walk away from Christianity, and there are any number of possibilities. After all, man has not changed biologically since primitive times; it is his religion that has changed, and it can easily change again. And if you do not think that such changes make a difference, get acquainted with some Sikhs and some Mussulmans of the same Punjabi stock; you will find them quite different sorts of people.

There is an important difference between Flew's parable and my own which we have not yet noticed. The explorers do not *mind* about their garden; they discuss it with interest, but not with concern. But my lunatic, poor fellow, minds about dons; and I mind about the steering of my car; it often has people in it that I care for. It is because I mind very much about what goes on in the garden in which I find myself, that I am unable to share the explorers' detachment.

C: Basil Mitchell

Flew's article is searching and perceptive, but there is, I think, something odd about his conduct of the theologian's case. The theologian surely would not deny that the fact of pain counts against the assertion that God loves men. This very incompatibility generates the most intractable of theological problems—the problem of evil. So the theologian *does* recognize the fact of pain as counting against Christian doctrine. But it is true that he will not allow it—or anything—to count decisively against it; for he is committed by his faith to trust in God. His attitude is not that of the detached observer, but of the believer.

Perhaps this can be brought out by yet another parable. In time of war in an occupied country, a member of the resistance meets one night a stranger who deeply impresses him. They spend that night together in conversation. The Stranger tells the partisan that he himself is on the side of the resistance—indeed that he is in command of it—and urges the partisan to have faith in him no matter what happens. The partisan is utterly convinced at that meeting of the Stranger's sincerity and constancy and undertakes to trust him.

They never meet in conditions of intimacy again. But sometimes the Stranger is seen helping members of the resistance, and the partisan is grateful and says to his friends, "He is on our side."

Sometimes he is seen in the uniform of the police handing over patriots to the occupying power. On these occasions his friends murmur against him, but the partisan still says, "He is on our side." He still believes that, in spite of appearances, the Stranger did not deceive him. Sometimes he asks the Stranger for help and receives it. He is then thankful. Sometimes he asks and does not receive it. Then he says, "The Stranger knows best." Sometimes his friends, in exasperation, say "Well, what *would* he have to do for you to admit that you were wrong and that he is not on our side?" But the partisan refuses to answer. He will not consent to put the Stranger to the test. And sometimes his friends complain, "Well, if *that's* what you mean by his being on our side, the sooner he goes over to the other side the better."

The partisan of the parable does not allow anything to count decisively against the proposition "The Stranger is on our side." This is because he has committed himself to trust the Stranger. But he of course recognizes that the Stranger's ambiguous behaviour *does* count against what he believes about him. It is precisely this situation which constitutes the trial of his faith.

When the partisan asks for help and doesn't get it, what can he do? He can (*a*) conclude that the stranger is not on our side or (*b*) maintain that he is on our side, but that he has reasons for withholding help.

The first he will refuse to do. How long can he uphold the second position without its becoming just silly?

I don't think one can say in advance. It will depend on the nature of the impression created by the Stranger in the first place. It will depend, too, on the manner in which he takes the Stranger's behaviour. If he blandly dismisses it as of no consequence, as having no bearing upon his belief, it will be assumed that he is thoughtless or insane. And it quite obviously won't do for him to say easily, "Oh, when used of the Stranger the phrase 'is on our side' *means* ambiguous behaviour of this sort." In that case he would be like the religious man who says blandly of a terrible disaster "It is God's will." No, he will only be regarded as sane and reasonable in his belief, if he experiences in himself the full force of the conflict.

It is here that my parable differs from Hare's. The partisan admits that many things may and do count against his belief, whereas Hare's lunatic who has a *blik* about dons doesn't admit that anything counts against his *blik*. Nothing *can* count against *bliks*. Also the partisan has a reason for having in the first instance committed himself, viz. the character of the Stranger; whereas the lunatic has no reason for his *blik* about dons—because, of course, you can't have reasons for *bliks*. This means that I agree with Flew that theological utterances must be assertions. The partisan is making an assertion when he says, "The Stranger is on our side."

Do I want to say that the partisan's belief about the Stranger is, in any sense, an explanation? I think I do. It explains and makes sense of the Stranger's behaviour: it helps to explain also the resistance movement in the context of which he appears. In each case it differs from the interpretation that the others put upon the same facts. "God loves men" resembles "the Stranger is on our side" (and many other significant statements, e.g. historical ones) in not being conclusively falsifiable. They can both be treated in at least three different ways: (1) As provisional hypotheses to be discarded if experience tells against them; (2) As significant articles of faith; (3) As vacuous formulae (expressing, perhaps, a desire for reassurance) to which experience makes no difference and which makes no difference to life.

The Christian, once he has committed himself, is precluded by his faith from taking up the first attitude: "Thou shalt not tempt the Lord thy God." He is in constant danger, as Flew has observed, of slipping into the third. But he need not; and, if he does, it is a failure in faith as well as in logic.

D: Antony Flew

It has been a good discussion: and I am glad to have helped to provoke it. But now—at least in *University*—it must come to an end: and the Editors of *University* have asked me to make some concluding remarks. Since it is impossible to deal with all the issues raised or to comment separately upon each contribution, I will concentrate on Mitchell and Hare, as representative of two very different kinds of response to the challenge made in "Theology and Falsification."

The challenge, it will be remembered, ran like this. Some theological utterances seem to, and are intended to, provide explanations or express assertions. Now an assertion, to be an assertion at all, must claim that things stand thus and thus; *and not otherwise.* Similarly an explanation, to be an explanation at all, must explain why this particular thing occurs; *and not something else.* Those last clauses are crucial. And yet sophisticated religious people—or so it seemed to me—are apt to overlook this, and tend to refuse to allow, not merely that anything actually does occur, but that anything conceivably could occur, which would count against their theological assertions and explanations. But in so far as they do this their supposed explanations are actually bogus, and their seeming assertions are really vacuous.

Mitchell's response to this challenge is admirably direct, straightforward, and understanding. He agrees "that theological utterances must be assertions." He agrees that if they are to be assertions, there must be something that would count against their truth. He agrees, too, that believers are in constant danger of transforming their would-be assertions into "vacuous formulae." But he takes me to task for an oddity in my "conduct of the theologian's case. The theologian surely would not deny that the fact of pain counts against the assertion that God loves men. This very incompatibility generates the most intractable of theological problems, the problem of evil." I think he is right. I should have made a distinction between two very different ways of dealing with what looks like evidence against the love of God: the way I stressed was the expedient of qualifying the original assertion; the way the theologian usually takes, at first, is to admit that it looks bad but to insist that there is—there must be—some explanation which will show that, in spite of appearances, there really is a God who loves us. His difficulty, it seems to me, is that he has given God attributes which rule out all possible saving explanations. In Mitchell's parable of the Stranger it is easy for the believer to find plausible excuses for ambiguous behaviour: for the Stranger is a man. But suppose the Stranger is God. We cannot say that he would like to help but cannot: God is omnipotent. We cannot say that he would help if he only knew: God is omniscient. We cannot say that he is not responsible for the wickedness of others: God creates those others. Indeed an omnipotent, omniscient God must be an accessory before (and during) the fact to every human misdeed, as well as being responsible for every non-moral defect in the universe. So, though I entirely concede that Mitchell was absolutely right to insist against me that the theologian's first move is to look for an *explanation,* I still think that in the end, if relentlessly pursued, he will have to resort to the avoiding action of *qualification.* And there lies the danger of that death by a thousand qualifications, which would, I agree, constitute "a failure in faith as well as in logic."

Hare's approach is fresh and bold. He confesses that "on the ground marked out by Flew, he seems to me to be completely victorious." He therefore introduces the concept of *blik.* But while I think that there is room for some such concept in philosophy, and that philosophers should be grateful to Hare for his invention, I nevertheless want to insist that any attempt to analyze Christian religious utterances as expressions or affirmations of a *blik* rather than as (at least would-be) assertions about the cosmos is fundamentally misguided. *First,* because thus interpreted they would be entirely unorthodox. If Hare's religion really is a *blik,* involving no cosmological assertions about the nature and activities of a supposed personal creator, then surely he is not a Christian at all? *Second,* because thus interpreted, they could scarcely do the job they do. If they were not even intended as assertions then many religious activities would become fraudulent, or merely silly. If "You ought *because* it is God's will" asserts no more than "You ought," then the person who prefers the former phraseology is not really giving a reason, but a fraudulent substitute for one, a dialectical dud cheque. If "My soul must be immortal *because* God loves his children, etc." asserts no more than "My soul must be immortal," then the man who reassures himself with theological arguments for immortality is being as silly as the man who tries to clear his overdraft by writing his

bank a cheque on the same account. (Of course neither of these utterances would be distinctively Christian: but this discussion never pretended to be so confined.) Religious utterances may indeed express false or even bogus assertions: but I simply do not believe that they are not both intended and interpreted to be or at any rate to presuppose assertions, at least in the context of religious practice; whatever shifts may be demanded, in another context, by the exigencies of theological apologetic.

One final suggestion. The philosophers of religion might well draw upon George Orwell's last appalling nightmare *1984* for the concept of *doublethink.* "*Doublethink* means the power of holding two contradictory beliefs simultaneously, and accepting both of them. The party intellectual knows that he is playing tricks with reality, but by the exercise of *doublethink* he also satisfies himself that reality is not violated" (*1984,* p. 220). Perhaps religious intellectuals too are sometimes driven to doublethink in order to retain their faith in a loving God in face of the reality of a heartless and indifferent world. But of this more another time, perhaps.

8.3 The Origins of the Question

Much Western philosophical reflection on the problem of religious language centers on the problem of God-talk. How can we speak meaningfully about God? This is because the theistic model has permeated religion so deeply in the West that many philosophers simply assume that the problem of religious language eventually boils down to the problem of speaking meaningfully about God. However, there is a lot more to religious language than God-talk.

Western philosophers, under the influence of the logical positivists and the later Wittgenstein (see the Introduction to Chapter 8) have not only assumed that the meaningfulness of God-talk is the central problem but also that there are many different and distinct ways of talking, such as science, poetry, fiction, philosophy, and religion. Not only must religious ways of speaking be analyzed, but also we must learn how they are different from and similar to the other ways in which we speak. Religion, in short, is just one way of talking. This seems so obvious to us in the secularized Western culture in which we live that we must stop to think that the ways in which we divide up language (and for that matter our world) are human constructions. Things can be classified (if classified they must be) in a variety of different ways. Perhaps, in some sense, all of language is religious?

Thomas P. Kasulis, professor of comparative philosophy at Northland College in Wisconsin, is the author of the next selection. He focuses on four different theories of language found in Japanese philosophy and argues that the Western discussion of the problem of religious language can benefit from the insights these theories offer.

Reading Questions

1. What is the assumption behind most contemporary Western approaches to the problem of religious language?
2. What is Kūkai's theory of language?
3. According to Shinran, how should one read sacred texts, and how does his view differ from literalism as it is normally understood?
4. How does Dōgen restrict the idea of a distinctively religious language?
5. What does Motoori Norinaga mean by *kokoro*?
6. What conclusions does Kasulis draw from his study of traditional Japanese theories of language?
7. Do you agree with the author's concluding remark that philosophy must reexamine itself before it can understand religious discourse? Why or why not?

The Origins of the Question*

THOMAS P. KASULIS

WHAT IS THE NATURE of religious language? Of the various types of language use, speech acts, or language games, which best apply to the way we use language in religious contexts? These are some of the primary questions in the philosophy of religion as practiced in the West today. There is no consensus on how these questions should be answered, but the questions still tend to frame the arena within which the discussions and disagreements occur.

The early positivists like A. J. Ayer, for example, applied these questions to religious discourse in a way that influenced much of the Anglo-American philosophy of religion to follow. Using an impoverished understanding of the kinds of discourse, Ayer assumed that religious language had to be one of two kinds. Either it asserted empirically verifiable propositions or it merely expressed emotions without making any claim to truth. In short, religious language either represented bad science (which is to say, superstition) or it was no more than a series of propositionally meaningless "oohs!" and "ahs!"

Subsequent philosophers tried to save religious discourse from this oversimplified critique. There were a variety of approaches. Some looked harder at the idea of verifiability, noting that certain religious claims were indeed empirically verifiable although only after death or at the Last Days, for example. This is admittedly an odd set of conditions for verifiability, but in theory no different from meaningful scientific claims whose truth cannot yet be determined because of the lack of sophisticated enough equipment or the proper set of conditions.

*From "The Origins of the Question: Four Traditional Japanese Philosophies of Language" by Thomas P. Kasulis. In *Culture and Modernity: East-West Philosophic Perspectives,* edited by Eliot Deutsch. Copyright © 1991 by University of Hawaii Press. Reprinted by permission. Footnotes edited.

Other defenders of religious discourse examined more closely the notion of assertion. Our analytic epistemological categories were enriched by comparing the assertions characteristic of belief, knowledge, and faith. Still others rethought the problem of reference. Perhaps religious assertions were not about external states of affairs, but rather about internal, personal dispositions to act or behave in certain ways. According to this view, verifiability lies in correlating religious statements with religious behavior. Related to this line of thinking, some philosophers of religion used J. L. Austin's theories to pursue the performative dimensions of religious language: religious sentences often do something as well as say something.

Our point is to note that even with all this variety, and it is merely a small sampling of the diverse analyses of religious language, basically the same questions are being asked. Of the kinds of discourse, which do we use in making religious statements? Of the kinds of knowledge, which do we find in religious contexts? As we shall now see, the twentieth-century European continental approaches have not been significantly different in this regard.

Probably the most significant movement in continental thought to influence the philosophy of religion in this century has been the philosophy and theology of symbols. The semiotic philosophers denied special status to scientific forms of knowing. For Neo-Kantians like Ernst Cassirer and theologians like Paul Tillich, science was only a single, non-privileged instance of human knowing based on the manipulation of symbolic structures. Following the thrust of Cassirer's work, Susanne Langer called for a reevaluation of such human phenomena as art and ritual, finding epistemic implications in what the positivists had excluded from philosophical consideration.[1]

We note, however, that even in the case of the philosophies of symbols the enterprise has been, as it was for the analytic philosophers, to locate religious language, or religious claims to knowledge, within the larger categories of language or knowledge itself. We continue to ask: what is the nature of religious language? what kinds of language use are found within religious discourse?

where does religious discourse fit under the broader theories of language and knowledge?

We do not take the time to reexamine the questions themselves, however. Where do the questions come from? What do they assume? For example, our contemporary Western line of inquiry seems to assume that some forms of language are religious and some are not. In other words, we assume that language itself is not religious, but only some kinds of language are religious. On the surface that assumption is innocent enough. It seems an obvious truth. But is it really so?

The historian of Western philosophy might point out that for Thomas Aquinas, for example, this "truth" was not so obvious. In fact, he explicitly denied it. For him all words ultimately came from the "inner word" or "word of the heart," the point of contact between the individual and the divine. This suggests that *all* language is sacred, not that religious language is only one category of linguistic expression alongside others.

If we look comparatively at the history of religions, we find the assumption that language in itself is sacred to be more the norm than the exception. The *Rg Veda* upholds speech *(vāc)* as the supreme principle or deity of sustenance (see, for example, X.125.4). The *Tao Te Ching* says it is the *named* which is the mother of the variegated universe of things. In Genesis, God says "let there be . . ." when creating things, even though there is no one to hear the words other than the divine ear itself. The Gospel of John says that the Word is in the creation of all things. Of course, we might discount all this as the reflection of an archaic and now antiquated world view. But that is precisely the point. The modern Western assumption that language is not intrinsically spiritual is just that—a modern Western assumption.

It would seem that in at least our historical and cultural context, we should be able to ignore the issue of the origin of language and simply take the presence of language as our starting point. Or can we? Wilbur Marshall Urban makes the following observation:

> It is often maintained that origins do not affect validity, but notoriously they do and nowhere more clearly than in this sphere of language. It

is, as we have seen, almost universally assumed that what speech was originally made for determines in some significant way what it is capable of doing now. . . . In any case, . . . historical origins may not affect values, but metaphysical concepts of ultimate origin certainly do.

So our question now becomes: what difference does it make to a philosophy of religious language whether we assume that the origin of language is itself spiritual? This brings us to our comparative enterprise. Let us now briefly examine four traditional Japanese philosophies of religious language, showing how they related the question of spiritual origins to the secondary question of distinguishing religious from nonreligious functions of ordinary language. We may then conclude with observations about what this comparative analysis can teach us about our current situation in the Western philosophy of religion.

Let us begin with the metaphysics of language developed by Kūkai (744–835), Japan's first major philosophical thinker and the founder of Japanese Shingon Buddhism. At the heart of Kūkai's philosophy was his theory about the nature of words. From the Shingon standpoint, each thing in the universe is a "symbolic expression" *(monji)* of the *dharmakāya buddha*. The universe as a whole is the "symbolic embodiment" *(samayashin)* of the *dharmakāya* as the specific Buddha Dainichi Nyorai (Sanskrit: *Mahāvairocana*). Contrary to the exoteric schools, which understand the *dharmakāya* to be the *abstract* identity between the Buddha and reality. Shingon maintains that the identity is *concrete* and *personal*. It is helpful to think about this relation on three levels: the cosmic, the microcosmic, and the macrocosmic: that is, the supersensible, the subsensible, and the sensible planes of reality.

On the cosmic level, the universe is just Dainichi Nyorai's act or function *(yū)*. Dainichi is in an enlightened state, mentally envisioning reality (the *maṇḍala*), verbally intoning the sacred sounds *(mantra)*, and physically enacting the sacred gestures *(mudrā)*. The universe is, therefore, the natural expression of Dainichi's self-enjoyment *(jijuyā sammai)*. The *dharmakāya* is just being itself and in its so doing, the universe is as

it is. What we know as the cosmos is actually Dainichi's mental, verbal, and bodily activity, the three intimacies *(sanmitsu)*. On this cosmic level, the goal of the Shingon Buddhist is to recognize the universe as the stylized expression, the intimation, of these three intimacies.

On the microcosmic level, Dainichi's enlightened activity is manifest as subperceptible resonances *(kyō)*. These resonances harmonize into various structural configurations: physically as the five (or according to Kūkai's later thought, six) elements, mentally as the five wisdoms (and the buddhas associated with each), and phonetically as the base units of all language. In terms of the latter, at the subperceptible, inaudible level every word is necessarily a "truth word" *(shingon)* in that it is a surface (macrocosmic) manifestation of a microcosmic expression within Dainichi's enlightened activity.

On the macrocosmic level, the realm of perceptible reality, we are ordinarily oblivious to the cosmic and microcosmic dimensions. Shingon practice aims at revealing Dainichi's activity by making one more intimately aware of one's own activity. Through the ritualized practice of the *maṇḍalas*, *mudrās*, and *mantras*, one realizes that one's own participation is itself Dainichi's act. Since it is the domain most directly related to language, let us consider the practical aspects of mantric practice.

Shingon ritual recognizes five (or six) seed *mantras* that, when properly intoned, attune the practitioner to the elemental resonances out of which all language is constituted. Through mantric practice, one knows directly the truth words *(shingon)* inaudible to ordinary hearing. This is intended to enrich the practitioner's awareness in two ways. First, one recognizes these microcosmic resonances to be the imperceptible building blocks of the universe. In this respect, the ordinary macrocosmic world becomes the surface appearance of a deeper spiritual reality. Second, that deeper microcosmic level is not the world of quantum mechanics, an atomistic system probabilistically structured. Rather, there is a pattern to the microcosmic resonances, a pattern which is ultimately the self-expressive force of the cosmic buddha, Dainichi Nyorai.

In terms of our concern about the religious nature of language, therefore, we can say the following. Kūkai's esoteric Buddhist metaphysics maintained that all things in the universe are the Buddha's spiritual expressions. Everything we experience is only a manifestation of a microcosmic resonance or vibration, which in turn is nothing but the self-expression of the personal being that cosmically constitutes the universe. Language, therefore, is in one respect no different from any other phenomenon—it is a symbolic expression of the absolute spiritual principle. In another respect, however, language (as well as other formal structures such as art, bodily postures, conceptual frameworks) has a special function. Language may not only express spirituality: it may also *refer* to it. It is through these formal structures that we initially come to know about the cosmic and microcosmic realities behind the macrocosmic world experienced through the ordinary use of the senses. For Kūkai, the phenomena of the world, just as they are, are telling us something, but only through teachings formulated in language, diagrams, art, and postures do we become attuned to what they are telling us. We become capable of harmonizing with the style of the universe's self-expression only through our exposure to the teachings of Shingon Buddhism.

In this regard we can say that Kūkai found a dual relationship between language and spirituality. On one level, all language (indeed everything whatsoever) is inherently religious. Without the spiritual presence of the Buddha Dainichi, there would be no language. On another level, however, we can distinguish truly spiritual forms of language use (what Kūkai would think of as esoteric teachings) from secularized forms of linguistic expression (the exoteric teachings). Only the former point to language's sacred foundation as they simultaneously express that foundation. Sacred words (epitomized by the *mantra*) express the sacred as sacred, whereas ordinary words merely express the sacred as something else. Sacred language directs us to the root of language and, therefore, to the root of reality.

Of course, Kūkai's view technically represents only Shingon Buddhism and Shingon has not been a dominant tradition in Japan for over a thousand years. Yet, the esoteric Buddhist world view also influenced the Tendai Buddhist tradition and, by extension, the popular schools arising in the Kamakura period such as Pure Land, Zen, and Nichiren—themselves all originally offshoots of Tendai. We can here briefly examine aspects of Shinran's and Dōgen's views of religious language to see how Kūkai's theory about the religious nature of language prevailed, although in a transformed (sometimes radically transformed) mode.

Let us begin with Shinran (1173–1262), the founder of Shin Buddhism or, more technically Jōdo Shinshū, the "True Pure Land School." The relevant issue for him was how we should try to read a religious text so that we may enter into its true meaning. In his *Kyōgyō-shinshō* Shinran, following T'an-luan, writes:

> The openings of the sutras declare: "thus" [*sutras* typically begin with the phrase "thus have I heard"]. This clarifies the fact that faith is what makes possible our entrance.

The important point in this rather trenchant passage is Shinran's association of "faith" or "entrusting" *(shinjin)* with "thus" *(nyoze)*. In his articulation of the faith experience in Shin Buddhism, Shinran emphasized that faith can never be self-consciously willed or calculated *(hakarai.)* Rather, it must be a surrender to the natural *(jinen)* presence of the "other-power" *(tariki),* that is, the compassion of Amida Buddha which prepares the way for our enlightenment. Amida's compassion is immediately available to us in all things, but we must allow ourselves to be open to it. If we depend on our own power, Shinran maintained, the ego would obstruct any progress toward enlightenment.

This presents an interesting problem for Shinran's hermeneutic theory. Since he follows the traditional stance that he himself does not know the nature of Amida or his soteriological role but rather that it "has been made known" to him through the *sutras* and the teachings of the Pure Land patriarchs, it is crucial that Shinran have an infallible way of reading and understanding such texts. He cannot trust his own ability to "figure things out" (*hakarai*) since that would be an instance of trying to save himself through his "own power" (*jiriki*). Hence, he must be a literalist who protects himself at all times from eisegesis, from reading his own ideas into the text.

Normally, when we think of literalist interpreters, we envision scholars who pore over the philological, historical, and contextual components of the text or, alternatively, fundamentalists who believe that the text is patently obvious and one should simply read it naively. Shinran would have good reasons for rejecting either of these models of literalism, however. The scholarly approach itself smacks of *hakarai*, the ability to figure things out by trusting one's own knowledge and technical skills. The fundamentalist approach, on the other hand, overlooks the pernicious presence of ego and its ability to delude us in our attempts to "just see what the text says."

Shinran's readings of the texts clearly fit neither model of literalism. In the opening of his *Ichinen tanen mon'i,* for example, he quotes a passage from Shan-tao, a passage that surely means by any ordinary reading of the Chinese: "May everyone always desire that *at the time of death* [the Pure Land] will appear before them" and interprets it to say instead: "Everyone should always, *up to the time of death,* desire that [the Pure Land] will appear before them."

The key to Shinran's position is in how he understands "other-power" to inform his reading of a text. Shinran's position is that one must submit to the text, but not to its letters; one must yield to the spiritual power behind it, the power of Amida's Vow. For Shinran, the Shin Buddhist reader should approach the text without preconceptions, without special technical skills, and without the confidence that one can understand. We should see the text as something open to our entering into it.

This explains why Shinran's reading emphasizes the terms "thus" (*nyoze*), "faith" (*shin*), and "enter" (*nyū*) in T'an-luan's statement. In Shinran's understanding of the power of Amida's Vow, *shinjin* or faith is the dynamic through which thusness and the thus-come (*nyorai,* that is, the Buddha Amida) work naturally through the person so that the person may enter the Pure Land. By approaching the text with *shinjin,* the reader trusts not the text but the compassionate vow of Amida Buddha to help us.

How can we trust ourselves to be honest? How can we trust ourselves not to deceive ourselves? According to Shinran, we can't. Faith, which includes the denial that I can figure out things on my own, must inform the reading of the text from the start as well as follow from it. A religious reading requires of the reader that one not trust oneself: such a misplaced trust is simply own-power, *jiriki.* The only effective form of trust is the trust in Amida's Vow, and that trust is nothing other than the natural function of the Vow's power itself. From the *tariki* standpoint, *I* do not read the text; the text expresses itself to me and through me.

What does this mean in broader philosophical terms? Shinran's point is that there is no such thing as a religious text *per se,* but only religious *readings* of sacred texts. More precisely, if a text is read nonreligiously, it is not a religious text. If it is read religiously, it may or may not be a religious text, depending on whether it possesses the capacity to affect the reader's spiritual self-reflection. Interestingly, if the reader leaves the reading with the sense of "now I know the answer," the text read is not religious. The point of the religious text is to make us more acutely aware of our inadequacy, our failings, our limitations. Similarly, a reading that leaves the reader in utter despair also fails to qualify as religious because it has not instilled the reader with the sense of "other-power" essential to the faith necessary in spiritual development. Indeed, according to Shinran, without such faith, the text cannot be read religiously.

Now let us consider Dōgen (1200–1253), the founder of the Japanese Sōtō Zen tradition. We have seen that in both Kūkai and Shinran there was a metaphysical assumption that all language is expressive of the sacred power of the Buddha, but that religious language is distinctive in its ability to refer to that fact and to lead the audience to recognize that truth. We find a similar situation in Dōgen. For Dōgen, like Kūkai, all of reality is the self-expression of the Buddha. In Dōgen's terminology, this is the ubiquitous nature of the Buddha's "expression" (*dōtoku*).

Dōgen even states that mountains and rivers, just as they are, are *sūtras*.

Dōgen's approach to religious language differs from that of many other Zen masters. First, some interpreted the traditional dictum that Zen be "outside letters" to mean that the Zen transmission from master to disciple must be nonverbal. Dōgen explicitly denied this interpretation. One focus of the nonverbalist interpretation was the traditional Zen story of the transmission of insight from the historical buddha, Śākyamuni, to his disciple Mahākāśyapa. The story states that the Buddha, seated before a group gathered for a lecture on the Dharma, silently twirled a flower and winked. Only Mahākāśyapa reacted—by smiling. Pleased with his response, the Buddha said he would transmit the treasury of the correct Dharma-eye *(shōbōgenzō)* directly to Mahākāśyapa.

In his *Shōbōgenzō* fascicle "Mitsugo," Dōgen gives his own interpretation of the story. He notes that many would take the Buddha's behavior to mean that esoteric, nonverbal transmission is superior to the verbal. That is, one might think the twirling and winking were *mitsugo* or esoteric language. Dōgen rejects that reading. First he points out that only after the nonverbal exchange did Śākyamuni speak about transmitting the Dharma. It seems, then, that the transmission itself did not take place with the silent exchange. As Dōgen states:

> If Śākyamuni dislikes the verbal and prefers to twirl the flower, he should save the twirling for after (speaking). (13:58)

If the Zen transmission can be verbal, Dōgen must explain how a particular verbalization may have a spiritual function. Here it is significant to see how he reinterprets the classical sense of the term "*mitsugo*," a word that would ordinarily be translated "esoteric language" in the Shingon or Tendai schools and have the connotations of an extraordinary, secret, ritualistic communication directly linking the minds of master and student. In contrast, Dōgen considers *mitsu* to be part of our everyday experience. He writes:

> The *mitsu* words, meanings, and actions [in other words, the three 'intimacies' discussed by esotericists like Kūkai] of the Buddha's truth *(buppō)*

are not the way [the anti-verbalists argue]. On the occasion when you meet someone, you hear and express *mitsu* words. When you know yourself, you know *mitsu* action. (13:58–59)

In other words, Dōgen maintains that *mitsugo* is not a mystical and recondite form of transmission at all. If it is true that, as Dōgen says, "on the occasion when you meet someone, you hear and express *mitsugo*," *mitsugo* must be instead the very basis of interpersonal communication. It is what makes conversation a meeting ground for human intimacy. Dōgen, in fact, says as much:

> This word *mitsu* indicates the fact of *intimacy (shinmitsu)*. . . . Intimate action is not knowledge of self and other [such that] I alone can know my private self and do not understand each other private person. Because [as we say] "intimacy is what is near you," everything exists through intimacy; each half exists through intimacy. Personally investigate such facts with clarity and diligence in your practice. (13:59)

For Dōgen, it seems, language becomes religious when the speaker and audience are each involved in their respective practices, and the expression *(dōtoku)* of that combined practice is verbalized as intimate language. To make this point, Dōgen again modifies the traditional understanding of a classical Zen term, *kattō*, a word which usually indicates a deluded person's "entanglement" in words. Since he rejects the idea that verbalization is necessarily deluded and an obstruction to the transmission of enlightenment, Dōgen added a positive meaning to the term *kattō*, attaching the nuance of "intertwining" to the verbal exchange of master and disciple. In his *Shōbōgenzō* fascicle "*Kattō*," Dōgen explores this point, explaining how one must "use *kattō* (intertwining) to cut through *kattō* (entanglement)." That is, the master uses words to entangle both the student and the master, and together they use the words to cut through that entanglement.

> Therefore, the very utterances are lines that leap out of themselves; student and master personally practice together. The very listenings are lines that leap out of themselves; student and master practice together. The common personal investigation of master and disciple is the patriarchal intertwin-

ing *(kattō)*. The patriarchal intertwining is the life of (Bodhidharma's) skin-flesh-bones-marrow. (Shākyamuni's) very twirling of the flower and winking are the intertwining.[2] (12:428)

Dōgen's general interpretation of religious language can be summarized as follows. Like Kūkai and Shinran, Dōgen believed every phenomenon is an expression of the buddha. In this respect, every event—verbal or nonverbal—has a spiritual source. Therefore, Dōgen restricts the idea of distinctively religious language *(mitsugo)*—language that refers to as well as expresses spirituality—to the context of language arising within the intertwining of a master's and student's mutual practice, that is, language within the context of *kattō*. For Dōgen, it should be noted, Zen practice is not the means to Zen enlightenment, but rather is identified with it. Dōgen uses the term *shushō*, "practicing enlightenment" or "cultivating the authentication" of the enlightenment already within us. The event of truly religious language arises only when the people in dialogue are in the process of expressing *(dōtoku suru)* their authentic selves and, as Dōgen says at one point, when "each person brings one's own half of the intimacy." Religious language only occurs when both people are referring to, as well as expressing, their radical enlightenment *(hongaku)*. According to Dōgen's theory of *dōtoku,* every statement, indeed every phenomenon, is expressive of a radical spirituality filling the cosmos, but only the religious language of *mitsugo* points out the expressive process and brings both speaker and audience into the awareness of that omnipresent process.

Obviously, Dōgen's primary model of religious language is oral, but his own unorthodox readings of traditional terms and classical passages suggests that he believed even written texts can exemplify *kattō*. Indeed, in another essay, I argued that such a point of view influenced his unusual writing style in his major work *Shōbōgenzō*.

As our final historical example, let us turn to the case of Motoori Norinaga (1730–1801), a major philosopher in the Shintō tradition and crucial to the revival of Shintō as a national religion in the nineteenth and twentieth centuries. Motoori was a philologist who turned his attention to deciphering one of the earliest texts recorded in Japa-

nese, the *Kojiki*. The *Kojiki* was first recorded in the eighth century and it supposedly preserved the most ancient Japanese stories of the creation, stories that had been preserved only in the oral tradition up to then. The orthography used in recording those stories, however, had not been used for a millennium and much of it was unintelligible to Motoori's contemporaries.

Motoori's purpose in spending most of his adult life decoding the text went beyond philology, however. Motoori was a fundamentalist who believed the *Kojiki* to be the actual words of the gods *(kami)* spoken at creation. Hence, the ancient Japanese language (the *Yamato no kotoba*) was not simply the earliest language, but the *Ursprache* of all languages. This devotional attitude led Motoori to believe in a rather intriguing theory of religious language.

In his study of the ancient Japanese language, Motoori identified with the perspective of the Native Studies *(kokugaku)* scholars who emphasized that the same term, *koto*, originally meant both "word" and "thing." This semantic range assumed a parallelism or even interdependent relation between the linguistic and the ontological. This resonance between word and referent was sometimes called *kotodama*, the "spirit of words/things." The Native Studies scholars made that notion central to their reconstruction of the original Japanese world view.

Of course, the nativists generally conceded that words today may refer in only a crude, indefinite way to nonlinguistic realities, but for them this was proof that the primal power of verbal expression has been lost. Motoori hoped to recapture it, however. His line of thought was as follows. Insofar as the *Kojiki* is the story of origins and is the earliest extant text written in Japanese, it must describe what had originally been orally transmitted about how word-things *(koto)* came into being. In the unfolding of the words-things found in the *Kojiki,* therefore, we find the reenactment, not merely the description, of creation itself. That is, if the *Kojiki*'s words are internally related with realities, when you capture the full resonance and semantic range of the word, you also capture the reality as well. To uncover the meaning of the ancient words is to participate ritually in the creation itself.

This theory of the Yamato language was in accord with Motoori's theory of poetry. For him, a poetic text is not simply the expression of fact; it also is a direct expression of *kokoro*. *Kokoro* is a term ordinarily embracing both heart and mind, the seat of personal intentionality both emotional and intellectual. Motoori did not, however, limit this term to the feelings of the experiencer alone, as being only subjective as opposed to objective. There is also *kokoro* in things (*mono no kokoro*) and events (*koto no kokoro*). If a person has sensitivity (*kokoro ga aru hito*—a person with heart), he or she will be aware of the *kokoro* of things as well. An affective knowledge occurs when the event's *kokoro* and the person's *kokoro* are expressions of the total affective context. According to Motoori, this affective resonance between the *kokoro* of the person and thing is called in classical literature *mono no aware,* literally (following Motoori's analysis of the word), "the ah-ness of things." The *aware* is the natural expression (like "ah") of being so in touch with a thing or event that we are in turn touched by it.

In this way, Motoori connected the spiritual and aesthetic into a single theory of the power of word-things. When the *kokoro* of the reader or the poet is in accord with the *kokoro* of things and events, the creative act of spirituality is enacted or reenacted: the words and realities find their completeness of expression in each other. It was, incidentally, this view of language (*kotoba*) as the budding of leaves (*ha* or *ba*) springing from the thing-words (*koto*) that Heidegger discussed in his "A Dialogue on Language between a Japanese and an Inquirer," in his *On the Way to Language.*

In summation, although devoutly Shintō in his perspective, Motoori was in accord with his Buddhist predecessors in believing the origin of language to be a spiritual event, an event whose significance is lost in ordinary discourse. Only when the heart-mind-intention (*kokoro*) of the individual is attuned to the spiritual power of language (*kotodama*), does the discourse both express and refer to that spiritual source.

To conclude this essay, we can now focus on some general principles in this analysis that reflect on our initial discussion about the philoso-

phy of religious language in our contemporary Western context. First, we have noted how all four of our traditional Japanese philosophers believed that language itself is sacred in its very source. Modern Western philosophies of language, of course, are not interested in the issue of origins, but as Urban argued, insofar as a philosopher makes an assumption about what language is for, there is at least a metaphysical if not historical assumption about why there is language at all, about whence language derives. Of twentieth-century Western philosophers, perhaps only Heidegger has made this metaphysical question about language central to his philosophical ruminations. It may be more than historical accident that modern Japanese philosophers have gravitated more toward Heidegger's work than that of any other twentieth-century Western thinker.

We also noted at the outset that the idea that language and things came into being together, emerging out of a common spiritual principle, seems to be remarkably widespread among the world's religions. Given this context, it is strange to limit our philosophical analysis of religious language to assertional functions: representatives of those traditional religions would argue we have already robbed the language of its spiritual basis. At least our four classical Japanese philosophers would agree with such a criticism. Perhaps religious language is meant to be about not what already is, but rather about the source of the what-is, that process which makes the what-is into the what-it-is. This circumlocution is reminiscent of Heidegger's odd phrase: the "thinging of things," a phrase which tries to capture the phenomenological fact that the things of experience come into being as experiential content in an organismic, rather than static, manner.

Second, our four classical Japanese philosophers have each, in his own way, argued that religious discourse is not a text, but the hearing or reading of a text. What makes a text or an utterance religious is not simply where it came from, the context in which it was expressed, or the nature of the object to which it refers. The audience and its state of heart or mind is a necessary condition for the religious character of the expression. This relation between the religious discourse and the audience is reciprocal. On one hand, the religious language has a performative function: it is meant to do something to or for the audience. Yet, on the other hand, it is the audience which imbues the discourse with its power. The religious language has power only insofar as the audience gives it its specialness. The members of one religious tradition are often left cold when they read the text of another tradition. As Kūkai, Dōgen, Shinran, and Motoori all insisted, the audience must participate with, or enter into, or become entangled in, or intend the text with the proper attitude.

Our final point concerns wisdom and its relation to philosophizing. One of the trends of modern Western philosophy has been the increasing movement away from the classic Greco-Roman and medieval emphasis on wisdom toward the almost exclusive focus on knowledge. The study of wisdom—both practical and intellectual—has given way to narrowly defined epistemological concerns. In doing so, philosophy has become the love of knowledge instead of the love of wisdom. The problem has been compounded ever since modern philosophy has turned its attention to religion, losing sight of the fact that religion also has more to do with wisdom than knowledge. If our postmodern philosophy of religion is going to deal more fruitfully with the nature of religious discourse, it would seem that philosophy must first reexamine itself and once again love that aspect of human life from which it derives its name—*sophia*. Only then might we again stand in a place where we can hear what religious discourse really has to say.

NOTES

1. Our survey could continue, showing in particular how some of these ways of doing philosophy of religion have run aground. The analytic approach has exhausted its repertoire of simplistic forms of language use and has moved increasingly into the area of figures of speech, metaphors, and so forth. There is still so much analysis to be done in these areas that the philosopher of religion cannot simply call on any agreed body of analysis as a tool to use in evaluating religious discourse in any sophisticated way. On the other side of the English Channel, the poststructuralist deconstructionists have detached symbolic forms from their claim to any Neo-Kantian transcendental necessity or their claim of being based in a "natural kinds" realism. Symbols, it seems, refer only to other symbols in some form of culturally, socially, and historically relative episteme.

2. The phrase "skin-flesh-bones-marrow" refers to the transmission of enlightenment from Bodhidharma, the founder of the Zen tradition in East Asia to his disciple Hui-k'o. For Dōgen's unorthodox interpretation of this story see his discussion in "*Kattō*" or my discussion of that interpretation in "Dōgen on How to Read *Shōbōgenzō*," in William LaFleur, ed., *Dōgen Studies* (Honolulu: University of Hawaii Press, 1987).

8.4 Symbols All Around

What if we see the world with only one eye? What if there is more to it than we first see? What if symbols are more than words written in a book? What if everything from rain to insects "speaks" a spiritual language? What are the boundaries of religious language? What are the boundaries of language? Is language only what is said or written down? What about gestures? Does shaking my head up and down count as language?

Philosophers trained in the European and Anglo-American traditions are used to reading. They see language displayed on the page in front of them, or they hear it as they discuss what meaning is and whether one can say anything at all about God. The religions they know the most about come in books. The divine revelation is there, written down, for all to analyze and argue about. There are creeds that further explain what is meant. Of course such philosophers are aware that art, hymns, poetry, architecture, gesture, dance, singing, and much more carry meaning. However, when it comes down to the bottom line, it is sentences uttered or written to which they turn their attention.

This fascination with what is written and this focus on some allegedly revealed text or dogmas officially passed by the votes of bishops obscure the fact that these written documents represent a very narrow range of religious expression. Many cultures—cultures that have been and are deeply religious—have existed for centuries without written texts or creeds. As a consequence, they have learned to find religious meaning elsewhere. They have learned to see with two eyes. They live in a symbolically rich world. The earth, wind, stones, sun, and animals all speak to them about the meaning and purpose of life. They don't have to read a book about the Great Spirit to hear what the sacred tells them.

Lame Deer (1903–1984) was a Lakota Sioux medicine man (see Reading 4.2 for background on the Lakota Sioux), and he tells us, in the following selection, about what we might call "natural religious symbols." He develops nothing like a "theory of religious language" as most philosophers would use the term, but his understanding of religious symbolism is clearly informed by a profound sense of the spiritual meaning of ordinary things. Not only is all language religious, but everything is a religious "language" in the sense that it communicates to us the purpose of human life and defines the place we occupy in a reality wider and more meaningful than we normally imagine.

Reading Questions

1. What do the following symbolize: bubbling water, fire, meat, and steam?
2. How does Lame Deer understand symbols?
3. How does Lame Deer understand the circle, and how does this contrast with his view of the square?
4. What is the relationship, according to Lame Deer, between *Wakan Tanka* and everything else?
5. What sort of powers do medicine men have, and where do they get them?
6. Do you see any similarities between Lame Deer's views on symbols and the Japanese views on religious language discussed by Kasulis in the previous selection? If so, what are they?

Symbols All Around*

JOHN FIRE/LAME DEER

WHAT DO YOU SEE here, my friend? Just an ordinary old cooking pot, black with soot and full of dents.

It is standing on the fire on top of that old wood stove, and the water bubbles and moves the lid as the white steam rises to the ceiling.

*Reprinted with the permission of Simon & Schuster from *Lame Deer Seeker of Visions* by John Fire/ Lame Deer and Richard Erdoes. Copyright © 1972 by John Fire/Lame Deer and Richard Erdoes.

Inside the pot is boiling water, chunks of meat with bone and fat, plenty of potatoes.

It doesn't seem to have a message, that old pot, and I guess you don't give it a thought. Except the soup smells good and reminds you that you are hungry. Maybe you are worried that this is dog stew. Well, don't worry. It's just beef—no fat puppy for a special ceremony. It's just an ordinary, everyday meal.

But I'm an Indian. I think about ordinary, common things like this pot. The bubbling water comes from the rain cloud. It represents the sky. The fire comes from the sun which warms us all—men, animals, trees. The meat stands for the four-legged creatures, our animal brothers, who gave of themselves so that we should live. The steam is living breath. It was water; now it goes up to the sky, becomes a cloud again. These things are sacred. Looking at that pot full of good soup, I am thinking how, in this simple manner, Wakan Tanka takes care of me. We Sioux spend a lot of time thinking about everyday things, which in our mind are mixed up with the spiritual. We see in the world around us many symbols that teach us the meaning of life. We have a saying that the white man sees so little, he must see with only one eye. We see a lot that you no longer notice. You could notice if you wanted to, but you are usually too busy. We Indians live in a world of symbols and images where the spiritual and the commonplace are one. To you symbols are just words, spoken or written in a book. To us they are part of nature, part of ourselves—the earth, the sun, the wind and the rain, stones, trees, animals, even little insects like ants and grasshoppers. We try to understand them not with the head but with the heart, and we need no more than a hint to give us the meaning.

What to you seems commonplace to us appears wondrous through symbolism. This is funny, because we don't even have a word for symbolism, yet we are all wrapped up in it. You have the word, but that is all.

Look at this belt. My grandmother made it. You say it is beautiful and this makes me glad, because I want to give it to you. But it is more than just beautiful; it tells a story. All you see is a geometric pattern of beads—lines, triangles and diamond shapes—but these are a tale of my grandfather's deeds. This diamond shape

represents a feather given to a warrior to wear after doing a brave thing like counting coup: These rectangles with one line missing

represent horses' tracks. They stand for the ponies captured from the enemy. This shape

means a horse killed in battle and its rider rescued by my grandfather. These two triangles

are arrows shot at the enemy. This belt tells of a battle. . . .

Symbolism helped us to "write" without an alphabet. By way of symbols we can even describe abstract thoughts precisely so that all may understand them. Two hands like this, open, reaching for each other,

is our sign for peace. A man holding a peace pipe

means a prayer.

This is a medicine man. His eyes are closed; he is having a vision, an insight. The wavy lines coming down on his head is the spirit power descending to him. A man surrounded by dots like this means he is afraid, things are closing in on him.

You know, it always makes me laugh when I hear young white kids speak of some people as "squares" or "straights"—old people, hardened in their ways, in their minds, in their hearts. They don't even have to be old. You can be an "old square" at eighteen. Anyway, calling these people "squares"—an Indian could have thought it up. To our way of thinking the Indians' symbol is the circle, the hoop. Nature wants things to be round. The bodies of human beings and animals have no corners. With us the circle stands for the togetherness of people who sit with one another around the campfire, relatives and friends united in peace while the pipe passes from hand to hand. The camp in which every tipi had its place was also a ring. The tipi was a ring in which people sat in a circle and all the families in the village were in turn circles within a larger circle, part of the larger hoop which was the seven campfires of the Sioux, representing one nation. The nation was only a part of the universe, in itself circular and made of the earth, which is round, of the sun, which is round, of the stars, which are round. The moon, the horizon, the rainbow—circles within circles within circles, with no beginning and no end.

To us this is beautiful and fitting, symbol and reality at the same time, expressing the harmony of life and nature. Our circle is timeless, flowing; it is new life emerging from death—life winning out over death.

The white man's symbol is the square. Square is his house, his office buildings with walls that separate people from one another. Square is the door which keeps strangers out, the dollar bill, the jail. Square are the white man's gadgets— boxes, boxes, boxes and more boxes—TV sets, radios, washing machines, computers, cars. These all have corners and sharp edges—points in time,

white man's time, with appointments, time clocks and rush hours—that's what the corners mean to me. You become a prisoner inside all these boxes.

More and more young white people want to stop being "straight" and "square" and try to become round, join our circle. That is good.

From birth to death we Indians are enfolded in symbols as in a blanket. An infant's cradle board is covered with designs to ensure a happy, healthy life for the child. The moccasins of the dead have their soles beaded in a certain way to ease the journey to the hereafter. For the same reason most of us have tattoos on our wrists— not like the tattoos of your sailors—daggers, hearts and nude girls—but just a name, a few letters or designs. The Owl Woman who guards the road to the spirit lodges looks at these tattoos and lets us pass. They are like a passport. Many Indians believe that if you don't have these signs on your body, that Ghost Woman won't let you through but will throw you over a cliff. In that case you have to roam the earth endlessly as a *wanagi*—a ghost. All you can do then is frighten people and whistle. Maybe it's not so bad being a *wanagi*. It could even be fun. I don't know. But, as you see, I have my arms tattooed.

Every day in my life I see symbols in the shape of certain roots or branches. I read messages in the stones. I pay special attention to them, because I am a Yuwipi man and that is my work. But I am not the only one. Many Indians do this.

Inyan—the rocks—are holy. Every man needs a stone to help him. There are two kinds of pebbles that make good medicine. One is white like ice. The other is like ordinary stone, but it makes you pick it up and recognize it by its special shape. You ask stones for aid to find things which are lost or missing. Stones can give warning of an enemy, of approaching misfortune. The winds are symbolized by a raven and a small black stone the size of an egg. . . .

A stone fits right into our world of symbols. It is round and endless. Its power is endless too. All round things are kin to each other, like *wagmuha*—the gourd, the holy rattle—which has 405 little stones inside it, pebbles collected from anthills.

Nothing is so small and unimportant but it has a spirit given to it by Wakan Tanka. Tunkan is what you might call a stone god, but he is also part of the Great Spirit. The gods are separate beings, but they are all united in Wakan Tanka. It is hard to understand—something like the Holy Trinity. You can't explain it except by going back to the "circles within circles" idea, the spirit splitting itself up into stones, trees, tiny insects even, making them all *wakan* by his ever-presence. And in turn all these myriad of things which makes up the universe flowing back to their source, united in the one Grandfather Spirit. . . .

I am a medicine man—a *wićaśa wakan*. "Medicine man"—that's a white man's word like squaw, papoose, Sioux, tomahawk—words that don't exist in the Indian language. I wish there were better words to make clear what "medicine man" stands for, but I can't find any, and you can't either, so I guess medicine man will have to do. But it doesn't convey the many different meanings that come to an Indian's mind when you say "medicine man."

We have different names for different men doing different things for which you have only that one puny name. First, we distinguish the healer—*pejuta wićaśa*—the man of herbs. He does not cure with the herbs alone; he must also have the *wakan* power to heal. Then we have the *yuwipi*, the tied-one, the man who uses the power of the rawhide and the stones to find and to cure. We also speak of the *waayatan*—the man of vision who can foretell events which will happen in the future, who has been given the power to see ahead. Things that have come true according to such a man's prediction are called *wakinyanpi*. This word also means the winged-ones, those who fly through the air, because the power to foretell the future comes from them.

Then there is the *wapiya*—the conjurer—what you might call a witch doctor. If he is a good man he does the *waanazin*—the shooting at the disease, the drawing up and sucking out of your body evil things which have been put into a person by a bad spirit, such as a particular kind of gopher that will shoot sharp blades of grass and tiny bits of porcupine quills from his hole in the ground into your body, causing it to break out in boils.

If such a conjurer is bad, he himself will put a sickness into you which only he can cure—for a price. There are some fakers among this group of men. They give a little medicine to a soldier boy which is supposed to protect him from harm, make him bulletproof and ensure his coming home safely. If he comes back in one piece, they collect. If he doesn't—well, that's just too bad.

Another kind of medicine man is the *heyoka*—the sacred clown—who uses his thunder power to cure some people. If you want to stretch the word out like a big blanket to cover everybody, even a peyote roadman could squeeze underneath it and qualify as a medicine man. But the more I think about it, the more I believe that the only real medicine man is the *wićaśa wakan*—the holy man. Such a one can cure, prophesy, talk to the herbs, command the stones, conduct the sun dance or even change the weather, but all this is of no great importance to him. There are merely stages he has passed through. The *wićaśa wakan* has gone beyond all this. He has the *wakanya wowanyanke*—the great vision. Sitting Bull was such a man. When he had his sun-dance vision at Medicine Deer Rock he saw many blue-coated soldiers fall backward into the Indian camp and he heard a voice telling him, "I give you these, because they have no ears." Sitting Bull knew then that the Indians would win the next battle. He did not fight himself, he commanded no men, he did not do anything except let his wisdom and power work for his people.

The *wićaśa wakan* wants to be by himself. He wants to be away from the crowd, from everyday matters. He likes to meditate, leaning against a tree or rock, feeling the earth move beneath him, feeling the weight of that big flaming sky upon him. That way he can figure things out. Closing his eyes, he sees many things clearly. What you see with your eyes shut is what counts.

The *wićaśa wakan* loves the silence, wrapping it around himself like a blanket—a loud silence with a voice like thunder which tells him of many things. Such a man likes to be in a place where there is no sound but the humming of insects.

He sits facing the west, asking for help. He talks to the plants and they answer him. He listens to the voices of the *wama kaśkan*—all those who move upon the earth, the animals. He is as one with them. From all living beings something flows into him all the time, and something flows from him. I don't know where or what, but it's there. I know. . . .

In order to be a medicine man one should find the visions there, in nature. To the west a man has the power from the buffalo. From the north he gets the power from the thunder-beings. From the east his strength comes from the spirit horse and the elk. From the south he has the ghost power. From above, from the sky, he will receive the wisdom of the great eagle. From beneath, from the earth, he will receive the mother's food. This is the way to become a *wićaśa wakan,* to learn the secret language, to speak about sacred things, to work with the stones and herbs, to use the pipe.

Much power comes from the animals, and most medicine men have their special animal which they saw in their first vision. One never kills or harms this animal. Medicine men can be buffalo, eagle, elk or bear dreamers. Of all the four-legged and winged creatures a medicine man could receive a vision from, the bear is foremost. The bear is the wisest of animals as far as medicines are concerned. If a man dreams of this animal he could become a great healer. The bear is the only animal that one can see in a dream acting like a medicine man, giving herbs to people. It digs up certain healing roots with its claws. Often it will show a man in a vision which medicines to use. . . .

8.5 Metaphorical Theology

Can religious language become idolatrous? Can it reinforce the power and dominance of one group over another? Can religious language disguise power relations? Can it mislead people into thinking something is sacred when it is not?

These are just some of the issues that Sallie McFague, professor of theology at Vanderbilt University, discusses in the following selection. She returns to some of the themes we explored in Reading 8.1, but with a few new twists. As a theologian, her concerns reflect an interest in how to do theology in contemporary culture. That culture has found much religious language irrelevant for a variety of reasons. Although her primary interests are theological, she is keenly aware of the historical and cultural context in which theology is done. She believes that at one time in history, treating religious language from a primarily "symbolic" or "sacramental" viewpoint made sense. But we live in a different time and must take the differences between the past and the present into account when we consider religious language. When we do take the differences into account, understanding religious language as metaphoric makes the most sense, or so McFague argues.

Context is important. Our understanding of language must be contextualized. When it is we see how culture, history, class, and gender have influenced how we think about God. Masculine and patriarchal metaphors permeate our language and our thought. Can we find new metaphors that avoid the problems associated with traditional patriarchal notions and still speak meaningfully of God?

We are so used to associating truth, reality, and literal language that we automatically become suspicious of talk about metaphoric language. If it is metaphoric, then it must somehow be untrue, or the extralinguistic reality of what is being referred to must be sacrificed. Although McFague does not here directly address issues of truth and realism, she does not assume that her emphasis on metaphoric religious language necessarily implies an abandonment of religious realism. For example, although the many parables Jesus told about the kingdom of God are highly metaphoric and should not be taken literally, they nevertheless "do tell us something about the rule of God."

Reading Questions

1. What is the problem of religious language for us today?
2. Why does religious language become both idolatrous and irrelevant apart from a religious context?
3. What are the *primary context* and the *interpretative context* for religious language?
4. Explain what the phrase "idolatry of religious language" means.
5. What is the feminist critique of religious language?
6. What is the *analogia entis,* and how is it related to symbolic sacramentalism?
7. What is the "Protestant Principle," and why is it important for our understanding of religious language?
8. What is a metaphor, and how does it differ from a symbol?
9. What is the difference between *primary* and *secondary* religious language?
10. What is a model, and what role does it play in metaphorical theology?
11. What is a "root-metaphor"?
12. What are the tasks of metaphorical theology?
13. List two or three criticisms of McFague's views on religious language.

Metaphorical Theology*

SALLIE McFAGUE

There is a God. There is no God. Where is the problem? I am quite sure that there is a God in the sense that I am sure my love is no illusion. I am quite sure there is no God in the sense that I am sure there is nothing which resembles what I can conceive when I say that word.[1]

Simone Weil, in her book *Waiting for God,* states the problem of religious language in the classic way. As a religious person, she is certain that her love for God is not an illusion, but she is equally certain that none of her conceptions of the divine resembles God. Her comments are in the great tradition of deeply religious people, and especially the mystics of all religious traditions, who feel conviction at the level of experience, at the level of worship, but great uncertainty at the level of words adequate to express the reality of God.

Augustine, the great Bishop of Hippo, notes that even the person who says the most about God is but "dumb," and yet, he adds, our only alternatives are to speak in halting, inadequate words or to remain silent. The Judeo-Christian tradition, more than many other religious traditions, has chosen not to remain silent. In fact,

*Reprinted from *Metaphorical Theology: Models of God in Religious Language,* by Sallie McFague, copyright © 1982 by Fortress Press. Used by permission of Augsburg Fortress.

this tradition and especially Christianity, and within Christianity especially Protestantism, has focused on and at times been obsessed by words, both "the Word of God" and human words about God.

The Problem of Religious Language

Increasingly, however, religious language is a problem for us, a problem of a somewhat different kind than the classical one. For most of us, it is not a question of being sure of God while being unsure of our language about God. Rather, we are unsure both at the experiential and the expressive levels. We are unsure at the experiential level because we are, even the most religious of us, secular in ways our foremothers and forefathers were not. We do not live in a sacramental universe in which the things of this world, its joys and catastrophes, harvests and famines, births and deaths, are understood as connected to and permeated by divine power and love. Our experience, our daily experience, is for the most part non-religious. Most of us go through the days accepting our fortunes and explaining our world without direct reference to God. If we experience God at all it tends to be at a private level and in a sporadic way; the natural and public events of our world do not stand for or image God.

Certainly we cannot return to the time of the sacramental universe; but apart from a *religious context* of some kind, religious language becomes both idolatrous and irrelevant. It becomes *idolatrous* because without a sense of awe, wonder, and mystery, we forget the inevitable distance between our words and the divine reality. It becomes *irrelevant* because without a sense of the immanence of the divine in our lives, we find language about God empty and meaningless. It is no accident, then, that the mystics in all religious traditions have been the most perceptive on the question of religious language. Aware as they are of the transcendence of God, they have not been inclined to identify our words with God; in fact, their tendency is more often to refuse any similarity between our words and the divine reality. Simone Weil stands foursquare in this tradition

when she says there is "nothing" which resembles her thoughts about God. The mystics, however, have also been the most imaginative and free in their language about God, finding all sorts of language relevant. As Augustine notes, we must use all the best images available to us in order to say *something* about the divine. The mystics have also not restricted their language about God to biblical or traditional imagery, for the experience of God, the certainty and the immediacy of it, has been the basis for new and powerful religious language.

The *primary context,* then, for any discussion of religious language is worship. Unless one has a sense of the mystery surrounding existence, of the profound inadequacy of all our thoughts and words, one will most likely identify God with our words: God *becomes* father, mother, lover, friend. Unless one has a sense of the nearness of God, the overwhelming sense of the way God pervades and permeates our very being, one will not find religious images significant: the power of the images for God of father, mother, lover, friend will not be appreciated. Apart from a religious context, religious language will inevitably go awry either in the direction of idolatry or irrelevancy or both.

There is, however, another critical context for religious language, one that has not been as central in the classical tradition and that does not surface in the quotation by Weil. In the broadest sense, we could call this the *interpretive context.* It is the context that recognizes that we who attempt to speak about God are social, cultural, and historical beings with particular perspectives influenced by a wide range of factors. The interpretive context within religious faiths has usually been limited to the "tradition," meaning the church or another institution which has set the interpretive precedents for what is proper (orthodox) or improper (heretical) religious language. In the last two hundred years, however, the interpretive context has increased greatly as people have realized the relativity of perspectives. With the introduction of historical criticism of religious texts, we became aware of the relativity of the words and images in sacred Scriptures, that these texts were written by limited people who expressed their experiences of divine reality in the manners and mores of their historical times.

Most recently, we have become conscious, by deepening our awareness of the *plurality* of perspectives, of dimensions of interpretation which had been largely submerged. That is to say, it is not only our time and place in history that influences our religious language, but also our class, race, and sex; our nationality, education, and family background; our interests, prejudices, and concerns. We have become aware, for instance, of the varying interests that determined the perspectives of New Testament writers. They not only saw their religious experience through the glasses of first-century Palestine but also through the refractions provided by their own individual histories and concerns. Consciousness of the relativity and plurality of interpretations forces us to recognize that religious language is not just the halting attempts by "Christians" to say something appropriate about God, but is the halting attempts by specific individuals: by Paul, a first-century convert from Judaism, who had great empathy with the problems of Jewish Christians but little sympathy for women or slave Christians; by Julian of Norwich, a medieval woman mystic, who spoke of "our tender Mother Jesus"; by Reinhold Niebuhr, a twentieth-century preacher from Detroit, whose experience with American capitalism caused him to see human sinfulness as the basis for political "realism"; by Mary Daly, a twentieth-century, Catholic-educated feminist, who sees the history of the world's religions as an exercise in misogyny. If we lose sight of the relativity and plurality of the interpretive context, our religious language will, as with the loss of the religious context, become idolatrous or irrelevant. It will become idolatrous, for we will absolutize one tradition of images for God; it will become irrelevant, for the experiences of many people will not be included within the canonized tradition.

The issues that emerge, then, from both the worship and the interpretive contexts of religious language, are *idolatry* and *irrelevance:* either we take our language about God literally or we find it meaningless. Another way to phrase these issues is to ask the questions: How does religious language refer to God and which religious images are central? Is there a way of speaking of religious language as referring to God without identifying it with the divine? Are there images which are central to a religious tradition *and* are there revolutionary possibilities within that tradition aiding new images to emerge? These are very complex questions, for they focus on the heart of language—its truth and its meaning. Does religious language refer to anything; if so, to what and how? Does religious language mean anything; if so, what and to whom? Our route to suggesting modest answers to these questions will be slow and indirect, as I believe is appropriate to the subject matter; but a beginning can be made by illustrating the issues of idolatry and irrelevance, truth and meaning, through contemporary movements within our culture that find them especially problematic.

The Idolatry of Religious Language

On the issue of the truth of religious language, there are continuing, powerful, conservative religious movements which insist on the literal reference of language to God. Religious conservatism is a widespread tendency within contemporary culture, not restricted to groups which call themselves "evangelicals" or "fundamentalists." This tendency is linked with fear of relativizing Scripture through historical criticism and a refusal to accept a plurality of interpretive perspectives. The Bible, says this movement, *is* the Word of God; the Bible is inerrant or divinely inspired; the words and images of the Bible are the authoritative and appropriate words and images for God. The Bible is a sacred text, different from all other texts, and not relative and pluralistic as are all other human products. The Bible becomes an idol: the fallible, human words of Scripture are understood as referring correctly and literally to God. Even where these sentiments are not expressed clearly or in such extreme fashion, religious literalism remains a powerful current in our society. And it does not stem only from a fear of relativism and plurality. It also derives from the understanding of what counts as "true" in our culture. What is "true" in our positivistic, scientifically oriented society is what corresponds with "reality," with the "facts." Translated into artistic terms, this means realistic art; the "true" painting or sculpture is a copy of what it represents. Translated into religious terms, "true" religious language is also a copy of what it represents; in other words, a literal or realistic representation of God's nature. If the Bible says that God is "father" then God is literally, really, "father"; the word "father" and the associations of that word truly refer to God's nature. In the same way that the law of gravity refers to the way things really are in the world, so "father" refers to the way God really is.

But there is, I believe, an even deeper reason why religious literalism runs rampant in our time. It is not only that many people have lost the practice of religious contemplation and prayer, which alone is sufficient to keep literalism at bay, or that positivistic scientism has injected a narrow view of truth into our culture. While both are true, it is also the case that we do not think in symbols in the way our forebears did. That is to say, we do not see the things of this world as standing for something else; they are simply what they are. A symbolic sensibility, on the contrary, sees multilayered realities, with the literal level suggestive of meanings beyond itself. While it may have been more justified for people in earlier times to be biblical literalists since they were less conscious of relativity, as symbolic thinkers, they were *not* literalists. From the third century on, the "fourfold method of exegesis"—in which three levels of interpretation followed the literal level—permitted and encouraged the exercise of the imagination in the interpretation of Scripture. While many of the "anagogical" and "tropological" interpretations were fanciful, the abandonment of the four levels in the Protestant Reformation, with the claim that the text was self-explanatory, eventually resulted in literalism.[2] The claim can be made that our time is *more* literalistic than any other time in history. Not only were double, triple, and more meanings once seen in Scripture (and Scripture considered richer as a consequence), but our notion of history as

the recording of "facts" is alien to the biblical consciousness. The ancients were less literalistic than we are, aware that truth has many levels and that when one writes the story of an influential person's life, one's perspective will color that story. Our is a literalistic mentality; theirs was a symbolical mentality. There can be no return to a symbolical mentality in its earlier forms; we no longer believe in four levels of scriptural exegesis or in a three-tiered universe.

Nor can many of us return to a symbolical mentality in its sacramental form; for instance, belief that natural and human objects and events are "figures" of the divine. For a traditional sacramental sensibility, the bread and wine of the Eucharist are symbols of divine nurture; they do not merely "point to" spiritual food, but really and truly *are* spiritual food. The things of this world participate in and signify what transcends our world. The sacramental sensibility depends upon a belief that everything is connected, that the beings of this world are analogously related to God (Being-Itself), and hence can be sacramentally related to God. The analogy of being by which all that is *is* because of its radical dependence on God ties everything together in a silent ontological web which reverberates with similarity within dissimilarity out to its farthest reaches. Even a corpse, says Augustine, is like God to the extent that it still has some degree of order left in its decaying flesh and emerging skeleton. In such a universe, everything holds together, everything fits, everything is related.

For a genuine symbolical sensibility such as Dante embraced in his *Divine Comedy*, the symbol—the finite object which signifies the infinite by participating in it—is neither literalized nor spiritualized. It does not become an idol or a mere sign. In our time, however, when there is skepticism concerning the unity of all that is, symbols tend either to be literalized (as in fundamentalism or the doctrine of transubstantiation) or spiritualized (as in Feuerbach or Protestant liberalism).

The medieval sacramental sensibility is not ours, either in theory or practice. Our time is characterized by disunity, by skepticism that anything is related to anything else, and by secularity. If there is to be any fresh understanding of the truth of images as a counter to literalistic truth, it will have to be one that takes seriously the characteristics of the contemporary sensibility.[3]

Before we leave this preliminary overview of literalism and the truth of religious language, it is necessary to add a word from social anthropology about *why* people cling to religious systems with such fervor, especially if they appear threatened by a secularized, relativistic, and pluralistic culture. As Clifford Geertz points out, human beings are "unfinished" at birth and must construct and order their world in ways that no other animals must do. Monkeys and bees are born into a monkey or bee "world" respectively—which is simply there for them. Having to construct our world, we are necessarily (if only subconsciously) protective of it and extremely anxious if it is threatened. We depend, says Geertz, so deeply on our constructions for our most basic sense of sanity that any threat to them is a threat to our very being.[4] Thus, one can conclude that people will be less open, less imaginative, less flexible during times of threat. They will be more literalistic, absolutist, dogmatic when the construction which orders their world is relativized, either through pluralistic perspectives from within the tradition or competing systems from without. Given the pressures against the traditional Christian imagistic system from, for instance, both the liberation theologies and from other world religions, this retreat into literalistic, absolutist hibernation is no surprise.

But literalism will not do. Much of this essay will be devoted to trying to show why it will not do and what the alternative is. Two thoughtful theologians point us in the right direction on the matter of religious language, the first with a straightforward admonition, the second with an analogy of religious language with poetic. British theologian Ian T. Ramsey has written:

> Let us always be cautious of talking about God in straightforward language. Let us never talk as if we had privileged access to the diaries of God's private life . . . so that we may say quite cheerfully why God did what, when and where.[5]

This admonition is never necessary for deeply religious people or persons aware of their own relative and limited perspectives. Old Testament scholar Phyllis Trible has written:

> To appropriate the metaphor of a Zen sutra, poetry is "like a finger pointing to the moon." It is a way to see the light that shines in darkness, a way to participate in transcendent truth and to embrace reality. To equate the finger with the moon or to acknowledge the finger and not perceive the moon is to miss the point.[6]

Or, to rephrase Trible's words for our subject, either to equate human words with the divine reality or to see no relationship between them is inappropriate. Rather, the proper way is "like a finger pointing to the moon." Is *this* the way "to participate in transcendent truth and to embrace reality"? I would agree with Trible that it is; I would call it the "metaphorical" way and will be elaborating on it as the form of religious language.

The Irrelevance of Religious Language

Turning now to the second problem facing religious language in our time—irrelevancy—we note that it also is a widespread phenomenon. In a secularized culture where the practice of regular public and private prayer is not widespread, this is bound to be the case. For many, the images in the Bible have sentimental significance from childhood days and happier times; for some, the biblical language creates a world of its own in sharp distinction from the evil modern world. But for many people, religious language, biblical language, has become, like a creed repeated too many times, boring and repetitious. We are essentially indifferent to it. And this is true despite the fact that biblical imagery is often vivid, powerful, shocking, and revolutionary. But all of the reasons given thus far for the "meaninglessness" of religious language have probably always been current. What distinguishes our time is various groups of people who are saying that traditional religious language is meaningless to them because it excludes them in *special* ways. In a more general sense, religious language in the Judeo-Christian tradition excludes us all, for it is largely biblical language; hence, its assumptions concerning social, political, and cultural matters are not ours. Entering the biblical world for many people is like going into a time warp in which one is transported to a world two thousand years in the past. We are aware of significant connections since both worlds are inhabited by human beings, but the images, problems, issues, and assumptions are different. In one way or another, we are all excluded from the biblical world and the tradition that has been formed from it: few if any of us identify easily or enthusiastically with images of demons, vineyards, Messiah and Son of man, kings, Pharisees, and so on. But the issues are much sharper and more painful for some groups: it is not simply that they do not identify; rather, they feel *specifically* excluded. The indifference and irrelevance that many people feel with regard to religious language is clarified by the critique of the more revolutionary groups, for their particular difficulties with religious language highlight issues that point directly to some of its basic characteristics. The feminist critique of religious language is especially relevant in this regard, for more than any of the other liberation theologies, feminist theology has focused on language, its power and its abuses. Three points in this critique stand out as significant.

First, feminists generally agree that whoever names the world owns the world. The Genesis story, according to the traditional, patriarchal interpretation, sees Adam naming the world without consulting Eve. For many feminists, this is a model of Western culture, including Christianity, which has been and still is a "man's world."[7] The feminist critique of religious language is an extremely sophisticated one, for it is based on a recognition of the fundamental importance of language to human existence. With Ludwig Wittgenstein, feminists would say, "The limits of one's language are the limits of one's world," and with Martin Heidegger, "Language is the house of being." We do not so much use language as we are used by it. Since we are all born into a world which is already

linguistic, in which the naming has already taken place, we only own our world to the extent that the naming that has occurred is our naming. Feminist theologians are claiming that the world of Western religion is not their world; it was named by men and excludes women. The world of Western religion can become a world for women only if it is open to their naming. New naming, changes in language, are, however, no minor matters, for if one believes that language and "world" are coterminous, then changes in the one will involve changes in the other, and such changes are often revolutionary. The current resistance to inclusive or unbiased language, for instance, both at the social and religious level, indicates that people know instinctively that a revolution in language means a revolution in one's world.

Second, feminists are saying that the particular problem they have with Western religious language is its patriarchal character. It is not just that "God the father" is a frequent appellation for the divine, but that the entire structure of divine-human and human-human relationships is understood in a patriarchal framework.[8] "God the father," as we shall see, has become a model which serves as a grid or screen through which to see not only the nature of God but also our relations to the divine and with one another. "Patriarchy" then is not just that most of the images of the deity in Western religion are masculine—king, father, husband, lord, master—but it is the Western way of life: it describes patterns of governance at national, ecclesiastical, business, and family levels. We shall investigate this model in some detail at a later time, for it is one of the most prominent in the Judeo-Christian tradition. But the point I am stressing now is the total, overarching character of patriarchalism which contributes to the sense of exclusion on the part of women and hence prompts their criticism of the irrelevance of much of Western religious language to them. They say the model of "God the father" has become an idol. When a model becomes an idol, the hypothetical character of the model is forgotten and what ought to be seen as *one* way to understand our relationship with God has become identified as *the* way. In fact, as happens when a model becomes an idol, the distance between image and reality collapses: "father" becomes God's "name" and patriarchy becomes the proper description of governing relationships at many levels. The transformation of the paternal model into the patriarchal is an important case in point concerning what can happen to models when *one* dominates. Feminist theologians are insisting that many models of God are necessary, among them feminine models, in order both to avoid idolatry and to include the experience of all peoples in our language about God.

Third, feminist theologians are saying that religious language is not only religious but also human, not only about God but also about us. The tradition says that we were created in the image of God, but the obverse is also the case, for we imagine God in *our* image. And the human images we choose for the divine influence the way we feel about ourselves, for these images are "divinized" and hence raised in status. For instance, earthly kingship gains in importance when the image of king is applied to God.[9] On the contrary, images that are excluded are not legitimated and honored; for instance, as feminists have pointed out, the paucity of feminine imagery for God in the Judeo-Christian tradition means a lower self-image for women in that tradition. The relationship between feminine imagery for the divine and the status of women in a society has been well documented in the history of religions.[10] One of the functions, therefore, of religious language is "naming ourselves" as we "name" God. Those who are conscious of being excluded from a religious tradition are most likely to recognize this important and often forgotten function of religious language.

In a number of ways, then, feminist theologians (and a similar case could be made by black and third world theologians) have shown why religious language is not meaningful in our time. Language which is not our language, models which have become idols, images which exclude our experience are three common failings of religious language, but they are especially evident to groups of people who feel excluded by the classical tradition of a religious faith.

Can Religious Language Be Revitalized?

If idolatry and irrelevance are the critical issues for religious language in our time, what remedies are possible for its revitalization? The crisis is too deep for patchwork solutions, for the problem lies in our most basic sense of "how things hold together." That is, many of us no longer believe in a symbolic, sacramental universe in which the part stands for the whole, the things of this world "figure" another world, and all that is is connected by a web of being. No longer believing in connections of this sort and hence afraid that our images refer to nothing, we literalize them, worshiping the icon in our desperation. Furthermore, we find them irrelevant for they connect us to nothing transcending ourselves: they are "just symbols." The question that looms before us is, I believe, a critical one for religious faith and expression: is it possible to have significant religious language, language that is true and meaningful, without classic sacramentalism? If we can no longer believe in a "figural" world—our world as a whole and in all its parts as a symbol of another world, a microcosm of it—can we still believe that our words about the divine are significant?

Let us consider this question more carefully. What are the characteristics of the classic sacramental perspective? The basis of the sacramental universe within Christianity (and there are similar perspectives in other religions) is the incarnation: the sense of divine immanence in the Hebrew tradition is brought to its apotheosis in the Johannine assertion that "the Word became flesh and dwelt among us." The full presence of God in an otherwise ordinary person, Jesus of Nazareth—as the Chalcedonian statement puts it, "fully God and fully man"—was the basis for a thoroughgoing sacramentalism. If God can be fully present in a particular human being, then all creation has the potential for serving as a symbol of divine immanence.[11] The natural and human orders of creation are not flat but two-dimensional: each thing is itself, but as itself, it is also something else—"news of God" as Gerard Manley Hopkins says. The world is alive with the presence of God; it "figures," shows forth, the divine in all its myriad particularity. Sacramentalism of this sort tends to be static and focused on the natural, not the historical, order. Incarnationalism, as the word indicates, is centered on the body, the flesh, not on human being as restless, moving, growing. The most extreme example of sacramentalism, the eucharistic doctrine of transubstantiation, illustrates clearly both the static and fleshly characteristics of the perspective. The bread and wine *become* the body and blood of Christ: two items of the naturalistic order are changed into what they symbolize. Actually, in this extreme case symbolization gives over to realism; the symbol is consumed by what it represents. But elsewhere in the symbolic perspective, the two dimensions exist in a hierarchical order of macrocosm-microcosm, spirit-body, Christ-church, man-woman, and so on. All is ordered, statically and hierarchically, with the body always "below," but permeated by spirit and capable of expressing and imaging spirit.[12]

In such a universe, of course, the meaning and truth of religious language are no problem. If the entire earthly order is a "figure" of the divine order, if each and every scrap of creation, both natural and human, participates in and signifies the divine order according to its own particularities, its own way of being in the world, then all that is "refers" to Being-Itself and has "meaning," both in itself and as a symbol. Everything is connected hierarchically; hence, everything here below is meaningful both in itself and as a symbol of the divine.

Symbolic sacramentalism received systematic interpretation and ordering in the medieval doctrine of *analogia entis,* the analogy of being. This doctrine says, in essence, that every existing thing participates in Being-Itself, but analogously. That is, being is differentiated absolutely, so that while everything is connected as beings immediately and radically dependent on God, each thing has, is, its own act of being and hence is radically particular. The analogy of being does not paint

the world all the same color; on the contrary, it stresses the glory of difference. Beneath the distinctions, however, everything is connected and this is the reason why everything in such a universe can be a symbol of everything else and, most especially, of God, who created everything out of the divine plenitude as a mirror and a reflection of the divine self. The analogical way, the symbolic way, rests on a profound *similarity* beneath the surface dissimilarities; what we see and speak of must be the differences, but we rest in the faith that all is empowered by the breath of God, Being-Itself.[13] The vision of God, the goal of all creation, is the belief that one day all of creation shall be one. The many shall return to the One, for the many are in secret one already.[14]

Now, try as we might, many if not most of us cannot work ourselves back into this mentality. If the destiny of religious language rests on a return to the traditional sacramental universe, if the significance of imagistic language depends on a belief that symbols participate in a transcendent reality, the future for religious language is grim. I do not believe either is the case—that we must or can return to such a sacramental universe or that the significance of images rests on symbolic participationism. In fact, we have not had a classic sacramental mentality for a long time (even though it hangs on in many quarters and, improperly understood, is the source of much literalistic realism in religious language). In effect, however, we have not had such a sensibility since at least the Protestant Reformation. One way to describe what occurred in the Reformation is a profound questioning of the symbolic mentality, a loosening of the connections between symbol and its reference. The eucharistic debate between Luther and the proponents of transubstantiation on the one hand, and between Luther and Zwingli on the other hand, reveals as much. Luther took a mediating position between the bread and wine as one with the body and the blood and these elements as a mere sign recalling them.[15] To Luther, the bread and the wine were still symbols of Christ's body and blood, still participated in that reality, but in a way that I would call "metaphorical," for the assertions "This is my body" and

"This is my blood" were not viewed as identity statements, but as including a silent but present negative. One critical difference between symbolic and metaphorical statements is that the latter always contain the whisper, "it is *and it is not.*"

I suggest, therefore, that one of the distinctive characteristics of Protestant thought is its insistence on the "and it is not." It is the iconoclastic tendency in Protestantism, what Paul Tillich calls the "Protestant Principle," the fear of idolatry, the concern lest the finite ever be imagined to be capable of the infinite. We see it in Martin Luther's "masks" of God, that God is revealed and veiled in all symbols; in John Calvin's notion of divine "accommodation" by which God stoops to our level by speaking in signs and images; and in an extreme form in Karl Barth's concept of *analogia fidei,* which insists that our language refers to God only as God from time to time causes our words to conform to the divine being.

The Protestant tradition is, I would suggest, "metaphorical"; the Catholic, "symbolical" (or "analogical" for contemporary Catholicism). I do not mean to suggest a hard and fast distinction here, but only a characteristic sensibility. The Protestant sensibility tends to see dissimilarity, distinction, tension and hence to be skeptical and secular, stressing the transcendence of God and the finitude of creation. The Catholic sensibility tends to see similarity, connection, harmony and, hence, to be believing and religious, stressing the continuity between God and creation. These caricatures are not meant to be directly related to the Protestant and Catholic ecclesiastical institutions or even to the theologies supported by these bodies. Not only are many Protestants "catholic" and many Catholics "protestant," but it is obvious that either tendency without the other would be insupportable. They are complementary. However, a sacramentalism of the medieval sort—the classic Catholic mentality—is not viable today, nor is it supported by most Catholics who seek a revitalization of this tradition. The most sophisticated revitalizations of the symbolic, sacramental tradition interpret it analogically, that is, in a way that stresses many of the characteristics of the metaphorical sensibility: its emphasis on the neg-

ativities, on the distance between image and what it represents, on its refusal of easy harmonies. Obversely, a Protestant sensibility which failed to see any connections or unity between God and the world would be totally negative and agnostic. A metaphorical perspective *does* see connections but they are of a tensive, discontinuous, and surprising nature.

One of the interesting and important characteristics of contemporary ecumenical theology is that it is neither traditionally Catholic nor Protestant, emphasizing neither easy continuities nor radical discontinuities, but some form of both. However, as David Tracy points out in his recent book, *The Analogical Imagination,* there are characteristic differences in the Christian community between those for whom experience in the world engenders primarily a sense of wonder and trust and those for whom it engenders primarily a need for healing and transformation.[16] The first moves from an awareness of harmony, taking the negativities into account, while the second moves from an awareness of the negativities, reaching toward a future harmony. They are two "ways," one not necessarily better than the other; it is the contention of this essay, however, that the Protestant sensibility is more characteristic of our time and is the place from which many of us must start. What we seek, then, is a form of theology, a form for our talk about God both at the primary religious level of images and the secondary theological level of concepts, which takes the Protestant sensibility seriously.

Metaphorical Theology

If modernity were the only criterion, our task would be relatively easy. But such is never the case in theology. Christian theology is always an interpretation of the "Gospel" in a particular time and place. So the other task of equal importance is to show that a *metaphorical theology* is indigenous to Christianity, not just in the sense that it is permitted, but is called for. And this I believe is the case. The heart of the Gospel in the New Testament is widely accepted to be the "kingdom of God"; what the kingdom is or means is never expressed but indirectly suggested by the parables of the kingdom.[17] The parables are by no means the only form in the New Testament which deals with the kingdom and we must be cautious lest we make an idol of them. However, as the dominant genre of Jesus' teaching on the kingdom, they suggest some central, albeit indirect, clues to its reality. As a form of religious language, the parables of the New Testament are very different from symbolic, sacramental language. They do not assume a believing or religious perspective on the part of the listeners to whom they are addressed; they do not assume continuity between our world and a transcendent one; they do not see similarity, connection, and harmony between our ways and the ways of God. On the contrary, they are a secular form of language, telling stories of ordinary people involved in mundane family, business, and social matters; they assume a non-believing or secular attitude on the part of their audience; they stress the discontinuity between our ways and the ways of the kingdom; they focus on the dissimilarity, incongruity, and tension between the assumptions and expectations of their characters and another set of assumptions and expectations identified with the kingdom. In other words, they are a form peculiarly suited to what I have called the Protestant sensibility.

They are so suited because they are metaphors, not symbols. They are metaphorical statements about religious matters, about what both transcends and affects us at the deepest level of our existence. What is it about a religious metaphorical statement which makes it more powerful than a symbolical statement? The answer to this question centers on the nature of metaphor and especially of metaphorical statements. To many people "metaphor" is merely a poetic ornament for illustrating an idea or adding rhetorical color to abstract or flat language. It appears to have little to do with ordinary language until one realizes that most ordinary language is composed of "dead metaphors," some obvious, such as "the arm of the chair" and others less obvious, such as "tradition," meaning "to hand over or hand down." Most simply, a metaphor is seeing one thing *as* something else, pretending "this" is

"that" because we do not know how to think or talk about "this," so we use "that" as a way of saying something about it. Thinking metaphorically means spotting a thread of similarity between two dissimilar objects, events, or whatever, one of which is better known than the other, and using the better-known one as a way of speaking about the lesser known.

Poets use metaphor all the time because they are constantly speaking about the great unknowns—mortality, love, fear, joy, guilt, hope, and so on. Religious language is deeply metaphorical for the same reason and it is therefore no surprise that Jesus' most characteristic form of teaching, the parables, should be extended metaphors. Less obvious, but of paramount importance, is the fact that metaphorical thinking constitutes the basis of human thought and language. From the time we are infants we construct our world through metaphor; that is, just as young children learn the meaning of the color red by finding the thread of similarity through many dissimilar objects (red ball, red apple, red cheeks), so we constantly ask when we do not know how to think about something, "What is it like?" Far from being an esoteric or ornamental rhetorical device superimposed *on* ordinary language, metaphor *is* ordinary language. It is the *way* we think. We often make distinctions between ordinary and poetic language, assuming that the first is direct and the second indirect, but actually both are indirect, for we always think by indirection. The difference between the two kinds of language is only that we have grown accustomed to the indirections of ordinary language; they have become conventional. Likewise, conceptual or abstract language is metaphorical in the sense that the ability to generalize depends upon seeing similarity within dissimilarity; a concept is an abstraction of the similar from a sea of dissimilars. Thus, Darwin's theory of the survival of the fittest is a high-level metaphorical exercise of recognizing a similar pattern amid an otherwise incredibly diverse set of phenomena.

The primary answer to the question of why religious metaphorical statements are so powerful is that they are in continuity with the way we think ordinarily. We are not usually conscious of the metaphorical character of our thought, of seeing "this" in terms of "that," of finding the thread of similarity amid dissimilars, but it is the only way a child's world can be constructed or our worlds expanded and transformed. Of course, there are important differences between ordinary and religious metaphorical statements which we shall fully note, but the first thing is to insist on their continuity. Symbolic statements, on the other hand, are not so much a way of knowing and speaking as they are sedimentation and solidification of metaphor. For in symbolical or sacramental thought, one does not think of "this" *as* "that," but "this" as *a part of* "that." The tension of metaphor is absorbed by the harmony of symbol.

Another way to discern the distinction between metaphorical and sacramental thinking is to say that in metaphorical statements we always make judgments. That is, we make assertions; we say "I am thinking about 'this' in terms of 'that'." The only times we do not think this way is when we have already accepted a particular way of thinking of something. When we already know something, that is, when we have accepted a perspective on something, then we see and think about it "directly," or so it seems. Actually, it is not the case that anything can be known or thought of directly or literally; rather, we have simply acquired a way of looking at it which is acceptable to us. Even as simple a statement as "this is a chair" means only that I have made a judgment that I will think about this object *as* a chair because there is sufficient similarity between this object and other objects which I have called "chairs" in the past that I believe my assertion is justified. The example may appear ridiculous but it was chosen because it illustrates metaphorical thinking at its most common, continuous, and instantaneous level. It is the same *kind* of thinking as the assertion "Jesus is the savior," inasmuch as here again one is making a decision to think of one thing in terms of another; in both cases, a judgment is involved that similarity is present. The differences between the two statements are vast and important, such as the degree of existential involvement and the much greater ignorance

of the subject matter, as well as the novelty of the assertion in the second statement. The point to stress, however, is that human thought is of a piece, it is indirect, and it involves judgments.[18]

We have remarked that metaphor finds the vein of similarity in the midst of dissimilars, while symbol rests on similarity already present and assumed. But the difference is even more marked: metaphor not only lives in the region of dissimilarity, but also in the region of the unconventional and surprising. Both humor and the grotesque are distinctly metaphorical.[19] Humor is the recognition of a *very* unlikely similarity among dissimilars and we laugh because we are surprised to discover that such unlikes are indeed alike in at least one respect. A great many jokes take the form, "How is a ——— like a ———?" Likewise, the grotesque forces us to look at radical incongruity, at what is outside, does not fit, is strange and disturbing. Both are extreme metaphorical forms which point up a crucial characteristic of metaphor: good metaphors shock, they bring unlikes together, they upset conventions, they involve tension, and they are implicitly revolutionary. The parables of Jesus are typically metaphorical in this regard, for they bring together dissimilars (lost coins, wayward children, buried treasure, and tardy laborers with the kingdom of God); they shock and disturb; they upset conventions and expectations and in so doing have revolutionary potential. In this regard, one could characterize symbolic, sacramental thinking as priestly and metaphorical thinking as prophetic. The first assumes an order and unity already present waiting to be realized; the second projects, tentatively, a possible transformed order and unity yet to be realized.[20]

Perhaps the most striking evidence of the revolutionary character of the New Testament parables is the redefinition they give to conventional understandings of the monarchical, hierarchical metaphors of "kingdom" and "rule." God's "kingdom," we discover from the parables, is not like any worldly reign; in fact, its essence is its opposition to the power of the mighty over the lowly, the rich over the poor, the righteous over the unrighteous. It is a *new* rule which is defined by the extraordinary reversal of expectations in the parables as well as in the life and death of Jesus.

The characteristics of metaphorical thinking we have suggested—ordinariness, incongruity, indirection, skepticism, judgment, unconventionality, surprise, and transformation or revolution—especially as they are realized in Jesus' parables, have persuaded many people to think of Jesus as a parable of God.[21] That is to say, the life and death of Jesus of Nazareth can be understood as itself a "parable" of God; in order to understand the ways of God with us—something unfamiliar and unknown to us, about which we do not know how to think or talk—we look at that life as a metaphor of God. What we see through that "grid" or "screen" is at one level an ordinary, secular story of a human being, but also a story shot through with surprise, unconventionality, and incongruities which not only upset our conventional expectations (for instance, of what a "savior" is and who gets "saved"), but also involve a judgment on our part—"Surely this man is the Christ." In contrast to incarnational christology, however, parabolic christology does not involve an assumption of continuity or identity between the human and the divine; it is not a "Jesusolatry," a form of idolatry. It is, I believe, a christology for the Protestant sensibility and the modern mentality.

All the foregoing comments on metaphor, parable, and Jesus as a parable require considerable elaboration. Perhaps, however, these brief introductory remarks are sufficient for us to attempt to advance a case for a metaphorical theology. If metaphor is the way by which we understand as well as enlarge our world and change it—that is, if the only way we have of dealing with the unfamiliar and new is in terms of the familiar and the old, thinking of "this" as "that" although we know the new thing is both like *and* unlike the old—if all this is the case, then it is no surprise that Jesus taught in parables or that many see him as a parable of God. For he introduced a new, strange way of being in the world, a way that could be grasped only through the indirection of stories of familiar life which both "were and were not" the kingdom. And he himself was in the

world in a new, strange way which was in many respects an ordinary life but one which also, as with the parables, called the mores and conventions of ordinary life into radical question.

A metaphorical theology, then, starts with the parables of Jesus and with Jesus as a parable of God. This starting place does not involve a belief in the Bible as authoritative in an absolute or closed sense; it does not involve acceptance of a canon or the Bible as "the Word of God." In fact, such a perspective reverses the direction of authority suitable both to Scripture and to the Protestant sensibility. For what we have in the New Testament are confessions of faith by people who, on the basis of their experience of the way their lives were changed by Jesus' Gospel and by Jesus, *gave* authority to him and to the writings about him. The New Testament writings are foundational; they are classics; they are a beginning. But if we take seriously the parables of Jesus and Jesus as a parable of God as our starting point and model, then we cannot say that the Bible is absolute or authoritative in any sense except the way that a "classic" text is authoritative: it continues to speak to us. What must always be kept in mind is that the parables as metaphors and the life of Jesus as a metaphor of God provide characteristics for theology: a theology guided by them is open-ended, tentative, indirect, tensive, iconoclastic, transformative. Some of these characteristics appear "negative," in the sense that they qualify any attempts at idolatry, whether this be the idolatry of the Bible, of tradition, of orthodoxy, or of the Church. In such a theology *no* finite thought, product, or creature can be identified with God and this includes Jesus of Nazareth, who as parable of God both "is and is not" God. Against all forms of literalistic realism and idolatry, a metaphorical theology insists that it is not only in keeping with the Protestant sensibility to be open, tentative, and iconoclastic but that these are the characteristics of Jesus' parables and of Jesus' own way of being in the world.

On the other hand, metaphorical theology is not just a modern version of the *via negativa* or an exercise in iconoclasm. It not only says "is not" but "is," not only no but yes. If the parables of Jesus and Jesus himself as a parable of God are genuine metaphors, then they give license for language about life with God; they point to a real, an assumed similarity between the metaphors and that to which they refer. The many parables of the kingdom tell us something about the rule of God, of what it means to live in the world according to God's way. Jesus as a parable of God tells us actually and concretely (though, of course, indirectly) about God's relationship to us. In other words, a metaphorical theology is "positive" as well as "negative," giving license for speech about God as well as indicating the limits of such speech. Such a theology, as is true of all theologies, must be concerned not only with *how* we speak of God but *what* we say of God. On the question of how we speak of God, a metaphorical theology is firmly opposed to literalism and idolatry of all kinds; on the question of what we say about God, metaphorical theology again turns to the parables and to Jesus as a parable for beginning, foundational clues.

The parables of the New Testament are united by a number of characteristics, of which one of the most outstanding is their concern with *relationships* of various kinds. What is important in the parables is not *who* the characters are (a static notion) but *what they do* (a dynamic one). The plot is always the heart of a parable, what a character or several characters decide in matters having to do with their *relationships with each other*. Whether one thinks of the parable of the Prodigal Son, the Good Samaritan, the Unjust Steward, or the Great Supper, it is relationships and decisions about them that are critical.[22] Just as the central Old Testament religious language is relational—focused on the covenant between God and Israel; so the central New Testament language is relational—focused on persons and their way of being in the world in community. Likewise, if we look at Jesus as a parable of God, we have no alternative but to recognize personal, relational language as the most appropriate language about God. Whatever more one may wish to say about him, he was a person relating to other persons in loving service and transforming power.

I have emphasized the word "person" for two reasons. First, as we were made *in the image of God* (Gen. 3:27), so we now, with the model of Jesus, have further support for imagining God in *our* image, the image of persons. This means that personal, relational images are central in a metaphorical theology—images of God as father, mother, lover, friend, savior, ruler, governor, servant, companion, comrade, liberator, and so on. The Judeo-Christian tradition has always been personalistic and relational in its religious languages. This need not be seen as crude anthropomorphism, but as foundational language, the dominant model, of God-talk. Such language, however, is not the only appropriate religious language: no *one* model can ever be adequate. We find—both in Scripture and in our tradition—naturalistic, impersonal images balancing the relational, personal ones: God as rock, fortress, running stream, power, sun, thunder, First Cause, and so on. This Judeo-Christian tradition has had a decidedly personalistic rather than naturalistic tendency, with appalling consequences for the exploitation of the natural environment. This tradition is personalistic, however, not in an individualistic but in a relational sense, and it is therefore appropriate and required that a revolutionary hermeneutic of this tradition broaden relationship to its widest dimensions, including the entire natural world. In any case, a metaphorical theology will insist that *many* metaphors and models are necessary, that a piling up of images is essential, both to avoid idolatry and to attempt to express the richness and variety of the divine-human relationship.

The second reason for stressing the word "person" is to underscore, in as strong and definitive a way as possible, that it is not patriarchal language which is licensed by Jesus as parable of God. The Christian tradition, and the Jewish as well, have been and still are deeply patriarchal. We will be giving substantial time to this issue, for the profound penetration of the patriarchal model not only in theology but also in the structures of Western culture makes it a critical one for any metaphorical theology to consider. What is stressed in the parables and in Jesus' own life focuses on persons and their relationships; therefore, the dominance of the patriarchal model in the Christian tradition must be seen as a perversion in its hegemony of the field of religious models and its exclusion of other personal, relational models. The dominance of the patriarchal model is idolatrous in its assumption of privileged appropriateness. To put the issue in its simplest form, God's name is not "father" although many Christians use "God" and "father" interchangeably as if "father" were a literal description of God.

A metaphorical theology, then, will emphasize personal, relational categories in its language about God, but not necessarily as the tradition has interpreted these categories. On the contrary, if one looks to the parables and Jesus as a parable to gain some preliminary understanding of what "person" means and what "relationship" means, both applied to us and to God, one finds not a baptizing of conventional hierarchies of relationships, whether these be of class, race, sex, or whatever, but a radical transformation of our expectations. For instance, if we are to say "God is father" it is both true *and* untrue, and even where true, it is different from conventional views of patriarchal fatherhood. If we are to call ourselves "children" in relationship to God, this is a limited and in some respects false image. There are personal, relational models which have been suppressed in the Christian tradition because of their social and political consequences; they are, however, as appropriate as the fatherhood model and are necessary both to qualify it and to include the images of personal, relational life of large numbers of people whose experiences have been excluded from traditional Christian language. To mention but two examples in passing, "mother" and "liberator" are metaphors of profound personal relationships with vast potential as models for God. They arise out of the depths of human relational existence and are licensed by the parabolic dimension of the New Testament, not in a literal way (the words do not appear), but in the sense that the characteristics

we associate with "mother" and "liberator" fit with (and, of course, also do not fit with) the surprising rule of God as we have it in the parables and the parable of Jesus.

But a metaphorical theology cannot stop with metaphors, with the parables and the life and death of Jesus as extended metaphors of God's rule. Metaphor, parables, and Jesus as parable *fund* theology, but are not theology. If we wish to be precise, we must make a distinction between primary and secondary religious language, between metaphorical and conceptual language. But it is impossible to keep the distinction clear because most primary religious language is implicitly conceptual and most secondary theological language is latently imagistic. The parables of Jesus cry out for interpretation—not for *one* interpretation, but nonetheless for answers to the question, "What does this parable mean?" The richness of imagistic language means that it will always spawn many interpretations. Likewise, the biblical story of Jesus' life and death, an extended metaphor itself and packed with many supporting metaphors (Jesus as Messiah, as Son of man, as Suffering Servant, and so on), is not just a story but is already highly interpreted. What the story *means* is the perspective from which it is told and not something tacked on to pure, unadulterated images. Or if we think of Paul's letters, we see a mixture of images and concepts, the images moving in the direction of concepts in the sense that, for instance, when Paul tells us we are buried with Christ so that we might rise with him, he also tells us what this means (baptism, or the newness of the Christian life). Or if one considers the Nicene Creed, one sees a mixture of imagistic and conceptual language: the phrase "God of God, Light of Light, Very God of Very God, Begotten not made, Being of one substance with the Father" and so on was deemed necessary to interpret the imagistic language "one Lord Jesus Christ" and "Son of God." Whether the interpretations are good ones, are appropriate, or are still meaningful to us is beside the point. What is critical at the moment is that *some* interpretation is necessary; imagistic language does not just tolerate interpretation but *demands* it.

Thus, metaphorical theology does not stop with metaphors but must deal with the entire gamut of religious/theological language. Robert Funk has noted that it is a tortuous route between Jesus' parables and systematic theology.[23] Indeed it is, but that route must be traversed, for to stop at the level of images, of metaphor, of story is inevitably to give over either to baptizing certain images (usually biblical ones) as alone appropriate or to finding religious images sterile and meaningless. In other words, in terms of the twin issues of idolatry and irrelevance in religious language, *moving beyond* metaphors is necessary both to avoid literalizing them and to attempt significant interpretations of them for our time. It is impossible just to tell "the simple story of Jesus" and it was not told that way in the first place, for the many "stories" of Jesus in the New Testament are each told within several layers of interpretation.

In the continuum of religious language from primary, imagistic to secondary, conceptual, a form emerges which is a mixed type: *the model.* The simplest way to define a model is as a dominant metaphor, a metaphor with staying power. Metaphors are usually the work of an individual, a flash of insight which is often passing. But some metaphors gain wide appeal and become major ways of structuring and ordering experience. Thus, T. S. Eliot's Wasteland or W. H. Auden's Age of Anxiety became perspectives from which modern culture was perceived. There are many kinds of models—scale models, picture models, analogue and theoretical models, as well as root-metaphors which are similar to models but of wider range. For our preliminary purposes, however, the main point is that models are a further step along the route from metaphorical to conceptual language. They are similar to metaphors in that they are images which retain the tension of the "is and is not" and, like religious and poetic metaphors, they have emotional appeal insofar as they suggest ways of understanding our being in the world. The example we have used before, "God the father," comes readily to mind: it is a metaphor which has become a model. As a model it not only retains characteristics of metaphor

but also reaches toward qualities of conceptual thought. It suggests a comprehensive, ordering structure with impressive interpretive potential. As a rich model with many associated commonplaces as well as a host of supporting metaphors, an entire theology can be worked out from this model. Thus, if God is understood on the model of "father," human beings are understood as "children," sin is rebellion against the "father," redemption is sacrifice by the "elder son" on behalf of the "brothers and sisters" for the guilt against the "father" and so on.[24]

Models, as is true of metaphors but in an organic, consistent, and comprehensive manner, give us a way of thinking about the unknown in terms of the known. As Max Black says, a model gives us a "grid," "screen," or "filter" which helps us to organize our thoughts about a less familiar subject by means of seeing it in terms of a more familiar one. He gives the example of seeing a military battle in terms of a chess game. The chess model will help to understand tactics and the movement of armies; as he shrewdly notes, however, it also "screens out" certain other aspects of battle—for instance, we will not think of blood and death if we use only the chess analogy.[25] Models are necessary, then, for they give us something to think about when we do not know what to think, a way of talking when we do not know how to talk. But they are also dangerous, for they exclude other ways of thinking and talking, and in so doing they can easily become literalized, that is, identified as *the* one and only way of understanding a subject. This danger is more prevalent with models than with metaphors because models have a wider range and are more permanent; they tend to object to competition in ways that metaphors do not. In many Old Testament psalms the psalmist will pile up metaphors for God in a riotous *melée*, mixing "rock," "lover," "fortress," "midwife," "fresh water," "judge," "helper," "thunder" and so on in a desperate attempt to express the richness of God's being. But models do not welcome such profusion; even in the case of models of the same *type* (for instance, "God the mother" along with "God the father") there is often great resistance. This is due, in part, to the literalization of models and it is probably the single greatest risk in their use.

It should be evident by now, however, that in all matters except the most conventional (where widely accepted perspectives or models are already operating), thinking by metaphor and hence by models is not optional but necessary. And this is true in the sciences as well as in the humanities. It is sometimes supposed that science deals with its subject matter directly, empirically; science is "factual" whereas poetry and religion are "spiritual, emotional, or imaginative." Unlike them, science does not need the indirection of metaphor but can move inductively from empirical observations to theory and from theory to verification in the "real" world. This positivistic view of science is fortunately no longer the only force in science; rather, what one finds is that much of the most interesting and suggestive work on models is being done by scientists, especially physicists. Relatively little has been written by theologians on models in religion; however, the literature on models in science is enormous, going back a good twenty-five years. As physics comes increasingly to deal with invisibles such as subatomic particles, behaviors of entities that must be imagined rather than observed, it finds itself in a position similar to poetry and religion in that it must attempt to understand the unknown in terms of known models. Also, as more and more conclusions in physics (as well as in many of the other sciences) are expressed in mathematical formulas, models become the only way of connecting scientific knowledge both with ordinary language and with other domains of science. Finally, and most importantly, scientists need models for discovering the new; to think of the new in terms of the old, so long as one does not collapse the two, can often, through the dialectic of similarity and dissimilarity, provide a breakthrough.

There are other uses of models in science as well. But the critical point for our preliminary purposes is to note the widespread acceptance of models in science as well as in many other disciplines. One finds thinking by models in biology, computer science, education theory, political science, ethics, psychology, sociology, and so on. The self-conscious use of models, in regard to both their benefits and their risks, is a common phenomenon in most fields of study. What this means, among other things, is that poetry and religion, the two fields which have always known they must think via metaphor (and as a consequence have been denied by many as dealing in knowledge—truth and meaning), now find that their way of metaphor and indirection is widely accepted as necessary in all creative, constructive thought. A scientist doing a routine experiment does not need models, but a scientist devising an experiment to test a hypothesis may very well need to try out various models in order to locate what is unfamiliar about the present case. And so it is in all creative ventures. What we do not know, we must simulate through models of what we do know.

Because of the centrality of models in science and the amount of analysis available on scientific models, we will be looking carefully at some of this material for possible insights into the ways models function in theology. We will discover, for instance, that as interpretive, explanatory devices religious models share structural characteristics with scientific models; but because models in religion emerge from existential experience, they have affectional dimensions as do poetic metaphors. But a metaphorical theology cannot stop at the level of models. To be sure, considerable interpretive activity takes place at such a stage: as dominant metaphors, models manifest priorities within a religious tradition; as organizing networks of images, they are well on the way to systematic thought; as comprehensive ways of envisioning reality, they implicitly raise questions of truth and reference; as metaphors that control the ways people envision both human and divine reality, they cannot avoid the issue of criteria in the choice of certain models and the exclusion of others. A further step of interpretation, however, is called for: conceptual interpretation and criticism.

Concepts and theories arise from metaphors and models; they are an attempt to generalize at the level of abstraction concerning competing and, at times, contradictory metaphors and models. By "concept" we mean an abstract notion; by "theory" we mean a speculative, systematic statement of relationships underlying certain phenomena. A concept is an idea or thought; a theory organizes ideas into an explanatory structure. Concepts, unlike metaphors, do not create new meaning, but rely on conventional, accepted meanings. Theories, unlike models, do not systematize one area in terms of another, but organize concepts into a whole. These definitions are only minimally helpful, however, for they are too neat and compartmentalized for a metaphorical theology. If our thesis holds that *all* thought is indirect, then all concepts and theories are metaphorical in the sense that they too are constructions; they are indirect attempts to interpret reality, which never can be dealt with directly. Concepts and theories, however, are at the far end of the continuum and rarely expose their metaphorical roots. These distinctions mainly show the different functions of metaphor, model, and concept or theory in the *one* task of interpreting our being in the world.

Conceptual language tends toward univocity, toward clear and concise meanings for ambiguous, multileveled, imagistic language. In this process something is lost and something is gained: richness and multivalency are sacrificed for precision and consistency. Conceptual thought attempts to find similarities among the models while models insist on dissimilarities among themselves. The relationship, however, is symbiotic. Images "feed" concepts; concepts "discipline" images. Images without concepts are blind; concepts without images are sterile. In a metaphorical theology, there is no suggestion of a hierarchy among metaphors, models, and concepts: concepts are not higher, better, or more necessary than images, or vice versa. Images are never free of the need for interpretation by concepts, their critique of competing images, or their demythologizing of literalized models. Concepts are never free of the need for funding by images, the affectional and existential richness of images, and the qualification against conceptual pretensions supplied by the plurality of images. In no sense can systematic thought be said to *explain* metaphors and models so that they be-

come mere illustrations for concepts; rather, the task of conceptual thought is to generalize (often in philosophical language, *the* generalizing language), to criticize images, to raise questions of their meaning and truth in explicit ways.

An example of the movement from parable toward conceptual thought can be illustrated briefly by the career of "the kingdom of God." I would call "the kingdom of God" the root-metaphor of Christianity which is supported and fed by many extended metaphors, the various parables. No *one* parable is adequate as a way of seeing the kingdom, and all the parables together undoubtedly are not either, but they are all that is provided. Many extended metaphors are necessary to give meaning to the model of the kingdom; taken together they display certain common features which are not illustrations of the kingdom so much as exemplifications of it. The process of understanding and interpreting these common features is not deductive or inductive but dialectical: "the rule of God" at this stage *is* all of the parabolic exemplifications. In the hands of Paul and his notion of "justification by faith," however, we move to a higher level of interpretation by a concept generalizing on that rule. Paul Ricoeur points out, and I believe rightly, that Paul's notion is in continuity with the foundational language of "the kingdom of God" and the underlying parables, but it is less particular, more generalized; less concrete, more abstract; less imagistic, more univocal. Ricoeur calls Paul's concept a "translation language," a semi-conceptual mode of discourse which remains under the control of the hermeneutical potential of metaphor *because* it preserves the tension of the foundational language.[26]

For another example of the relationship among metaphors, models, and concepts, one must remember that metaphors and models of God will range widely and have various degrees of dominance within a tradition: person, king, rock, mother, savior, father, fortress, lover, liberator, helper, and many more. We must ask questions of these models. Which ones are dominant? Why should certain ones be dominant? Are they consistent? Are the central models comprehensive? To whom are they significant? To whom are they meaningless or objectionable? Are they fruitful in the sense that they help us to understand our lives better, and are they commensurate with other matters we hold to be important? Do they fit with lived experience or do they have to be rationalized in order to be held? All of these questions and more fall under the heading of the critique of metaphors and models that is the task of conceptual thought.

Systematic thought also tries to organize all the dominant models in a tradition into an overarching system with a key model of its own. For instance, for Paul it was justification by grace through faith; for Augustine, the radical dependence of all that is on God; for Aquinas, the analogy of being whereby each creature participates in and glorifies God through realizing its proper finite end; for Schleiermacher, the feeling of absolute dependence; for Barth, the election of all people to salvation in the election of Jesus Christ before the foundation of the world. Each of these is a radical model, which could be called a "root-metaphor": "a root-metaphor is the most basic assumption about the nature of the world or experience that we can make when we try to give a description of it."[27] Each root-metaphor is a way of seeing "all that is" through a particular key concept. It is also thinking by models and, as is evident, even these root-metaphors are still metaphors: at the highest level of abstraction and generalization one does not escape metaphor (the exceptions are symbolic logic and higher mathematics which do not pretend to refer to reality as lived).

Therefore, we will focus on *models* because, as mediators between metaphors and concepts, they partake of the characteristics of each and are an especially fruitful type of expression to investigate for a metaphorical theology. The aim of a metaphorical theology, as we recall, is to envision ways of talking about the relationship between the divine and the human which are nonidolatrous but relevant: ways which can be said to be true without being literal; ways which are meaningful to all peoples, the traditionally excluded as well as the included. Such a theology, I believe, is appropriate to the Protestant sensibility and I have suggested clues to its character from the parables of Jesus and Jesus as parable. In this framework, moreover, models are critical because models are dominant *metaphors:* they retain the tension of metaphor—its "is and is not" quality which refuses all literalization. Models are also *dominant* metaphors: they are dominant within a tradition both because they have earned that right as "classics" which speak to people across many ages and because they have usurped that right to the false exclusion of other metaphors. Both their right and their usurpation of right must be taken into account.

The tasks of a metaphorical theology will become clear: to understand the centrality of models in religion and the particular models in the Christian tradition; to criticize literalized, exclusive models; to chart the relationships among metaphors, models, and concepts; and to investigate possibilities for transformative, revolutionary models.[28] The goal of this analysis can then be thought of as an attempt to question the *didactic* tradition of orthodoxy over the more flexible, open, *kerygmatic* point of view epitomized in the parables and Jesus as parable. What must be done in a metaphorical theology is to open up the relationships among metaphor, model, and concept for the purpose both of justifying dominant, founding metaphors as true but not literal *and* of discovering other appropriate dominant metaphors which for cultural, political, and social reasons have been suppressed.

The final task of a metaphorical theology will be a reforming, transforming one. As metaphorical, such theology can never be simply a baptizing of the tradition, for that would mean giving up the *tension* which is at the heart of metaphor. The classic models of the Christian tradition have been and still are hierarchical, authoritarian ones which have been absolutized. As feminist theologians have become increasingly aware, the orthodox tradition did a thorough job of plumbing the depths of one such model, the patriarchal, as a way of being articulate about God. Feminists have become conscious of the profound structural implications of this model as a form of ecclesiastical, social, political, economic, and personal oppression. The problem does not lie with the model itself of "God the father," for it is a profound metaphor and as true as any religious model available, but it has established a hegemony over the Western religious consciousness which it is the task of metaphorical theology to break. The "outsiders" to the mainline Christian tradition—women, blacks, third world people—are questioning the hierarchical, authoritarian, patriarchal models of Western theology. If Christianity is a universal religion (and not a tribal one for white, middle-class males), such voices are legitimate and necessary. As an example of one such voice, we will look at new religious images and models being suggested by women and we will do so in the spirit of openness to the future and to the unity that lies in the future, a spirit appropriate to a metaphorical theology. As Ursula LeGuin, a fantasy and science-fiction writer, says, truth lies in the imagination.[29] This may be only half a truth, but it is the half we most often forget.

NOTES

1. Simone Weil, *Waiting for God* (New York: Harper & Row, 1973), p. 32.

2. See Frank Kermode, *The Classic: Literary Images of Permanence and Change* (New York: Viking Press, 1975).

3. James Hillman in *Re-Visioning Psychology* (New York: Harper & Row, 1977) claims Protestantism denied the imagination and myth and killed off fantasy. See the article by Lucy Bregman, "Religious Imagination: Polytheistic Psychology Confronts Calvin," *Soundings* 63 (1980): 36–60. Bregman also suggests an intriguing list that includes the "left" and "right" brains, equating literalism with the left and symbolism with the right.

Rational	Imaginative
Technology	Art
Literal	Symbolic
History	Myth
Western	Eastern, primitive
Masculine	Feminine
Left-brain	Right-brain
Reformation	Renaissance
Repressive	Liberating
Sacred text	Myth
Work ethic	Spontaneous pleasure

4. Clifford Geertz, "Religion as a Cultural System," in *Reader in Comparative Religion*, 2d ed. rev., ed. William Lessa and Evon Vogt (New York: Harper & Row, 1965), p. 209.

5. Ian T. Ramsey, *Religious Language* (New York: Macmillan Co., 1963), p. 107.

6. Phyllis Trible, *God and the Rhetoric of Sexuality,* Overtures to Biblical Theology (Philadelphia: Fortress Press, 1978), p. 16.

7. The following quotation by Carol Christ and Judith Plaskow is an excellent summary of the feminist critique of language and the importance of naming.

> Consciousness-raising . . . leads to a critique of culture and to the tasks of transforming or recreating it. Feminists have called their task a "new naming" of self and world. It is through naming that humans progress from childhood to adulthood and learn to understand and shape the world about them. Under patriarchy, men have reserved to themselves the right to name, keeping women in a state of intellectual and spiritual dependency. Mary Daly suggests that the Genesis creation story, in which Adam names the animals and woman, is the paradigm of false naming in Western culture. If the world has been named by Adam without Eve's consultation, then the world has been named from the male point of view. As women begin to name the world for themselves, they will upset the order that has been taken for granted throughout history. They will call themselves and the world into new being. Naming women's experience thus becomes the model not only for personal liberation and growth, but for the feminist transformation of culture and religion (Carol Christ and Judith Plaskow, eds., *Womanspirit Rising: A Feminist Reader in Religion* [New York: Harper & Row, 1979], p. 7).

8. The reasons for patriarchy undoubtedly derive in part from the fact that as Elaine Pagels, along with many other scholars, points out, the God of Israel, unlike most other deities in the ancient Near East, shared his power with no female divinity. She writes,

> he scarcely can be characterized in any but masculine epithets: King, Lord, Master, Judge, and Father. Indeed, the absence of feminine symbolism of God marks Judaism, Christianity, and Islam in striking contrast to the world's other religious traditions, whether in Egypt, Babylonia, Greece, and Rome, or Africa, Polynesia, India, and North America. Jewish, Christian, and Islamic theologians, however, are quick to point out that God is not to be considered in sexual terms at all. Yet the actual language they use in worship and prayer conveys a different message and gives the distinct impression that God is thought of in exclusively *masculine* terms ("What Became of God the Mother? Conflicting Images of God in Early Christianity," in *Womanspirit Rising,* ed. Christ and Plaskow, p. 107).

9. This point is made at length in the classic study by Peter Berger, *The Social Reality of Religion* (London: Faber & Faber, 1969).

10. See, for example, Rita M. Gross, ed., *Beyond Androcentrism: New Essays on Women and Religion* (Missoula, Mont.: Scholars Press, 1977).

11. Incarnational theology, based on "the Word became flesh," eventuated in the orthodox christology

which has always been cryptically Docetic. In spite of the formula, "fully God and fully man," the human partnership was never taken with full seriousness, for again and again the church has been unwilling to deal with such matters as growth and change in Jesus of Nazareth as evidenced by its uneasiness about admitting the possibility of sin in him. An incarnational christology is inevitably static and nature-oriented, rather than dynamic and human-oriented. A thoughtful debate on incarnational christology can be found in John Hick, ed., *The Myth of God Incarnate* (Philadelphia: Westminster Press; London: SCM Press, 1977).

12. There are of course many fine studies of sacramentalism and it is not necessary or appropriate here to list them. A particularly interesting one, however, is Mary Douglas's *Natural Symbols* (New York: Pantheon Books, 1970) because she sees a direct connection both in primitive and advanced cultures between attitudes toward the body and the ability to think sacramentally. She finds Protestantism especially alienated in this regard, for its stress on inner experience, denigration of ritual, and rejection of mediating institutions make it impossible to see the body and hence the world from a symbolic perspective. I find her analysis of our problematic situation—one in which all connections have been broken—illuminating, but her solution—a return to organic sacramentalism with the full paraphernalia of medieval orthodox incarnationalism—insupportable.

13. The medieval doctrine of analogical predication rests on the analogy of being. We can predicate human characteristics of God (goodness, wisdom, etc.) because our being was created by and is dependent upon God's being. In the order of knowing, we proceed from the creature to the creator for we must start from the concrete and empirical; in the order of being we proceed from the creator to the creature, for God possesses the characteristics we attribute absolutely and truly, thought we do not know the *mode* in which they are realized in the divine being. The two prominent types of analogical predication in medieval philosophy were analogy of attribution and of proper proportionality. Both are necessary for one provides the *content*, the other the *form*, of predication. The analogy of attribution allows that we can attribute certain qualities to God because God is the ground of being and hence everything that is participates in God—*what* we say, therefore, is based on the creature as caused by, dependent upon, the creator. The analogy of proper proportionality insists that we do not know *how* such qualities are realized in God and hence this form of analogy serves as a negation of all forms of literalism and idolatry. Another way of expressing the necessity and relationship of the two types is to say that analogies of attribution are "models" licensing certain language for God and analogies of proper proportionality are "qualifiers" insisting on the necessary distance in all talk of God. In order to say *anything* we must use models from concrete, human experience, but in order to say anything *appropriately*, we must qualify our language for we do not know how these terms refer to God. For a fuller elaboration of models and qualifiers see the works of Ian T. Ramsey.

14. The Neoplatonic background of this synthesis is obvious, but so is the Aristotelian. The stress on the independence of each particular thing and the insistence that each glorifies God *only* as it seeks its own rightful end is the contribution of Aristotle; the stress on the relationship of the many to the One as an emanation and a return is from Neoplatonism via Augustine. The issue here (and the interpretation of *analogia entis*) is very complex; my suggestions are meant not as a contribution to that debate but solely to depict in a general way some of the characteristics of a sacramental mentality. For a careful interpretation along the above lines, see Etienne Gilson, *The Christian Philosophy of St. Thomas Aquinas* (New York: Random House, 1956).

15. For a fine discussion and elaboration of this point see Erich Heller, *The Disinherited Mind: Essays in Modern German Literature and Thought* (Cleveland: World Publishing, 1961), pp. 261–68.

16. David Tracy's impressive new work, *The Analogical Imagination: Christian Theology and the Culture of Pluralism* (New York: Crossroad; London: SCM Press, 1981), presents a contemporary interpretation of the analogical sensibility that in no way falls into either heavy sacramentalism or easy harmonies oblivious of the negativities. In fact, his view of the analogical imagination is in many ways identical with my understanding of the metaphorical sensibility. At one point he quotes Aristotle on *metaphor* as support for the analogical imagination:

> The power of the analogical imagination was honored by Aristotle in his famous dictum "to spot the similar in the dissimilar is the mark of poetic genius." That same power—at once participatory in the originating event of wonder, trust, disclosure and concealment by the whole, and positively distancing itself from that event by its own self-constituting demands of critical reflection—releases the analogical imagination of the systematic theologian to note the profound similarities-in-difference in all reality (p. 410).

As Tracy notes, all post-Enlightenment attempts to revive analogy as a basic Christian sensibility must take with absolute seriousness the skepticism, relativity, negativities, and indeed chaos that characterize contemporary life at intellectual, personal, and political levels. Nonetheless, I believe there is a difference between even Tracy's analogical imagination and what I am calling the metaphorical sensibility: the former, as Tracy says, is in the tradition of "manifestation," a tradition in which a sense of trust, wonder, grace is primary even when profoundly aware of the suffering, evil, and discontinuity that pervade that basic harmony. The other two traditions which he notes as comprising Christianity—

"proclamation" and "prophetic action"—are less conscious of that underlying grace, more conscious of the distance between the human and the divine and of the negativities of existence. It is my contention that while all three perspectives are necessary for a full Christian theology, the proclamation/prophetic is not only a necessity for many people in our time but is also an authentic Christian perspective. The different perspectives, as Tracy notes, need to be intensified and articulated in their concrete particularity, as long as such intensification and articulation are carried on in conversation and openness to the other perspectives.

Another case in point is the work of David Burrell who, in his book *Analogy and Philosophical Language* (New Haven, Conn.: Yale Univ. Press, 1973) comes out in favor of metaphor as lying behind analogy and serving as the justification for analogy. His main thesis is to show with the help of Wittgenstein that ordinary language is deeply metaphorical; hence, the use of analogy in predicating of God is not a medieval, esoteric exercise but an extension of ordinary usage. What lies behind analogical predication for Burrell, then, is not *analogia entis* or the analogy of attribution but the metaphorical character of ordinary language—its dialectical, multi-faceted nature in which borrowings and cross-sortings, judgments of aptness and appropriateness are all common characteristics. Analogical predication of God is, says Burrell, the same *kind* of language.

17. Leander Keck voices the position of many New Testament exegetes in the following statement: "The whole network of words, deeds, and death which we call 'Jesus' was pulled into a pattern by the magnetic power of the kingdom and hence reflected the impingement of that kingdom on his life and work. This was not simply a matter of Jesus working out the implications of a root idea. Rather, it was a matter of being grasped by a perception in such a way that the whole career became a celebration of the kingdom's coming and thereby its vanguard as well" (*A Future for the Historical Jesus: The Place of Jesus in Preaching and Theology* [Philadelphia: Fortress Press, 1981], pp. 218–19).

18. Jean Piaget's pattern of "assimilation" and "accommodation" to define the character of learning is similar to what we have presented. Hugh Petrie writes of Piaget's theory, "during assimilation, we learn by changing experience to fit our concepts and modes of understanding. During accommodation, we learn by changing our concepts and modes of understanding to fit our experience" ("Metaphor and Learning," in *Metaphor and Thought,* ed. Andrew Ortony [New York and Cambridge: Cambridge Univ. Press, 1979], p. 440). In assimilation, we stay with existing frameworks, with the familiar; but in accommodation, we pass from the known to the unknown—we change our concepts—and this process is accomplished by

means of metaphor: "The crucial use of metaphor is our moving from one conceptual scheme with its associated way of knowing to another conceptual scheme with *its* associated way of knowing" (p. 460). Thus, metaphor is not just heuristic or illustrative, but epistemologically necessary if new learning is to take place. What we discover is an anomaly; the old framework no longer can encompass our experience and only metaphor—which connects both with what we already know *and* with what we are groping to know—provides the movement that is the distinctive mark of learning.

19. See Kenneth Burke, *Permanence and Change: An Anatomy of Purpose* (New York: New Republic, 1935).

20. I am indebted to F. W. Dillistone for his distinction between analogical and metaphorical thinking. Of analogy he writes: "In any organic system the single member is related to the whole according to some pattern of order and proportion; no figure of speech is more fitted to express this relation than analogy" (*Christianity and Symbolism* [London: William Collins, 1955], p. 152). He notes that one can move from the known to the unknown because the part participates in the whole and is similar to it. Analogical thought is positive, comprehensive, and systematic. Analogy has links with the simile, metaphor with the contrast. Metaphor focuses attention on variety and the openness of reality, and on dissimilarity rather than similarity. Metaphor holds together similarity and dissimilarity in a resolution:

> The resolution is not final, for there are ever wider areas of conflict to embrace. But every metaphor which holds together two disparate aspects of reality in creative tension assumes the character of a prophecy of the final reconciliation of all things in the kingdom of God. It is the favorite tool of all the great poets. . . . Through it the imagination performs its task, the task which Coleridge describes as dissolving, diffusing, dissipating in order to recreate, as reconciling opposite or discordant qualities, as struggling to idealise and to unify. Through it the prophet leaps outside the circle of present experience, the realm of the factual and the commonsense, the typical and the regular. He parts company with those who are travelling the surer and steadier road of analogical comparison. By one act of daring he brings into creative relationship the apparently opposite and contrary and, if his metaphorical adventure proves successful, gains new treasure both for language and for life (Ibid., p. 161).

Finally, Dillistone notes that while analogy tends toward petrification, metaphor moves toward renovation and that Jesus was a metaphorical thinker, disrupting the old by seeing it in a new light.

21. Among the several New Testament critics who see Jesus as a parable of God are Leander Keck and John Donahue. Keck writes: "Jesus concentrated on parabolic speech because he himself was a parabolic event of the kingdom of God" (*A Future for the Historical Jesus,*

p. 244). Donahue writes: "Responding to the parable of Jesus in Mark is engagement in the ultimate paradox of the Christian life ("Jesus as the Parable of God in the Gospel of Mark," *Interpretation* 32 [1978]: 386). Both exegetes substantiate their claim by a comparison of Jesus' life with the characteristics of parables: their metaphoricity, mundanity, realism, strangeness, indirection, shocking disclosive power, and existential engagement.

22. Not all parables are of this sort: the kingdom parables of the buried treasure, lost coin, and mustard seed are not, for instance, but as we shall see, relational language, while the dominant model for God, ought to be balanced and is balanced in the Bible by non-relational, impersonal, naturalistic language.

23. Robert W. Funk, "The Parables: A Fragmentary Agenda," in *Jesus and Man's Hope,* 2 vols., ed. Donald G. Miller and Dikran Y. Hadidian (Pittsburgh: Pittsburgh Theological Seminary, 1971), vol. 2, pp. 287–303.

24. One thoroughgoing version of such a theology is in Sigmund Freud's *Moses and Monotheism* (New York: Alfred A. Knopf, 1947) where the Judeo-Christian tradition is reduced to an exercise in which adherents attempt to rid themselves of latent guilt from the tribal horde's murder of the father of the clan. The Oedipus complex is the individual's version, while Western religion deals with the same issue of coming to terms with guilt from the childhood of the race. But one does not need to accept Freud's somewhat esoteric views on the subject, for there are many examples of mainline Christian theologies where the dominant categories are familiar ones derived from the structural possibilities of patriarchy. The imagistic language in both the trinitarian and christological controversies is principally "Father" and "Son" with the relationships between God and Jesus of Nazareth largely determined by the potential of these images.

25. See Max Black's fine chapters 3 and 13 in his *Models and Metaphors* (Ithaca, N.Y.: Cornell Univ. Press, 1962).

26. Paul Ricoeur, "Biblical Hermeneutics," *Semeia* 4 (1975): 138.

27. The term "root-metaphor" is Stephen Pepper's from his book *World Hypotheses* (Berkeley and Los Angeles: Univ. of California Press, 1942). The quotation is from Earl R. MacCormac, *Metaphor and Myth in Science and Religion* (Durham, N.C.: Duke Univ. Press, 1976), p. 93.

28. I have used the term "metaphorical theology" rather than "parabolic theology" because the latter limits theological discourse to the primary level. I have tried to show that, to varying degrees, all constructive thought is implicitly or explicitly metaphorical (which is not to say that "everything is metaphor," for much philosophical as well as most scientific and ordinary language is at most mainly dead metaphor and does not function as alive metaphorical language). Hence, metaphorical theology can refer to the entire spectrum from parable to concept, though by using this term stress is put on the foundational, primary language that I believe is appropriate and necessary to theology. Moreover, by retaining the term "metaphorical," the characteristics of metaphor that I find critical to a theology in keeping with the Protestant sensibility, are constantly called to mind—tentativeness, open-endedness, secularity, projected rather than realized unity, tension, transformation, revolution, skepticism, and so on.

29. Ursula K. LeGuin, *The Language of the Night: Essays on Fantasy and Science Fiction,* ed. Susan Wood (New York: G. P. Putnam's Sons, 1979), p. 159.

Suggestions for Further Reading

Alston, William P. "Can We Speak Literally of God?" In *Is God God?,* edited by Axel D. Steuer and James Abingdon. Nashville, TN: Abingdon Press, 1981.

Ayer, A. J. *Language, Truth and Logic.* New York: Dover, 1936.

Bartsch, H. W., ed. *Kerygma and Myth.* London: S.P.C.K., 1957.

Blackstone, William T. *The Problem of Religious Language.* Englewood Cliffs, NJ: Prentice-Hall, 1963.

Bultmann, Rudolph. *The Scope of Demythologizing.* New York: Harper & Row, 1968.

Cabezón, José Ignacio. *Buddhism and Language: A Study of Indo-Tibetan Scholasticism.* Albany, NY: State University of New York Press, 1994.

Deloria, Vine, Jr. *God Is Red.* New York: Grosset and Dunlap, 1973.

Diamond, Malcolm, and Litzenburg, Thomas V., Jr., eds. *The Logic of God: Theology and Verification.* Indianapolis: Bobbs-Merrill, 1975.

Douglas, Mary. *Natural Symbols.* New York: Pantheon Books, 1970.

Ferré, Frederick. *Language, Logic and God.* New York: Harper & Row, 1969.

Hepburn, Ronald W. *Christianity and Paradox.* London: Watts, 1958.

———. "Demythologizing and the Problem of Validity." In *New Essays in Philosophical Theology,* edited by Antony Flew and Alasdair MacIntyre. New York: Macmillan, 1955.

High, D. M. *Language, Persons and Belief.* New York: Oxford Univeristy Press, 1967.

———. *New Essays on Religious Language.* Oxford: Clarendon Press, 1969.

Jaspers, Karl, and Bultmann, Rudolph. *Myth and Christianity: An Inquiry into the Possibility of Religion Without Myth.* Translated by Norbert Guterman. New York: Farrar, Straus & Giroux, 1958.

Jung, Carl G., *et al. Man and His Symbols.* Garden City, NY: Doubleday, 1964.

Knox, John. *Myth and Truth.* Charlottesville, VA: University Press of Virginia, 1964.

MacQuarrie, John. *God-Talk.* New York: Harper & Row, 1968.

Martin, James A., Jr. *The New Dialogue Between Philosophy and Theology.* New York: Seabury Press, 1966.

Martin, Michael. "The Verification Challenge." In *A Companion to Philosophy of Religion,* edited by Philip L. Quinn and Charles Talliaferro. Cambridge, MA: Blackwell, 1997.

Mascal, E. L. *Existence and Analogy.* New York: Longmans, 1949.

Mitchell, Basil, ed. *Faith and Logic.* London: George Allen & Unwin, 1959.

———, ed. *The Philosophy of Religion.* London: Oxford University Press, 1971.

Overholt, Thomas W., and Callicott, J. Baird, eds. *Clothed-in-Fur and Other Tales.* Washington, DC: University Press of America, 1982.

Parsons, Elsie Clews. *Pueblo Indian Religion.* 2 vols. Chicago: University of Chicago Press, 1939.

Ramsey, Ian T. *Religious Language.* London: Student Christian Movement Press, 1957.

Randall, John Herman, Jr. *The Role of Knowledge in Western Religion.* Boston, MA: Beacon Press, 1958.

Santoni, Ronald E., ed. *Religious Language and the Problem of Religious Knowledge.* Bloomington: Indiana University Press, 1968.

Scharfstein, Ben-Ami. *Ineffability: The Failure of Words in Philosophy and Religion.* Albany, NY: State University of New York Press, 1993.

Schlick, Moritz. "Meaning and Verification." *Philosophical Review* 45 (1936).

Soskice, Janet Martin. *Metaphor and Religious Language.* Oxford, England: Oxford University Press, 1985.

———. "Religious Language." In *A Companion to Philosophy of Religion,* edited by Philip L. Quinn and Charles Talliaferro. Cambridge, MA: Blackwell, 1997.

Storm, Hyemeyohsts. *Seven Arrows.* New York: Ballantine Books, 1972.

Tedlock, Dennis, and Tedlock, Barbara. *Teachings from the American Earth.* New York: Liveright, 1975.

Tracy, David. *The Analogical Imagination: Christian Theology and the Culture of Pluralism.* New York: Crossroad Publishing, 1988.

Trigg, Roger. "Theological Realism and Antirealism." In *A Companion to Philosophy of Religion,* edited by Philip L. Quinn and Charles Talliaferro. Cambridge, MA: Blackwell, 1997.

Underhill, Ruth. *Papago Indian Religion.* New York: Columbia University Press, 1946.

Urmson, J. O. *Philosophical Analysis.* Oxford: Clarendon Press, 1956.

CHAPTER 9

Do Faith and Reason Conflict?

Introduction

IS HUMAN REASON ABLE to discover religious truth? Is logic adequate to sort out what is true and what false in religious matters? Can philosophical thinking help us determine which claims about ultimate reality are true? Do humans need some sort of revelation? Do we need some type of disclosure from the divine side in order to know religious truth? When an alleged revelation says one thing, and reason leads to a different conclusion, which should we believe? Do you need evidence for your religious beliefs? Is it rational to believe something true on the basis of insufficient evidence? Is there a higher kind of knowledge gained through meditation that transcends critical reason and requires no proof? What is faith? What is reason? What is true, and how can we determine it?

As you can see from the foregoing questions, the problem of the relationship between religious faith and reason is not one problem but a whole set of problems. The title of this chapter both reveals and conceals a host of problems and issues.

Let us begin with some history. In the West, Greek philosophy developed a reliance on reason and logical thinking as the best way to determine what is true. Hebrew culture, in contrast, developed a reliance on divine revelation as the best way to determine what is true. The encounter between the Greek reliance on the authority of reason and the Jewish reliance on the authority of revelation led to tensions. Some Jews, such as Philo of Alexandria (30 B.C.E.–50), developed an allegorical method for interpreting the Hebrew Scriptures (what Christians call the Old Testament) in order to reconcile Greek philosophy and Jewish thought. Other Jews were less hospitable to Greek philosophy and found it a threat to their own traditions.

This tension between the authority of reason as exemplified in Greek philosophy and the authority of revelation as exemplified in certain sacred books carried over into Christianity. St. Paul counsels, "See to it that no one make a prey of you by philosophy" (Col. 2.8). A century later, the Christian theologian Tertullian (c. 160–230) found Paul's advice helpful in his fight against Gnostic Christians. Tertullian was convinced that Gnostics perverted the true faith with heresy. Their "false" interpretations of the Christian gospel were due, Tertullian argued, to Greek philosophy. Among other things, the Gnostics argued that a divine being could not really die and hence rise from the dead. Philosophy teaches that it is a contradiction to assert that a divine being dies, because to be divine means to be immortal. Those who told such stories must be liars or misled. Tertullian responded that such stories must be true, because no one would deliberately make up such fantastic tales hoping to be believed. Their very rational absurdity testifies to the veracity of the witnesses. Hence he declared that he believed such testimony because it was absurd. *Credo quia absurdum* (I believe because it is absurd), he declared, adding that "it is certain because it is impossible."

Within the same "revealed" book, however, where St. Paul's caution against philosophy occurs, another writer, St. John, uses an important Greek philosophical notion, the *logos* (word, reason), to explain who Christ was and is. Christ is the creative word and reason (*logos*) of God. Many early Christian theologians, following John's lead, found many Greek philosophical concepts useful in defending and defining the central doctrines of Christianity.

St. Augustine (354–430), regarded as one of the greatest theologians of the formative years of Christian theology, found Greek philosophy indispensable for understanding Christian revelation. "*Fides quaerens intellectum*" (faith in search of understanding) was the key, Augustine thought, to the reconciliation of faith and reason. Philosophy provided the tools for understanding revelation. Even outside the realm of religious questions, faith plays a vital role in reaching rational understanding. No understanding is possible for someone who persists in skepticism and refuses to believe anything. Even the philosopher must begin with the faith that reason can lead to truth.

The debate about the relationship between faith and reason spilled over into Islamic philosophy and theology. According to Islam, the *Qur'an* sets forth the final revelation of Allah's will. The *Qur'an* embodies the truth. However, what if what the *Qur'an* says differs from what the philosophers say? Some Islamic thinkers such as al-Ghazali (450–505) argued, in effect, so much the worse for philosophy. We should trust God's word over the word of mere mortals. Others argued for ways to harmonize philosophy and Islamic belief. If the *Qur'an,* in its literal meaning, contradicts philosophic reason, then the *Qur'an* must be interpreted allegorically. What appears to be a real contradiction turns out to be only apparent when the *Qur'an* is allegorically (rightly?) understood.

With the advent of modern science in the West, the debate about the relationship between faith and reason intensified. Some argued that science demands that nothing be believed until there is sufficient evidence for it. Because there is not sufficient evidence for religious beliefs (such as the belief that God exists), we should withhold assent until such evidence is available. But faith cannot always wait. Religious faith is vitally important to your salvation, and if you wait, you wait at the peril of your soul. If faith brings eternal life and unfaith eternal damnation, which option is best? Further, there are many circumstances in which it is wiser to risk error rather than the loss of a possible truth. When it comes to religion, a little cognitive risk may be in order.

The demand for evidence to support belief may itself be misguided. There are many things we believe without sufficient evidence, and it would be silly, if not irrational, not to believe them. Take the existence of other minds. You have no direct access to another's mind. You cannot think their thoughts or feel their emotions. Yet it is absurd to go through life thinking that everybody but you is a robot who has no inner conscious life. You may never be able to prove that other minds exist, but that does not mean it is not rational for you to believe so.

So far our focus has been on the West, but what about the East? Did the debate about the relationship between reason and faith develop in the same way? The short answer is no (with some notable exceptions). There were tensions in Chinese thought between those who wished to use logic and those who wished to rely on intuition. Among the Buddhists there was considerable skepticism about the value of metaphysical speculation when it came to matters of salvation. However, the separation and antagonism between religion and philosophy that characterize much Western thought are, on the whole, not characteristic of the East. Hinduism is a case in point. Hindu thinkers early recognized that there are a variety of ways to obtain knowledge. Perception or sense experience provides knowledge of the material world in which we live. Inference and logical reasoning provide another avenue to knowledge. The testimony of those who know by intuitive insight provides yet another. Meditative insight offers still another way. All of these ways are reasonable, if we define reason broadly enough.

It should be noted that the word *faith* is ambiguous. Sometimes it is used to mean faith in revelation, where revelation is understood as revealed propositions about religious matters (God, the afterlife, salvation). Hence faith amounts to *belief that* such statements are true. At other times *faith* is used in the sense of trust. In this sense, faith is not believing that some statement such as "God exists" is true but is equivalent to trusting in God and living accordingly. At other times "faith" is used to refer to a religious attitude of being ultimately concerned.

The word *reason* also is often used in different senses. Sometimes it refers to the reasoning process by which we figure out solutions to problems. Sometimes it means providing evidence or good reasons for the truth of some proposition. At other times it refers rather generally to many different intellectual processes we think of as rational.

As you read these selections, you will need to pay close attention to how these words are used. Also you need to keep in mind that the debate about faith and reason has, at least in the West, been strongly influenced by the idea that revelation discloses to humans information about matters that they cannot discover on their own (that is, by the use of reason). Hence revelation requires for its reception a special faculty, "faith," that is distinct from reason. This dichotomy has structured much of the philosophical debate and has made us think that religious faith cannot be reasonable or, at least, is something that falls outside the category of reason. Unfortunately, this dichotomy has been reinforced on the nonreligious side by those who maintain that nothing should be believed beyond that for which we have sufficient evidence. I hope these readings convince you that the situation is far more complex than this simple dichotomy indicates.

9.1 On the Harmony between Faith and Reason

Thomas Aquinas (see Reading 3.2) criticized some of his Christian theological colleagues by calling them Averroists. They have subsequently become known as the
Latin Averroists, and the "Averroism" they supposedly espoused has been characterized as the doctrine of "double-truth." According to this doctrine, there are two
truths: the truth taught by the philosophers and derived from demonstrative reasoning (deductive arguments) and the truth taught by divine revelation. These truths are
different and hence can never conflict.

This teaching alarmed Aquinas because he thought that truth had to be one.
If there was no unity to truth, then a fundamental law of logic, the law of non-
contradiction, made no sense. According to this law, a proposition (p) cannot be
both true and false. If it is true that God created the world out of nothing (as Christian, Jewish, and Islamic theology taught), then it must be false that the world is
eternal (as Aristotle taught), and vice versa. If the doctrine of double-truth prevailed,
then both propositions, even though they are contradictory, could be true. This is
logically absurd, or so Aquinas thought.

Why, however, did Aquinas label the doctrine of double-truth Averroism? The
term refers to the Latin name of Abu al-Walid Muhammad Ibn Ahmad Ibn Rushd, born
in 1126 in Cordova, Spain. He was the last of the great Islamic Aristotelian philosophers of the Middle Ages. Averroes wrote numerous commentaries on Aristotle and
found himself embroiled in controversies of one sort or another with other Islamic
thinkers. In the text that follows, he specifically refers to the Mu'tazilites and the
Ash'arites. Both used philosophical arguments to explicate and justify doctrines
derived from the *Qur'an*. Averroes also refers to Abu Nasr (Alfarabi), Ibn Sina
(Avicenna—see Reading 2.3), and Abu Ḥamid (Al-Gazali).

Al-Gazali had opposed Aristotelian philosophy on the grounds that it taught
doctrines contrary to divine revelation (see his *The Incoherence of the Philosophers*).
Averroes responded in his book *The Incoherence of the Incoherence.* This debate reflects the way the controversy about the relationship of faith and reason developed
in Islamic thought. The concern focused on the possible contradictions between
"truths" derived from philosophical reasoning (called demonstrative truth) and
"truths" derived from the *Qur'an* (called scriptural truth). The term *Peripatetic philosophers* refers to the Aristotelians.

Although Christian thinkers such as Aquinas thought that Averroes taught a
double-truth doctrine in an attempt to reconcile faith and reason, he did not. Granted,
he does teach that faith and reason cannot conflict. This is the case, however, not because there are two truths but because there is only one truth found in both revelation
and reason. If this is so, then any conflict must be apparent only, and it is the task of the
philosopher to show how the truth of faith and the truth of reason are in harmony.

Reading Questions

1. Why does Averroes maintain that "Demonstrative truth and Scriptural truth cannot conflict"?
2. Summarize the argument that Averroes presents for interpreting scripture allegorically if its meaning appears to conflict with demonstrative truth.

3. Why does scripture have a double meaning?
4. How does Averroes answer the objection that there are some things in scripture that Muslims have unanimously agreed to take in their apparent meaning and that demonstrative truth must yield to this unanimity?
5. How does Averroes reconcile the apparent contradiction between philosophers who hold that the world is pre-eternal (did not originate) and theological claims that it is not pre-eternal (did originate)?
6. Into what class of scripture do texts about the future life fall and why?
7. Why does Averroes hold that the "unlearned classes" must take scripture in its apparent rather than its allegorical meaning?
8. Do Averroes' arguments convince you that there is no real conflict between faith and reason? Why or why not?

On the Harmony between Faith and Reason*

AVERROES

Chapter Two. Philosophy Contains Nothing Opposed to Islam

Demonstrative truth and scriptural truth cannot conflict.

Now since this religion is true and summons to the study which leads to knowledge of the Truth, we the Muslim community know definitely that demonstrative study does not lead to [conclusions] conflicting with what Scripture has given us; for truth does not oppose truth but accords with it and bears witness to it.

If the apparent meaning of Scripture conflicts with demonstrative conclusions it must be interpreted allegorically, i.e. metaphorically.

This being so, whenever demonstrative study leads to any manner of knowledge about any being, that being is inevitably either unmentioned or mentioned in Scripture. If it is unmentioned there is no contradiction, and it is in the same case as an act whose category is unmentioned, so that the lawyer has to infer it by reasoning from Scrip-

ture. If Scripture speaks about it, the apparent meaning of the words inevitably either accords or conflicts with the conclusions of demonstration about it. If this [apparent meaning] accords there is no argument. If it conflicts there is a call for allegorical interpretation of it. The meaning of "allegorical interpretation" is: extension of the significance of an expression from real to metaphorical significance, without forsaking therein the standard metaphorical practices of Arabic, such as calling a thing by the name of something resembling it or a cause or consequence or accompaniment of it, or other things such as are enumerated in accounts of the kinds of metaphorical speech.

If the lawyer can do this, the religious thinker certainly can. Indeed these allegorical interpretations always receive confirmation from the apparent meaning of other passages of Scripture.

Now if the lawyer does this in many decisions of religious law, with how much more right is it done by the possessor of demonstrative knowledge! For the lawyer has at his disposition only

*From *Averroes on the Harmony of Religion and Philosophy,* translated by G. F. Hourani, London: Luzac Oriental, Ltd., © 1961.

reasoning based on opinion, while he who would know [God] [has at his disposition] reasoning based on certainty. So we affirm definitely that whenever the conclusion of a demonstration is in conflict with the apparent meaning of Scripture, that apparent meaning admits of allegorical interpretation according to the rules for such interpretation in Arabic. This proposition is questioned by no Muslim and doubted by no believer. But its certainty is immensely increased for those who have had close dealings with this idea and put it to the test, and made it their aim to reconcile the assertions of intellect and tradition. Indeed we may say that whenever a statement in Scripture conflicts in its apparent meaning with a conclusion of demonstration, if Scripture is considered carefully, and the rest of its contents searched page by page, there will invariably be found among the expressions of Scripture something which in its apparent meaning bears witness to that allegorical interpretation or comes close to bearing witness.

All Muslims accept the principle of allegorical interpretation; they only disagree about the extent of its application.

In the light of this idea the Muslims are unanimous in holding that it is not obligatory either to take all the expressions of Scripture in their apparent meaning or to extend them all from their apparent meaning by allegorical interpretation. They disagree [only] over which of them should and which should not be so interpreted: the Ash'arites for instance give an allegorical interpretation to the verse about God's directing Himself and the Tradition about His descent, while the Hanbalites take them in their apparent meaning.

The double meaning has been given to suit people's diverse intelligence. The apparent contradictions are meant to stimulate the learned to deeper study.

The reason why we have received a Scripture with both an apparent and an inner meaning lies in the diversity of people's natural capacities and the difference of their innate dispositions with regard to assent. The reason why we have received in Scripture texts whose apparent meanings con-

tradict each other is in order to draw the attention of those who are well grounded in science to the interpretation which reconciles them. This is the idea referred to in the words received from the Exalted (III, 7), "He it is who has sent down to you the Book, containing certain verses clear and definite" [and so on] down to the words "those who are well grounded in science."

In interpreting texts allegorically we must never violate Islamic consensus, when it is certain. But to establish it with certainty with regard to theoretical texts is impossible, because there have always been scholars who would not divulge their interpretation of such texts.

It may be objected: "There are some things in Scripture which the Muslims have unanimously agreed to take in their apparent meaning, others [which they have agreed] to interpret allegorically, and others about which they have disagreed; is it permissible, then, that demonstration should lead to interpreting allegorically what they have agreed to take in its apparent meaning, or to taking in its apparent meaning what they have agreed to interpret allegorically?" We reply: If unanimous agreement is established by a method which is certain, such [a result] is not sound; but if [the existence of] agreement on those things is a matter of opinion, then it may be sound. This is why Abū Hāmid, Abul-Ma'ālī, and other leaders of thought said that no one should be definitely called an unbeliever for violating unanimity on a point of interpretation in matters like these.

That unanimity on theoretical matters is never determined with certainty, as it can be on practical matters, may be shown to you by the fact that it is not possible for unanimity to be determined on any question at any period unless that period is strictly limited by us, and all the scholars existing in that period are known to us (i.e. known as individuals and in their total number), and the doctrine of each of them on the question has been handed down to us on unassailable authority, and, in addition to all this, unless we are sure that the scholars existing at the time were in agreement that there is not both an apparent and an inner meaning in Scripture, that knowledge of any question ought not to be kept secret from anyone, and that there is only one way for people to understand Scripture. But it is recorded in Tradition that many of the first believers used to hold that Scripture has both an apparent and an inner meaning, and that the inner meaning ought not to be learned by anyone who is not a man of learning in this field and who is incapable of understanding it. Thus, for example, Bukhārī reports a saying of 'Ali Ibn Abī Tālib, may God be pleased with him, "Speak to people about what they know. Do you want God and His Prophet to be accused of lying?" Other examples of the same kind are reported about a group of early believers. So how can it possibly be conceived that a unanimous agreement can have been handed down to us about a single theoretical question, when we know definitely that not a single period has been without scholars who held that there are things in Scripture whose true meaning should not be learned by all people?

The situation is different in practical matters: everyone holds that the truth about these should be disclosed to all people alike, and to establish the occurrence of unanimity about them we consider it sufficient that the question [at issue] should have been widely discussed and that no report of controversy about it should have been handed down to us. This is enough to establish the occurrence of unanimity on matters of practice, but on matters of doctrine the case is different.

> Ghazālī's charge of unbelief against Fārābī and Ibn Sinā, for asserting the world's eternity and God's ignorance of particulars and denying bodily resurrection, is only tentative, not definite.

You may object: "If we ought not to call a man an unbeliever for violating unanimity in cases of allegorical interpretation, because no unanimity is conceivable in such cases, what do you say about the Muslim philosophers, like Abū Nasr and Ibn Sinā? For Abū Hāmid called them both definitely unbelievers in the book of his known as *The disintegration* [*The Incoherence of the Philosophers*], on three counts: their assertions of the pre-eternity of the world and that God the Exalted does not know particulars" (may He be

Exalted far above that [ignorance]!), "and their allegorical interpretation of the passages concerning the resurrection of bodies and states of existence in the next life."

We answer: It is apparent from what he said on the subject that his calling them both unbelievers on these counts was not definite, since he made it clear in *The book of distinction* that calling people unbelievers for violating unanimity can only be tentative.

> Such a charge cannot be definite, because there has never been a consensus against allegorical interpretation. The *Qur'ān* itself indicates that it has inner meanings which it is the special function of the demonstrative class to understand.

Moreover, it is evident from what we have said that a unanimous agreement cannot be established in questions of this kind, because of the reports that many of the early believers of the first generation, as well as others, have said that there are allegorical interpretations which ought not to be expressed except to those who are qualified to receive allegories. These are "those who are well grounded in science"; for we prefer to place the stop after the words of God the Exalted (III, 7) "and those who are well grounded in science," because if the scholars did not understand allegorical interpretation, there would be no superiority in their assent which would oblige them to a belief in Him not found among the unlearned. God has described them as those who believe in Him, and this can only be taken to refer to the belief which is based on demonstration; and this [belief] only occurs together with the science of allegorical interpretation. For the unlearned believers are those whose belief in Him is not based on demonstration; and if this belief which God has attributed to the scholars is peculiar to them, it must come through demonstration, and if it comes through demonstration it only occurs together with the science of allegorical interpretation. For God the Exalted has informed us that those [verses] have an allegorical interpretation which is the truth, and demonstration can only be of the truth. That being the case, it is not possible for general unanimity to be established about allegorical interpretations, which God has made peculiar to scholars. This is self-evident to any fair-minded person.

> Besides, Ghazālī was mistaken in ascribing to the Peripatetics the opinion that God does not know particulars. Their view is that His knowledge of both particulars and universals differs from ours, in being the cause, not an effect, of the object known. They even hold that God sends premonitions in dreams of particular events.

In addition to all this we hold that Abū Hāmid was mistaken about the Peripatetic philosophers, in ascribing to them the assertion that God, Holy and Exalted, does not know particulars at all. In reality they hold that God the Exalted knows them in a way which is not of the same kind as our way of knowing them. For our knowledge of them is an effect of the object known, originated when it comes into existence and changing when it changes; whereas Glorious God's Knowledge of existence is the opposite of this: it is the cause of the object known, which is existent being. Thus to suppose the two kinds of knowledge similar to each other is to identify the essences and properties of opposite things, and that is the extreme of ignorance. And if the name of "knowledge" is predicated of both originated and eternal knowledge, it is predicated by sheer homonymy, as many names are predicated of opposite things: e.g. *jalal* of great and small, *ṣarīm* of light and darkness. Thus there exists no definition embracing both kinds of knowledge at once, as the theologians of our time imagine. We have devoted a separate essay to this question, impelled by one of our friends.

But how can anyone imagine that the Peripatetics say that God the Glorious does not know particulars with His eternal Knowledge, when they hold that true visions include premonitions of particular events due to occur in future time, and that this warning foreknowledge comes to people in their sleep from the eternal Knowledge which orders and rules the universe? Moreover, it is not only particulars which they say God does not know in the manner in which we know them, but universals as well; for the universals known to us are also effects of the nature of existent being,

while with His Knowledge the reverse is true. Thus the conclusion to which demonstration leads is that His Knowledge transcends qualification as "universal" or "particular." Consequently there is no point in disputing about this question, i.e. whether to call them unbelievers or not.

> On the question of the world, the ancient philosophers agree with the Ash'arites that it is originated and coeval with time. The Peripatetics only disagree with the Ash'arites and the Platonists in holding that past time is infinite. This difference is insufficient to justify a charge of unbelief.

Concerning the question whether the world is pre-eternal or came into existence, the disagreement between the Ash'arite theologians and the ancient philosophers is in my view almost resolvable into a disagreement about naming, especially in the case of certain of the ancients. For they agree that there are three classes of beings: two extremes and one intermediate between the extremes. They agree also about naming the extremes; but they disagree about the intermediate class.

[1] One extreme is a being which is brought into existence from something other than itself and by something, i.e. by an efficient cause and from some matter; and it, i.e. its existence, is preceded by time. This is the status of bodies whose generation is apprehended by sense, e.g. the generation of water, air, earth, animals, plants, and so on. All alike, ancients and Ash'arites, agree in naming this class of beings "originated." [2] The opposite extreme to this is a being which is not made from or by anything and not preceded by time; and here too all members of both schools agree in naming it "pre-eternal." This being is apprehended by demonstration; it is God, Blessed and Exalted, Who is the Maker, Giver of being and Sustainer of the universe; may He be praised and His Power exalted! [3] The class of being which is between these two extremes is that which is not made from anything and not preceded by time, but which is brought into existence by something, i.e. by an agent. This is the world as a whole. Now they all agree on the presence of these three characters in the world. For the theologians admit that time does not precede it, or rather this is a necessary

consequence for them since time according to them is something which accompanies motion and bodies. They also agree with the ancients in the view that future time is infinite and likewise future being. They only disagree about past time and past being: the theologians hold that it is finite (this is the doctrine of Plato and his followers), while Aristotle and his school hold that it is infinite, as is the case with future time.

Thus it is clear that [3] this last being bears a resemblance both to [1] the being which is really generated and to [2] the pre-eternal Being. So those who are more impressed with its resemblance to the pre-eternal than its resemblance to the originated name it "pre-eternal", while those who are more impressed with its resemblance to the originated name it "originated". But in truth it is neither really originated nor really pre-eternal, since the really originated is necessarily perishable and the really pre-eternal has no cause. Some—Plato and his followers—name it "originated and coeval with time," because time according to them is finite in the past.

Thus the doctrines about the world are not so very far apart from each other that some of them should be called irreligious and others not. For this to happen, opinions must be divergent in the extreme, i.e. contraries such as the theologians suppose to exist on this question; i.e. [they hold] that the names "pre-eternity" and "coming into existence" as applied to the world as a whole are contraries. But it is now clear from what we have said that this is not the case.

> Anyhow, the apparent meaning of Scripture is that there was a being and time before God created the present being and time. Thus the theologians' interpretation is allegorical and does not command unanimous agreement.

Over and above all this, these opinions about the world do not conform to the apparent meaning of Scripture. For if the apparent meaning of Scripture is searched, it will be evident from the verses which give us information about the bringing into existence of the world that its form really is originated, but that being itself and time extend continuously at both extremes, i.e. without interruption. Thus the words of God the Exalted (XI, 7) "He it is Who created the heavens and the earth in six days, and His throne was on the water," taken in their apparent meaning imply that there was a being before this present being, namely the throne and the water, and a time before this time, i.e. the one which is joined to the form of this being, namely the number of the movement of the celestial sphere. And the words of the Exalted (XIV, 48), "On the day when the earth shall be changed into other than earth, and the heavens as well," also in their apparent meaning imply that there will be a second being after this being. And the words of the Exalted (XLI, II), "Then He directed Himself towards the sky, and it was smoke," in their apparent meaning imply that the heavens were created from something.

Thus the theologians too in their statements about the world do not conform to the apparent meaning of Scripture but interpret it allegorically. For it is not stated in Scripture that God was existing with absolutely nothing else: a text to this effect is nowhere to be found. Then how is it conceivable that the theologians' allegorical interpretation of these verses could meet with unanimous agreement, when the apparent meaning of Scripture which we have mentioned about the existence of the world has been accepted by a school of philosophers!

> On such difficult questions, error committed by a qualified judge of his subject is excused by God, while error by an unqualified person is not excused.

It seems that those who disagree on the interpretation of these difficult questions earn merit if they are in the right and will be excused [by God] if they are in error. For assent to a thing as a result of an indication [of it] arising in the soul is something compulsory, not voluntary: i.e. it is not for us [to choose] not to assent or to assent, as it is to stand up or not to stand up. And since free choice is a condition of obligation, a man who assents to an error as a result of a consideration that has occurred to him is excused, if he is a scholar. This is why the Prophet, peace on him, said, "If the judge after exerting his mind makes a right decision, he will have a double reward; and if he makes a wrong decision he will [still] have a single reward." And what judge is more important than he who makes judgements about being, that it is thus or not thus? These judges are the scholars, specially chosen by God for [the task of] allegorical interpretation, and this error which is forgivable according to the Law is only such error as proceeds from scholars when they study the difficult matters which the Law obliges them to study.

But error proceeding from any other class of people is sheer sin, equally whether it relates to theoretical or to practical matters. For just as the judge who is ignorant of the [Prophet's] way of life is not excused if he makes an error in judgement, so he who makes judgements about beings without having the proper qualifications for [such] judgements is not excused but is either a sinner or an unbeliever. And if he who would judge what is allowed and forbidden is required to combine in himself the qualifications for exercise of personal judgement, namely knowledge of the principles [of law] and knowledge of how to draw inferences from those principles by reasoning, how much more properly is he who would make judgements about beings required to be qualified, i.e. to know the primary intellectual principle and the way to draw inferences from them!

Texts of Scripture fall into three kinds with respect to the excusability of error. [1] Texts which must be taken in their apparent meaning by everyone. Since the meaning can be understood plainly by demonstrative, dialectical and rhetorical methods alike, no one is excused for the error of interpreting these texts allegorically. [2] Texts which must be taken in their apparent meaning by the lower classes and interpreted allegorically by the demonstrative class. It is inexcusable for the lower classes to interpret them allegorically or for the demonstrative class to take them in their apparent meaning. [3] Texts whose classification under the previous headings is uncertain. Error in this matter by the demonstrative class is excused.

In general, error about Scripture is of two types: either error which is excused to one who is a qualified student of that matter in which the error occurs (as the skillful doctor is excused if he commits an error in the art of medicine and the skillful judge if he gives an erroneous judgement), but not excused to one who is not qualified in that subject; or error which is not excused to any person whatever, and which is unbelief if it concerns the principles of religion, or heresy if it concerns something subordinate to the principles.

This [latter] error is that which occurs about [1] matters, knowledge of which is provided by all the different methods of indication, so that knowledge of the matter in question is in this way possible for everyone. Examples are acknowledgement of God, Blessed and Exalted, of the prophetic missions, and of happiness and misery in the next life; for these three principles are attainable by the three classes of indication, by which everyone without exception can come to assent to what he is obliged to know: I mean the rhetorical, dialectical and demonstrative indications. So whoever denies such a thing, when it is one of the principles of the Law, is an unbeliever, who persists in defiance with his tongue though not with his heart, or neglects to expose himself to learning the indication of its truth. For if he belongs to the demonstrative class of men, a way has been provided for him to assent to it, by demonstration; if he belongs to the dialectical class, the way is by dialectic; and if he belongs to the class [which is convinced] by preaching, the way for him is by preaching. With this in view the Prophet, peace on him, said, "I have been ordered to fight people until they say 'There is no god but God' and believe in me", he means, by any of the three methods of attaining belief that suits them.

[2] With regard to things which by reason of their recondite character are only knowable by demonstration, God has been gracious to those of His servants who have no access to demonstration, on account of their natures, habits or lack of facilities for education: He has coined for them images and likenesses of these things, and summoned them to assent to those images, since it is possible for assent to those images to come about through the indications common to all men, i.e. the dialectical and rhetorical indications. This is the reason why Scripture is divided

into apparent and inner meanings: the apparent meaning consists of those images which are coined to stand for those ideas, while the inner meaning is those ideas [themselves], which are clear only to the demonstrative class. These are the four or five classes of beings mentioned by Abū Hāmid in *The book of the distinction*.

[1] But when it happens, as we said, that we know the thing itself by the three methods, we do not need to coin images of it, and it remains true in its apparent meaning, not admitting allegorical interpretation. If an apparent text of this kind refers to principles, anyone who interprets it allegorically is an unbeliever, e.g. anyone who thinks that there is no happiness or misery in the next life, and that the only purpose of this teaching is that men should be safeguarded from each other in their bodily and sensible lives, that it is but a practical device, and that man has no other goal than his sensible existence.

If this is established, it will have become clear to you from what we have said that there are [1] apparent texts of Scripture which it is not permitted to interpret allegorically; to do so on fundamentals is unbelief, on subordinate matters, heresy. There are also [2] apparent texts which have to be interpreted allegorically by men of the demonstrative class; for such men to take them in their apparent meaning is unbelief, while for those who are not of the demonstrative class to interpret them allegorically and take them out of their apparent meaning is unbelief or heresy on their part.

Of this [latter] class are the verse about God's directing Himself and the Tradition about His descent. That is why the Prophet, peace on him, said in the case of the black woman, when she told him that God was in the sky, "Free her, for she is a believer." This was because she was not of the demonstrative class; and the reason for his decision was that the class of people to whom assent comes only through the imagination, i.e. who do not assent to a thing except in so far as they can imagine it, find it difficult to assent to the existence of a being which is unrelated to any imaginable thing. This applies as well to those who understand from the relation stated merely

[that God has] a place; these are people who have advanced a little in their thought beyond the position of the first class, [by rejecting] belief in corporeality. Thus the [proper] answer to them with regard to such passages is that they belong to the ambiguous texts, and that the stop is to be placed after the words of God the Exalted (III, 7) "And no one knows the interpretation thereof except God." The demonstrative class, while agreeing unanimously that this class of text must be interpreted allegorically, may disagree about the interpretation, according to the level of each one's knowledge of demonstration.

There is also [3] a third class of Scriptural texts falling uncertainly between the other two classes, on which there is doubt. One group of those who devote themselves to theoretical study attach them to the apparent texts which it is not permitted to interpret allegorically, others attach them to the texts with inner meanings which scholars are not permitted to take in their apparent meanings. This [divergence of opinions] is due to the difficulty and ambiguity of this class of text. Anyone who commits an error about this class is excused, I mean any scholar.

> The texts about the future life fall into [3], since demonstrative scholars do not agree whether to take them in their apparent meaning or interpret them allegorically. Either is permissible. But it is inexcusable to deny the fact of a future life altogether.

If it is asked, "Since it is clear that scriptural texts in this respect fall into three grades, to which of these three grades, according to you, do the descriptions of the future life and its states belong?" we reply: The position clearly is that this matter belongs to the class [3] about which there is disagreement. For we find a group of those who claim an affinity with demonstration saying that it is obligatory to take these passages in their apparent meaning, because there is no demonstration leading to the impossibility of the apparent meaning in them—this is the view of the Ash'arites; while another group of those who devote themselves to demonstration interpret these passages allegorically, and these people give the most diverse interpretations of them. In this class must be counted Abū Hāmid and many of the Sūfīs; some of them combine the two interpretations of the passages, as Abū Hāmid does in some of his books.

So it is likely that a scholar who commits an error in this matter is excused, while one who is correct receives thanks or a reward: that is, if he acknowledges the existence [of a future life] and merely gives a certain sort of allegorical interpretation, i.e. of the mode of the future life not of its existence, provided that the interpretation given does not lead to denial of its existence. In this matter only the negation of existence is unbelief, because it concerns one of the principles of religion and one of those points to which assent is attainable through the three methods common to "the white man and the black man."

> The unlearned classes must take such texts in their apparent meaning. It is unbelief for the learned to set down allegorical interpretations in popular writings. By doing this Ghazālī caused confusion among the people. Demonstrative books should be banned to the unqualified, but not to the learned.

But anyone who is not a man of learning is obliged to take these passages in their apparent meaning, and allegorical interpretation of them is for him unbelief because it *leads* to unbelief. That is why we hold that, for anyone whose duty it is to believe in the apparent meaning, allegorical interpretation is unbelief, because it leads to unbelief. Anyone of the interpretative class who discloses such [an interpretation] to him is summoning him to unbelief, and he who summons to unbelief is an unbeliever.

Therefore allegorical interpretations ought to be set down only in demonstrative books because if they are in demonstrative books they are encountered by no one but men of the demonstrative class. But if they are set down in other than demonstrative books and one deals with them by poetical, rhetorical or dialectical methods, as Abū Hāmid does, then he commits an offence against the Law and against philosophy, even though the fellow intended nothing but good. For by this

procedure he wanted to increase the number of learned men, but in fact he increased the number of the corrupted not of the learned! As a result, one group came to slander philosophy, another to slander religion, and another to reconcile the [first] two [groups]. It seems that this [last] was one of his objects in his books; an indication that he wanted by this [procedure] to arouse minds is that he adhered to no one doctrine in his books but was an Ash'arite with the Ash'arites, a Sūfī with the Sūfīs and a philosopher with the philosophers, so that he was like the man in the verse:

> One day a Yamanī, if I meet a man of
>   Yaman,
> And if I meet a Ma'addī, I'm an 'Adnānī.

The *imāms* of the Muslims ought to forbid those of his books which contain learned matter to all save the learned, just as they ought to forbid demonstrative books to those who are not capable of understanding them. But the damage done to people by demonstrative books is lighter, because for the most part only persons of superior natural intelligence become acquainted with demonstrative books, and this class of persons is only misled through lack of practical virtue, unorganized reading, and tackling them without a teacher. On the other hand their total prohibition obstructs the purpose to which the Law summons, because it is a wrong to the best class of people and the best class of beings. For to do justice to the best class of beings demands that they should be known profoundly, by persons equipped to know them profoundly, and these are the best class of people; and the greater the value of the being, the greater is the injury towards it, which consists of ignorance of it. Thus the Exalted has said (XXXI, 13). "Associating [other gods] with God is indeed a great wrong."

> We have only discussed these questions in a popular work because they were already being publicly discussed.

This is as much as we see fit to affirm in this field of study, i.e. the correspondence between religion and philosophy and the rules for allegorical interpretation in religion. If it were not for the publicity given to the matter and to these questions which we have discussed, we should not have permitted ourselves to write a word on the subject; and we should not have had to make excuses for doing so to the interpretative scholars, because the proper place to discuss these questions is in demonstrative books. God is the Guide and helps us to follow the right course!

Chapter Three. Philosophical Interpretations of Scripture Should Not Be Taught to the Majority. The Law Provides Other Methods of Instructing Them.

> The purpose of Scripture is to teach true theoretical and practical science and right practice and attitudes.

You ought to know that the purpose of Scripture is simply to teach true science and right practice. True science is knowledge of God, Blessed and Exalted, and the other beings as they really are, and especially of noble beings, and knowledge of happiness and misery in the next life. Right practice consists in performing the acts which bring happiness and avoiding the acts which bring misery; and it is knowledge of these acts that is called "practical science". They fall into two divisions: (1) outward bodily acts; the science of these is called "jurisprudence"; and (2) acts of the soul such as gratitude, patience and other moral attitudes which the Law enjoins or forbids; the science of these is called "asceticism" or "the sciences of the future life." To these Abū Hāmid turned his attention in his book: as people had given up this sort [of act] and become immersed in the other sort, and as this sort [2] involves the greater fear of God, which is the cause of happiness, he called his book

"*The revival of the sciences of religion*". But we have digressed from our subject, so let us return to it.

> Scripture teaches concepts both directly and by symbols, and uses demonstrative, dialectical and rhetorical arguments. Dialectical and rhetorical arguments are prevalent because the main aim of Scripture is to teach the majority. In these arguments concepts are indicated directly or by symbols, in various combinations in premises and conclusion.

We say: The purpose of Scripture is to teach true science and right practice; and teaching is of two classes, [of] concepts and [of] judgements, as the logicians have shown. Now the methods available to men of [arriving at] judgements are three: demonstrative, dialectical and rhetorical; and the methods of forming concepts are two: either [conceiving] the object itself or [conceiving] a symbol of it. But not everyone has the natural ability to take in demonstrations, or [even] dialectical arguments, let alone demonstrative arguments which are so hard to learn and need so much time [even] for those who are qualified to learn them. Therefore, since it is the purpose of Scriptures simply to teach everyone, Scripture has to contain every method of [bringing about] judgements of assent and every method of forming concepts.

Now some of the methods of assent comprehend the majority of people, i.e. the occurrence of assent as a result of them [is comprehensive]: these are the rhetorical and the dialectical [methods]—and the rhetorical is more comprehensive than the dialectical. Another method is peculiar to a smaller number of people: this is the demonstrative. Therefore, since the primary purpose of Scripture is to take care of the majority (without neglecting to arouse the élite), the prevailing methods of expression in religion are the common methods by which the majority comes to form concepts and judgements. . . .

9.2 A Wager

Are you a gambling person? Do you like to bet? Are you willing from time to time to wager a few dollars in the hope of making a lot more? Would you make the following wager? You bet that God exists; that is, you decide to believe that God exists even though you have no real evidence that God does. Instead of money, you put on the gaming table a lifestyle. You ensure that your life conforms to the will of God and therefore sacrifice some earthly pleasures. If you win the bet (it turns out God does exist), then you gain eternal happiness in heaven. If you lose (God does not exist), then you have lost some earthly pleasures. How do you wager?

Let me offer you another wager. You bet that God does not exist; that is, you decide to believe that God does not exist even though there is no real evidence that God does not. You put on the gaming table your eternal happiness in heaven. If you win this wager (it turns out God does not exist), then you have kept your freedom to live without sacrificing earthly pleasures. If you lose this wager (God does exist), then you have lost eternal happiness in heaven. Which wager (God exists or God does not) has better odds?

Blaise Pascal (1623–1662), a French mathematician, physicist, and philosopher, thought that the first wager (to believe that God exists) is by far the best because it promises an infinite gain with the possibility of only a finite loss. We should reject the second wager (to believe that God does not exist) because it offers only a finite gain and the possibility of an infinite loss.

You might say that you do not really like either bet. Because there is no evidence to indicate which is most likely (that God exists or that God does not), you would prefer not to enter this lottery. However, this lottery is different. Not betting—that is, suspending belief about God's existence—is equivalent to betting God does not exist. This is one wager you cannot refuse, or so Pascal thinks.

Reading Questions

1. Why, according to Pascal, can reason decide nothing with respect to God's existence and nature?
2. Explain Pascal's wager in your own words.
3. How does Pascal respond to the objection that one may be wagering too much?
4. How does Pascal respond to the objection of the people who say they cannot force themselves to believe?
5. Do you find Pascal's wager convincing? Why or why not?
6. Can we will to believe things that evidence does not force us to believe? For example, can you will yourself to sincerely believe that the earth is flat? Why or why not?
7. Do you think that belief in God's existence is both necessary and sufficient for eternal happiness? Why or why not?

A Wager*

BLAISE PASCAL

Infinite—nothing.—Our soul is cast into a body, where it finds number, time, dimension. Thereupon it reasons, and calls this nature, necessity, and can believe nothing else.

Unity joined to infinitely adds nothing to it, no more than one foot to an infinite measure. The finite is annihilated in the presence of the infinite, and becomes a pure nothing. So our spirit before God, so our justice before divine justice. There is not so great disproportion between our justice and that of God, as between unity and infinity.

The justice of God must be vast like His compassion. Now, justice to the outcast is less vast and ought less to offend our feelings than mercy towards the elect.

We know that there is an infinite, and are ignorant of its nature. As we know it to be false that numbers are finite, it is therefore true that there is an infinity in number. But we do not know what it is. It is false that it is even, it is false that it is odd: for the addition of a unit can make no change in its nature. Yet it is a number, and every number is odd or even (this is certainly true of every finite number). So we may well know that there is a God without knowing what He is. Is there not one substantial truth, seeing there are so many things which are not the truth itself?

We know then the existence and nature of the finite, because we also are finite and have extension. We know the existence of the infinite, and are ignorant of its nature, because it has extension like us, but not limits like us. But we know neither the existence nor the nature of God, because He has neither extension nor limits.

But by faith we know His existence; in glory we shall know His nature. Now, I have already shown that we may well know the existence of a thing, without knowing its nature.

Let us now speak according to natural lights.

If there is a God, He is infinitely incomprehensible, since, having neither parts nor limits, He has no affinity to us. We are then incapable of knowing either what He is or if He is. This being so, who will dare to undertake the decision of the question? Not we, who have no affinity to Him.

Who then will blame Christians for not being able to give a reason for their belief, since they profess a religion for which they cannot give a reason? They declare, in expounding it to the world, that it is a foolishness, *stultitiam;* and then you complain that they do not prove it! If they proved it, they would not keep their words; it is in lacking proofs, that they are not lacking in sense. "Yes, but although this excuses those who offer it as such, and take away from them the blame of putting it forward without reason, it does not excuse those who receive it." Let us then examine this point, and say, "God is, or He is not." But to which side shall we incline? Reason can decide nothing here. There is an infinite chaos which separates us. A game is being played at the extremity of this infinite distance where heads or tails will turn up. What will you wager? According to reason, you can do neither the one thing nor the other; according to reason, you can defend neither of the propositions.

Do not then reprove for error those who have made a choice; for you know nothing about it. "No, but I blame them for having made, not this choice, but a choice; for again both he who chooses heads and he who chooses tails are equally at fault, they are both in the wrong. The true course is not to wager at all."

—Yes; but you must wager. It is not optional. You are embarked. Which will you choose then; Let us see. Since you must choose, let us see which interests you least. You have two things to

---

*From *Thoughts* by Blaise Pascal, translated by W. F. Trotter. New York: Collier & Son, 1910.

lose, the true and the good; and two things to stake, your reason and your will, your knowledge and your happiness; and your nature has two things to shun, error and misery. Your reason is no more shocked in choosing one rather than the other, since you must of necessity choose. This is one point settled. But your happiness? Let us weigh the gain and the loss in wagering that God is. Let us estimate these two chances. If you gain, you gain all; if you lose, you lose nothing. Wager them without hesitation that He is.—"That is very fine. Yes, I must wager; but I may perhaps wager too much."—Let us see. Since there is an equal risk of gain and of loss, if you had only to gain two lives, instead of one, you might still wager. But if there were three lives to gain, you would have to play (since you are under the necessity of playing), and you would be imprudent, when you are forced to play, not to chance your life to gain three at a game where there is an equal risk of loss and gain. But there is an eternity of life and happiness. And this being so, if there were an infinity of chances, of which one only would be for you, you would still be right in wagering one to win two, and you would act stupidly, being obliged to play, by refusing to stake one life against three at a game in which out of an infinity of an infinitely happy life to gain. But there is here an infinity of an infinitely happy life to gain, a chance of gain against a finite number of chances of loss, and what you stake is finite. It is all divided; wherever the infinite is and there is not an infinity of chances of loss against that of gain, there is no time to hesitate, you must give all. And thus, when one is forced to play, he must renounce reason to preserve his life, rather than risk it for infinite gain, as likely to happen as the loss of nothingness.

For it is no use to say it is uncertain if we will gain, and it is certain that we risk, and that the infinite distance between the *certainty* of what is staked and the *uncertainty* of what will be gained, equals the finite good which is certainly staked against the uncertain infinite. It is not so, as every player stakes a certainty to gain an uncertainty, and yet he stakes a finite certainty to gain a finite uncertainty, without transgressing

against reason. There is not an infinite distance between the certainty staked and the uncertainty of the gain; that is untrue. In truth, there is an infinity between the certainty of gain and the certainty of loss. But the uncertainty of the gain is proportioned to the certainty of the stake according to the proportion of the chances of gain and loss. Hence it comes that, if there are as many risks on one side as on the other, the course is to play even; and then the certainty of the stake is equal to the uncertainty of the gain, so far is it from the fact that there is an infinite distance between them. And so our proposition is of infinite force, when there is the finite to stake in a game where there are equal risks of gain and of loss, and the infinite to gain. This is demonstrable; and if men are capable of any truths, this is one.

"I confess it, I admit it. But still is there no means of seeing the faces of the cards?"—Yes, Scripture and the rest, &c.—"Yes, but I have my hands tied and my mouth closed: I am forced to wager, and am not free. I am not released, and am so made that I cannot believe. What then would you have me do?"

"True. But at least learn your inability to believe, since reason brings you to this, and yet you cannot believe. Endeavour then to convince yourself, not by increase of proofs of God, but by the abatement of your passions. You would like to attain faith, and do not know the way; you would like to cure yourself of unbelief, and ask the remedy for it. Learn of those who have been bound like you, and who now stake all their possessions. These are people who know the way which you would follow, and who are cured of an ill of which you would be cured. Follow the way by which they began; by acting as if they believe, taking the holy water, having masses said, &c. Even this will naturally make you believe, and deaden your acuteness."—"But this is what I am afraid of."—And why? What have you to lose?

But to show you that this leads you there, it is this which will lessen the passions, which are your stumbling-blocks.

The end of this discourse.—Now what harm will befall you in taking this side? You will be faithful, honest, humble, grateful, generous, a sincere friend, truthful. Certainly you will not have those poisonous pleasures, glory and luxury; but will you not have others? I will tell you that you will thereby gain in this life, and that, at each step you take on this road, you will see so great certainty of gain, so much nothingness in what you risk, that you will at last recognize that you have wagered for something certain and infinite, for which you have given nothing.

"Ah! This discourse transports me, charms me," &c.

If this discourse pleases you and seems impressive, know that it is made by a man who has knelt, both before and after it, in prayer to that Being, infinite and without parts, before whom he lays all he has, for you also to lay before Him all you have for your own good and for His glory, so that strength may be given to lowliness. . . .

9.3 The Ethics of Belief

Should you believe something to be true even though you have insufficient evidence that it is true? Do you have a moral obligation to refrain from believing something true or false if the available evidence is not sufficient? Suppose you lend your old car to a friend. You have not checked the brakes in some time, but you dismiss all doubts about the brakes from your mind, confident that they will work because they have in the past. Suppose your friend crashes and dies as a result of faulty brakes. Are you to blame? Suppose your friend does not crash and die. Are you to blame for putting her life in danger? If you do not have sufficient evidence that the brakes are in working order, then according to William K. Clifford (1845–1879), you are to blame no matter what happens.

Clifford, a British mathematician interested in philosophical and religious topics, wrote an essay entitled "The Ethics of Belief." This essay became widely influential in the Victorian period for its presentation of an argument in favor of agnosticism in religious matters. If we do not have sufficient evidence supporting either the existence or the nonexistence of God, then we ought to refrain from believing one way or the other.

Clifford's argument reflects an epistemological position usually called evidentialism. Evidentialism holds that we should not accept any statement as true unless we have good evidence to support its truth. Thus, for example, I should not believe that God exists unless or until I have sufficient evidence supporting this belief. Such evidence must meet appropriate *epistemic* standards such as consistency and relevance. *Practical* standards such as aiding me in accomplishing certain goals or possibly resulting in my eternal happiness will not do.

Reading Questions

1. What do the examples of the shipowner and the commission show?
2. What, according to Clifford, is the relationship between belief and action?
3. Do you agree with Clifford's contention that all of us have a duty to question our beliefs? Why or why not?
4. Do you agree with Clifford's claim that it is "wrong always, everywhere, and for anyone, to believe anything upon insufficient evidence"? Why or why not?
6. What do you think Clifford means by "sufficient evidence"? How much evidence is sufficient?

The Ethics of Belief*

WILLIAM K. CLIFFORD

A SHIPOWNER was about to send to sea an emigrant-ship. He knew that she was old, and not over-well built at the first; that she had seen many seas and climes, and often had needed repairs. Doubts had been suggested to him that possibly she was not seaworthy. These doubts preyed upon his mind, and made him unhappy; he thought that perhaps he ought to have her thoroughly overhauled and refitted, even though this should put him to great expense. Before the ship sailed, however, he succeeded in overcoming these melancholy reflections. He said to himself that she had gone safely through so many voyages and weathered so many storms that it was idle to suppose she would not come safely home from this trip also. He would put his trust in providence, which could hardly fail to protect all these unhappy families that were leaving their fatherland to seek for better times elsewhere. He would dismiss from his mind all ungenerous suspicions about the honesty of builders and contractors. In such ways he acquired a sincere and comfortable conviction that his vessel was thoroughly safe and seaworthy; he watched her departure with a light heart, and benevolent wishes for the success of the exiles in their strange new home that was to be; and he got his insurance-money when she went down in mid-ocean and told no tales.

What shall we say of him? Surely this, that he was verily guilty of the death of those men. It is admitted that he did sincerely believe in the soundness of his ship; but the sincerity of his conviction can in no wise help him, because *he had no right to believe on such evidence as was before him*. He had acquired his belief not by honestly earning it in patient investigation, but by stifling his doubts. And although in the end he may have felt so sure about it that he could not think otherwise, yet inasmuch as he had knowingly and willingly worked himself into that frame of mind, he must be held responsible for it.

Let us alter the case a little, and suppose that the ship was not unsound after all; that she made her voyage safely, and many others after it. Will that diminish the guilt of her owner? Not one jot. When an action is once done, it is right or wrong forever; no accidental failure of its good or evil fruits can possibly alter that. The man would not have been innocent, he would only have been not found out. The question of right or wrong has to do with the origin of his belief, not the matter of it; not what it was, but how he got it; not whether it turned out to be true or false, but whether he had a right to believe on such evidence as was before him.

There was once an island in which some of the inhabitants professed a religion teaching neither the doctrine of original sin nor that of eternal punishment. A suspicion got abroad that the professors of this religion had made use of unfair means to get their doctrines taught to children. They were accused of wresting the laws of their country in such a way as to remove children from the care of their natural and legal guardians; and even of stealing them away and keeping them concealed from their friends and relations. A certain number of men formed themselves into a society for the purpose of agitating the public about this matter. They published grave accusations against individual citizens of the highest position and character, and did all in their power to injure these citizens in the exercise of their professions. So great was the noise they made, that a Commission was appointed to investigate the facts; but after the Commission had carefully inquired into all the evidence that could be got, it appeared that the accused were innocent. Not only had they been accused on insufficient

*From *Lectures and Essays,* Vol. II London: Macmillan, 1897, pp. 177–188. Footnotes deleted.

evidence, but the evidence of their innocence was such as the agitators might easily have obtained, if they had attempted a fair inquiry. After these disclosures the inhabitants of that country looked upon the members of the agitating society, not only as persons whose judgment was to be distrusted, but also as no longer to be counted honourable men. For although they had sincerely and conscientiously believed in the charges they had made, yet *they had no right to believe on such evidence as was before them*. Their sincere convictions, instead of being honestly earned by patient inquiring, were stolen by listening to the voice of prejudice and passion.

Let us vary this case also, and suppose, other things remaining as before, that a still more accurate investigation proved the accused to have been really guilty. Would this make any difference in the guilt of the accusers? Clearly not; the question is not whether their belief was true or false, but whether they entertained it on wrong grounds. They would no doubt say, "Now you see that we were right after all; next time perhaps you will believe us." And they might be believed, but they would not thereby become honourable men. They would not be innocent, they would only be not found out. Every one of them, if he chose to examine himself *in foro conscientiae,* would know that he had acquired and nourished a belief, when he had no right to believe on such evidence as was before him; and therein he would know that he had done a wrong thing.

It may be said, however, that in both of these supposed cases it is not the belief which is judged to be wrong, but the action following upon it. The shipowner might say, "I am perfectly certain that my ship is sound, but still I feel it my duty to have her examined, before trusting the lives of so many people to her." And it might be said to the agitator, "However convinced you were of the justice of your cause and the truth of your convictions, you ought not to have made a public attack upon any man's character until you had examined the evidence on both sides with the utmost patience and care."

In the first place, let us admit that, so far as it goes, this view of the case is right and necessary; right, because even when a man's belief is so fixed that he cannot think otherwise, he still has a choice in regard to the action suggested by it, and so cannot escape the duty of investigating on the ground of the strength of his convictions; and necessary, because those who are not yet capable of controlling their feelings and thoughts must have a plain rule dealing with overt acts.

But this being premised as necessary, it becomes clear that it is not sufficient, and that our previous judgment is required to supplement it. For it is not possible so to sever the belief from the action it suggests as to condemn the one without condemning the other. No man holding a strong belief on one side of a question, or even wishing to hold a belief on one side, can investigate it with such fairness and completeness as if he were really in doubt and unbiased; so that the existence of a belief not founded on fair inquiry unfits a man for the performance of this necessary duty.

Nor is that truly a belief at all which has not some influence upon the actions of him who holds it. He who truly believes that which prompts him to an action has looked upon the action to lust after it; he has committed it already in his heart. If a belief is not realized immediately in open deeds, it is stored up for the guidance of the future. It goes to make a part of that aggregate of beliefs which is the link between sensation and action at every moment of all our lives, and which is so organized and compacted together that no part of it can be isolated from the rest, but every new addition modifies the structure of the whole. No real belief, however trifling and fragmentary it may seem, is ever truly insignificant; it prepares us to receive more of its like, confirms those which resembled it before, and weakens others; and so gradually it lays a stealthy train in our inmost thoughts, which may some day explode into overt action, and leave its stamp upon our character forever.

And no one man's belief is in any case a private matter which concerns himself alone. Our lives are guided by that general conception of the course of things which has been created by society for social purposes. Our words, our phrases, our forms and processes and modes of thought, are common property, fashioned and perfected from age to age;

an heirloom which every succeeding generation inherits as a precious deposit and a sacred trust to be handed on to the next one, not unchanged but enlarged and purified, with some clear marks of its proper handiwork. Into this, for good or ill, is woven every belief of every man who has speech of his fellows. An awful privilege, and an awful responsibility, that we should help to create the world in which posterity will live.

In the two supposed cases which have been considered, it has been judged wrong to believe on insufficient evidence, or to nourish belief by suppressing doubts and avoiding investigation. The mason of this judgment is not far to seek: it is that in both these cases the belief held by one man was of great importance to other men. But forasmuch as no belief held by one man, however seemingly trivial the belief, and however obscure the believer, is ever actually insignificant or without its effect on the fate of mankind, we have no choice but to extend our judgment to all cases of belief whatever. Belief, that sacred faculty which prompts the decisions of our will, and knits into harmonious working all the compacted energies of our being, is ours not for ourselves, but for humanity. It is rightly used on truths which have been established by long experience and waiting toil, and which have stood in the fierce light of free and fearless questioning. Then it helps to bind men together, and to strengthen and direct their common action. It is desecrated when given to unproved and unquestioned statements, for the solace and private pleasure of the believer; to add a tinsel splendour to the plain straight road of our life and display a bright mirage beyond it; or even to drown the common sorrows of our kind by a self-deception which allows them not only to cast down, but also to degrade us. Whoso would deserve well of his fellows in this matter will guard the purity of his belief with a very fanaticism of jealous care, lest at any time it should rest on an unworthy object, and catch a stain which can never be wiped away.

It is not only the leader of men, statesman, philosopher, or poet, that owes this bounden duty to mankind. Every rustic who delivers in the village alehouse his slow, infrequent sentences, may help to kill or keep alive the fatal superstitions which clog his race. Every hard-worked wife of an artisan may transmit to her children beliefs which shall knit society together, or rend it in pieces. No simplicity of mind, no obscurity of station, can escape the universal duty of questioning all that we believe.

It is true that this duty is a hard one, and the doubt which comes out of it is often a very bitter thing. It leaves us bare and powerless where we thought that we were safe and strong. To know all about anything is to know how to deal with it under all circumstances. We feel much happier and more secure when we think we know precisely what to do, no matter what happens, than when we have lost our way and do not know where to turn. And if we have supposed ourselves to know all about anything, and to be capable of doing what is fit in regard to it, we naturally do not like to find that we are really ignorant and powerless, that we have to begin again at the beginning, and try to learn what the thing is and how it is to be dealt with—if indeed anything can be learnt about it. It is the sense of power attached to a sense of knowledge that makes men desirous of believing, and afraid of doubting.

This sense of power is the highest and best of pleasures when the belief on which it is founded is a true belief and has been fairly earned by investigation. For then we may justly feel that it is common property, and holds good for others as well as for ourselves. Then we may be glad, not that *I* have learned secrets by which I am safer and stronger, but that *we men* have got mastery over more of the world; and we shall be strong, not for ourselves, but in the name of Man and in his strength. But if the belief has been accepted on insufficient evidence, the pleasure is a stolen one. Not only does it deceive ourselves by giving us a sense of power which we do not really possess, but it is sinful, because it is stolen in defiance of our duty to mankind. That duty is to guard ourselves from such beliefs as from a pestilence, which may shortly master our own body and then spread to the rest of the town. What would be thought of one who, for the sake of a sweet fruit, should deliberately run the risk of bringing a plague upon his family and his neighbours?

And, as in other such cases, it is not the risk only which has to be considered; for a bad action is always bad at the time when it is done, no matter what happens afterwards. Every time we let ourselves believe for unworthy reasons, we weaken our powers of self-control, of doubting, of judicially and fairly weighing evidence. We all suffer severely enough from the maintenance and support of false beliefs and the fatally wrong actions which they lead to, and the evil born when one such belief is entertained is great and wide. But a greater and wider evil arises when the credulous character is maintained and supported, when a habit of believing for unworthy reasons is fostered and made permanent. If I steal money from any person, there may be no harm done by the mere transfer of possession; he may not feel the loss, or it may prevent him from using the money badly. But I cannot help doing this great wrong towards Man, that I make myself dishonest. What hurts society is not that it should lose its property, but that it should become a den of thieves; for then it must cease to be society. This is why we ought not to do evil that good may come; for at any rate this great evil has come, that we have done evil and are made wicked thereby. In like manner, if I let myself believe anything on insufficient evidence, there may be no great harm done by the mere belief; it may be true after all, or I may never have occasion to exhibit it in outward acts. But I cannot help doing this great wrong towards Man, that I make myself credulous. The danger to society is not merely that it should believe wrong things, though that is great enough; but that it should become credulous, and lose the habit of testing things and inquiring into them; for then it must sink back into savagery.

The harm which is done by credulity in a man is not confined to the fostering of a credulous character in others, and consequent support of false beliefs. Habitual want of care about what I believe leads to habitual want of care in others about the truth of what is told to me. Men speak the truth to one another when each reveres the truth in his own mind and in the other's mind; but how shall my friend revere the truth in my mind when I myself am careless about it, when I believe things because I want to believe them, and because they are comforting and pleasant? Will he not learn to cry, "Peace," to me, when there is no peace? By such a course I shall surround myself with a thick atmosphere of falsehood and fraud, and in that I must live. It may matter little to me, in my cloud-castle of sweet illusions and darling lies; but it matters much to Man that I have made my neighbours ready to deceive. The credulous man is father to the liar and the cheat; he lives in the bosom of this his family, and it is no marvel if he should become even as they are. So closely are our duties knit together, that whoso shall keep the whole law, and yet offend in one point, he is guilty of all.

To sum up: it is wrong always, everywhere, and for anyone, to believe anything upon insufficient evidence. . . .

9.4 The Will to Believe

Consider the following case: A mountain climber finds herself on a ledge from which she can escape only by making a leap, a very long leap, to another ledge. If she believes she should not make the leap unless she has sufficient evidence that she can succeed, then she will stay on the ledge and perhaps perish. If she believes she can succeed, then she will give it her all and have a much better chance of making it, although she may not make it and may fall into the abyss.

William James (1842–1910), one of the leading advocates of a philosophy known as American pragmatism, uses an example like this one in an essay called "The Sentiment of Rationality" (1879) to show that there are cases where believing beyond the evidence is the best course of action. Perhaps religious belief is like the case of the mountain climber. Perhaps taking the "leap of faith" is the best course of action even if the evidence is insufficient.

James expands on this idea in an influential and controversial essay entitled "The Will to Believe." The title is misleading, as James himself admitted, because he argues for the "right" to believe, not for the notion that just willing something to be so makes it so. In this essay, James criticizes Clifford (see Reading 9.3) and the evidentialist position.

James argues that belief beyond the evidence is justified in at least three situations. First, when you are confronted with a "genuine option" that *cannot* be decided on evidential grounds, you have a right to decide the issue according to your "passional nature." Second, when faced with a situation where belief in a fact (recall the mountain climber) is necessary for the existence of that fact, you have the right to believe beyond the evidence. Third, in a situation where belief in a true proposition is necessary for getting at the evidence in support of its truth, you are entitled to believe.

James is not arguing that we have the right to believe anything we wish. When we have sufficient evidence, that is the end of the matter. Belief is and should be dictated by the evidence. However, life is not always so tidy, especially when it comes to religious and moral matters.

Reading Questions

1. What is a genuine option?
2. What is James's thesis?
3. How does James's attitude differ from Clifford's with respect to "our first and great commandments as would-be knowers"?
4. Create some of your own examples of cases "where a fact cannot come at all unless a preliminary faith exists in its coming"?
5. What is "the religious hypothesis," and what reasons does James provide in support of the conclusion that we should not keep our "willing nature out of the game"?
6. Who do you think is right, James or Clifford? Why?

The Will to Believe *

WILLIAM JAMES

I

Let us give the name of *hypothesis* to anything that may be proposed to our belief; and just as the electricians speak of live and dead wires, let us speak of any hypothesis as either *live* or *dead*. A live hypothesis is one which appeals as a real possibility to him to whom it is proposed. If I ask you to believe in the Mahdi, the notion makes no electric connection with your nature—it refuses

* From William James, *The Will to Believe and Other Essays in Popular Philosophy* (New York: Henry Holt and Co., 1912), pp. 1–31. Footnotes deleted.

to scintillate with any credibility at all. As an hypothesis it is completely dead. To an Arab, however (even if he be not one of the Mahdi's followers), the hypothesis is among the mind's possibilities: it is alive. This shows that deadness and liveness in an hypothesis are not intrinsic properties, but relations to the individual thinker. They are measured by his willingness to act. The maximum of liveness in an hypothesis means willingness to act irrevocably. Practically, that means belief; but there is some believing tendency wherever there is willingness to act at all.

Next, let us call the decision between two hypotheses an *option*. Options may be of several kinds. They may be—1, *living* or *dead;* 2, *forced* or *avoidable;* 3, *momentous* or *trivial;* and for our purposes we may call an option a *genuine* option when it is of the forced, living and momentous kind.

1. A living option is one in which both hypotheses are live ones. If I say to you: "Be a theosophist or be a mahomedan," it is probably a dead option, because for you neither hypothesis is likely to be alive. But if I say "Be an agnostic or be a Christian," it is otherwise: trained as you are, each hypothesis makes some appeal, however small, to your belief.

2. Next, if I say to you: "Choose between going out with your umbrella or without it," I do not offer you a genuine option, for it is not forced. You can easily avoid it by not going out at all. Similarly, if I say "Either love me or hate me," "Either call my theory true or call it false," your option is avoidable. You may remain indifferent to me, neither loving nor hating, and you may decline to offer any judgment as to my theory. But if I say "Either accept this truth or go without it," I put on you a forced option, for there is no standing place outside of the alternative. Every dilemma based on a complete logical disjunction, with no possibility of not choosing, is an option of this forced kind.

3. Finally, if I were Dr. Nansen and proposed to you to join my North Pole expedition, your option would be momentous; for this would probably be your only similar opportunity, and your choice now would either exclude you from the North Pole sort of immortality altogether or

put at least the chance of it into your hands. He who refuses to embrace a unique opportunity loses the prize as surely as if he tried and failed. *Per contra,* the option is trivial when the opportunity is not unique, when the stake is insignificant, or when the decision is reversible if it later prove unwise. Such trivial options abound in the scientific life. A chemist finds an hypothesis live enough to spend a year in its verification: he believes in it to that extent. But if his experiments prove inconclusive either way, he is quit for his loss of time, no vital harm being done. . . .

II

The next matter to consider is the actual psychology of human opinion. When we look at certain facts, it seems as if our passional and volitional nature lay at the root of all our convictions. When we look at others, it seems as if they could do nothing when the intellect had once said its say. Let us take the latter facts up first.

Does it not seem preposterous on the very face of it to talk of our opinions being modifiable at will? Can our will either help or hinder our intellect in its perceptions of truth? Can we, by just willing it, believe that Abraham Lincoln's existence is a myth, and that the portraits of him in *McClure's Magazine* are all of someone else? Can we, by any effort of our will, or by any strength of wish that it were true, believe ourselves well and about when we are roaring with rheumatism in bed, or feel certain that the sum of the two one-dollar bills in our pocket must be a hundred dollars? We can say any of these things, but we are absolutely impotent to believe them; and of just such things is the whole fabric of the truths that we do believe in made up—matters of fact, immediate or remote, as Hume said, and relations between ideas, which are either there or not there for us if we see them so, and which if not there cannot be put there by any action of our own.

In Pascal's *Thoughts* there is a celebrated passage known in literature as Pascal's wager. In it he tries to force us into Christianity by reasoning as if our concern with truth resembled our concern with the stakes in a game of chance. Translated freely his words are these: You must either believe or not believe that God is—which will you do? Your human reason cannot say. A game is going on between you and the nature of things which at the day of judgment will bring out either heads or tails. Weigh what your gains and your losses would be if you should stake all you have on heads, or God's existence: If you win in such case, you gain eternal beatitude; if you lose, you lose nothing at all. If there were an infinity of chances, and only one for God in this wager, still you ought to stake your all on God; for though you surely risk a finite loss by this procedure, any finite loss is reasonable, even a certain one is reasonable, if there is but the possibility of infinite gain. Go, then, and take holy water, and have masses said; belief will come and stupefy your scruples—*Cela vous fera croire et vous abêtira*. Why should you not? At bottom, what have you to lose?

You probably feel that when religious faith expresses itself thus, in the language of the gaming-table, it is put to its last trumps. Surely Pascal's own personal belief in masses and holy water had far other springs; and this celebrated page of his is but an argument for others, a last desperate snatch at a weapon against the hardness of the unbelieving heart. We feel that a faith in masses and holy water adopted wilfully after such a mechanical calculation would lack the inner soul of faith's reality; and if we were ourselves in the place of the Deity, we should probably take particular pleasure in cutting off believers of this pattern from their infinite reward. It is evident that unless there be some pre-existing tendency to believe in masses and holy water, the option offered to the will by Pascal is not a living option. Certainly no Turk ever took to masses and holy water on its account; and even to us Protestants these means of salvation seem such foregone impossibilities that Pascal's logic, invoked for them specifically, leaves us unmoved. As well might the Mahdi write to us, saying "I am the Expected One whom God has created in his effulgence. You shall be infinitely happy if you confess me; otherwise you shall be cut off from the light of the sun. Weigh, then, your infinite gain if I am genuine against your

finite sacrifice if I am not!" His logic would be that of Pascal; but he would vainly use it on us, for the hypothesis he offers us is dead. No tendency to act on it exists in us to any degree.

The talk of believing by our volition seems, then, from one point of view, simply silly. From another point of view it is worse than silly, it is vile. When one turns to the magnificent edifice of the physical sciences, and sees how it was reared; what thousands of disinterested moral lives of men lie buried in its mere foundations; what patience and postponement, what choking down of preference, what submission to the icy laws of outer fact are wrought into its very stones and mortar; how absolutely impersonal it stands in its vast augustness—then how besotted and contemptible seems every little sentimentalist who comes blowing his voluntary smoke-wreaths, and pretending to decide things from out of his private dream! Can we wonder if those bred in the rugged and manly school of science should feel like spewing such subjectivism out of their mouths? The whole system of loyalties which grow up in the schools of science go dead against its toleration; so that it is only natural that those who have caught the scientific fever should pass over to the opposite extreme, and write sometimes as if the incorruptibly truthful intellect ought positively to prefer bitterness and unacceptableness to the heart in its cup.

"It fortifies my soul to know
That, though I perish, Truth is so—"

sings Clough, whilst Huxley exclaims: "My only consolation lies in the reflection that, however bad our posterity may become, so long as they hold by the plain rule of not pretending to believe what they have no reason to believe because it may be to their advantage so to pretend [the word 'pretend' is surely here redundant], they will not have reached the lowest depths of immorality." And that delicious *enfant terrible* Clifford writes: "Belief is desecrated when given to unproved and unquestioned statements, for the solace and private pleasure of the believer. . . . Whoso would deserve well of his fellows in this matter will guard the purity of his belief with a very fanaticism of jealous care, lest at any time it should rest on an unworthy object, and catch a stain which can never be wiped away. . . . If [a] belief has been accepted on insufficient evidence [even though the belief be true, as Clifford on the same page explains], the pleasure is a stolen one. . . . It is sinful, because it is stolen in defiance of our duty to mankind. That duty is to guard ourselves from such beliefs as from a pestilence, which may shortly master our own body and then spread to the rest of the town. . . . It is wrong always, everywhere, and for anyone, to believe anything upon insufficient evidence."

III

All this strikes one as healthy, even when expressed, as by Clifford, with somewhat too much of robustious pathos in the voice. Free-will and simple wishing do seem, in the matter of our credences, to be only fifth wheels to the coach. Yet if anyone should thereupon assume that intellectual insight is what remains after wish and will and sentimental preference have taken wing, or that pure reason is what then settles our opinions, he would fly quite as directly in the teeth of the facts. . . .

Evidently, then, our non-intellectual nature does influence our convictions. There are passional tendencies and volitions which run before and others which come after belief, and it is only the latter that are too late for the fair; and they are not too late when the previous passional work has been already in their own direction. Pascal's argument, instead of being powerless, then seems a regular clincher, and is the last stroke needed to make our faith in masses and holy water complete. The state of things is evidently far from simple; and pure insight and logic, whatever they might do ideally, are not the only things that really do produce our creeds.

IV

Our next duty, having recognized this mixed-up state of affairs, is to ask whether it be simply reprehensible and pathological, or whether, on the contrary, we must treat it as a normal element in making up our minds. The thesis I defend is, briefly stated, this: *Our passional nature not only lawfully may, but must, decide an option between propositions, whenever it is a genuine option that cannot by its nature be decided on intellectual grounds; for to say, under such circumstances, "Do not decide, but leave the question open," is itself a passional decision—just like deciding yes or no— and is attended with the same risk of losing the truth. . . .*

VII

There are two ways of looking at our duty in the matter of opinion—ways entirely different, and yet ways about whose difference the theory of knowledge seems hitherto to have shown very little concern. *We must know the truth;* and *we must avoid error*—these are our first and great commandments as would-be knowers; but they are not two ways of stating an identical commandment, they are two separable laws. Although it may indeed happen that when we believe the truth *A,* we escape as an incidental consequence from believing the falsehood *B,* it hardly ever happens that by merely disbelieving *B* we necessarily believe *A.* We may in escaping *B* fall into believing other falsehoods, *C* or *D,* just as bad as *B;* or we may escape *B* by not believing anything at all, not even *A.*

Believe truth! Shun error!—these, we see, are two materially different laws; and by choosing between them we may end by colouring differently our whole intellectual life. We may regard the chase for truth as paramount, and the avoidance of error as secondary; or we may, on the other hand, treat the avoidance of error as more imperative, and let truth take its chance. Clifford, in the instructive passage which I have quoted, exhorts us to the latter course. Believe nothing, he tells us, keep your mind in suspense forever, rather than by closing it on insufficient evidence incur the awful risk of believing lies. You, on the other hand, may think that the risk of being in error is a very small matter when compared with the blessings of real knowledge, and be ready to be duped many times in your investigation rather than postpone indefinitely the chance of guessing true. I myself find it impossible to go with Clifford. We must remember that these feelings of our duty about either truth or error are in any case only expressions of our passional life. Biologically considered, our minds are as ready to grind out falsehood as veracity, and he who says "Better go without belief forever than believe a lie!" merely shows his own preponderant private horror of becoming a dupe. He may be critical of many of his desires and fears, but this fear he slavishly obeys. He cannot imagine anyone questioning its binding force. For my own part, I have also a horror of being duped; but I can believe that worse things than being duped may happen to a man in this world: so Clifford's exhortation has to my ears a thoroughly fantastic sound. It is like a general informing his soldiers that it is better to keep out of battle forever than to risk a single wound. Not so are victories either over enemies or over nature gained. Our errors are surely not such awfully solemn things. In a world where we are so certain to incur them in spite of all our caution, a certain lightness of heart seems healthier than this excessive nervousness on their behalf. . . .

VIII

Wherever the option between losing truth and gaining it is not momentous, we can throw the chance of *gaining truth* away, and at any rate save ourselves from any chance of *believing falsehood*, by not making up our minds at all till objective evidence has come. In scientific questions, this is almost always the case; and even in human affairs in general, the need of acting is seldom so urgent that a false belief to act on is better than no belief at all. Law courts, indeed, have to decide on the best evidence attainable for the moment, because a judge's duty is to make law as well as to ascertain it, and (as a learned judge once said to me) few cases are worth spending much time over: the great thing is to have them decided on *any* acceptable principle, and got out of the way. But in our dealings with objective nature we obviously are recorders, not makers, of the truth; and deci-

sions for the mere sake of deciding promptly and getting on to the next business would be wholly out of place. Throughout the breadth of physical nature facts are what they are quite independently of us, and seldom is there any such hurry about them that the risks of being duped by believing a premature theory need be faced. The questions here are always trivial options, the hypotheses are hardly living (at any rate not living for us spectators), the choice between believing truth or falsehood is seldom forced. The attitude of sceptical balance is therefore the absolutely wise one if we would escape mistakes. . . .

The question next arises: Are there not somewhere forced options in our speculative questions, and can we (as men who may be interested at least as much in positively gaining truth as in merely escaping dupery) always wait with impunity till the coercive evidence shall have arrived? It seems *a priori* improbable that the truth should be so nicely adjusted to our needs and powers as that. In the great boarding-house of nature, the cakes and the butter and the syrup seldom come out so even and leave the plates so clean. Indeed, we should view them with scientific suspicion if they did.

IX

Moral questions immediately present themselves as questions whose solution cannot wait for sensible proof. A moral question is a question not of what sensibly exists, but of what is good, or would be good if it did exist. Science can tell us what exists; but to compare the *worths*, both of what exists and of what does not exist, we must consult not science, but what Pascal calls our heart. Science herself consults her heart when she lays it down that the infinite ascertainment of fact and correction of false belief are the supreme goods for man. Challenge the statement and science can only repeat it oracularly, or else prove it by showing that such ascertainment and correction bring man all sorts of other goods which man's heart in turn declares. The question of having moral beliefs at all or not having them is decided by our will. Are our moral preferences true or false, or are they only odd biological phenomena, making things good or bad for *us,* but in themselves indifferent? How can your pure intellect decide? If your heart does not *want* a world of moral reality, your head will assuredly never make you believe in one. . . .

Turn now from these wide questions of good to a certain class of questions of fact, questions concerning personal relations, states of mind between one man and another. *Do you like me or not?*—for example. Whether you do or not depends, in countless instances, on whether I meet you half-way, am willing to assume that you must like me, and show you trust and expectation. The previous faith on my part in your liking's existence is in such cases what makes your liking come. But if I stand aloof, and refuse to budge an inch until I have objective evidence, until you shall have done something apt, as the absolutists say, *ad extorquendum assensum meum,* ten to one your liking never comes. How many women's hearts are vanquished by the mere sanguine insistence of some man that they *must* love him! he will not consent to the hypothesis that they cannot. The desire for a certain kind of truth here brings about that special truth's existence; and so it is in innumerable cases of other sorts. Who gains promotions, boons, appointments, but the man in whose life they are seen to play the part of live hypotheses, who discounts them, sacrifices other things for their sake before they have come, and takes risks for them in advance? His faith acts on the powers above him as a claim, and creates its own verification.

A social organism of any sort whatever, large or small, is what it is because each member proceeds to his own duty with a trust that the other members will simultaneously do theirs. Wherever a desired result is achieved by the co-operation of many independent persons, its existence as a fact is a pure consequence of the precursive faith in one another of those immediately concerned. A government, an army, a commercial system, a ship, a college, an athletic team, all exist on this condition, without which not only is nothing achieved, but nothing is even attempted. A whole train of passengers (individually brave enough) will be looted by a few highwaymen, simply because the latter can count on one another, while each passenger fears that if he makes a movement of resistance, he will be shot before anyone else backs him up. If we believed that the whole carfull would rise at once with us, we should each severally rise, and train-robbing would never even be attempted. There are, then, cases where a fact cannot come at all unless a preliminary faith exists in its coming. *And where faith in a fact can help create the fact,* that would be an insane logic which should say that faith running ahead of scientific evidence is the "lowest kind of immorality" into which a thinking being can fall. Yet such is the logic by which our scientific absolutists pretend to regulate our lives!

X

In truths dependent on our personal action, then, faith based on desire is certainly a lawful and possibly an indispensable thing.

But now, it will be said, these are all childish human cases, and have nothing to do with great cosmical matters, like the question of religious faith. Let us then pass on to that. Religions differ so much in their accidents that in discussing the religious question we must make it very generic and broad. What then do we now mean by the religious hypothesis? Science says things are; morality says some things are better than other things; and religion says essentially two things.

First, she says that the best things are the most eternal things, the overlapping things, the things in the universe that throw the last stone, so to speak, and say the final word. "Perfection is eternal"—this phrase of Charles Secrétan seems a good way of putting this first affirmation of religion, an affirmation which obviously cannot yet be verified scientifically at all.

The second affirmation of religion is that we are better off even now if we believe her first affirmation to be true.

Now let us consider what the logical elements of this situation are *in case the religious hypothesis in both its branches be really true.* (Of course, we must admit that possibility at the outset. If we are to discuss the question at all, it must involve a living option. If for any of you religion be a hypothesis that cannot, by any living possibility be true, then you need go no farther. I speak to the "saving remnant" alone.) So proceeding, we see, first, that religion offers itself as a *momentous* option. We are supposed to gain, even now, by our belief, and to lose by our non-belief, a certain vital good. Secondly, religion is a *forced* option, so far as that good goes. We cannot escape the issue by remaining sceptical and waiting for more light, because, although we do avoid error in that way *if religion be untrue,* we lose the good, *if it be true,* just as certainly as if we positively chose to disbelieve. It is as if a man should hesitate indefinitely to ask a certain woman to marry him because he was not perfectly sure that she would prove an angel after he brought her home. Would he not cut himself off from that particular angel-possibility as decisively as if he went and married someone else? Scepticism, then, is not avoidance of option; it is option of a certain particular kind of risk. *Better risk loss of truth than chance of error*—that is your faith-vetoer's exact position. He is actively playing his stake as much as the believer is; he is backing the field against the religious hypothesis, just as the believer is backing the religious hypothesis against the field. To preach scepticism to us as a duty until "sufficient evidence" for religion be found, is tantamount therefore to telling us, when in the presence of the religious hypothesis, that to yield to our fear of its being error is wiser and better than to yield to our hope that it may be true. It is not intellect against all passions, then; it is only intellect with one passion laying down its law. And by what, forsooth, is the supreme wisdom of this passion warranted? Dupery for dupery, what proof is there that dupery through hope is so much worse than dupery through fear? I, for one, can see no proof; and I simply refuse obedience to the scientist's command to imitate his kind of option, in a case where my own stake is important enough to give me the right to choose my own form of risk. If religion be true and the evidence for it be still insufficient, I do not wish, by putting your extinguisher upon my nature (which feels to me as if it had after all some business in this matter), to forfeit my sole chance in life of getting upon the winning side—that chance depending, of course, on my willingness to run the risk of acting as if my passional need of taking the world religiously might be prophetic and right.

All this is on the supposition that it really may be prophetic and right, and that, even to us who are discussing the matter, religion is a live hypothesis which may be true. Now to most of us religion comes in a still farther way that makes a veto on our active faith even more illogical. The more perfect and more eternal aspect of the universe is represented in our religions as having personal form. The universe is no longer a mere *It* to us, but a *Thou,* if we are religious; and any relation that may be possible from person to person might be possible here. For instance, although in one sense we are passive portions of the universe, in another we show a curious autonomy, as if we were small active centres on our own account. We feel, too, as if the appeal of religion to us were made to our own active good-will, as if evidence might be forever withheld from us unless we met the hypothesis half-way. To take a trivial illustration: just as a man who in a company of gentlemen made no advances, asked a warrant for every concession, and believed no one's word without proof, would cut himself off by such churlishness from all the social rewards that a more trusting spirit would earn—so here, one who should shut himself up in snarling logicality and try to make the gods extort his recognition willy-nilly, or not get it at all, might cut himself off forever from his only opportunity of making the gods' acquaintance. This feeling, forced on us we know not whence, that by obstinately believing that there are gods (although not to do so would be so easy both for our logic and our life) we are doing the universe the deepest service we can, seems part of the living essence of the religious hypothesis. If the hypothesis *were* true in all its parts, including this one, then pure intellectualism, with its veto on our making willing advances, would be an absurdity; and some participation of our sympathetic nature would be logically required. I, therefore, for one, cannot see my way to accepting the agnostic rules for truth-seeking, or wilfully agree to keep my willing nature out of the game. I cannot do so for this plain reason, that *a rule of thinking which would absolutely prevent me from acknowledging certain kinds of truth if those kinds of truth were really there, would be an irrational rule*. That for me is the long and short of the formal logic of the situation, no matter what the kinds of truth might materially be.

I confess I do not see how this logic can be escaped. But sad experience makes me fear that some of you may still shrink from radically saying with me, *in abstracto,* that we have the right to believe at our own risk any hypothesis that is live enough to tempt our will. I suspect, however, that if this is so, it is because you have got away from the abstract logical point of view altogether, and are thinking (perhaps without realizing it) of some particular religious hypothesis which for you is dead. The freedom to "believe what we will" you apply to the case of some patent superstition; and the faith you think of is the faith defined by the schoolboy when he said, "Faith is when you believe something that you know ain't true." I can only repeat that this is misapprehension. *In concreto,* the freedom to believe can only cover living options which the intellect of the individual cannot by itself resolve; and living options never seem absurdities to him who has them to consider. When I look at the religious question as it really puts itself to concrete men, and when I think of all the possibilities which both practically and theoretically it

involves, then this command that we shall put a stopper on our heart, instincts and courage, and *wait*—acting of course meanwhile more or less as if religion were *not* true—till doomsday, or till such time as our intellect and senses working together may have raked in evidence enough—this command, I say, seems to me the queerest idol ever manufactured in the philosophic cave. Were we scholastic absolutists, there might be more excuse. If we had an infallible intellect with its objective certitudes, we might feel ourselves disloyal to such a perfect organ of knowledge in not trusting to it exclusively, in not waiting for its releasing word. But if we are empiricists, if we believe that no bell in us tolls to let us know for certain when truth is in our grasp, then it seems a piece of idle fantasticality to preach so solemnly our duty of waiting for the bell. Indeed we *may* wait if we will—I hope you do not think that I am denying that—but if we do so, we do so at our peril as much as if we believed. In either case we *act*, taking our life in our hands. No one of us ought to issue vetoes to the other, nor should we bandy words of abuse. We ought, on the contrary, delicately and profoundly to respect one another's mental freedom—then only shall we bring about the intellectual republic; then only shall we have that spirit of inner tolerance without which all our outer tolerance is soulless, and which is empiricism's glory; then only shall we live and let live, in speculative as well as in practical things. . . .

9.5 Is Belief in God Rational?

If you do not have evidence to support your belief that tigers are bigger than domestic cats, then is your belief that they are bigger rational? If you do not have evidence that other minds exist, then is your belief that they do exist rational? If you do not have evidence that God exists, then is your belief that God does exist rational? If you do not have evidence that ultimate reality is non-dual, then is your belief that it is non-dual rational?

If you are an evidentialist such as William K. Clifford (see Reading 9.3), then you would argue that it is not only not rational but also ethically wrong to believe any proposition that is not sufficiently justified by the evidence. Evidentialism is one form of a more general epistemological view called foundationalism. According to foundationalism, a belief is rational if it is supported by good reasons—that is, by other beliefs that constitute evidence for it. These other beliefs, in turn, must be supported by good reasons. In order to prevent an infinite regress, foundationalism holds that there are some beliefs or propositions that are basic to noetic structures (belief systems). They form its foundations and hence do not need to be supported by additional good reasons. The query "How do you know that?" comes to an end when these basic propositions or beliefs are reached.

What sorts of propositions are basic? Foundationalists differ in their answer, but generally speaking, those who hold the so-called strong foundationalist position admit only three types of basic beliefs: 1) propositions that express a direct deliverance of sense experience, i.e., "There is a tree over there"; 2) propositions that are incorrigible for me in the sense that they express an immediate state of my consciousness, i.e., "I seem to see a printed page"; and 3) propositions that are self-evidently true to any person who understands them, i.e., "All unmarried men are bachelors."

Could there be other kinds of basic beliefs? The strong foundationalists think not. However, Alvin Plantinga, John A. O'Brian Professor of Philosophy and director of the Center for Philosophy of Religion at the University of Notre Dame and author of the next selection, thinks there may be. He argues that there is no good reason to exclude belief in God from the list of properly basic beliefs of some noetic structure and that it is hence a belief that is rational, even if one has little evidence to support it.

Plantinga's argument is subtle and, in part, based on a detailed critique of both evidentialism and strong foundationalism. It will require careful reading. The effort is worth it, however, because the issue is basic to a philosophical analysis of religion.

Reading Questions

1. What is the difference between believing *that* God exists and believing *in* God?
2. What is the difference between the "natural theologian" and the "natural atheologian"?
3. What is a noetic structure?
4. What is foundationalism, and what sorts of propositions belong to the foundation of a noetic structure according to foundationalism?
5. What is Plantinga's argument for the conclusion that there is "no reason at all for believing that belief in God cannot be basic in a rational noetic structure"?
6. If belief in God can be properly basic, as Plantinga claims, why cannot belief in Santa Claus or in the Great Pumpkin also be properly basic? Or can it?

Is Belief in God Rational?*

ALVIN PLANTINGA

OUR QUESTION . . . is whether belief in God is rational. This question is widely asked and widely answered. Many philosophers—most prominently, those in the great tradition of natural theology— have argued that belief in God *is* rational; they have typically done so by providing what they took to be

*From *Rationality and Religious Belief,* edited by C. F. Delaney. © 1979 by University of Notre Dame Press, Notre Dame, IN. Reprinted by permission. Footnotes deleted.

demonstrations or *proofs* of God's existence. Many others have argued that belief in God is irrational. If we call those of the first group "natural theologians," perhaps we should call those of the second "natural atheologians." (That would at any rate be kinder than calling them "unnatural theologians.") J. L. Mackie, for example, opens his statement of the problem of evil as follows: "I think, however, that a more telling criticism can be made by way of the traditional problem of evil. Here it can be shown, not merely that religious beliefs lack rational support, but that they are positively irrational. . . ." And a very large number of philosophers take it that a central question—perhaps *the* central question—of philosophy of religion is the question whether religious belief in general and belief in God in particular is rationally acceptable. . . .

The nineteenth-century philosopher W. K. Clifford provides a splendid if somewhat strident example of the view that the believer in God must have evidence if he is not to be irrational. Here he does not discriminate against religious belief; he apparently holds that a belief of any sort at all is rationally acceptable only if there is sufficient evidence for it. And he goes on to insist that it is wicked, immoral, monstrous, and perhaps even impolite to accept a belief for which one does not have sufficient evidence:

> Whose would deserve well of his fellows in this matter will guard the purity of his belief with a very fanaticism of jealous care, lest at any time it should rest on an unworthy object, and catch a stain which can never be wiped away.

He adds that if a

> belief has been accepted on insufficient evidence, the pleasure is a stolen one. Not only does it deceive ourselves by giving us a sense of power which we do not really possess, but it is sinful, because it is stolen in defiance of our duty to mankind. That duty is to guard ourselves from such beliefs as from a pestilence which may shortly master our body and spread to the rest of the town.

And finally:

> To sum up: it is wrong always, everywhere, and for anyone to believe anything upon insufficient evidence.

(It is not hard to detect, in these quotations, the "tone of robustious pathos" with which William James credits him.) Clifford finds it utterly obvious, furthermore, that those who believe in God do indeed so believe on insufficient evidence and thus deserve the above abuse. A believer in God is, on his view, at best a harmless pest and at worst a menace to society; in either case he should be discouraged.

Now there are some initial problems with Clifford's claim. For example, he doesn't tell us how *much* evidence is sufficient. More important, the notion of evidence is about as difficult as that of rationality: What is evidence? How do you know when you have some? How do you know when you have sufficient or enough? Suppose, furthermore, that a person thinks he has sufficient evidence for a proposition p when in fact he does not—would he then be irrational in believing p? Presumably a person can have sufficient evidence for what is false—else either Newton did not have sufficient evidence for his physical beliefs or contemporary physicists don't have enough for *theirs*. Suppose, then, that a person has sufficient evidence for the false proposition that he has sufficient evidence for p. Is he then irrational in believing p? Presumably not; but if not, having sufficient evidence is not, contrary to Clifford's claim, a necessary condition for believing p rationally.

But suppose we temporarily concede that these initial difficulties can be resolved and take a deeper look at Clifford's position. What is essential to it is the claim that we must evaluate the rationality of belief in God by examining its relation to *other* propositions. We are directed to estimate its rationality by determining whether we have *evidence* for it—whether we know, or at any rate rationally believe, some other propositions which stand in the appropriate relation to the proposition in question. And belief in God is rational, or reasonable, or rationally acceptable, on this view, only if there are other propositions with respect to which it is thus evident. . . .

Suppose we say that the assemblage of beliefs a person holds, together with the various logical and epistemic relations that hold among them, constitutes that person's *noetic structure*. Now what the Cliffordian really holds is that for each person S there is a set F of beliefs such that a proposition *p* is rational or rationally acceptable for S only if *p* is evident with respect to F—only if, that is, the propositions in F constitute, on balance, evidence for *p*. Let us say that this set F of propositions is the *foundation of S's noetic structure*. On this view every noetic structure has a foundation; and a proposition is rational for S, or known by S, or certain for S, only if it stands in the appropriate relation to the foundation of S's noetic structure.

Suppose we call this view *foundationalism*. It is by no means peculiar to Clifford; foundationalism has had a long and distinguished career in the history of philosophy, including among its adherents Plato, Aristotle, Aquinas, Descartes, Leibniz, Locke, and, to leap to the present, Professor Roderick Chisholm. And from the foundationalist point of view, our question must be restated: Is belief in God evident with respect to the foundations of my noetic structure? Clifford, as I say, takes it to be obvious that the answer is *no*. But *is* this obvious? To restate my earlier question: Might it not be that my belief in God is itself in the foundations of my noetic structure? Perhaps it is a member of F, in which case, of course, it will automatically be evident with respect to F.

Here the Cliffordian foundationalist goes further. Not just *any* belief can properly be in the foundations of a person's noetic structure; to be in F a belief must meet some fairly specific conditions. It must be capable of functioning foundationally; it must be capable of bearing its share of the weight of the entire noetic structure. The propositions in F, of course, are not inferred from other propositions and are not accepted on the basis of other propositions. I know the propositions in the foundations of my noetic structure, but not by virtue of knowing *other* propositions; for these are the ones I start with. And so the question the foundationalist asks about belief in God—namely, what is the evidence for it?—is not properly asked about the members of F; these items don't require to be evident with respect to *other* propositions in order to be rationally believed. Accordingly, says the foundationalist, not

just any proposition is capable of functioning foundationally: to be so capable, with respect to a person S, a proposition must not need the evidential support of other propositions: it must be such that it is possible that S know *p* but have no evidence for *p*.

Well, suppose all this is so; what kind of propositions *can* function foundationally? Here, of course, different foundationalists give different answers. Aristotle and Aquinas, for example, held that *self-evident* propositions—ones like *all black dogs are black*—belong in the foundations. Aquinas, at least, seems also to hold that propositions "evident to the senses," as he puts it—propositions like *some things change*—belong there. For he believed, of course, that the existence of God is demonstrable; and by this I think he meant that God's existence can be deduced from foundational propositions. He holds, furthermore, that God's existence can be demonstrated "from his effects"—from sensible objects; and in each of the five ways there is a premise that, says Aquinas, is "evident to the senses." I therefore believe Aquinas meant to include such propositions among the foundations. You may think it strange, incidentally, to count Aquinas among the Cliffordians. On this point, however, he probably belongs with them; he held that belief in God is rational only if evident with respect to the foundations. Of course he differs from Clifford in holding that in fact God's existence *is* evident with respect to them; he thinks it follows from members of F by argument forms that are themselves in F. This, indeed, is the burden of his five ways.

According to Aquinas, therefore, self-evident propositions and those evident to the senses belong in the foundations. And when he speaks of propositions of the latter sort, he means such propositions as

(1) there's a tree over there,

(2) there is an ash tray on my desk,

(3) that tree's leaves have turned yellow,

and

(4) this fender has rusted through.

Other foundationalists—Descartes, for example—argue that what goes into the foundations, in addition to self-evident propositions, are not propositions that, like (1)–(4), entail the existence of such material objects as ashtrays, trees, leaves, and fenders, but more cautious claims; for example:

(5) I seem to see a red book,
(6) it seems to me that I see a book with a red cover,
(7) I seem to see something red,

or even, as Professor Chisholm put it,

(8) I am appeared redly to.

The foundationalist who opts for propositions like (5)–(8) rather than (1)–(4) has a *prima facie* plausible reason for doing so: Belief in a proposition of the latter sort seems to have a sort of immunity from error not enjoyed by belief in one of the former. I may believe that there is a red ashtray on my desk, or that I see a red ashtray on my desk, when the fact is there is no red ashtray there at all: I am color-blind, or hallucinating, or the victim of an illusion of some sort or other. But it is at the least very much harder to see that I could be wrong in believing that I *seem* to see a red ashtray on my desk—that, in Chisholm's language, I am appeared redly (or red-ashtrayly) to. There are plenty of possible worlds in which I mistakenly believe that there is a red book on my desk; it is at least plausible to hold that there are no possible worlds in which I mistakenly believe that I seem to see a red book there. And this immunity from error may plausibly be taken to provide a reason for distinguishing between propositions like (5)–(8) and (1)–(4), admitting the former but not the latter to the foundations.

There is a small problem here, however: Every necessarily true proposition—every proposition true in all possible worlds—is such that there is no possible world in which I mistakenly believe it. Yet presumably the foundationalist will not be inclined to hold that every necessary proposition I believe is in the foundations of my noetic structure. Consider, for example, Goldbach's Conjecture that every even number greater than two is the sum of two primes. This proposition is either necessarily true or necessarily false, although it

isn't presently known which. Suppose it is in fact true, and I believe it, but not because I have found a proof of it; I simply believe it. The foundationalist will presumably hold, in this case, that my belief in Goldbach's Conjecture is necessarily true but not a good candidate for the foundations. Here I truly believe but do not know the proposition in question; so it does not belong among the foundations, and this despite the fact that there is no possible world in which I mistakenly believe it.

Presumably, then, the Cliffordian will not hold that just any necessarily true belief is automatically among the foundations. He may argue instead that what characterizes propositions like (5)–(8) is not just that it is not possible to believe them mistakenly, but that it is not possible to be mistaken about them. That is to say, a proposition of this sort is like a necessary proposition in that it is not possible for me to believe it mistakenly; it is unlike a necessary proposition, however, in that it is also not possible for me to believe its *denial* mistakenly. If I believe that I am appeared to redly, then it follows that I *am* appeared to redly; but if I believe that I am not appeared to redly, it follows equally that I am not thus appeared to. We might say that propositions meeting this condition are *incorrigible* for me; perhaps we can explain this notion thus:

(9) *p* is incorrigible for *S* at *t* iff there is no possible world in which *S* mistakenly believes *p* at *t* and no possible world in which *S* mistakenly believes not-*p* at *t*.

According to our paradigm Cliffordian, then, a belief is properly in the foundations of my noetic structure only if it is either self-evident or incorrigible for me. So suppose we take a look at self-evidence. What is it? Under what conditions is a proposition self-evident? What kinds of propositions are self-evident? Examples would include very simple arithmetical truths such as

(10) 2 + 1 = 3,

simple truths of logic such as

(11) no man is both married and unmarried,

perhaps the generalizations of simple truths of logic, such as

(12) for any proposition p, the conjunction of p with its denial is false.

and certain propositions expressing identity and diversity; for example

(13) Redness is distinct from greenness,
(14) the property of being prime is distinct from the property of being composite,

and

(15) the proposition *all men are mortal* is distinct from the proposition *all mortals are men.*

There are others; Aquinas gives as examples

(16) the whole is greater than the part,

where, presumably, he means by "part" what we mean by "proper part," and, more dubiously,

(17) man is an animal.

Still other candidates—candidates which may be less than entirely uncontroversial—come from many other areas: for example

(18) if p is necessarily true and p entails q, then q is necessarily true,
(19) if e^1 occurs before e^2 and e^2 occurs before e^3, then e^1 occurs before e^3,

and

(20) it is wrong to cause unnecessary (and unwanted) pain just for the fun of it.

What is it that characterizes these propositions? According to the tradition, the outstanding characteristic of a self-evident proposition is that one simply sees it to be true upon grasping or understanding it. Understanding a self-evident proposition is sufficient for apprehending its truth. Of course this notion must be relativized to *persons;* what is self-evident to you might not be to me. Very simple arithmetical truths will be self-evident to nearly all of us; but a truth like $17 + 18 = 35$ may be self-evident only to some. And of course a proposition is self-evident to a person only if he does in fact grasp it; so a proposition will not be self-evident to those who do not apprehend the concepts involved in the proposition. As Aquinas says, some propositions are self-evident only to the learned; his example is the truth that immaterial substances do not occupy space. Among those

propositions whose concepts not everyone grasps, some are such that anyone who *did* grasp them would see their truth; for example,

(21) A model of a first order theory T assigns truth to the axioms of T,

Others—$17 + 13 = 30$, for example—may be such that some but not all of those who apprehend them also see that they are true.

But how shall we understand this "seeing that they are true"? Those who speak of self-evidence explicitly turn to this visual metaphor and expressly explain self-evidence by reference to vision. There are two important aspects to the metaphor and two corresponding components to the idea of self-evidence. First, there is the *epistemic* component: a proposition p is self-evident to a person S only if S has *immediate* knowledge of p—i.e., knows p, and does not know p on the basis of his knowledge of other propositions. Consider a simple arithmetic truth such as $2 + 1 = 3$ and compare it with one like $24 \times 24 = 576$. I know each of these propositions; and I know the second but not the first on the basis of computation, which is a kind of inference. So I have immediate knowledge of the first but not the second. The epistemic component of self-evidence, therefore, is immediate knowledge; it follows, of course, that any proposition self-evident to a person is true. . . .

Now suppose we return to the main question: Why shouldn't belief in God be among the foundations of my noetic structure? Let us say that a proposition is *basic* for a person S if and only if it is in the foundations of S's noetic structure; our question, then, is this: Can belief in God be properly basic for a person? If not, why not? The answer, on the part of our hypothetical Cliffordian, was that even if this belief is *true,* it does not have the characteristics a proposition must have to deserve a place in the foundations. There is no room in the foundations for a proposition that can be known only on the basis of other propositions. A proposition is properly basic for a person only if he knows it immediately—i.e., knows it, and does not know it on the basis of other propositions. The proposition that God exists, however, is at best truly believed, not known, and even if it were known, it wouldn't be known immediately. The only propositions that meet this condition of immediate knowledge are those that are self-evident or incorrigible. Since this proposition is neither, it is not properly basic for anyone; that is, no well-formed, rational noetic structure contains this proposition in its foundations.

But why should the theist concede these things? Suppose he grants that there is a foundation to his noetic structure: a set F of propositions such that (1) he knows each member of F *immediately* and (2) whatever else he knows is evident with respect to the members of F. Suppose he concedes, further, that he does know other things, and knows them on the basis of his knowledge of these basic propositions. Suppose, in a particularly irenic and conciliatory frame of mind, he concedes still further that much of what he believes, he believes but does not know; and that the rationality of these beliefs is to be tested or measured by way of their connections with those propositions that are basic for him. Why should he not combine these concessions with the claim that his belief in God is properly basic for him?

Because, says the Cliffordian, belief in God is neither self-evident nor incorrigible. But now we must look more closely at this fundamental principle of the foundationalist's position:

(22) a proposition *p* is properly basic for a person *S* if and only if *p* is either self-evident to *S* or incorrigible for *S*;

that is, the foundations of a well-formed, rational noetic structure will contain propositions that are self-evident or incorrigible and will not contain any propositions that do not meet this condition.

We should note that self-evidence looms particularly large in the foundationalist scheme of things; in a way, his acceptance of what is incorrigible rests on self-evidence. For how does one know that a proposition *is* incorrigible for someone? How does one know that there are any incorrigible propositions at all? How does the foundationalist know that, e.g.,

(23) S is in pain

is incorrigible for *S*? (23) is incorrigible for *S* if and only if it isn't possible that *S* mistakenly believe either (23) or its negation; and that *this* is so, if indeed it is so, is presumably, according to the foundationalist, itself self-evident. So self-evidence plays a peculiarly fundamental role for the foundationalist; a proposition is properly basic, he holds, only if it is self-evident or incorrigible; and that a given proposition falls into the latter category (if indeed it does) will be itself self-evident.

And here we must ask a question that has been clamoring for attention. How does the foundationalist know—how does anyone know—that, indeed, a given proposition *is* self-evident? How do we tell? Isn't it possible that a proposition should seem to me to be self-evident when in fact it is not? Consider an analogy. Suppose the theist claims that a proposition *p* is properly basic for a person *S* if *S* knows *p* *immediately;* and suppose he adds that one of the things he immediately knows is that God exists. The Cliffordian foundationalist, presumably, will want to reply as follows: you *say* you have immediate knowledge of this proposition, but perhaps you are mistaken; perhaps you only *believe* and do not *know* that God exists; perhaps, indeed, God does *not* exist. How do you know that you have immediate knowledge of this proposition? What leads you to think so? . . .

We must distinguish, therefore, what appears to be self-evident from what really is. Suppose we say that a proposition *seems* or *appears* self-evident to a person if he understands . . . it. How, then, does the foundationalist determine which propositions really *are* self-evident for him? By noting, of course, which ones appear self-evident to him; he has nothing else to go on. Of course he cannot sensibly hold that *whatever* appears self-evident, really is . . . . Perhaps, however, he can retreat to a weaker principle; perhaps he can hold that whatever seems self-evident has, as we might put it, the presumption of self-evidence in its favor. What appears to be self-evident ought to be taken to self-evident unless there are reasons to the contrary—unless, for example, it appears self-evident that the proposition in question conflicts with *other* apparently self-evident propositions. And perhaps he will support this injunction by appeal to some such principles as

(24) Whatever seems self-evident is very likely true

or

(25) most propositions that *seem* self-evident *are* self-evident (and hence true).

But why should we accept (24) and (25)? Why does the foundationalist accept them? We should note, first of all, that neither of these propositions seems self-evident. One who understands them can nonetheless wonder whether they are true and in fact reject them. . . . Impressed with evolutionary theory, for example, we might suppose that the disposition to find these propositions self-evident is a trait emerging in the course of a long evolutionary development—a trait that has a certain survival value, but is at best fortuitously connected with truth, so that many or most of the propositions that appear self-evident to us are in fact false. Or, remembering our Descartes, we might speculate that we have been created by a being who delights in deception and produces in us a powerful tendency to accept certain false propositions as self-evident. Or we might speculate, in a Kierkegaardian vein, that our noetic endowment, once pristine and totally reliable, has been corrupted by some primal cataclysm befalling the human race. So (24) and (25) are not themselves apparently self-evident.

The important point here, however, lies in a different direction. Suppose these principles—(24) and (25)—*were* apparently self-evident. That is, suppose the proposition

(26) most propositions that display the phenomenological feature are true

itself displayed this feature. Would that be a relevant answer to the question of what reason, if any, there is for believing that most propositions displaying this feature are true? It is hard to see how. The question is whether a proposition's displaying this feature is a reason for thinking it true; to reply that (26) itself displays this feature is simply to invite the question again. Here the appeal to self-evidence seems entirely unsatisfactory. It is as if the

theist were to reply to the question: "Why believe in God?" by pointing out that God requires us to believe in Him, and requires us to believe only what is true. This may indeed be so; but it does not supply a reason for belief for anyone who does not already believe. Similarly, the claim that (24) and (25) are apparently self-evident, may or may not be true; but it can serve as a reason for accepting them only for someone who already accepts them. And hence it cannot serve as a reason, for the foundationalist, for accepting them.

The fact of the matter is, I think, that the foundationalist has no reason at all for accepting (24) and (25). They do not appear to be self-evident: and of course they are not incorrigible. But if the foundationalist *does* have a reason for them, that reason must trace back, ultimately, to the foundations; that is, the foundationalist has a reason, on his own view, for (24) and (25) only if they are evident with respect to propositions that are properly basic for him—propositions that are self-evident or incorrigible. It is hard to see how (24) or (25) could be evident with respect to such propositions.

Accordingly, the foundationalist accepts (24) and (25) but has no reason for so doing. He isn't *obliged* to accept them; there are alternatives. He simply commits himself to them. We might say that he commits himself to the trustworthiness of his noetic equipment. More elegantly, he commits himself to the reliability of his epistemic endowment. If, with an older tradition, we think of reason as an organ, or power, or faculty—the faculty whereby we discern what is self-evident—then the foundationalist commits himself to the basic reliability of reason. He doesn't do so, of course, as a result of (broadly speaking) scientific or rational investigation; he does so in advance of such investigation. For he has no reasons for accepting (24) and (25); but he does accept them, and he uses them to determine the acceptability of *other* propositions. In other words, (24) and (25) are members of the foundation of his noetic structure.

The foundationalist, therefore, commits himself to the basic reliability of reason. I do not say this by way of criticism; it is a commitment I share. The theist is by no means obliged to reject this commitment. Augustine, indeed, argued that reason is ultimately reliable just because God has created us and is not a deceiver. He has created us in such a way that certain propositions appear self-evident to us; and because he is a God of goodness and truth, he would not create us in such a way that *false* propositions should appear self-evident. Had Augustine been apprised of the Russell paradoxes, he might have expressed himself more guardedly; but his basic point remains. One who believes in God can certainly accept (24) and (25); and he, unlike the foundationalist, can give a reason for doing so.

Since the theist can properly concur with the foundationalist on (24) and (25), he can agree with the latter that apparently self-evident and incorrigible propositions are properly basic for *S*. But the foundationalist *credo*, we have seen, contains *two* elements, a positive and a negative. The foundationalist holds, positively, that

(27) self-evident and incorrigible propositions are properly basic for *S*,

and he adds, negatively, that

(28) *only* propositions of those sorts are properly basic for *S*.

But why should we accept this negative element? What is there to be said in favor of it? Do we have anything more than the foundationalist's word for (28)?

The fact is we have *less* than the foundationalist's word for it. For, as we have seen, it seems that he himself accepts (24) and (25) as basic; these are among the foundations of his noetic structure. But (24) and (25) are neither self-evident nor incorrigible; hence he appears to be hoist with his own petard. A similar point may be made with respect to (28) itself. (28) is neither self-evident nor incorrigible; nor does it appear to follow from propositions that are. It is, however, basic for the foundationalist. So he holds that self-evident and incorrigible propositions are the only viable candidates for the foundations of his noetic structure, but he himself accepts as basic (24) or (25), and (28), none of which meets this condition. But suppose we waive this point for the moment and leave the foundationalist to

try to see how to achieve coherence here. Is there any reason to believe (28)? If so, what is it? (28) certainly does not appear to be self-evident; it is certainly not incorrigible. It is very hard to see, furthermore, that it either follows from or is evident with respect to propositions that *are* self-evident or incorrigible. So it is hard to see that there is any reason for accepting (28), even from a roughly foundationalist point of view. Why then should we accept it? Why should the theist feel any obligation to believe it?

The answer, I believe, is that there is no reason at all for accepting (28); it is no more than a bit of intellectual imperialism on the part of the foundationalist. He means to commit himself to reason and to nothing more; he therefore declares irrational any noetic structure that contains more—belief in God, for example—in its foundations. But here there is no reason for the theist to follow his example; the believer is not obliged to take his word for it. So far we have found no reason at all for excluding belief in God from the foundations; so far we have found no reason at all for believing that belief in God cannot be basic in a rational noetic structure. To accept belief in God as basic is clearly not irrational in the sense of being proscribed by reason or in conflict with the deliverances of reason. The dictum that belief in God is not basic in a rational noetic structure is neither apparently self-evident nor apparently incorrigible. Nor does it seem to be a deductive consequence of what is self-evident or incorrigible. Is there, then, any reason at all for holding that a noetic structure including belief in God as basic is irrational? If there is, it remains to be specified.

It is worth noting, by way of conclusion, that the mature believer, the mature theist, does not typically accept belief in God tentatively, or hypothetically, or until something better comes along. Nor, I think, does he accept it as a conclusion from other things he believes: he accepts it as basic, as a part of the foundations of his noetic structure. The mature theist *commits* himself to belief in God; this means that he accepts belief in God as basic. Our present inquiry suggests that there is nothing contrary to reason or irrational in so doing.

9.6 Intellect and Intuition

The debate about the relationship between faith and reason is influenced strongly by the Western theistic context and the experience of Western society with critical reason. The tension between the authority of an alleged divine revelation and the authority of philosophical reason, the central role that faith plays as both a virtue and a means to salvation, the demand for sufficient evidence, and the critical methods of biblical interpretation shape the faith/reason controversy in the West. Faith, in this context, frequently comes to mean believing that a proposition (such as God exists) is true on insufficient evidence.

If we move beyond the Western theistic context, then the rules of the game dramatically change. Let us look at one example. In Advaita Vedanta (see Reading 2.2), the authoritative scriptures known as the *Vedas* are said to be "authorless." They do reveal transcendental truths, but God does not disclose these truths. Hence there is no demand to have faith in a divine revelation because there is no such revelation. However, there is a revelation of a sort—an authorless revelation.

This seems quite odd to Western minds until one knows that among the ways of gaining knowledge, according to Vedanta, is testimony. Testimony is a valid means of knowing if the source of the testimony is truthful and accurate. However, if a testimony has no author, then the validity of the testimony itself becomes even stronger because no question can be raised about the truthfulness of the author. To say that the testimony contained in the *Vedas* is authorless turns out, in Vedanta philosophy, to be a virtue, not a vice.

The *Vedas* are an eternal truth, or so it is claimed. They reflect the wisdom of ancient seers who gained this truth intuitively, by a type of higher sight. Although we are to have faith in what the seers saw and transmitted, this faith is only preliminary to our own seeing. In other words, there is a direct means to a higher knowledge that transcends lower knowledge that each of us can use. Various methods of meditation, including meditation on the testimony of scripture, were devised and taught to students who wished to find out for themselves. These methods can, it is claimed, facilitate the experiential insight into the truth of scripture that is vital for salvation (release from suffering and the round of reincarnation).

In the next selection, Sarvapalli Radhakrishnan (1888–1975) distinguishes different ways of knowing, claiming that the deepest religious truth is the result of creative intuition. Sarvapalli Radhakrishnan had a distinguished philosophical and educational career in addition to a political career that culminated in his serving as president of India from 1962 to 1967. For him the issue is not one of finding a satisfying relationship between faith and reason, but of recognizing that reason comes in different forms and that religious truth is as much a product of intellect as are other kinds of truth.

Reading Questions

1. What is the difference between the Eastern emphasis on creative intuition and the Western emphasis on critical intelligence?
2. What is the difference between sense experience and discursive reasoning?
3. What is intuitive knowing, and how is knowledge of the self an illustration of it?
4. Do you agree with Radhakrishnan that there is an intuitive knowledge that cannot be fully expressed in propositional form and that requires no proof? Why or why not?

Intellect and Intuition*

RADHAKRISHNAN

IF ALL KNOWLEDGE were of the scientific type, the contemporary challenge to religion would seem to be conclusive. The problem thus narrows itself to the reality of intuitive knowledge and the conditions of its validity. Is there or is there not knowledge which by its nature cannot be expressed in propositions and is yet trustworthy?

1. The Eastern Emphasis on Creative Intuition

The alleged dialogue between Socrates and the Indian philosopher suggests that for the whole Western tradition man is essentially a rational being, one who can think logically and act in a utilitarian manner. The Western mind lays great stress on science, logic and humanism. Hindu thinkers as a class hold with great conviction that we possess a power more interior than intellect by which we become aware of the real in its intimate individuality, and not merely in its superficial or discernible aspects. For the Hindus a system of philosophy is an insight, a *darśana*. It is the vision of truth and not a matter of logical argument and proof. They believe that the mind can be freed by gradual training from the influences of speculative intellect as well as past impressions, and that it can unite itself with the object whose nature is then fully manifested. They contend that we can control destiny by the power of truth. Knowledge means power. The lack of this knowledge is the root of all trouble. *Vidyā is mokṣa: avidyā is saṁsāra.* Intuitive realization is the means to salvation. He who knows is saved directly and immediately, and by means of that knowledge. Intuitive insight is identical with freedom. "Whoever knows 'I am Brahman' becomes this all." "He who knows that supreme Brahman becomes that Brahman itself." We cannot know Brahman fully and truly unless we partake of its essence, become one with it. To know God is to become divine, free from any outside influence likely to cause fear or sorrow. Brahman, which symbolizes the absolute reality, means also holy knowledge, intuitive wisdom. Intuitive wisdom becomes personified as the first principle of the universe. The acceptance of the authority of the Vedas by the different systems of Hindu thought is an admission that intuitive insight is a greater light in the abstruse problems of philosophy than logical understanding. Śaṁkara, for example, regards *anubhava* or integral experience as the highest kind of apprehension. While it may not be clear and distinct, it is sure and vivid. Buddha emphasizes the importance of *bodhi* or enlightenment. His impatience with metaphysical subtleties is well known. The sophistries of the intellect were, according to him, hindrances to the higher life. Knowledge of reality is to be won by spiritual effort. One cannot think one's way into reality, but only live into it. In early Buddhism, *prajñā* or intuitive insight represents the highest activity of the human mind. The general tendency of Hindu and Buddhist thought is to take hold of the aspiration of the human soul after a higher life, and treat this fact as the key to the interpretation of the universe, and all critical philosophy took this into account.

2. Western Emphasis on Critical Intelligence

While the dominant feature of Eastern thought is its insistence on creative intuition, the Western systems are generally characterized by a greater adherence to critical intelligence. This distinction

*From *An Idealist View of Life* by S. Radhakrishnan. (London: George Allen & Unwin, Ltd. 1932 [1961]). Reprinted by permission of HarperCollins Publishers Limited. Footnotes deleted.

is not to be pressed too closely. It is relative and not absolute. It describes the chief tendencies, and there are in fact many exceptions. It is only a question of the distribution of emphasis.

If we may trust the Pythagorean tradition, the method and achievements of Greek philosophy were largely affected by the example of mathematics. Socrates is credited by Aristotle with two things, inductive arguments and universal definitions. Whatever is real must have a definable form. Things are in virtue of their forms. The classification of moral concepts is the first step to any improvement in practice. Suggested definitions are tested by Socrates with reference to actual facts. For Plato, geometry was the model science. Even God geometrizes. Aristotle invented the science of logic. For him, man is preeminently a rational animal. Logic for the Greeks is not so much a science of discovery as one of proof. The civic life of the ancient Greeks centred round the assembly and the law courts, where intellectual subtlety and mental dexterity are most in demand. The great aim was to secure victory in debate, and the chief means to it was to master the technique of argument. More prominence was given to the expression and communication of thought than to its discovery and growth. There is an intimate relation between grammar and logic in Aristotle's *Organon*. The tendency to stereotype thought in conventional ways grew up. The canons of formal logic would be of excellent use, when all truths are discovered and nothing more remained to be known, but logic cannot dictate or set limits to the course of nature and progress of discovery.

I have no doubt that this summary description is quite inadequate to the complexity and richness of Greek thought. The non-mathematical side of Plato's teaching is perhaps his most important contribution. For Plato, noesis is the highest kind of knowledge, immediate and supra-intellectual. He believed in what he called dialectic or the conversation of the soul with itself, which is not scientific knowledge. Aristotle speaks of the absolute self-knowledge of God, a pure activity which knows no law and no end outside itself. This is not the place to discuss the alleged influence of Eastern thought on the Orphic mysteries and Pythagoras, and through them on Plato's philosophy. Pythagoras and Plato may owe to Indian thought more than the Hellenists are willing to admit. Speaking generally, however, it is not incorrect to hold that the Greeks attempted to give an explanation of the problem of certainty in terms of logical reason, and failed to justify the logical postulates themselves.

Plotinus and the Neo-Platonists were convinced that logical knowledge alone was inadequate. Neo-platonism which originated in Alexandria, where Oriental modes of thought were not unknown, presented a more organic view and grounded logical processes on the certainty of immediate experience. But the post-scholastic philosophers fell back upon a purely rationalistic approach to certainty, and the attempt to ground philosophy in science became more popular with the growth of natural sciences, which were actually engaged in pushing back the frontiers of knowledge through observation and experimental verification. Though the methodology of the sciences studied the processes by which beliefs grew and thoughts evolved, its actual interest was more in the grammar of discovery than the life of it. The latter by its very nature sets limits to logical exposition.

For Descartes, with whom modern European philosophy takes a new direction, truth means clearness and distinctness. Whatever can be expressed in mathematical form is clear and distinct. Descartes sets forth a system of universal concepts of reason which are derived from a consideration of certain fundamental, logical and mathematical relationships. In a famous sentence he observes, "I was especially delighted with mathematics. I was astonished that foundations so strong and solid should have had no loftier superstructure raised on them." His conception of universal mathematics and faith that all things are mutually related as the objects of geometry imply a strictly mechanical world. For Spinoza, even Ethics should be treated by the geometrical method. For Leibniz, again, the monads or perceiving minds differ in nothing other than the *form* of perception, for each monad resembles the others as regards the content of its perception. Each reflects the total universe from its own special angle. But the lowest monads, the plant and the animal ones, have dim and confused modes of perception. Divine cognition consists in completely distinct and adequate ideas. We, human beings, are in between. Our ideas of sense qualities are confused, those of logic and mathematics distinct. We attempt to transform the former into the latter kind, factual presentations into notions conceived by reason. The accomplishment of this ideal means for Leibniz the setting forth of a general system of the possible forms of thought and the universal laws of connection which these laws obey. Such a plan was outlined by Leibniz and became the foundation, in a sense, of symbolic logic which reached its great development in the works of Boole and Peano, Frege, Russell and others.

Kant's fundamental aim was to lead philosophy into the safe road of science, and he inquired into the possibility of philosophy as a science with the intention of formulating its conditions. The "nature" with which we deal in science and everyday life is due to the work of the understanding which arranges the multiplicity of sense in an orderly world according to a logic which Kant distinguished as synthetic from the traditional formal or analytical logic. His successors took over this logic of synthesis and utilized it for the purpose of resolving the imperfections of Kant's system. The tendency in Kant to postulate an intelligible world as the foundation of ethics is dismissed as irrelevant, and the world of things in themselves declared a poetic fiction. In Hegel, logic ceases to be a mere theory of thought, but becomes an account of reality. It is an abstract representation of an actual process by which the absolute spirit reveals itself as the universe in the different forms which the universe assumes to human consciousness, nature, history, society, art and religion. "What is rational is real and what is real is rational." Hegel's view of history as the manifestation of spirit in the threefold moments of thesis, antithesis and synthesis is an intellectual scheme which largely forced the facts into conformity with

an *a priori* formula. Hegel's influence is continued in the later idealists. "No fact," says Edward Caird, "which is in its nature incapable of being explained or reduced to law can be admitted to exist in the intelligible universe." For the Hegelians, reality is essentially knowable in the logical way. While Bosanquet is more Hegelian in his outlook, Bradley is more Kantian. For Bradley, thought moves within the realm of relationships and can never grasp or positively determine the ultimate reality. The realists are the worshippers of logic and the scientific method. Faith in the logical intellect as the supreme instrument of knowledge has led the realistic thinkers to devote their major energies to the precise formulation of specialized problems. The Behaviourists insist on the close relation between thinking and talking, and reduce thinking to a matter of language or expression. In the words of Max Müller, "To think is to speak low. To speak is to think aloud."

From the Socratic insistence on the concept to Russell's mathematical logic, the history of Western thought has been a supreme illustration of the primacy of the logical. Rationalism is deep in our bones, and we feel secure about scientific knowledge and sceptical about religious faith. If "there is no higher faculty than those involved in ordinary knowledge," if "the truth of religion" or the validity of religious experience is to be established, "as reasonable inference from discursive knowledge about the world, human history, the soul with its faculties and capacities; and above all from knowledge of the inter-connections between such items of knowledge," then it will be difficult for us to be certain about God. But the tradition of religion holds that those who have known God by acquaintance and not by hearsay have known him not as a valid conclusion from logical reasoning but by the constraining authority of experience. But is the authority of the latter valid, trustworthy?

3. *Different Ways of Knowing*

While all varieties of cognitive experience result in a knowledge of the real, it is produced in three ways, which are sense experience, discursive reasoning and intuitive apprehension. Sense experience helps us to know the outer characters of the external world. By means of it we obtain an acquaintance with the sensible qualities of the objects. Its data are the subject-matter of natural science which builds up a conceptual structure to describe them.

Logical knowledge is obtained by the processes of analysis and synthesis. The data supplied to us by perception are analysed and the results of the analysis yield a more systematic knowledge of the object perceived. This logical or conceptual knowledge is indirect and symbolic in its character. It helps us to handle and control the object and its workings. Conceptual explanations alter with the growth of experience and analysis. They are dependent on our perceptions, our interests, and our capacities. Both sense knowledge and logical knowledge are the means by which we acquire for practical purposes a control over our environment. . . .

6. *Intuitive Knowing*

There is a knowledge which is different from the conceptual, a knowledge by which we see things as they are, as unique individuals and not as members of a class or units in a crowd. It is nonsensuous, immediate knowledge. Sense knowledge is not the only kind of immediate knowledge. As distinct from sense knowledge or *pratyakṣa* (literally presented to a sense), the Hindu thinkers use the term *aparokṣa* for the non-sensuous immediate knowledge. This intuitive knowledge arises from an intimate fusion of mind with reality. It is knowledge by being and not by senses or by symbols. It is awareness of the truth of things by identity. We become one with the truth, one with the object of knowledge. The object known is seen not as an object outside the self, but as a part of the self. What intuition reveals is not so much a doctrine as a consciousness; it is a state of mind and not a definition of the object. Logic and language are a lower form, a diminution of this kind of knowledge. Thought is a means of partially manifesting and presenting what is concealed in this greater self-existent knowledge. Knowledge is

an intense and close communion between the knower and the known. In logical knowledge there is always the duality, the distinction between the knowledge of a thing and its being. Thought is able to reveal reality, because they are one in essence; but they are different in existence at the empirical level. Knowing a thing and being it are different. So thought needs verification.

There are aspects of reality where only this kind of knowledge is efficient. Take, e.g., the emotion of anger. Sense knowledge of it is not possible in regard to its superficial manifestations. Intellectual knowledge is not possible until the data are supplied from somewhere else, and sense cannot supply them. Before the intellect can analyse the mood of anger, it must get at it, and it cannot get at it by itself. We know what it is to be angry by being angry. No one can understand fully the force of human love or parental affection who has not himself been through them. Imagined emotions are quite different from felt ones.

The great illustration of intuitive knowledge given by Hindu thinkers is the knowledge of self. We become aware of our own self, as we become aware of love or anger, directly by a sort of identity with it. Self-knowledge is inseparable from self-existence. It seems to be the only true and direct knowledge we have: all else is inferential. Śaṁkara says that self-knowledge which is neither logical nor sensuous is the presupposition of every other kind of knowledge. It alone is beyond doubt for "it is of the essential nature of him who denies it." It is the object of the notion of self (*asmatpratyayaviṣaya*), and it is known to exist on account of its immediate presentation. It cannot be proved, since it is the basis of all proof. It is the light which is not nature, which is not man, but which made them both. All experience—cognition, affection, or conation—is always an experience to an "I." An "I" is implicit in all awareness. This "I" is not the body, however intimate the connection of the body with the "I" may be. The body is something which can be perceived by the senses. We do not say "I am the body," but only "I have a body." As part of the empirical consciousness, the reality of the body is that of the empirical world. We say "I see or hear," and not the eye sees or the ear hears. The "I" implicit in all knowledge is not something inferred from experience, but something lived and known by experience. It is experienced as a fundamentally simple existent, and is not to be confused with the self as conceived. What is immediately apprehended is different from what is conceptually constructed. The self immediately known in experience is known as a "that" and not a "what." We have in this immediate apprehen-

sion a knowledge of acquaintance with being, and not knowledge about its essence or nature. What is immediately apprehended is known as unique, as subject of all experience while everything else is object. There is no real but only a logical distinction between subject and object in the immediate intuitive awareness of the self as real being. "That which knows and that which is known (reason and the world of reason) are really the same thing." . . .

9.7 Kierkegaard on Rationality

Søren Aabye Kierkegaard (1813–1855) came to be known as the "gloomy Dane" and the "father of existentialism." Neither title is entirely accurate, but it is true that he saw his task as "reintroducing Christianity into Christiandom." He studied both philosophy and theology but did not take up a career in the established Lutheran Church of Denmark because he could not abide either the Hegelianism that permeated the theological and philosophical thinking of the day or the tepid sort of Christianity preached and practiced. Therefore, he became a modern-day Socrates standing as the "lone individual" against the "crowd" and reminding people via his writings that they have forgotten not only how to exist authentically but also what genuine Christianity is.

For Kierkegaard, intellectual reflection characteristic of the Hegelian system cannot motivate action. Only a decision, a "leap" informed by the passions (what he called "inwardness" or "subjectivity") can bring reflection to an end and eventuate in action. This leap must be made in faith (a "willing to be oneself") and it is made possible by trusting the power that "created the self."

Kierkegaard's emphasis on the "leap of faith," when combined with another theme, "truth is subjectivity," has led some scholars to classify him (oh, how he would hate that!) as a fideist. Fideism is difficult to characterize in general. It is often associated with the view that religious beliefs are not subject to independent rational assessment and, in that sense, contrasted with evidentialism (see Reading 9.3). There are many varieties of fideism. William James's (see Reading 9.4) views, along with Pascal's (see Reading 9.2), are sometimes called "voluntaristic fideism" because both are alleged to argue that assent to religious beliefs is an act of the will. Wittgensteinian fideism, yet another brand (see the Introduction to this chapter), supposedly argues that religious faith is a "total way of life" that can be understood only by living it. Existentialist fideism is yet another variety that is alleged to argue that religious faith is a blind leap based on a criterionless choice. Kierkegaard's views have often been associated with existentialist fideism.

As you well might imagine, existentialist varieties of fideism have been criticized for being irrational and relativistic. If no criteria govern my choice, then it seems that it makes little difference what I choose religiously (theism, atheism, agnosticism, non-theism or something else). One choice is as good as another.

Marilyn Gaye Piety, who has been a Visiting Scholar at the Department of Søren Kierkegaard Research of the University of Copenhagen, argues in the next selection that although Kierkegaard did emphasize choice, he by no means thought this choice either irrational or without criteria. There are a variety of ways in which we can interpret our experiences and live our lives, and we do occasionally choose between competing interpretations of our existence. Just because such choices may be informed by our "passions" does not mean that they are irrational or without criteria. What might the criteria be? Read and see what Piety thinks Kierkegaard would answer.

Reading Questions

1. Describe the impasse that the contemporary debate on human rationality has reached. From what does this impasse result?
2. How does Piety's account of Kiekegaard's criterion for the move from the aesthetic viewpoint to the ethical illustrate her claim that passion permeates our self-understanding at such points where we choose between frameworks?
3. Why, given Piety's interpretation of Kierkegaard, would dispassionate choice between frameworks be less rational than a passionate choice?
4. What is the criterion for choosing the Christian interpretation?
5. What is the "theoretical skeleton" of Kierkegaard's view of rationality "stripped of the religious assumptions"?
6. Do you agree with Piety about the advantages of Kierkegaard's interpretation of rationality over traditional conceptions? Why or why not?

Kierkegaard on Rationality*

MARILYN GAYE PIETY

THE IDEA has been advanced that human behavior, or more specifically, choice, can only be understood as rational within a particular conceptual framework. Proponents of this view contend that any possible system of justification must be understood as relative to a particular framework or system of values and hence that it is not possible to make rational choices *between* frameworks. Charles Taylor argues, on the other hand, that movement between frameworks can be rational. He bases this argument, however, on the claim that such movement is a natural or evolutionary development and not the result of a *choice*.[1] The contemporary debate on this issue has reached the point where it appears we must consider

either that it is not possible to choose rationally between frameworks, *or* that there is rational movement between frameworks, but that this movement is not the result of a choice.

Taylor contends that the transition from one framework to another is effected through what he refers to as "error reducing moves."[2] That is, he asserts that insofar as a given framework may involve certain incoherences, and insofar as an individual may be motivated to reduce these incoherences, his effort to do this may actually eventuate in the production of, or transition to, a new framework. He asserts that the situation of Luther with respect to traditional Catholicism could be understood as exemplifying a movement of this sort.

*Reprinted with permission from *Faith and Philosophy*, Vol. 10 (July 1993): 365–379.

Taylor argues, however, that such a transition from one framework to another is not the result of an appeal to some criterion that is *independent* of the two frameworks in question, but rather that it is the natural result of the desire of the individual for a more coherent scheme for interpreting his existence. Taylor does not see the individual as *choosing* between competing systems of interpretation, but rather as developing new systems through an effort to reduce the incoherences or errors inherent in the old systems. Thus, while many theorists are disposed to see the movement from one framework to another as fundamentally irrational, Taylor sees it as rational. Taylor is in agreement with the former group, however, in that he is not willing to allow that there are any criteria independent of the two frameworks in question, such that an appeal to these criteria would justify, or show to be rational, the *choice* of one over another.

It would appear that the *impasse* at which the contemporary debate on the nature of human rationality has arrived is the result of the tendency of philosophers, despite their efforts to the contrary, to cling to the old Enlightenment view of disinterested and dispassionate reasoning as the paradigm of that rationality. I shall argue that Kierkegaard provides us with a picture of an *interested* and *impassioned* reason which enables us to see how it is possible for the transition from one framework to another to be *both* rational *and* the result of a choice and that insofar as it does this, it represents a more "reasonable" picture of reason than the one that has been traditionally offered by metaphysics.

I

The view that choice can only be understood as rational relative to a particular conceptual framework is precisely the one that provides the foundation for Alasdair MacIntyre's charge in *After Virtue*[3] that Kierkegaard considers moral commitment to be "the expression of a criterionless choice,"[4] or a choice between "incompatible and incommensurable moral premises, a choice for

which no rational justification can be given." MacIntyre refers to this position as Kierkegaard's "discovery" and identifies it as his primary contribution to the history of moral or ethical philosophy; a contribution which MacIntyre claims marks the beginning of the "distinctively modern standpoint" on the nature of moral debate. MacIntyre is undoubtedly correct in his identification of the distinctively modern standpoint on such debates. He is not correct, however, as will become clear in the pages which follow, in his ascription of this view to Kierkegaard.

Kierkegaard's frameworks may be designated "aesthetic," "ethical," "religious" and "paradoxically religious" or "Christian."[5] That is, Kierkegaard's individual views existence from within one or the other of these alternative schemes of interpretation. The aesthetic individual, for example, views existence as defined aesthetically. He interprets the value of the phenomena of his existence—including his own actions—as derivative of, or reducible to, their aesthetic significance. Thus an aesthete values actions not insofar as they exemplify morally uplifting principles, but rather insofar as they are immediately compelling, interesting, or sensuously gratifying.

The difficulty, as MacIntyre so forcefully pointed out, is that different frameworks represent significantly different systems of values, hence what may serve as a criterion for choice within an ethical framework will very likely not enjoy the same status within an aesthetic framework.[6] The moral superiority of an ethical over an aesthetic interpretation of existence cannot serve, for an aesthete, as a criterion for choosing it over his present interpretation, because such "superiority" is not considered by an aesthete to be of any positive value. This situation is, of course, mirrored by that of the ethicist; hence one might conclude from this, as indeed MacIntyre does conclude, that such a choice between frameworks as Kierkegaard has B recommending to A in *Either-Or,* cannot be a rational one.

MacIntyre focuses upon the transition from an aesthetic to an ethical view of existence. It is clear, however, from Kierkegaard's own description of this transition, that MacIntyre has not properly understood Kierkegaard's position. The aesthetic stage of existence is also referred to by Kierkegaard as the stage of immediacy. To be an aesthete, for Kierkegaard, means to have an understanding of existence which interprets it in terms of what appears, in an immediate sense, to be true about it. Such an individual has his consciousness, according to Kierkegaard—and in particular his consciousness of suffering—in the dialectic of fortune and misfortune.[7] Thus Kierkegaard argues that misfortune or suffering is, for this individual,

> like a narrow pass on the way; now the immediate individual is in it, but his view of life must essentially always tell him that the difficulty will soon cease to hinder because it is a foreign element. If it does not cease, he despairs, by which his immediacy ceases to function, and the transition to another understanding of existence is rendered possible.[8]

What happens to the aesthete is that, in his despair, it seems to him as if there is a discrepancy between his suffering—insofar as it is persistent—and the interpretation of existence in which suffering is viewed as having merely accidental significance. Thus the aesthete, using the persistence of his suffering as a criterion for choosing between a view of existence in which suffering is considered merely accidental and a view in which it is seen as essential, may reject the aesthetic interpretation in favor of an ethical one. Such an individual adopts an ethical framework, not because it promises to *alleviate* his suffering, but because it provides an interpretation of his existence which sees suffering as something essential to that existence, and thus provides a more adequate—or one might even say more rational—account of his subjective experience.

It may be that there are other criteria, or other aspects of subjective experience apart from suffering, that could serve as criteria for choosing between competing interpretations of existence on Kierkegaard's view. Suffering is, however, the criterion which Kierkegaard himself chooses to focus upon when examining the nature of the transition from one stage of existence to another in the *Postscript*[9] and it will become apparent, in the pages

which follow, that this criterion alone is enough to expose the erroneous nature of MacIntyre's interpretation of Kierkegaard and his subsequent charge that Kierkegaard was an irrationalist.

II

Insofar as one framework or interpretation of existence may be spoken of as more adequate than another—that is, insofar as it may be spoken of as providing a more satisfactory account of the nature of the subjective experience of a particular individual—it is entirely reasonable to consider that it is more rational.[10] What is likely less clear, however, is precisely *how* the individual comes to consider that one interpretation is more adequate than another. In this instance we are concerned specifically with how it is that the individual comes to consider that the persistence of suffering is too great for the aesthetic interpretation of existence to be plausible, for it appears that it would be entirely possible for an individual to persist in suffering while *simultaneously* persisting in the belief that the suffering was indeed accidental and that in the next moment, with a change of fortune, it would stop.

Objectively, there is no incoherence in the idea that an aesthetic individual may experience persistent suffering. The accidental may indeed be persistent. The aesthetic interpretation of existence is not contradicted by the occurrence of what is, within this framework, the improbable persistence of suffering. Such statements of probability or improbability as a given framework expresses

> cannot be strictly contradicted by any event [e.g., the persistence of suffering] however improbably this event may appear in its light. The contradiction must be established by a *personal* [my italics] act of appraisal.[11]

The question is: Whence arises this "personal act of appraisal"; or when and how does the individual come to consider the persistence of his suffering to be too great and hence too improbable, within the aesthetic framework, for that interpretation of existence to be correct?

It is at this point that Kierkegaard's views concerning the role of passion in human reason come into play. It is widely recognized by Kierkegaard scholars that, as Heinrich Schmidinger expresses it: "*Subjektives Engagement ist . . . immer mit Leidenschaft und Pathos verbunden.*"[12] It has also been observed, however, that Kierkegaard considers passion to be opposed to reflection,[13] hence it is often believed that subjective engagement, according to Kierkegaard, is purely emotional, or devoid of any intellectual component.

This view is the result of a failure to appreciate that the intellectual dimension of human experience is not reducible, for Kierkegaard, to reflection. Reflection is indeed dispassionate or disinterested, according to Kierkegaard.[14] He also speaks of "abstract" or "systematic" thought as disinterested.[15] This would appear, however, to be a rather abbreviated or short hand way of emphasizing that the object of such thought is not the self, for he states elsewhere that all knowledge "is interested,"[16] whether the object of interest is something outside the knower, as is the case in metaphysics, or whether it is the knower himself, as is the case in ethics and religion.

Kierkegaard often equates passion and interest.[17] It is thus reasonable to assume that, if knowledge is interested, then it is also passionate, or involves passion at some level. But if knowledge involves passion, then it would appear that passion is not essentially opposed to reason, but rather plays an important part in the activity of the knower as such. If this is the case, then the passionate nature of subjective engagement does not preclude the possibility that such engagement could be rational. Hence the "personal act of appraisal" in question is not a merely arbitrary, capricious or emotional reaction to a phenomenon or particular set of phenomena; it is the result of a rational assessment of this phenomenon, or these phenomena, where the reason in question is of a passionate or interested sort.

The difficulty is that very few scholars appreciate the way in which passion informs reason, on Kierkegaard's view. In order to throw some light on this issue I shall depart for a moment from the examination of Kierkegaard's texts and turn instead to the consideration of the views of a more contemporary philosopher on this same issue. Michael Polanyi, whose views on probability I quoted above, is concerned in his book *Personal Knowledge* with how it is that apparently objectively meaningless probability statements become subjectively meaningful guides for interpreting reality.[18] Polanyi maintains that there is an area of extremely low probability—i.e., what we would refer to in everyday speech as an area of high improbability—that we find generally unacceptable. The occurrence of an event that is associated with this level of improbability leads us, he argues, to reject the interpretation of existence within which this event is considered so improbable and to search for a new interpretation where events such as the one in question are considered more probable. Polanyi goes on to point out, however, that any attempt to *formalize* the precise degree of improbability that we find unacceptable and which, when connected to a particular phenomenon within a given theory or interpretation of existence, would lead us to reject that view as false "is likely to go too far unless it acknowledges in advance *that it* [i.e., the formalization] *must remain within a framework of personal* [i.e., impassioned subjective] *judgement.*"[19]

The metaphysical tradition has led us to believe that such impassioned subjective judgement is vastly inferior—if indeed it has any claim to legitimacy at all—to dispassionate objective judgement. In a situation such as the one described above, however, a purely dispassionate or objective perspective would lead to no judgement at all, but rather to a sort of skeptical *epoche*. That is, viewed purely objectively, the occurrence of a highly improbable event says nothing about the truth or falsity of the framework within which it is viewed as improbable; it neither supports it, nor discredits it, so it fails to provide us with a foundation—i.e., an *objective* foundation—for any judgement whatsoever concerning the status of the framework.

It is clear, though, that not only do we often make such judgements, we appear to be *compelled* to make them simply by virtue of the kind of creatures we are. The difficulty is that there appear to be no fixed guidelines in relation to these judgements. But to say that there are no *fixed* guidelines is not to say that there are no guidelines at all. Passion, which has traditionally been considered to be in essential opposition to reason, permeates our understanding—or attempts to understand—our situation at such points and it is this passion, according to Kierkegaard, which serves as a guide to the judgements we make in these situations.

III

The metaphysical tradition has been reluctant to appreciate the way in which passion informs our understanding of ourselves and the phenomena of our experience, hence it is to Polanyi, a chemist turned philosopher—i.e., a metaphysical interloper—that we must turn for the explicitly formulated observation that some of the most meaningful of our assertions in science are only possible as the result of a collaboration of reason and passion and that these assertions will thus always and necessarily "have a passionate quality attached to them."[20]

Passion is admittedly not an easy concept to elucidate. Some effort at elucidation is necessary, however, because it is precisely passion that, according to Kierkegaard, informs the understanding of an individual in such a way that extra-framework criteria, or reasons for choosing between competing interpretations of existence, may come to exist for him.

A *positive* account of the meaning of "passion" is difficult, if not impossible, to provide. An impression of this meaning may be provided, however, if the expression is understood to be contrasted with such expressions as "dispassion" or "disinterestedness." Polanyi claims that passion is to be found in our "personal *participation*"[21] with the phenomenon whose probability is in question. Such participation might be understood to exemplify an essentially interested, as opposed to disinterested, relation to this phenomenon. It is just such an *interested* stance which Kierkegaard believes is *appropriate* with respect to the subjective phenomenon of suffering.[22] That is, Kierkegaard maintains that we have an essential interest in

determining or choosing the proper interpretation of existence. Our eternal blessedness, or eternal damnation is, according to Kierkegaard, ultimately dependent upon this choice. But if we do not take such an interested stance in relation to the phenomena of our subjective experience, then it will never be possible for us to choose between various interpretations of existence[23]—and, in particular, to choose the *correct* one—for the criteria for such choices can only exist for the *interested* observer. It is for this reason that Kierkegaard argues in the *Postscript* that Christianity has "nothing whatever to do with the systematic zeal of the personally *indifferent* [my italics] individual," but assumes rather "an infinite personal passionate *interest* [my italics]" on the part of the individual as "*conditio sine qua non.*"[24]

Thus it becomes clear that the discernment of a discrepancy between the aesthetic interpretation of existence, which sees suffering as accidental, and the persistence of the suffering which the individual experiences, is the result of an impassioned or subjective judgement on the part of that individual. The greater the degree of passion with which the consciousness of the individual is informed, the less high the degree of the improbability of the suffering need be, in order for the individual to seize upon that improbability as grounds for rejecting the interpretation of existence within which the particular account of suffering is contained.[25]

Picture the aesthete who experiences persistent suffering, but does not despair—i.e., he does not judge that his subjective experience discredits the interpretation of existence which views it as improbable. What distinguishes such an individual from one who does despair? It would appear that the individual who does not despair, fails to do so because he considers the phenomena of his existence—or of his subjective experience—objectively, which is to say, dispassionately; while the individual who does despair, does so precisely because he considers these same phenomena subjectively or passionately.

It is one thing, however, to observe that a choice between competing interpretations of existence is only possible if one takes a passionate or interested stance relative to the phenomena of one's subjective experience, and another to argue that such a stance justifies rather than merely explains this choice. Passion, for Kierkegaard, is the very essence of human existence. It is well known that Kierkegaard proposes that subjectivity is truth,[26] but it is not so well known that he also proposes that subjectivity is passion.[27] To be dispassionate, or insufficiently passionate, for Kierkegaard, is to be indifferent to existence, and this, in turn, amounts to being insufficiently human. It is for this reason that Kierkegaard considers the choice of an ethical over an aesthetic interpretation of existence to be justified, rather than merely explicable. That is, a passionate perspective relative to the phenomena of one's subjective experience is the only sort of perspective that is in keeping, on Kierkegaard's view, with the essence of the individual. A dispassionate perspective would not cohere with that essence.

Thus passion emerges as the catalyst of the exchange of one perspective of existence for another. That is, passion breaks down the apparent coherence or descriptive adequacy of a particular interpretation of existence. Unless the consciousness of the individual is informed with a sufficient degree of passion, the persistence of his or her suffering cannot serve as a criterion for rejecting the aesthetic in favor of the ethical interpretation of existence.

It is, of course, possible to be *too* passionate. If the consciousness of the individual is informed with too much passion, the resultant interpretation of existence may cross over into the pathological. Such a phenomenon is actually addressed by Kierkegaard and referred to by him in the *Postscript* as subjective madness (*subjective Galskab*).[28] It is important to note, however, that it is not possible to formalize the precise degree of passion which is sufficient to break down the aesthetic interpretation of existence so that the choice of another interpretation becomes possible, and yet not so great as to qualify the individual as pathological. It is precisely this resistance of passion, or of an understanding which is informed with passion, to such formalization that serves as a stumbling block to metaphysics. But

this is simply our situation as human beings and part of the task of philosophy is to help us to achieve a more profound understanding of that situation.

IV

I have restricted my explication of the nature of the transition from one stage of existence to another to the transition from the aesthetic to the ethical stage. I have done this because this was the transition that MacIntyre examined and which he used in an effort to support his charge that Kierkegaard was an irrationalist. It should be clear now that Kierkegaard's own interpretation of the nature of this transition will not support MacIntyre's charge. Opponents of the view I am propounding might argue, however, that while it appears possible to consider the choice between any of the non-Christian interpretations as rational, the same thing cannot be said concerning the choice to adopt a Christian framework. It is tempting to interpret Kierkegaard such that it appears the transition to the Christian stage of existence is the result of a choice for which there can be no criterion.

We can see, however, from the quotation below, that there is a criterion for choosing the Christian interpretation; this criterion is precisely the phenomenon of the consciousness of sin. That is, Kierkegaard contends that

> Christianity is only related to the consciousness of sin. Any other attempt to become a Christian for any other reason is quite literally lunacy; and that is how it should be.[29]

Just as the ethical interpretation of existence provided a more adequate account of human suffering to the aesthete whose consciousness was informed with a sufficient degree of passion, so does the Christian interpretation provide a more adequate account of the subjective experience of the individual whose consciousness is informed with an even greater degree of passion.

Such passion arises, again, from an *interested* stance toward the question of which of the possible interpretations of existence is correct. The more extreme the interpretation presented to the individual, the more passionate—as opposed to dispassionate—must his or her self examination be. That is, when an individual is presented with an interpretation of existence such as that offered by Christianity, an interpretation which makes his or her *eternal blessedness* or *eternal damnation* dependent upon its acceptance, then the proper response is not a casual concern as to the truth of this interpretation, but rather a deep and impassioned introspection in which the individual repeatedly asks himself: "Could this be the real nature of my existence?" "Does this interpretation of my existence make the most sense—i.e., more sense than any other interpretation—of my subjective experience?"[30]

V

With this we have a simple model of Kierkegaard's theory concerning the nature of human rationality. We must distinguish, however, what is essential to Kierkegaard's position as he understood it, and what is essential for the purposes of defending Kierkegaard against the charge of irrationalism as that charge was leveled against him by MacIntyre. It is important to appreciate that Kierkegaard's own understanding of the position described above involved a foundation of religious belief which is separable from the position itself. Kierkegaard would no more consider the persistence of an individual who has the good luck not to suffer in an aesthetic interpretation to be justified than we would consider the racism of an ignorant person to be justified. That is, just as we would consider that an ignorant person *should* know better than to be racist, Kierkegaard would consider that a fortunate person *should* know better than to persist in an aesthetic interpretation of existence.

Existence, for Kierkegaard, is characterized by sin and part of the way in which sin manifests itself is in the inability of the individual to sustain emotional equilibrium in the face of misfortune or adversity. It is this inability which accounts for the suffering in question. The difficulty is that this inability itself stems from an excessive attachment to worldly pleasure or comfort.[31] As long as the existence of an individual is characterized by such attachment, suffering is still present in it, *in potentia*. Hence, while suffering justifies the choice of an ethical over an aesthetic interpretation of existence, on Kierkegaard's view, the absence of suffering does not have the same significance. The absence of suffering does not justify the endorsement of an aesthetic view of existence because suffering is always present in the existence of an individual *in potentia,* so to speak, in the form of sin. Any individual who is sufficiently reflective to appreciate the tenuous nature of happiness on the aesthetic interpretation, would find his or her existence, no matter how "fortunate," characterized by an anxiety or fear of potential adversity which would itself constitute a kind of suffering. The only way to avoid such anxiety, on Kierkegaard's view, would be to avoid reflection.

We may argue that different levels of reflection are natural for different sorts of people and that it is even possible for certain individuals to live lives almost entirely devoid of reflection. Kierkegaard's religious convictions compel him to assume, however, that the activity of reflection is universally human and that whatever differences there may be in the degree of reflection which characterize various individuals, even the least reflective individual can only avoid recognizing the tenuous nature of happiness on the aesthetic view of existence by *willfully refusing* to reflect upon the significance of this view. And this willful refusal, on Kierkegaard's view, constitutes, in turn, a flight from the acknowledgement of oneself as sinful.

It is not necessary, however, that one share Kierkegaard's religious views in order to appreciate the force of his claim concerning the possibility of extra-framework criteria for choosing between competing interpretations of existence. If this were necessary, then the charge of irrationalism could still be leveled against him. That is, the support for his position would ultimately rest upon a foundation of dogma that could not itself be chosen for any reason, for it would only be relative to this foundation that reasons for such choices could exist.

One of the most important aspects of Kierkegaard's position is that experience is distinguished from the various interpretations which may be supplied to it. The medium of experience, according to Kierkegaard, is *actuality,* while the medium of such interpretations is *ideality.* That is, the interpretations represent clusters of concepts (hence the origin of the appellation "conceptual framework") and the medium of concepts is abstract, in contrast to the medium of experience, which is concrete.[32]

We can keep the view that subjective experience, insofar as it is actual, may be distinguished from a particular conceptual framework or ideal interpretation that is supplied to it and the claim that this experience can provide criteria for choosing between such frameworks, without having to accept the view that experience, properly defined, will always incline one toward a *particular* interpretation of existence. This is what one might refer to as the theoretical skeleton of Kierkegaard's view of rationality as it appears when stripped of the religious assumptions which gave the view its more specific definition in Kierkegaard's works.[33]

Taylor's contention that the transition from one interpretation of existence to another is effected through a move of error reduction is consistent with much of what Kierkegaard says concerning such transitions. On Kierkegaard's view, one rejects the aesthetic framework in favor of an ethical one precisely because a passionate interpretation of the persistence of one's suffering leads one to consider that there is an error in the aesthetic framework—the "error" in question being the view that suffering is of merely accidental significance or the result of misfortune. The difference between Taylor and Kierkegaard is that on Kierkegaard's account, the errors are not inconsistencies *within* a particular framework—for as we have seen, the persistence of suffering is not, objectively, inconsistent with the interpretation of existence which views such persistence as improbable—but are errors relative to the individual's subjective or impassioned *experience.*

One could express Kierkegaard's views in secular terms by substituting for "guilt consciousness" or "[t]he anguished conscience" what Taylor has identified as a "need for meaning."[34] Taylor contends that individuals are faced today with the problem of attempting to imbue their existence with some significance that goes beyond the expression and fulfillment—or lack thereof—of their daily needs.

Thus if one is more comfortable with the expression "need for meaning" than with Kierkegaard's overtly religious expression like "guilt consciousness," an individual could be understood as adopting a particular framework because he perceived that that framework promised to imbue his existence with the meaning of which he felt a lack. In this way an ethical interpretation of existence could be seen as supplying meaning to the suffering of an individual that the aesthetic interpretation was unable to supply.[35]

Concluding Comments

It should now be clear that the charge of irrationalism leveled against Kierkegaard by MacIntyre is based upon a misunderstanding of the relation between the aesthetic and the ethical interpretations of existence on Kierkegaard's view. Not only is Kierkegaard's philosophy not irrationalist in the way in which MacIntyre and others have claimed, his conception of the nature of human rationality is one which can be of great help in relation to the contemporary debate on the nature of human rationality. The view that "rational" decisions need not always be the result of purely objective or dispassionate speculation and that hence emotional or non-rational phenomena may serve as criteria for such choices is clearly one which would be of use to contemporary theorists.

Kierkegaard's interpretation of human rationality provides us with a positive alternative to the traditional conception of reason as disinterested and dispassionate. But it is not *simply* an alternative to this more traditional conception. It is an alternative with an *advantage.* That is, it provides us with a way to get beyond the *impasse* at which the contemporary debate on the issue has arrived, by reminding us that there are some areas of inquiry where "an objective indifference can . . . learn nothing at all,"[36] or as Nagel expressed it in *The View From Nowhere,* where "the truth is not to be found by traveling as far away from one's personal perspective as possible,"[37] and hence where being "rational" means taking a passionate or interested stance in relation to the phenomena in question.

Kierkegaard's view of rationality possesses a further advantage over the traditional view in that it provides us with a more descriptively adequate account of our understanding of ourselves and of the phenomena of our subjective experience. That is, it does not preclude the possibility that our movement from one interpretation of existence to another may take place as a natural or evolutionary development rather than as the result of a choice, but it also allows us to make sense of the experience, that we at least occasionally have, that we *choose* to adopt a particular interpretation of existence, that there are good *reasons* for adopting this interpretation and that we choose to adopt it *for* those reasons and not simply as a matter of pure caprice.

What we have in Kierkegaard's picture of the role of passion in reason is a more "reasonable" picture of reason than the one that has been offered to us by the metaphysical tradition. It is a picture of reason that involves a positive incorporation of what we essentially are, subjects situated in and passionately engaged with the flux which constitutes our temporal existence. Finally, it is a picture that allows us to justify rationally the weight that we seem *compelled,* simply by virtue of the kind of creatures we are, to attribute to our subjective experience.

NOTES

1. Charles Taylor, "Inescapable Frameworks," in *Sources of the Self* (Cambridge: Harvard University Press, 1989), pp. 3–24.

2. See note 1 above.

3. Alasdair MacIntyre, *After Virtue* (Notre Dame, Indiana: University of Notre Dame Press, 1984), pp. 36–62.

4. This and all subsequent quotations of MacIntyre are taken from page 38 of *After Virtue.*

5. There is some disagreement among Kierkegaard scholars as to the precise number of stages or interpretations of existence that are to be found in Kierkegaard's works. There is general agreement, however, that there are at least the four stages listed here, although there may be perhaps more than these four.

6. It is possible that the status of certain choices as rational will remain constant across frameworks. Candidates for such constancy, however, would most likely be very mundane or innocuous sorts of choices (e.g., the choice of an aspirin to alleviate headache pain).

7. *Concluding Unscientific Postcript,* translated by David F. Swenson and Walter Lowrie (Princeton: Princeton University Press, 1941), p.388/*Søren Kierkegaards Samlede Vaerker,* edited by A. B. Drachman, J. L. Heiberg and H. O. Lang (Copenhagen: Gyldendal, 1901–06), Vol. VII, pp. 376–77.

8. *Postscript,* p. 388/*Samlede Vaerker,* Vol. VII, p. 377.

9. See notes 7 and 8.

10. The failure of many philosophers to appreciate this point is very likely the result of what Thomas Nagel has pointed out is an "ambiguity in the idea of the rational." That is, Nagel observes that "'[r]ational' may mean either rationally required or rationally acceptable" (*The View From Nowhere* [New York: Oxford University Press, 1986], p. 200).

11. Michael Polanyi, *Personal Knowledge* (Chicago: University of Chicago Press, 1958), p. 24.

12. Heinrich Schmidinger, *Das Problem des Interesses und die Philosophie Sören Kierkegaards* (Freiberg/München: Verlag Karl Alber, 1983), p. 218.

13. Marold Westphal, *Kierkegaard's Critique of Religion and Society* (Macon, Georgia: Mercer University Press, 1987), p. 46.

14. *Philosophical Fragments; Johannes Climacus,* edited and translated by Howard and Edna H. Hong (Princeton: Princeton University Press, 1985), p. 170/*Søren Kierkegaards Papirer,* edited by P. A. Heiberg, V. Kuhr, E. Torsting and N. Thulstrup (Copenhagen: Glydendal, 1968–78), Vol. IV B 1, p. 149.

15. *Postscript,* p. 278/*Samlede Vaerker,* Vol. VII, p. 296; Søren Kierkegaard's Journals and Papers, translated by Howard V. and Edna H. Hong (Bloomington: Indiana University Press, 1967–78), Vol. 5 5621/*Papirer,* Vol. IV B 1, p. 149.

16. *Journals and Papers,* Vol. 2 2283/*Papirer,* Vol. IV C 99; *Journals and Papers,* Vol. 1 891/*Papirer,* Vol. IV B 13: 18.

17. See Schmidinger, op. cit., p. 254.

18. The purpose of Polanyi's claim that probability statements are objectively meaningless is to point out that such statements are essentially ambiguous. Probability statements relating to the behavior of electrons, for example, convey to the researcher that an electron *may* or *may not* be found in a particular spot at a par-

ticular time. Since this is something of which the scientist is undoubtedly already aware, even without the aid of the probability statement, Polanyi suggests that this ambiguity may lead one to conclude that probability statements do not *really* say anything. He argues, however, that there is "some meaning in assigning a numerical value to the probability of our finding an electron at a certain place on a particular occasion" (p. 21), but this meaning, he goes on to argue is to be found in "our personal participation in the event to which the probability statement refers" (p. 21).

19. Ibid., p. 29. The "passionate" or "impassioned" quality of our judgments, statements or assertions is the theme of the section of *Personal Knowledge* entitled "The Nature of Assertions" (pp. 27–30).

20. Op. cit., p. 27.

21. Ibid., p. 24.

22. For a comprehensive treatment of the significance of the concept of interest in Kierkegaard's philosophy, see: Heinrich M. Schmidinger, op. cit.

23. One might argue that a completely arbitrary choice would still be possible. This is not Kierkegaard's position, however. Kierkegaard believes that we inherit an aesthetic interpretation of existence simply by being human and that we will never adopt any other perspective without a specific reason for doing so; and such a reason cannot arise, on his view, unless we take an interested stance toward the phenomena of our subjective experience.

24. *Postscript,* p. 19 / *Samlede Vaerker,* Vol. VII, p. 6.

25. This situation is perhaps best illustrated by referring to the example of little children. Young children have not yet learned to view their situations dispassionately (and, in general, the younger the children, the more this is true of them), hence their judgments are often informed with a very high degree of passion. Children thus often seize upon even the slightest improbability as grounds for rejecting either the event with which the improbability is associated, or the framework within which the event in question is viewed as improbable. Children playing a game, for example, often refuse to accept that the same person can win even twice in a row. When faced with such a phenomenon they will often attempt either to show that the child in question has not actually won (i.e., that his evaluation of his situation was not correct) or that he cheated.

26. *Postscript,* pp. 169–244 / *Samlede Vaerker,* Vol. VII, pp. 157–211.

27. *Postscript,* p. 117 / *Samlede Vaerker,* Vol. VII, p. 106.

28. *Postscript,* p. 175 / *Samlede Vaerker,* Vol. VII, p. 163.

29. *Journals and Papers,* Vol. 1 492 / *Papirer,* Vol. IX A 414. The translation above is from a book called *The Diary of Søren Kierkegaard,* edited by Peter P. Rhode (Secaucus, NJ: Citadel Press, 1960), p. 150, and not from the Hong and Hong translation of Kierkegaard's *Journals and Papers.* The Hong translation is not substantially different. I have chosen the former translation, however, because I believe it is a little more readable.

30. This is one of the reasons that Kierkegaard had so little patience with organized Christianity, or, more specifically, with the Lutheran church in Denmark. That is, the version of Christianity offered to Danes by the Danish church was so denatured that the impassioned consciousness would reject it and hence the possibility of the individual's coming to believe the truth of Christianity would be precluded. *See Postscript,* pp. 323–43 / *Samlede Vaerker,* Vol. VII, pp. 312–33.

31. The expression "worldly" should not be equated with "material." "Worldly" is a much broader determination which encompasses all human pleasures, including intellectual and emotional ones, conceived independently of any religious significance they might have.

32. It is important to acknowledge, however, that the conceptual framework to which an individual subscribes helps to define his experience. This point was clearly not lost on Kierkegaard, as is demonstrated by his observation that "the true conception of despair is indispensable for conscious despair" (*The Sickness Unto Death,* translated by Howard V. and Edna H. Hong [Princeton: Princeton University Press, 1980], p. 47 / *Samlede Vaerker,* Vol. XI, p. 160). An individual's experience must still, according to Kierkegaard, be assumed to be substantially independent of the remark which helps to define it, or else it cannot have the role in transition from one framework to another that it is described by him as having. This putative independence is strengthened by Nagel's claim that "we don't ascribe such states [e.g., suffering] only to creatures who have mental concepts: we ascribe them to children and animals, and believe that we ourselves would have experiences even if we didn't have the language" (op. cit., p. 23).

33. This move should not be disturbing to anyone who shares Kierkegaard's religious convictions because saying that experience, properly defined, will not necessarily incline one toward a particular interpretation of existence does not make it so. If Kierkegaard is correct, then, of course, all roads will lead to Rome, so to speak (i.e., all experience, properly defined, will incline one toward a particular interpretation of existence). This is not, however, a matter for philosophers, but is rather between each individual and his or her own experience. That is, it is a matter for each individual as such, and this, according to Kierkegaard, is exactly as it should be.

34. See note 1 above. Such a substitution does not entail that a "need for meaning" is equivalent to "guilt consciousness," but merely that they are criteria of the same kind. That is, both expressions are qualifications

of subjective experience, although their content may be quite different.

35. One could not conclude from this, however, that the ethical interpretation is *objectively* more meaningful than the aesthetic interpretation. A foundation of something on the order of Kierkegaard's religious convictions is necessary to sustain that sort of claim. It is enough, however, that one interpretation of existence is *subjectively* more meaningful than another in order for the choice of that interpretation to be viewed as a rational one for the individual in question.

36. *Postscript,* p. 51 / *Samlede Vaerker,* Vol. VII, p. 39.
37. Op. cit., p. 27.

Suggestions for Further Reading

Abraham, William J., and Holtzer, Steven. *The Rationality of Religious Belief: Essays in Honor of Basil Mitchell.* New York: Oxford University Press, 1987.

Alston, William P. *A Realist Conception of Truth.* Ithaca, NY: Cornell University Press, 1996.

Ballie, John. *The Idea of Revelation in Recent Thought.* New York: Columbia University Press, 1956.

Blanshard, Brand. *Reason and Belief.* London: George Allen & Unwin, 1974.

Brunner, Emil. *Revelation and Reason.* Philadelphia: Westminster Press, 1946.

Crosson, Frederick, ed. *The Autonomy of Religious Belief.* Notre Dame, IN: University of Notre Dame Press, 1981.

Davis, Stephen. *Faith, Skepticism and Evidence.* Lewisburg, PA: Bucknell University Press, 1978.

Delaney, C. F., ed. *Rationality and Religious Belief.* Notre Dame, IN: University of Notre Dame Press, 1978.

Deutsch, Eliot, and van Buitenen, J. A. B. *A Source Book of Advaita Vedanta.* Honolulu: The University Press of Hawaii, 1971.

Farmer, H. H. *Revelation and Religion.* London: Nisbet, 1954.

Fiorenza, Elisabeth Schüssler. *In Memory of Her: A Feminist Theological Reconstruction of Christian Origins.* New York: Crossroad, 1986.

Grant, Jacquelyn. *White Women's Christ and Black Women's Jesus: Feminist Christology and Womanist Response.* Atlanta, GA: Scholars Press, 1989.

Green, Ronald M. *Religious Reason: The Rational and Moral Basis of Religious Belief.* New York: Oxford University Press, 1978.

Hegel, G. W. F. *Faith and Knowledge.* Albany, NY: State University of New York Press, 1977.

Hester, Marcus, ed. *Faith, Reason, and Skepticism.* Philadelphia, PA: Temple University Press, 1992.

Hick, John. *Faith and Knowledge.* Ithaca, NY: Cornell University Press, 1957.

James, William. *Pragmatism.* Cambridge, MA: Harvard University Press, 1975.

Jaspers, Karl. *Philosophical Faith and Revelation.* New York: Harper & Row, 1967.

Jordan, Jess, and Howard-Snydor, Daniel, eds. *Faith, Freedom, and Rationality: Philosophy of Religion Today.* Lanham, MD: Rowman and Littlefield, 1996.

Kellenberger, J. *Religious Discovery, Faith and Knowledge.* Englewood Cliffs, NJ: Prentice-Hall, 1972.

LaCugna, Catherine Mowry, ed. *Freeing Theology: The Essentials of Theology in Feminist Perspective.* San Francisco: HarperCollins, 1993.

Martin, C. B. *Religious Belief.* Ithaca, NY: Cornell University Press, 1959.

Mavrodes, George I. *Belief in God: A Study in the Epistemology of Religion.* New York: Random House, 1970.

———. *Revelation in Religious Belief.* Philadelphia: Temple University Press, 1988.

McCarthy, Gerald D., ed. *The Ethics of Belief Debate.* Atlanta, GA: Scholars Press, 1986.

Mitchell, Basil. *Faith and Logic: Oxford Essays in Philosophical Theology.* London: George Allen & Unwin, 1959.

Niebuhr, H. Richard. *The Meaning of Revelation.* New York: Macmillan, 1959.

Nielsen, Kai. "On the Logic of Revelation." *Sophia* 9 (1970): 8–13.

Penelhum, Terence. *Religion and Rationality.* New York: Random House, 1971.

———. "Is a Religious Epistemology Possible?" In *Knowledge and Necessity,* edited by Godfrey N. A. Vesey. London: Macmillan, 1970.

Perrett, Roy W., ed. *Indian Philosophy of Religion.* Dordrecht, The Netherlands: Kluwer Academic Publishers, 1989.

Phillips, D. Z. *Religion Without Explanation.* Oxford, England: Basil Blackwell, 1976.

Plantinga, Alvin, and Wolterstorff, Nicholas, eds. *Faith and Rationality: Reason and Belief in God.* Notre Dame, IN: University of Notre Dame Press, 1983.

Rescher, Nicholas. *Pascal's Wager.* Notre Dame, IN: University of Notre Dame Press, 1985.

Russell, Letty M., ed. *Feminist Interpretation of the Bible.* Philadelphia: Westminster, 1985.

Schilpp, Paul Arthur, ed. *The Philosophy of Sarvepalli Radhakrishnan.* The Library of Living Philosophers. New York: Tudor Publishing Co., 1952.

Sharma, Arvind. *The Philosophy of Religion and Advaita Vedanta: A Comparative Study in Religion and Reason.* University Park, PA: The Pennsylvania State University Press, 1995.

Smart, Ninian. *Philosophers and Religious Truth.* London: SCM, 1964.

Ross, James F. "Rational Reliance." *Journal of the American Academy of Religion.* Vol. LXII/3 (Fall 1994):769–798.

Swinburne, Richard. *Faith and Reason.* Oxford: Clarendon Press, 1981.

Thomas, George F. *Philosophy and Religious Belief.* New York: Scribner's, 1970.

Wernham, James C. S. *James's Will-to-Believe Doctrine: A Heretical View.* Toronto: McGill-Queen's, 1987.

Winch, Peter. "Understanding Primitive Society." In *Ethics and Action.* London: Routledge and Kegan Paul, 1972.

Zaehner, Robert Charles. *Philosophers and Religious Truth.* 2d ed. New York: Macmillan, 1969.

CHAPTER 10

Humanism, Science, and Miracles

Introduction

AS THE TITLE OF this chapter indicates, we will be dealing with three different topics. The connections among these topics may not be immediately obvious, so allow me to say something about how they are connected.

There are many different varieties of humanism: theistic, nontheistic, agnostic, and atheistic. What these humanisms have in common is an emphasis on the importance of human beings treating one another in a humane way. Most religions are humanistic. They teach love and care for others, and they advocate a just society. Atheistic humanism, in contrast to some of the other varieties, argues that such humane virtues cannot be achieved until we purge the supernaturalistic, superstitious, and theistic elements from religion. To urge us to love God above all else shifts our focus from the love of other humans—or so Feuerbach argued (see Reading 10.1). God-talk is used to drug people into accepting their lower social and economic status and hence quell the urge to work for a more just society—or so Marx thought (see Reading 10.2). According to Feuerbach and Marx, the truly humane elements of the religious impulse cannot explicitly emerge and have real impact on changing society until the concept of God is subjected to critical analysis.

I shall concentrate on atheistic humanism here because so much of this text concerns theistic and nontheistic viewpoints. Granted, we have seen something of a "negative" atheism that focuses exclusively on a critique of theistic views. But there is also a "positive" atheism; an atheism that see atheism as a virtue because of its positive benefits for humanity.

Science shares the humanistic spirit in the sense that it reflects the confidence in human reason and the need for free inquiry that humanism represents. Humanism is more than a set of moral values related to love and justice. It also acknowledges the need for humans to be free from all forms of oppression, including the oppression of thought, in order that the humane life might be realized and scientific inquiry into the nature of things might continue unimpeded by prejudice.

We should, however, not assume that science is by nature atheistic or more supportive of a nontheistic than of a theistic viewpoint. The scientific spirit supports free inquiry, but there is no rule that says such inquiry must necessarily end in atheism.

Traditional philosophy of religion construes the conflicts that have erupted between science and religion as conflicts between theism and science. This perspective betrays a double bias: first that the scientific perspective is unique to Western culture and second that religion amounts to belief in theism. Two of the selections that follow (Readings 10.3 and 10.4) take exception to this perspective.

The issue of miracles is, likewise, often framed in an exclusively theistic context. Within traditional philosophy of religion in the West, the debate is usually cast in terms of the so-called "violations" of the laws of nature. Any science (Eastern or Western) would view unexplained events (and miracles appear to be such events at the least) as a challenge. These are anomalies and hence problems to be solved. Do theistic religions resist these solutions? Is preserving the mystery of unexplained events more important? After all, if their mystery can be maintained, then do we not have some proof that the divine may still be operating in our world or perhaps proof that yogis have developed psychic powers that science cannot fathom? But are psychic powers "miracles" in a strict sense? For that matter, are miracles unexplained events? Don't we explain them by calling them miracles? Instead of saying, "Gravity caused that event" we say "The gods caused that event."

10.1 God Is a Projection

The book of Genesis in the Hebrew Bible (the Old Testament) says that God made humans in God's image. Ludwig Feuerbach (1804–1872) came to believe the reverse. Humans, he maintained, made God in their images.

Feuerbach studied theology and philosophy with some of the intellectual giants of nineteenth-century German thought, including Georg Hegel (1770–1831). Hegel argued that Absolute Spirit (*Geist*) becomes fully self-consciousness by projecting itself outward, so to speak. This projection constitutes the events of history, especially the history of ideas. Feuerbach undertook a "transformational criticism" of Hegel's ideas and argued that *Geist* does not project itself as the ideas developed in the course of human history but rather that humans project *Geist*. Hence God (the religious term for *Geist*) is a projection of an idealized humanity. Humans project into a spiritual realm what they take to be their highest and best virtues, thereby creating God in their own images.

Technically Feuerbach is an atheist, because he thinks that God does not exist apart from human projection. However, to see him only as an atheist who challenges the claim that God exists is to miss the religious motivation of his thought. Feuerbach thought of himself as a second Martin Luther (1483–1546). Just as Luther had given birth in the Protestant Reformation to a new form of Christianity, so Feuerbach hoped to give birth to a new and truer form of Christianity, a form he called "realized Christianity" (although some critics have labeled it "atheistic or secular humanism").

Feuerbach argues that a correct analysis of religion in general, and of Christianity in particular, reveals that religion amounts to a symbolic and mythical expression of an unconscious self-estrangement that constitutes one of the basic problems of human existence. Humans are, even if they are unaware of it, divided selves. There is a division or estrangement between our actual selves and our idealized selves—between what we are and what we ought to be (recall the cartoons with a devil on one shoulder and an angel on the other whispering advice). Religion is an elaborate metaphor reflecting this alienation between the real and the ideal. On the one hand, we project our idealized perfection (what we ought to be) as a divine being (God), and on the other, we project our own existence as one of total imperfection and sin in comparison with this perfect being. When this "hidden truth" of Christianity and other religions is made plain (and Feuerbach's program was to make it plain by bringing it into view through critical philosophical analysis), then humanity will be freed *from* its estrangement and freed *for* a "realized Christianity"—a humanized religion that has at its core the love of neighbor (all humanity), not the love of an illusory God.

Feuerbach's critique of religion and his atheism are meant not to destroy religion but to transform it. Although Feuerbach is well aware of the differences among religions, he believes that in all the so-called higher religions there is a common core of teaching, best exemplified in Jesus' teaching to love all humanity. However, this common core of moral teaching has been obscured by supernaturalistic elements. Thus, for example, in Christianity, the supernaturalistic dogmas about God, the Trinity, Christ's divinity, and so on have deflected human love from its true object (other humans) to God. His so-called atheistic or secular humanism has as its goal nothing less than to remove this obscurity and redirect human love and concern to its proper object, humanity itself.

Realized Christianity has an added advantage, Feuerbach thought. It removed the stumbling blocks in the way of a harmonious relationship between religion and science. Once the conflicts, both actual and potential, between science and religion are removed, the two could cooperate in promoting free inquiry and humanitarian goals.

Marian Evans translated the following selection into English. She used the pen name George Eliot because in 1854 it was not socially acceptable for females to engage in literary, philosophical, and theological pursuits. She experienced first hand the oppressive patriarchal culture that a masculine supernaturalism reinforced. However, she got Feuerbach published in English in spite of such prejudices and, like Feuerbach, hoped for a humanism without a distracting theism.

Reading Questions

1. What is the "proposition" that Feuerbach applies to religion, and what are its implications?
2. What constitutes the historical progress of religion, and what does it reveal about the nature of religion?
3. Do you agree with Feuerbach's claim that to "deny all the qualities of a being is equivalent to denying the being himself"? Why or why not?
4. Why is the distinction between God as he is in himself and God as he is for me a skeptical distinction, according to Feuerbach?
5. According to Feuerbach, what does the *true* atheist deny?

6. What phenomenon characterizes the very "core of religion"?

7. What is the mystery of religion, according to Feuerbach, and what is its root?

8. Do you agree or disagree with Feuerbach's argument that God is only *a* feeling because God is known only *in* feeling? Why or why not?

God Is a Projection*

LUDWIG FEUERBACH

RELIGION IS THE DREAM of the human mind. But even in dreams we do not find ourselves in emptiness or in heaven, but on earth, in the realm of reality; we only see real things in the entrancing splendour of imagination and caprice, instead of in the simple daylight of reality and necessity. Hence I do nothing more to religion—and to speculative philosophy and theology also—than to open its eyes, or rather to turn its gaze from the internal towards the external, i.e., I change the object as it is in the imagination into the object as it is in reality.

Introduction

THE ESSENCE OF RELIGION CONSIDERED GENERALLY

In the perceptions of the senses consciousness of the object is distinguishable from consciousness of self; but in religion, consciousness of the object and self-consciousness coincide. The object of the senses is out of man, the religious object is within him, and therefore as little forsakes him as his self-consciousness or his conscience; it is the intimate, the closest object. "God," says Augustine, for example, "is nearer, more related to us, and therefore more easily known by us, than sensible, corporeal things" (*De Genesi ad litteram,* l. v. c. 16). The object of the senses is in itself indifferent—independent of the disposition or of the judgment; but the object of religion is a selected object; the most excellent, the first, the supreme being; it essentially presupposes a critical judgment, a discrimination between the divine and the non-divine, between that which is worthy of adoration and that which is not worthy. And here may be applied, without any limitation, the proposition: the object of any subject is nothing else than the subject's own nature taken objectively. Such as are a man's thoughts and dispositions, such is his God; so much worth as a man has, so much and no more has his God. Consciousness of God is self-consciousness, knowledge of God is self-knowledge. By his God thou knowest the man, and by the man, his God; the two are identical. Whatever is God to a man, that is his heart and soul; and conversely, God is the manifested inward nature, the expressed self of a man,—religion the solemn unveiling of a man's hidden treasures, the revelation of his intimate thoughts, the open confession of his lovesecrets.

But when religion—consciousness of God—is designated as the self-consciousness of man, this is not to be understood as affirming that the religious man is directly aware of this identity; for, on the contrary, ignorance of it is fundamental to the peculiar nature of religion. To preclude this misconception, it is better to say, religion is man's earliest and also indirect form of self-knowledge.

*From *The Essence of Christianity* by Ludwig Feuerbach, translated by George Eliot. Gloucester, MA: Peter Smith Publishers, 1854.

Hence, religion everywhere precedes philosophy, as in the history of the race, so also in that of the individual. Man first of all sees his nature as if *out of* himself, before he finds it in himself. His own nature is in the first instance contemplated by him as that of another being. Religion is the childlike condition of humanity; but the child sees his nature—man—out of himself; in childhood a man is an object to himself, under the form of another man. Hence the historical progress of religion consists in this; that what by an earlier religion was regarded as objective, is now recognized as subjective; that is, what was formerly contemplated and worshipped as God is now perceived to be something *human*. What was at first religion becomes at a later period idolatry; man is seen to have adored his own nature. Man has given objectivity to himself, but has not recognized the object as his own nature: a later religion takes this forward step; every advance in religion is therefore a deeper self-knowledge. But every particular religion, while it pronounces its predecessors idolatrous, excepts itself—and necessarily so, otherwise it would no longer be religion—from the fate, the common nature of all religions: it imputes only to other religions what is the fault, if fault it be, of religion in general. Because it has a different object, a different tenor, because it has transcended the ideas of preceding religions, it erroneously supposes itself exalted above the necessary eternal laws which constitute the essence of religion—it fancies its objects, its ideas, to be superhuman. But the essence of religion, thus hidden from the religious, is evident to the thinker, by whom religion is viewed objectively, which it cannot be by its votaries. And it is our task to show that the antithesis of divine and human is altogether illusory, that it is nothing else than the antithesis between the human nature in general and the human individual; that, consequently, the object and contents of the Christian religion are altogether human.

Religion, at least the Christian, is the relation of man to himself, or more correctly to his own nature (i.e., his subjective nature); but a relation to it, viewed as a nature apart from his own. The divine being is nothing else than the human being, or, rather, the human nature purified, freed from the limits of the individual man, made objective—i.e., contemplated and revered as another, a distinct being. All the attributes of the divine nature are, therefore, attributes of the human nature.

In relation to the attributes, the predicates of the Divine Being, this is admitted without hesitation, but by no means in relation to the subject of these predicates. The negation of the subject is held to be irreligion, nay, atheism; though not so the negation of the predicates. But that which has no predicates or qualities, has no effect upon me; that which has no effect upon me has no existence for me. To deny all the qualities of a being is equivalent to denying the being himself. A being without qualities is one which cannot become an object to the mind, and such a being is virtually non-existent. Where man deprives God of all qualities, God is no longer anything more to him than a negative being. To the truly religious man, God is not a being without qualities, because to him he is a positive, real being. The theory that God cannot be defined, and consequently cannot be known by man, is therefore the offspring of recent times, a product of modern unbelief. . . . On the ground that God is unknowable, man excuses himself to what is yet remaining of his religious conscience for his forgetfulness of God, his absorption in the world: he denies God practically by his conduct,—the world has possession of all his thoughts and inclinations,—but he does not deny him theoretically, he does not attack his existence; he lets that rest. But this existence does not affect or incommode him; it is merely negative existence, an existence without existence, a self-contradictory existence,—a state of being which, as to its effects, is not distinguishable from non-being. The denial of determinate, positive predicates concerning the divine nature is nothing else than a denial of religion, with, however, an appearance of religion in its favor, so that it is not recognized as a denial; it is simply a subtle, disguised atheism. The alleged religious horror of limiting God by positive predicates is only the irreligious wish to know nothing more of God, to banish God from the mind. Dread of limitation is dread of existence.

There is, however, a still milder way of denying the divine predicates than the direct one just described. It is admitted that the predicates of the divine nature are finite, and more particularly, human qualities, but their rejection is rejected; they are even taken under protection, because it is necessary to man to have a definite conception of God, and since he is man he can form no other than a human conception of him. In relation to God, it is said, these predicates are certainly without any objective validity; but to me, if he is to exist for me, he cannot appear otherwise than as he does appear to me, namely, as a being with attributes analogous to the human. But this distinction between what God is in himself, and what he is for me destroys the peace of religion, and is besides in itself an unfounded and untenable distinction. I cannot know whether God is something else in himself or for himself than he is for me; what he is to me is to me all that he is. . . . In the distinction above stated, man takes a point of view above himself, i.e., above his nature, the absolute measure of his being; but this transcendentalism is only an illusion; for I can make the distinction between the object as it is in itself, and the object as it is for me, only where an object can really appear otherwise to me, not where it appears to me such as the absolute measure of my nature determines it to appear—such as it must appear to me.

Scepticism is the arch-enemy of religion; but the distinction between object and conception—between God as he is in himself, and God as he is for me—is a sceptical distinction, and therefore an irreligious one.

Wherever, therefore, this idea, that the religious predicates are only anthropomorphisms, has taken possession of a man, there has doubt, has unbelief, obtained the mastery of faith. And it is only the inconsequence of faint-heartedness and intellectual imbecility which does not proceed from this idea to the formal negation of the predicates, and from thence to the negation of the subject to which they relate. If thou doubtest the objective truth of the predicates, thou must also doubt the objective truth of the subject whose predicates they are. If thy predicates are anthropomorphisms, the subject of them is an anthropomorphism, too. If love, goodness, personality, etc., are human attributes, so also is the subject which thou presupposest, the existence of God, the belief that there is a God, an anthropomorphism—a presupposition purely human. Whence knowest thou that the belief in a God at all is not a limitation of man's mode of conception? . . .

Thou believest in love as a divine attribute because thou thyself lovest; thou believest that God is a wise, benevolent being because thou knowest nothing better in thyself than benevolence and wisdom; and thou believest that God exists, that therefore he is a subject—whatever exists is a subject, whether it be defined as substance, person, essence, or otherwise—because thou thyself existed, art thyself a subject. Thou knowest no higher human good than to love, than to be good and wise; and even so thou knowest no higher happiness than to exist, to be a subject; for the consciousness of all reality, of all bliss, is for thee bound up in the consciousness of being a subject, of existing. God is an existence, a subject to thee, for the same reason that he is to thee a wise, a blessed, a personal being. The distinction between the divine predicates and the divine subject is only this, that to thee the subject, the existence, does not appear an anthropomorphism, because the conception of it is necessarily involved in thy own existence as a subject, whereas the predicates do appear anthropomorphisms, because their necessity—the necessity that God should be conscious, wise, good, etc.,—is not an immediate necessity, identical with the being of man, but is evolved by his self-consciousness, by the activity of his thought. I am a subject, I exist, whether I be wise or unwise, good or bad. To exist is to man the first datum; it constitutes the very idea of the subject; it is presupposed by the predicates. Hence man relinquishes the predicates, but the existence of God is to him a settled, irrefragable, absolutely certain, objective truth. But, nevertheless, this distinction is merely an apparent one. The necessity of the subject lies only in the necessity of the predicate. Thou art a subject only in so far as thou art a human subject; the certainty and reality of thy existence lie only in the certainty and reality of thy human attributes. What the subject is lies only in the predicate; the predicate is the *truth* of the subject—the subject only the personified, existing predicate, the predicate conceived as existing. Subject and predicate are distinguished only as existence and essence. The negation of the predicates is therefore the negation of the subject. What remains of the human subject when abstracted from the human attributes? Even in the language of common life the divine predicates—Providence, Omniscience, Omnipotence—are put for the divine subject. . . .

Religion is that conception of the nature of the world and of man which is essential to, i.e., identical with, a man's nature. But man does not stand above this his necessary conception; on the contrary, it stands above him; it animates, determines, governs him. The necessity of a proof, of a middle term to unite qualities with existence, the possibility of a doubt, is abolished. Only that which is apart from my own being is capable of being doubted by me. How then can I doubt of God, who is my being? To doubt of God is to doubt of myself. Only when God is thought of abstractly, when his predicates are the result of philosophic abstraction, arises the distinction or separation between subject and predicate, existence and nature—arises the fiction that the existence of the subject is something else than the predicate, something immediate, indubitable, in distinction from the predicate, which is held to be doubtful. But this is only a fiction. A God who has abstract predicates has also an abstract existence. Existence, being, varies with varying qualities.

Thus what theology and philosophy have held to be God, the Absolute, the Infinite, is not God; but that which they have held not to be God is God: namely, the attribute, the quality, whatever has reality. Hence he alone is the true atheist to whom the predicates of the Divine Being,—for example, love, wisdom, justice,—are nothing; not he to whom merely the subject of these predicates is nothing. And in no wise is the negation

of the subject necessarily also a negation of the predicates considered in themselves. These have an intrinsic, independent reality; they force their recognition upon man by their very nature; they are self-evident truths to him; they prove, they attest themselves. It does not follow that goodness, justice, wisdom, are chimeras because the existence of God is a chimera, nor truths because this is a truth. The idea of God is dependent on the idea of justice, of benevolence; a God who is not benevolent, not just, not wise, is no God; but the converse does not hold. The fact is not that a quality is divine because God has it, but that God has it because it is in itself divine; because without it God would be a defective being. Justice, wisdom, in general every quality which constitutes the divinity of God, is determined and known by itself independently, but the idea of God is determined by the qualities which have thus been previously judged to be worthy of the divine nature; only in the case in which I identify God and justice, in which I think of God immediately as the reality of the idea of justice, is the idea of God self-determined. But if God as a subject is the determined, while the quality, the predicate, is the determining, then in truth the rank of the godhead is due not to the subject, but to the predicate.

Now, when it is shown that what the subject is lies entirely in the attributes of the subject; that is, that the predicate is the true subject; it is also proved that if the divine predicates are attributes of the human nature, the subject of those predicates is also of the human nature. But the divine predicates are partly general, partly personal. The general predicates are the metaphysical, but these serve only as external points of support to religion; they are not the characteristic definitions of religion. It is the personal predicates alone which constitute the essence of religion—in which the Divine Being is the object of religion. Such are, for example, that God is a Person, that he is the moral Lawgiver, the Father of mankind, the Holy One, the Just, the Good, the Merciful. It is, however, at once, clear, or it will at least be clear in the sequel, with regard to these and other definitions, that, especially as applied to a personality, they are purely human definitions, and that consequently man in religion—in his relation to God—is in relation to his own nature; for to the religious sentiment these predicates are not mere conceptions, mere images, which man forms of God, to be distinguished from that which God is in himself, but truths, facts, realities. Religion knows nothing of anthropomorphisms; to it they are not anthropomorphisms. It is the very essence of religion, that to it these definitions express the nature of God. They are pronounced to be images only by the understanding, which reflects on religion, and which while defending them yet before its own tribunal denies them. But to the religious sentiment God is a real Father, real Love and Mercy; for to it he is a real, living, personal being, and therefore his attributes are also living and personal. Nay, the definitions which are the most sufficing to the religious sentiment are precisely those which give the most offence to the understanding, and which in the process of reflection on religion it denies. Religion is essentially emotion; hence, objectively also, emotion is to it necessarily of a divine nature. Even anger appears to it an emotion not unworthy of God, provided only there be a religious motive at the foundation of this anger.

But here it is also essential to observe, and this phenomenon is an extremely remarkable one, characterizing the very core of religion, that in proportion as the divine subject is in reality human, the greater is the apparent difference between God and man; that is, the more, by reflection on religion, by theology, is the identity of the divine and human denied, and the human, considered as such, is depreciated. The reason of this is, that as what is positive in the conception of the divine being can only be human, the conception of man, as an object of consciousness, can only be negative. To enrich God, man must become poor; that God may be all, man must be nothing. But he desires to be nothing in himself, because what he takes from himself is not lost to him, since it is preserved in God. Man has his being in God; why then should he have it in himself? Where is the necessity of positing the same

thing twice, of having it twice? What man withdraws from himself, what he renounces in himself, he only enjoys in an incomparably higher and fuller measure in God. . . .

In brief, man in relation to God denies his own knowledge, his own thoughts, that he may place them in God. Man gives up his personality; but in return, God, the Almighty, infinite, unlimited being, is a person; he denies human dignity, the human *ego;* but in return God is to him a selfish, egotistical being, who in all things seeks only himself, his own honor, his own ends, he represents God as simply seeking the satisfaction of his own selfishness, while yet he frowns on that of every other being; his God is the very luxury of egoism. Religion further denies goodness as a quality of human nature; man is wicked, corrupt, incapable of good; but, on the other hand, God is only good—the Good Being. Man's nature demands as an object goodness, personified as God; but is it not hereby declared that goodness is an essential tendency of man? If my heart is wicked, my understanding perverted, how can I perceive and feel the holy to be holy, the good to be good? . . . Either goodness does not exist at all for man, or, if it does exist, therein is revealed to the individual man the holiness and goodness of human nature.

Man—this is the mystery of religion—projects his being into objectivity, and then again makes himself an object to this projected image of himself thus converted into a subject; he thinks of himself as an object to himself, but as the object of an object, of another being than himself. Thus here. Man is an object to God. That man is good or evil is not indifferent to God; no! He has a lively, profound interest in man's being good; he wills that man should be good, happy—for without goodness there is no happiness. Thus the religious man virtually retracts the nothingness of human activity, by making his dispositions and actions an object to God, by making man the end of God—for that which is an object to the mind is an end in action; by making the divine activity a means of human salvation. God acts, that man may be good and happy. Thus man, while he is apparently humiliated to the lowest degree, is in truth exalted to the highest. Thus, in and through God, man has in view himself alone. It is true that man places the aim of his action in God, but God has no other aim of action than the moral and eternal salvation of man; thus man has in fact no other aim than himself. The divine activity is not distinct from the human.

Appendix

Man has his highest being, his God, in himself; not in himself as an individual, but in his essential nature, his species. No individual is an adequate representation of his species, but only the human individual is conscious of the distinction between the species and the individual; in the sense of this distinction lies the root of religion. The yearning of man after something above himself is nothing else than the longing after the perfect type of his nature, the yearning to be free from himself, i.e., from the limits and defects of his individuality. Individuality is the self-conditioning, the self-limitation of the species. Thus man has cognizance of nothing above himself, of nothing beyond the nature of humanity; but to the individual man this nature presents itself under the form of an individual man. Thus, for example, the child sees the nature of man *above itself* in the form of its parents, the pupil in the form of his tutor. But all feelings which man experiences toward a superior man, nay, in general, all moral feelings which man has towards man, are of a religious nature. *Man feels nothing towards God which he does not also feel toward man. Homo homini deus est.* Want teaches prayer; but in misfortune, in sorrow, man kneels to entreat help of man also. Feeling makes God a man, but for the same reason it makes man a God. How often in deep emotion, which alone speaks genuine truth, man exclaims to man: Thou art, thou hast been my redeemer, my saviour, my protecting spirit, my God! We feel awe, reverence, humility, devout admiration, in thinking of a truly great, noble man; we feel ourselves worthless, we sink into nothing, even in the presence of human greatness. The purely, truly human emotions are

religious; but for that reason the religious emotions are purely human; the only difference is that the religious emotions are vague, indefinite; but even this is only the case when the object of them is indefinite. Where God is positively defined, is the object of positive religion, there God is also the object of positive, definite human feelings, the object of fear and love, and therefore he is a positively human being; for there is nothing more in God than what lies in feeling. If in the heart there is fear and terror, in God there is anger; if in the heart there is joy, hope, confidence, in God there is love. . . . Thus even in religion man bows before the nature of man under the form of a personal human being; religion itself expressly declares—and all anthropomorphisms declare this in opposition to Pantheism,—*quod supra nos nihil ad nos;* that is, a God who inspires us with no human emotions, who does not reflect our own emotions, in a word, who is not a man—such a God is nothing to us, has no interest for us, does not concern us.

It is clear from what has been said, that only where in truth, if not according to the subjective conception, the distinction between the divine and human being is abolished, is the objective existence of God, the existence of God as an objective, distinct being abolished—only there, I say, is religion made a mere matter of feeling or conversely, feeling the chief point in religion. The last refuge of theology therefore is feeling. God is renounced by the understanding; he has no longer the dignity of a real object, of a reality which imposes itself on the understanding; hence he is transferred to feeling: in feeling his existence is thought to be secure. And doubtless this is the safest refuge; for to make feeling the essence of religion is nothing else than to make feeling the essence of God. And as certainly as I exist, so certainly does my God exist. The certainty of God is here nothing else than the self-certainty of human-feeling, the yearning after God is the yearning after unlimited, uninterrupted, pure feeling. In life the feelings are interrupted; they collapse; they are followed by a state of void, of insensibility. The religious problem, therefore, is to give fixity to feeling in spite of the vicissitudes of life, and to separate it from repugnant disturbances and limitations: God himself is nothing else than undisturbed, uninterrupted feeling, feeling for which there exists no limits, no opposite. If God were a being distinct from thy feeling, he would be known to thee in some other way than simply in feeling; but just because thou perceivest him only by feeling, he exists only in feeling—he is himself only feeling.

10.2 Religion Is an Opiate

Do you think that ideas make the world go 'round? Do you think that if we can change the way people think, then we can change the way they act? Do you think that changing individuals will lead to a change in society?

Karl Marx (1818–1883) answered "No" to all these questions. Marx, after studying Hegel's dialectical idealism (the theory that the development of ideas determines historical events), reacted by developing dialectical materialism (the theory that the development of economics determines historical events).

As a student in Berlin, Marx came under the influence of Feuerbach (see Reading 10.1). He agreed with Feuerbach (and Hegel) that a basic problem of human existence is alienation—a divided and estranged self that contributes to the loss of our humanity. However, unlike Hegel and Feuerbach, he thought the causes of alienation were economic. Capitalism alienates workers from the value of their labor by paying them less than they deserve in order to provide more profit for the stockholders. Alienation is a social and economic problem, not just a personal and psychological problem. Religion is an elaborate system of ideas and rituals developed by the ruling economic classes (the rich) in order to keep the workers (the poor) content. It is a drug, an opiate, promising "pie in the sky by and by" as compensation for the lack of material rewards here and now.

Feuerbach, Marx contends, thinks that a critical interpretation of Christianity is the primary philosophical goal. Once we realize that God amounts to no more than the projection of an idealized human nature, a true realized Christianity will result. But matters are not so simple. Marx argues that the real point of philosophical criticism is not to *interpret* the world but to *change* it. Thus Marx went on to develop an economic and political philosophy of revolution that urges workers to take concrete steps to overthrow capitalism and its supporting ideologies, such as Christianity, and to replace them with communism.

Communism, as imagined by Marx, is a classless society (no gap between rich and poor) and a society free from governmental control and restrictions. There is no need for government because people will spontaneously do what a humanitarian ethic teaches—love of neighbor. This humanitarian society is possible, Marx thought, only when a theistically controlled society passes into history. Marx's atheism (or what used to be called Godless communism) was intended to make way for a humanitarian community of care and concern. Marx also thought it would enable the benefits of scientific inquiry to flow freely in society, thereby improving the lives of people. With no religious establishment or church constantly doing battle with the latest scientific theory, such as evolution, science would be able to pursue the truth unhindered by popular superstitions and oppositions. Like Jesus, Marx thought the truth would set us free.

Communism remains a noble ideal. It has never, as Marx envisioned it, existed, in spite of the fact that many countries have instituted what they call communism and have paid lip service to Marx's ideas. The so-called fall of communism that we have recently witnessed does not prove that Marx was wrong, only that his ideas have never really been put into practice. Perhaps it is impossible to do so. Perhaps his dream of a classless society in which all citizens enjoy freedom and economic security is an unrealizable utopia. Maybe it is too much like the idealized kingdom of God proclaimed in the Jewish and Christian testaments. According to that account, only God can bring about such a kingdom. Humans cannot do it. Maybe Marx just got impatient.

Reading Questions

1. According to Marx, what mistake does Feuerbach make in his book *The Essence of Christianity*?
2. What is the human essence, according to Marx, and what is the essence of social life?
3. Why does Marx claim that the "criticism of religion is the premise of all criticism"?
4. What is the basis of irreligious criticism?
5. In what sense is religious distress the expression of a real distress?
6. Where does the criticism of religion end, and what is its categorical imperative?
7. Do you agree or disagree with Marx's claim that philosophers such as Feuerbach only interpret the world but that the real point is to change it? Why?

Religion Is an Opiate*

KARL MARX

THE CHIEF DEFECT of all hitherto existing materialism—that of Feuerbach included—is that the thing [*Gegenstand*], reality, sensuousness, is conceived only in the form of the *object* [*Objekt*] or of *contemplation* [*Anschauung*], but not as *human sensuous activity, practice,* not subjectively. Hence it happened that the *active side*, in contradistinction to materialism, was developed by idealism—but only abstractly, since, of course, idealism does not know real, sensuous activity as such. Feuerbach wants sensuous objects, really differentiated from the thought-objects, but he does not conceive human activity itself as *objective* [*gegenständliche*] activity. Hence, in the *Essence of Christianity,* he regards the theoretical attitude as the only genuinely human attitude, while practice is conceived and fixed only in its dirty-judaical form of appearance. Hence he does not grasp the significance of "revolutionary," of "practical-critical," activity.

The question whether objective [*gegenständliche*] truth can be attributed to human thinking

*From "Theses on Feuerbach" and "Contribution to the Critique of Hegel's Philosophy of Right" by Karl Marx in *K. Marx and F. Engels On Religion*. Moscow: Foreign Languages Publishing House [n. d.], pp. 68–72, 41–42, 50–52. Reprinted by permission. Footnotes deleted.

is not a question of theory but a *practical* question. In practice man must prove the truth, that is, the reality and power, the this-sidedness [*Diesseitigkeit*] of his thinking. The dispute over the reality or non-reality of thinking which is isolated from practice is a purely *scholastic* question.

The materialist doctrine that men are products of circumstances and upbringing, and that, therefore, changed men are products of other circumstances and changed upbringing, forgets that it is men that change circumstances and that the educator himself needs educating. Hence, this doctrine necessarily arrives at dividing society into two parts, of which one is superior to society (in Robert Owen, for example).

The coincidence of the changing of circumstances and of human activity can be conceived and rationally understood only as *revolutionizing practice.*

Feuerbach starts out from the fact of religious self-alienation, the duplication of the world into a religious, imaginary world and a real one. His work consists in the dissolution of the religious world into its secular basis. He overlooks the fact that after this work is completed the chief thing still remains to be done. For the fact that the secular foundation detaches itself from itself and establishes itself in the clouds as an independent realm is really only to be explained by the self-cleavage and self-contradictoriness of this secular basis. The latter must itself, therefore, first be understood in its contradiction, and then revolutionized in practice by the removal of the contradiction. Thus, for instance, once the earthly family is discovered to be the secret of the holy family, the former must then itself be criticized in theory and revolutionized in practice.

Feuerbach, not satisfied with *abstract thinking,* appeals to *sensuous contemplation;* but he does not conceive sensuousness as *practical,* human-sensuous activity.

Feuerbach resolves the religious essence into the *human* essence. But the human essence is no abstraction inherent in each single individual. In its reality it is the ensemble of the social relations.

Feuerbach, who does not enter upon a criticism of this real essence, is consequently compelled:

1. To abstract from the historical process and to fix the religious sentiment [*Gemüt*] as something by itself and to presuppose an abstract—*isolated*—human individual.
2. The human essence, therefore, can with him be comprehended only as "genius," as an internal, dumb generality which merely *naturally* unites the many individuals.

Feuerbach, consequently, does not see that the "religious sentiment" is itself a *social product,* and that the abstract individual whom he analyzes belongs in reality to a particular form of society.

Social life is essentially *practical.* All mysteries which mislead theory to mysticism find their rational solution in human practice and in the comprehension of this practice.

The highest point attained by *contemplative* materialism, that is, materialism which does not understand sensuousness as practical activity, is the contemplation of single individuals in "civil society."

The standpoint of the old materialism is "civil" society; the standpoint of the new is *human* society, or socialized humanity.

The philosophers have only *interpreted* the world, in various ways; the point, however, is to *change* it. . . .

For Germany the *criticism of religion* is in the main complete, and criticism of religion is the premise of all criticism.

The *profane* existence of error, is discredited after its *heavenly oratio pro aris et focis* has been rejected. Man, who looked for a superman in the fantastic reality of heaven and found nothing there but the *reflexion* of himself, will no longer be disposed to find but the *semblance* of himself, the non-human [*Unmensch*] where he seeks and must seek his true reality.

The basis of irreligious criticism is: *Man makes religion,* religion does not make man. In other words, religion is the self-consciousness and self-feeling of man who has either not yet found himself or has already lost himself again. But *man* is no abstract being squatting outside the world. Man is *the world of man,* the state, society. This state, this society, produce religion, *a reversed world-consciousness,* because they are a *reversed world.* Religion is the general theory of that world, its encyclopaedic compendium, its logic in a popular form, its spiritualistic *point d'honneur,* its enthusiasm, its moral sanction, its solemn completion, its universal ground for consolation and justification. It is the *fantastic realization* of the human essence because the *human essence* has no true reality. The struggle against religion is therefore mediately the fight against *the other world,* of which religion is the spiritual *aroma.*

Religious distress is at the same time the *expression* of real distress and the *protest* against real distress. Religion is the sigh of the oppressed creature, the heart of a heartless world, just as it is the spirit of a spiritless situation. It is the *opium* of the people.

The abolition of religion as the *illusory* happiness of the people is required for their *real* happiness. The demand to give up the illusions about its condition is the *demand to give up a condition which needs illusions.* The criticism of religion is therefore *in embryo the criticism of the vale of woe,* the *halo* of which is religion.

Criticism has plucked the imaginary flowers from the chain not so that man will wear the chain without any fantasy or consolation but so that he will shake off the chain and cull the living flower. The criticism of religion disillusions man to make him think and act and shape his reality like a man who has been disillusioned and has come to reason, so that he will revolve round himself and therefore round his true sun. Religion is only the illusory sun which revolves round man as long as he does not revolve round himself.

The task of history, therefore, once the *world beyond the truth* has disappeared, is to establish the *truth of this world.* The immediate *task of philosophy,* which is at the service of history, once the *saintly form* of human self-alienation has been unmasked, is to unmask self-alienation in its *unholy forms.* Thus the criticism of heaven turns into the criticism of the earth, the *criticism of religion* into the *criticism of right* and the *criticism of theology* into the *criticism of politics.* . . .

The weapon of criticism cannot, of course, replace criticism of the weapon, material force must be overthrown by material force; but theory also becomes a material force as soon as it has gripped the masses. Theory is capable of gripping the masses as soon as it demonstrates *ad hominem,* and it demonstrates *ad hominem* as soon as it becomes radical. To be radical is to grasp the root of the matter. But for the man the root is man himself. The evident proof of the radicalism of German theory, and hence of its practical energy, is that it proceeds from a resolute *positive* abolition of religion. The criticism of religion ends with the teaching that *man is the highest essence for man,* hence with the *categoric imperative to overthrow all relations* in which man is a debased, enslaved, abandoned, despicable essence, relations which cannot be better described than by the cry of a Frenchman when it was planned to introduce a tax on dogs: Poor dogs! They want to treat you as human beings!

Even historically, theoretical emancipation has specific practical significance for Germany. For Germany's *revolutionary* past is theoretical, it is the *Reformation.* As the revolution then began in the brain of the *monk,* so now it begins in the brain of the *philosopher.*

Luther, we grant, overcame bondage out of *devotion* by replacing it by bondage out of *conviction.* He shattered faith in authority because he restored the authority of faith. He turned priests into laymen because he turned laymen into priests. He freed man from outer religiosity because he made religiosity the inner man. He freed the body from chains because he enchained the heart.

But if Protestantism was not the true solution of the problem it was at least the true setting of it. It was no longer a case of the layman's struggle against the *priest outside himself* but of his struggle against *his own priest inside himself,* his *priestly nature.* And if the Protestant transformation of the German laymen into priests emancipated the lay popes, the *princes,* with the whole of their priestly clique, the privileged and philistines, the philosophical transformation of priestly Germans into men will emancipate the *people.* But *secularization* will not stop at the *confiscation of church estates* set in motion mainly by hypocritical Prussia any more than emancipation stops at princes. The Peasant War, the most radical fact of German history, came to grief because of theology. Today, when theology itself has come to grief, the most unfree fact of German history, our *status quo*, will be shattered against philosophy. On the eve of the Reformation official Germany was the most unconditional slave of Rome. On the eve of its revolution it is the unconditional slave of less than Rome, of Prussia and Austria, of country junkers and philistines.

Meanwhile, a major difficulty seems to stand in the way of a *radical* German revolution.

For revolutions require a *passive* element, a *material* basis. Theory is fulfilled in a people only insofar as it is the fulfilment of the needs of that people. But will the monstrous discrepancy between the demands of German thought and the answers of German reality find a corresponding discrepancy between civil society and the state and between civil society and itself? Will the theoretical needs be immediate practical needs? It is not enough for thought to strive for realization, reality must itself strive towards thought.

But Germany did not rise to the intermediary stage of political emancipation at the same time as the modern nations. It has not yet reached in practice the stages which it has surpassed in theory. How can it do a *somersault*, not only over its own limitations, but at the same time over the limitations of the modern nations, over limitations which it must in reality feel and strive for as for emancipation from its real limitations? Only a revolution of radical needs can be a radical revolution and it seems that precisely the preconditions and ground for such needs are lacking.

If Germany has accompanied the development of the modern nations only with the abstract activity of thought without taking an effective share in the real struggle of that development, it has, on the other hand, shared the *sufferings* of that development, without sharing in its enjoyment or its partial satisfaction. To the abstract activity on the one hand corresponds the abstract suffering on the other. That is why Germany will one day find itself on the level of European decadence before ever having been on the level of European emancipation. It will be comparable to a *fetish worshipper* pining away with the diseases of Christianity.

10.3 The Scientific Spirit and Method in Chinese Philosophy

It is not hard to find examples of conflicts between science and religion in Western history. The Inquisition of the Roman Catholic Church warned Galileo (1564–1642) in 1616 not to teach the Copernican theory of the solar system. The Roman Catholic Church saw this theory as a threat to Christian faith because it asserted, contrary to what Scripture seems to imply, that the earth revolved around the sun. Does not Scripture declare that God made the sun stand still so Joshua could pursue a battle?

In 1632 Galileo published a work supporting the Copernican view in spite of the warning; he was brought to trial in 1633. The Roman Catholic Church has since acknowledged its error in the case of Galileo, and many of its clergy and lay-people have made distinguished contributions to the sciences.

The religious controversy over the Copernican theory seems to us today to be a quaint historical incident. Very few people would wish to throw you in prison for saying the earth is a planet that revolves around the sun. But mention the theory of evolution and you might evoke some strong responses. Since Darwin published *On the Origin of Species* in 1859, many believers have thought his views directly contradict the story of the origin of human life found in Genesis. Today the supporters of "creation science" do battle with the supporters of evolution over what should be taught in the public schools. Did human animals originate by a gradual process of evolution from simpler forms of life, or did God directly create them in the divine image and from the dust of the earth?

Conflicts between religion and science are not unique to Western history. Hu Shih, chancellor of the National Beijing University from 1938 to 1942 and president of the Academia Sinica until his death in 1962, reminds us in the next selection that such conflicts can also be found in Chinese history. Although some scholars have argued that the conflicts between religion and science are unique to the theistic religions of the West, Shih argues that they are mistaken. The scientific spirit did develop in China and within such religious philosophies as Confucianism and Taoism. Shih shows that the opposition between religion and science is too simplistic. Religions themselves, especially as their philosophical implications are worked out, exhibit a scientific attitude. This does not mean that conflict cannot arise between religious and scientific claims. One begins to suspect, however, that such conflicts may have more to do with political and social issues of power than with differing intellectual perspectives.

Reading Questions

1. What is Northrop's theory about why science never developed in the East, and what, according to Shih, is wrong with that theory?
2. What is the historical approach to the comparative study of philosophy?
3. According to Shih, in what ways do Confucius and Lao Tzu embody a scientific spirit?
4. In what way did Wang Ch'ung's scientific attitude come into conflict with the state religion of the Han Empire? Can you think of a comparable example from Western history? If so, what is it?

The Scientific Spirit and Method in Chinese Philosophy*

HU SHIH

I.

In the course of the past conferences on East-West philosophy, the question has been raised as to whether there was science in the East, and why the East developed little or no science.

To the first question, some of the answers seem definitely in the negative. "So the West generated the natural sciences, as the East did not," said Professor Wilmon Henry Sheldon. And Professor Filmer S. C. Northrop said, "there is very little science [in the East] beyond the most

*From *Philosophy and Culture East and West: East-West Philosophy in Practical Perspective,* edited by Charles A. Moore. Copyright © 1962 by the University of Hawaii Press, pp. 199–208. Reprinted by permission. Footnotes deleted.

obvious and elementary information of the natural history type."

To the second question as to why there was very little or no science in the East, the answers vary. But the most challenging and provocative answer has come from Northrop, who declares, "A culture which admits only concepts by intuition is automatically prevented from developing science of the Western type beyond the most elementary, inductive, natural history stage." As defined by Northrop, concepts by intuition are those "which denote, and the complete meaning of which is given by, something which is immediately apprehended." This is Northrop's theory:

> Formal reasoning and deductive science are not necessary if only concepts by intuition are used in a given culture. If what science and philosophy attempt to designate is immediately apprehended, then obviously all that one has to do in order to know it is to observe and contemplate it. The methods of intuition and contemplation become the sole trustworthy modes of inquiry. It is precisely this which the East affirms and precisely why its science has never progressed for long beyond the initial natural history stage of development to which concepts by intuition restrict one.

This theory is concisely expressed in these words: "The East used doctrine built out of concepts by intuition, whereas Western doctrine has tended to be constructed out of concepts by postulation."

I have no intention to go into the details of this Northropean theory, which must have been familiar to us who have followed our philosopher-friend all these 20 years.

I only wish to point out that this theory of bifurcation of East and West is unhistorical and untrue as far as the intellectual history of the East is concerned.

In the first place, there is no race or culture "which admits only concepts by intuition." Indeed, there is no man who "admits only concepts by intuition." Man is by nature a thinking animal, whose daily practical needs compel him to make inferences for better or for worse, and he often learns to make better and surer inferences. It has

been truly said that inference is the business man never ceases to engage in. And, in making inferences, man must make use of all his powers of perception, observation, imagination, generalization and postulation, induction and deduction. In that way, man develops his common sense, his stock of empirical knowledge, his wisdom, his civilization and culture. And, in the few centers of continuous intellectual and cultural tradition, man of the East and of the West, in the course of time, has developed his science, religion, and philosophy. I repeat, there is no culture "which admits only (the so-called) concepts by intuition," and which "is automatically prevented from developing science of the Western type."

In the second place, I wish to point out that, in attempting to understand the East and the West, what is needed is a historical approach, a historical attitude of mind, rather than a "technical terminology for comparative philosophy." Northrop includes among his examples of "concepts by postulation" these items: Centaurs, the opening sentence of the Fourth Gospel, the concept of God the father, the Christianity of St. Paul, of St. Augustine, and St. Thomas Aquinas, as well as the atoms of Democritus, the atomic models of Bohr's and Rutherford's classical atomic physics, and the space-time continuum of Einstein's physics. Surely, one can find a thousand imaginary concepts in the mythological and religious literature of India and China that can compare with the Greek concept of "Centaurs." And, surely, one can point to many scores of religious ideas in India and China that can compare with the concept of God contained in the first sentence of the Fourth Gospel. Are we not justified in calling a halt to such "bifurcating" terminology, which tends to emphasize a difference between East and West which historically does not exist?

I would like very much, therefore, to present here what I mean by the historical approach to the comparative study of philosophy. Briefly, the historical approach means that all past differences in the intellectual, philosophical, and religious activities of man, East and West, have been *historical* differences, produced, conditioned, shaped, grooved, and often seemingly perpetuated by geographical, climatic, economic, social and political, and even individual or biographical factors, all of which are capable of being studied and understood historically, rationally, and intelligently. Through this historical approach, patient and fruitful studies and researches can then be conducted, always seeking to be understood, never merely to laugh, or to cry, or to despair. It may be that, through this historical approach, we may find that, after all, there are more similarities than differences in the philosophies and religions of East and West; and that whatever striking differences have existed are no more than differences in the degree of emphasis brought about by a peculiar combination of historical factors. It may be that, through this historical approach, we may better understand the rise and rapid development of what has been called "science of the Western type"—not as an isolated or exclusive creation of any chosen people, but only as the natural product of an unusually happy combination of many historical forces. It may be that, as a result of patient historical researches, we may better understand that none of those historical forces, nor a combination of them, will ever "automatically prevent" or permanently incapacitate any race or culture from learning, adopting, developing—and even excelling in—the intellectual activities historically initiated and developed by any other race.

To say that any culture "is automatically prevented from developing science of the Western type" is to despair prematurely. But to seek to understand what historical forces have conspired to give the nations of Europe the glory of leading the entire world by at least fully four hundred years in the development of modern science, and, on the other hand, what other historical forces or what combinations of such forces have been largely responsible for retarding or even crushing such scientific development by any race or culture throughout historic times, not excepting the Graeco-Roman-Christian culture throughout the Middle Ages—that would be a legitimate ambition not unworthy of such a learned assembly of philosophers and historians of philosophy.

II.

It is in the direction of suggesting some such a historical approach to comparative philosophy that I have prepared this paper with the rather immodest title: "The Scientific Spirit and Method in Chinese Philosophy."

I have deliberately left out the scientific *content* of Chinese philosophy, not merely for the obvious reason that that content seems so insignificant compared with the achievement of Western science in the last four centuries, but also because I am of the opinion that, in the historical development of science, the scientific spirit or attitude of mind and the scientific method are of far more primary importance than any practical or empirical results of the astronomer, the calendar-reformer, the alchemist, the physician, or the horticulturist.

This point of view has been eloquently presented by Dr. James B. Conant, former President of Harvard University, and a first-rank scientist in his own right, in his Lectures, *On Understanding Science*. Let me, therefore, quote him:

> Who were the precursors of those early investigators who in the sixteenth and seventeenth centuries set the standards for exact and impartial inquiries? Who were the spiritual ancestors of Copernicus, Galileo and Vesalius? Not the casual experimenter or the artful contrivers of new mechanical devices who gradually increased our empirical knowledge of physics and chemistry during the Middle Ages. These men passed on to subsequent generations many facts and valuable methods of attaining practical ends but not the spirit of scientific inquiry.
>
> For the burst of new ardor in disciplined intellectual inquiry we must turn to a few minds steeped in the Socratic tradition, and to those early scholars who first recaptured the culture of Greece and Rome by primitive methods of archaeology. In the first period of the Renaissance, the love of dispassionate search for the truth was carried forward by those who were concerned with man and his works rather than with inanimate or animate nature. During the Middle Ages, interest in attempts to use the human reason critically and without prejudice, to probe deeply without fear and favor, was kept alive by

those who wrote about human problems. In the early days of the Revival of Learning, it was the humanist's exploration of antiquity that came nearest to exemplifying our modern ideas of impartial inquiry. . . .

Petrarch, Boccaccio, Machiavelli, and Erasmus, far more than the Alchemists, must be considered the precursors of the modern scientific investigator. Likewise, Rabelais and Montaigne who carried forward the critical philosophic spirit must be counted, it seems to me, among the forerunners of the modern scientists.

I believe that the position taken by President Conant is essentially correct. It is interesting to note that he gave his lectures a sub-title: "An Historical Approach."

From this historical standpoint, "the love of dispassionate search for the truth," the "interest in attempts to use the human reason critically and without prejudice, to probe deeply without fear and favor," "the ardor in disciplined intellectual inquiry," "the setting of standards for exact and impartial inquiry"—these are characteristics of the spirit and method of scientific inquiry. It is these aspects of the scientific spirit and method, as they are found in the intellectual and philosophical history of China, that shall form the main body of my paper.

III.

To begin with, there was undoubtedly a "Socratic tradition" in the intellectual heritage of ancient China. The tradition of free question and answer, of free discussion, independent thinking, and doubting, and of eager and dispassionate search for knowledge was maintained in the school of Confucius (551–479 B.C.). Confucius often described himself as one who "learns without satiety and teaches without being wearied," and as one who "loves antiquity and is earnest in seeking to know it." On one occasion, he spoke of himself as one "who is so eager to know that he forgets to eat, whose cares are lost in moments of rapturous triumph, unmindful of the coming of old age."

That was the man who founded and molded the orthodoxy of the Chinese intellectual life of

the past twenty-five centuries. There was much in Confucius that reminds us of Socrates. Like Socrates, Confucius always professed that he was not a "wise man" but a man who loved knowledge. He said: "He who knows does not rank with him who loves knowledge; and he who loves knowledge does not rank with him who really delights in it."

An interesting feature in the Confucian tradition is a deliberate encouragement of independent thinking and doubt. Thus Confucius spoke of his most gifted student, Yen Hui, "Hui is no help to me: he is always satisfied with what I say." But he also said, "I often talk to Hui for a whole day, and he, like a dullard, never raises an objection. But when he is gone and I examine his private life, I find him fully capable of developing [my ideas]. Hui is no dullard." Confucius apparently wanted no docile disciples who would feel pleased with everything he said. He wanted to encourage them to doubt and raise objections. This spirit of doubt and questioning was best shown in Mencius, who openly declared that to accept the whole *Book of History* as trustworthy is worse than to have no *Book of History* at all, and that, of the book *Wu-ch'eng* (a section of the *Book of History*), he would accept no more than two or three (bamboo) pages. Mencius also suggested a free and independent attitude of mind as a necessary prerequisite to the understanding of the *Book of Odes* (*Shih ching*).

The best-known Confucian dictum is: "Learning without thinking is labor lost; thinking without learning is perilous." He himself, however, seemed to be always inclined to the side of learning. He said of himself: "I have often spent a whole day without food and a whole night without sleep—to think. But it was of no use. It is better to study." "Study as if life were too short and you were on the point of missing it." "He who learns the truth in the morning, may die in the evening without regret." That was China's Socratic tradition.

Intellectual honesty was an important part of this tradition. "Yu," said Confucius to one of his students, "shall I tell you what knowledge is? To hold that you know a thing when you know it, and to hold that you do not know when you really do not know: that is knowledge." When on another occasion the same student asked Confucius how to serve the spirits and the gods, Confucius said, "We have not yet learned to serve men, how can we serve the spirits?" The questioner then asked about death, and the Master said, "We do not yet know life, how do we know death?" This was not evading the questions; it was an injunction to be intellectually honest about things one does not really know. Such an agnostic position about death and the gods and spirits has had lasting influence on Chinese thought in subsequent ages. That, too, was China's Socratic tradition.

In recent decades, doubt has been raised about the historicity of the man Lao Tzu, or Lao Tan, and about the authenticity and the dating of the ancient book known as the *Book of Lao Tzu*. But I, for one, still believe that Confucius was at one time a student of and apprentice to the older philosopher, Lao Tzu, whose influence in the direction of a naturalistic conception of the universe and of a *laissez-faire* (*wu-wei*) philosophy of government can be observed in the thinking of Confucius himself.

To have postulated a naturalistic view of the universe at so early a date (the sixth century B.C.) was a truly revolutionary act. The ancient Chinese notion of *T'ien* (Heaven) or *Ti* (Supreme God), as represented in the songs and hymns of the *Book of Odes,* was that of a knowing, feeling, loving, and hating supreme ruler of men and the universe. And the fate of men was also supposed to be in the hands of all kinds of gods and spirits. In place of such an anthropomorphic deity or deities, an entirely new philosophic concept was proposed.

> There is something of indeterminate
>   origin,
> And born before heaven and earth.
> Without voice and without body,
> It stands alone and does not change;
> It moves everywhere but is never
>   exhausted.
> It may be regarded as the mother of the
>   universe.
> I do not know its name:
> I call it "the Way" (*Tao*),
> And perforce designate it "the Great"
>   (*ta*).

So the new principle was postulated as the Way (Tao), that is, a process, an all-pervading and everlasting process. The Way becomes so of itself (*tzu-jan*), and all things become so of themselves.

"The Way (Tao) does nothing, yet it leaves nothing undone." That is the central idea of this naturalistic conception of the universe. It became the cornerstone of a political theory of non-activity, non-interference, *laissez faire* (*wu-wei*). "The best ruler is one whose existence is scarcely noticed by the people." And the same idea was developed into a moral philosophy of humility, of non-resistance to evil and violence. "The supreme good is likened to water which benefits all things and resists none." "The weak and yielding always wins over the hard and strong." "There is always the Great Executioner that executes. [That is the great Way, which does nothing but leaves nothing undone.] To do the executing for the Great Executioner is like doing the chopping for the master carpenter. He who does the chopping for the master carpenter rarely escapes injuring his own hand."

Such was the naturalistic tradition formed by Lao Tzu, the teacher of Confucius. But there was a fundamental difference between the teacher and his student. Confucius was a historically minded scholar and a great teacher and educator, whereas Lao Tzu was a nihilist in his conception of knowledge and civilization. The ideal utopia of Lao Tzu was a small State with a small population, where all the inventions of civilization, such as ships carriages "which multiplied human power by ten times and a hundred times are not to be put in use; and where the people would restore the use of knotted cords instead of writing!" "Always let the people have no knowledge, and therefore no desires." How different is this intellectual nihilism from Confucius' democratic philosophy of education, which says, "With education there will be no classes!"

But the naturalistic conception of the universe, as it was germinated in the *Book of Lao Tzu* and more fully developed in subsequent centuries, has been a most important philosophical heritage from the Classical Age. Naturalism itself best ex-emplifies the spirit of courageous doubt and constructive postulation. Its historical importance fully equals that of the humanist heritage left by Confucius. Whenever China had sunk deep into irrationality, superstition, and otherworldliness, as she has done several times in her long history, it was always the naturalism of Lao Tzu and the philosophical Taoists, or the humanism of Confucius, or a combination of the two, that would arise and try to rescue her from her sluggish slumbers.

The first great movement "to use the human reason critically and to probe deeply without fear and favor" in the face of the State Religion of the Han Empire was such a combination of the naturalistic philosophy of Taoism and the spirit of doubt and intellectual honesty that was the most valuable heritage handed down from Confucius and Mencius. The greatest representative of that movement of criticism was Wang Ch'ung (A.D. 27–*ca.* 100), author of a book of 85 essays called *Lun-heng,* "Essays in Criticism."

Wang Ch'ung spoke of his own essays in these words, "One sentence sums up my essays: I hate falsehood." "Right is made to appear wrong, and falsehood is regarded as truth. How can I remain silent! . . . When I read current books of this kind, when I see truth overshadowed by falsehood, my heart beats violently, and my brush trembles in my hand. How can I be silent! When I criticize them, I examine them in my reasoning power, check them against facts, and show up their falsehood by setting up proofs."

He was criticizing the superstitions and falsehoods of his age, of which the greatest and most powerful were the central doctrines of Catastrophes (*tsai*) and Anomalies (*i*), which the State Religion of the Han Empire, under the name of Confucianism, interpreted as warnings sent by a benevolent and all-seeing God (*T'ien*) to terrify the rulers and governments so that they might repent and reform their acts of misrule. This religion of Han Confucianism had been formulated by a number of philosopher-statesmen of the second and first centuries B.C., who were justifiably worried by the real problem of how to deal with the unlimited power of the absolute monarchy in a vast unified empire, and who, consciously or semiconsciously, had hit upon the religious weapon and had worked out an elaborate theology of "reciprocal relationship between Heaven (*T'ien*) and the rulers of men" which seemed to have been able to hold the absolute sovereigns in awe throughout the several centuries of the Han dynasties.

This theology of the State Religion of catastrophes and anomalies was best expressed by Tung Chung-shu (*ca.* 179–*ca.* 104 B.C.), who spoke like a prophet and with authority: "The action of man, when it reaches the highest level of good and evil [that is, when it becomes government action affecting vast numbers], will flow into the course of Heaven and Earth and cause reciprocal reverberations in their manifestations." "When a State is on the verge of ruin, Heaven will cause catastrophes [such as floods, famines, great fires] to befall earth as warnings to the ruler. When these are not hearkened to, Heaven will cause strange anomalies [such as sun eclipses, comets, unusual movements of planets] to appear to terrify the ruler into repentance. But, when even these anomalies fail to check his misrule, then ruin will come. All this shows that Heaven is always kind to the ruler and anxious to protect him from destruction." This theology of intimate reciprocal reverberations between Heaven and the rulers of men was supposedly based on an elaborate interpretation of the pre-Confucian *Book of History* and the Confucian *Ch'un-ch'iu* Annals (*Spring and Autumn Annals,* which recorded numerous unusual events on earth and in the heavens, including thirty-six eclipses of the sun and five earthquakes between 722 and 481 B.C.). But the canonical Classics of established Confucianism were not enough for the support of this fanatic and fantastic theology, which had to be reinforced by an ever-increasing crop of apocryphal works known as the *wei* (woofs or interweaving aids to the Canon) and the *ch'an* (prophecies), which are collections of bits of empirical knowledge intermixed with hundreds of astrological fantasies.

It is a historical fact that this State Religion of pseudo-Confucianism, at the height of its glory, was taken so seriously that many a Prime Minister was dismissed and one was forced by the Emperor to commit suicide, all because of the belief in Heaven's warning in the form of catastrophes and abnormalities. One of the three great medieval religions was in full sway over the empire.

It was against the basic idea of a reciprocal responsive relationship between a teleological God and the rulers of men that Wang Ch'ung was directing his main criticism. He was criticizing the theology of the established religion of the empire. The world view with which he set out to attack the current theology was the naturalistic philosophy of Lao Tzu and the Taoists. He said:

> The Way Tao of Heaven is that it does nothing and all things become so by themselves. If Heaven were to give warnings to men or mete out punishments, that would be "doing" things and not things "becoming so of themselves." . . . Those who hold that catastrophic and abnormal occurrences were purposeful warnings from Heaven are in reality degrading the dignity of the great Heaven by interpreting natural phenomena in terms of human action. They are therefore not convincing at all.

For, he pointed out,

> Heaven is most exalted, and man is tiny. Man's place between heaven and earth is like that of a flea inside one's clothes, or that of an ant in an anthill. . . . Surely it is absolutely impossible for man with his tiny body of seven feet to hope to bring about any response from the vast atmosphere of the great firmament.

That is why Wang Ch'ung said that the doctrine of reciprocal response between Heaven and man was in reality "degrading the dignity of the great Heaven."

And he offered to prove that man and all things in the universe were *never purposefully* (*ku*) produced by Heaven and Earth, but were *accidentally* (*ngou, ou*) so, of themselves:

> It is wrong to hold that man is born of Heaven and Earth purposely. Certain fluids are combined, and man is born accidentally. . . . All things are formed of fluid (*ch'i*), and each species reproduces itself. . . . If it were true that Heaven purposely produced all living things in the world, then Heaven should make them all love each other and not allow them to injure or prey on each other. . . . But there are tigers and wolves, poisonous snakes and insects, which prey on man. Can we say that it is the purpose of Heaven to create man for the use of those ferocious and poisonous animals?

The first century of the Christian era was a period of calendar reform under the Han Empire. And Wang Ch'ung made full use of the astronomical knowledge of his age to expose the folly of the current theological doctrine of catastrophes and anomalies as warnings from Heaven against the evil acts or policies of the rulers of the empire. He said:

> There is one eclipse of the sun in about forty-one or forty-two months, and there is one eclipse of the moon in about six months. Solar and lunar eclipses are regular occurrences which have nothing to do with government policies. And this is true of the hundreds of anomalies and thousands of calamities, none of which is necessarily caused by the action of the rulers of men.

But Wang Ch'ung more frequently cited facts of everyday experience as proofs or evidences in his numerous criticisms of the superstitions or falsehoods of his age. He offered five "tests" (*nien*) to prove that thunder was not the wrath of Heaven but only a kind of fire generated by the friction of the *yin* and *yang* fluids in the air. And he produced many a proof to support his thesis that there were no ghosts or spirits. One of those proofs is most ingenious and so far irrefutable: "If a ghost is the spirit of the dead man, then the ghost should be seen only in naked form and could not be seen with clothes on his body. For surely the cloth or silk can have no soul or spirit to survive destruction. How can it be explained that ghosts have never been seen in naked form, but always with clothes on?"

So much for my favorite philosopher, Wang Ch'ung. I have told his story to show how the spirit of courageous doubt and intellectual honesty of the Classical Age of Chinese philosophy could survive centuries of oblivion and would arise to carry on the fight of human reason against ignorance and falsehood, of creative doubt and constructive criticism against superstition and blind authority. To dare to doubt and question without fear and favor is the spirit of science. "To check falsehoods against facts and to expose them by setting up proofs" constitute the procedure of science. . . .

10.4 Religion and Science in the Global Age

Have you ever thought about the universe expanding into nothing until everything flies apart? Maybe, according to some scientific theories, it will implode back into itself so that everything becomes incredibly dense and compact. In either case, no trace of life will remain. Nothing of human history, culture, philosophy, or religion will be left. Not even a whisper or fading echo of human hopes and joys will be heard.

If the universe is as physical science describes it today, and if there is no other reality than this physical universe and its history, then there seems little hope that any human achievements will endure. The universe is indifferent to us. It responds to our pleas for recognition with a cold silence.

Religions have tried to humanize the universe and to help people feel there is more to life than a slide into absolute oblivion. One way in which some religions have humanized the universe is to posit a God who created it, sustains it, and cares for it. What if there is no such God? Is all hope lost?

There may be no real conflict between scientific and religious versions of reality. Granted, conflicts between science and religion have erupted in the course of human history. However, there is a difference between *real* and *apparent* conflicts. Some argue that because God created the physical universe, the more we find out about it, the more we find out about God. Others argue that religion is an expression of the poetic imagination. Its myths, symbols, and stories should no more be treated as science than Shakespeare's plays should be thought of as chemistry textbooks. There can be no real conflict between apples and oranges. Still others urge us to think of religion as providing information about the supernatural, whereas science offers information about the natural. This is a kind of "separate but equal" argument. Yet many find the attempts to isolate science and religion into non-conflicting realms misguided. The relationship between science and religion is far more complex.

This complexity increases when we begin to think of religion in nontheistic terms. Very often the philosophical discussions of the relationship between religion and science are based on a theistic assumption. What if we add a global perspective?

Masao Abe, author of the next essay, is Professor Emeritus of Nara University in Japan. He has taught in both Japan and the United States. His thought is strongly influenced by Kitaro Nishida, the leading figure of the Kyoto School of Japanese philosophy (see Reading 1.5) and reflects ideas that originated in Buddhist thought. Abe believes that the Buddhist perspective can make a positive contribution to the debate about the relationship of religion and science and can help us to move beyond thinking of these issues in a strictly theistic context.

Reading Questions

1. What are the basic characteristics of modern science, according to Abe?
2. In what sense was Christian theology an important catalyst in the development of science?
3. Do you agree with Abe that science can answer the "how" questions but only religion can answer the "why" questions?
4. What is the difference between a mechanistic and a teleological view, and why is the mechanistic view hostile to religion?

5. Why is the theistic answer to the "why" question incompatible with a mechanistic viewpoint, and why cannot process theology overcome the "nihility without God" opened up by science?
6. Why is Buddhism compatible with modern science?
7. What does Abe mean by "without why"?
8. What is the crucial task for Buddhism, and why must science and religion be harmonized?

Religion and Science in the Global Age*

MASAO ABE

IT IS ALMOST IMPOSSIBLE to deal with a problem of the magnitude of "Religion and Science in the Global Age" in its full scale and depth. Nevertheless I would like to discuss what I consider essential to the issue and elucidate it from a Buddhist point of view.

Modern science may be said to be a human enterprise through which man and nature are investigated as objectively as possible, that is, without subjective judgement. It is *fundamentally* free from any anthropocentric interest such as value, meaning and purpose. This mode of science was methodologically established by the Cartesian idea of *Mathēsis ūniversālis* and the Baconian method described in *Novum Organum*. It was a complete replacement of the Aristotelian teleological–biological standpoint by an approach based on mathematics and physics. The present form of science is the radical development of this approach.

In the eighteenth and nineteenth centuries in the West, serious conflicts arose between Christianity and science, as epitomized by the controversy surrounding Charles Darwin. It could be argued that Christian theology acted as an important catalyst in the development of modern science, for the idea of God as ruler of the universe made people sympathetic to the idea that God had arranged things in an orderly way and that there were natural laws which could be discovered if one looked hard enough. However, the assertion that science could not have arisen without the stimulus of theological ideas certainly does not demonstrate that those theological ideas have any genuine basis in reality.

In our time it is sometimes said that those who still maintain that there is a conflict between religion and science are rather naïve and old-fashioned, since contemporary theologians, having as a rule abandoned the view that the Holy Scriptures are literally the word of God, are well disposed toward dialogue and mediation between Christianity and science. Simultaneously it is suggested that the peculiar characteristics of twentieth-century science render it far less inimical to religion than was the science of the nineteenth century. I do not think, however, that this is really the case. While on the surface the problem may seem to have diminished, it is clear at a deeper level that science poses a serious threat to religion.

Let us examine the essential character of both science and religion. At the risk of oversimplification, one may say that science is concerned

* From *Zen and Western Thought* by Masao Abe, edited by William R. LaFleur. Copyright © 1985 by Masao Abe, edited by William R. LaFleur. University of Hawaii Press, pp. 241–248. Reprinted by permission. Most footnotes deleted.

with the answer to the question "how" whereas religion is concerned with the answer to the question "why." As used here, "how" refers to the process of cause and effect or "means" while "why" refers to meaning, purpose, or *raison d'être*. Science can provide an answer to the question of how a flower blooms, or how man comes to exist. It cannot, however, give an answer to the question of why a flower blooms or why man comes to exist. It can explain the cause of a given fact but not the meaning or ground of that fact. It is religion, not science that can offer an answer to the question "why."

Pre-modern science, which was based on the Aristotelian teleological–biological approach, gave a teleological answer to the question "how," for everything in the universe was then understood organically, that is, in terms of living entities. And a teleological answer to the question "how" was not necessarily incompatible with a religious answer to the question "why." The teleological view of the world offered by ancient physics was rather harmonious with the theistic view of man and nature as explained in Christianity. With the advent of modern science, however, the situation changed radically. Modern science, which is based on mathematics and physics, gives a non-teleological and mechanistic response to the question "how," and such a mechanistic answer to the question "how" is quite incompatible with the religious answer to the question "why." This is especially the case with a theistic religion such as Christianity, which is inextricably rooted in the notion of a personal God who is the Creator, Redeemer, and Judge of the universe. The modern scientific mechanistic view of the world is entirely indifferent to human existence. In the mechanistic view, not only physical matter, but also biological life and even the human psyche and spirit are reduced to entirely lifeless mechanistic phenomena. This is evident in contemporary molecular biology, experimental psychology, and genetics.

Unlike the teleological and biological view of nature in pre-modern science, the mechanistic view of the world of modern science grasps everything in the universe as lifeless, that is, in an entirely inhuman and insensitive manner. Such a mechanistic view of the world is not only incompatible with but also inimical to religion, which is concerned with the "why" question of the final meaning or ultimate ground of human existence in the world. It is inimical to religion because it deprives everything of its meaning, value, aim, and purpose. It may be said that the mechanistic answer to the question "how" as seen in modern science has "horizontally" severed the religious answer to the question "why." In so saying, I have in mind an image, in which a vertical line, representing religion which seeks for the ultimate ground of human existence, is severed by a horizontal line, representing science which is mainly concerned with the cause and effect of things in the universe. As a result, man is left hanging. It is now a serious task for religion, which is primarily concerned with the ultimate meaning of human life, to find a way to embrace the meaning-negating science which prevails in the modern world.[1]

The modern scientific mechanistic view of the world has created a still more serious problem for religion. It has brought forth atheism and radical nihilism. The mechanistic world view destroyed the "spiritual" basis on which all the teleological systems in religion hitherto rested, and opened up nihility at the base of the world, leaving no place for God. This abyss of nihility was also opened up at the bottom of human existence. The existentialism developed by Jean Paul Sartre, who insists that one's subjectivity can be established only in the realization of that nihility, is a direct consequence of the awareness of the nihility brought about by modern science. Contemporary atheism is not merely a materialistic atheism, but rather a more radical, existential atheism which tries to take "nihility without God" as the basis of Subjective freedom. In this regard, we must pay special attention to Friedrich Nietzsche, who proclaimed the arrival of nihilism about a century ago through his sharp insight into the nature of science and human destiny.

In his book, *Beyond Good and Evil*, Nietzsche presents his unique idea of the three stages of human history as follows:

Once upon a time men sacrificed human beings to their God, and perhaps just those they loved the best . . . then, during the moral epoch of mankind, they sacrificed to their God the strongest instincts they possessed, their "nature"; *this* festal joy shines in the cruel glances of ascetics and "anti-natural" fanatics. Finally, what still remained to be sacrificed? . . . Was it not necessary to sacrifice God himself? To sacrifice God for nothingness—this paradoxical mystery of the ultimate cruelty has been reserved for the rising generation; we all know something of this already.

To the first stage, Nietzsche ascribes the sacrifice of all primitive religions and also the sacrifice of the Emperor Tiberius in the Mithra-Grotto of the Island of Capri. It may be said that this first stage corresponds to the time of the Old Testament which records the story of this kind of sacrifice in the case, for example, of Abraham and Isaac. It would also be safe to say that the second stage represents the time of the New Testament and following Christian era in which the death and sacrifice of Jesus is seen as the redemption of original sin inherent in human nature. The third historic stage in which we "sacrifice God for nothingness" announces the advent of nihilism in the Nietzschean sense.

It may be said that we have already arrived at the third historic stage which Nietzsche described above. As he predicted, we are now experiencing the "nihility without God" which has been opened up by modern science at the base of the traditional notion of God. How to cope with this "nihility without God" is the most urgent problem emerging from the conflict between science and religion.

In this regard, the following two points must be emphasized if religion is to remain viable in its dialogue and confrontation with science:

1. It is necessary for each religion to re-examine the basis of its world view. For any religion, its world view is not like clothes that one can change whenever one pleases. A world view is to religion what water is to a fish. It is the indispensable condition through which religion can actually come into existence. Water is neither the life of the fish as such, nor its body, yet it is fundamentally linked to both. For a religion to change its world view is a matter no less fatal to it than for a fish to change from salt water to fresh.

2. What is even more crucial and important is that each religion re-examine and reinterpret that tradition's understanding of God or the "ultimate" and His or its relation to human beings and the world. With regard to this second point, Buddhism, which is fundamentally non-theistic, is in a somewhat different situation from Christianity, which is basically theistic. As I mentioned before, religion provides an answer to the question "why." Christianity gives a theistic answer to the question "why," in terms of the "will of God," the "rule of God," and accompanying notions such as creation, incarnation, redemption and last judgement. On the other hand, Buddhism provides a non-theistic answer to the question "why" through its emphasis on "dependent co-origination," "no-self," "Emptiness," "suchness" and so forth.

Theistic answers to the question "why" in Christianity, such as the "will of God" and the "rule of God" are incompatible with the modern scientific answer to the question "how." This is because the former strongly emphasize the personality of the ultimate while the latter is essentially impersonal. The personal God and his personal relationship to human beings are quite incompatible with the mechanistic view of the world. To overcome this incompatibility, various theological attempts have been made in the realm of Christianity. One of the most remarkable of these attempts is that of Process Theology, as exemplified by the efforts of John Cobb and others.

Process Theology is based on the philosophy of Whitehead, which in turn is based on critical consideration of modern science and mathematics. According to Process Theology, the ultimate is not the personal God, but creativity, which is somewhat impersonal. Both God and the world are equally understood as outcomes of the principle of creativity. God and the world as thus understood are mutually interpenetrating in terms of concrescense in which individual occasions of experience are dynamic acts of becoming. The notion of the ultimate as creativity in Process Theology is certainly less alien to the modern scientific mechanistic view of the world than the traditional Christian notion of a personal God. However, I wonder if it is *really* compatible with modern science. In order for a theology to be completely compatible with modern science, it must be of a thoroughly mechanistic and impersonal nature while fully retaining a teleological and personal nature as well. In other words, a dialectical unity of completely mechanistic—impersonal and completely teleological—personal natures is necessary for such a theology. Although Process Theology includes both mechanistic and teleological aspects by setting forth efficient and final causation, it combines these two aspects somewhat in a parallel manner, not in a dialectical or paradoxical way. That is to say, it is partially mechanistic and partially teleological. And however much the momentariness of events which constitute the process is emphasized, in the basic notion of "process" the teleological nature takes precedence over the mechanical nature. This is clearly seen when creativity as the ultimate is understood to be realizable only in actual instances of the *many becoming one,* and when creativity is possible only through an open future and closed past, that is, through the irreversibility of unidirectional time. I wonder if Process Theology can legitimately overcome the "nihility without God" which is opened up at the bottom of contemporary human existence by the modern scientific mechanistic view of the world.

In Buddhism, the non-theistic response to the question "why," as expressed through the notions of "dependent co-origination," "Emptiness" and "suchness," is compatible with the modern scientific mechanistic answer to the question "how," because these Buddhist notions, though deeply religious, are somewhat impersonal. To say they are impersonal does not mean Buddhism is indifferent to human affairs. On the contrary, Buddhism as a religion is essentially concerned with human salvation. In this respect, there is no difference between Christianity and Buddhism, for both traditions are equally concerned with salvation. However, the *foundation* on which salvation becomes possible is understood differently. In Christianity that foundation is understood as something personal, that is, as the personal relationship between man and God. On the other hand, in Buddhism, the foundation of salvation is not something personal, but impersonal and common to all beings. Human *salvation* and *its foundation,* though inseparable, must be distinguished. This distinction is important because the present conflict between science and religion is to a great extent related to the foundation of salvation.

The Buddhist notion of "dependent co-origination" insists that everything is interdependent with every other thing, both in regard to its existence and its ceasing to be. Nothing is self-existent and independent. For instance, bigness and smallness are interdependent; there is no such thing as bigness self-existing apart from smallness or smallness self-existing apart from bigness. Bigness is bigness and smallness is smallness, and yet they are completely interdependent. In the same way, good and evil are interdependent. It is illusory to think of the good as self-existing apart from evil or to think of evil as self-existing apart from the good. Good is good; evil is evil. There is a distinction. Yet good and evil are completely interdependent. Again, in the same way, the absolute and the relative are interdependent.

It is erroneous to conceive of the absolute as self-existing apart from the relative or to conceive of the relative as self-existing apart from the absolute. The absolute is the absolute and the relative is the relative, and yet the absolute and the relative are completely interdependent. And so, everything is interdependent; nothing is independent. This is the Buddhist notion of dependent co-origination. Accordingly, dependent co-origination or interdependence itself is neither absolute nor relative. Since it is neither absolute nor relative, it is also called "Emptiness." This is not, however, a mere emptiness. On the contrary, precisely because they are interdependent, the absolute is really the absolute and the relative is really the relative; good is really good and evil is really evil; bigness is really bigness and smallness is really smallness. Everything is just as it is. The differences between things are clearly realized. And yet their interdependence is realized as well. This is why "Emptiness" is also called as-it-is-ness or suchness. Emptiness is not a mere emptiness, but rather fullness in which the distinctiveness of everything is realized in a thoroughgoing manner.

I hope it is now clear that "dependent co-origination," "Emptiness" and "suchness" are simply different verbal expressions of one and the same Reality. In Buddhism, the ultimate is not God or creativity but "dependent co-origination." Buddhism is a religion which teaches us how to awaken to this truth of dependent co-origination. One who awakens to this truth is called a Buddha.

In "dependent co-origination," "Emptiness" and "suchness," everything is realized as reciprocal and reversible. There is nothing one-sided or unidirectional. Accordingly, the Buddhist notion of "dependent co-origination" as the ultimate is completely free from any teleological character. In this respect, it is compatible with modern science. Yet it is not merely mechanistic, for it is an answer to the religious question "why." In brief, Buddhism is neither teleological nor mechanistic.

Christianity provides a positive answer to the question "why" in terms of the will of God. Even when human reason does not understand why something happens in a certain way, faith in God accepts it as a trial or the mercy of God. In contrast, Buddhism, in answer to the question "why," responds with "it is so without why" or "it is just as it is." "Without why" as an answer to the question "why" is quite compatible with the modern scientific mechanistic answer to the question "how." But, the Buddhist answer "without why" does not indicate agnosticism or nihilism. It is not a negative answer in the sense of abandoning inquiry into "why." It is rather a positive and affirmative answer which is realized within a thoroughgoing inquiry into "why" and reached by breaking through the question "why." In short, the Buddhist answer "without why" does not signify agnosticism as the mere absence of a positive answer to the question "why," but, rather, indicates a great affirmation of Reality which cannot be analyzed by the question "why" and hence is beyond it.

The crucial task for Buddhism is this: how can Buddhism on the basis of "without why" as its ultimate ground, formulate a *positive direction* through which ethics and history can develop? In other words, how can *a new teleology* be established on the ground of "suchness," which is neither teleological nor mechanical? Here I must limit myself to suggesting that the Mahayana notion of "compassion," which is inseparably connected with "wisdom," and the idea of the "Bodhisattva," which is based on "Emptiness" and "suchness," can provide the foundation for such a Buddhist teleology.

Science without religion is dangerous, for it necessarily entails a complete mechanization of humanity. On the other hand, religion without science is powerless in that it lacks an effective means by which to actualize religious meaning in the contemporary world. Science and religion must work together harmoniously. It is an urgent task for us who approach the global age to find a way to integrate the two.

NOTE

1. In this paper I am not arguing that science as such brings forth atheism and nihilism. I am rather arguing that the *modern scientific world view* which is impersonal and mechanistic has brought forth atheism and nihilism. Natural science is not incompatible with religion, but scientific ideologies or scientism which absolutizes scientific truth as the *only* truth is incompatible with religion. When discussing scientific world views in this paper, I am mainly concerned with scientific ideologies or the scientific way of thinking in relation to religion.

10.5 Of Miracles

Consider the following examples:

1. Someone who has been pronounced dead comes back to life.
2. A person correctly predicts a future earthquake.

3. After praying, and having hands laid on him, a man recovers from asthma, never to be bothered again.

4. A woman dreams that a white elephant enters her womb. She gives birth to a son who becomes a major religious leader.

5. An illiterate person enters into trance states and recites words supposedly from God in the most beautiful and perfect language.

6. The birth of a white buffalo, a sacred figure, is correctly predicted by a wise elder. The death of its father only a few days later is also correctly predicted.

7. A person's cancer suddenly goes into remission and no one can explain why.

8. A large tiger suddenly disappears from a cage in full view of hundreds of people.

9. A child is baptized.

10. Water is changed into wine.

Are all of these events examples of miracles or only some of them? Which ones are examples of miracles? How do the examples you picked differ from those you identified as not miraculous? What distinguishes a miracle from a magic trick? Is a miracle the same thing as a rare and extraordinary event for which we now have no explanation?

One of the enduring questions in the philosophical and theological debate about miracles centers on how can we best define a miracle. Another question has to do with the very possibility of miracles. Is it logically possible for miracles to happen? If it is logically possible, have they happened? What sort of evidence would be good enough to convince a skeptic? If miracles do occur, what do they mean? Do they prove anything?

In David Hume's day (1711–1776), people were much concerned with miracles. John Tillotson (1630–1694), Archbishop of Canterbury and one of the most influential preachers of the day, argued that the miracles recorded in the Bible provided proof of the truth of Christianity. John Locke (1632–1704), a widely respected English philosopher, echoes Tillotson's thoughts when, in his *The Reasonableness of Christianity,* he argues that the performance of miracles by Jesus provides rational proof that Jesus is the Messiah.

Both Tillotson and Locke lived in an age that regarded reason as the final arbitrator of truth. For them, defending Christian belief on rational grounds was paramount. Miracles, they thought, provided such grounds. Earlier generations of Christians had been less sure about what miracles prove or even whether one could use them as proof. Martin Luther, for example, was convinced that Satan as well as God could do miracles. Miracles can be signs of divine grace (hence, for Luther, a sacrament such as baptism is a miracle), but we should be cautious when appealing to them as proofs, because Satan can always fool us.

Hume also thought we ought to be cautious. He noted that the Anglican Bishop Tillotson had not only defended Christianity by citing Christ's miracles but also had attacked Roman Catholic beliefs, especially the belief that the bread and wine are transubstantiated into the body and blood of Christ during the Mass. Tillotson argued that this claim ran counter to our sense experience (it still looks and tastes like bread and wine). Further, he maintained, no argument can prove some doctrine true unless that argument is stronger than the difficulties and objections to it. Tillotson knew of no such argument supporting transubstantiation that could outweigh the testimony of our senses.

Hume thought that this was a good argument. He also thought that Tillotson stumbled on an argument that could be generalized to cover the cases of all alleged miracles. Thus, in his general work on epistemology entitled *Enquiry Concerning Human Understanding,* Hume penned a mere 20-page section on miracles. The debate about miracles has not been the same since. Hume's little essay is the most influential philosophical essay on miracles that has been written in the West. It has caused bitter debate. Many think that what Hume has to say is definitive. Others argue that Hume is sadly mistaken. Read it, and see what you think.

Reading Questions

1. What does Hume mean by "a wise man . . . proportions his belief to the evidence"?
2. Our assurance of the truth of any argument from the "testimony of men" is subject to what principle, according to Hume?
3. How does Hume define a miracle, and why does he claim that there is "a direct and full proof, from the nature of the fact, against the existence of any miracle"?
4. What reasons does Hume provide to support his claim that there has never been a miraculous event for which we could have full confidence in its truth?
5. Do you think Hume is right or wrong when he argues that there cannot be evidence strong enough to convince reasonable people that miraculous violations of the laws of nature have occurred? Why?

Of Miracles*

DAVID HUME

Part I.

I flatter myself, that I have discovered an argument . . . which, if just, will, with the wise and learned, be an everlasting check to all kinds of superstitious delusion, and consequently, will be useful as long as the world endures. For so long, I presume, will the accounts of miracles and prodigies be found in all history, sacred and profane.

Though experience be our only guide in reasoning concerning matters of fact; it must be acknowledged, that this guide is not altogether infallible, but in some cases is apt to lead us into errors. One, who in our climate, should expect better weather in any week of June than in one of December, would reason justly, and conformably to experience; but it is certain, that he may happen, in the event, to find himself mistaken. However, we may observe, that, in such a case, he would have no cause to complain of experience; because it commonly informs us beforehand of the uncertainty, by that contrariety of events, which we may learn from a diligent observation. All effects follow not with like certainty from their supposed causes. Some events are found, in all countries and all ages, to have been constantly conjoined together: Others are found to have been more variable, and sometimes to disappoint

*From *An Enquiry Concerning Human Understanding* by David Hume. Oxford, England: Oxford University Press, 1748.

our expectations; so that, in our reasonings concerning matter of fact, there are all imaginable degrees of assurance, from the highest certainty to the lowest species of moral evidence.

A wise man, therefore, proportions his belief to the evidence. In such conclusions as are founded on an infallible experience, he expects the event with the last degree of assurance, and regards his past experience as a full *proof* of the future existence of that event. In other cases, he proceeds with more caution: He weighs the opposite experiments; He considers which side is supported by the greater number of experiments: to that side he inclines, with doubt and hesitation; and when at last he fixes his judgement, the evidence exceeds not what we properly call *probability*. All probability, then, supposes an opposition of experiments and observations, where the one side is found to overbalance the other, and to produce a degree of evidence, proportioned to the superiority. A hundred instances or experiments on one side, and fifty on another, afford a doubtful expectation of any event; though a hundred uniform experiments, with only one that is contradictory, reasonably beget a pretty strong degree of assurance. In all cases, we must balance the opposite experiments, where they are opposite, and deduct the smaller number from the greater, in order to know the exact force of the superior evidence.

To apply these principles to a particular instance; we may observe, that there is no species of reasoning more common, more useful, and even necessary to human life, than that which is derived from the testimony of men, and the reports of eye-witnesses and spectators. This species of reasoning, perhaps, one may deny to be founded on the relation of cause and effect. I shall not dispute about a word. It will be sufficient to observe that our assurance in any argument of this kind is derived from no other principle than our observation of the veracity of human testimony, and of the usual conformity of facts to the reports of witnesses. It being a general maxim, that no objects have any discoverable connexion together, and that all the inferences, which we can draw from one to another, are founded merely on our expe-

rience of their constant and regular conjunction; it is evident, that we ought not to make an exception to this maxim in favour of human testimony, whose connexion with any event seems, in itself, as little necessary as any other. Were not the memory tenacious to a certain degree; had not men commonly an inclination to truth and a principle of probity; were they not sensible to shame, when detected in a falsehood: Were not these, I say, discovered by *experience* to be qualities, inherent in human nature, we should never repose the least confidence in human testimony. A man delirious, or noted for falsehood and villany, has no manner of authority with us.

And as the evidence, derived from witnesses and human testimony, is founded on past experience, so it varies with the experience, and is regarded either as a *proof* or a *probability*, according at the conjunction between any particular kind of report and any kind of object has been found to be constant or variable. There are a number of circumstances to be taken into consideration in all judgements of this kind; and the ultimate standard, by which we determine all disputes, that may arise concerning them, is always derived from experience and observation. Where this experience is not entirely uniform on any side, it is attended with an unavoidable contrariety in our judgements, and with the same opposition and mutual destruction of argument as in every other kind of evidence. We frequently hesitate concerning the reports of others. We balance the opposite circumstances, which cause any doubt or uncertainty; and when we discover a superiority on any side, we incline to it; but still with a diminution of assurance, in proportion to the force of its antagonist.

This contrariety of evidence, in the present case, may be derived from several different causes; from the opposition of contrary testimony; from the character or number of the witnesses; from the manner of their delivering their testimony; or from the union of all these circumstances. We entertain a suspicion concerning any matter of fact, when the witnesses contradict each other; when they are but few, or of a doubtful character; when they have an interest in what they affirm;

when they deliver their testimony with hesitation, or on the contrary, with too violent asseverations. There are many other particulars of the same kind, which may diminish or destroy the force of any argument, derived from human testimony.

Suppose, for instance, that the fact, which the testimony endeavors to establish, partakes of the extraordinary and the marvellous; in that case, the evidence, resulting from the testimony, admits of a diminution, greater or less, in proportion as the fact is more or less unusual. The reason why we place any credit in witnesses and historians, is not derived from any *connexion,* which we perceive *a priori,* between testimony and reality, but because we are accustomed to find a conformity between them. But when the fact attested is such a one as has seldom fallen under our observation, here is a contest of two opposite experiences; of which the one destroys the other, as far as its force goes, and the superior can only operate on the mind by the force, which remains. The very same principle of experience, which gives us a certain degree of assurance in the testimony of witnesses, gives us also, in this case, another degree of assurance against the fact, which they endeavour to establish; from which contradition there necessarily arises a counterpoize, and mutual destruction of belief and authority.

I should not believe such story were it told me by Cato, was a proverbial saying in Rome, even during the lifetime of that philosophical patriot. The incredibility of a fact, it was allowed, might invalidate so great an authority.

The Indian prince, who refused to believe the first relations concerning the effects of frost, reasoned justly; and it naturally required very strong testimony to engage his assent to facts, that arose from a state of nature, with which he was unacquainted, and which bore so little analogy to those events, of which he had had constant and uniform experience. Though they were not contrary to his experience, they were not conformable to it.

But in order to encrease the probability against the testimony of witnesses, let us suppose, that the fact, which they affirm, instead of being only marvellous, is really miraculous; and suppose also, that the testimony considered apart and in itself, amounts to an entire proof; in that case, there is proof against proof, of which the strongest must prevail, but still with a diminution of its force, in proportion to that of its antagonist.

A miracle is a violation of the laws of nature; and as a firm and unalterable experience has established these laws, the proof against a miracle, from the very nature of the fact, is as entire as any argument from experience can possibly be imagined. Why is it more than probable, that all men must die; that lead cannot, of itself, remain suspended in the air; that fire consumes wood, and is extinguished by water; unless it be, that these events are found agreeable to the laws of nature, and there is required a violation of these laws, or in other words, a miracle to prevent them? Nothing is esteemed a miracle, if it ever happen in the common course of nature. It is no miracle that a man, seemingly in good health, should die on a sudden: because such a kind of death, though more unusual than any other, has yet been frequently observed to happen. But it is a miracle, that a dead man should come to life; because that has never been observed in any age or country. There must, therefore, be a uniform experience against every miraculous event, otherwise the event would not merit that appellation. And as a uniform experience amounts to a proof, there is here a direct and full *proof,* from the nature of the fact, against the existence of any miracle; nor can such a proof be destroyed, or the miracle rendered credible, but by an opposite proof, which is superior.

The plain consequence is (and it is a general maxim worthy of our attention), "That no testimony is sufficient to establish a miracle, unless the testimony be of such a kind, that its falsehood would be more miraculous, than the fact, which it endeavours to establish; and even in that case there is a mutual destruction of arguments, and the superior only gives us an assurance suitable to that degree of force, which remains, after deducting the inferior." When anyone tells me, that he saw a dead man restored to life, I immediately consider with myself, whether it be more probable, that this person should either deceive or be deceived, or that the fact, which he relates, should really have happened. I weigh the one miracle against the other; and according to the superiority, which I discover, I pronounce my decision, and always reject the greater miracle. If the falsehood of his testimony would be more miraculous, than the event which he relates; then, and not till then, can he pretend to command my belief or opinion.

Part II.

In the foregoing reasoning we have supposed, that the testimony, upon which a miracle is founded, may possibly amount to an entire proof, and that the falsehood of that testimony would be a real prodigy: But it is easy to shew, that we have been a great deal too liberal in our concession, and that there never was a miraculous event established on so full an evidence.

For *first,* there is not to be found, in all history, any miracle attested by a sufficient number of men, of such unquestioned good-sense, education, and learning, as to secure us against all delusion in themselves; of such undoubted integrity, as to place them beyond all suspicion of any design to deceive others; of such credit and reputation in the eyes of mankind, as to have a great deal to lose in case of their being detected in any falsehood; and at the same time, attesting facts performed in such a public manner and in so celebrated a part of the world, as to render the detection unavoidable: All which circumstances are requisite to give us a full assurance in the testimony of men.

Secondly. We may observe in human nature a principle which, if strictly examined, will be found to diminish extremely the assurance, which we might, from human testimony, have, in any kind of prodigy. The maxim, by which we commonly conduct ourselves in our reasonings, is, that the objects, of which we have no experience, resemble those, of which we have; that what we have found to be most usual is always most probable; and that where there is an opposition of arguments, we ought to give the preference to such as are founded on the greatest number of past observations. But though, in proceeding by this rule, we readily reject any fact which is unusual and incredible in an ordinary degree; yet in advancing farther, the mind observes not always the same rule; but when anything is affirmed utterly absurd and miraculous, it rather the more readily admits of such a fact, upon account of that very circumstance, which ought to destroy all its authority. The passion of *surprise* and *wonder,* arising from miracles, being an agreeable emotion, gives a sensible tendency towards the belief of those events, from which it is derived. And this goes so far, that even those who cannot enjoy this pleasure immediately, nor can believe those miraculous events, of which they are informed, yet love to partake of the satisfaction at secondhand or by rebound, and place a pride and delight in exciting the admiration of others.

With what greediness are the miraculous accounts of travellers received, their descriptions of sea and land monsters, their relations of wonderful adventures, strange men, and uncouth manners? But if the spirit of religion join itself to the love of wonder, there is an end of common sense; and human testimony, in these circumstances, loses all pretensions to authority. A religionist may be an enthusiast, and imagine he sees what has no reality: he may know his narrative to be false, and yet persevere in it, with the best intentions in the world, for the sake of promoting so holy a cause: or even where this delusion has not place, vanity, excited by so strong a temptation, operates on him more powerfully than on the rest of mankind in any other circumstances; and self-interest with equal force. His auditors may not have, and commonly have not, sufficient judgement to canvass his evidence: what judgement they have, they renounce by principle, in these sublime and mysterious subjects: or if they were ever so willing to employ it, passion and a heated imagination disturb the regularity of its operations. Their credulity increases his impudence: and his impudence overpowers their credulity.

Eloquence, when at its highest pitch, leaves little room for reason or reflection; but addressing itself entirely to the fancy or the affections, captivates the willing hearers, and subdues their understanding. Happily, this pitch it seldom attains.

But what a Tully or a Demosthenes could scarcely effect over a Roman or Athenian audience, every *Capuchin,* every itinerant or stationary teacher can perform over the generality of mankind, and in a higher degree, by touching such gross and vulgar passions.

The many instances of forged miracles, and prophecies, and supernatural events, which, in all ages, have either been detected by contrary evidence, or which detect themselves by their absurdity, prove sufficiently the strong propensity of mankind to the extraordinary and the marvellous, and ought reasonably to beget a suspicion against all relations of this kind. This is our natural way of thinking, even with regard to the most common and most credible events. For instance: There is no kind of report which rises so easily, and spreads so quickly, especially in country places and provincial towns, as those concerning marriages; insomuch that two young persons of equal condition never see each other twice, but the whole neighborhood immediately join them together. The pleasure of telling a piece of news so interesting, of propagating it, and of being the first reporters of it, spreads the intelligence. And this is so well known, that no man of sense gives attention to these reports, till he find them confirmed by some greater evidence. Do not the same passions, and others still stronger, incline the generality of mankind to believe and report, with the greatest vehemence and assurance, all religious miracles?

Thirdly. It forms a strong presumption against all supernatural and miraculous relations, that they are observed chiefly to abound among ignorant and barbarous nations; or if a civilized people has ever given admission to any of them, that people will be found to have received them from ignorant and barbarous ancestors, who transmitted them with that inviolable sanction and authority, which always attend received opinions. When we peruse the first histories of all nations, we are apt to imagine ourselves transported into some new world; where the whole frame of nature is disjointed, and every element performs its operations in a different manner, from what it does at present. Battles, revolutions, pestilence, famine and death, are never the effect of those natural causes, which we experience. Prodigies, omens, oracles, judgements, quite obscure the few natural events, that are intermingled with them. But as the former grow thinner every page, in proportion as we advance nearer the enlightened ages, we soon learn, that there is nothing mysterious or supernatural in the case, but that all proceeds from the usual propensity of mankind towards the marvellous, and that, though this inclination may at intervals receive a check from sense and learning, it can never be thoroughly extirpated from human nature.

It is strange, a judicious reader is apt to say, upon the perusal of these wonderful historians, *that such prodigious events never happen in our days.* But it is nothing strange, I hope, that men should lie in all ages. You must surely have seen instances enough of that frailty. You have yourself heard many such marvellous relations started, which, being treated with scorn by all the wise and judicious, have at least been abandoned even by the vulgar. Be assured, that those renowned lies, which have spread and flourished to such a monstrous height, arose from like beginnings; but being sown in a more proper soil, shot up at last into prodigies almost equal to those which they relate. . . .

I may add as a *fourth* reason, which diminishes the authority of prodigies, that there is no testimony for any, even those which have not been expressly detected, that is not opposed by an infinite number of witnesses; so that not only the miracle destroys the credit of testimony, but the testimony destroys itself. To make this the better understood, let us consider, that, in matters of religion, whatever is different is contrary; and that it is impossible the religions of ancient Rome, of Turkey, of Siam, and of China should, all of them, be established on any solid foundation. Every miracle, therefore, pretended to have been wrought in any of these religions (and all of them abound in miracles), as its direct scope is to establish the particular system to which it is attributed; so has it the same force, though more indirectly, to overthrow every other system. In destroying a rival system, it likewise destroys the credit of those miracles, on which that system was established; so that all the prodigies of different religions are to be regarded as contrary facts, and the evidences of these prodigies, whether weak or strong, as opposite to each other. According to this method of reasoning, when we believe any miracle of Mahomet or his successors, we have for our warrant the testimony of a few barbarous Arabians: And on the other hand, we are to regard the authority of Titus Livius, Plutarch, Tacitus, and, in short, of all the authors and witnesses, Grecian, Chinese, and Roman Catholic, who have related any miracle in their particular religion; I say, we are to regard their testimony in the same light as if they had mentioned that Mahometan miracle, and had in express terms contradicted it, with the same certainty as they have for the miracle they relate. This argument may appear over subtle and refined; but is not in reality different from the reasoning of a judge, who supposes, that the credit of two witnesses, maintaining a crime against any one, is destroyed by the testimony of two others, who affirm him to have been two hundred leagues distant, at the same instant when the crime is said to have been committed. . . .

10.6 Miracles

Many philosophers have assumed that Hume's arguments (see Reading 10.5) put to rest, once and for all, the use of miracles in Christian apologetics (defense of the faith). Gone are the days when some Christians can use miracles against other Christians and against other religions in the attempt to support the superiority of their own version of things. We now know much more about nontheistic traditions, and to define a miracle as an act of God is to rule out, by definition alone, events that nontheists might point to as confirmations of their views. For example, yogis in India often claim to have achieved certain powers, called *siddhis,* by yogic practice. These may range from the well-documented control of blood pressure, heart rate, and pain to claims about levitation, remembering past lives, and omniscience. Are these miracles or what some today call psychic phenomena? In any case, they are often used as evidence that the practice of yoga can produce extraordinary abilities. However, most yogis emphasis that the main goal of the practice of yoga is spiritual enlightenment, not *siddhis.* The debate on miracles is a good example of how philosophy of religion can at times be the philosophy of theism masquerading as something much broader. Any attempt to revive the case that miracles prove the truth of Christianity must take the claims of other religions into account.

In addition, the claims of science, or at least our present understanding of natural law, must be taken into account. Philosophical analysis of the concept of a natural law has become more sophisticated since Hume's day. However, the question remains whether the notion of a *violation* of natural law makes any sense. We can violate social laws. Speeding tickets prove that. But social laws are not natural laws, and we must be very cautious about drawing analogies between them.

Is it any longer possible to accept Hume's definition of a miracle as an event that violates the laws of nature and is caused by God? To add the "caused by God" part is to rule inadmissible the very possibility of miracle claims playing any significant role in nontheistic religions or to proclaim chauvinistically that even if such religions do not believe God caused their miracles, he did so nonetheless. To Hume's credit, he allowed for a broader notion by saying cause by "the Deity or by the interposition of some invisible agent." Gods many be one thing, invisible agents quite another.

In the following selection, Richard Swinburne, Nolloth Professor of Philosophy of the Christian Religions at the University of Oxford, discusses what he takes to be the key issues in the present debate about miracles. Definition is one of them. How we define the term will largely set the agenda for asking and answering other questions. But is a coherent definition possible? Swinburne thinks so. If so, then we can move on to other issues.

The ideas that Swinburne explores here are part of his introduction to a volume of readings on miracles. Hence he refers briefly to the writings of others included in the volume and alludes to his own arguments that are developed at length elsewhere. One such allusion occurs in conjunction with his discussion of Antony Flew's claim that no historical evidence could ever outweigh the scientific evidence. Swinburne thinks Flew is just plain wrong about this, because the claim that some formula expresses a law of nature and the claim that some historical event occurred for certain reasons are similar in kind. If similar in kind, then they are strong or weak claims for the same reasons. For example, formulas are sometimes shown to express a law of nature because they provide the most coherent and the simplest explanation of many apparently different events. In the same way, formulations of historical theories about events are accepted because they provide the most coherent and the simplest account.

Whether you find this a convincing argument may have something to do with your views about the nature of physical science and about social sciences like history. Whether you find something a miracle may have something to do with what Swinburne calls "background evidence." Are you inclined to believe that miracles happen? If you are, then investigating alleged cases of such happenings makes sense. If you are not so inclined, then you may find this discussion irrelevant. As you read Swinburne's analysis, your inclinations should become clear to you, if they are not so already.

Reading Questions

1. How does Swinburne define the term *miracle*?
2. Given his definition, could there be such a thing as a miracle in a nontheistic religious tradition? Why or why not?
3. What are the two major challenges to the coherence of his definition, and how does he respond?
4. Critically reflect on Hume's and Flew's discussion of the possibility of historical evidence existing for the occurrence of miracles. Do you think there could be such evidence? Why or why not?
5. What role does *background evidence* play in the philosophical discussion of miracles?
6. Under what circumstances should reports of miracles in different religions cancel out each other's evidential force?
7. What do you think? Is it *possible* for miracles to happen? And if it is, could we have evidence that confirms our belief that some event is a miracle? Why or why not?

Miracles*

RICHARD SWINBURNE

What Is a Miracle?

Many people understand by a *miracle* (and by words normally so translated into English) an event of an extraordinary kind brought about by a god and of religious significance. But some of the terms in this definition can be interpreted in various ways, which we must now distinguish. Further, *miracle* is sometimes used in a wider or a narrower sense than any of the senses that result from giving a precise meaning to some of the vague terms of this initial definition. These we must clarify.

"An Event of an Extraordinary Kind"

What counts as "of an extraordinary kind" depends on what is one's understanding of what happens ordinarily. Thus, on the view of Aristotle inherited by most medieval thinkers, each object belonged to a kind, and objects of each kind had natures specific to objects of that kind. An object's nature determined how it behaved naturally—that is, when not acted upon by another object. Thus it belonged to the nature of a plant to take in nourishment, grow, and subsequently decay, and its doing these things was natural behavior for it. Other objects, however, in virtue of their natures could make an object do what it would not do naturally (when that behavior of the latter object was its moving, that motion was said to be violent motion). A plant could not by its nature move across the Earth, but a human being could carry it across the Earth, thereby subjecting it to violent motion. A human's nature was such that he or she had the power of producing such motion in the plant. So the occurrences in the world, that is, the changes

of state of objects, were either occurrences that were natural behaviors of the objects concerned or were produced by other objects who by nature had the power to produce such occurrences. On the medieval view in general, objects had no option but to exercise their power in certain circumstances (plants will thrive in a favorable climate, and raindrops cannot but fall from the sky), but some objects (rational agents such as men or women) often have a choice whether or not to exercise their powers.

St. Thomas Aquinas (c. 1225–74) claimed that to be a miracle an event had to be such as to be beyond the natural power of any created thing to produce.... It was in consequence of this understanding of "extraordinary" that Aquinas held that God, as alone uncreated, could alone work miracles. Others, however, and especially Pope Benedict XIV (1675–1758), whose work *De Miraculis* forms a standard statement of Roman Catholic doctrine, more naturally allow that something is a miracle whose production exceeds "the power of visible and corporeal nature only" (1.1.12). Hence, on Benedict's view angels could work miracles. He further held that humans could work miracles if they were for an instant given powers (by an agent able to bestow such powers) beyond their nature.

However, talk about objects having natures in virtue of which they exercise certain powers is talk that belongs to ancient rather than modern science. Since the seventeenth century we have come to think of the behavior of things as governed not by their nature or by other objects in virtue of their nature but by laws of nature, or natural laws, which declare which events must or must probably follow other events. (This new way of talking is not one forced on people by any new scientific discovery, but is simply a different and

---

* *Miracles* by Swinburne, Richard, © 1989. Reprinted by permission of Prentice-Hall, Inc., Upper Saddle River, NJ.

sometimes more convenient way of setting forth our knowledge of the behavior of things.)

Natural laws may be universal or statistical in form. Universal laws are of the form "so-and-sos necessarily do (or are) such-and-such"; statistical laws are of the form "so-and-sos do (or are) such-and-such with such-and-such probability." Universal laws state what must happen; statistical laws state what has a certain in-built probability (in the sense of propensity) of happening in a particular case. Paradigm examples of universal laws are Newton's three laws of motion and his law of gravitation, which together state how bodies of different masses having certain initial arrangements and velocities subsequently have certain other arrangements and velocities. Since the eighteenth century many people, especially scientists, have believed that natural laws governed all events of all kinds. From the eighteenth to the beginning of the twentieth century most people believed that all natural laws were universal, so that the preceding state of the universe invariably determined in all its detail what its subsequent state was to be. This view may be called physical determinism. Yet since the development of quantum theory in this century, many scientists have come to hold that the fundamental natural laws are statistical. These are the laws governing the behavior of the fundamental particles, such as photons, electrons, and mesons, out of which the ordinary familiar objects that surround us are composed. It is a consequence of such laws, for example, that all photons approaching a potential barrier of a certain kind have a certain probability of passing through it and a certain probability of being reflected. There is no necessity about what an individual photon will do. However, although the probability of some small-scale event is often not especially close to one or zero, probabilities on the small scale often produce near-necessities on the large scale. So although one is far from certain what an individual fundamental particle will do, idiosyncrasies cancel out, and one can be pretty near certain to within a minute margin of error what a large number of such particles will do—which is why the behavior of ordinary size objects is in general so consistent (just as it fol-lows that if it is equally probable that a coin will fall heads or tails on any one occasion, then in a million throws very nearly half of the throws will be heads and very nearly half will be tails).

Given talk of natural laws, an event that goes against them or "violates" them would seem to be an event "of an extraordinary kind." (This notion of "violation" is examined in more detail later on.) If the laws are universal, such an event would be one whose nonoccurrence is predicted by the laws. If the laws are statistical, an event whose occurrence the laws rendered as highly improbable would seem to be an event of "an extraordinary kind." These seem to be the most natural modern equivalents of an event whose production exceeds the power of visible and corporeal nature. Many have certainly understood an event of this kind to be well on the way to being a miracle.

It is possible, of course, that people may think that L is a law of nature when it is not, and so may wrongly suppose that an event that violates L is a violation of a law of nature. Putting the matter in Aquinas's terminology of the powers of objects, he comments that the ignorant may not realize that it is within the natural power of a magnet to attract iron (102.1). And because of the progress of science, even the scientifically educated of a period in history may think that some apparent regularity is a law of nature when really it is not, and so they would suppose that some event E violates natural laws when it does not. Because of the difficulty sometimes involved in discerning whether an event is a violation of a law of nature, some have thought that what matters is whether an event seemed to those involved to be such a violation, not whether it really was. The fact that it appears thus, given perhaps that other conditions are also fulfilled, makes an event a miracle. Yet although the term is occasionally used in such a subjective sense, I do not think that this use is in fact at all common. For if something previously believed to be a violation of natural laws and for that reason a miracle is shown in fact to be in accord with natural laws, we are apt to say that it was not a miracle after all, not that it is now no longer a miracle.

However, there are other events that occur in perfect accord with natural laws, and yet are so "extraordinary" that many might consider them candidates for being miracles. These are extraordinary coincidences. Even given determinism, what happens is not solely a function of which laws operate. Laws state the subsequent effect of certain initial conditions, and what happens is a function as much of the initial conditions as of the laws. The state of the world today, given determinism, is a consequence of its state yesterday, and its state yesterday a consequence of its state the day before, and so on. (If there was an initial moment of the universe, then its subsequent state is, given the laws, a consequence of its initial state.) Now in any period of history, events of certain kinds are very frequent and events of other kinds very rare, and which are frequent and which are rare are, for any given set of natural laws, a consequence of a past state of the universe (which will not itself have been determined solely by the laws, but by yet earlier states, if such there were). Whereas the laws alone determine which event succeeds which, their coincidence (which event happens at the same time as which other event) depend also on initial states. Some coincidences will be normal, some abnormal or extraordinary. Some philosophers and theologians have wanted to allow the extraordinary coincidence as an event of an extraordinary kind, which was a candidate for being a miracle, and ordinary talk would seem to allow this usage. . . .

"An Event Brought About by a God"

The second condition stated in my original definition was that to be a miracle an event must be brought about by a god. I understand by a god a nonembodied rational agent of great power. By a rational agent I mean someone who has beliefs and acts intentionally (that is, for reasons). By saying the agent is "nonembodied" I mean that (except perhaps temporarily and by their own choice) the agent has no body; that is, there is no one material object through which alone the agent can act on the world and acquire justified beliefs about it. By the agent being of great power

I mean that he or she can produce effects far beyond the normal powers of humans.

This second condition may be made more tight or more loose. On a tighter definition an event would be a miracle only if brought about by God, not by any god. By God I mean the God of the Christians, Jews, and Moslems. (Since the defining properties by which Christians, Jews, and Moslems pick out the object of their worship are very similar—omnipotence, omniscience, perfect goodness, and so on—it is natural to say that Christians, Jews, and Moslems worship the same God. They do, of course, differ in their beliefs about what other properties that God has: Christians, unlike Moslems, for instance, believe that he is three "persons" in one "substance," and that he redeemed the world through Christ.) By Aquinas's definition of "miracle," only God can work miracles.

The second condition can be made looser by allowing any agent, not necessarily a god, to work miracles. It does not seem obviously self-contradictory to suppose that some embodied rational agent such as a human being worked a miracle. Benedict allowed that a human could work a miracle if temporarily given superhuman power.

"An Event of Religious Significance"

The third requirement in my definition for an event being a miracle is that it should have religious significance. If a god intervened in the natural order to make a feather land here rather than there for no deep ultimate purpose, or to upset a child's box of toys just for spite, these events would not naturally be described as miracles. To be a miracle an event must contribute significantly toward a holy divine purpose for the world.

On a wide understanding of religious significance, an event will have religious significance if it is a good event and a contribution to or foretaste of the ultimate destiny of the world. Thus the healing of a sick person will, by the Christian view, be of religious significance, since the world's ultimate destiny is, according to the Christian view, a state where evil, including sickness, is no more. But narrower views of religious significance are possible. For Benedict XIV, it is required of miracles "that they serve to confirm The Catholic Faith, or to demonstrate the sanctity of some man" (1.4.6). One way in which an extraordinary event could "confirm" a doctrine would be if it occurred in answer to prayer asking for confirmation of the doctrine as, if it occurred, did Elijah's purported miracle on Mount Carmel (1 Kings 18).

Elijah challenged the prophets of Baal: "Call ye on the name of your god, and I will call on the name of the Lord: and the god that answereth by fire let him be God." The prayer of the prophets of Baal got no response, but in answer to Elijah's prayer "the fire of the Lord fell, and consumed the burnt offering, and the wood, and the stones, and the dust," soaked in water, "and licked up the water that was in the trench." Another way in which an extraordinary event could confirm a doctrine could be by symbolizing it. If Jesus fed the five thousand in the wilderness with the five loaves and two fishes (see John 6:1–14), he was repeating on a larger scale an event believed to have been performed by Elisha (2 Kings 4:42 ff.), and thus, by the Jewish understanding, symbolizing his being a new and greater Elisha.

So then, religious significance can be understood in a wider or narrower sense. But in order to be a miracle, an event must surely have religious significance in some sense. Extraordinary events lacking religious significance are more appropriately characterized as magical or psychic phenomena rather than as miracles. It is for this reason that many ancient writers on miracles have written that a miracle is not an event contrary to nature but an event beyond nature. The point of this remark is that whereas an event that is a miracle is not in accordance with the nature of the objects involved in it, it is nevertheless in accordance with the divinely ordained natural order as a whole. It is indeed, Aquinas would argue, contrary to the nature of the sea that it "open up and offer a way through which people may pass," but its doing so at the time of the Israelite exodus from Egypt was part of the divine plan for the human race, and so in a sense it was very much a natural event. Miracles are events with a point in the overall scheme of things, and so in a sense are very much regular.

For a few modern writers any event of great religious significance is, as such, a miracle. It is not necessary for them that it be an event of an extraordinary kind brought about by a god or a human using abnormal powers (in the senses earlier described). A definition of this kind is offered by the Protestant theologian Paul Tillich (1886–1965). But although one may have good reason for recommending that *miracle* be used in this sense in the future, it is important to note that it is not the traditional sense; and if used in this new sense, *miracle* would take over a job often done previously by the word *sign* (or words so translated into English). When Ezekiel joined two sticks (Ezekiel 37:15–28) to show that God would unite into one people the tribes of Israel and Judah, there was nothing above nature in his physical movements, although his action had great religious significance. By a Tillichian definition, Ezekiel would have done a miracle, but it seems more natural to say that he performed a sign, although there was nothing miraculous in what he did.

As well as being used in the ways described above, the word *miracle* is sometimes used by people who do not wish to make any religious point. "It was a miracle" may sometimes mean simply that the event was highly unexpected and highly desirable. This use of *miracle* seems very much a derivative one, and is of no interest for the philosophy of religion.

By our initial definition, a miracle is an event of an extraordinary kind, brought about by a god, and of religious significance. We have seen how these conditions in our definition may be understood in narrower or wider ways, and how one or more of these conditions may be dropped, so that different senses of *miracle* result. The concepts of "extraordinary coincidence" or "religious significance" do not seem to raise any philosophical problems peculiar to the topic of miracles. The notion of a coincidence is perfectly comprehensible, and, given a religious system established on good grounds, the concept of religious significance seems perfectly comprehensible and applicable. (To examine the grounds for postulating such a system would be to go beyond the narrow confines set for this book, but some readings on this topic are listed in the Bibliography.) The main philosophical problems arise with the other concepts to which we have referred.

For the rest of this introduction, I shall understand a miracle in the sense of a *violation of a law of nature by a god*. I say this because all the philosophical problems peculiar to the topic of miracles arise with this definition, and because when we rightly add that a miracle has to be "of religious significance," we do get what is, I think, the most common understanding of this notion in the major religions over the past two millennia. In particular, Christians have generally claimed that from time to time God brings about miracles in this sense, and that evidence of violations in circumstances where God might be expected to bring them about is evidence (among other evidence) that God exists. The importance for Christian apologetic of the occurrence of miracles in this way made the Scottish philosopher David Hume (1711–76) understand *miracle* in just such a sense. Hume wrote that "a miracle may be accurately defined, as a transgression of a law of nature by a particular volition of the Deity, or by the interposition of some invisible agent" (p. 28, n. 3).

As we shall see, Hume argued that it is most unlikely that there can be good evidence for the occurrence of miracles in this sense.

The Coherence of the Definition

Recent philosophical writing has produced two separate challenges to the coherence of this definition of a miracle—as a violation of a law of nature by a god—suggesting that it contains some internal inconsistency, so that there could not possibly be such a thing as a miracle. The first challenge states that the notion of a "violation" of a law of nature (at any rate of a universal law) is incoherent. For a purported universal law of nature allegedly states what necessarily (and so always) happens, and if there was exception to a

purported law, it would not really be a law at all. Discovering a body that levitated (rose upward despite being made of matter that normally in that environment fell downward) would show that the "law" of gravity was not a law, and so it had not been violated. (This argument does not show that there cannot be a "violation" of a statistical law, for statistical laws do allow occasional improbable events to occur.) Alastair McKinnon presents this objection very forcefully. The notion of a "violation" requires careful definition to avoid such an objection. I try to meet this objection by understanding a "violation" of a law of nature as a "nonrepeatable counterinstance" to it, i.e., an exception that would not be repeated under similar circumstances. . . . If the levitation would not automatically occur again under similar circumstances, it would violate the law of gravity, without showing that it is not a law—on my suggested understanding of the "necessity" of a law of nature. This gives us a coherent and applicable sense of *miracle*.

The second challenge to the coherence of our definition arises from the consideration that to say that a miracle was (among other things) an event caused by a god is to say that it has a cause. In citing its cause, we explain its occurrence. But, the objection goes, explaining anything at all consists of showing that its occurrence was in accordance with some law of nature. So whatever can be explained is no violation of a law; and there cannot be such a thing as a caused violation. Patrick Nowell-Smith argued against an opponent on these lines:

> Let him consider the meaning of the word "explanation" and let him ask himself whether this notion does not involve that of a law or hypothesis capable of predictive expansion. And then let him ask himself whether such an explanation would not be natural, in whatever terms it was couched, and how the notion of "the supernatural" could play any part in it.

The defender of the coherence of our definition must claim that there is a way of explaining events other than the "scientific" way in terms of initial conditions and laws of nature. The defender must say that when we explain the results of intentional actions in terms of the purposes or intentions of agents, their beliefs, and capacities, we are using a quite different pattern of explanation from the scientific. When we explain the motion of my hand by my moving it, seeking to execute a purpose (to wave goodbye), in virtue of a belief (that you would see my hand moving and interpret it as such a wave) and a capacity (to cause the motion of my hand), we do seem to be using a very different pattern of explanation from the scientific, and yet one that really does explain why my hand moved. Whether such a "personal explanation" is quite different from a scientific explanation is, however, a controversial issue in the philosophy of mind. A simple defense is given of the view that personal explanation, and so causality by a personal agent ("agent causality"), is different in kind from the scientific. If it isn't, there could not be a violation of a law of nature, caused by some agent.

Historical Evidence for the Occurrence of Miracles

If our definition of *miracle* survives these challenges to its coherence, the next question is whether there could be good historical evidence that a miracle had occurred. All modern discussion of this matter takes off from the famous Section 10 of Hume's *Enquiry Concerning Human Understanding* (in this volume).

Part 1 of Section 10 is devoted to showing on philosophical grounds that the evidence against the occurrence of any purported miracle is normally likely to be extremely strong and to outweigh by far the evidence in favor of the occurrence. When he is conducting any enquiry, Hume claims, and, in particular, any historical inquiry "a wise man . . . proportions his belief to the evidence" (p. 24). If it be claimed that some particular event *E* happened, an investigator will weigh the evidence in favor of *E* having happened against the evidence that *E* did not happen. The evidence will include memories, the testimony of witnesses, and our experience of what generally happens. Thus a judge or detective will weigh the

evidence of one witness that Jones robbed the safe against the evidence of two witnesses that he was not in the vicinity at the time in question and evidence that Jones had never robbed a safe before. The more unusual the alleged event, the heavier is the evidence against it having happened. This is so because it is a basic principle of reasoning about matters of fact (often called by philosophers inductive reasoning) that the more often an event of a certain type *A* has been followed by an event of some type *B*, the more reason we have for expecting that the next event of type *A* will be followed by an event of type *B*. And the more often an event of type *A* has not been followed by an event of type *B*, the less reason we have to expect that the next one will be. Hence, the more often Jones is known in certain circumstances to have robbed safes, the more reasonable it is to assume that in similar circumstances he robbed another one. The more often rods of a certain constitution have broken when subjected to a certain strain, the more reasonable it is to expect that another one will. The evidence of what usually happens counts heavily against the testimony of witnesses that something abnormal did occur. A fortiori, if we have evidence that on all other known occasions an event of type *A* has been followed by an event of type *B*, then the evidence is very heavy against the claim that on one particular occasion an event of type *A* was not followed by an event of type *B*. Evidence of very many such particular observations establishes those general and apparently invariable correlations that we term laws of nature. Consequently, all such observations count against a claim that there has been one exception to this pattern. And it would take a great deal of evidence on the other side, the testimony of many reliable witnesses, to overcome this weight.

Thus very many astronomical and mechanical data that have been observed are instances of Newton's laws of motion. It is a consequence of Newton's laws that, given the present and past positions of sun and planets, the sun (relative to the Earth) never stays still. Consequently, the innumerable observations that substantiate Newton's laws are counter evidence to the claim in the Book of Joshua that for one day, while the Israelites conquered the Amorites, the sun stayed still (Joshua 10:13).

The question of a violation of a law of nature arises only when we suppose that we have actually got a law of nature. All the evidence that L is a law of nature is evidence against the claim that it was violated on a particular occasion. Because of the vast amount of evidence needed to establish L as a law of nature, it is most unlikely, Hume is in effect arguing, that there will be enough detailed historical evidence to outweigh it and to show that on a particular occasion an event E occurred, which L predicted would not occur. And if there were evidence to show that L did not operate on more than one occasion, that will suggest that L is not a law of nature at all.

Hume's argument is a powerful one; there is a useful modern commentary and development of it in a selection from J.L. Mackie. Whether we accept it depends on the principles for weighing the evidence of what normally happens (itself established by historical evidence) against historical evidence of what did happen on a particular occasion. Historical evidence may include one's own apparent memories, the testimony of many witnesses, and traces. One may apparently remember having seen E occur. More usually, a number of witnesses may report having seen E occur. And sometimes there may be traces, that is, the physical effects that would have been caused by E if E did, in fact, occur. Thus there may be a photograph of what happened, or footprints and fingerprints may corroborate testimony. Hume's official position is that, although historical evidence could outweigh the evidence of what normally happens to produce a balance of evidence in favor of the occurrence of a miracle, this is most unlikely. The only kind of historical evidence that Hume considered was testimony, and he claimed that "no testimony is sufficient to establish a miracle, unless the testimony be of such a kind that its falsehood would be more miraculous" (i.e., more improbable) "than the fact, which it endeavours to establish, and even in that case there is a mutual destruction of arguments, and the superior only gives us

an assurance suitable to that degree of force, which remains, after deducting the inferior." But although this is his official position, it seems that when Hume, in Part II of Section 10, comes to consider some particular cases, his standards are so high that no historical evidence could ever outweigh the evidence of what normally happens, to establish the occurrence of a miracle.

Discussion of Hume's argument is unfortunately complicated by an aspect of it that I have so far not brought up. For reasons arising from other parts of his philosophy (see his *Enquiry Concerning Human Understanding,* Sections 4, 5, and 7), Hume regarded laws of nature merely as true statements about what always happens, not as statements about what happens with physical "necessity" or probability. But there is a difference between what always happens and what necessarily happens—it may be a mere coincidence that all A's are B, rather than it being a necessity in nature that A's have to be B. But the more evidence we have that some regularity (e.g., A's being B) holds in very many diverse circumstances, that is evidence that it is a law of nature that A's are B, that being A causes something to be B, and so evidence that that regularity will operate in any other circumstances. Antony Flew argues that Hume's failure to recognize this distinction makes his argument less compelling than it should be, and that taking account of the distinction shows us that no historical evidence of what happened on one occasion could ever outweigh the scientific evidence from a well-established law of nature as to what must have happened on that occasion. I discuss the principles for weighing conflicting evidence and dispute this conclusion of Flew.

The calculus of probability is a valuable tool for analyzing weight of evidence. David Owen applies a well-known theorem of that calculus, Bayes' theorem, to bring out very clearly the principles involved in weighing evidence that a law of nature held on some occasion against the testimony of one witness that it did not. He concludes that if the witness is to be believed, "the reliability of the witness must be greater than the probability that the law of nature holds." He then asks, not unreasonably, "what witness is so reliable?" He does not, however, consider in detail the difference made if there are a number of independent witnesses whose testimony agrees, nor does he consider kinds of historical evidence other than testimony.

Background Evidence From an Overall World View

Laws of nature determine what necessarily happens (or happens with high physical probability): If some law fails to operate on some isolated occasion (i.e., there is a nonrepeatable counterinstance to it), that can only be because its operation has been suspended. But if there is no God or gods, laws of nature are the ultimate determinants of what happens, and the sudden failure of a law of nature to operate merely through chance, to allow a nonrepeatable exception to it to occur, is hardly to be expected. The "necessity" involved in natural laws is a physical push that will virtually invariably force things to conform to the law.

Violations are most unlikely to occur unless they are miracles. Any evidence that there is no God would give even stronger reason to believe that on a given occasion there was no violation of natural laws. A very considerable amount of detailed historical evidence would be needed in order to substantiate the conclusion that a violation occurred, in the face of such opposing evidence. (But if there were such evidence, it would show that the laws of nature were not omnideterminant and so would give grounds for believing that there is a God.)

If there is a God, then ex hypothesi, it is God who keeps in operation the laws of nature. They are not the ultimate determinants of what happens. God can suspend their operation, i.e., violate them, and intervene in the natural order if and when he chooses. Any evidence that there is a God, and any grounds for thinking that God would be expected to intervene in the natural order in certain circumstances such as those in which some reported violation *E* occurs, will be evidence that *E* occurred. Less will be needed by way of detailed historical evidence to overcome

the evidence of what normally happens. Background evidence from one's overall world view rightly conditions one's judgment about particular cases. As I have noted, the force of other evidence for and against the existence of God cannot be discussed here; suffice it to have shown its relevance. If there is a God, then by definition he will have the power to intervene in the natural order. But is it at all likely that God will do so? After all, why should he intervene in an order of things that he has himself created presumably exactly as he wished to create it?

Tillich and many others have argued that God would not intervene in his created order, and hence they preferred a definition of *miracle,* which allowed there to be instances of miracles, despite natural laws never being violated. More conservative religious believers have held that God does intervene in his created order from time to time, to respond to human needs or prayers, to which it is good that he should be sensitive as they occur. A violation in such circumstances would be "of religious significance."

Two kinds of circumstances in particular have seemed to be suited for a divine intervention. God might be expected to intervene to put his seal on the testimony of some particular prophet, to confirm a doctrine in other words. If a violation occurs, which some prophet predicts that God will bring about and which forwards the recognition of his doctrine, that would put God's seal on that doctrine. For God alone can bring about a violation of natural laws. If he does so, as predicted by a prophet so as to forward the recognition of that prophet's doctrine, God is reasonably taken (in the absence of counterevidence) to be giving his blessing to that doctrine and so declaring it true. Unless God is to violate natural laws, how can humans know whether some doctrine is true except by the natural light of their own reason, and is that going to be good enough to discover deep metaphysical truths? Christians have normally claimed that the miracles reported in connection with the life and death of Jesus Christ, and above all the reported miracle of his Resurrection, have this function of showing that Christ was God's special messenger and that what he said was true. That background evidence of the existence of God is crucial for the assessment of historical evidence, and that God might be expected to bring about miracles to confirm a revelation such as that of Christ was argued against Hume by William Paley (1743–1805).

Religious believers have also held that God might be expected to intervene in the natural order in answer to petitionary prayer. If God is to take humans seriously, he must interact with them and that involves changing things in the world in response to their requests. Eleonore Stump argues this . . . . But if petitionary prayer is something to which God responds by interfering in nature, does not this imply that miracles would have to occur rather more frequently than there is any evidence to suppose that they do? . . .

Do Miracles Occur?

This volume is concerned with how arguments for or against the occurrence of a particular miracle ought to go. But in order to bring the discussion down to earth a bit, it does contain one passage that claims that there is good evidence from history to suppose that miracles do occur and another that claims that there is good reason to suppose that they do not.

The first passage is the defense by Richard Purtill of the plausibility of Christian claims for the occurrences of the miracles reported in the New Testament. The other passage is Part II of Hume's Section 10, where he produces four arguments designed to show that "there never was a miraculous event established" in the way that he argued in Part I would be needed to show the occurrence of a miracle. Hume claims that "there is not to be found, in all history, any miracle attested by a sufficient number of men, of such unquestioned good sense, education, and learning, as to secure us against all delusion in themselves" (p. 29). Secondly, he observes that people in general love to gossip about the marvelous and surprising, and that religious people do not hesitate to tell falsehoods to propagate what they believe to be basically true. Thirdly, Hume also claims that "it forms a strong presumption against all

supernatural and miraculous relations, that they are observed chiefly to abound among ignorant and barbarous nations" (p. 31).

These three points are purported factual claims and no one would dispute that in so far as they are correct, they tend to diminish the worth of tales of miracles. Whether they are correct is an issue beyond the main focus of this book, but it is important to note that whether they are correct or not depends, sometimes crucially, on how Hume's terms are to be understood, e.g., what is to count as "sufficient" men, "unquestioned" good sense, and an "ignorant and barbarous nation"? Nations ignorant and barbarous in some respects are often very cultured, learned, and morally sensitive in other respects.

Hume's fourth argument in Part II is an important one. He points out that miracles are reported in the context of many different religious systems, and he then goes on to claim that a report of a miracle in one such context counts against the occurrence of a miracle in a different context. The argument is that if a miracle of ancient Greco-Roman religion occurred as described, that is evidence that the gods of the Greeks and Romans exist, and if a Christian miracle occurred as described, that is evidence that the God of Christians exists. But if the gods of the Greeks and Romans exist, the God of the Christians does not, and conversely. Therefore the evidence in favor of a Greco-Roman miracle is evidence against the existence of the God of the Christians, and hence evidence against the occurrence of Christian miracles, and conversely. And so, generally, reports of miracles, Hume claims, tend to cancel out each other's evidential force. Whether Hume is right in this claim depends on two empirical considerations. First, it must be that the miracles "wrought in each religion" would be if they occurred, evidence for theological propositions of each religion incompatible with those of the other religion. Some reported miracles are certainly of this kind. The Resurrection of Christ, if it occurred as predicted by Christ, apparently setting a seal on his teaching, does support some detailed doctrine. Some equally striking violation of a natural law in response to a prayer that it happen to prove that Christ was not sent by God would indeed, if it occurred, fit the Humean pattern of conflict. But miracles that would be merely answers to individual prayers for help, rather than confirmations of doctrine, do not seem to fit the Humean pattern. If most alleged miracles occurred as reported, they would show at most the power of a god or gods and their concern for the needs of humans, and little more specific in the way of doctrine, which would weaken the force of Hume's point considerably.

Secondly, it must be the case that those miracles wrought in the context of different religious systems, which do give support to incompatible doctrines, have similar support from historical evidence. It may be claimed, as, for example, by Purtill, that Christian miracles of this type (and above all "the" Christian miracle of the Resurrection) are well authenticated, to an extent in which doctrine-supporting miracles of other religions are not. At that point the argument about miracles must move to details of history. . . .

Suggestions for Further Reading

Banner, Michael C. *The Justification of Science and the Rationality of Religious Belief.* New York: Oxford University Press, 1990.

Barbour, Ian G. *Science and Religion: New Perspectives on the Dialogue.* New York: Harper & Row, 1968.

Basinger, David, and Basinger, Randall. *Philosophy and Miracle: The Contemporary Debate.* Lewiston, NY: Mellen Press, 1986.

Bonansea, Bernardino M. *God and Atheism.* Washington, DC: Catholic Univeristy Press, 1979.

Broad, C. D. "Hume's Theory of the Credibility of Miracles." *Proceedings of the Aristotelian Society* 17 (1916–1917).

Brown, Colin. *Miracles and the Critical Mind.* Grand Rapids, MI: William B. Eerdmans Publishing Company, 1984.

Coulson, Charles Alfred. *Science and the Idea of God.* Cambridge, England: Cambridge University Press, 1958.

Dampier, William Cecil. *A History of Science and Its Relations with Philosophy and Religion.* Cambridge, England: Cambridge University Press, 1948.

Flew, Antony. "Miracles." In *Encyclopedia of Philosophy,* edited by Paul Edwards. New York: Macmillan, 1966.

Geisler, Norman L. *Miracles and Modern Thought.* Grand Rapids, MI: Sondervan, 1982.

Geivett, Douglas, and Habermas, Gary R., eds. *In Defense of Miracles: A Comprehensive Case for God's Action in History.* Downers Grove, IL: InterVarsity Press, 1997.

Holmes, Rolston. *Science and Religion: A Critical Survey.* Philadelphia: Temple University Press, 1987.

Houston, J. *Reported Miracles: A Critique of Hume.* New York: Cambridge University Press, 1994.

Kurtz, Paul. *In Defense of Secular Humanism.* Buffalo, NY: Prometheus Press, 1983.

Lewis, C. S. *Miracles.* New York: Macmillan, 1947.

Marx, Karl. *Selected Essays.* Freeport, NY: Books for Libraries Press, 1968.

———. *The Communist Manifesto.* New York: Norton, 1988.

Miles, T. R. *Religion and the Scientific Outlook.* London: George Allen & Unwin, 1959.

Nielsen, Kai. *Philosophy and Atheism: In Defense of Atheism.* Buffalo, NY: Prometheus Books, 1985.

Peacocke, A. R. *Creation and the World of Science.* New York: Oxford University Press, 1979.

Purtill, R. L. *Thinking About Religion.* Englewood Cliffs, NJ: Prentice-Hall, 1978.

Raines, John C., and Dean, Thomas. *Marxism and Radical Religion: Essays Toward a Revolutionary Humanism.* Philadelphia: Temple University Press, 1970.

Russell, Bertrand. *Atheism: Collected Essays, 1943–1949*. New York: Arno Press and the *New York Times,* 1972.

———. *Why I Am Not a Christian, and Other Essays on Religion and Related Subjects.* Edited by Paul Edwards. New York: Simon and Schuster, 1957.

———. *Religion and Science.* London: Oxford University Press, 1961.

Stein, Gordon. *An Anthology of Atheism and Rationalism.* Buffalo, NY: Prometheus Books, 1980.

Swinburne, Richard. *The Concept of Miracle.* London: Macmillan, 1970.

Zurdeeg, Willem F. *Science and Creationism: A View from the National Academy of Sciences/Commitee on Science and Creationism.* Washington, DC: National Academy Press, 1984.

CHAPTER 11

Are All Religions True?

Introduction

SUPPOSE THERE WERE ONLY one religion in the world. Let's call it the religion of Bliss. Suppose further that most people were Blissians. They participated in its rituals and conducted their lives, for the most part, according to its teachings. There were some dissenters, some anti-Blissians, but very few.

One consequence of this imaginary situation would probably be that the teachings of Bliss would seem true. There would be no real alternatives, no other religions teaching different doctrines or disputing the truth of Bliss. No one would have to worry about what attitude to take toward rival religions. It would not be necessary. Blissians would have a monopoly on religious truth.

We do not live in such a world. Instead we live in a world with diverse religious traditions that have been and are in conflict. We cannot avoid contact with people of other faiths, and the very existence of such religious pluralism calls into question the truth of each. In the diverse religious world in which we live, we must develop some view about how our religion, if we profess one, relates to the others.

One possibility is to claim that only members of our religion will be saved because only our religion teaches the true path to salvation. Truth belongs to us exclusively. Another possibility is to claim that, although other religions teach some truth and although adherents to other religions can be saved, *our* religion teaches the *full* truth. It is the fulfillment of what the others have only dimly glimpsed. This sort of inclusivism seems more charitable than the exclusive attitude, but it is not so charitable as a third possibility often called pluralism. According to pluralism, all religions are valid paths to salvation.

If we adopt a pluralistic attitude, we need some sort of explanation of why the teachings of all these valid religions appear so different and often seem to conflict. One possibility is to argue that the differences are real but that they involve trivial matters. On important issues there is basic agreement. Another possibility is to argue that the differences are not real but merely apparent. On the surface the different religions seem to contradict each other, but when properly understood, they do not. Or one might admit real differences even on important matters but claim this does not affect the salvific value of each of the great traditions.

In addition to the attitudes of exclusivism, inclusivism, and pluralism, one might argue that today religions interpenetrate one another. Religions no longer exist isolated from one another, but in mutual relationship. What others believe and do helps me better understand my own religion.

We live, as it were, in a religious supermarket with competing brand names and products. Suppose we are shopping. How do we decide what to buy? Do we judge all the other religions by the standards of our own religion? Do we judge the other religions by their own standards? Do we develop some neutral set of rational criteria that enable us to judge impartially and fairly the truth claims of each?

Perhaps this whole business of judging the truth of other religions is misguided. Perhaps it simply cannot be done, or even if it could, it would miss the point. Perhaps we should concentrate on cooperation among the various religions on important moral and social issues, such as helping the poor and stopping violence and war.

Maybe the question "Are all religions true?" is misleading. It is certainly ambiguous. Does it mean that the teachings of the various religions are true? Does it mean that the rituals and rites practiced by the various religions are effective? Does it mean that the social organizations of the various religions are conducive to building community? If we restrict its meaning to the teachings alone, does the question mean that before a religion is true, all (every single one) of its teachings (however trivial) must be true? Further, the question seems to presuppose that there is some sort of religious truth that humans are capable of discovering. Perhaps there is no such thing as objective, absolute truth. What we call "truth" is nothing more than human constructions and conventions that reflect cultural values and biases. Perhaps truth is localized and relative to particular historical periods. After all, many different religions and societies have managed to flourish and survive on this planet while responding to the problems of human existence in very different ways. Perhaps what works for each is the only truth there is.

11.1 Four Attitudes

Consider the following cases:

CASE 1. I believe my religion teaches what is true. If what it teaches is true, then opposing views must be false. Hence there is no salvation for anyone apart from my religion.

CASE 2. I believe my religion teaches what is true. Other religions also teach things that agree with my religion, so other religions must contain some truth as well. However, only my religion teaches the full truth that the others only partially realize. Nevertheless, adherents to other religions may attain salvation insofar as they follow implicitly the path explicitly taught in my religion.

CASE 3. I believe my religion teaches what is true. I also believe other religions teach what is true. Therefore, the different religions must be different paths leading to the same goal, just as there are different paths up a mountain leading to the same summit. Each is right; they just constitute different ways of getting to the same end.

CASE 4. I believe all religions are seeking understanding. This search is enriched in a process of interpenetration, integration, and mutual appreciation. No human is a island and it is the same with religion. We come to understand ourselves, by understanding others.

Raimundo Panikkar was born in 1918 in Spain. He lived in India for many years and became a citizen of India. There he became intimately acquainted with the Indian religious traditions, although he eventually became a Roman Catholic priest and a professor of religious studies at the University of California in Santa Barbara. Because of his multicultural background and interests, he has been deeply involved in interreligious dialogues for a number of years, seeking to promote mutual understanding among the world's religions. His experience has taught him that people often enter such dialogues with four distinct attitudes. In the following selection, he characterizes these attitudes.

The first attitude he calls exclusivism; case 1 above reflects that viewpoint. Only my religion provides salvation and truth. Case 2 illustrates the second attitude, which Panikkar labels inclusivism. This attitude is clearly more tolerant and generous than the first, but it still singles out one religion (mine) as the best or highest among all the rest. The third attitude, illustrated by case 3 and labeled parallelism by Panikkar (it is also frequently called pluralism), is more tolerant. It neither restricts truth and salvation to one religion nor insists that one religion is better than all the rest. Case 4 reflects an attitude Pannikkar calls interpenetration. We approach other religions with the conviction that the more we know about and understand other religions, the more our own is enriched.

There are problems with each of these views, and Panikkar describes some of them. There are also other possible views that he does not discuss. For example, imagine a case 5 that maintains that none of the religions is a bearer of truth or salvation. This is a skeptical attitude and is distinct from the other four. However different the other four are, they all ascribe some value to religion. The skeptical attitude may also find some value (such as social utility) in religion, but it finds neither truth nor a means of salvation.

Reading Questions

1. What is exclusivism, and what are its difficulties?
2. What is inclusivism, and what are its difficulties?
3. What is parallelism, and what are its difficulties?
4. What is interpenetration, and what are its difficulties?
5. Does any of these four views reflect your own attitude? Which? Why?

Four Attitudes*

RAIMUNDO PANIKKAR

THE CHAPTERS THAT FOLLOW do not elaborate a theory of the religious encounter. They are part of that very encounter. And it is out of this praxis that I would like to propose the following *attitudes* and *models* for the proper rhetoric in the meeting of religious traditions.

I do not elaborate now on the value of these attitudes or the merits of these models. This would require studying the function and nature of the metaphor as well as developing a theory of the religious encounter. I only describe some attitudes and models, although I will probably betray my sympathies in the form of critical considerations. The dialogue needs an adequate rhetoric—in the classical sense of the word.

1. Four Attitudes

A. EXCLUSIVISM

A believing member of a religion in one way or another considers his religion to be true. Now, the claim to truth has a certain built-in claim to exclusivity. If a given statement is true, its contradictory cannot also be true. And if a certain human tradition claims to offer a universal context for truth, anything contrary to that "universal truth" will have to be declared false.

If, for instance, Islam embodies the true religion, a "non-Islamic truth" cannot exist in the field of religion. Any long standing religious tradition, of course, will have developed the necessary distinctions so as not to appear too blunt. It will say, for instance, that there are degrees of truth and that any "religious truth," if it is really true, "is" already a Muslim one, although the people concerned may not be conscious of it. It will further distinguish an objective order of truth from a subjective one so that a person can be "in good faith" and yet be in objective error, which as such will not be imputed against that person, etc.

This attitude has a certain element of heroism in it. You consecrate your life and dedicate your entire existence to something which is really worthy of being called a human cause, to something that claims to be not just a partial and imperfect truth, but a universal and even absolute truth. To be sure, an absolute God or Value has to be the final guarantee for such an attitude, so that you do not follow it because of personal whims or because you have uncritically raised your point of view to an absolute value. It is God's rights you defend when asserting your religion as "absolute religion." This does not imply an outright condemnation of the beliefs of all other human beings who have not received the "grace" of your calling. You may consider this call a burden and a duty (to carry vicariously the responsibility for the whole world) more than as a privilege and a gift. Who are we to put conditions on the Almighty?

On the other hand, this attitude presents its difficulties. First, it carries with it the obvious danger of intolerance, hybris and contempt for others. "We belong to the club of truth." It further bears the intrinsic weakness of assuming an almost purely logical conception of truth and the uncritical attitude of an epistemological naiveté. Truth is many-faceted and even if you assume that God speaks an exclusive language, everything depends on your understanding of it so that you may never really know whether your interpretation is the *only* right one. To recur to a superhuman instance in the discussion among two religious beliefs does

*A shorter version was first published in *The Intrareligious Dialogue* by R. Panikkar. Copyright © 1978 by Raimundo Panikkar. New York: Paulist Press. This longer version was published by Asian Trading Corporation in 1984. Reprinted by permission.

not solve any question, for it is often the case that God "speaks" also to others, and both partners relying on God's authority will always need the human mediation, so that ultimately God's authority depends on Man's interpretation (of the divine revelation).

As a matter of fact, although there are many *de facto* remnants of an exclusivistic attitude today, it is hardly defended *de jure*. To use the Christian *skandalon*, for instance, to defend Christianity would amount to the very betrayal of that saying about the "stumbling block." It would be the height of hypocrisy to condemn others and justify oneself using the scandal of God's revelation as a rationale for defending one's own attitude: divine revelation ceases to be a scandal for you (for you seem to accept it without scandal)—and you hurl it at others.

B. INCLUSIVISM

In the present world context one can hardly fail to discover positive and true values—even of the highest order—outside of one's own tradition. Traditional religions have to face this challenge. "Splendid isolation" is no longer possible. The most plausible condition for the claim to truth of one's own tradition is to affirm at the same time that it includes at different levels all that there is of truth wherever it exists. The inclusivistic attitude will tend to reinterpret things in such a way as to make them not only palatable but also assimilable. Whenever facing a plain contradiction, for instance, it will make the necessary distinctions between different planes so as to be able to overcome that contradiction. It will tend to become a universalism of an existential or formal nature rather than of essential content. A doctrinal truth can hardly claim universality if it insists too much on specific contents because the grasping of the contents always implies a particular "*forma mentis.*" An attitude of tolerant admission of different planes will, on the contrary, have it easier. An umbrella pattern or a formal structure can easily embrace different thought-systems.

If Vedanta, for example, is really the end and acme of all the Vedas, these latter understood as

the representation of all types of ultimate revelation, it can seemingly affirm that all sincere human affirmations have a place in its scheme because they represent different stages in the development of human consciousness and have a value in the particular context in which they are said. Nothing is rejected and all is fitted into its proper place.

This attitude has a certain quality of magnanimity and grandeur in it. You can follow your own path and do not need to condemn the other. You can even enter into communion with all other ways of life and, if you happen to have the real experience of inclusivity, you may be at peace not only with yourself, but with all other human and divine ways as well. You can be concrete in your allegiances and universal in your outlook.

On the other hand, this attitude also entails some difficulties. First, it also presents the danger of hybris, since it is only you who have the privilege of an all-embracing vision and tolerant attitude, you who allot to the others the place they must take in the universe. You are tolerant in your own eyes, but not in the eyes of those whose challenge your right to be on top. Furthermore it has the intrinsic difficulties of an almost alogical conception of truth and a built-in inner contradiction when the attitude is spelt out in theory and praxis.

If this attitude allows for a variegated expression of "religious truth" so as to be able to include the most disparate systems of thought, it is bound to make of truth a purely relative. Truth here cannot have an independent intellectual content, for it is one thing for the parsi and another for the Vaiṣṇava, one thing for the atheist and another for the theist. So, it is also another thing for you—unless you jump outside the model because it is you who have the clue, you who find a place for all the different world views. But then your belief, conception, ideology, intuition or whatever name we may call it, becomes a supersystem the moment that you formulate it: you seem to understand the lower viewpoints and put them in their right places. You cannot avoid claiming for yourself a superior knowledge even if you deny that your conviction is another viewpoint. If you "say," furthermore, that your position is only the ineffable fruit of a mystical insight, the moment that you put it into practice nothing prevents another from discovering and formulating the implicit assumptions of that attitude. Ultimately you claim to have a fuller truth in comparison with all the others who have only partial and relative truths.

As a matter of fact, although there are still many tendencies in several religious traditions that consider themselves all-inclusive, there are today only very few theoretical and philosophical formulations of a purely inclusivistic attitude. The claim of pluralism today is too strong to be so easily bypassed.

C. PARALLELISM

If your religion appears far from being perfect and yet it represents for you a symbol of the right path and a similar conviction seems to be the case for others, if you cannot dismiss the religious claim of the other nor assimilate it completely into your tradition, a plausible alternative is to assume that all are different creeds which, in spite of meanderings and crossings, actually run parallel to meet only in the ultimate, in the *eschaton,* at the very end of the human pilgrimage. Religions would then be parallel paths and our most urgent duty would be not to interfere with others, not to convert them or even to borrow from them, but to deepen our own respective traditions so that we may meet at the end, and in the depths of our own traditions. Be a better Christian, a better Marxist, a better Hindu and you will find unexpected riches and also points of contact with other people's ways.

This attitude presents very positive advantages. It is tolerant, it respects the others and does not judge them. It avoids muddy syncretisms and eclecticisms that concoct a religion according to our private tastes; it keeps the boundaries clear and spurs constant reform of one's own ways.

On the other hand, it too is not free of difficulties. First of all, it seems to go against the historical experience that the different religious and human traditions of the world have usually emerged from mutual interferences, influences and fertilizations. It too hastily assumes, furthermore, that every human tradition has in itself all the elements for further growth and development; in a word, it assumes the self-sufficiency of every tradition and seems to deny the need or convenience of mutual learning, or the need to walk outside the walls of one particular human tradition—as if in every one of them the entire human experience were crystallized or condensed. It flatters every one of us to hear that we possess *in nuce* all we need for a full human and religious maturity, but it splits the family of Man into watertight compartments, making any kind of conversion a real betrayal of one's own being. It allows growth, but not mutation. Even if we run parallel to each other, are there not *sangams, prayāgs,* affluents, inundations, natural and artificial dams, and above all, does not one and the same water flow "heavenwards" in the veins of the human being? Mere parallelism eschews the real issues.

Notwithstanding, this attitude presents on the other hand more prospects for an initial working hypothesis today. It carries a note of hope and patience at the same time; hope that we will meet at the end and patience that meanwhile we have to bear our differences. Yet when facing concrete problems of interferences, mutual influences and even dialogue one cannot just wait until this *kalpa* comes to an end or the *eschaton* appears. All crossings are dangerous, but there is no new life without *maithuna.*

D. INTERPENETRATION

The more we come to know the religions of the world, the more we are sensitive to the religiousness of our neighbour, all the more we begin to surmise that in every one of us the other is somehow implied, and vice-versa, that the other is not so independent from us and is somehow touched by our own beliefs. We begin to realize that our neighbour's religion does not only challenge and may even enrich our own, but that ultimately, the very differences which separate us are somewhat potentially within the own world of my religious convictions. We begin to accept that the other religion may complement mine and we may even entertain the idea that in some particular cases it may well supplement some of my beliefs provided that my religiousness remains an undivided whole. More and more we have the case of Marxists accepting Christian ideas, Christians subscribing to Hindu tenets, Muslims absorbing Buddhist views, etc. and all the way remaining Marxists, Christians and Muslims. But there is still more than this. It looks as if we were today all intertwined and that without these particular religious links my own religion would be incomprehensible for me and even impossible. Religions are unununderstandable without a certain background of "religion". Our own religiousness is seen within the framework of our neighbor's. Religions do not exist in isolation, but over against each other. There would be no Hindu consciousness were not for the fact of having to distinguish it from Muslims and Christians, for example. In a word, the relation between religions is neither of the type of exclusivism (only mine), or inclusivism (the mine embraces all the others), or parallelism (we are running independently towards the same goal), but one at a *sui generis perichoresis* or *circumincessio*, i.e. of a mutual interpretation without the loss of the proper peculiarities of each religiousness.

The obvious positive aspect of this attitude is the tolerance, broadmindedness and mutual confidence that it inspires. No religion is totally foreign to my own; within our own religion we may encounter the religion of the other; we all need one another; in some way we are saying not just the same but mutually complementing and correcting things. And even when religions struggle for supplementation, they do it within a mutually acknowledged religious frame.

On the other hand, this attitude is also not free from dangers. First of all, one has to ask if this is not a little wishful thinking. Are we so sure of this interpenetration? Do "Karma" and "Providence" interpenetrate or exclude each other? On what grounds can we establish it? Is this attitude not already a modification of the selfunderstanding of the traditions themselves? This could be answered by justifying the role of creative hermeneutics. Each interpretation is a new creation. But can we say that such hermeneutics really exist in all the minutiae of the world religions? Or is it not a kind of new religiousness which makes a selective use of the main tenets of the traditions while neglecting the others? There may be a religious universe but is it sufficiently broad as to allow for insuperable incompatibilities?

But again this attitude may offer perspectives which the others lack. It may put us on a way which is open to all and which nobody should feel reluctant to enter. It can contribute to the spiritual growth of the partners: even interpreting other beliefs as exaggeration or distortions of our own we touch a more fundamental frame of reference, and without losing our identity, we weaken our assertive ego. It can contribute to a mutual enrichment within a synthesis. The values of the other tradition are not merely juxtaposed to those of our tradition but truly assimilated and integrated to our beliefs and in our own being. It is an open process. . . .

11.2 Conflicting Truth Claims

Consider the following statements:

1. Ultimate reality is personal.
2. Ultimate reality is impersonal.
3. After we die we will be reincarnated.
4. After we die we will not be reincarnated but will go to heaven or hell.
5. The Bible is the final revelation of God's will.

6. The Qur'an is the final revelation of God's will.
7. We need to be redeemed from sin.
8. We need to find release from suffering.
9. We need to find liberation from ignorance.

All of these are claims made by different religions. Could all of these statements be true? Clearly they could all be false, but it seems unlikely that they could all be true, because some appear to contradict others. If I claim the Bible is the final revelation of God's will and you claim that it is not, one of us must be wrong, or so it would seem.

John Hick, author of the next selection, recently retired from Claremont Graduate School after a long and distinguished career teaching philosophy of religion in both England and the United States. One of his primary concerns has been to develop a theory of religion that would harmonize the conflicting claims of the different world religions. He has proposed a pluralistic hypothesis to account for religious differences. Behind all the personal gods and impersonal absolutes proposed by religious thinkers stands *the Real in itself*. This Real is experienced in different ways in different traditions. If this hypothesis is correct, then how do we account for the differing and often contradictory claims that different religions make? Can all religions somehow be reflecting the same reality when they speak of it in such different and conflicting ways?

Reading Questions

1. What is the skeptical argument that arises from the conflicting truth claims of the various religions?
2. How does the proposal to treat each religion as a distinct form of life with its own language game avoid the problem of conflicting truth claims?
3. What is the difference between "doctrinal disagreements" and "basic religious disagreements"?
4. What is "illicit reification," and how does it affect the concept of religion?
5. What are three areas of differences among religions, what is an example of each, and how does Hick propose that they be overcome?
6. What is Hick's hypothesis about the unity underlying religions?
7. What is the Kantian distinction between noumenal and phenomenal, and how does Hick use this to show how the *personae* and *impersonae* might be related?
8. Do you find Hick's hypothesis plausible? Why or why not?

Conflicting Truth Claims*

JOHN HICK

Many Faiths, All Claiming to Be True

Until comparatively recently each of the different religions of the world had developed in substantial ignorance of the others. There have been, it is true, great movements of expansion which have brought two faiths into contact: above all, the expansion of Buddhism during the last three centuries B.C. and the early centuries of the Christian era, carrying its message throughout India and Southeast Asia and into China, Tibet, and Japan, and then, the resurgence of the Hindu religion at the expense of Buddhism, with the result that today Buddhism is rarely to be found on the Indian subcontinent; next, the first Christian expansion into the Roman Empire; then the expansion of Islam in the seventh and eighth centuries C.E. into the Middle East, Europe, and later India; and finally, the second expansion of Christianity in the missionary movement of the nineteenth century. These interactions, however, were for the most part conflicts rather than dialogues; they did not engender any deep or sympathetic understanding of one faith by the adherents of another. It is only during the last hundred years or so that the scholarly study of world religions has made possible an accurate appreciation of the faiths of other people and so has brought home to an increasing number of us the problem of the conflicting truth claims made by different religious traditions. This issue now emerges as a major topic demanding a prominent place on the agenda of the philosopher of religion.

The problem can be posed very concretely in this way. If I had been born in India, I would probably be a Hindu; if in Egypt, probably a Muslim; if in Sri Lanka, probably a Buddhist; but I was born in England and am, predictably, a Christian. These different religions seem to say different and incompatible things about the nature of ultimate reality, about the modes of divine activity, and about the nature and destiny of the human race. Is the divine nature personal or nonpersonal? Does deity become incarnate in the world? Are human beings reborn again and again on earth? Is the empirical self the real self, destined for eternal life in fellowship with God, or is it only a temporary and illusory manifestation of an eternal higher self? Is the Bible, or the Qur'an, or the Bhagavad Gita the Word of God? If what Christianity says in answer to such questions is true, must not what Hinduism says be to a large extent false? If what Buddhism says is true, must not what Islam says be largely false?

The skeptical thrust of these questions goes very deep; for it is a short step from the thought that the different religions cannot all be true, although they each claim to be, to the thought that in all probability none of them is true. Thus Hume laid down the principle "that, in matters of religion, whatever is different is contrary; and that it is impossible the religions of ancient Rome, of Turkey, of Siam, and of China should, all of them, be established on any solid foundation." Accordingly, regarding miracles as evidence for the truth of a particular faith, "Every miracle, therefore, pretended to have been wrought in any of these religions (and all of them abound in miracles), as its direct scope is to establish the particular religion to which it is attributed; so has it the same force, though more indirectly, to overthrow every other system." By the same reasoning, any ground for believing a particular religion to be true must operate as a ground for believing every other religion to be false; accordingly, for any particular

*From *The Philosophy of Religion*, 3d ed. by John Hick. © 1983. Reprinted by permission. Prentice-Hall, Inc., Upper Saddle River, NJ. Footnotes deleted.

religion there will always be far more reason for believing it to be false than for believing it to be true. This is the skeptical argument that arises from the conflicting truth claims of the various world faiths.

W. A. Christian's Analysis

In his book *Meaning and Truth in Religion*, W. A. Christian begins with the idea of a "proposal for belief." Belief is here distinguished from knowledge; if I look at my watch and tell you the time, or if I look out of the window and report that it is raining, I am giving information, not making a belief proposal in Christian's sense. The context in which proposals for belief are made is that of common interest in a question to which neither party knows the answer, and in relation to which there is accordingly scope for theories that would provide an answer. Such a theory, offered for positive acceptance, is a proposal for belief. The following are examples of well-known religious belief-proposals:

> *Jesus is the Messiah.*
> *Atman is Brahman.*
> *Allah is merciful.*
> *All the Buddhas are one.*

These examples are drawn respectively from Christianity, Hinduism, Islam, and Buddhism. It is clear that these belief-proposals are all different; but are they incompatible? Do they, as put forward by these different faiths, conflict with one another?

Consider first what looks like a very direct religious disagreement. Christians say that (A) "Jesus is the Messiah," whereas Jews say that Jesus is not the Messiah and the Messiah is still to come. But William Christian points out that when we take account of what each party means by the term "Messiah" it turns out that they are not directly contradicting one another after all. For "Jews mean by 'the Messiah' a nondivine being who will restore Israel as an earthly community and usher in the consummation of history. Christians mean a promised savior of mankind from sin. Two different Messiah concepts are being ex-

pressed; hence two different propositions are being asserted." Thus the Jew's denial that Jesus is the Messiah does not contradict the Christian's assertion that Jesus *is* the Messiah.

This could suggest the following view: the concepts used in the belief-proposals of a particular religion are peculiar to that religion. Christians use the concept of the Messiah (= divine savior); Jews, the concept of Messiah (= human agent of God's purposes); Buddhists, the concept of Nirvana; Hindus, the concept of Brahman; and Muslims, for example, the concept of the Sharia. Each of these ideas, as it occurs within these religions, gains its meaning from its use within the context of that religion and is thus peculiar to it and has meaning only as part of its discourse. Hence there cannot be a case of two religions employing the same concept and saying contradictory things about it. The Christian, for example, does not say that Allah is not merciful, for Allah is not a Christian concept and Christian discourse does not include any statements about Allah. Or again, the Muslim does not say that Atman is not Brahman, for the question does not arise within the circle of Islamic discourse.

This position could be developed along lines for which some have found inspiration in the later writings of Wittgenstein. Each religion, one might say, is a "form of life" with its own "language-game." Christian language—employing such distinctively Christian concepts as Incarnation, Son of God, and Trinity—derives its meaning from the part that it plays in the Christian life. The criteria of what it is appropriate to say, and thus of what is to be accepted as true, are peculiar to this realm of discourse. These rules of the Christian language-game treat the Bible and Christian tradition as important sources of knowledge. But nothing that is said in the context of Christian faith can either agree or disagree with anything that is said within the context of another religion. The Christian and, say, the Buddhist, are different people, belonging to different religious communities and traditions and speaking different religious languages, each of which has meaning within the context of a different religious form of life; accordingly there is no question of their making rival belief-proposals. Such a theory has the great attraction that it avoids entirely the otherwise vexing problems of the apparently conflicting truth claims made by different religions.

However, William Christian goes on to show that any such solution would be only apparent. Returning to our original example, it is true that Jews and Christians mean different things by "the Messiah" and thus that when the one says that Jesus is not the Messiah and the other that he *is,* they are not directly contradicting each other. However, we can go beyond these two Messiah concepts. We can speak of "the one whom God promised to send to redeem Israel," it being left open whether this is a human or a divine being. We then have the belief-proposal (B), "Jesus is the one whom God promised to send to redeem Israel," this being a proposal that the Christian accepts and the Jew rejects. At this point there is a real disagreement between them about the truth concerning Jesus, a disagreement that was only temporarily masked by noting the different concepts of Messiah that were in use. Indeed, if there were no such genuine and substantial disagreement, it would be difficult to account for the original splitting off of Christianity from Judaism and for the religious polemics that followed. The persisting disagreement does not have to involve any hostility or bitterness; it does not have to prevent Christians and Jews from rejoicing in all that they have in common; and it is compatible with close friendship and cooperation between them. But it is also clear that they do in fact hold different and incompatible beliefs about the nature and significance of Jesus—as also about a large number of other related matters.

Thus, whereas (A) "Jesus is the Messiah" has different meanings for Christian and Jew, when we go behind this formula to (B) "Jesus is the one whom God promised to send to redeem Israel," we find that at this point there is direct Jewish-Christian disagreement. Furthermore, W. A. Christian points out that this process can be carried further to uncover differences between Christian and Jew on the one hand and, say, Sto-

ics on the other. For it is a presupposition of (B) that (C) "The being who rules the world acts in history," for that being is said to "promise," to "send," and to "redeem Israel." However, a Stoic would deny that the Divine does any of these things or indeed acts in history in any way. He thinks of the Divine quite differently, so that the question, "Has God acted in history in such-and-such a manner?" can never arise: since the world-ruler does not act in history at all, there is no scope for debate as to whether or not the world-ruler has acted by sending Jesus.

This process of formulating presuppositions that become the loci of religious disagreement can go yet further. The Jew, the Christian, and the Stoic all hold that there is a Being who rules the world: according to Jew and Christian, that Ruler acts in history, whereas according to the Stoic, not. But there are other faiths that would deny the presupposition that (D) "The source of all being rules the world." The Neoplatonist, for example, denies this, as does the Buddhist and the Hindu of the Advaita-Vedānta school . . . .

William Christian further points out that besides religious disagreements of this kind, in which different predicates are affirmed of the same subject (he calls these "doctrinal disagreements"), there are others in which different subjects are assigned to the same predicate; these latter he calls "basic religious disagreements." For example, the theist says that "God is the ground of being," but the pantheist says that "Nature is the ground of being." Other basic religious predicates attributed to different subjects in different religions are "the supreme goal of Life" (this is the Beatific Vision in Christianity, Nirvana in Buddhism); "that on which we unconditionally depend" (Allah in Islam, the God and Father of our Lord Jesus Christ in Christianity); "more important than anything else" (knowledge of one's true nature in Hinduism, worship of Jahweh in Judaism); "ultimate" (the Absolute, or Brahman, in Hinduism; Truth in humanism); "holy" (God in the theistic faiths, man in humanism). William Christian offers a complex and interesting theory of the relation between basic religious proposals and doctrinal proposals, but we are concerned at the moment only with his demonstration of how disagreements between religions may be located by one's uncovering the presuppositions of statements that might at first seem to have meaning only in the context of a particular religion, and thus not to be candidates for either agreement or disagreement on the part of other religions. We have seen that there are real disagreements concerning religious belief-proposals; that is to say, there are many belief-proposals that are accepted by the adherents of one religion but rejected by those of another.

So far, then, the problem posed at the beginning of this chapter has refused to be banished. There is, however, another approach to it which deserves to be considered.

Critique of the Concept of "A Religion"

In his important book *The Meaning and End of Religion*, Wilfred Cantwell Smith challenges the familiar concept of "a religion," upon which much of the traditional problem of conflicting religious truth claims rests. He emphasizes that what we call a religion—an empirical entity that can be traced historically and mapped geographically—is a human phenomenon. Christianity, Hinduism, Judaism, Buddhism, Islam, and so on are human creations whose history is part of the wider history of human culture. Cantwell Smith traces the development of the concept of a religion as a clear and bounded historical phenomenon and shows that the notion, far from being universal and self-evident, is a distinctively Western invention which has been exported to the rest of the world. "It is," he says, summarizing the outcome of his detailed historical argument, "a surprisingly modern aberration for anyone to think that Christianity is true or that Islam is—since the Enlightenment, basically, when Europe began to postulate religions as intellectualistic systems, patterns of doctrine, so that they could for the first time be labeled 'Christianity' and 'Buddhism,' and could be called true or false." The names by which we know the various "religions" today were in fact (with the exception of

"Islam") invented in the eighteenth century, and before they were imposed by the influence of the West upon the peoples of the world no one had thought of himself or herself as belonging to one of a set of competing systems of belief concerning which it is possible to ask, "Which of these systems is the true one?" This notion of religions as mutually exclusive entities with their own characteristics and histories—although it now tends to operate as a habitual category of our thinking—may well be an example of the illicit reification, the turning of good adjectives into bad substantives, to which the western mind is prone and against which contemporary philosophy has warned us. In this case a powerful but distorting conceptuality has helped to create phenomena answering to it, namely the religions of the world seeing themselves and each other as rival ideological communities.

Perhaps, however, instead of thinking of religion as existing in mutually exclusive systems, we should see the religious life of mankind as a dynamic continuum within which certain major disturbances have from time to time set up new fields of force, of greater or lesser power, displaying complex relationships of attraction and repulsion, absorption, resistance, and reinforcement. These major disturbances are the great creative religious moments of human history from which the distinguishable religious traditions have stemmed. Theologically, such moments are seen as intersections of divine grace, divine initiative, divine truth, with human faith, human response, human enlightenment. They have made their impact upon the stream of human life so as to affect the development of cultures; and what we call Christianity, Islam, Hinduism, Buddhism, are among the resulting historical-cultural phenomena. It is clear, for example, that Christianity has developed through a complex interaction between religious and non-religious factors. Christian ideas have been formed within the intellectual framework provided by Greek philosophy; the Christian church was molded as an institution by the Roman Empire and its system of laws: the Catholic mind reflects something of the Latin Mediterranean temperament, whereas the Protestant mind reflects something of the northern Germanic temperament, and so on. It is not hard to appreciate the connections between historical Christianity and the continuing life of humanity in the western hemisphere, and of course the same is true, in their own ways, of all the other religions of the world.

This means that it is not appropriate to speak of a religion as being true or false, any more than it is to speak of a civilization as being true or false. For the religions, in the sense of distinguishable religiocultural streams within human history, are expressions of the diversities of human types and temperaments and thought forms. The same differences between the eastern and western mentality that are revealed in characteristically different conceptual and linguistic, social, political, and artistic forms presumably also underlie the contrasts between eastern and western religion.

In *The Meaning and End of Religion* Cantwell Smith examines the development from the original religious event or idea—whether it be the insight of the Buddha, the life of Christ, or the career of Mohammed—to a religion in the sense of a vast living organism with its own credal backbone and its institutional skin. He shows in each case that this development stands in a questionable relationship to that original event or idea. Religions as institutions, with the theological doctrines and the codes of behavior that form their boundaries, did not come about because the religious reality required this, but because such a development was historically inevitable in the days of undeveloped communication between the different cultural groups. Now that the world has become a communicational unity, we are moving into a new situation in which it becomes both possible and appropriate for religious thinking to transcend these cultural-historical boundaries. But what form might such new thinking take, and how would it affect the problem of conflicting truth claims?

Toward a Possible Solution

To see the historical inevitability of the plurality of religions in the past and its noninevitability in the future, we must note the broad course that has been taken by the religious life of mankind. The human being has been described as a naturally religious animal, displaying an innate tendency to experience the environment as religiously as well as naturally significant and to feel required to live in it as such. This tendency is universally expressed in the cultures of primitive people, with their belief in sacred objects, endowed with *mana,* and in a multitude of spirits needing to be carefully propitiated. The divine reality is here crudely apprehended as a plurality of quasi-animal forces. The next stage seems to have come with the coalescence of tribes into larger groups. The tribal gods were then ranked in hierarchies (some being lost by amalgamation in the process) dominated, in the Middle East, by great national gods such as the Sumerian Ishtar, Amon of Thebes, Jahweh of Israel, Marduk of Babylon, the Greek Zeus, and in India by the Vedic high gods such as Dyaus (the sky god), Varuna (god of heaven), and Agni (the fire god). The world of such national and nature gods, often martial and cruel and sometimes requiring human sacrifices, reflected the state of humanity's awareness of the divine at the dawn of documentary history, some three thousand years ago.

So far, the whole development can be described as the growth of natural religion. That is to say, primitive spirit worship expressing man's fears of the unknown forces of nature, and later the worship of regional deities—depicting either aspects of nature (sun, sky, etc.) or the collective personality of a nation—represent the extent of humanity's religious life prior to any special intrusions of divine revelation or illumination.

But sometime after 1000 B.C. a golden age of religious creativity, named by Jaspers the Axial Period, dawned. This consisted of a series of revelatory experiences occurring in different parts of the world that deepened and purified people's conceptions of the divine, and that religious faith can only attribute to the pressure of the divine reality upon the human spirit. To quote A. C. Bouquet, "It is a commonplace with specialists in the history of religion that somewhere within the region of 800 B.C. there passed over the populations of this planet a stirring of the mind, which, while it left large tracts of humanity comparatively uninfluenced, produced in a number of different spots on the earth's surface prophetic individuals who created a series of new starting points for human living and thinking." At the threshold of this period some of the great Hebrew prophets appeared (Elijah in the ninth century; Amos, Hosea, and the first Isaiah in the eighth century; and then Jeremiah in the seventh), declaring that they had heard the word of the Lord claiming their obedience and demanding a new level of righteousness and justice in the life of Israel. During the next five centuries, between about 800 and 300 B.C., the prophet Zoroaster appeared in Persia; Greece produced Pythagoras, and then Socrates and Plato, and Aristotle; in China there was Confucius, and the author or authors of the Taoist scriptures; and in India this creative period saw the formation of the Upanishads and the lives of Gotama the Buddha, and Mahavira, founder of the Jain religion, and around the end of this period, the writing of the *Bhagavad Gita*. Even Christianity, beginning later, and then Islam, both have their roots in the Hebrew religion of the Axial Age, and can hardly be understood except in relation to it.

It is important to observe the situation within which all these revelatory moments occurred. Communication between the different groups of humanity was then so limited that for all practical purposes human beings inhabited a series of different worlds. For the most part people living in China, in India, in Arabia, in Persia, were unaware of the others' existence. There was thus, inevitably, a multiplicity of local religions that were also local civilizations. Accordingly the great creative moments of revelation and illumination occurred separately within the different cultures and influenced their development, giving them the coherence and confidence to expand into larger units, thus producing the vast religiocultural entities that we now call the world religions. So it is that until recently the different streams of religious experience and belief have flowed through different cultures, each forming and being formed by its own separate environment. There has, of course, been contact between different religions at certain points in history, and an influence—sometimes an important influence—of one upon another; nevertheless, the broad picture is one of religions developing separately within their different historical and cultural settings.

In addition to noting these historical circumstances, we need to make use of the important distinction between, on the one hand, human encounters with the divine reality in the various forms of religious experience, and on the other hand, theological theories or doctrines that men and women have developed to conceptualize the meaning of these encounters. These two components of religion, although distinguishable, are not separable. It is as hard to say which came first, as in the celebrated case of the hen and the egg; they continually react upon one another in a joint process of development, experience providing the ground of our beliefs, but these in turn influencing the forms taken by our experience. The different religions are different streams of religious experience, each having started at a different point within human history and each having formed its own conceptual self-consciousness within a different cultural milieu.

In the light of this it is possible to consider the hypothesis that the great religions are all, at their experiential roots, in contact with the same ultimate divine reality but that their differing experiences of that reality, interacting over the centuries with the differing thought forms of differing cultures, have led to increasing differentiation and contrasting elaboration—so that Hinduism, for example, is a very different phenomenon from Christianity, and very different ways of experiencing and conceiving the divine occur within them. However, now that in the "one world" of today the religious traditions are consciously interacting with each other in mutual observation and dialogue, it is possible that their future developments may move on gradually converging courses. During the next centuries each group will presumably continue to change, and it may be that they will grow closer together, so that one day such names as "Christianity," "Buddhism," "Islam," and "Hinduism" will no longer adequately describe the then current configurations of man's religious experience and belief. I am not thinking here of the extinction of human religiousness in a universal secularization. That is of course a possible future, and indeed many think it the most likely future to come about. But if the human creature is an indelibly religious animal he or she will always, even amidst secularization, experience a sense of the transcendent by which to be both troubled and uplifted. The future I am envisaging is accordingly one in which the presently existing religions will constitute the past history of different emphases and variations, which will then appear more like, for example, the different denominations of Christianity in North America or Europe today than like radically exclusive totalities.

If the nature of religion, and the history of religion, is indeed such that a development of this kind begins to take place in the remaining decades of the present century and during the succeeding twenty-first century, what would this imply concerning the problem of the conflicting truth claims of the different religions in their present forms?

We may distinguish three aspects of this question: differences in modes of experiencing the divine reality; differences of philosophical and theological theory concerning that reality or concerning the implications of religious experience; and differences in the key or revelatory experiences that unify a stream of religious experience and thought.

The most prominent and important example of the first kind of difference is probably that between the experience of the divine as personal and as nonpersonal. In Judaism, Christianity, Islam, and the important strand of Hinduism which is focused by the *Bhagavad Gita,* the Ultimate is apprehended as personal goodness, will, and purpose under the different names of Jahweh, God, Allah, Krishna, Shira. Whereas in Hinduism as interpreted by the Advaita Vedānta school, and in Theravada Buddhism, ultimate reality is apprehended as nonpersonal. Mahayana Buddhism, on the other hand, is a more complex tradition, including, for example, both nontheis-

tic Zen and quasi-theistic Pure Land Buddhism. There is, perhaps, in principle no difficulty in holding that these personal and nonpersonal experiences of the Ultimate can be understood as complementary rather than as incompatible. For if, as every profound form of religion has affirmed, the Ultimate reality is infinite and therefore exceeds the scope of our finite human categories, that reality may be both personal Lord and nonpersonal Ground of being. At any rate, there is a program for thought in the exploration of what Aurobindo called "the logic of the infinite" and the question of the extent to which predicates that are incompatible when attributed to a finite reality may no longer be incompatible when referred to infinite reality.

The second type of difference is in philosophical and theological theory or doctrine. Such differences, and indeed conflicts, are not merely apparent, but they are part of the still developing history of human thought; it may be that in time they will be transcended, for they belong to the historical, culturally conditioned aspect of religion, which is subject to change. When one considers, for example, the immense changes that have come about within Christian thought during the last hundred years, in response to the development of modern biblical scholarship and the modern physical and biological sciences, one can set no limit to the further developments that may take place in the future. A book of contemporary Christian theology (post-Darwin, post-Einstein, post-Freud), using modern biblical source criticism and taking for granted a considerable demythologization of the New Testament world view, would have been quite unrecognizable as Christian theology two centuries ago. Comparable responses to modern science are yet to occur in many of the other religions of the world, but they must inevitably come, sooner or later. When all the main religious traditions have been through their own encounter with modern science, they will probably have undergone as considerable an internal development as has Christianity. Besides, there will be an increasing influence of each faith upon every other as they meet and interact more and more freely within the "one world" of today.

In the light of all this, the future that I have spec-ulatively projected does not seem impossible.

However, it is the third kind of difference that constitutes the largest difficulty in the way of re-ligious agreement. Each religion has its holy founder or scripture, or both, in which the divine reality has been revealed—the Vedas, the Torah, the Buddha, Christ and the Bible, the Qur'an. Wherever the Holy is revealed, it claims an ab-solute response of faith and worship, which thus seems incompatible with a like response to any other claimed disclosure of the Holy. Within Christianity, for example, this absoluteness and exclusiveness of response has been strongly de-veloped in the doctrine that Christ was uniquely divine, the only Son of God, of one substance with the Father, the only mediator between God and man. But this traditional doctrine, formed in an age of substantial ignorance of the wider reli-gious life of mankind, gives rise today to an acute tension. On the one hand, Christianity tradition-ally teaches that God is the Creator and Lord of all mankind and seeks mankind's final good and salvation; and on the other hand that only by re-sponding in faith to God in Christ can we be saved. This means that infinite love has ordained that human beings can be saved only in a way that in fact excludes the large majority of them; for the greater part of all the human beings who have been born have lived either before Christ or outside the borders of Christendom. In an at-tempt to meet this glaring paradox, Christian theology has developed a doctrine according to which those outside the circle of Christian faith may nevertheless be saved. For example, the Sec-ond Vatican Council of the Roman Catholic Church, 1963–1965, declared that "Those who through no fault of theirs are still ignorant of the Gospel of Christ and of his Church yet sincerely seek God and, with the help of divine grace, strive to do his will as known to them through the voice of their conscience, those men can at-tain to eternal salvation." This represents a real movement in response to a real problem; never-theless it is only an epicycle of theory, complicat-ing the existing dogmatic system rather than going to the heart of the problem. The epicycle is designed to cover theists ("those who sincerely seek God") who have had no contact with the Christian gospel. But what of the nontheistic Buddhists and nontheistic Hindus? And what of those Muslims, Jews, Buddhists, Hindus, Jains, Parsees, etc., both theists and nontheists, who have heard the Christian gospel but have pre-ferred to adhere to the faith of their fathers?

Thus it seems that if the tension at the heart of the traditional Christian attitude to non-Chris-tian faiths is to be resolved, Christian thinkers must give even more radical thought to the prob-lem than they have as yet done. It is, however, not within the scope of this book to suggest a plan for the reconstruction of Christian or other religious doctrines.

A Philosophical Framework for Religious Pluralism

Among the great religious traditions, and partic-ularly within their more mystical strands, a dis-tinction is widely recognized between the Real or Ultimate or Divine *an sich* (in him/her/its-self) and the Real as conceptualized and experienced by human beings. The widespread assumption is that the Ultimate Reality is infinite and as such ex-ceeds the grasp of human thought and language, so that the describable and experienceable objects of worship and contemplation are not the Ulti-mate in its limitless reality but the Ultimate in its relationship to finite perceivers. One form of this distinction is that between *nirguna* Brahman, Brahman without attributes, beyond the scope of human thought, and *saguna* Brahman, Brahman with attributes, encountered within human expe-rience as Ishvara, the personal creator and gover-nor of the universe. In the west the Christian mys-tic Meister Eckhart drew a parallel distinction between the Godhead (*Deitas*) and God (*Deus*). The Taoist scripture, the *Tao Te Ching*, begins by affirming that "The Tao that can be expressed is not the eternal Tao." The Jewish Kabbalist mys-tics distinguished between En Soph, the absolute divine reality beyond all human description, and the God of the Bible; and among the Muslim Sufis, Al Haqq, the Real, seems to be a similar concept to En Soph, as the abyss of Godhead underlying the self-revealing Allah. More recently Paul Tillich has spoken of "the God above the God of theism." A. N. Whitehead, and the process theologians who follow him, distinguish between the primordial and consequent natures of God; and Gordon Kaufman has recently distinguished between the "real God" and the "available God." These all seem to be somewhat similar (though not identical) distinctions. If we suppose that the Real is one but that our human perceptions of the Real are plural and various, we have a basis for the hypothesis, suggested tentatively in the previous section, that the different streams of religious experience represent diverse awarenesses of the same limitless transcendent reality, which is perceived in characteristically different ways by different human mentalities, forming and formed by different cultural histories.

Immanuel Kant has provided (without intending to do so) a philosophical framework within which such a hypothesis can be developed. He distinguished between the world as it is *an sich,* which he called the noumenal world, and the world as it appears to human consciousness, which he called the phenomenal world. His writings can be interpreted in various ways, but according to one interpretation the phenomenal world *is* the noumenal world as humanly experienced. The innumerable diverse sensory clues are brought together in human consciousness, according to Kant, by means of a system of relational concepts or categories (such as "thing" and "cause") in terms of which we are aware of our environment. Thus our environment as we perceive it is a joint product of the world itself and the selecting, interpreting, and unifying activity of the perceiver. Kant was concerned mainly with the psychological contribution to our awareness of the world, but the basic principle can also be seen at work on the physiological level. Our sensory equipment is capable of responding to only a minute proportion of the full range of sound and electromagnetic waves—light, radio, infrared, ultraviolet, X, and gamma—which are impinging upon us all the time. Consequently, the world as we experience it represents a particular selection—a distinctively human selection—from the immense complexity and richness of the world as it is *an sich.* We experience at a certain macro/micro level. What we experience and use as the solid, enduring table would be, to a micro-observer, a swirling universe of discharging energy, consisting of electrons, neutrons, and quarks in continuous rapid activity. We perceive the world as it appears to beings with our particular physical and psychological equipment. Indeed, the way the world *appears* to us is the way the world *is for us* as we inhabit and interact with it. As Thomas Aquinas said long ago, "The thing known is in the knower according to the mode of the knower."

Is it possible to adopt the broad Kantian distinction between the world as it is in itself and the world as it appears to us with our particular cognitive machinery, and apply it to the relation between the Ultimate Reality and our different human awarenesses of that Reality? If so, we shall think in terms of a single divine noumenon and perhaps many diverse divine phenomena. We may form the hypothesis that the Real *an sich* is experienced by human beings in terms of one of two basic religious concepts. One is the concept of God, or of the Real experienced as personal, which presides over the theistic forms of religion. The other is the concept of the Absolute, or of the Real experienced as nonpersonal, which presides over the various nontheistic forms of religion. Each of these basic concepts is, however, made more concrete (in Kantian terminology, schematized) as a range of particular images of God or particular concepts of the Absolute. These images of God are formed within the different religious histories. Thus the Jahweh of the Hebrew Scriptures exists in interaction with the Jewish people. He is a part of their history and they are a part of his; he cannot be abstracted from this particular concrete historical nexus. On the other hand, Krishna is a quite different divine figure, existing in relation to a different faith-community, with its own different and distinctive religious ethos. Given the basic hypothesis of the reality of the Divine, we may say that Jahweh and Krishna (and likewise, Shiva, and Allah, and the

Father of Jesus Christ) are different *personae* in terms of which the divine Reality is experienced and thought within different streams of religious life. These different *personae* are thus partly projections of the divine Reality into human consciousness, and partly projections of the human consciousness itself as it has been formed by particular historical cultures. From the human end they are our different images of God; from the divine end they are God's *personae* in relation to the different human histories of faith.

A similar account will have to be given of the forms of nonpersonal Absolute, or *impersonae,* experienced within the different strands of non-theistic religion—Brahman, Nirvana, Sunyata, the Dharma, the Dharmakaya, the Tao. Here, according to our hypothesis, the same limitless ultimate Reality is being experienced and thought through different forms of the concept of the Real as non-personal.

It is characteristic of the more mystical forms of awareness of the Real that they seem to be direct, and not mediated—or therefore distorted—by the perceptual machinery of the human mind. However, our hypothesis will have to hold that even the apparently direct and unmediated awareness of the Real in the Hindu *moksha,* in the Buddhist *satori,*

and in the unitive mysticism of the West, is still the conscious experience of a human subject and as such is influenced by the interpretative set of the cognizing mind. All human beings have been influenced by the culture of which they are a part and have received, or have developed in their appropriation of it, certain deep interpretative tendencies which help to form their experience and are thus continually confirmed within it. We see evidence of such deep "sets" at work when we observe that mystics formed by Hindu, Buddhist, Christian, Muslim, and Jewish religious cultures report distinctively different forms of experience. Thus, far from it being the case that they all undergo an identical experience but report it in different religious languages, it seems more probable that they undergo characteristically different unitive experiences (even though with important common features), the differences being due to the conceptual frameworks and meditational disciplines supplied by the religious traditions in which they participate.

Thus it is a possible, and indeed an attractive, hypothesis—as an alternative to total skepticism—that the great religious traditions of the world represent different human perceptions of and response to the same infinite divine Reality.

11.3 Religious Pluralism and Advaita Vedanta

For centuries many religions could live isolated, for the most part, from others. When they did come in contact, their relationship tended to be characterized by warfare and conflict rather than by harmony and tolerance. Today that isolation is no longer possible. Telecommunications, modern travel, and immigration have resulted in ever greater contact. Will this cause greater religious conflict than in the past? Or will the religions learn ways to get along?

Centuries ago, in India, different religions could not live in isolation. There was constant contact, and ways of dealing with others had to be worked out. Long before modern philosophers began to wrestle with the issue of conflicting religious truth claims, Indian philosophers grappled with the same problem.

In the next selection, Arvind Sharma, Birks Professor of Comparative Religion at McGill University, compares Hick's views on conflicting truth claims with the views worked out in Advaita Vedanta (see Reading 2.2). Sharma finds both similarities and differences, but the similarities are striking enough for Sharma to conclude that there are "very strong family resemblances" between Hick's hypothesis and the Advaita Vedanta view.

Some might question whether such comparisons are really possible. The language, culture, tradition and philosophical assumptions of an ancient Indian philosophy, such as Advaita Vedanta, are so very different from the modern situation and the framework in which Hick is operating that comparing their views may be like comparing apples and watches. In other words, the incommensurability between the two is so great that there may be no sure way of translating claims that Hick makes about *the Real in itself* and claims that Shankara makes about Brahman. The fact that both assert that ultimate reality is beyond our ordinary experience further complicates matters.

Reading Questions

1. How does the parable of the blind man and the elephant illustrate a point different from Hume's contention that in religious matters, "whatever is different is contrary"?
2. What are the key points of the Advaitic view of Reality?
3. What is the Advaitin response to the Christian's analysis of religious disagreements, and why do doctrinal disagreements within Vedanta *not* lead to intolerance?
4. How does the Advaitin respond to Smith's analysis of religions as cumulative traditions?
5. How does Advaita Vedanta respond to the three differences among religions identified by Hick?
6. What five points does Sharma make in comparing Hick's philosophical framework with Advaita Vedanta?
7. Do religions give different names to the same ultimate reality? What do you think and why?

Religious Pluralism and Advaita Vedanta*

ARVIND SHARMA

Introduction

It is sometimes claimed that whereas in the past great movements of religious expansion such as those of Buddhism, Christianity and Islam did involve contact among followers of different religions, such contact for the most part represented "conflicts rather than dialogues." It is only during the past few centuries that such contact has stimulated inquiry into the actual beliefs and practices of various religions in a less combative atmosphere and has "brought home to an increasing number of us the problem of the conflicting truth claims made by different religious traditions."

Although this may be true globally, it seems that India had to face the issue of religious

*From Arvind Sharma, *The Philosophy of Religions and Advaita Vedanta: A Comparative Study in Religions and Reason.* University Park: The Pennsylvania State University Press, 1995, pp. 211–224. Copyright © 1995 The Pennsylvania State University. Reproduced by permission of the publisher. Footnotes deleted.

pluralism—and that of the conflicting truth claims inherent in such a situation—at least as far back as the sixth century B.C.E. This may or may not be what Heinrich Zimmer had in mind when he wrote: "We of the Occident are about to arrive at a crossroads that was reached by the thinkers of India some seven hundred years before Christ," but conflicting truth claims were certainly an element in the situation Indian thinkers had to reckon with at the time. This point is well illustrated by the following parable:

Buddha, the Blessed One, gives of the blind men and the elephant to illustrate that partial knowledge always breeds bigotry and fanaticism. Once a group of disciples entered the city of Śrāvasti to beg alms. They found there a number of sectarians holding disputations with one another and maintaining "This is the truth, that is not the truth. That is not truth, this is the truth." After listening to these conflicting views, the brethren came back to the Exalted One and described to him what they had seen and heard at Śrāvasti.

Then said the Exalted One:

"These sectarians, brethren, are blind and unseeing. They know not the real, they know not the unreal; they know not the truth, they know not the untruth. In such a state of ignorance do they dispute and quarrel as they describe. Now in former times, brethren, there was a Rājā (king) in this same Śrāvasti. Then, brethren, the Rājā called to a certain man, saying: 'Come thou, good fellow! Go, gather together all the blind men that are in Śrāvasti!'

" 'Very good, Your Majesty,' replied that man, and in obedience to the Rājā, gathered together all the blind men, took them with him to the Rājā, and said: 'Your Majesty, all the blind men of Śrāvasti are now assembled.'

" 'Then, my good man, show the blind men an elephant.'

" 'Very good, Your Majesty,' said the man and did as he was told, saying: 'O ye blind men, such as this is an elephant.'

"And to one he presented the head of the elephant, to another, the ear, to another a tusk, the trunk, the foot, back, tail and tuft of the tail, saying to each one that was the elephant.

"Now, brethren, that man, having presented the elephant to the blind men, came to the Rājā and said: 'Your Majesty, the elephant has been presented to the blind men. Do what is your will.'

"Thereupon, brethren, the Rājā went up to the blind men and said to each: 'Have you studied the elephant?'

" 'Yes, Your Majesty.'

" 'Then tell me your conclusions about him.'

"Thereupon those who had been presented with the head answered 'Your Majesty, an elephant is just like a pot.' And those who had only observed the ear replied: 'An elephant is just like a winnowing basket.' Those who had been presented with the tusk said it was a ploughshare. Those who knew only the trunk said it was a plough. 'The body,' said they, 'is a granary; the foot, a pillar; the back, a mortar; the tail, a pestle; the tuft of the tail, just a besom.'

"Then they began to quarrel, shouting, 'Yes, it is!' 'No, it isn't!' 'An elephant is not that!' 'Yes it is like that!' and so on, till they came to fisticuffs about the matter.

"Then, brethren, that Rājā was delighted with the scene.

"Just so are these sectarians who are wanderers, blind, unseeing, knowing not the truth, but each maintaining it is thus and thus."

The parable is significant in that it follows a direction opposite to the one taken by the Western philosophy of religion, which has evolved on the principle laid down by Hume "that, in matters of religion, whatever is different is contrary." The parable here illustrates that whatever is contrary is not necessarily contradictory. John H. Hick elaborates Hume's point made in relation to miracles—that while it constitutes the proof of one religion it must constitute the disproof of another—thus: "By the same reasoning, any ground for believing a particular religion to be true must operate as a ground for believing every other religion to be false; accordingly, for any particular religion there will always be far more reason for believing it to be false than for believing it to be true."

Advaita Vedānta takes a different view on this point because it emphasizes experience rather than belief. "To say that God exists means that spiritual experience is attainable." Because it is attainable in different forms, each attainment confirms rather than contradicts attainment or expression of it. It is Hume's assumption that different attainments represent different and contradictory beliefs but "Hindu thinkers warn against rationalistic self-sufficiency" in these matters which takes the form of dogma and maintain that different attainments represent different apprehensions of the one Reality, which is infinite, so that "toleration is the homage which the finite mind pays to the inexhaustibility of the Infinite." This is recognized by Śaṅkara, who contended with other schools of thought but also proclaimed the insufficiency of any one school of thought in relation to the divine.

The key points to be noted here in the Advaitic vision of Reality are as follows: (1) The Absolute is beyond human words and may be brought within the limits of comprehension in many diverse but not necessarily mutually negating ways. (2) This Absolute or the Real is one, which explains the "attitude of acceptance of other cults." In this context the following line of the RgVeda (1.164.46) is often invoked: "The Real is one, the learned call it by various names, Agni, Yama, Mātariśvan." (3) The Real is known through experience, and the experience of a modern Hindu mystic such as Rāmakṛṣṇa (1836–86) confirms the view that various religions represent different approaches to the same Reality. Thus the Advaitin position tends to be very different from that of Hume, as is obvious from the statement of S. Radhakrishnan on this very point.

It is sometimes urged that the descriptions of God conflict with one another. It only shows that our notions are not true. To say that our ideas of God are not true is not to deny the reality of God to which our ideas refer. Refined definitions of God as moral personality, and holy love may contradict cruder ones which look upon him as a primitive despot, a sort of sultan in the sky, but they all intend the same reality. If personal equation does not vitiate the claim to objectivity in sense perception and scientific inquiry, there is no reason to assume that it does so in religious experience.

W. A. Christian's Analysis

W. A. Christian analyzes religious disagreements among world religions as consisting of basically two kinds: (1) "doctrinal disagreements," in which "different predicates are affirmed of the same subject"—for example, Jesus was "the One whom God promised to send to redeem Israel," a statement about which Jews and Christians substantially differ, as over the statement that "Jesus is the Messiah," over which they may be seen to only nominally differ on account of different conceptions of the Messiah, and (2) "basic religious disagreements," in which "different subjects are assigned to the same predicate," as when the *ultimate* is regarded as God in Christianity, Brahman in Hinduism, and Tao in Taoism.

The Advaitin response to Christian's analysis is basically consistent with its position described earlier: that whether it is a case of affirming different predicates of the same subject or of assigning different subjects to the same predicate, the language-barrier in relation to Brahman is never overcome.

Within this broad limitation, however, in Advaita Vedānta "doctrinal disagreements" play a more important role than "basic religious disagreements." Advaita has little difficulty with different predicates being assigned to the same subject. Thus Śaṅkara quotes the following text in his Aitareya-Upaniṣad Bhāṣya: "Some speak of it as Agni, some as Manu, Prajāpati, Indra, others as Prāṇa, yet others as the eternal Brahman."

But the situation is different in the case of doctrinal disagreements. Just as one can speak of the Messiah in the context of Judaism and Christianity, one can speak of Brahman in the context of the Vedantic tradition. Advaita accords primacy to *nirguṇa* Brahman, but some other schools of Vedānta accord primacy to *saguṇa* Brahman. In fact, "The main issue that was debated by the Vedantins who came after Śaṅkara was whether *Brahman* is *nirguṇa* or *saguṇa*." Troy Wilson Organ graphically illustrates the difference involved in the two approaches: water is water, no doubt, but it is quite different when experienced as H_2O or as a cold splash on one's face.

This doctrinal disagreement within Vedānta, however, has characterized it from the earliest times to the present, and has continued through the centuries *without compromising tolerance* within it in any marked degree. This is because the issue arises at the level of the ultimate. No school of Vedānta rejects the validity of either the *saguṇa* or *nirguṇa* formulation: the issue is of relative priority rather than absolute truth. Indeed, Gauḍapāda, a famous predecessor of Śaṅkara, says that Advaita Vedānta "is pleasing to all, has no dispute with anyone, and is not hostile to anyone."

W. C. Smith's Analysis

Just as W. A. Christian probed the nature of belief in the context of conflicting truth claims, W. C. Smith probes the nature of religion itself. He concludes that it represents the Western habit of "turning good adjectives into bad substantives" through "illicit reification," which manifested itself after the Enlightenment in the form of raising the question about the truth or falsity of a religion as an intellectual system. Religions should really be viewed as cumulative traditions. As he puts it, "It is not appropriate to speak of a religion as being true or false, any more than it is to speak of a civilization as being true or false."

It seems that Smith is arguing against a religion being related to theories of truth on the one hand and advocating a Wittgensteinian "culture-game" theory on the other. Both of these are questionable from an Advaitin point of view. The correspondence theory is hard to verify in relation to religions, but even if it is accepted that the various religions represent distinct "truth-systems" in accordance with the coherence theory, so to speak, and are "relative," even then what is true of one may not be true of another. It is true that Smith blunts this last point by arguing that religions are to be viewed as culture-systems rather than truth-systems. However, the followers of the religions regard them as making truth claims, and from that point of view the problem persists.

The "culture-game" theory on the model of the "language-game" does have the merit of avoiding the truth-falsehood issue but opens up the Santayanan point that "religions are not true or false but better or worse." Here again Smith would not like to force the issue—but the Advaitin would—of whether the issue is veridical or functional. If the question of whether religion is true or false is *not* asked, then the question of whether it is good (useful) or bad (useless) needs to be asked. A modern Advaitin, S. Radhakrishnan, for instance, states: "Let us frankly recognize that the efficiency of a religion is to be judged by the development of religious qualities such as quiet confidence, inner calm, gentleness of the spirit, love of neighbour, mercy to all creation, destruction of tyrannous desires, and the aspiration for spiritual freedom, and there are no trustworthy statistics to tell us that these qualities are found more in efficient nations."

The point here is not that these virtues cannot be quantitatively measured but rather that they form the qualitative propaedeutic for the study of Advaita according to Śaṅkara.

John H. Hick's Analysis

John H. Hick distinguishes among three kinds of differences among the religions of the world: (1) differences in modes of experiencing the divine Reality, especially as personal or impersonal; (2) philosophical and theological differences; and (3) differences in the "key or revelatory experiences that unify a stream of religious experience and thought." Hick seems to think that differences in the first two categories are not hard to overcome. He writes, for instance, that the personal and impersonal modes of encountering reality could be "understood as complementary rather than as incompatible." Similarly, in the philosophical and theological realms the various religions may converge in the future as they face the challenges of critical scholarship, science, and globalization together and overcome or moderate their historical specificities. It is the differences of the third kind which Hick sees as constituting "the largest difficulty in the way of religious agreement. Each religion has its holy founder or scripture, or both, in which the divine Reality has been revealed—the Vedas, the Torah, the Buddha, Christ and the Bible, the Qur'an. Wherever the Holy is revealed, it claims an absolute response of faith and worship, which thus seems incompatible with a like response to any other claimed disclosure of the Holy."

Advaita Vedānta seems to confirm Hick's view on the first point—that the personal and impersonal approaches to the divine may be viewed as complementary. It also seems to confirm his second point—that modernity will reduce religious differences. In this matter Advaita Vedānta may well have anticipated modern developments. We may now examine the third kind of difference, which according to Hick may prove to be a major obstacle in resolving conflicting truth claims. The issue here turns on the founder and scripture of the tradition.

Advaita Vedānta dispenses with the issue of the founder in accepting the Vedas as *apauruṣeya;* that is, as possessing neither a human nor divine author. But what about its claim that only the Vedas can supply humanity with saving knowledge?

Some scholars, K. Satchidananda Murty among them, have argued very strongly that salvation must be mediated through the Vedas in the context of Advaita Vedānta. This does seem to be the general position, despite problems, but it is not entirely clear whether this is a substantial or a nominal position and even whether the position within Advaita Vedānta might not be more charitable than it has been made out to be.

In this context Brahmasūtra 1.1.4 is significant, as it declares that the Upaniṣads, are to be interpreted *tat tu samanvayāt* (on the principle of harmony). The well-known modern thinker, S. Radhakrishnan has suggested that "today the *samanvaya* or harmonization has to be extended to the living faiths of mankind"—and, one might add, to the *scriptures* of all the living faiths of mankind. Such an approach might have the effect of rendering the third difficulty identified by Hick more tractable.

A Philosophical Framework for Religious Pluralism in John H. Hick and Advaita Vedānta: A Comparison

John H. Hick then goes on to propose a philosophical framework for religious pluralism, the basic principle of which is that we can "think in terms of a single divine noumenon and perhaps many diverse divine phenomena." In elaborating this position Hick makes several remarks that are quite significant from the point of view of Advaita Vedānta: (1) Hick identifies the "similar (though not identical) distinctions" found within the major religious traditions between the Real as such and the Real as experienced by human beings.

> In the west the Christian mystic Meister Eckhart drew a parallel distinction between the Godhead (*Deitas*) and God (*Deus*). The Taoist scripture, the *Tao Te Ching*, begins by affirming that "the Tao that can be expressed is not the eternal Tao." The Jewish Kabbalist mystics distinguished between En Soph, the absolute divine reality beyond all human description, and the God of the Bible; and among the Muslim Sufis, Al Haqq, the Real, seems to be a similar concept to En Soph, as the abyss of Godhead underlying the self-revealing Allah. More recently Paul Tillich has spoken of "the God above the God of theism." A. N. Whitehead, and the process theologians who follow him, distinguish between the primordial and consequent natures of God; and Gordon Kaufman has recently distinguished between the "real God" and the "available God."

Hick draws on Immanuel Kant's concept of "the world as it is *an sich,* which he called the noumenal world, and the world as it appears to human consciousness, which he calls the phenomenal world." Taking his cue from this, Hick forms "the hypothesis that the Real *an sich* is experienced by human beings in terms of one of the two basic religious concepts" ("the Real as such and the Real as experienced by human beings"), which when experienced are "made more concrete (in Kantian terminology, schematized) as a range of particular images of God or particular concepts of the Absolute." Thus, on the one hand, are the *different* images of God as found in the various theistic religions explained and on the other the different forms of nontheistic religions which refer to the Absolute—"Brahman, Nirvana, Sunyata, the Dharma, the Dharmakaya, the Tao."

Hick further maintains that although it is sometimes claimed of the absolutistic experience that it is unmediated, unlike the theistic, by the human mind, "our hypothesis will have to hold that even the apparently direct and unmediated awareness of the Real in the Hindu *moksha,* in the Buddhist *satori,* and in the unitive mysticism of the West, is still the conscious experience of the human agent and as such is influenced by the interpretative set of the cognizing mind." Ultimately, Hick concludes that "it is a possible, and indeed an attractive hypothesis—as an alternative to total skepticism—that the great religious traditions of the world represent different human perceptions of and response to the same infinite divine Reality."

The reader will recognize that this position is very similar to the one developed by modern Advaitin thinkers. However, the difference between the position advocated by John H. Hick and the position of the Advaitin on these points needs to be clarified.

1. The reader will notice, and Hick specifically mentions, the similarity of the distinctions between Godhead and God, and so on, to the distinction drawn between *nirguṇa* and *saguṇa* Brahman in Advaita. Here the point to be kept in mind from the Advaitic point of view is that "God as immanent (saguṇa) and God as transcendent Reality (nirguṇa) are not two any more than the man on the stage and the man outside the stage are two." This is an allusion to Śaṅkara's analogy of the actor—a shepherd who appears on the stage in the *role* of a king is not two people, a shepherd and a king. In other words, Advaita would insist, the *nirguṇa* and *saguṇa* refer to two aspects of the *same* Reality.

2. Immanuel Kant's concept of *Ding an sich* must be used with some caution in the context of

Advaita. This becomes clear from certain observations made by M. Hiriyanna while concluding a discussion of *nirguṇa* Brahman:

> Here naturally arises the question whether such an entity is not a sheer abstraction. Śaṁkara recognizes the force of this objection. It is, indeed, the very objection he seems to have raised against a certain other monistic view (*sattādvaita*) of Upanishadic teaching which was in vogue in his time, viz. that Brahman is universal Being. Śaṁkara's monism differs from it in that it views the ultimate reality not as objective, but as identical *at bottom* with the individual self (*ātmādvaita*). This altered conception secures the maximum certainty to the reality of Brahman, for nothing can possibly carry greater certitude with it than one's belief in the existence of oneself. "A man," it has been said, "may doubt of many things, of anything *else;* but he can never doubt of his own being," for that very act of doubting would affirm its existence. It is thus eventually through something in ourselves that, according to Śaṁkara, we are able to judge of reality and unreality. Such a view does not mean that the self is known to us completely. Far from it. But, at the same time, it does not remain wholly unknown, being our own self—a fact which distinguishes the advaitic ultimate from not only the universal Being referred to above, *but also (to mention a Western parallel) the thing-in-itself of Kant.*

In Advaita, the thing-in-itself is knowable in a metempirical way, as the *ātman,* though there is considerable controversy surrounding the issue of how it is known. In this debate the role of the *mind* is one of the points at issue. According to one school, for instance, *direct* knowledge of the ultimate Reality, Brahman, is possible because as "Brahman, which is to be known, is not different from the knower (the subject) immediate knowledge is possible." Another view is that "though the knowledge of Brahman derived from scripture is not itself immediate, Brahman is immediate; and Brahman is immediately experienced by mind only."

Although the latter position is closer to Hick's, neither position would agree with his statement that the experience is "*influenced*" by the interpretative set of the cognizing mind," as the dispute between them is over the mechanics of Realization alone. What is crucial to note here is the possibility of "immediate knowledge not involving sense-perception. The empirical self, for instance, is immediately known, but it cannot be said to be *presented* to any sense. Hence the word pratyakṣa, which literally means 'presented to a sense,' is here replaced by the wider term aparokṣa or 'not mediate.'" It is also important to note, in a broader context, the pervasive significance of the Ātman = Brahman identity in Advaita.

However, although the *experience* as such is not influenced by the cognizing mind—because, in the technical jargon of Advaita, the internal organ (*antaḥkaraṇa*) is merged with nescience (*avidyā*), *of which it is a product,* before the latter is sublated, leading to Brahman-*experience*—our *knowledge* of it may be influenced by the internal organ "for no knowledge, whether mediate or immediate, is possible in the absence of the internal organ," although the self, *ātman,* is ontologically prior to the "false identity of the self and the not-self," which presupposes *avidyā* or ignorance."

3. The previous discussion clarifies the view whether, from the point of view of Advaita, one can agree with Hick that "even the apparently direct and unmediated awareness of the Real . . . is still the conscious experience of the human subject and as such is influenced by the interpretative set of the cognizing mind." The Advaitic position would seem to suggest that the awareness of the Real is unmediated and direct, but when it becomes recognized *as* the conscious experience of the subject it is influenced by the mind-set. On the analogy of sleep it may be pointed out that our personality has nothing to do with the *state* of deep sleep; "None of the features of sleep . . . is 'known' at the time, for no knowledge, whether mediate or immediate, is possible in the absence of the internal organ. But they are nevertheless realized then as shown by the fact of their being recalled afterwards." At the stage of recall the internal organ is again active and the mind-set now comes into play.

4. The Advaitin philosophical framework, nevertheless, for religious pluralism, is very similar to

Hick's and shares its attractive features. It is, however, capable of an extension that is possible while one is functioning from within an Advaitic framework but perhaps not possible if one is operating within the framework suggested by Hick. Nor is it entirely clear whether the new position represents any advance or possesses any advantage over that advocated by John H. Hick. It, however, needs to be taken into account as it does actually appear in the history of Advaita Vedānta. It is rooted in the Advaitic position that in the final analysis only one ultimate reality exists, which is called *Brahman* or *ātman*. But if there is really only one reality, are we left with any other position to even contend with? Thus a modern exponent of Advaita Vedānta can affirm that

> Advaita is *non-dual-ism*. Reality, according to its insight, is non-dual, not-two. Advaita does not profess to formulate conceptually what Reality is. It is not, therefore, a system of thought, an *ism*. It is not a school among schools of philosophy. It does not reject any view of Reality; it only seeks to transcend all views, since these are by their very nature restricted, limited, and circumscribed. The pluralisms, theistic or otherwise, imagine that they are opposed to Advaita. But Advaita is not opposed to any of the partial views of Reality.

Such an affirmation is in keeping with the tradition of Advaita Vedānta, for an early exponent of it, Gauḍapāda (seventh century C.E.) declared: "The dualists (i.e. pluralists) are conclusively firm in regard to the status of their respective opinions. They are in conflict with one another. But, Advaita is in no conflict with them. Advaita, verily, is the supreme truth; dvaita is a variant thereof. For the dualists, there is duality either way (i.e. both in the Absolute and in the phenomenal manifold). With that (duality) this (non-duality) is not in conflict."

Such a view has the merit of being nonconflictual, but at the cost of dismissing the other party out of hand. This is apparent in a remark Śaṅkara makes in his commentary on the verses of Gauḍapāda quoted above. Śaṅkara writes: "As one who is mounted on a spirited elephant does not drive it against a lunatic who stands on the ground and shouts, 'Drive your elephant against me who also am seated on an elephant,' because he (the former) has no notion of opposition, even so (is the case with the non-dualist). Thus, in truth, the knower of *Brahman* is the very self of the dualists. For this reason, our view is not in conflict with theirs."

In point of fact, however, Śaṅkara did engage other schools in debate and dialogue. Perhaps if it is realized that Śaṅkara is talking here from a metempirical point of view, whereas all discourse is carried on within the empirical realm, the contradiction is converted into a paradox.

5. The founder and the scriptures loom large as an issue in Hick's agenda, but Advaita Vedānta deals in the eternal rather than the historical. It could be argued that it apotheosizes the Veda; however, the Veda also belongs to the realm of *mithyā;* moreover, some say that the Vedas are endless, which creates room for the acceptance of other scriptures. Finally, experience takes precedence over the Vedas, on which their own claim to validity really rests. Thus what John H. Hick identifies as the main obstacles to the accommo-

dation of conflicting truth claims turn out to be less problematical in the case of Advaita Vedānta.

Conclusion

Despite these divergences there is little doubt that there exists a very strong family resemblance in the philosophical frameworks offered by John H. Hick and Advaita Vedānta for resolving conflicting truth claims. This becomes quite clear from such Advaitic statements as the following found in the Yogavāśiṣtha (III.1.12; III.5, 6, 7; V.8.19):

> Many names have been given to the Absolute by the learned for practical purposes such as Law, Self, Truth.
>
> It is called Person by the Sāṃkhya thinkers, Brahman by the Vedāntins, pure and simple consciousness by the Vijñānavādins, Śūnya by the Nihilists, the Illuminator by the worshippers of the Sun. It is also called the Speaker, the Thinker, the Enjoyer of actions and the Doer of them.
>
> Śiva for the worshippers of Śiva, and Time for those who believe in Time alone.

11.4 The Transcendent Unity of Religions

Many people have distinguished the esoteric (hidden, secret, inner, spiritual) aspect of religions from the exoteric (public, historical, institutional) aspect. Some have come to believe that the esoteric side of religions expresses and embodies a *philosophia perennis*—an ancient wisdom about a divine Reality that constitutes an absolute unity transcendent to the empirical reality we know. This Perennial Philosophy, some claim, can be found in rudimentary and fragmentary forms in the myths of pre-literate peoples and in more fully developed forms in all of the major world religions.

Frithjof Schuon, born in Basel, Switzerland, in 1907 and author of the next selection, became interested in the *philosophia perennis* at an early age and has devoted a lifetime to its study. He studied Sufism in Algeria and Morocco and was strongly influenced by the Algerian Sufi Ahmad Al-Allawi. He became convinced that there exists a universal, ancient, and sacred wisdom that has shaped and informed all of the diverse religious traditions. He became particularly attracted to the Islamic Sufi tradition because of its mystical spirituality and its claim that in Allah is revealed the transcendent unity of all reality. If there is such a unity, then it must constitute the transcendent unity of religions.

On the exoteric level, religions are diverse. They make what appear to be contradictory claims. They regard certain religious founders and prophets as unique givers of truth and salvation. The exoteric, however, is finite, relative, particular, and perspectival. The esoteric has to do with what is infinite, absolute, universal, and integral. The true unity of religions is in the esoteric dimension. Those who understand the esoteric (those who know the ancient *philosophia perennis*) see that the conflicts and differences among the diverse traditions are really superficial. Beneath the surface lies a wondrous unity that mystics of all ages and all faiths proclaim—or so Schuon argues.

Many question whether there is such a thing as a *philosophia perennis* (a term first coined by the German philosopher Leibniz, 1646–1716). Still others wonder whether it can be at the core of all religions. In part, the arguments are historical. What sort of evidence do we have, and what does it prove? In part the arguments are philosophical. Can one simply ignore what appears to be genuine religious diversity and disagreement by reinterpreting it as an exoteric expression of a hidden unity and truth?

Although Schuon does believe there is agreement among diverse traditions about the ideas of the Perennial Philosophy, he also believes that the true unity of religions must be ultimately located at a deeper level—the level of the divine unity itself. Here is found the transcendent unity not only of religions but of all reality. Ultimately, all diversity and plurality are but accidental variations on a unitary divine theme.

You might wonder whether Schuon somewhat arbitrarily elevates one particular philosophical notion of the divine to the status of highest truth and relegates the rest to a lesser, exoteric status. Read and see what you think.

Reading Questions

1. What does philosophy ignore, according to Schuon?
2. What, according to Schuon, is the difference between a dogmatic affirmation and a speculative formulation?
3. Do you agree with Schuon's assertion that "if God were on the side of one religious form only," then its persuasive force would be such that "no man of good faith would be able to resist it"? Why or why not?
4. How does Schuon support his claim that anyone who tries to prove the truth of one religion to the exclusion of others cannot provide such a proof?
5. If, as Schuon asserts, "pure and absolute Truth can only be found beyond all its possible expressions," then it would seem that we can never state this *Truth*. If we cannot, then how do we know that what Schuon claims about "absolute Truth" is true?

The Transcendent Unity of Religions*

FRITHJOF SCHUON

THE TRUE AND COMPLETE understanding of an idea goes far beyond the first apprehension of the idea by the intelligence, although more often than not this apprehension is taken for understanding itself. While it is true that the immediate evidence conveyed to us by any particular idea is, on its own level, a real understanding, there can be no question of its embracing the whole extent of the idea, since it is primarily the sign of an aptitude to understand that idea in its completeness. Any truth can in fact be understood at different levels and according to different conceptual dimensions, that is to say, according to an indefinite number of modalities that correspond to all the possible aspects, likewise indefinite in number, of the truth in question. This way of regarding ideas accordingly leads to the question of spiritual realization, the doctrinal expressions of which clearly illustrate the dimensional indefinitude of theoretical conceptions.

Philosophy, considered from the standpoint of its limitations—and it is the limitations of philosophy that confer upon it its specific character—is based on the systematic ignoring of what has been stated above. In other words, philosophy ignores what would be its own negation; moreover, it concerns itself solely with mental schemes that, with its claim to universality, it likes to regard as absolute, although from the point of view of spiritual realization these schemes are merely so many virtual or potential and unused objects, insofar at least as they refer to true ideas; when, however, this is not the case, as practically always occurs in modern philosophy, these schemes are reduced to the condition of mere devices that are unusable from a speculative point of view and are therefore without any real value. As for true ideas, those, that is to say, that more or less implicitly suggest aspects of the total Truth, and hence this Truth itself, they become by that very fact intellectual keys and indeed have no other function; this is something that metaphysical thought alone is capable of grasping. So far as philosophical or ordinary theological thought is concerned, there is, on the contrary, an ignorance affecting not only the nature of the ideas that are believed to be completely understood, but also and above all the scope of theory as such; theoretical understanding is in fact transitory and limited by definition, though its limits can only be more or less approximately defined.

The purely "theoristic" understanding of an idea, which we have so termed because of the limitative tendency that paralyzes it, may justly be characterized by the word "dogmatism"; religious dogma in fact, at least to the extent to which it is supposed to exclude other conceptual forms, though certainly not in itself, represents an idea considered in conformity with a theoristic tendency, and this exclusive way of looking at ideas has even become characteristic of the religious point of view as such. A religious dogma ceases, however, to be limited in this way once it is understood in the light of its inherent truth, which is of a universal order, and this is the case in all esoterism. On the other hand, the ideas formulated in esoterism and in metaphysical doctrines generally may in their turn be understood according to the dogmatic or theoristic tendency, and the case is then analogous to that of the religious dogmatism of which we have just spoken. In this connection, we must again point out that a religious dogma is not a dogma in itself but solely by the fact of being considered as such and through a sort of confusion of the idea with the form in which it is clothed; on the other

---

hand, the outward dogmatization of universal truths is perfectly justified in view of the fact that these truths or ideas, in having to provide the foundation of a religion, must be capable of being assimilated in some degree by all men. Dogmatism as such does not consist in the mere enunciation of an idea, that is to say, in the fact of giving form to a spiritual intuition, but rather in an interpretation that, instead of rejoining the formless and total Truth after taking as its starting point one of the forms of that Truth, results in a sort of paralysis of this form by denying its intellectual potentialities and by attributing to it an absoluteness that only the formless and total Truth itself can possess.

Dogmatism reveals itself not only by its inability to conceive the inward or implicit illimitability of the symbol, the universality that resolves all outward oppositions, but also by its inability to recognize, when faced with two apparently contradictory truths, the inward connection that they implicitly affirm, a connection that makes of them complementary aspects of one and the same truth. One might illustrate this in the following manner: whoever participates in universal Knowledge will regard two apparently contradictory truths as he would two points situated on one and the same circumference that links them together by its continuity and so reduces them to unity; in the measure in which these points are distant from, and thus opposed to one another, there will be contradiction, and this contradiction will reach its maximum when the two points are situated at the extremities of a diameter of the circle; but this extreme opposition or contradiction only appears as a result of isolating the points under consideration from the circle and ignoring the existence of the latter. One may conclude from this that a dogmatic affirmation, that is to say, an affirmation that is inseparable from its form and admits no other, is comparable to a point, which by definition, as it were, contradicts all other possible points; a speculative formulation, on the other hand, is comparable to an element of a circle, the very form of which indicates its logical and ontological continuity and therefore the whole circle or, by analogical trans-

position, the whole Truth; this comparison will, perhaps, suggest in the clearest possible way the difference that separates a dogmatic affirmation from a speculative formulation.

The outward and intentional contradictoriness of speculative formulations may show itself, it goes without saying, not only in a single, logically paradoxical formula such as the Vedic *Aham Brahmasmi* ("I am Brahma")—the Vedantic definition of the yogi—or the *Ana 'l-Ḥaqq* ("I am the Truth") of Al-Ḥallāj, or Christ's words concerning His Divinity, but also, and for even stronger reasons, as between different formulations each of which may be logically homogeneous in itself. Examples of the latter may be found in all sacred Scriptures, notably in the Koran: we need only recall the apparent contradiction between the affirmations regarding predestination and those regarding free will, affirmations that are contradictory only in the sense that they express opposite aspects of a single reality. However, apart from these paradoxical formulations—whether they are so in themselves or in relation to one another—there also remain certain theories that, although expressing the strictest orthodoxy, are nevertheless in outward contradiction one with another, this being due to the diversity of their respective points of view, which are not chosen arbitrarily and artificially but are established spontaneously by virtue of a genuine intellectual originality.

To return to what was said above about the understanding of ideas, a theoretical notion may be compared to the view of an object. Just as this view does not reveal all possible aspects, or in other words, the integral nature of the object, the perfect knowledge of which would be nothing less than identity with it, so a theoretical notion does not itself correspond to the integral truth, of which it necessarily suggests only one aspect, essential or otherwise.[1] In the example just given, error corresponds to an inadequate view of the object whereas a dogmatic conception is comparable to the exclusive view of one aspect of the object, a view that supposes the immobility of the seeing subject. As for a speculative and therefore intellectually unlimited conception, this may be compared to the sum of all possible views of the object in question, views that presuppose in the subject a power of displacement or an ability to alter his viewpoint, hence a certain mode of identity with the dimensions of space, which themselves effectually reveal the integral nature of the object, at least with respect to its form, which is all that is in question in the example given. Movement in space is in fact an active participation in the possibilities of space, whereas static extension in space, the form of our bodies, for example, is a passive participation in these same possibilities. This may be transposed without difficulty to a higher plane and one may then speak of an "intellectual space," namely, the cognitive all-possibility that is fundamentally the same as the Divine Omniscience, and consequently of "intellectual dimensions" that are the internal modalities of this Omniscience; Knowledge through the Intellect is none other than the perfect participation of the subject in these modalities, and in the physical world this participation is effectively represented by movement. When speaking, therefore, of the understanding of ideas, we may distinguish between a dogmatic understanding, comparable to the view of an object from a single viewpoint, and an integral or speculative understanding, comparable to the indefinite series of possible views of the object, views that are realized through indefinitely multiple changes of point of view. Just as, when the eye changes its position, the different views of an object are connected by a perfect continuity, which represents, so to speak, the determining reality of the object, so the different aspects of a truth, however contradictory they may appear and notwithstanding their indefinite multiplicity, describe the integral Truth that surpasses and determines them. We would again refer here to an illustration we have already used; a dogmatic affirmation corresponds to a point that, as such, contradicts by definition every other point, whereas a speculative formulation is always conceived as an element of a circle that by its very form indicates principally its own continuity, and hence the entire circle and the Truth in its entirety.

It follows from the above that in speculative doctrines it is the point of view on the one hand and the aspect on the other hand that determine the form of the affirmation, whereas in dogmatism the affirmation is confused with a determinate point of view and aspect, thus excluding all others. . . .

Exoteric doctrine as such, considered, that is to say, apart from the "spiritual influence" that is capable of acting on souls independently of it, by no means possesses absolute certitude. Theological knowledge cannot by itself shut out the temptations of doubt, even in the case of great mystics; as for the influences of Grace that may intervene in such cases, they are not consubstantial with the intelligence, so that their permanence does not depend on the being who benefits from them. Exoteric ideology being limited to a relative point of view, that of individual salvation—an interested point of view that even influences the conception of Divinity in a restrictive sense—possesses no means of proof or doctrinal credentials proportionate to its own exigencies. Every exoteric doctrine is in fact characterized by a disproportion between its dogmatic demands and its dialectical guarantees: for its demands are absolute as deriving from the Divine Will and therefore also from Divine Knowledge, whereas its guarantees are relative, because they are independent of this Will and based, not on Divine Knowledge, but on a human point of view, that of reason and sentiment. For instance, Brahmins are invited to abandon completely a religion that has lasted for several thousands of years, one that has provided the spiritual support of innumerable generations and has produced flowers of wisdom and holiness down to our times. The arguments that are produced to justify this extraordinary demand are in no wise logically conclusive, nor do they bear any proportion to the magnitude of the demand; the reasons that the Brahmins have for remaining faithful to their spiritual patrimony are therefore infinitely stronger than the reasons by which it is sought to persuade them to cease being what they are. The disproportion, from the Hindu point of view, between the immense reality of the Brahmanic tradition and the insufficiency of the Christian counterarguments is such as to prove quite sufficiently that had God wished to submit the world to one religion only, the arguments put forward on behalf of this religion would not be so feeble, nor those of certain so-called "infidels" so powerful; in other words, if God were on the side of one religious form only, the persuasive power of this form would be such that no man of good faith would be able to resist it. Moreover, the application of the term "infidel" to civilizations that are, with one exception, very much older than Christianity and that have every spiritual and historic right to ignore the latter, provides a further demonstration, by the very illogicality of its naive pretensions, of the perverted nature of the Christian claims with regard to other orthodox traditional forms.

An absolute requirement to believe in one particular religion and not in another cannot in fact be justified save by eminently relative means, as, for example, by attempted philosophico-theological, historical, or sentimental proofs; in reality, however, no proofs exist in support of such claims to the unique and exclusive truth, and any attempt so made can only concern the individual dispositions of men, which, being ultimately reducible to a question of credulity, are as relative as can be. Every exoteric perspective claims, by definition, to be the only true and legitimate one. This is because the exoteric point of view, being concerned only with an individual interest, namely, salvation, has no advantage to gain from knowledge of the truth of other religious forms. Being uninterested as to its own deepest truth, it is even less interested in the truth of other religions, or rather it denies this truth, since the idea of a plurality of religious forms might be prejudicial to the exclusive pursuit of individual salvation. This clearly shows up the relativity of form as such, though the latter is nonetheless an absolute necessity for the salvation of the individual. It might be asked, however, why the guarantees, that is to say, the proofs of veracity or credibility, which religious polemists do their utmost to produce, do not derive spontaneously from the Divine Will, as is the case with religious demands. Obviously such a question has no

meaning unless it relates to truths, for one cannot prove errors; the arguments of religious controversy are, however, in no way related to the intrinsic and positive domain of faith; an idea that has only an extrinsic and negative significance and that, fundamentally, is merely the result of an induction—such, for example, as the idea of the exclusive truth and legitimacy of a particular religion or, which comes to the same thing, of the falsity and illegitimacy of all other possible religions—an idea such as this evidently cannot be the object of proof, whether this proof be divine or, for still stronger reasons, human. So far as genuine dogmas are concerned—that is to say, dogmas that are not derived by induction but are of a strictly intrinsic character—if God has not given theoretical proofs of their truth it is, in the first place, because such proofs are inconceivable and nonexistent on the exoteric plane, and to demand them as unbelievers do would be a pure and simple contradiction; secondly, as we shall see later, if such proofs do in fact exist, it is on quite a different plane, and the Divine Revelation most certainly implies them, without any omission. Moreover, to return to the exoteric plane where alone this question is relevant, the Revelation in its essential aspect is sufficiently intelligible to enable it to serve as a vehicle for the action of Grace, and Grace is the only sufficient and fully valid reason for adhering to a religion. However, since this action of Grace only concerns those who do not in fact possess its equivalent under some other revealed form, the dogmas remain without persuasive power—we may say without proofs—for those who do possess this equivalent. Such people are therefore "unconvertible"—leaving aside certain cases of conversion due to the suggestive force of a collective psychism, in which case Grace intervenes only *a posteriori*, for the spiritual influence can have no hold over them, just as one light cannot illuminate another. This is in conformity with the Divine Will, which has distributed the one Truth under different forms or, to express it in another way, between different humanities, each one of which is symbolically the only one. It may be added that if the extrinsic relativity of exoterism is in conformity with the Divine Will, which affirms itself in this way according to the very nature of things, it goes without saying that this relativity cannot be done away with by any human will.

Thus, having shown that no rigorous proof exists to support an exoteric claim to the exclusive possession of the truth, must we not now go further and admit that even the orthodoxy of a religious form cannot be proved? Such a conclusion would be highly artificial and, in any case, completely erroneous, since there is implicit in every religious form an absolute proof of its truth and so of its orthodoxy; what cannot be proved, for want of absolute proof, is not intrinsic truth, hence the traditional legitimacy, of a form of the universal Revelation, but solely the hypothetical fact that any particular form is the only true and legitimate one, and if this cannot be proved it is for the simple reason that it is untrue.

There are, therefore, irrefutable proofs of the truth of a religion; but these proofs, which are of a purely spiritual order, while being the only possible proofs in support of a revealed truth, entail at the same time a denial of the pretensions to exclusiveness of the form. In other words, he who sets out to prove the truth of one religion either has no proofs, since such proofs do not exist, or else he has the proofs that affirm all religious truth without exception, whatever the form in which it may have clothed itself.

The exoteric claim to the exclusive possession of a unique truth, or of Truth without epithet, is therefore an error purely and simply; in reality, every expressed truth necessarily assumes a form, that of its expression, and it is metaphysically impossible that any form should possess a unique value to the exclusion of other forms; for a form, by definition, cannot be unique and exclusive, that is to say, it cannot be the only possible expression of what it expresses. Form implies specification or distinction, and the specific is only conceivable as a modality of a "species," that is to say, of a category that includes a combination of analogous modalities. Again, that which is limited excludes by definition whatever is not comprised within its own limits and must

compensate for this exclusion by a reaffirmation or repetition of itself outside its own boundaries, which amounts to saying that the existence of other limited things is rigorously implied in the very definition of the limited. To claim that a limitation, for example, a form considered as such, is unique and incomparable of its kind, and that it excludes the existence of other analogous modalities, is to attribute to it the unicity of Existence itself; now, no one can contest the fact that a form is always a limitation or that a religion is of necessity always a form—not, that goes without saying, by virtue of its internal Truth, which is of a universal and supraformal order, but because of its mode of expression, which, as such, cannot but be formal and therefore specific and limited. It can never be said too often that a form is always a modality of a category of formal, and therefore distinctive or multiple, manifestation, and is consequently but one modality among others that are equally possible, their suprapformal cause alone being unique. We will also repeat—for this is metaphysically of great importance—that a form, by the very fact that it is limited, necessarily leaves something outside itself, namely, that which its limits exclude; and this something, if it belongs to the same order, is necessarily analogous to the form under consideration, since the distinction between forms must needs be compensated by an indistinction or relative identity that prevents them from being absolutely distinct from each other, for that would entail the absurd idea of a plurality of unicities or Existences, each form representing a sort of divinity without any relationship to other forms.

As we have just seen, the exoteric claim to the exclusive possession of the truth comes up against the axiomatic objection that there is no such thing in existence as a unique fact, for the simple reason that it is strictly impossible that such a fact should exist, unicity alone being unique and no fact being unicity; it is this that is ignored by the ideology of the "believers," which is fundamentally nothing but an intentional and interested confusion between the formal and the universal. The ideas that are affirmed in one religious form (as, for example, the idea of the Word or of the Divine Unity) cannot fail to be affirmed, in one way or another, in all other religious forms; similarly the means of grace or of spiritual realization at the disposal of one priestly order cannot but possess their equivalent elsewhere; and indeed, the more important and indispensable any particular means of grace may be, the more certain is it that it will be found in all the orthodox forms in a mode appropriate to the environment in question.

The foregoing can be summed up in the following formula: pure and absolute Truth can only be found beyond all its possible expressions; these expressions, as such, cannot claim the attributes of this Truth; their relative remoteness from it is expressed by their differentiation and multiplicity, by which they are strictly limited.

NOTE

1. In a treatise directed against rationalist philosophy, Al-Ghazzālī speaks of certain blind men who, not having even a theoretical knowledge of an elephant, came across this animal one day and started to feel the different parts of its body; as a result each man represented the animal to himself according to the part that he touched: for the first, who touched a foot, the elephant resembled a column, whereas for the second, who touched one of the tusks, it resembled a stake, and so on. By this parable Al-Ghazzālī seeks to show the error involved in trying to enclose the universal within a fragmentary notion of it, or within isolated and exclusive aspects or points of view. Shri Ramakrishna also uses this parable to demonstrate the inadequacy of dogmatic exclusiveness in its negative aspect. The same idea could, however, be expressed by means of an even more adequate example: faced with any object, some might say that it "is" a certain shape, while others might say that it "is" such and such a material; others again might maintain that it "is" such and such a number or such and such a weight, and so forth.

11.5 Whose Objectivity? Which Neutrality?

What criteria should we use in sorting out the conflicting truth claims among the various religions? Do we have a set of principles and procedures for going about deciding who is right and who is wrong? If we lack such principles, why? Is it impossible to decide such conflicts? Or maybe it is possible, but we just have not figured out how to do it yet.

Can we appeal to religious experience in order to settle conflicts? When it comes to questions of truth, how should we interpret such experiences? Should we appeal to historical facts? Does proving that Jesus lived (or the Buddha or Muhammad) prove anything about the truth of their messages?

Perhaps we should use a pragmatic criterion. Does faith *x* help people live better lives? How do we determine that? If it does, how does this bear on its truth? It may help me get through some really depressing moments to believe that angels are watching over me and keeping me from harm, but does that prove angels exist?

The list of questions and suggestions could go on and on. When it comes to settling disputed claims to truth among the world's religions, there are many more questions than answers. There are, however, several different options, and a careful exploration of each might give us some guidance. One of the biggest problems is the issue of objectivity. Is it really possible to be objective when judging different religions?

Gavin D'Costa, professor of religion at the University of Bristol, explores some of the options in the next selection. He is quite skeptical of claims to neutrality. Objectivity is illusive, he thinks, when it comes to deciding religious truth. Should we give up and stop trying? D'Costa thinks not. Can he convince you?

Reading Questions

1. What four options are available for judging the truth claims of religions?
2. What two axioms does D'Costa hope to establish?
3. According to D'Costa, what is wrong with Netland's two definitions and eight principles?
4. What is Ward's argument, and what is wrong with it?
5. What does D'Costa conclude about the impasse regarding conflicting truth claims?
6. Do you think D'Costa's conclusion is correct? Why or why not?

Whose Objectivity? Which Neutrality?*

GAVIN D'COSTA

I

There is an impasse in the discussion as to how to judge a religion other than one's own. On the one hand judging another religion by the criteria and standards of one's own tradition has become a highly problematic exercise. The metaphor used by some critics for such an approach is that of jingoistic flag-waving. Criticisms of this strategy are numerous and interdisciplinary in their nature. For instance, it is argued that such an enterprise is part and parcel of the political–economic imperialism of western (Christian) history. Such geo-political–religious imperialism is intolerable in a post-colonial age. Sociologically, anthropologically, and philosophically it has been argued that disparate traditions are quite simply incommensurable, each operating with their own rules and grammar. Hence, to judge one religion against another is like judging the goodness of an apple against a vacuum cleaner. The degree of incommensurability varies, so that at the lower end of the scale, the appropriate analogy is that of judging the goodness of apples against oranges. Such criticisms involve a range of disputed questions such as the possibility of successful translation of one language into another alien and different language, the epistemological logocentricism of western philosophical thought, and so on. I should state before proceeding that despite such criticisms I am a supporter of a nuanced form of this first strategy. I shall return to this point in due course.

If, on the one hand, judging another religion by one's own is deemed problematic, the alternative has proven equally so. Here it is maintained that it is inappropriate to use criteria from one's own religion to judge another religion. One may judge another religion by that religion's criteria alone or one should desist from such a task altogether as it is conceptually impossible. However, critics point out that if one judges another religion purely by its own criteria then the whole problem of conflicting truth claims is bypassed which was in fact the reason for trying to find criteria for judgement. Judging religions by their own criteria may be helpful in some contexts, but it takes us no further in trying to arbitrate

*From "Whose Objectivity? Which Neutrality? The Doomed Quest for a Neutral Vantage Point from Which to Judge Religions" by Gavin D'Costa. *Religious Studies 29.* Copyright © 1993 Cambridge University Press, 79–95. Reprinted by permission. Footnotes deleted.

between two rival religious claims. Critics also point out that total incommensurability is self defeating and such relativism is finally conceptually indefensible. Such relativism effectively ghettoises religions by emasculating any public relevance they may claim. In response, relativising the relativisers means that those who stipulate against religions making judgements on other religions commit the very error they are opposed to by carrying out judgements on all religions.

Stalemate? There are two other options. One would be to question the necessity of such a task and re-centre attention on more pressing issues such as poverty and hunger, political exploitation of women and minorities, child abuse, and the global destruction of parent earth (an inverse form of child abuse). This could be labelled the liberationist/pragmatic strategy that moves the focus away from conflicting doctrines and truth claims and tries to focus on common social and environmental problems. While the agenda is unquestionably urgent, such a pragmatic strategy does not really circumvent the problem. Questions of "justice" and "virtue" are involved in addressing such social and moral problems, and inevitably critiques of a tradition other than one's own, as well as one's own, will be required in trying to eradicate "child abuse" or "exploitation" of women. Hence, such a strategy meets the same difficulty, for most religions circumscribe their world and thereby define the activities that can and should go on within those boundaries. Religions are not just doctrinal entities, but traditions which fuse and hold together doctrine, practice, liturgy, ritual and so on. Philosophically, such an emphasis on morality as the uncontroversial bridge to avoid the impasse described above stems from an impoverished form of Enlightenment natural ethics which assumes incontestable universal moral norms that would be adhered to by all sensible persons. It should also be said that such a pragmatic approach is sometimes suggested by those who are frankly indifferent to religions and essentially wish to impose a humanistic agenda homogeneously upon all religions.

So what of the fourth option which could deliver us from this impasse? This strategy is subtle and interesting and in limited respects a variant on the above. It is also deceptively straightforward. It is the path of neutrality. Find neutral, commonly acceptable criteria which could not sensibly be rejected by any thinking adherent of any religious tradition. Apply these criteria and one will find a way through the impasse and provide a basis for judging true from false religions. Utopian? Just such a strategy has been suggested by two philosophers of religion: Keith Ward and Harold Netland in *A Vision to Pursue* and *Dissonant Voices* respectively. Ward and Netland could not, of course, refer to each other's work, but one might expect from both of them a consensus on criteria, or at least an agreement in principle with each other's criteria. It would be less fair to expect agreement on the outcome of the application of their criteria for this of course would be quite a complicated task. However, when we turn to their two books we find something surprising, although perhaps quite predictable. Not only are their criteria very different, but Ward suggests all religions would achieve worthwhile scores and thereby supports a form of pluralism (p. 191f), while Netland on the other hand suggests that Christianity alone "satisfies the requirements of all the . . . criteria" (p. 193) and hence, alone amongst the traditions, is true. Such an outcome should alert us to the inherent problem in such allegedly neutral strategies. What I wish to do is critically examine each of their proposals to show that such strategies are futile. In so doing, I will be implicitly arguing for a version of the first position outlined above.

I also hope to show the truth of two axioms. The first is that *in relation to the increased specificity of an alleged neutral proposal its neutrality diminishes.* The second is that *in relation to the decreased specificity of an alleged neutral proposal its usefulness diminishes.* The underlying logic of these two axioms is that whatever criteria are specified they are always and necessarily tradition specific. To give them the status of tradition-transcending robs them of the specificity that ensures their critical cutting edge. And the degree to which they have a critical cutting edge, the more they are rendered tradition specific so they cannot be deemed neutral and capable of acceptance by *all* sensible persons. The implication of this claim would be that by definition any claim to break the impasse by means of the neutrality route is doomed to failure because it is illusory.

II

Harold Netland's proposals are advanced in an interesting defence of Christian "exclusivism" (there is no salvation outside faith in Christ). I do not wish to discuss Netland's book here but am only concerned with his allegedly universally acceptable and binding proposals for determining the truth or falsity of competing religious worldviews. Netland's proposals come after a convincing and robust criticism against relativist strategies (mainly Hick and Knitter—but he would probably add Ward to his list) and less convincing criticisms of fideist strategies. He is dissatisfied with both for their inability to settle questions of truth. He notes that his proposals are not exhaustive and in need of further explication (p. 183), but what he offers is sufficient for discussion. He advances eight principles (P), which are dependent on two prior definitions (D) of religion. I quote from his summary (pp. 192–3):

> D1: p is a defining belief of R if and only if being an active participant in good standing within the religious community of R entails acceptance of p.
>
> D2: A religion R is true if and only if all of its defining beliefs are true; if any of its defining beliefs are false, then R is false.
>
> P1: If a defining belief p of a religion R is self-contradictory then p is false.
>
> P2: If two or more defining beliefs of R are mutually contradictory at least one of them must be false.
>
> P3: If a defining belief p of R is self-defeating it cannot reasonably be accepted as true.
>
> P4: If the defining beliefs of R are not coherent in the sense of providing a unified perspective of the world, then R cannot plausibly be regarded as true.
>
> P5: Any religious worldview which is unable to account for fundamental phenomena associated with a religious orientation or which cannot provide adequate answers to central questions in religion should not be accepted as true.
>
> P6: If a defining belief p of R contradicts well-established conclusions in other domains, and if R cannot justify doing so, then p should be rejected as probably false.
>
> P7: If a defining belief p of R depends upon a belief in another domain (e.g. history) which there is good reason to reject as false, then there is good reason to reject p as probably false.
>
> P8: If one or more defining beliefs of R are incompatible with widely accepted and well-established moral values and principles; or if R includes among its essential practices or rites activities which are incompatible with basic moral values and practices, then there is good reason for rejecting R as false.
>
> P9: If the defining beliefs of R entail the denial of the objectivity of basic moral values and principles; or if they entail the denial of the objective distinction between right and wrong, good and evil, then there is good reason for rejecting R as false.
>
> P10: If R is unable to provide adequate answers to basic questions about the phenomenon of moral awareness this provides good reason for rejecting R as false.

Before turning to the proposals, it should be noted that it seems odd for an evangelical Christian like Netland, who insists that faith in Christ is required for salvation, to propose such a scheme. It would appear that his exclusivist claim should in fact be that salvation is only granted to those who accept his ten principles and two definitions, for he writes that "I should state that the reason I believe one is *justified* in accepting the Christian faith as *true* is because it is the only worldview that satisfies the requirements of all the above criteria" (p. 193, my emphases)—not apparently, because of who Jesus was and who his community proclaimed him to be. The truth of revelation is subject to the truth of the ten principles and two definitions! But let us turn to his proposals.

Netland acknowledges that regarding his definition D1 (p is a defining belief of R if and only if being an active participant in good standing within the religious community of R entails acceptance of p) there is a difficulty in that religions heatedly debate what beliefs precisely constitute "defining beliefs," but he does not think this problematic in terms of the overall logic of his proposals. However, it may be argued that it is for the following reasons. Firstly, precisely because within any one religion there is considerable debate as to what its defining beliefs may be, it is spurious to suggest a cohesive and unified referent to the term "religion." In this respect there are many Christianities and many Buddhisms, both now and in times past, so that in principle the application of the evaluating criteria would have to be applied to *every possible* manifestation of *every possible* religious tradition before Netland's claim that "the [*sic*] Christian faith . . . is the only worldview that satisfied the requirements of all the above criteria" (p. 93) could be seen to be true. While he prefaces this claim that "although this cannot be argued here" I would maintain that while such a task is in principle possible, in practice it would be virtually impossible. It would require *a posteriori* studies using Netland's principles which to my knowledge has not even been started, let alone suggesting that it could be achieved by a single person in a single lifetime. Hence, while this does not jeopardize Netland's overall aim in principle, it suggests a misplaced confidence in his claiming Christianity to be the winner, on such terms, of the judging competition.

Furthermore, while Netland tends to reify religion into a single unified substance, the interesting philosophical and theological factor is precisely the phenomena of change and transformation within religious tradition. William Christian has shown very clearly that besides holding defining beliefs, religious persons also have the mechanisms by which they control, establish and discern defining beliefs and may in one period change what counts as a defining belief for very good theological or philosophical reasons, without thereby changing or denying the "same" religious adherence. The point about this was that even within a unified denomination we can see that there are mechanisms by which it can demote "defining beliefs" to the status of peripheral beliefs without necessary self-contradiction.

Hence, D2 could be rendered tautologous in stipulating that "A religion R is true if and only if all of its defining beliefs are true; if any of its defining beliefs are false, then R is false." Historically, short of changing religion, in times of credibility crisis regarding a defining belief, religious thinkers would tend to relegate that belief in status, rather than hold it as a defining belief with self-consciousness of its error. Again, this does not bear immediately on the question of neutral criteria, but suggests the difficulty with embarking on any evaluating exercise outside of a tradition-specific starting-point.

Finally, what if the defining beliefs of a religion were avowedly fideistic or relativist and such were their subsequent definitions of "truth"? In practice, relativism seems to be quite a recent phenomenon amongst liberal western educated members of religions, but fideism has a distinguished pedigree within different traditions. Fideistic predestination, for example, is evident in Madhava's theology and in Augustine's later thought. This raises the difficulty of the very definition of religion being non-neutral and acceptable to all, for Netland has concealed in his proposal an unstated D3: that is, "Truth is propositional and realist and religions can only define themselves in this way." Hence, what masquerades as an apparently *neutral definition* of religion is in fact a *prescriptive evaluation* of what constitutes genuine true religion, before we even get to the principles which are supposed to perform precisely the task of discerning genuine true religion. This is hardly a promising start.

Let us now turn to the principles that Netland offers and for the moment grant that the project of defining religion is trouble-free. Netland's first and second principles, which rely on notions of identity, non-contradiction and excluded middle, are a promising start for literate, speculative, self-reflective traditions. (I'm not sure the Azande would subscribe to entering this scheme so that they could be evaluated.) I think that here Netland genuinely isolates tradition-transcending principles which would be acceptable to many literate, speculative, self-reflecting persons in different religions. But without looking at the way in which such principles are applied and used from within a specific tradition, they do not really help in settling disputes over truth, except in discerning muddles. Take two examples. If we apply P1 and P2 (if a defining belief p of a religion R is self-contradictory then p is false; and if two or more defining beliefs of R are mutually contradictory at least one of them must be false) to a Zen koan, "listen to the sound of one hand clapping," a koan which is essential as a means to realizing satori, Netland would rule Zen out because such a statement is meaningless in his terms. But Zen Buddhists accept such rules of logic only to show that satori transcends logical conceptuality and definition. A Mādhyamika Buddhist such as Nāgārjuna, who also accepts such rules of logic only to show why no logical system can be held, would also be disqualified by Netland. In fact, Netland may also end up dismissing certain scientists for claiming that light is both a wave and not a wave, or an Einstein for suggesting that the speed at which we observe an object travelling would be both the same and different, depending on our observational position.

The problem here is that these principles do not help in the task of evaluation. One must observe the ways in which they are used within different communities, where such principles may be accepted but are subordinated to more fundamental truths of revelation by which they are regulated. So that while conversation between Netland, Nāgārjuna and Einstein could be possible in accepting the validity of the principle of identity, non-contradiction and excluded middle, the way in which they would each utilize and understand logic would be quite different, yet internally consistent and defensible. Netland is partly aware of this for he notes that some would say that the notions of nirvāna, satori and the Trinity are all contradictory and adds "whether any of these doctrines is indeed self-contradictory is of course a separate and complex question" (p. 184). But is it a separate question? I think Netland here moves too quickly, for whether they are indeed self-contradictory is established by the way that a specific tradition regards and utilizes these principles. Isolating the principles

outside of a particular context does not really get us very far. Recall my axioms: in relation to the increased specificity of an alleged neutral proposal its neutrality diminishes and secondly, in relation to the decreased specificity of an alleged neutral proposal its usefulness diminishes. The latter might be applied to P1 and P2 without claiming that they are entirely without merit, although one must acknowledge their limited provenance, namely literate, speculative, self-reflecting persons within religions and their limited provenance, namely subordination to truths of revelation or meditative experience.

Of P3 (if a defining belief p of R is self-defeating it cannot reasonably be accepted as true) it may be observed that it amounts to no more than P1, for "self-defeating" is by Netland's own definition tantamount to self-contradiction. He writes of self-defeating statements that they "cannot be true because they provide the grounds for their own refutation" (p. 184) and the example he gives, that of thorough-going relativism being self-refuting, is obviously an example of self-contradiction. P4 (if the defining beliefs of R are not coherent in the sense of providing a unified perspective on the world, then R cannot plausibly be regarded as true) amounts to coherence *within* a religious system and as with P1 and P2 Netland does, I believe, isolate a tradition-transcending criterion which would be acceptable to most literate, speculative, self-reflecting persons within different religions. As he notes himself, "coherence of a worldview in and of itself is not sufficient to guarantee truth of a worldview, but lack of coherence does provide good reason for its rejection" (p. 186). It should also be noted that the notions of coherence may vary as we will see below in relation to the notion of "adequacy."

P5 seems to amount to a tautologous criterion for judgement, for it dismisses a religion which is "unable to account for fundamental phenomena associated with religious orientation" and one "which cannot provide adequate answers to central questions in religion." The reason for suggesting tautology here is that "fundamental phenomena" are not something self-evident to any neutral on-looker who can then judge between different explanations of these same phenomena and then choose the best. Rather, religious world views actually define and select what they perceive to be fundamental phenomena and their very power lies in the answers they give to the type of question they perceive. Take for example the central way in which the question of God is not seen as necessary for enlightenment by the Buddha and does not need to feature in the notion of dukkha, its cause and the means to remove it. The "fundamental phenomena" here are radically and differently constructed from those perceived by a Richard Swinburne who in suffering sees the problem of evil because of a belief in a loving God, and must then "answer" this problem by defending a good and loving God. While Buddhists and Christians share the same physical world it would pre-judge a whole range of questions to suggest they interpret/experience and experience/interpret the world in a common way, implying common fundamental phenomena or even a sense of what counts as an "adequate" answer to very different questions. Adequacy, for example, is intrinsically a theological and philosophical notion highly dependent on the tradition within which the term is used. For instance, certain Christian critics of free-will theodicies (adequate answers to the question of evil in the face of a loving God, a non-question for a Buddhist) will find the free-will defence entirely inadequate on the grounds that the attempted justification of suffering is un-Christian. Such a position is advanced by Kenneth Surin. Now defenders of the free-will argument like Swinburne can argue endlessly, but such critics as Surin will *a priori* refuse their overall vision for they have, one might say, incommensurable criteria of adequacy. Critics may try and show why such defences are internally problematic, as does Surin, but ultimately they have different senses of "adequacy," such that Swinburne will be satisfied with a rationally plausible answer while Surin requires that the answer, if "adequate," must satisfy the child being burnt to death in the ovens of Auschwitz. Again, Netland is aware of such problems for he writes that "there is not always agreement concerning just what phenomena fall

within the reference range of a religious worldview and what constitutes a satisfactory answer to the basic questions of religion. This fact, however, does not call into question the legitimacy of the criterion itself but simply indicates the difficulty of applying it to particular religious worldviews" (p. 187). But this final sentence avoids the problem, as I have tried to show, for this criterion does not actually mean anything without the specification that Netland seems to think is an entirely separate question. Netland further perpetuates the kind of essentialism about "religion," the "world" and "common questions" in a manner that is quite ahistorical in assuming such cohesive, reified and unitary entities.

P6 to P10 begin to bear features of "thick" description where tradition specific characteristics are much more obvious and unmask the alleged neutrality of the proposals. P6 and P7 use "well-established conclusions in other domains," such as science, history and archaeology, upon which to judge the claims of religion, either in the case of direct contradiction (P6) or dependency (P7). The difference between P6 and P7 could be a difference of degree rather than of kind. But that is not relevant, for more importantly Netland situates his criteria very clearly in a specific tradition. Netland's neutrality is that of the enlightened western secularist where there is a distinct separation between theological "science" and the historical, scientific and archaeological sciences, each one given sovereign reign within its own field and ever increasingly the latter group given sovereign reign over religious territory. But such presuppositions are very tradition specific. Admittedly with the internationalization of western secular culture many societies and religions are going through some similar fragmentationary processes, although it must be noted, they react very differently. For example, in some Islamic thought there is no autonomy granted to secular sciences in the way presupposed by Netland such that religious truth is determined and controlled by secular truths. The same could be said for some forms of Chinese and early Indian thought where "scientific theories" were actually part of religious worldviews, for example in the evolutionary framework of Sāmkhya-Yoga where Netland's distinction between science and religion would not make sense, let alone be applicable. And one can also find resurgent within some forms of Christianity a strong resistance to such fragmentation coming from both conservative evangelicals, who oppose scientific theories of evolution and from radical post-modernists, who oppose scientific notions of history. Here again, I am not suggesting that Netland's criterion is entirely unhelpful, but that without tradition-specific specification it is unuseable, and insofar as it can be used, betrays its neutrality.

P8 and P9 are perhaps the most blatantly nonneutral and given my first axiom that in relation to the increased specificity of an alleged neutral proposals its neutrality diminishes, it is not surprising that these principles are the ones which might take us on some distance in actually carrying out a process of judgement. P8 states: "If one or more defining beliefs of R are incompatible with widely accepted and well-established moral values and principles; or if R includes among its essential practices or rites activities which are incompatible with basic moral values and practices, then there is good reason for rejecting R as false." This unashamedly privileges western secular tastes and sensibilities in deeming religions true in accordance with their conformity to current notions of good taste and decency. Netland seems unaware of the huge and questionable set of assumptions implicit in this criterion. Firstly, he is guilty of the now consistent danger of "essentialism"; assuming some homogeneous coherence and consensus on moral values, principles and practices. But this begs the question as to which society will Netland turn to find this alleged consensus: the Azande, the Aztec, the Crusader Christians of the middle ages, Tibetan Buddhism before the entry of the Chinese, present-day Saudi Arabia, present-day England, present-day Chicago, or where? And when he has chosen that society, which group's morality is he to take as normative, and what about the plurality of moral values, principles and practices that he will inevitably find? Strangely, Netland seems to ignore such intractable difficulties, but rather cites ex-

amples of this allegedly neutral common morality: "Thus, a religious world view which includes child sacrifice or cannibalism as an essential rite or adopts as a basic tenet the inherent superiority of whites over blacks should, for this reason, be rejected as probably false" (p. 190). These are a curious set of examples, because in present day Chicago and England it would seem that public morality as a whole accepts as a basic moral value the right to choose what the Roman Catholic Church views as "child sacrifice": abortion. And in certain parts of Protestant Northern Ireland, there are still leaflets circulated where the communion rite of the Catholic mass is seen as cannibalism and "God's vicar on Earth" as "Satan's representative."

The point I am making is this. There are no sets of basic moral values which are neutral and acceptable to all people, and as soon as one tries to specify some their historical and tradition-specific nature becomes evident. Prohibition on suicide in one tradition amounts to martyrdom in another, avoiding meat only on a Friday in one tradition amounts to a six-day species-genocide in the eyes of another. My view does not in itself exclude the possibility of overlap, family resemblances, and so on. However, I would question the possibility that there is a homogeneous neutral publicly acceptable morality. Furthermore, if such an entity were found there seems to be no good reason to advance such a criterion as deciding the truth or falsity of a religion. For nearly all religious traditions the logic operates in the reverse direction. For example, in some forms of Judaism, Islam and Christianity, good and bad are defined from the basis of revelation and certain streams of privileged tradition stemming from that revelation, and this has then often been the basis for criticising the societies in which Jews, Christians and Muslims then find themselves. Netland's P8 suggests a reverse logic which is difficult to defend historically.

P9 has especially interesting results for its specifies that "if the defining beliefs of R entail the denial of the objectivity of basic moral values and principles; or if they entail the denial of the objective distinction between right and wrong, good and evil, then there is good reason for rejecting R as false." Here, more than almost anywhere else, the tradition-specific nature of Netland's proposals becomes evident. He gives no grounds for assuming that it is universally acceptable that such a realist view of ethics is the case, or why it is uncontroversial that there is an objective distinction between right/wrong, good/evil. This obvious weakness would allow those groups who do not agree with these assumptions to question (quite rightly given Netland's project) whether such proposals are objective neutral criteria for evaluating religions. One can imagine an Advaitin specifying that any religion that viewed the distinction between evil/good as an objective one could not be true because it undermines the absolute undifferentiated nature of Brahman, which is of course beyond the provisional duality of good and evil. Netland would no doubt reply that this was rather loading the dice. But oddly, he does the same with a curious air of innocence. Hence, he concludes that a

> strong case can be made for the view that Advaita Vedanta Hinduism and Zen Buddhism— insofar as they make a fundamental ontological distinction between levels of reality and truth and maintain that the highest Reality and Truth is absolutely undifferentiated unity, allowing no distinctions whatever—are incompatible with moral objectivity. It is hard to see how Advaita Vedanta or Zen can accommodate an objective distinction between good and evil, right and wrong (p. 190).

and hence they are probably false religions. It is also clear that such a proposal would be far from acceptable to most Advaitins or Zen Buddhists. Needless to say, the battlefield over the question is entirely misconstrued by Netland. He wins, so to speak, on very loaded and pre-judged terms which settle the question of religious truth before it has actually been discussed properly. This hardly overcomes the impasse regarding questions of conflicting truth claims, but rather propounds an answer of neutral criteria which we have seen to be far from neutral.

Little need be said about P10 (if R is unable to provide adequate answers to basic questions about the phenomenon of moral awareness, this provides good reason for rejecting R as false.) As with my criticisms of P5, it must be urged that the notion of "adequacy" is far from clear and involves strong theological and philosophical judgements as to what it constitutes. And as with my criticisms of P5, it must also be asked whether there is any agreed phenomenon of "moral awareness" or whether Netland simply once again creates essences out of a complex multiform phenomenon. Zen Buddhists clearly think that they do provide "adequate answers" and that the "inadequate" answers are given by theists (who are dualists) like Netland and their notions of adequacy are not derived from classical logic, but from the basic experience of satori, which conceptually defies the norms of classical logic.

If Netland's attempt to frame neutral criteria by which to judge religions is deeply problematic, as I hope to have shown, will Ward's fare any better? The logic of my criticisms suggests that the answer must be "no" for the two axioms have so far proven true: in relation to the increased specificity of an alleged neutral proposal its neutrality diminishes and that in relation to the decreased specificity of an alleged neutral proposal its usefulness diminishes.

III

Keith Ward's proposals are advanced in the context of his vision of Christianity in the twenty first century. He follows in the tradition of John Hick's pluralism, adopting a unitarian Christology and wishing to forge peaceful and harmonious relations between religions by means of overcoming exclusivist Christologies. As with Netland's book, I am concerned solely to assess his proposed neutral criteria by which to judge religions. Ward suggests that there are "certain common features of being human" (p. 178) such that it will be possible to specify "the criteria of excellence which are appropriate to human beings and the nature of the goal which is proper to humanity as such" (p. 179). Hence Ward wishes to establish that there "is a set of fundamental values which are given by the very nature of human being itself, and which are not merely conventional or matters of arbitrary and wholly subjective preference" (p. 179). Once more, we see a curious logic whereby religions will be told what constitutes their truthfulness in terms of some foundational Archimedes point outside of all religious traditions. This Archimedian point is that of a Kantian form of natural theology.

Ward, like Netland, criticises relativist and fideist positions and sees the way out of the impasse regarding conflicting truth claims in the provision of universal criteria. These are established by conditions for the possibility of reflectively using the concept of "value." This allegedly avoids the difficulties of dealing with the very different types of values held, but probes deeper, into the transcendental arguments from the notion of value. Ward notes analogies here with Kant's transcendental arguments for the possibility of scientific and mathematical knowledge. But this analogy should alert us to two possible dangers. Firstly, that in specifying general conditions for being able to hold values nothing specific is said about the content of values and their possible conflicts, which is ultimately the issue at stake. The point is not that every one has and is able to make truth claims, but rather that the truth claims themselves, if taken seriously, often conflict. Second, Kant operates within a very specific tradition and the history of philosophy since testifies to the controversy as to whether he had attained for pure and practical reason the transcending role he claimed for it. There are strong philosophical counter-traditions questioning the entire Kantian project which is germane for indicating the problem of any alleged neutral starting point.

What is Ward's argument? I hope I convey it correctly for at times in his text the different steps and stages are not always clear. Firstly, he argues that the notion of "value" presupposes preference and choice, and that value, if it is worthy of being sought, must be an intrinsically worthwhile

state of consciousness. Secondly, he argues that "happiness" is a basic value which admittedly "does not show what sort of conscious state happiness is" (p. 182), and that such happiness can be found in different ways, although one must qualify it by stating that it "is always wrong to cause sorrow or suffering, in the absence of further justifying factors" (p. 182). Thirdly, to seek to make choices to attain happiness, a further basic value is presupposed: that of knowledge. Hence, with qualifications, it can be said that it "is an unequivocally good thing to have the capacity to know what can be chosen and how best to achieve it" (p. 184). Knowledge is not simply a grasp of the facts, but a "deep sensitivity to and appreciation of beauty and order and a compassionate empathy with the sufferings of all creatures" and involves "an understanding of the nature of things and the explanation for their existence, so far as this is available" (p. 184). Fourthly, choice, happiness, and knowledge presuppose freedom to make such choices. Ward summarises his argument thus: "if I value anything at all, I have a good reason to value the realization of intrinsically satisfying conscious states, the capacity of knowing which states are actual and possible, of reasoning about how to obtain them, and of being free to realize them. These basic values are presupposed by the analysis of value in terms of rational preference" (p. 186). In order to render this as a universally applicable truth, Ward adds a fifth value, which he calls "justice; which simply reminds us that whatever is a basic value for us is one for anyone like us in the relevant aspects" (p. 186), meaning that if pursuing the attainment of values is good for x, and all factors being equal for y, then justice requires that it is good for y similarly to pursue the attainment of values.

In keeping with the Kantian transcendental nature of the argument, it should be noted that all Ward has provided (if his argument is correct) are certain formal, rather than material, elements constitutive of human beings as value seeking. Realizing intrinsically satisfying conscious states, knowing about such states, being able to know how to obtain them and being free to do so, are all formal properties of moral agents, specifying nothing whatsoever about the contents of the moral vision they hold. But Ward goes on to say that in so much as these conditions hold, one can claim to have arrived at an "autonomous," "objective" and "absolute" "standard or test for the acceptability of values. Any values which frustrate or destroy any of the set of basic values are less acceptable than values which, in a particular context, can be seen as encouraging the realization of the set of basic values" (p. 187). But can material choices actually effect the formal conditions required for making choices? Is Ward guilty of a category confusion? I think that he is guilty because what he calls "the set of basic values" are not actually material choices available, but the conditions for making any material choices. If it is otherwise, then these cannot be transcendental conditions for value-seeking that Ward claims them to be. Precisely because the "basic set of values" are conditions for choice-making and value-seeking they cannot specify the material contents of choice-making and value-seeking. Hence, they can hardly apply as criteria for granting truthfulness to material choices, but only as stating the necessary conditions for material choices.

In fact it should be noted that even the way in which Ward has specified the transcendental conditions of value seeking human beings is not neutral. For instance, he presupposes some very tradition specific notions of rationality and knowledge. Rationality is defined as "the capacity to discern the true nature of things and the deepest patterns of intelligibility in the world" (p. 184), a definition which smacks of traditional theistic natural theology. What of the Nāgārjunas of this world, who far from noting that the nature of things constitutes deep patterns of intelligibility in the world, note rather that nothing within this world is properly intelligible and therefore nothing within this world is properly satisfying? The same could be said for Śankara's Advaita Vedānta, for on the ultimate level of truth the world is actually unintelligible (anirvicanya) and has no proper status (māyā). A similar criticism could be advanced regarding Ward's definition

of knowledge which requires an "appreciation of beauty and order," an aspect of deep illusion according to most Buddhists. And similarly, for Ward's concession that while happiness can admittedly be found in different ways, he would qualify it by saying it "is always wrong to cause sorrow or suffering, in the absence of further justifying factors" (p. 102). But the notions of "sorrow" and "suffering" are in danger of being essentialised (*à la* Netland), for surely such terms are actually defined and have their meaning within tradition-specific contexts, not in a general and universal sense as implied by Ward? Suffering and sorrow, for a Buddhist, constitute the marks of dukkha and are part of the nature of empirical existence, whereas within certain forms of Christianity they are not essential to empirical existence and exist as a result of sin. Hence, at one level to be freed of the illusion of God as an essential being is to be freed from suffering and sorrow (within Buddhism), while entirely the opposite could be the case with Christianity. The list of differing constructions and construals given to this term could be multiplied and the point I am making is simple. I wish to stress that there is no neutral language and concepts and hence, even within Ward's formal definition, there is no neutrality. But let us for the moment grant Ward's argument a potential coherence to see how he further slips from stating common *formal* requirements to equating these with common *material* goals, compounding his category mistake.

Having rejected any seeking of values that destroys those absolute values which presuppose the conditions for seeking value, Ward goes on to distinguish between being *merely* human (being capable of pursuing these values) and being *fully* human (realising these values as fully as possible) (p. 188). So where does religion enter the picture? Ward's answer is that the religions all share a common "structure" which consists "in a maximal instantiation of the five basic values" (p. 189). But at this level of generality Ward's criteria do not really take us very far in resolving any conflicts concerning "maximal instantiation," for herein lies the problem of conflicting truth claims, and he seems to partially recognize this when he adds "and one can see how different faiths interpret such a maximal case in different ways" (p. 189). This amounts to saying that all religions have in common is a desire to achieve a way of life in which adherents are fulfilled and of course this is not saying very much regarding the evaluation of what counts as fulfilling or not. How, for instance, is martyrdom discerned as authentic or inauthentic in the cases of St Peter, the Jonestown disciples, and the followers of Hizballah (the Party of God)? All persons in the above cases may fully believe that they are achieving a "maximal instantiation" of pursuing that which is most valuable. It is at this point that Ward most clearly jumps the tracks and introduces a concealed assumption that actually negates the thrust of his argument from neutrality.

He begins to argue that while different faiths may interpret maximal cases in different ways, the differences "are subtle differences of interpretation" (p. 189) and have a commonality of content; that is "a turning-away from selfishness by relating individuals to a supreme objective value which is their ultimate goal" (p. 188). Or again, he says "there is agreement on the need to move from self towards a supreme objective value and an agreement on the sort of value this will be which forms a deeper structure underlying particular differences of interpretation" (p. 190). But this is surely a classical case of a category mistake; the confusion of the categories of form and content. Ward simply jumps from assuming a common structure (a movement towards a supreme objective value) to conflating that structure with content, and therefore a common goal. Hence, rather than attempting a solution to the problem, Ward dissolves it by not taking conflicting claims seriously. It is worth quoting at length the following passage which demonstrates this:

> It might be better to see the different faiths, not as in radical opposition but as having a range of agreed values, but varying ways of interpreting them in the light of a developing understanding of the world. There is an important sense in which differing faiths are engaged in a common pursuit of supreme value, though they conceive this in diverse ways. The theist will seek to transcend self by achieving a conscious relationship to God which enables her to share and reflect the supreme perfections of God. She seeks to make her will one with the divine will. The Buddhist seeks to transcend selfish desire, to make her nature one with the Buddha nature. The Vedantin seeks to realize her self as one with the Self of all, unlimited being, consciousness and bliss. Is there so much difference here? Are the deep agreements not more important that the countless unsettlable disputes which litter the libraries of professional dogmatists? (p. 190).

Presuming "professional dogmatists" is a term of abuse, I must plead guilty to being such a character, for it seems to me that the reverse of what Ward observes is the case. There seems to be very deep disagreements of content, even if there is a commonality of structure within different religions. For example (if one can generalize for the moment) the Christian's entire morality and pursuit of supreme value is based on difference and participation, difference from God but finally participation in his love, charity and goodness. Difference, distinction and participation are all upheld as ontological categories by means of the doctrine of the Trinity. The Advaitin on the other hand is entirely orientated towards unity without difference and oneness without duality: the "experience" of anubhava in which Brahman is realized as the sole existent, one without a second. Not only is the goal different, but so is the entire basis of morality and what counts as the ultimate truth for the Christian and Advaitin. And Rāmānuja and Madhva, as Vedāntins, certainly felt that the errors of Śankara were serious enough to condemn his teachings, to criticise his false understanding of Brahman and thereby the basis of Śankara's ethics. Without even drawing the Buddhist in at this point, and the differences between different schools of Buddhism are considerable, the "countless unsettlable disputes" are far from insignificant. It seems that the deep structure actually testifies to something very different from what Ward sees. Despite various commonalities in formal structure, and perhaps commonalities in values at varying levels of theory and practice, at a fundamental level there are substantial ontological differences that cannot be dissolved. This it should be recalled is the purpose of the exercise: to adjudicate between such differences. But Ward's strategy is to relegate such differences to "subtle differences of interpretation" and one suddenly realizes that the transcendental argument for the condition of value-seeking, has dropped entirely out of sight. And this is not insignificant.

Ward's allegedly neutral path of adjudication is, it seems to me, independent of the conclusions which he draws for two basic reasons. The first is that he commits a category mistake in applying his argument. From a similarity of formal structure, he assumes a common goal. Secondly, the criteria are not in fact neutral for Ward has already decided earlier in the book (and has begun to do so in his earlier work: *Images of Eternity*, 1987) that religions present "iconic" visions, where "iconic" plays a similar function to John Hick's category of "myth"; that is, something is "revealed" but it cannot be held to be an absolute truth and it must always be open to correction and transformation. Hence, disputes between the ultimate nature of reality can always be relegated to complementary perspectives and not finally taken seriously at all. It is curious that those wishing better relationships between religions and who are anxious to dispose of exclusivist claims, end up inadvertently not respecting the integrity of the different traditions and the seriousness and absoluteness of their claims and thereby erect a new exclusivism.

IV

I have endeavoured to achieve certain limited goals. Firstly, I have tried to show that the impasse in the problem of conflicting truth claims cannot be met by means of advancing neutral criteria for adjudicating between religions. As has been demonstrated by my examination of Ward and Netland, it can be argued that in relation to the increased specificity of an alleged neutral proposal its neutrality diminishes and secondly, in relation to the decreased specificity of an alleged neutral proposal its usefulness diminishes. In Netland's case we saw that his criteria were either so underspecified as to be incapable of the task, or so overspecified to be obvious form of tradition-specific (at least theistic) criteria that they could not count as performing the task they were set up to perform. In Ward's case we saw that his criteria were far from neutral and when they actually achieve results in application, they only did so by changing their nature through a category mistake.

Where does this leave us in the impasse regarding conflicting truth claims? Slightly better off I think, in avoiding certain options. In arguing implicitly that one cannot start from other than a tradition-specific starting point I hope to have shown the necessity for pursuing the question along the avenues set out in the first of the options outlined at the beginning of the paper. However, it remains to be shown how one can profitably counter the various objections to such an approach and to argue that this is in fact the only credible way in which to judge religions other than one's own.

11.6 A Problem for Radical Pluralism

If I hold that my religion has an exclusive monopoly on the truth and that all others are wrong, I assume there is such a thing as religious truth. If I hold that my religion is inclusive of the truth found in all religions insofar as it articulates such truth in its fullest extent, I assume there is such a thing as religious truth. If I think that all religions are true and that all present a plurality of valid paths to salvation, I assume that there is religious truth. If I go even further and adopt a more radical position, arguing that every religion ought to learn from and include within its own traditions the truth discovered in the other traditions, I assume that there is religious truth.

What if there is no such thing as THE TRUTH? What if all religions construct diverse human responses to the pressures of life, making sense of human experience as best they can given their historical and social locations? There may be no absolute and objective Truth, but only localized, constructed, cultural methods for coping with the problems of human existence. Perhaps we should not assume there is religious truth but only that there are varied responses to the issues and problems of being human.

Purusottama Bilimoria, who teaches religion and philosophy at Deakin University in Australia and is the author of the next selection, raises the question of whether the assumption of truth behind the various responses to religious plurality is appropriate. He suggests a "critical pluralism" that recognizes that there is no such thing as THE TRUTH in any absolute sense. Rather, he acknowledges various traditions struggling to construct meaning as best they can in a world that is often hostile.

If religious truth is a humanly constructed idea, if it is an artifact of human existence, then a type of hopeless relativism appears to engulf us. What is true for you is false for me, and what is true for me is false for you. Where does this leave us? If my religion teaches that human sacrifices must be made in order to ensure that the sun will come back and give us life, should you say, "Well, that's true for you, but in my religion it is false"? Should you then go on to say, "Nevertheless, go ahead, sacrifice those people. After all, truth is a humanly constructed notion, localized in time and place and unique to various experiences and traditions"?

Reading Questions

1. What is a more radical form of pluralism according to Bilimoria?
2. What is the implicit assumption of radical pluralism?
3. Why is the "ontotheological-metaphysical" presupposition questionable?
4. How does deconstructive a/theology reconceive God?
5. What is the post-onto/theocentric challenge?
6. If a new kind of critical pluralism is built around the idea that all conceptions of truth are equally constructed human artifacts and that there is no TRUTH in any absolute sense, then how could that critical pluralism escape being just another constructed truth like exclusivism, inclusivism, pluralism, and radical pluralism?

A Problem for Radical Pluralism*

PURUSOTTAMA BILIMORIA

Preamble

An aspect of Max Charlesworth's practical philosophy has engaged the following set of problems: If a culture X takes its episteme, theological (or, secular) framework and set of values to be paradigmatic or in some ways privileged, then what does this mean for the different religious worldviews, values and ideals of other cultures, and of the sub-cultures within it? How is it possible in a pluralistic society where people have very differing ethical views to reach any kind of community consensus on significant moral issues? What if they also have altogether differing views about the foundations of ethics or morality and the nature of the ethical enterprise, and about the precise relationship of ethics to law? Further, the ethical views of certain minority communities are based on or derived from *religious* foundations which may be radically different from, sometimes in conflict with, those of the majority society (whether quasi-religious or secular). What then are the implications for any due process in legal discourse about the claims of one group over another—e.g. Australian Aboriginal claim to their "sacred" land iconically linked with the Ancestor Spirits as against British Australian law?

Max Charlesworth's discursive handling of the questions and issues that arise in this confrontation have helped inspire wide-ranging discussions and even reviews of customary practices and opinions. But this matter is best left for more detailed treatment at another occasion. I want merely to pose a question for one facet of these problems, for the problem precipitated by pluralism, albeit religious/theological pluralism . . . .

I. Religious Pluralism

The contemporary Swiss-German theologian Hans Küng has suggested that the "boundary between the true and false today, even as Christians see it, no longer runs simply between Christianity and other religions, but at least in part *within* each of the religions."

The conventional discourse on religious pluralism has hitherto been framed in terms of the encounter of Christianity with "other" or "non-Christian" religions and the kind of response Christians might or might not make to people of non-Christian persuasion in all their diversity and complexity. The positions and attitudes adopted within the pluralist ("dialogue-ic") paradigm have ranged from forms of "exclusivism" (that all religions have some worth, but Christianity offers the only valid path, *extra ecclesiam nulla salus*), "inclusivism" (that other religions have great spiritual depth and revelations, but are not sufficiently salvific), and "pluralism" (that the truth-content of faith can have a variety of articulations each of which is legitimate), with shades in between. Ernest Troeltsch, William Hocking and Paul Tillich first suggested the idea of pluralism, although with differing interpretations and implications of the claim to finality or normativity for Christians. The consensus in more recent times seems to gravitate towards *pluralism* in one or the other of its interpretations. The more popular understanding of religious pluralism, as articulated by W. C. Smith, John Hick, Paul Knitter, D'Costa among others, maintains that "other religions are equally salvific paths to God, and Christianity's claim that it is the only path (exclusivism), or the fulfilment of other paths (inclusivism) should

*From "A Problem for Radical (onto-theos) Pluralism" by Purusottama Bilimoria, *Sophia* 30 (1991):21–33. Reprinted by permission. Footnotes deleted.

be rejected for good theological and phenome-nological grounds."

In other words, the traditional universalism and absolutism attached to the Christian posi-tion is bracketed and the independent validity of other religions—even in their "otherness" or *alterity*—is now recognised. Much thought has been given as to how the differences between re-ligions, the great diversity of beliefs, practices, rites and symbolisms, might be reconciled or a *rapprochement* brought about among them. And there has been much optimism about learning from other religions and the mutual enrichment or upliftment that can be experienced anew in "dialogues and conversations" with people whose religious instincts appear not to have been scorched by centuries of internal theological dis-putes, doubts and argumentations, and by the rapid shifts that the modern (beginning with Western) societies have made towards secularism, scientism and technocratic utopianism.

A corollary of this mitigated position is a more radical form of pluralism which argues that the established and dogmatic traditions should turn over to and enmesh (integrate) themselves as much as practicable with the cur-rency of other, possibly less dogmatic, ("world" and "primal") traditions with radically different (maybe more ancient) historical roots and wealth of outlook on nature, on the human condition, on the cosmos, on liberation, and so on. While during the colonial-imperial phase the distant and marginalised traditions were infiltrated, ex-propriated and recast to look more like the dominant tradition (e.g. Christianity in Hindu-Muslim India, typified in R. Panikkar's earlier The Hidden Christ of India), the trend now is to reverse the process and appropriate the "other" traditions into one's own tradition in the intra-religious context. (Which, of course, echoes a process already operative in the intra-traditions context, e.g. bhakti or devotionalism appropri-ated into the mainstream ritualistic Brahmanism that led to the emergence of Hinduism vis-à-vis Buddhism and Jainism.) Pluralism becomes a means of preserving the old in the guise of the new or other.

This task, it is urged, is a matter of some ur-gency now that there is widespread recognition of the historical contingency of every cultural artifact—as surely religion is one—as well as our growing awareness of the unavoidable "preju-dices" and the questionable assumption under-girding the privileged or paradigmatic access to the "Ultimate" claimed in each religion. To-gether the religions may be able to heal the scars left by the clashes of disparate cultures, and inject some sanity, hope and insightful wisdom towards preventing nature and humankind from the threat of human-engendered destruction, if not also work toward the betterment of human beings as indeed the goal of each religion appears, in princi-ple at least, to be absolutely committed to.

Thus, Christianity could be Judaised, Judaism Hinduised, Hinduism Islamised, Islam Bud-dhised, Buddhism Koori-ised, and so on. Imagine the prospect that Australia presents for such a "crucible of a radical spirituality," situated as it is in the Pacific-Asia region with an indigenous (ab-original) tradition that goes back some 50,000 years, and is now a home for a plethora of ethnic and culturally diverse groups that have brought their own faith-traditions to its shores! This would seem to be the challenge of what goes under the rubric of "radical pluralism," which, while it ac-knowledges the historical relativity of each reli-gion, nevertheless accedes to the intrinsic inten-tionality or drift towards the essential truth, the *telos,* as well as submitting to the fundamental in-tegrity, insights, virtues and spirituality of each tra-dition. Even if the form of relativism it implicitly admits to is merely "provisional," there appears to prefigure here an assumption that truth might just be plural; or, more likely, that truth is one but that it conceals itself behind a kaleidoscopic facade.

There are versions of radical pluralism that, pushed to further degrees of ambivalence, at-tempt to ride over the limitations imposed by the excluded middle, contrary to Parmenides' intu-ition; thus in calling for the non-exclusion of other truths from one's own, we have a simul-taneity of "One and Many." But there is a more serious suggestion that supervenes on the dis-tinction that some want to draw between truth in science, in religion, in ethics, in human disciplines, in personal orientations, and so on. And this turns on a revision of the classical (Aristotelian) notion of truth (culminating in science as its key model). Thus, it follows that, if religions are plural, truth must also be plural.

II. Plurality of Truth

The question of how one might legitimate the claim to a variety of truth qua truth aside, there is another problem which the pluralist paradigm seems least self-conscious of. As the post-modern critics are at pains to point out, radical pluralism continues to trade on the implicit assumption that there is such a thing as religious truth, or that there is an "ultimate something" that answers to the description of truth in each religion. In short, the assumption is that there is some one *ultimate* being or reality, the universal spirit as the absolute (*logos, onto-theos*), which transcendentally sediments as the core intentionality of all religions. The ultra-radical pluralist might say that because the ultimate reality is ineffable and language presents a barrier to this hidden reality, the best we can do is to pursue the different names of the absolute (as we would if we were looking for the "ultimate ice cream" or playing different "language-games"). The pluralist approach, then, in conceding to different paradigms of the ultimate reality, unequivocally affirms that there is an absolute of which each religious truth is an attempted articulation. The term "God" names the "ultimate reality" in Western religious traditions; the terms "Brahman" in Hinduism, and "*nirvana/śūnyatā* (emptiness)" in conjunction with "*Dharma/dharmakāya*" and "refuge in Buddha" in Buddhism, have analogous function to that of the term "God."

In other words, religious truths are, if not simply a variety of reflecting articulations of the ultimate truth, modes of representations of the one true Ultimate (ens realissimum). It is only that we are not yet able to decide as to which of these is the final manifestation or decisive articulation, or as to which captures best the distinctive mark of the Ultimate: the truth of truths (the "highest

truth" *à la* neo-Vedānta discourse). Perhaps history in its *n*th fulfilment, or another (or the deferred) revelation, or a prophet, or avatāra, or total submission, etc., will in due course disclose it to us.

III. The Questionable Presupposition

It is the very ontotheological-metaphysical presupposition just sketched, whether it is based on the identity of God and being (intuited through reason as in philosophical theology and argued in philosophy of religion) or based on revelation and faith as in the discourse of theology, or on the scriptural evocation of Brahman, and so on, that has now become suspect. Reason itself (more persistently since Kant) has come in the firing line as being an insufficient tool to explain and defend the claims supposedly derived from sources more transcendental to it. Theoretical reason knows only this world of "appearance," and not the whatever-in-itself. For Kant, the postulate of God, just as the ideas of the "world" and "self," is a matter of reasonable trust (and not quite a matter of faith), intended to guide and govern our wisdom and tenets. Thus if reason is not universal in all matters—or not universal at all—there can be no truth, still less religious truth, that can lay claim to being universal.

Thus it seems that while the earlier form of absolutism that underpinned the exclusive (and to an extent, inclusive) truth—claim of one religion over the others (i.e. in respect of being in possession of the truth, regardless of its content—and this applies, *pari pasu*, to strong forms of Judaism, Hinduism, Islam, and Buddhism) is rejected, the absolutism *in* the truth-content (i.e. the meta-*écrit* in respect of the ontology of God, Brahman, Allah, Buddha-nature, the Dreaming, etc.) is not really set aside or bracketed sufficiently. For, to reject the latter kind of absolutism would be to risk undermining the very doctrinal formations and foundations of religious discourse altogether. But it is precisely this *foundationalism* that has for so long stood its own ground within religion, and returned to in the thinking of great philosophers like Plato,

Śankara, Hegel, Schleiermacher, Rahner, *et al.*, which now has come under the hermeneutics of suspicion.

This critique is not simply a rehearse of the attack of positivists and sundry philosophers, although it takes notice of it, but has come about in part as a result of the problems raised regarding the formation and function of God as an onto-theological concept in the history of Western thought, by Nietzsche, Heidegger, Kierkegaard, Barth with other German theologians, later Wittgenstein and French deconstructionists. The metaphysical presupposition or prejudgment implicitly determining much of religious thought anywhere in respect of the ever constant presence, the *sacra arché* and spiritual telos or its inspirations to a transcendentalised utopia, is increasingly thrown into the open as a possible source of all that has gone wrong in the current historical situation. Thus the facticity and particularity of Western thought in respect of its presupposition and faith in the historical uniqueness of its development has been brought home by Heidegger, Gadamer and Derrida among others, who have in their own inimitable ways tried to address the "crisis" (and *décadence*) now upon the very foundations of (modern) European culture, thought, ethics, and religion. The illusion of the apparent universality and necessity of the metaphysical flight has apparently been dispelled by reaching back to the ground of metaphysics and the specific thinking, or the unthought, on which it has been based. Metaphysics is looked upon as a "*supplément*" (addition and substitution) for naive discourse "about things." The thought of Being or "truth" is tantamount to an "intrusion within language's closure upon itself." Grammatology (the science of writing) shakes this complacency, and reveals the inconsistencies in the codes and signifiers which served to maintain the constancy of the logos, the absolute *arché* or *telos* that never was.

IV. Deconstruction in Theology

Similar critical reflections have occurred and are perhaps continuing in Eastern traditions as well, which in the particular case of Buddhism may be traced back to Nāgārjuna's (2nd cent BCE) dialectical critique of Brahmanic metaphysics and orthopraxy, continued in Vijñāñāvada's ambivalence over the Absolute of Vedānta, and more recently in Nishitani's work on *No-thingness* (combining Buddhist and Heideggerian insights for a critique of "Eastern modernity").

In the Anglo-American world there have been echoes of this problematic in the so-called "Death of God" theology (with Robinson's *Honest to God* assault) and in the deconstructionist twist it (has) received in the hands of Thomas Altizer Jr., Carl Raschke, Robert Scharlemann, and Mark C. Taylor. Even though, it may be pointed out, that while in deconstructive a/theology the project of revealing the "absence" and "NOTHNESS" of the theistic image of deity is meticulously completed, there is implicit in its discourse a "leap" (transgression) beyond the text (the "Word," which writing both forgets and wrenches from its *unconscious*) to the projected (often interiorised into the equally abnegated self) return of the "noncentred whole," the "Wholly Other." It is in the *otherness,* the *Alterity,* of God which theism had forgotten and which lay buried beneath the metaphysical speculations, that the "traces" can be retrieved. This "absent" God is discernible only in the "space" marked by the *uncertainty* of its *différance* (read as Hegel's subversion of absolute idealism in the notion of absolute negativity). The play on "*difference*" harkens back via Derrida to Heidegger's uncovering of the "ontological difference," that is, the difference between being and entities, as well as to his larger task of the "destruction" (*Destruktion*) of the history of ontology. A "spacing" is then made possible which does not tolerate an identity (total self-presence) that closes in upon itself. While the entitative notion of God as the transtemporal or metaphysical entity ("being as Being") is arrested (and dismembered), along with all the conventional signifiers attuned to this traditional conception, God is re-conceived (re-constituted) as the being that is not God or, better still, when God is not being God. It is in its *totaliter aliter,* without remainder, as the "negated presence" rather than absolute nihilism, that truth arises as the "ghost" that continues to dance on the tomb of the dead (Crucified) God: "a self-consciousness which itself becomes absolute by passing through the death of God."

Bonhoeffer (already in conversation with followers of Mahatma Gandhi who had raised doubts about the historicity of Jesus) is particularly important in this regard for being perhaps the earliest of such "deconstructionists" to have issued the challenge to Christianity to rethink its traditional self-understanding. As he wrote from his prison cell: "Religious people speak of God when human perception is (often just from laziness) at an end, or human resources fail: it is really always the *Deux ex machina* they call to their aid, either for the so-called solving of insoluble problems or as support in human failure—always, that is to say, helping out human weakness or on the borders of human existence. Of necessity, that can only go on until men can, by their own strength, push those borders a little further, so that God becomes superfluous as a *Deus ex machina*." Of course, while in one sense Bonhoeffer was, as the saying goes, pulling the rug from under the feet of the Church, in another sense he was preparing Christianity for a radically different conception of the "ultimate" in his rejection of the metaphysical and theological notion of deity, and in his concern with the secular world. This challenge is still being worked out for its fuller implications in Christian theology (particularly with Barthian thesis of the historical reality of revelation that cuts across theism and atheism, believers and unbelievers alike); and it has had a tremendous impact on "third world" theology as well (especially on liberation theology). But in other ways, the discourse has not moved much beyond the acceptance of Christ as the incarnation of truth [or the erased term] in history.

There is a further difficulty with deconstructive a/theology. While it does make considerable overtures towards, particularly Buddhist tradition (most evident in Altizer's recent writings with unmistakeable Buddhistic signifiers), the concepts from varying traditions are treated as "remains, what is left over, to be used or discarded at the whim of the theologian," without giving full regard to their context, or to the damning indictment their further *reductio* might entail for what a/theology would not withstand, viz. its own self-destruction. Thus "Buddhist nothingness," "śunya," the "utter self-emptying and emptiness of . . ." abound in the rhetorical fits of a/theology. Once emptied, however, the "space" is quickly filled up again—not on account of the spectre of relativism, but in the anxiety of stark nihilism, the *abyss* that might swallow everything/being and itself too. But why does a/theology evade this ultimate consequence of its own deconstituting endeavour? If a/theology is to be true to the dual *aporias* of pluralism and radical deconstruction, must it not countenance the possibility of its own structural subversion, capitulation? Indeed, there is already some disquiet among deconstructive theologians as they criticise each other's *excesses,* quasi-transcendentalisms, false inversions (e.g. of the *Geist in the structure and language of the Unconscious*), and misappropriation of the role of interpretation in the deconstructive enterprise.

V. The Post-onto/theocentric Challenge

In the light of the foregoing analysis, the challenge staring us in the face in the late hour of the 20th century may be formulated thus: We might well be content and adapt ourselves to living in a pluralist milieu wherein each one accepts and tolerates the respective "faith-path" chosen by adherents of other religions, but can we accept that there is therefore a plurality of "absolutes"? That alongside God, there is in the deepest (or "highest") reality, also Allah, Brahman, the Dreaming, Buddha-nature (or the converse)? That these are not simply different manifestations of the same "One and Only One," or "Not-Two, nor-Many," "Not Another" (*non aliud*) being or truth, but are Ultimates in their own right? Or, we might be forced to ask, where does radical pluralism draw the line before the legitimacy it accords to each religion transgresses the boundary of the truth-claim with respect to the "Ultimate" in each religion? The question is not about the different ways in which the Ultimate is conceived (e.g. as the absolute in identity, in relativity, in *identity-in-difference,* in non-difference, in utter *difference,* or its "*altar-ity,*" and so on), but it is about the presupposition that beyond the indefinite dissemination of the signs there is a referent (a signified), some constant, whether in its "pleroma" (infinite, "fullness") or its "emptiness" ("non-beingness," "nothingness"), that answers to the description? (Even if that absolutising is intransitive, i.e. without subject or predicate.)

And what response can a sanguine religious pluralism make to those (within religion and outside religion, say, in philosophy and science) who reject the idea or possibility of any "absolute" altogether as a hopelessly futile metaphysical project in whose traps religions fell and have remained entangled? This critique, then, disqualifies any and all claims to universal truth in or across religions: all religious truth is henceforth considered to be local, partial, and constructed. Here all truth stands de-absolutised. So the differences in myth and doctrine across religions are not differences in truth-claims nor are they "alternative maps, in different projections, of the universe . . ." but are simply different ways of making sense of the existential facticity of life and different ways of dealing with this non-transcendental or relative subjectivity in the day to day activities and concerns of people. (While Hick appears to be saying something close to this, for him the *soteriological* significance, and its afterlife verification, nonetheless leads us away from the relative to some unarticulated notion of the absolute, once again.)

Again, it is insisted, the differing orientations are not simply variations on the same invariant objective truth, but categorically distinct historical experiences which resist reduction to a unitary symbolic process, or revelation, or way of knowing. It resists reduction to even anything like a common denominator of the rather safe and pervasively non-cognitive "numinous" that Otto sought on the cognitive model provided by Kant's epistemology, much less to the spiritual unity or its *telos* in transcendental subjectivity as pursued by theologians inspired by the Cartesian-Husserlian project in phenomenology.

Hence to rescue religion and maintain genuine plurality of spiritual life-worlds, some argue, one ought seriously to consider rejecting belief in the Absolute (of any kind or form) altogether, and any claim to the universal and normative for all and sundry. For it is this belief, fundamental to most if not all religions, rather than the confrontations of differences in conceptions of the absolute and the practices and histories of the religious traditions amidst us, that gives rise to intolerance, competition, self-righteousness, dogmatism, barbarism and such adverse conducts as the other history of religions has made amply evident.

Indeed, it would be argued in such a critique that overall what is more important to emphasise is the fact of the differences *qua difference* in the cluster of social-historical phenomena, and irreducibly so. And that there need be assumed nothing in particular, or of a general kind, of which these are differences; that is to say, at no point in the inquiry should one presume to have arrived at an understanding of some common "Archimedean centre" ("the centre of the centre"), from which the lines of differentiation have, as it were, shot out. This predilection towards finding the core central myth, the universal arche(type), the projected confirmation in eschatology/soteriology/orthopraxy, and such other epithets ("name of the names") that express this universalist proclivity across the differences in the religious orientations (described to us profusely by anthropologists and religious dialogists) ought to be indefinitely deferred, suspended, or even erased. Nor need this be a cause for celebration, but possibly a sombre lamentation that such a goal is, in the final analysis, unattainable.

The Jainas in India pre-empted this move by suggesting that it is neither possible *nor necessary* to have an absolute view on anything, still less on matters of "ultimate concern," such as whether there is or is not an absolute. (Pyrrho perhaps imbibed "imperturbability" and "*epoche*" in matters ultimate from the Jainas when he accompanied Alexander to India.) Genuine tolerance and "conversation," the Jainas preached, is only possible when "one-sidedness" (*ekānta*) in thinking is clearly set aside. (Jaina philosophy, it may be noted in passing, provided a seven-term dialectic which allowed the possibility of holding, that from varying points of view: "x is," "x is not," "x both is and is not," "x is inexpressible," "x is both not and inexpressible," "x is, is not, and is also inexpressible.")

The challenge in the "post-modern" human condition targets at the underfoot of radical pluralism in suggesting that there is neither one "absolute" or "decisive" truth-content (logos, presence) in religion (contrary to the exclusivist presupposition), nor a plurality of expressions or articulations inscripting the same deep truth-content (contrary to the inclusivists assumption). Indeed, it argues that all conceptions of truth are equally constructed artifacts, which have thus to be contextualised and understood in the horizons of the disparate and possibly unique experiences, tradition and aspirations of each cultural group.

If the arguments on which this challenge is pivoted go through, then what kind of *pluralism* is possible, without risking ambiguity, equivocation, deep uncertainty and *angst* that characterise radical pluralism? Is "critical pluralism" that can countenance and come to terms, albeit creatively rather than destructively, with the kinds of problems and questions raised, a real possibility? Might this be the direction or turn we could more fruitfully take in our reflections at this juncture of the history of reflections on religion and particularly on the confrontations of vastly different traditions, denominations and sub-cultures within and between the religions of the world? . . .

Suggestions for Further Reading

Adler, Mortimer J. *Truth in Religion: The Plurality of Religions and the Unity of Truth.* London: Collier Macmillan, 1990.

Anderson, Sir James Norman Dalrymple. *Christianity and World Religions: The Challenge of Pluralism.* Downers Grove, IL: Inter-Varsity Press, 1984.

Bilimoria, Purushottama, ed. "Tradition and Pluralism." *Sophia: A Journal for Philosophical Theology and Cross-Cultural Philosophy of Religion* 34 (March–April):1995.

Chatterjee, Margaret. "Reflections on Religious Pluralism in the Indian Context." In *Culture and Modernity: East–West Philosophic Perspectives,* edited by Eliot Deutsch. Honolulu: University of Hawaii Press, 1991.

Christian, William. *Oppositions of Religious Doctrines.* New York: Herder and Herder, 1972.

Cobb, John. *Beyond Dialogue.* Philadelphia: Fortress Press, 1982.

Connolly, William E. *The Bias of Pluralism.* New York: Atherton Press, 1969.

Coward, Harold G. *Pluralism: Challenge to World Religions.* Maryknoll, NY: Orbis Books, 1985.

———. *Religious Pluralism and the World Religions.* Madras, India: Radhakrishnan Institute, University of Madras, 1983.

———, ed. *Modern Indian Responses to Religious Pluralism.* Albany: State University of New York Press, 1987.

Copleston, Frederick Charles. *Religion and the One: Philosophies East and West.* New York: Crossroad, 1982.

Das, Bhagavan. *The Essential Unity of All Religions.* Wheaton, IL: The Theosophical Society, 1939.

D'Costa, Gavin. *Theology and Religious Pluralism: The Challenge of Other Religions.* New York: Basil Blackwell, 1986.

———, ed. *Christian Uniqueness Reconsidered: The Myth of a Pluralistic Theology of Religions.* Maryknoll, NY: Orbis Books, 1990.

Dean, Thomas. *Religious Pluralism and Truth: Essays on Cross-Cultural Philosophy of Religion.* Albany: State University of New York Press, 1995.

Donovan, Peter. "The Intolerance of Religious Pluralism." *Religious Studies* 26 (June 1993):217–229.

Hick, John, ed. "Religious Pluralism." *Faith and Philosophy* 4 (October 1988).

———. *God and the Universe of Faiths.* London: Macmillan, 1973.

———. *God Has Many Names.* Philadelphia: Westminster Press, 1980.

———. *Problems of Religious Pluralism.* New York: St. Martin's Press, 1985.

———. *Truth and Dialogue in World Religions.* Philadelphia: Westminster Press, 1974.

———. *An Interpretation of Religion: Human Responses to the Transcendent.* New Haven: Yale University Press, 1989.

Huxley, Aldous. *The Perennial Philosophy.* New York: Harper & Row, 1945.

Knitter, Paul F. *No Other Name? A Critical Survey of Christian Attitudes Toward the World Religions.* Maryknoll, NY: Orbis Books, 1985.

Kraemer, H. *The Christian Message in a Non-Christian World.* London: Edinburgh House Press, 1938.

———. *Why Christianity of All Religions?* London: Lutterworth Press, 1962.

Lipner, Julius. "Truth-Claims and Inter-religious Dialogue." *Religious Studies* 12 (1976): 217–230.

Nasr, Seyyed Hossein. *Knowledge and the Sacred.* Albany, NY: State University of New York Press, 1989.

Newman, Jay. *Foundations of Religious Tolerance.* Toronto: University of Toronto Press, 1982.

Radhakrishnan, S. *Eastern Religions and Western Thought.* 2d edition. London: Oxford University Press, 1940.

Rouner, Leroy S., ed. *Religious Pluralism.* Notre Dame, IN: University of Notre Dame Press, 1984.

Senor, Thomas D., ed. "Part II Religious Pluralism" (articles by Plantinga, van Inwagen, Runzo, and Mavordes defending exclusivism or critiquing pluralism) in *The Rationality of Belief and the Plurality of Faith: Essays in Honor of William P. Alston.* Ithaca, NY: Cornell University Press, 1995.

Smart, Ninian. *A Dialogue of Religions.* SCM Press, 1960.

Smith, Huston. *The Forgotten Truth; The Primordial Tradition.* New York: Harper & Row, 1976.

Smith, William Cantwell. *Religious Diversity.* Edited by Willard G. Oxtoby. New York: Harper & Row, 1976.

———. *Towards a World Theology.* Philadelphia: Westminster Press, 1981.

Stetson, Brad. *Pluralism and Particularity in Religious Belief.* Westport, CT: Praeger, 1994.

Tillich, Paul. *Christianity and the Encounter of the World Religions.* New York: Columbia University Press, 1963.

Ward, Keith. "Truth and the Diversity of Religions." *Religious Studies* 26 (March 1990):1–18.

———. *Religion and Revelation.* Oxford, England: Clarendon Press, 1994.

Yandell, Keith. "Religious Experience and Rational Appraisal." *Religious Studies* 8 (June 1974).

Yearley, Lee H. *New Religious Virtues and the Study of Religion.* Phoenix, AZ: Arizona State University Press, 1994.